The Catechism of Catholic Ethics

A work of Roman Catholic moral theology

The Catechism of Catholic Ethics

A work of Roman Catholic
moral theology

by

Ronald L. Conte Jr.

"Yet, for all the days of your life,
have God in your mind.
And be careful that you never consent to sin,
nor overlook the precepts of the Lord our God."
(Tobit 4:6)

The Catechism of Catholic Ethics
A work of Roman Catholic moral theology
Copyright © 2010 by Ronald L. Conte Jr.

This book is copyrighted in all electronic and printed versions. All rights reserved.

Quotations from Sacred Scripture are from the Catholic Public Domain Version of the Bible, original edition, translated, edited, and published by Ronald L. Conte Jr.

Chronology: This book is the fruit of many years of work and prayer, many years of studying the teachings of Sacred Tradition, Sacred Scripture, and the Magisterium, of writing Roman Catholic theology, and most importantly, of living the Catholic Christian Faith. In discussing the Faith over the course of many years with my fellow Catholics, I noticed a lack of knowledge among even devout persons on the subject of ethics, especially on the basic principles that underlie every moral decision. After writing a number of articles on Catholic ethics, I saw that a more comprehensive approach was needed. Work on this book began while I was still working on completing my translation of the Bible (the CPDV). After completing the translation, in spring of 2009, I was able to devote more time to the project. The majority of the book was written from spring of 2009 to early 2010.

Written, edited, and published by: Ronald L. Conte Jr.

Publication of first edition: March, 2010

ISBN-13: 978-0-9802249-6-2

Table of Contents:

Introduction	vii
1. The Basis for Morality	1
2. The Eternal Moral Law	9
3. The Three Fonts of Morality	16
[A. Intention, B. Moral Object, C. Circumstances]	
4. The Principle of Double Effect	50
5. Judgment and Moral Certitude	62
6. Conscience	71
7. Degrees of Sin and of Culpability	81
8. Interior Acts and Exterior Acts	92
9. Positive and Negative Precepts	99
10. The End Does Not Justify the Means	124
11. Tradition, Scripture, Magisterium	137
12. Doctrine and Discipline	164
13. Imperfection and Perfection	216
14. Types of Evil	229
15. Direct and Voluntary Deprivations	250
16. Proper Moral Definitions	255
17. Theft and Lying	260
18. Types of Murder	275
19. Just and Unjust Violence	286
20. Just and Unjust War	325
21. Slavery	337
22. Abortion and Contraception	349
23. Assisted Reproductive Technology	368
24. Sexual Sins	387
25. Marital Sexual Ethics	465
26. Sets of Acts	510
27. Incomplete Acts	518
28. Cooperation with Evil	528
29. Temptation	606
30. Grace and Salvation	642
Afterword	727

Anima Christi

Soul of Christ, sanctify me.

Body of Christ, save me.

Blood of Christ, inebriate me.

Water from the side of Christ, wash me.

Passion of Christ, strengthen me.

O good Jesus, hear me.

Within your wounds, hide me.

Permit me never to be separated from you.

From the malicious enemy, defend me.

In the hour of my death, call me,

and bid me come to you,

so that I may praise you,

with all your Saints and Angels,

forever and ever. Amen.

Introduction

.001.
[Daniel]
{10:21} "But, in truth, I announce to you what is expressed in the scripture of truth...."

The Reader of This Book

This book was not written for every Catholic, but only for a certain type of Catholic.

I know what my fellow Catholics are like. Some are meek and humble, seeking the truths of faith and morals in all that is taught, explicitly and implicitly, in Sacred Tradition and in Sacred Scripture, and by the Magisterium. These faithful souls are willing to learn the Faith ever better, and to have their understanding of the Faith improved and corrected. They will accept a sound theological argument, based on Tradition, Scripture, Magisterium. They continually cooperate with grace as they continually strive to become more like Christ, and to grow in knowledge of the Christian Faith.

These humble Catholics rejoice whenever they find any book of sound Catholic instruction, on faith, morals, and salvation, which can help them understand their Faith in ever greater depth and breadth. Catholics such as this will be truly joyful to have this book, which presents the teachings of Sacred Tradition, Sacred Scripture, and the Magisterium on the basic principles of Catholic moral theology, and their application, in a manner that is accessible to the ordinary layperson. I offer this book to them, in order to assist them to understand the eternal moral law, to avoid sin, to live a moral life, and to become truly pleasing to God in every way.

.002. Although this book is not infallible, many of the teachings in this book are infallible, since these are the infallible teachings of Sacred Tradition, of Sacred Scripture, and of the Sacred Magisterium (which teaches infallibly by solemn definitions of the Pope, solemn definitions of Ecumenical Councils, and the ordinary and universal Magisterium). The faithful and reasonable Catholic will use this book as a resource to obtain a better understanding of the moral truths of Divine Revelation found in Tradition, Scripture, Magisterium, which same truths on morality are also accessible to reason alone through natural law. The faithful and reasonable Catholic will not regard this book as infallible in itself, but will use this book as a one of many means to seek and to find the truths that are of God who is Wisdom and Truth.

To the faithful and reasonable Catholic, I say that this book contains infallible teachings of the Church, non-infallible teachings of the Church, the theological insights of Saints, and sound (but fallible) theological opinion. This book also has insights into moral theology rarely found in other sources. Use this book to achieve a better understanding of the moral teachings of the Catholic Faith. And

Introduction

stand corrected whenever this book offers you a more profound understanding of morality, firmly based on Tradition, Scripture, Magisterium.

.003. But do not be influenced by those persons who adhere to the majority opinion in all things, who disregard or denigrate the truths of Sacred Tradition and Sacred Scripture, who interpret the teachings of the Magisterium so as to weaken or nullify them, who seek to make the teachings of the Catholic Faith ever more narrow and ever more shallow, so as free themselves from the light yoke of Christ, and so as to justify their own sinful lives.

[Exodus]
{23:2} You shall not follow the crowd in doing evil. Neither shall you go astray in judgment, by agreeing with the majority opinion, apart from the truth.

I know what my fellow Catholics are like. Some among my fellow Catholics will not accept much of what this book teaches, on the excuse that we should (they suppose) only believe the explicit written teachings of the Magisterium. If we should live solely by the written letter of magisterial documents, then how did the early Christians live so faithfully, with few, if any, magisterial documents? And how did they succeed in spreading the Gospel of the one holy Catholic and Apostolic Church, to so many nations, to the great benefit of all future generations? They lived as we ought to live, by faith and reason, by Tradition, Scripture, Magisterium together. So it is not possible, at any time during the pilgrim journey of the Church on earth, to live solely by the written doctrinal decisions of the Magisterium. For in order to understand these doctrines, and to bind them together as one Faith, and to apply them to our lives, we must necessarily make substantial use of theological opinion and of our own pious but fallible understanding. It is not possible for the faithful to live the moral teachings of the Catholic Faith solely based on the letter of written magisterial documents, without including their own pious yet fallible understanding of Tradition, and of Scripture, and of those magisterial teachings. Therefore, this book does not go astray by using theological opinion to explain, to expound, and to apply the teachings of Tradition, Scripture, Magisterium on the moral law.

I know what my fellow Catholics are like. Some few among my fellow Catholics will make sweeping condemnations of this book, on one pretext or another. For some Catholics reject any teaching that is not in agreement with the version of Catholicism found in their own minds. They are not seeking truth in Sacred Tradition, and in Sacred Scripture, and from the Magisterium. They have accepted a limited, and to some extent erroneous, set of ideas about the Catholic Faith. And they are neither willing to learn anything more, nor to have their errors corrected. They automatically assume to be false anything contrary to their own limited understanding (and misunderstanding) of Catholicism. They have ceased to seek the truths of Christ in the Sacred Deposit of Faith. This book will be rejected by such persons on the basis of various excuses and claims.

.004. Whoever treats this book with contempt, treats Christ with contempt. For this book, though fallible, is of Christ and of His Divine Revelation and of His Church. Whoever treats this book with respect, treats Christ with respect. For this book, though fallible, is a small and weak reflection of the Living Word of

Introduction

God, the Living Truth, who is Jesus Christ. Read Matthew 25:40, 45; Mark 6:11; 9:35-40; Luke 9:2, 5; John 13:20.

This book is not for those Catholics who have decided that the Catholic Faith is nothing other than what they have already understood and accepted. This book is not for those Catholics who, after accepting the Catholic Faith, have closed their minds and hearts to any further understanding or correction. This books is not for those Catholics who assume that any idea must be false, if it is contrary to their own understanding, or if it is an idea they had not heard before. This book is not for those Catholics who condemn every theological argument contrary to their own understanding, without making any theological argument of their own. This book is not for those Catholics who judge the orthodoxy of a book, not based on Tradition, Scripture, Magisterium, but based on whether or not the book conforms to their own limited understanding, or to the majority opinion.

This book is a catechism on the subject of the moral teachings of the Roman Catholic Faith. The book was written to instruct those faithful Catholics who are willing to change their lives to conform ever more closely to the moral teachings of Christ as found in Tradition, Scripture, Magisterium. This catechism is a balm for the wounds of the Church, which has been grievously harmed by ignorance of sound moral doctrine, by the spread of false moral doctrines, and by the sinful influence of secular society.

.005. What is a Catechism?

A catechism is an instructional book, and, in the context of the Roman Catholic faith, it is a book for teaching the truths of the Catholic Faith. Any priest or theologian, any knowledgeable member of the Church, might write a catechism on one topic or another within Catholic theology, or on Catholicism in general. Many such books have been written in the history of the Church. Some are called catechisms in the title, others are catechisms in fact, but not in title. Most of these books were not written by Bishops and are not official documents of the Magisterium.

In the history of the Church, from time to time, one Bishop or another has written an instructional text for his diocese, or a group of local Bishops have written, or commissioned to be written, a catechism or similar catechetical text for their jurisdiction. Sometimes these texts are issued by the ordinary Magisterium, and if so their teachings are generally non-infallible. However, any catechism might contain teachings that are infallible, because they have been previously established as infallible by the Magisterium. Now these catechetical texts often contain discipline in addition to doctrine (teachings). While doctrine falls under the teaching authority of the Church, discipline falls under the temporal authority.

Among those catechisms issued by the Magisterium, certain few texts stand above the others.

Introduction

In 1562, the Council of Trent ordered that an official catechism be written, primarily for use by priests; this work is called the Roman Catechism. The work was completed in 1566, a few years after the Council of Trent ended, and was translated into many different languages for use throughout the Church. The Roman Catechism is relatively brief compared to the current official Catechism of the Catholic Church.

In 1866, the local Bishops in America met, in the Second Plenary Council of Baltimore, and decided that a catechism would be written, similar in form to the Roman Catechism (of Trent). This work is called the Baltimore Catechism. It remained a popular text throughout the Church, even until the late 20th century, when the Catechism of the Catholic Church was published.

The 1994 official Catechism of the Catholic Church is a unique book in Church history; it is the longest and most comprehensive Catechism issued by the Holy See. There have been only a few other Catechisms issued by the Magisterium in the history of the Church. Its companion book, called the Compendium of the Catechism, is a summary of the teachings found in the official Catechism, but presented in a simpler and more abbreviated form. Both of these books are very useful to all Catholics. No teaching in the Catechism is infallible merely by being in the Catechism, but many of its teachings are infallible, having been taught infallibly by a Pope, or by an Ecumenical Council, or by the Universal Magisterium.

In addition, there are have been many catechisms written by theologians or priests, but not issued by the Magisterium.

For example, in the late 1500's, Saint Robert Bellarmine wrote one small catechism for children, and another for teachers of religion; these were written by him as a private theologian. His catechisms were approved by the temporal authority of the Church, but were not issued by the Magisterium. His subsequent authority as a Cardinal, and his later canonization as a Saint, caused this catechism to be held in high regard by the faithful for many years.

.006. In more recent years, a number of theologians have written general catechisms, of varying quality and usefulness. The worldwide Church on earth has a great need for instructional texts, not only for children, but also for adults. Throughout the history of the Church, many of the faithful from all walks of life have risen up to fill this need, in one way or another. Most catechisms are not documents of the Magisterium, but rather are texts written by members of the faithful in order to instruct and correct their fellow Catholic Christians. Writing a catechism is one of many ways that lay persons exercise their right and duty to spread the Gospel, which is called the apostolate of the laity.

Second Vatican Council: "The apostolate of the laity derives from their Christian vocation and the Church can never be without it."[1]

---

[1] Second Vatican Council, Apostolicam Actuositatem, Decree on the Apostolate of the Laity, n. 1.

Introduction

"The Church was founded for the purpose of spreading the kingdom of Christ throughout the earth for the glory of God the Father, to enable all men to share in His saving redemption, and that through them the whole world might enter into a relationship with Christ. All activity of the Mystical Body directed to the attainment of this goal is called the apostolate, which the Church carries on in various ways through all her members. For the Christian vocation by its very nature is also a vocation to the apostolate."[2]

"The laity derive the right and duty to the apostolate from their union with Christ the head; incorporated into Christ's Mystical Body through Baptism and strengthened by the power of the Holy Spirit through Confirmation, they are assigned to the apostolate by the Lord Himself."[3]

"The individual apostolate, flowing generously from its source in a truly Christian life (cf. John 4:14), is the origin and condition of the whole lay apostolate, even of the organized type, and it admits of no substitute. Regardless of status, all lay persons (including those who have no opportunity or possibility for collaboration in associations) are called to this type of apostolate and obliged to engage in it.... Then by the apostolate the spoken and written word, which is utterly necessary under certain circumstances, lay people announce Christ, explain and spread His teaching in accordance with one's status and ability, and faithfully profess it."[4]

The laity have the right and the duty to spread the Gospel, by both the spoken and written word, and by all of the means of social communication. Catechisms, whether or not they have the word catechism in the title, are one means of spreading the Gospel message. For all the lay faithful have been assigned by Christ Himself to be little apostles, spreading the Word of God in accord with each person's particular gifts and circumstances, helping their fellow Christians to learn the truths given to the Church by God through Sacred Tradition, Sacred Scripture, and the Magisterium. It is the task of all the faithful, but especially of theologians, to meditate upon the teachings of Tradition, Scripture, Magisterium, to seek an ever better understanding of the Faith, and to benefit the Church by sharing those insights with one another.

.007. The Character of This Catechism

This book is titled 'The Catechism of Catholic Ethics' because it is in fact a catechetical book, i.e. an instructional book, which teaches the reader on the subject of Catholic ethics. The Catechism of Catholic Ethics is a work of Roman Catholic moral theology, and like all sound theology, this book presents not only the definitive teachings of the Magisterium, but also sound theological opinion.

Suppose that a theologian attempted to write a catechism containing only the explicit written teachings of the Magisterium. He might include in the book only a series of quotes from magisterial documents, and nothing else. But then the

---

[2] Second Vatican Council, Apostolicam Actuositatem, n. 2.
[3] Second Vatican Council, Apostolicam Actuositatem, n. 3.
[4] Second Vatican Council, Apostolicam Actuositatem, n. 16.

Introduction

ordinary lay reader would easily misunderstand any such collection of quotes, if these are offered without additional explanation and interpretation. Therefore, this explanation and interpretation is needed, so that the reader may understand the teachings of the Magisterium. But any explanation or interpretation of magisterial teachings is not, per se, of the Magisterium, but is instead a commentary in the realm of theological opinion. So it benefits the reader to have theological opinion along with the definitive teachings of the Magisterium in any catechism.

Suppose that a theologian attempted to write a catechism containing the definitive teachings of the Magisterium, along with only the minimum explanation and interpretation needed to allow those teachings to be understood. But the teachings of the Catholic Faith are not solely from the Magisterium, but are from Sacred Tradition, and from Sacred Scripture, as well as from the Magisterium. Such a book would be ignoring the sources of Divine Revelation themselves, Sacred Tradition and Sacred Scripture. So it is important for every catechism not only to cite and explain magisterial documents, but also to cite and explain Sacred Scripture, as well as the writings of the Fathers, Doctors, and Saints of the Church, which are one type of expression, and one means of transmission, of Sacred Tradition. The error of attempting to base the Faith on the Magisterium alone is similar to the error of attempting to base the Faith on Scripture alone. The teachings of the Catholic Faith have a threefold basis: Tradition, Scripture, Magisterium. Catholics are bound by the moral law to believe all of the truths of Sacred Tradition and Sacred Scripture directly, as well as they are able to understand these truths, even if a particular truth has not been explicitly taught by the Magisterium.

Second Vatican Council: "It is clear, therefore, that Sacred Tradition, Sacred Scripture and the teaching authority [i.e. the Magisterium] of the Church, in accord with God's most wise design, are so linked and joined together that one cannot stand without the others, and that all together and each in its own way under the action of the one Holy Spirit contribute effectively to the salvation of souls."[5]

Another problem with this approach of keeping theological commentary in a catechism to a minimum is that the Magisterium has not answered every question on faith and morals. There are many important questions on faith and morals whose answers come from theology, based on an interpretation and application of the explicit and implicit teachings of Tradition, Scripture, Magisterium, but without a particular explicit magisterial teaching corresponding to each and every point. The faithful would understand the Catholic Faith with much less breadth and depth if theological arguments, conclusions, and opinions, were excluded from their consideration of the Faith. The faithful would understand the Catholic Faith only as isolated intellectual propositions if they abandoned all theological inquiry, arguments, assertions, conclusions, and opinions, if they abandoned the search for truth by a direct study of Tradition and Scripture, and if they adhered only to the explicit written

---

[5] Second Vatican Council, Dei Verbum, n. 10.

Introduction

teachings of the Magisterium (as indeed many wolves among the sheep claim that we must do).

.008. Theological opinions, assertions, terminology, distinctions, arguments and conclusions, as well as the pious opinions of all the faithful, based on faith and reason, based on a direct study of Tradition and Scripture, are necessary to properly understand the teachings of the Magisterium, both explicit and implicit, to join the teachings of the Magisterium with the teachings of Sacred Tradition and Sacred Scripture as one Faith, to apply these teachings to the various circumstances of life in this world, and to increase continually our understanding of the mysteries of the Faith. Those who propose the contrary, who claim that we are to live only by the explicit written teachings of the Magisterium, who disdain theological opinion, who say we are to wait for the Magisterium to decide every question, such as these have gone astray from the true Faith of the one holy Catholic and Apostolic Church, and into the error of the Pharisees.

Therefore, this catechism offers teachings on morality from the explicit and implicit teachings of Sacred Tradition, Sacred Scripture, and the Magisterium, along with that theological interpretation and commentary necessary to explain and apply those teachings, and also offers theological insights, all in order to assist the faithful in understanding Roman Catholic ethics with ever greater breadth and depth. However, this catechism is not primarily a work of theological opinion, but rather is fundamentally a work of instruction in the teachings of the Catholic Faith on morality. No one can reject every teaching in this book without committing abject heresy. No one can reject the majority of the teachings in this book, especially on the basic principles of morality, without committing heresy. All of the fundamental principles of morality found in this book are the teachings of the Roman Catholic Faith.

This catechism presents the basic principles of Catholic moral teaching, along with the application of those principles to specific areas of morality. These basic principles should not be the subject of disagreement among faithful and reasonable Catholics. The teaching of the Magisterium as well as the teaching of Tradition and Scripture, are sufficiently clear and definitive on all of the basic principles of morality. The particular expression of these principles might legitimately vary from one person to another, but the basic truths themselves are indisputable. Now amid the faithful flock of Jesus Christ, there will always be some wolves in sheep's clothing who attempt to obscure these basic principles in order to prevent their own sins from coming to light, in order that they may gain the approval of their audience, and in order that they may exalt themselves and do whatever they please, without regard for true morality. But for those Catholics who live in imitation of Christ, by the light of Tradition, Scripture, Magisterium, and by the use of both faith and reason, these basic ethical principles are the foundation of their moral life.

.009. The Catechism of Catholic Ethics is not primarily a work of speculative theology. Now in one sense all theology is speculative, since even a straightforward explanation of definitive magisterial teaching must include assertions beyond the explicit definitions of the Magisterium. But in another sense, speculative theology is that theology which proposes new insights into the Sacred Deposit of Faith, hidden within Tradition and Scripture, beyond a mere explanation of, and commentary on, magisterial teaching. However, this book is mainly concerned with presenting the clear and definitive teaching of Sacred Tradition, Sacred Scripture, and the Magisterium on morality, and with using sound moral theology to expound those definitive teachings. The particular way of phrasing and presenting these ideas may be, to some extent, new. But the teachings themselves are the ancient teachings of the Christian Faith, even as ancient as that time when the Ten Commandments were written by God on tablets of stone, and were entrusted to Moses and the Israelites.

This book also devotes extensive space to the application of these basic moral principles to various areas of morality. In many cases, the Magisterium has explicit and definitive teachings on the morality of a particular type of act. In other cases, the application of the basic principles of ethics taught by the Magisterium is relatively simple and clear. However, on some points, faithful and reasonable Catholics might disagree, not with the basic principles of ethics, and not with any particular definitive teaching, but with the particular judgment of the prudential order used to apply these principles to particular circumstances. Such disagreements are not contrary to the unity of charity which binds all the sheep into one flock, under one Shepherd.

Pope John XXIII: "Differences of opinion in the application of principles can sometimes arise even among sincere Catholics. When this happens, they should be careful not to lose their respect and esteem for each other. Instead, they should strive to find points of agreement for effective and suitable action, and not wear themselves out in interminable arguments, and, under pretext of the better or the best, omit to do the good that is possible and therefore obligatory."[6]

In addition to teachings on morals, this book also presents teachings on faith that are useful in the area of morality. This includes teachings on the nature of Sacred Tradition, Sacred Scripture, and the Magisterium, and on the spiritual authority and temporal authority of the Church. Although the Magisterium can and certainly does teach by means of reason from natural law, every moral truth is also found, at least implicitly, in the Sacred Deposit of Faith (which is comprised solely of Sacred Tradition and Sacred Scripture). Therefore, the nature of these three sources of truth, Tradition, Scripture, Magisterium, is relevant to the topic of morality. All the moral teachings of the Church are able to be understood by reason and perceived from natural law, but these same moral truths are more easily attained and more firmly held when they are obtained from Divine Revelation.

.010. The Wisdom of the Faithful

It is not always clear whether a teaching of the Magisterium has been taught infallibly, or only non-infallibly. It is not always clear if an idea is a teaching of the Magisterium, or a theological opinion. In addition, some theologians distinguish several different levels of theological opinion. But it is easily a matter

---

[6] Pope John XXIII, Mater et Magistra, n. 238.

Introduction

of dispute as to which level of theological opinion applies to any idea. If a theologian were to attempt to label every assertion by its certitude, as either infallible, non-infallible, or on one of several levels of opinion, these labels would also vary in their certitude and would often be a matter of dispute.

Some of the faithful claim that all the teachings of the Magisterium are infallible, and they also denigrate the role of theological opinion; in this way, they attempt to make the Faith seem more secure and more certain. But by no means, in this life, can we have absolute certitude on every question of faith and morals. Now by faith in the teachings of the Magisterium, we can be certain of particular truths and of the path to salvation. But only when we have the Beatific Vision of God in Heaven will our knowledge of the Roman Catholic Faith be absolute, and entirely certain. In the mean time, we must live by faith and reason, adhering to infallible teachings, as well as to non-infallible teachings (which might contain some limited error), and making substantial use of fallible theological opinion. For without the non-infallible and the fallible, the infallible by itself would not be sufficient to guide us to salvation.

So I entrust this book to the wisdom of the faithful. May they consider the contents of this catechism in accord with the law of charity. May they evaluate it, by both faith and reason, in the light of Tradition, and Scripture, and the Magisterium. May the mind of the faithful be led by the grace of God to use all that is true and good in this book in order to understand and to live the moral teachings of the Christian faith. I will leave it to the good judgment of the reader to determine which points are infallible teachings, which are non-infallible teachings, and which are sound theological opinions. The faithful and reasonable Catholic will accept all that is true and useful within this book. There are also some theological assertions in this book which might be a matter of pious disagreement among the faithful. I trust that the grace of God will guide us all to an ever fuller understanding of His Revelation in Sacred Tradition and Sacred Scripture. May the grace and peace of Jesus Christ be with all His faithful disciples.

.011. The Imprimatur

The Church has two types of authority, spiritual and temporal. The spiritual (teaching) authority of the Church, called the Magisterium, issues teachings on matters of faith, morals, and salvation. The temporal authority of the Church issues rules and rulings, which are judgments of the prudential order. These temporal decisions may well be based on doctrine, but they are not in themselves doctrine, but discipline. While the spiritual authority of the Church may teach either infallibly or non-infallibly, the temporal authority of the Church is fallible.

The imprimatur is a temporal decision of proper authority in the Church, usually of the local ordinary (the Bishop in charge of a diocese). The imprimatur permits a work on doctrine or discipline to be published. The word 'imprimatur' means 'let it be published'.

Usually a theologian has the role (called 'censor') of assisting the local Bishop in deciding whether or not to grant the imprimatur. If he considers that there is nothing that might stand in the way of the granting of the imprimatur, he grants the nihil obstat. The phrase 'nihil obstat' means 'nothing stands in the way.' No work should claim to have only the nihil obstat, without also having the imprimatur, because the nihil obstat is not essentially authoritative, but advisory. Often a Bishop does not read the work that receives, or fails to receive, the imprimatur. He relies on the advice of the censor who has reviewed the work. However, if a Bishop so wishes, he can review the work himself and give only the imprimatur; the nihil obstat in such a case would be unnecessary.

The 'imprimi potest' is the permission from a religious superior to a member of that religious order to publish a work. The phrase 'imprimi potest' means 'it is able to be published.' Only a work written by a member of a religious community requires the imprimi potest. A work by a diocesan priest or deacon, or by a lay theologian or other lay person, does not need and cannot obtain an imprimi potest.

Some works have the following text after the imprimatur and nihil obstat: "The nihil obstat and imprimatur are official declarations that a book or pamphlet is free of doctrinal and moral error. No implication is contained therein that those who have granted the nihil obstat and imprimatur agree with the opinions expressed." It is always true that the nihil obstat and imprimatur do not necessarily imply that the Bishop or the censor agree with any theological opinions in the work. A work with the imprimatur may contain theological opinion and theological errors.

In principle, the imprimatur is granted only if the work is free from that particular type of theological error which would contradict the teaching of the Magisterium on faith and morals. But since the imprimatur is issued by the temporal authority of the local Bishop, not by the teaching authority, all such decisions are fallible. In practice, some good works of theology lack the imprimatur, and some poor works of theology have somehow been granted the imprimatur. Some works with the imprimatur nevertheless contain errors on faith and morals. It would be imprudent for the faithful to assume that every book with the imprimatur was free from all theological error, or to assume that a book without the imprimatur was not a reliable source of sound doctrine on faith and morals.

.012. The Needs of the Church

In one sense, the Church is always pure, holy, true, just, faithful, loving, wise, and full of every virtue. For Christ is the head of the Church, and the Church is His body, and the Church is enlivened and guided by the Holy Spirit. But in another sense, as regards the individual members of the Church on earth, each is a sinner, and many members substantially fail to believe and to live according to the truths of the Catholic Faith. And it is in this sense that the Church today is in a dire condition. Sinful secular society has had a strong influence over many members of the Church, to the detriment of their eternal salvation. Many Catholics do not believe all that the Catholic Faith teaches. Those who do believe often fail to act in accord with those beliefs. Many objective mortal sins are found among the sheep of Christ's flock.

Introduction

There is also a dire lack of knowledge among the members of the Church on matters of faith, morals, and salvation. Many of the Church's teachings are entirely unknown, or substantially misunderstood, by most of the faithful. They know trivial facts about their favorite entertainment shows or musical groups, but they do not know even the most basic teachings of the Church on any subject. They spend several hours a day entertaining themselves with television and other forms of media. But they seldom read the Bible, or a book by a Saint, or any book of theology. Ignorance about the teachings of the Catholic Faith prevails among most members of the Church on earth today. To make matters worse, many Catholics have confused serious doctrinal errors with the teachings of the Church. Their limited understanding of Church teaching is adulterated by many false ideas, which they mistakenly think are correct belief.

Many modern-day theologians have done little to correct, and some have even worsened, this situation. This fault is "partly on account of the multiplication of useless questions, articles, and arguments"[7] as St. Thomas complained about the theologians of his day. Many theologians write obscure articles, in obscure journals, going on at great length about trivial matters that are of no use at all to the Christian striving to live in imitation of Christ and Mary. Other theologians teach in an accessible manner, but they teach only what their audience wishes to hear. Some theologians teach in an entertaining manner, but their teaching is superficial. Worse of all are those theologians who are blind guides, who teach what is contrary to the truths of faith and morals taught by Christ through Tradition, Scripture, Magisterium. Few theologians in the world today teach the truth, in a way that is accessible and comprehensible to the ordinary Catholic, in contradiction to the popular sins and heresies of the day, with good insight into the Catholic Faith based not only on study, but also on living the Faith from day to day.

In addition to the grievous harm done by certain theologians who present inaccurate and false teachings, the Church today is plagued by ignorant and arrogant persons who teach without first having learned. If they were ignorant but also humble, then they would seek knowledge before teaching, and then their teaching would be useful. If they were arrogant but knowledgeable, then at least their teaching would be generally correct, which again would be of some use. But since they are both arrogant and ignorant, they teach falsehoods and refuse all correction and learning. They assume that correct Catholic teaching is nothing other than the ideas in their own uneducated mind. Whatever seems right to them, they assume that the same is Catholic teaching. When confronted by sources in Tradition, Scripture, Magisterium, demonstrating that their teaching is contrary to the teaching of the Church, they conclude that the Church should change Her teaching.

Persons such as this have little interest in reading the writings of the Saints, Fathers, and Doctors of the Church, and no interest at all in reading the writings of ordinary theologians. They have not taken the time to read the documents of

---

[7] St. Thomas Aquinas, Summa Theologica, Introduction.

Introduction

Popes and Councils. They teach without knowledge, and they despise anyone who attempts to teach or to correct them. They do not seem to care that their teaching is ignorant and false. They assert numerous false doctrines, even to the extent of heresy. They present endless arguments to support whatever falsehood they have asserted, but their arguments are faulty, or baseless, or heretical, or even completely absurd. Some of these persons do not even offer an argument to support their many false assertions. Persons like this have been multiplied in the Church today.

.013. And as a result, very many Catholics today do not understand even the most basic teachings of the Catholic Faith on morality. They do not know how to determine if a sin is venial or mortal. They do not understand that some acts are intrinsically evil, and therefore never moral, regardless of intention or circumstances. They do not understand the basic terminology of moral theology. Perhaps they are able to say that the end does not justify the means, but when evaluating the morality of a choice before them, they often use the end to justify the means without realizing it. They have never heard of the three fonts of morality. They have no idea what a moral object is. They cannot distinguish between formal cooperation, immediate material cooperation, and mediate material cooperation, because they have never heard of these concepts.

They do not understand the principle of double effect, nor do they know what the sin of scandal is. They have never heard of positive and negative precepts. They do not understand the difference between direct abortion and indirect abortion. When facing a question concerning the morality of an act, they have no idea how to determine if the act is moral or not. They mistakenly think that conscience is supreme, even above Church teaching on morality. There is a widespread lack of understanding on morality among the faithful, not only on particular magisterial decisions on particular ethical questions, but more importantly on the basic principles of morality found throughout Sacred Tradition and Sacred Scripture, and upon which the Magisterium itself relies in answering particular moral questions.

If the Magisterium has explicitly stated that a particular act is immoral, they might know that the act is immoral, but not why it is immoral. If the Magisterium has not explicitly stated that a particular act is immoral, they have no idea where to begin in order to evaluate the morality of that act. Some even think that they are free to ignore the clear and definitive teachings of Sacred Tradition and Sacred Scripture on morality, as long as the Magisterium has not explicitly stated a decision on a particular question. They feel bound by explicit magisterial statements, but not by the basic moral principles of the eternal moral law, not by Sacred Tradition, not by Sacred Scripture, and not by all that is necessarily implied by the explicit teachings of the Magisterium.

Some Catholics almost completely ignore Catholic teaching on morality, instead relying on whatever is the common secular norm. The majority opinion in secular society, on almost any issue of morality, is often also the majority opinion among those who call themselves Catholic, in contradiction to, or in ignorance of, the teachings of the Faith. Perhaps this is one reason why so many

Introduction

Catholic accept and use contraception, as if this were moral, despite the definitive teaching of the Church against contraception. They have accepted secular society as their teacher on morality; they do not consider the Church to be their teacher.

.014. The Purpose of this Book

The purpose of this book is to offer to the faithful a clear and concise presentation of the teachings of Sacred Tradition, Sacred Scripture, and the Magisterium on the basic principles of morality, along with sound theological opinion and a multitude of examples of the application of those principles. This book does not attempt to answer every moral question. Instead, by teaching the faithful to understand and to apply the basic principles of morality, the faithful should be able to answer almost any moral question, in any area of life, by their own faith and knowledge. For all of the teachings of the Faith on morality are based on these basic principles.

It is more useful to teach the reader to understand and to apply the basic principles of ethics, than to attempt to answer a large number of specific questions on morality. No list of specific questions and answers on morality can address every possible ethical situation. But with a sound understanding of the basic principles of morality, the reader can then apply these principles in order to answer specific ethical questions and to solve moral dilemmas. Give a man a fish and he will eat for a day; teach a man to fish and he will eat for a lifetime. So do not be surprised if this book does not contain a particular answer to each and every particular moral question. Instead, let this book teach you the basic principles of morality and how to apply them. Then you will be able to find the answers to your moral questions by faith and reason.

The examples of moral and immoral acts in this book are hypothetical. They are not descriptions of particular real persons or events. However, similar types of moral dilemmas have certainly occurred many times in human history. The purpose of each example is to illustrate the basic principles of morality and their application.

.015. About the Author

The author of this book, The Catechism of Catholic Ethics, is Ronald L. Conte Jr., a Roman Catholic lay theologian and Bible translator.

My work in theology includes writings in moral theology, dogmatic theology, and speculative theology. Previous to writing this catechism, I wrote a number of articles on morality, including articles on various topics in sexual ethics. I also wrote a series of articles on Sacred Tradition, Sacred Scripture, and the Magisterium. I have written several books on eschatology, as well as numerous articles refuting the doctrinal errors and other false claims of various alleged private revelations. I have written a comprehensive book of New Testament Biblical chronology, and a book of speculative theology, concerned mainly with the Virgin Mary and the Most Holy Trinity.

Introduction

My books on eschatology are titled: The Bible and the Future of the World, The Secrets of Medjugorje and Garabandal Revealed, The First Part of the Tribulation, and my forthcoming book, The Second Part of the Tribulation. My work of New Testament Biblical chronology is titled: Important Dates in the Lives of Jesus and Mary. And my book of speculative theology is titled: New Insights into the Deposit of Faith.

Ronald L. Conte Jr. is also the sole translator and editor of the Catholic Public Domain Version (CPDV) of the Sacred Bible.

I translated the Latin Bible (specifically the Pope Sixtus V and Pope Clement VIII Latin Vulgate) into modern English, using the Challoner Douay Bible as a guide. This translation is called the Catholic Public Domain Version. I have placed the entire translation in the public domain, for use by all the faithful as they see fit. The Catholic Public Domain Version adheres to the Vatican Norms for Bible Translation issued by the Congregation for the Doctrine of the Faith in 1997, under then Cardinal Ratzinger. In accord with those norms, the CPDV does not impose inclusive language on the text. The CPDV is a fairly literal translation of the Latin source text, and does not loosely rephrase any verse or passage. The Old Testament was translated in the light of the New Testament, and both Testaments were translated in the light of Roman Catholic teaching.

I have used the internet extensively in my theology work: to make my translation of the Bible freely and widely available, to publish theology writings, to discuss the Faith with my fellow Catholics, and to reach out to the faithful around the world.

.016. About the Section Numbers

Numbers, beginning and ending with a period, are used in this book to mark different sections. The reason for this numbering is to permit uniform referencing of this work. At a later time, this book might be printed in different formats, with larger or smaller print, or with larger or smaller page sizes, so that references by page number would differ from one edition to another. Also, at a later time, the author might elect to place the book on the internet, on a series of web pages, where citations by page number would not apply. The use of this numbering system does not imply anything about the contents.

.017. About the Cover images

The front cover image is a photo of a stained glass window which depicts Adam and Eve, after they sinned and fell from grace, as they are being expelled from Paradise by an Angel with a flaming sword. The text across the window says: LIGNUM VITÆ MICHÆLUS ADAM HEVA which translates as "Tree of life, Michael, Adam, Eve." The text is difficult to read because of the unusual script, and also because the letter 'S' at the end of Michaelus and the letter 'H' at the start of Heva are each covered by a foot in the design of the window. The Latin text for Genesis 3:20 gives the spelling of Eve's name as 'Heva.'

The back cover image is of the Crucifixion, the source of all grace for repentance and forgiveness. At the foot of the Cross are Mary and the Apostle John. The other woman pictured is probably Saint Mary Magdalene; her position at he foot of the Cross calls to mind her anointing of His feet a short time before His Crucifixion. "And standing beside the cross of Jesus were his mother, and his mother's sister, and Mary of Cleophas, and Mary Magdalene." (Jn 19:25). His mother's sister is the older sister of the Virgin Mary. Mary of Cleophas is her daughter, the Virgin Mary's niece. Beside the Cross in the image is the soldier who pierced the side of Christ, Cassius Longinus. In the image, he has not yet pierced Christ's side.

The entire moral law is implicit in the single act of Christ dying for our salvation on the Cross.

Introduction

Chapter 1
The Basis for Morality

.018.
God alone is good.
The goodness of God is the basis for all morality.

[Luke]
{18:19} Then Jesus said to him: "Why do you call me good? No one is good except God alone."

[2 Maccabees]
{1:24} And the prayer of Nehemiah was held in this way: "O Lord God, Creator of all, terrible and strong, just and merciful, you alone are the good King.
{1:25} You alone are excellent, you alone are just, and all-powerful, and eternal, who frees Israel from all evil, who created the chosen fathers and sanctified them."

Everything created by God has goodness, but God alone is Goodness. Only God is perfect and infinite Goodness, by His very Nature.

Saint Thomas Aquinas: "God alone is good essentially.... and He is not directed to anything else as to an end, but is Himself the last end of all things. Hence it is manifest that God alone has every kind of perfection by His own essence; therefore He Himself alone is good essentially."[8]

God is offended by all bad acts because He is good. Acts that are moral are good before God. Acts that are immoral are not good before God. An immoral act is a bad act; it is an evil act. Evil is always contrary to good.

The Nature of God determines whether a knowingly chosen act is either good or evil. All that is good is in some way like God, and all that is evil is in some way contrary to God. All moral acts in some way resemble the very Nature of God, and all immoral acts in some way oppose the very Nature of God. The eternal unchanging Goodness of God is what makes one act moral and another act immoral. Good acts can never become evil, and evil acts can never become good, because God is eternal unchanging Goodness itself.

.019. The term 'act' or 'human act' in moral theology refers specifically to those types of acts by human persons which are, or can be, knowingly chosen. The term 'evil' or 'moral evil' refers to any morally illicit act, i.e. to any sin, even to the smallest semi-deliberate venial sin. The term 'licit' in moral theology refers to the moral law, such that whatever is licit is not a sin, and whatever is illicit is a sin.

An internal (or interior) act is an act that is confined to the heart and mind (the will and intellect). An external (or exterior) act is an act that reaches beyond the heart and mind (the will and intellect). An exterior knowingly chosen act

---

[8] Saint Thomas Aquinas, Summa Theologica, I., Q. 6. A. 3.

includes the interior use of will and intellect, since any knowing choice is made by the will and intellect. If an exterior act is not knowingly chosen, then the act is not an actual sin, but it may be an objective sin.

Example: Coveting your neighbor's wife is an internal (or interior) act. Committing adultery with your neighbor's wife is an external (or exterior) act. The exterior act of adultery includes the interior knowing choice of the act. An act of adultery may well be accompanied by other interior acts, such as an interior act of coveting your neighbor's wife. Each of these acts is gravely immoral, and each has its own culpability.

.020. Types of Sin

Sin is nothing else but an immoral act. Actual sin is a knowingly chosen immoral act. Any knowingly chosen act, moral or immoral, is made by the free will based on knowledge within the intellect (the mind). All knowingly chosen acts are either morally good or morally bad. Each and every knowingly chosen act must be good in order to avoid sin.

This knowledge pertains to whether or not the act is moral. If an individual acts without the knowledge (or sincere belief) that the act is immoral, then he acts without knowledge and without culpability. This knowledge is prior to the chosen act; any knowledge obtained after the chosen act does not affect the culpability of a past act.

This choice is a choice of the free will, based on the knowledge (or sincere belief) of the morality of the act. If an individual acts without a choice of the free will, then he acts without choice and without culpability. Whenever anyone freely chooses to commit an act, which he knows (or sincerely believes) at the time is immoral, he sins. Any substantial reduction in knowledge of the morality of the act, or in freedom of choice, substantially reduces culpability.

An objective sin is an act that is immoral, without consideration as to whether or not it was knowingly chosen. An objective sin is also an actual sin, if it is done by a knowing choice. A merely objective sin is an objective sin that is done without the knowledge that the act was immoral, or without a free choice of the will. Each and every actual sin includes culpability (guilt) before God for that sin. A merely objective sin includes no culpability, because the act was not knowingly chosen. A sin can be an actual sin, but not an objective sin, if the act is moral, but the individual freely committed the act in the belief that it was immoral. A sin can be an objective sin, but not an actual sin, if the act is immoral, but the individual committed the act in the belief that it was moral, or without free choice.

.021. A venial sin is an act that is not so gravely immoral before God as to be entirely incompatible with true love of God and neighbor. An actual venial sin does not include sufficient culpability to take away the state of grace from the soul, nor to deserve eternal damnation. A venial sin is always in some way contrary to true love of God and neighbor, but to a substantially limited extent.

An actual venial sin always includes some culpability and some lack of cooperation with grace, and always deserves some degree of punishment.

A mortal sin is an act that is so gravely immoral before God as to be entirely incompatible with true love of God and neighbor. An actual mortal sin includes sufficient culpability to take away the state of grace from the soul, and to deserve eternal damnation.

Saint Thomas Aquinas: "Therefore when the soul is so disordered by sin as to turn away from its last end, viz. God, to Whom it is united by charity, there is mortal sin; but when it is disordered without turning away from God, there is venial sin."[9]

Pope John Paul II: "And when through sin, the soul commits a disorder that reaches the point of turning away from its ultimate end, God, to which it is bound by charity, then the sin is mortal; on the other hand, whenever the disorder does not reach the point of a turning away from God, the sin is venial. For this reason venial sin does not deprive the sinner of sanctifying grace, friendship with God, charity and therefore eternal happiness, whereas just such a deprivation is precisely the consequence of mortal sin."[10]

Mortal sin differs from venial sin both by degree and by type. Any mortal sin is more serious than any venial sin, so they differ by degree. Mortal sins are greater in degree, since they offend God more. But mortal sin is also a different type of sin, the type that deserves eternal punishment. No one is ever sent to Hell merely for unrepentant venial sins. But one unrepentant actual mortal sin is sufficient to condemn the person to eternal punishment in Hell.[11]

.022. Whosoever dies in a state of grace is saved and will have eternal life in Heaven. Whosoever dies not in a state of grace is condemned and will have eternal death in Hell. Repentance from any and all actual mortal sins, prior to death, is absolutely required for eternal life (eternal salvation).

The matter of an act is the objective morality of the act, apart from knowledge and choice. If an act was not freely chosen, or if an act was not chosen in the knowledge that the act is immoral, then there is no actual sin. But objectively, the act may still be immoral. When we consider the matter of the act, we are considering whether or not the act is an objective sin. Whenever an objective sin is knowingly chosen, then that objective sin is also an actual sin.

An objective mortal sin is any act that is gravely immoral, without consideration as to whether or not it was knowingly chosen. An objective mortal sin is also an actual mortal sin, if the act was done with full knowledge (or belief) that the act was gravely immoral, and by a fully deliberate choice. A merely objective mortal sin is an objective mortal sin that is not also an actual mortal sin, because the act

---

[9] St. Thomas Aquinas, Summa Theologica, I-II, Q. 72, A. 5.
[10] Pope John Paul II, Reconciliation and Penance, n. 17; he cites St. Thomas Aquinas, Summa Theologica, I-II, Q. 72, A. 5.
[11] Pope Benedict XII, On the Beatific Vision of God; Council of Florence, 6 July 1439.

was done without full knowledge that the act was gravely immoral, or without a fully deliberate choice of the free will.

An objective mortal sin is without any culpability, if the act was done without any knowledge that the act was immoral, or without any deliberate choice of the free will. An objective mortal sin has substantially reduced culpability, to the extent of an actual venial sin, if the act was done with substantially less than full knowledge that the act was gravely immoral, or by substantially less than a fully deliberate choice. Relatively minor reductions in culpability, due to a less than substantial reduction in knowledge or deliberation, are not sufficient to prevent a knowingly chosen objective mortal sin from being also an actual mortal sin.

.023. Knowledge

When a lack of knowledge is willful, as when an individual deliberately and substantially refuses to seek knowledge pertaining to morality, either generally or with regard to a particular act, the objective sin is also an actual sin, despite the lack of knowledge, since the lack of knowledge is substantially culpable.

When there is a substantial lack of knowledge that the act is immoral, despite substantial sincere efforts by the individual to find the truth of morality as it pertains to that act and to acts in general, then the culpability is substantially reduced, even in some cases to the extent of no culpability at all. This complete reduction of culpability is called invincible ignorance. It occurs when the individual did not know and could not know, within the particular limitations of that individual's life, that the act was immoral.

Example: A non-Catholic pregnant woman chooses to have a direct abortion to save her own life, not realizing that direct abortion is always gravely immoral, even to save the life of the mother. If she truly had no knowledge at all that this particular choice was immoral, then she would lack culpability, even though direct abortion is always objectively gravely immoral. So in this case, the act would be an objective mortal sin, but not an actual mortal sin. Hypothetically, she could have known that this type of abortion is gravely immoral by accepting the teachings of the Catholic Church. But within the limits of her knowledge and sincere beliefs at the time, and within the extent and limit of her ability to reason about morality (which in all of us is harmed by original sin, past personal sins, and the sinfulness of society), she could not have known that the act was gravely immoral. So in this case, the ignorance was invincible.

Invincible ignorance applies within the limits of the individual's ability to find the truth about a particular moral decision within a particular situation. The ignorance need not be absolutely invincible. The entire moral law is accessible to reason and theoretically can be attained by reason alone. Yet the ignorance is still invincible and the act still lacks all culpability, if the individual could not attain to the correct understanding of the morality of a particular act within their current limitations at the time of the act. Absolute perfection in seeking moral truth is not required to have invincible ignorance.

But sincere and substantial incorrect knowledge (mistaken belief) does not always excuse the individual from culpability with regard to sin. If the individual sincerely but mistakenly believes that an act is immoral, and yet he knowingly chooses the act despite this belief, then he sins.

Example: A physician believes, incorrectly, that indirect abortion is always gravely immoral, and despite this incorrect sincere belief, he still performs a treatment that constitues an indirect abortion, in order to save the life of the mother, when also the prenatal's life cannot be saved. The act is not objectively immoral, but it is still an actual mortal sin, because he believed that the act was gravely immoral, yet he freely chose to do that act. His sincere lack of correct knowledge does not excuse the act, because he freely chose to do what he sincerely believed to be immoral.

.024. Also, if the person does not know that the act is immoral, but does not care if the act is immoral, then he sins. It is always a sin to act without concern for good or evil. Ignorance as to whether or not an act is moral is not invincible ignorance if, as the Second Vatican Council taught, the person "cares but little for truth and goodness."[12] The sincere search for moral truth by the conscience is essential for a human person to avoid sin.

In some cases, a person may have an inner conflict as to whether or not an act is moral. To some extent, the individual may know in their heart that a particular act is morally wrong. But then, when reasoning about the morality of the act, he concludes that it is moral. This individual argues to himself that the act is justified, but he knows, to a limited extent in his conscience, perhaps in a way that is beyond expression in words, that the act is immoral. In such cases, there is a type of knowledge that the act is immoral, so the free choice of such an act would be an actual sin. The culpability may be substantially reduced, if the person is sincerely conflicted about whether or not the act is moral, thinking in his mind that it is moral, but knowing to a limited extent in his heart that it is not moral.

Examples of partial knowledge that an act is a sin: (1) The person knows to some extent in his heart that the act is a sin, but he reasons incorrectly in his mind that it is moral. (2) The person reasons that the act is moral, but with some degree of insincerity. (3) The person thinks that the act is moral, but with substantial reason for doubt.

But if the individual fully realizes in his heart that the act is immoral, and if his reasoning about the morality of the act is merely a rationalization, (an insincere use of reason, not seeking truth, but seeking an excuse to act apart from morality) then the knowledge would be full. In such cases, if the choice (deliberation) is also full, and the sin is objectively gravely immoral, then the knowing choice of that act would be an actual mortal sin.

---

[12] Second Vatican Council, Gaudium et Spes, n. 16.

.025. Free Will

Human persons are able to sin because they have free will. An actual sin is any act that is known (or believed) to be immoral and is freely chosen. A lack of knowledge (pertaining to the morality of the act) reduces culpability. A lack of free choice also reduces culpability. When there is a complete lack of freedom in choosing, or when no choice at all was made, then no actual sin was committed and there is no culpability.

A free choice is a deliberate choice. Deliberation is not a length of time in considering what to choose. No particular length of time in deliberating is needed for culpability. Deliberation is the resolve of the will to knowingly commit the act. If a person is fully resolved to commit an act, then the deliberation is full. Although full deliberation often involves a length of time in considering the act, all that is needed for full deliberation is a full resolve to act.

Deliberation is based on knowledge, for a person cannot be resolved to choose an act, unless he knows what he is choosing. If a person is fully resolved to commit an act, but he does not know that the act is immoral, then there is no culpability, because the free choice was not the choice of an act known (or believed) to be immoral. But in such a case, the reduction of culpability is from a lack of knowledge, not from a lack of free choice. Knowledge and free choice are closely related and interdependent, but distinct.

In many cases, the knowing choice of an immoral act is semi-deliberate. The person might have an inner conflict as to whether or not to choose an act. And if a choice is then required by the situation, the person might make a quick decision (to choose an act known to be immoral) without full deliberation (full resolve). This type of semi-deliberate choice reduces culpability. For a sin to be an actual mortal sin, both the knowledge and the free choice must be full, and the sin must be known (or believed) to be objectively a serious sin (an objective mortal sin).

Often, semi-deliberate sins are interior sins of the mind and heart. The human person in the fallen state is susceptible, due to concupiscence (a tendency toward sin resulting from original sin) to passing sinful thoughts. The consent (free choice) to such thoughts often does not have full resolve (full deliberation). If the interior sin is an objective mortal sin, the culpability would be reduced to that of an actual venial sin, if the choice (deliberation) is substantially less than full. If the sin is an objective venial sin, the culpability would be reduced to a less serious venial sin because the choice (deliberation) is substantially less than full.

.026. Types of Knowledge and Choice

An actual sin is a knowingly chosen immoral act. This knowledge is specifically the knowledge of the immorality of the chosen act, and this choice is specifically the free choice by the will of the known immoral act.

A mere objective sin is also an immoral act, an act that is objectively immoral. But with mere objective sin, either there is no knowledge that the act is immoral, or there is no free choice. Even so, a mere objective sin always includes the choice of the act, and the knowledge of which act is being chosen. Even if the choice was not a free choice, the person chose to act. Even if the knowledge was not knowledge that the act was immoral, the person knew which act was being chosen. Otherwise, the act is not an actual sin, and is not an objective sin, and is not truly an act at all (as that term is used in moral theology).

There are two types of knowledge which apply to the morality of acts: the mere knowledge as to which act is being chosen, and the knowledge as to whether or not that act is moral. There are two types of choice which apply to the morality of acts: the mere choice of a particular act, and the exercise of free will in the choice of that particular act.

An actual sin includes both types of knowledge. The person knows which act he is choosing, and he also knows that the act is immoral. An actual sin also includes both types of choice. The person chooses a particular act, and he makes that choice by an exercise of his free will.

A mere objective sin includes one or both types of knowledge, and one or both types of choice, but not all four. A lack of knowledge that the chosen act is immoral, or a lack of free will in the choosing of that act, causes the immoral act to be merely an objective sin, and not also an actual sin. An actual sin includes all four: both types of knowledge and both types of choice. A mere objective sin includes two or three of those four: either both types of knowledge and a choice that is not free, or both types of choice but only the knowledge as to which act is chosen.

But if there is no choice at all, not even a choice without freedom, or if there is no knowledge at all, not even the knowledge of which act is being chosen, then there is no sin at all, neither actual sin, nor objective sin. If there is no choice at all, or if there is no knowledge at all, then there is no act, and therefore there is no sin at all, neither actual sin, nor objective sin. For every sin is an act. If there is evil but there is no act, then the evil is merely physical evil (harm or disorder), and not moral evil. (See the chapter on Types of Evil.)

Examples: (1) A woman freely chooses to procure a direct abortion, knowing that abortion is gravely immoral; her sin is an actual mortal sin. (2) A woman procures a direct abortion, because the pregnancy endangers her life, mistakenly thinking that direct abortion is moral when the mother's life is in danger. If she sincerely did not know that direct abortion is intrinsically evil and always gravely immoral, even when the mother's life is in danger, and if she sincerely believed that the act was moral, without substantial negligence in seeking moral truth, then her sin is an objective mortal sin, but not an actual mortal sin. (3) A woman is pregnant and has a miscarriage. There was no human act, i.e. no knowingly chosen act at all, and so this is neither an actual sin, nor a mere objective sin. The death of the prenatal child is a type of harm (physical evil), because it is the loss of an innocent human life, but there is no sin.

Examples: (1) A man deliberately chooses to ingest poison in order to commit suicide, knowing that suicide is gravely immoral; his sin is an actual mortal sin. (2) A terminally-ill man ingests poison in order to commit suicide, mistakenly believing that suicide can be moral in some circumstances. In truth, suicide is intrinsically evil and always gravely immoral. If he was sincere in his mistaken belief, without substantial negligence in seeking moral truth, then his act was an objective mortal sin, but not an actual mortal sin.

(3) A man knowingly chooses to have a salad for dinner. He does not know that the mushrooms in the salad are poisonous; he dies as a result of eating that salad. The act of ingesting the mushrooms would seem to be a knowingly chosen act. But the man only chose to ingest what he believed to be food. A person can only exercise free will based on knowledge in the intellect. He did not know that the mushrooms were poisonous, and so the act of ingesting the poison was not a knowingly chosen act in any sense of the term. He did not choose to ingest poison, neither as an act of free will, nor even as a choice that was lacking in true freedom or full consent. He did not possess either of the two types of knowledge, specifically, knowledge of which act is being chosen, or knowledge of the morality of the chosen act. His act of ingesting the mushrooms was neither an actual sin, nor an objective sin. His act was not moral evil, despite the harm (physical evil) that occurred. His knowing choice to ingest what he believed was food was a moral act. He did not commit the knowingly chosen act of ingesting poison.

Examples: (1) A man knowingly chooses to drive while intoxicated. He chooses this act despite his knowledge that the lives of other persons, and his own life, will be placed in danger, to some degree. Fortunately, no one is killed or harmed. Yet this act is an actual sin. The man anticipated that grave harm could possibly result from his choice, and he knowingly chose to act with disregard for this harm. Even though the harm did not occur, the sinful choice is the same. The seriousness of the sin depends on the likelihood that the grave harm would occur.

(2) A man incorrectly judges that he is sober enough to drive, but he crashes the vehicle and kills someone. If he was sincere in his mistaken judgment that grave harm was very unlikely because he did not have much to drink, he avoided actual sin. He did not knowingly choose an immoral act. However, his judgment of the circumstances, especially the likely bad consequences, was in error; his choice was an objective sin.

(3) A man drives his car without any negligence. A person suddenly runs out in front of the vehicle, and the driver has no opportunity to stop before the car hits and kills the person. In this case, the driver did not choose a sinful act, neither an actual sin, nor a merely objective sin. There was no choice to kill, nor was there any knowledge that driving the car, at that time, in that place, would likely result in a death. Therefore, the death of the pedestrian is a type of harm (physical evil), not moral evil. For morality only pertains to knowingly chosen acts. If there is no choice at all, or no knowledge at all, then there is no immoral act, not even objectively.

Chapter 2
The Eternal Moral Law

.027.
God Exists. God is Good. God is Love. God is Wisdom. God is Justice. God is Mercy. God is Truth. God is One. In God, existence, goodness, love, wisdom, justice, mercy, truth, and all that is truly and absolutely good, are One and are the very Nature of God. Every immoral act is contrary to the will and nature of God. Every moral act is in harmony with the will and nature of God. The moral law is inherent to the Nature of God.

The moral law is not a set of written laws, although any requirement of the moral law can be written down. The moral law is not a set of decisions made by God about good and evil. The moral law is not a particular set of just laws, although all just laws are based on the moral law. The moral law is not the implementation of justice in particular cases. The moral law is justice itself. All that is contrary to the moral law is contrary to justice itself. All that is in agreement with the moral law is in agreement with justice itself. Although the whole moral law, in any and all of its requirements, can be understood by reason alone, and can be expressed in particular laws and implemented in particular cases, the moral law as a whole is greater than reason and greater than any set of written laws.

The moral law is justice itself. God is Justice. Therefore, God is the moral law. All injustice is contrary to the very Nature of God. All justice is in agreement with the very Nature of God. Nothing is immoral unless it is immoral before God. Nothing is moral unless it is moral before God. Whoever rejects the moral law, rejects God. Whoever accepts the moral law, accepts God. Whoever follows the moral law, obeys God. Whoever follows the moral law, imitates God.

[Ephesians]
{5:1} Therefore, as most beloved sons, be imitators of God.

[Matthew]
{5:48} "Therefore, be perfect, even as your heavenly Father is perfect."

Saint Thomas Aquinas: "Wherefore as the type of the Divine Wisdom, inasmuch as by It all things are created, has the character of art, exemplar or idea; so the type of Divine Wisdom, as moving all things to their due end, bears the character of law. Accordingly the eternal law is nothing else than the type of Divine Wisdom, as directing all actions and movements."[13]

Since God is Wisdom, and Justice, and Love, and Mercy, and Goodness itself, God is the moral law. And so the moral law is also referred to as the eternal law of God. For the eternal moral law is nothing other than the Just Nature of God. God is Justice, and so God is the eternal moral law. Whoever knows the moral law, knows God. Whoever loves the moral law, loves God. Ignorance of the moral law is ignorance of God. Hatred of the moral law is hatred of God.

---

[13] St. Thomas Aquinas, Summa Theologica, I-II, Q. 93, A. 1.

The Eternal Moral Law

Whoever would love God, must first know God, and whoever would know God, must first know the moral law. Knowledge of God without knowledge of morality is ignorance of God.

Saint Thomas Aquinas: "So then no one can know the eternal law, as it is in itself, except the blessed who see God in His Essence. But every rational creature knows it in its reflection, greater or less. For every knowledge of truth is a kind of reflection and participation of the eternal law, which is the unchangeable truth, as Augustine says (De Vera Relig. xxxi)."[14]

The moral law is justice itself. God is the eternal moral law because the very Nature of God is infinitely just. The moral law is not any written set of laws; the moral law is the Justice of God, which is His very Nature. Only those who have the Beatific Vision of God know the eternal moral law as it is in itself. The whole moral law is accessible to reason, not in the sense that reason can entirely comprehend God who is infinite Justice, but only in the sense that reason is able to comprehend any and all requirements of the moral law, including general principles and particular moral decisions.

.028. The moral law is eternal and universal and unchanging. The moral law applies to all persons, at all times, in all circumstances, without any exception. The moral law is eternal and universal and unchanging, because God is eternal and universal and unchanging. God is all-knowing, and present everywhere, and eternal, and unchanging. The moral law did not change when the Old Testament covenant was established. The moral law did not change when the New Testament covenant was established. The moral law did not change when one Ecumenical Council or another issued its teachings. The moral law will not change when Christ Returns. The moral law will not change when God takes away heaven and earth, and makes a new heaven and a new earth. The moral law is unchanging because God is unchanging. The moral law is eternal because God is eternal.

The moral law is universal, applying to all persons, at all times, in all places, in all situations. There is no context in which the moral law changes, or in which the principles of morality are different, or in which nothing is immoral, or in which the moral law does not apply, or in which the moral law applies only in a limited way, or only to a limited extent. All the principles of the moral law are universal, applying to all persons, at all times, in all places, in all situations.

The moral law is a type of law. The moral law is the archetype of all law. The moral law is the one law above all other laws, from which all particular just laws are derived. The moral law is ultimately the law of justice itself. God is Justice. God is the eternal moral law.

All that applies to just laws in general also applies to the moral law, with the provision that the moral law exceeds all other laws by being the eternal Justice of God. No law has any legitimate authority, and no law is recognized as a law in

---

[14] St. Thomas Aquinas, Summa Theologica, I-II, Q. 91, A. 2.

the eyes of God, unless it is based upon the eternal moral law. And all human persons are subject to the moral law equally.

Pope John Paul II: "It makes no difference whether one is the master of the world or the 'poorest of the poor' on the face of the earth. Before the demands of morality we are all absolutely equal."[15]

.029. An unjust law is not a law.

All unjust laws are contrary to the eternal moral law, and therefore contrary to God, who is Justice, who is the eternal moral law. Whoever obeys the moral law, obeys God. Whoever disobeys the moral law, disobeys God. Whoever obeys justice, obeys God. Whoever disobeys justice, disobeys God.

Saint Augustine: "For it seems to me that an unjust law is no law at all."[16]

Pope Leo XIII: "For laws are to be obeyed only insofar as they conform with right reason and thus with the eternal law of God."[17]

Saint Thomas Aquinas: "Human law is law only in virtue of its accordance with right reason: and thus it is manifest that it flows from the eternal law. And in so far as it deviates from right reason it is called an unjust law; in such case it is no law at all, but rather a species of violence."[18]

An unjust law is not a law.

All just laws are (1) reasonable, (2) of proper authority, (3) for the common good, (4) promulgated, and (5) enforced.

Saint Thomas Aquinas: "Thus from the four preceding articles, the definition of law may be gathered; and it is nothing else than an ordinance of reason, for the common good, made by him who has care of the community, and promulgated."[19]

But elsewhere Saint Thomas also states that violations of law (human or Divine) are punished. Therefore, the definition of just law includes enforcement, by means of the punishment (and threat of that punishment) of those who offend against the law.

Saint Thomas Aquinas: "for the sinner acts against his reason, and against human and Divine law. Wherefore he incurs a threefold punishment; one, inflicted by himself, viz. remorse of conscience; another, inflicted by man; and a third, inflicted by God."[20]

---

[15] Pope John Paul II, Veritatis Splendor, n. 96.
[16] St. Augustine, On Free Choice of the Will, n. 5.
[17] Pope Leo XIII, Rerum Novarum, n. 72.
[18] St. Thomas Aquinas, Summa Theologica, I-II, Q. 93, A. 3.
[19] St. Thomas Aquinas, Summa Theologica, I-II, Q. 90, A. 4.
[20] St. Thomas Aquinas, Summa Theologica, I-II, Q. 87, A. 1.

.030. (1) An unreasonable law is not a law.

The Justice of God is wise, and the Wisdom of God is just. Since God is Justice and Wisdom, the eternal moral law is always inherently just and reasonable. Therefore, every unreasonable law is contrary to the eternal moral law. An unreasonable law is necessarily an unjust law. Laws are only just when they are reasonable. And it is by means of reason that created persons perceive moral truths about justice.

Saint Thomas Aquinas: "Therefore all laws, in so far as they partake of right reason, are derived from the eternal law. Hence Augustine says (De Lib. Arb. i, 6) that 'in temporal law there is nothing just and lawful, but what man has drawn from the eternal law.' "[21]

The eternal moral law of God is always inherently just and reasonable and wise and loving and merciful. For the moral law is that eternal justice which is the very Nature of God. God is the source of reason and wisdom and justice and all that is good. As a result, the moral law is always accessible to reason, and always in accord with reason. And reason is able to perceive and to understand each and every requirement of the eternal moral law.

(2) A law not made by proper authority is not a law.

Laws are issued by the person (or group of persons) that has legislative authority. God is the supreme legislator of the moral law. However, the moral law is not merely issued by God. The moral law is justice itself, and justice is inherent to the very Nature of God. Is God bound by the moral law? God is the eternal moral law, and since He cannot do anything contrary to His own Divine Nature, God can never do anything unjust or immoral. God never violates the moral law, for He cannot contradict Himself. God never requires His creatures to violate the moral law, for He cannot deny Himself.

[2 Timothy]
{2:13} If we are unfaithful, he remains faithful: he is not able to deny himself.

God is justice, and His justice is love. God is love, and His love is merciful. God is mercy, and His mercy is just. In God, mercy and love and justice are One, and are the very Nature of God.

(3) A law contrary to the common good is not a law.

The moral law is ordered by love of God and neighbor, and therefore following the moral law is always good in God's eyes and always ultimately best for everyone. However, in the short-sighted understanding of sinful human persons, sometimes what is moral seems contrary to the common good, and sometimes what is immoral seems in accord with the common good. But in truth, whatever is immoral is not only an offense against God, who is infinite love, but also harmful to humanity.

---

[21] St. Thomas Aquinas, Summa Theologica, I-II, Q. 93, A. 3.

The saying is true: "An injustice anywhere is an injustice everywhere."[22] Even if an offense against the moral law would seem to have no effect on anyone, except the person who commits the offense, the rest of humanity suffers because that person (in rejecting cooperation with grace) has less to offer his neighbor. Every offense against the moral law is a rejection of the grace of God. Every immoral act is done apart from the grace of God.

Every human person is a part of the human race. Each human person's knowingly chosen acts necessarily affect the rest of humanity. "No man is an Island, entire of itself; every man is a piece of the Continent, a part of the main.... Any man's death diminishes me, because I am involved in mankind...."[23] And any man's sin diminishes other men, because God made humanity to be one family, with God as their Father. Therefore, any and all acts contrary to the moral law are contrary to the common good.

.031. (4) An unpromulgated law is not a law.

Canon Law 7: "A law is established when it is promulgated."[24]

Saint Thomas Aquinas: "It is laid down in the Decretals, dist. 4, that 'laws are established when they are promulgated.'"[25]

Therefore, if a law is not promulgated, it is not established as a law. The moral law must be promulgated (made known) in order to be a type of law. The moral law is the eternal Justice of God, and so this eternal moral law has always existed; thus, in one sense, its promulgation is eternal. But, in another sense, the moral law was promulgated, specifically to humanity, when human nature was first created. For the human person perceives moral truth by means of free will and reason (intellect), which are gifts to the human person from God. Reason perceives moral truth by knowledge of the goodness and the good order found in all of creation, especially in created persons.

Natural law is the promulgation of the eternal moral law in all creation, especially in created persons, both in the nature of each created thing, and in the ordered relationship between created things. Moral goodness is inherent to, and understandable from, all Creation, especially created persons. The nature of created persons is more like the Nature of God than any other created thing. And so the natural law is most clearly perceived within the nature of created persons and within the proper relationships between created persons.

Saint Thomas Aquinas: "Augustine says (De Lib. Arb. i, 6) that 'knowledge of the eternal law is imprinted on us.'"[26]

Saint Thomas Aquinas: "The natural law is a participation in us of the eternal law...."[27]

---

[22] Samuel Johnson, 1709-1784.
[23] John Donne, Devotions upon Emergent Occasions, Meditation XVII.
[24] Code of Canon Law for the Latin Church (1983), Canon 7.
[25] St. Thomas Aquinas, Summa Theologica, I-II, Q. 90, A. 4.
[26] St. Thomas Aquinas, Summa Theologica, I-II, Q. 91, A. 2.

This imprinting of the eternal moral law upon human persons is inherent to human nature itself; it is not merely an addition to, or one aspect of, human nature. For all that God created is inherently good, and therefore all that God created is a reflection of God, who is Goodness itself. Human persons are said to be made in the image of God because free will and reason make created persons more like God than other created things. Thus the natural law is first and foremost found in human nature itself.

The eternal moral law is God, and so perfect knowledge of that law is only obtained with perfect knowledge of God in the Beatific Vision of the very Nature (Essence) of God.[28] But the moral law can also be known by the use of reason to consider all that God has created, i.e. the goodness and good order of natural things. All that is good in Creation is a reflection of God who is Just. Therefore, justice is inherent to all created things, to the natural order of all created things, and especially to the hearts and minds of all created persons. Free will and reason, and our understanding of the natural world and its proper order, give us the ability to understand what is just and what is unjust. Thus, the natural law is the promulgation of the moral law into the very nature of all created things, especially created persons. The eternal moral law is the Just Nature of God, and the eternal moral law is promulgated in the nature of created things, especially created persons.

Saint Thomas Aquinas: "The natural law is promulgated by the very fact that God instilled it into man's mind so as to be known by him naturally."[29]

But the natural law is no different than the moral law, except that the natural law is the means by which we know the moral law. Therefore, the natural law is the promulgation of the moral law, so that this eternal moral law may be known naturally by created persons.

[Romans]
{2:14} For when the Gentiles, who do not have the law, do by nature those things which are of the law, such persons, not having the law, are a law unto themselves.
{2:15} For they reveal the work of the law written in their hearts, while their conscience renders testimony about them, and their thoughts within themselves also accuse or even defend them,
{2:16} unto the day when God shall judge the hidden things of men, through Jesus Christ, according to my Gospel.

The natural law is nothing other than the promulgation of the eternal moral law by God within the nature and order of Creation. Therefore, the natural law is also universal and immutable.[30]

---

[27] St. Thomas Aquinas, Summa Theologica, I-II, Q. 96, A. 2.
[28] St. Thomas Aquinas, Summa Theologica, I-II, Q. 91, A. 2.
[29] St. Thomas Aquinas, Summa Theologica, I-II, Q. 90, A. 4.
[30] Pope John Paul II, Veritatis Splendor, n. 51, 53. The Pontiff defends the "universality and immutability" of the natural law.

.032.
(5) An unenforceable law is not a law. An unenforced law is not a law. If a law is either unenforceable or unenforced, it is not a law.

The entire moral law is enforceable and is enforced by God, who judges justly and who punishes sinners. God knows and judges even the hidden things of men, even interior sins, deep within the heart and mind, which seem to be unknown outside of the person who sins. Therefore, even interior sins are an offense against the moral law. And every type and degree of sin can and will be punished by God. If we repent and do penance, that penance suffices as the just punishment due for our sins. If we repent but do not do sufficient penance, we will be punished by God in Purgatory. If we do not repent from actual mortal sin, we will be punished by God in Hell.

All knowingly chosen good acts are in accord with the moral law. All knowingly chosen bad acts are contrary to the moral law. Nothing illicit under the moral law is good. Nothing licit under the moral law is bad. All morality and all just law is of the eternal moral law. All immoral acts are:

(1) unreasonable before God,
(2) contrary to the authority of God,
(3) contrary to the common good as intended by God,
(4) contrary to the requirements of the moral law made known by God,
(5) punishable by God.

Chapter 3
The Three Fonts of Morality

.033.

A font is a source, or basis, or cause for the morality of an act. An act is immoral if any one or more of these fonts is bad. An act is moral only if all of the fonts of morality are good. There are three fonts of morality.

FIRST FONT: The intended end (or purpose) for which the act is chosen.

SECOND FONT: The inherent ordering of the act itself toward its moral object. This ordering constitutes the moral species, i.e. the essential moral nature, of the chosen act.

THIRD FONT: The circumstances pertaining to the morality of the act, especially the consequences.

Catechism of the Catholic Church: "The morality of human acts depends on: -- the object chosen; -- the end in view or the intention; -- the circumstances of the action. The object, the intention, and the circumstances make up the 'sources,' or constitutive elements, of the morality of human acts."[31]

Compendium of the Catechism: "The morality of human acts depends on three sources: *the object chosen*, either a true or apparent good; *the intention* of the subject who acts, that is, the purpose for which the subject performs the act; and *the circumstances* of the act, which include its consequences."[32]

USCCB Catechism: "Every moral act consists of three elements: the objective act (what we do), the subjective goal or intention (why we do the act), and the concrete situation or circumstances in which we perform the act.... All three aspects must be good -- the objective act, the subjective intention, and the circumstances -- in order to have a morally good act."[33]

There is no other basis for the morality of an act apart from these three fonts. For any act to be moral, all three fonts must be good. If any one font is bad, the act is immoral, even if the other fonts are good. Each and every knowingly chosen act is judged solely by the three fonts of morality. The three fonts of morality are the sole determinant of the morality of each and every knowingly chosen act, without any exception whatsoever. Whoever contradicts this teaching has overturned the very foundation of every moral teaching in the one holy Catholic and Apostolic Church.

.034. The term 'fonts' is derived from a Latin word (fons, fontis) meaning 'spring,' or 'source,' or 'principle cause.' The morality of any act springs forth from the three fonts as from a figurative wellspring of water, as from one

---

[31] Catechism of the Catholic Church, n. 1750.
[32] Compendium of the Catechism of the Catholic Church, n. 367.
[33] United States Catholic Catechism for Adults, U.S. Conference of Catholic Bishops, July 2006, p. 311-312.

threefold principle cause. These three fonts can be summarized using various terminology:

[1] the intention, or end, or purpose, or motive, of the person
[2] the moral object, or object, or species, or nature, of the act itself
[3] the circumstances, or consequences, of the intentionally chosen act

The first font is of the person; the second font is of the act; the third font is of the act chosen by the person. The first font is the subjective intention of the person; the second font is the objective morality of the act itself; the third font is the result of the intentionally chosen act.

Pope John Paul II: "These are the acts which, in the Church's moral tradition, have been termed 'intrinsically evil' (*intrinsece malum*): they are such *always and per se,* in other words, on account of their very [2] object, and quite apart from the ulterior [1] intentions of the one acting and the [3] circumstances. Consequently, without in the least denying the influence on morality exercised by circumstances and especially by intentions, the Church teaches that 'there exist acts which *per se* and in themselves, independently of circumstances, are always seriously wrong by reason of their object'."[34]

All three fonts must be good for an act to be moral. If any one font is bad, then the act as a whole is immoral.

Saint Thomas Aquinas: "Nothing hinders an action that is good in one of the ways mentioned above, from lacking goodness in another way. And thus it may happen that an action which is good in its [2] species or in its [3] circumstances is ordained to an evil [1] end, or vice versa. However, an action is not good simply, unless it is good in all those ways: since 'evil results from any single defect, but good from the complete cause,' as Dionysius says (Div. Nom. iv)."[35]

.035. The Source of This Doctrine on the Fonts

The division of morality into three fonts (sources, principle causes) is a particular way of expressing an eternal truth of the moral law. This truth is found in both Divine Revelation (Tradition and Scripture) and in natural law.[36] The Christian Faith has always understood and taught that [1] bad intention causes any act to be a sin, [2] that certain kinds of acts, by their very nature, are inherently immoral, [3] that it is a sin to choose even a good act, with good intention, if more harm is done than good in the consequences of the act.

This threefold truth is implicit in the moral teachings of the Old Testament. And even apart from Divine Revelation, by the light of natural law (i.e. by the use of free will and reason to understand the goodness and good order in all of nature, especially in created persons), all men and women of good will are capable of understanding this truth about good and evil, right and wrong. However, this

---

[34] Pope John Paul II, Veritatis Splendor, n. 80; inner quote is from Pope John Paul II, Reconciliatio et Paenitentia, n. 17.
[35] Saint Thomas Aquinas, Summa Theologica, I-II, Q. 18, A. 4.
[36] Pope John Paul II, Veritatis Splendor, n. 12, 28, 82.

truth has not always been expressed by this explicit division into three numbered or named fonts, with this same terminology. This particular expression of eternal moral truth developed over time, based largely on the work of Saint Thomas Aquinas in the Summa Theologica.

.036. The Order and Numbering of the Fonts

Saint Thomas Aquinas describes all morality as depending only on these factors: the intended end of the person, the moral object of the chosen act, and the circumstances of the intentionally chosen act.

"Is the good or evil of a human action derived from its object?"
"Is it derived from a circumstance?"
"Is it derived from the end?"[37]

However, the term 'fonts' and their numbering developed later. Over time, various moral theologians have presented the three fonts of morality with differing terminology, and in differing order. Some use a numbering (first, second, third); but others do not. The Catechism of the Catholic Church and the Compendium do not number the fonts, but give the order as: object, intended end, circumstances. This order differs from the order used by Saint Thomas. Pope John Paul II's encyclical on morality, 'Veritatis Splendor,' does not use any particular order or numbering for the three fonts. So the very same doctrine on morality may be presented in different ways.

This book uses the order: [1] intention, [2] moral object, [3] circumstances. However, no particular order or numbering is necessary to the truths that are expressed by the three fonts of morality. All the truths of faith and morals may be expressed in various ways, using various terms, without altering in the least the eternal truths that are being presented, whether in one particular manner or another. Doctrine is independent of terminology. Terminology is useful in expressing doctrine. But terminology is not doctrine. And no particular terminology is essential to doctrine. (The reason for the particular order and numbering of the fonts used in this book is explained below.)

.037. The Three Fonts and the Human Will

Although we can understand, objectively, whether an act is moral or immoral without choosing that act, the morality of all human acts is based fundamentally on the human will. All three fonts spring forth from the choice of the free will. But these three have a natural order in relation to the human will and to one another. This natural order results in the font of intention being numbered first, moral object second, and the consequences third.

The first choice made by the will, in any moral or immoral act, is the intention, which is the end or purpose for which the act is chosen. The intended end motivates the subsequent choice of the act itself. The person chooses one act and not another, as a means to achieve a particular intended end. The choice of an act with its moral object is subsequent (logically and usually chronologically) to

---

[37] Saint Thomas Aquinas, Summa Theologica, I-II, Q. 16, A. 2, 3, 4.

the choice of an intended end. The choice of an intended end, and of a particular act, then results in the consequences, which occur subsequent (logically and usually chronologically) to the chosen act. The choice of intention occurs first, and next this intention motivates the choice by the human will of a particular act with its moral object. The consequences of the intentionally chosen act occur last, as a result of the other two fonts. So the order used in this book is in accord with the natural order of the three fonts: [1] the intention of the person, [2] the chosen act with its moral object, [3] and the consequences.

All morality begins with the subject (the human person). The font of intention resides in the subject. It is natural to place this font first, before the chosen act, because the intention of the subject subsequently results in the choice of an act.

The morality of the second font resides in the chosen act itself, not in the subject. Since the act itself, with its moral object, is chosen by the subject based on the intended end, this font proceeds from the first font of intention, and is naturally considered second.

The third font of consequences results from the other two fonts. Without an intention giving rise to a chosen act, no consequences can occur. So the second font proceeds from the first, and the third font proceeds from the first and the second.

.038. The Three Fonts and the Trinity

There is an analogy to be found between the three fonts of morality and the Trinity. The threefold nature of the fonts is a reflection of the one threefold Nature of God, the Most Holy Trinity.

The first font of intention does not proceed from the other fonts, just as the First Person, the Father, does not proceed from the Son or the Spirit. The intention is the beginning of the morality of any act, just as the Father is the beginning of the Three Persons.

The second font proceeds from the first font, just as the Son proceeds from the Father. The choice of the act (with its moral object) is based on the logically prior choice of the intended end. An act is chosen to achieve an end; the intended end is therefore prior to the act chosen to fulfill that end. But the second font of the chosen act (with its moral object) does not proceed from the circumstances, just as the Son does not proceed from the Spirit.

The third font of consequences proceeds from the first two fonts together, just as the Spirit proceeds from the Father and Son together (as from one principle). The third font does not proceed separately from the intention and then from the act, but it proceeds from the intention and the chosen act together, as from one principle.

The second font consists of the chosen act itself, with its essential moral nature as determined by the moral object of that act. The second font is a union of the chosen act itself, with its inherent moral meaning, and the moral object. The Son became incarnate, so that His one Person would be a union of a human nature, which is body and soul, with the eternal Divine Nature. An analogy can be made between the second font and the Incarnation. The concrete chosen act is analogous to the body, and the moral meaning inherent to that act is analogous to the soul. Body and soul together constitute human nature. Every good moral object is not only ordered toward a good proximate end, but is also capable of being ordered toward the Good Ultimate End, God. A good moral object is analogous to the Divine Nature. And so the union of the act (and its inherent moral meaning) with the moral object is analogous to the union of the human nature of Christ with His Divine Nature at the Incarnation.

So again, the order and numbering of the three fonts is fittingly presented as: [1] intention, [2] object, [3] consequences. This order is neither arbitrary, nor contrary to doctrine. But neither is this order essential to doctrine. The truths of the moral law expressed in the form of the three fonts is not fundamentally changed if a different order and numbering of the fonts is used.

.039.
A. FIRST FONT OF MORALITY: Intention

[Proverbs]
{24:8} Whoever intends to do evil shall be called foolish.
{24:9} The intention of the foolish is sin.

[Psalms]
{55:6} All day long, they curse my words. All their intentions are for evil against me.
{118:118} You have despised all those who fell away from your judgments. For their intention is unjust.

Sacred Tradition and Sacred Scripture have always taught that a person sins if his intention is unjust. Intention by itself can cause an act to be immoral. For when the free will knowingly chooses an intention that is contrary to the moral law, and therefore contrary to the Just Nature of God, the human person sins. Each and every immoral intention is contrary to true love of God, neighbor, and self, even if that intention remains hidden in the depths of the heart and mind. For evil intentions are not hidden from the eyes of God.

[Isaiah]
{1:16} Wash, become clean, take away the evil of your intentions from my eyes. Cease to act perversely.
{29:15} Woe to you who use the depths of the heart, so that you may hide your intentions from the Lord. Their works are done in darkness, and so they say: "Who sees us?" and "Who knows us?"

The first font of morality is the intention of the person who chooses to act. When a human person has an immoral intention, he sins, even if the other two fonts of morality, his chosen act and its consequences, are good. Anyone who chooses a good act, with only good consequences, but also with an evil intention, commits a sin. A good act chosen with an immoral intention is a sin, even if only good consequences result. For if the first font of morality is bad, then the overall act, including all three fonts, is a sin.

All three fonts must be good for the overall act to be moral. There are no exceptions whatsoever to this principle of morality. One bad font is sufficient to make the overall act, including all three fonts, immoral. To avoid sin, each and every knowingly chosen act must be good under all three fonts of morality. Whenever any one font is bad, the overall act is a sin.

The first font is also called the purpose, or motive, or end, or intended end. Every intention is directed at a particular end. The person chooses an act in order to achieve that intended end; this end is the purpose or motive for the choice of that act. Therefore, every intention is a knowing choice of a particular end. But when an individual acts, he intends to achieve a particular end by a particular means, and so both the end and the means are included in one intention.

Saint Thomas Aquinas: "…the will is moved to the means for the sake of the end: and thus the movement of the will to the end and its movement to the means are one and the same thing." [38]

Therefore, if a person intends to achieve an end, even a moral end, by an immoral means, the intention is sinful. The intention to achieve a good end does not justify the use of an immoral means. In order for the first font of intention to be good, all that is intended must be moral. The intention includes the end or purpose for which the act is done, and the intended means to that end.

.040. An intention is a knowing choice of a particular means for a particular end (or purpose). Every intention is an exercise of the free will, enlightened by knowledge, toward a particular end, by a particular means. The free will cannot intend without knowledge provided by the intellect. Every intention is a knowing choice; it is an act of the will and intellect. But every knowing choice is a choice of something, which is called the end. And that end is reached in some manner, which is called the means.

Examples: (1) A physician intends the end of relieving the suffering of a patient, by means of euthanasia. The intended end is good, but the intended means is intrinsically evil, and so the intention is immoral. The one intention includes both the end and the means. (2) A physician intends the end of relieving the suffering of a patient, by means of a medication that relieves pain, but does not cause death. Both the intended end and the intended means are good, and so the intention is moral.

For any intention to be good, everything that is intended must be moral, including the end and the means to that end. For whoever intends evil, sins against God.

Pope John Paul II: "Furthermore, an intention is good when it has as its aim the true good of the person in view of his ultimate end." [39]

---

[38] St. Thomas Aquinas, Summa Theologica, I-II, Q. 12, A. 4; see also A. 1-3.

The goodness of an intended end is always evaluated based on the threefold commandment to love God, neighbor, self. The entire moral law is based on this commandment, and so every good intention must be in harmony with this threefold love. Any intended immorality, in the end or in the means, is contrary to true love of God, neighbor, self.

Therefore, it is true that an intention is immoral when a person intends either a means, or an end, that is morally evil. However, it is also true that the human person never intends evil in and of itself, that is, evil for the sake of evil. An immoral intention is always directed at an end that is either a lesser good in contradiction to a greater good, or an apparent good; no one can intend evil itself directly.[40] For evil is essentially a deprivation of some good, and a deprivation is non-existent; it is a lack of some good. (For more on this point, see the chapter on Types of Evil.)

.041.
B. SECOND FONT OF MORALITY: Moral Object

The second font is the knowingly chosen act itself, with its inherent moral meaning, as determined by its moral object. The moral object is the end toward which the act itself is inherently directed. The act itself is the knowingly chosen act of the human person, considered apart from intention and circumstances. The inherent moral meaning of an act is its essential moral nature; it is the type of act, in terms of morality.

Certain kinds of acts are intrinsically evil because these acts are inherently directed at an end, i.e. a moral object, that is evil. The intrinsic ordering of the act itself, by its very nature, toward an evil moral object makes that act necessarily always immoral.

The terms used to describe the second font, such as object or moral object, moral nature or moral species, intrinsic evil, and similar terms, have developed over time within the Church, both in theological writings and in magisterial documents. But the truth that certain kinds of knowingly chosen acts are always immoral, by the very nature of the act, is an eternal truth. This truth has been found in Sacred Tradition and Sacred Scripture since Divine Revelation was given to humanity. This truth has been found in natural law since nature and humanity were created. The eternal moral law, which is the Justice of God, has always contained the truth that certain kinds of acts are intrinsically evil, and therefore contrary to the good, just, loving, merciful Nature of God.

[Matthew]
{19:17} And he said to him: "Why do you question me about what is good? One is good: God. But if you wish to enter into life, observe the commandments."

---

[39] Pope John Paul II, Veritatis Splendor, n. 82.
[40] Saint Thomas Aquinas, Summa Theologica, I-II, Q. 18, A. 4; he cites pseudo-Dionysius, On the Divine Names, chap. 4, section 19. Cf. Compendium, n. 367.

{19:18} He said to him, "Which?" And Jesus said: "You shall not murder. You shall not commit adultery. You shall not steal. You shall not give false testimony."

Certain kinds of acts, such as murder, adultery, theft, lying, are inherently immoral by the very nature of the act itself; such acts are intrinsically evil because they have an evil moral object. In other words, the act by its very nature is ordered toward an end (the moral object) that is contrary to the goodness of God, and therefore contrary to true love of God, neighbor, self. This threefold love of God, neighbor, self is the basis for all the commandments.

[Mark]
{12:29} And Jesus answered him: "For the first commandment of all is this: 'Listen, O Israel. The Lord your God is one God.
{12:30} And you shall love the Lord your God from your whole heart, and from your whole soul, and from your whole mind, and from your whole strength. This is the first commandment.'
{12:31} But the second is similar to it: 'You shall love your neighbor as yourself.' There is no other commandment greater than these."

All the fonts are evaluated as to their morality based on the commandments to love God, and to love your neighbor as yourself.

.042. The Second Font

Every knowingly chosen act includes all three fonts of morality. In one sense, we use the term 'act' to refer to the overall act, with all three fonts: [1] intention, [2] moral object, and [3] circumstances. If any one font is immoral, then the overall act is immoral. One bad font corrupts the entire knowingly chosen act.

But when considering the second font, we consider the act narrowly; this is the chosen act itself, apart from intention and circumstances. The second font considers only the act itself, not intention or circumstances, which are the other two fonts. The act itself is chosen by the human person, in order to achieve the intended end. But the second font does not include the intended end.

Every knowingly chosen act has a moral meaning inherent to the act itself. This moral meaning is inseparable from the act itself, for it is essential to the very nature of the act. This essential moral nature is also called the species, or moral species, of the act itself. It is the intrinsic moral meaning of the chosen act before the eyes of God, in the light of the eternal moral law, which is the Justice of God. This meaning is inherent to, and inseparable from, the act chosen by the human will.

This essential moral meaning is determined by the moral object toward which the act, by its very nature, is directed. The moral object determines the morality of the second font by determining the essential moral nature of the chosen act itself. Every knowingly chosen act is inherently ordered toward an end, in terms of morality, called the moral object. The moral object is not the end intended by the person, nor is it the 'end result' or consequences of the act. The moral object is the end toward which the act itself is inherently directed. This inherent ordering of the act itself toward its moral object determines the moral meaning (or moral nature) of the act itself. However, it is the inherent ordering of the chosen act toward its moral object, not the attainment of that moral object, which determines the morality of the second font.

Any act that is inherently ordered toward a good moral object, toward a moral object that is in harmony with true love of God and neighbor, is an inherently good act. Any act that is inherently ordered toward a bad moral object, toward a moral object that is in conflict with true love of God and neighbor, is an inherently bad act. This type of immoral act is said to be intrinsically evil, or intrinsically morally disordered. Each and every intrinsically evil act is always immoral, by its very nature, regardless of intention or circumstances.

Pope John Paul II: "It is a matter of prohibitions which forbid a given action *semper et pro semper* [always and in each instance], without exception, because the choice of this kind of behavior is in no case compatible with the goodness of the will of the acting person, with his vocation to life with God and to communion with his neighbor."[41]

.043. The Act Itself

Morality concerns human acts, which are acts chosen by the free will based on knowledge in the intellect. Such acts do not exist apart from persons choosing to act. When a person freely chooses an immoral act, knowing that it is immoral, he commits an actual sin. Even when a person chooses an immoral act without knowledge that it is immoral, or without full deliberation, the act was chosen by the will, and that act has an objective morality. A person might be mistaken in his knowledge concerning the morality of the chosen act, but he at least knows which act he is choosing. Moral and immoral acts only occur when a person chooses to act. The term 'act' in moral theology must be understood to refer to acts that are knowingly chosen by the human will, or (when considering whether or not an act ought to be chosen) to refer to acts that can be knowingly chosen by the human will. Morality concerns knowingly chosen acts of the human will.

In Veritatis Splendor, Pope John Paul II uses the terms: 'concrete act,' 'concrete action,' 'concrete behavior,' 'concrete choice,' 'particular act,' 'human act,' 'human actions,' 'concrete kind of behavior,' 'specific kinds of behavior,' and similar phrases, all to describe any act of the human person chosen by the will and intellect. Such knowingly chosen acts can be interior or exterior. An interior act is confined to the mind and heart, e.g. a lustful thought. An exterior act reaches beyond the mind and heart, e.g. an act of adultery. But an exterior knowingly chosen act always includes an interior act of the human will, knowingly choosing the act. Such acts can be acts of commission, in which the human person chooses to do something (i.e. to engage in an action or behavior), or acts of omission, in which the human person chooses not to do something (i.e. to refrain from an action or behavior). Although an act of omission (which when immoral is called a sin of omission) would seem to be not an act, there is always the interior act of deciding to refrain from acting. Such an interior act of deciding

---

[41] Pope John Paul II, Veritatis Splendor, n. 52.

is either moral or immoral. The term 'act itself' refers this same concept of the particular act chosen by the human will, which Pope John Paul II calls by these various phrases.

The morality of each and every human act is determined by all three fonts of morality. The term 'act itself' refers to the second font, considered distinctly from the other two fonts; it is the act chosen by the human will, apart from the intention (the purpose for which the act was chosen), and apart from the circumstances surrounding the chosen act. The act itself is the particular action (interior or exterior) chosen by the human will.[42] The term 'overall act' refers to all three fonts of morality, including [1] the intention of the person who chooses the act, [2] the moral meaning inherent to the chosen act itself, as determined by the moral object, and [3] the circumstances of the chosen act, especially the consequences.

.044. The Inherent Moral Meaning of Human Acts

All human acts (acts that are, or can be, knowingly chosen) have an inherent moral meaning before God. There are no knowingly chosen acts which are devoid of morality, or beyond the reach of the moral law, or irrelevant as to their morality, or good without regard to the eternal moral law. The eternal moral law is universal. All knowingly chosen acts are under the moral law. All knowingly chosen acts have an inherent moral meaning.

Even if the chosen act is an exterior physical action, all such exterior acts include an interior act of the will and intellect, an act of the human person knowingly choosing the physical action. By choosing any act, the human person is also choosing the moral meaning inherent to that same act. An exterior act, such as killing an innocent human person, or having sexual relations outside of marriage, or choosing to assert a falsehood, or taking what belongs to another, cannot be reduced to a mere physical action which would have no inherent moral meaning, or which would take its morality solely from intention and circumstances. Each and every knowingly chosen act of a human person has an inherent moral meaning before God. In addition to intention and circumstances, the inherent moral meaning of the act itself must be considered when evaluating the morality of any act. All knowingly chosen acts have an inherent moral meaning before God, which is the moral nature (or moral species) of the act itself. By its moral nature, an act is either morally good in itself, or morally bad in itself.

Pope John Paul II: "But the consideration of these [3] consequences, and also of [1] intentions, is not sufficient for judging the moral quality of a concrete choice. The weighing of the goods and evils foreseeable as the consequence of an action is not an adequate method for determining whether the choice of that concrete kind of behavior is 'according to its species,' or 'in itself,' morally good or bad, licit or illicit. The foreseeable consequences are part of those circumstances of the

---

[42] Cf. Peter J. Kreeft, Catholic Christianity, p. 183. "What makes any act good or evil? ... (a) the act itself, (b) the motive, and (c) the situation."

act, which, while capable of lessening the gravity of an evil act, nonetheless cannot alter its [2] moral species."[43]

The term 'species,' or 'moral species,' refers to the essential moral nature of the chosen act. The inherent moral meaning of an act is its moral nature or moral species. In order to avoid sin, all three fonts of morality must be good: [1] the intention must be good, [2] the inherent moral meaning of the act itself must be good, [3] the reasonably foreseeable good consequences must outweigh the reasonably foreseeable bad consequences. But intention and circumstances can never change the inherent moral meaning of the act itself. If the inherent moral meaning of an act is evil, then the choice of that act is a sin.

Pope John Paul II: "Only the act in conformity with the good can be a path that leads to life. The rational ordering of the human act to the good in its truth and the voluntary pursuit of that good, known by reason, constitute morality. Hence human activity cannot be judged as morally good merely because it is a means for attaining one or another of its goals, or simply because the subject's intention is good. Activity is morally good when it attests to and expresses the voluntary ordering of the person to his ultimate end and the conformity of a concrete action with the human good as it is acknowledged in its truth by reason. If the object of the concrete action is not in harmony with the true good of the person, the choice of that action makes our will and ourselves morally evil, thus putting us in conflict with our ultimate end, the supreme good, God himself."[44]

How do we determine if the chosen act is in itself good or evil? What is the basis for the inherent moral meaning (the essential moral nature or moral species) of the particular chosen act? The chosen act is good, 'according to its species,' or 'in itself,' if the act is inherently ordered toward a good end. The chosen act is evil, 'according to its species,' or 'in itself,' if the act is inherently ordered toward a bad end. The end toward which the act itself is inherently directed is called the 'object,' or 'moral object.' If the moral object is good, then the inherent moral meaning of the act is good; if the moral object is bad, then the inherent moral meaning of the act is bad. When the moral object is bad, nothing can cause the overall act to become good, not the best of intentions, and not the most dire of circumstances. For every act with a bad moral object is intrinsically evil.

.045. The Moral Object

The 'object' or 'moral object' of the act itself determines its inherent moral meaning before God. When the moral object is bad, the act itself is intrinsically evil, and the second font is bad. When the moral object is good, the act itself is intrinsically good, and the second font is good (but all three fonts must be good for the overall act to be moral). Some acts are intrinsically disordered, and other acts are intrinsically ordered; the intrinsic moral order, or intrinsic moral disorder, of any act is determined by its moral object.

---

[43] Pope John Paul II, Veritatis Splendor, n. 77.
[44] Pope John Paul II, Veritatis Splendor, n. 72.

The moral object defines the act itself, under the moral law, before the eyes of God. This is not a legalistic or secular definition of an act, but rather the definition of the act in the light of faith and reason; it is the moral definition (or moral meaning) of the act. The inherent moral meaning of an act is its essential moral nature, which is independent of intention and circumstances. The moral object determines this intrinsic moral meaning (or essential moral nature) of the act itself.

Every knowingly chosen act has an inherent moral meaning, which is inseparable from the act itself. The act itself always includes the moral meaning intrinsic to that act, which is its essential moral nature (or moral species). And each and every act of the human person (an act that is, or can be, knowingly chosen) has a moral object, under the eternal moral law, before the eyes of God.

The moral meaning inherent to the act itself is determined by this object, or end, toward which the act is ordered. If an act is ordered toward an evil moral object, then the act is evil. If an act is ordered toward a good moral object, then the act is good. Although this object or end may seem extrinsic to, or separate from, the act itself, it is the very ordering of the act toward that end which constitutes the intrinsic moral nature of the act, not the attainment of that end.

This inherent ordering of the act is either good or evil. When an act is ordered toward an evil end, it is incapable of being ordered ultimately to God, who is infinite Justice, who is our final end. Thus the moral object is sometimes called the 'proximate end,' as distinguished from our ultimate end, God. Any act with a bad moral object is called 'intrinsically evil,' and not merely 'evil,' because the ordering toward that evil moral object is intrinsic to the very nature of the act itself. Intrinsically evil acts are also called intrinsically disordered because all such acts, by their very nature, lack the good order intended by God for the knowingly chosen acts of created persons.

The moral object is the end toward which the act is inherently ordered. But even if the act never attains that end, the act is nevertheless inherently directed toward that end. It is precisely this ordering toward a good or evil end (the moral object) that determines whether the act is good or evil 'according to its species,' or 'in itself.' An act possesses its moral object merely by being inherently ordered toward that moral object. The essential moral nature (or species) of the act is absolutely identical to this inherent ordering toward a good or evil moral object.

An act is intrinsically evil merely because it is ordered toward an evil end, regardless of whether or not the act achieves that end. An intrinsically disordered act is evil solely because it is ordered toward an evil moral object. This moral disorder of intrinsically evil acts is independent of intention, independent of circumstances, independent of other knowingly chosen acts, and independent of whether or not the act attains its object. Each and every human act, by its very nature, is ordered toward either a good moral object, or an evil moral object. The moral object is distinct, but not entirely separate, from the act that is ordered toward that object. For each and every human act possesses its moral object merely by being inherently ordered toward that end, even if it does not attain that moral object as an achieved end. In this way, the moral object determines the inherent moral meaning of the act itself.

Analogy: An arrow is directed toward a target, just as an act is directed toward its moral object. Even if the arrow does not reach its target, the arrow is nevertheless ordered toward that target.

.046. Even if a human act does not achieve its moral object, the act nevertheless possesses its moral object by being ordered toward that end. An act still possesses the same essential moral nature, as determined by the moral object, even when it does not attain that moral object, because the act knowingly chosen by the will is inherently ordered toward that end. And since the inherent moral meaning of the act is determined by the moral object, the moral object can be said to be inherent to the act, regardless of whether or not the moral object is attained.

The moral object is not the end intended by the person who acts. The moral object is the end toward which the act, by its very nature, is ordered. The moral object is not the purpose or intention for which the act is done. The moral meaning of the act before God is inherent to the act itself, regardless of intention. The person who acts is choosing both the act and its inherent ordering toward its moral object. The intended end chosen by the person who acts does not determine the moral object. Sometimes the intended end and the moral object (a type of end) are the same; sometimes they differ. But in no case does the intention of the person who chooses the act determine the moral object. The moral object is inherent to the very nature of the chosen act, regardless of the intention of the person who chooses the act, and regardless of the circumstances. By the very fact that the human person chooses any act, he necessarily also chooses the inherent moral nature (or moral species) of the act, which is determined by its moral object.

Pope John Paul II: "Reason attests that there are objects of the human act which are by their nature 'incapable of being ordered' to God, because they radically contradict the good of the person made in his image. These are the acts which, in the Church's moral tradition, have been termed 'intrinsically evil' (*intrinsece malum*): they are such *always and per se*, in other words, on account of their very object, and quite apart from the ulterior intentions of the one acting and the circumstances. Consequently, without in the least denying the influence on morality exercised by circumstances and especially by intentions, the Church teaches that 'there exist acts which *per se* and in themselves, independently of circumstances, are always seriously wrong by reason of their object.' "[45]

When the moral object is evil (bad, immoral), the act is called intrinsically evil (or intrinsically disordered) because the act, by its very nature, is ordered toward an end that is incompatible with love of God, who is Goodness itself, who is our final end. Whenever the moral object of an act is bad, then the second font is bad and the act is intrinsically evil. The moral object (or proximate end) of an act is bad whenever it is incapable of being ordered to God, our ultimate end. The

---

[45] Pope John Paul II, Veritatis Splendor, n. 80. Interior quote is from Pope John Paul II, Reconciliation and Penance, n. 17.

moral object is bad whenever it is incompatible with the goodness that God intends for human life, because this goodness and life should always be directed toward God as our final end. The moral object is bad whenever it is contrary to the moral law, which orders all our knowingly chosen acts in accord with the will of God and toward God as our final end.

.047. The term 'object' or 'moral object' has a specialized meaning derived from philosophy, as developed and applied especially by St. Thomas Aquinas.[46] While the intention resides in the subject (the person who knowingly chooses an act), the moral object resides in the act itself.[47] A good or bad intention has no effect at all on the moral object of the act itself. Intention is entirely in the first font; the moral object is entirely in the second font. The moral object is inherent to the act chosen by the will and intellect. But the end intended by the person who acts, and the moral object (a type of end) toward which the chosen act itself inherently tends, are distinct. The person who acts intends a particular end or purpose. But the act itself is also tends toward a particular end (the moral object). Sometimes these two ends are the same. But if the intention changes to seek a different end, the moral object is unaffected. The moral object is inherent to the act itself. In no case is the moral object determined by the intention of the person who acts.

Examples: (1) A man intends to pay his rent (the intended end), by stealing money from a neighbor (the chosen act). This act is directed toward the object of depriving another person of what belongs to him. The moral object of theft is contrary to love of God and neighbor, and so the moral object is evil, making the chosen act intrinsically evil. The essential moral nature of this act is that of theft. Thus the second font is bad, and the overall act is always immoral.

In this example, the first font includes a good intended end, to pay rent that is owed for housing, as well as an immoral intended means, to obtain that rent by an intrinsically evil act. So even though the intended end is good, the intention to use an immoral means to that end causes the intention to be evil. And so the first font is also bad. The intention to use an immoral means is always a bad intention.

Now the number of various exterior acts that can be used to commit theft, in all its varies forms, is endless. Yet the moral object in every case is the same, to deprive another person of their property. So as long as the particular concrete act has the same moral object, it necessarily also has the same moral nature. For the moral object determines the essential moral nature (the moral species) of the act.

(2) A person intends to impress his friends (the intended end) by committing an act of theft. Although this intention differs from the first example, the chosen act remains inherently directed toward the same moral object, i.e. the same end, to take what belongs to another. The change in intention from the first case to the second does not change the moral object. Even though the intended end is now directed toward the end of improving one's reputation among a group of (immoral) persons, the moral object of the act is unaffected by that intention.

---

[46] Summa Theologica, I-II, Q. 18, A. 6.
[47] Catechism of the Catholic Church, n. 1752.

Every moral object is independent of intention. No intention whatsoever can cause an evil moral object to become good. A change in intention cannot cause the act of theft, or any other intrinsically evil act, to become moral.

(3) A physician intends to heal a patient by giving the patient a treatment. The treatment is inherently directed toward the healing of the patient. The intended end and the moral object are the same: to heal the patient. The intention is good. The moral object is good, and therefore the inherent moral meaning of the act itself is good. Sometimes the intended end and the moral object are the same.

(4) Another physician gives another patient the same treatment for the same illness; the treatment still has the same moral object, the healing of the patient. But this physician intends to make as much money as he can, regardless of the needs of his patients. The intended end and the moral object are different. The intention is bad, but the moral object is good. Whenever any one font is bad, the person who commits the act (the overall act with all three fonts) commits a sin.

Notice that whether the intention is the same as the moral object, or different, the intention has no effect on the moral object. The moral object is always independent of intention. Even when the intention is immoral, the moral object may be good.

However, if the moral object of the act itself is evil, and if the person intends to use this act, known to be immoral, as a means to a good end, such an intention is sinful. For whoever intends evil, as a means or as an end, sins against God, who is the infinite fullness of all Goodness. But if the person intends to use an immoral means to a good end, while sincerely and mistakenly thinking that the means is moral, the intention is still objectively immoral, but, due to a lack of knowledge, such an intention would not, by itself, cause the act to be an actual sin.

.048. The Intended End versus the Moral Object

The purpose for which an act is done (first font) and the moral object (second font) are both types of ends. When both the intended end and the moral object are good, the intended end is often the same as the moral object. When a human person cooperates with grace in choosing an act, grace enables and guides the human will to have a good intention and to choose an act with a good moral object. The good moral object of a chosen act is often the same as the good intended end because all good ends (intended ends and moral objects) are ultimately ordered to God as the final end of all that is good.

Even so, the intention never determines the moral object, and a change in intention never changes the moral object. A good intention cannot cause an evil moral object to become good; neither can an evil intention cause a good moral object to become evil.

Examples: (1) A person chooses to feed the hungry in order to help his neighbor and ultimately in order to please God. The act itself of feeding the hungry has the moral object (proximate end) of helping one's neighbor, and (like all good moral objects) also is directed toward our ultimate end, God. In this case, the intended end and the moral object are the same. Notice that an intention can have more than one end.[48]

(2) A person chooses to feed the hungry in order to do penance for his past sins, and ultimately in order to please God. The act itself of feeding the hungry has the moral object (proximate end) of helping one's neighbor, and also is directed toward God, our ultimate end. In this case, the intended end and the moral object are both good, and are both ultimately directed toward God, but they differ in their proximate end. All good intentions and all good acts are ultimately directed toward God, who is Goodness itself. And so, every good act, done with a good intention, will have the same ultimate end in both the intention and the moral object. But the proximate intended end and the moral object may or may not be the same when both fonts are good.

(3) A person chooses to feed the hungry, but with the intended end of obtaining worldly honor (cf. Mt 6:2). Despite this bad intention, the act itself of feeding the hungry still has the good moral object of helping those in need. In this case, the intended end and the moral object are different; one is bad and the other is good.

If the intended end is good, but the intended means is an act with an evil moral object, then the intention is objectively immoral. Every intrinsically evil act is always immoral, under the second font, due to an evil moral object. But every intention to commit an intrinsically evil act, whether as an intended means or as an intended end, is also always immoral, under the first font. In order for the first font to be good, all that is intended must be morally good. When an intrinsically evil act is intended as an immoral means to a good end, the chosen act itself and its moral object remain evil. Neither can such an intention, to use an intrinsically evil act as an immoral means to a good end, be considered a good intention. For even when the intended end is good, the intention to use an evil means to that good end is an immoral intention. The end does not justify the means. A good intended end does not justify an immoral intended means.

.049. Intrinsically Evil Acts Are Always Immoral

When the moral object is evil, the second font is bad and the act itself is intrinsically evil and always immoral. Intrinsically evil acts are always immoral, even if the intended end, in the first font, is good, and even if the consequences, in the third font, are good. The overall act is always immoral whenever any one font is bad. And so every intrinsically evil is always immoral, regardless of the intention (first font) or the circumstances (third font).

Examples: (1) A woman is pregnant and also has a severe chronic illness; the pregnancy will endanger her life. She procures a direct abortion, not intending the death of the prenatal, but intending to save her own life. Her intended end of saving her own life is good, and the circumstances are dire. Yet this concrete act of direct abortion has the moral object of the direct and voluntary killing of an innocent human being, which is murder. Even though she does not intend the death of the prenatal as an end, the act itself is inherently ordered toward that

---

[48] Saint Thomas Aquinas, *Summa Theologica*, I-II, Q. 12, A. 1-4.

evil end, which is its moral object. Any and all acts of direct abortion are intrinsically evil and always gravely immoral, regardless of intention and circumstances, because the moral object (murder) is evil.

(2) Another woman is pregnant, and she procures a direct abortion because she does not want the emotional and financial burden of another child in her life. Despite the difference in intention between these two cases, this direct abortion has the same moral object as all direct abortions have, the killing of an innocent human being. The end (the moral object) toward which the act is inherently ordered is unaffected by the intended end of the person who chooses the act. The choice of any act of direct abortion is necessarily also a choice of the inherent moral meaning of that act, as determined by its moral object. If the inherent moral meaning of an act is evil, then it is always immoral to choose that act.

(3) A person lies, in a small matter, order to save innocent persons from being murdered. The act of lying has the evil moral object of asserting a falsehood. Lying is intrinsically evil and always immoral because God is Truth. All lying offends God and is contrary to the moral law. A good intended end and good consequences, even the saving many innocent lives, cannot cause an intrinsically evil act to become good. The lie in this case is a venial sin, but it is still a sin. The best intended end and the most dire of circumstances can never cause what is inherently evil to become good.

Although it might seem, from a worldly point of view, that one ought to commit a venial sin if many innocent lives would be saved, from a heavenly point of view, this is not the truth. For no innocent human life is truly lost to God. All who die in a state of grace live forever in eternal happiness in Heaven. And so, not a single resident of Heaven considers even a slight venial sin to be justified by any intention or circumstance, not even by the saving of many innocent lives. Nor should we on earth, who have the hope of eternal life in Heaven, claim to justify even small sins for any reason. We should always imitate Christ in all our moral decisions. Christ would not commit even the slightest venial sin for any reason, not to save His own life, not to save many lives, not to redeem the whole world from Hell.

Saint Catherine of Siena: "The light of discretion (which proceeds from love, as I have told thee) gives to the neighbor a conditioned love, one that, being ordered aright, does not cause the injury of sin to self in order to be useful to others, for, if one single sin were committed to save the whole world from Hell, or to obtain one great virtue, the motive would not be a rightly ordered or discreet love, but rather indiscreet, for it is not lawful to perform even one act of great virtue and profit to others, by means of the guilt of sin."[49]

Nothing whatsoever can cause an intrinsically evil act to become morally licit. Intention and circumstances have no effect on the moral object of the chosen act. Other chosen acts have no effect on the moral object of the particular chosen act. Each knowingly chosen act is good only if all three fonts are good. If any one

---

[49] The Dialogue of Saint Catherine of Siena, n. 42. In this quote, God is speaking to St. Catherine by means of a private revelation.

font is bad, the act is immoral, despite any goodness in the other two fonts, and despite any goodness in other knowingly chosen acts.

Each knowingly chosen act has its own inherent moral object. One knowingly chosen act has no effect on the moral object of a different knowingly chosen act, since the moral object is inherent to each particular act. No knowingly chosen act is without its own moral object, because every knowingly chosen act has its own inherent moral meaning before God. One act does not borrow the moral object of another act, nor can the moral object of one act cancel, or change, or outweigh the moral object of another act. Whenever the moral object is evil, the act which is inherently ordered toward that moral object is also evil; and no intention or circumstance or other acts or other considerations whatsoever can cause that same act to become moral.

Even if an intrinsically evil act were done with a good intended end, in circumstances where only good consequences resulted, the act itself would still be immoral because the moral meaning of the act is inherent to, and inseparable from, the act itself. Intrinsically evil acts are, by their very nature, ordered toward an evil moral object (an evil end). Whenever the moral object is evil (bad, immoral), the choice of such an act is always a sin, even with the best intended end, and even in the most dire of circumstances. The moral object is always independent of intention, always independent of circumstances, and always independent of other knowingly chosen acts. The moral object determines the inherent moral nature (or species) of the act itself. When the moral object is evil, then the act is evil by its very nature.

Pope John Paul II: "The Church proposes the example of numerous Saints who bore witness to and defended moral truth even to the point of enduring martyrdom, or who preferred death to a single mortal sin. In raising them to the honor of the altars, the Church has canonized their witness and declared the truth of their judgment, according to which the love of God entails the obligation to respect his commandments, even in the most dire of circumstances, and the refusal to betray those commandments, even for the sake of saving one's own life."[50]

.050. If the person intends a good end by means of an act that is intrinsically evil, the intended means is bad. For an intention to be good, everything that is intended, including the intended end and the intended means to that end, must be good. A knowingly chosen intrinsically evil act (the second font) also has an objectively immoral intended means (in the first font), regardless of the intended end of the choice, because the intended means is an intrinsically evil act.

All intrinsically evil acts have at least some bad consequences, even if these are not readily apparent, such as the harm done to the soul of the individual committing the act and to the souls of those who are influenced by the act, and the harm done by the loss of the graces that the individual and others would have received if the individual had chosen to cooperate with God's grace instead of committing the intrinsically evil act. Each and every objective sin, and

---

[50] Pope John Paul II, Veritatis Splendor, n. 91.

especially every actual sin, and most especially every actual mortal sin, harms the Church and the world in some way and to some extent, and also denies graces to the souls in Purgatory. (Whenever we do good in cooperation with grace in this life, the holy souls in Purgatory benefit, because we are all part of one and the same Church, which includes the communion of all its members.)

If an individual intends a good end by means of an intrinsically evil act, then the first font (intention) is bad because the intended means is an intrinsically evil act, and the second font is bad because the inherent moral meaning of the act is intrinsically evil, and the third font has some bad consequences because all evil does some harm to God's good creation. Now in the third font, perhaps the good consequences might outweigh the bad consequences. But even so, the overall act (including all three fonts) would still be immoral.

Whenever the act itself is intrinsically evil, the second font of morality is bad. Whenever the second font of morality is bad, the act itself is intrinsically evil. The second font of morality considers whether or not the act itself, in its inherent moral meaning, is evil (bad, immoral); if so, then the second font is bad, and the act itself is intrinsically evil, and the overall act, including intention and circumstances, is immoral. Intrinsically evil acts are always immoral, regardless of intention or circumstances. Whenever any one, two, or three of the fonts of morality is immoral, the overall act is immoral. An intrinsically evil act can never be moral because the act cannot be separated from its inherent moral meaning (as determined by its moral object). Intention and circumstances cannot make an intrinsically evil act moral, because all three fonts must be good for the overall act to be moral.

Pope John Paul II: "The doctrine of the object as a source of morality represents an authentic explicitation of the Biblical morality of the Covenant and of the commandments, of charity and of the virtues. The moral quality of human acting is dependent on this fidelity to the commandments, as an expression of obedience and of love. For this reason -- we repeat -- the opinion must be rejected as erroneous which maintains that it is impossible to qualify as morally evil according to its species the deliberate choice of certain kinds of behavior or specific acts, without taking into account the intention for which the choice was made or the totality of the foreseeable consequences of that act for all persons concerned."[51]

The term 'explicitation' in the Latin text of this document is 'pate factionem,' which refers to an explanation that 'opens' or 'makes accessible' (pate) a truth by 'division' into parts (factionem). The three fonts explain morality by dividing it into its constituent elements. When the moral object (second font) of an act is evil, the act itself is intrinsically evil and always immoral, regardless of intention (first font) or consequences (third font).

.051. Nothing can cause an intrinsically evil act to become moral. Intention and circumstance cannot make an intrinsically evil act moral, because the act itself is inherently ordered toward an evil moral object. Intention is the first font, and

---

[51] Pope John Paul II, Veritatis Splendor, n. 82.

circumstances is the third font, but all three fonts must be good for the overall act to be moral. If the second font is bad, the act is immoral, even if the other two fonts are good. The other two fonts may make the overall act more or less evil, but they cannot cause an intrinsically evil act to become moral. All three fonts must be good for any act to be moral.

All intrinsically evil acts are defined, in their essential moral nature, solely under the second font.

Examples: The difference between abortion and infanticide is found in the circumstance of whether the death occurs before or after birth; this difference is in the third font. The difference between euthanasia and other types of murder is found in the intention to use euthanasia in order to relieve suffering; this difference is in the first font. However, the essential moral nature of abortion, of infanticide, and of euthanasia, is that of murder. So even though the particular type of murder depends upon the other fonts, that which determines the essential moral nature of the act is entirely in the second font. Murder is an intrinsically evil act. The circumstances might may make one murder abortion and another infanticide; or the intention may make one murder euthanasia and another not. But the moral meaning inherent to the act itself (as determined by its moral object) is in the second font alone. Thus intention and circumstance can never make any type of murder moral, because these two fonts have no effect on the inherent ordering of the act itself toward its moral object. The moral object of any act entirely and solely determines the second font of morality, and is entirely unaffected by the other two fonts.

The moral object of the act determines the essential moral nature (the moral species) of the act itself. In no case and in no way can the act itself be separated from the moral meaning inherent to that same act.

Analogy: In this analogy, the act itself is compared to the body, and the moral meaning inherent to the act is compared to the soul. The human person is composed of body and soul; death is the separation of body and soul. All human persons include both a physical body and a soul. All human acts include both the act itself and the inherent moral meaning of the act. The soul cannot be separated from the body without death. The moral meaning inherent to any act cannot be separated from the act itself. If any analysis of the morality of an act separates the inherent moral meaning of the act from the act itself, then that analysis is dead (i.e. the analysis fails).

Examples: (1) A man steals money from his neighbor. The moral meaning inherent to the act of physically taking the money is that of theft. The physical act of taking the money cannot be said to have no moral meaning, or to have only the moral meaning found in intention and circumstance. For an act cannot be separated from the meaning inherent to that act. All knowingly chosen acts have an inherent moral meaning before God. Stealing is always immoral, regardless of intention or circumstances. The act itself and its inherent moral meaning are inseparable.

(2) A man commits adultery with his neighbor's wife. The act of having sexual relations with another man's wife cannot be separated from the moral meaning inherent to the act, which is that of adultery. Adultery can never be moral, no matter what the intention or circumstances are, because the moral meaning inherent to the act is evil. Adultery can never be good, nor can it ever be morally neutral, because an act cannot be separated from the intrinsic moral meaning of that act. The moral meaning inherent to an act of adultery and the act itself are inseparable.

.052. The inherent moral meaning of each act is determined by its moral object. In order to discover what the moral object is, one must consider the act itself. It would be impossible to know the moral object without knowing which act is being knowingly chosen. Therefore, it is not possible to correctly evaluate the second font without considering both the act itself and its moral object. The morality of the second font is found in the ordering of the act itself toward its moral object. This ordering (toward a moral object) is absolutely identical to the inherent moral meaning (i.e. the moral nature, or moral species) of the act. The moral object determines the inherent moral meaning because the inherent moral meaning is nothing other than the ordering of the act itself toward its moral object. This inherent moral meaning is never separate from the act itself because the moral nature of the act is identical to this ordering toward a moral object, and nothing can be separated from its own essential nature. Even if the moral object is never attained, the act itself remains inherently ordered toward its moral object, and so the moral nature of the act does not change.

Example: A man asks a question of a priest. A question seeks an answer as its end. But the moral object is not any end, but the end of the act itself in terms of morality. So the end in terms of morality (i.e. the moral object) depends on the content of the answer that is sought by the question. The content of the answer that is sought by the question is not in the circumstances, because it is the moral object of the act itself. A man asks a question of a priest, seeking knowledge of the sins confessed to that priest by another person. This question has the moral object of breaking the seal of the confessional. Even if the priest says nothing, turns away, and departs, so that the end (moral object) that is sought is never obtained, the question inherently seeks this moral object of breaking the seal of the confessional, and so the act of asking this question is intrinsically evil.

One can never justify any intrinsically evil act by claiming that the meaning inherent to the act has been changed by any intention, or by any circumstance, or by any other acts, or by any factor or context whatsoever. Nothing can change the inherent moral meaning of the second font concerning any particular act (i.e. the concrete act, the chosen type of behavior), because that moral meaning is inherent to, and inseparable from, the act itself. Nothing can change the moral object of a particular act, because that particular act is inherently ordered toward its moral object.

Pope John Paul II: "Consequently, circumstances or intentions can never transform an act, intrinsically evil by virtue of its object, into an act 'subjectively' good or defensible as a choice."[52]

Pope John Paul II: "No circumstance, no purpose, no law whatsoever can ever make licit an act which is intrinsically illicit, since it is contrary to the Law of God which is written in every human heart, knowable by reason itself, and proclaimed by the Church."[53]

The Catechism of the Catholic Church: "It is therefore an error to judge the morality of human acts by considering only the intention that inspires them or the circumstances (environment, social pressure, duress or emergency, etc.) which supply their context. There are acts which, in and of themselves, independently of circumstances and intentions, are always gravely illicit by reason of their object; such as blasphemy and perjury, murder and adultery. One may not do evil so that good may result from it."[54]

Whenever the second font is bad, the act itself is necessarily intrinsically evil because the second font considers only the essential moral nature of the act (i.e. the inherent moral meaning) as determined by the moral object. An intrinsically evil act remains immoral regardless of intention (first font) and regardless of circumstance (third font). But it is always the case that, if any one font is bad, the overall act is immoral. This principle whereby the overall act is immoral whenever any one font is bad, regardless of the other two fonts, is not unique to intrinsically evil acts. Whenever any one font is bad, the other two fonts can never justify the overall act.

.053. Degree

Intrinsically evil acts are always immoral, because the moral object of the act is contrary to the moral law. A change in degree does not change the inherent ordering of that act toward its moral object.[55] This inherent ordering of any act toward its moral object constitutes the moral nature (or moral species) of the act itself. A change in degree cannot make an intrinsically evil act moral, because the essential moral nature of the act remains the same.

Analogy: Consider a large amount of water compared to a small amount of water. Each possesses the nature of water. Having a lesser amount does not change its nature. And the same applies to the moral nature inherent to any act.

Example: Lying is intrinsically evil and always immoral, even to a small degree. One lie may be a venial sin, and another lie may be a mortal sin. But lying remains immoral regardless of the degree. An evil intention makes a lie more serious in degree. A good intention makes a lie less serious in degree. Circumstances may make one lie more serious, or another lie less serious. But lying is intrinsically evil and always immoral, regardless of intention or

---

[52] Pope John Paul II, Veritatis Splendor, n. 81.
[53] Pope John Paul II, Evangelium Vitae, n. 62.
[54] CCC, n. 1756.
[55] Summa Theologica, I-II, Q. 18, A. 11.

circumstance. Even a small lie has an inherent moral meaning that is contrary to the love of God, who is Truth.

An intrinsically evil act may be a mortal sin, or it may be a venial sin. Intrinsically evil acts are always immoral, but such acts are not always gravely immoral. An intrinsically evil act is necessarily always gravely immoral only if the moral object makes the act so gravely disordered that choosing such an act turns the human person away from his ultimate end, God. When the moral object makes the act not only intrinsically evil, but also gravely immoral, then intention and circumstances cannot cause the overall act to be less than an objective mortal sin. Otherwise, if the moral object makes the act intrinsically evil, but not necessarily gravely immoral, then the intention and circumstances determine whether the intrinsically evil act is an objective mortal sin or an objective venial sin.

Examples: (1) Direct abortion is both intrinsically evil and always gravely immoral, because its moral object is the direct and voluntary killing of an innocent human being. Even with the best of intentions and in the most dire of circumstances, direct abortion is always an objective mortal sin. The moral object of direct abortion is gravely contrary to love of God and neighbor.

(2) Euthanasia is both intrinsically evil and always gravely immoral, because its moral object is the direct and voluntary killing of an innocent human being. Even with the best of intentions and in the most dire of circumstances, euthanasia is always an objective mortal sin; its moral object causes the act to be always an objective mortal sin because the choice of such an act is necessarily also the choice of the inherent moral meaning of that act, as determined by the moral object. And the moral object of murder is entirely incompatible with the threefold love of God, neighbor, self.

(3) Lying is intrinsically evil, but not necessarily gravely immoral. The moral object of lying is not so fundamentally disordered, apart from a consideration of intention and circumstances, as to be necessarily and always an objective mortal sin. Lying to one's neighbor is not inherently so gravely disordered as to deserve eternal Hellfire, nor so as to cause the human person to turn entirely away from true love of God and neighbor. A gravely immoral intention, or gravely immoral consequences, can make a particular lie an objective mortal sin. But the second font by itself does not make the act of lying gravely immoral.

A change in degree does not change the moral object of an act from good to evil, or from evil to good. The moral object is never good in one degree, and evil in another degree. The intention and circumstances may affect the degree of sinfulness of the overall act, but such a change in degree does not affect the moral object. If any act is entirely moral in one degree, but immoral in another degree, then the act cannot be intrinsically evil, because a change in degree does not change the inherent moral nature of the act as determined by the moral object. A change in degree cannot cause a bad moral object to become good, nor a good moral object to become bad.

.054. Independence

The three fonts of morality are independent of one another. The intention cannot change the moral object of the act itself. The circumstances cannot change the moral object of the act itself. The inherent moral meaning of the act itself is determined solely by the moral object, not by intention or circumstances.

The first font of morality is the intention of the subject (the person who acts). The person intends a particular end, by a particular means. By contrast, the moral object is the end toward which the act itself is inherently ordered. The intended end of the subject has no effect at all on the end toward which the act itself is intrinsically directed. The intended end and the moral object may sometimes be directed toward the same end. But in no case does the intention determine the moral object, and in no case does a change in intention change the moral object.

No act ever derives its moral object from the intention of the person who acts, but only and always from the good or evil end toward which the chosen act itself is inherently directed. If an intrinsically evil act is used for a good purpose (i.e. a good intended end), the moral object of that act remains evil and the act itself remains always immoral. Similarly, the moral object is never derived from the circumstances, such that the same act would have a different moral object in a different circumstance. The inherent moral meaning of any act is determined solely by the moral object toward which that act is inherently ordered, independent of the intention of the person, and independent of the circumstances or context of the situation.

Good or bad circumstances, even when extremely dire, have no effect at all on the moral object of the act itself. Circumstance is entirely in the third font; the moral object is entirely in the second font. Circumstances can never change the essential moral nature (or moral species) of the act itself, which is entirely determined by the moral object.

Pope John Paul II: "The weighing of the goods and evils foreseeable as the consequence of an action is not an adequate method for determining whether the choice of that concrete kind of behavior is 'according to its species', or 'in itself', morally good or bad, licit or illicit. The foreseeable consequences are part of those circumstances of the act, which, while capable of lessening the gravity of an evil act, nonetheless cannot alter its moral species."[56]

.055. The Moral Object is a Type of End

The moral object is the end in terms of morality, not the end in terms of intention, and not the end in terms of consequences. The moral object is a type of end toward which the act itself is inherently ordered, but in terms of morality, not in terms of concrete or tangible results. The moral object is not the end intended by the person who acts, but rather the moral end toward which the act itself is inherently directed.

---

[56] Pope John Paul II, Veritatis Splendor, n. 77.

Examples: (1) A man takes money belonging to another person. The moral object of this act of theft is the deprivation of goods from their owner, which is contrary to love of neighbor. As a consequence, he can now buy items that he could not buy before. His intended end may have been the same as this consequence (this end result), to be able to buy items. There is nothing to prevent the intended end and the anticipated consequences from being the same. However, the intended end in the first font, and the consequences in the third font, are different types of ends from the moral object of the second font.

(2) A man and a woman have natural sexual relations before marriage. One result (or consequence) of the sexual act is sexual climax and pleasure. But the moral object of this act of pre-marital sex is the deprivation of the marital meaning from the sexual act. Pleasure of any kind is not an act, but a result. Pleasure of any kind is not a moral object, because pleasure by itself is neither moral, nor immoral. Some bad acts result in pleasure of one type or another. Some good acts result in pleasure of one type or another. The moral object is the end in terms of morality, not the intended end, and not a consequential end.

(3) A woman tells a lie to her neighbor. The lie has the effect of deceiving the neighbor. This deception might be intended as a means to some end; it is also one of the consequences. Even so, the moral object of lying is not deception, but the deprivation of truth from an assertion. Even if the person telling the lie does not expect the deception of the listener to be a likely consequence, or even if the person telling the lie does not intend deception, God is still offended, because God is Truth. Lying is contrary to the very Nature of God. The intention to deceive is in the first font. The consequence that a person is deceived is in the third font. But the direct and voluntary assertion of a falsehood is in the second font. The second font is independent of intention and circumstances; therefore, lying is independent of deception.

(4) A surgeon attempts to save a patient's life by high-risk surgery; there is no other way to save this patient's life. The patient dies during the operation. This result of his act, the death of an innocent person, is the same as the result of a successful act of murder. But the moral object is not at all the same. The moral object is not a consequence (or result) of the chosen act, but rather the moral end toward the act is inherently ordered. The good moral object of this act of surgery is to save the patient's life. The reasonably anticipated risk of death is in the third font, not the second font. The intention to save the patient's life is in the first font. In this case, as is often the case with morally good acts, the intended end and the moral object are the same.

The moral end is the end in terms of morality (an end which may be either moral or immoral), not the concrete result of the chosen act. The end in terms of morality is determined by the proper relation of created things to one another and to God. Each and every moral object that is contrary to true love of God, or true love of neighbor, or true love of self, is an evil moral object. The moral object of an intrinsically evil act can always be expressed as a direct and voluntary deprivation of some good, and specifically as a deprivation of some good related to true love of God, neighbor, self.

The moral object is often confused with either the intended end, or with the consequences of the chosen act. The moral object is not the end intended by the person, nor is it the immediate or subsequent consequences of the chosen act. The tangible concrete results of an act are distinct from the moral end of the act. In fact, many persons sin precisely because they seek some tangible concrete end (as part of the consequences), without due regard for the inherent moral meaning of their chosen acts as determined by the moral object. The moral object is the end in terms of morality, i.e. within the moral order created by God. If you are not considering the act itself, apart from intention and circumstances, and in terms of the inherent moral meaning of the act before God, you will not be able to perceive the moral object.

The moral object is logically subsequent, but not necessarily chronologically subsequent, to the chosen act itself.

The moral object is not the future consequences of the chosen act; the moral object is in the second font, not the third font. For some acts, the moral object is chronologically subsequent to the act itself. For other acts, the moral object occurs at the same time as the chosen act (chronologically concurrent). But the moral object never occurs prior to the chosen act, since the act is ordered toward the moral object as to an end.

Examples: (1) A man deliberately fires a rifle at his innocent neighbor, murdering him. The moral object is to deprive an innocent human being of life. The deprivation of the life of the innocent man occurs subsequent to the chosen act of firing the rifle. In this case, the moral object is chronologically subsequent to the concrete act (the act itself).

(2) A man breaks into his neighbors house and steals some valuables. The moral object is to deprive the owner of his goods. This deprivation occurs during the end of the concrete act. First the man travels to his neighbor's house, then he breaks in, next he finds the valuables, and lastly he leaves with those valuables.

(3) A neighbor loans his valuables to a man, who at first takes the goods in trust (without any sin or crime). The man later decides to keep the valuables for himself. The act of theft occurs when he makes that decision, and the moral object of the deprivation of the owner's goods also occurs at the very same time. In this case, the moral object is chronologically concurrent (occurring at the same time) to the act itself. Previously, the owner was not deprived of his goods, since they were held in trust by agreement. As soon as the man holding those goods in trust decides to take ownership away from his neighbor, the act of theft has occurred and the moral object is attained.

(4) A man has natural sexual relations with his wife. The moral object is threefold: unitive, procreative, and marital. The act is inherently ordered toward union, which occurs during the act; toward procreation, which occurs after the act (sometimes days later); and toward expressing and strengthening the marriage, which occurs both during and after the act. Every knowingly chosen act is inherently ordered toward its moral object. But regardless of whether the moral object is achieved during or after the chosen act, or even if it is not

achieved at all, the inherent ordering of the act (toward its moral object) is always during the act itself, since it is the very nature of the act.

In order to determine the inherent moral meaning of the act itself, we must consider the end toward which the act is ordered. If we do not consider this end in terms of morality, but only in terms of intention and consequences, then we have cast aside true and absolute moral values. The moral object is often misunderstood because persons who live worldly lives are not accustomed to thinking of acts in terms of morality. The moral object of each act must be understood in order to know if the second font is moral.

.056.
C. THIRD FONT OF MORALITY: Circumstances

[Romans]
{12:17} Render to no one harm for harm. Provide good things, not only in the sight of God, but also in the sight of all men.
...
{13:10} The love of neighbor does no harm.

The third font of morality is the circumstances pertaining to the morality of the act, especially the consequences.

In moral theology, the word 'circumstances' refers solely to those known factors (past, present, or future) that pertain to the morality of the act, apart from intention, and apart from the essential moral nature of the act itself. Any factor that seems like a circumstance (in the secular definition of the word), but which has no moral bearing on the act, would not be a circumstance as that word is defined in moral theology. Any factor that seems like a circumstance, but which pertains to the morality of the first or second fonts, would not be a circumstance as that word is defined in moral theology. The circumstances of an act include everything that pertains to the morality of the act, other than the first two fonts.

The circumstances are the person's knowledge of any past, present, or future factors that affect the morality of the act. A judgment of the prudential order is used to evaluate the circumstances, including the moral weight of any applicable knowledge of the past, of the present, and of the future foreseeable consequences. This knowledge by a human person of past, present, and future circumstances is limited, because the human person is not all-knowing. Only what can be reasonably known or anticipated falls under the third font.

Knowingly chosen acts have future consequences, which human reason can anticipate, to a limited extent. The totality of the foreseeable consequences for all persons affected by the act are evaluated as to whether or not the good consequences morally outweigh the bad consequences. This evaluation of the moral consequences, as they can be reasonably anticipated, is based solely on any knowledge of past and present circumstances, in so far as these may affect the future consequences. The past is unaffected by our moral choices. And once a situation is present before us, our next knowingly chosen act only affects the future (even if the future is the very next moment). Therefore, only the future is affected by our moral choices. The totality of the reasonably anticipated future consequences of any knowingly chosen act is considered in the third font, so as to determine if the third font is good or bad. But the future is anticipated based on the application of reason to our knowledge of past circumstances and of the present situation. The third font is the anticipated future consequences of the act, but this anticipation is necessarily based on knowledge of the past and present. Therefore, we can say that the third font is only the future consequences, with the understanding that these consequences are anticipated based on knowledge of past and present circumstances; or we can say that the third font is the past, present, and future circumstances together, with the same understanding.

But it is important to understand that the good and bad consequences are to be evaluated by their weight under the moral law, which is based on love of God and neighbor. This evaluation considers the moral weight of the consequences: the consequences for all persons affected by the chosen act, in terms of morality, i.e. in terms of love of God and neighbor. The weight of the consequences must not be evaluated in terms of selfish interest, nor of merely material benefit. The moral weight of the third font is based on the true spiritual love of God, neighbor, self, and is not based on a selfish love, nor merely on the material and temporal benefits and detriments to neighbor and self. The moral weight of the good and bad consequences includes material and temporal consequences, but must also transcend these to include all spiritual consequences, such as any benefit or harm to the souls and spiritual lives of all persons affected by the act.

If the moral weight of the good consequences is greater than the moral weight of the bad consequences, then the third font is good, despite some bad consequences. If the moral weight of the bad consequences is greater than the moral weight of the good consequences, then the third font is bad, despite some good consequences. Whenever the third font is bad, the overall act is immoral. When the third font is good, the other two fonts must also be good for the overall act to be moral.

Example: A man intends to quit his job in order to find work that provides him with a better living; both his current and intended occupations are moral. The act of quitting one job to go to another job is moral; it is not intrinsically evil to leave one type of work for another. However, the circumstances are such that there is a likelihood that he will not obtain the new job, or if he obtains it, there is a likelihood that he will not keep it, and his family depends on him for their livelihood. One of the foreseeable consequences is a substantial and likely risk of harm because he might not be able to support his family. The intention (to obtain a better living) and the act itself (changing jobs) are both good. But in these circumstances, the bad consequence of substantial risk to his family outweighs the good consequence of possibly making a better living. The act would not be moral in those circumstances, even though the first two fonts are good, because of the reasonably anticipated bad consequences to other persons.

The future consequences of an act determine the morality of the third font. However, these future consequences are anticipated based on past and present circumstances.

Examples: A police officer encounters a man holding a gun. (1) If the officer has no knowledge of past criminal activity by this man, and in the present situation the man is behaving in a non-threatening manner, then the officer would not be justified in using deadly force. The officer reasonably anticipates, based on knowledge of the past and present, that he will not be harmed if he refrains from using deadly force. (2) If the officer recognizes the man as a known violent criminal, who is suspected of killing another police officer in the recent past, and the man is behaving in a threatening manner, then the officer may be justified in using deadly force. The officer may reasonably anticipate that he will die or be seriously harmed, if he does not use deadly force. But his reasonable anticipation of future consequences is based on his knowledge of past and present circumstances.

.057. Our evaluation of possible future consequences always follows from our knowledge of past and present circumstances. In this life, human persons have no direct knowledge of the future. Instead, human reason anticipates the possible or likely future consequences, based on our knowledge of the past and the present.

Examples: (1) A physician prescribes a moral treatment, knowing, from past cases and past studies, the usefulness of the treatment and its risks. He also knows the past medical history and the present symptoms of the patient. The physician can reasonably anticipate that the treatment will be useful to the patient, and that the potential for harm, such as in side effects, is outweighed by the good effect on health. It is moral for the physician to give the patient that treatment. (2) But in the same situation, suppose that, after the patient receives the medication, he dies from a previously unknown allergy to that medication. The patient and the physician had no way of knowing that the medication would cause that harmful effect. The physician did not sin by giving that medication to that patient, even though the patient died as a result. The act of giving the patient that medication was moral because the third font includes only the totality of the foreseeable consequences and any knowledge of past or present circumstances, but not any unknowable factors.

Neither was it a merely objective sin for the physician to give that medication to that patient. Whatever is not knowable by the person who acts is not in the third font at all, not even objectively. The entire moral law is accessible to reason. And whether or not an intention (first font) or a moral object (second font) is evil is always knowable. But reason is not always able to know every fact in every circumstance, nor every future consequence, because human persons are not all-knowing. Thus, if a fact is not known, then that fact cannot make the act an actual sin, and if a fact is not knowable, then that fact cannot make the act even an objective sin. Whatever is unknowable by the human person is not in the third font. The physician knew that with any medication there is a risk of adverse side effects, and even a small risk of death. But he need only weigh what is known, including the known degree of risk. When the actual outcome in a particular case is not foreseeable, it does not affect the morality of the act, even objectively. (If the physician had known that the patient was severely allergic to that particular medication, then the act of giving that medication to that patient would be morally a different act.)

Ignorance in the third font differs from invincible ignorance. Invincible ignorance applies when an objective sin is not also an actual sin because the limitations that apply to a particular human person, at a particular point in time, prevent him from knowing that which is generally accessible to reason and a part of the moral law. In cases of invincible ignorance, the deficiency in knowledge makes an objective sin not also an actual sin. Invincible ignorance applies to the third font when the individual makes a sincere error in evaluating the moral weight of the known past, present, and future circumstances. But when a factor, which would be in the third font if it was knowable, is an unknowable past or present circumstance, or an unforeseeable future consequence, then that factor cannot cause the act to be either an actual sin, or an objective sin. Whatever is unknowable in the third font is not under the moral law.

Examples: (1) A soldier kills an enemy combatant in a just military action during a just war. The first two fonts are good. The soldier had no way of knowing that this particular enemy combatant had knowledge of enemy battle plans, which would have come to light if the combatant had been captured instead of being killed, and which therefore would have saved many lives. This unforeseeable consequence is not in the third font and does not affect the morality of the act, even objectively. The act is moral because the first two fonts are good, and in the known past, present, and future circumstances, the good outweighed the bad.

(2) A soldier kills an innocent civilian, mistakenly thinking that he is an enemy combatant. The soldier had no way of knowing that this person was an innocent civilian. The act of killing this person was not an actual mortal sin, but it was an objective mortal sin, because the knowledge that was lacking determines the second font, not the third. Killing an innocent human being is an intrinsically evil act, and so nothing can make the act objectively moral. Invincible ignorance prevents an objective sin from being also an actual sin, but it cannot cause an objectively immoral act to become good.

.058. The intention of a particular end is always known to the person who acts, because intention by definition is a type of knowing free choice. Invincible ignorance never applies to an intended end, since a person always knows (or is readily able to know) his own purpose for acting. Invincible ignorance may apply to the first font if the person did not know that the intended means was intrinsically evil, and so he did not know that the intention of that means was objectively immoral. Invincible ignorance may apply to the second font, if the person did not know that the chosen act was intrinsically evil; in such a case the act would not be an actual sin, but would still be an objective sin. (But culpable ignorance is not invincible.) However, in the third font, invincible ignorance applies to the judgment of the moral weight of the circumstances, and does not apply to any unknowable past or present circumstances, nor to any unforeseeable future consequences.

Even if the first two fonts are good, if, in the evaluation of the third font, the bad consequences outweigh the good, then the third font is bad and the overall act is immoral. Whenever any one font of morality is bad, the overall act is immoral, and cannot be done without sin. But if the circumstances change, so that the good consequences now outweigh the bad, and the first two fonts are also good, then the act would be moral. The circumstances are the reasonably foreseeable future consequences (based on knowledge of past and present circumstances) that pertain to the morality of the act. Any consequence that cannot be reasonably anticipated is not in the third font and does not affect the morality of the chosen act.

The third font differs from the first and second fonts in that good and bad are weighed, and some bad circumstances can be tolerated, to some degree. In the first font, no degree of bad intention can occur without sin. Any type or degree of bad intention makes an act a sin (at least a venial sin). In the second font, if the moral object of the act is bad, then the act which is ordered toward that object is intrinsically evil and always a sin (at least a venial sin). A change in degree does not change the inherent moral nature of the act.

In the first font, a bad intended end is an immoral intended end. In the second font, a bad moral object is an evil moral object; it is immoral. Any immorality in the first or second font makes the font immoral and the act immoral. But in the third font, the bad consequences are not necessarily immoral; they are bad in the sense of harm, and not in the sense of morally bad. Only when the bad consequences outweigh the good consequences is the third font morally bad. That is why some bad consequences can be tolerated in the third font, whereas no bad intended end and no bad moral object can be tolerated in the first and second fonts. The term 'bad' in the consequences of an act refers to the harm that is done. It is not moral to do more harm than good. But it is moral to do more good than harm.

.059.
COMPARISON OF THE THREE FONTS

Harm in the Three Fonts

In the first font, if any type of harm or immorality is intended as an end, then the first font is immoral. In the second font, if the act itself is inherently directed at any type of harm or immorality as an end (the moral object), then the act is intrinsically evil and the second font is immoral. Although harm differs from immorality, it is never moral to intend harm as an end, nor to choose an act that is inherently directed at harm as an end. For all harm is contrary to the fullness of goodness in created things as intended by God.

However, some harm may be tolerated, in the first font, but only in the means, and only in view of a greater good in the end. Similarly, in the third font, some harm may be tolerated in the bad consequences, but only in view of a greater good in the good consequences. The type of bad (or evil) that is harm differs from the type of bad (or evil) that is immoral. (See the chapter on Types of Evil.) No immorality is tolerable in any of the three fonts of morality; any immorality in any font makes the overall act immoral. However, moral evil differs from harm. Some harm can be tolerated in the intended means and in the consequences, in view of a greater good.

Example: (1) A physician intends to amputate a limb to save a life. In the first font, the intended means is bad in the sense of harm, but it is not bad in the sense of immoral. Any immorality in the intended means or intended end would make the first font immoral. Also, if harm were intended as an end, the first font would be immoral. So if the physician intended to amputate a limb as his intended end, such an intention would be immoral. But since the physician only intends this harm as an intended means to a greater good in the intended end (saving a life), the intended means is moral. This weighing of the harm in the intended means compared to the good in the intended end is similar to the weighing of harm (bad consequences) compared to benefit (good consequences) in the third font. A physician could not morally intend to amputate a limb in order to achieve only a small benefit to health. The good done in the intended end would then not morally outweigh the harm used as a means to that end. An immoral means is never justified by a good end. No immorality is ever justified at all. But some degree of harm in the intended means can be tolerated if the good in the intended end is greater.

Even though the three fonts of morality are independent of one another, there is a certain relationship between them. The good and bad consequences are often related to the intention. A person often chooses an act with the intention of obtaining the good consequences of that act. However, if the act is chosen with the intention of obtaining the bad consequences as an intended end, such an intention is always immoral. In such a case, the first font is bad, but the third font might still be good, if the good consequences outweigh the bad. Thus, bad consequences may be intended as a means to a greater good, but never as an end. And this is in agreement with the evaluation of the third font, such that bad consequences are tolerated in view of greater good consequences.

Venial and Mortal Sin in the Three Fonts

Mortal sin differs from venial sin by both degree and type. Several venial sins together are more serious than one venial sin, but a series of venial sins can never add up to a mortal sin. In order to be a mortal sin, the act must be a different type of sin, not merely a greater degree of sin. Therefore, the fonts also cannot be added together so that two or three venial fonts in the same act would constitute a mortal sin. If each font by itself would make the act only a venial sin, the overall act can be only a venial sin. If one font makes the act a venial sin, any additional immorality in the other fonts makes the act a more serious sin, but never to the extent of a mortal sin, unless at least one of the fonts by itself would make the act a mortal sin. For mortal sin is a different type of act.

Similarly, if any one font makes the act a mortal sin, the other fonts cannot reduce the act to less than a mortal sin. The other fonts can affect the seriousness of the sin within the type of sin, making a venial sin more or less sinful (but still venial), or making a mortal sin more or less sinful (but still mortal). But the other fonts cannot change the type of the sin from mortal to venial. Even one gravely immoral font makes the overall act a mortal sin.

.060. Changing the Morality of a Font

The third font may be moral despite some degree of bad circumstances (if the good outweighs the bad), or immoral despite some degree of good circumstances (if the bad outweighs the good). A difference in degree may change the morality of the third font, because in the circumstances a person weighs both the benefits and the harm in order to determine which is greater. But if the circumstances change, so that the good now outweighs the bad, or the bad now outweighs the good, then the morality of the third font changes. A good act done with good intention is immoral if the bad consequences outweigh the good. But at another time, in different circumstances, the good might now outweigh the bad for the same good act with the same good intention. Thus, a change in circumstances may change the morality of the third font.

The first font is immoral if the intention of the subject (the person who acts) is immoral. But if the other two fonts are good, and if the only reason that the act is immoral is that the intention is bad, the person may cooperate with grace to change his intention, thus making the same act with the same consequences now moral. Thus, a change in intention may change the morality of the first font.

However, the second font is immoral if the act itself is intrinsically, by the very nature of the act, directed at an evil end (the moral object). Nothing can change this type of act from evil to good. A different act may be chosen, one that has a good moral object instead of an evil moral object. But each and every good act is fundamentally different in its essential moral nature from each and every evil act. The only way to change the moral object is to choose a fundamentally different type of act. As long as the moral object remains evil, the chosen act cannot become moral.

The person who acts may change his intention, by the grace of God, from evil to good. The person may wait for the circumstances to change, so that the good now outweighs the bad. Or the person might choose a good act, or a series of good acts, that will change the circumstances of a different act, so that now the good outweighs the bad. But unlike the other two fonts, the second font cannot be changed by a change in intention, nor by a change in circumstances, but only by changing the fundamental type of act that is chosen. The person who acts cannot change the moral object of an evil act from evil to good. The only way to change the moral object is to choose a different act with a different moral object.

Three Types of Ends

Each font pertains to a different type of end. The first font is the end intended by the person in choosing the act. The first font also includes the intended means, which is itself a type of end; a means is an intermediate end. Every intended means and every intended end ought to be ordered toward God as our ultimate end. So every intention in every act should be a means to God, our final end.

The morality of the second font is determined by the moral object, which is the end, in terms of morality, toward which the chosen act is inherently directed. The morality of the third font is determined by the reasonably anticipated end results of the chosen act, i.e. the good and bad consequences. The consequences of any act are a type of end.

There is nothing to prevent any font from having more than one end. A single act may have more than one moral object. A good act may have more than one good moral object. An intrinsically evil act may have more than one evil moral object. But whenever an act has more than one moral object, a single evil moral object causes the act itself to be intrinsically evil and always immoral. Similarly, if a person has more than one intention in choosing a single act, any immorality in the intention causes the first font to be bad. Only the third font can tolerate some bad consequences and still be good, because bad consequences are not moral evil, but physical evil (harm or disorder).

The morality of each font is determined by the ends pertaining to that font. All good ends are capable of being directed toward God as our final end. Whenever any end in any font is not capable of being ordered toward God, that font is bad and the chosen act is immoral. And the evaluation of each font, as to whether or not its end can also be a means to God as the final end, is based on the love of God, which implies both the love of neighbor and a true ordered love of self. Therefore, the love of God, neighbor, self is the basis for the three fonts of morality.

Chapter 4
The Principle of Double Effect

.061.

The principle of double effect is the natural result of a proper understanding of the three fonts of morality; it is not additional to the three fonts, but rather is found within these fonts. Under the principle of double effect, an act is moral if the first two fonts are good and if, in the third font, the good outweighs the bad. When the intention, including the intended means and the intended end, is good, and when the act itself is good (due to a good moral object), then the morality of the overall act depends on the circumstances. But if the moral weight of the circumstances depends on two effects (i.e. consequences) of the act, one good and the other bad, the act is moral if the good outweighs the bad, and immoral if the bad outweighs the good.

So the principle of double effect is nothing other than the proper application of the three fonts of morality to a particular class of acts, those in which the first two fonts are good, and in which the third font has both good and bad consequences (i.e. effects). This principle also applies if there are multiple good and multiple bad consequences. In any case, as long as the first two fonts are good and, in the third font, the totality of the good consequences outweighs the totality of the bad consequences, the act is moral. As long as the third font has good and bad circumstances, and the good outweighs the bad, and the other two fonts are good, then the act is justified under the principle of double effect. If all three fonts are good, and there is nothing bad in the circumstances, then the act would be moral; but this would not be classified under the principle of double effect, if there are only good effects.

.062. Intention and Bad Consequences

There is a provision of the principle of double effect which states that the bad consequences must not be intended (as an end). But this is merely a proper application of the three fonts of morality. It is not moral to intend any type of harm, such as found in the bad consequences of an act, as an end. And whenever the intention is immoral, the overall act is immoral, regardless of the other two fonts. If the bad consequences in the third font are intended as an end, then the first font is immoral.

However, the bad consequences in the third font may be intended as a means to an end, because the bad consequences are not moral evil, but only a type of harm or disorder. An immoral means cannot be used, even to obtain a moral end. But a means that is bad in the sense of harm or disorder can be tolerated as a bad consequence that is outweighed by the good consequences of the same act.

Examples: (1) A judge gives a sentence of death to a criminal convicted of a very serious crime. The judge intends the death of a human person, which is a type of serious harm. But, according to Saint Thomas Aquinas, it is moral for him to intend this harm as a means to protect the common good.[57] For he is acting similarly to a physician who amputates a limb to save a life. The loss of the life of even a criminal is a bad consequence in the third font. But since this person is guilty of serious crimes, this loss is bad in the sense of harm, but it is not intrinsically evil. The proper use of the death penalty is not immoral because the person killed is guilty, not innocent. A bad means may be intended in order to achieve a greater good end, but only if the bad means is bad in the sense of harm, and not bad in the sense of immoral.

The principle of double effect justifies the use of the death penalty in certain cases. The intended end is the justice of safeguarding the common good. The intended means is the death of the guilty convicted criminal; this means is not immoral; it is bad in the sense of harm, but not in the sense of morally bad. The act itself is an act of defending the community and dispensing justice to the guilty. The good consequences of protecting the common good must outweigh the bad consequences of the loss of a human life. If so, then all three fonts are good, and the judge may morally give the death penalty in such cases.

(2) Jesus allowed His own death, intending His death to be a means to the good end of our salvation. He could have prevented His own death, by calling on His Father and His Angels (Mt 26:53). Jesus did not cause His own death, for suicide is intrinsically evil and always gravely immoral. Nor did He intend His own death as an end, which would be immoral. But He did permit His own death, with the intention of accomplishing the good end of our salvation. Thus a bad (but moral) means may be intended for the sake of a greater good end.

[Matthew]
{26:53} Or do you think that I cannot ask my Father, so that he would give me, even now, more than twelve legions of Angels?
{26:54} How then would the Scriptures be fulfilled, which say that it must be so?"

(3) Jesus chose to be baptized by John the Baptist, despite the disorder of having a finite creature baptize the Savior, who is infinite God, and from whom all Baptism has its effectiveness. Every disorder is a type of harm. But this disorder was not immoral, and was not intended as an end, but as a means to a greater good end, the establishment of the Sacrament of Baptism.

[Matthew]
{3:13} Then Jesus came from Galilee, to John at the Jordan, in order to be baptized by him.
{3:14} But John refused him, saying, "I ought to be baptized by you, and yet you come to me?"
{3:15} And responding, Jesus said to him: "Permit this for now. For in this way it is fitting for us to fulfill all justice." Then he allowed him.

(4) Jesus used violence when removing the buyers and sellers from the Temple. Now violence is not necessarily immoral, but it is a type of harm or disorder. For

---

[57] Saint Thomas Aquinas, Summa Theologica, II-II, Q. 64, A. 7.

God did not create any persons for the sake of violence, and violence is only ever necessary because of the sinfulness of human persons. Jesus intended to use (moderate, limited) violence as a means to the good end of stopping the sins of buying and selling in the Temple of God. Thus, the use of violence may be intended as a moral (but harmful) means to a greater good end.

[Matthew]
{21:12} And Jesus entered into the temple of God, and he cast out all who were selling and buying in the temple, and he overturned the tables of the money changers and the chairs of the vendors of doves.
{21:13} And he said to them: "It is written: 'My house shall be called a house of prayer. But you have made it into a den of robbers.' "

[John]
{2:14} And he found, sitting in the temple, sellers of oxen and sheep and doves, and the moneychangers.
{2:15} And when he had made something like a whip out of little cords, he drove them all out of the temple, including the sheep and the oxen. And he poured out the brass coins of the moneychangers, and he overturned their tables.
{2:16} And to those who were selling doves, he said: "Take these things out of here, and do not make my Father's house into a house of commerce."

.063. But violence is also a bad consequence, since it is by definition a type of harm. Therefore, a bad consequence can be morally intended as a means to a good end, for bad consequences are not bad in the sense of immoral, but only in the sense of harm or disorder. The consequences of an act are only immoral if the totality of the bad consequences outweighs the totality of the good consequences. Otherwise, some bad consequences may be tolerated, and may even be intended as a means to a greater good end. Neither is this use of bad consequences a justification of the means by the end, since this means is not bad in the sense of immoral. Whatever is immoral cannot be justified at all, not even by reference to a good end. But bad consequences are not immoral in themselves.

However, a bad consequence in the third font, whether in the case of the principle of double effect or in any case at all, may never be intended as an end, even if this consequence is not in itself immoral, even if the good consequences outweigh the bad. The reason is that the intention of a bad consequence as an end, rather than as a means, is not capable of being ordered toward God as our final end. In other words, true love of God, neighbor, self is not compatible with the choice by the human will of any type of harm or disorder (bad consequences) as an end.

If the good consequences outweigh the bad, but if those bad consequences are intended as an end, then the third font is good, but the first font is bad. A bad intention makes the first font of morality bad, not the third. So for the principle of double effect to make an act good, the bad consequences must not be intended as an end. But it is always the case that all three fonts must be good for the overall act to be moral.

The Principle of Double Effect

If there is any immoral intention, then the first font is bad and the overall act is immoral, regardless of the other two fonts. If the moral object is bad, then the act is intrinsically evil, and the second font is bad, and the overall act is immoral, regardless of the other two fonts. If the bad circumstances outweigh the good circumstances, then the third font is bad, and the overall act is immoral, regardless of the other two fonts. Even under the principle of double effect, the overall act is only moral if all three fonts are good. So the principle of double effect is not an exception to the three fonts, but merely its proper application.

.064. Killing in Self-defense

In the Summa Theologica, Saint Thomas Aquinas considers the question: "Whether it is lawful to kill a man in self-defense?" The act of killing in self-defense is the classic example of the principle of double effect. This act has two very weighty effects, the loss of one person's life, and the saving of another person's life.

Saint Thomas Aquinas: "I answer that, Nothing hinders one act from having two effects, only one of which is intended, while the other is beside the intention. Now moral acts take their species according to what is intended, and not according to what is beside the intention, since this is accidental as explained above (II-II, 43, 3; I-II, 12, 1). Accordingly the act of self-defense may have two effects, one is the saving of one's life, the other is the slaying of the aggressor. Therefore this act, since one's intention is to save one's own life, is not unlawful, seeing that it is natural to everything to keep itself in 'being,' as far as possible."[58]

St. Thomas did not explicitly analyze morality in terms of the three fonts. However, the three fonts are implicit to his work, and so we are able to better understand his teaching by applying each of the three fonts.

These two effects, that one person dies and another lives, are in the third font; these are the good and bad consequences of the chosen act of self-defense. The good effect of saving the life of an innocent person (one's self, or even another innocent person) outweighs the bad effect of the death of a guilty person. When deadly force is used in self-defense (or in defense of others), it is used to repel an unjust attack. Therefore, one person is guilty of an unjust attack, and the other person is innocent. So the saving of the innocent life has greater moral weight. Therefore, the third font is good.

In the above quote, when St. Thomas refers to intention, he is actually referring to the second font, not the first. For the act itself is always a deliberately chosen act, i.e. an intentionally chosen act. The moral species (or essential moral nature) of the second font is determined by the moral object of the deliberately chosen act. In an act of self-defense, the intentionally chosen act has the object of defending innocent life. But every moral object is inherent to the chosen act, which is in the second font. The moral object is never inherent to, nor is it determined by, the intended end or purpose, which is in the first font.

---

[58] Saint Thomas Aquinas, Summa Theologica, II-II, Q. 64, A. 7.

"The innocent and the just you shall not kill." (Ex 23:7). "And they put them to death, and innocent blood was saved on that day." (Dan 13:62).

The innocent may not be killed, but the guilty may be killed in some cases, such as to save the innocent from death, if all three fonts are good. Acts of self-defense have a good moral object, because the chosen act is inherently directed at the end of defending the innocent. And this act is a particular fulfillment of the commandment to love your neighbor: "you shall love your neighbor as yourself." (Mt 19:19). Therefore, an act of self-defense has a good second font. But in order to be moral, any act of self-defense must also be good under the first font of intention. So if the bad consequences are intended as an end, then the first font is immoral. However, the bad consequence of the death of the aggressor may be intended as a means, not as an end.

.065. Saint Thomas gives two types of examples of intention, the immoral intention where the death of the aggressor is intended as an end (such as out of private animosity), and the moral intention of the death of the aggressor as a means to justice and the common good.

Saint Thomas Aquinas: "it is not lawful for a man to intend killing a man in self-defense, except for such as have public authority, who while intending to kill a man in self-defense, refer this to the public good, as in the case of a soldier fighting against the foe, and in the minister of the judge struggling with robbers, although even these sin if they be moved by private animosity."[59]

The judge, by public authority, sentences someone to death, and morally intends that the convicted criminal die, but this death is intended as a means, not as an end. If he were motivated out of private animosity, so that he intended the death as an end, then his intention would be immoral. Similarly, intending to kill a man in self-defense is an immoral intention only if the death is intended as an end. The death of the aggressor may be morally intended as a necessary means to the good end of self-defense, just as similarly occurs in the case of a just judge, or of a soldier fighting in a just war. The judge morally intends the death of the convicted criminal, as a means to the end of defending the common good. The soldier morally intends the death of the enemy combatant, as a means to the end of defending the nation. Bad consequences may be intended as a means to a good end. For bad consequences are bad in the sense of harm or disorder, not in the sense of immorality.

Notice that, even when deadly force has a good moral object in the second font, as in the case of a soldier defending his country, or a law enforcement officer defending the community, or an individual defending himself or his family, the first font of intention must also be good. Whoever intends evil, sins against God. If the intention is immoral, then the moral object would remain good, but the overall act would be a sin. Similarly, if the good consequences of an act of killing in self-defense, or in a just war, or in the use of the death penalty, were outweighed by the bad consequences, then the act would be immoral under the third font, even if the first and second fonts are good. An act of self-defense can

---

[59] Saint Thomas Aquinas, Summa Theologica, II-II, Q. 64, A. 7.

be moral under the second font, but also immoral under the first or third fonts. For the fonts are independent of one another. It is not sufficient for an act of killing to have a good moral object (self-defense, defense of the community, defense of the nation), the other two fonts must also be good for the act to be moral. The intention must be good, and the good consequences must outweigh the bad consequences.

Saint Thomas Aquinas: "And yet, though proceeding from a good intention, an act may be rendered unlawful, if it be out of proportion to the end. Wherefore if a man, in self-defense, uses more than necessary violence, it will be unlawful: whereas if he repel force with moderation his defense will be lawful, because according to the jurists [Cap. Significasti, De Homicid. volunt. vel casual.], 'it is lawful to repel force by force, provided one does not exceed the limits of a blameless defense.' "[60]

In the quote above, St. Thomas considers the case of a good act of self-defense, with good intention, but where the force used is disproportionate. But in terms of the three fonts of morality, this must be understood to refer only to the proportion of the good and bad consequences. This proportionality is not based on the amount of force, but on the amount of harm done by that force, which must be outweighed by the good done by the same act. So if deadly force is needed for self-defense, it does not change the proportionality of the third font if a larger weapon or a more forceful weapon is used (such as a gun instead of a knife), as long as the harm done is the same, i.e. the death of the aggressor. Whether or not a use of force is considered to be moderate or disproportionate depends on the moral weight of the consequences, not specifically on the amount of force used in self-defense.

Saint Thomas Aquinas: "Nor is it necessary for salvation that a man omit the act of moderate self-defense in order to avoid killing the other man, since one is bound to take more care of one's own life than of another's."[61]

The moral law is based on love of God, neighbor, and self. This threefold love has a certain order, in that our love of God is first, our love of neighbor is second (since we are to be selfless, not selfish), and our love of self is third. However, when our neighbor is guilty of an attack against the innocent (against one's self or one's neighbor), the duty to the innocent outweighs the duty to show love even to the guilty. And this remains true even if the innocent person is one's self. However, even the death of a guilty person is a bad consequence to be weighed in the third font of morality. For all human persons are made in the image of the Most Holy Trinity.

.066. Equal Moral Weight

In any knowingly chosen act, if the good and bad consequences are of equal moral weight, and if the first and second fonts are good, then the act is moral. The good intention (first font) is pleasing to God. The chosen good act (second

---

[60] Saint Thomas Aquinas, Summa Theologica, II-II, Q. 64, A. 7.
[61] Saint Thomas Aquinas, Summa Theologica, II-II, Q. 64, A. 7.

font) is pleasing to God. For all that is good is pleasing to God, who is Goodness itself. The circumstances (third font) include good and bad consequences of equal moral weight, and so the third font does not offend God. For the bad consequences are not in themselves morally bad, but are bad in the sense of harm or disorder. And this harm is balanced by good consequences of the same moral weight. Therefore, even though the good and bad circumstances are judged to be of equal moral weight, the goodness of the first two fonts, with the equality of the moral weight in the third font, makes the overall act moral.

Example: (1) The lives of two adults are in grave danger, but the rescuer can only save one life. The intention to save a life is good; the loss of the other life is not intended. The act itself of saving one life is good, since it is a particular fulfillment of the commandment to love your neighbor. In the circumstances, there are two effects, one good and the other bad, specifically, that one person lives and the other person dies. In this situation, the act of rescuing one adult, allowing the other adult to die, is moral. The first two fonts are good. The good and bad effects are equal, since one innocent life is saved while another innocent life is lost. The good effect is intended and the bad effect is not intended. The act is moral because the first two fonts are pleasing to God, and because the third font is not offensive to God, since the moral weight of the good and bad consequences are equal.

.067. Other Examples

The principle of double effect applies whenever there are both good and bad consequences to an act. The evaluation of an act under this principle is nothing other than the proper evaluation of the act under all three fonts of morality.

FIRST FONT: Is the intended end good? The intention of a bad end causes any act to be immoral. Any bad consequences cannot be intended as an end. And everything intended as either an end or a means must be morally good. An intrinsically evil act cannot be intended as a means. Bad consequences can only be intended as a means, not as an end.

SECOND FONT: Is the moral object of the deliberately chosen act good? If the moral object is evil, then the chosen act is intrinsically evil and always immoral. The principle of double effect cannot justify an intrinsically evil act. The moral object must be good, or the second font and the overall act will be immoral.

THIRD FONT: If the first and second fonts are both good, and there are both good and bad consequences, then the act might be moral under the principle of double effect, despite the bad consequences. If the first or the second fonts are bad, then the overall act is immoral. If there are no bad consequences, then all three fonts are good and the act is moral (but this would not be an example of the principle of double effect).

If the first and second fonts are both good, and if there are both good and bad consequences in the third font, then the moral weight of the consequences must be judged in order to determine the morality of the act. If the consequences are equal in weight, or if the good outweighs the bad, then the act is moral. If the

The Principle of Double Effect

bad consequences outweigh the good consequences, then the overall act is immoral because the third font is bad.

Examples: (1) A woman is pregnant and has cancer. She is in the early stages of pregnancy, but her cancer is advancing rapidly. If she attempts to wait until her prenatal child is viable outside the womb and can be delivered, both she and the prenatal will die before viability. If she has the treatment, there is a good chance that her life can be saved, but the cancer treatment will kill the prenatal.

In this example, the intended end is to save the life of the woman; the intended means is a moral act, the treatment of the disease of cancer. The chosen act of taking this cancer treatment has the good moral object of saving a life. This act is not intrinsically evil because it is inherently directed at the saving of life, not the destruction of life. The good consequence is the likelihood of saving the mother's life. The bad consequence is the unintended death of the prenatal. But since there was no way to save the prenatal's life, the good consequence of saving an innocent life, one that can be saved, outweighs the bad consequence of failing to save an innocent life, one that cannot be saved. This act of taking the cancer medication is moral under the principle of double effect, despite the unintended death of the prenatal. (In such cases, the death of the prenatal is sometimes referred to under the term 'indirect abortion.' Although direct abortion is intrinsically evil and always gravely immoral, 'indirect abortion' is not truly abortion and so is sometimes moral.)

(2) A citizen is voting and has a choice between two candidates. But the consequences of voting for either candidate have both good and bad effects. Both candidates have positions on issues, likely to affect legislation, that are only partly in agreement with Catholic teaching. A vote for either candidate will have both good and bad effects.

The voter must have only good intention in his voting choice. For example, he cannot intend that abortion become legal, or remain legal, or become more widely available. He cannot intend that the economy be changed for the sake of his own selfish benefit, to the harm of others. He cannot intend anything contrary to the common good. However, if the only font causing your act to be immoral is the first font of intention, then cooperate with grace so as to change your intention. The faithful of Jesus Christ should intend only good, because Jesus intends only good, and because God is Good, by His very Nature.

Voting for a candidate is not intrinsically evil. The moral object is the election of a human person to represent a group of citizens. This moral object is good, not evil because representative democracy is not evil; it is directed toward the common good and capable of being directed toward God as the ultimate Good. Even if a candidate is particularly unfit for this type of service, the act of voting for him is not inherently directed at an evil end. So when voting for a candidate, the second font is good. Therefore, if the intention is good, the morality of this type of choice depends on an evaluation of the good and bad consequences of the act of voting for each candidate.

Unfortunately, the effect of voting for almost any candidate today has substantial good and bad effects. Therefore, the principle of double effect applies, to determine if the good effects of any particular act of voting outweigh the bad effects. A voter can morally vote for a particular candidate if the voter has only good intentions, and if the voter judges that this way of voting will do the most good and the least harm, such that the good consequences outweigh the bad. Such an evaluation is complex, depending on the various issues, their moral weight, the likelihood that an issue will be affected by the vote, the likelihood that the candidate can be elected, and other factors. Faithful and reasonable Catholics may disagree as to the evaluation of the moral weight of a complex set of consequences with both good and bad effects.

(3) A person tells a small lie, for a good intended end, with both good and bad effects. In this example, the chosen act of lying is intrinsically evil and always immoral. The principle of double effect can never justify an act that is inherently directed at an evil moral object. All such acts are intrinsically evil and always sinful. The good intended end might seem to make the first font good, but the person intends to reach this good end by the intrinsically evil means of lying, and so the intended means is morally bad, causing the first font to be immoral. Both the first and second fonts in this example are immoral, so the act would be a sin even if the good effects outweigh the bad. If it is also the case that the bad effects outweigh the good, then the sin is more serious. Lying is always immoral, but it is not always gravely immoral. The first and third fonts can make one lie gravely immoral, and another lie only a venial sin.

(4) A woman has a hysterectomy (operation removing the uterus) in order to treat a grave medical problem. The intended end is good, to obtain good health. The moral object is the same as the intention, i.e. to obtain good health. The operation has two effects, the good effect of improved health, and the bad effect of rendering the woman infertile. In this case, the good effect of health outweighs the bad effect of infertility. For if the problem went untreated, the woman's life might be endangered, or at least infertility would still result, from the medical disorder itself. So this type of medical treatment, with good and bad effects, may be justified under the principle of double effect, depending on the evaluation of the complex risks and benefits, as well as any other medical options, in one particular case or another.

.068. The Sin of Scandal

Moral theology uses the term 'scandal' with a specialized meaning.

[Mark]
{9:41} "And whoever will have **scandalized** one of these little ones who believe in me: it would be better for him if a great millstone were placed around his neck and he were thrown into the sea."

Saint Jerome: "As this word 'scandalum' (offense or stumbling block) is of such frequent use in ecclesiastical writings, we will shortly explain it. We might render it in Latin, 'offendiculum,' or 'ruina,' or 'impactio'. And so when we read, 'Whoever shall scandalize,' we understand, whoever by word or deed has given an occasion of falling to any."[62] [St. Jerome is commenting on Matthew 15:12, but quoting from Mark 9:41.]

Saint Thomas Aquinas: "Scandal is, therefore, fittingly defined as 'something less rightly done or said, that occasions another's spiritual downfall.' "[63]

The sin of scandal occurs when, as a consequence of one person's knowingly chosen act, another person is influenced toward sin. The influence toward sin is generally by bad example, as may occur when a sin becomes publicly known. In some cases, the other person might be influenced to misunderstand a teaching of the Church on a matter of faith or morals. All such misunderstandings tend toward sin, because the truths of faith and morals, properly understood, always lead us to God and away from sin. Therefore, St. Jerome explains that the sin of scandal is any word or deed (i.e. any exterior act) that might have the bad consequence of leading another person into spiritual downfall, which includes any sin, but especially mortal sin.

That scandal can be a sin is clear from the words of our Lord (Mk 9:41). Yet it is not possible in a sinful world for there to be no scandals, i.e. no influences of one sinner on another toward sin. Even so, those who influence others toward sin are doing harm to their neighbor. Speaking particularly about influencing young innocent persons toward serious sin, Jesus speaks using a harsh figure that is mild in comparison to the offense itself.

[Luke]
{17:1} And he said to his disciples: "It is impossible for scandals not to occur. But woe to him through whom they come!
{17:2} It would be better for him if a millstone were placed around his neck and he were thrown into the sea, than to lead astray one of these little ones."

However, speaking generally, scandal is a consequence in the third font. And so, if a good act (second font) with good intention (first font) has both good and bad consequences (third font), then the act might be moral under the principle of double effect. Therefore, Jesus did not commit the sin of scandal, even though the Pharisees were scandalized by the good deeds and true preaching of Jesus.

[Matthew]
{15:12} Tunc accedentes discipuli eius, dixerunt ei: Scis quia Pharisæi audito verbo hoc, **scandalizati sunt**?
{15:12} Then his disciples drew near and said to him, "Do you know that the Pharisees, upon hearing this word, **were offended** [i.e. scandalized]?"

The Pharisees would have sinned less if Jesus had not arrived and preached during their lifetimes. For they would not have committed the sin of rejecting the Messiah. But this bad consequence, like all bad consequences, must be weighed against the good consequences in the third font. The good consequences of

---

[62] St. Jerome, quoted in the Catena Aurea (Golden Chain) of St. Thomas Aquinas; Gospel of Matthew 15:12; translated by Parker and Rivington, London, 1842.
[63] Saint Thomas Aquinas, Summa Theologica, II-II, Q. 43, A. 1.

Jesus' public Ministry far outweigh the bad consequence of presenting an occasion of scandal to the Pharisees.

[John]
{7:1} Then, after these things, Jesus was walking in Galilee. For he was not willing to walk in Judea, because the Jews were seeking to kill him.
{7:2} Now the feast day of the Jews, the Feast of Tabernacles, was near.
…
{7:6} Therefore, Jesus said to them: "My time has not yet come; but your time is always at hand.
{7:7} The world cannot hate you. But it hates me, because I offer testimony about it, that its works are evil.
{7:8} You may go up to this feast day. But I am not going up to this feast day, because my time has not yet been fulfilled."
{7:9} When he had said these things, he himself remained in Galilee.
{7:10} But after his brothers went up, then he also went up to the feast day, not openly, but as if in secret.

When Jesus used mental reservation, by saying that he was not going to the feast because the time was not yet right, He did not commit the sin of scandal, though some persons might have misunderstood Him and might have incorrectly concluded that He lied. For scandal is only a sin if the bad consequences outweigh the good. The good consequence of avoiding an attempt on his life, and the good consequence of giving us an example of the proper use of mental reservation, outweigh any scandal that might occur if someone misunderstands His words.

St. Thomas plainly states that scandal can occur without sin on the part of the person who gives scandal. Such is the case with any scandal resulting from the good deeds of Jesus Christ, or of the Saints who lived in imitation of Him.

.069. Saint Thomas Aquinas: "Yet there can be passive scandal, without sin on the part of the person whose action has occasioned the scandal, as for instance, when a person is scandalized at another's good deed."[64]

Passive scandal refers to a good act with good intention, which may result in, but does not necessitate, the spiritual downfall on the part of some other persons. In such cases, a person does not necessarily sin when there is a bad consequence that some other persons are scandalized. If all three fonts are good, including the totality of good and bad consequences in the third font, then the act would be moral, despite the bad consequence of passive scandal.

But 'active scandal' occurs when one person sins, and that sin also influences others to sin; active scandal includes sin by definition. However, even in active scandal, the consequence of influencing other persons to sin could possibly be outweighed by good consequences in the third font. Although the act itself might be a sin under the first or second fonts (e.g. lying), and therefore be called 'active scandal,' the third font itself might be moral, even if the scandal of others results,

---

[64] Saint Thomas Aquinas, Summa Theologica, II-II, Q. 43, A. 2.

if this bad consequence is outweighed by the good consequences in the third font. The three fonts of morality always determine the morality of each and every knowingly chosen act, without any exception whatsoever.

Therefore, the principle of double effect must take into account the possibility of the sin of scandal. If the chosen act might influence other persons to sin, even if only because they have misunderstood (as occurs in passive scandal), then this bad consequence must be weighed with all the other good and bad consequences. Sometimes the additional bad consequence of scandal is enough to cause the totality of the bad consequences to outweigh the totality of the good consequences, making the third font, and the overall act, immoral. The principle of double effect does not justify an act if the bad consequences outweigh the good. However, in some cases, even if there is a danger of some persons being scandalized (influenced toward sin), the good consequences might still outweigh the bad consequences. The principle of double effect can justify a good act with good intention, even with the bad consequence of scandal, as long as the good consequences have sufficient moral weight.

Chapter 5
Judgment and Moral Certitude

.070.
A judgment of the prudential order is needed when weighing the circumstances, including the foreseeable good and bad consequences. This judgment takes the teachings of the Church on faith and morals, and the moral law as perceived by reason, and then uses reason to apply these teachings to an evaluation of particular circumstances. Such judgments are necessary, since neither Divine Revelation (Tradition and Scripture), nor the Magisterium of the Church, can list every possible set of circumstances, with every possible combination of various factors, and then state the correct moral decision for each; such a list would be endless.

Catechism of the Catholic Church: "Prudence disposes the practical reason to discern, in every circumstance, our true good and to choose the right means for achieving it."[65]

Prudence is applied wisdom. Prudential judgment uses reason, enlightened and guided by love and faith and hope, to evaluate the available information about the circumstances, as this applies to morality. Reason applies the teachings of the Faith to the particulars of the situation.

Judgments of the prudential order, as applied to the third font, are limited: by incomplete or incorrect knowledge of past circumstances (since we are not all-knowing), by misunderstandings of the present circumstances (since we are sinners whose hearts and minds are clouded by sin), by an incomplete ability to anticipate future consequences (since we cannot literally foresee the future), and by an imperfect ability to evaluate the totality of factors affecting the morality of the circumstances (since our use of reason is imperfect, due to our fallen state, our tendency toward sin, our past personal sins, and the influence of sinful society). But again it should be noted that if any circumstance or consequence is truly and entirely unable to be known or anticipated by the use of reason, such a circumstance or consequence has no effect on the morality of the act. Whatever is truly and entirely unknowable is not under the moral law, since the entire moral law is accessible to reason.

Even when the search for moral truth is sincere, the knowledge that is used to evaluate the circumstances is often limited. The morality of a knowingly chosen act is based upon the knowledge available at the time to the particular individual. Given a certain limit to the knowledge of the circumstances, an act may not be an actual sin. But if new knowledge is obtained over time, then the proper judgment may change as well, and the act may then be an actual sin. If the act is moral given the limited knowledge available, then the person may act, and he acts without actual sin. Certainly, there is an objective truth, in the eyes of God who knows all things, as to whether or not the act is objectively moral. But the

---
[65] Catechism of the Catholic Church, 1835.

morality of the act, for a particular individual human person, as either an actual sin, or a morally permissible act, is based on the available knowledge.

Example: (1) A physician intends to benefit a patient by the use of a moral medical treatment; the first and second fonts are good. There are two applicable medications; the first has fewer side effects, and the second has more. Both are usually equally capable of treating this illness. The second medication has the same good consequences as the first; it is effective at treating this illness. But the second has more bad consequences, in the form of harmful side effects. In this circumstance, the physician should give the first medication; it would not be moral to give the second medication because of the greater harm to the patient (unless other circumstances apply). The knowledge is limited because the physician does not know how either medication will effect this particular patient. A medication that is better in general for most patients, may be worse for a particular patient.

(2) A physician treats the patient with the first medication, and it is not effective. New knowledge has now been obtained, and so the circumstances have changed. Now it would be moral to use the second medication, despite the greater side effects, because the first medication is now known to be ineffective. A change in knowledge is a change in circumstances, because the circumstances include only what is known (or can be reasonably concluded, or reasonably anticipated), not what is unknown or unforeseeable. This consequence, that the first medication would not be effective for this particular patient, was not initially known, and so this knowledge was not initially in the circumstances. The initial moral judgment was not wrong; it was the correct judgment given the limited knowledge, and so it was moral.

.071. There will often be a legitimate, though limited, range of faithful and reasonable opinions among Catholics on the application of Catholic moral teaching to the circumstances pertaining to various particular moral decisions. Such faithful and reasonable disagreement occurs because this application (particularly in the third font) requires a judgment of the prudential order, that is, a discernment of the various circumstances, which may be complex, and their moral meaning and moral weight, in order to determine, in particular cases, whether or not an act is moral. The limit of this faithful difference of opinion is that all Catholics must adhere to every required belief of the Catholic Faith on morality, and that they must apply those teachings with a reasonable judgment formed in the light of love of God and neighbor, faith in the teachings of the Church, and hope for eternal life. A sincere use of prudential judgment is always an exercise of both faith and reason.

Pope John XXIII: "Differences of opinion in the application of principles can sometimes arise even among sincere Catholics. When this happens, they should be careful not to lose their respect and esteem for each other. Instead, they should strive to find points of agreement for effective and suitable action, and not wear themselves out in interminable arguments, and, under pretext of the better or the best, omit to do the good that is possible and therefore obligatory."[66]

Colorado Catholic Conference: "In some moral matters the use of reason allows for a legitimate diversity in our prudential judgments. Catholic voters may differ, for example, on what constitutes the best immigration policy, how to provide universal health care, or affordable housing. Catholics may even have differing judgments on the state's use of the death penalty or the decision to wage a just war. The morality of such questions lies not in what is done (the moral object), but in the motive and circumstances. Therefore, because these prudential judgments do not involve a direct choice of something evil, and take into consideration various goods, it is possible for Catholic voters to arrive at different, even opposing judgments."[67]

Cardinal Joseph Ratzinger: "Not all moral issues have the same moral weight as abortion and euthanasia. For example, if a Catholic were to be at odds with the Holy Father on the application of capital punishment or on the decision to wage war, he would not for that reason be considered unworthy to present himself to receive Holy Communion. While the Church exhorts civil authorities to seek peace, not war, and to exercise discretion and mercy in imposing punishment on criminals, it may still be permissible to take up arms to repel an aggressor or to have recourse to capital punishment. There may be a legitimate diversity of opinion even among Catholics about waging war and applying the death penalty, but not however with regard to abortion and euthanasia."[68]

Abortion and euthanasia are intrinsically evil and always gravely immoral. Therefore, no judgment of the prudential order is applied to determine when such acts are immoral; they are always immoral. But war in general is not intrinsically evil. A judgment of the prudential order is needed to determine whether a particular war is just or unjust. The use of the death penalty by proper authority is not intrinsically evil. A judgment of the prudential order is needed to determine whether the death penalty should be used in a particular case, or whether a particular government should have recourse to the death penalty given the particular circumstances, at that time, in that nation or state.

Notice that then-Cardinal Ratzinger (now Pope Benedict XVI) even allows for a difference of judgment between the Pope and an individual lay person. The teachings of the Roman Pontiff as an act of the Magisterium (the teaching authority of the Church) are binding. But his judgments of the prudential order are not teachings and are not strictly binding. The official judgments and prudential decisions of the temporal authority of the Church, as well as the personal judgments or prudential decisions of the Pope or any Bishop, are not teachings and are not required beliefs. And so a devout Catholic might faithfully

---

[66] Pope John XXIII, Mater et Magistra, n. 238.
[67] Colorado Catholic Conference, Moral Principles for Catholic Voters, p. 2
[68] Cardinal Joseph Ratzinger, Worthiness to Receive Holy Communion, General Principles (sent by Cardinal Ratzinger to Cardinal McCarrick, Archbishop of Washington, D.C., and made public in July, 2004), n. 3;
http://www.priestsforlife.org/magisterium/bishops/04-07ratzingerommunion.htm

and reasonably disagree with a particular judgment or prudential decision, without sin. Judgments of the prudential order, even by the Holy Father, are fallible; but so, too, are the same types of judgments by any individual.

.072. Grace and Morality

The faithful are guided by the three theological virtues (love, faith, hope) when they judge the morality of any act. Whoever has the three theological virtues has sanctifying grace. Whoever dies in a state of sanctifying grace certainly will have eternal life in Heaven. Whoever dies without sanctifying grace certainly will have eternal death in Hell. No one can do anything truly substantially selflessly good without sanctifying grace. Partial cooperation with actual grace, in acts of limited goodness, are possible in persons without sanctifying grace. Nothing of true and lasting goodness is done without the grace of God.

Love: True love of God and neighbor, not merely as an intellectual proposition, but as a virtue continually exercised in our lives, is a sure guide whenever any decision on morals is needed, especially when the moral weight of particular circumstances must be evaluated by faith and reason. However, a distorted idea of love is sometimes used to justify immoral acts. True love of God and neighbor is always in conformity with the teachings of Tradition, Scripture, Magisterium, and is never in conflict with any principle or requirement of the eternal moral law. True spiritual love is always a cooperation with the grace of God. A true and pure spiritual love, as distinguished from various lesser uses and misuses of the word, is also called charity.

[1 Corinthians]
{13:4} Charity is patient, is kind. Charity does not envy, does not act wrongly, is not inflated.
{13:5} Charity is not ambitious, does not seek for itself, is not provoked to anger, devises no evil.
{13:6} Charity does not rejoice over iniquity, but does rejoice in truth.
{13:7} Charity suffers all, believes all, hopes all, endures all.

Faith: A living faith is always a cooperation with the grace of God. Without sanctifying grace, faith is a mere intellectual adherence to particular ideas, and not a living faith. Some persons, who have fallen into a state of actual mortal sin and so have lost sanctifying grace, may still retain a type of true faith, but this type of faith is not alive, but dead. They do not have the fullness of the theological virtue of faith. They have no true spiritual love, no faith that is lived in selfless good works (prayer, self-denial, works of mercy), and no grace-filled hope that leads to eternal life. However, this type of faith retains a certain usefulness, in that the person knows by this faith that he must repent and confess, in order to return to sanctifying grace, to a faith that is fully alive. And partial cooperation with grace, even while in a state of actual mortal sin, allows this dead faith to perceive and to follow the path to return to living faith. This living faith includes seeking truth, believing truth, living according to truth, adhering to truth despite adversity, and being faithful to God and neighbor. A living faith always cooperates with reason, guides and enlightens reason, and believes beyond reason. Living faith is evidenced by works showing love of God and neighbor, and hope for eternal life. A full living faith flows from love of God and neighbor.

Hope: The theological virtue of hope is always a cooperation with the grace of God. True hope trusts in God and in all that is good. Hope flows from love and faith. What is the reason that we should not commit the smallest sin, even in the most dire of circumstances? The reason is that we have the hope of eternal life. So no matter how dire the circumstances may be in this life, sin is never justified because those dire circumstances are limited to life in this passing world.

.073. Moral Certitude

Moral certitude is a degree of certitude, based on currently available limited knowledge, sufficient to act in good conscience, i.e. without actual sin. Moral certitude is not absolute certitude. It is inherent to the fallen state that human persons have limited knowledge and a fallible use of reason when making judgments of the prudential order. A person need not have absolute certitude as to the best course of action before acting. The certitude possessed is morally sufficient if the individual makes use of available knowledge, and then chooses to act, or to refrain from acting, in conformity with the moral law, as it is understood by faith and reason. Use of moral certitude applies especially to the third font, since numerous different factors in the circumstances must be evaluated as to the totality of their moral weight.

Evaluating the consequences often involves a judgment about the degree of risk and the degree of possible harm. There may not be absolute certitude as to the exact set of consequences that will result from an act. However, there may be moral certitude that a certain degree of risk, and a certain degree of harm, is present. In such cases, the consequences in third font are evaluated based on the likelihood of possible harm and the extent of that harm, versus the likelihood of possible benefit and the extent of that benefit.

If there is a slight likelihood of great harm, or a great likelihood of slight harm, the bad consequences have only a slight moral weight. If there is a slight likelihood of great good, or a great likelihood of slight good, the good consequences have only a slight moral weight. Many daily activities carry some minor risk, such as crossing the street, or taking a short drive. But since the possibility of great harm is slight, the act need only offer a correspondingly minor benefit to be moral. However, the substantial possibility of grave harm would have substantial moral weight, even though the harm is only a risk and not a certainty.

Example: (1) A man decides to drive his vehicle while tired. His intention is good, in that he intends to get to his home. Driving a vehicle while tired is not intrinsically evil. Whether or not it is moral is a matter of degree, and this degree is in the circumstances. If he is extremely tired, so that there is a substantial risk of causing serious harm, then the act would be immoral. If he is not so tired as to present any significant risk of harm, then the act would be moral. So in the third font, there is a judgment to be made of the risk of bad consequences. This depends on how likely it is that his tiredness will result in an accident causing grave harm. If he is very tired, and the drive is long, the risk of grave harm in the consequences is greater. Even though the man cannot know in advance whether or not he will do harm with his vehicle, he is able to judge the degree of likelihood and the degree of possible harm, not with absolute certitude, but with moral certitude.

But when an act is immoral due to the great likelihood of great harm, even if the likely grave harm does not happen to occur, the morality of the act is unchanged. The morality of the act is based on the known likelihood of harm at the time that the decision to act was made, and is not based on the specific subsequent outcome. Since the person is only able to judge in advance, with moral certitude, the likelihood of the bad consequences, not the exact actual outcome, the morality is based on that likelihood (i.e. the risk of bad consequences).

Example: (2) A man decides to drive his vehicle, even though he knows that he is so tired there is a risk of serious harm (since he might fall asleep at the wheel, crash his vehicle, and cause injury or death). Even if he successfully drives the vehicle home without any harm, the act was still a sin, because the morality of the third font is based on what can be known, the known degree of risk, and not on the particular outcome in a particular case, which cannot be known in advance.

Similarly, when an act is moral due to the very small risk of great harm, even if the unlikely great harm happens to occur, the morality of the act is unchanged. Even though great harm resulted, the act was moral because the great harm was very unlikely, and so was outweighed by the likely good consequences.

Example: (3) A physician intends to cure a patient with a medication, which includes a small risk of grave harm (death), and where the benefits are substantial and very likely, and the risk is very small. If, by chance in a particular case, the patient dies, even though the likelihood of this outcome was very small, the act of giving the patient this medication was moral, because the physician had no way of knowing the outcome in this particular case. He correctly judged the known risk of serious harm to be small, and the benefits to be much more substantial than the risk, and so his decision to act was moral.

If physicians never treated patients, except when there was no risk at all of harm, there would be no medications, no treatments, and certainly no surgery, since nearly every medication and treatment has at least a very small risk of serious harm. There is a great benefit to society in general, and to particular persons, in accepting a limited amount of risk in exchange for more weighty benefits. Without this concept of acting despite bad consequences or the risk of bad consequences, very many good acts done with good intention could not be done, and society as well as individuals would suffer a very great loss from the inability to act despite limited bad consequences or a mere possibility of harm.

As long as the good circumstances are judged with moral certitude to outweigh the bad circumstances, the third font is moral. This is true even though the future consequences are not entirely knowable, and even when an unlikely bad consequence happens to occur. Judgment with moral certitude is based only on what is knowable. Whatever is truly and entirely unknowable does not affect the morality of an act.

.074. A judgment is also made when weighing one risk against another, in cases where a person is choosing between two possible acts, and both acts have significant risks.

Examples: (4) A woman is pregnant and has cancer. If she is treated for the cancer, the treatment will certainly kill the prenatal, but will likely cure the woman. If she attempts to delay treatment until the prenatal is viable (i.e. able to be delivered and live), there is a great likelihood that both the mother and the prenatal will die before the prenatal can be saved. There is a corresponding small possibility that the prenatal's life might be saved. But even in the unlikely event that the child is saved, the mother will still likely die (having waited too long to treat the cancer). In this case, it would not be moral for the woman to delay treatment. The great risk of losing two lives is not justified by the slight possibility that one life may be saved. It is not only moral for her to accept the treatment for cancer, despite the indirect and unintended death of the prenatal, it is also required by the moral law. For there is no significant likelihood that the prenatal's life can be saved. And the slight chance of saving the prenatal (with the loss of the mother's life) is outweighed by the great likelihood that the mother's life can be saved if she receives the treatment.

(5) A woman is pregnant and has cancer, but the prenatal is only a few weeks away from viability. If she is treated for the cancer immediately, the treatment will certainly kill the prenatal, and will likely cure the woman. If the woman delays the treatment for cancer until after the prenatal is viable and delivered, both lives will likely be saved, but with a modest increase in risk to the mother (since treatment is delayed). In this case, the modest increase in risk to the mother is outweighed by the great likelihood that the prenatal's life can also be saved. Therefore, in these circumstances, it would not be moral for the woman to have the cancer treatment immediately. The only moral course of action would be to delay treatment until after the prenatal is viable and is delivered.

Judgment and moral certitude applies, in the above discussed examples, especially when the prenatal is neither far from viability, nor close to viability. A delay before treatment would then present a degree of risk to the mother's life which may be difficult for the physician to judge. He would make use of knowledge from past medical cases and from the present medical condition of the woman, along with a judgment about the possible future consequences. The woman must also make a judgment as to the moral weight of the consequences.

There is no definitive principle of the moral law, nor any definitive teaching of the Magisterium, that will provide an absolute answer, in every set of circumstances, about the moral weight of the good and bad circumstances in the third font of morality. A judgment is needed, and the certitude of that judgment is moral certitude, not absolute certitude. In many such cases, the individual uses faith and reason to make a judgment, which may or may not be objectively correct (before God who is all-knowing), but which is nevertheless made in good conscience, with moral certitude, and without actual sin.

If the person intends an immoral means or an immoral end, the chosen act is always immoral because the first font is bad. If the person chooses an act that is intrinsically evil, then the act is always immoral because the second font is bad. Tradition, Scripture, and the Magisterium have teachings as to which intentions are evil and which acts are evil. When the Faith teaches that an intention or an act is evil, then there is no judgment of the prudential order to apply; it is an article of faith that the act is immoral. If there is no clear teaching in Tradition, Scripture, or the Magisterium about a particular intention or a particular act (as to whether or not it is evil), then a judgment of the prudential order applies faith and reason to determine if either of the first two fonts are bad.

But it is in the third font that a judgment of the prudential order is most often needed. In some cases, the correct judgment is so clear from faith and morals, from applying the basic principles of morality, that there should be no difference in judgment among faithful and reasonable Catholic Christians. If the bad consequences include the likely death of several persons, and the good consequences are small, no reasonable person could sincerely judge the act to be moral. But in many cases, there can be a faithful and reasonable diversity of judgment, because the set of good and bad circumstances are complex and difficult to weigh. This diversity occurs especially when the circumstances include a possibility, rather than a near certainty, as to the good and bad consequences. The degree of possibility can be difficult to judge.

.075. Influences on Judgment

Not only do judgments of the prudential order vary from one faithful and reasonable person to another, but such judgments also vary over time for the same person. A faithful and reasonable child, and that same person as a teenager, and as a young adult, and as an older adult, and as a elderly adult, will make different judgments on morality. Even supposing that this same person, at each stage of life, exercises faithful and reasonable judgment, certain factors may improve this person's judgment over time, such as: an increase in understanding of the moral law, an increase in knowledge of the teachings of the Catholic Faith, greater experience in the events of human life, greater emotional and intellectual maturity, and other factors.

However, some factors may worsen a person's judgment to some extent, from time to time, such as: the limited ability to reason found in the very young, the difficulties of going through the teenage years, a decrease in mental acuity with old age, stressful situations at any age (loss of job, loss of family member, financial problems, etc.), the influence of other sinners, the influence of sinful secular society, as well as various physical, psychological, and other factors.

Even in the absence of factors with substantial influence, judgments of the prudential order by the same person may vary over time because the individual fallen human person has limited knowledge, imperfect use of reason, and imperfect cooperation with the grace of God. Minor variations or lapses in judgment have only a minor effect on the morality of a decision, causing that decision to be either imperfect but not sinful, or sinful but only to a venial extent.

A minor lapse in judgment does not, by itself, constitute an actual mortal sin. Some lapses in judgment may be culpable, if they procede from an insincerity in seeking, or a willful turning away from, moral truth. But not every lapse in judgment is culpable, since it is inherent to the condition of fallen humanity that our knowledge of morality, our use of reason, and our cooperation with grace are all imperfect and changing. Some failures to cooperate with grace, to a limited extent, are imperfections, not sins. Only God is perfect and unchanging.

However, grave lapses in judgment may have grave culpability, even to the extent of an actual mortal sin. Some persons refer to acts of pre-marital sex, or of adultery, as so-called indiscretions. In truth, every sexual act outside of marriage is an objective mortal sin. And no gravely immoral acts, in any area of morality, are mere indiscretions. A person who freely and knowingly chooses a gravely immoral act is culpable for that mortal sin. The minor lapses and variations in judgment that are inherent to the fallen state are not sufficient to excuse grave sin, for the moral law is accessible even to sinners, and even to unbelievers.

Some grave errors in judgment may have substantially reduced culpability, so that an objective mortal sin becomes an actual venial sin. But this would only occur if there were factors beyond the control of the individual person, which substantially reduced his knowledge or freedom of choice, impairing his ability to make a correct moral judgment.

Chapter 6
Conscience

.076.
Conscience itself is the ability of free will and reason to seek and to understand moral truth. The exercise of conscience is an act of will and intellect by which the human person seeks knowledge of moral truth.[69] The fruit of conscience is the understanding of moral truth obtained by this search. Thus conscience is threefold: the ability to search for moral truth, the act of searching, and the knowledge obtained by the search.

All human persons have a conscience because all human persons have free will (the ability to choose) and reason (the ability to understand). Conscience is not separate from, nor additional to, free will and reason. Conscience is inherent to the very nature of free will and reason. Whoever possesses and is able to exercise free will and reason, necessarily also possesses and is able to exercise conscience. For conscience itself is the ability of free will and reason to attain moral truth. And the entire moral law is accessible to reason. The use of conscience is the use of free will and reason to seek moral truth. And the fruit of conscience is the understanding of moral truth obtained by that use of free will and reason.

The purpose of conscience is to obtain knowledge, so as to know wrong from right. A person who desires to do good and to avoid evil must first discern which acts are good and which acts are evil. This discernment of good and evil applies to general concepts, as well as to particular intentions, acts, and circumstances. The general search for moral truth seeks an understanding of the principles of morality. The particular search for moral truth applies those principles to particular intentions, acts, and circumstances. In both cases, the human person seeks knowledge of the eternal moral law. The substantial omission of either a general or a particular search for moral truth results in a bad conscience before the eyes of God.

If a person knowingly chooses to act without a sincere search for moral truth, then he acts in bad conscience. If a person knowingly chooses to act regardless of moral truth, then he acts in bad conscience. The choice to act regardless of morality is always an immoral choice. If a person knowingly chooses to act in contradiction to knowledge obtained by the search for moral truth, then he acts in bad conscience. The choice to act in contradiction to moral truth is always an immoral choice. If anyone knowingly chooses to act, either without a sincere search for moral truth, or in contradiction to the knowledge obtained by that search, then he acts in bad conscience.

Cardinal Ratzinger: "Conscience is not an independent and infallible faculty. It is an act of moral judgment regarding a responsible choice. A right conscience is one duly illumined by faith and by the objective moral law and it presupposes, as well, the uprightness of the will in the pursuit of the true good."[70]

---

[69] Cf. St. Thomas Aquinas, Summa Theologica, I, Q. 79, A. 13.
[70] Cardinal Ratzinger, Instruction on the Ecclesial Vocation of the Theologian, n. 38.

.077. Whenever a person knowingly chooses an immoral act, he acts in bad conscience and he sins. Every act done in bad conscience is necessarily an actual sin. Every actual sin is necessarily done in bad conscience.

If an immoral act is done with the sincere but mistaken belief that the act is moral, the act is done in good conscience, and is not an actual sin. For this belief to be sincere, the person must exercise his conscience by sincerely seeking knowledge of moral truth, in general and in particular. This exercise of conscience is necessary for any knowingly chosen act to be moral; otherwise, the first font of morality is bad. Whenever the intent is to act without concern for morality, the intent is immoral.

All actual sins are done in bad conscience because all actual sins are freely chosen, either in the knowledge or belief that the act is immoral, or without due concern for the morality of the act. If, after a sincere search for moral truth, the person truly believes the act to be objectively moral, then the act is done in good conscience, even if the act is objectively immoral.

Any act freely chosen despite the knowledge or belief that the act is sinful, or without concern for whether the act is moral, is done in bad conscience. Any act freely chosen in the knowledge or belief that the act is moral, with due regard for whether the act is moral, is done in good conscience. Any act done in good conscience is not an actual sin, but may be an objective sin (if the person did not realize that the act was objectively immoral). This due regard for whether or not the chosen act is moral is found in the first font, in the intention of the person choosing the act. Whoever acts with amoral intent (not caring about good and evil), commits immorality.

This due regard for the morality of an act depends on the seriousness of the act. A person should not expend great effort to determine the morality of a minor matter, nor should a person expend only a little effort to determine the morality of a grave matter. The degree of regard for the morality of an act should be in proportion to the degree of seriousness of the act within the course of human life as intended by God.

.078. The exercise of conscience refers to an interior act, not an exterior act. Reading a book to obtain knowledge of morality is not per se an exercise of conscience, although this exterior act may well be accompanied by an interior act seeking knowledge of moral truth. A knowingly chosen exterior act is moral only when the accompanying interior act of will and intellect (the knowing choice) is also moral. A good deed done with bad intent is a sin. A good deed done in the mistaken belief that the deed is immoral is a sin.

The fruit of conscience is the knowledge gained by the search for moral truth. If the knowledge gained indicates that the person has sinned, especially seriously and without repentance, then the person is said to be in a state of bad conscience. If the knowledge gained indicates that the person has not sinned, or that he has sinned, repented, and been forgiven, then the person is said to be in a state of good conscience.

Conscience

Many persons in the world today are not in good conscience. They rationalize their moral choices, so as to claim to be doing good when doing evil. They seek certain limited goods offered by the world, without also seeking knowledge of moral truth. They lack a continuing concern to do good and to avoid evil. Then, too, many of the persons who do seek some knowledge of moral truth also subjugate this search to their own temporal needs and desires. They speak and act as if moral truth were relative and subjective and dependent upon their own ideas and desires. And some persons in the world today have even rejected entirely the use of conscience.

Joseph Ratzinger: "The fact is that under the pretext of goodness, people neglect conscience. They place acceptance, the avoidance of problems, the comfortable pursuit of their existence, the good opinion of others and good-naturedness above truth in the scale of values."[71]

The secular world offers many falsehoods on morality, many pretexts and rationalizations, many false opinions, and much disorder in the scale of values. To be in good conscience, all Catholics must form and guide their consciences in the light of Catholic teaching on morality, found in Tradition, Scripture, Magisterium, and in the light of reason. Often, Catholic teaching on morality will be in opposition to the ideas of modern society. All Catholics are required to place the teachings of the Faith above any contrary claims made by secular or non-Catholic sources.

To be in good conscience, all Catholics must place the teachings of Tradition, Scripture, Magisterium above even their own reasoning. Certainly, reason is necessary in order to understand the teachings of the Catholic Faith and in order to apply these teachings to each person's life. Faith works in harmony with reason. But faith is also greater than reason. Reason is the servant of Faith, not its master. Therefore, if the Catholic Faith definitively teaches that an act is immoral, no Catholic would be in good conscience if he reasoned, in opposition to a clear and definitive teaching of the Church, that the act was moral.

Example: Many Catholics do not understand with their reason why contraception is intrinsically evil and always gravely immoral. Among these are some Catholics who nevertheless, based on faith, believe Church teaching against contraception, in contradiction to their own reasoning. But some other Catholics place their own reasoning above faith, and so they reject Catholic teaching against contraception. Despite their firm conviction based on their own faulty reasoning, they are not in good conscience, because their mistaken belief is freely chosen in contradiction to the known definitive teaching of the Catholic Church on morality. The intentional disregard or rejection of the clear and definitive teaching of the Catholic Faith on morality is always an actual sin, and is always in bad conscience.

---

[71] Joseph Ratzinger, Salt of the Earth, p. 68.

.079. Primacy of conscience

The human conscience has primacy, the first place in decisions of morality, only within certain limits. The primacy of conscience applies to a good conscience, formed in the light of moral truth from faith and reason.

A good conscience must seek moral truth, in general and in particular, with a selfless and sincere love of God and neighbor. A good conscience must not contradict, and must be formed in the light of, the clear and definitive teachings of the Catholic Faith on morality. A good conscience must be guided by the hope for eternal life, so that the passing temptations and difficulties of this life do not lead a person to sin. Therefore, a good conscience is based on love, faith, and hope. No conscience is above love, faith, and hope. No conscience has primacy above love, faith, and hope.

When a conscience is guided by love, faith, and hope, such a good conscience has primacy above other considerations.

Such a good conscience takes precedence in moral decisions over the opinions of secular society, over the opinions of family, friends, or co-workers, over the opinions of persons with secular authority, and over the opinions of persons with excellent reputations and credentials.

Such a good conscience takes precedence in moral decisions over the personal opinions of Bishops, priests, religious, theologians, and even over the personal opinion of the Pope. The Pope and the Bishops are never infallible in their personal opinions, but only when their teachings under the Magisterium meet certain criteria. The Pope is prevented by God from committing the sin of apostasy, heresy, or schism. But the Pope and the Bishops are not prevented by God from erring in their personal opinions, even on matters of faith and morals. A faithful Catholic should reasonably give some weight to the personal opinion of the Pope, or of a Bishop or group of Bishops, on moral matters, since they are knowledgeable about morality. But a good conscience will not treat personal opinion as if it were equivalent to the clear and definitive teaching of Tradition, Scripture, Magisterium. A moral decision may be in good conscience, even if that decision contradicts the personal opinion of some Church leaders, as long as that decision is based on the three pillars of the one holy Roman Catholic Faith: Tradition, Scripture, Magisterium.

Such a good conscience takes precedence in moral decisions over judgments of the prudential order made under the temporal authority of the Church. The temporal authority of the Church is fallible, and may err even to a significant extent. When a moral decision is made in good conscience, based on the higher principles of Tradition, Scripture, Magisterium, that decision may sometimes conflict with the temporal authority of the Church, either because a particular judgment of the temporal authority did not take into account every particular circumstance, or because a particular judgment was in error. Since the temporal authority of the Church is fallible, and does not teach faith and morals, but rather makes judgments of the prudential order, a faithful Catholic may sometimes act in contradiction to the temporal authority of the Church, in good conscience, without sin.

.080. If your conscience is based on love, faith, and hope (which includes faith in the teachings of Tradition, Scripture, Magisterium), then your sincere reasonable decisions on what is moral in particular circumstances are in good conscience, and are without actual sin. But the claim that one is in good conscience does not justify disregarding the search for moral truth, theological arguments based on Tradition, Scripture, Magisterium, and the holy words and examples of the lives of the Saints. An insincere conscience is not a good conscience. A conscience based on rationalization is not based on faith or reason.

If your conscience includes some limited degree of insincerity, or some limited degree of negligence in seeking moral truth, then your moral decisions might not be entirely in good conscience. If so, then your insincerity or negligence is itself a venial sin, and you might also sin venially by acting based on that insincerity or negligence. However, some limited faults and failings in seeking moral truth may reach only to the extent of imperfection, and not to the extent of even venial sin.

If your conscience includes a substantial degree of insincerity, or if you substantially ignore or reject the search for moral truth in any grave matter, then your moral decisions are not in good conscience. If so, then your substantial insincerity, negligence, or rejection of moral truth is itself a mortal sin, and you might also sin mortally by acting based on this insincerity, negligence, or rejection, in any grave matter.

A knowingly chosen interior act of insincerity or neglect in the search for moral truth, if it is to a limited degree, is itself an actual venial sin. A knowingly chosen interior act of insincerity or neglect in the search for moral truth, to a substantial degree, or its compete rejection, in any grave matter, is itself an actual mortal sin. Insincerity or neglect of conscience is itself a sin. This same insincerity or neglect of conscience also leads to further sins, since anyone who acts in bad conscience sins by intending to act without due regard for the moral law. The complete rejection of morality, or the complete refusal to exercise conscience in the search for moral truth, is always an actual mortal sin.

Any sin of the insincerity, neglect, or rejection of morality is always an actual sin, either venial or mortal. No one could unknowingly or unwillingly be insincere or neglectful concerning morality, because by definition these sins include a knowing choice. The whole moral law is open to reason, and the search for moral truth is the first and most essential principle of morality. Therefore, if anyone ignores, neglects, or rejects the search for moral truth itself, he sins venially, if to a limited degree or in a small matter, or he sins mortally, if to a substantial degree and in a grave matter.

A person might sin against their conscience by a venial sin, or by a mortal sin. Some limited degree of selfishness or insincerity in seeking moral truth would be a venial sin. Substantial insincerity in seeking moral truth, so that what is sought is a mere rationalization, whether in general or in a particular case where the matter is grave, would be a mortal sin. Also any person who completely abandons concern for whether or not his acts are moral, who makes no attempt to do what is good and to avoid doing what is evil, has committed an actual mortal sin in his mind and heart by choosing to completely abandon the search for moral truth.

.081. Whether or not an act is objectively sinful is independent of conscience. A knowingly chosen act done in good conscience is not an actual sin, but it may or may not be an objective sin. A knowingly chosen act done in bad conscience is an actual sin, but it may or may not be an objective sin. A good conscience might mistakenly consider an objectively immoral act to be moral, or an objectively moral act to be immoral. A bad conscience might mistakenly consider an objectively immoral act to be moral, or an objectively moral act to be immoral.

Whether or not an act is objectively sinful is above conscience. If a person in good conscience mistakenly believes that an objectively immoral act is moral, the act remains objectively immoral. If a person in good conscience mistakenly believes that an objectively moral act is immoral, the act remains objectively moral. Moral truth is not relative to conscience, even when a mistaken good conscience is without culpability in doing what is objectively sinful. Moral truth is not relative. Moral truth is nothing other than the unchanging eternal justice of the very Nature of God.

Minor failures to be entirely sincere and perfectly selfless are common among fallen human persons. Such minor faults are not sufficient to cause the person to be in bad conscience, nor even, if minor in extent, to cause the person to sin even venially. Such minor failures are imperfections, not sins. Only when the failure is contrary to the love of God and neighbor, to a limited extent, is the failure a venial sin. And only when the failure is contrary to love of God and neighbor, to a full extent, is the failure a mortal sin.

Any substantial insincerity in seeking moral truth would cause any decision, even if objectively correct, to be sinful due to the substantial and willful rejection of moral truth. Even when all three fonts are objectively good, if a person decides that the fonts are good by a willful turning away from the sincere search for truth, then he sins, since his evaluation of the three fonts is substantially dishonest. He does not truly know or sincerely believe that all three fonts are objectively good; he does not truly care if any of the fonts are bad. His evaluation of the fonts is a rationalization of the act, and not a sincere belief that the act is morally good. He is therefore willing (if only implicitly) to do the act even if it is immoral, and so he sins.

When there are different opinions as to whether or not an act is moral, if a person chooses which opinion to accept and which act to do, not based on a sincere search for truth, but instead based on what is easier, or more familiar, or more pleasing to self, or more pleasing to others, or easier to justify to others, such a person does not act in good conscience. Even if the opinion chosen by such a person is the correct opinion, or an incorrect opinion asserted by someone else in good conscience, he sins by acting in bad conscience. For he has not chosen the act in the knowledge or sincere belief that it was moral, but only on the excuse that someone else said it was moral.

.082. Examination of conscience

Pope John Paul II: "First of all, an indispensable condition is the rectitude and clarity of the penitent's conscience. People cannot come to true and genuine repentance until they realize that sin is contrary to the ethical norm written in their innermost being; until they admit that they have had a personal and responsible experience of this contrast; until they say not only that 'sin exists' but also 'I have sinned'; until they admit that sin has introduced a division into their consciences which then pervades their whole being and separates them from God and from their brothers and sisters. The sacramental sign of this clarity of conscience is the act traditionally called the examination of conscience, an act that must never be one of anxious psychological introspection, but a sincere and calm comparison with the interior moral law, with the evangelical norms proposed by the Church, with Jesus Christ himself, who is our teacher and model of life, and with the heavenly Father, who calls us to goodness and perfection."[72]

By an examination of conscience, the human person searches for knowledge of particular past sinful acts in his own life. This knowledge of the truth that one has sinned may be already on the conscience, in the sense that the person already knows that a past act was sinful, in which case the examination of conscience brings that knowledge to present consideration by the mind. Or this knowledge may be obtained by means of the examination of conscience, in the sense that, while examining one's past moral choices, a comparison with the moral law (by faith and reason) newly reveals that a past choice was a sinful choice.

Pope John Paul II: "Examination of conscience is therefore one of the most decisive moments of life. It places each individual before the truth of his own life. Thus he discovers the distance which separates his deeds from the ideal which he had set for himself."[73]

The examination of conscience can reveal actual sin, acts freely chosen in the knowledge that the act was immoral, and it can reveal merely objective sin, acts committed either without free choice or without the knowledge that the act was immoral. Only actual sin includes culpability before God. But the discovery of merely objective sin assists the individual in transforming his life to become more like the life of Jesus Christ, and more pleasing to God. Even the non-culpable commission of a merely objective sin (especially objective mortal sin) is a type of moral disorder before the eyes of God. For all such acts are objectively contrary to that goodness and justice and love which is the very Nature of God. Every human person should strive to rid his life first of every actual mortal sin, then also of every merely objective mortal sin, and finally of as much venial sin as possible, especially those venial sins that are fully deliberate.

---

[72] Pope John Paul II, Reconciliation and Penance, n. 31, III.
[73] Pope John Paul II, Incarnationis Mysterium, n. 11.

Many methods of examination of conscience have been suggested and may be used. One method is to examine past moral choices categorized by interior sins of the heart and mind versus exterior sins of word and deed. Another approach is to consider sins of commission versus sins of omission. Still another approach is to consider each of the ten commandments, and search for any sins even distantly related to one of the commandments. For example, any sexual sin at all would be related to the commandment not to commit adultery, and any lie or dishonesty at all would be related to the commandment not to bear false witness against your neighbor. Another approach is to consider one's known weaknesses and known tendencies toward certain sins ('old sins'), to know if any of these types of sins have been committed since the individual's last good confession; and next to consider any new sins into which one might have fallen. Other approaches may be used, as the individual sees fit in examining the moral choices of his life. Or the individual may simply permit himself to be guided, without any method, by the grace of God in examining his moral choices and sins.

.083. The Guidance and Formation of Conscience

Conscience is threefold: the ability of free will and reason to search for moral truth, the act of searching, and the understanding obtained by the search. Conscience is an ability inherent to the very nature of free will and reason. The whole moral law is open to reason, and so reason is able to guide free will to moral truth. The existence of God is also open to reason (Romans 1:19-20). By reason alone, man can know that God exists, that He created all else that exists, and that He is good. Therefore, reason guides the conscience toward belief in God, and this faith in God, by His grace, is also a guide of conscience. Faith and reason are the guides of conscience.

Pope Benedict XVI: "Faith, which grants a share in God's perfect knowledge, helps reason to realize its full potential."[74]

Faith does not stand alone, for a living faith is always accompanied by love and hope. And love, faith, hope are always in the grace of God. The moral truths obtained by reason are obtained by the exercise of free will and intellect, which, as created by God, are good and are able to seek and find moral truth. But the moral truths obtained by faith are obtained from Divine Revelation, that is, from Sacred Tradition, Sacred Scripture, and the Church's living Magisterium. In a sense, the truths obtained by reason are obtained from within, and the truths obtained by faith are obtained from without. But the knowledge obtained from Divine Revelation is greater and more certain that the knowledge obtained by human will and intellect alone. And so, faith is greater than reason in the search for moral truth.

As conscience is guided by faith and reason, urged forward through many difficulties by the sincere desire of the will to know moral truth, the ability to find moral truth improves. Conscience becomes formed in accord with objective moral truth, so as to more quickly and more easily seek and obtain additional

---

[74] Pope Benedict XVI, Audience of 16 December 2009 on John of Salisbury.

moral truths. As one moral truth is discovered and understood and accepted, then subsequent moral truths are obtained more quickly and more easily. For all moral truths are one, and that One Truth is the merciful Justice which is the very Nature of God.

Conscience seeks two types of moral truths: general and particular. The general moral truths are principles, for example: that all stealing is immoral, or that all sin should be avoided, or that the love of God and neighbor should guide all our actions. The particular moral truths are decisions about the morality of particular acts in our lives, either of past acts that may or may not have been moral, or of future acts that we are considering as to their morality. As the conscience finds both types of truths, further insight is obtained into general moral principles and into the morality of particular acts.

The formation of conscience occurs by the continual sincere use of conscience, guided by faith and reason. Over time, the sincere search for moral truth by faith and reason results in a conscience that is ever more knowledgeable about moral truth, and ever more ready to adhere to the known truths of the moral law. But since every precept of the moral law flows from true love of God and neighbor, the conscience is formed not only by continually making good moral decisions, but also by practicing love of God and neighbor through prayer, self-denial, and works of mercy. As the Christian continually lives in imitation of Jesus Christ, his conscience is continually formed to become more like the conscience of Jesus Christ.

A bad conscience is also guided and formed. If the individual places reason above faith, then incorrect decisions on morality are multiplied. If the individual allows their conscience to be turned aside by selfish desires and worldly concerns, the search for moral truth becomes ever more difficult. The more a person sins, the harder it is for him to distinguish good from evil, moral truth from moral falsehood. As falsehoods on morality are accepted and accumulate, the individual's understanding of morality moves further and further from truth. These errors on morality are culpable when the person freely chooses rationalizations and selfishness over truth and love of God and neighbor. If this process of moving ever further from moral truth continues, mortal sins are committed ever more easily and more frequently, even without repentance. The end result is seen throughout human history, when human persons commit acts of severe immorality against God and against one another.

Second Vatican Council: "In the depths of his conscience, man detects a law which he does not impose upon himself, but which holds him to obedience. Always summoning him to love good and avoid evil, the voice of conscience when necessary speaks to his heart: do this, shun that. For man has in his heart a law written by God; to obey it is the very dignity of man; according to it he will be judged. Conscience is the most secret core and sanctuary of a man. There he is alone with God, Whose voice echoes in his depths. In a wonderful manner conscience reveals that law which is fulfilled by love of God and neighbor. In fidelity to conscience, Christians are joined with the rest of men in the search for truth, and for the genuine solution to the numerous problems which arise in the life of individuals from social relationships. Hence the more right conscience holds sway, the more persons and groups turn aside from blind choice and strive to be guided by the objective norms of morality. Conscience frequently errs from invincible ignorance without losing its dignity. The same cannot be said for a man who cares but little for truth and goodness, or for a conscience which by degrees grows practically sightless as a result of habitual sin."[75]

---

[75] Second Vatican Council, *Gaudium et Spes*, n. 16.

Chapter 7
Degrees of Sin and of Culpability

.084.

Pope John Paul II: "Every actual (personal) sin is a real abuse of freedom, contrary to the will of God. The degree of this abuse may vary. The different degrees of guilt of the sinner also depend on this. In this sense one must apply a different measure for actual sins, when it is a question of evaluating the degree of evil contained in them. From this, too, derives the difference between 'grave' sin and 'venial' sin. Grave sin is also 'mortal' because it brings about the loss of sanctifying grace in the one who commits it."[76]

Sin is divided into two main degrees, mortal and venial. Actual mortal sin is entirely incompatible with love of God and neighbor, and deserves eternal punishment. Actual venial sin is not entirely incompatible with love of God and neighbor, and does not deserve eternal punishment. The difference between actual venial sin and actual mortal sin is as great as the difference between eternal life and eternal death, between Heaven and Hell. The most important distinction of degrees of sin is between mortal sin and venial sin.

Actual sin is a knowingly chosen immoral act. Actual sin requires three elements: (1) knowledge, (2) choice, (3) the matter of the act. The objective morality of the act is referred to as the matter of the act. If the act is objectively morally disordered, the matter of the act is immoral.

There are different degrees of mortal sin, and different degrees of venial sin. Some sins are more serious, since they have a greater moral disorder, and other sins are less serious, since they have a lesser moral disorder. Some sins offend God more than other sins, because they are more in conflict with the goodness that God intends for created persons. All Creation and especially all created persons are a reflection of the goodness of God. Sins that are more disordered are more thoroughly in opposition to the goodness of God. All that is sin is contrary to the very Nature of God, who is goodness, justice, love, mercy, who is all that is good. The more thoroughly an act is in conflict with the goodness of God, the more sinful is the act. This concept applies to both mortal sins and venial sins.

.085. There are degrees of mortal sin.

Some mortal sins are more serious, since they have a greater moral disorder, and other mortal sins are less serious, since they have a lesser moral disorder. But all mortal sins are gravely disordered. Some mortal sins offend God more than other mortal sins, because they are more thoroughly in conflict with His Goodness and with the goodness that He intends for all Creation.

Examples: (1) A man steals a significant amount of money from his neighbor, so that the loss causes serious harm; this theft is a mortal sin. But the same type of

---

[76] Pope John Paul II, General Audience, 29 October 1986; http://www.vatican.va/holy_father/john_paul_ii/audiences/alpha/data/aud19861029en.html

sin, theft, becomes more serious if more harm is done. (2) A man steals all of the money that his neighbor, a poor widow, had to live on; she has no family left to help her and now cannot pay for food, medicine, or shelter. This second theft is a more serious mortal sin because more harm is done in the consequences of the knowingly chosen act.

(3) A married couple use a barrier method of contraception (not an abortifacient method). This use of artificial contraception is intrinsically evil and always gravely immoral; it is a mortal sin. (4) A married couple conceive a child, and then they agree to abort the child. Direct abortion is intrinsically evil and always gravely immoral; it is a mortal sin. However, more harm is done by abortion than by contraception (abortifacient contraception is a separate case) because abortion kills an innocent human person, whereas mere contraception does not. Therefore, abortion is a more serious mortal sin than the mortal sin of contraception. (Abortifacient contraception sometimes works by killing a conceived human person, rather than by preventing conception, in which case the abortifacient contraception is a type of abortion and is more serious.)

(5) A man and a woman have natural sexual relations outside of marriage; this sexual sin is a mortal sin. (6) If a man and a woman have unnatural sexual relations outside of marriage, the sin is objectively a more serious mortal sin. This sin has a greater degree of moral disorder because the one act is both sex outside of marriage and an unnatural sexual act. (7) If a man rapes a woman, outside of marriage, by means of an unnatural sexual act, the act has an even greater degree of moral disorder, because the one act is rape, and an unnatural sexual act, and sex outside of marriage. (8) If a husband rapes his wife by means of an unnatural sexual act, the act has a still greater degree of moral disorder, because the one act is rape, and an unnatural sexual act, and a serious offense against the institution of marriage established by God.

Any sexual sin committed within marriage is more sinful than the same sexual sin committed outside of marriage because the sin additionally offends against the institution of marriage established by God at the beginning of the creation of the human race. Moreover, any sexual sin committed in a marriage where the husband and wife have the true Sacrament of Marriage is more offensive to God than the same sexual sin committed in a merely natural marriage, because the sin additionally offends against a Sacrament, as well as against the institution of natural marriage.

Three elements together are needed for an act to be an actual mortal sin: (1) full knowledge (that the act is gravely immoral), (2) full consent (i.e. resolve, deliberation, choice), (3) and the matter of the act must be gravely immoral. The matter of the act is everything pertaining to the morality of the act, in all three fonts, other than consent and knowledge. Actual sin is a knowingly chosen immoral act. Actual mortal sin is a knowingly chosen immoral act in which the knowledge is full, the choice is full, and the immorality is grave (in a sense, full).

The first two elements, consent and knowledge, are components of the first font of morality, intention. For a sin to be an actual mortal sin, the intention must include full consent and full knowledge, since every intent is a knowing choice.

However, the matter of the act includes the other components of the first font, the intention to use a particular means and to achieve a particular end, as well as the entirety of the other two fonts. If either the intended means or the intended end is gravely immoral, or if the moral object is gravely immoral, or if the bad consequences outweigh the good consequences to a grave extent, then the act is an objective mortal sin.

If an objective mortal sin is knowingly chosen with full consent and full knowledge, then that objective mortal sin is also an actual mortal sin. If the matter of the act is not sinful, or if the matter is only an objective venial sin, but if the person knowingly chooses the act in the sincere belief that the matter is gravely immoral, then the act is an actual mortal sin, even when the act is not an objective mortal sin.

.086. There are degrees of venial sin.

Some venial sins are more serious, but still only venial, because they have a greater moral disorder than other venial sins. Some venial sins offend God more than other venial sins because they are more in conflict with the goodness of God and the goodness that He intends for Creation and for created persons.

Examples: (1) A wife has prepared dinner for her husband; she asks him what he had for lunch. He had the same food that she has prepared for dinner, but in order to avoid hurting her feelings, he lies about what he ate for lunch. This lie is a venial sin. (2) But if he also had previously promised his wife that he would no longer lie to her in order to spare her feelings, and now he lies again, it is a more serious sin, but still venial, because the one act is both a lie and the breaking of a promise. (This promise concerns only a venial matter, so breaking this promise is venial, not mortal.) There is more moral disorder in the second case, and so the sin is more serious, but in both cases the matter is not grave.

The elements that make an actual venial sin more or less serious, but still a venial sin, are of the same type as for an actual mortal sin, but to a lesser degree: (1) knowledge, (2) consent, (3) the matter of the act. All three elements must be present for any act to be an actual sin. A venial sin must have some degree of knowledge that the act is immoral in order to be an actual sin. If there is no knowledge (or sincere belief) that the act is immoral, then the act might be an objective sin, but it is not an actual sin. A venial sin must have some degree of consent in order to be an actual sin. If there is no degree of free consent, the act might be an objective sin, but it is not an actual sin. Any sin must be a knowingly chosen immoral act in order to be an actual sin. The matter of the act refers to the objective morality of the act that is knowingly chosen. If the matter of the act is objectively moral, then the act is not an objective sin. If the matter of the act is mistakenly but sincerely believed to be immoral, and if the act is knowingly chosen, then the act is an actual sin.

Thus all three elements must be present for a knowingly chosen act to be an actual sin (with the provision that an objectively moral act is still an actual sin if the person knowingly chooses the act in the sincere belief that the matter is objectively immoral). But for the act to be an actual venial sin, and not an actual mortal sin, at least one of these three elements must be substantially limited: (1) knowledge to a limited degree, or (2) consent to a limited degree, or (3) the matter of the act must be limited, i.e. not gravely disordered. When any of the three elements required for actual mortal sin are substantially reduced or absent, then that act is not an actual mortal sin (even if it is objectively gravely immoral). When any of the elements required for an actual venial sin are absent, then that act is not an actual venial sin (even if it is objectively a venial sin).

A venial sin can be more or less serious, but still venial, without any of the three elements of actual mortal sin. But when an actual venial sin has one or two (but not all three) of the elements of actual mortal sin, it is a more serious venial sin. A venial sin chosen with full knowledge that the act is immoral is more serious than the same venial sin with less than full knowledge of the immorality of the act. Full knowledge is one element of actual mortal sin. A fully deliberate venial sin is more serious than the same venial sin with less than full deliberation (consent). Full deliberation is one element of actual mortal sin. If an objective mortal sin is chosen without full knowledge or without full deliberation, that sin is not an actual mortal sin, but is an actual venial sin. However, an actual venial sin whose matter is objectively grave (objectively morally disordered) is more serious than the same knowledge and choice of an objective venial sin. Gravely immoral matter is an element of actual mortal sin. Only when all three elements of mortal sin are present is an act an actual mortal sin. But when one or two of the elements of actual mortal sin (full knowledge, or full consent, or a gravely disordered matter) are present, the actual venial sin is more serious.

An actual venial sin is more serious if the sin is objectively a mortal sin. An objective mortal sin can be an actual venial sin, if the gravely immoral act is not done with full knowledge and with full consent. An actual venial sin that is objectively gravely immoral is more serious than an actual venial sin that is objectively venial, because any act that is an objective mortal sin is more thoroughly in opposition to the goodness of God. An objective mortal sin offends God more, and does more harm to one's neighbor, than an objective venial sin.

.087. The matter of a sin is the moral order or disorder of the act objectively before God. The matter of the sin is the sin considered in its objective elements within the three fonts. In the first font, the objective matter is the intention to use a particular means to a particular end; the matter of the first font is distinct from consent and knowledge. So the first font has both objective elements (intended means and end) and subjective elements (consent and knowledge). In the second font, the entire font is objective and is determined by the moral object toward which the act itself is inherently directed. In the third font, the entire font is objective and is determined by the moral weight of the good and bad consequences. Even though a judgment of the individual is used to evaluate the third font, there is an objective moral truth before God as to its morality.

Acts that depart from the proper moral order intended by God for humanity, to such an extent as to be entirely incompatible with true love of God and neighbor, are objective mortal sins (their matter is gravely disordered). Acts that depart from the proper moral order intended by God for humanity to a substantially limited extent are objective venial sins (the matter is disordered, but not gravely disordered). God intends all human acts to conform to good moral order, because all Creation, and especially all created persons, are made in the image of God, who is Goodness itself. All mortal sins depart seriously from the moral order intended by God; hence their matter is called objectively grave. All venial sins depart from the moral order intended by God to a substantially limited extent; hence their matter is called objectively venial.

This third criteria for an act to be an actual mortal sin, called the matter of the act, is based upon the objective morality of all three fonts, but not including deliberation and knowledge (which are the first two criteria for an act to be an actual mortal sin).

If, in the first font, the knowing choice is directed at an end, or by a means, that is gravely immoral, or if, in the second font, the moral object is gravely immoral, or if, in the third font, the bad consequences outweigh the good consequences to an extent that is gravely immoral, then the matter of the act is grave. If any one font is objectively gravely immoral, then the overall act (including all three fonts) is objectively gravely immoral, and is an objective mortal sin. If an objective mortal sin is done with full knowledge and with full deliberation, then the act is an actual mortal sin. If all three of these elements are not present together, then the act is not an actual mortal sin, but may be an actual venial sin.

Concerning objective sin, if one of the fonts is objectively gravely immoral, it is not possible for the goodness of the other two fonts to outweigh the bad font, such that the overall act would be either objectively reduced to a venial sin, or objectively not a sin. Certainly, even if one or two fonts are objectively gravely immoral, the goodness of another font can diminish the immorality of the overall act, making an objective mortal sin a less serious mortal sin, but the overall act would remain gravely immoral. The reason that any font is objectively gravely immoral is that it is entirely incompatible with true love of God and neighbor. Whenever any one font is in such a state of total moral opposition to the goodness of God, then the addition of two good fonts does not change the moral opposition to God of the other font.

Whenever any one font is immoral to a grave extent, then the overall act is a mortal sin. Even if the other two fonts are very good, one gravely immoral font is sufficient to make the act a mortal sin, and the goodness of the other two fonts cannot reduce the objective immorality of the overall act to that of an objective venial sin.

Examples: (1) The best intention and the most dire circumstances cannot cause direct abortion to be anything less than an objective mortal sin.

(2) A good work of mercy, such as donating money to the Church, and the good consequences that result from that donation, cannot cause the overall act to be anything less than a mortal sin, if the intention is gravely immoral, such as to deceive the leaders of the Church in order to obtain power within the Church (cf. Acts 5).

(3) A good act done with good intent, such as correcting one's employer for a manifest venial sin, would be a mortal sin if the reasonably anticipated bad consequences outweighed the good consequences to a grave extent. So if the correction results in the loss of one's job and the inability to provide the necessities of life for your family, the grave harm (third font) would cause this good act (second font) done with good intent (first font) to be an objective mortal sin.

.088. The morality of each font is independent of the other fonts. A good intention cannot cause an evil moral object to become good. A good intention cannot cause evil consequences to become good. A good moral object cannot cause an evil intention to become good. A good moral object cannot cause evil consequences to become good. A good consequence cannot cause an evil intention to become good. A good consequence cannot cause an evil moral object to become good. All this is true because all that is evil before the eyes of God is certainly evil, and all that is good before the eyes of God is certainly good. Nothing can cause evil to become good, or good to become evil. For all the goodness in Creation is of God, who is eternal and unchanging Goodness, and all evil is opposed to God, who never does evil in the least. The absolute separation of good and evil is essential to every general principle of morality and to every particular application of morality. The rejection of this absolute separation thoroughly corrupts a proper understanding of moral truth. If good could become evil, or if evil could become good, then the moral law would have no force at all. If good could become evil, or if evil could become good, then God would not exist. For the Goodness of God is the same as His very Existence.

[Psalms]
{5:5} In the morning, I will stand before you, and I will see. For you are not a God who wills iniquity.
...
{50:5} For I know my iniquity, and my sin is ever before me.
{50:6} Against you only have I sinned, and I have done evil before your eyes. And so, you are justified in your words, and you will prevail when you give judgment.
...
{118:11} I have hidden your eloquence in my heart, so that I may not sin against you.

[Isaiah]
{5:20} Woe to you who call evil good, and good evil; who substitute darkness for light, and light for darkness; who exchange bitter for sweet, and sweet for bitter!

Therefore, whenever any one font of morality is objectively gravely immoral, the goodness of the other two fonts can never cause the overall act to be objectively less than grave. The good or evil in one font does not change the good or evil in another font. The goodness of any one or two fonts can lessen the gravity of the overall act, because the overall act includes all three fonts. If any two fonts are gravely immoral, this offends God less than if all three fonts were gravely immoral, and more than if only one font is gravely immoral. But this difference can only make a mortal sin more or less serious as a mortal sin. As long as any one font is gravely disordered, the overall act remains objective mortal sin, no matter how good the other two fonts may be, because the act remains fundamentally incompatible with true love of God and neighbor. Therefore, if one font is sufficiently grave to be an objective mortal sin, then the other fonts can never reduce the morality of the overall act to that of an objective venial sin.

Pope John Paul II: "If acts are intrinsically evil, a good intention or particular circumstances can diminish their evil, but they cannot remove it. They remain 'irremediably' evil acts; per se and in themselves they are not capable of being ordered to God and to the good of the person. 'As for acts which are themselves sins (cum iam opera ipsa peccata sunt),' Saint Augustine writes, 'like theft, fornication, blasphemy, who would dare affirm that, by doing them for good motives (causis bonis), they would no longer be sins, or, what is even more absurd, that they would be sins that are justified?' Consequently, circumstances or intentions can never transform an act intrinsically evil by virtue of its object into an act 'subjectively' good or defensible as a choice."[77]

.089. Only when a knowingly chosen act has all three elements, (1) full consent, (2) full knowledge, (3) objectively grave matter, only then is the act an actual mortal sin. However, when an actual venial sin has one or two of these elements of actual mortal sin, that venial sin is more serious, because it is closer to the great offense of an actual mortal sin.

Saint Catherine of Siena: "The light of discretion (which proceeds from love, as I have told thee) gives to the neighbor a conditioned love, one that, being ordered aright, does not cause the injury of sin to self in order to be useful to others, for, if one single sin were committed to save the whole world from Hell, or to obtain one great virtue, the motive would not be a rightly ordered or discreet love, but rather indiscreet, for it is not lawful to perform even one act of great virtue and profit to others, by means of the guilt of sin."[78]

Here Saint Catherine teaches that nothing can cause a sinful act to become moral. Even if one single venial sin were committed to save the entire planet from destruction, or to save the entire human race from Hell, that sin would remain immoral. Good cannot cause evil to become good, and evil cannot cause good to become evil. Sin remains sin no matter what else is said or done.

Example: A person tells a venial lie (not a mortal sin). Lying is intrinsically evil and therefore always immoral. But suppose that the person lies with a good intended end and with some good consequences. The moral object remains evil, the good intended end remains good, and the good consequences remain good.

---

[77] Pope John Paul II, Veritatis Splendor, n. 81; inner quote is from St. Augustine, Contra Mendacium, VII, 18: "When, however, the works in themselves are evil, such as thefts, fornications, blasphemies, or other such; who is there that will say, that upon good causes they may be done, so as either to be no sins, or, what is more absurd, just sins?"
[78] The Dialogue of Saint Catherine of Siena, n. 42. In this quote, God is speaking to St. Catherine by means of a private revelation.

Even within the same act, whatever is good in that act remains good, and whatever is evil in that act remains evil. Otherwise, there would be no moral law.

.090. Degrees of Culpability

If a person is in the process of considering whether or not to choose a particular act, the act is not yet chosen. There is no culpability if an individual considers an immoral act, but decides not to commit the act. Once an immoral act is chosen, the only factors that can diminish or increase culpability are those that are within the three fonts of morality. These three fonts determine if an act is sinful, the degree of sin, and the degree of culpability. The whole moral law can be understood in terms of these three fonts.

Culpability pertains to actual sin. The degree of culpability is the degree of guilt for actual sin. The degree of culpability differs from the degree of objective sin. An act that is objectively a mortal sin may have substantially reduced culpability, if the person did not know that the act was gravely immoral (but thought the act to be somewhat immoral), so that the culpability is reduced to that of an actual venial sin, not an actual mortal sin. In some cases, due to invincible ignorance, a person may have no culpability despite having freely chosen to do what is gravely immoral, if, with sincerity and without negligence in seeking moral truth, he did not realize that the act was at all sinful.

Culpability is guilt before God for knowingly chosen immoral acts (actual sins). If an act was not knowingly chosen, i.e. not freely chosen with knowledge that the act was immoral, then there is no culpability. All actual sins, and only actual sins, include culpability. A merely objective sin, no matter how gravely immoral, would have no culpability if the gravely immoral act was not knowingly chosen, i.e. not freely chosen in the knowledge that the act was immoral.

.091. Both venial and morals sins have culpability. All culpable sins deserve some punishment from God. The culpability of a mortal sin is much greater than the culpability of a venial sin. The greater the degree of sin, the greater the degree of culpability, if the act is knowingly chosen. Some actual mortal sins have a greater culpability and other actual mortal sins have a lesser culpability; but all actual mortal sins have culpability to a grave extent. Some actual venial sins have a greater culpability and other actual venial sins have a lesser culpability; but all actual venial sins have substantially limited culpability.

The degree of culpability is determined by the degree of sinfulness in the matter of the act, and by the degree of knowledge in the intellect that the act was sinful, and by the degree of consent in the free will to the sinful act. The matter is the objective elements of the act in all three fonts. Knowledge and choice are the subjective elements of the act, which are only in the first font. The person who knowingly chooses an act is the subject.

There are three types of cases where there is no culpability. (1) If the matter of the act is not sinful, then the knowingly chosen act is not a sin and has no culpability, but only if the person understands that the matter of the act is not a sin. (2) If the person sincerely but mistakenly believed that the act was not at all sinful, then the knowingly chosen act is not an actual sin, even though it is an objective sin. (3) If the person did not act by a choice of the free will, then the act is not an actual sin, and there is no culpability.

There are three types of cases where culpability is diminished: (1) If the matter is objectively less sinful, then the culpability is also reduced to the same extent, but only if the person understood the act to be objectively less sinful. (2) If the person had some degree of misunderstanding in the knowledge of the morality of the act, mistakenly but sincerely thinking the act to be less sinful. (3) If the person chose the act with less free choice of the will (i.e. less than a fully deliberate choice); this is called semi-deliberate. Some semi-deliberate acts have a greater degree of deliberation, and some have a lesser degree of deliberation.

There are three types of cases where culpability is increased: (1) If the matter is objectively more sinful, then the culpability is also greater to the same extent, but only if the person understood the act to be objectively more sinful. (2) If the person had some degree of misunderstanding in the knowledge of the morality of the act, mistakenly but sincerely thinking the act to be more sinful. (3) If the person chose the act with closer to full deliberation, or with full deliberation, in the free will; some semi-deliberate acts are more deliberate (but not full) and others are less deliberate.

.092. There are a number of factors that might affect the knowledge or free choice of a sinful act, so as to increase or decrease culpability. The following are some examples of various factors that may reduce the culpability of a knowing choice. This is not an exhaustive list, but only select examples.

Physical impairments to the brain reduce culpability if either the ability to understand the morality of a choice, or the ability to freely choose, are reduced. Examples would include any injury, illness, or congenital problem that substantially affects mental functioning, as well as any type of intoxication (legal or illegal drugs, or alcohol). This reduction in knowledge and free choice does not affect knowingly chosen acts prior to intoxication, including the knowing choice to become intoxicated.

Psychological limitations reduce culpability if either the ability to understand the morality of a choice, or the ability to freely choose, are reduced. Examples would include psychological problems (transient or chronic), such as anxiety, depression, addiction, post traumatic stress disorder, schizophrenia, or psychosis. Even when a psychological problem is not a diagnosable mental illness, there may be substantial reduction in culpability. Examples would include: being abused as a child, being fearful because of some serious threat or danger, being oppressed by chronic pain or chronic stress. Examples of psychological limitations would also include factors due to age: the very young, because of limited ability to understand right from wrong, and the very old, because of decreased mental functioning with changes to the brain in old age.

Spiritual problems reduce culpability if either the ability to understand the morality of a choice, or the ability to freely choose, are reduced. One's own past personal sins can affect judgment as to what is sinful to some degree, reducing culpability. Examples would include a person who committed many objective mortal sins of a particular type prior to converting to the Catholic Faith. Then, after conversion, the person more easily falls back into that same type of sin, because his past sins make it more difficult for him to perceive the degree of sinfulness of the act, and more difficult to choose with full freedom. Examples would also include living in a sinful world, where the lack of understanding of morality, and many false claims about morality, are widely disseminated, making it more difficult for the conscience to correctly know the degree of sinfulness of the act. Examples would also include having a number of close family members or friends who sin seriously and who neither repent, nor even acknowledge that the acts are sinful. All these influences make it more difficult for the individual to perceive that an act is immoral, or to perceive the degree of sinfulness of the act, and more difficult to choose freely the right course of action. Examples would include the sins of some Catholics, which make it more difficult for other persons to understand accurately the teachings of the Church on morals. And examples would include the failings of leaders and teachers within the Church who teach incorrect or inaccurate doctrine on morals.

All of these factors may reduce culpability by a substantially affecting the knowledge or free choice of acts that are objectively immoral.

.093. But the matter of the act, under all three fonts, also affects the degree of sinfulness of the act. And, if the person understands this greater or lesser degree of sinfulness in the matter of the act, it also affects the degree of culpability. There is less culpability in acts that are known to be less sinful, and more culpability in acts that are known to be more sinful.

If an act is immoral under the second or third fonts, the overall act is more sinful with a worse intention and less sinful with a better intention. But no intention, no matter how good, can cause an act that has even one bad font to be moral. One bad font is sufficient to make the whole act immoral.

If an act is immoral under the first or second fonts, the overall act is more sinful if the bad consequences outweigh the good consequences, and this sinfulness increases by degrees with any increase in the moral weight of the bad consequences. Such an act is less sinful if the good consequences outweigh the bad consequences, and increasingly less sinful with any increase in the moral weight of the good consequences. But if any one font is bad, nothing can cause the overall act to be moral.

If an act is immoral under the first or third fonts, the overall act is more sinful whenever the chosen act is intrinsically evil (i.e. immoral under the second font). Also, some intrinsically evil acts are inherently grave sins (e.g. abortion, murder), whereas other intrinsically evil acts (e.g. lying, theft) are not inherently grave, but are either venial or mortal depending on the intention and the circumstances.

However, these possible increases and decreases in culpability and in sinfulness have limits. When one font makes an act a sin, the other fonts may cause the act to be more or less sinful, but only to a certain extent. If one font causes an act to be a sin, the other two fonts, no matter how good, cannot make the overall act moral. And nothing can cause an act that is an objective mortal sin due to grave immorality in one font, from being less than an objective mortal sin overall. If one font causes an act to be an objective mortal sin, the other two fonts, no matter how good, cannot make the overall act less than an objective mortal sin.

Examples: Lying is intrinsically evil and always immoral. The other fonts can affect the degree of morality of the overall act. A lie is less serious if it is done with a good intended end, or if the good consequences outweigh the bad consequences. A lie is more serious if it is done with an immoral intended end, or if the bad consequences outweigh the good consequences. (1) Lying under oath during a trial with the intention of sending an innocent person to prison is a mortal sin, because the intention and the bad consequences are each gravely morally disordered. (2) Lying about whether or not the food that someone cooked for you tastes good, with the intention of sparing their feelings, is immoral; for all lying is intrinsically evil. But the good intention and the substantially limited bad consequences are not gravely disordered, and so this lie is a venial sin.

.094. Lying is always a sin, but some lies are venial sins and other lies are mortal sins, depending on the intention and the circumstances. However, even if a particular intention or a particular circumstance causes a lie to be somewhat more serious, the act might still be an objective venial sin if it is not so seriously disordered as to be fundamentally contrary to true love of God and neighbor.

A theft that is a mortal sin may be less serious, but still mortal, if the theft does less harm to the owner of the goods. A theft that is a venial sin may be more serious, but still venial, if the theft does more harm to the owner of the goods, but that harm is still relatively small. Theft is always a sin, but some thefts are venial sins, and other thefts are mortal sins, depending on the intention and the circumstances. The first and third fonts can cause an intrinsically evil act of theft to be more or less serious, but they cannot cause theft to be moral.

It is also possible for any sin, which would otherwise be a venial sin, to become an actual mortal sin, if it is chosen with an evil intention. Any act chosen with malicious intent, or hateful intent, or lustful intent, or any other gravely immoral intention, is a mortal sin, even if the act itself and its consequences are good, or even if the act itself and its consequences would have made the act only a venial sin. A gravely disordered intention makes any chosen act gravely immoral. If a good act is done with only good consequences, the overall act is nevertheless gravely immoral if the intention is gravely immoral. Also, intention is never chosen without free choice, nor without knowledge of one's own intention, and so an immoral intention is always an actual sin, and a gravely immoral intention is always an actual mortal sin.

Chapter 8
Interior Acts and Exterior Acts

.095.
In the second font, the act itself can be either an interior act or an exterior act. An interior act is an act limited to the heart and mind, i.e. to the will and intellect. An exterior act is any act that goes beyond will and intellect. This distinction is implicit in the ten commandments.

[Deuteronomy]
{5:18} And you shall not commit adultery.
...
{5:21} You shall not covet your neighbor's wife....

There are two separate commandments, one for the external act of adultery, and the other for the internal act of being willing to commit adultery. Even if the act is limited to the heart and mind, and is never carried out in any exterior way, the act of desiring to commit adultery (of consenting with the free will to the act of adultery) is a serious sin against God. Thus, the ten commandments divides sinful acts into those that are internal and those that are external.

This distinction of interior and exterior sins is also found in the Penitential Rite of holy Mass: "I confess to Almighty God, and to you my brothers and sisters, that I have sinned through my own fault, in my thoughts and in my words, in what I have done, and in what I have failed to do...."[79]

Our sins in thought are interior sins, and our sins in word or deed are exterior sins. All sins, interior and exterior, are subject to the eternal moral law. Each and every sin, whether interior or exterior, must be good under all three fonts of morality in order to be moral.

[Matthew]
{5:27} You have heard that it was said to the ancients: 'You shall not commit adultery.'
{5:28} But I say to you, that anyone who will have looked at a woman, so as to lust after her, has already committed adultery with her in his heart.
{5:29} And if your right eye causes you to sin, root it out and cast it away from you. For it is better for you that one of your members perish, than that your whole body be cast into Hell.

Jesus condemns both the exterior act of adultery, and the interior act of lust. The exterior act of merely looking at a woman is not a sin. Admiring beauty in a woman is not adultery of the heart. Only if the man consents to lust with the will and intellect does he commit adultery of the heart. Jesus describes lust as adultery of the heart because any act of lust is a willingness to commit an illicit sexual act, including any gravely immoral sexual act, the primary example of

---

[79] Penitential Rite, English translation of The Roman Missal, International Committee on English in the Liturgy, Inc.

which is adultery. If the person is not willing to commit the immoral sexual act, then even if there is some degree or type of sin, the sin is not lust.

This interior act of consenting to an illicit sexual act is an actual mortal sin only if it is done with full consent and full knowledge that the act is gravely immoral (or without caring if the act is gravely immoral). As is the case with any interior sin, a mere passing thought or temptation, to which one does not consent, would not be a sin at all. And if the consent or knowledge is substantially less than full, the interior act would be an actual venial sin, not an actual mortal sin.

.096. How do we distinguish whether a thought about a sinful act is an objective mortal sin, an objective venial sin, or not a sin at all?

Adultery is intrinsically evil and always gravely immoral. The act of adultery is an objective mortal sin. If the act of adultery is chosen with full knowledge and full consent, then it is an actual mortal sin. But a thought about adultery is not the same as an act of adultery. A person may think about the ten commandments, and about the mortal sin of adultery, without himself sinning. Therefore, thoughts about adultery, or about sexual acts in general, or about any sinful act, are not necessarily sinful thoughts. A thought about adultery is not inherently ordered toward the commission of the act of adultery. Nor are thoughts about any act inherently ordered toward the doing of the act itself. Thinking is not the same as doing. Thus, consent to a thought about an act does not imply consent to the act itself, and consent to a thought about an intrinsically evil act is not itself intrinsically evil.

However, if the consent to the thought includes a willingness to commit the intrinsically evil act, then the interior act of consent to that act is intrinsically evil. For every intrinsically evil act, even one that is exterior (e.g. murder, fornication, theft), always includes an interior knowing choice of the act by the will and intellect. If the will and intellect make fundamentally the same choice, but without the exterior act, then the sin is fundamentally the same sin. And so, if any exterior act is intrinsically evil and gravely immoral, then even the interior consent alone to the same act is also intrinsically evil and gravely immoral. But this refers to actual consent to the sinful act, not merely consent to thoughts about the sinful act.

If a person thinks about an exterior sinful act, with an interior consent to the act, not merely with consent to thoughts about the act, then he has committed an interior sin of the same type as the exterior sin. If the exterior act to which he consents is an intrinsically evil act, then the interior consent to the act is intrinsically evil. If the exterior act to which he consents is inherently gravely immoral, then the interior consent to the same act is inherently gravely immoral. If the exterior act to which he consents is only a venial sin, then the interior consent to the same act is only a venial sin. If the exterior act to which he consents is a sin, but not intrinsically evil, then the interior consent to the same act is a sin, but not intrinsically evil.

However, the exterior commission of a sinful act generally has more bad consequences than the mere interior consent to the same act. Therefore, the exterior sin is overall more sinful. If the exterior sin is a grave matter solely because of these exterior bad consequences, then the interior consent to the same sin would be a venial matter because these bad consequences are lacking. Keep in mind, though, that a gravely immoral intention can make any interior or exterior act whatsoever into a mortal sin. Thus, a sin that is solely interior may be an actual mortal sin, because of bad intention, even if the same sin carried out in the exterior (and without a gravely immoral intention) is only venial. Any actual mortal sin will have worse consequences than any actual venial sin, but this includes the interior consequences to the soul.

If there is no interior consent to the sinful act, but only consent to thoughts about the sinful act, then the interior act is not necessarily a sin. Such an interior consent to thoughts about sinful acts may be without sin, as when someone studying ethics thinks about the sinful acts discussed in examples. Or there may be some sinfulness found in consent to thoughts about sinful acts, if the person dwells on such thoughts in a selfish or disordered manner. If there is some sinfulness, the sin may be either venial or mortal. Thus consent to thoughts about a sinful act may be: not a sin, or a venial sin, or a mortal sin.

.097. The same is true when the acts that are considered in thought are entirely moral acts. The consent to such thoughts may be moral. But there may be some sinfulness found in consent to thoughts about moral acts, if the person dwells on such thoughts in a selfish or disordered manner. As long as the consent to the thoughts is not consent to the act itself, the moral object of the act itself is only interior (dependent upon the nature of the thoughts by themselves). But whenever the consent is consent to the exterior act, not merely to thoughts about the act, the interior act has the same moral object as the exterior act. And even if that moral object is never achieved, the interior act is still inherently ordered toward that moral object, and so the inherent moral meaning of the interior act is still determined by that moral object.

Examples: (1) A man thinks about becoming a famous sports player, and receiving money and fame. The acts being considered are not necessarily sinful. But the consideration of these acts may include the sins of selfishness, or pride, or a disordered desire for money. So the exterior acts being considered are not sins, but they are considered in a sinful manner, and so the interior act is a sin. (2) A man thinks about being married and having sexual relations with his wife. The sexual act being considered is moral, but the manner of considering the act may be selfish, with a disordered desire for sexual relations above other more important goods, or apart from true love of spouse. (3) A woman thinks about an attractive man that she sees, and she fantasizes about sexual relations with him. If she has no willingness to commit the illicit sexual act (of relations outside of marriage), then her thoughts are not intrinsically evil, and not necessarily gravely immoral. Her consent is to the thoughts, and not to the act. Even so, she might sin venially, or she might sin mortally. For any knowingly chosen act can be a mortal sin, if done with a gravely disordered intention, or with gravely disordered consequences.

.098. The Summa Theologica of Saint Thomas Aquinas considers the same question of consent to thought about an exterior act, as compared to consent in thought to the exterior act itself. His terminology can be difficult to understand and so I've added some explanatory notes [in brackets]. The terms 'delight' and 'delectation' refer to enjoyment, but also imply consent with the will to thoughts in the mind.

Saint Thomas Aquinas: "Accordingly a man who is thinking of fornication, may delight in either of two things: [1] first, in the thought itself, [2] secondly, in the fornication thought of.

"[1] Now the delectation [enjoyment] in the thought itself results from the inclination of the appetite to the thought; and the thought itself is not in itself a mortal sin; sometimes indeed it is only a venial sin, as when a man thinks of such a thing for no [good] purpose; and sometimes it is no sin at all, as when a man has a [good] purpose in thinking of it; for instance, he may wish to preach or dispute about it. Consequently such affection or delectation in respect of the thought of fornication is not a mortal sin in virtue of its genus [i.e. not intrinsically evil], but is sometimes a venial sin and sometimes no sin at all: wherefore neither is it a mortal sin to consent to such a thought [i.e. not a mortal sin under the second font of morality].

"[2] But that a man in thinking of fornication takes pleasure in the act thought of, is due to his desire being inclined to this act. Wherefore the fact that a man consents to such a delectation, amounts to nothing less than a consent to the inclination of his appetite to fornication [consenting to the exterior act itself]: for no man takes pleasure except in that which is in conformity with his appetite. Now it is a mortal sin, if a man deliberately chooses that his appetite be conformed to what is in itself a mortal sin [i.e. a sin that is inherently gravely immoral]. Wherefore such a consent [in thought] to delectation in a mortal sin, is itself a mortal sin..."[80]

In the first case, Saint Thomas considers consent to taking enjoyment in the thought itself. For example, one might think about the act of murder. There may be some enjoyment in thinking about murder, such as the enjoyment of learning about the ten commandments, or even the enjoyment of reading an entertaining murder mystery novel. So in some cases consent to such thoughts about murder is not a sin. In other cases, a person might sin by thinking about murder, such as by thinking about forms of entertainment (movies, books, etc.) which are excessively violent, or by the enjoyment of thoughts about killing one's enemies, yet with no willingness to commit the act. Such an interior sin, when it lacks consent to the sinful exterior act, is not a mortal sin under the second font because it is not intrinsically evil (not in itself immoral). This same interior act may be a venial or a mortal sin, depending on the other two fonts, but it does not have the same moral object as the exterior act.

In the second case, Saint Thomas considers consent in thought to the sinful act itself. Such interior consent without the exterior act is the same interior consent

---

[80] Saint Thomas Aquinas, Summa Theologica, I-II, Q. 74, n. 8.

as occurs with the exterior act. Therefore, this consent has the same moral object (even if the exterior act never occurs). For the act itself never takes its morality from the achievement of the moral object, but from the inherent ordering of the chosen act toward that moral object. Thus an act which is solely interior, and which includes consent to the moral object of the exterior act, takes its morality from that moral object. For the interior act is inherently directed to that moral object as to an end. Therefore, interior consent to an exterior intrinsically evil act is also intrinsically evil. For consent to any act always includes consent to its moral object. If the consent is to a moral object that is necessarily a mortal sin (such that the second font makes the matter grave), then the interior act is a mortal sin. For the knowing choice of the human person is the same when the interior consent is by itself, as when the interior consent is accompanied by its exterior act.

.099. The same considerations apply to other interior sins. But this is not a new or different set of principles of morality for interior acts. In every case, regardless of the subject matter of the thoughts and desires of the heart and mind, the three fonts of morality and all the basic principles of morality still hold true.

FIRST FONT: When we apply the three fonts of morality to an internal act, the first font is still the intention. The intention is sinful in the case of an internal act if the individual intends either an immoral end or an immoral means.

Examples: (1) A person is thinking about the means that he might use to steal from his employer. His intended end is to find a way to commit the theft without being caught; his intention is immoral. (2) A person is thinking about a clever means to steal, so as to write a fictional story. His intended end is not to steal, but to entertain; his intention is not immoral.

(3) A person is considering what to say to his employer regarding a mistake that he has made in his work. If he considers various words that he might use in the explanation, intending to deceive, then his intention is sinful. The employer has a right to know about this mistake, since it pertains to the work of his business. (4) A person withholds information from his employer, omitting information to which the employer has no right, with the intention of protecting someone else's privacy, not with the intention to deceive. Lying is intrinsically evil and always immoral, but the mere withholding of information to which the other person has no right is not lying.

SECOND FONT: For any interior act, the act itself is always of both will and intellect. The will can only choose based on knowledge in the intellect. An interior act, whether moral or immoral, is always a choice of the will of what is known by the intellect. Although we refer to some sins as desires, a sinful desire is always a choice of the will based on knowledge in the intellect. A person cannot desire what he does not know. Mere emotions, such as anger, or mere passing thoughts of sinful acts, are not even objective sins, unless there is an act of free will and intellect (a knowing choice); these are not actual sins unless the choice is free and the knowledge reveals the immorality of the chosen act.

The moral object of the interior act is the end toward which the interior act is directed. But even if that interior act would require an accompanying exterior act in order to achieve the moral object, and that exterior act is absent, the inherent moral meaning of the interior act is nevertheless determined by that moral object. For every act remains inherently ordered toward its moral object, even when the moral object is not achieved. When a man commits adultery of the heart, he sins grievously, even though he has not obtained the object of the gravely disordered desire to which he has consented. Whenever an interior sin has an evil moral object, the interior sin is intrinsically evil and always immoral.

THIRD FONT: Both moral and immoral interior acts have consequences.

Good interior acts, such as interior prayer and interior self-denial (e.g. refraining from selfish thoughts), have good effects, not only on the soul of the individual, but also on the lives of other persons. Many of the Saints lived in isolation from the world and from other persons, and yet they benefited the Church and the world greatly by their interior life of prayer and self-denial. All persons who are in a state of grace share in one holy communion, united by the Spirit of God and led by Jesus Christ. The state of grace in the soul is the presence of the Holy Spirit, in love, faith, and hope. One and the same Holy Spirit unites all who are in a state of grace by His presence. Therefore, all who are in a state of grace are one in the love of God. Good knowingly chosen acts that occur in cooperation with grace are a benefit to all who are one in grace.

Bad interior acts, such as heresy, idolatry, blasphemy, hatred, malice, lust, and other sins, have bad effects, not only on the soul of the individual, but also on the lives of other persons. For actual venial sins harm the soul by beginning to turn us away from God and from all that is good. And actual mortal sins harm the soul grievously by turning us entirely away from God and from all that is good, depriving us of the life of grace in the soul and of the communion of the saints. (The term 'saints' refers to all who are in a state of grace.) In addition to harming ourselves, our knowingly chosen immoral acts also harm other persons. For they are denied the graces that they would have received if we had chosen to do good, instead of evil. And if we commit actual mortal sin, they are denied the benefits if we had remained in a state of grace, in the communion of the saints.

.100. In addition, when the individual is harmed by his own sins, eventually this harm will show itself in exterior acts. A person who continually sins interiorly will eventually sin in the exterior as well. For both interior and exterior acts proceed from the same mind and heart. These exterior sins will also do harm to other persons. Thus even the most well-hidden interior sins have bad consequences, both seen and unseen.

[Matthew]
{5:21} You have heard that it was said to the ancients: 'You shall not murder; whoever will have murdered shall be liable to judgment.'
{5:22} But I say to you, that anyone who becomes angry with his brother shall be liable to judgment.

Interior Acts and Exterior Acts

Jesus compares an exterior sin to an interior sin. The moral law prohibits not only exterior sins, such as violence against the innocent, but also interior sins, such as anger against the innocent. If a man kills, he is liable to judgment in order to determine whether or not the killing was justified. If a man consents to anger in his heart and mind, he is liable to judgment in order to determine whether or not the anger was justified. A righteous anger is not sinful, for even Jesus was justly angry when he saw people treating the sanctuary like a marketplace, buying and selling (John 2:14-16).

[Matthew]
{15:19} For from the heart go out evil thoughts, murders, adulteries, fornications, thefts, false testimonies, blasphemies.
{15:20} These are the things that defile a man.....

In His teaching, Jesus refers to both interiors sins and exterior sins. Evil thoughts are interior sins. The sin of blasphemy can be interior or exterior. Even if these thoughts are not carried out in any exterior way, the interior consent to evil thoughts is a sin. Jesus places evil thoughts in the same set of sins as murder, adultery, fornication, theft, false testimony, and blasphemy because evil thoughts can be actual mortal sins, and because interior mortal sins can lead to exterior mortal sins.

Chapter 9
Positive and Negative Precepts

.101.

[Psalms]
{33:17} But the countenance of the Lord is upon those who do evil, to perish the remembrance of them from the earth.

[1 John]
{3:4} Everyone who commits a sin, also commits iniquity. For sin is iniquity.

[James]
{4:17} Therefore, he who knows that he ought to do a good thing, and does not do it, for him it is a sin.

The eternal moral law forbids both sins of commission and sins of omission. During holy Mass, the people pray an act of contrition for sin: "in my thoughts and in my words, in what I have done, and in what I have failed to do...."[81] The sins of commission are found "in what I have done" and the sins of omission are found "in what I have failed to do." Both sins of commission and sins of omission are contrary to the moral law.

Whenever any precept of the moral law forbids an act, the precept is called a negative precept. The negative precepts ('you shall not') require the human person to refrain from acting; to commit such an act is a sin. Sins against negative precepts are generally sins of commission, because sin occurs when the forbidden act is committed. With negative precepts, refraining from acting is moral, and acting is immoral. However, there is nothing to prevent a sin of omission from being contrary to a negative precept. For example, the negative precept against euthanasia ('you shall not murder') can be violated by the omission of ordinary and necessary care, such as food and water.

Whenever any precept of the moral law requires an act to be done, the precept is called a positive precept. The positive precepts ('you shall') require the human person to act; to refrain from acting is a sin. Sins against positive precepts are generally sins of omission, because it is sinful to omit the required act. With positive precepts, acting is moral, and refraining from acting is immoral. However, there is nothing to prevent a sin of commission from being contrary to a positive precept. For example, the positive precept to worship the Lord God and to serve Him alone (Deut 6:13; Mt 4:10) is violated by the sin of commission of adding the worship of false gods to the worship of the Lord. And since all negative precepts are derived from the two greatest commandments, to love God above all, and to love your neighbor as yourself, every sin against a negative precept is also a sin against a positive precept.

.102. Negative precepts are binding always and in each instance. If it is a sin to knowingly choose a particular act, then that act can never morally be done. Even

---

[81] USCCB, peoplesparts.pdf, the wording quoted is the same in both the new and revised text, Revised Order of the Mass, Third Edition.

immoral acts that are not intrinsically evil are always immoral, in the sense that whenever the same act has the same fonts of morality, such that one or more fonts are bad, the overall act will always be immoral. A good act (with a good moral object), with only good consequences, but done with bad intention, is always immoral, as long as the intention remains the same. A good act, done with good intention, but with bad consequences that outweigh the good consequences, is always immoral, as long as the consequences remain the same. Whenever any one or more fonts is bad, the overall act is always immoral, as long as the fonts remain the same.

"In moral theology negative precepts (i.e., prohibitions) are considered to bind in each and every case. Thus, 'do not murder' would bind *semper et pro semper*. Positive precepts, such as 'help the poor,' bind *semper* (always) but not *pro semper* (in each instance), as there are many instances in which someone may not be able to be engaged in the direct work of helping the poor (for example, when one is studying, recreating, sleeping, etc.)."[82]

Negative precepts are always binding, in general and in particular. Each and every negative precept is forbidden always (in general) and in each instance (in particular). There are no instances in which it is moral to commit murder, or adultery, or theft, or lying, or to act with bad intention, or to act when the bad consequences outweigh the good consequences.

Pope John Paul II: "God's commandments teach us the way of life. The negative moral precepts, which declare that the choice of certain actions is morally unacceptable, have an absolute value for human freedom: they are valid always and everywhere, without exception. They make it clear that the choice of certain ways of acting is radically incompatible with the love of God and with the dignity of the person created in his image. Such choices cannot be redeemed by the goodness of any intention or of any consequence; they are irrevocably opposed to the bond between persons; they contradict the fundamental decision to direct one's life to God."[83]

.103. Positive precepts are binding always, but not in each instance; they bind in general, but not in particular. The positive precept to keep holy the Sabbath applies on the Sabbath day (Sunday, or the Saturday vigil) and on holy days of obligation (which are a type of Sabbath), but not on every day. Even on the Sabbath, while we are asleep, we are not fulfilling this precept. The positive precept to worship the Lord your God is always binding, on every day, and yet we are not required, under penalty of sin, to perform acts of worship continually, but only from time to time. The positive precept to honor your father and mother is always binding in general, but we may choose the particular times, occasions, and ways of fulfilling this precept. The positive precept to give alms is always binding in general, but we may choose when and how to give to those in need.

---

[82] James T. Bretzke, Consecrated phrases: a Latin theological dictionary, (Liturgical Press, 1998), p. 129-130.
[83] Pope John Paul II, Evangelium Vitae, n. 75.

Therefore, on some occasions, we may omit fulfilling a positive precept, without sin, in favor of fulfilling that precept on another occasion, or in another way.

Pope John Paul II: "It is right and just, always and for everyone, to serve God, to render him the worship which is his due and to honor one's parents as they deserve. Positive precepts such as these, which order us to perform certain actions and to cultivate certain dispositions, are universally binding; they are 'unchanging.' They unite in the same common good all people of every period of history, created for 'the same divine calling and destiny.' These universal and permanent laws correspond to things known by the practical reason and are applied to particular acts through the judgment of conscience. The acting subject personally assimilates the truth contained in the law. He appropriates this truth of his being and makes it his own by his acts and the corresponding virtues. The negative precepts of the natural law are universally valid. They oblige each and every individual, always and in every circumstance. It is a matter of prohibitions which forbid a given action *semper et pro semper*, without exception, because the choice of this kind of behavior is in no case compatible with the goodness of the will of the acting person, with his vocation to life with God and to communion with his neighbor. It is prohibited -- to everyone and in every case -- to violate these precepts. They oblige everyone, regardless of the cost, never to offend in anyone, beginning with oneself, the personal dignity common to all."[84]

Ability affects the fulfillment of positive precepts, but not negative precepts. We are always able to refrain from committing a sin against a negative precept, by refraining from murder, adultery, theft, lying, etc. We are not always able to fulfill every positive precept at all times. Each person has a limited amount of time and ability and resources to use in fulfilling the positive precepts.

.104. Omitting Fulfillment of Positive Precepts

There are three types of instances in which a person may omit fulfilling a positive precept, without committing a sin:

1. A person may omit fulfilling a positive precept, without committing a sin, when the person chooses to fulfill the positive precept in another way, or at another time.

Example: You receive numerous requests for donations to charities from many different groups. You are free to give money to one charity and not to another, even though no negative precept requires you to refrain from giving to a particular charity. Even when an act is not prohibited by a negative precept, it may be omitted in favor of fulfilling the positive precept in some other way, or at some other time.

[2 Corinthians]
{3:17} Now the Spirit is Lord. And wherever the Spirit of the Lord is, there is liberty.

---

[84] Pope John Paul II, Veritatis Splendor, n. 52.

Positive and Negative Precepts

There are a myriad of different ways that one might fulfill the positive precept to love your neighbor. The human person is free to choose, without sin, among these many ways. This is the most common reason why a person might not fulfill a positive precept in a particular instance. For the Spirit of the Lord does not command us, as if we were slaves, as to exactly what we should do in each and every moment, and in each and every act. We are prohibited from sin, and we are required to do good works in love. But we are free to choose the acts of love that we will do within the various circumstances of our lives.

2. A person may omit fulfilling a positive precept, without committing a sin, when a negative precept prohibits a particular way of fulfilling a positive precept because the circumstances make the act a sin.

First Font: A person has control over his own intention, and so if a bad intention prohibits the fulfillment of a positive precept, the person should change his intention. So while acting with a bad intention is always prohibited by negative precept, this is not an absolute obstacle to the particular fulfillment of any positive precept, since the person can cooperate with grace in order to change to a good intention and then the act can be done.

Second Font: An intrinsically evil act never fulfills a positive precept, neither in general, nor in particular, because God is not divided against Himself. He cannot both will an act to be done to fulfill a positive precept, and forbid the very same act under a negative precept. Intrinsically evil acts are always immoral, and are never justified on the claim that the intrinsically evil act somehow fulfills a positive precept, whether in general or in particular. All intrinsically evil acts are prohibited under negative precept, and such acts can never fulfill a positive precept in any way.

Third font: A negative precept may sometimes prohibit, due to the circumstances, a particular instance of the fulfillment of a positive precept. If the intention and the act itself (with its moral object) are good, then the act may perhaps be a particular way of fulfilling a positive precept. But this same act, in some circumstances, may have more bad consequences than good consequences. In such cases, the particular fulfillment of the positive precept will be prohibited by negative precept. The person must then find some other way to fulfill that positive precept, by choosing the same act in other circumstances, or by choosing a different act, perhaps at another time.

Examples: (1) A group of persons are in need of money. A husband and wife would like to donate, but they do not have sufficient financial resources to do so. Such a donation would harm their own family, and such harm would be a sin prohibited under negative precept (because the bad consequences outweigh the good consequences). But the husband and wife can still fulfill the positive precept of helping those in need by prayer and self-denial, or by donating at another time, when circumstances permit.

(2) A person is ill with a contagious disease (e.g. the flu), and so he cannot attend Mass on Sunday. If he attends, he will harm his neighbors by the consequences of his act, in that they may become ill. The negative precept to refrain from

doing more harm than good in the consequences of our acts prohibits this particular way of fulfilling the positive precept to keep holy the Sabbath. However, the person can still keep the Sabbath holy in other ways, such as by prayer and the reading of Sacred Scripture at home. And after he recovers, he can then fulfill this positive precept by attending Mass again.

(3) Your neighbor is drowning, but you are unable to swim and the water is deep. Suppose that there is no other way for you to rescue him except to jump into the water. But if you do so, there is very little chance that you will save him, and the most likely result is that you will drown with him. You are prohibited by a negative precept from jumping into the water because you will likely die, and your neighbor will likely not be saved, and so the bad consequences outweigh the good consequences. Therefore, you are not obligated to fulfill the positive precept of helping those in need in this particular way, at this particular time.

The negative precepts never prohibit any of the positive precepts directly, since both negative and positive precepts are of the one moral law, which is of God, who never contradicts Himself. A negative precept may only ever prohibit a particular way of fulfilling a positive precept, i.e. the positive precept in particular, and not the positive precept in general. This conflict between a negative precept and a particular way of fulfilling a positive precept occurs due to the circumstances.

3. A person may omit fulfilling a positive precept, without committing a sin, when the person is unable to fulfill the positive precept in a particular way due to circumstances, even though the particular act is not a sin.

Each person must refrain from any and all sinful acts at all times; this is possible because refraining from a prohibited act does not take time or resources or physical ability. All that is required is grace and free will. But the fulfillment of the positive precepts requires time, ability, and resources. Now we all have some time and some ability and some resources (however meager) to use in the fulfillment of positive precepts. And so no one is absolutely excluded from this obligation due to a lack of time, ability, or resources. We can help others by praying for them, by offering acts of self-denial for them, by kind words and whatever kind deeds we are able to do. But in some instances, a person may be unable to fulfill a particular positive precept in a particular circumstance. There is no sin in this type omission, because the positive precepts do not require continual fulfillment at all times, in all circumstances.

Pope John Paul II: "In the case of the positive moral precepts, prudence always has the task of verifying that they apply in a specific situation, for example, in view of other duties which may be more important or urgent. But the negative moral precepts, those prohibiting certain concrete actions or kinds of behavior as intrinsically evil, do not allow for any legitimate exception."[85]

---

[85] Pope John Paul II, Veritatis Splendor, n. 67.

.105. But if you are inclined to think that you often lack what is needed to fulfill the positive precepts, consider this example from the lives of Louis Joseph Martin and Zélie Guérin Martin, the parents of Saint Therese of Lisieux:

"Charity in all its forms was a natural outlet to the piety of these simple hearts. Husband and wife set aside each year a considerable portion of their earnings for the Propagation of the Faith; they relieved poor persons in distress, and ministered to them with their own hands. On one occasion Monsieur Martin, like a good Samaritan, was seen to raise a drunken man from the ground in a busy thoroughfare, take his bag of tools, support him on his arm, and lead him home. Another time when he saw, in a railway station, a poor and starving epileptic without the means to return to his distant home, he was so touched with pity that he took off his hat and, placing in it an alms, proceeded to beg from the passengers on behalf of the sufferer. Money poured in, and it was with a heart brimming over with gratitude that the sick man blessed his benefactor."[86]

Although at times it may seem as if we are powerless to help those in need, there is always the power of prayer, of self-denial, and of the most humble acts of mercy. For it is not the most powerful acts that are great before God, but rather the acts that are done with the most love. It is by acts of love that we fulfill all the positive precepts. Without love, no positive precept is truly fulfilled in the eyes of God.

Saint Therese of Lisieux: "O my Jesus, I love Thee! I love my Mother, the Church; I bear in mind that 'the least act of pure love is of more value to her than all other works together.' "[87] (The inner quote is from Saint John of the Cross.)

[Tobit]
{4:7} Give alms from your substance, and do not turn away your face from any pauper. For so it shall be that neither will the face of the Lord be turned away from you.
{4:8} In whatever way that you are able, so shall you be merciful.
{4:9} If you have much, distribute abundantly. If you have little, nevertheless strive to bestow a little freely.
{4:10} For you store up for yourself a good reward for the day of necessity.
{4:11} For almsgiving liberates from every sin and from death, and it will not suffer the soul to go into darkness.
{4:12} Almsgiving will be a great act of faith before the most high God, for all those who practice it.

.106. Required Fulfillment of Positive Precepts

There is only one type of instance in which a person is required to fulfill a positive precept in a particular instance: in order to avoid sin against a negative

---

[86] T. N. Taylor, Prologue, The Autobiography of Saint Thérèse of Lisieux, PDF ebook version, p. 5.
[87] Saint Therese, The Autobiography of Saint Thérèse of Lisieux, PDF ebook version, p. 101.

precept. Although negative precepts never prohibit positive precepts in general, at times a negative precept will require the fulfillment of a positive precept in a particular instance. In such cases, the requirement to fulfill a positive precept in a particular instance is of the negative precept, not specifically of the positive precept. Positive precepts only require fulfillment in general, not in particular. In such a case, the negative precept is requiring an act to be done, rather than requiring an act to be avoided, and so the negative precept is prohibiting a sin of omission.

Some sins of omission are sins against negative precepts.

Pope John Paul II: "For a correct moral judgment on euthanasia, in the first place a clear definition is required. Euthanasia in the strict sense is understood to be an action or omission which of itself and by intention causes death, with the purpose of eliminating all suffering."[88]

Murder is defined (by Pope John Paul II in the same encyclical) as "the direct and voluntary killing of an innocent human being...."[89] Abortion is murder in the circumstance where the innocent person is a prenatal; infanticide is murder in the circumstance where the innocent person is an infant. Euthanasia is murder with the intention of eliminating all suffering. Now while the type of murder may vary depending on the first font of intention, and on the third font of circumstances, every type of murder is intrinsically evil under the second font, since it is the direct and voluntary killing of an innocent human being. The essential moral definition of murder is solely under the second font, even if the particular type of murder varies depending on the other fonts. For all murder is intrinsically evil.

And all murder is prohibited by negative precept: "You shall not murder." (Mt 19:18).[90] For the negative precepts specify acts that we are prohibited from doing. Every type of murder, including euthanasia, is prohibited by negative precept. But Pope John Paul II clearly defines euthanasia, a type of murder, as either a sin of commission, or a sin of omission. And when this sin is an omission, the omission cannot be merely in the first or third fonts, since all types of murder and all intrinsically evil acts are defined, as to their essential moral nature, under the second font. For euthanasia, like every type of murder, is intrinsically evil. Therefore, some intrinsically evil acts are sins of omission, and some sins of omission are sins against a negative precept, rather than sins against a positive precept.

Examples: (1) A physician commits the sin of euthanasia by deciding to omit an ordinary intervention needed to keep a patient alive, such as food, water, or ordinary medical care. This sin of omission is a type of murder. But even when an act of murder is not euthanasia (i.e. not done with the intention of relieving all suffering), the murder may still be a sin of omission.

---

[88] Pope John Paul II, Evangelium Vitae, n. 65.
[89] Pope John Paul II, Evangelium Vitae, n. 57.
[90] In the Latin Vulgate, Jesus states the commandment as: "Non homicidium facies" which translates as "You shall not murder."

(2) The ancient Greeks and Romans used to commit infanticide by leaving the infant without any care, exposed to the elements of nature. The Roman Senate once passed a law (which was never filed and so never made effective) requiring all male newborns, in Rome, for one year, to be left unattended until they died.[91] The same type of infanticide by omission was sometimes practiced in order to eliminate daughters. These are acts of murder by the omission of ordinary and necessary care.

(3) A man sees his neighbor drowning, and he can easily rescue him by throwing him a flotation device, and by shouting for help. The man deliberately chooses to omit saving his neighbor, knowing that the result will be the death of an innocent human being. Again, this is an act of murder by a sin of omission; the act is intrinsically evil and is contrary to a negative precept: "You shall not murder." (Mt 19:18).

Murder by omission, and other intrinsically evil sins of omission against negative precepts, must be direct and voluntary acts. Although it may seem as if a sin of omission is not direct, since the omitted act is not done, all intrinsically evil acts are direct in that the chosen act is directly related (inherently ordered) to its moral object. A sin of omission is the knowingly chosen act of deciding not to do what is required. A sin of omission always includes the interior voluntary act of deciding not to do what the eternal moral law requires be done. Thus, even a sin of omission may be a direct and voluntary immoral act.

.107. The Ten Commandments

The ten commandments can be divided into positive and negative precepts. The traditional numbering and order of the ten commandments is as stated in the Catechism of the Catholic Church (with references to Scripture added).[92]

1. I am the LORD your God: you shall not have strange gods before me. (Exodus 20:2-6; Deuteronomy 5:6-10)
2. You shall not take the name of the LORD your God in vain. (Exodus 20:7; Deut 5:11)
3. Remember to keep holy the LORD'S Day. (Exodus 20:8-11; Deut 5:12-15)
4. Honor your father and your mother. (Exodus 20:12; Deut 5:16)
5. You shall not kill. (Exodus 20:13; Deut 5:17)
6. You shall not commit adultery. (Exodus 20:14; Deut 5:18)
7. You shall not steal. (Exodus 20:15; Deut 5:19)
8. You shall not bear false witness against your neighbor. (Exodus 20:16; Deut 5:20)
9. You shall not covet your neighbor's wife. (Exodus 20:17; Deut 5:21)
10. You shall not covet your neighbor's goods. (Exodus 20:17; Deut 5:21)

---

[91] Suetonius, Lives of the Caesars, II, The Deified Augustus, XCIV, (Loeb Classical Library, Suetonius, Volume I), p. 287. They were reacting to a prophecy that a male child born in that year would become emperor. See also, Finegan, Handbook of Biblical Chronology, n. 509, which cites: Perowne, Life and Times of Herod, n. 172.
[92] The Catechism of the Catholic Church, n. 2051.

Positive and Negative Precepts

The Old Testament lists the ten commandments in both the Book of Exodus and the Book of Deuteronomy.

[Exodus]

{20:1} And the Lord spoke all these words:

{20:2} "I am the Lord your God, who led you away from the land of Egypt, out of the house of servitude.

{20:3} You shall not have strange gods before me.

{20:4} You shall not make for yourself a graven image, nor a likeness of anything that is in heaven above or on earth below, nor of those things which are in the waters under the earth.

{20:5} You shall not adore them, nor shall you worship them. I am the Lord your God: strong, zealous, visiting the iniquity of the fathers on the sons to the third and fourth generation of those who hate me,

{20:6} and showing mercy to thousands of those who love me and keep my precepts.

{20:7} You shall not take the name of the Lord your God in vain. For the Lord will not hold harmless one who takes the name of the Lord his God falsely.

{20:8} Remember that you are to sanctify the day of the Sabbath.

{20:9} For six days, you will work and accomplish all your tasks.

{20:10} But the seventh day is the Sabbath of the Lord your God. You shall not do any work in it: you and your son and your daughter, your male servant and your female servant, your beast and the newcomer who is within your gates.

{20:11} For in six days the Lord made heaven and earth, and the sea, and all the things that are in them, and so he rested on the seventh day. For this reason, the Lord has blessed the day of the Sabbath and sanctified it.

{20:12} Honor your father and your mother, so that you may have a long life upon the land, which the Lord your God will give to you.

{20:13} You shall not murder.

{20:14} You shall not commit adultery.

{20:15} You shall not steal.

{20:16} You shall not speak false testimony against your neighbor.

{20:17} You shall not covet the house of your neighbor; neither shall you desire his wife, nor male servant, nor female servant, nor ox, nor donkey, nor anything that is his."

[Deuteronomy]

{5:6} 'I am the Lord your God, who led you away from the land of Egypt, from the house of servitude.

{5:7} You shall not have strange gods in my sight.

{5:8} You shall not make for yourself a graven image, nor the likeness of anything, which is in heaven above, or on earth below, or which abides in the waters under the earth.

{5:9} You shall not adore and you shall not worship these things. For I am the Lord your God, a jealous God, repaying the iniquity of the fathers upon the sons to the third and fourth generation to those who hate me,

{5:10} and acting with mercy in thousands of ways to those who love me and keep my precepts.

{5:11} You shall not use the name of the Lord your God in vain. For he will not go unpunished who takes up his name over an unimportant matter.
{5:12} Observe the day of the Sabbath, so that you may sanctify it, just as the Lord your God has instructed you.
{5:13} For six days, you shall labor and do all your work.
{5:14} The seventh is the day of the Sabbath, that is, the rest of the Lord your God. You shall not do any work in it, nor shall your son, nor daughter, nor man servant, nor woman servant, nor ox, nor donkey, nor any of your cattle, nor the sojourner who is within your gates, so that your men and woman servants may rest, just as you do.
{5:15} Remember that you also were servants in Egypt, and the Lord your God led you away from that place with a strong hand and an outstretched arm. Because of this, he has instructed you so that you would observe the Sabbath day.
{5:16} Honor your father and mother, just as the Lord your God has instructed you, so that you may live a long time, and so that it may be well with you in the land, which the Lord your God will give to you.
{5:17} You shall not murder.
{5:18} And you shall not commit adultery.
{5:19} And you shall not commit theft.
{5:20} Neither shall you speak false testimony against your neighbor.
{5:21} You shall not covet your neighbor's wife, nor his house, nor his field, nor his man servant, nor his woman servant, nor his ox, nor his donkey, nor anything out of all that is his.'

The very first assertion, stated just prior to the giving of these ten fundamental precepts, is the even more fundamental statement of truth, that truth which is the basis for all the commandments and the entire moral law: "I am the LORD your God." All the commandments, positive and negative, are based on the existence and Nature of God, who is Goodness and Truth. The ten commandments are an expression of the Nature of God. God exists, and He is Good and Just. Therefore, these commandments, which flow from his Nature, are good and just.

Every sin that is a direct and voluntary violation of one of the ten commandments is an intrinsically evil act. Each of the ten commandments, whether a positive precept or a negative precept, whether forbidding an interior sin or an exterior sin, whether forbidding a sin of commission or a sin of omission, each of the ten commandments prohibits one or another intrinsically evil act. The moral object of each of these sins is a deprivation of some good related to love of God and neighbor. And so each of these sins against the ten commandments is intrinsically evil.

However, we can also derive all other sins from these ten commandments, and not every sin is intrinsically evil. Therefore, sins that are merely derived from the ten commandments, not directly forbidden by these ten, may or may not be intrinsically evil. For example, from the commandment not to bear false witness against your neighbor (a gravely immoral intrinsically evil act), we derive the prohibition against all lying (also intrinsically evil, but not always grave), and also the misuse of mental reservation (which is not intrinsically evil, and may or may not be grave).

.108.
1. The Lord is God; therefore, you shall worship Him.

The first commandment is the supreme positive precept, from which are derived all other positive and negative precepts. The truth that the Lord is the one and only God implies that we must worship and serve Him alone. From this positive precept, to worship God, follows several related negative precepts: do not have false gods, do not make graven images representing false gods, do not adore or worship false gods and their images. The worship of false gods is presented in its parts: choosing to accept a false god in general, performing particular acts related to that acceptance, whether it is making a graven image or any other worship-related act, and these two types of errors constitute false adoration and false worship, which is contrary to the Truth that the Lord alone is God. This commandment also forbids apostasy, heresy, and schism, each of which constitutes a rejection of true religion, by which God is known and worshipped.

Then this commandment closes with the same assertion of truth, that the Lord is God, and with a further truth, that the one God is strong, zealous (i.e. active, not passive), just, and merciful. His commandments are like His Nature, strong, active, just, and merciful. The Lord is God, and He is Good, and His precepts flow from His Nature. Therefore, we must love Him and His precepts. For whoever loves and keeps the precepts of the eternal moral law, loves and keeps the Lord God.

[John]
{14:21} Whoever holds to my commandments and keeps them: it is he who loves me. And whoever loves me shall be loved by my Father. And I will love him, and I will manifest myself to him."

All the other positive and negative precepts flow from this first positive precept, to worship the Lord God; and this supreme positive precept itself flows from the one supreme Truth, the Lord God. Keeping the commandments, both the positive precepts and the negative precepts, is an essential part of the true worship of God. Jesus teaches us that to keep the commandments of the eternal moral law is to love God. Whoever loves the eternal moral law, loves God. Whoever obeys the eternal moral law, obeys God.

The positive precept to worship God includes every type of true worship, such as prayer to God, fasting and self-denial for God, and works of mercy toward our neighbor done out of love for God. Every sincere act of prayer, self-denial, or mercy, done with interior cooperation with grace, is a way of worshiping of God, and of fulfilling this first and greatest commandment.

2. The Lord is God; therefore, you shall worship Him; therefore, you shall not take His name in vain.

The second commandment is a negative precept, you shall not take the name of the Lord your God in vain. This precept follows from the first precept. You shall worship the Lord God; therefore, you shall not take his name in vain. This commandment prohibits sins such as: blasphemy, swearing falsely by the name of God, and breaking vows to God (such as the vows of poverty, chastity, and obedience, or the marital vows). By extension, this commandment also prohibits all sacrilege and all irreverence toward whatever is holy: Sacred Tradition, Sacred Scripture, the Magisterium, the Virgin Mary, the Saints and holy Angels, the sanctuaries of churches, etc. The second commandment not only prohibits the various ways of taking the Lord's name in vain, but also the related acts of any type of irreverence toward whatever is holy. And since human nature is made in the image of God, any malice toward our fellow human beings is, by extension, prohibited by this commandment.

Every negative precept follows from a positive precept, because all positive and negative precepts are derived from the supreme positive precept, to worship the Lord God. Living a moral life is a type of worship of God. Living an immoral life is a type of offense against the worship of God. God exists and He is Good; therefore, we must worship Him, and become like Him, by keeping all His precepts. For all the precepts of the moral law flow from the very Nature of God Himself.

3. The Lord is God; therefore, you shall worship Him; therefore, you shall keep holy the Sabbath.

The third commandment is a positive precept, to keep holy the Sabbath. Like all precepts, this precept flows from the supreme precept, to worship the Lord, for He alone is God. The Sabbath is a day dedicated to the Lord because He is God. In addition, a number of related negative precepts can be derived from the positive precept to keep holy the Sabbath, such as the precept not to commit a sacrilege against the Sabbath, not to treat every day as the same, and not to exalt any non-Sabbath day as if it were a Sabbath day (but the holy days of the liturgical calendar are a type of Sabbath). Also, a number of related positive precepts are derived from the third commandment, such as to perform certain works that are fitting to the Sabbath day: to rest, to be quiet and peaceful and cheerful, to enjoy the company of family and friends, to enjoy food and drink, to be kind and merciful to others, etc.

[Nehemiah]
{8:9} Then Nehemiah (the same is the cupbearer) and Ezra, the priest and scribe, and the Levites, who were interpreting for all the people, said: "This day has been sanctified to the Lord our God. Do not mourn, and do not weep." For all of the people were weeping, as they were listening to the words of the law.
{8:10} And he said to them: "Go, eat fat foods and drink sweet drinks, and send portions to those who have not prepared for themselves. For it is the holy day of the Lord. And do not be sad. For the joy of the Lord is also our strength."
{8:11} Then the Levites caused the people to be silent, saying: "Be quiet. For the day is holy. And do not be sorrowful."

4. The Lord is God; therefore, you shall worship Him; therefore, you shall honor your father and your mother.

The positive precept to worship God implies the fourth commandment, also a positive precept, to honor your father and mother. The human race was created by God, beginning with Adam, who is the father of the world, and Eve, who is the mother of all the living. When we honor our father and mother, we also honor all our ancestors, even back to Adam and Eve, who were each directly created by God. And so, in this way, we honor the creation of humanity by God, and our own procreation by our parents and by God.

[Wisdom]
{10:1} This is he, who was formed first by God, the father of the world, who was alone when created; she preserved him,
{10:2} and led him out of his offense, and gave him the power to maintain all things.

[Genesis]
{3:20} And Adam called the name of his wife, 'Eve,' because she was the mother of all the living.

When we honor our father and mother, we also honor God, who created the human race, and who ordained that all human beings should be procreated by a father and a mother. For the relationship between parent and child is a reflection of the relationship between God and each human person. All created persons are from God, who is the Father of all, and so we are each and all children of God. Therefore, we must honor our parents.

A number of related positive precepts are derived from this positive precept, such as to honor and respect all our ancestors and family members, to assist our parents and family members in need, and to respect all those whose authority is a reflection of the authority of God.

.109.
5. The Lord is God; therefore, you shall worship Him; therefore, you shall not murder.

The Hebrew text of this verse for the fifth commandment, in both Exodus and Deuteronomy, literally says "You shall not murder," not "You shall not kill." And in the Gospel text, in the Latin Vulgate, in one place Jesus says "Non homicidium facies," which translates as "You shall not murder," and in another place, He says "Non occides," which translates as "You shall not kill."

[Matthew]
{19:18} Dicit illi: Quæ? Iesus autem dixit: Non homicidium facies: Non adulterabis: Non facies furtum: Non falsum testimonium dices:
{19:18} He said to him, "Which?" And Jesus said: "You shall not murder. You shall not commit adultery. You shall not steal. You shall not give false testimony."

[Luke]
{18:20} Mandata nosti: Non occides: Non mœchaberis: Non furtum facies: Non falsum testimonium dices: Honora patrem tuum, et matrem.
{18:20} You know the commandments: You shall not kill. You shall not commit adultery. You shall not steal. You shall not give false testimony. Honor your father and mother."

Now the text of the Old Testament passages for this commandment have often been translated as "You shall not kill," despite the well-known meaning of the Hebrew text "You shall not murder." So there are two possible translations, "You shall not murder," and "You shall not kill." Certainly, the commandment itself is "You shall not murder." For both Exodus and Deuteronomy, subsequent to commanding "You shall not murder," also command the use of the death penalty for certain crimes. And the Catholic Faith has always taught that killing in self-defense, in just war, and the use of the death penalty are not intrinsically evil, and are sometimes moral depending on intention and circumstances. Therefore, the commandment is not "You shall not kill," but "You shall not murder."

However, in a holy and peaceful world, or even in a sinful world if everyone would at least avoid mortal sin, there would be no need for killing in self-defense, no need for war, and no need for the death penalty. The 'Our Father' prayer teaches us to seek such holiness and peace, even in this sinful life:

[Matthew]
{6:9} Therefore, you shall pray in this way: Our Father, who is in heaven: May your name be kept holy.
{6:10} May your kingdom come. May your will be done, as in heaven, so also on earth.
{6:11} Give us this day our life-sustaining bread.
{6:12} And forgive us our debts, as we also forgive our debtors.
{6:13} And lead us not into temptation. But free us from evil. Amen.

If God's name is kept holy, and if His kingdom is established even among sinners, and if His will is done even imperfectly by sinners, then we would be free from evil, at least to such an extent that we would no longer need to kill. So while the commandment is "You shall not murder," the ideal is "You shall not kill." The human race is, or at least should be, in the process of moving from the mere requirement not to murder, to the ideal not to kill at all. Therefore, both translations are correct, each in its own way.

The difference between murder and killing is that murder is the direct and voluntary killing of an innocent human person. Therefore, the negative precept prohibiting murder (not to kill the innocent) also prohibits related sins against the innocent, such as any kind of violence against the innocent, false or arbitrary imprisonment (again, of the innocent), and any similar sins against the innocent. This commandment not only implies that the innocent should not be treated as if they were guilty, but also that the guilty should not be treated as if they were innocent.

[Daniel]
{13:53} judging unjust judgments, oppressing the innocent, and setting free the guilty....

6. The Lord is God; therefore, you shall worship Him; therefore, you shall not commit adultery.

The positive precept to worship God implies the sixth commandment, that we should not commit adultery. For both natural marriage and the holy Sacrament of Marriage are ordained by God. The relationship between husband and wife is a reflection of the relationship between God and Creation, and a reflection of the relationship between Christ and His Church. A serious offense against marriage is a serious offense against God. For in the beginning, God created man and woman, and He ordained that these two should be joined in marriage and become as one flesh (Genesis 1:27; 2:24).

From the negative precept not to commit adultery are derived other negative precepts, those that forbid every kind of sexual sin, including any kind of sexual act that is non-unitive, or non-procreative, or non-marital. Also derived from the negative precept against adultery is any kind of adultery of the heart, and any kind of lust.

7. The Lord is God; therefore, you shall worship Him; therefore, you shall not commit theft.

Like all commandments, the seventh commandment flows from the first precept, to love and worship God. For God is the first owner of all things. And God did not create and then abandon His creation. God created, and He still possesses, His creation. All created things were brought into existence, and still continue in existence, by the power of God.

[Romans]
{11:36} For from him, and through him, and in him are all things. To him is glory, for all eternity. Amen.

[Colossians]
{1:16} For in him was created everything in heaven and on earth, visible and invisible, whether thrones, or dominations, or principalities, or powers. All things were created through him and in him.
{1:17} And he is before all, and in him all things continue.

The ownership of any created thing, of any type of property, by any created person, is a reflection of the greater and more thorough ownership of all Creation by God. For God not only created all things and owns all things, He causes all things to continue to exist. When we respect the ownership rights of other persons, we are respecting the First Owner of all things. Therefore, any act of theft is also an offense against the worship of God. Every sin is in some way, to some extent, a sin against the first and greatest commandment, to worship God.

The sins related to the negative precept of theft include the positive precept to respect all created things, and to respect ownership rights, and the negative precept to refrain from doing harm to the property of other persons.

8. The Lord is God; therefore, you shall worship Him; therefore, you shall not speak false testimony against your neighbor.

The commandment to worship God also implies the eight commandment, not to bear false witness. The God we worship is Truth. God is not merely truthful; He is Truth. The very Nature of God is Truth, Love, Justice, Mercy, etc. Therefore, all lies offend God. The particular lie of bearing false witness against your neighbor is the most serious type of lying. But all lying is contrary to the Nature of God, who is Truth.

By extension this commandment also prohibits the related sins of any type of lying, sins of the misuse of mental reservation, sins of deceitfulness, hypocrisy, and any other type of falseness before God or neighbor, or even within ourselves. This commandment also prohibits the sin of ignoring important truths for selfish reasons. Also prohibited by this commandment is the sin of omission of failing to seek truth in one's life, especially truths pertaining to faith, morals, and salvation. Truth must be valued by us in this life because God is Truth.

.110.
9. The Lord is God; therefore, you shall worship Him; therefore, you shall not covet your neighbor's wife.
10. The Lord is God; therefore, you shall worship Him; therefore, you shall not covet your neighbor's goods.

These two commandments are interrelated, and so they are stated together in Scripture as one sentence and one verse.

[Exodus]
{20:17} You shall not covet the house of your neighbor; neither shall you desire his wife, nor male servant, nor female servant, nor ox, nor donkey, nor anything that is his."

[Deuteronomy]
{5:21} You shall not covet your neighbor's wife, nor his house, nor his field, nor his man servant, nor his woman servant, nor his ox, nor his donkey, nor anything out of all that is his.'

The negative precept of the ninth commandment prohibits adultery of the heart. It is not sufficient for salvation for us to merely refrain from the exterior sins, such as adultery. We must also refrain from the interior sins, such as adultery of the heart. And by extension, this negative precept also prohibits every type of lust (the interior consent, not merely to thoughts about sinful sexual acts, but to the acts themselves). The expression of this commandment in both Exodus and Deuteronomy also extends the commandment to the coveting of other persons.

The coveting of your neighbor's house can be understood in two ways: first, as the coveting of the members of the household (under the ninth commandment); second, as the coveting of the house itself and all the possessions that are related to it (under the tenth commandment). The coveting of persons that is prohibited is any type of lust, not only lust for a neighbor's wife, but also lust directed at any persons at all. For all lust is contrary to true love of God, neighbor, and self.

Your neighbor's servant is coveted, sinfully, either by the desire for illicit sexual acts, or by the inordinate desire to have these servants as one's own servants (or employees). Even if you hire your neighbor's employee away from him by offering better wages (a moral exterior act), the interior act of desiring what belongs to your neighbor without regard for the harm that might be done by taking away your neighbor's employee is contrary to true love of neighbor, and so is a sin against this negative precept.

This negative precept against lust (the ninth commandment) teaches us that interior sins can be just as immoral as exterior sins, such as the interior sins of being willing to commit an act of theft, even if the exterior act of theft is never done, of being willing to commit an act of lying, even if the lie is never told, of being willing to commit an act of murder, even if the murder is never done, etc.

The ninth commandment not only prohibits the sexual coveting of lust, but also any other type of coveting related to persons. If you covet your neighbor's wife by treating her as your close friend, without lust, this act still harms the marriage relationship of your neighbor with his wife, and so it is inordinate and sinful. Or if you covet your neighbor's children by treating them as if they were your children, this harms the parent-child relationship of your neighbor. And the same is true for the other persons of your neighbor's household. There is a proper order to the relationships between human persons, in the family, in the Church, and in society. Any sin against this proper order is an offense against the true worship of God, who created and ordered humanity according to His own good will.

In these ninth and tenth commandments, the wife and servants and other persons of the household are not being treated as possessions. For if they were viewed as possessions, then there would be no need to divide this verse into two commandments. But instead, there are separate commandments for coveting persons, by the sin of lust or in other ways, and for coveting possessions.

.111. The Two Great Commandments

Jesus refers to the ten commandments in the Gospels. The New Testament does not nullify or change the eternal moral law at all. The ten commandments and the entire moral law are still in force.

[Matthew]
{19:16} And behold, someone approached and said to him, "Good Teacher, what good should I do, so that I may have eternal life?"
{19:17} And he said to him: "Why do you question me about what is good? One is good: God. But if you wish to enter into life, observe the commandments."
{19:18} He said to him, "Which?" And Jesus said: "You shall not murder. You shall not commit adultery. You shall not steal. You shall not give false testimony.
{19:19} Honor your father and your mother. And, you shall love your neighbor as yourself."

[Luke]
{18:18} And a certain leader questioned him, saying: "Good teacher, what should I do to possess eternal life?"

{18:19} Then Jesus said to him: "Why do you call me good? No one is good except God alone.
{18:20} You know the commandments: You shall not kill. You shall not commit adultery. You shall not steal. You shall not give false testimony. Honor your father and mother."

Notice that Jesus does not need to restate all ten commandments. The ten commandments are interrelated, and are an expression and summary of the eternal moral law. God could have given us fewer than ten commandments, or more than ten, because these ten are not the whole moral law, but are a way of pointing to the whole moral law. All the ten commandments flow from the truth that the Lord is God, and from the supreme commandment to worship God. Even this one greatest commandment by itself is sufficient to imply all other positive and negative precepts. But when Jesus is asked which commandment is greatest, He states two commandments, rather than one.

[Matthew]
{22:36} "Teacher, which is the great commandment in the law?"
{22:37} Jesus said to him: " 'You shall love the Lord your God from all your heart, and with all your soul and with all your mind.'
{22:38} This is the greatest and first commandment.
{22:39} But the second is similar to it: 'You shall love your neighbor as yourself.'
{22:40} On these two commandments the entire law depends, and also the prophets."

To love God with your entire self is to worship God. The positive precept to love God is the first and greatest commandment, from which all other positive and negative precepts flow. To love any person or thing other than God, in this same way and to this same extent, is the sin of idolatry. True worship must be offered to God alone. The theological term used for the worship that is due solely to God is 'latria' (from the Greek, latreia). By comparison, the proper veneration due to the Virgin Mary, and to the Saints and holy Angels, and to other holy persons is termed 'dulia' (from the Greek, doulia). But it would be the sin of idolatry to adore the Virgin Mary, or the Saints or Angels, or any other persons or things.

Jesus could have answered with this one commandment, to love God above all else. For all the other precepts of the moral law are necessarily implied by this one precept. But He stated a second commandment, to love your neighbor as yourself. Yet He did not say 'You shall love your neighbor from all your heart, and with all your soul and with all your mind.' For love of neighbor is fundamentally different from love of God. We love God in worship; we love our neighbor in respect, not worship. Anyone who distorts love of neighbor into a total love with the entire soul, heart, mind, and body is turning love of neighbor into the false love of idolatry. We must love God above all created persons, even ourselves, and above all created things. True love of neighbor is ordered within, but below, the love of God.

Catechism of the Catholic Church: "Love toward oneself remains a fundamental principle of morality."[93]

True love of neighbor includes an ordered love of self, for the term 'neighbor' refers to all human persons, including one's self. And Jesus did not merely say to love your neighbor, but to love your neighbor as yourself, implying that we must also love ourselves. Thus the greatest commandments can also be stated as three: a worshipful love of God, a selfless love of neighbor, and an ordered love of self. All other positive and negative precepts follow from this single threefold positive precept (which is one yet three, like the Trinity), to love God, neighbor, self.

[1 John]
{4:21} And this is the commandment that we have from God, that he who loves God must also love his brother.

[Galatians]
{5:14} For the entire law is fulfilled by one word: "You shall love your neighbor as yourself."

This true love of God, neighbor, and self compels us to worship God, to assist our neighbor in knowing and loving God, and to seek our own holiness and our own salvation in God. For Sacred Tradition and Sacred Scripture have always taught each of the faithful to consider his or her own holiness and salvation as one of the most important goods in life. But if we know that we should seek our own salvation, then we also know that we should assist our neighbors in seeking their own salvation, all for the greater glory of God.

[Matthew]
{7:12} Therefore, all things whatsoever that you wish that men would do to you, do so also to them. For this is the law and the prophets.

[Luke]
{6:31} And exactly as you would want people to treat you, treat them also the same.

Jesus summed up all the commandments by the single commandment to love your neighbor. For true love of neighbor implies true love of God. An honest person, who never lies, is a person who loves God and neighbor. A faithful person, who truly loves their spouse, is a person who loves God and neighbor. Even a person who truly loves himself, not in a selfish and disordered way, but in a way that seeks holiness and salvation, is a person who loves God and neighbor. All the commandments are one commandment. The entire moral law is one law. Every part of the moral law implies the whole moral law.

[1 John]
{4:20} If anyone says that he loves God, but hates his brother, then he is a liar. For he who does not love his brother, whom he does see, in what way can he love God, whom he does not see?

---

[93] Catechism of the Catholic Church, n. 2264.

{4:21} And this is the commandment that we have from God, that he who loves God must also love his brother.

[Romans]
{13:8} ... For whoever loves his neighbor has fulfilled the law.

The teaching of Jesus to love our neighbor is not a new commandment. This same teaching is implied by the commandment to worship God, and is implied by each and all of the ten commandments. The commandment to love your neighbor is even stated in the Old Testament, in a number of different places, with a number of different wordings, including:

[Tobit]
{4:16} Whatever you would hate to have done to you by another, see that you never do so to another.

[Proverbs]
{14:21} Whoever despises his neighbor, sins.

[Sirach]
{27:18} Love your neighbor, and be united with him faithfully.

But in another sense, this commandment to love one another is renewed in Christ. For Christ calls us to an even greater love of neighbor than ever before, such that we would strive to love one another even as Christ has loved us. The newness of this commandment is found in the revelation of Jesus Christ. But since Christ is also revealed (yet hidden) in the Old Testament, this same commandment is not new in an absolute sense. And since Christ is revealed in all Creation (for all things were created through Him and for Him), this same commandment is not entirely new, but was always implicit in natural law, and was always within the eternal moral law, which is the Justice of Christ, the Word of God.

[John]
{13:34} I give you a new commandment: Love one another. Just as I have loved you, so also must you love one another.

This new commandment does not, in any way nor to any extent, nullify or change the eternal moral law as summed up in the ten commandments, and as implied by the supreme commandment to worship God. All the commandments of the moral law, as expressed in natural law and in the Old Testament, are still in force. For the eternal moral law is unchanging.

[John]
{14:15} If you love me, keep my commandments.
...
{14:21} Whoever holds to my commandments and keeps them: it is he who loves me. And whoever loves me shall be loved by my Father. And I will love him, and I will manifest myself to him."

Positive and Negative Precepts

If anyone claims that any positive or negative precept of the eternal moral law has been added to, subtracted from, or changed; or that Christians have a type of freedom which includes a loosening of the eternal moral law; or that the temporal authority of the Church and its decisions are above, or can make exceptions to, the eternal moral law; or that God can contradict Himself by acting contrary to the eternal moral law; then it is proof that such a one has gone astray from the true teaching of Christ and of His Church.

[Matthew]
{5:19} Therefore, whoever will have loosened one of the least of these commandments, and have taught men so, shall be called the least in the kingdom of heaven. But whoever will have done and taught these, such a one shall be called great in the kingdom of heaven.

.112. Venial Offenses Against Grave Obligations

Concerning positive precepts, a grave failure to fulfill a grave requirement of the moral law is an objective mortal sin. But a substantially-limited failure to fulfill a grave requirement of the moral law is only a venial sin. So a sin of omission is only a mortal sin if the chosen omission was a grave failure of a grave obligation.

Concerning negative precepts, a grave violation of a grave prohibition of the moral law is an objective mortal sin. But a substantially-limited violation of a grave prohibition of the moral law is only a venial sin. So a sin of commission is only a mortal sin if the chosen act was a grave violation of a grave prohibition.

The reason for this limitation is that sin is only mortal if the choice of the soul is sufficient (given the conditions of actual mortal sin) to turn the soul away from God, to deprive the soul of sanctifying grace, to be entirely incompatible with love of God, neighbor, self, and to deserve eternal Hellfire.

Saint Thomas Aquinas: "Therefore when the soul is so disordered by sin as to turn away from its last end, viz. God, to Whom it is united by charity, there is mortal sin; but when it is disordered without turning away from God, there is venial sin."[94]

Pope John Paul II: "And when through sin, the soul commits a disorder that reaches the point of turning away from its ultimate end, God, to which it is bound by charity, then the sin is mortal; on the other hand, whenever the disorder does not reach the point of a turning away from God, the sin is venial. For this reason venial sin does not deprive the sinner of sanctifying grace, friendship with God, charity and therefore eternal happiness, whereas just such a deprivation is precisely the consequence of mortal sin."[95]

Whenever any sin is substantially-limited, it is not a mortal sin since the choice of that sin is not sufficient to turn the soul away from friendship with God, nor to break the bond of charity, nor to lose sanctifying grace and eternal happiness.

---

[94] St. Thomas Aquinas, Summa Theologica, I-II, Q. 72, A. 5.
[95] Pope John Paul II, Reconciliation and Penance, n. 17; he cites St. Thomas Aquinas, Summa Theologica, I-II, Q. 72, A. 5.

Such a limitation might occur from a lack of full consent, or from a lack of full knowledge of the grave immorality of an act; this type of limitation causes an objective mortal sin to be either an actual venial sin, or not a culpable sin at all. Or such a limitation might occur in the objective matter of the sin, as when the obligation is grave, but the offense against that obligation is substantially limited; this type of limitation causes a sin against a grave obligation under a positive or negative precept to be only a venial sin.

Examples: (1) A husband has a grave obligation to be faithful to his wife. If he violates that grave obligation to a grave extent, such as by an act of adultery, or by abandoning his wife, then he commits a grave sin. But if he violates that grave obligation in a substantially-limited way, such as by flirting with another woman, or by not giving his wife enough time and attention, then he commits a venial sin, not a mortal sin. And the same is true for all the requirements of the moral law, both the acts are required, and the acts are prohibited.

(2) We each have a grave obligation under the moral law to honor our father and mother. An extensive failure to honor one's parents is a grave sin. So if an adult has living parents who are in grave need, but he abandons them, not giving them help that he is able to give, then he commits a mortal sin because his omission is a grave failure of a grave obligation. But if he merely does not call or visit his parents as often as he should, then his offense is only a venial sin because his omission is a substantially-limited failure of a grave obligation.

(3) A couple are dating, but are unmarried. They have a grave obligation to be chaste in their acts prior to marriage. If they fail in that grave obligation to a grave extent, such as by having premarital sexual relations, it is a mortal sin. But if they fail in their grave obligation to chastity to a substantially-limited extent, such as by being overly passionate in kissing and hugging (but without lust), it is only a venial sin.

When the obligation is grave, but the failure is not grave, then the sin is only venial. The limited nature of any failure to fulfill a positive precept, or to refrain from violating a negative precept, prevents the sin from being so disordered as to turn the soul that knowingly chooses such an act entirely away from God. Even if the obligation or prohibition is a grave matter, if the sin against that obligation or prohibition is substantially-limited, then the moral weight of the sin itself is venial, not mortal. The charity of God inherent to sanctifying grace is entirely incompatible with mortal sin. But when a failure or violation (a sin of omission or commission) is substantially-limited, the chosen act is not incompatible with remaining in a state of sanctifying grace. Despite the grave moral weight of the obligation or prohibition, only when the sin itself is also grave (under at least one of the three fonts of morality) does the act become an objective mortal sin.

.113. Missing Mass

Catechism of the Catholic Church: "The Sunday Eucharist is the foundation and confirmation of all Christian practice. For this reason the faithful are obliged to participate in the Eucharist on days of obligation, unless excused for a serious reason (for example, illness, the care of infants) or dispensed by their own pastor. Those who deliberately fail in this obligation commit a grave sin."[96]

But a substantially-limited deliberate failure in this or any grave obligation is not a mortal sin. Therefore, only those persons who fail to a grave extent to fulfill this grave obligation commit a mortal sin by missing Mass. Attending Mass on Sundays and holy days is only one part of the grave obligation to worship God and to keep holy the Sabbath. The failure to attend Mass, on one particular Sunday or holy day of obligation, is a substantially-limited violation of the positive precepts to worship God and to keep holy the Sabbath. For attending Mass is only one of many ways that we worship God and keep holy the Sabbath.

Missing Mass may be a mortal sin, or a venial sin, or not a sin at all. Missing Mass for a just reason is not a sin at all. The Catechism gives illness and the care of infants as examples of reasons that allow a person to miss Mass without sin. These examples are not grave reasons, but only just reasons. Examples of grave reasons for missing Mass include a severe illness, or the danger of death, or any situation in which grave harm would occur if one attends. But only a just reason (weighty or substantial, but not grave) is needed to miss Mass without sin.[97] Since only a just reason, not a grave reason, is needed to exempt one from the obligation, the matter of missing Mass on one occasion cannot be a grave matter. For only a grave reason excuses one from a grave obligation.

Also, the Catechism notes that a pastor (the priest who is the head of the parish) may excuse someone from the obligation to attend Mass on a particular occasion; if so, then the person who misses Mass would not be guilty of sin at all. And no limits or guidance is given in Canon Law (Canon 1245) or in the Catechism as to the conditions for such a dispensation granted by a pastor, except that it is obviously limited to particular occasions and is not a continuing dispensation. If the duty to attend Mass were such that missing Mass even once were a grave failure of a grave obligation, then a dispensation could not be granted by a parish priest at his own discretion. A parish priest cannot dispense someone from a grave obligation merely by his own judgment.

Therefore, while the obligation to worship God, to keep holy the Sabbath, and to attend Mass regularly is a grave obligation, missing Mass on occasion with a just reason is not a sin, and missing Mass on occasion for little or no reason is only a venial sin. The believing and practicing Catholic who regularly attends Mass (on Sundays and holy days), and who worships God and keeps the Sabbath holy in other ways as well, fulfills his grave obligation. If the same Catholic then misses Mass on occasion for little or no reason, his failure is venial; it is not a grave failure that would result in the loss of sanctifying grace, separation from the charity of God, and the punishment of eternal Hellfire.

---

[96] Catechism of the Catholic Church, n. 2181.
[97] Note that the Decree of the Apostolic Penitentiary of the Holy See (29 June 2002) establishing a plenary indulgence for Divine Mercy Sunday considers that the faithful might miss Mass on that Sunday "for a just cause," and yet still receive the plenary indulgence. This would not be possible if missing Mass without sin required a grave cause, nor if missing Mass for merely a just cause were a grave sin.

Many Catholics, throughout the history of the Church, have had difficulty in attending Mass. Transportation and communication were limited. In many areas, there were a limited number of Catholic parishes. It was not possible for every Catholic to attend Mass every Sunday and every holy day. And when traveling, especially in past times, it was even more difficult to attend Mass. So the practice of the faithful throughout most of history was not to treat attendance at Mass as an absolute necessity, under pain of mortal sin, for each Sunday and holy day. The grave obligation to worship God and to keep holy the Sabbath has been the continual practice of the Church from the time of Christ, and of the Jews from Old Testament times. But attending Mass on Sundays and holy days is only one of many ways to fulfill that positive precept.

Canon law has a provision (Canon 920) requiring each Catholic to receive Communion at least once a year. But if every Catholic is required under pain of mortal sin to attend Mass every Sunday and every holy day, why would the Church require reception of Communion only once a year? It is a reflection of the understanding that worshipping God and keeping holy the Sabbath are not always fulfilled by means of attendance at Mass. It is a reflection of the historical practice of the faithful to attend Mass less often than every Sunday and holy day. And still today, in many areas of the world, some of the faithful have great difficulty attending Mass every Sunday and holy day. And so the Canon remains in force which requires reception of Communion at least once a year.

However, if a Catholic abandons worshiping God or abandons keeping holy the Sabbath, he certainly commits an objective mortal sin. And if a Catholic misses Mass frequently for little or no reason, or if he abandons going to Mass altogether, he certainly commits an objective mortal sin. These are grave failures to fulfill grave obligations, and so the failure is a mortal sin, not merely a venial sin. Abandoning the worship of God is sufficiently grave to deprive the soul of sanctifying grace and to deserve eternal Hellfire. Rejection of the precept to keep holy the Sabbath is sufficiently grave to deprive the soul of sanctifying grace and to deserve eternal Hellfire. Abandoning attendance at Mass or missing Mass frequently without reason is sufficiently grave to deprive the soul of sanctifying grace and to deserve eternal Hellfire. But the conditions distinguishing actual mortal sin from objective mortal sin also apply.

Examples: (1) A Catholic usually attends Mass on Sundays and Holy Days of obligation. If he misses Mass on occasion for a just reason, he does not sin at all. Just reasons for missing Mass include illness, caring for someone else who is ill, caring for young children, requirements of work, the difficulty of getting to Mass while traveling, or reasons of similar weight.

(2) The same Catholic misses Mass on one occasion for little or no reason. He oversleeps, or he does not feel motivated to attend Mass, or he has a social event he wishes to attend, or he wishes to watch a sports event. His reason for missing Mass is not a just reason; these and other similar reasons lack sufficient moral weight. His failure to attend Mass on such an occasion is a venial sin.

(3) A Catholic decides that he is no longer going to practice the Catholic Faith by attending Mass, or that he is only going to attend Mass on special occasions, such as Christmas, Easter, and the weddings and funerals of family members. Such a substantial failure to fulfill the grave obligation to attend Mass is a mortal sin.

Chapter 10
The End Does Not Justify The Means

.114.
[Romans]
{3:8} And should we not do evil, so that good may result? For so we have been slandered, and so some have claimed we said; their condemnation is just.

Sacred Scripture teaches that we may not do evil, even if much good will result. Saint Paul the Apostle condemned the idea that we should do evil so that good would result. Those who claim that we are morally permitted to do evil so that good may result are justly condemned for teaching a falsehood about the eternal moral law. And those who do evil so that good may result are justly condemned for this violation of the eternal moral law.

Sacred Congregation for the Doctrine of the Faith: "It is never permitted to do something which is intrinsically illicit, not even in view of a good result: the end does not justify the means."[98]

The term 'intrinsically illicit' is another way of saying intrinsically evil; licit and illicit in this context refers to what is permitted or forbidden under the moral law. Intrinsically evil acts are always immoral, regardless of your intention and regardless of the circumstances. An intrinsically evil act is immoral, even if the good consequences of committing the act are very good, and even if the bad consequences of not committing the act are very bad. Regardless of the degree of good or bad in the consequences (in the third font), intrinsically evil acts are always immoral (in the second font). In order to be good, all three fonts of an act must be good; any one bad font makes the act immoral.

In the case of an intrinsically evil act done for the purpose of obtaining good consequences, the intended end is good, but the intention to use an intrinsically evil means to achieve that end is an immoral intention. A good intended end does not justify an immoral intended means. Any immorality in the intention, whether in the end or in the means, makes the first font bad. The intention to use an intrinsically evil act as a means is a sinful intention.

.115. When a person commits an intrinsically evil act in order to obtain the good consequences of that act, at times the bad consequences will outweigh the good, causing the third font also to be bad. For those persons who mistakenly think that the end justifies the means often do not weigh all the good and bad consequences. But even if the good consequences greatly outweigh the bad consequences, making the third font undoubtedly good, the chosen act remains intrinsically evil and always immoral. For good consequences and good intentions have no effect on the moral object of the chosen act. And it is never the case that an intrinsically evil act has no bad consequences at all. The doing of evil always has a bad effect: on the soul of the person who chose the evil act, on the souls of other persons who are deprived of graces they would have received if

---

[98] Sacred Congregation for the Doctrine of the Faith, Dignitas Personae, n. 21.

the person had chosen to do good, and on the Church and the world in general, because evil is chosen instead of good.

Pope Paul VI: "Though it is true that sometimes it is lawful to tolerate a lesser moral evil in order to avoid a greater evil or in order to promote a greater good, it is never lawful, even for the gravest reasons, to do evil that good may come of it (cf. Rom 3:8) -- in other words, to intend directly something which of its very nature contradicts the moral order, and which must therefore be judged unworthy of man, even though the intention is to protect or promote the welfare of an individual, of a family or of society in general."[99]

The toleration of a lesser moral evil to avoid a greater evil, or to promote a greater good, refers to the third font of morality. Some bad consequences (a type of evil) can be tolerated in the third font, if the good consequences outweigh the bad. And to some extent, we must tolerate moral evil in other persons, for we are all sinners; if we do not tolerate some lesser moral evil in others, we could not tolerate anyone (not even ourselves). But when we tolerate lesser moral evil done by others, we are not the ones choosing to do evil. It is always contrary to the eternal moral law to choose to do moral evil, regardless of which font causes the chosen act to be immoral. Not only intrinsically evil acts, which are immoral under the second font, are prohibited by the moral law, but also any act done with immoral intention, and any act having bad consequences that outweigh the good consequences (so that the third font is immoral).

Any act which 'of its very nature contradicts the moral order' is an intrinsically evil act. All intrinsically evil acts are direct and voluntary; they are intentionally chosen acts that are inherently directed at an evil moral object. Therefore Pope Paul VI says "to intend directly." And the essential moral nature of any such chosen act is determined by the moral object. All evil moral objects contradict the moral order, which is based on love of God, neighbor, self. Such acts are unworthy of human persons because we are all made in the image of God, who is the foundation and source of all morality. A good intention, such as to protect or promote the welfare of our neighbor or of the common good, cannot cause an evil moral object to become good. And even very weighty good consequences cannot cause an evil moral object to become good.

Pope John Paul II: "…the end never justifies the means."[100]

Pontifical Council for the Family: "…one cannot do evil for a good end. The end does not justify the means."[101]

Catechism of the Catholic Church: "The end does not justify the means."[102]

---

[99] Pope Paul VI, Humanae Vitae, n. 14.
[100] Message of his Holiness Pope John Paul II for the Celebration of the World Day of Peace, 1 January 2004, n. 8.
[101] Cardinal Alfonso López Trujillo, Pontifical Council for the Family, 3. c.
[102] Catechism of the Catholic Church, n. 1753.

Catechism of the Catholic Church: " 'An evil action cannot be justified by reference to a good intention' (cf. St. Thomas Aquinas, Dec. praec. 6). The end does not justify the means."[103]

Sacred Scripture and the Magisterium of the Church both clearly and definitively teach that the end does not justify the means. It is a sin of heresy against the moral teachings of the Catholic Faith to believe or to teach that the end justifies the means. If any argument in moral theology is explicitly or implicitly based on the idea that the end justifies the means, then that argument is not only false, but is based on heresy.

If the intention (first font) is to use an act with an evil moral object (second font), as a means to obtain a certain good consequences (third font), then the act is immoral. Every intrinsically evil act is always immoral, even when the intended end and the resulting consequences are good. The second font is bad, and so the overall act is necessarily immoral. The use of an intrinsically evil act as an immoral means to a good intended end, or to obtain good consequences, does not change the act itself, which remains immoral.

.116. The reason that a good end cannot justify an immoral means is that immorality is never justified. Immoral ends are not justified. Immoral means are not justified. A good act remains always good. An evil act remains always evil. Nothing can change good into evil, or evil into good. Even God, who is infinite Goodness, cannot change evil into good, or good into evil. Neither can God do evil so that good may result. And God is incapable of justifying even the slightest immoral means for the sake of the greatest good end. For to do so would be to deny Himself.

It is true, considering the first font by itself, that a good intended end does not justify a bad intended means. An intention is immoral whenever a person intends to use an immoral means to a good end. And it is also true, considering the third font by itself, that the good consequences must outweigh the bad consequences for the third font to be good. If the bad consequences outweigh the good consequences, then the good consequences cannot justify the third font by itself, even though the good consequences are a type of end.

Catechism of the Catholic Church: "There are concrete acts that it is always wrong to choose, because their choice entails a disorder of the will, i.e., a moral evil. One may not do evil so that good may result from it."[104]

The term 'concrete acts' is also found in Veritatis Splendor; this term refers to the act itself, i.e. the act knowingly chosen by the human person. The human will chooses an act based on knowledge in the intellect. A concrete act may be an interior decision (a type of act) not to commit another act. A concrete act may be an interior act, or an exterior act. Both morally good acts and morally bad acts are concrete acts.

---

[103] Catechism of the Catholic Church, n. 1759; inner quote is from St. Thomas Aquinas, De Decem Praeceptis [On the Ten Commandments].
[104] Catechism of the Catholic Church, n. 1761.

The concrete act, i.e. the act itself, is in the second font. The act itself is always wrong to knowingly choose whenever the moral object is evil. Every knowingly chosen act is inherently directed toward its moral object. The inherent ordering of the act itself toward its moral object cannot be separated from the act itself. Therefore, a concrete act with an evil moral object is inherently evil. The knowing choice of such an act is always a disorder of the will, that is, a use of the free will to choose moral evil. A good intended end, and any good that might result in the consequences (a type of end) cannot change the moral object, and cannot justify the knowing choice of that inherently evil act as a means to a good end, nor for any reason at all.

The end never justifies the means. The morality of the chosen act is not determined solely by the morality of the intended end, nor solely by the morality of the end result (the consequences). An intrinsically evil act is never justified by good intention, nor by good consequences. A good end does not cause an evil means to become good. It is never moral to do evil, with the intention of obtaining good consequences. It is never moral to do evil, not for any reason, not even so that some great good will result.

.117. Implicit Denial of This Doctrine

The end does not justify the means. This is a very simple and clear teaching, definitively taught by Sacred Scripture and by the Magisterium. It is one of many required beliefs of the Catholic Faith on ethics. Yet the implicit denial of this doctrine is one of the most common mistakes in ethics, not only in secular society, but even among some Catholic Christians. Though it is rare to find a Catholic who will openly claim that the end justifies the means, often this doctrine is implicitly denied by the type of argument that is offered on various moral questions. Many persons will present arguments that in effect are using the end to justify the means, without realizing it.

But in secular society, the idea that the end justifies the means is very commonly found in discussions on morality on a wide range of topics. Again, even in secular society, most persons who use the end to justify the means do not openly state that the end justifies the means. But this false idea is implicit to the argument that they are presenting.

Examples

(1) Is the denial of fundamental human rights justified to protect national security? Is the torture of human persons justified if it will prevent a terrorist attack?

On the topic of terrorism, some persons claim that we are justified in denying known or suspected terrorists fundamental human rights, or that we are justified in using any degree or type of torture against them. The justification is then said to be national security, or the prevention of a severe terrorist attack, or simply the saving of many lives. This argument claims that the means (the denial of fundamental human rights, torture) is justified by the intended end, which is also said to be the most weighty consequential end, of saving lives.

To the contrary, the end of saving lives does not justify any act, used as a means to that end, which is immoral. Even if the means is an act that is not intrinsically evil, but is immoral under the first or third fonts, such an immoral act cannot be justified by reference to a good end. No immorality is ever justified. And if the act itself is intrinsically evil, then nothing can justify the knowing choice of such an act, regardless of the intention or the circumstances, no matter how many lives are saved.

Therefore, if a human person is a known or suspected terrorist, he cannot morally be denied fundamental human rights, such as food, medical care, freedom of worship, and the right to a fair trial before a proportional punishment for his crimes. A known or suspected terrorist cannot be morally held indefinitely without trial, nor under inhumane living conditions. All human persons, regardless of what crimes or sins they may have committed, must be treated as human persons.

(2) Is embryonic stem cell research (ESCR) justified if it will cure many diseases, eliminate much suffering, and save many lives?

Some persons claim that the destruction of human embryos which occurs as a direct result of embryonic stem cell research is justified by the many diseases that will be cured, and by the many lives that will be saved.

To the contrary, even if it were true that ESCR would result in treatments and cures that would eliminate much suffering and save many lives, this good end would not justify the evil means of the direct and voluntary killing of innocent human persons that occurs when human embryos are used, and thereby destroyed, in this type of research. The direct and voluntary killing of an innocent human person of any age is murder, which is intrinsically evil and always gravely immoral. Even if very good consequences result from only a single act of murder, the act remains a grave evil because the human being killed is an innocent human person, made in the image of God. The killing of human persons that results from ESCR is intrinsically evil and gravely immoral under the second font of morality. No intended end in the first font, and no consequential end in the third font, can change the morality of the second font, which in this case is gravely immoral.

Moreover, it is clear from the current state of medical research (2009) that embryonic stem cell research is also immoral under the third font of morality. Currently, any claim about the good which might possibly be accomplished through embryonic stem cell research can also be made about stem cells that are obtained ethically, i.e. without the killing of a prenatal. The pluripotency that is desired for research is found in all types of stem cells. So the good consequences that might possibly occur through this type of research is no more likely to occur from ESCR, than from ethical types of stem cell research (e.g. adult stem cells or iPSCs). But all types of stem cells are not equal in their consequences.

Embryonic stem cells (ESCs) have dna that differs from the patient's own dna, and so any tissue that is produced might be rejected by the patient's body; this is a bad consequence not found with other types of stem cell research. Also, ESCs are obtained by killing a human embryo; not only is this immoral under the second font, but the death of the innocent prenatal is also a bad consequence (in the third font) not found with other stem cell types.

By comparison adult stem cells and induced pluripotent stem cells (iPSCs) have the same dna as the patient, since they are taken, or derived, from the patient's own cells; this makes the cells produced more likely to be accepted by the patient's body; this is a good consequence not found with ESCR. And no human embryos are killed in the process of obtaining or making either adult stem cells or iPSCs; again, this is a good consequence not found with ESCR.

In any area of morality, when evaluating the third font, the good and bad consequences of alternate choices must be weighed. So if there is a way to obtain the same good consequences (medical research that might result in treatments and cures), with fewer bad consequences or no substantial bad consequences (no death to innocent human persons; no medical problems to the patient due to differences in dna), then it would not be moral to choose the act that has the substantially greater bad consequences, and the same good consequences.

Therefore, embryonic stem cell research is gravely immoral, not only under the second font, due to the destruction of human embryos, but also under the third font, since the other types of stem cell research have greater good consequences, and far less bad consequences. The good end of treating and curing diseases does not justify a means that is intrinsically evil under the second font (killing the innocent). Neither does that same good end justify the use of a means in which the bad consequences outweigh the good consequences under the third font.

(3) Was the bombing of Hiroshima and Nagasaki justified in order to end the war sooner and save many lives?

Even today, many persons still claim that the direct targeting of the cities of Hiroshima and Nagasaki with nuclear bombs during World War 2 was justified because the war ended sooner and very many lives were saved. They consider that, if the bombing of those cities did not take place, further military action would be necessary, including perhaps an invasion of the main island of Japan, resulting in many more civilian and military deaths.

To the contrary, the direct and voluntary killing of innocent civilians during warfare is a type of murder. All murder is intrinsically evil and always gravely immoral. And intrinsically evil acts are never justified by good intention, nor by dire circumstances. The good end of saving millions of lives does not justify an intrinsically evil means, even if that means is the murder of only one person.

In addition to the many deaths, many innocent human persons were severely injured by this direct targeting of civilians with nuclear bombs. The direct and deliberate harming of innocent human persons is also intrinsically evil. Again, the good end of saving many lives does not justify an intrinsically evil means, regardless of whether that means is murder of the innocent, or the direct and deliberate harm of the innocent. The number of innocent persons saved cannot be weighed against the number of innocent persons directly and deliberately killed or maimed, because intrinsically evil acts are always immoral. The number saved and the number harmed may affect the moral weight of the third font, but not the second. For it is never moral to do evil so that good may result.

The number of lives lost or saved affects the third font of morality, but not the second. When choosing between two acts, one that has fewer deaths and more lives saved, and another that has more deaths and fewer lives saved, the act with the fewer deaths and greater number of lives saved has the better third font. But even when we solely consider the third font, it is not sufficient for one act to be better than another; each chosen act must be moral in itself, under each font. So if one act has a better third font than another act, but the better act still has more bad consequences than good consequences in the third font, that seemingly better act is still immoral. If both acts are immoral, neither act can be done.

(4) Was the fire-bombing of Tokyo justified in order to end the war sooner and save many lives?

The bombing of Tokyo during World War 2 was not a nuclear bomb, and not all civilians in the city were killed. However, the act itself of fire-bombing a mass center of population was deliberately directed at the killing and maiming of innocent civilians, not at any particular military target. The intended end (the purpose) was to demoralize the civilian population to undermine support for the war. But regardless of the intended end, the means to that end was intrinsically evil and always gravely immoral because innocent human persons were directly and deliberately killed or harmed.

The good end of saving innocent lives does not justify the intrinsically evil means of killing or harming innocent lives. The intended end and the consequential end of saving of a great number of innocent lives can never justify an intrinsically evil act. The fact that the bombing of Tokyo was not a nuclear bomb does not cause the act to become moral. The act itself of directly and deliberately killing the innocent is intrinsically evil and always gravely immoral.
.118.
(5) Is one sin justified if by committing that sin a person avoids a greater sin?

The end of avoiding a greater sin does not justify committing a lesser sin as a means to that end.

Actual sin is a knowingly chosen immoral act. All immoral acts are evil, to one degree or another. Nothing can cause an evil act to become good. The distinction and separation between moral good and moral evil is as complete and unchangeable as the distinction and separation between Heaven and Hell. Nothing can turn Hell into Heaven, and nothing can turn Heaven into Hell. Every good act remains good, and every sinful act remains sinful. A sin does not become good by being used as a means to avoid a greater sin. For a good end does not justify an immoral means.

The intended end of avoiding a greater sin does not justify the commission of a lesser sin. Good intention is not sufficient to make an act moral. All three fonts of morality must be good. If an act is intrinsically evil, nothing can make that act good, not even a purpose and circumstance such that, by committing one sin, a person supposedly avoids a greater sin.

Furthermore, God always gives sufficient grace and providence so that no one is required to commit one sin in order to avoid another sin. All actual sin is culpable because all actual sin is avoidable, by the grace of God. Therefore, the question is flawed in that it assumes that the only way to avoid one sin is to commit a lesser sin. It is always possible to avoid any particular actual sin.

(6) Is direct abortion justified to save the life of the mother, when the prenatal's life cannot be saved?

The good end of saving the life of the mother does not justify the direct and voluntary killing of an innocent human person. The end of saving a life, or even of saving many lives, does not justify an evil means, such as the murder of an innocent prenatal. Direct abortion is intrinsically evil and always gravely immoral. Intrinsically evil acts never become moral, even when the intended end is very good and the circumstances are dire.

A good end cannot cause an evil means to become good because evil and good are in complete opposition. The separation between good and evil is one of the most fundamental principles of all morality. To claim that evil acts can become good, or that good acts can become evil, is to reject the eternal and unchanging Nature of God, who is Justice and Goodness, who is the source of all morality.

(7) Is lying justified in order to keep your job and support your family?

The good end of retaining a job and of supporting your family does not justify any act that is intrinsically evil. Lying is always immoral because the act itself is inherently directed at an end, its moral object, which is contrary to God who is Truth. Lying is not capable of being ordered toward God as our ultimate end, because God is Truth, and all lying is inherently opposed to truth. All lies offend God. So a good end cannot cause the intrinsically evil act of lying to become good.

No matter how dire the circumstances of this life might be, we must always remember that we have the hope of eternal life with God, who is Goodness itself. So we cannot justify the knowing choice of any act that is evil before God on the basis of the passing circumstances of this life. Although very grave consequences might occur when we choose not to sin, those consequences cannot harm our eternal life as long as we continue to do good and avoid doing evil. Every dire circumstance shall pass away and be forgotten. Therefore, we cannot justify the smallest sin on the basis of the most dire circumstance. The love of God, and faith in Jesus Christ, and hope for eternal life must be our guide through all the difficulties of this life.

(8) Is it moral to directly attack an enemy military target during a just war if the civilians casualties are overwhelming?

In this example, the intention is good, to attack the enemy during a just war. The act itself is moral because deadly force is directed only at an enemy military target, and the civilians deaths are not direct or deliberate. The second font is good because use of deadly force against the enemy in a just war is moral, and because the civilians deaths are in the third font. Since the second font is good, this is not an example of an intrinsically evil act being used as the evil means to a good end. However, the third font must also be good for the act to be moral.

If the bad consequences of a number of civilian deaths outweighs the good consequences of destroying an enemy military target, then the act is immoral under the third font. In this case, the end of obtaining the good consequences does not justify the means, specifically, an act that is immoral under the third font, not the second.

If the destruction of a particular military target will end the war sooner, and will save many lives, then these weighty good consequences would be sufficient to outweigh a number of indirect civilian deaths. In this case, the end is not justifying the means, but rather both the end and the means are moral. It is moral to do a good act (attacking a military target during a just war; no direct attack on innocents), with good intention (saving lives), and in which the good consequences of saving many lives outweighs the bad consequences of some unintended indirect civilian deaths. So this act is good under all three fonts and therefore this act may be used as a good means to a good end. But if any font makes an act immoral, that act cannot be done, not even to obtain good consequences.

(9) Is contraception justified if a pregnancy would endanger the life of the woman?

The end of saving an innocent human life does not justify an intrinsically evil means. The use of contraception is intrinsically evil under the second font of morality. Nothing in the first or third fonts, not the best of intentions, not the most dire of circumstances, can cause an intrinsically evil act to become moral.

However, the woman's life need not be in danger. She can morally refrain from sexual relations, so that her life is not in danger. Also, it may be possible, in consultation with a physician knowledgeable about natural family planning, to use NFP so strictly as to have very little risk of pregnancy and still have marital relations for at least a few consecutive days out of each month (starting some length of time after ovulation, and ending when the next cycle begins). The patient and physician would still have to weigh this small risk of death from pregnancy (which would vary from one patient to another) against the moral value of a married couple being able to have marital relations.

.119. (10) Is the use of condoms justified in order to prevent disease transmission between a husband and wife?

In this case, the act itself is the use of a contraceptive during sexual relations; such an act is intrinsically evil, and therefore always immoral. An intrinsically evil means is not justified by any end whatsoever. It is false to claim that the act itself is the prevention of disease transmission; that result is a good consequence in the third font and the intended end in the first font, but it is not the moral object in the second font. The chosen act is to have contracepted sexual relations, and all contraceptive acts are intrinsically evil. The good end of preventing disease transmission does not justify an intrinsically evil act.

Unfortunately, many people have a strong tendency to over-value sexual acts. When a situation occurs that might cause them to be unable to continue to have sexual relations, they are willing to accept any excuse or rationalization that will prevent the loss of their sexual activity. But the eternal moral law does not permit sin of any kind in order to obtain any good end, not even the over-valued good end of sexual relations.

If there is a grave reason for a husband and wife to refrain from all marital relations, then they do not sin by living without any sexual relations. But if they use a contraceptive as a means to be able to have marital relations, then they are putting the good end of marital relations above the Good that is God. All sinful acts, whether they are immoral in their means or in their ends, offend God. All moral acts please God. No good in this passing life is so good as to justify a sin against God, the ultimate Good.

Neither is it true that the good intention and the difficulty of the circumstances transforms the intrinsically evil act of contracepted sexual relations into a morally good act of preventing disease. The couple are knowingly choosing to have sexual relations while using a contraceptive that is inherently directed at frustrating the procreative meaning of sexual relations. The intention and the circumstances do not have any affect on the moral object of the second font.

Pope John Paul II: "Consequently, circumstances or intentions can never transform an act, intrinsically evil by virtue of its object, into an act 'subjectively' good or defensible as a choice."[105]

Pope John Paul II: "No circumstance, no purpose, no law whatsoever can ever make licit an act which is intrinsically illicit, since it is contrary to the Law of God which is written in every human heart, knowable by reason itself, and proclaimed by the Church."[106]

.120. (11) Are unnatural sexual acts justified between a husband and wife, as long as these acts are used as a type of foreplay?

Foreplay is a means to an end; acts of foreplay prepare for the act of natural marital relations. Since the end does not justify the means, every act used as foreplay must be good under all three fonts of morality, as those fonts spring up from each particular act. One act cannot be justified by the fonts of a different act. If an act is intrinsically evil and always immoral when done apart from natural marital relations, then the same act remains intrinsically evil when done with natural marital relations, even when used as a means to prepare for the end of

---

[105] Pope John Paul II, Veritatis Splendor, n. 81.
[106] Pope John Paul II, Evangelium Vitae, n. 62.

natural marital relations. The end of natural marital relations open to life does not cause the means used to prepare for that act to change from evil to good. Nor is it correct to say that acts of foreplay have no morality of their own, but somehow derive their morality from the end. The idea that the means takes its morality from the end is merely a different way of saying that the end justifies the means.

Any sexual act that is intrinsically evil apart from natural marital relations, remains intrinsically evil when done before, during, or after marital relations. The end of natural marital relations open to life does not justify the means to that end. Nor can the good fonts of one act change the fonts of another act. An act with an evil moral object cannot be made moral by being combined in some way with another act.

If a husband and wife commit an unnatural sexual act (e.g. an act of oral, anal, or manipulative sex) as a means to the end of natural marital relations open to life, the means is intrinsically evil and always gravely immoral, even though the end is good and moral. The end does not cause the means to become good. The end does not change the morality of the means. The end does not exempt the means from the moral law.

Every unnatural sexual act is intrinsically evil, even within marriage, because this type of sexual act does not have both the unitive and procreative meanings joined in the same act. In order to be moral, each and every sexual act must be marital, unitive, and procreative.

Pope Paul VI: "The Church, nevertheless, in urging men to the observance of the precepts of the natural law, which it interprets by its constant doctrine, teaches that each and every **marital** act must of necessity retain its intrinsic relationship to the procreation of human life. This particular doctrine, often expounded by the magisterium of the Church, is based on the inseparable connection, established by God, which man on his own initiative may not break, between the **unitive** significance and the **procreative** significance which are both inherent to the marriage act."[107]

Unnatural sexual acts are deprived of the procreative meaning in the moral object, therefore all such acts are intrinsically evil. Unnatural sexual acts are also not truly unitive, in the moral sense of the word, and not truly marital, in the moral sense of the word. Even if an unnatural sexual act is not consummated (not continued to the point of sexual climax), and is followed by an act of natural marital relations open to life, the unnatural sexual act remains intrinsically evil because the moral object remains unchanged. Sexual climax may be an intended end, and a consequential end, but it is not the moral object; and so the lack of sexual climax in an unnatural sexual act does not change the moral object from evil to good. The moral object of each and every sexual act must be marital and unitive and procreative; this threefold moral object is required for any sexual act to be moral. The lack of one or more of these three meanings causes the moral

---

[107] Pope Paul VI, Evangelium Vitae, n. 11-12.

object to be evil. Therefore, the end of natural marital relations open to life does not justify the use of unnatural sexual acts, consummated or non-consummated, as an intrinsically evil means to that good end.

Neither is it correct to say that the unnatural sexual act is merely a part of one continuous act, so that the totality of what occurs in the marital bedroom is morally evaluated as one act. This approach is merely another form of the heretical claim that the end justifies the means. In this approach, one or more acts, used as a means to the end of natural marital relations, and that end itself, are claimed to be one continuous act, so that the good fonts of the act of natural marital relations open to life in effect are claimed to justify any and all sexual acts that occur before, during, or after the act of natural marital relations. This claim cleverly attempts to justify the means by the end, by claiming that the end and the means are one and the same act. To the contrary, the idea that the end and the means are one continuous act cannot be used to justify an evil means for the sake of a good end.

First, each knowingly chosen act must be moral under all three fonts, as those fonts spring up from that act. It is obvious that a set of acts in the marital bedroom are not one continuous act, since the couple knowingly chooses each act, are able to commit the acts in varying order, and are able to include or omit any particular act. Second, this patently false claim is merely used to combine the end and the means, so that the end can be used as a way to justify the means. But the Church infallibly teaches through the Universal Magisterium that the end never justifies the means. Third, this approach of combining a set of acts, the means and the end, and of claiming that the set is one continuous act, so that all the acts are justified by the good end, is never used (even by those who support this false claim) in other areas of morality. It is only used in the area of sexual ethics, so as to justify certain types of sexual acts, which are promoted by secular society as good, but which the Church has always condemned and never allowed, not even between husband and wife.

(12) Is the use of unnatural sexual acts justified if a spouse cannot reach sexual climax in any other way?

The good end of having sexual climax within marital relations does not justify the use of an intrinsically evil means. Unnatural sexual acts are not procreative, and not truly unitive, and not even truly marital. For God who created male and female, and who joined them in holy matrimony, does not intend that their bodies and their marriage be used in any unnatural manner. And so this type of sexual act is always gravely immoral. The good end of giving pleasure to one's spouse does not justify the means used to reach that end.

Sexual climax is a good consequence (in the third font) of natural marital relations. Although pleasure is not the primary end of marital relations, it is one of the lesser good ends. But as in all areas of morality, the means to any good end must also be good. Natural marital relations open to life is a good means, which has many good results. A husband and wife may seek these good results as ends, including the procreation of children, the expression and strengthening of love and of the marriage, the quieting of concupiscence (i.e. sexual desire), and the pleasure that occurs as a result of a good act of natural marital relations open to life. However, a husband and wife may not seek any good end by an evil means. They may not seek the good end of procreation by means of in vitro fertilization or artificial insemination. They may not seek the good end of quieting concupiscence by acts of masturbation. They may not seek the good end of sexual pleasure by means of unnatural sexual acts. Although sinful secular society promotes the seeking of every kind of pleasure as if this were among the greatest goods, we know from the teaching of Christ that every kind of pleasure in this life is like sand compared to the overflowing happiness of Heaven, and even compared to the peace and joy that we have in this life when we imitate Christ.

Unnatural sexual acts are intrinsically evil, and therefore are not justified by the end of seeking to give sexual pleasure to one's spouse, nor by any end or reason whatsoever.

.121. Summary

The doctrine that the end does not justify the means is very well established in Catholic teaching, and yet often implicitly denied. Each of these claims: (1) that the end changes the morality of the means, (2) that the end determines the morality of the means, (3) that the end exempts the means from the moral law, is merely a different form of the heretical claim that the end justifies the means. Often these ideas are not explicitly stated, but are inherent to the argument being presented.

If the end justifies the means, then any immoral act whatsoever could be justified by merely directing that act toward a particular good end. The entire moral law would then become meaningless and ineffective. The result of claiming that the end justifies the means is to claim that any act at all becomes moral when directed at a good end. If the end justifies the means, then nothing is always immoral, and all of the Church's teaching on morality would fall apart.

To the contrary, a good end does not change the morality of the means. To be moral, the means must be good under all three fonts, as those fonts apply to that particular act. The fact that an act is the means to a good end does not determine the morality of the act. We should not work toward evil ends, but even when the end is good, the means must also be entirely moral.

Any act at all, in any area of morality, any act that is intrinsically evil to do by itself, remains intrinsically evil when done as a means to a good end, or when done before, during, or after other acts. Nothing can cause an intrinsically evil act to become moral. Nothing can cause an intrinsically evil act to transform into another type of act, one that is moral. The Church teaches that even the most noble of intentions and the most dire of circumstances cannot justify the commission of an intrinsically evil act. Each and every act, including any acts used as a means to a good end, must be moral under all three fonts of morality in order to be good before God. Any bad font makes that act immoral, even if the other fonts are good, even if the act is done as a means to a good end, even if the act is done before, during, or after another act, one that is moral.

Chapter 11
Tradition, Scripture, Magisterium

.122.
Doctrines

The doctrines of the Church are teachings on matters of faith, morals, salvation. Our faith leads us to live a life of good morals, which leads to eternal salvation. Theology on matters of faith is called dogmatic theology; theology on matters of morality is called moral theology; theology on matters of salvation is called soteriology.[108]

The doctrines of the Church are found in Sacred Tradition, Sacred Scripture, and the teachings of the Magisterium. These are the three pillars of truth in the Catholic Faith: Tradition, Scripture, Magisterium. The faithful are required by the moral law to believe in the teachings of Sacred Tradition, and of Sacred Scripture, and of the Magisterium. The Catholic Faith is not based solely on the teachings of the Magisterium, but on the teachings of all three sources. This threefold source of truth has been the basis for the Catholic Faith since the time of Christ. In the early Church, when there were few if any magisterial documents, the teachings of the Living Magisterium were known by the preaching of the Apostles and their successors, the Bishops. And the faithful did not live by magisterial teachings alone, but also by the teachings of Sacred Tradition and Sacred Scripture.

Sacred Tradition and Sacred Scripture teach the truths of Divine Revelation without error, and so both Tradition and Scripture are entirely inerrant. The Magisterium is able to teach either infallibly (no possibility of error), or non-infallibly (limited possibility of error). But this infallibility found in Tradition, Scripture, Magisterium is not merely the absence of error, but also the presence of subtle and profound truths, divinely revealed by God who is Truth, on matters of faith and morals, for the purpose of our salvation.

And this fullness of truth in Divine Revelation is a reflection of the Word of God, Jesus Christ, the Second Person of the Most Holy Trinity, the eternal Son of the eternal Father. The Son proceeds from the Father like one Word, with infinite fullness, uttered as Truth from Truth. So also does the Holy Spirit, who is Truth, inspire the truths of Sacred Tradition and Sacred Scripture, as if these truths of Divine Revelation were one Word, uttered by the Holy Spirit, as an expression of the Word of God, the Son of the Father. The Sacred Deposit of Faith is a reflection of the Truth that is the living Word of God, Jesus Christ. Therefore, this Divine Revelation, found in Sacred Tradition and Sacred Scripture, is both entirely inspired and entirely inerrant. All that is asserted as true, on any subject, by Tradition or Scripture, is certainly inspired by God and is certainly true.

---

[108] Teachings on salvation are usually categorized as teachings of faith, and so soteriology is usually categorized under dogmatic theology.

.123. Sacred Tradition

Second Vatican Council: "This plan of revelation is realized by deeds and words having in inner unity: the deeds wrought by God in the history of salvation manifest and confirm the teaching and realities signified by the words, while the words proclaim the deeds and clarify the mystery contained in them. By this revelation then, the deepest truth about God and the salvation of man shines out for our sake in Christ, who is both the mediator and the fullness of all revelation."[109]

Sacred Tradition itself is "the deeds wrought by God in the history of salvation." These deeds include the creation of the universe, and all that it contains, including the creation of humanity, as well as the all deeds of God in the history of the Israelites during the Old Testament time period. Preeminent among the deeds wrought by God in salvation history are the deeds of the New Testament time period. These are the deeds of God Incarnate, Jesus Christ, throughout His Life, and especially during His Ministry, His Passion, and His salvific death on the Cross, as well as His Resurrection and the sending of the Holy Spirit on the Church at Pentecost. Although Sacred Scripture contains words about the salvific act of Christ, Sacred Tradition includes the deed itself. Thus Sacred Tradition includes the source of salvation itself, not merely words about that salvation, and that source is the deeds of the Son of God at His Passion and Crucifixion.

First Vatican Council: "Now this supernatural revelation, according to the belief of the universal church, as declared by the sacred council of Trent, is contained in written books and unwritten traditions...."[110]

Sacred Tradition itself is unwritten because it is deeds, not words about deeds. These deeds of God in salvation history can be described in words, but the Catholic Faith is not based solely on the words of Revelation, but also on the deeds of Revelation, deeds which reveal truths about God and morality, deeds which accomplish our salvation. These truths can be expressed in words, but they are never fully contained or fully expressed in words alone.

Tradition itself is often confused with the transmission of Tradition. Sacred Tradition itself, which is the deeds of God in salvation history, especially the deeds of Christ, is distinct from the transmission of Sacred Tradition. All the teachings of Sacred Tradition are infallible truths, because God never errs in His deeds. But Sacred Tradition is transmitted by means of us poor sinners, who frequently err; and yet the Spirit of God preserves the truths of Sacred Tradition unstained by our own sins and faults. Similarly, all the teachings of Sacred Scripture are infallible truths, yet any individual manuscript, translation, or edit may contain errors particular to that edition. Thus the Apostles, who were each sinners, were still able to transmit the infallible truths of Sacred Tradition throughout their generation and to the next generation.

---

[109] Second Vatican Council, Dei Verbum, n. 2; from Chapter I, "Revelation Itself."
[110] First Vatican Council, Chapter 2, On Revelation.

.124. Sacred Tradition is transmitted in many ways, not only by the Apostles, who lived the truths of Sacred Tradition that they learned from Christ Himself, but also by all the faithful of every generation, in so far as they live in imitation of Christ. And just as Sacred Tradition itself is the deeds of God in salvation history, so also the primary means of transmission of Sacred Tradition is the deeds of the people of God. Sacred Tradition itself is unwritten because it is the deeds themselves. Sacred Scripture contains words about those deeds; but the deeds themselves also teach us directly. Similarly, the deeds of all faithful Christians teach other Christians, and even the whole world, about the truths of Sacred Tradition directly, even at times without any words. The deed of a martyr dying, without a word, for the sake of Christ, in imitation of Christ's own death, is part of the transmission of Sacred Tradition. And even the least unknown Christians help to transmit Sacred Tradition by living as Christ lived.

Second Vatican Council: "Now what was handed on by the Apostles includes everything which contributes toward the holiness of life and increase in faith of the peoples of God; and so the Church, in her teaching, life and worship, perpetuates and hands on to all generations all that she herself is, all that she believes."[111]

The deeds of the Church also transmit Sacred Tradition. So the truths of Sacred Tradition are transmitted, even apart from the spoken or written word, by the deeds of the Sacraments, and the Mass, and other liturgical services, and by all the deeds of the people of God gathered as one Body of Christ. The deeds of God, especially the deeds of Christ, the Son of God, in salvation history are primarily transmitted by the lives of every Christian, and by the faith life of the Church, the body of believers on earth. For the holy Catholic Christian Faith is no mere set of holy words, but a holy way of life, the Way of Christ. The truths of the Faith are transmitted primarily by being lived.

But Sacred Tradition is also transmitted by the written and spoken word. On this point, the distinction between Sacred Tradition itself and the transmission of Sacred Tradition is essential. Sacred Tradition is infallible. The written and spoken words used to help transmit Tradition (in addition to deeds as the primary means of transmission) are not infallible; they are the words of all faithful Christians as they explain the faith to one another, and to the subsequent generations.

All the deeds of the faithful and of the Church itself, from the greatest deeds, such as a holy Saint dying as a martyr for Christ, to even the least deeds, such as a poor Christian offering his daily sufferings to Christ on the Cross, or a small child praying an Our Father and a Hail Mary, all the deeds of all the faithful, are part of the transmission of Sacred Tradition. For this reason, Sacred Tradition is fittingly called the Living Tradition, for its transmission is by the lives of all the faithful of every generation. Sacred Tradition is lived.

Second Vatican Council: "The holy people of God shares also in Christ's prophetic office; it spreads abroad a living witness to Him, especially by means

---

[111] Second Vatican Council, Dei Verbum, n. 8.

of a life of faith and charity and by offering to God a sacrifice of praise, the tribute of lips which give praise to His name. The entire body of the faithful, anointed as they are by the Holy One, cannot err in matters of belief. They manifest this special property by means of the whole peoples' supernatural discernment in matters of faith when 'from the Bishops down to the last of the lay faithful' they show universal agreement in matters of faith and morals. That discernment in matters of faith is aroused and sustained by the Spirit of truth. It is exercised under the guidance of the sacred teaching authority, in faithful and respectful obedience to which the people of God accepts that which is not just the word of men but truly the word of God."[112]

When all the faithful "show universal agreement in matters of faith and morals" they "cannot err". This infallibility of the body of the faithful is not a teaching authority similar to that of the Magisterium, exercised only by the Pope and the Bishops. Truly, this infallibility found in the body of all the faithful is an example of the Living Tradition. Sacred Tradition is infallible. But since Tradition is unwritten, we often do not notice when those around us, or even we ourselves, are manifesting the truths of that Living Tradition. When all the faithful are in agreement on what to believe and how to live, from the teachings and life of Christ, this is an example of Tradition being transmitted by the lives of the body of believers.

.125. The deeds and words of every faithful Christian, in so far as these adhere to the example and teaching of Christ, help to transmit Tradition. This includes the written and spoken words used by the faithful to transmit the truths of Divine Revelation throughout a generation, and to future generations. These words are not infallible because they are not Sacred Tradition itself; these words are a means for the transmission of Sacred Tradition. But the Holy Spirit guides and protects the expression of Sacred Tradition within the Church, so that the truths of Divine Revelation will neither be lost, nor corrupted, even though it is we poor sinners who transmit the infallible truths of Sacred Tradition.

Sacred Tradition is not an oral tradition, but rather it is a set of truths expressed by the deeds of God, and the deeds of the Son of God, in salvation history. And those truths are transmitted mainly by our deeds, but also by our spoken and written words. These are the words of all the faithful as they explain and defend the Faith throughout the history of the Church, from the time of the Apostles and the early Church Fathers, and throughout every century, continuously and unbroken to the present day and beyond.

The Catholic Faith is lived; it is not a set of words alone, but of deeds and words. Our deeds, in so far as we imitate Christ, each and everyone of us, are a means of the transmission of Sacred Tradition. When our deeds in our life, and even in our death, are like the life and death of Christ, then we are expressing, in part, the truths of Sacred Tradition which are unwritten truths that extend even beyond words. The truths of Divine Revelation are found in the deeds of Sacred Tradition and in the words of Sacred Scripture. Similarly, the lives of faithful

---

[112] Second Vatican Council, Lumen Gentium, n. 12.

Christians contain both deeds and words: our deeds in imitation of Christ, and our understanding and expression of the words of Christ. For all of Sacred Tradition and all of Sacred Scripture is Christ speaking to us.

All the teachings of Sacred Tradition are infallible truths, because God never errs in His deeds, just as He never errs in His words. The teachings of Sacred Tradition are infallible and immutable truths. They cannot be changed by any authority, not by the Magisterium, not by Christ Himself. For these truths are an expression of the Living Truth who is God. And God is eternal and unchanging Truth.

.126. The letter and the spirit of Sacred Tradition

Certainly, Sacred Tradition itself is unwritten deeds, and is mainly transmitted by the deeds of our lives and of the Church as the body of believers, in imitation of the deeds of Christ. But the spoken and written word also serve to help transmit the truths of Sacred Tradition. These spoken and written words are not themselves infallible because they are not themselves Sacred Tradition. They are a means of transmission of Sacred Tradition. All the faithful without exception are able, in so far as their words express what has been handed down, to assist in transmitting Sacred Tradition by the spoken and written word. A parent teaching a child the truths of Sacred Tradition is using words to transmit what has been handed down. But preeminent among the words that transmit Sacred Tradition are the words of the Fathers, Doctors, and Saints of the Church.

However, these words are not Sacred Tradition itself, and so these words are fallible. The words of Sacred Scripture are infallible because those words are Sacred Scripture itself. But the words used to transmit the unwritten truths of Sacred Tradition, truths expressed by God in the deeds of salvation history, especially the deeds of Christ our Savior, these words are not Sacred Tradition itself, and so these words are not infallible. Therefore, we must distinguish between Sacred Tradition itself, which is infallible, and the words (along with the deeds) used to transmit those infallible truths.

If we treat every word of every Father, Doctor, and Saint of the Church as if it were infallible, then we would be putting the letter above the spirit of Sacred Tradition. For the spirit of Sacred Tradition is the truths that are transmitted by means of words and deeds, the words and deeds of saints and sinners. But the words of the Fathers, Doctors, and Saints are not infallible.

Even Saint Joseph erred, though without sin, in thinking that he should dismiss the Virgin Mary, his betrothed, and not keep her as his virgin wife (Matthew 1:18-20). Even Saint John the Baptist erred, though without sin, in thinking that perhaps Jesus was not the Messiah, but was merely someone preparing for the Messiah (Luke 7:18-20). Similarly, the Fathers, Doctors, and Saints of the Church have sometimes erred on matters of faith and morals, and these errors have been, or may be, corrected by the Magisterium.

Since Sacred Tradition is not the words of the Fathers of the Church, but the deeds of God, we offend God when we reduce Sacred Tradition to nothing other than the words of the Fathers. Neither should we expect that all doctrines on faith and morals should have been expressed explicitly by the early Church Fathers. Every doctrine on faith and morals is found, at least implicitly in Sacred Tradition. Every doctrine on faith and morals is found, at least implicitly in Sacred Scripture. But not every doctrine is found, even implicitly in the words of the early Church Fathers. Sacred Tradition is greater than their words.

Also, we must not fall into the error of thinking that Sacred Tradition is only the words used for its transmission. In Sacred Tradition, God expresses truths by means of deeds. So we err seriously when we consider Sacred Tradition to be only the words used in its transmission, rather than the unwritten truths expressed by the deeds of God. And this then leads to the error of reducing Sacred Tradition to the letter of the written word, which is always less than the fullness of truth expressed in the deeds of God in salvation history.

.127. The Grievous Error of ultra-Traditionalists

By traditionalists is meant, not those faithful Catholics who seek to live in accord with the doctrines of Sacred Tradition, Sacred Scripture, and the Magisterium, but rather those ultra-traditionalists who have rejected the Magisterium (especially Vatican II and the recent Popes) on the basis of a claim that the Magisterium has gone astray from Tradition. Such persons arrogantly set themselves up as judges over every Pope and over every Council, to decide if a Pope or Council has (supposedly) gone astray. They lack the ability to judge Popes and Councils, they lack the authority to judge Popes and Councils, and they also judge unjustly.

These lost souls claim that the Second Vatican Council and all the Popes since that time have fallen into heresy. But Christ Himself taught that His Church can never go astray, and that the faith of Peter, who is the Rock on which She is founded, can never fail.

[Matthew]
{16:18} "And I say to you, that you are Peter, and upon this rock I will build my Church, and the gates of Hell shall not prevail against it.
{16:19} And I will give you the keys of the kingdom of heaven. And whatever you shall bind on earth shall be bound, even in heaven. And whatever you shall release on earth shall be released, even in heaven."

{22:32} "But I have prayed for you, so that your faith may not fail, and so that you, once converted, may confirm your brothers."

The infallible Universal Magisterium teaches that the Church is indefectible.[113] Therefore, the Church can neither go astray Herself, nor lead the faithful away from the path of salvation. But if the Pope, who is the Vicar of Christ and the visible head of the Church on earth, either by himself or with the body of

---

[113] cf. Pope John Paul II, Ut Unum Sint, n. 98; Pope Benedict XV, Ad Beatissimi Apostolorum, n. 19; Pope St. Pius X, Jucunda Sane, n. 8; Catechism of the Catholic Church, n. 1108.

Bishops, whether gathered in an Ecumenical Council or dispersed through the world, could go astray from the true Faith into heresy, then the Rock on which the Church is founded, who is Peter and his successors, would fail, and salvation would be lost, and the gates of Hell would prevail. Therefore, it is impossible for either the body of Bishops with the Pope as their head, or the Pope by himself, to fall into heresy.

By virtue of the promise of Christ that Peter's faith will not faith, and that he will strengthen the faith of his brother bishops (Mt 22:32), no Pope can possibly fall into apostasy, heresy, or schism, and neither can the body of Bishops, those who remain in communion with one another and subject to the Pope as their head, fall as a body into those same sins. For these three sins are each a type of utter failure of faith. Therefore, the grace of God entirely prevents apostasy, heresy, and schism in each and every valid successor to Peter, and in the body of Bishops united to him. Neither is this grace contrary to free will, for the man who accepts his valid election as Pope does so by an act of his free will, and thereby cooperates with grace to receive the gift to be, not only the visible head of the Church on earth, but also the head of the body of Bishops and the seat of the Magisterium. And the Bishops also freely cooperate with grace, so as to receive, as a body with a head, a similar gift, when they freely choose to remain in communion with one another and to remain subject to the Roman Pontiff as to the Vicar of Christ, the Head of the Church.

.128. Sacred Scripture

All the teachings of Sacred Scripture are infallible truths, because God never errs in His words, just as He never errs in His deeds. The teachings of Sacred Scripture are infallible and immutable truths. They cannot be changed by any authority, not by the Magisterium, not by Christ Himself. For these truths are an expression of the Living Truth who is God. And God is eternal and unchanging Truth.

The Council of Florence: "It [the holy Roman church] professes that one and the same God is the author of the old and the new Testament -- that is, the law and the prophets, and the gospel -- since the saints of both testaments spoke under the inspiration of the same Spirit. It accepts and venerates their books, whose titles are as follows." [The Council then lists all the books of the Old and New Testament, and includes the Lamentations of Jeremiah with the book of Jeremiah.][114]

The Council infallibly taught that God is the author of all the books of the Bible, in the Old and New Testaments, by the inspiration of the Holy Spirit. The Council also infallibly listed the Canon of Scripture as all the books of the Catholic Bible, including the deuterocanonical books.

The Council of Trent: "The sacred and holy, ecumenical, and general Synod of Trent ... following the examples of the orthodox Fathers, receives and venerates with an equal affection of piety, and reverence, all the books both of the Old and

---

[114] The Council of Florence, Session 11 (4 February 1442).

of the New Testament -- seeing that one God is the author of both -- as also the said traditions, as well those appertaining to faith as to morals, as having been dictated, either by Christ's own word of mouth, or by the Holy Spirit, and preserved in the Catholic Church by a continuous succession.... [The Council then lists all the books of the Old and New Testament, and includes the Lamentations of Jeremiah with the book of Jeremiah.] But if any one receive not, as sacred and canonical, the said books entire with all their parts, as they have been used to be read in the Catholic Church, and as they are contained in the old Latin vulgate edition; and knowingly and deliberately contemn the traditions aforesaid; let him be anathema."[115]

The Council uses the figure of dictation in order to indicate that the inspiration of the Holy Spirit determines all that is in these books, "entire with all their parts." These books are entirely inspired, sacred, and canonical, with all their parts. This teaching is infallible, as indicated by the anathema against anyone who rejects the teaching.

First Vatican Council: "The complete books of the old and the new Testament with all their parts, as they are listed in the decree of the said council and as they are found in the old Latin Vulgate edition, are to be received as sacred and canonical. These books the church holds to be sacred and canonical, not because she subsequently approved them by her authority after they had been composed by unaided human skill, nor simply because they contain revelation without error, but because, being written under the inspiration of the holy Spirit, they have God as their author, and were as such committed to the church."

The Council infallibly taught that the "complete books" of the Old and New Testaments "with all their parts" are sacred and canonical, and they contain revelation from God "without error" because they have been written in their entirety "under the inspiration of the Holy Spirit." The total inspiration of Sacred Scripture implies the total inerrancy of Sacred Scripture. For God is the author of every part of every book of Sacred Scripture.

.129. Therefore, it is contrary to the infallible teaching of the Councils of Florence, Trent, and Vatican I to drop any verse or any part of any verse from the canon of Sacred Scripture for any reason. All the opinions and arguments of all scholars put together cannot withstand the infallible teaching of even a single Council. Yet here are three Councils teaching this same solemn definition of the Canon of Sacred Scripture as consisting in all the books "with all their parts."

Pope Leo XIII: "But it is absolutely wrong and forbidden, either to narrow inspiration to certain parts only of Holy Scripture, or to admit that the sacred writer has erred.... For all the books which the Church receives as sacred and canonical, are written wholly and entirely, with all their parts, at the dictation of the Holy Spirit; and so far is it from being possible that any error can co-exist with inspiration, that inspiration not only is essentially incompatible with error, but excludes and rejects it as absolutely and necessarily as it is impossible that God Himself, the supreme Truth, can utter that which is not true. This is the

---

[115] The Council of Trent, Session 4 (8 April 1546).

ancient and unchanging faith of the Church, solemnly defined in the Councils of Florence and of Trent, and finally confirmed and more expressly formulated by the Council of the Vatican."[116]

The phrase "at the dictation of the Holy Spirit" is a figure indicating, not literal dictation, but rather a fullness of inspiration such that all the books of the Bible contain all those things and only those things that the Spirit wills. All the books of Sacred Scripture, with all their parts, are inspired, sacred, and canonical. Those who claim that the Bible contains any kind of error are in effect claiming that either Sacred Scripture is not entirely inspired in all its parts, or that God inspired error; neither can be true. The Magisterium definitively teaches that all of Sacred Scripture is inspired, and that inspiration is necessarily and absolutely incompatible with every error. God who is Supreme Truth "cannot utter that which is not true," for He cannot deny Himself. And all of Sacred Scripture is God speaking to us.

Every teaching that is "the ancient and unchanging faith of the Church" is an infallible teaching and a required belief. And every teaching that has been "solemnly defined" by an Ecumenical Council is also an infallible teaching and a required belief. Therefore, this teaching on the total inspiration and total inerrancy of Sacred Scripture is an infallible dogma, which all Catholics are required to believe with a divine and catholic faith, i.e. with full and unreserved agreement as a matter of faith. All contrary opinions are "absolutely wrong and forbidden," and constitute at least material heresy against the Catholic Faith.

Pope Pius X published a Syllabus of Errors, in which he condemned the idea that: "Divine inspiration does not extend to all of Sacred Scriptures so that it renders its parts, each and every one, free from every error."[117]

All of Sacred Scripture is inspired by God, therefore all of Sacred Scripture is free from every error. The opinion that any part of the Bible contains error of any kind was condemned by Pope Pius X, just as this same opinion was condemned by Pope Leo XIII.

Pope Benedict XV: "St. Jerome's teaching on this point serves to confirm and illustrate what our predecessor of happy memory, Leo XIII, declared to be the ancient and traditional belief of the Church touching the absolute immunity of Scripture from error: So far is it from being the case that error can be compatible with inspiration, that, on the contrary, it not only of its very nature precludes the presence of error, but as necessarily excludes it and forbids it as God, the Supreme Truth, necessarily cannot be the Author of error."[118]

Again, any teaching that is "the ancient and traditional belief of the Church" on a matter of faith, such as the inerrancy of Sacred Scripture, is an infallible teaching and a required belief of the Catholic Faith. The immunity of Sacred Scripture from error is absolute. All that is inspired is inerrant, because God who

---

[116] Pope Leo XIII, Providentissimus Deus, n. 20.
[117] Pope Pius X, Lamentabili Sane, n. 11.
[118] Pope Benedict XV, Spiritus Paraclitus, n. 16.

is Truth cannot inspire error of any kind. Inspiration by the Holy Spirit necessarily precludes every error. And this teaching is an infallible dogma of the Catholic Faith.

Pope Benedict XV: "But although these words of our predecessor leave no room for doubt or dispute, it grieves us to find that not only men outside, but even children of the Catholic Church -- nay, what is a peculiar sorrow to us, even clerics and professors of sacred learning -- who in their own conceit either openly repudiate or at least attack in secret the Church's teaching on this point."[119]

Any teaching of the Church that leaves "no room for doubt or dispute" is a teaching that all Catholics are required to believe. Those persons, even clerics (ordained persons) and scholars, who reject the inerrancy of Sacred Scripture are rejecting the teaching of the Church. Their arguments and their credentials cannot stand against the infallible teaching of the Church on the total inspiration and total inerrancy of Sacred Scripture.

Pope Benedict XV: "Divine inspiration extends to every part of the Bible without the slightest exception, and that no error can occur in the inspired text...."[120]

.130. Inspiration implies inerrancy. Since this inspiration is total, extending to every part of the Bible "without the slightest exception," then this inerrancy must also be total, allowing for no errors at all in the inspired text. If anyone claims that Sacred Scripture contains any error, on any subject matter at all, in any part of the Bible, such a person is attacking the clear and definitive teaching of the Magisterium on Divine Revelation.

Pope Pius XII: "...they put forward again the opinion, already often condemned, which asserts that immunity from error extends only to those parts of the Bible that treat of God or of moral and religious matters."[121]

The Magisterium has often condemned the opinion that the inerrancy of Sacred Scripture extends only to matters of faith and morals, or only to matters that pertain to salvation. This condemned opinion continues to be asserted and to spread throughout the Church today. Some persons recently have been presenting this condemned opinion as if it were the teaching of the Church, or as if it were a tenable opinion of faithful Catholics. But it is a fact that the Magisterium has definitively, repeatedly, and strongly condemned this erroneous opinion.

Pope Pius XII: "The sacred Council of Trent ordained by solemn decree that 'the entire books with all their parts, as they have been used to be read in the Catholic Church and are contained in the old vulgate Latin edition, are to be held sacred and canonical.' In our own time the Vatican Council, with the object of condemning false doctrines regarding inspiration, declared that these same books were to be regarded by the Church as sacred and canonical 'not because, having

---

[119] Pope Benedict XV, Spiritus Paraclitus, n. 18.
[120] Pope Benedict XV, Spiritus Paraclitus, n. 21.
[121] Pope Pius XII, Humani Generis, n. 22.

been composed by human industry, they were afterwards approved by her authority, nor merely because they contain revelation without error, but because, having been written under the inspiration of the Holy Spirit, they have God for their author, and as such were handed down to the Church herself.' When, subsequently, some Catholic writers, in spite of this solemn definition of Catholic doctrine, by which such divine authority is claimed for the 'entire books with all their parts' as to secure freedom from any error whatsoever, ventured to restrict the truth of Sacred Scripture solely to matters of faith and morals, and to regard other matters, whether in the domain of physical science or history, as 'obiter dicta' [said in passing] and -- as they contended -- in no wise connected with faith, Our Predecessor of immortal memory, Leo XIII in the Encyclical Letter Providentissimus Deus, published on November 18 in the year 1893, justly and rightly condemned these errors and safe-guarded the studies of the Divine Books by most wise precepts and rules."[122]

Pope Pius XII taught the same doctrine found in a solemn decree of the Council of Trent, and in the teaching of the First Vatican Council, that all the books of the Bible, with all their parts, are inspired, sacred, and canonical, not only "because they contain revelation without error, but because, having been written under the inspiration of the Holy Spirit, they have God for their author." The entire Bible is inspired by the Holy Spirit, and is sacred and canonical; therefore, the entire Bible, by divine authority, has a "freedom from any error whatsoever."

He also again condemned the same false opinion previously condemned by other Popes, the claim that inerrancy only applies to faith and morals, or to religious matters, and that all assertions in the realm of science or history need not be considered accurate or true. Pope Pius XII reiterated, adding his own authority to that of prior Popes, that these errors are justly and rightly condemned. All the assertions of Sacred Scripture, on matters of faith, morals, salvation, science, history, and all other topics, fall under the dogma of total inspiration and total inerrancy.

Pope Pius XII: "This teaching, which Our Predecessor Leo XIII set forth with such solemnity, We also proclaim with Our authority and We urge all to adhere to it religiously."[123]

.131. This teaching on the total inerrancy of Sacred Scripture is an infallible teaching of the Magisterium, solemnly proclaimed by Ecumenical Councils and by Popes, and all the faithful are obliged to adhere to it as a matter of faith.

Pope Pius XII: "For as the substantial Word of God became like to men in all things, 'except sin,' (Heb 4:15) so the words of God, expressed in human language, are made like to human speech in every respect, except error."[124]

For Sacred Scripture is an expression of the Word of God, the Second Person of the Most Holy Trinity. Just as the Word of God made flesh cannot contain sin,

---

[122] Pope Pius XII, Divino Afflante Spiritu, n. 1.
[123] Pope Pius XII, Divino Afflante Spiritu, n. 4.
[124] Pope Pius XII, Divino Afflante Spiritu, n. 37.

neither can the written Word of God (in Sacred Scripture) or the unwritten Word of God (in Sacred Tradition) contain any error. The claim that either Sacred Tradition or Sacred Scripture contains error is in effect a claim that Jesus Christ, the living Word of God, contains error. For the Holy Spirit inspired Sacred Tradition and Sacred Scripture to be a perfect reflection of the living Word of God, who is Jesus Christ.

The Second Person of the Trinity is like a single Word uttered by the Father, a Word that so fully expresses who the Father is, that this Word is a distinct Person, equal in Divinity to the Father. Similarly, all of Sacred Scripture is like one Word uttered by God. No part of Sacred Scripture can be false, since the total inspiration of all the books of the Bible with all their parts makes these many words truly one inspired Word uttered by the Holy Spirit, as a reflection of Jesus Christ, the living Word of God the Father.

Pope Pius XII: "Hence the Catholic commentator, in order to comply with the present needs of biblical studies, in explaining the Sacred Scripture and in demonstrating and proving its immunity from all error, should also make a prudent use of this means, determine, that is, to what extent the manner of expression or the literary mode adopted by the sacred writer may lead to a correct and genuine interpretation; and let him be convinced that this part of his office cannot be neglected without serious detriment to Catholic exegesis. Not infrequently -- to mention only one instance -- when some persons reproachfully charge the Sacred Writers with some historical error or inaccuracy in the recording of facts, on closer examination it turns out to be nothing else than those customary modes of expression and narration peculiar to the ancients, which used to be employed in the mutual dealings of social life and which in fact were sanctioned by common usage."[125]

The faithful commentator on Sacred Scripture has an obligation to demonstrate and support the teaching of the Faith on the absolute immunity from all error of the inspired text. Only after accepting this dogma of total inspiration and total inerrancy can the faithful Catholic go on to discuss the manner of expression, figures of speech, and literary modes used to express the truths of Sacred Scripture. The claim that any passage is exempt from this immunity from error, on the grounds that the passage is one or another type of literary genre, is incompatible with the inspired inerrancy of Scripture. Literary genres, figures of speech, and various manners of expression are used to express truths; these factors do not exempt any passage from inerrancy. The claim that the assertion of falsehoods is part of a literary genre is likewise incompatible with the inspired inerrancy of Scripture. Pope Pius XII teaches that Sacred Scripture has an "immunity from all error," which includes freedom from historical errors, and freedom from error by inaccuracy. Literary genres are not exempt from inspiration and therefore not exempt from inerrancy.

Catechism of the Catholic Church: "According to an ancient tradition, one can distinguish between two senses of Scripture: the literal and the spiritual, the latter

---

[125] Pope Pius XII, Divino Afflante Spiritu, n. 38.

being subdivided into the allegorical, moral and anagogical senses. The profound concordance of the four senses guarantees all its richness to the living reading of Scripture in the Church. The literal sense is the meaning conveyed by the words of Scripture and discovered by exegesis, following the rules of sound interpretation: 'All other senses of Sacred Scripture are based on the literal.' "[126]

.132. Sacred Scripture has two main senses or levels of meaning: the literal and the spiritual. The literal level of meaning includes figures of speech, so it may be called the literal/figurative sense of Scripture. The spiritual sense is based on the literal/figurative sense.

Saint Thomas Aquinas: "The parabolical [figurative] sense is contained in the literal, for by words things are signified properly [literally] and figuratively. Nor is the figure itself, but that which is figured, the literal sense. When Scripture speaks of God's arm, the literal sense is not that God has such a member, but only what is signified by this member, namely operative power. Hence it is plain that nothing false can ever underlie the literal sense of Holy Writ."[127]

Both literal assertions and figures of speech are used to express truths. It is not possible for the literal/figurative level of meaning to express a falsehood as a means to the assertion of a truth on the spiritual level of meaning. For the spiritual sense is entirely based on, and derived from, the literal/figurative sense. If the literal/figurative sense were false, then the spiritual sense would also be false. But the dogma of inerrancy requires us to believe that no sense of Scripture is false, neither the literal, nor the spiritual.

Second Vatican Council: "Those divinely revealed realities which are contained and presented in Sacred Scripture have been committed to writing under the inspiration of the Holy Spirit. For holy mother Church, relying on the belief of the Apostles (see John 20:31; 2 Tim. 3:16; 2 Peter 1:19-20, 3:15-16), holds that the books of both the Old and New Testaments in their entirety, with all their parts, are sacred and canonical because written under the inspiration of the Holy Spirit, they have God as their author and have been handed on as such to the Church herself. In composing the sacred books, God chose men and while employed by Him they made use of their powers and abilities, so that with Him acting in them and through them, they, as true authors, consigned to writing everything and only those things which He wanted."[128]

The Second Vatican Council reiterates the teaching of the Council of Trent that all the books of the Bible, "in their entirety, with all their parts," are inspired, sacred, and canonical. Although the Council of Trent did use the phrase "all their parts," Vatican II adds the phrase "in their entirety," which expresses and further emphasizes that no part of Sacred Scripture is exempt from inspiration. The inerrancy that is inherent to inspiration is expressed in a new way: that the sacred authors consigned to writing all those things and only those things that

---

[126] Catechism of the Catholic Church, 115 to 116; inner quote from Saint Thomas Aquinas, Summa Theologica, I, Q. 1, A. 10.
[127] Saint Thomas Aquinas, Summa Theologica, I. Q. 1, A. 10.
[128] Second Vatican Council, Dei Verbum, n. 11.

God willed. Now God cannot will error or falsehood, and so this teaching is entirely in accord with the above cited teachings of Popes and Councils on total inspiration and total inerrancy.

Second Vatican Council: "Therefore, since everything asserted by the inspired authors or sacred writers must be held to be asserted by the Holy Spirit, it follows that the books of Scripture must be acknowledged as teaching solidly, faithfully and without error that truth which God wanted put into sacred writings (5) for the sake of salvation. Therefore 'all Scripture is divinely inspired and has its use for teaching the truth and refuting error, for reformation of manners and discipline in right living, so that the man who belongs to God may be efficient and equipped for good work of every kind' (2 Tim. 3:16-17, Greek text)."[129]

.133. The above text is often misquoted in order to reassert the error, already often condemned by Popes and Councils, that inerrancy is limited to truths pertaining to faith and morals, or pertaining to salvation: "without error that truth which God wanted put into sacred writings for the sake of salvation." But this quote is taken out of context. The Council first asserted the dogma of total inspiration, and then, in the same sentence as the partial quote (as it is so often used), next asserted that everything asserted by the inspired authors "must be held to be asserted by the Holy Spirit." But as was taught plainly in the quotes above from several Popes, God cannot inspire error. And the Council did not limit what is asserted by the Holy Spirit to only those things that were asserted on salvation, or on faith or morals, by the inspired authors. Instead, the Council taught that everything asserted by the sacred authors of the books of the Bible is asserted by the Holy Spirit.

The phrase "for the sake of salvation" correctly describes the purpose that the Holy Spirit had in inspiring the text of the Bible, but does not limit the scope of those truths. Certainly, the most important inspired truths are those that pertain to faith, morals, and salvation. But this does not imply that on other matters the Holy Spirit inspired falsehoods, nor does it imply that on other matters the assertions of the sacred authors are not inspired.

[Matthew]
{5:17} "Do not think that I have come to loosen the law or the prophets. I have not come to loosen, but to fulfill.
{5:18} Amen I say to you, certainly, until heaven and earth pass away, not one iota, not one dot shall pass away from the law, until all is done.
{5:19} Therefore, whoever will have loosened one of the least of these commandments, and have taught men so, shall be called the least in the kingdom of heaven. But whoever will have done and taught these, such a one shall be called great in the kingdom of heaven."

Not one iota or dot can pass away from the law and the prophets, that is, from Sacred Scripture, because all of Scripture is inspired and inerrant. If it were not, then much more than an iota or a dot could pass away from it. Whoever says that Sacred Scripture contains errors, thereby implies that these supposedly-

---
[129] Vatican II, Dei Verbum, n. 11.

erroneous parts of Scripture, now that they have been discovered, are null and void, as if they had passed away from the law and the prophets (as the Old Testament is often called). But this claim contradicts the words of our Lord.

[John]
{10:35} ... Scripture cannot be broken

If Scripture contains any falsehoods on any subject, then it is broken; but Christ Himself said that Scripture cannot be broken, that is, Scripture cannot be wrong or false or incorrect, or in any way broken as pertains to truth.

[2 Timothy]
{3:16} All Scripture, having been divinely inspired, is useful for teaching, for reproof, for correction, and for instruction in justice,
{3:17} so that the man of God may be perfect, having been trained for every good work.

All Scripture is inspired, therefore, all Scripture is inerrant. If there were any errors in Scripture on any subject, then all Scripture would not be useful for teaching and reproof and correction and instruction. If Scripture contains errors that need to be corrected, then Scripture would not be useful for correction, but would instead be the object of correction. And those persons who reject the dogma of total inspiration and total inerrancy often treat Scripture as if it were in need of their correction; not content to reject the inspired Word of God, they also exalt themselves as if they were above the Word of God.

.134. The Canon of Sacred Scripture

Both the Council of Florence and the Council of Trent defined the Canon of Sacred Scripture as 72 books.[130] They counted the Lamentations of Jeremiah and the Book of Jeremiah as one book, whereas today it is common to count them separately, making 73 books, but the Canon is the same. The Council of Trent and the First Vatican Council both taught that this Canon includes all the books of the Bible, in their entirety, with all their parts, as they are found in the old Latin Vulgate Bible. The Second Vatican Council also taught that this same Canon includes all the books and all their parts.

Council of Trent: "But if any one receive not, as sacred and canonical, the said books entire with all their parts, as they have been used to be read in the Catholic Church, and as they are contained in the old Latin vulgate edition; and knowingly and deliberately contemn the traditions aforesaid; let him be anathema."[131]

First Vatican Council: "The complete books of the old and the new Testament with all their parts, as they are listed in the decree of the said council [the

---

[130] Council of Florence, Session 11 on 4 February 1442; Council of Trent, 4th Session on 8 April 1546.
[131] Council of Trent, 4th Session on 8 April 1546.

Council of Trent] and as they are found in the old Latin Vulgate edition, are to be received as sacred and canonical."[132]

Second Vatican Council: "For holy mother Church, relying on the belief of the Apostles (see John 20:31; 2 Tim. 3:16; 2 Peter 1:19-20, 3:15-16), holds that the books of both the Old and New Testaments in their entirety, with all their parts, are sacred and canonical because written under the inspiration of the Holy Spirit, they have God as their author and have been handed on as such to the Church herself."[133]

Therefore, every verse and every part of every verse, found in the old Latin Vulgate Bible, is to be retained in all future translations and editions of the Bible, under pain of the anathema of the Council of Trent, and under pain of all of the penalties that fall upon those who embrace abject heresy.

In recent decades, some Biblical scholars have claimed that certain parts of the Canon of Sacred Scripture, a verse or a part of a verse, found in the old and Latin Vulgate, are nevertheless not sacred and not canonical, and are to be removed from the text of editions of the Bible, or relegated to footnotes and annotations. This heretical practice directly contradicts the infallible dogma of the Councils of Trent, Vatican I, and Vatican II, that the Canon of Sacred Scripture includes all the books, in their entirety, with all their parts.

If a scholar can drop any phrase or verse from the Bible, even if on the basis of scholarship and with the agreement of most other scholars, then faith would be deprived of its certitude which is based on the authority of the holy Word of God. For then every verse would be suspect as being either a verse that scholars may remove from the text at a later time, or a verse whose meaning will change if part of the verse is latter removed. And this process of removing parts of Sacred Scripture was begun in earnest only in recent times (in the 20th century), implying that for nearly two thousand years the Church was teaching from a Canon of Scripture that contained some non-sacred, non-canonical, non-inspired verses or parts of verses, as if the Church were teaching the truths necessary to salvation from an unreliable source. And this claim in turn implies that the Living Tradition, which used this Canon, in its entirety, for so many centuries, was also in error.

And as a result, scholarship is thereby placed above Divine Revelation found in Sacred Scripture. For whatever Sacred Scripture might teach can be changed or nullified by a scholarly decision to change the text, or to remove a part of the text. Some scholars have gone so far as to suggest removing the last half of John 6, the ending of Mark's Gospel, the story of the woman caught in adultery in John 8, as well as various other verses and parts of verses (some of which have been removed from recent editions of the Bible) in the Old and New Testaments. Once scholars are given control over the Canon, to remove whatever they wish, in contradiction to the decisions of the above-cited Councils, the authority of

---

[132] First Vatican Council, Chapter 2, On Revelation.
[133] Second Vatican Council, Dei Verbum, n. 11.

Sacred Scripture is quickly eroded, since any verse or passage might later be removed, or changed in meaning by the removal of a portion of the passage.

And as a result, scholars are placed above the Magisterium. For the Magisterium teaches the truths found in Sacred Tradition and Sacred Scripture.[134] But if scholars can determine and change the content of Sacred Scripture, then they are in effect above the Magisterium. When the Magisterium teaches a truth from Sacred Scripture, the scholar might claim that the teaching is incorrect because the passage of Sacred Scripture is to be altered by removal of some portion, or by removal of the entire section. Therefore, the teaching of the Council of Trent, and of subsequent Councils, which affirms that the Canon of Sacred Scripture includes all the books, in their entirety, with all their parts, as found in the old Latin Vulgate Bible, is not only true and wise and prudent, but also necessary to protect the Faith itself from erosion and ruin. The idea that the majority opinion of scholars should prevail over the definitive teaching of the Magisterium in an Ecumenical Council is an heretical idea.

And the dropping of any verse, or of any significant part of a verse, implies that the Canon is open, which is contrary to the teaching of the Church. The Canon of Sacred Scripture is closed. Therefore, no verses or parts of verses can be added, and no verses or parts of verses can be removed. To remove any verse or substantial part of any verse implies the heretical claim that the Canon is open.

The temporal authority of the Church approves of Bible translations; but the infallible Magisterium of three Councils has taught that the Canon is closed. This Canon consists of the books, named by Trent and found in the old Latin Vulgate, in their entirety with all their parts. If we accept that verses can be dropped, because that some editions with dropped verses have the approval of the temporal authority of the Church, then we are in effect claiming that the temporal authority can nullify or overrule the infallible teaching authority; such a claim is also a heresy.

Therefore, no matter how many scholars agree, and no matter what reasons they offer to support their claim, no passage or verse, nor any meaningful portion of any verse, however brief, may be removed from the Canon of Sacred Scripture, if it is found in the old Latin Vulgate.

.135. The letter versus the spirit of Sacred Scripture

Sacred Scripture is lived. If all the written books of the Bible disappeared from the world, Sacred Scripture would still exist in the lives of all the faithful. The Holy Spirit inspired the human authors of Scripture, and He inspired the written words themselves, and He continues to protect the Sacred Deposit of Faith, in both Sacred Tradition and Sacred Scripture, as it is passed on from generation to generation. But what is inspired is not mere letters, but the truths expressed by the letters. And these truths must be lived by the faithful in order to enliven the Church. For the text of Sacred Scripture is not an object to be dissected and manipulated by scientific or scholarly study. Instead, these written words are an

---

[134] Second Vatican Council, Dei Verbum, n. 10.

expression by the Holy Spirit of the Living Word, the Second Person of the Most Holy Trinity. And the truths taught by means of these inspired words must be lived in order to accomplish the purpose of salvation intended by God the Father.

The words of Sacred Scripture are a reflection of Christ; they are a representation of Him; they teach truths from Him. These truths were written by the Holy Spirit; they are like one Word uttered by God, like the Son uttered by the Father.

The sacred authors, writing under inspiration of the Holy Spirit, wrote all those things and only those things that God willed. And these inspired and inerrant writings are not only inerrant in the original manuscripts. For no original manuscripts have survived to the present day. If inerrancy were limited to the original manuscripts, then inerrancy would not have survived to the present day. To the contrary, the inerrant truths expressed in Sacred Scripture were not lost with the original manuscripts. For the Holy Spirit protects both Sacred Tradition and Sacred Scripture, the one Sacred Deposit of Faith, as it is transmitted from generation to generation. Therefore, no truths are lost or changed, and no falsehoods are added, to either Sacred Tradition or Sacred Scripture.

Bible copyists, translators, and editors do not act under inspiration. And since inerrancy follows from inspiration, their work is not inerrant. Any particular edition of the Bible may have errors particular to that edition, errors introduced by a copyist (or printer in modern times) or translator or editor. But this type of error is not of Sacred Scripture itself, and does not harm inerrancy, since by comparison with other editions such particular errors can be detected. When Sacred Tradition is transmitted from generation to generation, the means of transmission is by the words and deeds of fallible sinners. Yet the Holy Spirit protects the truths of Sacred Tradition itself, so that this transmission by means of us poor sinners does no harm to the truths of the Sacred Deposit of Faith. Similarly, when Sacred Scripture is transmitted from generation to generation by various copies, translations, and editions of the Bible, the means of transmission is the fallible work of sinners. Yet the Holy Spirit protects the truths of Sacred Scripture itself, so that this transmission by means of us poor sinners does no harm to the truths of the Sacred Deposit of Faith.

.136. The Magisterium

The Magisterium is the ability and authority of the Church to teach the revealed truths found in the Deposit of Faith, as well as the truths found in natural law. The Deposit of Faith consists solely of Sacred Tradition and Sacred Scripture, which is Divine Revelation from God. Everything taught by Tradition or Scripture is entirely true and infallible. The Magisterium is a gift to the whole Church, but is exercised only by the Pope and the Bishops.

The Pope and the Bishops, in exercising the gift of the Magisterium, use both faith and reason in order to teach the revealed truths of Sacred Tradition and Sacred Scripture. Any truth found explicitly or implicitly in Sacred Tradition or Sacred Scripture may be taught by the Magisterium. The implicit truths have a necessary connection with the explicit truths. The implicit truths are not readily apparent, but are necessarily implied by the explicitly stated, or readily apparent, truths. The implicit truths have a necessary connection with Revelation; they are strictly and intimately connected with Revelation. They are contained in Divine Revelation in the sense that Sacred Tradition and Sacred Scripture necessarily imply these truths. For example, Sacred Scripture does not explicitly teach the doctrines of the Immaculate Conception and of the Assumption, but these truths are nevertheless necessarily implied by what is explicitly stated about the role of Mary as the Mother of our Savior, and about salvation through Him.

The Magisterium can also teach the truths found in natural law. However, all truths found in natural law, which are certainly accessible to reason alone, are also found in the Sacred Deposit of Faith. And all these truths are more easily attained and more profoundly understood through faith and reason applied to Divine Revelation, than through reason applied to nature (to all Creation) alone.

Pope Paul VI: "No member of the faithful could possibly deny that the Church is competent in her magisterium to interpret the natural moral law. It is in fact indisputable, as Our predecessors have many times declared, that Jesus Christ, when He communicated His divine power to Peter and the other Apostles and sent them to teach all nations His commandments, constituted them as the authentic guardians and interpreters of the whole moral law, not only, that is, of the law of the Gospel but also of the natural law. For the natural law, too, declares the will of God, and its faithful observance is necessary for men's eternal salvation."[135]

.137. The one Magisterium may be exercised in either of two ways, infallibly under the Sacred Magisterium, or non-infallibly under the Ordinary Magisterium. The teaching of the Magisterium is always either infallible or non-infallible, never fallible. All non-infallible teachings have only a limited possibility of error. The errors that are possible are more than trivial or insignificant. But in no case and at no time is the Magisterium capable of teaching an error or a set of errors which, individually or together, would lead the faithful away from the path of salvation.

All infallible teachings of the Magisterium have no possibility of error. These infallible teachings are irreformable, because all of these teachings are entirely true, and are a reflection of that eternal unchanging truth that is God. God is eternal and unchanging Truth. Therefore, the infallible teachings of the Magisterium cannot be changed or nullified; they are expressions of eternal truth. Everything taught under the ability and authority of the Sacred Magisterium is entirely true and infallible.

The Sacred Magisterium can never be exercised under any circumstances whatsoever apart from the Pope. Even if all the Bishops of the Church agree on a matter of faith or morals, apart from the Roman Pontiff who is the head of the body of Bishops, they cannot exercise the infallible Sacred Magisterium. Any group of Bishops by themselves, and each individual Bishop, can only exercise the non-infallible Ordinary Magisterium.

---

[135] Pope Paul VI, Humanae Vitae, n. 4.

.138. The infallible Sacred Magisterium can be exercised in any of three ways.

I. Papal Infallibility

The Pope has, in and of himself, by virtue of his office, the full ability and authority of the Sacred Magisterium. Therefore, the Pope can exercise the Sacred Magisterium without the participation of any of the Bishops. The criteria under which the Pope exercises Papal Infallibility are five, as defined and taught by the First and Second Vatican Councils.

First Vatican Council:

1. "the Roman Pontiff"
2. "speaks ex cathedra" ("that is, when in the discharge of his office as shepherd and teacher of all Christians, and by virtue of his supreme apostolic authority….")
3. "he defines"
4. "that a doctrine concerning faith or morals"
5. "must be held by the whole Church"[136]

Second Vatican Council:

1. "the Roman Pontiff"
2. "in virtue of his office, when as the supreme shepherd and teacher of all the faithful, who confirms his brethren in their faith (cf. Lk 22:32),"
3. "by a definitive act, he proclaims"
4. "a doctrine of faith or morals" ("And this infallibility…in defining doctrine of faith and morals, extends as far as the deposit of revelation extends")
5. "in accordance with revelation itself, which all are obliged to abide by and be in conformity with"[137]

Whenever the teaching of the Roman Pontiff falls short of meeting all of these criteria, then his teaching is non-infallible. If anyone claims that the teaching of the Pope is always infallible regardless of these criteria, or that his teaching is infallible under a greater or lesser set of conditions, then he contradicts the infallible definition of the First Vatican Council on Papal Infallibility, and he falls under the anathema of the Council.

First Vatican Council: "If anyone, God forbid, should presume to contradict this our definition, let him be anathema."[138]

II. Ecumenical Councils (the body of Bishops gathered with the Pope as their head)

It is not necessary for every Bishop to participate in order for a such a gathering to exercise the infallible Sacred Magisterium. However, the body of Bishops must be sufficiently represented. A gathering of local Bishops from only one nation or one area would not be representative of the body of Bishops and of the

---

[136] First Vatican Council, Pastor Aeternus, chapter 4.
[137] Second Vatican Council, Lumen Gentium, n. 25.
[138] First Vatican Council, Pastor Aeternus, chapter 4.

universal Church which they authoritatively teach and guide. All such gatherings must occur under the authority, teaching, and guidance of the Pope. No matter how many Bishops gather together, and no matter what they say, the Bishops cannot exercise the Sacred Magisterium apart from the Pope. For the Pope has a special charism from God to oversee the Bishops whenever they exercise the Sacred Magisterium. Without such oversight, the Bishops cannot exercise any type of infallibility under the Magisterium.

.139. An Ecumenical Council is the body of Bishops with the Pope as their head. Each and every valid Ecumenical Council possesses the full authority given by Christ to the Pope and the body of Bishops. Therefore, a Council can exercise both the teaching authority and the temporal authority. And the teaching authority may be exercised by a Council either infallibly or non-infallibly. The temporal decisions of a Council are not teachings; they are decisions of the prudential order on matters of discipline, not doctrine. Such decisions are changeable and revocable. A Council's non-infallible teachings, like all non-infallible teachings, have a limited possibility of error, and so also have a limited possibility of reform. A Council's infallible teachings, like all infallible teachings, have no possibility of error and are irreformable.

The Pope is not personally infallible; rather, it is his teaching that is infallible when it meets certain criteria. Similarly, Ecumenical Councils are not in and of themselves infallible; rather, it is their teaching that is infallible when it meets certain criteria. Although there is no formal definition telling us when a Council is teaching infallibly, we can apply the criteria of papal infallibility, with slight modification, to the infallibility exercised by a Council.

1. the body of bishops gathered with the Pope as their head
2. speak ex cathedra (by their office as shepherds and teachers of the Church)
3. they define
4. that a doctrine concerning faith or morals
5. must be held by the whole Church

Not every teaching of every Council is infallible. This is particularly clear in the more ancient councils, when infallible teachings were distinguished as separate Canons with attached anathemas for those who would reject the teaching. But there were also various teachings that were non-infallible, such as the introductory material before a set of infallible Canons, and various exhortations to holiness, outside of the infallible Canons.
.140.
III. The Universal Magisterium (i.e. the ordinary and universal Magisterium)

Second Vatican Council: "Although the individual bishops do not enjoy the prerogative of infallibility, they nevertheless proclaim Christ's doctrine infallibly whenever, even though dispersed through the world, but still maintaining the bond of communion among themselves and with the successor of Peter, and authentically teaching matters of faith and morals, they are in agreement on one position as definitively to be held."[139]

---

[139] Second Vatican Council, Lumen Gentium, n. 25.

This particular type of exercise of the Sacred Magisterium is often called 'ordinary and universal' because it takes place in the course of the daily teaching and witness of the Bishops dispersed throughout the world yet united with the Pope, and not in the course of a particular gathering or a particular document. First, many Bishops, individually or in local groups, in various ways, at various times, exercise the non-infallible Ordinary Magisterium on a particular point of doctrine. Eventually, this non-infallible teaching becomes taught universally, both by Bishops throughout the world, and by the Pope as their head. When such a teaching, which initially was taught under the non-infallible Ordinary Magisterium, is finally taught definitively by the Bishops dispersed through the world and by the Roman Pontiff as the head of the Bishops, then this ordinary teaching becomes a universal teaching, and therefore infallible. For the whole body of Bishops led by the Pope cannot err when they are in agreement on one position of faith and morals definitively to be held by all the faithful.

The Universal Magisterium is exercised when the Bishops dispersed through the world, and the Pope also, teach one and the same doctrine, from the Deposit of Faith, as a required belief for all the faithful. Such an exercise occurs over time within the daily preaching and witness of the Bishops and the Pope. It may find various written expressions in various times and forms, but those particular expressions are not themselves an infallible exercise of the Sacred Magisterium. The universality of such a definitive teaching is what moves the teaching from falling initially under the non-infallible Ordinary Magisterium to fall finally under the infallible Sacred Magisterium.

The Universal Magisterium cannot be exercised apart from the Pope because the Pope is the head of the body of Bishops. If no Pope has ever taught or witnessed to a particular teaching, then it is not a teaching of the Universal Magisterium, nor does it fall under any exercise of the Sacred Magisterium.

.141. Infallibility and the Full Assent of Faith

Pope John Paul II summarized the three ways that the Magisterium teaches infallibly in talk he gave to the U.S. Bishops. The phrase *charisma veritatis certum* means a 'charism of certain truth.' In other words, the Magisterium has a divine gift to be able to know and teach the truth with certitude, i.e. infallibly. I've added my numbering of the three modes of infallibility in brackets in the quote below.

Pope John Paul II: "This magisterium is not above the divine word but serves it with a specific *charisma veritatis certum*, which includes the charism of infallibility, present not only in [1] the solemn definitions of the Roman Pontiff and [2] of Ecumenical Councils, but also in the [3] universal ordinary magisterium, which can truly be considered as the usual expression of the Church's infallibility."[140]

All infallible teachings required the full assent of faith.

---

[140] Address of Pope John Paul II to the Bishops from the United States on their 'Ad Limina' visit, 15 October 1988, n. 4.

Cardinal Ratzinger: "When the Magisterium of the Church makes an infallible pronouncement and solemnly declares that a teaching is found in Revelation, the assent called for is that of theological faith. This kind of adherence is to be given even to the teaching of the ordinary and universal Magisterium when it proposes for belief a teaching of faith as divinely revealed."[141]

First Vatican Council: "Therefore, by divine and catholic faith all those things are to be believed which are contained in the Word of God as found in Scripture and Tradition, and which are proposed by the Church as matters to be believed as divinely revealed, whether by her solemn judgment or in her ordinary and universal magisterium."[142]

The solemn judgment of the Magisterium refers to solemn definitions by a Pope or by an Ecumenical Council. All such solemn definitions of doctrine on matters of faith and morals are infallible. In addition, the teachings of the Universal Magisterium are infallible. And all infallible teachings must be believed with theological faith, that is, with divine and catholic faith.

Canon Law quotations are from the Code of Canon Law for the Latin Church, unless otherwise stated.[143]

Canon 750, n. 1. "A person must believe with divine and Catholic faith all those things contained in the word of God, written or handed on, that is, in the one deposit of faith entrusted to the Church, and at the same time proposed as divinely revealed either by the solemn magisterium of the Church or by its ordinary and universal magisterium which is manifested by the common adherence of the Christian faithful under the leadership of the sacred magisterium; therefore all are bound to avoid any doctrines whatsoever contrary to them."

Canon 751 "Heresy is the obstinate denial or obstinate doubt after the reception of baptism of some truth which is to be believed by divine and Catholic faith; apostasy is the total repudiation of the Christian faith; schism is the refusal of submission to the Supreme Pontiff or of communion with the members of the Church subject to him."

Canon 1364, n. 1. "... an apostate from the faith, a heretic, or a schismatic incurs a latae sententiae excommunication.... n. 2. If contumacy [obstinacy; refusal to submit to authority] of long duration or the gravity of scandal demands it, other penalties can be added, including dismissal from the clerical state."

All infallible teachings must be believed with the full assent of faith, i.e. by an exercise of the theological virtue of faith. Otherwise, the baptized person falls into the sin of formal heresy and under its penalties.

---

[141] Cardinal Ratzinger, Instruction on the Ecclesial Vocation of the Theologian, n. 23.
[142] First Vatican Council, Chapter 3, On faith.
[143] Code of Canon Law for the Latin Church, first promulgated in 1983. http://www.vatican.va/archive/

Second Vatican Council: "In matters of faith and morals, the bishops speak in the name of Christ and the faithful are to accept their teaching and adhere to it with a religious assent. This religious submission of mind and will must be shown in a special way to the authentic magisterium of the Roman Pontiff, even when he is not speaking ex cathedra...."[144]

.142. All non-infallible teachings require the religious submission of will and intellect. Since non-infallible teachings are non-irreformable, and are subject to a limited possibility of error, the full assent of faith is not required. The assent required by non-infallible teachings is religious assent, which differs by type and degree.

Individual Bishops cannot teach infallibly, but they can teach non-infallibly, and so their teaching requires religious assent. This same assent must be shown in a special way, i.e. to a higher degree, to the non-infallible teachings of the Pope.

Canon 750, n. 2. "Each and every thing which is proposed definitively by the magisterium of the Church concerning the doctrine of faith and morals, that is, each and every thing which is required to safeguard reverently and to expound faithfully the same deposit of faith, is also to be firmly embraced and retained; therefore, one who rejects those propositions which are to be held definitively is opposed to the doctrine of the Catholic Church."

The rejection of a non-infallible teaching is not the sin of heresy. A Catholic who rejects a non-infallible teaching is opposing a doctrine of the Church. But heresy only occurs when the teaching being opposed is an infallible teaching.

Canon 752 "Although not an assent of faith, a religious submission of the intellect and will must be given to a doctrine which the Supreme Pontiff or the college of bishops declares concerning faith or morals when they exercise the authentic magisterium, even if they do not intend to proclaim it by definitive act; therefore, the Christian faithful are to take care to avoid those things which do not agree with it."

Canon 753 "Although the bishops who are in communion with the head and members of the college, whether individually or joined together in conferences of bishops or in particular councils, do not possess infallibility in teaching, they are authentic teachers and instructors of the faith for the Christian faithful entrusted to their care; the Christian faithful are bound to adhere with religious submission of mind to the authentic magisterium of their bishops."

Whenever a teaching is non-infallible, the type and degree of assent required is not the full assent of faith, but the lesser degree and different type of assent called the religious submission of intellect and will. The full assent of faith is required for infallible teachings because these teachings are certainly true, and are important to salvation. The religious submission of will and intellect is required for non-infallible teachings, despite the possibility of error, because the errors possible are limited and because the teachings are helpful to salvation.

---

[144] Second Vatican Council, Lumen Gentium, n. 25.

.143. The Ordinary Magisterium

Any teaching of the Magisterium that does not fall under the infallible Sacred Magisterium necessarily falls under the non-infallible Ordinary Magisterium. The term non-infallible means that these teachings admit a limited possibility of error, but never to such an extent that any error or set of errors could lead the faithful away from the path of salvation.

Pope John Paul II: "With respect to the non-infallible expressions of the authentic magisterium of the Church, these should be received with religious submission of mind and will."[145]

Cardinal Ratzinger: "When the Magisterium, not intending to act 'definitively', teaches a doctrine to aid a better understanding of Revelation and make explicit its contents, or to recall how some teaching is in conformity with the truths of faith, or finally to guard against ideas that are incompatible with these truths, the response called for is that of the religious submission of will and intellect. This kind of response cannot be simply exterior or disciplinary but must be understood within the logic of faith and under the impulse of obedience to the faith."[146]

The non-infallible teachings of the Magisterium have a limited possibility of error. The errors that are possible in non-infallible teachings are limited such that no error or set of errors can possibly lead the faithful away from the path of salvation. The non-infallible teachings of the Magisterium are non-irreformable.[147] They can contain errors, and those errors can and eventually will be corrected. But all non-infallible teachings have only a limited possibility of error, and so they have only a limited ability to be reformed (changed). The limit of the possibility of error sets the limit of the possibility of reform.

Any individual Bishop, or the Pope, or any gathering of Bishops (with or without the Pope) can exercise the non-infallible Ordinary Magisterium. Even though the Pope has the ability to teach infallibly under papal infallibility, he most often teaches under the non-infallible Ordinary Magisterium. Even though Ecumenical Councils and similar gatherings have the ability to teach infallibly, they also can and do teach, to one extent or another, under the non-infallible Ordinary Magisterium.

.144. The letter versus the spirit of Magisterial teachings

The teachings of the Magisterium are not merely a set of written doctrines; there are explicit teachings given in writing, but there are also teachings that are implicit in those writings. More importantly, the teachings of the Magisterium are lived by the faithful. Even without any documents of the Magisterium, as was the case in the early Church, the Magisterium is exercised by the Pope and the Bishops, and these teachings of the Magisterium are lived by the faithful.

---

[145] Address of Pope John Paul II to the Bishops from the United States on their 'Ad Limina' visit, 15 October 1988, n. 5.
[146] Cardinal Ratzinger, Instruction on the Ecclesial Vocation of the Theologian, n. 23.
[147] Cardinal Ratzinger, Instruction on the Ecclesial Vocation of the Theologian, n. 28.

The spirit of the Magisterial teachings is found in the truths of the Magisterium expressed by the written word, and the truths of the Magisterium implied by the written words, and in the truths of the Magisterium lived by the faithful. No one who believes only the written letter will even be able to properly understand those written explicit teachings. For the truths of the Faith taught by the Magisterium are understood not so much by reading about those truths, but by living those truths. And in order to live these explicit written teachings, we must also perceive and accept all that is implied by those written teachings. Otherwise, we could never apply the teachings of the Magisterium to the particular circumstances of our daily lives.

Neither is it possible to live the teachings of the Magisterium, explicit and implicit, without also accepting and living the teachings of Sacred Tradition and Sacred Scripture. The faithful have always learned the truths of the faith from Sacred Tradition, and from Sacred Scripture, and from the Magisterium, not from any one or two of these three alone. And how would the Christians of the early Church have known the Faith, if they could only wait for the letter of Magisterial teachings to be issued? They would have been unable to live as Christians if they did not learn the truths of the Faith, not only from the Magisterium, but also directly from Sacred Tradition and Sacred Scripture.

And so it is a grievous error against the Sacred Deposit of Faith to consider that the teachings of the Catholic Church are only the teachings of the Magisterium, and not also all the teachings explicit and implicit, of both Sacred Tradition and Sacred Scripture. For the Church truly possesses, as a gift from God for all humanity, this Deposit of Divine Revelation, which consists solely of Sacred Tradition and Sacred Scripture. These truths, held in trust by the Church, are expressed in a threefold manner, in Sacred Tradition and in Sacred Scripture and by the Magisterium. To reduce the source of truth from these three to only one, the Magisterium, is analogous to reducing the Trinity to One Person. Those who believe only in the teachings of the Magisterium, and not also in the teachings of Tradition and Scripture, commit much the same error as the Protestants, who believe only in Sacred Scripture, and not also in Tradition and the Magisterium.

.145. The Unity of Tradition, Scripture, Magisterium

Second Vatican Council: "Sacred tradition and Sacred Scripture form one sacred deposit of the word of God, committed to the Church. Holding fast to this deposit the entire holy people united with their shepherds remain always steadfast in the teaching of the Apostles, in the common life, in the breaking of the bread and in prayers (see Acts 2:42, Greek text), so that holding to, practicing and professing the heritage of the faith, it becomes on the part of the bishops and faithful a single common effort."

"But the task of authentically interpreting the word of God, whether written or handed on, has been entrusted exclusively to the living teaching office of the Church, whose authority is exercised in the name of Jesus Christ. This teaching office is not above the word of God, but serves it, teaching only what has been handed on, listening to it devoutly, guarding it scrupulously and explaining it faithfully in accord with a divine commission and with the help of the Holy Spirit, it draws from this one deposit of faith everything which it presents for belief as divinely revealed."

"It is clear, therefore, that sacred tradition, Sacred Scripture and the teaching authority of the Church, in accord with God's most wise design, are so linked and joined together that one cannot stand without the others, and that all together and each in its own way under the action of the one Holy Spirit contribute effectively to the salvation of souls."[148]

The Protestant error of sola scriptura, that is, of basing the teachings of the faith on Sacred Scripture alone, has two companion errors, found in those who adhere to Tradition apart from Scripture and Magisterium, and in those who adhere solely to the teachings of the Magisterium, apart from Tradition and Scripture. The true Catholic Faith is based on Sacred Tradition, Sacred Scripture, and the Living Magisterium. All those who reject any one or two of these three, and all those who severely denigrate one or two of these three, have fallen into a grievous heresy, which undermines all other teachings. For the truths of Divine Revelation are secured by these three pillars: Sacred Tradition, Sacred Scripture, and the Magisterium. If any of these three pillars are absent or substantially shortened, then the Faith will topple to the ground in ruins.

---

[148] Second Vatican Council, Dei Verbum, n. 10, in its entirety.

Chapter 12
Doctrine and Discipline

.146.
Discipline is not Doctrine

The Church has two types of authority, the teaching authority, called the Magisterium, which teaches doctrine, and the temporal authority, which issues rules and rulings. There are two types of decisions made by the Church: decisions on doctrine by the teaching authority, and decisions on discipline (rules and rulings) by the temporal authority. The teaching authority teaches on matters of faith and morals. The temporal authority makes judgments of the prudential order, generally requiring an evaluation of particular circumstances. Temporal decisions pertain to the particulars of person, time, and place, and not specifically to teachings on faith or morals. A judgment by the temporal authority on a matter of discipline is usually based on, or related in some way, to doctrines on faith and morals. But the two types of authority are distinct.

The doctrines of the Church on morals are truths of the unchanging eternal moral law. These truths on morals are not able to be changed, nor does anyone have the authority to make exceptions to the eternal moral law. For the eternal moral law is the unchanging Justice of God. There are no exceptions to any of the truths of the moral law on just acts and sinful acts, on good and evil. That which is good will always be good, and that which is evil will always be evil. Acts that offend God will always be immoral, and acts that please God will always be moral. For God is unchanging eternal Goodness. Even Christ cannot change the Nature of God, which is His own Divine Nature, and so even Christ cannot change the eternal moral law.

The doctrines of the Church on matters of faith, morals, and salvation are unchanging eternal truths. All these truths are given to the Church in Divine Revelation, the Sacred Deposit of Faith, also called the Word of God, which is comprised solely of Sacred Tradition and Sacred Scripture. But all of Divine Revelation is an expression of the Living Word, the Second Person of the Most Holy Trinity. And the Trinity is eternal and unchanging Truth.

However, the disciplines of the Church, the practices, rules, and rulings of the temporal authority of the Church, are changeable. The Church has two types of authority, the teaching authority (called the Magisterium) and the temporal authority. The teaching authority issues doctrines on faith, morals, and salvation. The temporal authority issues rules and rulings; the temporal authority governs the practices of the Church. The teaching authority of the Church teaches either infallibly (no possibility of error) or non-infallibly (limited possibility of error). But the temporal authority of the Church does not teach, and so its temporal decisions are fallible. The decisions of the temporal authority can never be infallible because these decisions are not teachings of truth; infallibility pertains to truth.

As a result, the practices (whether established by law or by custom), and rules (laws of the temporal authority, not the moral law), and rulings (judgments in particular cases) of the Church can be changed; they can be added to, subtracted from, or dispensed entirely. Such a change or dispensation can apply to particular persons or situations, or can apply generally. A dispensation from a temporal law can be temporary, or can continue indefinitely. The disciplines of the Church are temporal, not eternal like the moral law, and they can be changed in various ways, or they can be nullified entirely. These are not doctrines of truth, which can never change. God is Truth and God is unchanging; therefore, truths never change. But God is not practices, rules, and rulings, and so the disciplines of the Church may change. Even the Old Testament temporal laws (e.g. dietary laws, animals sacrifices, etc.), which were established by Divine Revelation from God directly to the Jewish people, are not eternal, are not unchangeable, and have been dispensed by Christ. All practices, rules, rulings, and the like, which are not direct expressions of the moral law, are changeable and dispensable.

.147. The Temporal Authority of the Church

[Matthew]
{28:18} And Jesus, drawing near, spoke to them, saying: "All authority has been given to me in heaven and on earth.
{28:19} Therefore, go forth and teach all nations, baptizing them in the name of the Father and of the Son and of the Holy Spirit,
{28:20} teaching them to observe all that I have ever commanded you. And behold, I am with you always, even to the consummation of the age."

Jesus Christ has been given "all authority in heaven and on earth" by the Father. It should be clear to reason alone that God has authority over all Creation, including heaven, angels, the material universe, all living things, all humanity. Therefore, God has authority over all of human society, over every nation, government, business, and family, over every group of human persons and every individual human person. And since Christ is God, Jesus Christ has this same authority, given to Him by the Father (John 5:18-27).

Pope Boniface VIII: "Urged by faith, we are obliged to believe and to hold that there is One Holy Catholic and truly Apostolic Church. And this we firmly believe and simply confess: outside of Her, there is neither salvation, nor the remission of sins, just as the Bridegroom in the Canticles proclaims: 'One is my dove, my perfect one. One is her mother; elect is she who bore her.' [Canticles 6:8]. And this represents the one mystical body, whose head is Christ, and truly God [is the head] of Christ. [1 Corinthians 11:3] In Her, there is one Lord, one faith, one baptism. [Ephesians 4:5]"[149]

---

[149] Pope Boniface VIII, Unam Sanctam, 18 November 1302; author's translation of the Latin, n. 1. Primary source for Latin text:
Cardinal Henry Edward Manning, (Archbishop of Westminster, England), The Vatican Decrees in their Bearing on Civil Allegiance, (Catholic Publication Society: New York, 1875), p. 172-173.

The Church is no mere collection of human persons, but a Divine Institution, which is made truly Divine by having the Son of God as her head and the Spirit of God as her life and guide. The Church is not the body of the faithful alone, but the body of the faithful with Jesus Christ as their head. The body is not separated from the head, for then it would be dead. The Church is not merely the body of Christ, but the body united to Christ, the head. Therefore, the authority possessed by the Church is the full authority of Christ, because Christ is the head of the Church.

Pope Boniface VIII: "We are instructed in the Gospel sayings that in Her and within Her power, there are two swords, specifically, the spiritual and the temporal. For the Apostles say, 'Behold, there are two swords here,' that is, in the Church. But when the Apostles were speaking, the Lord did not respond, 'it is too much,' but 'it is sufficient.' [Luke 22:38] Certainly, whoever denies that the temporal sword is in the power of Peter, misunderstands the word of the Lord, saying: 'Put your sword into its sheath.' [Matthew 26:52]"[150]

Now this full authority can be divided into two types, spiritual and temporal. The spiritual authority of the Church is the teaching authority, also called the Magisterium. But this Magisterium possesses both the authority to teach and the ability to teach. And this ability is of the Holy Spirit, who enlivens and guides the Magisterium, as well as the whole Church. For we adhere to the teachings of the Magisterium not only because they are authoritative, but most of all because they are true. And it is the truth of these teachings that gives the teachings their authority. For Christ is Truth, and so the teachings of His Church have the authority of Truth.

The temporal authority of the Church does not teach truth, but instead makes decisions of the prudential order, i.e. rules and rulings. The decisions that fall under the temporal authority of the Church include Canon Law, rules for religious orders, norms for liturgical services, rules about indulgences, rulings in particular cases in dioceses and in the Church more broadly, and the like. For the Church not only teaches, but She also governs, since She has both types of authority given to Her by Christ, the spiritual and the temporal.

Now the temporal authority, in principle, is not limited to merely governing the institution of the Church, as if the Church were merely one of many institutions among men. The temporal authority of Christ extends over all Creation, including all humanity. Therefore, the Church in truth has both spiritual and temporal authority over all human persons, and over all of society, even over those portions of society which do not acknowledge Her authority. For Christ is God, and God has chosen the one Church to be the sole source of salvation for the whole world.

Christ Himself exercised both the teaching authority and the temporal authority. His teaching authority is clear to any reader of the Gospels. And the crowds, those who heard Him speak in person, also perceived this teaching authority.

---

[150] Pope Boniface VIII, Unam Sanctam, 18 November 1302; author's translation of the Latin, n. 4.

[Matthew]
{7:28} And it happened, when Jesus had completed these words, that the crowds were astonished at his doctrine.
{7:29} For he was teaching them as one who has authority, and not like their scribes and Pharisees.

But Christ also exercised the temporal authority. For example, when He sent out the Twelve (Matthew 10:9-10), He gave some rules to them for the journey; and similarly again, when He sent out the seventy-two (Luke 10:4-5), He did the same. These rules have never been understood by the Church as teachings of the eternal moral law, but rather as practical decisions to address the particulars of time and place. And this same type of authority is also exercised by the Church, when She makes rules for religious orders, for priests and deacons, and for the laity, as to how they will proceed along their journey with Christ.

.148. Of these two authorities, the teaching authority is more important than the temporal authority. For Christ Himself placed teachings above rulings, even though He has full authority to rule over all Creation. And His use of His teaching authority during His Ministry far exceeded His use of His temporal authority. So it is that the Church most often prefers to correct sinners by teaching, rather than by making rules or by dispensing penalties. But in truth the Church has both types of authority.

Now this doctrine of the two types of authority is found in Sacred Scripture. The two swords of Peter represent these two types of authority given to the Church, the spiritual (teaching) authority and the temporal authority.[151]

[Luke]
{22:38} So they said, "Lord, behold, there are two swords here." But he said to them, "It is sufficient."

[John]
{18:10} Then Simon Peter, having a sword, drew it, and he struck the servant of the high priest, and he cut off his right ear. Now the name of the servant was Malchus.
{18:11} Therefore, Jesus said to Peter: "Set your sword into the scabbard. Should I not drink the chalice which my Father has given to me?"

Sacred Scripture, as explained by Pope Boniface VIII, teaches that the Church has two types of authority, spiritual and temporal.[152] It has long been the case that some persons, particularly in secular society, deny that the Church has any temporal authority over society in general, over nations, over non-Catholics. But the Pope teaches that anyone who denies that this temporal sword is in the power of the Church, and especially in the power of the visible head of the Church on earth, Peter and his successors, is contradicting the words of the Lord.

---

[151] See also: Johann Peter Kirsch, Unam Sanctam, The Catholic Encyclopedia, Vol. 15. (New York: Robert Appleton Company, 1912).
[152] Pope Boniface VIII, Unam Sanctam, n. 4.

Even some Catholics in effect deny the temporal authority of the Church when they treat all rules and rulings, all decisions of the prudential order, as if these proceed from the Magisterium, as if the Church has only the authority of the Magisterium and not also the temporal authority. Then this fundamental error leads to other errors, such as treating discipline as if it were doctrine, such as berating fellow Catholics who believe and live the doctrines of the Faith but have transgressed only relatively minor points of discipline, or such as thinking that they are saved by exterior actions, without interior cooperation with grace. The error of not acknowledging that the Church has two distinct types of authority may also lead to the error of concluding that all temporal decisions are infallible. But in truth only the spiritual authority (i.e. the teaching authority called the Magisterium) can teach infallibly, or non-infallibly. The temporal authority does not teach at all, but only acts by judgment and reason; the temporal authority is fallible and can err. But this is not acknowledged by those Catholics who deny that the Church has two swords, or who do not distinguish between the two.

.149. The Church has both spiritual authority and temporal authority over the whole world, over heaven and earth, over all nations and all individuals, because Christ, as the Son of God, was given this authority by the Father. The Church exercises this authority with Christ as Her head and with the Holy Spirit as Her guide. However, the Church chooses, in general, not to exercise, directly, her temporal authority over non-Catholics, and over secular governments, even in Catholic nations. Instead, She prefers to teach, rather than to rule; She prefers to exhort to holiness, rather than to dispense penalties. That is why Christ told Peter to place his sword into its scabbard. The temporal authority of the Church toward secular society is sheathed, at least to some extent.

Pope Boniface VIII: "Therefore, both are in the power of the Church, namely, the spiritual sword and the material. But indeed, the latter is to be exercised on behalf of the Church; and truly, the former is to be exercised by the Church. The former is of the priest; the latter is by the hand of kings and soldiers, but at the will and sufferance of the priest. Now one sword ought to be under the other sword, and so the temporal authority is to be subject to the spiritual authority. For though the Apostle said: 'there is no authority except from God and those who have been ordained by God,' [Romans 13:1] still they would not have been ordained unless one sword were under the other sword. And so what is inferior should be led forward by another, to what is highest. For, according to blessed Dionysius, it is a law of divine power that what is lowest is to be led forward by what is intermediate, to what is highest."[153]

Although the Church possesses both types of authority over all humanity, She permits secular governments to exercise temporal authority to a certain extent. But in principle (though governments often deny it), the Church still retains this authority; it is exercised, on behalf of the Church, by various secular authorities; and it should be exercised at the will and permission of the priest. Here the term priest refers, not primarily to the parish priest, but to the Pope, who is the high

---

[153] Pope Boniface VIII, Unam Sanctam, 18 November 1302; author's translation of the Latin, n. 4-5.

priest of the Church, and to the Bishops (for a Bishop is a kind of priest). So priest is used as a figure for the Church and her leaders, just as the phrase 'kings and soldiers' is used as a figure for secular authorities in general, including leaders who are neither kings nor soldiers. Pope Boniface taught that even the authority of secular society is derived from, and remains a part of, the authority of the Church.

And so, in principle, the Church exercises Her temporal authority over secular society through the secular leaders, that is, indirectly. And She exercises Her temporal authority over Herself and Her members directly (e.g. through Canon Law, liturgical norms, etc.). But the Church always exercises Her spiritual (teaching) authority directly, by the Pope and the Bishops. The Church never exercises her spiritual authority through secular authorities. For Saul was chosen by God to be the first king of Israel. And yet when even a king chosen by God acted as if he were a priest, his act was condemned by God (1 Samuel 13:7-14).

But at all times, no matter how the temporal authority is exercised, this temporal authority is subordinate to the spiritual (teaching) authority, because God is Truth, and the spiritual authority teaches doctrinal truths, which are a reflection of the very Nature of God. Certainly every good discipline is solidly based on doctrine. But this only further proves that discipline is subordinate to doctrine, since discipline is dependent on doctrine, and not the other way around.

In the present time, secular society exercises temporal authority, in the form of governments and laws, and, unfortunately, often does so with complete disregard for both the teaching authority and the temporal authority of the Church. However, in principle, every temporal authority, even in secular society, acts on behalf of the Church and under the power of the Church. And every secular authority ought to obey the Church, for Christ is the head of the Church, and the Father has given Him all authority in heaven and on earth.

.150. These two swords of Peter provide sufficient authority for the Church to accomplish all that God wills. Yet when Peter took a sword and struck with violence, Jesus commanded him to put his sword back into its sheath. On the literal level of meaning, Peter was not exercising any authority of the Church, but was acting rashly based on emotion, not based on faith or reason. But on the spiritual level of meaning, the figure of the sword and its use against someone who opposes the Church represents the use of the temporal authority of the Church against those who are outside the visible structure of the Church. The Church does in fact possess both spiritual and temporal authority over the whole world, over every nation and every human person. But in ordering Peter to sheath his temporal sword, Christ has in effect ordered the Church, generally speaking, not to exercise Her temporal authority, directly, over those who are outside the Church. And this is so that the Church, like Christ, would appeal to all humanity by grace and good works, by faith and reason, by teachings and exhortations, rather than by the temporal authority, which the Church truly possesses, but which they do not acknowledge.

Even so, the temporal authority of the Church is not sheathed with regard to Catholics throughout the world. It is the will of God for the Church to exercise both spiritual and temporal authority over all Catholics. This exercise of authority is seen in Canon Law, in decisions of the prudential order by the Holy See, and by Bishops' Conferences, and by local Bishops. But as clearly seen in the words and example of Christ, the Church must always place the teaching authority above the temporal authority. For when the disciples of Christ wanted to make Him king, so as to rule over them mainly by temporal authority, He fled from them.

[John]
{6:14} Therefore, those men, when they had seen that Jesus had accomplished a sign, they said, "Truly, this one is the Prophet who is to come into the world."
{6:15} And so, when he realized that they were going to come and take him away and make him king, Jesus fled back to the mountain, by himself alone.

Therefore, the Church must always place Her teaching authority above her temporal authority. For when Christ could have ruled more by commanding than by teaching, He fled. He did not merely walk away. He did not merely verbally correct these men who wanted Him to rule by temporal authority. He fled from them, so that He was alone. For Jesus Christ is Truth, but He is not rules and rulings. So teaching the truth is more important than issuing rulings and enforcing rules (though the latter is a practical necessity in many instances).

.151. These two types of authority held by the Church are sometimes represented under the figure of two swords, and other times under the figure of two keys. The symbol of two keys crossed, one gold and one silver, is found in the papal coat of arms of Popes Benedict XVI, John Paul II, John Paul I, Paul VI, John XXIII, Pius XII, and other Popes, as well as in the Vatican coat of arms and the Vatican flag. The gold key represents the spiritual authority, and the silver key represents the temporal authority. The figure of gold is used for the spiritual authority, as opposed to silver for the temporal authority, because the spiritual authority is more important than the temporal authority. However, the Church, and especially the Pope as the Vicar of Christ, has always possessed both types of authority.

Pope Boniface VIII: "And so, to whatever extent the spiritual power excels beyond the worldly, in both dignity and rank, we must, to the same extent, clearly admit that the spiritual surpasses the temporal."[154]

In imitation of Christ, and by His command to Peter to sheath his sword, instead of pressing secular society to obey her commands, the Church prudently sheaths her temporal sword with regard to those who are formally outside the Church (non-Catholics). She prefers to teach and to exhort them, appealing by reason and also by faith (to whatever extent they will accept teachings based on faith). She prefers not to assert her temporal authority over non-Catholics, offering the truth with humility and meekness. Nevertheless, it is an undeniable truth of the Catholic Faith that Christ has full authority over heaven and earth, including over all nations and all human persons, and that Christ has given both spiritual and temporal authority to the Church, authority exercised to the fullest extent by

---

[154] Pope Boniface VIII, Unam Sanctam, 18 November 1302; author's translation, n. 6.

Peter and his successors. For when Christ comes as Judge, He judges all nations and all persons, not merely Christians. And outside the Church, there is no salvation.

Pope Boniface VIII: "For truth is the witness that the spiritual authority holds [the ability] to establish the earthly authority, and to judge if it might not have been good. And this, concerning the Church and the authority of the Church, the prophecy of Jeremiah verifies: 'Behold, today I have appointed you over nations and kingdoms' [Jeremiah 1:10] and the rest that follows."[155]

Even though much of the world is non-Christian, Christ and His Church, with the Roman Pontiff as Her visible head representing Christ, has authority from God the Father over all nations and all human persons. And this authority includes not only the spiritual authority to teach, but also the temporal authority, to govern. And this governing extends to every nation and every human person, such that the Church truly has authority from God above all nations, which no nation has a right to ignore or to contradict. No claim of freedoms or rights, and no claim of separation of Church and State, can possibly supercede the authority that Christ, the Son of God, gave to His Church over all persons and all nations. For though the Church permits the State to be, in some sense and to some extent, separate, by this permission the Church does in no way and to no extent nullify or lessen Her true temporal authority over the State given irrevocably by God.

.152. An example of this permission of limited separation of Church and State is found in Pope Clement V's document 'Meruit,' which was also reiterated by the Fifth Lateran Council. That document allows the French government, and by implication other secular governments, to continue to govern over secular matters, with the assurance that the Church would continue along the path chosen by Her Savior, to keep her temporal sword sheathed in many respects. But in no way does this document, or others like it, nullify or lessen the temporal authority of the Church. The Church is merely acting as Pope Boniface VIII described, permitting kings and soldiers to exercise temporal authority over secular society on behalf of the Church, and at the will and sufferance of the Church.[156] Thus the Church exercises her spiritual authority directly, and She exercises her temporal authority both directly, over Her members and their actions, and indirectly, by means of secular governments over secular society.

Pope Boniface VIII: "Moreover, that every human creature is to be subject to the Roman pontiff, we declare, we state, we define, and we pronounce to be entirely from the necessity of salvation."[157]

This necessity for salvation does not imply that non-Catholics are not saved, but rather that the plan of God in salvation history gives an absolutely essential role to the Church and to the head of the Church on earth, the Pope, not only in the salvation of Catholics, but also in the salvation of all those who may be saved despite being formally outside the Church. For the Church, with Christ as Her

---

[155] Pope Boniface VIII, Unam Sanctam, 18 November 1302; author's translation, n. 6.
[156] Pope Boniface VIII, Unam Sanctam, 18 November 1302, n. 4.
[157] Pope Boniface VIII, Unam Sanctam, 18 November 1302.

head, is the only means of salvation by which human persons may be saved, including those before Christ became Incarnate, and those who remain as non-Catholics or as non-Christians after Christ died for our salvation. Even if they do not realize it, those who are visibly outside the Church are saved, by the mercy of God, through the Church, by being in some mystical and hidden manner within the Church. Outside the Church, there is no salvation; but wherever the Holy Spirit is, there is the Church.

Fourth Lateran Council: "There is indeed one universal church of the faithful, outside of which nobody at all is saved, in which Jesus Christ is both priest and sacrifice."[158]

Pope John Paul II: "Since Christ brings about salvation through his Mystical Body, which is the Church, the way of salvation is connected essentially with the Church. The axiom 'extra ecclesiam nulla salus' -- 'outside the Church there is no salvation' -- stated by St. Cyprian (Epist. 73, 21; PL 1123 AB), belongs to the Christian tradition. It was included in the Fourth Lateran Council (DS 802), in the Bull 'Unam Sanctam' of Boniface VIII (DS 870) and the Council of Florence (Decretum pro Jacobitis, DS 1351). The axiom means that for those who are not ignorant of the fact that the Church has been established as necessary by God through Jesus Christ, there is an obligation to enter the Church and remain in her in order to attain salvation (cf. LG 14). For those, however, who have not received the Gospel proclamation, as I wrote in the Encyclical 'Redemptoris Missio,' salvation is accessible in mysterious ways, inasmuch as divine grace is granted to them by virtue of Christ's redeeming sacrifice, without external membership in the Church, but nonetheless always in relation to her (cf. Redemptoris Missio, n. 10). It is a mysterious relationship. It is mysterious for those who receive the grace, because they do not know the Church and sometimes even outwardly reject her. It is also mysterious in itself, because it is linked to the saving mystery of grace, which includes an essential reference to the Church the Savior founded. In order to take effect, saving grace requires acceptance, cooperation, a 'yes' to the divine gift. This acceptance is, at least implicitly, oriented to Christ and the Church. Thus it can also be said that 'sine ecclesia nulla salus' -- 'without the Church there is no salvation.' Belonging to the Church, the Mystical Body of Christ, however implicitly and indeed mysteriously, is an essential condition for salvation."[159]

Pope Boniface VIII: "Moreover, that every human creature is to be subject to the Roman pontiff, we declare, we state, we define, and we pronounce to be entirely from the necessity of salvation."[160]

Now this pronouncement of Pope Boniface VIII is not a new idea; this Pope was the first to define the teaching formally, but the Church has always regarded the role of Peter and his successors as essential to God's plan of salvation. For Christ

---

[158] Fourth Lateran Council, Confession of Faith.
[159] Pope John Paul II, All Salvation Comes through Christ, General Audience, 31 May 1995.
[160] Pope Boniface VIII, Unam Sanctam, n. 9; author's translation of the Latin.

Himself instituted Peter as the rock on which the Church is founded. So of course that rock and foundation cannot be permanently taken away from the Church. The role of the Roman Pontiff as the visible head of the Church is necessary for the sake of our salvation.

.153. The particular wording of this definition of doctrine is based on the teaching of Saint Thomas.

Saint Thomas Aquinas: "For it is revealed that to be subject to the Roman Pontiff is from the necessity of salvation.... And [Saint] Maximus [the Confessor] in the epistle to those of the East directly says: 'We state that the universal Church has been united and founded upon the rock of the confession of Peter, [and] according to the definition of salvation, in Her, by the necessity of salvation, our souls are to remain, and to her [our souls] are to be obedient, keeping her faith and confession.' "[161]

The question has persisted, since this Papal Bull of Pope Boniface VIII in 1302, as to the meaning of the phrase 'de necessitate salutis,' which is translated literally as 'from the necessity of salvation,' and more loosely as 'necessary to salvation.' This teaching of the Pope is based on the teaching of St. Thomas, and the rest of that section from the work of St. Thomas provides some clarification. The role of Peter and his successors is not only integral to the Church, but also part of Her very foundation, and one of the causes of Her unity. Thus the role of the Roman Pontiff is essential to the Church, and the Church is that one ark of salvation which is essential to the salvation offered to all humanity. Therefore, it follows that rejection of the Roman Pontiff is rejection of the Church, and that acceptance of the Roman Pontiff is necessary to the acceptance of the Church, of the Church's role in salvation, and therefore of salvation itself. And since the Petrine role is as the visible head of the Church, acceptance of this role implies subjection to the Pope.

The phrasing 'de necessitate salutis' used by Pope Boniface is also used by St. Thomas in the Summa Theologica on the necessity of the Sacraments: 'utrum omnia sint de necessitate salutis,' i.e. 'whether all [the Sacraments] are from the necessity of salvation.' Saint Thomas Aquinas distinguishes two types of necessity. The first type of necessity is absolute and specific; it is something necessary for each person, without which no person can be saved. For example, Baptism (formal or non-formal) is absolutely necessary for salvation, for each and every human person. But the second type of necessity only arises from the necessity of salvation, that is, generally, as something needed by the Church for Her work of salvation. For example, Holy Orders is necessary to the work of the Church for our salvation, but non-ordained persons can still be saved. And this second type is properly called 'necessary to salvation' since it is necessary to the salvific work of the Church, for outside of Her, there is no salvation.

Saint Thomas Aquinas: "First, a thing may be necessary so that without it the end cannot be attained; thus food is necessary for human life. And this is simple

---

[161] Saint Thomas Aquinas, Contra Errores Graecorum, pars 2, cap. 38; author's translation of the Latin found at: http://www.corpusthomisticum.org/oce.html

necessity of end. Secondly, a thing is said to be necessary, if, without it, the end cannot be attained so becomingly [fittingly]: thus a horse is necessary for a journey. But this is not simple necessity of end."[162]

St. Thomas explains that only the Sacrament of Baptism (or the desire for it) is absolutely necessary, such that without it the end of salvation cannot be attained. The Sacrament of Confession (or the desire for it) is necessary only if one has fallen into mortal sin. The Sacrament of Holy Orders is necessary, not for each individual, but so that the Church can function for the sake of the salvation of each individual. And the other Sacraments are necessary, not absolutely for each individual, but because they are necessary to the Church as a whole, and to the set of Sacraments as a whole, since "Confirmation perfects Baptism; Extreme Unction perfects Penance; while Matrimony, by multiplying them, preserves the numbers in the Church."[163]

Now in response to the 'first objection' on this question in the Summa, which asserts that all the sacraments are necessary to salvation ('de necessitate salutis'), St. Thomas agrees that all the Sacraments are necessary to salvation, but only if this is understood to include both types of necessity.

The text of the Fifth Lateran Council agrees that this necessity to salvation is not the first type, not absolute for each individual, but the second type, which arises out of the general necessity of salvation and the means of salvation chosen by God, specifically, the Church with Her visible had, the Roman Pontiff.

Fifth Lateran Council: "And since it *arises from the necessity of salvation* ('de necessitate salutis existat') that all the faithful of Christ are to be subject to the Roman Pontiff, just as we are taught by the testimony of the divine Scriptures and of the holy Fathers, and as is declared by the Constitution of Pope Boniface VIII of happy memory, which begins 'Unam Sanctam,' for the salvation of the souls of the same faithful, and by the supreme authority of the Roman pontiff and of this holy See, and by the unity and power of the Church, his spouse, the same Constitution, being approved by the sacred Council, we renew and approve."[164]

.154. The Latin grammatical construction used by Unam Sanctam ('de necessitate salutis') could be translated as 'necessary to salvation,' or as 'from the necessity of salvation.' The first translation tends to favor the first type of necessity, and the second translation favors the second type of necessity. But the phrasing used by the Fifth Lateran Council only allows for the second phrasing, and consequently for the second type of necessity. For the Fifth Lateran Council says 'arises [existat] from the necessity of salvation,' which cannot be translated as 'arises necessary to salvation' as this would not make sense grammatically. And so the teaching that subjection to the Roman Pontiff is entirely necessary to salvation is of the second type of necessity, namely, that this subjection is generally necessary for the work of salvation of the Church, and is necessary to

---

[162] Saint Thomas Aquinas, Summa Theologica, III, Q. 65, A. 4.
[163] Saint Thomas Aquinas, Summa Theologica, III, Q. 65, A. 4.
[164] Pope Leo X, Fifth Lateran Council, Session 11; author's translation of the Latin.

the individual, in order to avoid actual mortal sin, when the individual knows that Peter and his successors were established by Christ as the visible head of the Church. But this teaching does not imply that non-Catholics and non-Christians are unable to be saved (just as Pope John Paul II explains in the quote above).

[Matthew]
{16:16} Simon Peter responded by saying, "You are the Christ, the Son of the living God."
{16:17} And in response, Jesus said to him: "Blessed are you, Simon son of Jonah. For flesh and blood has not revealed this to you, but my Father, who is in heaven.
{16:18} And I say to you, that you are Peter, and upon this rock I will build my Church, and the gates of Hell shall not prevail against it.
{16:19} And I will give you the keys of the kingdom of heaven. And whatever you shall bind on earth shall be bound, even in heaven. And whatever you shall release on earth shall be released, even in heaven."

[2 Corinthians]
{13:10} Therefore, I write these things while absent, so that, when present, I may not have to act more harshly, according to the authority which the Lord has given to me, for edification and not for destruction.

[Titus]
{2:15} Speak and exhort and argue these things with all authority. Let no one despise you.

.155. The Temporal Authority of Canon Law

Canon Law quotations are from the Code of Canon Law for the Latin Church, unless otherwise cited.[165]

Certain provisions of Canon Law, the law issued by authority of the Holy See, are direct expressions of the moral law, or of articles of faith. Even if Canon Law did not contain a particular expression of the moral law, that same law would still be in force, because the moral law is universal and unchanging. Even if Canon Law did not contain a particular expression of an article of faith, that same doctrine would still be a required belief, having been taught by Sacred Tradition, Sacred Scripture, or the Magisterium. Those parts of Canon Law that directly express doctrines of faith or morals are not per se of Canon Law, but are incorporated into the Canons because the disciplines of the Church are based on the doctrines of the Church. Doctrine is not based on discipline, but discipline is based on doctrine.

The teaching authority of the Church is greater that the temporal authority of the Church. The doctrines of the Church are greater than the disciplines of the Church. For doctrines are expressions of eternal truth, and God is Truth. Disciplines are practices used as a means to live the doctrines on faith, morals,

---

[165] Code of Canon Law for the Latin Church, first promulgated in 1983.
http://www.vatican.va/archive/cdc/index.htm

and salvation. Disciplines give us particular forms for exterior acts directed toward worship of God and love of neighbor. But numerous different exterior acts can be used as a means to the same end.

The eternal moral law is absolute and unchanging, because truth is absolute and unchanging. But Canon Law can be changed, dispensed, or nullified. It is not possible to knowingly choose to violate the moral law without sin; by definition, sin is a knowingly chosen act contrary to the moral law. But it is possible to act contrary to Canon Law, or contrary to a rule or ruling of the temporal authority of the Church more generally, without sin.

The moral law permits all that is moral and forbids all that is immoral; its scope in morality is universal. But Canon Law has a limited scope. First, there are two different (but rather similar) sets of Canon Law, one for the Latin Rite of the Catholic Church (the Church generally in the West) and one for the Catholic Churches in the East. The moral law is universal, but Canon Law is not. Second, Canons can be dispensed by proper authority, usually by the local ordinary (the Bishop in charge of a particular diocese), and always by the Holy See (unless the Canon is a direct expression of a doctrine on faith or morals). In a few cases, the priest who is the pastor of a parish may dispense from a provision of Canon Law, or a lay person may dispense himself, for a just reason, or for a grave reason, depending on the Canon. Third, Canon Law can sometimes be overruled by custom, if the custom is longstanding and the circumstances require it.

Canon 5, n. 1. "Other contrary customs are also considered suppressed unless the Code expressly provides otherwise or unless they are centenary or immemorial customs which can be tolerated if, in the judgment of the ordinary, they cannot be removed due to the circumstances of places and persons."

Fourth, the Canons of the Church do not include every possible aspect of discipline or practice. They do not include most liturgical norms. Also, there are customs of practice in the Church which are beyond the law, about which Canon Law does not speak and has no say.

Canon 2 "For the most part the Code does not define the rites which must be observed in celebrating liturgical actions. Therefore, liturgical laws in force until now retain their force unless one of them is contrary to the canons of the Code."

Canon 5, n. 2. "Universal or particular customs beyond the law (praeter ius) which are in force until now are preserved."

Canons that are per se of Canon Law ('merely ecclesiastical laws'), not expressions of doctrine on faith or morals, are only binding on Catholics who have completed seven years of age (unless the Canon states a different age). Thus, Canon Law does not bind all Christians, only Catholic Christians, and is limited by the age of the individual. The moral law has no such limits to its scope.

Canon 11 "Merely ecclesiastical laws bind those who have been baptized in the Catholic Church or received into it, possess the efficient use of reason, and, unless the law expressly provides otherwise, have completed seven years of age."

Canons are sometimes limited by territory; the moral law is not limited by place or time.

Canon 12, n. 2. "All who are actually present in a certain territory, however, are exempted from universal laws which are not in force in that territory."

Canon law is subject to interpretation. When the law establishes a penalty or restriction in the exercise of rights, or when one provision makes exceptions to another provision, the interpretation must be narrow.

Canon 18 "Laws which establish a penalty, restrict the free exercise of rights, or contain an exception from the law are subject to strict interpretation."

Canon 27 "Custom is the best interpreter of laws."

Canon Law is subject to interpretation by custom, to nullification in particular cases by longstanding custom, to dispensations from proper authority in the Church. Canon Law, and every particular exercise of the temporal authority of the Church, is not universal, not eternal, not immutable, not infallible. Canon Law is subject to interpretation by those with authority to apply these laws; it is also subject to interpretation by the ordinary lay faithful. For example, some Canons forbid certain acts, unless there is, in some cases, a just reason, or in other cases, a grave reason. But in some Canons, it is the layperson who may decide if a just or grave reasons exists.

Canon 920, n. 1. "After being initiated into the Most Holy Eucharist, each of the faithful is obliged to receive holy communion at least once a year."

Canon 920, n. 2. "This precept must be fulfilled during the Easter season unless it is fulfilled for a just cause at another time during the year."

The individual member of the faithful may judge whether a just cause exists to fulfill this obligation at another time during the year.

Canon 919, n. 1. "A person who is to receive the Most Holy Eucharist is to abstain for at least one hour before holy communion from any food and drink, except for only water and medicine."

Canon 919, n. 3. "The elderly, the infirm, and those who care for them can receive the Most Holy Eucharist even if they have eaten something within the preceding hour."

The individual member of the faithful may judge whether their situation fits n. 3, permitting reception of Communion with a fast of less than one hour.

Canon 104 "Spouses are to have a common domicile or quasi-domicile; by reason of legitimate separation or some other just cause, both can have their own domicile or quasi-domicile."

The individual spouses may judge whether they have a just cause to live in separate domiciles.

.156. Canon Law does not stand on its own, as the eternal moral law does. Canon law, and every other exercise of the temporal authority of the Church, including all discipline, is entirely subservient to the doctrines of Sacred Tradition, Sacred Scripture, and the Magisterium. If any provision of the temporal authority, whether in Canon Law or otherwise, is contrary to a doctrine of Tradition, Scripture, Magisterium, then that law, rule, or ruling is null and void. Nothing contrary to Divine Revelation, nothing contrary to the moral law, nothing contrary to any true teaching on faith, morals, or salvation, has any force, even if issued by the temporal authority of the Church, whether issued by the Roman Pontiff, or the Holy See, or Canon Law, or a Bishops' Conference, or an individual Bishop, or any other temporal authority. God is Truth, but God is not rules and rulings.

It often happens with human laws in civil society, and sometimes with Canon Law, that a law which is generally just and useful becomes unjust in particular circumstances. And no law in civil society, nor in Church law, can foresee every particular set of circumstances. So this problem is unavoidable. In such cases, it might not be contrary to the eternal moral law to violate (ignore or set aside) that law in that circumstance.

The spirit of charity takes precedence over the letter of the law. The law of charity is greater than any provision of Canon Law, greater than any rule or ruling, and greater than any exercise of the temporal authority of the Church. This is the teaching of Christ. So if anyone places the letter of any rule or ruling above the law of charity, he rejects Christ, and he commits the sin of Pharisaism.

[Matthew]
{12:1} At that time, Jesus went out through the ripe grain on the Sabbath. And his disciples, being hungry, began to separate the grain and to eat.
{12:2} Then the Pharisees, seeing this, said to him, "Behold, your disciples are doing what is not lawful to do on the Sabbaths."
{12:3} But he said to them: "Have you not read what David did, when he was hungry, and those who were with him:
{12:4} how he entered the house of God and ate the bread of the Presence, which was not lawful for him to eat, nor for those who were with him, but only for the priests?
{12:5} Or have you not read in the law, that on the Sabbaths the priests in the temple violate the Sabbath, and they are without guilt?"

David violated a law of the Old Testament disciplines, which were given by God through Moses. These Old Testament disciplines were like a type of Canon Law given by Divine Revelation, for they were not doctrines, but only disciplines. These Old Testament disciplines, even during the time of the Old Testament, could be violated for a just cause, or for a grave cause, without sin. David and his men were in grave need of food, and so they could violate a discipline, without violating the eternal moral law. There are no exceptions to the moral law; whoever violates the moral law, commits a sin. But even the Old Testament disciplines given by God could be violated without sin, in some cases. And the same is true of Canon Law and of all the New Testament disciplines, including any particular exercise of the temporal authority of the Church.

Anyone who places the temporal authority of the Church above or equal to the teaching authority, or who places rules and rulings above or equal to the rule of charity, or who places disciplines above or equal to doctrines, is guilty of the sin of the Pharisees. Christ taught that even the Old Testament laws, i.e. laws that are of discipline, not the moral law, can be violated without sin, for a just reason, or for a grave reason. And Canon Law itself also repeatedly acknowledges that various acts that are forbidden by law can be done for a just reason, or for a grave reason, depending on the act and the circumstances.

An unjust law is not a law. A law that contradicts the law of charity is not a law. If any provision of Canon Law, as it applies to a particular circumstance, is contrary to the law of charity, that Canon can be violated without sin. If any particular rule or ruling of the temporal authority of the Church is contrary to the law of charity, to some extent, that rule or ruling lacks force to the same extent. Nothing contrary to the law of charity, which is the commandment to love God, neighbor, and self, can ever have the force of law in the eyes of God. Thus, it was possible for David and his men to violate temporal laws instituted by God in Divine Revelation, without sin. And it is also possible for the members of the Church to violate particular temporal rules or rulings of the Church, in so far as these are contrary to the law of charity, without sin.

[Galatians]
{4:30} And what does Scripture say? "Cast out the woman servant and her son. For the son of a servant women shall not be an heir with the son of a free woman."
{4:31} And so, brothers, we are not the sons of the servant woman, but rather of the free woman. And this is the freedom with which Christ has set us free.

.157. The Temporal Authority of Liturgical Norms

Jesus Christ established all Seven of the Sacraments, and He established the Mass, during which the Sacrament of the Eucharist is effected. But Christ did not establish the Mass with immutable specifics. He did not establish one set form of the Mass, never to be changed. The first Mass, and the only Mass at which Christ in person visibly consecrated the Eucharist, not through a priest, but directly with His own hands, took the form of a Passover supper, modified by Christ for the sake of this new Sacrament. No subsequent Mass permitted by the Church had that same form. And the form that the Church has permitted for the Mass has changed over time. The temporal authority of the Church possess the authority to change the form of the Mass.

Christ did not give to His Church the authority to choose one sole immutable form for the Mass. The teachings of the Church on faith, morals, and salvation are immutable; they are an expression of the Truth that is God, who is unchanging and eternal. But all disciplines, practices, rules, and rulings, all that is of the temporal authority of the Church, including the form of the Mass, is changeable, dispensable, and temporary. For in Heaven, there is no Mass; the

Mass is an imperfect foreshadowing of that perfect Heavenly banquet. Even after the general Resurrection, when the Resurrected Just are whole, in body and soul, there is no Mass. For the imperfect and the temporary shall pass away. All that is of the temporal authority of the Church shall pass away.

The Church has the authority from Christ to change the form of the Mass. The rules for the form of the Mass, and for other liturgical services, are called liturgical norms. These are not absolute truths on faith or morals, but are merely a set of practical decisions on the form that these services are to take. Liturgical norms are never immutable; they are always changeable. And since the temporal authority of the Church is fallible, the norms chosen at any particular time might be better or worse; they might be flawed in various ways. The Magisterium of the Church is able to teach either infallibly or non-infallibly; but the temporal authority of the Church is fallible. The Church, in both types of authority, teaching and temporal, and as a whole, is indefectible, and so no decision on doctrine or discipline can tear the Church, the Body of Christ, apart from her Head. But since decisions of the temporal authority are not beliefs, but are only rules and rulings, these decision are fallible.

Nothing that is of the temporal authority of the Church can be made unchangeable by the Church. When any Pope or Ecumenical Council decides a matter of the temporal authority, whether it is a provision of Canon Law, or a form for a liturgical service, or any temporal matter that is not a matter of doctrine, then any subsequent Pope or Ecumenical Council can change or nullify that same decision. If a Pope or Ecumenical Council teaches a doctrine infallibly, that teaching cannot be changed. Not even God can change truth, for God is unchanging Truth, and He cannot be unfaithful to Himself. But temporal matters are discipline, not doctrine. Therefore, any temporal decision can change or be nullified.

If the temporal decisions of each Pope could not be changed by subsequent Popes, then each successive Pope would have ever less authority. But Christ gave the same authority to each successor of Peter as to the Apostle Peter himself. It is contrary to the teachings of the Catholic Faith to claim, in effect, that each successive Pope has ever less authority. Therefore, the temporal decisions of any Pope or Ecumenical Council are never immutable, and can always be changed or nullified, by any subsequent Pope or Ecumenical Council.

And since the form of the Mass is of the temporal authority, the form of the Mass can change. Even if a Pope uses the strongest possible language to forbid anyone, even a subsequent Pope or Council, to change the form of the Mass, nevertheless a subsequent Pope or Council can change the form of the Mass. Otherwise, each Pope would lack a degree or type of authority that his predecessor possessed. To the contrary, each Pope's authority, by virtue of being a successor of Peter, is directly from Christ. And so this doctrine prevents any Pope from exercising the temporal authority in any way, and to any extent, which would diminish the authority of his successor.

.158. Doctrine and Discipline in the Sacraments

The Sacraments have two types of elements, (1) essential elements, which cannot be changed, not even by the Church, and (2) non-essential elements, which the temporal authority of the Church can change. The essential elements are immutable; the non-essential elements are mutable. The essential elements are unchangeable because they are part of the doctrine of the Faith concerning that Sacrament. The non-essential elements are changeable because they are part of the discipline of the Faith concerning that Sacrament.

Examples:

(1) Baptism: The Church lacks the authority to change the Sacrament of Baptism such that water is not used. Water is an essential element to this Sacrament. It is a teaching of the Church that the formal Sacrament of Baptism requires water.

Council of Trent: "CANON II. If any one says, that true and natural water is not of necessity for baptism, and, on that account, wrests, to some sort of metaphor, those words of our Lord Jesus Christ; Unless a man be born again of water and the Holy Ghost; let him be anathema."[166]

However, the Church does have the authority to make general rules for the Sacrament of Baptism, such as that the ordinary minister is an ordained person, and that non-ordained persons are not to baptize except in certain circumstances. If someone violates this rule of the temporal authority, and gives the Sacrament of Baptism, with all of the essential elements, but contrary to this non-essential element, the Sacrament is still valid, but illicit. The Sacrament would still have the full and proper effect on the individual. But the person who acted contrary to the rules of the temporal authority, acted illicitly.

(2) the Eucharist: The Church lacks the authority to change the Sacrament of holy Communion from the consecration of wheat bread and grape wine to some other matter, such as rice, or wheat without any gluten, or another type of food, or non-grape wine, or another type of drink. The use of wheat bread and grape wine is a matter of doctrine, not discipline.

However, the Church does have the authority to govern the norms for the Eucharistic prayer (other than the words of consecration), and to govern the norms for the Mass, and the norms for receiving Communion. Although some persons treat reception of Communion on the tongue as a type of dogma, this act is a practice, not a belief; it is a matter of discipline, not doctrine. Therefore, the Church does have the authority to permit reception of Communion in the hand. Although at the present time reception of Communion on the tongue is the norm, and reception in the hand is permitted, there is nothing to prevent proper authority in the Church from changing this practice.

(3) Marriage: The Church lacks the authority to dispense the Sacrament of Marriage to any persons other than one man and one woman. A valid

---

[166] The Council of Trent, Decree on the Sacraments, On Baptism, Canon II.

Sacrament of Marriage requires one man and one woman. The Church lacks the authority to change this infallible and immutable doctrine.

However, the Church does have the authority to cause a Sacrament such as Marriage to be valid or invalid based on particular conditions, which the Church can change or dispense, to some extent.

Canon 1108 n. 1. "Only those marriages are valid which are contracted before the local ordinary, pastor, or a priest or deacon delegated by either of them, who assist, and before two witnesses according to the rules expressed in the following canons and without prejudice to the exceptions mentioned in canons 144, 1112 n. 1, 1116, and 1127 n. 1-2."[167]

The other Canons mentioned give various other conditions, under the temporal authority, affecting the validity or licitness of the Sacrament. Notice that the temporal authority can effect whether or not the Sacrament is valid, as in the above example on Marriage, or it can effect whether or not the Sacrament is licit, as in the example above on Baptism.

(4) Holy Orders: The Church lacks the authority to give the Sacrament of Holy Orders, to the sacerdotal or episcopal degrees (i.e. as priest or bishop), to anyone other than men.[168]

However, the Church has the authority to permit some married men to be ordained as priests. Yet the Church does not have the authority to admit only married men to the priesthood; for Christ was unmarried, and all priests are representatives of Christ.

The temporal authority of the Church can make changes to other requirements, such as who may be ordained, the time and manner of preparation, and the form of the ceremony used to confer Holy Orders. But the temporal authority cannot change the requirement that only a Bishop may confer the Sacrament of Holy Orders.

Some aspects of the Sacraments are of doctrine, and therefore cannot be changed. Other aspects of the Sacraments, even those that affect validity, are of discipline, and therefore can be changed by the Church.

.159. Rulings of the Temporal Authority

Discipline includes not only Canon Law and liturgical norms, but also the rulings of persons in authority within Church in particular cases.

Canon Law is a fairly new aspect of discipline in the Church. The current Code for the Latin Church was issued in 1983; the previous Code was issued in 1917. But prior to that date, there was no formal Code of Canon Law. Instead, there were a set of rulings in particular cases, which often had implications, directly or indirectly, for other similar cases; such rulings had an effect similar to precedent

---

[167] Code of Canon Law for the Latin Church, Canon 1108, paragraph 1.
[168] Pope John Paul II, Ordinatio Sacerdotalis.

Doctrine and Discipline

in the laws of secular society. These rulings were called decretals. The term is most often used to refer to various collections, in the history of the Church, of decisions by the Holy See on matters of discipline. Prior to Canon Law, these decretals (collections of decrees) were used throughout the Church to determine correct discipline on the same or on related circumstances. The laws of the Church had their historical development in these collections of rulings in particular cases. And even subsequent to the establishment of Canon Law, any ruling of the Holy See on a particular temporal matter can be used as a type of precedent (absent a specific provision of Canon Law on the subject) to determine the discipline of the Church on related matters.

All such rulings on temporal matters by the Holy See, and also any lesser exercise of the temporal authority (such as by an individual Bishop or Bishops' Conference) is fallible, and is able to be subsequently reformed or nullified, or dispensed in particular cases. The rulings of the temporal authority are not teachings on truth, but decisions of the most prudent course of action, or decisions on the regulation of various temporal matters. These are judgments of the prudential order, not decisions on doctrine.

Consider the example of Saint Pio of Pietrelcina (Padre Pio). As his popularity increased among the faithful, his detractors became more adamant, and they poured out many false accusations against him:

"As his spiritual influence increased, so did the voices of his detractors. Accusations against Padre Pio poured in to the Holy Office (today the Congregation for the Doctrine of Faith). By June 1922, restrictions were placed on the public's access to Padre Pio...and he was ordered not to answer correspondence from people seeking spiritual direction.... Despite the restrictions and controversies, Padre Pio's ministry continued. From 1924 - 1931 various statements were made by the Holy See that denied the supernaturality of Padre Pio's phenomena. On June 9, 1931, the Feast of Corpus Christi, Padre Pio was ordered by the Holy See to desist from all activities except the celebration of the Mass, which was to be in private. By early 1933, Pope Pius XI ordered the Holy See to reverse its ban on Padre Pio's public celebration of Mass, saying, 'I have not been badly disposed toward Padre Pio, but I have been badly informed.' "[169]

The Pope and the Holy See erred in restricting the activities of this Saint, and they erred in publicly stating that his experiences were not supernatural (from God). The Pope attributed this error to having been misinformed (apparently by the numerous opponents of Padre Pio). It is clear that the prudential judgments of the Pope and of the Holy See are from the temporal authority of the Church, not from the Magisterium, and that all such judgments and decisions of the temporal authority are fallible. Such judgments are subject to error due to incorrect information, as well as incorrect judgment, in particular cases.[170]

---

[169] http://www.ewtn.com/padrepio/man/biography2.htm
[170] This example is taken from my book: Conte, *The First Part of the Tribulation*, revised edition, p. 421.

Not only the Pope and the Holy See, but also Bishops' Conferences and individual Bishops, may err in their exercise of the temporal authority. The Magisterium of the Church teaches either infallibly, or non-infallibly. But the temporal authority of the Church does not teach, and is fallible. The indefectibility of the Church prevents the fallible decisions of the temporal authority, and the limited errors possible in non-infallible teachings, from ever leading the faithful away from the path of salvation. But errors are still possible, to a limited extent in non-infallible teachings, and to a greater (but still limited) extent in decisions of discipline, rather than doctrine.

The ability of the Roman Pontiff to teach infallibly does not extend to decisions of discipline, since these are not teachings. When the Pope decides a matter of prudential judgment, not a decision on doctrine, he does not act infallibly. Therefore, it is possible for a faithful and reasonable Catholic to disagree with the Pope in a matter of judgment, without sinning.

Cardinal Ratzinger: "For example, if a Catholic were to be at odds with the Holy Father on the application of capital punishment or on the decision to wage war, he would not for that reason be considered unworthy to present himself to receive Holy Communion. While the Church exhorts civil authorities to seek peace, not war, and to exercise discretion and mercy in imposing punishment on criminals, it may still be permissible to take up arms to repel an aggressor or to have recourse to capital punishment. There may be a legitimate diversity of opinion even among Catholics about waging war and applying the death penalty, but not however with regard to abortion and euthanasia."[171]

Notice that then-Cardinal Ratzinger, now Pope Benedict XVI, does not consider that faithful Catholics must agree with every decision of the Pope. The legitimate diversity of opinion among Catholics that he discusses pertains to the doctrines of just war and of capital punishment. For a judgment of the prudential order is needed in order to decide if the war is just in particular circumstances, or if the use of the death penalty is moral in particular circumstances. And when the Pope makes such a judgment, faithful Catholics may disagree. This disagreement is not a difference of belief on doctrine, but a difference of prudential judgment about the facts and the assessment of those facts in temporal circumstances.

.160. Faithful Dissent versus Unfaithful Dissent

The Magisterium of the Church teaches not only by authority, but also by ability. If the Magisterium had no ability to teach the truth by the guidance of the Holy Spirit, then the Magisterium would have no authority. And this ability of the Magisterium is of the Holy Spirit; it is specifically the ability to understand and to teach the truths of faith and morals found in Sacred Tradition and Sacred Scripture, as well as the truths found in natural law. We believe these authoritative teachings of the Magisterium not merely because they have authority, but more so because they are true. God who is Truth is grievously

---

[171] Cardinal Joseph Ratzinger, Worthiness to Receive Holy Communion, General Principles; 2004 letter to Cardinal McCarrick.
http://www.priestsforlife.org/magisterium/bishops/04-07ratzingerommunion.htm

offended whenever any Catholic believes solely by authority, without regard for truth. For then it is as if God who is Truth were requiring His children to believe whatever is taught with authority, even if it is contrary to truth. Some Catholics take this attitude toward the Magisterium, thinking themselves to be more faithful, as if it matters little whether or not the teaching is true, as long as it is authoritative. This attitude quickly leads to other errors, for when a decision on doctrine by the Magisterium is treated as merely authoritative, the doctrine is easily misunderstood.

When Christ taught, He did not say that we should believe based mainly on His authority. Our Lord taught us to believe because these truths are from God, who is Truth. All that Christ taught He received from the Father. And Christ is the Living Word. Christ is a single all-encompassing Word of Truth uttered by the Father. Our Lord taught us to believe with obedience, not any assertion, but the Truths of the Faith that are from God. And this is not the mere external obedience of accepting whatever is ordered, but rather the holy obedience that is almost indistinguishable from love.

[John]
{14:6} Jesus said to him: "I am the Way, and the Truth, and the Life. No one comes to the Father, except through me.
{14:7} If you had known me, certainly you would also have known my Father. And from now on, you shall know him, and you have seen him."
...
{15:12} This is my precept: that you love one another, just as I have loved you.
{15:13} No one has a greater love than this: that he lay down his life for his friends.
{15:14} You are my friends, if you do what I instruct you.
{15:15} I will no longer call you servants, for the servant does not know what his Lord is doing. But I have called you friends, because everything whatsoever that I have heard from my Father, I have made known to you.

When the Magisterium teaches infallibly, in solemn definitions of the Pope, in solemn definitions of an Ecumenical Council, and by the Universal Magisterium, these teaches not only have the highest authority, they have the charism of certain truth. These teachings benefit from the divine gift of Christ to the Church in the Holy Spirit so that the teaching is certainly true. Furthermore, such teachings are on matters of faith or morals, which are taught for the benefit of the salvation of all the faithful. Knowing these truths of faith and morals with certitude, by both faith and reason, greatly assists the faithful in obtaining, retaining, and achieving eternal salvation. The authoritative requirement for the faithful to believe infallible teachings arises from the necessity of salvation. We are required to give the full assent of faith to all infallible teachings of the Magisterium because these teachings are necessary to our salvation.

This full assent of faith is also called theological faith, since it is the fullest exercise of the theological virtue of faith. This full assent of faith is also called a divine and catholic faith, since it is a gift of divine grace. For no one can believe with true faith except those who have been given and have accepted the grace of

God to believe. Mere human assent is not the full assent of faith. If you believe a teaching of the Catholic Faith merely because it makes sense to your own mind, merely because you arrived at the same conclusion on your own, then you do not believe out of faith. Those who believe by faith are able to accept teachings that are even beyond their own understanding based on reason alone.

Sacred Tradition and Sacred Scripture each infallibly teach the truths of Divine Revelation, which together form one Sacred Deposit of Faith. When the Magisterium teaches infallibly, it teaches from Sacred Tradition and Sacred Scripture. The source is infallible, because Sacred Tradition and Sacred Scripture are of the Holy Spirit. The teaching faculty of the Magisterium is also infallible due to the action of the same Holy Spirit. When the Magisterium teaches infallibly from the Sacred Deposit of Faith, this faculty is fittingly called the Sacred Magisterium. And the assent required of these teachings of the Sacred Magisterium is fittingly called sacred assent, or theological assent, or the full assent of faith, or a divine and catholic faith.

Therefore, the faithful may not faithfully dissent from infallible teachings. For there is no possibility of error in any infallible teaching of the Sacred Magisterium. However, the faithful must be careful not to misunderstand the meaning of an infallible teaching. Even the infallible teachings of the Magisterium are subject to proper interpretation in the light of the entire body of teachings of Tradition, Scripture, Magisterium. This is not to say that an infallible teaching could ever be in error, or in need of correction, or substantially altered in meaning by the interpretation. The goal of the interpretation of an infallible teaching is to understand the truth that is being asserted ever more fully, and to incorporate that truth into the entire body of teachings of the Faith. For this set of truths is truly One Truth, a reflection of the Living Word of God.

The Magisterium is One. The infallible Sacred Magisterium and the non-infallible Ordinary Magisterium are one faculty, one gift from God to the whole Church, exercised solely by the Roman Pontiff and the Bishops. Only solemn definitions of the Pope, solemn definitions of an Ecumenical Council, and teachings of the Universal Magisterium are infallible. All other teachings of the Magisterium are non-infallible, and non-irreformable, and subject to a limited possibility of error. Individual Bishops and local groups of Bishops are unable to exercise the infallible Sacred Magisterium by themselves, but only as a part of the whole body of Bishops with the Pope as their head. Individual Bishops and local groups of Bishops (e.g. Bishops' Conferences, local Synods), when teaching by themselves, may only exercise the Ordinary Magisterium.

Now a different type and degree of assent is required of the faithful for the non-infallible teachings of the Ordinary Magisterium. The non-infallible teachings allow for a limited possibility of error, and so they are non-irreformable. A more definitive decision of the Magisterium at a later time may possibly change or correct such a non-infallible teaching, at least in part. This possibility of error is not a probability of error. This limit is such that no error and no set of errors in non-infallible teachings of the Magisterium can ever reach to such an extent as to lead the faithful away from the path of salvation.

Truly, it would be much more difficult for the faithful to achieve salvation by relying solely on infallible teachings. For the infallible teachings, more so in the early Church, but also today, do not include every aspect of faith and morals. The non-infallible teachings are needed to expound and to connect and to apply the infallible teachings, so that the Faith can be lived. The exercise of the non-infallible teaching authority allows the Bishops, even individually, to guide the faithful along the path of salvation, and to respond to current questions and current threats pertaining to faith and morals, quickly and simply, without the need for the Pope, or the Pope and the body of Bishops, to respond with a definitive infallible pronouncement in answer to every question. Thus, the non-infallible ordinary Magisterium and its teachings are necessary to our salvation.

The non-infallible teachings are necessary to salvation, and they cannot err to such an extent as to lead us away from salvation. Therefore, the Magisterium, compelled by concern for our salvation, justly requires the faithful to give their religious submission of will and intellect to these teachings, despite the limited possibility of error. This type of assent is not the full assent of faith, but is a different type and lesser degree of assent, which might fittingly be called our ordinary assent to the teachings of the Ordinary Magisterium.

The difference between the full assent of faith to infallible teachings, and the religious submission of will and intellect to non-infallible teachings, is that the latter allows for some faithful dissent. The possible extent of this dissent is the same as the possible extent of error. For we are compelled by our love for God who is Truth, and for Christ our Savior who is the Way, the Truth, and the Life, to seek and to adhere to truth even, at times, when the non-infallible teaching authority teaches the contrary. Now there are some who claim that we should adhere to all teachings of the Magisterium, without any exception, being either blindly unwilling to know if any errors are present in non-infallible teachings, or adhering to whatever is taught regardless of those errors. This approach is a sinful rejection of truth, and an exaltation of the Magisterium to the extent of idolatry.

The Magisterium is a gift from God to the whole Church, given for the sake of our salvation. Christ did not choose the make the Magisterium always infallible in every teaching at all times, for He did not want the Magisterium to become like a god to be worshiped, but rather to be a servant to His faithful to assist them in achieving salvation. But we cannot achieve salvation if we abandon our personal search for truth, and replace it with blind obedience to the letter of the teachings of the Magisterium. For Jesus Christ "has made us suitable ministers of the New Testament, not in the letter, but in the Spirit. For the letter kills, but the Spirit gives life." (1 Cor 3:6). Therefore, we must follow the spirit of the teachings of the Magisterium, which is always to seek and to find the truths of Divine Revelation. Thus, by occasionally dissenting from a non-infallible teaching, we show true holy obedience to God and true spiritual faithfulness to the Magisterium, rather than the unfaithfulness of a blind obedience which either pretends that the Magisterium never errs, or offends by adhering to a known falsehood as if it were truth, or replaces faith in truth with obedience to the letter.

However, that dissent is unfaithful which rejects all non-infallible teachings, or which treats all non-infallible teachings as if they were opinion, or which rejects any infallible teaching, or which accepts any idea that is fundamentally incompatible with any infallible teaching, or with the body of non-infallible teachings.

.161. Faithful Disobedience versus Unfaithful Disobedience

The Church has two types of authority. Her doctrines are of the spiritual authority, and Her disciplines are of the temporal authority. Dissent refers to doctrine, where as disobedience refers to discipline. Judgments of the prudential order, i.e. judgments about temporal circumstances, fall under the temporal authority. When the Pope, or an Ecumenical Council, or any other lesser authority in the Church, makes a decision or judgment of the prudential order, the result is not doctrine, but discipline. A rejection or objection to discipline is disobedience, not dissent. And so dissent is contrary to doctrine, but disobedience is contrary to discipline.

The faithful are not required to agree with every judgment of the prudential order of the Pope or of lesser authorities in the Church. Such judgments fall under the temporal authority, not the teaching authority. Therefore, these judgments are neither infallible, nor non-infallible, but are fallible, except that the Church remains always indefectible. Decisions of the temporal authority can be erroneous, but never in such a manner or to such an extent that the Church would utterly fail, or would fall away from the path of salvation.

Cardinal Ratzinger: "Not all moral issues have the same moral weight as abortion and euthanasia. For example, if a Catholic were to be at odds with the Holy Father on the application of capital punishment or on the decision to wage war, he would not for that reason be considered unworthy to present himself to receive Holy Communion. While the Church exhorts civil authorities to seek peace, not war, and to exercise discretion and mercy in imposing punishment on criminals, it may still be permissible to take up arms to repel an aggressor or to have recourse to capital punishment. There may be a legitimate diversity of opinion even among Catholics about waging war and applying the death penalty, but not however with regard to abortion and euthanasia."[172]

In the above quote, Cardinal Ratzinger was writing at a time when he was the Prefect for the Sacred Congregation for the Doctrine of the Faith, prior to his election as Roman Pontiff. He plainly states that the ordinary lay Catholic may disagree with a judgment of the Pope as to whether or not capital punishment should be applied in a particular case, or whether or not a particular nation should go to war in a particular circumstance. Such decisions are not doctrines. The Church definitively teaches that some wars are just; the Church definitively teaches that the use of capital punishment is sometimes moral. The faithful Catholic may not disagree with these definitive teachings. But the judgment of the prudential order as to when to apply the death penalty, or whether or not a

---

[172] Cardinal Joseph Ratzinger, Worthiness to Receive Holy Communion, General Principles; 2004 letter to Cardinal McCarrick.

particular war is just, is not a doctrine. If the Pope renders a judgment in such cases, this is of the temporal authority, not the teaching authority. Notice that Cardinal Ratzinger allows that a lay Catholic is not obliged to agree with every judgment of the temporal authority. Therefore, faithful obedience to the temporal authority does not require agreement with every judgment or decision of the Pope, nor of lesser authorities, such as a Bishops' Conference, or the local Bishop.

A faithful Catholic may disagree with a teaching of the non-infallible Magisterium because such teachings may contain error. Similarly, a faithful Catholic may disagree with, and may even disobey, a rule, ruling, judgment, or decision of the temporal authority of the Church because such decisions are fallible and may contain error. God is Truth, and therefore the faithful are sometimes able to dissent or disobey, faithfully and reasonably, without sinning. A faithful Catholic may disagree with a judgment of the Pope, of the Holy See, of a Bishops' Conference, or of a local Bishop, and at times may faithfully and reasonably disobey.

The faithful are obliged by the Nature of God who is Truth to adhere to the infallible teachings of the Magisterium, because these teachings are certainly true. And the faithful are similarly obligated, generally, to adhere to the non-infallible teachings of the Magisterium, because these teaching are generally true, with only a limited possibility of error. But the same devotion to God who is Truth permits and even at times compels us to dissent from a non-infallible teaching, in the sincere belief, based on Sacred Tradition, or Sacred Scripture, or other teachings of the Magisterium, that the particular non-infallible teaching is in error. Otherwise, if we ignore truth in order to be blindly loyal to magisterial teachings, then we would commit the sin of idolatry, treating the Magisterium as an idol to be worshiped, instead of as a gift to the whole Church from God who is Truth. For the first commandment is to worship the Lord God, and to serve Him alone. And He is perfect and infinite Truth.

For much the same reason, the faithful are obligated by the Nature of God who is Justice, to obey the just decisions of the temporal authority of the Church. However, when a rule or ruling, or any judgment or decision, of the temporal authority is contrary to justice, or in conflict with the truths taught by Tradition, Scripture, Magisterium -- when it is either contrary to the common good, or would do more harm than good in a particular case -- then the faithful may disobey, without sin.

[Mark]
{2:23} And again, while the Lord was walking through the ripe grain on the Sabbath, his disciples, as they advanced, began to separate the ears of grains.
{2:24} But the Pharisees said to him, "Behold, why are they doing what is not lawful on the Sabbaths?"
{2:25} And he said to them: "Have you never read what David did, when he had need and was hungry, both he and those who were with him?

{2:26} How he went into the house of God, under the high priest Abiathar, and ate the bread of the Presence, which it was not lawful to eat, except for the priests, and how he gave it to those who were with him?"
{2:27} And he said to them: "The Sabbath was made for man, and not man for the Sabbath.
{2:28} And so, the Son of man is Lord, even of the Sabbath."

.162. The Old Testament contains both doctrines on faith and morals, and disciplines. Now these disciplines were issued by God Himself, and are part of Sacred Scripture. Yet David and his men were able to disobey this discipline, in a particular circumstances, without sin. So if the decisions of discipline issued by God in Sacred Scripture can be violated without sin, then certainly also the disciplines and decisions of the temporal authority of the Church can, at times, be disobeyed without sin. For the rules and rulings of the temporal authority of the Church are made for the benefit of man, and not man for the benefit of rules and rulings.

The rules of Canon Law (those that are per se of Canon Law, not those that are a direct expression of faith or morals) are for the common good of the Church. But there is nothing to prevent a rule that generally accomplishes the common good from doing more harm than good in particular circumstances. Similarly, the rule forbidding anyone to eat the bread of the Presence (an Old Testament foreshadowing of the Eucharist) was a just rule for the common good. However, in the particular circumstance when David and his men were unjustly sought to be put to death, and were hungry (without recourse to other sources of food), it would have been unjust to deny them this bread.

An unjust law is not a law. And even when a law or ruling is just in general, but unjust in a particular case, morally, that law or ruling (whether of secular society or of the Church) is not binding in that particular case. For God is Justice, but He is not rules and rulings. Now this applies to laws and rulings that are of the temporal authority, not to the eternal moral law. For God is Justice, and the eternal moral law is the unchanging Justice of God.

Therefore, a faithful and reasonable Catholic may at times disobey a rule or ruling of the temporal authority of the Church or a provision of Canon Law per se, and may at times disagree with, and argue against, a decision or judgment of the Church, in cooperation with the grace of God and without sin, so as to do what is just in all circumstances. Otherwise, if we blindly obey the temporal authority of the Church, without regard for justice, then we would commit the sin of idolatry, treating the temporal authority of the Church as an idol to be worshiped, instead of as a gift to the whole Church from God who is Justice. For the first commandment is to worship the Lord God, and to serve Him alone. And He is perfect and infinite Justice.

Perfect obedience to God requires, at times, disobedience to any authority that is less than God, including the Pope, the Holy See, a Bishops' Conference, a local Bishop, the pastor of a parish, a religious superior, and other temporal authorities in the Church. Now all this applies even though the person issuing the rule or ruling may be faithful and holy, acting under lawful authority within the Church.

The situation is substantially different though, when an authority in secular society, or even a person exercising temporal authority within the Church, (such as a committee of Bishops, or a local Bishop, or a religious superior, or a pastor of a parish) has gone thoroughly astray from truth and justice, departing from the required beliefs of the Catholic Faith, or departing from justice itself, or both. There is no obligation to obey anyone who has fully departed from truth and justice, for all true authority is from God (Rom 13:1), who is Truth, who is Justice. Anyone who has abandoned truth and justice has thereby lost all legitimate authority. A law not made by proper authority is not a law. And any person with authority, who goes fully astray from truth and justice, thereby loses his authority.

Now this situation happens much more often in secular society than with persons in authority in the Church. And within the Church, neither the Pope, nor the body of Bishops led by the Pope, can go astray from truth or justice to such an extent. But certain lesser authorities do at times go thoroughly astray from truth or justice, as when a Bishop, priest, deacon, or religious commits apostasy, heresy, or schism, or as when the same persons commit acts of grievous injustice (such as the abandonment of the vow of chastity in various sexual sins). And all the faithful are aware that even one of the Twelve Apostles, Judas Iscariot, went astray from truth and justice, and thereby lost his place as an Apostle, which place was then transferred to another person, one who was worthy (Acts 1). In such cases, when a person who has a role as a shepherd over the sheep, chooses instead to become like a wolf in sheep's clothing, then the faithful have no obligation to believe or obey such a person at all, even if the rule or order is in conformity with reason, but only the obligation (as always) to believe what the Church teaches and to obey the moral law (under all three fonts of morality), and to generally obey the rules and ruling of those authorities who have not gone astray. For the Shepherd doe not require the sheep to be obedient to wolves.

Saint Thomas Aquinas: "laws may be unjust in two ways: first, by being contrary to human good, through being opposed to the things mentioned above -- either in respect of the end, as when an authority imposes on his subjects burdensome laws, conducive, not to the common good, but rather to his own cupidity [desires] or vainglory -- or in respect of the author, as when a man makes a law that goes beyond the power committed to him -- or in respect of the form, as when burdens are imposed unequally on the community, although with a view to the common good. The like are acts of violence rather than laws; because, as Augustine says (De Lib. Arb. i, 5), 'a law that is not just, seems to be no law at all.' Therefore such laws do not bind in conscience, except perhaps in order to avoid scandal or disturbance, for which cause a man should even yield his right, according to Matthew 5:40-41: 'If a man...take away thy coat, let go thy cloak also unto him; and whosoever will force thee one mile, go with him other two.' "[173]

Compendium of the Social Doctrine of the Church: "whenever public authority -- which has its foundation in human nature and belongs to the order pre-ordained by God -- fails to seek the common good, it abandons its proper purpose and so de-legitimizes itself. Citizens are not obligated in conscience to follow the prescriptions of civil authorities if their precepts are contrary to the demands of the moral order, to the fundamental rights of persons or to the teachings of the Gospel."[174]

Saint Thomas Aquinas: "He who in a case of necessity acts beside the letter of the law, does not judge the law; but of a particular case in which he sees that the letter of the law is not to be observed."[175] For "necessity knows no law".[176]

Charity is true love of God, and neighbor, and self. The law of charity can overrule any rule. But the law of charity cannot overrule the moral law. For the law of charity is the eternal moral law.

.163. The Errors of the Pharisees of Today

[Matthew]
{3:7} Then, seeing many of the Pharisees and Sadducees arriving for his baptism, he said to them: "Progeny of vipers, who warned to you to flee from the approaching wrath?
{3:8} Therefore, produce fruit worthy of repentance.
{3:9} And do not choose to say within yourselves, 'We have Abraham as our father.' For I tell you that God has the power to raise up sons to Abraham from these stones.
{3:10} For even now the axe has been placed at the root of the trees. Therefore, every tree that does not produce good fruit shall be cut down and cast into the fire."

These particular Pharisees and Sadducees were not cooperating with grace interiorly, but were claiming to be saved based on their lineage from Abraham. They were not producing the good fruit that inevitably springs forth from all cooperation with grace. Similarly, some Catholics claim to be saved merely by being Catholic, or by being a conservative Catholic, or by being loyal to the Magisterium, or by performing exterior acts, such as attending daily Mass, praying the Rosary, fasting, giving alms. In truth, without the interior cooperation with grace, a Catholic cannot be saved, even if he or she does all of the aforementioned good acts. Some who attend daily Mass will not be saved, because they commit actual mortal sin and they do not repent. Some who pray the Rosary, fast, and give alms will not be saved, for the same reason. Cooperate

---

[173] Saint Thomas Aquinas, Summa Theologica, I-II, Q. 96, A. 4.
[174] Compendium of the Social Doctrine of the Church, Pontifical Council for Justice and Peace, n. 398-399.
[175] Saint Thomas Aquinas, Summa Theologica, I-II, Q. 96, A. 6.
[176] Saint Thomas Aquinas, Summa Theologica, I-II, Q. 96, A. 6.

with grace interiorly, so that all of your acts are done out of love of God and neighbor, and not merely to be seen by others, and then you will be on the sure path to salvation.

[Matthew]
{5:19} Therefore, whoever will have loosened one of the least of these commandments, and have taught men so, shall be called the least in the kingdom of heaven. But whoever will have done and taught these, such a one shall be called great in the kingdom of heaven.
{5:20} For I say to you, that unless your justice has surpassed that of the scribes and the Pharisees you shall not enter into the kingdom of heaven.
{5:21} You have heard that it was said to the ancients: 'You shall not murder; whoever will have murdered shall be liable to judgment.'
{5:22} But I say to you, that anyone who becomes angry with his brother shall be liable to judgment. But whoever will have called his brother, 'Idiot,' shall be liable to the council. Then, whoever will have called him, 'Worthless,' shall be liable to the fires of Hell.

The scribes and Pharisees followed the commandments only exteriorly, not also interiorly. They followed the letter of the law (at least in many respects), but not the spirit of the law. And so, even though they followed the exterior requirements of the law, even in the smallest parts, they were not just and were not on the path to salvation. For to be saved, the faithful Christian must not only avoid the exterior sins, but also the accompanying interior sins. The commandment "You shall not murder" also implies that you shall not commit any interior acts related to murder, such as malice, hatred, contempt, derision, or any unjust anger toward your neighbor. The Pharisees obeyed the commandments only exteriorly. Similarly, some Catholics claim to be following the teaching of the Church, but they have unjust anger, contempt, derision, and even hatred and malice, toward their neighbors.

{9:11} And the Pharisees, seeing this, said to his disciples, "Why does your Teacher eat with tax collectors and sinners?"

The Pharisees considered themselves to be good and other human persons to be evil. They rejected other human persons, not showing true love of neighbor, on the excuse that such persons erred by violating a rule, or by violating the moral law. To the contrary, Jesus died for all of us, while we were yet sinners. Although we can and should judge and condemn sinful acts, we should not judge and condemn any human person for whom Jesus died. Who knows if a great sinner, like Saul (himself a Pharisee), might soon repent and become a great Saint?

{9:14} Then the disciples of John drew near to him, saying, "Why do we and the Pharisees fast frequently, but your disciples do not fast?"

Fasting is done for a purpose, in order to bring us closer to God. Fasting is not an end in itself; it is a means to the end of greater devotion to God. The person who fasts more often is not necessarily holier than the person who fasts less often. We must not confuse the means with the end. God is our ultimate end. Those who turn various means within religion into ends in themselves, so that these things are no longer directed toward God as our final end, are committing the error of the Pharisees.

{12:10} And behold, there was a man who had a withered hand, and they questioned him, so that they might accuse him, saying, "Is it lawful to cure on the Sabbaths?"
{12:11} But he said to them: "Who is there among you, having even one sheep, if it will have fallen into a pit on the Sabbath, would not take hold of it and lift it up?
{12:12} How much better is a man than a sheep? And so, it is lawful to do good on the Sabbaths."
{12:13} Then he said to the man, "Extend your hand." And he extended it, and it was restored to health, just like the other one.
{12:14} Then the Pharisees, departing, took council against him, as to how they might destroy him.

.164. Other than the eternal moral law, which is the unchanging Justice of God, any law or rule or ruling or judgment or decision of authority, even of the temporal authority of the Church, is subject to exception and to possible faithful disobedience, whenever the justice of God requires a different course of action. Even certain exterior precepts in the Old Testament, which were established by Divine Revelation from God, those that are not doctrines of the moral law, but disciplines of the Old Testament, are subject to the law of charity. The love of God and neighbor permitted Jesus to do what might be considered a type of work on the Sabbath, without being truly unlawful or unjust. For whenever true charity, that is, true love of God and neighbor, is in conflict with a rule or ruling of temporal authority, the law of charity prevails over all lesser laws.

{12:38} Then certain ones from the scribes and the Pharisees responded to him, saying, "Teacher, we want to see a sign from you."

The Pharisees of today demand to see signs, that is, they demand to see credentials, proof of reputation, various types of approval, instead of seeking the truth wherever it may be found.

{15:1} Then the scribes and the Pharisees came to him from Jerusalem, saying:
{15:2} "Why do your disciples transgress the tradition of the elders? For they do not wash their hands when they eat bread."
{15:3} But responding, he said to them: "And why do you transgress the commandment of God for the sake of your tradition?...

The Pharisees of today exalt mere rules and rulings above the commandments and teachings of Divine Revelation. Instead, the faithful Catholic will give each good its proper place in Creation, with God above all Creation. The faithful Catholic puts doctrines on faith and morals above the rules and rulings of the temporal authority. The faithful Catholic knows how to judge the differing weights of various doctrines, and of various disciplines. For not doctrine has the same weight, and not every decision of the temporal authority has the same weight.

The faithful Catholic places Sacred Tradition and Sacred Scripture above the traditions of the present day. So if an idea is commonly accepted in secular society, or even among Catholics, and yet is contrary to Tradition, Scripture, Magisterium, the faithful Catholic will not adhere to the majority view, but will reject that idea. The faithful Catholic distinguishes and prefers the beliefs and practices of the one true Church over the majority view.

{15:12} Then his disciples drew near and said to him, "Do you know that the Pharisees, upon hearing this word, were offended?"
{15:13} But in response he said: "Every plant which has not been planted by my heavenly Father shall be uprooted.
{15:14} Leave them alone. They are blind, and they lead the blind. But if the blind are in charge of the blind, both will fall into the pit."

The Pharisees of today have exalted themselves to become teachers of the Catholic Faith, even though they themselves have badly misunderstood those teachings. They are blind to the true teachings of Tradition, Scripture, Magisterium, and yet they offer themselves as guides to others. Only those who are also blind to truth will follow them.

{16:12} Then they understood that he was not saying that they should beware of the leaven of bread, but of the doctrine of the Pharisees and the Sadducees.

The Pharisees and Sadducees of today are those Catholics who teach false doctrines. The Pharisees are some among conservative Catholics who teach various conservative errors. They think that the conservative theological opinion is necessarily the correct opinion. They broaden the infallibility of the Magisterium, as if the Magisterium were always infallible, never non-infallible. They do not distinguish fallible decisions of the temporal authority; they consider that all decisions, on discipline as well as doctrine, are infallible and are of the Magisterium. They promote blind obedience to the Bishops and the Holy See. They value exterior acts over interior cooperation with grace. But not all conservative Catholics are Pharisees. The Sadducees of today are some among liberal Catholics, who teach various liberal errors. They treat every conservative or traditional theological opinion as suspect. They think that the Second Vatican Council has liberated them from any and all past Church teachings that they dislike. They narrow the infallibility of the Magisterium, so that few if any teachings are infallible. But not all liberal Catholics are Sadducees.

{23:4} For they bind up heavy and unbearable burdens, and they impose them on men's shoulders. But they are not willing to move them with even a finger of their own.
{23:5} Truly, they do all their works so that they may be seen by men. For they enlarge their phylacteries and glorify their hems.
{23:6} And they love the first places at feasts, and the first chairs in the synagogues,
{23:7} and greetings in the marketplace, and to be called Master by men.

The Pharisees of today adhere to the letter of Church law, but not to the spirit of Church teaching and law, which is the spirit of charity. They value reputation and credentials above truth. The interpret Church doctrine and discipline harshly, as if Truth and Mercy were not one in God.

.165. The Pharisees of today use rules to contradict the moral law and the law of charity. Rules have a certain practical usefulness to accomplish good ends by good means in particular circumstances. But there is nothing to prevent either a rule from being poorly-written, so that its usefulness is at best limited, or a rule from being useless or harmful in a particular circumstance. Giving excessive weight to rules is Pharisaism. When anyone follows rules in contradiction to the Gospel and the moral law, such a person sins against God, who is the source of the Divine Revelation of the Gospel message and the source of the moral law. Christ taught us to put faith and morals above mere rules, and to live by faith and love and mercy, not by blind obedience.

Neither can it be said that, once a rule is made by competent authority in the Church, the rule becomes a part of the moral law. For the moral law is universal and unchanging, being in itself the very Nature of God, who is Goodness and Justice, and who is unchanging. Neither can it be said that, once a rule is made by competent authority in the Church, anyone breaking that rule must be sinning. For whoever adheres fully to the moral law completely avoids sin, and the moral law is universal and unchanging. Therefore, it is possible to disobey a rule or ruling of the temporal authority of the Church, without sin.

Now listen to what Christ said, not only about the Pharisees of His day, but prophetically about the Pharisees of future times:

[Matthew]
{23:13} So then: Woe to you, scribes and Pharisees, you hypocrites! For you close the kingdom of heaven before men. For you yourselves do not enter, and those who are entering, you would not permit to enter.
{23:14} Woe to you scribes and Pharisees, you hypocrites! For you consume the houses of widows, praying long prayers. Because of this, you shall receive the greater judgment.
{23:15} Woe to you, scribes and Pharisees, you hypocrites! For you travel around by sea and by land, in order to make one convert. And when he has been converted, you make him twice the son of Hell that you are yourselves.
{23:16} Woe to you, blind guides, who say: 'Whoever will have sworn by the temple, it is nothing. But whoever will have sworn by the gold of the temple is obligated.'
{23:17} You are foolish and blind! For which is greater: the gold, or the temple that sanctifies the gold?
{23:18} And you say: 'Whoever will have sworn by the altar, it is nothing. But whoever will have sworn by the gift that is on the altar is obligated.'
{23:19} How blind you are! For which is greater: the gift, or the altar that sanctifies the gift?
{23:20} Therefore, whoever swears by the altar, swears by it, and by all that is on it.

{23:21} And whoever will have sworn by the temple, swears by it, and by him who dwells in it.
{23:22} And whoever swears by heaven, swears by the throne of God, and by him who sits upon it.
{23:23} Woe to you, scribes and Pharisees, you hypocrites! For you collect tithes on mint and dill and cumin, but you have abandoned the weightier things of the law: judgment and mercy and faith. These you ought to have done, while not omitting the others.
{23:24} You blind guides, straining out a gnat, while swallowing a camel!
{23:25} Woe to you, scribes and Pharisees, you hypocrites! For you clean what is outside the cup and the dish, but on the inside you are full of avarice and impurity.
{23:26} You blind Pharisee! First clean the inside of the cup and the dish, and then what is outside becomes clean.
{23:27} Woe to you, scribes and Pharisees, you hypocrites! For you are like whitewashed sepulchers, which outwardly appear brilliant to men, yet truly, inside, they are filled with the bones of the dead and with all filth.
{23:28} So also, you certainly appear to men outwardly to be just. But inwardly you are filled with hypocrisy and iniquity.
{23:29} Woe to you, scribes and Pharisees, you hypocrites, who build the sepulchers of the prophets and adorn the monuments of the just.
{23:30} And then you say, 'If we had been there in the days of our fathers, we would not have joined with them in the blood of the prophets.'
{23:31} And so you are witnesses against yourselves, that you are the sons of those who killed the prophets.
{23:32} Complete, then, the measure of your fathers.
{23:33} You serpents, you brood of vipers! How will you escape from the judgment of Hell?

.166. From the Old Testament to the New Testament

The Jewish Faith, as described in the Old Testament, had both doctrines and disciplines.

All the truths taught by God in the Old Testament remain true: on faith, on morals, on salvation, and on all subjects about which Sacred Scripture makes an assertion. In particular, the moral law does not change, because the moral law is the Justice inherent to the very Nature of God. And God is unchanging. Therefore, all expressions of the moral law in the Old Testament remain in force. And all the truths about God and salvation and all other subjects remain true. Even though the Jews did not fully understand the plan of God for the Messiah and for salvation, yet all that Divine Revelation taught them remains entirely true. We Christians understand these truths much more profoundly than before Christ arrived. But no falsehoods were taught by Sacred Scripture in the Old Testament. The Old Testament disciplines have been dispensed; but the Old Testament doctrines on faith, morals, and salvation, have not changed.

Examples of doctrines in the Old Testament include that God is One, that God created heaven and earth, and the Ten Commandments. The eternal moral law does not change. The eternal moral law is the same in the Old Testament as in the New Testament. There is a more profound expression of the eternal moral law in the New Testament. But the eternal moral law has not changed; nothing has been added, nothing has been taken away, and nothing has been changed. The reader of the Catechism of the Catholic Church will notice that the section on morality is based on the Ten Commandments. The Old Testament teachings on morality remain true, and have not changed. Yet Christians understand morality more profoundly, and they are called now not only to live moral lives, but to imitate Christ in lives of self-sacrifice and great holiness. Thus we have the new Commandment:

[John]
{13:34} "I give you a new commandment: Love one another. Just as I have loved you, so also must you love one another."

We are called to love even beyond what is required by the moral law, so that we imitate Christ in all that we do. We are called even to reach toward that perfection which we as finite creatures can never attain, the perfect Goodness of God.

[Matthew]
{5:48} "Therefore, be perfect, even as your heavenly Father is perfect."

In one sense, this commandment to love as Christ loves is new. But in another sense, this new commandment is old. For all that Christ would explicitly teach by word and example, was always implicit in the Old Testament.

[1 John]
{2:7} Most beloved, I am not writing to you a new commandment, but the old commandment, which you had from the beginning. The old commandment is the Word, which you have heard.
{2:8} Then too, I am writing to you a new commandment, which is the Truth in him and in you. For the darkness has passed away, and the true Light is now shining.

We understand the eternal moral law, and all the truths of the Faith, better by knowing Christ, His teachings, and His self-sacrifice on the Cross. The entire moral law is implicit in the single act of Jesus Christ dying for our salvation on the Cross. All that is immoral is contrary to Christ's salvific death. All that is moral is in harmony with Christ's salvific death. Each and every teaching of Sacred Tradition, Sacred Scripture, and the Magisterium, on faith and morals and salvation, is implicit in the single act of the Son of God dying for our salvation on the Cross: "though one blood drop, which thence did fall, accepted, would have served, He yet shed all...."[177]

The Old Testament also contains disciplines; these are practices, not truths. The Old Testament practices are changeable and dispensable, and in fact have been

---

[177] John Donne, Upon The Annunciation and Passion Falling Upon One Day (March 25th, 1608).

dispensed by Christ. All the truths of the Old Testament remain true, but the practices have been dispensed and replaced, we might even say transformed, into the New Testament practices. The Old Testament practices foreshadowed Christ, and now that we know Christ more fully than anyone knew Him before His Incarnation, the Old Testament disciplines have given way to the disciplines of the New Testament, which are greater since they proceed from a fuller understanding of doctrine. All good discipline is based on doctrine.

.167. Examples of disciplines in the Old Testament include the dietary laws, the laws concerning ritual purity and impurity, also circumcision, animal sacrifices, and many other practices. This type of 'law' is not part of the doctrine of the moral law, but is a rule or discipline. Discipline is not doctrine. Every correct doctrine is an immutable truth. But every correct discipline is merely a practice, not a truth, and therefore is changeable and dispensable (i.e. it can be taken away). Now the Old Testament dietary laws, and the rules on ritual purity, and the rituals of animal sacrifice, and other disciplines, have been dispensed by Christ. However, all these disciplines were and still are a type of parable, a figure acted out in the lives of the Jewish people, which teach truths (on the spiritual level of meaning). And those teachings are still in effect. So the letter of those Old Testament disciplines has been dispensed, but the letter points to the spirit, for all good disciplines point to, and are ordered under, doctrines. The eternal moral law is that type of law which is doctrine, whereas many Old Testament laws are that type of law which is discipline, and which is therefore changeable and dispensable.

Saint Thomas Aquinas: "I answer that, As is clear from what has been said (101, 2; 102, 2), the legal ceremonies were ordained for a double purpose; the worship of God, and the foreshadowing of Christ. Now whoever worships God must needs worship Him by means of certain fixed things pertaining to external worship. But the fixing of the divine worship belongs to the ceremonies; just as the determining of our relations with our neighbor is a matter determined by the judicial precepts...."[178]

By judicial precepts, St. Thomas means the eternal moral law. Certainly, the moral law has not changed between the Old and New Testaments, for the moral law is eternal. By means of the New Testament, we understand the moral law more profoundly, but the moral law itself has not changed. As for the purpose of the ceremonial laws (e.g. dietary laws), these had a practical purpose in providing exterior actions to accompany the interior worship of God, making that interior worship easier. For the human person is soul and body, not soul alone; and so our worship of God must be in body as well as in soul. But just as the soul is greater than the body, so also is the interior worship greater than the exterior worship.

---

[178] Saint Thomas Aquinas, *Summa Theologica*, I-II, Q. 103, A. 1.

Saint Thomas Aquinas: "The Old Law is said to be 'forever' simply and absolutely, as regards its moral precepts; but as regards the ceremonial precepts it lasts forever in respect of the reality which those ceremonies foreshadowed."[179]

The Old Testament disciplines pointed to spiritual realities in Christ, which continue into New Testament times and forever. Therefore, the Old Testament passages of Sacred Scripture describing these ceremonial precepts are not useless to Christians; the spiritual level of meaning of those passages is still in force and is still a useful figure for understanding Christ and the Christian Faith.

.168. Dietary Laws

The dietary laws of the Old Testament are disciplines, not doctrines; they are not expressions of the unchanging moral law, but are changeable rules and practices. But the letter of these dietary rules also has a spiritual meaning. And this spiritual meaning is unchanging truth.

Before the Jewish Faith was established by God, human society knew only pagan religions, which did not distinguish moral good from moral evil. In order to avoid sin and to live a life pleasing to God, it is necessary for each and every human person to distinguish between good and evil every day. And so God wisely chose to give the Jewish people a living parable, in the form of the dietary laws, so that the Jews would have to consider the will of God in daily life, at every meal. In this way, they could more easily and more quickly incorporate into their lives the daily practice of distinguishing between acts that are good before God and acts that evil before God. So the distinction between clean and unclean foods was a metaphor, incorporated into daily life, for the distinction between good and evil.

God established the Jewish Faith, and He prepared the Jewish people, by grace and providence, and by Divine Revelation, for the arrival of the Messiah, the Son of God. But when Christ arrived and taught, and when He died and rose for our salvation, at that point in human history, the use of this practice of dietary laws, the use of the living metaphor for good and evil, was no longer necessary. This Old Testament discipline could be dispensed, and be replaced with the disciplines of the Catholic Christian faith.

In a sense the disciplines of the Old Testament, as a whole, have not so much been taken away as they have been transfigured into the New Testament disciplines. For we still distinguish between good and evil, between what is good before God and what is evil before God. And we still have exterior practices, and various rules and rulings, all of which are changeable, and all of which serve the higher things of the Faith.

.169. Tithing

[Luke]
{21:1} And looking around, he saw the wealthy putting their donations into the offertory.

---

[179] Saint Thomas Aquinas, Summa Theologica, I-II, Q. 103, A. 2.

{21:2} Then he also saw a certain widow, a pauper, putting in two small brass coins.
{21:3} And he said: "Truly, I say to you, that this poor widow has put in more than all the others.
{21:4} For all these, out of their abundance, have added to the gifts for God. But she, out of what she needed, has put in all that she had to live on."

The Old Testament discipline of tithing (along with all other disciplines of the Old Testament) has been dispensed by Christ. The early Church considered whether or not the Old Testament disciplines were still in force. Peter and the Apostles met and decided (Acts 15) that the Old Testament disciplines are not in force (but on certain specific points, see below). Tithing was not kept in force.

However, all the Old Testament disciplines without exception were a type of figure, expressing profound spiritual truths, and those truths are immutable doctrine. The practice of tithing (giving the set percentage of 10%) points toward a truth in the moral law, a positive precept, to give alms to those in need and to give alms to the Church, for the support and propagation of the Faith.

Now today some Catholics have attempted to reinstitute the practice of tithing, claiming that the Old Testament practice is still in force, that it is still binding, even though Christ dispensed the Old Testament disciplines. This claim implies that some of the Old Testament practices have not been dispensed; it is the same as if they are claiming that Christians must be circumcised, or must carry out animal sacrifices, or must follow the dietary laws. The idea that Catholic Christians today, or at any time since the death and resurrection of Christ, are obligated to give a set percentage of ten percent (or any other set percentage), based on the Old Testament law, is an heretical idea.

Instead, we are under the law of charity, and we are obligated, as a positive precept under the moral law, to give generously to the Church and to those in need, not by the letter of those Old Testament laws which have been dispensed by Christ and by His Church, but as the Spirit moves us, by the grace and providence of God.

[1 Timothy]
{6:17} Instruct the wealthy of this age not to have a superior attitude, nor to hope in the uncertainty of riches, but in the living God, who offers us everything in abundance to enjoy,
{6:18} and to do good, to become rich in good works, to donate readily, to share,
{6:19} to gather for themselves the treasure of a good foundation for the future, so that they may obtain true life.

[2 Corinthians]
{8:14} In this present time, let your abundance supply their need, so that their abundance may also supply your need, in order that there may be an equality, just as it was written:
{8:15} "He with more did not have too much; and he with less did not have too little."
...

{9:6} But I say this: Whoever sows sparingly will also reap sparingly. And whoever sows with blessings shall also reap from blessings:
{9:7} each one giving, just as he has determined in his heart, neither out of sadness, nor out of obligation. For God loves a cheerful giver.
{9:8} And God is able to make every grace abound in you, so that, always having what you need in all things, you may abound unto every good work,
{9:9} just as it was written: "He has distributed widely, he has given to the poor; his justice remains from age to age."

The faithful are called by God to give to those in need and to the Church, generously and cheerfully, not out of obligation, and not according to a set percentage under the Old Testament law. And this generous giving by the Christian is not only, nor mainly, a giving of money, but a giving of one's self fully, so that we help the Church and those in need by our prayers, by self-denial, and by all the works of mercy. Giving alms is only one of the many possible works of mercy, and works of mercy is only one of the three types of good works: (1) prayer, (2) self-denial, (3) works of mercy.

.170. Circumcision

[Philippians]
{3:3} For we are the circumcised, we who serve God in the Spirit and who glory in Christ Jesus, having no confidence in the flesh.

[Colossians]
{2:11} In him also, you have been circumcised with a circumcision not made by hand, not by the despoiling of the body of flesh, but by the circumcision of Christ.

The practice of circumcision is an Old Testament discipline that is no longer in force (Acts 15), but the spiritual meaning remains true and in force. Saint Stephen, the first martyr and one of the first deacons of the Church, teaches that circumcision remains in force on the spiritual level of meaning, as a figure indicating obedience to God.

[Acts]
{7:51} "Stiff-necked and uncircumcised in heart and ears, you ever resist the Holy Spirit. Just as your fathers did, so also do you do."

St. Stephen is not suggesting that Christians must be circumcised. Instead, he is continuing the spiritual meaning of circumcision, while laying aside the exterior practice. The spirit of circumcision still prevails in New Testament times, but the letter of the law on circumcision does not. Saint Paul taught this same approach to circumcision. For even during Old Testament times, the true meaning and usefulness of circumcision was the inward meaning, of which the outward practice was a symbol.

[Romans]
{2:26} And so, if the uncircumcised keep the justices of the law, shall not this lack of circumcision be counted as circumcision?
…

{2:28} For a Jew is not he who seems so outwardly. Neither is circumcision that which seems so outwardly, in the flesh.
{2:29} But a Jew is he who is so inwardly. And circumcision of the heart is in the spirit, not in the letter. For its praise is not of men, but of God.

True circumcision, in Old Testament as well as New Testament times, is of the spirit, not the letter. The outward sign of circumcision, useful in Old Testament times, and no longer necessary in New Testament times, was always merely an indicator of the spiritual meaning. And though the letter of the law concerning the discipline of circumcision is no longer in force, the spiritual meaning of devotion to God remains in force.

[Colossians]
{2:11} In him also, you have been circumcised with a circumcision not made by hand, not by the despoiling of the body of flesh, but by the circumcision of Christ.
...
{2:13} And when you were dead in your transgressions and in the uncircumcision of your flesh, he enlivened you, together with him, forgiving you of all transgressions,

All faithful Christians have a circumcision of the heart; they are circumcised in the figurative sense. The Old Testament practice is no longer in force, but the truths which that practice symbolized remain true. All the truths symbolized by the Old Testament disciplines are still true; they are still in force as spiritual truths.

The spiritual meaning of circumcision is threefold. First, the practice symbolizes a single-hearted devotion to God, in spiritual purity, required of all the faithful, of Jews in ancient times (and still today), and of all Christians. Though Christians lack the outward practice, the inward spiritual purity and single-hearted devotion is required of all Christians, men and women.

Second, the practice symbolizes that chastity (purity in the narrow sense of sexual purity) which avoids all sexual sins, not only adultery and all sexual acts outside of marriage, but also sexual sins within marriage. The sign of circumcision was given only to men, but the meaning applies to men and women.

Jewish women, as mothers, would be responsible for having their male children circumcised at only 8 days of age, an age when the infant would be almost always with his mother. And concerning adult men, a wife would know of her husband's circumcision, which would remind not only him, but also her, that devotion to God (the first meaning) implies faithfulness in all our acts, including those pertaining to sexuality (the second meaning). For each and every marital sexual act must be good under all three fonts of the eternal moral law of God. The mark of circumcision served to remind all Jews that God requires all persons to live a moral life, in all areas of life, including sexuality.

Third, the practice of circumcision symbolizes that God gives different roles to men and women, in the family, in the Faith, and in society. Circumcision was chosen as one of many symbols in the Jewish Faith in order to teach the Jews that God intends different roles for men than for women. Though men and women are equal by having the same human nature, they are given unequal roles. The fact that circumcision is given only to males shows this difference under the plan of God.

Now all three of these spiritual meanings of circumcision continue to prevail today within the Catholic Christian Faith. We are still all called to purity in soul, i.e. to have a single-hearted devotion to God. And this primary meaning of circumcision is the one used in the quotes above from St. Stephen in Acts, and from St. Paul in his Epistles. If anyone is pure in body, entirely a virgin in the bodily sense, but is not pure in heart and mind, that person is not worthy to be called a virgin. True virginity is purity in both body and soul, not in body alone, not in soul alone. Therefore, we are all called to the second meaning of spiritual circumcision, which is the chastity of the body. And no one can commit sexual sins with the body and yet be pure in soul. The interior knowing choice to commit a sexual sin in the body always corrupts the soul. So these two meanings are inseparable.

The third spiritual meaning of circumcision is still in force today. For the Church has always taught that men and women have been given different roles in the family, the Church, and society. For example, the husband is the head of the family; this is taught in Sacred Scripture (1 Corinthians 11; Ephesians 5), as well as by the Magisterium.[180] And in the Church, only men are given the roles of Pope, Bishop, and priest; the Church does not have the ability or the authority to ordain women to the priesthood or to the episcopate.[181] God's intention to give men and women different roles has always been a part of human nature, even from the very beginning before the Fall from grace. For Eve was not created at the same time as Adam, nor in the same manner, nor for the same purpose. But Eve was created second, from the side of Adam, in order to be a helper to Adam (Genesis 2:18-25). And Mary was created to be a helper to Christ.

But the practice of circumcision, the letter of the law of circumcision, is not needed by Christians today. For we have the spiritual meaning of circumcision by our faith in the teachings of Christ.

.171. Transfiguration of the Covenant

The Old Testament laws were part of the Old Testament Covenant. Certainly the moral law is still in force, since the eternal moral law is the Justice of God. But the disciplines of the Old Covenant are not in force. Yet it is not the case that the New Covenant has no discipline. The Church has two types of authority, the teaching authority, which issues doctrines on faith, morals, and salvation, as well as the temporal authority, which issues rules and rulings, that is, disciplines. The faithful depend upon both the beliefs and the practices of the Church in order to live the faith.

---

[180] Pope Pius XI, Casti Connubii, n. 29; see also Pope Leo XIII, Arcanum Divinae Sapientiae, n. 11.
[181] Pope John Paul II, Ordinatio Sacerdotalis.

But the Old Testament Covenant was issues by God in words that indicate it shall continue forever. In Genesis, God says to Abram (Abraham):

[Genesis]
{13:14} And the Lord said to Abram, after Lot was divided from him: "Lift up your eyes, and gaze out from the place where you are now, to the north and to the meridian, to the east and to the west.
{13:15} All the land that you see, I will give to you, and to your offspring even forever.
{13:16} And I will make your offspring like the dust of the earth. If any man is able to number the dust of the earth, he will be able to number your offspring as well."

If the Old Testament covenant is no longer in force, if it has been nullified or even replaced, then the offspring of Abraham would not be his countless spiritual offspring, including all faithful Christians. His offspring would then be a much smaller number. And the meaning of the passage would then be restricted from the broad promise of countless spiritual offspring, to the narrow promise of many merely physical descendents. But the Magnificat of the Virgin Mary in Sacred Scripture teaches that Christians are the spiritual descendents of Abraham:

[Luke]
{1:54} He has taken up his servant Israel, mindful of his mercy,
{1:55} just as he spoke to our fathers: to Abraham and to his offspring forever."

Therefore, the Old Testament covenant, which began with Abraham, continues for his spiritual descendents forever. There is no end to this covenant. So then how can we explain that there is also a New Testament covenant established by the Blood of Christ?

[Luke]
{22:20} Similarly also, he took the chalice, after he had eaten the meal, saying: "This chalice is the new covenant in my blood, which will be shed for you."

We cannot say that the Old Covenant has passed away, since God promised that covenant to Abraham and his (spiritual) descendents forever. And we cannot say that there are two covenants, the Old and the New, by which human persons are saved. For we know by faith that all who are saved have salvation by the Blood of Christ, who died for us on the Cross. Christ is the sole source of salvation, so there cannot be two covenants in force today. Neither can we say that the New Covenant has replaced the Old Covenant, since God promised Abraham that the Old Covenant would continue in his spiritual descendents forever.

The only solution to this theological dilemma is that the Old Covenant has been transfigured, has been transformed, into the New Covenant. All of the Old Covenant promises continue under the New Covenant, in a higher form. For example, the promise concerning the descendents of Abraham, which is true of his physical descendents, the Hebrew people, when they live by faith, is true to an even greater extent of all his spiritual descendents, Christians. And the disciplines of the Old Testament, which had their usefulness in their time, continue to be fulfilled in their spiritual meaning, in the spirit but not the letter of those practices. The promises God made to Abraham and to his descendents, which He said in truth would continue forever, do in truth continue forever, and to a much greater extent than Abraham ever imagined.

This transfiguration of the Old Testament covenant into the New Testament covenant is analogous to the change that occurs at the consecration of bread and wine into the Body and Blood of Christ. Both bread and wine are good things from God; so too is the Old Covenant a good thing from God. But the consecrated bread and wine, which is the Real Presence of Christ, is so much greater than words can express. Similarly, the New Covenant is so much greater than words can express, for God became a man and died for our salvation, and this is the fulfillment, with an exceedingly great superabundance, of every Old Covenant promise and of all the promises of the New Covenant.

Since even the Old Testament disciplines instituted by God by Divine Revelation are dispensable, then certainly the New Testament disciplines are also changeable and dispensable. Now as long as we are in this life, following Christ in body and soul, we need some disciplines, exterior rules for worship, to live as the people of God, to act harmoniously with one another, just as the Israelites needed in ancient times. We need both doctrine and discipline. The temporal authority of the Church has the authority to change various elements of discipline, and to dispense from various elements of discipline. But the Church lacks the authority to entirely dispense from all disciplines, so that the Faith would then be doctrine without discipline. In Heaven, no discipline is needed because all the faithful have the Beatific Vision of God. And after the general Resurrection, again no discipline is needed, for the same reason. But as long as we are in this life, the people of God need some practices, rules, and rulings, as a practical necessity in order to live out the doctrines of the Faith. Doctrine is always greater than discipline, but discipline is not entirely dispensable.

.172. The Force of Old Testament Disciplines

None of the Old Testament disciplines are still in force.

The Council of Florence: "It [the holy Roman church] firmly believes, professes and teaches that the legal prescriptions of the old Testament or the Mosaic law, which are divided into ceremonies, holy sacrifices and sacraments [mysteries, not Sacraments per se], because they were instituted to signify something in the future, although they were adequate for the divine cult of that age, once our Lord Jesus Christ who was signified by them had come, came to an end and the Sacraments of the new Testament had their beginning."[182]

The reason for the Old Testament disciplines in general was to teach a spiritual meaning by a living figure, by a metaphor that was lived in daily life. So in distinguishing between clean and unclean foods, the Israelites cultivated a daily habit of considering and following the will of God, and of distinguishing

---

[182] The Council of Florence, Session 11 (4 February 1442).

between what is acceptable before God and what is not. This was new to religion at the time. The pagan religions did not distinguish at all between good and evil. They had many gods, and a person might do something that supposedly pleased one god, but angered another. There was no sense of absolute right and wrong. So the various ceremonial precepts, i.e. the disciplines, of the Old Testament were useful to compel the Israelites to consider the will of God, at many times throughout the day, in many different areas of life.

In New Testament times, we still have disciplines, but they are the disciplines of the new covenant. Discipline is not doctrine, and so even the new disciplines are dispensable and changeable. For example, we abstain from meat on Fridays of Lent, but a dispensation can be granted for a just reason (e.g. when St. Patrick's feast falls on a Friday of Lent, if there are many Irish Catholics in a particular diocese).

The Council of Florence: "It [the holy Roman church] firmly believes, professes and teaches that every creature of God is good and nothing is to be rejected if it is received with thanksgiving, because according to the word of the Lord not what goes into the mouth defiles a person, and because the difference in the Mosaic law between clean and unclean foods belongs to ceremonial practices, which have passed away and lost their efficacy with the coming of the gospel. It also declares that the Apostolic prohibition [in Acts 15], to abstain from what has been sacrificed to idols and from blood and from what is strangled, was suited to that time when a single Church was rising from Jews and Gentiles, who previously lived with different ceremonies and customs. This was so that the Gentiles should have some observances in common with Jews, and occasion would be offered of coming together in one worship and faith of God and a cause of dissension might be removed, since by ancient custom blood and strangled things seemed abominable to Jews, and Gentiles could be thought to be returning to idolatry if they ate sacrificial food. In places, however, where the Christian religion has been promulgated to such an extent that no Jew is to be met with and all have joined the Church, uniformly practicing the same rites and ceremonies of the gospel and believing that to the clean all things are clean, since the cause of that Apostolic prohibition has ceased, so its effect has ceased. It condemns, then, no kind of food that human society accepts and nobody at all neither man nor woman, should make a distinction between animals, no matter how they died; although for the health of the body, for the practice of virtue or for the sake of regular and ecclesiastical discipline many things that are not proscribed can and should be omitted, as the Apostle says all things are lawful, but not all are helpful [1 Corinthians 6:12]."[183]

All the Old Testament disciplines have been dispensed. But all of the doctrines of the eternal moral law, including all those expressed in the Old Testament, are eternally in force. And the passages of Scripture detailing the Old Testament disciplines still retain their force on the spiritual level of meaning, for these disciplines foreshadowed the New Covenant under Christ, which is still in force.

---

[183] The Council of Florence, Session 11 (4 February 1442).

Now the New Testament does have its own disciplines. For the Christian Faith, like the Jewish Faith in the Old Testament, has both beliefs and practices, i.e. doctrines and disciplines. So it is true that the Old Testament disciplines have been transformed into the higher disciplines of the New Testament.

But as the Council of Florence points out, the early Church retained a few Old Testament disciplines, incorporating them into the New Testament disciplines, in order to avoid the sin of scandal to the Jews who had converted, or who might soon convert, to the Christian Faith.

[Acts]
{15:28} For it has seemed good to the Holy Spirit and to us to impose no further burden upon you, other than these necessary things:
{15:29} that you abstain from things immolated to idols, and from blood, and from what has been suffocated, and from fornication. You will do well to keep yourselves from these things. Farewell."

First, notice that idolatry and fornication are still prohibited. This is a way of indicating that all of the Old Testament laws which are really just expressions of the eternal moral law are still in force. Right and wrong have not changed. The Ten Commandments have not changed. But certain precepts from the Old Testament that are not moral doctrines, but only disciplines were temporarily retained, including not eating certain foods. But these very few Old Testament disciplines that continued (for a limited time) as New Testament disciplines have not become precepts of the moral law; these acts that are generally prohibited as a matter of discipline are not intrinsically evil. All the New Testament disciplines are changeable and dispensable by the authority of the Church. And the Council of Florence, in agreement with Saint Thomas Aquinas in the Summa Theologica, taught that those Old Testament disciplines which were temporarily continued in order to avoid the sin of scandal, have long since lapsed, because the reason for the discipline has lapsed. There is no longer the danger of scandal, since the Church no longer consists of both a large number of recent Jewish converts, and a large number of recent Gentile converts. All discipline lapses (loses its force) when the reason for the discipline lapses.

Saint Thomas Aquinas: "...these foods were forbidden literally, not with the purpose of enforcing compliance with the legal ceremonies, but in order to further the union of Gentiles and Jews living side by side. Because blood and things strangled were loathsome to the Jews by ancient custom; while the Jews might have suspected the Gentiles of relapse into idolatry if the latter had partaken of things offered to idols. Hence these things were prohibited for the time being, during which the Gentiles and Jews were to become united together. But as time went on, with the lapse of the cause, the effect lapsed also, when the truth of the Gospel teaching was divulged, wherein Our Lord taught that 'not that which enters into the mouth defiles a man' (Matthew 15:11); and that 'nothing is to be rejected that is received with thanksgiving' (1 Timothy 4:4)."[184]

---

[184] Saint Thomas Aquinas, Summa Theologica, I-II, Q. 103, A. 4.

But notice that the reason for the discipline was an underlying moral doctrine. The obligation to avoid scandal is a positive precept of the moral law. It is a sin to lead someone else into sin; this is called the sin of scandal. So, for example, Sacred Scripture instructs us through the words of Saint Paul that eating food that has been sacrificed to an idol is not an inherently immoral act. But Christians generally should not do so because of the sin of scandal, i.e. because of the possible harm to persons who might be influence by the example of acts which at least seem to approve of idolatry.

[1 Corinthians]
{8:7} But knowledge is not in everyone. For some persons, even now, with consent to an idol, eat what has been sacrificed to an idol. And their conscience, being infirm, becomes polluted.
{8:8} Yet food does not commend us to God. For if we eat, we will not have more, and if we do not eat, we will not have less.
{8:9} But be careful not to let your liberty become a cause of sin to those who are weak.
{8:10} For if anyone sees someone with knowledge sitting down to eat in idolatry, will not his own conscience, being infirm, be emboldened to eat what has been sacrificed to idols?
{8:11} And should an infirm brother perish by your knowledge, even though Christ died for him?
{8:12} So when you sin in this way against the brothers, and you harm their weakened conscience, then you sin against Christ.

Therefore, if any act is moral in itself (having a good moral object) and is done with good intention, the act is still a sin if the bad consequences, such as leading someone else into sin, outweigh the good consequences. The discipline instituted temporarily in Acts 15 is based on the doctrine of the sin of scandal. All binding discipline is based on doctrine. If any discipline has no basis in the doctrines of faith and morals, then that discipline is not binding.

The continuation of these very few Old Testament disciplines for a brief time teaches us that the Old Testament disciplines were neither in error, nor worthless. And this continuation also teaches us that the Old Testament disciplines are continuous with, and related to, the New Testament disciplines. For all discipline has the purpose of assisting us in worshiping God, and all discipline has a spiritual meaning referring to Christ. This continuation further teaches us that the Old Testament disciplines are still in force under their spiritual meaning.

.173. New Testament Disciplines

Even though the New Testament disciplines are greater than the Old Testament discipline, we cannot live solely by discipline. The doctrines of the Church on faith, morals, and salvation are essential to our journey to eternal life. Nor can we merely learn the letter of the doctrines, and follow the letter of the disciplines. For the Catholic Faith is lived, not only by exterior words and deeds, but also interiorly, by the life of grace in our souls, and by the worship of God from the depths of our hearts and minds. The letter of doctrine and discipline is necessary and useful. But the doctrines must be believed and lived in spirit, and even the exterior disciplines must be lived in spirit, and not merely fulfilled by exterior action. Without interior cooperation with grace, all our exterior actions are meaningless and futile.

We need practices to assist us in worshiping God, and in doing good works. We cannot live the Faith only interiorly. And so we attend Mass, we go to Confession, we pray out loud, we fast, we do works of mercy toward those in need, we avoid committing sins in our exterior words and deeds. These exterior acts must also be accompanied by their corresponding interior acts of cooperation with grace. If we attend Mass, but we withhold from God true worship of the spirit, of the heart and mind, so that we worship only exteriorly, then we have only the letter, but not the spirit, of the Faith. If we go to confession and list all our sins, but if we are not also repentant in soul, then we are not forgiven. For exterior acts by themselves cannot save. If we fast, and recite many prayers, and give money to charity, but not in cooperation with grace, not in true spiritual love of God and neighbor, then we do not benefit from the mere exterior act.

[Matthew]
{6:1} "Pay attention, lest you perform your justice before men, in order to be seen by them; otherwise you shall not have a reward with your Father, who is in heaven.
{6:2} Therefore, when you give alms, do not choose to sound a trumpet before you, as the hypocrites do in the synagogues and in the towns, so that they may be honored by men. Amen I say to you, they have received their reward.
{6:3} But when you give alms, do not let your left hand know what your right hand is doing,
{6:4} so that your almsgiving may be in secret, and your Father, who sees in secret, will repay you.
{6:5} And when you pray, you should not be like the hypocrites, who love standing in the synagogues and at the corners of the streets to pray, so that they may be seen by men. Amen I say to you, they have received their reward.
{6:6} But you, when you pray, enter into your room, and having shut the door, pray to your Father in secret, and your Father, who sees in secret, will repay you.
{6:7} And when praying, do not choose many words, as the pagans do. For they think that by their excess of words they might be heeded.
{6:8} Therefore, do not choose to imitate them. For your Father knows what your needs may be, even before you ask him.

The spirit of the Faith, that is, the interior, is absolutely essential to salvation. If we do all the proper exterior acts, but without cooperating with grace, then we will not benefit spiritually from those acts; they are useless. The Catholic Faith is lived by the virtues of love, faith, hope, and by all the virtues in cooperation with grace, in imitation of the Life of Christ. The mysteries of the Faith exceed all human language and understanding. Certainly, we have exterior disciplines, just as the Jews in ancient times had exterior disciplines. And certainly these New Testament disciplines are greater than the Old Testament disciplines. But neither type of discipline is useful to our salvation, unless the inner spiritual meaning is lived along with the exterior practices. The exterior is useful, and the interior is essential.

.174. The Letter versus the Spirit of the Law

[2 Corinthians]
{3:6} And he has made us suitable ministers of the New Testament, not in the letter, but in the Spirit. For the letter kills, but the Spirit gives life.

When we live in the Holy Spirit, we do not abandon or despise the letter of the law, such as the written words of Sacred Scripture, or the written words of Church doctrine, or the practices, rules, and rulings of the Church. But it is only by living in cooperation with grace that we can give life to the written words that describe the Catholic Faith. We worship God from the depths of our hearts and minds, from the depths of our souls, and this worship also manifests itself exteriorly. But exterior acts alone cannot save; interior acts in cooperation with grace are necessary for salvation. The letter without the spirit does not give eternal life.

The Apostle Paul, formerly Saul, was a devout practicing Jew, but he practiced only the letter of the Jewish Faith. When the Messiah arrived, Saul did not accept Him. When a group of persons murdered Saint Stephen, Saul cooperated in his death. When the Christian Faith began to spread, Saul persecuted the Church and delivered some Christians to imprisonment and death. Saul followed only the letter of the Old Testament law. He did not follow the teachings of God in the Old Testament in spirit. He lacked judgment and mercy and that living faith which can only exist along with love and hope. But at his conversion, Saul became the Apostle Saint Paul, a man who lived and taught the faith by interior grace as well as by exterior acts.

[Matthew]
{23:23} Woe to you, scribes and Pharisees, you hypocrites! For you collect tithes on mint and dill and cumin, but you have abandoned the weightier things of the law: judgment and mercy and faith. These you ought to have done, while not omitting the others.

The weightier things of the law are of the spirit: good judgment, mercy to others, and faith in God. But notice that Jesus does not teach us to abandon the letter of the law. The letter of the law is useful to the practice of the faith, but the spirit of the law gives life to faith. For the letter of the law practiced by itself results in a faith that is dead. But the spirit of the law, practiced with interior grace and exterior good works, keeps faith alive in true spiritual love and with hope for eternal life.

In Old Testament times, God gave the Israelites the letter of a law written by God Himself, including both doctrines on faith and morals, and Old Testament disciplines. But the Jews continued to sin, even seriously, for generation after generation. This example proves that no set of written laws, however just and prudent they may be, can cause a society to be good. Every society should have just and prudent laws. But just laws and good customs cannot cause society to be good; the people must choose to be good. As always, an inner cooperation with grace is necessary for every knowingly chosen good act to have eternal value. Nothing is good before God which is contrary to His will and grace.

Just laws cannot solve problems caused by sin. In the history of humanity, every just law has been broken. Thus, the letter of the law cannot succeed without the spirit of the law. And the spirit of the law is the law of charity, the unwritten law of cooperation between free will and grace. The negative and positive precepts of the eternal moral law are only truly fulfilled when the human person cooperates with grace. So, for example, if a man refrains from adultery as an exterior act, but interiorly he sins by lust, he has still broken the commandment against adultery. For he did not cooperate with grace interiorly. Thus, the letter of the law is necessary, but not sufficient.

[Matthew]
{5:17} Do not think that I have come to loosen the law or the prophets. I have not come to loosen, but to fulfill.
{5:18} Amen I say to you, certainly, until heaven and earth pass away, not one iota, not one dot shall pass away from the law, until all is done.

The letter is necessary. We know God by means of the letters of Sacred Scripture, and by the writings of the Saints, Fathers, and Doctors of the Church, and by the teachings of the Magisterium (which are usually written). The disciplines of the Church, the practices and rules and rulings, are necessary. But the letter is not sufficient. The letter alone does not give life.

The gift of sanctifying grace given at Baptism gives life. Our inner cooperation with grace, which is our cooperation with the Holy Spirit, retains life. If we do all the proper exterior works, but do not have that inner grace, then we are spiritually dead. But if we live according to the law of charity, then we will fulfill both the letter and the spirit of the law.

.175. The Letter of the Moral Law

The letter of the eternal moral law is a direct expression of immutable true doctrines, and so can never be dispensed. Every correct expression of the eternal moral law combines both the spirit and the letter of the law of that Justice, which is the very Nature of God. Therefore, it is not possible for the Church, nor even for Christ, to dispense from the eternal moral law. All the laws of the eternal moral law are immutable truths, true from all eternity, as unchanging as God is unchanging.

[Matthew]
{5:17} Do not think that I have come to loosen the law or the prophets. I have not come to loosen, but to fulfill.
{5:18} Amen I say to you, certainly, until heaven and earth pass away, not one iota, not one dot shall pass away from the law, until all is done.
{5:19} Therefore, whoever will have loosened one of the least of these commandments, and have taught men so, shall be called the least in the

kingdom of heaven. But whoever will have done and taught these, such a one shall be called great in the kingdom of heaven.
{5:20} For I say to you, that unless your justice has surpassed that of the scribes and the Pharisees you shall not enter into the kingdom of heaven.

The scribes and Pharisees fulfilled only the letter of the law, and not also the spirit of the law. Any Catholic who likewise fulfills only the letter of Church doctrine and discipline, and not also the spirit of the law, which is the law of true charity, any such person, whether Catholic or not, will not enter the kingdom of heaven.

There are no legal loopholes in the moral law.

Definitions of particular types of sins (e.g. lying, adultery, stealing, etc.) must necessarily use one wording or another. It may well be possible to find an act that should be categorized as stealing or lying, but which does not fit a particular wording of the definition of that sin in a particular magisterial document, interpreted in a legalistic or narrow manner. Even in such cases, that act should still be categorized as that sin. The proper question is not whether an act fits a particular wording in a particular definition of a sin, but whether or not that act has the same moral meaning, good or evil, as the defined act. In practice, a number of different wordings would be possible, reasonable, and useful to describe the very same act with its inherent moral object. And in practice, some useful wordings, describing a particular type of sin, might not be broad enough, especially when interpreted in a legalistic or narrow manner, to include all sins of that type. Even so, all that is contrary to the eternal moral law, which is the Justice of the very Nature of God, is in truth a sin, even if a particular letter of the law can be found which makes it seem as if the sinful act is permitted.

Examples: (1) Suppose that we define abortion as the killing of an innocent human being prior to birth, and infanticide as the killing of an innocent human being during infancy. Then how would we treat the killing of an innocent human being during birth (so-called partial birth abortion)? Even though this killing does not fit the particular wording used in this example (narrowly interpreted), the act has the same inherent moral object, the killing of an innocent human, and so the act could be categorized as either abortion or infanticide, despite the particular wording used in this example.

(2) You shall not bear false witness against your neighbor. The commandment does not seem to forbid bearing false witness 'in favor' of your neighbor, such as lying under oath to keep your guilty neighbor from being convicted of his crime. But Sacred Tradition has always interpreted this commandment as forbidding all lying. The wording of the commandment describes the worst case of lying, but despite the particular wording, all lying is prohibited by this commandment.

(3) You shall not commit adultery. The commandment does not seem to forbid pre-marital sex, since in that case neither person would be married. But Sacred Tradition has always interpreted this commandment as forbidding all sexual immorality. The wording of the commandment describes one of the worst (and

perhaps one of the most common) cases, but despite the particular wording, all sexual immorality is prohibited by this commandment.

Every human person is held by God to the full meaning of the moral law, despite any legalistic or narrow interpretation of the particular wording of any particular definition of a sin. If any type of sin is defined in such a way that one can find a substantially similar act that does not meet the exact wording of that particular definition, that act is still a sin, since if violates the spirit of the law, even if it seems to be allowed by the letter of the law.

Jesus himself gave examples of this type of misinterpretation of the letter of the law.

[Matthew]
{5:19} Therefore, whoever will have loosened one of the least of these commandments, and have taught men so, shall be called the least in the kingdom of heaven. But whoever will have done and taught these, such a one shall be called great in the kingdom of heaven.
{5:20} For I say to you, that unless your justice has surpassed that of the scribes and the Pharisees you shall not enter into the kingdom of heaven.
{5:21} You have heard that it was said to the ancients: 'You shall not murder; whoever will have murdered shall be liable to judgment.'
{5:22} But I say to you, that anyone who becomes angry with his brother shall be liable to judgment. But whoever will have called his brother, 'Idiot,' shall be liable to the council. Then, whoever will have called him, 'Worthless,' shall be liable to the fires of Hell.

Jesus interprets the commandment not to murder as prohibiting even the interior act of unjust anger against one's neighbor, as well as the exterior acts that are far short of murder, such as expressing that unjust anger merely in words. Sacred Tradition has always interpreted the commandment against murder to prohibit also unjust acts of violence that are short of murder, as well as interior sinful acts related to unjust violence against one's neighbor.

[Matthew]
{5:27} You have heard that it was said to the ancients: 'You shall not commit adultery.'
{5:28} But I say to you, that anyone who will have looked at a woman, so as to lust after her, has already committed adultery with her in his heart.

Jesus interprets the commandment not to commit adultery as prohibiting even the interior act of lust. The letter of the law prohibits the exterior act of adultery, but the spirit of the law prohibits all immoral sexual acts, and all interior acts of lust.

Jesus also condemns the misuse of the letter of a particular law or rule in order to justify immoral acts.

[Matthew]
{23:16} Woe to you, blind guides, who say: 'Whoever will have sworn by the temple, it is nothing. But whoever will have sworn by the gold of the temple is obligated.'
{23:17} You are foolish and blind! For which is greater: the gold, or the temple that sanctifies the gold?
{23:18} And you say: 'Whoever will have sworn by the altar, it is nothing. But whoever will have sworn by the gift that is on the altar is obligated.'
{23:19} How blind you are! For which is greater: the gift, or the altar that sanctifies the gift?
{23:20} Therefore, whoever swears by the altar, swears by it, and by all that is on it.
{23:21} And whoever will have sworn by the temple, swears by it, and by him who dwells in it.
{23:22} And whoever swears by heaven, swears by the throne of God, and by him who sits upon it.

The law of charity is above every rule. The law of charity can overrule any rule. The law of charity is the interpreter of every rule.

Chapter 13
Imperfection and Perfection

.176.
Not every failure to do the whole will of God is a sin.

We mere weak and mortal human beings are in a fallen state. We have concupiscence, that remnant of original sin which remains after baptism, and which manifests itself as a tendency toward sin. We have been adversely affected by our past personal sins and by the sinfulness of the world in which we live. We are sinners who lack the beatific vision of God, and so our knowledge and application of the eternal moral law is limited and flawed.

As a result, an individual often may fall short of doing the whole will of God, but without sin. Any act in which all three fonts are good is a moral act, even if the act is far from perfect. All knowingly chosen acts that are without sin are good in the eyes of God, even when such acts fail to do the whole will of God.

Examples: (1) An individual resolves to fast more strictly than is required during Lent. If he falls short of his resolution, but still does at least what is required, then he has not sinned, even though he has fallen short of his praiseworthy goal. (2) An individual resolves to go to daily Mass every day for a period of time. If he falls short of his resolution, but still does at least what is required, then he has not sinned, even though he has fallen short of his praiseworthy goal.

A perfect act entirely fulfills the will of God concerning that act. Most knowingly chosen acts by most human persons fall short of perfection. An imperfect act falls short of perfection, but not to such an extent as to be a sin. Some imperfect acts have no more goodness than needed to avoid sin, whereas other imperfect acts have more goodness than needed to avoid sin, but still fall short of complete harmony with the perfect will of God for that act. Thus, some acts are perfect, some acts are far from perfect yet avoid sin, and other acts fall somewhere between those two extremes. Sacred Scripture expresses this truth about perfection and imperfection in Saint Paul's letter to the Romans.

[Romans]
{12:2} And do not choose to be conformed to this age, but instead choose to be reformed in the newness of your mind, so that you may demonstrate what is the will of God: what is good, and what is well-pleasing, and what is perfect.

All knowingly chosen acts that avoid sin are good before God, and so the will of God includes all good acts. Some acts are perfect before God because they fulfill all that God wills for that act. A well-pleasing act falls short of perfection, so that the individual does less than the whole will of God, but is more pleasing to God than an act that merely avoids sin. All human acts that avoid sin are good. All human acts that avoid sin conform to the will of God to a sufficient extent, even when the particular act does not conform to the will of God perfectly, i.e. to a full extent.

Imperfection and Perfection

[Matthew]

{19:16} And behold, someone approached and said to him, "Good Teacher, what good should I do, so that I may have eternal life?"

{19:17} And he said to him: "Why do you question me about what is good? One is good: God. But if you wish to enter into life, observe the commandments."

{19:18} He said to him, "Which?" And Jesus said: "You shall not murder. You shall not commit adultery. You shall not steal. You shall not give false testimony.

{19:19} Honor your father and your mother. And, you shall love your neighbor as yourself."

{19:20} The young man said to him: "All these I have kept from my childhood. What is still lacking for me?"

{19:21} Jesus said to him: "If you are willing to be perfect, go, sell what you have, and give to the poor, and then you will have treasure in heaven. And come, follow me."

{19:22} And when the young man had heard this word, he went away sad, for he had many possessions.

The young man avoided sin, in that he fulfilled all the commandments, including loving his neighbor as himself. But when Jesus called him to be perfect, he declined. This young man did not commit a mortal sin by declining to be perfect. Christ did not say to him that one more thing was required in order to have eternal life, but only that one more thing was required for perfection. This young man was imperfect; he failed when called to perfection by Christ. But he still had eternal life, because he avoided mortal sin, even while being imperfect. Therefore, perfection in doing the will of God is best, but is not required for eternal life.

.177. A sinful act is an act that is contrary to the very Nature of God, for God is Justice and Love and Mercy and Goodness. A sinful act is an act that is contrary to true love of God and true love of neighbor, as these goods are properly understood by faith and reason. A sinful act is an act that is contrary to the eternal moral law. All knowingly chosen acts that are not at all sinful are good in the eyes of God. All Creation is good. Human nature is good, since we are made in the image of God. Therefore, all human acts, all knowingly chosen acts by human persons, if these acts at least avoid sin, are necessarily good before God. An act that fails to be perfect, but also avoids sin, is a good act.

Examples: (1) A person attends holy Mass on Sunday, fulfilling the obligation to worship God and to keep holy the Sabbath. (2) Another person does the same, and participates with greater devotion, but not whole-heartedly. (3) Still another person participates in holy Mass with a whole-hearted devotion. The person in the first example avoided sin. The second person avoided sin and did more to please God, but was not perfect. As for the third person, it is difficult to say if his participation in holy Mass was truly perfect, or merely closer to perfection than the other examples.

(4) A person donates money to those in need. He gives from money that he does not need, after he provides for all that he himself needs. His limited donations to charity are still good. He avoids a sin of omission by giving alms in this way. (5)

An elderly woman, a widow with no family to support, nor anyone to support her, gives to charity all that she has to live on. She has not only fulfilled her moral obligation to help those in need, she has done so with a perfection that is in imitation of Christ's perfect and total self-giving for our salvation.

[Mark]
{12:41} And Jesus, sitting opposite the offertory box, considered the way in which the crowd cast coins into the offertory, and that many of the wealthy cast in a great deal.
{12:42} But when one poor widow had arrived, she put in two small coins, which is a quarter.
{12:43} And calling together his disciples, he said to them: "Amen I say to you, that this poor widow has put in more than all those who contributed to the offertory.
{12:44} For they all gave from their abundance, yet truly, she gave from her scarcity, even all that she had, her entire living."

This woman is a widow; she could only morally give her entire living because she had no family to support. So if a man who is husband and father, or a woman who is wife and mother, gives not only from their excess, but more generously (e.g. cutting back on expenses, so as to give more to charity), they may be perfect in almsgiving without giving away the family's entire living. If they give away all that they have, so that they are no longer able to support their own family, this act is sin, not perfection. So perfection is not the greatest degree, but the most fitting degree in accord with the will of God.

Perfection, in some acts, by sinners in this mortal life, is not such a high standard as to be unattainable. All sinners are imperfect and also sinful, by definition. But some particular acts by sinners, those sinners who are in a state of grace and who are striving to do the will of God, can sometimes be perfect in the eyes of God. This is possible by the grace of God, and not by human effort alone. Sacred Scripture gives some examples of perfect and imperfect acts.

[1 Chronicles]
{12:38} All these men of war, equipped for the fight, went with a perfect heart to Hebron, so that they might appoint David as king over all of Israel. Then, too, all the remainder of Israel were of one heart, so that they might make David king.

Sacred Scripture does not say that these men of war were perfect in their entire lives, but only in their heart, in this particular intention of the heart, to make David king in accord with the will of God. They desired to have David as king because he was God's choice as king. Their intention was in perfect harmony with the will of God, in this particular purpose. The same was true for the rest of Israel who also desired David as king; they were perfect in this particular intention.

[2 Chronicles]
{25:1} Amaziah was twenty-five years old when he had begun to reign. And he reigned for twenty-nine years in Jerusalem. The name of his mother was Jehoaddan, from Jerusalem.

{25:2} And he accomplished good in the sight of the Lord. Yet truly, not with a perfect heart.
{25:3} And when he saw himself to be strengthened in his rule, he cut the throats of the servants who had killed his father, the king.
{25:4} But he did not put to death their sons, just as it was written in the book of the law of Moses, where the Lord instructed, saying: "The fathers shall not be slain because of the sons, nor the sons because of their fathers. Instead, each one shall die for his own sin."

King Amaziah did what was good in the eyes of God. As king, he had the authority to judge and to sentence the servants who had murdered the previous king, his father. And so his act of issuing a just sentence against them was good. Then he did not put to death their sons, which would have been a sinful act of revenge, not an act of justice, since they were not guilty of this crime. But Sacred Scripture reveals to us that his heart was not perfect. Perhaps he would have been perfect in heart if he had shown mercy to those servants, by not giving them the death penalty, despite their serious crime. Or perhaps his act was imperfect for other reasons. But since he did what was just, he avoided sin, and his actions were good, but not perfect, before God.

[1 Kings]
{15:14} But the high places, he did not take away. Yet truly, the heart of Asa was perfect with the Lord during all his days.

King Asa was perfect before God in his decision to follow the will of the Lord, as it was known to him through the Jewish law and the prophets in ancient times. Some of the Israelites worshipped in the high places, on hilltops and mountainsides throughout the country. This worship was directed at the Lord, but also incorporated some of the false ideas and rituals of pagan worship. King Asa did not worship in the high places, and so his own heart was perfect in his desire to worship God in accord with faith and reason. Yet he was not perfect his exercise of kingly authority. For he had the authority to correct those who went astray from true worship, by taking away the high places, and he did not do so. So here is an example of a human person who was perfect in one act (his decision to worship God uprightly), but imperfect or sinful in another act (his decision to omit correcting those who erred in their worship of God).

[Joshua]
{24:14} Now therefore, fear the Lord, and serve him with a perfect and very sincere heart. And take away the gods that your fathers served in Mesopotamia and in Egypt, and serve the Lord.

.178. If a person tries to avoid mortal sin, but does not try to avoid venial sin, he will commit many venial sins and some mortal sins. If a person tries to avoid both mortal sin and venial sin, he will commit fewer venial sins, but he will usually avoid mortal sin. If a person tries to be perfect and very sincere in doing God's will, he will often fall into imperfection, but less often into venial sin, and rarely if ever into mortal sin. If we wish to please God and to live a moral life, we cannot merely strive to avoid mortal sin. We must strive to do the will of God with a perfect and very sincere heart.

[Luke]
{7:19} And John called two of his disciples, and he sent them to Jesus, saying, "Are you he who is to come, or should we wait for another?"

Saint John the Baptist did not sin by asking Jesus who He was. For at that time, Jesus had not yet died and risen as the final revelation within His Ministry of His identity as the Savior and the Son of God. John asked this question early in the Ministry of Jesus. His uncertainty, at that point in time, about the role of Jesus in salvation history was an imperfection, not a sin. Even the holiest Saints of the Church fall short of perfection.

[Matthew]
{1:18} Now the procreation of the Christ occurred in this way. After his mother Mary had been betrothed to Joseph, before they lived together, she was found to have conceived in her womb by the Holy Spirit.
{1:19} Then Joseph, her husband, since he was just and was not willing to hand her over, preferred to send her away secretly.

Saint Joseph, patron of the universal Church and head of the Holy Family, was very holy and yet imperfect. He thought that perhaps the best course of action would be to send his betrothed, the Virgin Mary, away secretly, rather than to continue as her chaste husband. He erred, and was corrected by God, but he did not sin. Even the holiest Saints of the Church fall short of perfection.

Saint Teresa of Avila: "In small matters I followed my own inclinations, and I still do so, without paying any attention to what is most perfect."[185]

Imperfection in this life is very common, even among the holiest of Saints. Our imperfections should humble us to greater appreciation for the perfection that is God. We should strive for perfection, but not expect perfection.

[Matthew]
{5:48} "Therefore, be perfect, even as your heavenly Father is perfect."
...
{19:21} Jesus said to him: "If you are willing to be perfect, go, sell what you have, and give to the poor, and then you will have treasure in heaven. And come, follow me."

In both the Old and New Testament times, even for mere weak and mortal sinners, some perfection in this life is attainable. But Jesus presents this call to be utterly perfect, "even as your heavenly Father is perfect," not as a requirement for salvation, and not as a goal that can be completely attained in this life. Instead, this journey toward perfection begins in this life, but is only completed in Heaven. Then we will have the Beatific Vision of God, and we will no longer sin at all, and we will no longer stray from the perfect will of God in the least.

Saint Therese of Lisieux: "for the holiest souls will not be perfect till they are in heaven."[186]

---

[185] St. Teresa of Avila, The Way of Perfection, p. 55.

Imperfection and Perfection

.179. Perfection

In order to avoid sin, our will must be in agreement with the eternal moral law, so that we never knowingly choose an immoral act. For all sin is of the will. In order to be perfect, our will must be in full agreement with the perfect will of God, so that we never knowingly choose less than the whole will of God for each act. But in this life, we mere weak and mortal human beings are not entirely perfect in all that we do. Even when we sinners avoid sin concerning a particular choice, we often fall short of perfection.

Jesus is entirely perfect in His human nature because His human nature is thoroughly united to His perfect Divine Nature as one Divine Person. The human nature of Jesus was filled with every grace, from His Divine Nature, within the hypostatic union, from the first moment of His Incarnation, and throughout every moment thereafter. The human nature of Jesus is without original sin, and without personal sin, and without imperfection of any kind.

The Virgin Mary is the perfect disciple of her Divine Son Jesus Christ. She is merely human, not Divine. But her human nature is without original sin, and without personal sin, and without imperfection of any kind. For she was filled with every grace by the Holy Spirit, from the first moment of her existence at her Immaculate Conception, and throughout every moment thereafter. She always did God's whole will without any exception, and so she was always sinless and entirely perfect in every knowingly chosen act.

Even though the human natures of Jesus and Mary are each perfect, the human nature of Jesus is greater than the human nature of Mary. The place in Creation given to the human nature of Jesus is greater than the place given to the Virgin Mary. The entire human race, including the Virgin Mary, is offered eternal salvation through the human nature of Jesus, through His death and Resurrection. The human nature of the Virgin Mary is saved through the human nature of Jesus. Therefore, even when we consider only His human nature by itself, Christ is greater than Mary. Yet both are perfect.

.180. False Ideas about Perfection

The topic of the path to spiritual perfection could fill many volumes. Many Saints have written about the path to greater holiness. However, for the purposes of this volume on ethics, a caution against certain false ideas about perfection should be sufficient.

Fewer sins does not necessarily indicate a greater degree of perfection. An infant commits no personal sins. A holy Saint might still commit some venial sins in his or her adult life. But the Saint is held up as an example of holiness for all to imitate, and the infant is not. The baptized infant who dies, goes to Heaven, and so does the Saint. But the reward of the Saint is so much greater, because he or she has done many good works for the Lord in cooperation with the grace of

---

[186] St. Therese of Lisieux, Autobiography, PDF version, p. 90.

God. Spiritual perfection is found partly in avoiding sin; but it is also found in works of true love and mercy carried out in imitation of Christ.

Examples: (1) A Saint has a high degree of perfection by spending his days in a monastery meditating on God; he commits few venial sins. Then God calls this Saint to leave the contemplative life, so as to live an active life among worldly sinners, for their great benefit. In this next stage of his life, this Saint might have more venial sins than he did in the monastery, due to the difficulties of living among sinners in the world. But since he is doing the will of God, despite having more venial sins, he has a greater degree of perfection than if he remained in the monastery.

(2) The Virgin Mary is, always has been, and always will be, entirely sinless. But if we judge her holiness merely by the lack of sin, she would seem to have the same degree of holiness from her Immaculate Conception to her Assumption. Yet the most important deeds of her life, done in full cooperation with grace, were to be the mother of our Savior, and to suffer with Him at the foot of His Cross. As a young girl, prior to her fiat (her 'Let it be done' when God asked her to be the mother of the Messiah), she was not as holy as after her fiat. Each act that we do in cooperation with grace makes us holier. And after she suffered with Christ at the foot of His Cross, she was holier than before she suffered with him. For to suffer with Christ is the summit of holiness in this life.

Therefore, perfection is found not only in avoiding sin, but also in the acts that we do in cooperation with grace. Mary was perfect as a child, and perfect as an adult, and yet she increased in holiness, because perfection for an adult is greater than perfection for a child. Jesus and Mary are each sinless and perfect, yet the human nature of Jesus is greater than the human nature of Mary. One perfection can be greater than another perfection. A perfect act of martyrdom is greater than a perfect act of almsgiving. A perfect consent to the vow of chastity is greater than a perfect consent to the vow of holy matrimony.

A greater number of exterior works does not necessarily indicate a greater degree of perfection. We must not fall into the error of thinking that if we pray the Rosary, go to daily Mass, fast two or three times a week, donate a certain percentage of what we earn to charitable causes, etc., that we have become close to perfect. None of these exterior acts are at all meritorious in the eyes of God, except when accompanied by an interior cooperation with grace. And every cooperation with grace is an act of love toward God and neighbor. This true spiritual love is called charity.

[1 Corinthians]
{13:1} If I were to speak in the language of men, or of Angels, yet not have charity, I would be like a clanging bell or a crashing cymbal.
{13:2} And if I have prophecy, and learn every mystery, and obtain all knowledge, and possess all faith, so that I could move mountains, yet not have charity, then I am nothing.
{13:3} And if I distribute all my goods in order to feed the poor, and if I hand over my body to be burned, yet not have charity, it offers me nothing.

Neither recited prayer, nor fasting and self-denial, nor works of mercy, are truly good unless these acts are done in cooperation with grace. The intention of the will to knowingly choose good, rather than evil, is necessary for an act to be good before God. A good act (having a good moral object), done with only good consequences, is still a sin if it is done with a bad intention, such as selfishness or greed or lust or malice.

[Luke]
{18:9} Now about certain persons who consider themselves to be just, while disdaining others, he told also this parable:
{18:10} "Two men ascended to the temple, in order to pray. One was a Pharisee, and the other was a tax collector.
{18:11} Standing, the Pharisee prayed within himself in this way: 'O God, I give thanks to you that I am not like the rest of men: robbers, unjust, adulterers, even as this tax collector chooses to be.
{18:12} I fast twice between Sabbaths. I give tithes from all that I possess.'
{18:13} And the tax collector, standing at a distance, was not willing to even lift up his eyes to heaven. But he struck his chest, saying: 'O God, be merciful to me, a sinner.'
{18:14} I say to you, this one descended to his house justified, but not the other. For everyone who exalts himself will be humbled; and whoever humbles himself will be exalted."

Prayer is only a path to holiness if done in love, faith, and hope. Fasting is only a path to holiness if done in love, faith, and hope. Giving money to charity is only a path to holiness if done in love, faith, and hope. Works of mercy are only a path to holiness if done in love, faith, and hope. There is a false idea of perfection, found among the Pharisees of today, which considers perfection to consist solely in exterior acts, without an interior cooperation with grace.

[Matthew]
{23:27} Woe to you, scribes and Pharisees, you hypocrites! For you are like whitewashed sepulchers, which outwardly appear brilliant to men, yet truly, inside, they are filled with the bones of the dead and with all filth.
{23:28} So also, you certainly appear to men outwardly to be just. But inwardly you are filled with hypocrisy and iniquity.

Another idea of perfection correctly considers perfection to be found in doing the will of God, but errs to a great extent in finding God's will. This error is due to a lack of detachment from self and from the world. Such persons are only doing their own will. Sometimes even great sins are committed by persons who claim that they are doing the will of God. They may rationalize their actions by saying that it is the will of God, but such is not the case.

[John]
{16:2} They will put you out of the synagogues. But the hour is coming when everyone who puts you to death will consider that he is offering an excellent service to God.

Imperfection and Perfection

.181. Those who would seek perfection must have true spiritual detachment from self and from this world, in order to find the true will of God. We mere weak and mortal sinners must always consider the possibility that what we think is the will of God is not truly His will, but our own erroneous idea about His will.

Saint Teresa of Avila: "Let us now come to the detachment which we must practice, for if this is carried out perfectly it includes everything else."[187]

The Imitation of Christ: "He is truly wise who looks upon all earthly things as folly that he may gain Christ. He who does God's will and renounces his own is truly very learned."[188]

Another error considers perfection to be found in being "100% faithful to the Magisterium" of the Church. But the Magisterium teaches us to be faithful to Sacred Tradition and to Sacred Scripture, not to the Magisterium alone. Therefore, such persons err by narrowing the teachings of the Faith only to the teachings of the Magisterium. They also err by further narrowing the teachings of the Magisterium solely to the written explicit teachings of the Magisterium, and not also to all that is implied by those teachings. Thus they make the living Magisterium into a dead Magisterium. Often such persons misunderstand what the Magisterium teaches in its explicit written teachings. For having separated the teachings of the Magisterium from Sacred Tradition and Sacred Scripture, and having reduced the meaning of those teachings to only the dead letter and not the living Word, they are unable to properly understand even what is explicitly written. Finally, having convinced themselves that they are perfect in their understanding (of this narrowed, over-simplified, and erroneous version of Catholic teaching), nothing can dissuade them from their errors. They do not even consider the possibility that they have erred. They are like the Pharisees who strictly followed only the letter of the law, and not also the spirit of the law.

We must all be aware, in striving to do the will of God, that our knowledge of the will of God is fallible and limited. If we strive for perfection by doing God's will, but without taking account of our fallibility and limitations in knowing the will of God, we will go astray from the path to perfection and holiness. Many a Catholic thinks himself to be perfect, not because he does God's whole will, but because he does his own over-simplified and flawed version of God's will.

Saint Therese of Lisieux: "I used to think myself completely detached, but since Our Lord's words have become clear, I see that I am indeed very imperfect."[189]

Unless you are holier than Saint Therese of Lisieux, you are very imperfect.

.182. Prayer is important to the path of perfection and holiness, but without the inner cooperation with grace, the mere mental or verbal recitation of prayer is empty. Praying in cooperation with grace is sometimes called praying with the heart. But it would be an error to consider prayer with the heart to refer merely

---

[187] St. Teresa of Avila, The Way of Perfection, p. 41.
[188] Thomas a Kempis, The Imitation of Christ, Christian Classics Ethereal Library ebook edition, p. 8.
[189] St. Therese of Lisieux, Autobiography, PDF version, p. 80.

Imperfection and Perfection

to prayer with emotion. Devotion is not emotion. If we are not only to avoid sin, but also to follow the path of perfection by doing the whole will of God, we must pray regardless of whether the emotions of the moment are assisting or hindering our prayers. Perseverance in prayer, regardless of our emotions and our physical or psychological state, indicates cooperation with grace. We must not pray only when led to prayer by emotion.

Saint Teresa of Avila: "perfect souls are in no way repelled by trials, but rather desire them and pray for them and love them."[190]

Saint Therese of Lisieux: "He has been pleased to create great Saints, who may be compared to the lily and the rose, but He has also created lesser ones, who must be content to be daisies or simple violets flowering at His Feet, and whose mission it is to gladden His Divine Eyes when He deigns to look down on them. And the more gladly they do His Will the greater is their perfection."[191]

There is a false idea of perfection which considers the path to holiness to be the same for all persons. If one person goes to daily Mass, and another person attends Mass only on Sundays and holy days, it would be an error to conclude that the person going to daily Mass is necessarily holier or more perfect. If one person fasts three times in a week, and another person does not fast at all in that week, it would be an error to conclude that the person who is not fasting is necessarily less holy or less perfect. For perfection is found in doing the will of God, and the will of God is not the same for all persons. If it is God's will that you eat, but instead you fast, you are not more perfect, but less perfect. If it is God's will that you work in the world, but instead you sit in the church praying, you are not more perfect, but less perfect.

[Matthew]
{11:18} "For John came neither eating nor drinking; and they say, 'He has a demon.'
{11:19} The Son of man came eating and drinking; and they say, 'Behold, a man who eats voraciously and who drinks wine, a friend of tax collectors and sinners.' But wisdom is justified by her sons."

God wills that all persons avoid sin. The eternal moral law is the same for all persons. The law against sin is the same for all persons. But God wills different paths to perfection and holiness for different persons. Also, there is nothing to prevent something that is more perfect in general, from being less perfect in a certain circumstance. Thus virginity and celibacy are better than marriage, but for a particular person greater holiness may be found in marriage than in remaining unmarried. It is a false idea of perfection to consider the path to perfection to be the same for all persons. What is perfect for one person is far from perfect for another person.

.183. Another error considers perfection to be found in total obedience, not to God, but to human persons, such as to the Pope, the Bishops, a superior in a

---

[190] St. Teresa of Avila, The Way of Perfection, p. 116.
[191] St. Therese of Lisieux, Autobiography, PDF version, p. 9.

religious order, a spiritual director, or a wife's obedience to her husband, or child's obedience to his or her parents.

The Pope is the visible head of the Church on earth, but he is not God. Jesus Christ is God and is the one true Head of the universal Church. When the Pope teaches infallibly, either by himself or with the body of Bishops, we are required to give the full assent of faith to these infallible doctrines. When the Pope or the Bishops teach non-infallibly, we are required to give, not the full assent of faith, but the religious submission of will and intellect, which is a different degree and type of assent. And because the non-infallible teachings of the Magisterium are subject to a limited possibility of error, we may faithfully dissent, to an extent within the same limits, from non-infallible teachings. If someone decides to adhere to all non-infallible teachings, with the full assent of faith and with no possibility of dissent, regardless of whether or not such teachings are entirely true, this would be sin, not perfection. For such an approach entirely disregards truth, replacing the search for truth within Tradition, Scripture, Magisterium with a blind obedience to authority. The complete disregard for truth is not a greater degree of faith or perfection, but a grave sin. God is Truth. Whoever casts aside truth, casts aside God.

If someone were to adhere, in total obedience, to every decision of the fallible temporal authority of the Pope, or of the Bishops, this would be sin, not perfection. For such an approach substitutes blind obedience for truth and justice, and therefore such an approach is gravely contrary to the eternal moral law. The temporal authority of the Church is fallible. If anyone treats the temporal authority of the Church as if it were infallible, or worse, as if the temporal authority of the Church were greater than truth and justice, such a person sins gravely. Although such a person may think that he is more perfect, in truth he has fallen into sin, even into the mortal sin of idolatry. For morality is found in obedience to the eternal moral law, which is the Justice of God. And perfection is found in obedience to the will of God. But if anyone replaces obedience to God with blind obedience to any person or authority, even to the Pope or to the temporal authority of the Church, then he commits the sin of idolatry.

.184. The rules and rulings of the Church are fallible. The rules and rulings of the Church are not the same as the eternal moral law. If anyone treats rules and rulings, even those decided authoritatively and definitively by the Pope and the body of Bishops, as if these were identical to, or above, the eternal moral law, he commits the sin of idolatry. For the eternal moral law is the Justice inherent to the very Nature of God. God is the eternal moral law. God is not the rules and rulings of the Church. God is Truth, Love, Mercy, Justice, Goodness; but God is not rules. In so far as any rule or ruling is contrary to the eternal moral law, such a rule or ruling is not binding on any person. An unjust rule is not a rule; an unjust ruling is not binding.

True perfection consists in perfect obedience to the will of God. However, we must always remember that our own understanding of God's will is limited and flawed. Therefore, as concerns perfection and imperfection, the conclusion that God wills us to do one thing, rather than another, does not bind absolutely; for the will of God is not the same as our understanding of the will of God. We must always consider the possibility that we have erred in determining the will of God. We must sometimes be willing to refrain from doing what we thought was the will of God.

Another error considers perfection to be found in doing the same holy acts, in the same way and to the same extent, every day. The will of God is not the same for us on each and every day. On one day, He wills that we be filled with joy and peace; on another day, He wills that we endure a cross of sorrow or anguish. On one day, He wills that we pray more and do fewer exterior good works; on another day, He wills that we pray less and do more exterior good works. The amount of prayer, self-denial, and works of mercy that God wills for us in each day changes. On one day, such as a feast day in the Church, He wills that we feast; and on another day, such as a Friday of Lent, He wills that we fast. If you always pray the same prayers every day, you are not doing the whole will of God. If you always do the same acts of self-denial every day, you are not doing the whole will of God. If you always do the same works of mercy every day, you are not doing the whole will of God.

Another error considers perfection to be found in a false type of freedom, as if the human person were not bound to obey the entire moral law, or as if the baptized member of the Church were not bound to believe the teachings of Tradition, Scripture, Magisterium. The idea is false which considers true love to be free from obedience and from faith. Although a person may, on occasion and for sufficient reason, faithfully disobey or faithfully dissent, within certain limits, from the temporal authority or from a non-infallible teaching, he goes astray from true love, faith, and hope who disregards the eternal moral law, or the body of teachings of the Catholic Faith, or any infallible teaching (or any truth at all if he knows that it is true). Only a severely distorted notion of love would loosen all morals, or reject all authority, or ignore all truths, on the basis that love is greater. In God, justice and authority and truth and love are the same.

.185. Finally, as an example of perfection, consider Sacred Scripture. The Word of God contains all those things and only those things that God wills. Sacred Scripture is complex and subtle, emphasizing the breadth and depth of wisdom. Sacred Scripture lacks the superficial and false type of perfection found in being neat, and organized, and predictable. So, too, should our lives be complex and subtle, emphasizing wisdom, avoiding the mere appearance of perfection on the surface. Whoever would be perfect must be willing to appear to be far from perfect.

To avoid sin, one must obey the eternal moral law. To be perfect, one must obey both the eternal moral law and the whole will of God. But such perfection is not possible unless the human person is detached from the things of creation, in order to be attached to the Creator of all things.

Saint Teresa of Avila: "the soul that is perfect can be detached and humble anywhere."[192]

---

[192] St. Teresa of Avila, The Way of Perfection, p. 49.

Saint Teresa of Avila: "those who are perfect will surrender their wills like the perfect souls they are and will forgive others with the perfection that has been described."[193]

Although we cannot be entirely perfect in this life, we can continually strive to reform our lives and to conform to the perfect examples of Jesus and Mary. By the grace of God, it is possible for some of our acts to be perfect. But even when we fall far short of perfection, we are still able to avoid sin.

---

[193] St. Teresa of Avila, The Way of Perfection, p. 115.

Chapter 14
Types of Evil

.186.
Saint Thomas Aquinas: "by the name of evil is signified the absence of good."[194]

Evil is a privation of good. Any lack of goodness can be called evil, in some sense of the word. But how do we determine what is good?

The Infinite

God is infinitely Good. The infinite Goodness of the Nature of God is the basis for determining what is good, and what is a privation of good, i.e. evil.

Ss. Augustine and Aquinas: "God is truly and absolutely simple."[195]

God is good, and not evil, because existence is good and God exists. God is the perfect fullness of all existence. For all that is truly and perfectly good exists in God, not merely as a quality, but as His very Nature, in absolute perfect fullness. God is Goodness itself, and that goodness is the same as His very existence. In God, existence is love is truth is mercy is justice is all that is truly good.

God is not a being who acts, for then God would not be truly and absolutely simple. In God, being and doing are exactly the same. Otherwise, God would be divided into being and doing, divided into existence and goodness and love and other separate qualities, and He would then not be perfect simple existence. God is One Divine Eternal Act, the act of being all that God is, and of doing all that God does. In God being and doing are one. All that God is, and all that God does, is One and is the same as His very existence.

.187. Existence is good. Evil is a privation of good. If we hypothesize a God who would be pure evil, he would have to be a privation of all that is good, including existence. And so an evil God, by definition, would not exist. An evil God cannot exist, and the God who does exist must be good. Existence is good; all that is exists is good; goodness is a type of existence, a type of 'being'.

Neither can the good God who exists be good and yet do evil. For in God, being and doing are exactly the same. God exists. God is absolutely simple. Therefore, God is and does only good.

Evil is a privation of good. In God there is no privation of good at all. God is infinitely Good by His very Nature. His infinite existence is the same as His infinite goodness. If God were to cease from being good (which can never occur), He would literally cease to exist. In God, goodness and existence are literally absolutely identical. God is the perfect fulfillment of all that is truly good. The

---

[194] Saint Thomas Aquinas, Summa Theologica, I, Q. 48, A. 1.
[195] Saint Thomas Aquinas, Summa Theologica, I, Q. 3, A. 7. "On the contrary, Augustine says (De Trin. iv, 6,7): 'God is truly and absolutely simple.' I answer that, the absolute simplicity of God may be shown in many ways."

Types of Evil

Nature of God is pure simple perfect absolute infinite goodness. Therefore, all that God creates must be good.

.188. The Finite

God is Good; therefore, all that He creates must also be good.

[Genesis 1]
{1:1} In the beginning, God created heaven and earth.
...
{1:31} And God saw everything that he had made. And they were very good. And it became evening and morning, the sixth day.

God is good and infinite. All that God has created is good, but finite. The Nature of God is infinite goodness. The nature of each and every created thing is good, though to a finite extent. But no created thing is morally evil by its very nature. All creation is finite, but nothing in creation has moral evil as its nature. For the infinitely good God cannot create moral evil. All creation is natural and finite. Therefore, each created thing lacks goodness in the sense that what is finite lacks infinite goodness, and what is natural lacks any goodness that it is beyond its nature. But this type of lack of goodness is not moral evil (it is 'metaphysical evil', as explained below). Thus, there are other types of evil in addition to moral evil.

Created persons are made in the image of God. All created things are good, and so all created things are like God, to some limited extent. But created persons have free will and intellect; and as a result, they are able to love. The ability to knowingly and freely choose to love makes created persons more like God than all other created things. All created persons have a good nature, and the good nature of created persons is more like the Goodness of God than any other created thing.

Pure evil does not exist. The most evil human person that could be imagined, a man who has deliberately and knowingly abandoned all that is morally good, a man who does only wicked deeds, still has a human nature, and that human nature is good. The goodness of human nature itself is a witness against each and every human person who sins, whether he commits a few venial sins, or many mortal sins. For all who commit moral evil are contradicting their own nature, which is good. All created things were created by God who is Good. Therefore, whenever any created person chooses to do moral evil, he acts in hypocrisy, contradicting his own good nature and his own good Creator.

Even the fallen angels have a good angelic nature. The devils are evil in the sense that they choose to do moral evil; they have no love, no faith, no hope, no virtue, no grace. But their nature remains good, just as it was created by God. For in the beginning, when God created all that exists, He also created beings that are pure spirit without bodies, called angels. And all angels, when they were created, were sinless and entirely good. But they each had free will and intellect; they each were able to sin. And those who chose to sin, against the infinitely good God who created them, were choosing to do moral evil, while their nature remained good, and their Creator remained Infinite Goodness. Those angels who chose to sin, fell from grace and became fallen angels, also called devils or demons. But their angelic nature remains good, as a continuing witness against their evil deeds.

Thus, all moral evil is a type of hypocrisy, because the person who chooses moral evil has a good nature, and was created by a good God. Human nature is good. Angelic nature is good. All created persons are good. Moral evil is always a knowingly chosen act of a created person. Since the nature of each and every created person is good, the choice of moral evil is always a type of hypocrisy. There is a fundamental self-contradiction whenever anyone chooses to do any moral evil, from the smallest sin to the greatest sin. All evil is hypocrisy because God is good.

Any belief system or philosophy, any argument based on faith or reason, which concludes a falsehood or argues in favor of an immorality, is self-contradictory. For faith and reason are good, but falsehoods and immorality are evil. Every falsehood is a deprivation of truth. Every moral evil is a deprivation of moral good. The use of faith or reason to argue for falsehoods or immorality is itself a witness against those false or immoral conclusions, because faith and reason are inherently good, and they are a reflection of the Nature of God. But falsehoods and immorality are deprived of goodness.

Whoever sins, contradicts his own nature as well as his Creator. All moral evil is not only contrary to the moral law, but also contrary to the nature of the sinner. For all that God created is good by nature, even the worst sinners.

.189. Light and Darkness

Good and evil are comparable to light and darkness. A fire emits light, but no type of fire emits darkness. For darkness does not have existence; it is a lack of a type of existence, light. Similarly, evil is always a lack of some type of goodness, but within good created things. For pure evil is pure non-existence, which by definition does not exist. And all created things have a good nature. Therefore, evil cannot exist on its own; and every kind of evil must be a kind of deprivation of good, to a limited extent, within created things with good natures. A complete deprivation of good would be a complete lack of existence. And so pure evil does not exist.

Sacred Scripture uses the figure of light and darkness to refer to good and evil.

[John]
{1:5} And the light shines in the darkness, and the darkness did not comprehend it.

Light can understand darkness; goodness can understand evil. For darkness is an absence of light, and evil is an absence of goodness. By knowing what light is, we know what darkness is, an absence of light. And by understanding goodness, we understand its privation, evil. But darkness can understand neither darkness nor light; for in lacking light, darkness is unable to understand light, and unable to understand the privation of light, which is darkness. Those persons who are thoroughly immersed in sin do not understand good acts, and neither do they understand even their own sins. For they are living lives of darkness, without the light of truth and love, which, like all goodness, is of God, who is Goodness.

{3:19} "And this is the judgment: that the Light has come into the world, and men loved darkness more than light. For their works were evil.
{3:20} For everyone who does evil hates the Light and does not go toward the Light, so that his works may not be corrected.
{3:21} But whoever acts in truth goes toward the Light, so that his works may be manifested, because they have been accomplished in God."

Jesus refers to Himself as 'the Light' because light is a figure for goodness, and Jesus in His Divine Nature is Goodness itself. Those persons who prefer moral evil over moral good are, in a sense, loving darkness. They prefer the absence of the Light of Christ and His teachings. Whoever accepts goodness of any kind, to that same extent, he accepts God. For all that is good is of God, who is pure infinite Goodness. The better we understand Christ, the better we understand moral goodness, and its distinction from moral evil. For God is the source of all that is good, in every true sense of the word.

[Ephesians]
{5:8} For you were darkness, in times past, but now you are light, in the Lord. So then, walk as sons of the light.

[1 Peter]
{2:9} But you are a chosen generation, a royal priesthood, a holy nation, an acquired people, so that you may announce the virtues of him who has called you out of darkness into his marvelous light.

Saint Paul and Saint Peter each refer to the darkness of moral evil, which is a privation of goodness in knowingly chosen acts. Those human persons who live immersed in many serious sins are darkness, or are in darkness, in the sense that their chosen acts are evil. But they are not darkness in their nature, which remains good. Therefore, human persons may be called evil because of evil acts, but not because of their nature, which is good and which can repent and choose good acts. If the nature of human persons immersed in sin was evil, then they could not repent. But human nature is not evil in itself, since evil is a privation, and a complete privation would lack even existence.

Therefore, all 'evil' human persons are not pure evil, since they have a good nature. A human person is called evil when he knowingly and freely chooses to commit acts that are morally evil, especially mortal sins, and most especially numerous actual mortal sins. But a human person is able to use free will (which is good) and intellect (which is also good) to cooperate with grace, and to repent, and to choose good acts, freely and knowingly. So repentant sinners are said to be in the light, or even to be light, for they have become like God, who is the Light of truth and love in His own infinite Nature.

[1 John]
{1:5} And this is the announcement which we have heard from him, and which we announce to you: that God is light, and in him there is no darkness.
{1:6} If we claim that we have fellowship with him, and yet we walk in darkness, then we are lying and not telling the truth.
{1:7} But if we walk in the light, just as he also is in the light, then we have fellowship with one another, and the blood of Jesus Christ, his Son, cleanses us from all sin.

Light is a figure for goodness. God is light, meaning that He is Goodness itself. In God, there is no darkness, that is, no lack of goodness. He is perfect infinite goodness, as His very Existence. Human persons have a good nature, made in the image of our Creator, who is Goodness itself. So when human persons sin, they choose darkness, even though their nature and their Creator is light. Such is the inherent contradiction of all sin.

.190. Three Types of Evil

When evil is defined broadly, as any type of privation of good, there are three types of evil, based on the type of good that is lacking: (1) moral evil, (2) physical evil, (3) metaphysical evil.

(1) Moral evil is a deprivation of moral goodness in the acts of created persons. Moral goodness is the greatest good in Creation, and this moral goodness reaches its highest form in acts of true love of God and neighbor. The greatest evil is moral evil, which is a deprivation of the greatest good, and which is always contrary to true love of God and neighbor. Moral evil is sin, and sin is found only in created persons. Created persons can knowingly choose between the greatest good, knowingly chosen moral acts expressing true love of God and neighbor, and the greatest deprivation of good, knowingly chosen immoral acts contrary to true love of God and neighbor.

(2) Physical evil is a deprivation of any natural good in created things and in the relationship between created things. The good that is lacking ought to be present, in accord with the good nature of the created thing, and in accord with the plan of God for the good relationship between created things. Physical evil is contrary to the plan of God, and God only permits physical evil because of sin. Physical evil is any type of harm or disorder, including suffering; it is not necessarily literally 'physical.' There is harm and disorder in the world generally because there is sin in the world generally. But, in this life, those who suffer the most are not necessarily those who have sinned the most. Physical evil is related to moral evil in that physical evil results from moral evil (sin), and sometimes tends toward moral evil (the disorder called 'concupiscence' is a type of physical evil). But physical evil is not moral evil.

(3) Metaphysical evil is perhaps best understood as the lack of goodness inherent in all created things, merely because they are finite, as compared to God who is infinitely good. All created things are finite, and so each and every created thing lacks the infinite goodness of God. This type of lack of goodness is very different from moral evil. This limit to the goodness of finite created things is not moral

evil and is not related to moral evil. This limited goodness ought to cause us to seek infinite goodness, which is found only in the Divine Nature of God.

There is no lack of goodness that does not fit into one of the above three categories. All created things have at least metaphysical evil, i.e. finiteness. Only God is infinite Goodness, and only God is uncreated. Nothing exists except the Creator and His Creation. And nothing is infinitely good except the Creator. All Creation is lacking in goodness when compared to God.

The Catholic Encyclopedia: "According to the nature of the perfection which it limits, evil is metaphysical, physical, or moral. Metaphysical evil is not evil properly so called; it is but the negation of a greater good, or the limitation of finite beings by other finite beings. Physical evil deprives the subject affected by it of some natural good, and is adverse to the well-being of the subject, as pain and suffering. Moral evil is found only in intelligent beings; it deprives them of some moral good."[196]

.191.
I. Moral Evil

Moral evil is the worst type of evil because it is a deprivation of the greatest type of good. The greatest good in creation is found when created persons choose to cooperate with the grace of God in knowingly chosen good acts. All cooperation with the grace of God is a type of imitation of God, who is infinitely Good. The greatest good is found in acts that fulfill the threefold commandment to love God, neighbor, self.

Moral evil is a privation of goodness in knowingly chosen acts. Free will and intellect are the gifts that make created persons more like God than any other created thing. But this great gift of free will and intellect, when directed toward acts of deprivation rather than of goodness, results in the worst evil: moral evil.

Moral evil is sin, and sin is nothing else but a knowingly chosen immoral act. The goodness of the Nature of God, and the goodness that God intends for created persons, determines which acts are morally good, and which acts are morally evil. Sin is the knowing choice to use the greatest natural ability in all Creation, free will and intellect, to reject the greatest good in all Creation, true love of God, neighbor, self. All sin is contrary to the love of God, neighbor, self. The greatest deprivation is by definition the worst evil: sin. All sin is contrary to the eternal moral law.

The eternal moral law is nothing else but the Justice which is the very Nature of God. God is Justice and Goodness and Love. And so God cannot be evil, nor can He do evil, because He cannot contradict Himself. God cannot violate the eternal moral law because God is the eternal moral law, and He cannot deny His

---

[196] A. C. O'Neil, 'Sin,' The Catholic Encyclopedia, Vol. 14, (New York: Robert Appleton Company, 1912). http://www.newadvent.org/cathen/14004b.htm – Theologians use a number of different definitions of metaphysical evil; this work uses the simple and clear definition that metaphysical evil is finiteness.

own Nature. The one true God is the summit and source of all that is good. All moral evil is contrary to the very Nature of God.

Created persons, both angels and human persons, have a nature created by God. All that God has created is good. But created persons also have the good gift of reason and free will, which they are able to exercise in knowingly chosen evil acts, contrary to the moral order intended by God. And this moral order is a reflection of the Justice of God. So they freely choose to act in a way that is contrary to their own nature and contrary to the Nature of God, who is perfect and infinite Goodness. Such knowingly chosen immoral acts are called sin, or moral evil. All sin, from the smallest sin to the greatest sin, is moral evil. All moral evil is hypocrisy, since the person who does evil has a good nature and was created by God who is Good. And all moral evil is a privation of good, since the acts that constitute moral evil have an absence of the moral goodness intended by God, who is Justice and Love and Mercy and Truth. The privation of moral goodness is moral evil, and all moral evil is contrary to God, who is infinite Goodness and perfect Justice.

Actual sin is nothing else but a knowingly chosen immoral act, an act that is freely chosen in the knowledge that the act is immoral. All actual sin is of reason and free will. All actual sins are knowingly chosen acts. The privation of good is what causes any knowingly chosen act to be moral evil. Sin is evil because the chosen act lacks the goodness intended by God for the acts of created persons.

Every morally good act is like the very Nature of God. Everyone who knowingly chooses to cooperate with grace in a morally good act becomes like God, at least in that particular act. Sin is evil because the will of a person who chooses an immoral act lacks the goodness intended by God for created persons. Every morally evil act has a deprivation that is contrary to the very Nature of God; it is a deprivation of some good that is a reflection of the Nature of God; it is a deprivation of true love of God, neighbor, self. Everyone who knowingly chooses to commit a morally evil act becomes contrary to God, to some extent, at least in that particular act.

The privation of good in morally evil acts always pertains to the three fonts of morality. But which goods might be lacking in each of these fonts?

[Matthew]
{22:36} "Teacher, which is the great commandment in the law?"
{22:37} Jesus said to him: " 'You shall love the Lord your God from all your heart, and with all your soul and with all your mind.'
{22:38} This is the greatest and first commandment.
{22:39} But the second is similar to it: 'You shall love your neighbor as yourself.'
{22:40} On these two commandments the entire law depends, and also the prophets."

The privation of moral good, which is called moral evil, is always a lack of true and full love, and all that is required by love: of God, of neighbor, and of self. This love of self is not selfishness, but a detached, properly ordered, spiritual love of self. For if all human beings are our neighbors, then we too are neighbors to ourselves. Whatever is contrary to true love of God, and neighbor, and self is contrary to the eternal moral law. Moral evil is always a privation of true spiritual love of God, neighbor, self; it is a privation in the intention, or in the moral object of the chosen act, or in the consequences of the act.

.192.
FIRST FONT: The first font is immoral if the person intends either a means that is moral evil, or an end that is moral evil. However, the human person can never literally intend evil, i.e. evil in and of itself, for evil is a privation, and a privation does not exist. All goodness is a type of existence or 'being.' Thus, all evil is a deprivation of goodness, a lack of existence or 'being.' To intend evil in and of itself would be to intend an absence, which is not possible.

A human person can never choose evil as an end in itself because evil is a deprivation or absence. Although it might seem as if one person or another intends evil itself, strictly speaking such is not the case. Evil is a deprivation of good, and so the human person, even when sinning, is always choosing either a lesser good in contradiction to a greater good, or an apparent good. Even if the intended end is morally evil, and the chosen act is intrinsically evil, the human person is not choosing evil in and of itself as an intended end, but is choosing a lesser good in contradiction to a greater good, or an apparent good. But such a choice is made because of what the end is, despite what it is not.

Saint Thomas Aquinas: "The will is not always directed to what is truly good, but sometimes to the apparent good; which has indeed some measure of good, but not of a good that is simply suitable to be desired."[197]

When an intention is immoral (i.e. moral evil), either the intended end or the intended means lacks moral goodness. But this deprivation is not intended in and of itself. Rather, the person intends a lesser or an apparent good, that is contrary to the greater good of love of God and neighbor.[198] When a human person intends an immoral means or an immoral end, his will is directed toward a means or end that lacks moral goodness in a certain way, to a certain extent. An immoral intention, directed toward an end, is not directed toward the deprivation in and of itself, but toward a limited good in that end despite its deprivation. Similarly, when the intention is to make use of an immoral means, that intention is not directed to the deprivation, in and of itself, in the means, but toward whatever is good in the end, and to whatever is useful in the means to achieve that end, despite its moral deprivation.

Examples: (1) A person intends to become wealthy by means of some harm to his neighbor. He intends a limited good, the good things of a wealthy life, such as good food, clothing, housing, transportation, but in contradiction to the greater good of love of God and neighbor. This intention is moral evil, but what is per se intended is a good accompanied by a deprivation. Similarly, any human

---

[197] Saint Thomas Aquinas, Summa Theologica, I-II, Q. 19, A. 1.
[198] Saint Thomas Aquinas, Summa Theologica, I-II, Q. 18, A. 4; citing Dionysius, On the Divine Names, chap. 4, n. 19; cf. Compendium of the Catechism, n. 367-368.

person, who is said to be evil, has a good human nature, but that good human nature is accompanied by a deprivation in the form of immoral acts.

(2) A person intends to murder his neighbor (the means), to achieve the intended end of silencing his neighbor's religious or social or political views. The act of murder deprives an innocent human person of life. In this example, the act is chosen as the means because this particular deprivation achieves the intended end. But in this case the intended end is merely an apparent good, and is contrary to love of God and neighbor.

(3) A person intends to tell a lie in order to avoid losing his job. His chosen act is intrinsically evil, for lying has the deprivation of truth from an assertion as its moral object. This immoral means is chosen because it achieves a certain end. But this intended end is not the deprivation of truth in the assertion, but the choice of a limited good, retaining employment. This person intends to use an immoral means, a lie, to a good end, but this intended means is contrary to the love of God, who is Truth. This means is chosen because the deprivation in the means achieves a good end. But the intention is still immoral. In order to avoid sin in the first font, all that is intended must be morally good.

So a deprivation of moral goodness is never intended, in itself, as an end. For a deprivation is an absence, and an absence cannot be intended directly, per se. However, a deprivation can be intended as a evil means to an end, in the sense that a person chooses an immoral means precisely because its deprivation achieves the intended end. An immoral intention always includes some limited good or some apparent good in the end, which is chosen despite its moral evil, i.e. despite its contradiction with the greater good of that threefold love of God, neighbor, self, which is the basis for the moral law.

.193.
SECOND FONT: The second font is immoral if the chosen act is inherently directed toward an evil moral object, i.e. a end that is deprived of some good. The good that is lacking is always a good required by the love of God, neighbor, and self, which is the basis for the entire moral law.

An intrinsically evil act is morally evil because the act is inherently ordered toward an end that is deprived of a good which the eternal moral law requires to be present. A person with an immoral intention does not intend a moral deprivation, in and of itself, but instead intends an end with some limited goodness or apparent goodness, despite a moral deprivation. But an immoral act can be inherently directed toward the moral deprivation itself in the end, i.e. in an evil moral object. Acts can be intrinsically evil, but persons cannot be intrinsically evil. For the nature of every created person is good. But the nature of intrinsically evil acts is evil, and this is precisely because the act is ordered toward the moral deprivation itself in the end (in the evil moral object). Even so, no act is pure evil, for pure deprivation is non-existence.

Saint Thomas Aquinas: "We must therefore say that every action has goodness, in so far as it has being; whereas it is lacking in goodness, in so far as it is lacking in something that is due to its fullness of being; and thus it is said to be evil....

Evil acts in virtue of deficient goodness. For if there were nothing of good there, there would be neither being nor possibility of action. On the other hand, if good were not deficient, there would be no evil. Consequently, the action done is a deficient good, which is good in a certain respect, but simply evil."[199]

Examples: (1) A person chooses to deprive his neighbor of his goods; the chosen act is an act of theft. The deprivation of goods from the owner is the evil moral object. The intention may be to gain wealth, or to enjoy harming one's neighbor, or to repay a debt, or to buy certain goods, or to experience a thrill, or to impress immoral friends, or some other intended end. But the thief never intends the deprivation, in and of itself, as an end, but only as a means to some other end.

(2) A terminally ill person chooses to kill himself, committing suicide, as a way to relieve all suffering (euthanasia). The chosen act is a type of murder (it is both suicide and euthanasia), which is intrinsically evil and always gravely immoral. However, the person does not intended the deprivation of life from an innocent person (himself) as an intended end, in and of itself; he intends this deprivation as a immoral means to the good intended end of relieving all suffering. The act itself is inherently directed at the deprivation; but the intention is not directed at the deprivation per se, but at a lesser or apparent good, despite the deprivation.

Deprivations by themselves do not exist, and so they cannot be intended as an end. This truth does not imply that intended ends are never immoral. An intended end may be morally evil, but the human person does not intend the evil itself in that end, but only the limited good or apparent good that accompanies that deprivation.

Now if the intended end is good, but the chosen act is inherently ordered toward an evil moral object, then the choice of such an intrinsically evil act, even as an immoral means to a good end, is always a sinful choice, despite the good intended end. This point is important because often persons will claim that an intrinsically evil act is morally permissible because the harm inherent to the act itself, i.e. the deprivation in the evil moral object, is not the intended end. But it is always the case, when the moral object is evil, that the intended end is not directed toward the deprivation in the moral object as to an end. Such a claim cannot justify the choice of an act that is intrinsically evil and always immoral.

Good can be intended as an end, in and of itself, because goodness exists. A person who intends a good end certainly can intend the goodness itself. The person can intend a good end, by a good means, and can choose an act with a good moral object. For goodness is not a deprivation; all goodness is a type of existence or 'being'. And all moral goodness is capable of being ordered toward God as our ultimate good end. Moral goodness is chosen because it is good. But moral evil is chosen despite its deprivation of goodness.

.194.
THIRD FONT: The third font is the moral weight of the good and bad consequences of the act. When the bad consequences morally outweigh the good

---

[199] Saint Thomas Aquinas, Summa Theologica, I-II, Q. 18, A. 1.

consequences, then the third font is immoral, and the choice of that act is a sin (moral evil). However, the bad consequences by themselves are not bad in the sense of moral evil, but are bad in the sense of physical evil. The third font is morally good, despite any physical evil (i.e. the bad consequences), when the good consequences outweigh that physical evil (harm, disorder).

This distinction between moral evil and physical evil is therefore necessary to properly understand the third font. It is moral evil to knowingly choose an act that does more harm (physical evil) than good. But it is not moral evil (in the third font, at least) to knowingly choose an act that does more good than harm, even though that harm is a type of evil. For physical evil is not moral evil. But to intend any physical evil as an end is immoral, because all our ends must be capable of being directed toward God. There is no moral evil, no physical evil, and no metaphysical evil in God, who is infinitely Good, in the fullest and truest sense of the word 'good.'

The bad consequences in the third font are never, by themselves, moral evil. The third font is only ever immoral when the bad consequences outweigh the good. But in the case of passive scandal, a good act with good intention may have the bad consequence of leading some persons into sin (perhaps because the act is likely to be misunderstood, and so is likely to mislead). The sin of these other persons is moral evil. But the consequence whereby a good act with good intent might tend to lead someone else into sin is itself only 'physical' evil. And such passive scandal is only a sin if the bad consequences outweigh the good. For if either the first or second fonts were bad, the act would be active scandal, not passive scandal.

.195.
II. Physical Evil

Catholic moral theology sometimes applies the term 'evil' to privations of good other than the privation of moral goodness. This use of the term 'evil' does not refer to sin. Moral evil is sin. Other types of evil are not sin and have no culpability. Physical evil is not a knowing choice of an immoral act. Physical evil is not moral evil, and so there is no sin in mere physical evil. A knowing choice concerning some physical evil may or may not be a sin, depending on the three fonts of morality. But physical evil itself is not actual sin, is not mere objective sin, and is not moral evil.

[Matthew]
{6:34} "Therefore, do not be anxious about tomorrow; for the future day will be anxious for itself. Sufficient for the day is its evil."

Here Jesus is referring to the physical evils of each day, not to moral evil. Each day has many difficulties, problems, sufferings, losses, and harm, varying in type and degree. Concern for the physical evils of the present day is necessary and sufficient. We should not spend each day anxious about all possible future harm and disorder that might occur.

Types of Evil

The Lord God is infinite Goodness, and so He can never do moral evil. Yet Sacred Scripture says this: "Shall there be evil in a city, which the Lord hath not done?" (Amos 3:6, Challoner version). The note for this verse says: "*Evil in a city.* He speaks of the *evil* of punishments of war, famine, pestilence, desolation, &c., but not of the *evil* of *sin*, of which God is not the author."[200] Therefore, moral evil is not the only type of evil. And to make this distinction between moral evil and other types of evil clear, some translations use a different word to refer to the evil that is harm and not sin. The New Jerusalem Bible uses the word 'misfortune,' and the Catholic Public Domain Version uses the word 'disaster.' But the term used in moral theology for this type of evil is 'physical evil.'

The term 'physical evil' is somewhat inaccurate. Physical evil is not necessarily physical. A better term would be 'harm' or 'disorder.' Physical evil is a privation of a natural good, other than moral goodness, in created things, especially created persons. Physical evil results (a) when a good quality is absent, which ought to be present; or (b) when a good quality is present, but in a lesser form; or (c) when there is a disorder in the relationship between one created thing and another created thing; or (d) when there is a disorder in the relationship between a created person and God. Each of these types of physical evil (harm or disorder) is judged according to the proper nature, or according to proper relationship, as intended by God for Creation.

But if what is absent is not intended by God to be present, then that absence is not a type of physical evil. The fact that a stone lacks reason and free will is not a type of physical evil, for it is not the will of God for stones to have those faculties. However, if a human person is in a coma and so cannot exercise reason and free will, this is a type of disorder (physical evil). God intends human persons to be able to exercise their faculties of reason and free will. That an infant cannot yet exercise reason to a substantial extent is not a disorder, since it is natural for an infant not to have the full use of reason yet. If an infant is unbaptized, even though baptism is beyond what is natural, there is a disorder in the relationship between that infant and God. For God intends infants to be baptized. Created persons are the highest form of created thing, and so any physical evil in created persons is a greater privation than in lesser created things, according to the good that ought to be present in each according to its nature and the will of God.

Examples of physical evil: (1) injury or disease, (2) pollution in the environment, (3) the destruction of buildings due to an earthquake, (4) the disorder in society caused by a civil war, (5) the disorder in a family caused by the absence of one parent, (6) the harm to the Church caused by sins of heresy, (7) the lack of the state of grace in persons conceived in original sin, prior to baptism, (8) the lack of a state of grace in persons who have committed actual mortal sin, prior to repentance and forgiveness, (9) the harm done to the mystical Body of Christ (the Church) by any and all sin, (10) the lack of virtue in a person who has been lax in prayer and self-denial, (11) the disorder in a person who has an addiction, (12) any type of psychological disorder, (13) any type of spiritual disorder, (14) the lack of knowledge on matters of faith and morals among the faithful of

---

[200] The Holy Bible, Challoner Douay translation, 1899 Baltimore edition; Baronius Press.

the Church on earth, (15) unjust laws, (16) customs that are harmful to society, (17) inequities in the distribution of food, medical care, work, shelter, and other basic human necessities, (18) any type of suffering caused by sin, (19) the loss of innocent human life at any time from any cause, (20) the harm caused by the sin of abortion (including the death of the prenatal, the psychological and spiritual harm to the mother and the family, and the harm to society).

Physical evil is a type of harm or disorder. The term 'physical evil' does not refer only to physical harm, but to any type of harm or disorder that is contrary to the good nature and good order intended by God for created things. God intends only good for His Creation, and especially for created persons. Suffering and other types of harm and disorder result from sin. All physical evil results from moral evil. There is suffering and death in the world because of sin.

[Romans]
{5:12} Therefore, just as through one man sin entered into this world, and through sin, death; so also death was transferred to all men, to all who have sinned.

If there were no moral evil at all in the world, then there would be no bad consequences to any act. For all physical evil is related to moral evil. Such was the case for Adam and Eve, before the Fall from grace; there was no physical evil in Paradise. And such will be the case for all the Faithful after the General Resurrection; there will be no physical evil in the new heaven and the new earth.

[Revelation]
{21:1} I saw the new heaven and the new earth. For the first heaven and the first earth passed away, and the sea *[i.e. Purgatory]* is no more....
{21:4} And God will wipe away every tear from their eyes. And death shall be no more. And neither mourning, nor crying out, nor grief shall be anymore. For the first things have passed away.

When the harm of physical evil is caused by a knowingly chosen act, that harm is a bad consequence in the third font. These bad consequences, considered by themselves, are only a type of physical evil, not moral evil. Even if the bad consequence is that of scandal (when one person's choice influences others to sin), the harm done to the spiritual lives of others is a type of 'physical' evil. The sins of those influenced by scandal are moral evil, but the harm done by the person who presents the scandal is a bad consequence. And all bad consequences are a type of physical evil. Only when the bad consequences outweigh the good consequences is the third font (and therefore the overall act) morally evil.

If a person chooses an act in which all three fonts of morality are good, there may still be some bad consequences. Some bad consequences are tolerable because this type of evil is physical evil (harm or disorder), not moral evil. A bad consequence is not a knowingly chosen immoral act, but only the result of a knowingly chosen act, and so an act may be moral even if some physical evil results from that act. When the bad consequences (harm) outweigh the good consequences (benefit), then the knowing choice of such an act would be moral evil. The knowing choice of an act that does more harm than good is moral evil because the choice lacks a type of moral goodness that ought be found in human acts. All human acts should have (1) a good intention, (2) a good inherent moral meaning, and (3) more benefit than harm in the consequences. The lack of any one of these three goods causes the human act (a knowingly chosen act) to be moral evil, not merely physical evil, and therefore a sin.

.196. The Three Fonts and Physical Evil

The relationship between physical evil (harm or disorder) and knowingly chosen acts is the cause of moral evil. Sin is moral evil, but moral evil occurs when a person knowingly chooses, in any of the three fonts, physical evil. But this is only true if 'physical evil' is understood in its broadest sense, to include every kind of harm or disorder, including disorder in our relationship with God and neighbor. This truth can also be stated such that moral evil only occurs when we knowingly choose acts that are contrary to love of God, neighbor, self. All such acts involve physical evil, in the broadest sense.

FIRST FONT: It is always a sin to intend physical evil as an end. Though physical evil is not moral evil, the knowing choice of such a privation of good as an end is contrary to the justice of God. For by definition, physical evil is a privation of a good intended by God. However, it is sometimes moral to intend physical evil as a means to a good end. Moral evil is never justified; moral evil is not justified as an end, nor is it justified as a means to an end. However, physical evil is not moral evil. And so physical evil (harm or disorder) may be tolerated, or even intended as a means, if it is a necessary to a good end. An act with a good end, with some harm but no immorality in the means, is capable of being directed toward God as our final end. But an act with any immorality in the means or the end is not capable of being directed toward God as our final end. For all immoral acts are incompatible with love of God, neighbor, self.

The use of physical evil as an intended means to a good end is moral, as long as the good in the end outweighs the harm in the means. This is proven by many different examples, including examples from the life of Christ.

Examples: (1) Christ practiced and recommended fasting as a means to the good end of a holy life. Fasting is a type of physical evil, because the body is denied what is natural: healthy portions and types of food at various times during the day. (The denial to one's self of unhealthy types, or of excessive amounts, of food is not fasting, strictly speaking.) It is a sin to treat fasting as an end in itself. For a physical evil cannot be intended as an end. But it is virtuous to practice self-denial as a means to a greater good end. For fasting is not in itself moral evil, but physical evil. And certainly, when one fasts, this physical evil is intended as a means; the deprivation of food is not unintended.

(2) Physical evil includes suffering and death. Christ chose to use his suffering and death as a moral means to a good end, our salvation. This use of suffering and death was the intention of God, and God can never violate the moral law. Therefore, we may intend physical evil as a moral means to a good end, as long as the good in the end outweighs the physical evil in the means.

Types of Evil

(3) A soldier throws his body on a grenade in order to save the lives of his fellow soldiers. He does not directly and deliberately kill himself, and so his act is not the sin of suicide (second font). However, in the first font, he not only intends the good end of saving innocent lives, he also intends to use his moral act, which includes the physical evil of his own death, as the means to that good end. His death is not in the moral object, so his act is not intrinsically evil. His death is not intended as an end, but only as a necessary means to a greater good end; and the intended means is only physical evil, not moral evil. Therefore, his act is moral.

(4) A physician amputates a foot in order to save a life. The loss of the foot is a type of physical evil, but not moral evil. The intention to use this harm to a foot as a means is moral because it is directed toward the greater good of saving a life. The act itself has the moral object of saving a life, the same as the intended end. The good consequences outweigh the bad consequences in the third font. And so all three fonts are good. Thus the intention to use physical evil (not moral evil) as a means to a greater good end is a moral intention. Christ himself used a similar figure (cutting off a foot) in order to teach a spiritual truth.

[Matthew]
{18:8} So if your hand or your foot leads you to sin, cut it off and cast it away from you. It is better for you to enter into life disabled or lame, than to be sent into eternal fire having two hands or two feet.
{18:9} And if your eye leads you to sin, root it out and cast it away from you. It is better for you to enter into life with one eye, than to be sent into the fires of Hell having two eyes.

Certainly, Jesus was not saying that a hand, or foot, or eye, or other body part, should be cut off in order to avoid sin. But He also would not have used this figure if physical evil could not be morally intended as a means to a greater good.

(5) A man kills an attacker who presents an immediate threat to the lives of himself and his family. It would be immoral for the man to intend the death of the attacker as an end. For the death of any human person is a type of physical evil, and physical evil is by definition not in accord with the ends that God intends for Creation, especially for created persons. But in an act of self-defense, a man may intend the death of the attacker as a necessary means to a greater good, specifically, the safety of himself and his family. God intended the death of Christ as a means to the greater good of our salvation. Therefore, the intention of death as a means, when the act itself is not directed toward an evil moral object (such as any form of murder), may be moral, as long as all three fonts are good. The intention to use physical evil (but not moral evil) as a means to a good end is not necessarily immoral.

(6) A judge sentences a person convicted of a very serious crime to death. The judge intends the death of the convicted criminal, not as an end in itself, but only as a means to the end of justice and the common good. His intention is moral because the intended means is not an intrinsically evil act of murder, but a moral act of defense of the community and of the dispensation of justice.

(7) A soldier intends to kill an enemy combatant during a just war, not as an end in itself, but only as a means for the defense of the innocent in the nation defended by the war. His intended means is moral because he does not intend to use an intrinsically evil act, such as murder, as a means (or as an end). He is not intending moral evil as a means, but only physical evil.

From the above examples, it is abundantly clear that physical evil (any type of harm or disorder that is not a sin) may be intended as a necessary means to a greater good end, but not as an end in itself. Such an intended means does not make the first font immoral. And so, as long as all three fonts are good, the overall act will be moral, despite the toleration of some degree of physical evil in the intended means.

.197.
SECOND FONT: The knowingly chosen act cannot be inherently directed toward any physical evil as an end, i.e. as the moral object. For a moral object is only good when it is an end that is in accord with the love of God, neighbor, self. If an act is inherently directed at a physical evil as an end, then the act is intrinsically evil. Physical evil can sometimes be tolerated as a necessary means to a good end, because physical evil by itself is not moral evil. But if the physical evil is the moral object toward which the act is directed, then the act is not directed at a good end, and the end toward which it is directed is contrary to the will of God. For God never wills physical evil as an end. By definition, physical evil is a deprivation in the nature or order of created things as intended by God. Physical evil is a type of harm or disorder. God never intends harm or disorder as an end because He is infinitely Good. Therefore, such an act would be intrinsically evil.

Examples: (1) A physician directly kills a prenatal in order to save the life of the mother. The death of the prenatal is not the intended end; the good intended end is to save the life of the mother. The death of any human person is physical evil. Any deliberately chosen act that is directly ordered toward physical evil as to an end has an evil moral object and is intrinsically evil and always immoral. And the intention to use an intrinsically evil act as an immoral means to a good end is an immoral intention. Both the second and first fonts are bad; the act is immoral. The killing of the prenatal is direct abortion, a type of murder, and is therefore intrinsically evil and always gravely immoral.

(2) A physician treats a pregnant woman for cancer; the treatment saves the life of the mother, but results in the unintended death of the prenatal. The prenatal was in the early stages of development, and could not be saved. The death of the prenatal is physical evil. However, the act itself is inherently directed at the good of saving the mother's life. The death of the prenatal is an unintended bad consequence of an inherently good act. The moral object is not physical evil. The death of the prenatal is indirect abortion, not direct abortion. The act is moral.

In this case, the physical evil of the death of the prenatal cannot be intended even as a means. A physician may intend to cut of a limb as a means to the end of saving a life because the good of saving a life outweighs the physical evil of the loss of a limb, and because the means is not moral evil, but merely physical evil.

But no one may intend the death of one innocent person to save another, for then the second font would be intrinsically evil, and the means would not be mere physical evil, but also moral evil. A judge, in morally dispensing the death penalty, may intend the death of the convicted criminal, not as an end, but as a means to the defense of the community.[201] But in this case, the killing is not directed at the death of an innocent (which would be murder and always immoral), but at the just punishment of the guilty. Physical evil may be in the intended means, but only if that means is also moral.

(3) A man kills an attacker in defense of himself and his family. The act itself has the good moral object of protecting and defending innocent life. The physical evil of the death of the attacker is not the end toward which the act itself is inherently directed, and so the second font is good. This loss of human life, even of someone guilty of a gravely immoral attack, is still a type of physical evil, and so it may not be intended as an end, nor may the act itself be inherently directed toward that loss of human life as the moral object. But in the case of self-defense, when the moral object is good, and the death of the attacker is only intended as a means, not an end, then the intention and the act are both morally good.

The man may intend the use of deadly force (a physical evil) as a moral means to a good end, because the use of deadly force in self-defense is not moral evil, but only physical evil. But the death of even a guilty attacker cannot be intended as an end, and cannot be the end (moral object) toward which chosen act is inherently ordered; for then this physical evil of the death of a human person would also be moral evil. Furthermore, it would be absurd to claim that the death of the attacker is not intended even as a means, because if the man had no intention at all of using deadly force (or any type of force), he would not be able to act at all in self-defense. All human acts require intention.

THIRD FONT: In the third font, the good and bad consequences are weighed to determine if the bad consequences outweigh the good, making this font immoral. The bad consequences of an act are nothing else but physical evil; this includes any type of harm or disorder. The bad consequences by themselves do not constitute moral evil; for moral evil only results if an act is chosen in which the bad consequences morally outweigh the good consequences. Physical evil can be tolerated in the consequences of a knowingly chosen act, but only if the good consequences of the same act outweigh this harm or disorder. Thus the concept of physical evil is inherent to a proper understanding of the three fonts.

Physical evil sometimes results from even a good act done with good intention, because we live in a sinful and imperfect world. It is not possible for all our good and moral acts to be without any bad consequences. This truth is established by considering the life of Jesus Christ. He suffered and died; both suffering and death are examples of physical evil. Yet His life among us was entirely sinless and perfect. So neither can we expect, in this life, that our good acts with good intentions would have no bad consequences.

---

[201] Saint Thomas Aquinas, Summa Theologica, II-II, Q. 64, A. 7.

The bad consequences of our acts are not in themselves moral evil. If a bad consequence were intended as an end, the first font would constitute moral evil, but the third font might still be good, if the good consequences outweighed the bad. If a bad consequence were also in the moral object, the second font would constitute moral evil, but the third font would still be evaluated independent of the other two fonts. If a bad consequence includes leading someone else into sin, the act of the person who sins is moral evil, but this bad consequence considered in itself is not a sin, but physical evil.

.198.
III. Metaphysical Evil

All created things are finite, including angels, human nature, the human soul, and all material things. Even the human nature of Christ is finite, for He is like us in all things but sin, and we are each finite.

Only the Divine Nature is infinite Goodness. God alone is infinitely good. Now all that God created is truly good, but not infinitely good; created things have only limited goodness. And so each and every created thing, in one respect or another, is lacking in goodness, if only by being finite.

The term 'metaphysical evil' is used (seldom) in theology to refer to a privation of good that is neither moral evil (sin), nor physical evil (harm or disorder). Theologians disagree as to the proper definition of the term, but the term is perhaps most useful when it refers solely to privations of good that are due to the finiteness and natural limitations in created things. Only God has no privation of goodness whatsoever. All creation is good, but nothing in creation is infinitely good. Thus the finiteness of created things is a type of privation of good.

[Matthew]
{7:11} "Therefore, if you, though you are evil, know how to give good gifts to your sons, how much more will your Father, who is in heaven, give good things to those who ask him?"

Jesus used the word 'evil' to describe persons who were giving good gifts to their sons. These persons were not sinning, and so Jesus was not referring to moral evil. And they were not harming anyone, and so Jesus was not referring to physical evil. Instead, Jesus was using the term 'evil' to refer to what theologians call 'metaphysical evil.' He was making a comparison between human persons and God the Father. Metaphysical evil is the lack of goodness of finite created things compared to God, who is infinitely good. Compared to God, all created things, even good human persons doing good deeds, are lacking in goodness. And the difference in goodness between the Infinite Good that is God and any finite created good thing is a very great difference. Therefore, the term 'evil' is not as unfit for this description as it might seem at first.

[Matthew]
{19:17} And he said to him: "Why do you question me about what is good? One is good: God. But if you wish to enter into life, observe the commandments."

Types of Evil

This teaching of Christ, that only God is good, is the basis for the distinction called 'metaphysical evil'. Only God is the perfect fulfillment of all Goodness without any limitations whatsoever. All else that is called good is in some sense truly good, but is also truly lacking in goodness when compared to God. That is why Christ said that only God is truly Good, in the fullest sense of the word. And that is why theologians use the term 'metaphysical evil' for things that are truly good, but are also greatly lacking in goodness when compared to the infinitely good God.

[Romans]
{1:20} For unseen things about him have been made conspicuous, since the creation of the world, being understood by the things that were made; likewise his everlasting virtue and divinity, so much so that they have no excuse.

Now the concept of metaphysical evil is more useful than it might seem. The lack of infinite goodness in created things points us to the infinitely good Creator. In this way, our perception of the limitations in good created things leads us to seek the infinitely Good source of all that is good. And we are then able to understand that all good acts must be capable of being directed toward God as the highest Good and the Author of all lesser goods.

The human nature of Christ is finite; therefore, His human nature lacks infinite goodness and is included under the term 'metaphysical evil.' And this conclusion is implied by the above quote (Mt 19:17) from Scripture, in which Jesus says only God is Good. The human nature of Christ is not His Divine Nature, and so is not included in the assertion that only God is the infinite perfection of all that is Good.

Jesus has no moral evil in His human nature, nor in His Divine Nature. Jesus has no physical evil (harm or disorder) in His Divine Nature. For nothing that is evil in any sense of the word is found in the Divinity of God.

Jesus did have physical evil in His human nature; for He suffered and died, and both suffering and death are examples of physical evil. Therefore, we should understand that any physical evil in our lives, such as disease, or injury, or the many various types of disorders that afflict fallen humanity, are not moral evil for us, and do not prevent or detract from our salvation. In fact, just as Christ used the physical evil of His suffering and death to the good end of our salvation, so also can we offer all our sufferings to the Father through Christ, united with the sufferings of Christ, so as to participate in Christ's salvific work.

.199. The Blessed Virgin Mary

The Virgin Mary is finite. She is sinless, and so she has always been free from all moral evil. But she is not infinitely good, because she is not God. Therefore, she has that finiteness that is called metaphysical evil. And Mary also had that type of evil called physical evil; for, like her Saviour and Son Jesus Christ, she also suffered. She suffered at the foot of the Cross. And it is (currently) the ordinary non-infallible teaching of the Magisterium that the Virgin Mary died at the end of her life on earth and was raised from the dead by Christ, prior to her

Assumption (which is an infallible teaching).[202] The Virgin Mary suffered and died, and all suffering and death is a type of physical evil.

However, Mary did not have physical evil in the sense of imperfection; she was always entirely perfect throughout her entire life, from her Immaculate Conception to her Assumption. Imperfection is a type of physical evil because all that is imperfect lacks a particular type of goodness. For the will of God for each and every thing in creation is perfection, not imperfection. All imperfection falls short of the will of God, but without sin (moral evil). If an act is sinful, it is not called merely imperfect, but sin (moral evil). If an act is imperfect, it is not sinful, but it is less than intended by the perfect will of God. This lack of perfection is a lack of goodness, and so it is a type of evil. It is not metaphysical evil, because perfection is according to the nature of the created thing, as intended by God. The lack of a natural good is not metaphysical evil, but physical evil. Mary was entirely perfect, and so she did not have physical evil in the sense of imperfection.

The Blessed Virgin Mary was always sinless and perfect. God is also sinless and perfect. Yet Mary was humble before God because she knew well that the goodness of God is infinite, and that her own goodness as a created person is finite. The infinite goodness of God is infinitely greater than the finite goodness of the sinless perfect Virgin Mary. Therefore, Mary was perfectly humble, despite her sinlessness and perfection. How much more humble should we be, knowing that we were conceived with original sin, that we retain concupiscence after baptism has entirely wiped away original sin, that we commit many personal sins in our lives, that (even when we avoid sin) we are very imperfect, and that we, too, are finite creatures before an infinite God. We have much more reason to be humble, and yet Mary exceeds us all in the perfection of her humility.

Was Mary worthy to be the mother of God Incarnate? We can consider this question in three ways, according to the three types of evil. Mary had no sin at all, no moral evil. She was worthy in this sense. God caused Mary to be sinless, by means of her Immaculate Conception and by means of the fullness of grace given to her, throughout her life, directly from the Cross of Her Divine Son Jesus Christ. God made her worthy in this way. And Mary was entirely perfect throughout her entire life. The gift of her perfection, like the gift of her sinlessness, was also given to Mary directly from the Cross of Christ. Now although she could suffer, which is a type of physical evil, her suffering was like the suffering of our Savior, and was entirely in accord with the will of God as a moral means to a good end (assisting in the salvific work of Christ). And so she had no physical evil in the sense of imperfection. Therefore, Mary was worthy in this way also. So Mary was worthy to be the mother of the Savior by her sinlessness and her perfection.

However, her Divine Son Jesus Christ is God Incarnate. He has both a finite human nature and the infinite Divine Nature. Mary is finite, but Jesus as God is

---

[202] Pope Pius XII, Munificentissimus Deus, on her death: n. 14, 17, 18, 20, 21, 22, 40; and on her resurrection: n. 22, 28, 35.

infinite. In this sense, Mary was unworthy to be the mother of the Savior, for He is the infinite God made man. The finite is not worthy before the Infinite.

Did the Virgin Mary have shame? She had no shame due to sin, which is moral evil, because she was always sinless. We sinners should have shame at our sins. She had no shame due to any imperfection, a type of physical evil, because she was always perfect. We sinners, who often fall far short of the perfect will of God, should have shame at our imperfections. For the will of God for each of us is perfect, but we often do our own imperfect will instead. But Mary did have the third type of shame, corresponding to the third type of evil (metaphysical evil). For as a finite creature before the infinite God, she had shame, that is, she realized that her own perfect goodness is finite and therefore unworthy before the perfect infinite goodness of God. For the goodness of God is infinitely greater than the entire sum of all the finite goodness in all Creation, including the human nature of Christ, the Virgin Mary, all the Angels and Saints, all created persons, and all the rest of Creation.

Chapter 15
Direct and Voluntary Deprivations

.200.
Direct

Intrinsically evil acts are always morally direct.

Pope John Paul II: "Therefore, by the authority which Christ conferred upon Peter and his Successors, and in communion with the Bishops of the Catholic Church, I confirm that the direct and voluntary killing of an innocent human being is always gravely immoral. This doctrine, based upon that unwritten law which man, in the light of reason, finds in his own heart (cf. Rom 2:14-15), is reaffirmed by Sacred Scripture, transmitted by the Tradition of the Church and taught by the ordinary and universal Magisterium."[203]

Examples of the indirect killing of innocent human persons: (1) In a just war, a military leader orders the bombing of an enemy target, knowing that the attack will also likely result in some innocent persons being killed. This indirect killing is not intrinsically evil; it may or may not be moral, depending on intention and circumstances, but the act itself is not inherently directed toward the evil moral object of killing the innocent.

(2) City leaders decide to build a large complex bridge, knowing that the construction work is dangerous and that some deaths of construction workers will result. Some of the acts involved in building a bridge (or a skyscraper) may be dangerous, but these acts are not intrinsically evil. And the act of deciding to build a bridge does not have an evil moral object. The decision to build it may or may not be moral, depending on the intention, and whether or not the benefits outweigh the harm in the circumstances. But the second font is good.

(3) A disease epidemic threatens the lives of the citizens of a nation. Health and government officials decide to vaccinate a large percentage of the population. There are many factors to consider in the circumstances, but a large vaccination program might be anticipated to result in the deaths of some small percentage of the persons who receive the vaccine, due to adverse reactions. Even though the vaccine causes some deaths, in a way that might be termed 'physically direct,' these deaths are morally indirect because the chosen act itself of giving out vaccines is inherently directed at the moral object of preventing disease, not at the killing of the innocent. The deaths of these persons are in the third font, not the second. Such a vaccination program may or may not be moral, depending on intention, and on the weight of the good and bad consequences. But it is not intrinsically evil, even though some innocent persons will die as a result.

In moral theology, the term direct does not refer to physical directness, but rather to moral directness. If someone devises a clever complex physically-indirect means to kill an innocent human being, the act would still be morally direct, because the chosen act itself is inherently directed at the moral object of killing

---
[203] Pope John Paul II, Veritatis Splendor, 57.

an innocent human being. However, if someone knowingly chooses an act that indirectly results in the death of an innocent person, that act is not murder; such an act may or may not be moral, depending on intention and circumstances, but the act is not intrinsically evil because it is not inherently directed at the killing of the innocent person. Moral directness is an essential element in all intrinsically evil acts. If the chosen act is not morally direct, it is not intrinsically evil.

Intrinsically evil acts are always direct and voluntary, and always immoral. If a different act produces the same or similar results (in the consequences), but indirectly, then the different act is not intrinsically evil, but neither is it necessarily moral. Every intrinsically evil act is inherently directed at an evil end, called its moral object; it is in this sense that all intrinsically evil acts are direct (i.e. morally direct). The relationship between any act and its moral object is direct because the act itself is inherently ordered toward that moral object. But if a different act is not inherently ordered toward that same moral object, yet has the same end result as a consequence (in the third font, not the second), then that act is not directed at that result as to a moral object, and so the act is not intrinsically evil. The physical evil (harm) that results is indirect, since this evil is not the moral object toward which the act is inherently ordered, but rather results from that act indirectly, as a consequence.

Example of indirect abortion: (1) A woman is in the early stages of pregnancy, and she has cancer. The cancer is advancing rapidly. She cannot wait until the prenatal is viable and can be delivered, because by that time the cancer will have killed both mother and prenatal. The cancer treatment kills all cells that grow quickly, including cancer cells and the cells of the growing prenatal. The chosen act of treating the cancer has the moral object of saving the life of the mother, not of killing the prenatal. The death of the prenatal is not the end toward which the chosen act is inherently directed, but is an unintended bad consequence in the third font. The death of the prenatal would only be intrinsically evil if the knowingly chosen act was inherently directed at killing the prenatal. The cancer treatment does not distinguish between the cancer and the prenatal; the cancer treatment kills the growing cells of the cancer just as directly (i.e. 'physically' directly) as it kills the prenatal. But the knowingly chosen act of the human person, to give the mother a cancer treatment, is intrinsically directed at the health of the mother, not at the death of the prenatal. The death of the prenatal is unintended (first font) and is a bad consequence (third font). The death of the prenatal is not the moral object of the act itself (second font). The act itself is inherently directed at the health of the mother. This is all the more clear when we consider a case where a cancer patient is not pregnant, and is given essentially the same treatment.

Every knowingly chosen act is directly related to its moral object, and only indirectly related to its consequences. Intrinsically evil acts are always direct in their relation to their moral object. No act, good or evil, is ever indirectly related to its moral object. A different act may have the same result (e.g. the death of an innocent human being), without being intrinsically evil, if that result is in the consequences and is not the moral object. However, all intrinsically evil acts have some bad consequences, so that the evil moral object is always accompanied by some harm or disorder (physical evil) in the third font that is a result of the chosen act.

Examples: (1) Abortion, euthanasia, and other forms of murder have the death of the innocent as the moral object. But this death is also a bad consequence of the chosen act, and so it is both a moral evil and a physical evil (harm or disorder). (2) Theft has the taking (deprivation) of goods owned by another as the moral object, but this loss of goods is also a bad consequence. (3) Lying has the assertion of a falsehood as its moral object in the second font. But this deprivation of truth in an assertion is also a type of harmful disorder in the third font, because the expression of a falsehood by a person is contrary to the good order that God intends for Creation.

When an act is directly related to an evil moral object, that evil (a deprivation of good) is also a bad consequence. All moral evil results in some physical evil (harm or disorder) because all sin harms the goodness and good order in God's good creation.

.201. Voluntary

Intrinsically evil acts are always voluntary.

Both moral acts and immoral acts are voluntary (i.e. deliberately chosen, intentionally chosen). Morality is concerned with acts, known by reason (intellect), and chosen by free will. The will is the root of every moral act and of every immoral act. If any act is not at all voluntary, it cannot be immoral, nor it is even an act as that term is used in moral theology.

Pope John Paul II: "Every choice always implies a reference by the deliberate will to the goods and evils indicated by the natural law as goods to be pursued and evils to be avoided."[204]

Pope John Paul II: "Acting is morally good when the choices of freedom are in conformity with man's true good and thus express the voluntary ordering of the person towards his ultimate end: God himself.... The rational ordering of the human act to the good in its truth and the voluntary pursuit of that good, known by reason, constitute morality.... Activity is morally good when it attests to and expresses the voluntary ordering of the person to his ultimate end and the conformity of a concrete action with the human good as it is acknowledged in its truth by reason."[205]

All sin is voluntary; each sin is an immoral choice. Sin is determined by the three fonts of morality. Each of the three fonts of morality results from an exercise of will and intellect, in a knowing choice, by the human person. The first font is the intended end (and the intended means to that end) chosen by the will based on knowledge in the intellect. The second font is the inherent moral meaning of the knowingly chosen act as determined by its moral object. The third font is the consequences that result from that chosen act, in so far as these can be known

---

[204] Pope John Paul II, Veritatis Splendor, n. 67.
[205] Pope John Paul II, Veritatis Splendor, n. 72.

(reasonably anticipated) in advance, based on the past and present circumstances. A knowing choice, made by free will and reason (intellect), is fundamental and indispensable to each and every font of morality.

Even if the human person chooses an intrinsically evil act as a bad means to a good end, the act is nevertheless chosen by the will. The choice of an intrinsically evil act is always either an actual sin, or at least an objective sin. The person knows which act he is choosing, and so some type of knowledge and choice are involved in even a merely objective sin. And if the intrinsically evil act is chosen by an exercise of free will, and with knowledge of the immorality of the act, then it is also an actual sin. But if there is no choice at all, not even a choice lacking in freedom or deliberation, or if there is no knowledge at all, not even the mere knowledge of which act is being chosen, then there is no sin at all, not even objectively. Thus, all intrinsically evil acts are voluntary; they are chosen acts.

But this choice of an intrinsically evil act is not merely a choice of the act itself, but also of its inherent moral meaning as determined by its moral object. It is not possible for someone to choose the act itself, without choosing its inherent moral meaning. No one can say in truth that he has chosen an intrinsically evil act, but not the inherent moral meaning determined by its moral object. No one can say in truth that he has not sinned in choosing an intrinsically evil act, because he only chose the act itself, and not its inherent moral meaning. The choice of the act itself is necessarily always a choice also of the moral meaning which is inherent to, and inseparable from, that same act.

.202. Deprivation

Intrinsically evil acts always have a deprivation of good in the moral object. An act is intrinsically evil if it has an evil moral object. An evil moral object is deprived of some moral good that the eternal moral law requires to be present. An evil moral object is always a deprivation of some moral good required by the justice and goodness of God.

Examples: (1) Murder deprives an innocent human person of life. (2) False imprisonment deprives the innocent person of freedom. (3) Theft deprives an owner of his property. (4) Lying deprives assertions of truth. (5) Extra-marital sexual acts deprive the sexual act of the good of marriage. (6) Unnatural sexual acts deprive the sexual act of the procreative and unitive meanings. (7) Contraception deprives the sexual act of the procreative meaning. (8) Artificial procreation deprives procreation of the unitive meaning. (Other examples follow in the next chapter.)

Since intrinsically evil acts are always direct and voluntary, we need not repeat the phrase 'direct and voluntary' in every definition of every intrinsically evil act. However, even when not stated, it is always implied that intrinsically evil acts are morally direct (the act is directly related to its moral object) and voluntary (i.e. deliberate; the act is knowingly and intentionally chosen by the will and intellect). Neither do we need to state the particular deprivation of good with the term 'deprivation.' However, even when stated in other terms, it is always implied that intrinsically evil acts are a direct and voluntary deprivation of some good in the moral object of the act.

The good of which any evil moral object is deprived is always a good inherent to the threefold great commandment: to love God, neighbor, self. The first commandment, to love God above all else, implies that we must also love all that God created, especially created persons, and all that is good in the eyes of God. The second commandment, to love your neighbor as yourself, implies that we must also love God, for apart from God and His grace there is no true love, and all that is worthy of being loved within our neighbor is of God. This commandment also implies that you must love yourself in a way that is good before God, not in a disordered or selfish way. The emphasis of the commandment is on loving your neighbor, because each person is naturally inclined to be concerned at least for his own good. But all three are interrelated and indispensable. You cannot love God, and hate your neighbor or yourself. You cannot love your neighbor, and hate God or yourself. You cannot truly love yourself, in a detached and ordered way, and hate God or neighbor. Since all the other commandments flow from this one great commandment, all intrinsically evil acts are inherently contrary to true love of God, neighbor, self.

Therefore, every intrinsically evil act can be defined as a direct and voluntary deprivation of a good that is inherent to love of God, neighbor, self.

Chapter 16
Proper Moral Definitions

.203.
The Necessity of Proper Definitions

The proper moral definition of a knowingly chosen act must be given in terms of the three fonts of morality. Without a proper definition of each act in terms of morality, some moral acts will seem immoral, and some immoral acts will seem moral. Although an incorrect or imprecise definition may provide the correct moral decision in many cases, in some cases it will lead one into moral error and objective sin. When an act is properly defined in terms of the fonts of morality, the definition may well differ, to one extent or another, from the dictionary definition, the medical definition, the legal definition, or the common understanding of that act.

Examples: (1) Some persons define abortion as the termination of a pregnancy. They then define pregnancy as beginning with implantation in the uterus (i.e. when the placenta begins to form). Based on these improper definitions, the killing of a prenatal from conception up to the time of implantation is not considered by them to be an abortion. Also, they refer to certain drugs as 'emergency contraceptives,' when in fact these drugs often prevent implantation of the conceived prenatal, causing an early abortion. In this way, incorrect definitions are used to make abortion seem like contraception. Proper definitions are needed for a proper understanding.

(2) Many persons do not understand the difference between direct abortion and indirect abortion. As a result, they incorrectly believe that direct abortion is sometimes moral, or that indirect abortion is always immoral. Direct abortion is the direct and voluntary killing of an innocent human being, at any time from conception to birth. Direct abortion is intrinsically evil and always gravely immoral. But the related term, indirect abortion, does not refer to the direct and voluntary killing of a prenatal, but rather to the direct treatment of a medical condition in the mother, which indirectly results in the unintended death of the prenatal. This type of treatment is moral in some circumstances, such as to save the life of the mother, when the prenatal's life cannot be saved. Direct abortion is never moral, not even to save the life of the mother, not even if the prenatal's life cannot be saved. Indirect abortion to save the life of the mother is sometimes moral, when all three fonts of morality are good. Again, proper definitions are necessary in order to distinguish between moral and immoral acts.

(3) Some acts that are legally defined as theft are not morally defined as theft, but as expropriation, under a proper definition. Theft is intrinsically evil and always immoral; expropriation is sometimes moral, when all three fonts are good. This distinction between theft and expropriation is similar to the distinction between direct abortion and indirect abortion.

Second Vatican Council: "By its very nature private property has a social quality which is based on the law of the common destination of earthly goods....

Whenever, nevertheless, the common good requires expropriation, compensation must be reckoned in equity after all the circumstances have been weighed."[206]

The Council taught that expropriation is not always immoral, but also that it is not always moral. All three fonts must be good, including the moral weight of all the circumstances. Expropriation is not theft; theft is intrinsically evil, and expropriation is not intrinsically evil. However, expropriation is only moral with good intent and if the good consequences outweigh the bad consequences.

Saint Thomas Aquinas: "In cases of need all things are common property, so that there would seem to be no sin in taking another's property, for need has made it common.... Nevertheless, if the need be so manifest and urgent, that it is evident that the present need must be remedied by whatever means be at hand (for instance when a person is in some imminent danger, and there is no other possible remedy), then it is lawful for a man to succor his own need by means of another's property, by taking it either openly or secretly: nor is this properly speaking theft or robbery."[207]

The distinction between theft and expropriation clearly demonstrates the need for proper moral definitions in order to understand which acts are moral, and which acts are immoral. A proper definition in terms of morality helps us to determine which acts are good and which acts are evil. An improper definition hinders or prevents us from determining which acts are good and which acts are evil. The same is true for sexual acts; the proper definition of any sexual act, in terms of Catholic moral teaching, is necessary to determine the morality of the act correctly.

.204. The Relationship of the Fonts

The first and third fonts do not effect the essential moral nature of any chosen act, since that nature (or 'species') is determined by the moral object, which is in the second font. When a good act is done with bad intention, the act itself (second font) remains good and the intention (first font) remains bad. The first font of intention has no effect on the morality of the second font. When a good act is done with bad consequences, the act itself remains good and the consequences (third font) remain bad. The third font of the circumstances (especially the consequences) has no effect on the morality of the second font. Intention and circumstances affect the morality of the overall act (which includes all three fonts). But intention and circumstances have no effect on the second font, which is determined solely by the inherent ordering of the act itself toward its moral object.

The intention to use an intrinsically evil act as an immoral means to a good end makes the intention immoral. But the intention never changes the essential moral nature of the act itself. Good acts remain moral, and bad acts remain immoral, in the second font, regardless of good or bad intention in the first font,

---

[206] Second Vatican Council, Gaudium et Spes, n. 71.
[207] St. Thomas Aquinas, Summa Theologica, II-II, Q. 66, A. 7.

and regardless of good or bad circumstances in the third font. The morality of the first and third fonts (intention and circumstances) does not affect the essential moral nature of the chosen act, which is the second font.

.205. Broad versus Narrow Definitions

The moral definition of an act may be restricted to the second font alone. This type of moral definition describes only the inherent moral meaning of the act, i.e. its moral species or essential moral nature, as determined by its moral object. Any act with a bad moral object is an intrinsically evil act. All intrinsically evil acts are defined, as to their essential moral nature, solely under the second font. This narrower type of definition is useful because intrinsically evil acts are always immoral regardless of the other two fonts (intention and circumstance).

The moral definition of an act can also include all three fonts of morality. This broader type of definition is useful because the overall act is always immoral whenever any one or more fonts is bad. Some immoral acts are intrinsically evil, and so can be defined solely under the second font. But other immoral acts are not intrinsically evil, and therefore must necessarily be defined more broadly, so as to include intention or circumstances, or both.

Some intrinsically evil acts are further classified into subtypes based on intention or circumstances. So the narrow definition of the intrinsically evil act is solely under the second font, but the particular categorization of the act, within the set of acts that have the same essential moral nature, depends on the other fonts. Abortion, infanticide, suicide, and euthanasia are all types of murder. The second font in each case makes the act murder, and the other fonts determine the further classification of the act. Thus, some intrinsically evil acts, which are immoral under the second font, are further defined by intention or circumstances.

.206. Improper Definitions

Often a misunderstanding concerning the morality of an act is rooted in an improper definition, or in a misunderstanding of the proper definition, of the moral or immoral act being considered. A proper moral definition is necessary for a proper understanding of any knowingly chosen act. The proper definition of any act in terms of morality is according to the three fonts.

In many cases, a devout practicing Catholic Christian may understand that an act is immoral, even without a particular definition in mind for that particular act. But even a holy person risks committing an objective mortal sin if his understanding of morality is not based firmly on those distinctions (within the three fonts) needed to understand some of the more difficult moral decisions. So when someone mistakenly thinks that a moral act is immoral, or that an immoral act is moral, the misunderstanding often proceeds from an improper definition, or from a misunderstanding of the three fonts of morality.

Examples: (1) An entirely incorrect definition of lying could be phrased as: "Lying is the unjust telling of an untruth." This approach nullifies the teaching of the Faith that lying, as an intrinsically evil act, is always immoral. If a lie, or any other intrinsically evil act at all, is defined with the word 'unjust' in the definition, then whether or not the chosen act is intrinsically evil would depend upon a prior determination as to whether or not the act is unjust. But that determination would have to be made without the benefit of the teaching that intrinsically evil acts are always immoral, because the act is not said to be intrinsically evil until it is first judged to be unjust. In this approach, an unjust lie is said to be intrinsically evil, and a supposedly just lie is said not to be intrinsically evil, or rather is not defined as a lie at all. The result is that any lie can be claimed to be moral by the baseless claim that the lie is 'just' and therefore not a lie. Perhaps the evaluation as to the justice or injustice of the lie would claim to be based on intention and circumstances. But this approach still negates the definitive teaching of the Magisterium that intrinsically evil acts are always immoral.

(2) When lust is correctly defined, it is clear that even within marriage a husband and wife may not lust after each other. An incorrect definition of lust, which is called adultery of the heart by Christ (Mt 5:28), might lead to the incorrect conclusion that, when sexual relations occurs between husband and wife, no lust could possibly be present. And this error in the definition of lust could result in a husband and wife falling into serious sin. The correct definition of lust is of the heart and mind, such that no exterior act is necessary, and such that, even if the exterior act is moral (i.e. natural marital relations), the interior sin of lust might still be present. Lust is a willingness to commit any illicit sexual act. A husband commits the sin of lust toward his wife (or she toward him), if he uses her as a sexual object, merely for his own pleasure, so that in principle he is not having sexual relations with his wife, but with whatever source of sexual pleasure is available, or if he is willing to obtain pleasure in an illicit sexual act with his wife (even if the illicit act never occurs).

(3) Killing may be justified in self-defense (or by law enforcement officers in defense of the community, or by the justice system in a proper use of the death penalty, or in just warfare). A failure to properly define an act of self-defense versus an act of murder can result either in a claim that murder has occurred when the killing was justified, or in a claim that a killing was justified when the act was murder.

(4) The Church plainly teaches that expropriation is distinct from theft, and may be moral.[208] However, most governments have not written their laws such that expropriation would be distinguished from theft. An act that is theft under a legal definition may well be a moral act of expropriation. A reliance on the legal definition, instead of the moral definition, will sometimes result in an incorrect evaluation as to the morality of an act.

(5) In secular society, there is currently a discussion about the use of torture in interrogations of accused terrorists and other enemy combatants. However, it is very common for these discussions to offer no definition of torture at all, or to have such a broad definition that any slight use (or implied use) of force, even against persons known to be guilty of serious offences, is called torture. In truth, without a proper definition of torture under the three fonts of morality, any

---

[208] Second Vatican Council, Gaudium et Spes, n. 71.

statements as to the morality of torture are likely to be incorrect. Also, no act can be said to be intrinsically evil unless that act is defined as immoral under the second font. If there is no definition at all, then there is no basis for stating whether or not a particular act is intrinsically evil.

Chapter 17
Theft and Lying

.207.
Theft

Theft is narrowly defined as the direct and voluntary deprivation of goods owned by another person. Love of God and neighbor requires us to respect the right of our neighbor to own property. Under this definition, theft is intrinsically evil.

A broader definition of theft allows further classification, by intention and circumstances, into various types of theft, such as embezzlement, fraud, theft of intellectual property, etc. These acts are intrinsically evil, since they are types of theft, even though the type is determined by intention or circumstances, because the second font has an evil moral object.

Expropriation may seem to resemble theft, and in fact may be theft under a dictionary definition, or under a legal definition. But under a proper moral definition, expropriation is not theft because God is the First Owner of all goods. So if one person has an abundance of food, and other persons have no other reasonable way to obtain enough food to live, except by taking that person's food without his consent, then the act of taking the food (or other necessities of life) is not theft, and is not intrinsically evil. The right of ownership of any goods is first to God, who does not will that some persons starve, or are continually malnourished, when there is ample food available. God wills that the goods of this life be shared by all human persons, at least to the extent that any dire need can be met by what is available, but not to such an extent that no one may have true ownership of goods. The ownership of goods by human persons is good and moral because it is a reflection of the ownership of all Creation by God.

But even when the act itself is certainly expropriation, which has the good moral object of distributing the goods of creation to those in dire need, the overall act is only moral if all three fonts are good. And so expropriation with a bad intention, or when the bad circumstances outweigh the good, would not be moral. Neither is it moral to commit an intrinsically evil act, such as killing the innocent, or assaulting the innocent, in order to accomplish the expropriation.

The legal right of eminent domain, when properly applied, is a type of expropriation. The common good may require that private property be expropriated from the owner to the larger community. Just compensation is due to the owner, and the good consequences of taking the property must outweigh any bad consequences to the owner, his family, neighbors, employees, and everyone affected by the act. Although the act itself of taking of property by right of eminent domain may be a type of expropriation, the intention and the circumstances must also be good. Otherwise, even if the act itself is truly a type of expropriation, the overall act would be immoral.

In cases where individuals exercise a moral act of expropriation, violence against the innocent is not thereby justified. A moral act never justifies an immoral act; intrinsically evil acts are never justified, not by any intention, not in any circumstances, not by other moral or immoral acts. An act of violence might be justified against a person who is guilty of attempting to do serious harm to the innocent, in which case the violence would be self-defense or defense of others, and not an intrinsically evil act. A moral act of expropriation might be accompanied by a moral act of self-defense. But each and every act must be good under all three fonts, as each font springs from, and applies to, each particular act. Even if two acts occur at the same time, or one immediately after another, each act must be good under all three of its own fonts. A bad font makes any act immoral. A bad second font makes any act intrinsically evil and always immoral. But a good second font is not sufficient to make the overall act moral. All three fonts of morality must be good for any act to be moral.

.208. Robbery

Saint Thomas distinguishes theft from robbery: "Wherefore theft and robbery derive their sinful nature, through the taking being involuntary on the part of the person from whom something is taken. Now the involuntary is twofold, namely, through violence and through ignorance, as stated in Ethic. iii, 1. Therefore the sinful aspect of robbery differs from that of theft: and consequently they differ specifically."[209]

Although in other places, Saint Thomas sums up the difference between theft and robbery such that theft is done in secret and robbery is done in the open, it is clear from all that he says on the topic that robbery is done openly by the use of violence or the threat of violence.

Theft is narrowly defined, under the second font, as the direct and voluntary deprivation of goods owned by another. Robbery is also the direct and voluntary deprivation of goods owned by another. So the second font is the same in theft as in robbery. Therefore, robbery should be defined as a type of theft. The difference between robbery and simple theft is found in the third font. (Similarly, the differences between abortion and infanticide are found in the third font, but each is nevertheless a type of murder.) Robbery is theft by means of violence or the threat of violence. Therefore, robbery is properly defined as the direct and voluntary deprivation of goods owned by another person, by violent means. If robbery were committed without any violence, such as by stealth or deception, then it would no longer be robbery. But since the second font would be unchanged, the act would still remain a type of theft, which is intrinsically evil.

Any act of violence, or an act that threatens violence, even when it accompanies the type of theft called robbery, is a separate act, and so it must be evaluated on the basis of its own three fonts of morality. The first font of intention is to obtain the goods of another, which is an immoral intention. The act itself of violence (or of a threat of violence) against the innocent has the moral object to harm one's neighbor, which is contrary to the eternal moral law. Thus the moral object is evil and the act itself is intrinsically evil. The circumstances would depend on the particular example of robbery, but would generally include the harm done to

---

[209] St. Thomas Aquinas, Summa Theologica, II-II, Q. 66, A. 4; he cites Ethic. iii, 1, which is a work by Aristotle called Nicomachean Ethics.

.209. Usury

[Exodus]
{22:25} If you lend money to the poor of my people who live among you, you shall not coerce them like a collector, nor oppress them with usury.

[Psalm 14] (15)
{14:1} A Psalm of David. O Lord, who will dwell in your tabernacle? Or who will rest on your holy mountain?
{14:2} He who walks without blemish and who works justice.
{14:3} He who speaks the truth in his heart, who has not acted deceitfully with his tongue, and has not done evil to his neighbor, and has not taken up a reproach against his neighbors.
{14:4} In his sight, the malicious one has been reduced to nothing, but he glorifies those who fear the Lord. He who swears to his neighbor and does not deceive.
{14:5} He who has not given his money in usury, nor accepted bribes against the innocent. He who does these things will be undisturbed for eternity.

Usury can be divided into two types, one of which is intrinsically evil, and the other of which is not intrinsically evil, but is immoral because of the circumstances.

First, when usury is excessive interest charged when goods or money are loaned, the morality of the act depends on the degree of interest, which is a circumstance. It is immoral to charge excessive interest on goods or money loaned, even if the amount of interest is legal. The moral law may require you to lend money without interest to a family member or to another person, as an act of charity, in certain circumstances. But charging interest is not intrinsically evil, for Sacred Scripture permits lending at interest.

[Deuteronomy]
{23:19} You shall not lend money, or grain, or anything else at all, to your brother at interest,
{23:20} but only to a foreigner. For you shall lend to your brother whatever he needs without interest, so that the Lord your God may bless you in all your works in the land, which you shall enter so as to possess it.

The Israelites were not permitted to charge interest on money or goods lent to their fellow Israelites. The act of lending, in such a case, is an act of charity, or a type of almsgiving; the eternal moral law requires acts of charity and almsgiving. However, the Israelites were permitted to charge interest on money or goods lent to foreigners (i.e. to non-Jews). Sacred Scripture specifically permits this type of interest; therefore, charging interest cannot be intrinsically evil. Thus, usury does not refer to any type of interest charged against what is loaned, but to excessive interest.

Charging interest is moral because the person loaning the money or goods lacks the use of these until they are returned, and the money or goods may decrease in value (due to inflation, or wear and tear), and the lender assumes a degree of risk in making the loan. Therefore, it is just to compensate the lender (or creditor) for the time period of the use, for any loss in value of what is borrowed, and for the assumed risk. When the interest charged is excessive, then the act is immoral, but only because of degree (which is in the circumstances). Intrinsically evil acts are not moral in one degree and immoral in another degree. And so usury by excessive interest is immoral, but not intrinsically evil. A reduction in the degree of interest would make the very same act moral.

Second, when usury is a type of theft, then the act is intrinsically evil and always immoral, regardless of intention or circumstances. In this case, the lender (or creditor) requires both a payment for the goods, in an amount which meets or exceeds the value of the goods, and also the return of the goods. For example, a wealthy merchant would give a measure of wheat in exchange for a fee, and also require the return of the same amount of wheat at a later time (after the harvest). Since the price for the wheat was sufficient for its purchase, the wheat has been sold, and its ownership has been transferred to the buyer. The additional requirement to return the same amount of wheat constitutes a type of theft. In the past times, in some places, some secular laws supported this type of usury. But even when it is entirely legal, this type of usury is an act of theft, and is intrinsically evil and always immoral.

.210. Lying

[Sirach]
{7:13} Do not love a lie against your brother, nor should you act the same toward your friend.
{7:14} Do not be willing to devise a lie of any kind. For the practice of lying is not good.

[John]
{14:6} Jesus said to him: "I am the Way, and the Truth, and the Life. No one comes to the Father, except through me."

Lying is the direct and voluntary deprivation of truth from an assertion. Lying is intrinsically evil and is always immoral, regardless of intention or circumstances. If a person makes a false assertion without knowing that the assertion is false, then the act is not voluntary (i.e. not deliberate), and so the act is not intrinsically evil, is not a lie, and is not even an objective sin. In such a case, the deprivation of truth from the assertion is in the third font, not the second font. Whenever the deprivation of truth is morally indirect (e.g. mental reservation), or not voluntary (e.g. a false assertion made in ignorance), then the act is not lying at all. Lying is intrinsically evil. All intrinsically evil acts are the direct and voluntary deprivation of some good required by the love of God and neighbor. Any act that is not morally direct, or not voluntary (deliberately chosen, intentionally chosen), is not intrinsically evil.

Since God is Truth, all lying offends God, even with good intention, even without the intention to deceive, even with good consequences, even in dire circumstances, even in circumstances where other persons are not deceived or harmed. God is Truth, therefore all lying is immoral.

Some common definitions of lying are incorrect, because they do not define lying in such a way that its morality is independent of intention and circumstances. Lying is intrinsically evil; all intrinsically evil acts are immoral regardless of intention or circumstances. Therefore, a proper definition of lying should omit any mention of intention or circumstances.

Now some intrinsically evil acts are further divided into subtypes, by their intention or circumstances. For example, euthanasia is a subtype of murder; euthanasia is murder with the intention of relieving all suffering. But if we omit the intention, the act remains a type of murder and remains intrinsically evil. Therefore, even if one type of lying or another is defined with a mention of intention or circumstances, the essential moral nature of the act is independent of intention or circumstances. For example, the ten commandments forbid lying in the circumstance of bearing false witness against your neighbor. All lying is immoral. The particular example of lying stated in the ten commandments is a very grievous type of lying. In this case, the circumstances make the lie a serious sin, but lying in any circumstances is still immoral.

The Catechism of the Catholic Church defines lying as follows: " 'A lie consists in speaking a falsehood with the intention of deceiving.' "[210] This definition, quoted from Saint Augustine by the Catechism, is not sufficiently broad. Lying with the intention of deceiving is a subtype of lying. For all lying is intrinsically evil, and all intrinsically evil acts are immoral regardless of intention. The Catechism goes on to imply that lying is intrinsically evil: "Lying is the most direct offense against the truth....By its very nature, lying is to be condemned."[211]

However, a better and more comprehensive definition of lying will not include mention of intention or circumstances. Lying is the direct and voluntary deprivation of truth from an assertion. The same definition might also be stated in other terms, as the direct and voluntary assertion of a falsehood. However, this latter definition must be understood such that some false assertions are by way of omission. For example, if a witness swears in a court of law to tell "the truth, the whole truth, and nothing but the truth," and then subsequently omits a relevant substantive truth from his testimony, not only is the oath violated, but the testimony itself is a lie because the witness directly and deliberately deprived his testimony of truth, such that what was asserted was not a truthful description of events, but a lying description of events.

---

[210] Catechism of the Catholic Church, n. 2482; the text cites St. Augustine, De mendacio 4, 5: PL 40: 491.
[211] Catechism of the Catholic Church, n. 2483, 2485.

So at times even an omission may constitute a direct and voluntary deprivation of truth from an assertion. Similarly, euthanasia, which is also intrinsically evil, may also occur at times by an act of omission, rather than an act of commission.

.211. However, a similar act is a different type of sin: when a person remains silent even though the eternal moral law requires a particular truth to be expressed out of love for God and neighbor. In this case, the person sins, but the sin is not a lie. The sin of omission in this case is not a lie of omission because the act is not an assertion deprived of truth (as when a truth is omitted from testimony), but a decision to refrain from expressing any truth on that subject.

It immoral to tell a lie, even a small lie, even with good intention, even in order to avoid grave consequences. God is Truth, and lying is inherently contrary to truth. Lying is intrinsically evil, and intrinsically evil acts are always immoral.

St. Thomas Aquinas: "An action that is naturally evil in respect of its genus can by no means be good and lawful, since in order for an action to be good it must be right in every respect: because good results from a complete cause, while evil results from any single defect, as Dionysius asserts (Div. Nom. iv). Now a lie is evil in respect of its genus, since it is an action bearing on undue matter..... A lie is sinful not only because it injures one's neighbor, but also on account of its inordinateness.... Therefore it is not lawful to tell a lie in order to deliver another from any danger whatever."[212]

Suppose that a man tells a venial lie in order to keep several innocent persons from being unjustly put to death. The lie remains a venial sin, despite the good intentions and the good consequences. The good intention remains good; the good consequences remain good; the moral object remains immoral. A thousand good acts do not justify the smallest bad act, nor do a thousand bad acts corrupt the smallest good act. Nothing is more essential or more fundamental to the eternal moral law than the distinction and separation between good and evil. Good acts do not justify bad acts, and bad acts do not corrupt good acts. Whatever is good remains good; whatever is bad remains bad.

Furthermore, good does not come from evil. When a man tells a venial lie in order to achieve very good consequences, the good in the consequences does not come from the sin of lying, but from the grace and providence of God. Even though it is said that God brings good out of evil, this is a figure of speech. God brings all that is good from His own Goodness, including every grace, every providence, and every miracle. The lie that is told with the purpose of saving innocent lives is not itself the source of that good consequence, even though it may seem to be so from a worldly point of view. God's grace, providence, and miracles give us all that is good. Nothing truly good proceeds from intrinsically evil acts of any kind, whether venial or moral.

[Matthew]
{7:17} So then, every good tree produces good fruit, and the evil tree produces evil fruit.

---

[212] Saint Thomas Aquinas, Summa Theologica, II-II, Q. 110, A. 3.

{7:18} A good tree is not able to produce evil fruit, and an evil tree is not able to produce good fruit.

So in truth, the man should not lie in order to save lives, for the lives will be saved, if it is the will of God, by grace and providence and miracles, not by lying. If God permits their lives to be saved when the man tells a lie, they are saved not because he lied, but because God is merciful, giving great benefits even to us mere weak and mortal sinners.

Furthermore, all innocent souls, and all repentant souls, have the hope of eternal life. And so the bad consequence of death should not be considered to be so great as to compel us to commit even a small sin. For when the innocent are killed, despite all our efforts and prayers, they are with God in Heaven.

[Matthew]
{5:10} Blessed are those who endure persecution for the sake of justice, for theirs is the kingdom of heaven.
{5:11} Blessed are you when they have slandered you, and persecuted you, and spoken all kinds of evil against you, falsely, for my sake:
{5:12} be glad and exult, for your reward in heaven is plentiful. For so they persecuted the prophets who were before you.
{5:13} You are the salt of the earth. But if salt loses its saltiness, with what will it be salted? It is no longer useful at all, except to be cast out and trampled under by men.

Notice what our Lord says. Those who are persecuted for the sake of justice have a reward waiting for them in heaven. Their reward is plentiful, and eternal, and no one can take it away from them. But if we sin, supposedly in order to do good, we become like salt that has lost its saltiness. Those who suffer innocently will have a reward in heaven. And those who sin, no matter what the excuse, will be punished: either with a temporary punishment in this life or in Purgatory, or with an everlasting punishment in Hell.

Finally, God is infinite Goodness. Even the smallest sin is offensive to God who is infinite, and so even the smallest sin is not justified, not even for a weighty reason. For no reason for sinning outweighs the infinite Goodness who is God.

.212. The Three Fonts and Lying

The act of lying is intrinsically evil, and so a proper narrow definition of lying would be restricted to the second font. Lying is the deliberate and morally direct deprivation of truth from an assertion. A bad intention can make a lie more sinful. A good intention can make a lie less sinful. The circumstances can also make a lie more or less sinful, based on whether the consequences of the lie do more or less harm. But lying is never defined, in its essential moral nature, by the first or third fonts.

The intention to deceive does not make an act a lie. Persons commonly lie with the intent to deceive, but that intention is not what defines lying. Neither intention, nor circumstances, ever affect the definition of an act under the second font. The direct and deliberate assertion of a falsehood is what constitutes the lie;

all this is in the second font. One lie is told with the intention of deceiving, and another lie is told without that intention; but both are lies. One lie is told with the consequence that a person is misled, and another lie is told without that consequence; but both are lies. And consider that a person might also be misled or deceived by mental reservation, without any lie. So whether or not there is an intention to deceive, does not reveal whether or not a lie was told. And if it happens that no one is misled as a consequence of the lie, the act of lying remains intrinsically evil. The second font defines the essential moral nature of each and every intrinsically evil act. The first and third fonts can make an intrinsically evil act more or less sinful, but they do not define the act.

.213. Mental Reservation

For a time, some theologians used the term "strict mental reservation" to refer to a statement which is directly and deliberately false, but which is modified to become true by an unstated (mentally-reserved) qualification. However, this idea was subsequently condemned by Pope Innocent XI.[213] Since then, strict mental reservation has been held to be merely a type of lying. For in strict mental reservation, the assertion is directly and deliberately deprived of truth. And the unexpressed qualification does not affect the deprivation of truth in what is expressed (or asserted), because that qualification is unexpressed (not asserted). This act is entirely unlike true mental reservation, which asserts one truth, while reserving another truth. An act of strict mental reservation asserts a falsehood, and therefore is not true mental reservation, but is merely a lie. The proper definition of mental reservation excludes strict mental reservation, since that act fits the proper definition of lying.

Mental reservation is the expression of one truth, with the reservation (i.e. the omission) of a related truth. There are two types of limitations that may cause a statement to be a type of mental reservation: (1) the expression of a truth with the omission of a related truth, or (2) the expression of a truth with the omission of the true manner of interpretation. In the first case, there are two related truths; one is expressed and another is omitted. In the second case, the related truth that is omitted is merely the proper manner of interpretation of the expressed truth. Human language often has multiple possible meanings; this commonly-understood feature of language does not cause what is expressed to be a lie.

Examples: (1) Abraham stated that his wife Sarah was his sister (Gen 20:1-14). Two facts are true on this topic: first, that she is his sister (his half-sister, as we might say today), and second, that she is his wife. He stated the truth that she is his sister, and he omitted the truth that she is his wife. The omission of the truth that she is his wife does not cause the stated truth, that she is his sister, to be false.

(2) In the same case, Abraham's assertion that Sarah was his sister was a truth expressed with the omission of the proper interpretation. A brother and sister may have either one or two parents in common. Abraham omitted the proper interpretation, specifically that they have only one parent in common. His

---

[213] Pope Innocent XI, Santissimus Dominus, n. 26, 27.

statement was not a lie, since half-brothers and half-sisters are commonly called brother or sister without further qualification.

An act of mental reservation always consists of two parts: the act of expressing a truth, and a decision to omit another truth. The omitted truth is either a related but distinct truth, or the correct manner of interpretation of the expressed truth. No falsehood is asserted, and no truth is denied, in mental reservation. The direct and deliberate expression of a falsehood, or the direct and deliberate denial of a truth, are not types of mental reservation, but types of lying. The direct and deliberate assertion of a truth, or denial of a falsehood, are not types of mental reservation, but expressions of truth without mental reservation.

Every good moral object is a particular fulfillment of the threefold foundation of the moral law: love of God, neighbor, and self. And so the truth expressed must not be directed at harming one's neighbor; otherwise the expression of that truth, while not the sin of lying, would constitute the sin of words directed at the deliberate harm of an innocent person (a type of assault on the innocent by means of words, i.e. calumny). Similarly, the omission of the related truth must not be directed at the deliberate harm of the innocent. Otherwise the act is not properly defined as mental reservation, but as calumny by omission.

Mental reservation can be moral, despite the omission of a truth, because the obligation to avoid lying does not require all truths to be told at all times. The omission of a truth is only a lie when the omitted truth is required to make what is expressed true. If what is expressed can stand on its own as true, then the omission of a related truth does not constitute a lie. Strict mental reservation is properly understood to be a lie, because what is expressed cannot stand on its own as a truth. So in order for mental reservation to avoid being a lie, the omitted truth must not be required in order for what is expressed to be true. The expressed truth must be able to stand on its own as a truth.

Now when the omitted truth is the correct manner of interpretation of the expressed truth, the expressed truth must be capable of being understood with correct interpretation while standing on its own (without the need for what is omitted). Reason must be capable of understanding the expressed truth in is proper interpretation.

Example: (1) Jesus told some of his fellow Jews that He was not going to the Feast of Tabernacles in Jerusalem because for Him the time was not yet right (John 7:1-10). This statement on its own is capable of being understood properly, as a true expression. When the reason given for not going to a particular place is that the time in not right, this expression necessarily implies that when the time is right, the person might go to that place. The truth that is expressed includes an expressed limitation, in this case of time. Nothing is said or implied outside of that expressed limitation. And so the expressed truth stands on its own as true.

.214. The Three Fonts and Mental Reservation

Mental reservation, by definition, has a good moral object. However, an act with a good moral object may still be immoral, if it is done with bad intention, or in circumstances when the bad consequences outweigh the good. The three fonts of morality always apply. No act is moral unless all three fonts are good. But any single bad font is sufficient to make any act immoral.

Lying is the direct and voluntary deprivation of truth from an assertion. Lying is immoral because the moral object (in the second font) is evil. But with mental reservation, the deprivation of truth from an assertion is not the moral object of the act. With mental reservation, the assertion is true; the omission of a related truth, or the omission of the proper interpretation of the expressed truth, is not a lie because all that is expressed is able to stand on its own as a true assertion. When a listener misunderstands an assertion under mental reservation, the misunderstanding is a consequence in the third font; the second font remains good. But to be moral, every knowingly chosen act must be good under all three fonts.

Therefore, mental reservation is not intrinsically evil, but neither is it always moral. If a person uses mental reservation with immoral intention, then the act is a sin under the first font of intention. Or if a person uses mental reservation with good intent, but in circumstances where the harm (bad consequences) done by the use of mental reservation outweighs the good consequences, then the act is a sin under the third font. Mental reservation is only moral with good intent and when the good consequences outweigh the bad.

The intention in the first font of any act must be moral in both the intended end and the intended means. The moral use of mental reservation may include the intention to deceive the listener, but only as a bad (but not immoral) means to a greater good end. The third font tolerates some bad consequences, if these are outweighed by the good consequences, only because the bad consequences are not immoral, but are bad in the sense of harm or disorder. Similarly, the first font tolerates a bad intended means for the sake of a good intended end (such as a physician amputating a limb in order to save a life), but only if that means is not immoral, but is bad in the sense of harm or disorder, and only if the intended end is not bad in any sense and outweighs any harm done in the intended means. It is sometimes moral to intend the use of a type of harm or disorder as a means. But is it never moral to intend any type of harm or disorder as an end. For all our ends in this life (proximate ends) must be capable of being ordered toward God as our ultimate end, in eternal life.

One of the most common bad consequences of mental reservation is the deprivation of truth in mind of listeners, who may misunderstand the expressed truth. A person would not be justified in using mental reservation without regard for intention and consequences, because all three fonts must be good for any act to be moral. Since mental reservation often has the bad consequence of a listener being deceived, there must be a proportionately serious good consequence that outweighs this bad consequence. Otherwise, the use of mental reservation would be a sin, though not the sin of lying.

.215. Does the expression of a truth always have a good moral object?

Suppose that a priest states the truth in revealing the contents of a penitent's confession. Breaking the seal of the confessional is intrinsically evil and always gravely immoral. But stating a truth is not intrinsically evil. In such a case, the moral object of the act is two-fold: (1) a truth is expressed, and (2) the seal of the confessional is broken. Any act which has an evil moral object is an intrinsically evil act; this is true even if the act has more than one moral object, and even if only one of the moral objects is evil. Just as one bad font is sufficient to make the overall act immoral, so also one bad moral object is sufficient to make the act itself intrinsically evil. (This concept is important in sexual ethics, since sexual relations has a threefold moral object which is marital, unitive, and procreative. A deprivation of even one of these three is sufficient to make the act intrinsically evil and always gravely immoral.)

Mental reservation always expresses a truth, and the moral object of expressing a truth is always good. But since an act may have more than one moral object, that same act of expressing a truth (with or without a mental reservation) may have another moral object which is evil. In such a case, the mere expression of truth is not what causes the act itself to be intrinsically evil. And so mental reservation, and any expression of truth without a mental reservation, is not inherently wrong. But if the act of expressing a truth has a second moral object, that moral object may be evil, not because a truth was told, but because the act was inherently directed at another moral object, one that is evil, such as to harm the innocent in some manner.

Thus, mental reservation is not intrinsically evil, since its moral object is the expression of truth, but neither is the use of mental reservation always moral under the second font. For when the act of telling a truth has another moral object, one that is evil, then that same act is intrinsically evil. Mental reservation must be moral under all three fonts for the act to be moral. An act of mental reservation might be immoral because of a bad intention, or because the act is directed at a second moral object, one that is evil, or because the harmful consequences outweigh any good consequences.

.216. Deception

[Sirach]
{19:22} There is a certain cleverness, and it is unjust.
{19:23} And there is one who utters a careful word, explaining away the truth. There is one who humbles himself wickedly, for his interior is filled with deceit.

Deceit can be a sin, even if the person finds a clever way to deceive someone without lying. The commandment to love God not only forbids us from lying, but also forbids the misuse of mental reservation, such as when a person intends to deceive another person for a harmful purpose, or at any time when the bad consequences would outweigh the good. Even if the deceit is able to be accomplished without a lie, the act is still subject to all three fonts of morality. A particular act of deception might not be a lie under the second font, but it might still be a sin under the first or third fonts.

Suppose that someone uses mental reservation with the intention of avoiding serious harm to an innocent person. The intended end is not to deceive, but to do good to one's neighbor. The result that one person misunderstands or is deceived by the use of mental reservation may be an intended means in the first font, and a bad consequence in the third font, but it is outweighed by the good that results from avoiding harm to an innocent person. In such a case, the intention and the consequences are moral, but all this must be accomplished also with a good second font, i.e. without lying.

.217. Speak the Truth or Remain Silent

The commandment to love God not only forbids us from lying, and from the misuse of mental reservation, but also at times from telling certain truths to certain persons (without any mental reservation). Sometimes the positive precept to love our neighbor requires us to be silent, rather than to speak. The commandment to love our neighbor forbids us from telling the truth either with bad intention, or when more harm is done than good. If we are told a truth in confidence, and revealing that truth will do more harm than good, then the third font is bad, and the act is immoral.

In some circumstances, a human person has a moral obligation not to reveal a truth. A priest must never break the seal of the confessional, since this act would be intrinsically evil. And a physician should not reveal confidential medical information to those who have no right to that information, because of the harm done by violating the privacy of the patient.

In other circumstances, though it is not a sin to reveal a truth, a person may morally withhold the truth, if in his or her judgment a particular person or group has no right to know that truth. If your employer requires you to give an accounting of your work for him, he has a right to this type of truth. But if he requires you to give an accounting of your personal life, you may refuse to provide him with these truths, since he has no right to know. But even when a person has no right to know a truth, lying is not justified.

Lying is intrinsically evil and always immoral. Mental reservation is not intrinsically evil, because it is not a direct and voluntary deprivation of some good required by love of God, neighbor, self. If the moral object of an expression is good, then the expression is not a lie. The moral object of mental reservation is good because mental reservation expresses a truth. Mental reservation may include an equivocation, i.e. an expression of truth which might have more than one meaning. But the expression itself must stand on its own as a truth, in order to avoid lying.

If it is a sin to express a certain truth, one may use mental reservation to express a different truth, or one may remain silent. We are not obligated to answer every question, nor to correct every misunderstanding. We are not obligated to continually speak on every subject, nor to dispense every truth to every person. But we are morally obligated to withhold certain truths from certain persons who might use that information to do evil. And we are morally obligated to refrain from every kind of sin, including lying. For lying is intrinsically evil and always immoral; lying is never justified, no matter how good the intention, no matter how dire the circumstances. No one is justified in telling the smallest lie, nor in committing the smallest sin of any kind, even if one small sin would save the whole world from Hell.

[Luke]
{23:1} And the entire multitude of them, rising up, led him to Pilate.
{23:2} Then they began to accuse him, saying, "We found this one subverting our nation, and prohibiting giving tribute to Caesar, and saying that he is Christ the king."
{23:3} And Pilate questioned him, saying: "You are the king of the Jews?" But in response, he said: "You are saying it."
{23:4} Then Pilate said to the leaders of the priests and to the crowds, "I find no case against this man."
{23:5} But they continued more intensely, saying: "He has stirred up the people, teaching throughout all of Judea, beginning from Galilee, even to this place."
{23:6} But Pilate, upon hearing Galilee, asked if the man were of Galilee.
{23:7} And when he realized that he was under Herod's jurisdiction, he sent him away to Herod, who was himself also at Jerusalem in those days.
{23:8} Then Herod, upon seeing Jesus, was very glad. For he had been wanting to see him for a long time, because he had heard so many things about him, and he was hoping to see some kind of sign wrought by him.
{23:9} Then he questioned him with many words. But he gave him no response at all.
{23:10} And the leaders of the priests, and the scribes, stood firm in persistently accusing him.

Jesus was silent before Herod. Even though Herod had authority in secular society and was exercising that authority by questioning Jesus, our Lord chose to remain silent. The leaders of the Jewish priests and scribes also went to Herod, so that they could continue to accuse Jesus. But despite their many accusations, He chose to remain silent. However, when accused before Pilate, Jesus did give a response.

The example of Christ teaches us that we may wisely choose between speaking the truth, and remaining silent. In one circumstance, it might be unwise or even immoral to remain silent. In another circumstance, it might be unwise or even immoral to speak a particular truth. However, in all circumstances, lying is always immoral. Since the time of Christ, the Saints and martyrs have continued this example of Christ by sometimes replying to accusations, and other times remaining silent in the face of accusations.

In mental reservation, one truth is spoken, and another truth is reserved in silence. So mental reservation combines both speaking the truth, and withholding the truth in silence. The truth that is spoken must stand on its own as true. If the spoken statement by itself, without what is unspoken, is a deliberate falsehood, then the statement is a lie, not a type of mental reservation.

.218. Examples of Mental Reservation

[John]
{7:1} Then, after these things, Jesus was walking in Galilee. For he was not willing to walk in Judea, because the Jews were seeking to kill him.
{7:2} Now the feast day of the Jews, the Feast of Tabernacles, was near.
{7:3} And his brothers said to him: "Move away from here and go into Judea, so that your disciples there may also see your works that you do.
{7:4} Of course, no one does anything in secret, but he himself seeks to be in the public view. Since you do these things, manifest yourself to the world."
{7:5} For neither did his brothers believe in him.
{7:6} Therefore, Jesus said to them: "My time has not yet come; but your time is always at hand.
{7:7} The world cannot hate you. But it hates me, because I offer testimony about it, that its works are evil.
{7:8} You may go up to this feast day. But I am not going up to this feast day, because my time has not yet been fulfilled."
{7:9} When he had said these things, he himself remained in Galilee.
{7:10} But after his brothers went up, then he also went up to the feast day, not openly, but as if in secret.

Jesus used mental reservation by stating that He was not going to the feast because it was not yet time for him. This statement was true; he was not going because it was not yet time for Him to go to the feast in Jerusalem. The statement contains a limit to the assertion, based on time, implying that He might or might not go to the feast once His time had been fulfilled. Jesus omitted the truth about whether or not He would go at a later time. And in fact, later He did go to the feast.

Jesus had a serious reason for using mental reservation, in that the Jews were seeking to kill Him. And so Jesus neither sinned by lying, nor did He sin by misusing mental reservation. This is an example of the proper use of mental reservation. When mental reservation is used without a proportionately serious reason, then that act is a sin. Abraham also gave us an example of the proper use of mental reservation.

[Genesis]
{20:1} Abraham advanced from there into the southern land, and he lived between Kadesh and Shur. And he sojourned in Gerar.
{20:2} And he said about his wife Sarah: "She is my sister." Therefore, Abimelech, the king of Gerar, sent for her and took her.
{20:3} Then God came to Abimelech through a dream in the night, and he said to him: "Lo, you shall die because of the woman that you have taken. For she has a husband."
{20:4} In truth, Abimelech had not touched her, and so he said: "Lord, would you put to death a people, ignorant and just?
{20:5} Did he not say to me, 'She is my sister,' and did she not say, 'He is my brother?' In the sincerity of my heart and the purity of my hands, I have done this."

{20:6} And God said to him: "And I know that you have acted with a sincere heart. And therefore I kept you from sinning against me, and I did not release you to touch her.
{20:7} Now therefore, return his wife to the man, for he is a prophet. And he will pray for you, and you will live. But if you are not willing to return her, know this: you shall die a death, you and all that is yours."
{20:8} And immediately Abimelech, rising up in the night, called all his servants. And he spoke all these words in their hearing, and all the men were very afraid.
{20:9} Then Abimelech called also for Abraham, and he said to him: "What have you done to us? How have we sinned against you, so that you would bring so great a sin upon me and upon my kingdom? You have done to us what you ought not to have done."
{20:10} And remonstrating him again, he said, "What did you see, so that you would do this?"
{20:11} Abraham responded: "I thought to myself, saying: Perhaps there is no fear of God in this place. And they will put me to death because of my wife.
{20:12} Yet, in another way, she is also truly my sister, the daughter of my father, and not the daughter of my mother, and I took her as a wife.
{20:13} Then, after God led me out of my father's house, I said to her: 'You will show this mercy to me. In every place, to which we will travel, you will say that I am your brother.' "
{20:14} Therefore, Abimelech took sheep and oxen, and men servants and women servants, and he gave them to Abraham. And he returned his wife Sarah to him.

Abraham was afraid that some men, seeing that his wife Sarah was beautiful, would kill him to obtain her. His use of mental reservation was moral because he had a proportionately serious reason. Though they were husband and wife, Abraham stated that she was his sister; and Sarah stated that he was her brother. "Yet, in another way, she is also truly my sister, the daughter of my father, and not the daughter of my mother, and I took her as a wife." (Genesis 20:12). Here there are two truths, and only one is expressed; the other is reserved for a serious reason (the threat of death). Sarah was truly the sister, i.e. the half-sister, of Abraham. He omitted the truth that she was also his wife.

Mental reservation is not intrinsically evil. The chosen act has a twofold moral object: (1) to express a truth, and (2) to omit a related truth. Neither the expression of a truth, nor the omission of a truth, is intrinsically evil. Sometimes the moral law requires us to omit telling a particular truth to a particular person. For lying is not merely any omission of a truth; it is an assertion deprived of a truth. Christ was silent before Herod, omitting speaking the truth. In mental reservation, no falsehood is asserted to be true, and no truth is asserted to be false, so the twofold moral object of mental reservation is good. However, mental reservation is not always moral. Any act that is moral under the second font, might be immoral under the first or third fonts. The intention must be good, and the good consequences must outweigh any bad consequences.

Chapter 18
Types of Murder

.219.
Direct Homicide

Pope John Paul II: "Therefore, by the authority which Christ conferred upon Peter and his Successors, and in communion with the Bishops of the Catholic Church, I confirm that the direct and voluntary killing of an innocent human being is always gravely immoral. This doctrine, based upon that unwritten law which man, in the light of reason, finds in his own heart (cf. Rom 2:14-15), is reaffirmed by Sacred Scripture, transmitted by the Tradition of the Church and taught by the ordinary and universal Magisterium."[214]

Not all killing is murder, and not all killing is immoral. A certain type of killing, called murder, is intrinsically evil and always gravely immoral. But in order for a killing to be murder, the act must be "direct and voluntary" (morally-direct and deliberate) and must be directed at the killing of an innocent human being. Otherwise, the act is not murder. Murder is immoral under the second font, and is therefore intrinsically evil. Other types of killing, which are not immoral under the second font, may still be immoral under the first or third fonts.

All murder is intrinsically evil and always gravely immoral; murder is always an objective mortal sin because the moral object is not only immoral, but gravely immoral. Nothing in the first or third fonts of intention and circumstances can cause an act that is gravely immoral under the second font to become either a moral act, or objectively only venial. But an act that is gravely immoral under the second font may become a yet more serious sin due to additional immorality in the first or third fonts. Certain types of murder are made more serious by intention or circumstances.

If the intention is particularly malicious, then the act of murder is even more serious. If the person who is murdered is particularly defenseless and innocent, this circumstance causes the murder to be even more gravely immoral. If there is substantially greater harm when a particular person is killed, then this circumstance causes the act to become an even more serious sin. If the victim has a particular role in society, or the family, or the Church, such that much more harm is done by the murder of that person, then the act is a more serious sin.

Examples: (1) The murder of a prenatal, or infant, or child is a more serious murder because of the circumstance of the age of the victim. Such victims are particularly defenseless and innocent, making the sin even more serious. (2) The murder of a member of the clergy or religious life is a more serious murder due to the circumstance of the additional harm to the Church that occurs when a priest or religious is murdered. (3) The murder (assassination) of a political leader causes substantial harm to society, more so than the murder of an ordinary citizen, and so this circumstance makes the act an even more serious sin.

---

[214] Pope John Paul II, Evangelium Vitae, n. 57.

(4) The murder of the parents of several children is a more serious sin because of the substantial additional harm that is done in leaving the children as orphans. (5) The intention to kill someone out of hatred for their religious beliefs, or out of anger at the good that the person has done, adds a gravely immoral intention to the gravely immoral act of murder, causing the act to be even more sinful.

The murder of a father (patricide) or mother (matricide) by their child is the sin of murder, but the act is made more serious by the circumstance that the father and mother gave life to that child, and raised that child. And this act is made even more serious by another evil moral object in the second font, not only the moral object of killing an innocent human person, but also of violating to a severe degree the commandment to honor your father and mother. The positive precept to honor your father and mother is violated to a grave extent by the act of patricide or matricide.

Catechism of the Catholic Church: "The fifth commandment forbids direct and intentional killing as gravely sinful. the murderer and those who cooperate voluntarily in murder commit a sin that cries out to heaven for vengeance. Infanticide, fratricide, parricide, and the murder of a spouse are especially grave crimes by reason of the natural bonds which they break. Concern for 'eugenics' or public health cannot justify any murder, even if commanded by public authority."[215]

.220. Indirect Homicide

The definition of murder is the direct and voluntary killing of an innocent human person. Murder is intrinsically evil because the voluntarily chosen act is inherently directed toward an evil moral object, the killing of the innocent. But an act is not murder if the chosen act is not directed at the killing of the innocent, and only indirectly results in the death of the innocent. The death of the innocent is indirect when it is only a consequence in the third font, and not also the moral object in the second font. However, this is not sufficient to cause the act to be moral. As always, all three fonts must be good for the overall act to avoid sin.

Examples: (1) During a just war, the military bombs a legitimate enemy military target, but a number of innocent civilians are indirectly killed by the attack. The deaths of these innocents is indirect homicide, and not murder (which is direct homicide). The second font has the moral object of defending the nation in a just war by means of a direct attack against enemy soldiers, not against the innocent. However, to be moral, the intention must be good, e.g. to advance the war effort in defense of the nation, and the good consequences of attacking that target must morally outweigh the harm done by the death of innocents. If the harm done by the deaths of these innocents (the bad consequences) morally outweighs the good done in attacking an enemy target during a just a war, then the third font would be immoral, and the overall act would be a sin, but not the sin of murder. On the other hand, if all three fonts are good, then this indirect homicide would be moral.

---

[215] Catechism of the Catholic Church, n. 2268.

(2) A physician performs an operation, with the patient's consent, which presents a grave risk to the life of the patient. The patient dies during the operation. The physician did not commit murder, because the chosen act was directed at the good moral object of healing the patient. However, the overall act would only be moral if his intention were good, to heal the patient (rather than, say, to make money despite an unnecessary risk to a patient), and if the reasonably foreseen good consequences morally outweighs the bad consequences. If the patient would almost certainly die without the operation, and if the operation, despite a substantial risk of death, also offered a substantial chance of success, then the good consequences would outweigh the bad, and the act would be moral. The death of the patient could not be foreseen by the surgeon as a definitive result, but only as a risk. The chosen act was not inherently directed at that death, and so the death is morally indirect, and is in the third font, not the second font.

(3) Direct abortion is murder, but indirect abortion (though not always moral) is not murder. With direct abortion, the intentionally chosen act is inherently directed toward the death of the innocent prenatal. But with indirect abortion, the chosen act is directed at the health of the mother. Even so, for indirect abortion to be moral, the intention must be good; the death of the prenatal cannot be intended, and the good consequences must morally outweigh the bad consequences. So if there is a reasonable chance of saving the life of the prenatal, even with a moderate increase in risk to the life of the mother, then indirect abortion would not be moral. But if the prenatal's life cannot be saved, and if the mother's life can likely be saved, then indirect abortion would be moral.

(4) A man drives while inebriated, and accidentally kills another person. The act was not murder, because it was not deliberate (voluntary). The chosen act of driving while inebriated is not inherently directed at the death of the innocent. The death of innocent persons is certainly a likely consequence of the chosen act, but this death is therefore in the third font, not the second. This act is a serious sin, because the man chose to drive a vehicle, knowing the likely consequence that lives would be harmed or lost.

(5) The use of the death penalty by proper civil authority is not murder, if the person who is killed is determined to be guilty of a serious crime, beyond doubt, after all legitimate appeals are exhausted. Murder is the killing of the innocent, not the guilty. However, for a use of the death penalty to be moral, all three fonts must be good. The fact that a proper use of the death penalty is not immoral under the second font, as a type of murder, does not imply that every use of the death penalty is moral. An immoral intention, or a bad third font, would make the use of the death penalty in such cases immoral.

.221. In addition to unequivocally condemning direct homicide (murder) in all its forms, the Catechism of the Catholic Church also discusses and condemns any act of indirect homicide if the intention or the consequences cause the act to be immoral. For each and every knowingly chosen act is only moral if all three fonts are good.

Catechism of the Catholic Church: "The fifth commandment forbids doing anything with the intention of indirectly bringing about a person's death. The moral law prohibits exposing someone to mortal danger without grave reason, as well as refusing assistance to a person in danger. The acceptance by human society of murderous famines, without efforts to remedy them, is a scandalous injustice and a grave offense."[216]

The fifth commandment is: "You shall not murder." But by extension, this commandment also forbids sinful indirect homicide, including a sinful intention, such as intending the indirect death of the innocent. An example of this type of sinful intention would be indirect abortion in which the death of the prenatal is intended. Although indirect homicide is not murder, the intention must be good or the act is nevertheless a sin.

The Catechism next gives the example of an act that exposes a person to mortal danger without a grave reason. This act is sinful under the third font; it is not an act of murder under the second font. Placing someone's life in danger is a bad consequence, and is not moral unless the good consequences outweigh the bad. An example of this sin would be a physician who agrees to perform an operation that is unnecessary and involves a grave risk to the patient's life.

When indirect homicide is a sin, it can be either a sin of commission or a sin of omission. And so the Catechism gives the example of refusing assistance to a person in danger; such a refusal could be murder by omission, if the chosen act of refusal is directed at the death of the innocent. Or this refusal could be indirect homicide, as when a government chooses to omit applying resources to save lives, and instead uses those resources on less weighty concerns.

Similarly, when a deadly famine occurs, if those who have the resources to lift or alleviate the famine decide to omit this particular fulfillment of love of neighbor, they commit a grave sin. This might be the sin of murder by omission, such as when a government refuses to give relief from a famine to an area of a nation that is in revolt against the government, so that the chosen act of omission is directed at the deaths of those citizens because they do not support the government. Or this omission could be an example of sinful indirect homicide, if the resources for lifting or alleviating the famine are not withheld so as to cause death, but are unfairly distributed, so that the bad consequences of some innocent deaths are not outweighed by the good consequences of the particular plan of distribution.

Catechism of the Catholic Church: "Those whose usurious and avaricious dealings lead to the hunger and death of their brethren in the human family indirectly commit homicide, which is imputable to them. Unintentional killing is not morally imputable. But one is not exonerated from grave offense if, without proportionate reasons, he has acted in a way that brings about someone's death, even without the intention to do so."[217]

The Catechism also correctly condemns persons who commit acts of usury and avarice, not only for those particular sins, but also for the harm done, in the third

---

[216] Catechism of the Catholic Church, n. 2269.
[217] Catechism of the Catholic Church, n. 2269.

font of consequences. In some cases, this harm may even reach to such an extent that many innocent persons die. So, from all of these examples given in the Catechism, it is clear that, although indirect homicide is not murder under the second font, it might still be a grave sin under the first or third fonts.

"Unintentional killing is not morally imputable" as an act of murder, for murder is always direct and voluntary. The act of murder is intentionally chosen and is inherently directed at the death of the innocent. But even when the second font is not murder, all three fonts must be good for sin to be avoided. An immoral intention makes any act a sin. And if the bad consequences of any act outweigh the good consequences, then there are not "proportionate reasons" for the act, and the act is a sin under the third font. Notice that the above quoted paragraph from the Catechism puts into practice the teaching that any act is immoral if any one font is bad. If the third font is bad because the good consequences do not proportionately outweigh the bad, then the act is a sin, even if the intention is good and the chosen act is not murder.

.222. Euthanasia

Pope John Paul II: "Euthanasia in the strict sense is understood to be an action or omission which of itself and by intention causes death, with the purpose of eliminating all suffering."[218]

The expression "by intention" does not refer to the first font, but to the second font. The first font is the intention in the sense of the intended end, the purpose for which the act is done. In the above quoted definition, the first font is expressed as "the purpose of eliminating all suffering." The second font is the act itself, which is always an act deliberately chosen by the will. All intrinsically evil acts, including euthanasia, are intentionally chosen acts. Various terms are used to describe this same concept: chosen acts, deliberate acts, intentional acts, voluntary acts. These different phrasings all express the same truth, that the sinful act is chosen by the will. The purpose (intended end) for which the act is chosen is the first font; the inherent ordering of the deliberately chosen (intentionally chosen) act toward its moral object is the second font.

The essential moral nature of murder is defined solely under the second font: the morally-direct and deliberate killing of an innocent human being. The further classification of the act, as the type of murder called euthanasia, is found in the first font. Euthanasia is murder with the intention (the intended end or purpose) of relieving all suffering.

Pope John Paul II clearly and definitively teaches that euthanasia can be either a sin of commission, or a sin of omission. Since euthanasia is a type of murder, and murder is intrinsically evil, this teaching implies that other types of murder, and other intrinsically evil acts, may be either sins of commission, or sins of omission. An intrinsically evil act is not necessarily a sin of commission.

---

[218] Pope John Paul II, Evangelium Vitae, n. 65.

Pope John Paul II: "I confirm that euthanasia is a grave violation of the law of God, since it is the deliberate and morally unacceptable killing of a human person. This doctrine is based upon the natural law and upon the written word of God, is transmitted by the Church's Tradition and taught by the ordinary and universal Magisterium."[219]

The essential moral nature of the act itself is murder, which is the direct and voluntary (deliberate) deprivation of the life of an innocent human being. But this type of murder is distinguished from other types of murder by the first font, by the intention to eliminate all suffering. If the same concrete act were done with a different intention (such as to obtain an inheritance), the essential moral nature would not change; the act would still be properly and narrowly defined as murder. The type of murder may change with the intention or the circumstances, but as long as the moral object has not changed, the act itself still has the same essential moral nature, and is still murder, and is still intrinsically evil.

.223. Suicide

Suicide is murder in the circumstance where the person who is killing and the person who is being killed are the same person. Suicide is the direct and voluntary deprivation of the life of an innocent human being, when that human being is one's self. The second font makes the act itself murder. Even though the third font is used to define the particular type of murder, the essential moral nature of the act is independent of intention and circumstances. Suicide is intrinsically evil and always gravely immoral because it is a type of murder.

Example: A person commits suicide, for the purpose of eliminating their own suffering, because he or she is terminally ill. The essential moral nature of the act is murder, which is intrinsically evil and always gravely immoral. The intention makes this act the type of murder called euthanasia. The circumstances make this act also the type of murder called suicide. This one sin is properly defined as murder, but also as euthanasia, and also as suicide.

Suicide is a particularly grievous form of murder because the murderer is also the person who is killed. When someone murders another person, perhaps the victim was in state of grace and will have eternal life; and perhaps the murderer will later repent and also be saved. But suicide, once completed in death, does not allow for any subsequent repentance. Suicide is always an objective mortal sin. But if a particular act of suicide is also an actual mortal sin, then the person who committed suicide is condemned to Hell. For there is no opportunity to repent from actual mortal sin subsequent to death.

Certainly, some suicides are lessened in culpability due to factors that reduce freedom of choice, such as psychological disorders, or due to a lack of knowledge that suicide is always gravely immoral. If the reduction in culpability is sufficient to make the act merely an objective mortal sin, and not also an actual mortal sin, even if culpability to the extent of a venial sin remains, then the person who commits this sin may perhaps go to Heaven by way of Purgatory.

---

[219] Pope John Paul II, Evangelium Vitae, n. 65.

But even if the culpability is reduced to less than an actual mortal sin, if the person who commits suicide was not in a state of grace at death due to other unrepentant actual mortal sins, then he is still condemned to Hell. Therefore, suicide is particularly dangerous to the salvation of souls.

.224. Assisted Suicide

Pope John Paul II: "To concur with the intention of another person to commit suicide and to help in carrying it out through so-called 'assisted suicide' means to cooperate in, and at times to be the actual perpetrator of, an injustice which can never be excused, even if it is requested. In a remarkably relevant passage Saint Augustine writes that 'it is never licit to kill another: even if he should wish it, indeed if he request it because, hanging between life and death, he begs for help in freeing the soul struggling against the bonds of the body and longing to be released; nor is it licit even when a sick person is no longer able to live'."[220]

When a woman obtains an abortion, she often authorizes someone else to carry out the actual killing of the prenatal. In such cases, both she and the person who does the killing are guilty of this particular type of murder, abortion. Similarly, when one person obtains the assistance of another in order to commit suicide, both are guilty of murder. When the person who assists does so by a morally direct and deliberate act, he is not merely guilty of cooperation in the act of murder, but of murder itself. Murder is any direct and voluntary act which deprives an innocent human being of life. The act of murder can even be an act of omission, in which the act itself is a decision not to carry out another act, such as to provide ordinary and necessary care or assistance, as required by the moral law, to one's self or one's neighbor. Such murders of omission occur in cases of euthanasia, but are also possible in cases of suicide or assisted suicide, or homicide in general.

Examples: (1) A man decides to omit receiving necessary and ordinary medical care, knowing that this omission will result in his own death. This sin of omission is the sin of suicide. (2) A person decides to omit providing necessary and ordinary medical care to another, knowing that this omission will result in the person's death. This sin of omission is the sin of murder. If the intention is to eliminate all suffering, then the particular type of murder is euthanasia. (3) A person sees his neighbor drowning, and he could easily save him by throwing him a life-preserver; he deliberately decides to refrain from assisting his neighbor, knowing that this omission will result in the neighbor's death. This sin of omission is the sin of murder. (4) One person convinces another person to assist him in committing suicide by providing the necessary lethal combination of drugs and the means to deliver the drugs. Regardless of who actually injects the lethal drugs, these two persons are both guilty of murder because each one has committed a morally direct (even if physically indirect) and voluntary act, which is inherently ordered toward depriving an innocent human person of life.

---

[220] Pope John Paul II, Evangelium Vitae, n. 66; inner quote from Augustine, Epistulae, Corpus Scriptorum Ecclesiasticorum Latinorum, vol. 57, n. 320.

.225. Infanticide and Abortion

Second Vatican Council: "For God, the Lord of life, has conferred on men the surpassing ministry of safeguarding life in a manner which is worthy of man. Therefore from the moment of its conception life must be guarded with the greatest care, while abortion and infanticide are unspeakable crimes."[221]

Infanticide is defined as the direct and voluntary deprivation of life from an innocent human being, in the circumstance where the person is an infant. But regardless of the first font of intention, and the third font of circumstances (which includes the age of the person), the act remains an intrinsically evil act of murder under the second font.

As is true for euthanasia, this type of murder can be committed by an act of commission or omission. Infanticide by omission was a common practice in past centuries, in various cultures and areas of the world. Infants who were unwanted for one reason or another would be left without necessary and ordinary care in order to cause their deaths, killing the infant by a morally direct act of omission.

Other times, the infant would be placed outdoors, exposed to nature, killing the infant by an act of commission. In this case, the infant is not killed in a direct physical action, and so some cultures did not consider the act of exposing an infant to be a type of murder. But this method of killing an infant is morally direct, even if it is physically indirect. The act of leaving the infant exposed to the elements is inherently directed at the moral object of the death of an innocent human person; therefore, the act is a type of murder. Intrinsically evil acts are always morally direct; but they may or may not be physically direct.

Partial birth abortion, in which the innocent human being is killed during birth, could be categorized as infanticide, or as abortion. Regardless of categorization by type under the first or third fonts, all such acts are a type of murder, which is intrinsically evil and always gravely immoral, under the second font. It is interesting to note that a 1910 article from the Catholic Encyclopedia defines infanticide as "the killing of an infant before or after birth," thus categorizing abortion as a type of infanticide.[222] There is nothing wrong with this type of definition, since abortion and infanticide have the same essential moral nature, that of murder, and the difference in circumstances (the age of the person) does not affect the moral species of the act.

Abortion and infanticide are both types of murder. The difference found in the circumstances, as to whether the person is a prenatal or an infant, does not change the essential moral nature of the act. The same is true of all intrinsically evil acts; the essential moral nature of the act is never changed by intention or by circumstances. (See also the chapter: Abortion and Contraception.)

---

[221] Second Vatican Council, Gaudium et Spes, n. 51.
[222] James Joseph Walsh, 'Infanticide,' The Catholic Encyclopedia, Vol. 8. (New York: Robert Appleton Co., 1910) http://www.newadvent.org/cathen/08001b.htm

.226. Genocide

Genocide is properly defined as a type of murder. Genocide is a set of acts of murder, either with the intention of killing a large number of innocent persons of a particular group, or in the circumstances (regardless of intention) in which a large number of innocent persons of a particular group are killed. The common definition of the term genocide is more narrow, usually defined as the attempt to murder all members of a particular ethnic group, or at least all members of that ethnic group in a particular area. But morally the act is the same if the group is distinguished by politics, culture, religion, gender, age, or any other broad category. Thus abortion is sometimes correctly referred to as a type of genocide, because abortion is the murder of a large number of persons of a particular group, prenatals.

If someone commits a diverse set of acts, some acts might be intrinsically evil and gravely immoral, other acts might be intrinsically evil but not gravely immoral, some acts might be not intrinsically evil but still immoral, and other acts might be moral. And so, a morally diverse set of acts cannot be properly called intrinsically evil, even if some acts within the set are intrinsically evil, because other moral or immoral acts in the same set are not intrinsically evil. It would be misleading to use the term intrinsic evil to describe a set of acts, unless all the principle acts that define the set are intrinsically evil.

Since each principle act in the set of acts called genocide is an intrinsically evil act of murder, the set may be referred to as intrinsically evil. Usually, intrinsic evil refers to an individual act. But genocide is properly defined as a set of acts of murder, and each of the acts in this set is intrinsically evil and always gravely immoral. Therefore, the set of acts can be called intrinsically evil and always gravely immoral.

The intention to murder all or most members of a particular narrow group, such as all other persons who are in line to receive an inheritance, would not be genocide. These acts would be murders, but not the particular type of murder called genocide. In some cases, it might be difficult to distinguish whether the killing of a number of innocent persons should be called genocide or not. But each and every act of murder remains intrinsically evil and always gravely immoral, regardless of what type of murder it is.

The essential moral nature of each act is found in the second font of morality. Under the second font, each act within the set of murders called genocide is intrinsically evil and always gravely immoral. The other two fonts, intention and circumstances, may cause one set of murders to be genocide, and another set of murders to be still murder but not genocide. But the moral object is the same, and so the essential moral nature of each act is the same.

Genocide would be improperly defined as the killing of all members of an ethnic (or other) group, because genocide is not merely killing, but murder. Thus, when the Israelites were ordered by God to kill all members of the seven tribes who were living in the Promised Land before the Israelites, God was not ordering genocide, nor murder of any kind. God can never require or ask anyone to commit any intrinsically evil act. First, all lives belong to God, and so when God decides that it is time for someone to die, it is not murder. Second, God did not permit the Israelites to kill whomever they wished, nor to take whatever land they wished, nor to wipe out any tribe that troubled them. Only certain lands and peoples were delivered into the hands of the Israelites, upon the order of God and not by their own decision:

[Deuteronomy]
{2:4} And instruct the people, saying: You shall cross through the borders of your brothers, the sons of Esau, who live at Seir, and they will fear you.
{2:5} Therefore, take care diligently, lest you be moved against them. For I will not give to you from their land even as much as the step that one foot can tread upon, because I have given Mount Seir to Esau as a possession.
{2:6} You shall buy food from them for money, and you shall eat. You shall draw water for money, and you shall drink.
{2:7} The Lord your God has blessed you in every work of your hands. The Lord your God, dwelling with you, knows your journey, how you crossed through this great wilderness over forty years, and how you have been lacking in nothing.'
{2:8} And when we had passed through our brothers, the sons of Esau, who were living at Seir by the way of the plain from Elath and from Eziongeber, we arrived at the way which leads to the desert of Moab.
{2:9} And the Lord said to me: 'You should not fight against the Moabites, nor should you go to battle against them. For I will not give to you anything from their land, because I have given Ar to the sons of Lot as a possession.'
...
{2:36} from Aroer, which is above the bank of the torrent Arnon, a town which is situated in a valley, all the way to Gilead. There was not a village or city which escaped from our hands. The Lord our God delivered everything to us,
{2:37} except the land of the sons of Ammon, which we did not approach, and all that is adjacent to the torrent Jabbok, and the cities in the mountains, and all the places which the Lord our God prohibited to us."

.227. This type of killing is not genocide, even if the Israelites destroyed entire tribes, because this was done at the order of God. And since the Israelites refrained from fighting against certain other tribes, also on the order of God, it is clear that they were not merely killing whomever they wished to kill. Genocide is not merely the killing, but the murder, of a particular group of persons. Sacred Scripture reveals that these seven tribes were being put to death on the order of God for their many serious sins.

[Wisdom]
{12:1} O how good and gracious, Lord, is your spirit in all things!
{12:2} Therefore, those who wander afield, you correct, and, as to those who sin, you counsel them and admonish them, so that, having abandoned malice, they may believe in you, O Lord.
{12:3} For those ancient inhabitants of your holy land, who you abhorred,
{12:4} because they were doing works hateful to you, through unjust medicines and sacrifices,

{12:5} and the merciless murderers of their own sons, and the eaters of human entrails, and the devourers of blood apart from your community sacrament,

{12:6} and the sellers performing the ceremonies of helpless souls, you willed to destroy by the hands of our parents,

{12:7} so that they might worthily secure the sojourn of the children of God, in the land which is most beloved by you.

{12:8} Yet, so that you were lenient even to these men, you sent wasps, forerunners of your army, so that you might destroy them little by little,

{12:9} not because you were unable to subdue the impious under the just by war or by cruel beasts, or with a harsh word to exterminate them at once,

{12:10} but, in judging by degrees, you were giving them a place of repentance, not unaware that their nation is wicked, and their malice is inherent, and that their thinking could never be changed.

{12:11} For this offspring was accursed from the beginning. Neither did you, fearing anyone, give favor to their sins.

{12:12} For who will say to you, "What have you done?" Or who will stand against your judgment? Or who will come before you as a defender of unfair men? Or who will accuse you, if the nations perish, which you have made?

{12:13} For neither is there any other God but you, who has care of all, to whom you would show that you did not give judgment unjustly.

{12:14} Neither will king or tyrant inquire before you about those whom you destroyed.

{12:15} Therefore, since you are just, you order all things justly, considering it foreign to your virtue to condemn him who does not deserve to be punished.

{12:16} For your power is the beginning of justice, and, because you are Lord of all, you make yourself to be lenient to all.

Such is the wisdom of God, greater than the wisdom of this age, that He wills some persons and some groups of persons to be destroyed, either little by little, or all at once. But it is not for man to usurp the role of God in passing such a judgment. Thus genocide only occurs when there is the sin of murder, not merely any type of killing or death.

Chapter 19
Just and Unjust Violence

.228.
Self-defense

Murder is defined as the morally-direct and deliberate killing of an innocent human person. Killing in self-defense, or in defense of others, is not murder because the person who is killed is not innocent, but is guilty of a grave attack against the innocent. The moral object of murder is the killing of an innocent human being, but the moral object of self-defense is not the killing of the guilty attacker, but the defense of the innocent person who is being attacked. The death of the murder victim is the moral object in the second font, and is a consequence in the third font. The death of an attacker, when deadly force is used in self-defense, is in the third font, but not the second. For an act of murder is inherently ordered toward its moral object, the killing of the innocent, but an act of self-defense is inherently ordered toward a different moral object, the protection of the innocent.

Catechism of the Catholic Church: "Love toward oneself remains a fundamental principle of morality. Therefore it is legitimate to insist on respect for one's own right to life. Someone who defends his life is not guilty of murder even if he is forced to deal his aggressor a lethal blow."[223]

[Matthew]
{22:35} And one of them, a doctor of the law, questioned him, to test him:
{22:36} "Teacher, which is the great commandment in the law?"
{22:37} Jesus said to him: " 'You shall love the Lord your God from all your heart, and with all your soul and with all your mind.'
{22:38} This is the greatest and first commandment.
{22:39} But the second is similar to it: 'You shall love your neighbor as yourself.'
{22:40} On these two commandments the entire law depends, and also the prophets."

The single threefold commandment, upon which the whole moral law rests, is love of God, love of neighbor, love of self. Christ's command not only to love God, but also to love your neighbor as yourself, includes an ordered love of self. The right to self-defense is based on an ordered love of self, on a choice to defend the life given to you by God against an objectively unjust attack. The person who kills in self-defense obeys the command to love God and self, and does not disobey the command to love your neighbor, since true love of neighbor is in no way contrary to justice. When your neighbor attacks you with deadly force, compelling you to choose between your life and his, you may morally choose to defend your life, because you are innocent and he is guilty. The eternal moral law always distinguishes between the innocent and the guilty, since innocence is in harmony with the moral law, and guilt is not.

---

[223] Catechism of the Catholic Church, n. 2264.

But concerning self-defense, the terms innocent and guilty have a specialized meaning. The aggressor is guilty in the immediate situation of choosing a particular objectively immoral act that threatens the defender with grave harm. But the aggressor is not being judged as to the guilt or innocence of his life or of his soul. And the person who acts in self-defense may have sinned much at other times during his life, but he is innocent in terms of the immediate situation.

Examples: (1) Your neighbor on one side of the street is a very sinful man, who has publicly admitted to committing many mortal sins, and who openly states that he is unrepentant; he is guilty of many gravely immoral acts. But he never threatens you with any type of grave harm, and so you may not kill him. Though he is guilty of many sins and crimes, he is innocent of any grave aggression against you, and so to kill him would be to kill an innocent person. He is guilty of many things, but he is innocent of attacking you.

(2) Your neighbor on the other side of the street is a veritable living Saint; by all accounts he is full of every virtue, and no one accuses him of any offense. But one day, afflicted by a severe psychological illness, he attacks you with deadly force. You may morally kill him in self-defense (if there is no other way to save your own life), even though he is, as they say, 'not guilty by reason of insanity.' Your attacker is without any culpability in the sense of actual mortal sin; his soul and his life are innocent. But in the immediate situation he has chosen (in this case without free will) to assault your life with deadly force. He is committing an objective grave attack against you, though without the culpability of actual sin.

(3) A man is convicted of very serious crimes and given a life sentence; he admits to the crimes. In prison, he is attacked with deadly force by another prisoner. He may morally use deadly force to defend himself, despite his guilt in other acts in his life. This man, who is guilty of many things in his life, is innocent in the immediate situation. The act of self-defense does not judge the soul or life of the individual, but only judges the morality of the chosen act, under all three fonts.

.229. Types of Attacks

Under the eternal moral law, one may morally defend one's self, even with deadly force if necessary, when there is an aggression that threatens grave harm to one's own life or safety. Such acts of aggression (to which one may possibly reply with deadly force) include not only the grave harm of death, but also serious bodily injury, rape, kidnapping, and similar unjust aggression that would cause serious harm. However, human law varies greatly in which acts of force are permitted in which circumstances, even in self-defense. An act that is moral might not be legal, and illegally using deadly force has grave consequences.

Saint Thomas Aquinas: "It is written (Exodus 22:2): 'If a thief be found breaking into a house or undermining it, and be wounded so as to die; he that slew him shall not be guilty of blood.' Now it is much more lawful to defend one's life than one's house. Therefore neither is a man guilty of murder if he kill another in defense of his own life."[224]

St. Thomas taught that deadly force may sometimes be used in order to defend one's home. Though the passage he quotes from Exodus makes reference to a thief, the thief is not being killed for stealing, but for endangering the safety of the residents of the house. This distinction is made clear by the whole passage:

[Exodus]
{22:1} "If anyone will have stolen an ox or a sheep, and if he kills it or sells it, then he will restore five oxen for one ox, and four sheep for one sheep.
{22:2} If a thief will have been discovered breaking into a house, or digging under it, and he has received a mortal wound, he who struck him down will not be guilty of blood.
{22:3} But if he did this when the sun was risen, he has perpetrated a homicide, and he shall die. If he does not have the means to make restitution for the theft, he shall be sold.

A thief is generally punished with less than deadly force (Ex 22:1, 3). But the Old Testament law considers the resident who kills a thief at night to be innocent of murder, and the resident who kills a thief in the day to be guilty of murder. The thief breaking in at night expects that the residents are home asleep, and might be awakened by him. So the thief might have a weapon and the will to use it, in case he is confronted by the awakened residents. Therefore, theft at night is accompanied by an implied threat against the safety of the residents. But during the day, the thief might not expect anyone to be home, and so he might not be armed and willing to use force. Also, he is more easily frightened away during the day, since he does not have the cover of darkness. No one is asleep, so shouting may bring quick assistance from family, neighbors, or servants.

Now this is said in the context of the Old Testament law addressing the situation of the Israelites in ancient times. The modern situation might be different in its particulars, but the principles are the same. Deadly force is not justified to prevent simple theft, but may be justified if that theft is accompanied by violence, or the threat of violence, to such an extent as to cause grave harm. Robbery is defined as theft by means of violence, and if the violence or threat of violence is sufficiently grave, deadly force might be justified.

The grave harm prevented by the moral use of deadly force need not be mere bodily harm. For example, it may be moral to use deadly force to prevent or stop a rape. Although rape may cause some degree of bodily harm, most of the harm is psychological, emotional, and even spiritual. Grave harm to the whole person (soul, spirit, body) results from sexual assault; therefore, deadly force may be justified, if necessary to prevent or stop this grave type of assault.

Catechism of the Catholic Church: "Rape is the forcible violation of the sexual intimacy of another person. It does injury to justice and charity. Rape deeply wounds the respect, freedom, and physical and moral integrity to which every

---

[224] Saint Thomas Aquinas, Summa Theologica, II-II, Q. 64, A. 7.

person has a right. It causes grave damage that can mark the victim for life. It is always an intrinsically evil act."[225]

Self-defense is used, not merely to defend the body, but to defend the whole person. Therefore, deadly force can be used to defend against kidnapping, even if there is no specific additional threat of death or bodily harm, because the freedom and moral integrity of the individual is under a grave threat of harm. The same applies to serious crimes such as rape; though bodily harm might occur, it is the grave harm to the person as a whole that justifies self-defense in cases of rape. The eternal moral law applies to the whole person, not merely to the body.

This principle is particularly important also to other types of self-defense, such as when a nation uses deadly force to protect, not only the lives of its citizens, but also their moral integrity and their mental and spiritual well-being. Thus, just war defends not only lives, but also the freedom and way of life of a people. A nation uses deadly force in just war, not only against an aggressor that wishes to destroy, but also against one that wishes to enslave or to subjugate. A government may use deadly force in defense of a community in cases of looting (such as during a disaster), not only if lives are threatened, but if the general peace and security of the entire community is severely threatened. Similarly, the death penalty is justified, not only to prevent physical harm to citizens, but also to protect the peace and security of the entire community, as when persons who commit terrorist acts are put to death for their crimes.

.230. Legal versus Moral

The reader is **strongly cautioned** that laws permitting the use of deadly force, and the use of lesser degrees of force, vary greatly from one place to another. The interpretation and application of the law can also vary from place to place, and from time to time. Although it is moral to use deadly force in certain situations, often the laws of society permit the use of such force **in a narrower range of situations**. Prudence dictates that a person inform himself as to the laws of the society in which he lives, especially laws whose violation may result in grave consequences.

The eternal moral law is not the same as the written laws and the customs of human society. What is moral may be illegal, and what is immoral may be legal. Every human person is subject first and foremost to the authority of God, who is Justice itself. A human person should never violate the moral law. But there are situations in which a human person may morally violate human law. There are situations in which a human person is required by the moral law to act in violation of human law. However, when it is possible to obey human law without any immorality, it is usually more prudent and expedient to obey.

Although human law cannot change the moral law at all, the consequences of obeying or disobeying human law can effect the evaluation of the third font of morality. If it is legal and moral to use deadly force in self-defense in one set of

---

[225] Catechism of the Catholic Church, n. 2356.

circumstances, the good consequences may outweigh the bad consequences. But in other circumstances, if it is moral but illegal to use deadly force in self-defense, the bad consequences of committing a moral but illegal act may now outweigh the good consequences. And even if a particular act is both moral and legal, that act might be still not the wisest course of action. Some moral acts are more perfect and other moral acts are less perfect.

.231. The Three Fonts and Self-Defense

The three fonts of morality always apply to every knowingly chosen act. If a particular act using deadly force is not intrinsically evil, because the moral object is self-defense, not the taking of innocent life, the other fonts must also be good for the act of self-defense to be entirely moral. If someone kills in self-defense, but with bad intent, then he sins under the first font (intention). If someone kills in self-defense, but in circumstances when the bad consequences outweigh the good consequences, then he sins under the third font (consequences).

If a particular use of deadly force is self-defense, then that act is moral under the second font. The moral object of the act itself is to protect and defend innocent human life; this moral object is good. However, in order for the overall act to be moral, the first and third fonts must also be good. Any act done with bad intent is a sinful act under the first font. If the person who is using any type or degree of force in self-defense does so with bad intent, such as with the intention to do harm to someone out of revenge or hatred or jealousy or other immoral motives, then he sins; this is true even if the situation itself would permit the moral use of force in self-defense. The defender must not intend the death or injury of the attacker as an end. The defender may morally intend to use deadly force, or a lesser degree of force, as an intended means to accomplish his defense. But this is true only because the intended means is moral; moderate violence in self-defense is a moral means. But no one may justify an intrinsically evil act, neither murder, nor violence against the innocent, nor any other intrinsically evil act, on the basis of a good intended end or good consequences. Both the intended end and the intended means must be moral for the first font to be good.

In the third font, the good consequences of the act (a moral act of self-defense with good intent) must outweigh the bad consequences. Now when a degree of force is used in self-defense, the degree of force and the bad consequences are in the third font. The use of violence against human persons has bad consequences because all human persons are made in the image of God. Thus, if self-defense can be accomplished with three good fonts but without force, or without deadly force, then either no force or the lesser degree of force should be preferred. Even if a use of a particular degree of force is moral under all three fonts, if a lesser degree of force has the same good consequences, and fewer bad consequences, the act with the most good consequences and the least bad consequences should be preferred. However, for any act of self-defense that is good under the second font, and done with good intent under the first font, the degree of force used (which is in the third font) is at least morally permissible (even if far than perfect) if the good consequences outweigh the bad. The totality of the good and bad consequences for all persons affected by the chosen act must be weighed. If the good outweighs the bad, then the third font is moral. But using deadly force has weighty bad consequences that would be avoided if self-defense could be accomplished with less than deadly force.

The likelihood that particular good and bad consequences will result from any act of self-defense is a consideration in the third font. This evaluation must include the possible good and bad consequences of not using force, or of using less force. Even though we cannot know with certitude what all of the good and bad consequences will be from a moral act of self-defense, we can reasonably conclude the likelihood that the lives of one or more innocent persons will be protected from grave harm or death, and that the attacker will suffer some degree of harm from the use of violence in self-defense, even possibly death. The weight of the good and bad consequences includes the likelihood of each.

St. Thomas Aquinas: "If a man in self-defense uses more than necessary violence, it will be unlawful: whereas if he repels force with moderation, his defense will be lawful...."[226]

If the bad consequences from the use of excessive force outweigh the good consequences, then even if the act itself has the moral object of self-defense, the act is immoral under the third font. However, if the use of excessive force is such that a man is killed or gravely harmed when no grave response was justified, then the act itself (under the second font) is not a type of self-defense. For every man who is guilty of a crime or sin is also innocent beyond the extent of his guilt. So if an attacker assaults another man with relatively minor force, the man who is attacked morally may use only limited force in self-defense. If instead he uses deadly force, or an excessive degree of force that causes unnecessary grave harm, then his act does not have the moral object of self-defense, but has the moral object of violence against the innocent. For though his attacker is guilty of the lesser offense of assault with minor force, the attacker is also innocent of assault with grave force.

.232. Refusal to Defend Oneself

Jesus Christ did not defend Himself, when he was assaulted in various ways during His Passion, nor did He defend Himself against the unjust use of deadly force at His Crucifixion. If Christ had defended Himself, so as not to suffer and die, then our salvation would have been lost. Following this sacred example, many of the Saints have refused to defend themselves when they were attacked by word or deed, even to the extent of willingly accepting martyrdom. They did so not because they despised the life that God gave them, but because they wished to imitate Christ in self-sacrifice, even unto death, and because they had a firm hope in eternal life with God, which no one can take away.

Therefore, even when a person has a right to use force in self-defense, he is not always obligated to do so. In some circumstances, with good intent, a person can decide to omit acts of self-defense, permitting suffering and even death, in

---

[226] Saint Thomas Aquinas, Summa Theologica, II-II, Q. 64. A. 7; also quoted in Catechism of the Catholic Church, n. 2264.

imitation of Christ. However, the good consequences must outweigh the bad consequences for this act of omission (an interior act of deciding to omit self-defense) to be moral. So a man with a wife and children who need him generally could not morally omit self-defense, if he was able to defend himself. The harm done by his death to his wife and children would make such an omission a sin under the third font (consequences).

The life given to each of us by God is good, and God intends that we continue to live until natural death. This good gift is precious, and therefore each innocent person has a positive moral responsibility to protect and to defend his or her own life against unjust aggression. The eternal moral law generally requires innocent persons to defend themselves against grave unjust harm.

.233. Defense of Others

Catechism of the Catholic Church: "Legitimate defense can be not only a right but a grave duty for someone responsible for another's life. Preserving the common good requires rendering the unjust aggressor unable to inflict harm. To this end, those holding legitimate authority have the right to repel by armed force aggressors against the civil community entrusted to their charge."[227]

In addition to the responsibility to defend one's own life, human persons have a responsibility, in some circumstances, to use force in defense of other persons, even (if necessary) deadly force. The responsibility to defend the innocent against grave harm is ordered such that the first and foremost responsibility is to defend oneself: "since one is bound to take more care of one's own life than of another's."[228] Similarly, concerning the soul, each person's first responsibility is to his own salvation and holiness; efforts to assist in the salvation and holiness of other persons are secondary. And this is true even for a Bishop, priest, deacon, or religious: "the first duty of priests, that is, the duty of becoming holy themselves."[229]

We have a lesser but still at times grave moral obligation to act in the defense of other persons, especially close family members, or persons in immediate need who have no other means of defense. **Again, the reader is strongly cautioned that what is moral is not always legal.** Consult the laws in your locality, and consider the grave consequences that might result if you use force, deadly or otherwise, when it is moral but illegal.

We also each have some degree of responsibility to defend the larger community and the nation. Most persons fulfill that responsibility by paying taxes and by treating law enforcement officers and soldiers with respect. Some person fulfill that responsibility more fully and directly, by becoming police officers or soldiers.

---

[227] Catechism of the Catholic Church, n. 2265.
[228] Saint Thomas Aquinas, Summa Theologica, II-II, Q. 64. A. 7; also quoted in Catechism of the Catholic Church, n. 2264.
[229] Pope John XXIII, Sacerdotii Nostri Primordia, n. 97; quoting Pope Pius XII, Menti Nostrae, n. 60, see also n. 13.

Every legitimate government has a duty and a right to use force in defense of the community, by law enforcement officers and by soldiers. A law enforcement officer may morally use force, even deadly force, when necessary to protect the community from grave harm. A soldier may force, even deadly force, when necessary to protect the nation, not only during a just war, but in other types of just military actions against unjust aggressors, such as terrorist groups.

The threefold commandment to love God, neighbor, and self results in both the right and the duty of self-defense and defense of others. But since love of God is greater than love of neighbor or self, any use of force for legitimate defense must be good before God. All three fonts of morality must be good: (1) intention, (2) moral object, (3) consequences. Even when a person acts in legitimate defense of self or others, and with good intention, the good consequences must outweigh the bad consequences. Since we are all made in the image of God, the death of even a guilty person is a weighty bad consequence. Therefore, no person or authority should be too quick to use deadly force.

.234. Death Penalty

[Luke]
{19:27} "Yet truly, as for those enemies of mine, who did not want me to reign over them, bring them here, and put them to death before me."

Cardinal Dulles: "In the Old Testament the Mosaic Law specifies no less than thirty-six capital offenses calling for execution.... In his debates with the Pharisees, Jesus cites with approval the apparently harsh commandment, 'He who speaks evil of father or mother, let him surely die' (Matthew 15:4; Mark 7:10, referring to Exodus 21:17; cf. Leviticus 20:9). When Pilate calls attention to his authority to crucify him, Jesus points out that Pilate's power comes to him from above -- that is to say, from God (John 19:11). Jesus commends the good thief on the cross next to him, who has admitted that he and his fellow thief are receiving the due reward of their deeds (Luke 23:41)."[230]

Sacred Scripture plainly teaches, in both the Old and New Testaments, that the use of the death penalty (capital punishment) can be moral. But whether or not the death penalty is moral in a particular case depends on a proper definition of the act under the three fonts of morality. The first font, the intended end or purpose of the act, will vary depending on the particular intention of each person who is involved in supporting, or legislating, or applying the death penalty. If the only font causing the death penalty to be immoral were the intended end, then a change in intention would make the act moral. Whenever any act has a good moral object, it is possible for that act to be done with good intention; for the good intention could be the same as the good moral object. Therefore, if the use of the death penalty is not intrinsically evil, but instead has a good moral object, then the death penalty could possibly be carried out with a good intention. If a particular type of killing has an evil moral object, then no intention or circumstance would justify the act. So the various intended purposes of the death penalty will be discussed after we determine the moral object.

---

[230] Cardinal Avery Dulles, 'Catholicism & Capital Punishment,' First Things, April 2001.

The second font is determined by the moral object. The moral object of murder is the deprivation of life from an innocent human person. But the death penalty only takes the life of a person convicted of a serious crime. The moral object of the death penalty is similar to the moral object of the use of deadly force in self-defense, except that the whole community is defending itself against grave harm from the unjust acts of an individual or group. This moral object is good since it is a particular fulfillment of the commandment to love your neighbor. Capital punishment has the moral object of protecting and defending the lives of the innocent members of the community, for the common good, against gravely unjust acts. Therefore, the use of the death penalty is not a type of murder.

Saint Thomas Aquinas: "Now every individual person is compared to the whole community, as part to whole. Therefore if a man be dangerous and infectious to the community, on account of some sin, it is praiseworthy and advantageous that he be killed in order to safeguard the common good…. it is lawful to kill an evildoer in so far as it is directed to the welfare of the whole community, so that it belongs to him alone who has charge of the community's welfare…. a public authority is requisite in order to condemn him to death for the common good."[231]

The act itself of applying the death penalty is the killing of a human person who is guilty of criminal acts of grave harm. But the moral object of this act is the defense of the community against these gravely unjust acts, for the common good. Notice the requirement that the person who is killed be guilty of some serious sin, of some evil-doing. A human person cannot be put to death for the common good without being guilty to a grave extent of some crime against the community. The end of benefiting the common good would not justify the killing an innocent person as an immoral means to that good end; only a guilty person can possibly be killed, morally, under the death penalty.

Sacred Scripture teaches that the death penalty is not intrinsically evil, and that it may be moral if the criminal has deliberately and knowingly committed a crime that does grave harm. But not all crimes are sufficiently grave to warrant capital punishment.

[Acts]
{25:10} But Paul said: "I stand in Caesar's tribunal, which is where I ought to be judged. I have done no harm to the Jews, as you well know.
{25:11} For if I have harmed them, or if I have done anything deserving of death, I do not object to dying. But if there is nothing to these things about which they accuse me, no one is able to deliver me to them. I appeal to Caesar."

Saint Paul has done no harm, so he does not deserve the death penalty. But he admits that if he had done harm, and only to such an extent that death would be deserved, he would not object to dying. Paul does not consider the death penalty to be always immoral, but only immoral when grave harm has not been done. If

---

[231] Saint Thomas Aquinas, Summa Theologica, II-II, Q. 64, A. 2, 3.

the use of the death penalty were intrinsically evil, then Sacred Scripture would not present this good example as a lesson for us to imitate.

Catechism of the Catholic Church: "The State's effort to contain the spread of behaviors injurious to human rights and the fundamental rules of civil coexistence corresponds to the requirement of watching over the common good. Legitimate public authority has the right and duty to inflict penalties commensurate with the gravity of the crime.... The traditional teaching of the Church does not exclude, presupposing full ascertainment of the identity and responsibility of the offender, recourse to the death penalty, when this is the only practicable way to defend the lives of human beings effectively against the aggressor."[232]

Pope John Paul II: "It is clear that, for these purposes to be achieved, the nature and extent of the punishment must be carefully evaluated and decided upon, and ought not go to the extreme of executing the offender except in cases of absolute necessity: in other words, when it would not be possible otherwise to defend society."[233]

Intrinsically evil acts are always immoral. But the Catechism and Pope John Paul II teach that the use of the death penalty is not always immoral. Therefore, the use of the death penalty is not intrinsically evil; it is not immoral under the second font. However, we must still consider which intentions and which circumstances would make the use of the death penalty moral under all three fonts. The death penalty is immoral, in any particular case, whenever the bad consequences outweigh the good consequences in the third font.

.235. The Old Testament Circumstances

The Old Testament law includes many crimes for which the Israelites were commanded to put the guilty to death. Sacred Scripture is the inerrant Word of God, a written reflection of Christ, the Living Word. Therefore, any act commanded in the Old Testament law cannot be intrinsically evil. For God never requires anyone to commit any kind of moral evil. But we must also consider the circumstances of the Old Testament law.

Before the Jewish Faith was established by God, through Abraham and the Patriarchs and Moses, the world knew only pagan religions. These religions did not know that God is One; they believed in many gods. And they did not know that true worship must include doing good and avoiding evil. Their religion did not teach them good from evil to any substantial extent. They had the light of reason, but their perception of good and evil by reason alone was filled with many serious errors, due to original sin and personal sin.

So in order to establish the worship of the one true God, who is Goodness itself, and in order to incorporate a true and full morality into the lives of the Israelites and ultimately into the whole world, the penalties for doing evil had to be more

---

[232] Catechism of the Catholic Church, n. 2266-2267.
[233] Pope John Paul II, Evangelium Vitae, n. 56.

severe than would be required in another set of circumstances. And all this was necessarily to prepare the Israelites, so that the Messiah, who would offer salvation to all persons, could be born among a people who worshipped the one true God in truth and justice. For the salvation of all, some harsher penalties were necessary, in order to prepare the way for the Messiah among a people who (like all peoples) were sinful and resistent to change.

Once the Messiah, Jesus Christ, arrived and taught us, and once he died for our salvation, the harsher penalties of the Old Testament law were no longer necessary. The preparation for, and the arrival of, the Messiah had occurred. And greater graces were now available through the New Testament Sacraments than had been available previously, even to the people of the Promise, the Israelites. True morality had been established among the Jews, and next was offered by Christianity to all persons, Jews and Gentiles. The death penalty remains moral under the second font, but the circumstances have changed. There is less need for the death penalty now that Christ has arrived and has established the Church and the Sacraments.

Even the most strict Jews of the present day, who follow the Old Testament law very closely, do not put persons to death in accord with the Old Testament law. For they, too, seem to realize, in their hearts if not in their minds, that the Old Covenant has been transformed into the new Covenant, and that the harsher penalties are no longer necessary. And all this is in the circumstances of the third font. It cannot be true that the death penalty, which was moral under the second font in ancient times, is now no longer moral under the second font. For the eternal moral law does not change. But circumstances do change, and the moral law requires us to act in accord with all three fonts, including the circumstances.

It is false to claim that the death penalty in the Old Testament was not of God, or was added to the law by human persons, apart from the will of God, or was used because of a substantial misunderstanding of true morality. It is false to claim that the death penalty in the Old Testament is an example of an error in Sacred Scripture, or is no longer in force at all (as if the eternal moral law had changed). It is a heresy to claim that there are any false assertions in the inspired Word of God, Sacred Scripture.

Saint Thomas Aquinas: "It is unlawful to hold that any false assertion is contained either in the Gospel or in any canonical Scripture, or that the writers thereof have told untruths, because faith would be deprived of its certitude which is based on the authority of Holy Writ."[234]

The Old Testament law made use of the death penalty because capital punishment is not intrinsically evil, and because the circumstances were such that the good consequences far outweighed the bad consequences. The bad consequences are the harm done to the individual who loses his life, and to his family, and to the community, since even a criminal guilty of grave offenses is not entirely evil. The good consequences were that true morality was established within the human race, and particularly among the Israelites, to prepare for the

---

[234] Saint Thomas Aquinas, Summa Theologica, II-II, Q. 110, A. 3.

Messiah who would offer eternal life to all persons. These good consequences far outweighed the bad consequences.

.236. Serious Crimes Only

A guilty person who is punished with a sentence that exceeds the measure of the offense is punished unjustly. The moral object is then not the defense of the community. Therefore, the death penalty is not morally applied except in response to a grave offense. For every guilty person is innocent beyond the measure of his offense. To punish a person guilty of a lesser offense with a penalty fitting only to a grave offense is to punish a person beyond the extent of his guilt, into the extent of his innocence. Such a punishment is a type of unjust violence against the innocent, and is intrinsically evil.

Example: (1) A government decides that a large amount of taxpayer money will be saved by giving the death penalty instead of long prison sentences. Although all the persons who would be killed will have been convicted of serious crimes, they are not being punished with death to defend the community against grave harm. They are not being put to death because they were judged to be guilty of crimes that deserve death, but only to save money. And imprisonment was sufficient to defend the community in these cases. Therefore, in this example, the act itself is intrinsically evil, because it is directed at the moral object of the taking of innocent life. These prisoners were guilty, but not guilty unto death.

Catechism of the Catholic Church: "If, instead, bloodless means are sufficient to defend against the aggressor and to protect the safety of persons, public authority should limit itself to such means, because they better correspond to the concrete conditions of the common good and are more in conformity to the dignity of the human person."[235]

Even if a use of the death penalty is moral under all three fonts, there may be a lesser penalty with fewer bad consequences, and/or more good consequences, so that the lesser penalty is closer to the full will of God, is more in conformity with the truth that the human person is made in the image of God, and therefore is to be preferred.

.237. Moral and Immoral Purposes

In cases where the second and third fonts are good, such that the death penalty has a good moral object and the good consequences outweigh the bad, the intended end (or purpose) of the use of the death penalty may vary from one person to another. Numerous persons are involved in writing, promoting, and passing legislation that allows for the death penalty, and in deciding on, and carrying out, this penalty in each particular case. The intentions of these many persons will vary. Moral intentions are necessary, but not sufficient, for an act to be moral. And any immoral intention makes an act immoral, at least for anyone with that intention. So, even when capital punishment is moral under the second and third fonts, it may not be moral for particular persons under the first font.

---

[235] Catechism of the Catholic Church, n. 2267.

The number of possible immoral intentions for the death penalty are very many. It is not necessary to list every immoral intention, because the type of intention that makes any act immoral is the same for the death penalty. Sacred Scripture provides a number of examples of immoral intentions.

[Romans]
{1:29} having been completely filled with all iniquity, malice, fornication, avarice, wickedness; full of envy, murder, contention, deceit, spite, gossiping;
{1:30} slanderous, hateful toward God, abusive, arrogant, self-exalting, devisers of evil, disobedient to parents,
{1:31} foolish, disorderly; without affection, without fidelity, without mercy.
{1:32} And these, though they had known the justice of God, did not understand that those who act in such a manner are deserving of death, and not only those who do these things, but also those who consent to what is done.

Examples of immoral intentions include: malice, lust, avarice, envy, spite, hatred of God or of religion, hatred of one's fellow human beings, arrogance, and many other intentions. Reason is able to identify every immoral intention, for every kind of immorality is contrary to the threefold commandment to love God, neighbor, self. And so a comprehensive list of every possible evil intention is not necessary.

But notice that Saint Paul, in the above quote from the letter to the Romans, acknowledges that certain serious offenses are so serious as to deserve death. The death penalty is not murder because the offense itself is so severe as to deserve the penalty of death. And such an offense is also so serious that, if it were done with full knowledge and full deliberation, it would constitute an actual mortal sin, deserving of eternal punishment in Hell (which is figuratively called the second death; Rev 20:14). The punishment of the death penalty is less severe than the punishment of eternal Hellfire. The existence of Hell proves that the death penalty is not always immoral, for if a greater punishment is justified, then a lesser punishment cannot be said to be so severe as to be immoral.

The same kinds of offenses that deserve the death penalty also deserve eternal Hellfire. But for this very reason, the death penalty must be applied sparingly, and only for the most severe cases. For persons who commit serious crimes are often not in a state of grace as a result of their crimes, which are also serious sins. And to put them to death promptly would give them little time for repentance, making it more likely that they be sent to Hell forever. If instead of the death penalty, the convicted criminal is given a long jail sentence, there is a greater time period for repentance and salvation. Therefore, even when the death penalty is necessary to defend the community, if at all possible, the convicted and sentenced criminal should be given a jail sentence prior to the death penalty, perhaps as long as a year or more, so as to provide time for repentance.

.238. Moral Purposes

When the use of the death penalty is moral under the second and third fonts (moral object, and circumstances), which intended ends (purposes) are moral, so that the first font will also be moral?

Cardinal Dulles: "The purposes of criminal punishment are rather unanimously delineated in the Catholic tradition. Punishment is held to have a variety of ends that may conveniently be reduced to the following four: rehabilitation, defense against the criminal, deterrence, and retribution."[236]

Just Punishment

Cardinal Dulles: "Summarizing the verdict of Scripture and tradition, we can glean some settled points of doctrine. It is agreed that crime deserves punishment in this life and not only in the next. In addition, it is agreed that the State has authority to administer appropriate punishment to those judged guilty of crimes and that this punishment may, in serious cases, include the sentence of death."[237]

It is moral for those with proper authority in the State to intend the death penalty for the purpose of just punishment. (Dulles uses the term 'retribution' in the sense of the distribution of justice, not in the sense of retaliation.) For Sacred Scripture contains the command of God to the Israelites to apply the death penalty, not only when there is a grave danger of physical violence to the community, e.g. in cases of murder, but also when the crime itself is so serious as to deserve a correspondingly serious punishment.

[Romans]
{1:32} And these, though they had known the justice of God, did not understand that those who act in such a manner are deserving of death, and not only those who do these things, but also those who consent to what is done.

[Acts]
{25:11} "For if I have harmed them, or if I have done anything deserving of death, I do not object to dying...."

The Apostle Saint Paul teaches in the letter to the Romans that some sins are so severe as to deserve death because of the nature of the act itself. He does not say that those who commit these sins should be put to death solely when the protection of the lives of the community requires it. Rather, he says that the type of offense inherently deserves death. And even in his own case, Saint Paul states that he has no objection to receiving the death penalty, but only if his offense is either: (1) the type that causes grave harm, implying that the penalty protects against further harm, or (2) the type that deserves death because the offense itself is so grave that the fitting punishment is also similarly grave.

God Himself punishes all unrepentant actual mortal sins with eternal Hellfire. And yet this punishment is not the minimum necessary to protect the innocent from further harm. This eternal punishment is given by God because justice requires that the punishment fit the crime. The primary purpose of the punishment given by God to the souls in Hell is justice. Similarly, those holy souls who died in a state of grace, without any actual mortal sin on their conscience, still must be punished in Purgatory to whatever extent justice

---

[236] Cardinal Avery Dulles, 'Catholicism & Capital Punishment', First Things, April 2001.
[237] Cardinal Avery Dulles, 'Catholicism & Capital Punishment', First Things, April 2001.

requires punishment for sin not satisfied in this life. The purpose is to justly punish sin, not to protect the innocent or the community. God applies this punishment in Hell and in Purgatory, and He does so primarily in order to apply the punishment required by justice.

Now the State has all of its temporal authority, including the authority to judge and to punish criminals, solely from God through the Church (Romans 13:4).[238] Therefore, the State in exercising the authority of God when applying the death penalty can certainly do so, morally, for with the same intention as God, to dispense a grave but just punishment that is fitting to a grave and unjust offense.

Cardinal Dulles: "In principle, guilt calls for punishment. The graver the offense, the more severe the punishment ought to be. In Holy Scripture, as we have seen, death is regarded as the appropriate punishment for serious transgressions. Thomas Aquinas held that sin calls for the deprivation of some good, such as, in serious cases, the good of temporal or even eternal life."[239]

However, the State need not seek to punish every criminal to the full measure of punishment required by his crimes. For though the State has authority from God, this authority is limited. Only God is able to punish every sin, in this life, or in Hell, or in Purgatory, with perfect justice and mercy. Therefore, although the State can morally apply the death penalty in some severe cases for the purpose of just punishment, the State is not obligated to give the death penalty to every crime that inherently deserves a severe punishment. Moreover, the State lacks the authority to give a penalty to every sin that deserves punishment.[240] For the State is not God, is not all-knowing, is not infallible, is not perfectly just and merciful.

.239. Defense of the Innocent

Just as Saint Paul implies in Acts 25:11, another moral purpose for the use of the death penalty, in addition to justly punishing an offense, is the protection of the community from someone who has done serious harm. Pope John Paul II mentions both types of moral purposes for the death penalty.

Pope John Paul II: "The primary purpose of the punishment which society inflicts is 'to redress the disorder caused by the offence'. Public authority must redress the violation of personal and social rights by imposing on the offender an adequate punishment for the crime...."[241]

The Pontiff goes on to consider lesser punishments, which have the advantage of allowing for the rehabilitation of the offender, as well as the use of capital punishment, "when it would not be possible otherwise to defend society."[242]

---

[238] Pope Boniface VIII, Unam Sanctam, n. 4, 6, 8; author's numbering and translation.
[239] Cardinal Avery Dulles, 'Catholicism & Capital Punishment', First Things, April 2001.
[240] Saint Thomas Aquinas, Summa Theologica, I-II, Q. 96, A. 2.
[241] Pope John Paul II, Evangelium Vitae, n. 56; inner quote from Catechism of the Catholic Church, n. 2266.
[242] Pope John Paul II, Evangelium Vitae, n. 56.

The members of the community are innocent, not in the sense of sinless, but in the sense that the guilty criminal has done serious harm to them without justification. The death penalty ensures that the criminal cannot continue this harm to the innocent. Now in most cases of serious crimes, the criminal can be prevented from doing further harm by imprisonment, and a long prison sentence may well be sufficient also as a just punishment. And this punishment, as Pope John Paul II teaches, has the advantage of allowing for the repentance of the offender. But the Pontiff also allows that the use of the death penalty in severe cases in order to protect the community is a moral intention: "as a kind of 'legitimate defense' on the part of society."[243]

Examples of imprisonment being insufficient to protect society are rare, but also readily apparent. A prison inmate who has power within organized crime can sometimes order a murder, and direct his organization to commit other serious crimes, from within prison. It is nearly impossible to so thoroughly separate a prisoner from the rest of society that no communication would be possible with the outside world. And any such communication, for certain few criminal bosses, can be used to commit additional crimes.

But if we postulate an imprisonment with no communication at all, such a punishment would be unjust. For each human person is inherently a part of the larger community; the human race is one family. In some cases, imprisonment is not sufficient to protect the community, and the severe measures needed for such protection, other than the death penalty, would not be moral to use. For even convicted criminals must be treated as fellow human persons. To place each in his own small cell alone, with no communication with other persons, for a long time or for life, is a punishment which extends beyond the measure of the offense, and which does unjust violence to the integrity of the human person.

In other cases, the criminal might use his communication with other prisoners to recruit members for a criminal or terrorist organization. Even if the one criminal is imprisoned for life, he can spend that time recruiting prisoners who will be released soon. The result is that the community is not protected against continuing grave harm from that criminal. And again, the sentence of perpetual solitary confinement, which would be necessary to prevent such recruitment and thereby to defend society, would not be moral. One may not commit an injustice in order to accomplish justice. But the use of the death penalty would protect society and would be moral.

.240. Rehabilitation

Cardinal Dulles: "The sentence of death, however, can and sometimes does move the condemned person to repentance and conversion. There is a large body of Christian literature on the value of prayers and pastoral ministry for convicts on death row or on the scaffold.... By consenting to the punishment of death, the wrongdoer is placed in a position to expiate his evil deeds and escape punishment in the next life."[244]

---

[243] Pope John Paul II, Evangelium Vitae, n. 27.
[244] Cardinal Avery Dulles, 'Catholicism & Capital Punishment', First Things, April 2001.

The prisoner who looks forward to a long jail sentence, or to life in prison, is considering his life within a society of fellow criminals. He might be less willing or less likely to repent in this circumstance, since repenting from his crimes might earn him the hatred of the unrepentant inmates, and since he considers that his death and judgment by God is perhaps many years away. But the prisoner who is awaiting the death penalty, if, in the case of an ordered justice system, that penalty is applied neither too soon, nor with too much delay, is forced by circumstances to consider his own death. He is generally held apart from the other prisoners, and so he does not consider that repentance will be detrimental to his life in prison. The clergy who minister in prisons tend to give special attention to those who are awaiting death. And the result may be that the prisoner on death row cooperates with grace unto repentance and conversion. And if he next offers to God his own death as a just punishment for his sins and crimes, this act helps him to reduce or even entirely expiate the punishment that would otherwise be due in the next life. Thus, the just use of the death penalty does not contradict the concern for rehabilitation.

But rehabilitation is obviously also possible when the convicted criminal is imprisoned for a lengthy sentence. Although life among other criminals tends against that rehabilitation, various programs within the prison, efforts by clergy, and prayers by all the faithful, can certainly accomplish this reform of even a hardened criminal. Such repentance is not apparent in many cases, but is also not uncommon. Some prisoners repent only after a long time in prison; others repent more promptly. Therefore, the need for rehabilitation neither necessitates, nor rules out, the use of capital punishment.

.241. Deterrence

Criminals are not entirely devoid of reason. If any criminal had no use of reason at all, he would be found not guilty by reason of insanity, because he would have no way to know right from wrong without the ability to reason. Certainly, all sin is in some way contrary to reason; and crimes are generally also sins. But the criminal usually shows some use of reason, in that he plans the crime, and in that he tries to provide himself with greater gain and less risk. Some crimes in particular show a great deal of foresight and use of intellect, despite their lack of morality (cf. Luke 16:1-8). Therefore, the threat of a longer sentence for a more serious type of crime, and of the death penalty for the most serious types of crimes, does have an affect on some criminals in their choices. A criminal may choose to commit robbery without a gun, since the use of a weapon in a robbery increases the sentence. A criminal may choose to avoid crimes with the death penalty attached to them, because of the greater risk to himself. And this deterrence does not depend on the criminal making a moral decision, but a self-centered decision, that of self-preservation. Therefore, the death penalty can function as a deterrent, in some cases.

However, if the death penalty is used excessively in human law, such that many crimes include this penalty, then the criminal at some point may realize that he is facing death, because of the offenses he has already committed. He might then use deadly force against everyone who attempts to arrest him or who might later testify against him. In such cases of the excessive use of this penalty, the opposite effect to deterrence occurs; the penalty spurs the criminal to commit more crimes, of a more serious nature, not fewer crimes. A poorly-written death penalty law is worse than having no death penalty at all available as a punishment.

Also, for certain types of crimes, victims and witnesses might be less willing to make a complaint and/or testify if the death penalty is given too readily. Even the victim of a crime might not want the perpetrator to suffer an excessive penalty. So again, an overly broad use of the death penalty in human law may have a counter-productive effect, that of deterring witnesses and complainants, rather than deterring serious crime.

So from these considerations, it is clear that the deterrent effect is limited to well-written laws that apply the death penalty narrowly, only in the most severe cases. But neither can we dismiss the deterrent effect of the death penalty in all cases. For Sacred Scripture plainly teaches that the death penalty can be an effective deterrent.

[Deuteronomy]
{13:4} Follow the Lord your God, and fear him, and keep his commandments, and listen to his voice. Him shall you serve, and to him shall you cling.
{13:5} But that prophet or forger of dreams shall be put to death. For he has spoken so as to turn you away from the Lord your God, who led you away from the land of Egypt and who redeemed you from the house of servitude, and so as to cause you to wander from the way that the Lord your God has entrusted to you. And so shall you remove the evil from your midst.
{13:6} If your brother, the son of your mother, or your own son or daughter, or your wife who is in your bosom, or your friend, whom you love like your own soul, were willing to persuade you secretly, saying: 'Let us go, and serve foreign gods,' which neither you nor your fathers have known,
{13:7} gods from any of the surrounding nations, whether these are near or far away, from the beginning even to the end of the earth,
{13:8} you should neither agree with him, nor listen to him. And your eye should not spare him so that you take pity on him and conceal him.
{13:9} Instead, you shall put him to death promptly. Let your hand be upon him first, and after that, let the hands of all the people be sent forth.
{13:10} He shall be killed by being overwhelmed with stones. For he was willing to draw you away from the Lord your God, who led you away from the land of Egypt, from the house of servitude.
{13:11} So may all of Israel, upon hearing this, be afraid, so that nothing like this will ever be done again.

These verses from the Old Testament law are very instructive about the death penalty. One purpose for the penalty is described as: "so shall you remove the evil from your midst." Removing a source of great harm to the community, harm to the whole person, body and soul, in effect defends the innocent from the guilty (similar to self-defense). The false prophet who leads Israel away from the Lord God is guilty of serious harm to the soul. In order to protect the innocent in the community from grave harm of any kind, whether death, or serious bodily injury, or the loss of fundamental human rights, or grave spiritual harm, the death penalty is moral. But if the reader doubts that defense against grave spiritual harm can be a moral purpose, consider that in the war of the Maccabees, the invaders were willing to live in peace with the Jews, and do them no bodily harm, as long as they abandoned their religion. And Sacred Scripture allows that this war of the Maccabees was moral; God was with the Maccabees in their use of deadly force, because they acted justly and in accord with the will of God.

Notice, in the quote above, that the death penalty is to be applied without bias or favoritism. If even your closest family or friend is guilty unto death, the same penalty is to be applied for the same serious crimes. This necessity of absolute fairness in application of the penalty may affect the judgment of the faithful when deciding whether or not to support death penalty laws in a nation, based on the particular circumstances of that time and place.

.242. But on the topic of deterrence, Sacred Scripture plainly and repeatedly teaches that deterrence is a moral purpose to the death penalty.

[Deuteronomy]
{13:11} So may all of Israel, upon hearing this, be afraid, so that nothing like this will ever be done again.
...
{17:12} But whoever will be arrogant, unwilling to obey the order of the priest who ministers at that time to the Lord your God, and the decree of the judge, that man shall die. And so shall you take away the evil from Israel.
{17:13} And when the people hear about this, they shall be afraid, so that no one, from that time on, will swell with pride.

Again, the purpose is both to protect Israel from evil in the sense of harm, and to deter other persons from committing the same type of offense out of pride. And yet again the same book presents the same teaching a third time, as if to present a third witness.

{19:15} One witness shall not stand against another, no matter what the sin or outrage may be. For every word shall stand by the mouth of two or three witnesses.
{19:16} If a lying witness will have stood against a man, accusing him of a transgression,
{19:17} both of those whose case it is shall stand before the Lord in the sight of the priests and the judges who shall be in those days.
{19:18} And when, after a very diligent examination, they will have found that the false witness had told a lie against his brother,
{19:19} they shall render to him just as he intended to do to his brother. And so shall you take away the evil from your midst.
{19:20} Then the others, upon hearing this, will be afraid, and they will by no means dare to do such things.

The person who bears false witness, intending to cause an unjust punishment to be inflicted on his brother (his brother or neighbor in the broadest sense of the word) shall receive the same punishment he attempted to inflict. In this way, we see that the sin of perjury is greater or lesser depending on the seriousness of the accusation and its punishment. And this greater or lesser punishment given to the perjurer can extend even to the death penalty. If a person commits perjury that would have caused an innocent person to be given the death penalty, the just penalty for that crime of perjury can extend even to the penalty of death. And then Scripture concludes by saying that other persons, "upon hearing this, will be afraid, and they will by no means dare to do such things." This verse plainly teaches that just punishments, up to and including death, can be a deterrent. Therefore, the intention to use the death penalty as a deterrent is a moral intention.

But notice that the situation described by Sacred Scripture is that of a false witness during a criminal trial. Scripture acknowledges that some trials might have false witnesses, providing false testimony, and making it more difficult for the court to determine correctly whether the defendant is innocent or guilty. The likelihood of a false judgment in death penalty cases weighs in the third font, when the citizens of a nation or its leaders are judging whether or not the death penalty does more good than harm in particular circumstances.

.243. Differences of Judgment

The Church teaches that the death penalty is moral under the second font; it is not murder. And certainly the use of the death penalty in particular cases may be moral under all three fonts. But the voters and leaders of a nation must still determine whether the absence of this penalty in their laws will have more good consequences and fewer bad consequences than the presence of this penalty in their laws. Even when an act is moral, there may be another act that is more in conformity with the full will of God for human affairs, an act with fewer bad consequences and more good consequences.

It is a required belief of all Catholics, a belief infallibly taught by the Universal Magisterium, that the death penalty is not murder and can be moral. Anyone who claims that the death penalty is necessarily always immoral is contradicting the teaching of Sacred Tradition, Sacred Scripture and the Magisterium. But the faithful still need to judge whether a nation in its particular circumstances would be better served by using other types of punishments, instead of death.

Cardinal Joseph Ratzinger: "While the Church exhorts civil authorities to seek peace, not war, and to exercise discretion and mercy in imposing punishment on criminals, it may still be permissible to take up arms to repel an aggressor or to have recourse to capital punishment. There may be a legitimate diversity of opinion even among Catholics about waging war and applying the death penalty, but not however with regard to abortion and euthanasia."[245]

---

[245] Cardinal Joseph Ratzinger, Worthiness to Receive Holy Communion, General Principles (sent by Cardinal Ratzinger to Cardinal McCarrick, Archbishop of Washington, D.C., and made public in July, 2004), n. 3; http://www.priestsforlife.org/magisterium/bishops/04-07ratzingerommunion.htm

This legitimate diversity of opinion among the faithful occurs because the evaluation of the good and bad circumstances is complex, and is not based solely on faith in the definitive teachings of Divine Revelation, but also on a reasoned judgment of many different factors that would affect the consequences of an act. Therefore, a decision to support or oppose a particular use of the death penalty, or a particular death penalty law, depends in part on the particular circumstances of place and time. These circumstances vary greatly, and their evaluation allows for differing reasonable judgments.

Some of the circumstances that weigh against the use of the death penalty in the laws of a nation include: biases in the justice system against minorities; a track record of erroneous judgment (such as exoneration from death row by DNA evidence); the great difference in the quality of the defense available to a poor defendant compared to a wealthy one; the significant resources that the State can bring to bear on behalf of the prosecution compared to the limited resources of the defense; the influence of popular sentiment and the mass media on the jury; the great variation in judgments by different judges; and other factors.

Some of the circumstances that weigh in favor of the use of the death penalty in the laws of a nation include: the overall fairness of the justice system; resources available to poor defendants; recent court precedents narrowing the use of the death penalty; the presence in society of powerful criminal organizations and terrorist groups whose members might be able to do much harm even from within prison; the prevalence in society of very severe crimes, which call out for a just and proportionate punishment; and other factors.

The teaching authority of the Magisterium cannot substitute for the prudential judgment of the faithful in all the various circumstances affecting each moral decision. The faithful must make their own judgment of particular circumstances, so that their decisions will do the most good and the least harm. The faithful are not permitted to believe that the death penalty is always immoral. But neither are they permitted to believe that the death penalty is always moral or always best, regardless of circumstance or intention.

.244. Violence against the Innocent

Not all killing is immoral. Murder is not any type of killing, but the direct and voluntary killing of an innocent human being. The innocence of the person killed is essential to the definition of murder under the second font of morality. Thus, killing in self-defense is not intrinsically evil, and may be moral if all three fonts are good. But killing in self-defense is not necessarily moral, because the bad consequences might outweigh the good consequences.

Not all violence is immoral. Just as the use of lethal violence in self-defense may be moral, if all three fonts are good, so also the use of less than lethal violence may be moral, if all three fonts are good. Murder is immoral because the person killed is innocent. Violence against the innocent is immoral because the person harmed is innocent. Any act of direct and voluntary violence against the innocent is an intrinsically evil act.

Violence against the innocent deprives the victim of health, harming the person either physically, mentally, or spiritually. Violence against the innocent harms the human person. The whole person, not merely the body, must be free from harm in order to be free from violence. Although human law generally only recognizes physical and mental harm as a crime, the soul of a person can be seriously harmed by the direct and voluntary acts of other persons. And this type of deliberate harm is also contrary to true love of God and neighbor, and so it is also a sin. The moral law supercedes all human law and all social custom.

Any morally direct and deliberate act that harms an innocent human person is intrinsically evil and always immoral. As is true for lying, so also acts of harm to the innocent may be venial sins or mortal sins; the gravity of the sin depends on intention and circumstances. A small degree of deliberate and morally direct harm is a venial sin, unless it is made mortal by a malicious intention, or by some circumstance. Differences in degree are also in the circumstances.

Examples: (1) A physician gives a helpful treatment that causes pain to the patient. The moral object of his act is the health of the patient; the pain is an unintended consequence. This act is not intrinsically evil and is not a type of violence against the innocent.

(2) A parent punishes a child for an offense by striking the child in a way that causes some brief pain, but no lasting harm. The child is guilty of an offense, and the punishment does not exceed the measure of the guilt (also taking into account age), and so this act is not violence against the innocent.

(3) A government finds a person guilty of a minor crime. The convicted criminal is then given a severe sentence, such as a long imprisonment. Since the punishment exceeds the limits of the offense, it extends beyond the guilt of the criminal. Therefore, this long imprisonment is an act of violence against the innocent. For each person is innocent beyond the measure of his guilt. A person who is only guilty of a minor offense, is innocent of a serious offense.

(4) A military commander orders a military target to be attacked during a just defense of his nation. He knows that there is a likelihood that some innocent persons will be harmed. But since the act itself is against a legitimate military target during a just war, the second font is good and the act is not intrinsically evil; the harm done to the innocent is in the third font, not the second font. However, all three fonts must be good for any act to be moral.

.245. Maiming the Innocent

Maiming someone refers to a type of severe harm to a human person, either the physical harm of cutting off a body part (the most common use of the term), or of severely scarring the skin, or even of severely harming the person mentally or spiritually. Such harm is often irreparable in this life, but if modern medicine is able, or becomes able, to repair the harm, the second font would be the same. Maiming the innocent is a type of direct and voluntary harm to an innocent person. If the harm is less severe, and so is not classified as maiming, the act is nevertheless intrinsically evil (if it is the direct and voluntary harming of an innocent person). Thus, maiming is a subcategory of violence against the innocent. The degree and type of harm is in the third font, but what makes the act intrinsically evil is in the second font.

Maiming the guilty is permitted in the Old Testament in some cases:

[Exodus]
{21:24} an eye for an eye, a tooth for a tooth, a hand for a hand, a foot for a foot,
{21:25} a scrape for a scrape, a wound for a wound, a bruise for a bruise.

[Deuteronomy]
{25:11} If two men have a conflict between themselves, and one begins to do violence to the other, and if the other's wife, wanting to rescue her husband from the hand of the stronger one, extends her hand and grasps him by his private parts,
{25:12} then you shall cut off her hand. Neither shall you weep over her with any mercy.

Saint Thomas cites Sacred Scripture in maintaining that maiming the guilty is not intrinsically evil, in answer to the question: "Whether in some cases it may be lawful to maim anyone?"

"On the contrary, It is written (Exodus 21:24): 'Eye for eye, tooth for tooth, hand for hand, foot for foot.' .... Hence just as by public authority a person is lawfully deprived of life altogether on account of certain more heinous sins, so is he deprived of a member on account of certain lesser sins."[246]

Since the use of the death penalty is not intrinsically evil when a person is guilty of a serious crime, the use of less than lethal force against the guilty is also not intrinsically evil. But even in Old Testament times, maiming was a rare penalty. For when less than lethal punishment is fitting to the crime, other punishments, which do no irreparable harm and therefore are in greater harmony with the possibility of repentance and rehabilitation, are usually sufficient to the measure of the offense. Reparable harm is preferable over irreparable harm as a punishment, because great sinners sometime repent greatly. Irreparable harm for a serious offense is not intrinsically evil, since the harm is not irreparable to God.

Some persons in society today have suggested the use of castration against persons convicted of repeated serious sexual crimes. As a type of maiming of a guilty person, one which fits the seriousness and type of the crime (and which some claim will help prevent the crime from occurring again), this punishment is not intrinsically evil. However, in order to be moral, this punishment must be good under all three fonts. Generally, other lesser punishments should be used before maiming, if circumstances allow.

With any use of maiming as a punishment for any crime, as is true for other uses of violence against the guilty, the harm done must not exceed the measure of the guilt. Otherwise, that harm becomes an intrinsically evil act of violence against the innocent. For each guilty person is only guilty within the limits of his offense,

---

[246] St. Thomas Aquinas, Summa Theologica, II-II, Q. 65, A. 1.

and beyond that limit he is innocent. Therefore, maiming for other than a very serious offense would exceed the limits of the guilt, and so would be an intrinsically evil act of violence against the innocent.

Now God does not permit anyone to be harmed in any way that He Himself cannot repair, better than new, in Heaven for the soul, and in the general Resurrection for the body united to the soul. But this does not justify the sin of violence of any kind against the innocent. The term irreparable harm refers to the life of the individual in this world. But no harm is irreparable to God.

Perhaps the most common way that persons are maimed in modern society is during warfare, when a soldier is maimed by an attack from the enemy, or when an innocent civilian is maimed indirectly (though the target is an enemy combatant). When an innocent person is maimed by an act that is not morally direct and deliberate, the act is not intrinsically evil; but it may still be immoral under the first or third fonts. So if a government shows disregard for severe harm to civilians, such as in the placement of mines, or in the bombing of military targets near the civilian population, the harm done to the innocent may be a serious sin under the first and third fonts, even if the act is not intrinsically evil. When an enemy combatant is maimed in the just defense of a nation, the harm done is not in the second font, since the moral object of the act is the just defense of a nation, and not the maiming of even the guilty. But again the first and third fonts must also be good. A bad intention makes any act immoral. If the bad consequences outweigh the good consequences, the act is immoral.

.246. Torture

The term torture is used today with a wide variety of different meanings and ranges of meaning. Some persons use the term torture to describe any severe suffering, regardless of the cause. However, if the suffering does not result from a knowingly chosen act, the term would not describe a moral or immoral act. And if the chosen act is not morally-direct and voluntary, then the act is not intrinsically evil.

As a knowingly chosen act, torture is sometimes used to refer broadly to any deliberate infliction of severe suffering. Some persons even use the term torture to describe relatively moderate inflicted suffering. But although all deliberate acts are subject to the moral law, an overly-broad definition of torture cannot be said to be intrinsically evil. Some degree of suffering may be inflicted on a guilty person as a punishment for a crime, and for a severe crime, the punishment may be of a proportionate degree. The teaching of the Church has always permitted punishment of the guilty, not only by imprisonment, which afflicts the prisoner with substantial suffering in the loss of his freedom, but also by the death penalty. The suffering of the loss of life is among the most severe punishments that human persons can inflict.

God inflicts punishment on the guilty souls in Hell, and this is the deliberate infliction of severe suffering. Yet God cannot violate the moral law; for the eternal moral law is the Justice inherent to His very Nature, and He cannot contradict Himself. Therefore, the torture of the guilty souls in Hell is not intrinsically evil, and torture itself, broadly defined, is not intrinsically evil. The punishment of the guilty, whether in this life, or in Hell, or in Purgatory, inflicts suffering, even severe suffering, on the guilty. When torture is defined so broadly as to include proportionate punishment of the guilty, torture cannot be said to be intrinsically evil, nor always immoral.

Many common definitions of torture include a statement about the intention of the one who commits the act of torture. Torture is said to be done with the intention of extracting information, or of satisfying revenge, or of frightening opponents, or for other motives. But intrinsically evil acts are immoral regardless of intention. And so whenever any definition of torture depends upon intention for its morality, that act, so defined, is not intrinsically evil.

.247. Narrow Definition

Setting aside the more common uses of the term torture, a narrow definition of torture could be applied only to the innocent, regardless of intention. Murder is intrinsically evil because it is the direct and voluntary killing of an innocent human being, not merely any killing. Similarly, we can define torture narrowly as the direct and voluntary infliction of severe suffering on the innocent. But like the maiming of the innocent, this definition is a type of direct and deliberate violence against the innocent, which is intrinsically evil.

This narrow definition of torture would also include a punishment of the guilty that was both severe and excessive. For to punish the guilty beyond an extent proportional to their guilt is a type of violence against the innocent (and so it is no longer properly called punishment). Even a person who is guilty of a serious crime is innocent beyond the limits of that crime.

Example: A person is guilty of theft, but is innocent of murder. If he is punished with a severe punishment, fitting to the crime of murder, but not to that of theft, then the punishment is an infliction of severe suffering on an innocent person. For despite being guilty of theft, he is innocent of murder. Whenever a person is punished beyond the measure of their guilt, the punishment extends into their innocence.

God's punishment of the guilty in Hell, in Purgatory, and in this life would not fall under this narrow definition of torture. For even in Hell, God punishes the guilty no more than they deserve, and certainly less than they deserve. For God is not merely Just, but also Merciful. His justice is merciful, and His mercy is just.

This narrow definition of torture, as the direct and voluntary infliction of severe violence against the innocent, is intrinsically evil, despite having the circumstance of degree (because torture is severe) as part of its definition. For when the degree is too small to be called torture, the act remains intrinsically evil, as the direct and voluntary harm of the innocent. Similarly, the definition of the intrinsically evil act of euthanasia includes the intention (first font) to relieve all suffering; but when that intention is not present, the second font remains intrinsically evil, as a type of murder.

Examples: (1) A physician inflicts a small degree of suffering on a patient, by a direct and voluntary act, in order to test the ability of the nervous system to detect sharp pain versus dull pressure. Such an act is not intrinsically evil, because the moral object is the health of the patient, not the harm of the innocent. Suffering by itself is not torture, and is not immoral; for suffering is physical evil.

(2) A physician gives a patient a cancer treatment that he knows will inflict severe suffering on the patient. In this case, the suffering is not in the second font, but in the third. For the chosen act directly treats the disease, and the suffering is an unintended consequence. Therefore, this infliction of suffering does not fit the narrow definition of torture. The suffering was not direct and voluntary, but indirect and unintended. And so the suffering inflicted is not a type of violence.

(3) A military instructor puts his recruits through very difficult circumstances, deliberately choosing to inflict suffering on them (of one degree or another) as a means to prepare them for the difficulties of warfare. This act is not a type of violence, despite a considerable degree of suffering, as long as the act is not inherently contrary to the fundamental human rights of the recruits. The physical evil of suffering can be tolerated in the bad consequences of an act, if outweighed by good consequences, and it can be tolerated in the intended means, as long as the means and the end are both moral, and the good end outweighs the physical evil in the means. But suffering cannot be an intended end, nor can it be the moral object of the act itself. For physical evil as an end is incompatible with the love of God, neighbor, self.

All violence against the innocent is contrary to love of God and neighbor. But in moral theology, the term violence is used not so much to refer to physical force, but to harm to the human person. And so violence in moral theology pertains to morality; it includes harm of any kind, even non-physical. Thus, the Second Vatican Council condemned, and Pope John Paul II reiterated, that various types of physical and non-physical violence against the innocent are immoral.

Second Vatican Council: "whatever violates the integrity of the human person, such as mutilation, physical and mental torture and attempts to coerce the spirit; whatever is offensive to human dignity, such as subhuman living conditions, arbitrary imprisonment, [*arbitrary*] deportation, slavery, prostitution and trafficking in women and children; degrading conditions of work which treat laborers as mere instruments of profit, and not as free responsible persons: all these and the like..."[247]

Note that I've added 'arbitrary' before 'deportation.' Just as imprisonment of the guilty is not immoral, so also deportation of the guilty is not immoral. The proportionate punishment of the guilty is not a type of violence at all, as that term is used in moral theology. Imprisonment or deportation of the innocent is immoral, and is a type of violence. Arbitrary imprisonment or deportation is immoral because the term 'arbitrary' indicates that there was no prior determination of guilt.

---

[247] Second Vatican Council, Gaudium et Spes, n. 27; also quoted by Pope John Paul II, in Veritatis Splendor, n. 80.

The infliction of suffering is not, in and of itself, necessarily immoral. Murder is the killing of an innocent human person, but killing in general is not necessarily immoral. Murder and other types of violence against the innocent are intrinsically evil, but killing in general and the infliction of suffering in general is not intrinsically evil.

In its narrow definition, torture is intrinsically evil, because it is defined as a type of violence against the innocent. And in this same narrow definition, torture is always gravely immoral, because it is by definition severe (in the circumstances). If an act of torture were reduced in severity, so that it was no longer gravely immoral, the act would not be defined as torture; but that act would still be intrinsically evil, because the moral object would be unchanged. Similarly, perjury is lying in the circumstance that one is under oath (e.g. in a court of law). But if the same lie takes place in a different circumstance, it might not be perjury, and it even might not be gravely immoral, but it would still be intrinsically evil, for the moral object would be unchanged. So an intrinsically evil act can be defined under more than one font, even in such a manner that a change in the first or third font would cause the act to fall under a different definition, or would cause the act to be no longer gravely immoral. Yet the act remains intrinsically evil because the moral object is unchanged.

Now the more common uses of the word torture are too broad to fit within this narrow definition. And so such common uses of the word torture do not refer to acts that are necessarily intrinsically evil. Some acts that fit under the common broad use of the term torture would be intrinsically evil, but other acts that fit under the same common definition would not be intrinsically evil. A narrow and proper definition of the term torture is needed before the act can be correctly said to be intrinsically evil.

.248. Threats

A threat, in the most general sense of the word, is an expression of a willingness to commit an act that has some bad consequences. Since a bad consequence does not necessarily imply an immoral act, the term threat in the broadest sense includes both moral and immoral acts. A person might threaten to assault an innocent person (immoral), or threaten to kill an innocent person (immoral), or threaten to bring legal action (sometimes moral), or threaten to quit their job (sometimes moral). In each of these cases, there are two acts to consider: (1) the act of making the threat, and (2) the act that will occur if the threat is carried out.

As long as all three fonts of morality are good, the threat is moral. As long as all three fonts of morality are good, the threatened act is moral. There are no exceptions to the three fonts of morality. But the question arises, if the act is immoral, is the threat to commit that act also immoral? What is the relationship in terms of morality between an act and a threat to commit that same act?

If it is wrong to commit a particular act, then it is wrong to threaten to commit that same act. If the commission of an act offends God, then the threat to commit the same act also offends God. It is never the will of God for anyone to express a willingness to commit an act that is contrary to the will of God. For God cannot contradict Himself. Neither can He will that we act, or express a willingness to act, contrary to His own Goodness. The threat to commit a sinful act, is itself always a sinful act.

This truth is particularly clear for intrinsically evil acts. It is always immoral to commit an intrinsically evil act; therefore, it is always immoral to threaten to commit an intrinsically evil act. The moral object of the threat to commit an act is the same as the moral object of the commission of the act. Both the act and the threat to commit the act are inherently directed toward the same end, the same moral object. Therefore, the act and the threat each have the same inherent moral meaning. If the act is intrinsically evil, then the threat is intrinsically evil. These are two distinct acts, each with its own morality; but whenever two different acts have the same moral object, they necessarily have the same essential moral nature in the second font.

Examples: (1) A man threatens to murder his neighbor (second font), intending to frighten him (first font), not intending to commit the murder, expecting the result that the neighbor will stop bothering him (third font). The moral object is not the purpose of causing fear, which is an intention in the first font. The moral object is not the expected result, which is a consequence in the third font. The moral object is never determined or affected by intention or consequences. The act itself is inherently directed at an end, independent of intention and consequences, called the moral object. Even if the man does not intend to carry out the murder, the act itself remains the same, making a threat to kill an innocent person. The act itself of making this threat is inherently ordered toward the deprivation of the life of an innocent person.

The threat has the same moral object as the threatened act, even if the person has no intention of carrying out the threat. For the second font is not determined by intention. Neither is the second font is determined by the attainment of the moral object, but by the inherent ordering of the act itself toward that moral object. Threats are inherently ordered toward the moral object of the threatened act. Therefore, the mere threat to commit murder has the same moral object as the act of murder, even though, by itself the threat does not achieve that moral object. A threat to commit murder is contrary to the love of neighbor for the same reason that the act of murder is contrary to the love of neighbor: an evil moral object.

The gravity of the second font is therefore also the same; for the gravity of the second font is always solely determined by the moral object. When the moral object of two different acts is the same, then the gravity of the second font is the same. But the gravity of the overall act, including all three fonts, might not be the same.

In the above example, the threat by itself is less sinful than the threatened act, but only because the first and third fonts are not the same in the threat as in the act. For the intention, while immoral, has less culpability because it does not include the intention to carry out the murder. And the third font of the threat does not include the anticipated bad consequence of the death of an innocent person. But the moral object is the same. And since the moral object is evil, the act itself is intrinsically evil. Therefore, both murder and the mere threat to commit murder are intrinsically evil.

(2) A man threatens to lie under oath if an unjust lawsuit is brought against him by his neighbor. He has the good intended end of avoiding the harm that he anticipates will occur from the misuse of the legal system in this particular case (but his intended means is immoral). He anticipates the good consequence that much harm to himself will be avoided, and that little or no harm will come to his neighbor. However, the act of lying is intrinsically evil. Now the man has not lied, but rather he threatened to lie. And the threat to lie under oath makes the lie (and the threat) a more serious act. But the threat to lie has the same moral object as the lie itself. Both the act of threatening to lie, and the telling of a lie, are directed at the same end in terms of morality, an end incompatible with the love of God who is Truth. Threatening to lie offends God because lying offends God; threatening to lie offends God for the same reason that lying offends God: because God is Truth. Therefore, the moral object of the threat is the same as that of the act, and thus the essential moral nature (moral species) of the threat is the same as that of the act. Both lying and threatening to lie are intrinsically evil and always immoral.

.249. The gravity of the sin might be less for a threat than for the act that is threatened, since the bad consequences would typically be greater for the commission of an act than for the mere threat to commit the same act. But the threat to commit an immoral act is still immoral. However, if an act is not immoral under any of the three fonts, then it is generally not immoral to threaten to commit the same act, unless the threat itself has a substantially different intention or circumstances, not found in the commission of the act.

Consider an intrinsically evil act that fails to attain its moral object. If two persons separately attempt to commit murder, and only one succeeds, both have committed the same sin under the second font. The moral object of an attempt to commit murder is the same, regardless of whether or not the attempt succeeds. For it is not the attainment of the moral object that determines the second font, but the inherent ordering of the act itself toward that moral object. An attempted murder that fails and an attempted murder that succeeds are each inherently directed at the moral object of the deprivation of life from an innocent human person. Similarly, the threat to commit murder, a failed attempted murder, and a successful attempted murder all have the same moral object. Each act is inherently directed at the deprivation of life from an innocent human person. The failure to attain that death does not affect the moral object of the threat, nor of the failed attempt.

Whenever a threat to commit an intrinsically evil act is also a lie, that threat has two moral objects, the moral object of lying and the moral object of the threatened intrinsically evil act. Lying is never moral. And if the purpose of the lie is to cause serious harm, e.g. by means of the fear caused by the threat, then the lie is also grave. There is nothing to prevent a knowingly chosen act from having more than one intention, more than one moral object, and more than one consequence, in the three fonts of that one act.

If an act is not intrinsically evil, but is immoral due to intention or circumstances, then it is still immoral to threaten to commit that same act. Suppose that a threatened act has a good moral object, but is immoral due to intention. The threat to commit this act is itself a knowingly chosen act, with all three fonts. It is not possible to have a good intention in threatening to commit an act that has an immoral intention. To be moral, all that is intended must be good. Even if a person does not intend to commit the threatened act, the expression of the threat uses an immoral act, an act with a bad intention, as the intended means, making the first font of the threat immoral. And lying adds an additional sin to the threat. Now suppose that a threatened act has a good moral object, but is immoral because the bad consequences outweigh the good. The threat to commit this immoral act also has a bad intention, since the intention is to use an immoral act as a means by threatening to commit the act.

Any threat is moral if all three fonts are good. Any threat is immoral if any one font is bad. A threat to commit a sin, is itself a sin, at least because of intention. For even if the intended end in making the threat is good, the intended means of threatening to commit an immoral act makes the intention immoral. And if the threatened act is intrinsically evil, then the threat itself has the same evil moral object and so is also intrinsically evil.

If the bad consequences of making a threat outweigh the good consequences, then the threat itself is immoral, even if the intention and moral object are good in the threat, and even if all three fonts are good in the threatened act. The three fonts of morality always apply. The third font in the threat is evaluated based on the good and bad consequences of the threat itself, not of the subsequent act. The circumstances of the threat and of the act are generally related. But it is possible for the morality of the third font in the threat to differ from that of the threatened act. Each act has its own three fonts.

Examples: (1) The leaders of a nation discover that the leaders of another nation are preparing a war of aggression against them. The aggressor nation threatens warfare; this threat is immoral because they are threatening to commit a sinful act (unjust war); the aggressor nation is thereby threatening to kill the innocent. In response, the leaders of the defending nation threaten to use a measured degree of military force, against military targets, in defense of their nation; this threat is moral because it is good under all three fonts. Since just war is not intrinsically evil, the threat of a just war is not intrinsically evil. The moral object of a just war is the defense of the nation; the moral object of threatening to enter into a just war is the defense of the nation.

(2) An innocent person is confronted by criminals on the street who threaten him with serious physical harm or death; this threat has the evil moral object of violence against the innocent. The innocent person responds by taking out a gun and brandishing it; this threat is moral because the threatened act is one of moral self-defense. [Note that what is moral is not always legal; laws concerning weapons and self-defense vary greatly from one place to another.] The threat to

use deadly force is moral, if all three fonts are good. In some circumstances, the mere threat to use deadly force may be sufficient to accomplish self-defense; in this way, the bad consequence of killing even a guilty human person is avoided. The intention of self-defense is good; the moral object of self-defense is good; the consequence of avoiding killing anyone is also good. All three fonts are good and so this type of threat of violence would generally be moral. However, if it is illegal to brandish a weapon in self-defense, then the additional bad consequences from the illegal act might make the third font bad and the overall act immoral.

But concerning the act by the criminals, the threat to use deadly force is intrinsically evil and always immoral whenever the use of that deadly force would be intrinsically evil and always immoral. Thus the threat to use deadly force, in this example, by the criminals is not moral. If they use deadly force, they are committing murder; and so their threat to use deadly force is directed at the same moral object, murder.

(3) An employer threatens an employee with firing, unless he commits an unlawful and immoral act; this threat is immoral. The employee threatens to complain to law enforcement, or threatens to bring a lawsuit; both of these threats are moral, because the acts being threatened are moral.

.250. In all cases, the morality of any act depends on all three fonts. In all cases when the moral object is good, the intention and consequences must also be good for the overall act to be moral. The threat to commit an act, and the threatened act, always have the same moral object (though the threat might have an additional moral object, as happens, for example, if the threat is also a lie).

But even when the moral object is the same, the threat and the act may have different first and third fonts. Each is a distinct act. So it is even possible for the threat to be immoral, while the threatened act is moral. If the intention in the threat is immoral, the threat is immoral regardless of whether or not the threatened act is moral. If the consequences of making a threat are immoral, the threat is immoral regardless of whether or not the threatened act is moral. However, if the threatened act is immoral under any font, the threat itself must be immoral, at least by immoral intention, if not also by the moral object or the circumstances. And if someone makes a threat to commit an immoral act, without intending to commit the act, he also sins by lying.

Examples: (1) A particular lawsuit is moral in a particular case. The intention is to recover monetary damages from the defendant (respondent) for harm done. The act itself of taking someone to court for a civil case is not intrinsically evil. The good consequences of the act outweigh the bad. However, the threat to commit an act might have a different intention, and different circumstances. The intention may be to frighten someone into paying an unjust amount of money, or into agreeing to an unreasonable act. And while it is unlikely that the same sinful person who has an immoral intention in threatening an act will have a good intention in carrying out that act, it is possible.

Human persons often commit both moral and immoral acts. The fact that one act is immoral does not imply that the next act will be immoral. The fact that one act is moral does not imply that the next act will be moral. In every case without exception, each and every moral act is good under all three fonts, and each and every immoral act is bad under one or more fonts. The three fonts determine the morality of each and every knowingly chosen act, including the type of act that is a threat to commit another act.

(2) One nation prepares to commit unjust military aggression against another nation. The leader of the defending nation threatens a strong military response, which is a moral act; but his intention in making the threat is to give himself excessive political power (beyond what reason and reasonable laws allow). The circumstances might also be such that the bad consequences of this threat, that he obtains excessive power, outweighs any good consequences. So for the threat, the first and third fonts are bad, but the second font (the threat to use just force) is good. If next the nation is attacked, his intention may well be to defend the nation, which is a good intention. And the good consequences of defending the nation may well outweigh the bad consequences of the war. So in this case, the threat is immoral, but the threatened act is moral.

Each act must be evaluated under each of the three fonts, as those fonts rise up from, and apply to, each particular act. If two acts have the same moral object, then they have the same inherent moral meaning in the second font. But two distinct acts will not necessarily have the same intention or circumstances, even if they have the same moral object. It is always immoral to threaten to commit an immoral act, at least because the intention is bad. It is sometimes immoral to threaten to commit even a moral act, because the intention and circumstances are not necessarily the same in the threat as in the act.

.251. Punishment of the Guilty

If a human person is guilty of a serious crime, he might be killed, or imprisoned, or lose certain privileges within society as a defense against, and as a punishment for, his crime. But even a convicted criminal may not be punished by denying him any fundamental human rights. For human nature is good, and all human persons are made in the image of God. Also, the guilt of a crime has limits, beyond which the criminal is innocent. For example, a thief who has not also committed murder is innocent of the crime of murder; he can only be punished according to the type and extent of his offense. Therefore, even if a human person is guilty of some sin or crime, his just punishment must be limited to the offense. If a guilty person is punished beyond the type and extent of his guilt, then such a punishment is not justice, but is an intrinsically evil act of direct and deliberate violence against the innocent.

It is never moral to punish the guilty by killing or harming the innocent. The killing or harm of the innocent, by a direct and deliberate act, is intrinsically evil and always immoral. This type of harm or violence (as these terms are used in moral theology) is contrary to the integrity of the human person made in the image of God. But mere physical force is not necessarily harm or violence. A sport that involves violence in the literal sense does not usually involve violence in the moral sense of harm or violence to the integrity of the human person.

Certain types of punishments are intrinsically evil to use against even a guilty person. Rape is not a moral punishment for any crime, not even for severe sexual crimes. Rape is intrinsically evil and always gravely immoral; therefore, it is not justified by the intention to punish the guilty, nor by the circumstance that the criminal himself is a rapist, nor by any intention or circumstances whatsoever. The human person is made in the image of God; therefore, the rape of even a guilty person offends God seriously.

It is intrinsically evil and always gravely immoral to sell a human being. All human persons are made in the image of God. Every direct and deliberate selling of a human being, whether a prenatal, child, or adult, is intrinsically evil and always gravely immoral. Such acts are inherently and directly contrary to true love of God, since we all belong to Him as children (not as objects), and directly contrary to true love of neighbor and self. It is not moral even to sell one's self into slavery. Therefore, such an act cannot be a moral punishment.

[Genesis]
{37:18} And, when they had seen him from afar, before he approached them, they decided to kill him.
{37:19} And they said one to another: "Behold, the dreamer approaches.
{37:20} Come, let us kill him and cast him into the old cistern. And let us say: 'an evil wild beast has devoured him.' And then it will become apparent what his dreams will do for him."
{37:21} But Reuben, on hearing this, strove to free him from their hands, and he said:
{37:22} "Do not take away his life, nor shed blood. But throw him into this cistern, which is in the wilderness, and so keep your hands harmless." But he said this, wanting to rescue him from their hands, so as to return him to his father.
{37:23} And so, as soon as he came to his brothers, they very quickly stripped him of his tunic, which was ankle-length and woven of many colors,
{37:24} and they cast him into an old cistern, which held no water.
{37:25} And sitting down to eat bread, they saw some Ishmaelites, travelers coming from Gilead, with their camels, carrying spices, and resin, and oil of myrrh into Egypt.
{37:26} Therefore, Judah said to his brothers: "What will it profit us, if we kill our brother and conceal his blood?
{37:27} It is better that he be sold to the Ishmaelites, and then our hands will not be defiled. For he is our brother and our flesh." His brothers agreed to his words.
{37:28} And when the Midianite merchants were passing by, they drew him from the cistern, and they sold him to the Ishmaelites for twenty pieces of silver. And these led him into Egypt.

Reuben did not sin by suggesting that Joseph be put into an old (i.e. dried up) cistern. The act that he proposed was not intrinsically evil, and his intention was good, and, in that circumstance, he reasonably anticipated the likely good consequence of being able to save his brother. However, Judah did sin, even though he suggested the less sinful act of selling his brother, rather than killing him (for all except Reuben thought that casting him into the well would cause his death). The act of selling a human person is intrinsically evil and always gravely immoral.

Sacred Scripture permits punishments of the guilty by imprisonment, maiming (though rarely), or even death (depending on the offense), because these types of punishments are not intrinsically evil. It is not inherently immoral to imprison someone, or to cut off a limb (as physicians sometimes do), or to kill someone. Therefore, it is possible in some circumstances for such acts to be used as moral punishments. Even though a crime for which maiming would be a just and fitting punishment is rare, the punishment is not intrinsically evil.

Some punishments are just, and other punishments are unjust. Among the unjust punishments are any and all intrinsically evil acts, as well as any punishment which can sometimes be moral, but which is not proportionate to a particular offense. But all the punishments of this life are temporary. Only God can give the punishment of unending suffering in Hell. Therefore, it is better to suffer a punishment for a sin or crime in this life, than to suffer unceasingly in Hell in the next life.

.252. False Imprisonment

The direct and deliberate imprisonment of an innocent human being is intrinsically evil and always immoral. This act is the morally direct and deliberate deprivation of the freedom given by God to all human persons by virtue of the gift of freewill. The deprivation of this freedom is an evil moral object because this type of freedom follows from the gifts of reason and free will inherent to human nature, as created by God. Reason and freewill are the gifts that make human persons more like God than any other created thing. Imprisonment of the innocent deprives the human person of the full use of free will to govern the person's own life in accord with reason. The deprivation of the use of these gifts is an evil moral object because the love of God and neighbor requires human beings to be permitted to exercise free will in accord with reason. False imprisonment restricts this use of a gift from God without justification.

Guilty persons may be morally imprisoned, to the extent of their crime, because they chose to use free will contrary to reason. The entire moral law, and all just laws without exception, are in accord with reason. The basis for the immorality of unjust imprisonment is the same as for just imprisonment: reason and free will.

False imprisonment can occur in a number of different ways. Just as there are different forms of murder, each of which is intrinsically evil, there are also different forms of false imprisonment, each of which is intrinsically evil. Regardless of dictionary or legal definitions, regardless of intention or circumstances, all false imprisonment is intrinsically evil.

False imprisonment occurs when a person or group lacks the proper authority to imprison anyone (even the guilty), and yet they take it upon themselves to do so.

Kidnapping, hostage-taking, and unlawful detainment each include the offense of false imprisonment (under the moral definition of the term). Even if a trial is held, but not by proper authority, then the imprisonment that follows will be false.

False imprisonment also occurs when proper authority holds a trial that is directly and deliberately unjust in any fundamental way which takes away the ability of the trial to determine the truth of guilt or innocence. If a prison sentence follows after a fundamentally unjust trial, that imprisonment is intrinsically evil and gravely immoral. Note that a number of different types of injustices might be present in the law enforcement and trial which would not fit this definition, which would still be immoral, but which would not result in the imprisonment being false. As long as these injustices are limited, such that the trial as a whole is just, and is generally able to determine guilt or innocence, then these injustices would not cause any resultant imprisonment to be intrinsically evil and false.

If proper authority convicts a criminal by a just trial, and a just imprisonment occurs subsequently, that imprisonment becomes a false imprisonment if the person is held beyond the length of time justly due for that crime. Some persons have suggested that, for certain crimes, a person might be held indefinitely, after completing the entirety of a just sentence, in order to protect the community at large. This type of indefinite imprisonment is false imprisonment, because the punishment extends beyond the guilt of the offense. The punishment becomes unjust whenever the proper punishment for an offense is satisfied, but the punishment continues. But if an offense is so serious that a longer prison sentence is just, then the laws should be changed to give such a sentence, or the judges should consider the seriousness of the offense when the sentence is decided.

It is intrinsically evil and always gravely immoral to extend a prison sentence indefinitely, without any additional crime having been committed, no matter what the original offense was, and no matter how evil the criminal might seem to be. For God alone judges the whole person, at the particular judgment, and God alone sends some such persons to permanent imprisonment in Hell, or to temporary imprisonment in Purgatory. The power is not given to any authority on earth, not to the Church on earth, and not to any government or court, to judge and condemn the person, regardless of the acts. Earthly powers may judge certain acts to be sinful or criminal, but they may not judge the person (in the sense of judging the soul or the life of the person).

A sentence of life imprisonment can be given as a proportionate punishment for one very serious crime, or for a set of serious crimes. But it would be intrinsically evil to give a life sentence to someone, not because of the immorality of his crimes, but rather because the person was judged to be immoral. Such an approach usurps the authority of God at the particular judgment, and such a sentence is a type of false imprisonment. Intrinsically evil acts are never justified, not for any purpose, not in any circumstances.

Certain types of 'three strikes' laws, those which imprison someone for life if they have committed any three felonies, are fundamentally unjust, and often result in a type of false imprisonment. If any one crime, or the entire set of crimes taken together, deserves life imprisonment as a proportionate punishment for that offense or set of offenses, then the imprisonment would be just. But otherwise, an unjust and false imprisonment results. For the authority of governments and courts does not extend to judging the person, such that a person who commits three felonies would be judged to be an 'habitual offender,' and would be given a sentence based, not on his acts, but on that judgment of the person. When a life sentence in such cases is given, it is not because of the acts committed, but in effect because of a judgment about the person himself. Such a judgment of the person, rather than of the acts, is only lawfully made by God Himself, because He is all-knowing, infallible, perfect, merciful, and just. Courts may give proportionate punishments to convicted defendants for their criminal acts, but they may not extend that imprisonment, neither for a certain additional number of years, nor for life, except when the particular offenses deserve that particular sentence. The set of crimes cannot be taken as evidence of the immorality of the person, so that the person, rather than the acts of that person, would be judged and punished. God alone has this role.

Examples: (1) A person commits a serious felony, serves the prison sentence, commits a second serious felony, serves the second sentence. Then he commits a relatively minor crime, but one that is categorized as a felony; he is then given either a long imprisonment, or life in prison, under a three strikes law. In this case, the first two crimes were justly punished with proportionate lengths of time in prison. And the punishment given after the third offense was substantially out of proportion to the crime. This subsequent imprisonment after the third offense is a type of false imprisonment. The person is in effect being judged and condemned, not for the third offense which was relatively minor, not for the first two offenses which were already punished, but for supposedly being a habitual offender (i.e. a bad person). The courts lack the authority under the moral law to judge persons, and so any sentence based on such a judgment is immoral.

(2) A person commits three serious crimes, and upon being convicted of the third crime is given a sentence of life in prison. But the third crime is so serious that a sentence of life in prison is proportionate to the crime. In this case, the prison sentence that results is not false or unjust, even if the three strikes law itself is generally unjust. For the punishment is proportional to the crime.

.253. Arbitrary imprisonment

Arbitrary imprisonment is a type of false imprisonment where the person or group who imprisons does not consider whether the persons imprisoned are guilty or innocent. All persons in a group are rounded up and given a prison sentence, without regard to guilt or innocence. If proper authority imprisons persons without knowing that they are guilty, then they are in effect imprisoning the innocent. This sin is comparable to the person who asserts a claim, without any reason for believing that the claim is true, without caring if the claim is false;

such a person commits the sin of lying, even if the claim is, without his knowing it, true.

.254. Indefinite Imprisonment

Imprisoning a human person convicted of a serious crime for a long time, or even for life, is not intrinsically evil, because the person is not innocent, but guilty. However, the punishment must be proportional to the crime, and the determination of guilt must be in accord with reason. A long prison sentence is a lesser punishment than death, especially since the possibility of an appeal, or of a commutation of sentence, often remains for a long time after the prison term begins. However, the prison conditions must be reasonable and humane. It is always the case when punishing the guilty that an excessive punishment extends beyond the person's guilt into their innocence. For no matter what crime has been committed, human nature is created by God, in the image of God.

For certain types of serious crimes, or when serious crimes are repeated numerous times over a long period, a convicted criminal could be reasonably and fairly imprisoned for a long period of time, and with a later evaluation of the potential of that person to continue to commit such crimes, which could result in parole. The person is then freed from prison, but given some supervision. Such a punishment would not be immoral because the punishment fits the crime, and because the possibility of parole is merciful and encourages rehabilitation, one of the goals of imprisonment. The justice system has a responsibility and a right to imprison convicted criminals in such a way and for such a length of time as is needed to protect society, but also a responsibility and a right to reduce that time for sufficient cause. This type of sentence is, in one sense, indefinite, in that it may be shortened for a just reason.

However, indefinite imprisonment of a guilty person beyond the punishment due for the crime, or of a person who is innocent, or of a person who is denied a trial, or of a person whose trial is unreasonably delayed, is intrinsically evil, because the moral object is contrary to the Nature of God who is Just and Merciful, and contrary to the love of neighbor. In each of these cases, the moral object is the deprivation of the fundamental human rights of freedom from an innocent person. The guilty person is innocent beyond the measure of his offense. The person who is imprisoned without a trial, or for a long time prior to trial without a cause proportionate to the evidence and charges, is also innocent (in the sense that no determination of guilt has yet been made). The imprisonment of a person either known to be innocent, or in the absence of evidence of guilt, is intrinsically evil. It is moral for a defendant to be imprisoned awaiting trial, if a judge determines that there is sufficient evidence to support the charges, and either the crime is sufficiently serious or the person is a threat to others or a flight risk; in such a case, there is some evidence that the person is not innocent. However, a human person cannot morally be imprisoned for a long time awaiting trial, nor for an indefinite length of time with no trial forthcoming, even if there is some basis for an accusation against that person. For it is not uncommon for a person who has been accused of a serious crime to be exonerated at trial. Therefore, a long prison term awaiting trial, without a proportionate reason, is a type of false imprisonment, which is intrinsically evil.

In the case of enemy combatants captured on the battlefield during a just war, if they are known to be guilty of being enemy combatants, they may be detained for a limited period of time. However, if they are not accused of committing any war crimes, or any serious crimes at all, then it is immoral for them to be held indefinitely. Even if they are accused of serious crimes, it is immoral for them to be held indefinitely; they must be given a just trial. A military may justly imprison captured enemy combatants for a limited period of time, in humane prison conditions, if the war is just. For then the enemy combatants are objectively guilty of engaging in unjust warfare (i.e. as unjust aggressors).

But indefinite imprisonment without a trial is a type of false imprisonment, even for enemy combatants. For the extent of their guilt, merely for fighting in an unjust war of their nation, is limited, and so their time in prison must be limited. Unless they have committed particular war crimes or other serious offenses, neither indefinite imprisonment, nor life in prison, is proportionate to the offense of fighting in an unjust war. For citizens often misjudge their own nation's justification for war, perhaps mistakenly thinking that an unjust war is just. Therefore, even an enemy combatant cannot be imprisoned indefinitely.

.255. Unjust Prison Conditions

Suppose that a human person is accused of a serious crime, given a fair trial, found guilty, and sentenced to a fitting length of time in prison. If the prison conditions are inhumane, then the incarceration is immoral. There was nothing wrong with the trial and sentencing, but even a convicted criminal is a human person deserving of just treatment. The injustice committed by a criminal does not justify the immoral treatment of that human person.

A prison sentence generally consists of two parts, the length of time and the conditions during that length of time. An unjustly long prison sentence is a type of false imprisonment, since the sentence extends beyond the guilt of the prisoner. If the length of the sentence is just, the conditions of imprisonment must also be just. If the conditions are either inhumane, or if the conditions are generally humane, but include a type of punishment beyond what is fitting to the crime, then in either case the imprisonment is immoral.

It is common knowledge in modern society that prisoners are subject to possible physical or sexual abuse in prison. How can such a severe injustice be so well-known, and yet continue to be unaddressed for so many years? No prisoner, regardless of his or her crime, deserves to be subject to physical or sexual abuse. Every guilty person is innocent beyond the measure of his or her guilt. And sexual abuse in particular is never a just punishment, not even for someone convicted of committing the crime of sexual abuse to a severe extent. For the moral law, which is the Justice inherent to the Nature of God, requires injustice to be punished with justice, not with further injustice.

Inhumane prison conditions include any conditions that deny, or in effect deny, fundamental human rights to the prisoner. When any prison denies the fundamental human rights of the prisoners to a substantial extent, the set of acts by which those rights are denied fits the moral definition of slavery (regardless of whether or not the prisoners are forced to work). Even if fundamental human rights are denied to a limited extent, such a denial is intrinsically evil. Examples of inhumane prison conditions include: deprivation of sufficient food and water, deprivation of medical care, deprivation of safety (as when guards or other prisoners assault or abuse the prisoners), deprivation of communication, education, and even some entertainment, as well as the deprivation of any other basic human need. The food, drink, and other necessities provided to prisoners need not be of high quality, need not be particularly pleasing or comforting, and may be significantly more limited than what is found in general society. But the basic human needs of the prisoners must be met in order to avoid committing a grave injustice.

Unjust punishments, other than a sentence of excessive length, include: excessively arduous labor, an excessive number of work hours, excessive isolation of the prisoner from other persons (as occurs in 'supermax' prisons), excessive crowding of the prison, and other unjust conditions.

Governments, courts, and society in general, cannot justify the intrinsically evil acts of false imprisonment, indefinite or arbitrary imprisonment, and inhumane prison conditions, on the basis of the seriousness of the crime. Intrinsically evil acts are never justified, not even to protect society from serious crimes. A society is only just if its acts are just, and its acts are only just if it treats all human persons without exception in accord with the eternal moral law, which is based on the love of God, neighbor, self.

Chapter 20
Just and Unjust War

.256.
The Morality of War

A decision by the leaders of a nation to go to war, and certain fundamental acts within warfare, such as killing enemy combatants and attacking military targets, are not necessarily immoral. War, in general, is not intrinsically evil. For intrinsically evil acts are always immoral, but war is not always immoral.

If all warfare were immoral, then God would not have commanded the Israelites to go to war.

[Joshua]
{11:15} Just as the Lord had instructed his servant Moses, so did Moses instruct Joshua, and he fulfilled everything. He did not omit even one word out of all the commandments, which the Lord had commanded Moses.
{11:16} And so Joshua seized the entire land of the mountains, and of the south, and the land of Goshen, and the plains, and the western region, and the mountain of Israel, and its plains.
{11:17} As for the part of the mountain that ascends to Seir, as far as Baalgad, along the plain of Lebanon under mount Hermon, all their kings he seized, struck down, and killed.
{11:18} For a long time, Joshua fought against these kings.
{11:19} There was not a city that delivered itself to the sons of Israel, except the Hivites who were living at Gibeon. For he seized it all in warfare.
{11:20} For it was the sentence of the Lord that their hearts would be hardened, and that they would fight against Israel and fall, and that they did not deserve any clemency, and that they should perish, just as the Lord had commanded Moses.

If all warfare were immoral, then the Holy Spirit would not have inspired Psalms using battles and warfare as figures for the struggles of life.

[Psalms]
{17:32} For who is God, except the Lord? And who is God, except our God?
{17:33} It is God who has wrapped me with virtue and made my way immaculate.
{17:34} It is he who has perfected my feet, like the feet of deer, and who stations me upon the heights.
{17:35} It is he who trains my hands for battle. And you have set my arms like a bow of brass.
{17:36} And you have given me the protection of your salvation. And your right hand sustains me. And your discipline has corrected me unto the end. And your discipline itself will teach me.
{17:37} You have expanded my footsteps under me, and my tracks have not been weakened.

{17:38} I will pursue my enemies and apprehend them. And I will not turn back until they have failed.
{17:39} I will break them, and they will not be able to stand. They will fall under my feet.
{17:40} And you have wrapped me with virtue for the battle. And those rising up against me, you have subdued under me.
{17:41} And you have given the back of my enemies to me, and you have destroyed those who hated me.
{17:42} They cried out, but there was none to save them, to the Lord, but he did not heed them.
{17:43} And I will crush them into dust before the face of the wind, so that I will obliterate them like the mud in the streets.
{17:44} You will rescue me from the contradictions of the people. You will set me at the head of the Gentiles.
{17:45} A people I did not know has served me. As soon as their ears heard, they were obedient to me.

If all warfare were immoral, then Saint John the Baptist would have counseled soldiers to leave the military:

[Luke]
{3:14} Then the soldiers also questioned him, saying, "And what should we do?" And he said to them: "You should strike no one, and you should not make false accusations. And be content with your pay."

If all warfare were immoral, then Jesus would not have praised the centurion:

[Matthew]
{8:10} And, hearing this, Jesus wondered. And he said to those following him: "Amen I say to you, I have not found so great a faith in Israel."

If all warfare were immoral, then Saint Paul would not have used the figure of "a soldier in a good war" to describe spreading the Gospel in a sinful world.

[1 Timothy]
{1:18} This precept I commend to you, my son Timothy, in accord with the prophets who preceded you: that you serve among them like a soldier in a good war,
{1:19} holding to faith and good conscience, against those who, by rejecting these things, have made a shipwreck of the faith.

.257. Avoiding War

Though some wars are just, all war should be avoided if possible. For every just war would not occur at all, if there were not many mortal sins upon the earth. At Fatima, our Lady said: "Wars are a punishment for the sins of mankind."[248]

---

[248] Highlights of Our Lady of Fatima's Message to the World, http://www.salvemariaregina.info/Message.html

When God establishes His Kingdom on earth, then there will be no more tears (i.e. suffering) and no more death. Therefore, there will also be no more war, for every war brings suffering and death.

[Ecclesiastes]
{9:18} Wisdom is better than weapons of war.

[Revelation]
{21:1} I saw the new heaven and the new earth. For the first heaven and the first earth passed away, and the sea is no more.
{21:2} And I, John, saw the Holy City, the New Jerusalem, descending out of heaven from God, prepared like a bride adorned for her husband.
{21:3} And I heard a great voice from the throne, saying: "Behold the tabernacle of God with men. And he will dwell with them, and they will be his people. And God himself will be their God with them.
{21:4} And God will wipe away every tear from their eyes. And death shall be no more. And neither mourning, nor crying out, nor grief shall be anymore. For the first things have passed away."

Therefore, even just war should be avoided. If war in a particular case, taking into account all three fonts of morality, would be moral, this does not imply that the nation is obligated to go to war. A person is not obligated to perform an act merely because that act would be moral. Perhaps another moral act can be found which will do more good and less harm.

And yet, in some cases, a nation may be obligated to go to war. For example, if it is clear that nothing else would be effective, in a particular case, to protect many lives from death or severe harm, then those who are responsible for defending the nation would sin if they refused to protect the lives given to their care. A nation must not be too quick to go to war, nor too slow to go to war, for in either case much harm might result.

.258. Traditional Approach

Even a brief war involves many knowingly chosen acts by many persons. Some of these acts may be moral. Others of these acts may be immoral. Even if the decision to go to war was moral, subsequent acts during the war might be immoral. A just war does not justify all acts that occur during that war.

Catechism of the Catholic Church: "The Church and human reason both assert the permanent validity of the moral law during armed conflict."[249]

Each and every knowingly chosen act is subject to the eternal moral law. Each and every knowingly chosen act must be good under all three fonts of morality in order to avoid sin. There are no exceptions to the eternal moral law. The decision to go to war must be just under all three fonts. And once the war has begun, each and every knowingly chosen act must be moral under all three fonts.

---

[249] Catechism of the Catholic Church, n. 2312.

Second Vatican Council: "But it is one thing to undertake military action for the just defense of the people, and something else again to seek the subjugation of other nations. Nor, by the same token, does the mere fact that war has unhappily begun mean that all is fair between the warring parties. Those too who devote themselves to the military service of their country should regard themselves as the agents of security and freedom of peoples. As long as they fulfill this role properly, they are making a genuine contribution to the establishment of peace."[250]

The Fathers of the Council did not require Catholics to avoid military service, nor did they condemn all warfare. The Magisterium continues to teach that some wars are just wars. The traditional conditions in moral theology for a just war are summed up by Saint Thomas Aquinas, based largely on the work of Saint Augustine.

Saint Thomas Aquinas: "I answer that, In order for a war to be just, three things are necessary. First, the authority of the sovereign by whose command the war is to be waged.... Secondly, a just cause is required, namely that those who are attacked, should be attacked because they deserve it on account of some fault.... Thirdly, it is necessary that the belligerents should have a rightful intention, so that they intend the advancement of good, or the avoidance of evil."[251]

Saint Thomas specifies three conditions for a war to be moral. First, the intention must be good (first font). A good intention is required of all knowingly chosen acts; a bad intention makes any act immoral. The decision to go to war, and the acts that occur during that war, must be done with good intention. Any act done with bad intent is a sin. If, during the war, some acts are done with good intent, and other acts are done with bad intent, the acts done with bad intent are sins.

Second, the cause for the war must be just. The 'just cause' is not the purpose for going to war, which is in the first font, but rather the inherent ordering of the act (e.g. the act of deciding to go to war) toward a good moral object (second font). In the case of just war, the good moral object must be a particular fulfillment of the commandments to love God, and to love your neighbor as yourself. The most commonly cited moral object is the defense of the people of a nation, when that nation is being attacked. But other moral objects may also be good, such as one nation defending another nation from an attack by a third nation, or a clear immediate severe threat to a nation or group of nations, prior to any enemy attack. In these examples, the just cause is the defense of the innocent. Other moral objects are possible, such as the Israelites carrying out the sentence of God against the seven tribes in the Promised Land.

Third, Saint Thomas states (based on the work of Saint Augustine) that the persons who decide to go to war must have proper authority. This requirement is part of the third font. Some other conditions (in the third font) for a war to be just are stated in the Catechism:

---

[250] Second Vatican Council, Gaudium et Spes, n. 79.
[251] St. Thomas Aquinas, Summa Theologica, II-II, Q. 40, A. 1.

Catechism of the Catholic Church: "The strict conditions for legitimate defense by military force require rigorous consideration. The gravity of such a decision makes it subject to rigorous conditions of moral legitimacy. At one and the same time: the damage inflicted by the aggressor on the nation or community of nations must be lasting, grave, and certain; all other means of putting an end to it must have been shown to be impractical or ineffective; there must be serious prospects of success; the use of arms must not produce evils and disorders graver than the evil to be eliminated. The power of modern means of destruction weighs very heavily in evaluating this condition."[252]

However, these conditions are merely an explanation of how the third font of morality applies to the particular subject of war. As always, in the third font, the good consequences must outweigh the bad consequences. Concerning warfare, this evaluation of the third font considers: the damage (bad consequences) if the nation does not go to war; any means that might be used to avoid these bad consequences without going to war; the likelihood of success (good consequences) of the war compared to the other possible options; and overall the just war must do more good than harm (the good consequences must morally outweigh the bad). All of this is merely an evaluation of the third font of morality. The other two fonts must also be good.

The traditional requirement that the war be 'successful' must be understood in terms of morality, not in secular or military terms. A successful war does more good than harm, so that the good consequences outweigh the bad. A military victory of any kind is not necessary to the morality of a war. A nation might fight, knowing that it will lose, in order to obtain favorable conditions for a peace treaty, thus avoiding the complete subjugation of the nation and saving many lives. A nation might fight, knowing that it will lose, in order to substantially weaken the ability of an aggressor nation to continue to conquer other nations. If each successive nation does not fight because it cannot win, then all are conquered. But if one nation after another fights and loses, the aggressor nation continually loses military resources, eventually resulting in its defeat. And this defeat would be a type of success. A war is successful as long as the war does more good than harm in the reasonably anticipated overall consequences of the war.

.259. Just War and Unjust War

Second Vatican Council: "Certainly, war has not been rooted out of human affairs. As long as the danger of war remains and there is no competent and sufficiently powerful authority at the international level, governments cannot be denied the right to legitimate defense once every means of peaceful settlement has been exhausted. State authorities and others who share public responsibility have the duty to conduct such grave matters soberly and to protect the welfare of the people entrusted to their care. But it is one thing to undertake military action for the just defense of the people, and something else again to seek the

---

[252] Catechism of the Catholic Church, n. 2309.

subjugation of other nations. Nor, by the same token, does the mere fact that war has unhappily begun mean that all is fair between the warring parties."[253]

Cardinal Joseph Ratzinger: "While the Church exhorts civil authorities to seek peace, not war, and to exercise discretion and mercy in imposing punishment on criminals, it may still be permissible to take up arms to repel an aggressor or to have recourse to capital punishment."[254]

Some wars, even in modern times, may be just. War is not intrinsically evil; war is not always immoral. Even so, every just war includes very grave injustices, at least by one side in the conflict. If a nation undertakes a just war to defend itself against an unjust attack by an aggressor nation, the leaders of the aggressor nation have committed mortal sin by their decision to attack unjustly. Even on the side of the nation justly defending itself, during the war some individual soldiers might commit mortal sins. In the course of the severities of warfare, serious sins are often committed by individuals on both sides of the war. And so a just war is not without sins by some persons, even by many persons. If both sides in an impending conflict avoided all objective mortal sin, there would be no war ever again.

A just war is a set of acts. A war may reasonably be called a just war, even though some acts by some persons during the war are sins. We are all mere weak and mortal sinners. During the severities of war, some sins will be committed, even when a nation is justly defending itself. A war is called just, despite these sins, when certain conditions are met. In order to be properly defined as a just war, the principle acts of that war, by the side that is acting justly, must be moral. These principle acts may be divided into three types.

First, the act of deciding to go to war must be just. Even if this decision is made by one man, a war cannot occur unless many other men decide to obey his decision and follow his orders. And so the act of deciding to go to war is a set of acts by many persons. Herein lies a problem. What if the intention to go to war is good in some men, and bad in other men? Certainly, whoever acts with bad intent, sins. But a war may still be properly defined as a just war, despite some bad intent by some persons, if those principally responsible for the decision to go to war have a good intention, and if the war has a good moral object, such as the defense of the nation, and if the reasonably anticipated good consequences outweigh the bad. If the three fonts of morality are good concerning the decision to go to war, then the first condition for a just war is met.

Second, the principle acts used to conduct the war must be just. These acts may be further divided into two types: those ordered by the chain of command, and the customary or common practice of soldiers apart from any orders. For soldiers, even those who are obedient, do not have orders for every act in every situation during the war. They necessarily make some decisions on their own.

---

[253] Second Vatican Council, Gaudium et Spes, n. 79.
[254] Cardinal Joseph Ratzinger, Prefect of the Sacred Congregation for the Doctrine of the Faith, letter to Cardinal McCarrick, Archbishop of Washington, D.C., made public July 2004; http://www.ewtn.com/library/CURIA/cdfworthycom.htm

And some soldiers act contrary to their orders. If a decision to go to war is made with good intention, in order to defend the nation, the war would still be fundamentally unjust if the war is conducted by means of gravely immoral acts, either by order or by custom.

Again, there are many persons involved in the conduct of the war. Some unjust acts by some individuals would not cause the war to be unjust, as long as the war is generally conducted in a just manner, by order and by custom. Again, all three fonts of morality must be good. If the commanders of the war or the soldiers generally have a sinful intent, such as to kill enemy combatants out of hatred for an ethnic or religious group, then the war is unjust, even if the decision to go to war was in order to defend the nation. Or if the war is generally conducted by directly targeting innocents, then the moral object of such conduct is evil and the war is unjust. If a few soldiers target innocents, contrary to orders and contrary to the custom of most soldiers, then the war does not thereby become unjust; this is all the more clear when such soldiers are arrested, tried, and convicted for killing innocents. But even when an intention is good, and the moral object of the acts of warfare are good, the good consequences must outweigh the bad. If a war is conducted by targeting military targets only, but often in circumstances where the harm to innocents outweighs the good that is done, then the war is an unjust war. If any of the three fonts of morality are bad, in the way that the war is generally conducted, then the war cannot be called a just war.

The decision to go to war to justly defend the nation does not "mean that all is fair between the warring parties." A just war is not merely a war that defends a nation, but also a war that is conducted in a moral manner. And the morality of the decision to go to war, and of the principle acts in the conduct of the war, are determined by the three fonts of morality.

Other acts might occur during the war which are not fundamental to the decision to go to war, and which are not fundamental to the conduct of the war. Such acts may be moral or immoral, but they do not determine the morality of the war. Some soldiers might commit various personal sins, such as adultery or theft. Some few leaders may have sinful intent, such as to gain power. Some few soldiers might act with deliberate violence toward some civilians, apart from orders and the customary behavior of fellow soldiers. But these acts are not fundamental to the decision or conduct of the war, and so they do not make a war unjust. Neither would the good acts of a few soldiers cause a fundamentally unjust war to become a just war.

Third, the end of the war must be just. If a war begins as a just war, in defense of a nation, and uses just acts to conduct the war, then so far the war is just. But if the reason for beginning the war is resolved, in that the nation is now safe from attacks and threats of attack, the war should end. But if the war continues with now an unjust intention, or with an evil moral object, or if the bad consequences of continuing the war now outweigh the good consequences, or if the war is now conducted anew with principle acts that are unjust, then the war has become an unjust war. In order to be a just war from beginning to end, the war must be brought to an end in accord with the three fonts of morality. The intention must not change to an unjust intention, and the principle acts of the war must not change to acts that are intrinsically evil or otherwise immoral, and the war must end before more harm is done than good. For as any war continues, bad consequences continue to occur; therefore, a just war will end as soon as possible, so that the harm does not accumulate and outweigh any good that has been done.

If a person is guilty of a crime and is punished, this punishment is just; but if the punishment extends beyond the measure of the crime, then the punishment becomes an intrinsically evil act of violence against the innocent. Similarly, if a just war, undertaken to defend a nation, continues beyond the needs of defense, so as to subjugate or to utterly destroy the aggressor nation, or so as to directly kill innocent civilians, then the war has been extended beyond the measure of a just war, and has become an act of violence against the innocent.

.260. Unjust Acts During A Just War

In all cases without any exception, each and every knowingly chosen act must be good under all three fonts for the person to avoid sin. Even when a war is just, any and all immoral acts remain immoral. A just war does not justify immoral acts that occur during the war, whether these acts are venial sins or mortal sins, whether these acts do little harm or great harm.

Example: (1) The war of the United States against Japan during World War 2 was a just war, in that the U.S. was defending itself against military aggression by Japan (at Pearl Harbor) as well as defending other nations that were also attacked (by Germany as well as Japan). Most of the principle acts of the war were moral, as when the Allies attacked various military targets. However, the fire bombing of Tokyo, and the nuclear bomb attacks of Hiroshima and Nagasaki, were intrinsically evil and gravely immoral acts. The moral object of these acts was the direct and deliberate killing of innocent human persons. These were not primarily military targets, but civilian targets. The intention to demoralize the enemy, and the anticipated good consequence of saving lives by ending the war sooner, do not justify the intrinsically evil act of the murder of innocent human persons.

Second Vatican Council: "Any act of war aimed indiscriminately at the destruction of entire cities of extensive areas along with their population is a crime against God and man himself. It merits unequivocal and unhesitating condemnation."[255]

By this example, it is clear that a just war may include some gravely immoral principle acts. War is a set of acts. As always, each and every knowingly chosen act must be good under all three fonts for the act to be moral. If a set of acts includes some moral acts and some immoral acts, the good acts remain good and the bad acts remain bad. A war may be termed a just war, if all three fonts are good for the decision to go to war, and for the conduct during the war, and for the conclusion of the war (lest the war become unjust by continuing beyond

---

[255] Second Vatican Council, Gaudium et Spes, n. 80.

its purpose). However, if any person or group commits a sin during a just war, that sinful act remains immoral.

Because war is a set of acts, in some wars, it may be difficult to discern if the war is just or unjust. If the war is just in many ways, but if there are also substantially unjust principle acts during the war, some persons might reasonably call the war just, despite some unjust particular acts, and other persons might reasonably call the war unjust, despite some just particular acts. This difficulty occurs when evaluating the morality of any diverse set of acts. However, each particular act remains either moral or immoral, based on the three fonts of morality, as those fonts spring up from, and apply to, each particular act. Despite differing judgments as to the proper classification of the set of acts, good acts remain good, and bad acts remain bad. Good acts during an unjust war remain good; evil acts during a just war remain evil.

.261. A Just War That Becomes Unjust

A just war may become unjust in either of two ways: either because the conduct of the war changes; or because the war extends beyond the original justification of the decision to go to war, typically the defense of the people of a nation. Suppose that a nation undertakes a just war in defense of the people, and the nation conducts the war by principle acts that are also just. But if the nation begins to lose the war, and so they undertake a new approach, so as to conduct the war, by order or by custom, with gravely immoral principle acts, then the war becomes an unjust war. Or suppose that a nation conducts a just war, but when the purpose of defending the nation is accomplished, they continue the war in order to loot the aggressor nation, or in order to subjugate its people, or in order to take revenge on the aggressor nation. In such a case, what began as a just war now becomes an unjust war.

An individual knowingly chosen act is either moral or immoral. But a diverse set of acts may contain some moral and some immoral acts. The acts earlier in the set may be generally moral, but the acts later in the set may be generally immoral. There is nothing to prevent a just war from becoming an unjust war, because good acts do not justify subsequent bad acts.

There are two types of immoral acts, those that are intrinsically evil (when the second font is bad), and those that are immoral but not intrinsically evil (when the second font is good, but either or both of the first and third fonts are bad). A war might be unjust because the principle acts of the war are intrinsically evil, or because these principle acts are gravely immoral (under the first or third fonts) but not intrinsically evil. A just war might become an unjust war if the principle acts change from those that have a good moral object to those that have a bad moral object. Or a just war might become an unjust war, even if the moral object does not change, if perhaps the intention or the circumstances change. All three fonts must be good for any act to be moral. A good second font (moral object) does not justify a bad first or third font (intention or circumstances), even during a just war.

.262. Intrinsically Evil War

A war may be just or unjust. When an unjust war is immoral under the second font of morality, due to an evil moral object, then the war is also intrinsically evil. When an unjust war has a good moral object, but is immoral under the first or third fonts, then the war is unjust, but not intrinsically evil. An intrinsically evil war is a type of unjust war. Some unjust wars are intrinsically evil, and other unjust wars are not intrinsically evil. Warfare in general is not intrinsically evil, just as killing in general is not intrinsically evil. A particular type of killing called murder is intrinsically evil, just as particular types of war are intrinsically evil.

Since war is a set of acts, again the problem arises as to which intrinsically evil acts, committed in association with the war, cause the war as a whole to be properly termed intrinsically evil. Generally, if the decision to go to war has a bad moral object, then the war may be said to be both unjust and intrinsically evil. If the decision to go to war is inherently directed at the killing of innocents, the war is intrinsically evil. Now some innocent deaths will occur in the consequences of nearly any war, but the good consequence of defending an entire nation from grave harm may outweigh this common bad consequence. However, if the death of innocents is the moral object of the decision to go to war, then no intention and no circumstances can justify that war.

An act is intrinsically evil when its moral object is evil; all intrinsically evil acts are inherently ordered toward an evil moral object. If an act is intrinsically evil (e.g. murder, theft, lying), then the decision itself to commit such an act is also intrinsically evil. For a decision is a type of act. The decision to murder has the same moral object as the act of murder. The decision to steal has the same moral object as the act of theft. The decision to lie has the same moral object as the act of lying. Therefore, if a leader decides to undertake a war with principle acts that have an evil moral object, such as the direct and deliberate killing of innocents, then the decision itself is also intrinsically evil.

Examples: (1) A leader decides to undertake a nuclear war, the principle acts of which will target the cities of another nation. The act of killing the entire innocent population of a city is intrinsically evil, as a type of murder. The principle acts of this war are intrinsically evil and gravely immoral. Therefore, the decision to commit these intrinsically evil acts is itself intrinsically evil. And the war may be properly called, not only an unjust war, but also an intrinsically evil war.

(2) A nation undertakes a war in order to defend itself. However, during the war, the nation is in danger of being defeated. The leaders then decide to change the conduct of the war, so that cities and mass centers of civilian populations are directly and deliberately targeted. Although the war began as a just war, the principle acts have now changed and the war has become unjust. And since the direct and voluntary killing of innocent human persons is murder, these principle acts are intrinsically evil and gravely immoral. The intended end of defending an entire nation from destruction, and the dire circumstances threatening the loss of many innocent lives, do not justify the use of intrinsically evil acts in the conduct

of the war. A nation may not use intrinsically evil acts in order to accomplish the good intended end of self-defense.

Sometimes during a war, individual persons will commit serious crimes, including various intrinsically evil acts, such as murder, rape, theft, etc. Such acts by individuals do not make the war as a whole intrinsically evil. But these acts must be condemned and prosecuted by the nation or group of nations with the ability to do so. And the leaders of each nation and each military must not direct, encourage, or permit such gravely immoral and intrinsically evil acts while they conduct the war.

.263. War is intrinsically evil when either the decision to go to war, or the principle acts by which the war is conducted, are intrinsically evil. A decision to commit an intrinsically evil act is itself an intrinsically evil act. The principle acts of a war, whether by order or by the customary behavior of the soldiers, must not include intrinsically evil acts, such as murder, rape, assaulting the innocent, imprisoning the innocent, robbing the innocent of their land and possessions, or subjugating human persons into slavery.

Examples of intrinsically evil types of war: (1) a genocidal war, with genocide being defined as a type of murder, (2) a war principally directed against innocent civilians, such as a nuclear war which targets population centers, (3) a war in which soldiers rape the civilians around them, whether by order or by common practice, (4) a war in which the soldiers the rob and steal from the surrounding population. All of these examples would make a war intrinsically evil, if they are the principle acts of that war.

It may be difficult to categorize a war in which some principle acts are intrinsically evil and gravely immoral, and other principle acts are moral. Similarly, sometimes a man will do much good in his life, but also much harm, and so it is difficult to say what his life was like. Regardless of the categorization of the war, all immoral acts remain immoral, and all moral acts remain moral.

A war that uses lying as part of the method of doing war does not become intrinsically evil, even though lying itself is intrinsically evil. For lying is not the type of act that is inherent to warfare; neither lying nor telling the truth is a principle act of war. However, killing and the movement of troops among a population are inherent to warfare. Therefore, any war that makes substantial use of the killing of innocent civilians, or of rape or looting (as the troops move among a population) would be an intrinsically evil war.

On the one hand, modern warfare has the capability to lessen the harm done by war. The population of a modern nation often has substantial influence over its government, so as to participate in a decision to go to war, or to cease from war. Communication and dissemination of information is greater than at any time in history. Modern weapons have a capability for precise targeting, so that the killing of innocents may be more easily avoided. On the other hand, modern weapons are capable of killing very large numbers of persons very quickly. And modern technology for information and communication can also be used to do great harm. This misuse of modern weapons and technology is possible, even by a relatively small number of persons, when they attain positions of leadership or control in a nation.

Second Vatican Council: "The horror and perversity of war is immensely magnified by the addition of scientific weapons. For acts of war involving these weapons can inflict massive and indiscriminate destruction, thus going far beyond the bounds of legitimate defense."[256]

---

[256] Second Vatican Council, Gaudium et Spes, n. 80.

Chapter 21
Slavery

.264.

The definition of slavery determines its morality. If we define slavery very broadly, so as to include such forms as indentured servitude, and the requirement that imprisoned criminals work, then slavery, broadly defined, would neither be intrinsically evil, nor always immoral.

Cardinal Avery Dulles: "Radical forms of slavery that deprive human beings of all personal rights are never morally permissible, but more or less moderate forms of subjection and servitude will always accompany the human condition."[257]

In the same article, Dulles considers teachings related to slavery as found in Sacred Tradition, Sacred Scripture, and the Magisterium. He finds that Catholic teaching does not condemn slavery, under its broad definition, as intrinsically evil, nor as always gravely immoral. This is because slavery, broadly defined, includes various degrees of subjection or servitude which are not inherently contrary to love of God and neighbor, and which may be moral with good intention and in certain circumstances. Thus, in ancient times, indentured servitude was a useful (though flawed) way to obtain work and the necessities of life, for a human person who otherwise would be destitute.

However, when slavery is narrowly defined, in what Dulles calls its 'radical' form, then slavery is always immoral. And this is the reason that the Second Vatican Council was able to unequivocally condemn slavery, despite many sources in Tradition, Scripture, Magisterium which permit the broader form in some circumstances. The context of the condemnation indicates that the Council was referring to the narrow form of slavery (which is also the way that the term 'slavery' is used in modern language).

Second Vatican Council: "Furthermore, whatever is opposed to life itself, such as any type of murder, genocide, abortion, euthanasia or willful self-destruction, whatever violates the integrity of the human person, such as mutilation, torments inflicted on body or mind, attempts to coerce the will itself; whatever insults human dignity, such as subhuman living conditions, arbitrary imprisonment, deportation, slavery, prostitution, the selling of women and children; as well as disgraceful working conditions, where men are treated as mere tools for profit, rather than as free and responsible persons; all these things and others of their like are infamies indeed. They poison human society, but they do more harm to those who practice them than those who suffer from the injury. Moreover, they are supreme dishonor to the Creator."[258]

The above list of immoral acts includes some acts that are intrinsically evil, such as murder. The list also includes acts which may be moral or immoral,

---

[257] Cardinal Avery Dulles, 'Development or Reversal?', First Things, October 2005.
[258] Second Vatican Council, Gaudium et Spes, n. 27.

depending on intention and circumstances, but which are not intrinsically evil, such as deportation. A nation may morally deport a person who has committed a crime, or who has entered the nation contrary to a just law. Arbitrary deportation would be intrinsically evil, but not all deportation. Other items in the list are not necessarily human acts at all, such as living and working conditions. The use of human persons as tools for profit is an immoral intention; but the act itself is not specified in this case. So this list is not solely a list of intrinsically evil acts. Therefore, the inclusion of slavery on the list is not sufficient to conclude that the Council was teaching that slavery is intrinsically evil.

.265. The Magisterium has long condemned the severe form of slavery, which is slavery narrowly defined, and which excludes moderate forms such as indentured servitude or requiring convicted criminals to work.

Pope Leo XIII: "This zeal of the Church for liberating the slaves has not languished with the passage of time; on the contrary, the more it bore fruit, the more eagerly it glowed. There are incontestable historical documents which attest to that fact, documents which commended to posterity the names of many of Our predecessors. Among them Saint Gregory the Great, Hadrian I, Alexander III, Innocent III, Gregory IX, Pius II, Leo X, Paul III, Urban VIII, Benedict XIV, Pius VII, and Gregory XVI stand out. They applied every effort to eliminate the institution of slavery wherever it existed. They also took care lest the seeds of slavery return to those places from which this evil institution had been cut away."[259]

However, this type of unequivocal condemnation of slavery was only applied to the narrow form of slavery. Pope Pius X refers to slavery in the narrow sense as "slavery, properly so called." He thereby excludes such forms as indentured servitude, and various other degrees of subjection and servitude.

Pope Pius X: "It is true that soon afterwards the worst of these indignities -- that is to say, slavery, properly so called -- was, by the goodness of the merciful God, abolished; and to this public abolition of slavery in Brazil and in other regions the excellent men who governed those Republics were greatly moved and encouraged by the maternal care and insistence of the Church."[260]

But in the many condemnations by the Church of slavery properly so called, there is no particular formal definition of slavery, neither one that would constitute an intrinsically evil act, nor one that would be gravely immoral but not intrinsically evil. Therefore, we must consider whether slavery, defined narrowly, is intrinsically evil and always gravely immoral, or gravely immoral without being intrinsically evil. An act might be defined such that the first or third font is immoral, even gravely immoral, but without being immoral under the second font. Such a definition would make the act always immoral, but not intrinsically evil. Every act that is intrinsically evil is also always immoral. But some acts that are always immoral are not intrinsically evil.

---

[259] Pope Leo XIII, Catholicae Ecclesiae, Encyclical on Slavery in the Missions, n. 1.
[260] Pope Pius X, Lacrimabili Statu, Encyclical on the Indians of South America to the Archbishops and Bishops of Latin America, n. 1.

.266. Slavery Defined Narrowly

One problem with defining slavery narrowly, such that slavery would be intrinsically evil, is that slavery is a set of acts. Traditionally, the term intrinsically evil has been applied to individual acts, such as murder, theft, lying. Most of the past magisterial condemnations of slavery, while clearly teaching that slavery, properly so called, is gravely immoral, do not address the question of whether or not slavery is intrinsically evil. And yet, in Veritatis Splendor, Pope John Paul II implies that slavery is intrinsically evil.[261] It is a development of doctrine to apply the term intrinsic evil to a closely-related but diverse set of acts, such as slavery or certain types of war.

The narrow definition of slavery does not include indentured servitude, which is called slavery in some Bible translations. Neither does it include merely requiring a person to work. Also excluded is the use of the term slavery as a figure of speech, as when sin is referred to as a type of slavery, or as when very difficult work conditions are called slavery. The narrow definition is what Pope Pius X termed "slavery, properly so called."

Slavery is a set of acts. In order to enslave someone, a single act does not suffice. Slavery is a diverse set of acts. Similarly, war is a diverse set of acts. A single act is not a war; various different types of acts are combined to constitute a war. A person is brought into slavery and kept in slavery by a series of related acts, such as the passing of unjust laws allowing slavery, the threat of force and the use of force to obtain and retain slaves, the kidnapping of human persons, the sale of human persons, the degradation of the slave, forced labor, disgraceful working and living conditions, and numerous other acts; these acts are part of what is usually called slavery. But if a particular set of acts includes only a subset of these acts, the set would still properly be called slavery, as long as certain essential elements are included.

Although the entire set of acts common to slavery is broad and varied, the acts that are essential to slavery, narrowly defined, are few. These are the acts which are always present whenever slavery occurs, and without which slavery does not occur. Each of these various acts deprives the human person of his or her fundamental human rights. When a human person has all of his or her fundamental rights, slavery is not possible. Or if a group of persons, being held in slavery, subsequently have all of their fundamental rights returned, then they are no longer slaves. They can choose where to live, and what work to do; they are free to make decisions for their own lives. They cannot be kidnapped, or sold, or owned, or falsely imprisoned, without these rights being grievously violated. There is no way to enslave a group of persons who are able to exercise all of their fundamental human rights. Therefore, the deprivation of fundamental human rights is essential to slavery; without this deprivation, slavery cannot occur. Other types of acts may occur with these acts, but these other acts by themselves

---

[261] Pope John Paul II, Veritatis Splendor, n. 80; Dulles argues that this implied conclusion was not a development of doctrine, and was unintended by the Pontiff.

do not constitute slavery unless they are accompanied by the deprivation of fundamental human rights.

Is the deprivation of fundamental human rights by itself sufficient to the definition of slavery? Suppose that a human person is deprived of all fundamental human rights, but the more common elements of slavery are not present, such as forced labor or racism. Such a person is nevertheless the victim of a type of slavery. For the deprivation of fundamental human rights is not merely an essential element in slavery, it is the essential meaning of the term. To say that someone is a slave is to say that they are deprived of their fundamental human rights. To make someone a slave is to deprive them of their fundamental human rights. And so the use of the term slavery to refer to any set of acts by which a person is deprived of all fundamental human rights is fitting, even if the more common elements of slavery are lacking.

This definition results in certain sets of acts being termed slavery beyond common usage of the word. But it is not unusual for the terms of moral theology to differ substantially from common language.

Example: When human persons are created by in vitro fertilization, human cloning, or any other form of artificial procreation, the resulting prenatals are often treated as if they were objects to be owned, used, and destroyed. The set of acts which creates, stores, and makes use of these human persons, treating them as mere physical objects, is a type of slavery.

Cardinal Nguyên Van Thuân: "Embryonic cloning violates the fundamental norms of human rights law.... Here there is a risk of a new form of racism, for the development of these techniques could lead to the creation of a 'sub-category of human beings,' destined basically for the convenience of certain others. This would be a new and terrible form of slavery."[262]

.267. Formal Definition of Slavery

Slavery is a set of acts; each of the essential acts of slavery directly and deliberately deprives the human person of all fundamental human rights. Each of these acts is intrinsically evil, because each is a direct and voluntary deprivation of a good required by the eternal moral law, required by true love of God and neighbor. The set of acts called slavery may be said to be intrinsically evil because each of the acts essential to the set are intrinsically evil, even though some of the non-essential acts may be gravely immoral, but not intrinsically evil.

The moral object of slavery, properly so called, is the deprivation of human rights. Although the concrete acts that result in this deprivation are various, each act has the same moral object, and so each act in this diverse set of acts has the

---

[262] François-Xavier Cardinal Nguyên Van Thuân, Pontifical Council for Justice and Peace, Contribution to the World Conference Against Racism held in Durban, South Africa (2001), no. 21;
http://www.vatican.va/roman_curia/pontifical_councils/justpeace/documents/rc_pc_justpeace_doc_20010829_comunicato-razzismo_en.html
See also: http://www.usccb.org/prolife/tdocs/cloning.shtml

same essential moral nature. Similarly, murder may be committed by many different concrete acts, by various acts of commission or even by acts of omission, and a person might even commit a set of acts of murder of various types. Yet the moral object of murder is always the same, the direct and deliberate deprivation of life from an innocent human person. Similarly, though slavery is a diverse set of acts, each act that is essential to the set has the same moral object, the deprivation of fundamental human rights.

If a set of acts deprives the human person of only some fundamental human rights, is that set properly called slavery? The rights that are fundamental to the human person are distinct, but not separate. All of these fundamental human rights are immediately based on the nature of the human person as created by God and in the image of God. In the practical case, when human persons are deprived of some, but not all, of these rights, the ones that remain are necessarily restricted in their exercise, or otherwise adversely affected. For all fundamental human rights are closely-related, being based in one and the same human nature created by the One God. Then, too, in many cases the erosion of rights continues until all basic human rights are lost or severely restricted. And so the fundamental human rights are like a train with numerous sections linked together; they all move together. And so any deprivation of most, but not all, of the fundamental human rights is still properly called slavery.

Consider also that, if a group of persons has no fundamental human rights, being in a state of severe slavery, the restoration of only one right, or of even a few rights, does not end the slavery. Therefore, not all fundamental human rights need to be taken away for the term slavery to be properly and narrowly applied. But even if, in a particular case, an individual or a group is deprived of only a few fundamental human rights, while most others remain, and even if this deprivation could not fittingly be called slavery, the acts that deprive human person of their fundamental human rights are nevertheless intrinsically evil and always gravely immoral. Every deprivation of any fundamental human right is immoral regardless of intention or circumstances. As is true for each and every intrinsically evil act, the acts that are essential to slavery remain immoral regardless of intention or circumstances, including the circumstance of the degree of severity.

If a group of persons are in a state of slavery, as a result of any set or subset of acts whatsoever, and if, one by one or all at once, they are allowed to exercise their fundamental human rights, the slavery necessarily ends. It is not possible to enslave any person or group of persons without depriving them of basic human rights. This deprivation is essential to the moral definition of slavery.

The essential moral nature of each act that is essential to slavery is inherently directed at the deprivation of fundamental human rights. Without such a deprivation, slavery would not exist. Any set of acts that deprives human persons of their fundamental human rights is a type of slavery (even if it is not customary to use the term in that instance). Any set of acts that does not deprive human persons of their fundamental human rights is not slavery, even if every act in that set is gravely immoral, or intrinsically evil.

.268. Second Vatican Council: "At the same time, however, there is a growing awareness of the exalted dignity proper to the human person, since he stands above all things, and his rights and duties are universal and inviolable. Therefore, there must be made available to all men everything necessary for leading a life truly human, such as food, clothing, and shelter; the right to choose a state of life freely and to found a family, the right to education, to employment, to a good reputation, to respect, to appropriate information, to activity in accord with the upright norm of one's own conscience, to protection of privacy and rightful freedom, even in matters religious."[263]

These fundamental human rights are possessed by each and every human person simply because each human person is created by God and in the image of God. These fundamental human rights are universal and inviolable. It is directly and inherently contrary to love of God and love of neighbor to violate these rights. Therefore, the direct and deliberate deprivation of these rights is intrinsically evil. Slavery is essentially a deprivation of fundamental human rights.

Pope John Paul II stated the essential moral nature of slavery when he taught that slavery is "a grave violation of fundamental human rights."[264]

Second Vatican Council: "At the same time let them put up a stubborn fight against any kind of slavery, whether social or political, and safeguard the basic rights of man under every political system."[265]

Both Pope John Paul II and the Second Vatican Council taught that slavery is essentially a type of deprivation of human rights. Therefore, slavery is narrowly and properly defined as a set of acts which directly and deliberately deprive the human person of fundamental human rights, to a substantial extent. The acts that are essential to slavery are acts that directly and deliberately deprive human persons of their fundamental human rights. Therefore, slavery, though it is a set of acts, can be properly called intrinsically evil.

A fundamental human right is a right that is inherent to human nature as created and intended by God. Although sinful secular society will sometimes claim that certain grave sins are rights or freedoms, no human person has a right to sin. No intrinsically evil act, no gravely immoral act, and no sin whatsoever, is a right or freedom, as those terms are properly understood. True freedom is found in avoiding sin. If any so-called right or freedom is contrary to the eternal moral law, then it is not a right or freedom at all, but a sin.

.269. Greater and Lesser Degrees of Slavery

Intrinsically evil acts are always immoral, regardless of degree. The smallest lie is still intrinsically evil, as is the smallest theft. If slavery is intrinsically evil, then slavery must be immoral, even in the smallest degree. But since slavery is a set of

---

[263] Second Vatican Council, Gaudium et Spes, n. 26.
[264] Pope John Paul II, Letter to Archbishop Jean-Louis Tauran, Secretary for Relations with States, On the Occasion of the International Conference 'Twenty-First Century Slavery: The Human Rights Dimension to Trafficking in Human Beings', para. 2.
[265] Second Vatican Council, Gaudium et Spes, n. 29.

acts, it is only necessary for each essential act to be intrinsically evil and always immoral, regardless of degree. In every case when a set of acts is considered, each act must be evaluated on its own as to its morality. Now each of the essential acts of slavery directly and deliberately deprives the human person of fundamental human rights. These acts constitute the basis for slavery; without this denial of fundamental rights, slavery cannot occur. And every such deprivation of rights is immoral, even to a small degree. For these are the rights that are inherent to human nature itself, as created by God. Therefore, any act, small or great, that directly and deliberately deprives a human person, or a group of human persons, of their fundamental human rights is intrinsically evil.

But because slavery is a set of acts, it is possible for the set to be reduced to such an extent that the set of acts, or a single act by itself, is not fittingly called slavery. Even so, each individual act that is essential to slavery remains intrinsically evil. For if even a single act directly and deliberately deprives a single human person of one fundamental human right, even to a limited extent, that act is inherently contrary to love of God and neighbor. So when these acts occur to such a limited extent that the term slavery does not apply, the acts themselves are still intrinsically evil. Therefore, slavery may be termed intrinsically evil, even though the same acts to a lesser degree are not slavery.

Slavery is a set of acts that directly and deliberately deprive the human person of fundamental human rights, to a substantial extent. If these same acts occur such that fundamental human rights are lost or compromised only to a limited extent, even if the acts are no longer fittingly called slavery, the acts remain intrinsically evil. The same reasoning applies to other moral definitions of sets of acts that may be termed intrinsically evil, such as certain types of unjust war. Even if these same acts within the war were to occur to such a limited extent that the set of acts, or an individual act, could not be properly called a war, the individual acts remain intrinsically evil and always immoral.

Now when slavery does occur, it may be more or less severe. When the Israelites were in slavery in Egypt, the degree of oppression increased as time passed:

[Exodus]
{1:12} "And the more they oppressed them, so much more did they multiply and increase."

Eventually, the degree of slavery increased to the point of depriving the Israelite male children of life, allowing only the female children to live (perhaps retained for sexual exploitation). Thus the Israelite people, especially the children, were treated as objects to be used or disposed of, and not as human persons with fundamental rights.

{1:22} Therefore, Pharaoh instructed all his people, saying: "Whatever will be born of the male sex, cast it into the river; whatever will be born of the female sex, retain it."

Slavery

Therefore, slavery can exist in greater and lesser degrees. But even when the degree is so slight that the acts are no longer properly called slavery, these same acts remain intrinsically evil and always immoral.

.270. The Essential Acts of Slavery

A number of different types of acts may be deliberately and inherently directed at the deprivation of fundamental human rights. Not all of these acts need be present for slavery to occur. Any set or subset of these intrinsically evil and gravely immoral acts, each of which is inherently ordered toward the evil moral object of the deprivation of fundamental human rights, would constitute slavery, as long as the set deprives the human person of fundamental rights to a substantial extent.

These essential acts include the acts by which the human person is brought into the state of slavery, such as by kidnapping, or by the selling of a human person. Kidnapping is a gravely immoral and intrinsically evil act. The selling of a human person of any age or state of life, even if they are a prenatal or infant, even if they are a convicted criminal or a prisoner of war, is gravely immoral and intrinsically evil. In ancient times, when enemy combatants were captured during a war, they were sometimes transferred from military custody into slavery. Although the capture of enemy combatants during a war may be moral, the subsequent transfer of these human person into slavery deprives them of their fundamental human rights.

The acts by which the human person is brought into slavery are various. A person might be kidnapped into slavery, as when an adult or child is taken for use as a slave. A person might be sold into slavery, as when a parent sells a child into slavery. A soldier might be captured in warfare, and then sold as a slave. A civilian might be taken during a war and then brought into slavery without buying or selling. Although the acts that bring a person into slavery are various, each of these acts is intrinsically evil. The act of kidnapping (whether of an adult or child) and the act of selling a human person are both intrinsically evil acts. Although capturing an enemy combatant during war is not intrinsically evil, and the subsequent transfer of the captured soldier into slavery, might occur without selling, this transfer of a human person into slavery is intrinsically evil. So no matter which particular act or set of acts is used to bring a human person into slavery, these acts are intrinsically evil.

It is always the case when slavery occurs that the human person was somehow brought into the state of slavery by some act or set of acts that are necessarily intrinsically evil and always gravely immoral. A person is brought into a state of slavery when his or her fundamental human rights are taken away. If a man and a woman, who are both slaves, bear a child, and if by law or custom or force that child is immediately considered also a slave, the act by which the child becomes a slave is intrinsically evil. Any law, custom, use of force, or any other act that directly and deliberately brings a human person into a state of slavery, a state of deprivation of fundamental human rights, is an intrinsically evil and gravely immoral act. Such acts include passing such a law, enforcing such a law, obeying such a law, as well as instituting, promoting, or continuing such a custom, and any use of force or the threat of force to do the same.

Recall also that the term 'direct', when used in moral theology concerning intrinsically evil acts, refers to moral directness; these acts might be physically direct, or physically indirect. The acts that bring a person into slavery might even be non-physical, as when the customs and beliefs of a society so strongly promote the enslavement of a class of persons that even the enslaved individuals tend to believe that they have no rights. In such cases, even if no physical means is used, directly or indirectly, to deprive human persons of their rights, the non-physical acts by which this deprivation occurs (e.g. the teaching and promotion of these customs and beliefs) are intrinsically evil.

No human person is created by God in a state of slavery. No human person can be morally reduced to a state of slavery due to his or her crimes, sins, choices, state of life, or any other act or circumstance whatsoever. No human person can be brought into slavery unless an intrinsically evil and gravely immoral act, or set of acts, has been committed. Therefore, the acts by which a human person is brought into slavery, i.e. those acts which initially take away the person's fundamental human rights, are essential acts within the moral definition of slavery.

.271. Once a human person is brought into a state of slavery, they cannot continue in that state unless other sinful acts are committed which continue to deprive them of their fundamental human rights. If a person is brought into slavery, but subsequently is permitted to exercise all fundamental human rights, then that person is no longer a slave. In order for slavery to continue, subsequent intrinsically evil acts must be committed to retain them in a state of slavery, in a state of deprivation of human rights. Such acts may even be acts of omission. All such acts by which the human person is retained in the state of slavery are intrinsically evil and always gravely immoral.

Examples of these intrinsically evil acts include: false imprisonment, violence and threats of violence against the innocent, the passing and enforcement of pro-slavery laws, the teaching of beliefs and the promotion of customs that directly support slavery, the sin of omission of denying fundamental human rights, and any similar acts. All these acts are intrinsically evil, and all these acts have the moral object of denying fundamental human rights to the human person.

The essential acts of slavery are of two types: those that bring the person into the state of deprivation of fundamental human rights, and those that continue to bind the person in that same state. Each of these acts is morally direct, regardless of whether the act is physically direct, or physically indirect, or non-physical.

Examples of physically direct acts: (1) kidnapping a person into slavery, (2) keeping a person in slavery with chains or bars, (3) the use of force against persons to bring them into slavery, or to punish them if they attempt to free themselves from slavery.

Examples of physically indirect acts: (1) the threat of force, (2) the payment of money, goods, or promises in order to bring someone into slavery, or to retain them in slavery, (3) the deprivation of basic human needs, such as adequate food, clothing, shelter, etc., in order to keep someone in slavery, so that they lack the resources to exercise their fundamental human rights.

Examples of non-physical acts: (1) the decision to obey or to enforce pro-slavery laws, (2) the decision to believe in racism, or caste systems, or other ideas that denigrate one group of human persons, eroding or denying their fundamental human rights, (3) the decision to adhere to pro-slavery customs, (4) the decision to omit assisting a human person whose fundamental rights are being denied.

The essential acts of slavery are therefore those acts that deprive and continue to deprive any human person of their fundamental human rights. These acts are necessarily a set of acts. For slavery is a continuous state, in which the human person lacks his or her fundamental rights. And since these rights belong to that human person merely by virtue of being human, it is intrinsically evil and always gravely immoral to deny the exercise those rights. Therefore, slavery is a set of acts that deprive and continue to deprive human persons of their fundamental human rights.

.272. Related Acts

Now other sins and crimes might have been committed against a person while in a state of slavery. Some of these acts may be intrinsically evil, and others may be immoral, even gravely immoral, but not intrinsically evil. Some of these acts may be intrinsically evil, but not deprive the person of fundamental human rights. Each knowingly chosen act stands on its own as to its morality. But the acts that are essential to slavery are each and all intrinsically evil and gravely immoral deprivations of fundamental human rights.

Certain acts are common to slavery, but not essential to its moral definition. The absence of these common elements does not necessarily imply the absence of slavery; the presence of these common elements does not necessarily imply the presence of slavery.

Slavery can occur without forced labor. Forced labor is often a part of the state of slavery. However, many nations as well as the United Nations, now recognize (by the light of reason and natural law) that some forms of slavery exist without forced labor. For example, when children are sold for the purpose of sexual exploitation, this is a type of slavery, but without forced labor.[266]

In another example, when persons in a society are part of a denigrated social caste, the members of which are treated as if they have no human rights, this is a type of slavery. These persons are in a state of deprivation of human rights; that state exists regardless of whether or not they are given work. If at first they have some type of lowly work, but next they are deprived of all work, they would be

---

[266] It would be absurd to claim that the victim of sexual exploitation is performing some kind of work merely by being abused in this way.

in a worse state of slavery, because they would still lack their fundamental human rights and would also lack any means to support themselves. Therefore, forced labor is not essential to slavery.

Forced labor can occur without slavery. For example, compelling convicted criminals to work is not slavery under the narrow definition, and is not intrinsically evil. A parent may morally compel a child to do chores and to do homework. An employer morally compels his employees to work, by offering pay and by the threat of firing. A government may morally compel citizens to perform military service, or jury duty, or some other work necessary to the common good. Soldiers may be compelled to march. In various situations, some persons might be morally compelled to do difficult or unpleasant tasks. As is clear from these examples, forced labor by itself is not slavery, and forced labor is not intrinsically evil. In some circumstances, forced labor is immoral; in other circumstances, forced labor is moral. The morality of forced labor depends on the first and third fonts; merely compelling someone to work is not slavery and is not necessarily immoral. The forced labor of slavery is gravely immoral, but not by itself intrinsically evil.

Mistreatment of various kinds commonly accompanies slavery. However, mistreatment alone is not slavery, and so it is not essential to the moral definition of slavery. For example, a human person might be given inadequate provisions, such as food, clothing, shelter, medical care, etc. The immorality is due to the degree and type of provisions that are given to the person. But the act itself of giving another human person food, clothing, shelter, medical care is not inherently evil. Now when the particular type and degree of provisions have the effect of helping to subjugate the individual, then the act is immoral, because of intention and circumstances. The intention to subjugate or to mistreat is in the first font. The inadequacy of the provisions or of the treatment is in the third font, since whether or not the provisions is adequate depends on the particular circumstances, such as the quantity and quality of the provisions, and whether what is available is fairly distributed. On the other hand, if entirely adequate provisions are given to a slave, the condition of slavery has not ended; a well-fed slave is still a slave. Or if a slave is relatively well-treated, but still lacks fundamental human rights, the condition of slavery has not ended; a well-treated slave is still a slave. In order to end slavery, all human persons must be given all fundamental human rights.

Slavery, though intrinsically evil and gravely immoral, may be accompanied by some good acts that are only incidental to the slavery, and are not a part of the formal definition, such as the opportunity to earn one's freedom, or being treated fairly by some persons at some times. But even if a slave is treated in a moral manner on occasion, any good acts toward the slave do not justify the immoral acts, nor is slavery itself, as a set of intrinsically evil acts, justified by incidental good acts that may also occur.

.273. Summary on Slavery

Slavery is properly and narrowly defined as a set of intrinsically evil acts, each of which directly and deliberately deprives the human person of fundamental human rights. The concrete acts by which the human person is deprived of fundamental human rights are varied, and so the set of acts in particular cases is also varied. But each act in the set is intrinsically evil and gravely immoral, and each act is of the same type, depriving the human person of fundamental human rights. These acts are essential to slavery, such that slavery does not occur without a set of acts of this type. Therefore, the set of acts called slavery is intrinsically evil and always gravely immoral.

If slavery is intrinsically evil, then why has the Church not condemned slavery as intrinsically evil and always gravely immoral? The reason is that the term slavery, as it is often used in Tradition and Scripture, refers to the broad definition, which is not intrinsically evil. Also, the term intrinsically evil is usually applied to a single act that is inherently directed toward an evil moral object. But slavery, even when defined narrowly, is a set of acts. And so it is a development of doctrine to begin to use the term intrinsically evil to refer to a set of acts, such as an intrinsically evil war, or the narrow definition of slavery.

The acts by which any human person is deprived of their fundamental human rights are always intrinsically evil, because the moral object is contrary to true love of God, in whose image we are each made, and contrary to true love of neighbor. Therefore, even though this deprivation of human rights is accomplished through a varied set of acts, since the moral object of each of the essential acts of slavery is evil, it is correct to say that slavery is intrinsically evil.

When we consider any set of acts whatsoever, it is nevertheless always true that each and every knowingly chosen act is subject to the eternal moral law. Each act must be good under all three fonts in order to avoid sin. If someone performs an act of kindness toward a person trapped in slavery, that good act remains moral, despite the grave immorality of slavery. Or if someone were to commit some sin, whether venial or mortal, during a set of very good acts, that bad act remains immoral, despite the goodness of the other acts. The classification of a set of acts as slavery, or as an unjust and intrinsically evil war, or as a just war, or any other classification, does not justify immoral acts, nor does it corrupt moral acts. Every good act remains moral, and every bad act remains immoral, regardless of the other acts that occur before, during, or after the act.

Chapter 22
Abortion and Contraception

.274.

Pope John Paul II: "Therefore, by the authority which Christ conferred upon Peter and his Successors, in communion with the Bishops -- who on various occasions have condemned abortion and who in the aforementioned consultation, albeit dispersed throughout the world, have shown unanimous agreement concerning this doctrine -- I declare that direct abortion, that is, abortion willed as an end or as a means, always constitutes a grave moral disorder, since it is the deliberate killing of an innocent human being. This doctrine is based upon the natural law and upon the written Word of God, is transmitted by the Church's Tradition and taught by the ordinary and universal Magisterium."[267]

Direct abortion is the direct and voluntary deprivation of the life of an innocent human being, prior to birth. Many of the faithful use the simple term 'abortion' to refer to direct abortion. Thus they correctly say that abortion is always wrong. Theologians (and certain magisterial documents) distinguish between direct abortion and indirect abortion, but the latter is not what is usually called abortion by the faithful.

Indirect abortion is a knowingly chosen act, usually a medical treatment given to a pregnant woman, which indirectly results in the death of the prenatal. Indirect abortion is not intrinsically evil and not always immoral, because it is not direct and voluntary. But neither is indirect abortion always moral. By definition, abortion is only indirect when, in the second font, the chosen act is inherently ordered toward a good moral object (such as the treatment of illness or injury in the mother), and, in the third font, the death of the prenatal is a consequence of that morally good act. Indirect abortion, by definition, always has a good second font; direct abortion, by definition, always has a bad second font. But for indirect abortion to be moral, the intention and the circumstances must also be good. Sometimes indirect abortion is moral, and sometimes it is immoral, depending on intention and circumstances. The death of the prenatal must be unintended; the intention must be only to save the life of the mother. And the likelihood of saving each life, or of saving both lives, must be weighed. To be moral, the good consequences of the chosen act must outweigh the bad.

Examples: (1) A pregnant woman has cancer. In this case, indirect abortion would be moral, if there is no way to save the life of the prenatal, and if the mother's life could be saved by a treatment directed at the mother's health, not at the death of the prenatal. (2) A pregnant woman has cancer. In this case, indirect abortion would not be moral, if there was a way to save the life of the prenatal, perhaps by waiting some length of time until the prenatal is viable and can be delivered, and if the additional risk to the mother is moderate. Treating the cancer immediately would result in the death of the prenatal, a death that can be

---

[267] Pope John Paul II, Evangelium Vitae, n. 62.

avoided. But waiting to treat the cancer would likely result in both lives being saved, and so the bad consequences of the additional risk to the mother is outweighed by the good consequences of saving two lives.

Unfortunately, some medical texts still refer to a miscarriage as a 'spontaneous abortion.' Moral theology does not use the term abortion to refer to miscarriages. A miscarriage involves the death of a prenatal, but that death is not direct or voluntary, and so it is not a direct abortion. Neither is a miscarriage an indirect abortion, since there was no knowingly chosen act at all which would result even indirectly in the death of the prenatal. Miscarriages are not sin, neither actual sin nor objective sin. Miscarriages are not a punishment for sin. They are the result of being in the fallen state, such that all human persons are subject to the possibility of injury, illness, and various types of harm and misfortune.

There are a number of different medical terms used to describe the human being during development, such as zygote, blastocyst, embryo, fetus. The term prenatal is defined as any human being from conception to birth, and includes every stage of development, from the single cell zygote until birth is completed, and every stage, at every point in time, from conception to birth. Prenatals are always innocent; they can never be killed justly, as if in self-defense. The direct and voluntary killing of a prenatal is the intrinsically evil act of direct abortion, and is always gravely immoral.

.275. Embryonic Stem Cell Research

If embryonic stem cell research (ESCR) could be done without death or harm to the prenatal, then it might be moral. However, at the present time, ESCR necessarily involves the morally direct and deliberate killing of the prenatal, an innocent human being. All such acts, regardless of the purpose for which they are done, and regardless of the circumstances in which they are done, constitute intrinsically evil acts of murder. This type of murder should be classified as a type of abortion, since the person who is killed is a prenatal.

Pope John Paul II: "This evaluation of the morality of abortion is to be applied also to the recent forms of intervention on human embryos which, although carried out for purposes legitimate in themselves, inevitably involve the killing of those embryos.... The killing of innocent human creatures, even if carried out to help others, constitutes an absolutely unacceptable act."[268]

The Roman Pontiff prudently uses the term 'human creatures,' within this teaching, in order to forestall any spurious claim that such embryos are not really 'human persons' or 'human beings' due to the method of creation or the stage of development. The teaching of the Catholic Faith is that the direct and voluntary killing of any innocent human, from conception to birth, and throughout all stages of life, is the absolutely immoral act of murder.

This definition of murder includes the killing of embryos or prenatals at any stage of development, for any purpose whatsoever. The intention (in the first font)

---

[268] Pope John Paul II, Evangelium Vitae, n. 63.

to use ESCR to develop cures for diseases, to save lives, and to end suffering, does not justify the direct and voluntary killing of those innocent, very young, human beings. The basic principles of morality always apply. Intrinsically evil acts are never justified by intention or circumstance. Even when the intention is not to kill, but to save lives, if the chosen act is inherently directed at killing an innocent, then the act is deliberate (i.e. intentionally chosen).

.276. Abortifacient Contraception

Conception usually occurs in the lateral one third of the fallopian tube; the conceived prenatal begins to develop while moving along the tube into the uterus, and next becomes implanted in the uterine wall. The implanted prenatal continues to develop, and also induces the development of the placenta within the uterus.

Certain types of contraception sometimes work by killing the conceived prenatal. Such contraceptives are called 'abortifacient' because, even if they usually work by preventing conception, they are able to cause an abortion. Prevention of implantation of the conceived prenatal inevitably results in the death of the prenatal; this is perhaps the most common way that abortifacient contraceptives kill the prenatal. Barrier methods of contraception are not generally abortifacient, unless they include an abortifacient chemical contraceptive, such as a spermicide, with the barrier method. Some spermicides are solely contraceptive; others are abortifacient.[269]

The choice to use abortifacient contraception is always the objective mortal sin of direct and voluntary abortion, because the chosen act is inherently directed at the death of the prenatal. Even if the intention of the person who uses the abortifacient is only to prevent conception, the act itself is nevertheless inherently ordered toward the death of the prenatal. Even if, in a particular circumstance, a prenatal is not killed, the act itself remains inherently ordered toward the death of the prenatal.

Whenever a person chooses an act, that act is properly called voluntary or deliberate, regardless of intention or circumstances. The choosing of the act makes the act voluntary; the intention (or purpose) for which the act was chosen is a separate font and therefore a separate consideration. The determination as to whether the chosen act is an actual sin, or merely an objective sin, is also a separate consideration. The use of abortifacient contraception is always an objective mortal sin. If the person did not realize that the method was abortifacient, then that person would not be guilty of the actual mortal sin of abortion, but would still be guilty of the mortal sin of using contraception.

The use of abortifacient contraceptives is inherently directed at two moral objects, each of which is gravely immoral: (1) preventing conception, (2) causing the death of the prenatal. Even when an early abortion does not occur, the use of an abortifacient is immoral, both because the act is inherently directed at

---

[269] Contraception Journal, Volume 54, Issue 6, Pages 323-393 (December 1996). http://www.ncbi.nlm.nih.gov/pubmed/8968666

contraception, and because the act inherently is directed at killing an innocent. For it is not the attainment of the moral object that makes the act immoral, but the inherent ordering of the act toward that moral object. The use of any type of contraception is an objective mortal sin. The use of abortifacient contraception is a more serious objective mortal sin, because the act itself is more seriously disordered (the moral object has a greater opposition to love of God and neighbor), and because more harm occurs in the consequences (the possible death of one or more prenatals). Those persons who use contraception or abortifacient contraception, freely choosing an act that they know is gravely immoral, are guilty of actual mortal sin.

The intention to use contraception solely to prevent pregnancy, without any intention to cause an early abortion, does not change the fact that the chosen act (the use of an abortifacient contraceptive) is inherently directed at abortion as well as contraception. The intention of the person who uses the contraception is the first font of morality; but the inherent ordering of the chosen act toward its moral object is the second font. Some persons might possibly use an abortifacient contraceptive with invincible ignorance, being unaware of the ability of the contraceptive to cause an early abortion. But even in such cases, the use of abortifacient contraceptives is an objective mortal sin, because the act remains inherently directed, not only at preventing conception, but also at killing the prenatal if conception occurs.

.277. The copper IUD (intra uterine device) at times works by preventing the implantation of the conceived prenatal. This abortifacient effect is proven by the fact that the copper IUD is sometimes used as a form of so-called emergency contraception, which is said to be 99.9% effective when used within 10 days after sexual relations: "Inserting a copper IUD within 10 days of coitus is more expensive but more effective than hormone tablets; pregnancy rate is 0.1%."[270] Conception can occur up to five days after, but most often occurs within three days, of sexual relations.[271] Implantation occurs 5 to 8 days after conception.[272] The pregnancy rate would not be only 0.1% if the copper IUD (inserted within 10 days) merely prevented conception, since conception generally does not occur more than 5 days after sexual relations. Therefore, the copper IUD sometimes kills the conceived prenatal, and is an abortifacient device.[273]

---

[270] The Merck Manuals Online Medical Library, The Merck Manual for Healthcare Professionals; Emergency Contraception; (Content last modified August 2007).
http://www.merck.com/mmpe/sec18/ch255/ch255b.html#sec18-ch255-ch255b-776
[271] Institute for Reproductive Health, Georgetown University, Standard Days Method: Scientific Basis (Retrieved on July 3, 2009).
http://www.irh.org/RTP-SDM.htm.
[272] Merck Manual for Healthcare Professionals, Conception and Prenatal Development; (Content last modified November 2005).
http://www.merck.com/mmpe/sec18/ch258/ch258a.html
[273] Some studies have examined the levels of hCG (a protein produced by the placenta) in order to claim that IUDs are not abortive. But since the IUD kills the conceived prenatal before implantation, there would be no placental development and no hCG protein.

Abortion and Contraception

It is well-established in medicine that various chemical contraceptives sometimes work by preventing implantation. They harm the ability of the endometrium (the lining of the uterus) to receive the conceived prenatal. Under Catholic teaching, any chemical or device which prevents implantation of the conceived prenatal thereby causes an abortion. The conceived prenatal cannot survive without implantation. And so the prenatal is killed, in a manner that is morally direct, by any chemical or device which prevents implantation. Some researchers have objected to the use of the term abortifacient on the basis that these contraceptives usually work by preventing conception, and less often work by preventing implantation.[274] But the frequency or infrequency with which the death of the innocent prenatal occurs does not affect the moral object. The abortifacient contraceptive is inherently ordered toward two intrinsically evil moral objects: (1) the prevention of conception, and (2) the killing of the prenatal.

The use of abortifacient contraceptives of every kind is so widespread in modern society, especially in the wealthier nations, that is it possible that more abortions occur as a result of abortifacient contraceptives than at all the abortion clinics in the world. If the world outlawed all surgical abortions, but still permitted abortifacient contraception, a very large number of abortions would still occur. In order to end all abortion, the world must cease from all surgical abortions, and all abortifacient contraception, and all other abortive acts (including embryonic stem cell research).

.278. Life Begins at Conception

The origin of each human life, in body and soul, at conception, is important to the moral definition of abortion.

A. The Incarnation of Our Lord Jesus Christ

1. At the Incarnation, the Son of God assumed a human nature composed of a rational soul and a body.

Council of Ephesus: "For if it is necessary to believe that being God by nature he became flesh, that is man ensouled with a rational soul...."[275]

Council of Ephesus: "We confess, then, our lord Jesus Christ, the only begotten Son of God, perfect God, and perfect man of a rational soul and a body, begotten before all ages from the Father in his godhead, the same in the last days, for us and for our salvation, born of Mary the virgin, according to his humanity, one and the same consubstantial with the Father in godhead and consubstantial with us in humanity, for a union of two natures took place."[276]

---

[274] "In terms of the IUD, there is accumulating research evidence that the device works primarily by preventing fertilization and, less frequently, by interfering with implantation." http://www.ncbi.nlm.nih.gov/pubmed/12283786
[275] Council of Ephesus, Third Letter of Cyril to Nestorius, approved by the Council.
[276] Council of Ephesus, Formula of union between Cyril and John of Antioch, approved by the Council.

2. In His human nature, Jesus is consubstantial with us, and is like us in all respects except for sin. His human nature is like our human nature, and our human nature is like His human nature (except that he is sinless).

Council of Chalcedon: "So, following the saintly fathers, we all with one voice teach the confession of one and the same Son, our Lord Jesus Christ: the same perfect in divinity and perfect in humanity, the same truly God and truly man, of a rational soul and a body; consubstantial with the Father as regards his divinity, and the same consubstantial with us as regards his humanity; like us in all respects except for sin...." [277]

3. The Incarnation occurred only once, when the Divine Nature of the Eternal Son of God was united to his human nature, body and soul, which was the same moment when his human nature, body and soul, was created.

Saint Thomas Aquinas, citing Saint Gregory the Great: "On the contrary, Gregory says (Moral. xviii): 'As soon as the angel announced it, as soon as the Spirit came down, the Word was in the womb, within the womb the Word was made flesh.'" [278]

Saint Thomas Aquinas, citing Saint John of Damascus: "On the contrary, Damascene says (De Fide Orth. iii): 'At the very instant that there was flesh, it was the flesh of the Word of God, it was flesh animated with a rational and intellectual soul.'" [279]

Saint Thomas Aquinas: "On the contrary, Augustine says (De Fide ad Petrum xviii): 'Hold steadfastly, and doubt not for a moment that Christ's flesh was not conceived in the Virgin's womb, before being assumed by the Word.'" [280] [The work cited is now believed to have been written by Saint Fulgentius.]

4. It is contrary to the teaching of the Catholic Faith to claim that the soul of Jesus Christ was created before or after His body, or before or after His virgin conception, or before or after His Incarnation, or that the Incarnation occurred at a different time for His body than for His soul, or that His body or soul ever existed before the Incarnation, or apart from the Incarnation. For even after the death of Jesus Christ, and before His Resurrection, His Divine Nature remained always united, at all times, to His body and to His soul.[281]

5. It is contrary to the dogma of the Incarnation to claim that the creation of the body of Jesus Christ, and the creation of the soul of Jesus Christ, and the union of body and soul, and the Incarnation of the Divine Nature with His human

---

[277] Council of Chalcedon, Definition of the Faith; cf. Hebrews 4:15)
[278] St. Thomas Aquinas, Summa Theologica, III, Q. 33, A. 1; Saint Gregory and Saint Thomas are both Doctors of the Church.
[279] St. Thomas Aquinas, Summa Theologica, III, Q. 33, A. 2; Saint John of Damascus and Saint Thomas are both Doctors of the Church.
[280] St. Thomas Aquinas, Summa Theologica, III, Q. 33, A. 3; Saint Fulgentius was a Bishop in Africa and an ardent follower of St. Augustine.
[281] St. Thomas Aquinas, Summa Theologica, III, Q. 50, A. 2 and 3; he cites St. John of Damascus, De Fide Orthodoxa, III.

nature, did not occur all in one and the same instant, at the moment of the Incarnation, which was the same as the moment of the virgin conception of the whole human nature of Jesus Christ.

6. In His human nature, Jesus is "like us in all respects except for sin," and is "consubstantial with us in humanity." Therefore, like the human nature of Christ, each human being is conceived such that body and soul are created in the same instant, and with body and soul united. The body is not created before the soul, nor is the soul created before the body; body and soul are created, as one human being, in the same instant. And the union of body and soul occurs at the same instant that both body and soul are created.

7. Therefore, what is true for Jesus in His humanity is also true for us in our humanity: the life of each human being, with body and soul united, begins at conception.

.279.
B. The Immaculate Conception of the Virgin Mary

1. The Blessed Virgin Mary was preserved free from all effects of original sin.

Pope Pius IX: "We declare, pronounce, and define that the doctrine which holds that the most Blessed Virgin Mary, in the first instant of her conception, by a singular grace and privilege granted by Almighty God, in view of the merits of Jesus Christ, the Savior of the human race, was preserved free from all stain of original sin, is a doctrine revealed by God and therefore to be believed firmly and constantly by all the faithful."[282]

2. Original sin effects both body and soul.

Council of Trent: "If any one does not confess that the first man, Adam, when he had transgressed the commandment of God in Paradise, immediately lost the holiness and justice wherein he had been constituted; and that he incurred, through the offence of that prevarication, the wrath and indignation of God, and consequently death, with which God had previously threatened him, and, together with death, captivity under his power who thenceforth had the empire of death, that is to say, the devil, and that the entire Adam, through that offence of prevarication, was changed, in body and soul, for the worse; let him be anathema."[283]

Council of Trent: "If any one asserts, that the prevarication of Adam injured himself alone, and not his posterity; and that the holiness and justice, received of God, which he lost, he lost for himself alone, and not for us also; or that he, being defiled by the sin of disobedience, has only transfused death, and pains of the body, into the whole human race, but not sin also, which is the death of the soul; let him be anathema:--whereas he contradicts the apostle who says; By one

---

[282] Pope Pius IX, Ineffabilis Deus, the definition.
[283] Council of Trent, Fifth Session, Decree on Original Sin, n. 1.

man sin entered into the world, and by sin death, and so death passed upon all men, in whom all have sinned."[284]

3. Therefore, the Virgin Mary was preserved free from the effects of original sin in both her body and her soul.

4. This preservation from all effects of original sin, in body and in soul, occurred in the first instant of her conception:

Pope Pius IX: "in the first instant of her conception [in primo instanti suae conceptionis] ... preserved immune from every stain of original sin [ab omni originalis culpae labe praeservatam immunem]"[285]

5. Therefore, the body and soul of the Virgin Mary were created at the same time, at her conception. If her soul were created before or after her body, or before or after her conception, then she would not have been preserved free from all effects of original sin, in body and in soul, in the first instant of her conception. The dogma of the Immaculate Conception requires us to believe that the body and soul of the Virgin Mary were created at the same time, and in the first instant of her conception.

6. Every single member of the human race is a human being composed of both a soul and a body:

Council of Ephesus: "In the same sort of way a human being, though he be composed of soul and body, is considered to be not dual, but rather one out of two."[286]

Pope Pius XII: "A marvelous vision, which makes us see the human race in the unity of one common origin in God 'one God and Father of all, Who is above all, and through all, and in us all' (Ephesians 4:6); in the unity of nature which in every man is equally composed of material body and spiritual, immortal soul...."[287]

Pope Pius XII: "The soul is not a person, but the soul, joined to the body, is a person."[288]

7. The Virgin Mary is a descendent of Adam and Eve, and a member of the human race. Her human nature, body and soul, is like the human nature of every member of the human race, and our human nature is like her human nature (except that she is sinless).

Second Vatican Council: "At the same time, however, because she belongs to the offspring of Adam she is one with all those who are to be saved."[289]

---

[284] Council of Trent, Fifth Session, Decree on Original Sin, n. 2.
[285] Pope Pius IX, Ineffabilis Deus, the definition; see footnote 29 for the Latin text.
[286] Council of Ephesus, Third Letter of Cyril to Nestorius, read into the acts of the Council.
[287] Pope Pius XII, Summi Pontificatus, n. 38.
[288] Pope Pius XII, Munificentissimus Deus, n. 32.
[289] Second Vatican Council, Lumen Gentium, n. 53.

Second Vatican Council: "Thus Mary, a daughter of Adam, consenting to the divine Word, became the mother of Jesus, the one and only Mediator."[290]

Pope John Paul II: "The Second Vatican Council prepares us for this by presenting in its teaching the Mother of God in the mystery of Christ and of the Church. If it is true, as the Council itself proclaims, that 'only in the mystery of the Incarnate Word does the mystery of man take on light,' then this principle must be applied in a very particular way to that exceptional 'daughter of the human race,' that extraordinary 'woman' who became the Mother of Christ. Only in the mystery of Christ is her mystery fully made clear."[291]

Pope John Paul II: "Following tradition, the Council does not hesitate to call Mary 'the Mother of Christ and mother of mankind': since she belongs to the offspring of Adam, she is one with all human beings...."[292]

8. Therefore, the Virgin Mary is also consubstantial with us in humanity and like us in all respects except for sin.

9. Therefore, what is true of the Virgin Mary is also true of us, the soul of each and every human being (i.e. each and every descendent of Adam and Eve) is created at the same instant as the body, which is the first instant of conception.[293] If this were not true, then the Virgin Mary would not be like us in all respects except for sin, and she would not be "the offspring of Adam" and "one with all human beings."

10. Therefore, every human being, beginning at the first instant of conception, is a human person, having both a body and a soul.

11. The first instant of conception is the single cell stage of development.

Sacred Congregation for the Doctrine of the Faith: "Thus the fruit of human generation, from the first moment of its existence, that is to say from the moment the zygote has formed, demands the unconditional respect that is morally due to the human being in his bodily and spiritual totality. The human being is to be respected and treated as a person from the moment of conception; and therefore from that same moment his rights as a person must be recognized, among which in the first place is the inviolable right of every innocent human being to life."[294]

Sacred Congregation for the Doctrine of the Faith: "The human being must be respected -- as a person -- from the very first instant of his existence."[295]

---

[290] Second Vatican Council, Lumen Gentium, n. 56.
[291] Pope John Paul II, Redemptoris Mater, n. 4.
[292] Pope John Paul II, Redemptoris Mater, n. 23.
[293] This statement does not address questions concerning the creation of Adam and the creation of Eve.
[294] Cardinal Ratzinger, CDF, Donum Vitae, I, 1.
[295] Cardinal Ratzinger, CDF, Donum Vitae, I. 1.

12. Therefore, from the moment of conception, even when the human being is only a single cell, and at any time from conception to birth, the killing of a human being is the sin of abortion, which is a type of murder. For murder is the direct and voluntary killing of an innocent human being, and all human beings prior to birth are certainly innocent.

There should be no debate among the faithful about the time of 'ensoulment', or about when a prenatal becomes a human person. The dogmas of the Incarnation and of the Immaculate Conception necessarily imply that, in the very same instant, the body is created, and the soul is created, and body and soul are one. A human being, at any stage of life, in any condition whatsoever, has a body and a soul; every human being with a body and a soul is a human person. The soul in particular is made directly by God, in the image of God. Therefore, human life must be protected from the moment of conception. All prenatal human beings are innocent human persons created by God and in the image of God.

.280. Contraception

Pontifical Council for the Family: "The Church has always taught the intrinsic evil of contraception, that is, of every marital act intentionally rendered unfruitful. This teaching is to be held as definitive and irreformable."[296]

Intrinsically evil acts are always properly and narrowly defined under the second font alone, independent of the first and third fonts. The use of contraception is intrinsically evil. Therefore, a proper definition of contraception does not include intention or circumstances.

There are two types of sins related to contraception.

First, every non-procreative sexual act is intrinsically evil and always gravely immoral. This includes contracepted acts of natural marital relations, as well as all unnatural sexual acts. Second, any usage of contraception is intrinsically evil and always gravely immoral. So if a woman takes a birth control pill on a daily basis, she sins daily, even if she does not have sexual relations on a particular day. For she has knowingly chosen an act inherently directed at a gravely evil moral object.

To be moral, each and every sexual act must be unitive, procreative, and marital. The good moral object of every moral sexual act is threefold: unitive, procreative, and marital. All non-unitive sexual acts are intrinsically evil, due to the deprivation of the unitive meaning in the moral object. All non-procreative acts are intrinsically evil, due to the deprivation of the procreative meaning in the moral object. All non-marital sexual acts are intrinsically evil, due to the deprivation of the marital meaning in the moral object. (See the chapters on Sexual Sins and on Marital Sexual Acts.)

---

[296] Pontifical Council for the Family, Vademecum ['Go with me'] for Confessors concerning some Aspects of the Morality of Conjugal Life, n. 2-4.

Contraception is defined as any deliberate act, regardless of the intended end or the circumstances, which directly deprives the sexual act of its procreative meaning.

Pope Paul VI: "Similarly excluded is any action which either before, at the moment of, or after sexual intercourse, is specifically intended to prevent procreation -- whether as an end or as a means."[297]

Pope John Paul II, quoting Pope Paul VI: " 'every action which, either in anticipation of the conjugal act, or in its accomplishment, or in the development of its natural consequences, proposes, whether as an end or as a means, to render procreation impossible.' "[298]

Two different translations of the same text from Humanae Vitae are quoted above. Since the deliberate and morally-direct deprivation of the procreative meaning from any sexual act is what constitutes contraception, the intention of the person is not essential to the definition. The first translation of the text above uses the word 'intended,' but this should not be understood as if the first font of intention determined the morality of the act. All intrinsically evil acts are deliberate, and this is the meaning of 'specifically intended,' i.e. a deliberate act. (So if a married couple are infertile, there is no deliberate act of contraception; the natural sexual act is still inherently directed at procreation, even though this end is unable to be attained.) The second wording is better for understanding the distinction between the intention in the first font, and the fact that the act itself in the second font is a deliberately chosen act. It is the chosen action itself which inherently proposes a non-procreative moral object.

.281. All contraceptive acts render the use of the genital sexual faculty non-procreative. Contraceptive acts done "in anticipation of the conjugal act" would include taking a contraceptive pill or applying a contraceptive barrier before sexual relations. Contraceptive acts done in the "accomplishment" of the sexual act would include the withdrawal method of contraception, and any inherently non-procreative sexual act. Contraceptive acts done "in the development of its [the conjugal act's] natural consequences" would include methods that interfere with conception after intercourse, such as spermicides and pills that prevent ovulation. The "development of its natural consequences" refers to the biological process after intercourse whereby the sperm travel toward the fallopian tubes, and the ovum is released, so that conception might occur.

Both Pope Paul VI and Pope John Paul II taught that the use of contraception is intrinsically evil and always gravely immoral, "whether as an end or as a means." A contraceptive act is an end when the purpose is to prevent conception. But even if the contraceptive is used as a means to another end, such as when chemical contraceptives are used to treat a medical problem, or when a barrier method is used to prevent disease transmission, the use of the contraceptive is intrinsically evil. The intended end of the usage of a contraceptive is in the first font; the effects are in the third font. But the usage of contraception (i.e. the act

---

[297] Pope Paul VI, Humanae Vitae, n. 14.
[298] Pope John Paul II, Familiaris Consortio, n. 32, quoting Humanae Vitae, n. 14.

itself) remains inherently directed at depriving the sexual act of its procreative meaning. A good intended end and good anticipated consequences do not change the inherent moral meaning of the act itself. Contraceptive acts are intrinsically evil. Contraceptive acts include taking a birth control pill on a daily basis, or making use of a barrier contraceptive, or any type of direct sterilization, as well as every non-procreative sexual act.

Examples: (1) A married couple use a contraceptive in order to avoid conception. Contraception is an intended end. The moral object of the act of using contraception (such as taking a contraceptive pill) is the direct and voluntary deprivation of the procreative meaning from the sexual act. Each and every contraceptive act is intrinsically evil and always gravely immoral. Each and every non-procreative sexual act is intrinsically evil and always gravely immoral.

(2) A husband has a serious disease that can be transmitted to his wife by sexual intercourse. The couple uses a barrier method of contraception in order to have sexual relations and prevent disease transmission. The use of the contraceptive is a means to the intended end of disease prevention. However, the chosen act itself is intrinsically evil, since the sexual act is deprived of the procreative meaning by a morally-direct and deliberately-chosen act. The good intended end of preventing disease transmission does not justify the intrinsically evil means of using a contraceptive. The moral object of any act is not changed by a change in intention or circumstances.

(3) A husband and wife engage in non-procreative sexual acts (i.e. unnatural sexual acts) with the intention of having sexual pleasure without the possibility of conception. The intended end is to avoid conception. The act itself is sexual relations deprived of its procreative meaning. All non-procreative sexual acts are intrinsically evil because the moral object every sexual act must be unitive, and procreative, and marital. In this case, both the intended end (contraception) and the act itself (each unnatural sexual act) are intrinsically evil and gravely immoral.

(4) A husband and wife engage in several non-procreative sexual acts (i.e. unnatural sexual acts) because they wish have sexual pleasure. They do not intend to avoid conception, and they also include some acts of natural marital relations open to life. The intended end of the unnatural sexual act is pleasure, not contraception. However, each and every unnatural sexual act is inherently deprived of the procreative meaning. And so each and every unnatural sexual act is intrinsically evil and always gravely immoral. In order to be moral, each and every sexual act must be unitive, and procreative, and marital. Unnatural sexual acts, even between a husband and wife, are not procreative. Neither are such acts truly unitive or truly marital. The sexual act of natural marital relations open to life is good, but each and every unnatural sexual act is intrinsically evil and always gravely immoral. To be moral, each and every sexual act must be unitive, and procreative, and marital.

.282. However, the birth control pill, in and of itself, is not intrinsically evil. Only knowingly chosen acts are intrinsically evil. Physical objects, even if those objects are generally used to commit an intrinsically evil act, are not themselves intrinsically evil. In some cases, the use of the birth control pill for non-contraceptive medical purposes would be moral, if the woman is not sexually active, or if the woman is post-menopausal, as long as the medication does not deprive the sexual act of its procreative meaning. In such cases, the moral object is not the deprivation of the procreative meaning, but the health of the woman.

Examples: (1) A married woman is post-menopausal, and she is prescribed the same hormone found in birth control pills for medical purposes. In this case, the pill does not deprive the marital sexual act of its procreative meaning, since the woman is no longer fertile. Therefore, in this case, the use of this medication is not a contraceptive act, and is morally licit.

(2) A single woman, who does not engage in pre-marital sexual relations, is prescribed the birth control pill in order to treat a medical condition (such as irregular and painful periods). The use of the birth control pill to regulate her monthly cycle, while she is not sexually active, is not a contraceptive act, and is morally licit.

(3) A married woman is prescribed the birth control pill in order to treat a medical condition. She continues to engage in sexual relations with her husband while using this medication. There are two types of acts that occur in this situation: first, the chosen act of taking a medication which has a contraceptive effect; second, the chosen act of having marital relations while on this medication.

(a) The act of taking the medication: The intention is to treat a medical condition; the first font is good. In the second font, the act itself is inherently ordered toward treating a medical condition, and so the second font is good. The chosen act has good and bad consequences. The good consequence is that the medical problem is treated. The contraceptive effect of the medication is in the third font, not the second font, because the medication is inherently directed at treating an illness. The bad consequences are that this married woman would have to refrain from sexual relations, in order to avoid the sin of contracepted sexual acts as well as the sin of a possible early abortion (since birth control pills are abortifacient). These bad consequences may or may not outweigh the good consequence of treating a health problem, depending on the seriousness of the condition.

(b) The act of having sexual relations while on the medication. Suppose that this married woman takes the prescribed medication, and she judges that, in her particular circumstances, the good consequences outweigh the bad. The act of choosing to have sexual relations while on the birth control pill (or any similar medication with a contraceptive effect) is a distinct act, and so all three fonts for this act must also be good in order for that act to be moral. Even if taking the medication is not intrinsically evil because the moral object is good health, the choice to have marital relations while on that medication is morally distinct.

In this case, the first font of intention is to express love between the spouses; so the first font is moral. The chosen act (second font) is to engage in sexual relations while taking a medication with a contraceptive effect. In order to be moral, each and every act of sexual relations must have all three meanings in its moral object: unitive, procreative, and marital. But the medication has the effect of making sexual relations non-procreative. The married couple is able to refrain from marital relations, while the illness is being treated. If they choose to have sexual relations, they have chosen a sexual act knowing that the act has been deprived of the procreative meaning by the other chosen act of taking the medication. If they have marital relations, they commit a mortal sin against God, because they chose to have contracepted sexual relations. The act of taking of the medication has a good second font, because it is ordered toward treating an illness. But the act of choosing to have contracepted sexual relations has a bad second font. The couple must refrain from all marital relations while she is on this medication.

.283. Furthermore, this mortal sin of having marital relations while the wife is taking a chemical contraceptive is made even more serious by the fact that chemical contraceptives are generally abortifacient; they are able to cause an abortion. The married couple is choosing an act (sexual relations while using an abortifacient contraceptive) which not only deprives the sexual act of the procreative meaning, but also includes a certain likelihood that, if the contraception fails and a child is conceived, an abortion would occur. Such an abortion can by no means be considered an indirect abortion, since the couple knowingly chose an act that is inherently directed at the abortion (having sexual relations while taking an abortifacient). They could have refrained from relations while she was on the medication. Or she could have sought a different type of treatment (perhaps from a Catholic physician). The death of the prenatal in this case is in the second font. The act of having sexual relations while using an abortifacient contraceptive is inherently directed at the evil moral object of non-procreative sexual union, and also at the moral object of the death of an innocent human being. In the third font, the possible death of a prenatal child outweighs the good effect of a married couple enjoying sexual relations.

(4) A married woman is prescribed the birth control pill in order to treat a medical condition. She continues to engage in sexual relations with her husband while using this medication. She also uses Natural Family Planning at the same time. Now some persons have tried to justify the use of a chemical contraceptive for medical purposes, when NFP is also used. The problem with this approach is that NFP neither adds, nor takes away, the procreative meaning from natural marital relations. The chemical contraceptive deprives the sexual act of its procreative meaning, and using NFP does not restore that procreative meaning. Therefore, this case is the same as the previous case in terms of morality. Also, NFP is not 100% effective, and so the use of a chemical contraceptive that is also an abortifacient, along with NFP, still presents an unacceptable (though reduced) risk that a conceived children will be aborted by the medication.

.284. Direct and Voluntary Sterilization

Pope Paul VI: "Therefore We base Our words on the first principles of a human and Christian doctrine of marriage when We are obliged once more to declare that the direct interruption of the generative process already begun and, above all, all direct abortion, even for therapeutic reasons, are to be absolutely excluded as lawful means of regulating the number of children. Equally to be condemned, as the magisterium of the Church has affirmed on many occasions, is direct sterilization, whether of the man or of the woman, whether permanent or temporary."[299]

The term "generative process" is a translation of a single Latin word, "generationis," signifying the process by which procreation occurs. The generative process is the process by which new life is generated. The direct interruption of "the generative process already begun" refers to a type of contraception. The process is said to have "already begun" when sexual relations has already occurred. So "the generative process already begun" refers to the time period and events after sexual relations and prior to conception. (The sperm move toward the fallopian tubes; the ovum is released and moves down the fallopian tube.)

But once conception itself has occurred, any "interruption" is actually an abortion, which then falls under the next portion of the same sentence, absolutely condemning all direct abortions for any reason. Therefore, the condemnation of "the direct interruption of the generative process already begun" only refers to methods of contraception used after the sexual act (e.g. the use of spermicides or chemical contraceptives after sexual relations in order to prevent conception). Other methods of contraception, used before or during the act, are also condemned unequivocally in the same document (in the very next sentence).

Notice that the term direct is used in condemning abortion ("direct abortion"), and sterilization ("direct sterilization"), as well as contraception ("direct interruption"). Intrinsically evil acts are always morally direct and deliberately chosen. If a woman undergoes a medical procedure, necessary due to some illness or injury, and one of the consequences of this treatment is sterility, temporary or permanent, the effect is in the third font, not the second font, and so this effect is morally indirect, not morally direct. Thus, a medically-necessary procedure, such as a hysterectomy, is not intrinsically evil, because the resultant sterility is not direct and deliberate (voluntary), and may be moral if the fonts of intention and circumstances are also good.

Pope Paul VI: "On the other hand, the Church does not consider at all illicit the use of those therapeutic means necessary to cure bodily diseases, even if a foreseeable impediment to procreation should result there from -- provided such impediment is not directly intended for any motive whatsoever."[300]

The term "foreseeable impediment to procreation" refers to the bad consequence (sterility) of an intrinsically good act (treating disease or injury). The bad consequence of sterility is in the third font because it is a reasonably anticipated result of the chosen act. Thus the sterility that results is morally indirect. Even so, the good consequence of treating the disease or injury must outweigh the bad consequence of sterility; otherwise the act is immoral. The intention must also be

---

[299] Pope Paul VI, Humanae Vitae, n. 14.
[300] Pope Paul VI, Humanae Vitae, n. 15.

good; and it is especially noteworthy that one must not intend the bad result of sterility. A woman who has a hysterectomy as a type of direct sterilization, not in order to treat an illness or injury, sins gravely. A woman who has a hysterectomy in order to treat a serious illness or injury does not sin.

Any morally indirect act, including indirect abortion and indirect sterilization, is by definition not intrinsically evil, and any such act may be morally permissible, but only if the first and third fonts are also good (intention and circumstances). The next section considers an all too common case when what might be termed 'indirect contraception' is morally permissible.

.285. Medical Interventions After Rape

All contraceptive acts (e.g. taking a birth control pill), and all contracepted sexual acts (e.g. choosing to engage in sexual acts not inherently ordered toward procreation) are intrinsically evil because they are the deliberate choice of an act that is inherently directed at a moral object deprived of a good (the procreative meaning) required by the eternal moral law. The use of contraceptives is intrinsically evil because sexual relations is inherently directed at conception.

Consider that withdrawal is one type of immoral contraception (cf. Gen 38:9). But if someone interrupts a rape that is in progress, this interruption of the rape is moral. The interruption of the sexual act of rape does not constitute the withdrawal method of contraception because the contraceptive effect is not the moral object, but an effect in the consequences of the act. The moral object of the interruption is to end an injustice to one's neighbor; as an act of love of neighbor, interrupting a rape in progress has a good moral object. And in the third font, the good consequence of stopping an act of severe physical, emotional, and mental harm outweighs the bad consequence of the contraceptive effect.

Similarly, after a rape is completed, if a women enters a hospital emergency room and is given a non-abortifacient spermicide, this medical intervention has the moral object of interrupting the rape. For conception is the natural and inherent aim of sexual intercourse. Therefore, this medical intervention is inherently directed at interrupting a rape, and the contraceptive effect is in the third font, not the second font. Thus, a non-abortifacient intervention to prevent conception in cases of rape does not meet the definition of contraception in moral terms. Every physical act of natural intercourse, even a rape, naturally progresses toward conception because the sexual faculty was designed for that purpose. And so the use of an intervention, what would ordinary be called a contraceptive, to prevent conception after a rape is an interruption of the rape itself. In terms of the moral analysis of the second font, this intervention is similar to indirect abortion and indirect sterilization, and so it might be termed 'indirect contraception.'

It is moral to interrupt a rape, because the act of interrupting is not a contraceptive act, but a moral act based on the positive precept requiring one to assist a neighbor in need. Since sexual intercourse is inherently aimed at conception, an intervention to prevent conception in cases of rape is an interruption of the rape (in terms of morality) and is therefore not a morally direct act of contraception. For the progress toward conception is a continuation of, and an inherent part of, the act of sexual intercourse (which in this case is also rape). Therefore, such an intervention (e.g. use of spermicides) is not contraception per se and is moral, as long as the intervention is not abortifacient.

An abortifacient cannot be used in such a case. Once a new human life begins, the direct and voluntary killing of that innocent human person is intrinsically evil and always gravely immoral. And conception is, in a sense, the completion of the sexual act. Killing a child conceived by rape does not interrupt the rape, but rather represents a second and more serious crime after the rape, the crime of murder.

A woman who has been raped might have previously conceived a child by her husband. Medical tests for pregnancy are only able to detect pregnancy about 2 or 3 weeks after conception. So it is possible that a woman who tests negative for pregnancy might still have conceived a child by her husband, prior to the rape. Or, if there is some length of time before the woman obtains medical help, she may have conceived a child from the rape. In either case, the new human life deserves the full protection due to any innocent human person. And so an abortifacient contraceptive must not be used in order to interrupt the rape, due to the significant risk that a prenatal might have been conceived and might be killed.

Contraception is intrinsically evil and always gravely immoral, because sexual intercourse is inherently aimed at conception. But for the same reason, the use of an intervention to prevent conception in cases of rape is not direct contraception. The progress toward conception is an inherent part of the rape, and so it is moral to interrupt the rape with an intervention to prevent conception.

.286. Medical Interventions for Ectopic Pregnancy

An ectopic pregnancy is a pregnancy in which implantation and growth of the prenatal occurs in the wrong location, usually outside the womb (the uterus). Ectopic pregnancies usually occur in the fallopian tubes, but they can also occur where the fallopian tubes open to the uterus (the cornua), in the ovaries, in the cervix (the neck of the womb), or in the abdominal or pelvic cavity.

In a significant percentage of ectopic pregnancies, the prenatal dies on its own because of the difficulties of proper growth outside the womb. Sometimes the woman is unaware of the ectopic pregnancy until after the death of the prenatal. If the prenatal has already died, it can be removed by a simple surgical procedure. There is no moral issue with the removal of an already deceased prenatal.

If the prenatal has not yet died on his own, the most likely result of an ectopic pregnancy is nevertheless the eventual death of the prenatal, and a substantial risk of harm or death to the mother. These substantial bad consequences of leaving an ectopic pregnancy untreated are in the third font, and are generally not outweighed by any good consequences. And so, it would not be moral to leave an ectopic pregnancy untreated, if a moral and effective treatment were available.

The use of a drug to kill the developing prenatal is nothing other than the direct and voluntary killing of an innocent human person. Such an intervention constitutes a direct abortion. Every direct abortion is intrinsically evil and always gravely immoral. The good of saving the life of the mother does not make a direct abortion moral. The morality of all intrinsically evil acts is independent of intention and circumstances. No matter how good the intention and no matter how dire the circumstances, direct abortion is always gravely immoral, even to save the life of the mother.

Surgical removal of a living ectopic prenatal is considered by some theologians to be immoral because it is a direct act. Certainly, all intrinsically evil acts are morally direct, but mere physical directness does not constitute moral directness. In the case of indirect abortion, the medication kills the prenatal and treats the illness of the mother (e.g. cancer) both in a physically direct manner; but morally the medication directly treats the disease of the mother and only indirectly kills the prenatal. Thus the death of the prenatal is in the third font, causing indirect abortion to be not intrinsically evil, and not always immoral.

Surgical removal of the fallopian tube with the prenatal is considered by some theologians to be the correct treatment, based on the claim that the fallopian tube is diseased and the removal of the tube directly treats the disease and indirectly kills the prenatal. However, it is factually false to say that the fallopian tube is diseased. Ectopic pregnancies also occur in the abdomen, in the pelvic cavity, in the cervix of the uterus, in the cornua of the uterus, or even in the ovaries. No one claims that the abdomen is diseased and must be removed as a treatment, or that the pelvic cavity is diseased, or that the cervix, or cornua, or ovaries are diseased and must be removed. For by definition, an ectopic pregnancy is the implantation and development of the prenatal in the wrong location; the term 'ectopic' means 'out of place.' Therefore, the disease is certainly found in the fact that the prenatal is growing in the wrong location.

Morally, the ideal treatment would be to remove the prenatal from the wrong location, and implant the prenatal in the correct location in the uterus. Medically, this is not currently possible.[301] Doctors and researchers have a moral obligation to research and develop a procedure whereby an ectopic pregnancy can be transplanted into the womb. They should also develop a similar procedure for transferring a prenatal from the womb of a mother with a serious illness or injury to the womb of a woman who is healthy. This type of procedure is not outside of the reach of modern medical science.

Since this medical disorder consists entirely in the fact that the prenatal is in the wrong location, removing the prenatal from that location treats the disease in a manner that is morally direct. The death of the prenatal as a result of this removal is indirect. If and when a medical procedure is developed that can move the prenatal from the wrong location to the womb, then the moral treatment would be to first remove the prenatal from the wrong location, then to implant

---

[301] One physician succeeded, in one case, in moving the prenatal to the uterus; a healthy child was born. Numerous subsequent attempts to replicate this procedure failed.

the prenatal in the correct location. If the same prenatal in the same mother had been implanted in the correct location, then there would be no disorder at all. From these considerations, it is clear that the removal of the prenatal from the wrong location does not kill the prenatal in a morally direct manner. Although the death of the prenatal as a result of removal is (or at least seems) physically direct, the death is morally indirect, and therefore not intrinsically evil. The removal directly treats the medical disorder of ectopic pregnancy. The death of the prenatal is an unintended consequence.

The surgical removal of a living ectopic prenatal is moral when all three fonts are good. In the first font, a good intention would be to protect the life of the mother from serious harm and risk of death. In the second font, the moral object is to directly treat the disease of ectopic pregnancy by removing the prenatal from the wrong location. Surgical removal has the good moral object of treating and protecting the health of the mother. This moral object, like all good moral objects, is a particular fulfillment of the positive precept to love your neighbor. In the third font, the good consequence of saving the life of the mother outweighs the bad consequence of the death of the prenatal, but only because the prenatal's life cannot be saved, and the mother's life can be saved. Since all three fonts are good, the surgical removal of a living ectopic prenatal is moral.

Chapter 23
Assisted Reproductive Technology

.287.
Artificial Procreation

There are no exceptions to the eternal moral law. Science is not exempt from the moral law. Procreation is not exempt from the moral law.

Sacred Congregation for the Doctrine of the Faith: "By 'artificial procreation' or 'artificial fertilization' are understood here the different technical procedures directed towards obtaining a human conception in a manner other than the sexual union of man and woman."[302]

The moral object of natural marital relations open to life is procreative, unitive, and marital. This threefold moral object renders the marital sexual act inherently good and moral; thus, the second font of natural marital relations open to life is good. Any sexual act that is non-procreative, or non-unitive, or non-marital is intrinsically evil and always gravely immoral. The eternal moral law of God requires that each and every marital sexual act be both unitive and procreative.[303]

Any unitive act that is not also procreative and marital is intrinsically evil and always gravely immoral. Any procreative act that is not also unitive and marital is intrinsically evil and always gravely immoral. The eternal moral law of God requires that procreation occur within marriage and by means of sexual union. The separation of the unitive and procreative meanings is always immoral, even within marriage. Artificial procreation brings about conception apart from the marital sexual act. Therefore, all types of artificial procreation are intrinsically evil and always gravely immoral.

In medical terminology, the various forms of artificial procreation are each a type of "assisted reproductive technology" (ART). Whenever assisted reproductive technology involves a separation of procreation from natural sexual relations, the act is intrinsically evil and always gravely immoral. Whenever assisted reproductive technology involves the direct and voluntary killing of an innocent human being, at any stage from conception and thereafter, the act is a type of murder, specifically a type of abortion. The good intention of assisting a couple in bearing a child, and the circumstance that the couple is unable to bear a child in the natural manner, do not justify committing a gravely immoral intrinsically evil act. Assisted reproductive technology (ART) includes various types of acts; some are immoral, and others are moral.

ART includes medical interventions in cases of fertility which do not involve artificial procreation or abortion. For example, a woman with fertility problems might be successfully treated with hormone therapy. In this case, the act itself of taking a medication to treat infertility is moral; the act is not intrinsically evil, and so the second font is good. For the overall act to be moral, the intention

---

[302] Cardinal Ratzinger, CDF, Donum Vitae, I. n. 6.
[303] Pope Paul VI, Humanae Vitae, n. 11-12.

must also be good, and the good consequences must outweigh any bad consequences. The hormone therapy must not represent an undue risk to the mother, nor to the conceived children. Similarly, any surgical procedure used to correct infertility (such as opening blocked fallopian tubes) would not be intrinsically evil, but must also be good under the first and third fonts (intention and consequences).

.288. ART includes the various types of artificial insemination, each of which takes sperm from the man and places it into the woman's reproductive tract (the fallopian tubes, or uterus, or cervix, etc.). Every form of artificial insemination is a type of artificial procreation, which separates the unitive marital sexual act from procreation. All such techniques, and any similar techniques that might be invented, are intrinsically evil and always gravely immoral.

In vitro fertilization (IVF) takes the gametes (sperm and ovum) from a man and woman, and artificially combines them, so that conception occurs outside of the woman's body, usually in a petri dish or similar container. The older technique is to simply combine the sperm and ovum in a petri dish in order to achieve conception. A newer technique uses specialized tools and equipment to inject one sperm into one ovum; this type of IVF technique is called ICSI (Intra Cytoplasmic Sperm Injection). After conception occurs, either the zygote is transferred into a fallopian tube (called ZIFT, zygote intra-fallopian transfer), or further development of the zygote, to the embryo stage, occurs, prior to embryo transfer (ET). Regardless of the particular technique, in vitro fertilization is a type of artificial procreation, which is intrinsically evil and always gravely immoral because it separates the unitive sexual act from procreation.

In vivo fertilization takes the gametes (sperm and ovum) from a man and woman, and combines them, apart from the marital act, so that conception occurs (by medical intervention) inside the woman's body, such as in a fallopian tube (called GIFT, gamete intra-fallopian transfer). In vivo fertilization is also a type of artificial procreation, and is therefore intrinsically evil and always gravely immoral because it separates the unitive sexual act from procreation.

Regardless of the technique used, once a human being is conceived, from the first moment of conception at the single cell stage and thereafter, the human being is a human person, with body and soul, created in the image of God. All such very young human persons are innocent, and therefore they have a right to life. The direct and voluntary killing of any innocent human being is murder, and is always gravely immoral. The direct and voluntary destruction of any embryo, regardless of how or why the embryo was created, is morally no different than the murder of an innocent infant or young child.

Human cloning produces a new human life from the cells of one person, even from cells that are not gametes. Any such technique of producing new human life, that is, a human being at any stage of development, apart from the natural sexual act, is intrinsically evil and always gravely immoral. Human cloning is therefore also intrinsically evil and always gravely immoral. The purpose and the circumstances of any act of human cloning, or of any other form of artificial procreation, does not change the inherent moral meaning of the act itself.

Artificial procreation is always gravely immoral, regardless of whether it is done for therapeutic purposes, such as to provide material for medical research, or to prevent or treat illness or injury, or for reproductive purposes, i.e. to produce a new child, or for any other purpose whatsoever. Good intentions and dire circumstances can never justify an intrinsically evil act.

Now even if some new method of artificial procreation is invented, any and all methods of artificial procreation, methods which separate procreation from the unitive martial sexual act, no matter what form these methods might take, are gravely contrary to the eternal moral law of God. Each and every act of artificial procreation is intrinsically evil and always gravely immoral.

Sacred Congregation for the Doctrine of the Faith: "The process of IVF and ET must be judged in itself and cannot borrow its definitive moral quality from the totality of conjugal life of which it becomes part, nor from the conjugal acts which may precede or follow it."[304]

IVF is In Vitro Fertilization, which brings about conception outside of the body, and ET is Embryo Transfer, which places the conceived embryo inside the body.

Even if the persons contributing gametes to a method of artificial procreation are husband and wife, the act of artificial procreation remains immoral because the unitive and procreative meanings are separated into different acts. The presence of the marital meaning does not justify the separation of the unitive and procreative meanings into different acts. In artificial procreation, the act by which new life is conceived is separated, by man on his own initiative, from the unitive act.

Pope Paul VI: "This particular doctrine, often expounded by the magisterium of the Church, is based on the inseparable connection, established by God, which man on his own initiative may not break, between the unitive significance and the procreative significance which are both inherent to the marriage act."[305]

.289. The Congregation rejected the idea, also rejected by Pope Paul VI in Humanae Vitae, that a set of acts might be combined, or might be considered as if they were one so-called 'continuous act', so that one act which is unitive and another act which is procreative would be morally sufficient to provide both the unitive and the procreative meanings. An act of artificial procreation is not justified by a prior or subsequent act of unitive marital relations.

In all areas of human life, each and every act stands on its own as to its morality. Therefore, what is said by the Congregation about non-unitive procreative acts may also be applied to non-procreative sexual acts. Each and every sexual act "must be judged in itself and cannot borrow its definitive moral quality from the totality of conjugal life of which it becomes part, nor from the conjugal acts

---

[304] Cardinal Ratzinger, CDF, Donum Vitae, II. n. 5.
[305] Pope Paul VI, Humanae Vitae, n. 12.

which may precede or follow it."³⁰⁶ Therefore, an unnatural sexual act is not justified by a prior, subsequent, or concurrent procreative sexual act. To be moral, each and every act must be unitive and procreative and marital. A set of acts cannot be combined, so as to obtain this threefold moral object by separate acts.

Each sexual act must be unitive, and procreative, and marital. It is just as immoral for a husband and wife to choose to engage in sexual acts that are non-procreative (i.e. unnatural sexual acts), as it is for a husband and wife to engage in procreative acts that are non-unitive. Even if the marital meaning is in some sense present in non-procreative acts or in non-unitive acts, any such act is intrinsically evil and always gravely immoral, unless all three meanings are present: unitive, procreative, marital.

Furthermore, artificial procreation is not procreation in the manner intended by God for men and women within marriage. Therefore, not only is the unitive meaning absent from acts of artificial procreation, but the procreative and martial meanings, though in some sense present, are harmed by the lack of the unitive meaning. Similarly, all unnatural sexual acts between a husband and wife are not only immoral due to the lack of the procreative meaning, but they are not truly unitive and not truly marital.

.290. Even so, any and all human beings who are created by any type of artificial procreation whatsoever are human persons made in the image of God, and are deserving of the same full set of human rights as all other human persons. If sin should happen to prevail in this life, to such an extent that some number of human beings would be created by various methods of artificial procreation, the method of artificial procreation is evil, but the human beings so created are not evil, but rather are made in the image of God.

Sacred Congregation for the Doctrine of the Faith: "From the moment of conception, the life of every human being is to be respected in an absolute way because man is the only creature on earth that God has 'wished for himself' and the spiritual soul of each man is 'immediately created' by God; his whole being bears the image of the Creator."³⁰⁷

If a human being is procreated by the sin of rape, or by the sin of artificial procreation, or by any other sin, that sin and its guilt is not attributable to the human person who was created, but only to those persons who knowingly chose to commit those sins. The new human life that is created is innocent of all personal sins, even if the act resulting in his or her creation is a grave sin. For no matter what method is used to create the human body, the human soul is always directly created by God, and the whole person is made in the image of God.

---

[306] Cardinal Ratzinger, CDF, Donum Vitae, II. n. 5; the CDF was referring to procreative acts that lack the unitive meaning. The author is applying the quote to any sexual acts that lack the procreative or unitive or marital meanings.
[307] Cardinal Ratzinger, CDF, Donum Vitae, n. 5.

Pope Pius XII: "for the Catholic faith obliges us to hold that souls are immediately created by God."[308]

Pope John Paul II: "The various techniques of artificial reproduction, which would seem to be at the service of life and which are frequently used with this intention, actually open the door to new threats against life. Apart from the fact that they are morally unacceptable, since they separate procreation from the fully human context of the conjugal act, these techniques have a high rate of failure: not just failure in relation to fertilization but with regard to the subsequent development of the embryo, which is exposed to the risk of death, generally within a very short space of time. Furthermore, the number of embryos produced is often greater than that needed for implantation in the woman's womb, and these so-called 'spare embryos' are then destroyed or used for research which, under the pretext of scientific or medical progress, in fact reduces human life to the level of simple 'biological material' to be freely disposed of."[309]

Artificial procreation is intrinsically evil and always gravely immoral, under the second font, and it also has bad consequences in the third font. Artificial procreation can "open the door to new threats against life." As assisted reproductive technology is currently practiced in the United States and other developed nations, many deaths of conceived human beings accompanies each successful birth. When artificial procreation occurs by in vitro fertilization (IVF), at least several eggs are fertilized; some are selected for transfer to the womb ("fresh"); some are selected for cryopreservation ("frozen"). But it is apparent that the remainder are immediately destroyed; this destruction is a type of very early abortion (since the human being is prenatal). The embryos that are cryopreserved stand very little chance of reaching development in the womb and birth, even less so than those that are immediately transferred to the womb. The vast majority of the embryos that result from in vitro fertilization do not survive to birth. A large percentage do not successfully implant in the womb, so as to form a placenta. Those that do survive to form a placenta are in danger of death: from an increased risk of miscarriage, from so-called embryo reduction (which is nothing else but direct abortion to reduce the number of embryos), from the possibility of direct abortion apart from embryo reduction. So it is clear that artificial procreation, which is gravely immoral in itself, is often accompanied by other gravely immoral acts, especially direct abortion.

.291. Embryo Freezing

Sacred Congregation for the Doctrine of the Faith: "The freezing of embryos, even when carried out in order to preserve the life of an embryo -- cryopreservation -- constitutes an offense against the respect due to human beings by exposing them to grave risks of death or harm to their physical integrity and depriving them, at least temporarily, of maternal shelter and

---

[308] Pope Pius XII, Humani Generis, n. 36.
[309] Pope John Paul II, Evangelium Vitae, n. 14.

gestation, thus placing them in a situation in which further offences and manipulation are possible."[310]

The freezing of a human embryo after creation is a distinct act from the act of artificial procreation used to create the embryo. Each act must stand on its own as to its morality. The intention might be to preserve the embryo for later implantation, gestation, and ultimately a live birth; such an intended end is good. However, the intended means (freezing, thawing, embryo transfer to the womb) presents a grave and substantial risk of death to this very young human person; thus, the intended means is immoral. Any intended immorality makes the first font bad.

The second font is the act of freezing the embryo, also called cryopreservation. The moral object of the act is to preserve the embryo, not to destroy him or her. The preservation of human life is not intrinsically evil. So the second font is good.

Example: Suppose that a woman unfortunately chooses to use artificial procreation to create an embryo, intending to have physicians transfer the embryo to her womb promptly (giving the embryo the best chance for life). However, she is seriously injured or becomes seriously ill, so that the embryo cannot be implanted in her womb at the current time. If the only way to possibly save the life of the human embryo is cryopreservation, then the act is moral. Such an act is inherently directed at preserving life, and so the second font is good. The intrinsically evil act of artificial procreation is a morally distinct act. The immorality of artificial procreation does not determine the morality of subsequent acts.

Also, the requirement to love your neighbor would positively require the woman and her physician to save the life of the human embryo, if at all possible. The grave sin committed in creating this very young human person in no way implies that he or she has no right to life. All such very young human persons are innocent of the serious sin committed by other persons in creating them by artificial means. To permit an embryo, frozen or otherwise, to die by inaction, when one is able to act to save this human person's life, would be the sin of murder by omission.

The third font is the good and bad consequences of the cryopreservation. The good consequence is the possibility for later implantation and birth; the chance for life. But there are several grave bad consequences. First, the circumstances are such that implantation soon after procreation gives the best chance for a live birth. Choosing to freeze the embryo in that circumstance is the immoral choice of a greater risk of death over a lesser risk of death. Second, the current state of medical technology is such that a very large percentage of frozen embryos that are intended for later implantation and birth will die despite all efforts to the contrary. Third, the current state of law and society is such that the frozen embryos are treated as if they were mere objects to be owned, used, misused, or destroyed at will; they are not treated as human persons. Therefore, the freezing of human embryos is not intrinsically evil, but is gravely immoral under the first

---

[310] Cardinal Ratzinger, CDF, Donum Vitae, I. n. 6

and third fonts of morality, except when absolutely necessary to save the life of the embryo.

Notice that, in the above quote from the Congregation for the Doctrine of the Faith, the freezing of embryos is not called intrinsically evil. The reason given by the Congregation for the immorality of cryopreservation is a description of the third font: "exposing them to grave risks of death or harm to their physical integrity and depriving them, at least temporarily, of maternal shelter and gestation, thus placing them in a situation in which further offences and manipulation are possible."[311] All of these factors pertain to the circumstances, not to the moral object of the act.

It is praiseworthy that Italy passed a law (in 2004) making the freezing of human embryos illegal, except in exceptional circumstances in order to preserve the life of the embryos (when the created embryos cannot be implanted immediately). Also outlawed were gamete donation, the use of embryos for research, and reproductive cloning.[312] Unfortunately, the same nation still permits artificial procreation and many related immoral acts. It is also worth noting that some other nations have passed laws discouraging the implantation of more than one embryo at a time.[313] When more than one embryo is implanted (or transferred, as they say), the risk of death to each embryo rises. Although artificial procreation and various related procedures of assisted reproductive technology are gravely immoral and still currently legal (as of 2009), there is an implicit admission of this immorality in some of the more recent laws on the subject.

As concluded above, the cryopreservation of human embryos is not intrinsically evil, but is usually gravely immoral under the first and third fonts of morality. However, other knowingly chosen acts occur after freezing, and those acts must be evaluated at to their morality on their own.

.292. Cryopreservation and Slavery

As explained in the earlier section on slavery, the essential moral nature of slavery is found in the deprivation of fundamental human rights. The slave is deprived of his or her human rights. These are not those so-called rights that are often claimed by sinful secular society in opposition to the eternal moral law and the moral teachings of the Church. Instead, these fundamental human rights are truly from God, and they belong to each and every human person merely by virtue of being human. The slave is deprived of these rights, and as a result he or she is treated like a piece of property to be owned, transferred to another owner (with or without payment), used or misused, and disposed of at will or whim. But in truth, no human being owns another human being; all human beings are children of God. Again I say, all human persons are children of God; they are

---

[311] Cardinal Ratzinger, CDF, Donum Vitae, I. n. 6
[312] Andrea Boggio, 'Italy enacts new law on medically assisted reproduction,' Human Reproduction, March 24, 2005;
http://humrep.oxfordjournals.org/cgi/reprint/deh871v1.pdf
[313] Belgium and a few of the Scandinavian nations, according to numerous sources.

not even owned as property by God. Whoever claims to own another human being, regardless of that person's age or state of life, makes a false claim.

Although one can conceive of a situation in which it would be moral under all three fonts of morality to freeze an embryo, such is not the current situation in society. Embryos are treated as if there were mere property, to be owned, transferred to another owner, used or misused, and disposed of at will or whim. The act itself of freezing of an embryo is not intrinsically evil. But subsequent acts with regard to the embryo, by which the human being, at such a young age, is treated as if he or she were a non-human piece of property, and is deprived of literally all fundamental human rights whatsoever, are a set of intrinsically evil and gravely immoral acts. And since this set of acts deprives these young human persons of all fundamental human rights, this is certainly a type of slavery.

Although slavery, as it has been practiced in human history, commonly involved forced labor or discrimination based on ethnicity, such common factors are not absolutely essential to slavery. Any set of acts which directly and deliberately deprives the human person of all fundamental human rights is a type of slavery, not merely as a figure of speech, but literally and fully. In fact, this new type of slavery (by the gravely immoral acts of artificial reproductive technology), only recently invented by science and culture, is worse than even the severe forms of slavery in past times.

The human person who is frozen at the embryo stage of development, at an age measured in days, not in years or even in months, is literally unable to exercise reason or free will, and is given no right to continue to develop or to eventually be born. The frozen embryo is stored at either the clinic where the embryo was artificially procreated, or at another facility which might not even be owned by the same clinic. Many of these embryos remain stored indefinitely, with no plans to attempt to give them further development and birth. Some embryos have been in storage for decades. Some of the married couples who 'own' the embryos are no longer reachable by mail or phone. Some of the 'owners' have stopped paying the expensive yearly fee for storage, resulting in the embryos being abandoned and eventually destroyed. In some cases, divorce has resulted in a dispute of 'ownership,' which may take years to decide in court.[314]

Some of the embryos are used for "quality assurance activities," and a few are even used for "embryology training." Both of these types of 'uses' result in the direct destruction of the embryo. Some embryos are used for medical research, and this, too, inevitably results in their direct destruction. Some embryos are specifically marked for destruction, merely because the 'owners' signed the appropriate paperwork. All of the aforementioned acts that directly destroy a human embryo are properly defined under the moral law as acts of murder, specifically as types of abortions (since the human persons are prenatal). Each of these acts is inherently directed at the moral object of the deprivation of life from

---

[314] Hoffman et al., Cryopreserved embryos in the United States and their availability for research, Fertility and Sterility, vol. 79, no. 5, May 2003.

innocent human persons; each of these acts is nothing other than the direct and voluntary killing of an innocent human person, which is murder.[315]

But before being killed, these embryos suffer the slavery of being treated as objects, rather than as human persons. And the essential acts of this type of slavery are each intrinsically evil and always gravely immoral, because each deprives these very young and very innocent human persons of all fundamental human rights.

.293. Surrogate Motherhood

Like embryo freezing, surrogate motherhood is not intrinsically evil, but is gravely immoral as it is currently commonly practiced. Again, the Congregation for the Doctrine of the Faith does not use the term intrinsic evil, and the basis for the determination of immorality is in the third font, not the second font.

Sacred Congregation for the Doctrine of the Faith: "Surrogate motherhood represents an objective failure to meet the obligations of maternal love, of conjugal fidelity and of responsible motherhood; it offends the dignity and the right of the child to be conceived, carried in the womb, brought into the world and brought up by his own parents; it sets up, to the detriment of families, a division between the physical, psychological and moral elements which constitute those families. By 'surrogate mother' the Instruction means:
a) the woman who carries in pregnancy an embryo implanted in her uterus and who is genetically a stranger to the embryo because it has been obtained through the union of the gametes of 'donors'. She carries the pregnancy with a pledge to surrender the baby once it is born to the party who commissioned or made the agreement for the pregnancy.
b) the woman who carries in pregnancy an embryo to whose procreation she has contributed the donation of her own ovum, fertilized through insemination with the sperm of a man other than her husband. She carries the pregnancy with a pledge to surrender the child once it is born to the party who commissioned or made the agreement for the pregnancy."[316]

In answering the question as to whether or not surrogate motherhood is morally licit, the Congregation limits the definition of surrogate motherhood to specific circumstances; thus, the morality depends on the third font. The circumstances described are in fact the most common use of surrogate motherhood; certainly, in these circumstances, surrogate motherhood is gravely immoral. The parents have not only chosen to use artificial procreation, which is intrinsically evil, but also have chosen to harm the bond of maternal love, by raising the child in the womb of another woman, to harm conjugal fidelity by involving a human person outside of the marriage bond in the gestation of the child, to harm the child by depriving that child of being developed and raised with these elements of maternal love and marital fidelity. In these circumstances, surrogate motherhood is gravely immoral.

---

[315] See the various acts described in: Hoffman, Cryopreserved embryos…, May 2003.
[316] Cardinal Ratzinger, CDF, Donum Vitae, II. A. n. 3.

But while the Sacred Congregation has not been lax, in recent instructions, to condemn whatever is intrinsically evil with the explicit declaration that the act is intrinsically evil, there is no such determination in the above quoted document. Nor is it implied by the reason given for the immorality of surrogate motherhood that such an act is intrinsically evil. Instead, the reason and the very definition of surrogate motherhood are dependent on the circumstances.

However, one can easily present a different circumstance, which uses a broader definition of surrogate motherhood, and which not only shows that the second font is good, but that the first and third fonts may also be good.

Example: (1) A pregnant woman is in a vehicular accident, and as a result, she can no longer carry the prenatal. But the prenatal not far enough advanced in development to be delivered. If medical technology would someday be able, with the willing assistance of another woman, the prenatal might be transferred into the other woman's womb, and so be given life instead of death. In this example, the child was conceived by natural marital relations, and the use of another woman in raising the child in the womb is of necessity. The moral object of the act is the saving of the life of an innocent person; the act itself is the medical procedure that is morally direct in accomplishing this good object. So the second font is good. The circumstances are such that the good consequence of saving an innocent life outweighs the bad consequence that another woman must raise the child in the womb, for a brief time. The intention is only to save an innocent life. Thus, all three fonts are good and the act is moral.

(2) A man and woman unfortunately commit the sin of artificial procreation. The couple freeze and then abandon that embryo. The only means to bring that very young human person to life is by a medical procedure where the embryo is transferred to the womb of another woman, not the biological mother of the embryo. The act itself is a medical procedure with the moral object of allowing a human person to develop and be born. The moral object is good because it is a particular fulfillment of the commandment to love your neighbor. The intention is to give development and birth to a human person, and to avoid the eventual death that would result from many years of being frozen. The circumstances are such that the embryo cannot be transferred to the womb of the mother. Perhaps she has died, or is unwilling, or is too old for a reasonable chance of success. The bad consequence of being raised in the womb of another woman is outweighed by the circumstance that this is the only path to continued life for this person. Thus, all three fonts are good and the act is moral.

Therefore, surrogate motherhood is not intrinsically evil, and may be moral, with good intention and when the good consequences outweigh the bad.

.294. Embryo Adoption

The analysis of the morality of embryo adoption (or 'prenatal adoption') is similar to that of surrogate motherhood. Both types of acts involve the transfer of an embryo to the womb of a woman who is not the mother of the child. Both acts are directed at the good moral object of giving life to an innocent and very young human person. But embryo adoption more specifically refers to the circumstance in which a frozen embryo cannot be given continued development, birth, and the possibility of a normal lifespan, except by being borne by a woman other than the mother. Embryo adoption transfers the parental guardianship and care of a prenatal child (a human embryo, usually frozen) from one woman to a second woman. Therefore, it is similar to adoption, and it is also a type of surrogate motherhood. Just as surrogate motherhood is not intrinsically evil and may be moral in some circumstances, embryo adoption likewise is not intrinsically evil and may be moral in some circumstances. However, as we will see below, the current circumstances are very difficult.

Sacred Congregation for the Doctrine of the Faith: "It has also been proposed, solely in order to allow human beings to be born who are otherwise condemned to destruction, that there could be a form of 'prenatal adoption'. This proposal, praiseworthy with regard to the intention of respecting and defending human life, presents however various problems not dissimilar to those mentioned above. All things considered, it needs to be recognized that the thousands of abandoned embryos represent a situation of injustice which in fact cannot be resolved."[317]

The Congregation states that the intention (first font) is good. The second font would be bad if prenatal adoption were intrinsically evil, and this would make the moral analysis of the situation relatively simple; intrinsically evil acts are always immoral. But the CDF does not state that prenatal adoption is intrinsically evil. In fact, the Congregation states the good moral object of prenatal adoption, "to allow human beings to be born who are otherwise condemned to destruction." Also, the CDF does not state that non-abandoned frozen embryos are in an irresolvable situation. Again, this indicates that the second font of morality is good, and that the immorality depends on the circumstances. A complex set of circumstances, summed up by the phrase "all things considered," is what makes this situation morally intractable.

But it is an irrefutable principle of morality that a good act, done with good intention, that is immoral only due to the circumstances, becomes moral when that same good act, done with good intention, can be done in different circumstances, such that the good consequences now outweigh any bad consequences. Therefore, in some circumstances, frozen embryos may be morally given development and birth by transfer to the womb of either the biological mother (for non-abandoned embryos) or a surrogate mother (for abandoned embryos, and for those that cannot be given life by means of their biological mother due to age, illness, or injury).

All acts of artificial procreation are intrinsically evil and always gravely immoral. But once the human person is created, he or she has a right to life. The immorality of surrogate motherhood is based on the third font, specifically, the bad consequences that can be reasonably anticipated when a prenatal is raised in the womb of a woman other than the mother. But since this immorality is not intrinsically evil (under the second font), in some grave circumstances the good consequences may outweigh these bad consequences. So if the frozen embryo (or

---

[317] Sacred Congregation for the Doctrine of the Faith, Dignitas Personae, n. 19.

for some grave reason, the fresh embryo) has no path to continued development and birth other than embryo adoption and/or surrogate motherhood, the act may be moral. A medical intervention to give life to a frozen embryo is not intrinsically evil; the morality depends on the third font.

.295. The first font of intention is good, which is to respect and defend human life. A frozen embryo may have no possibility for development, birth, and a normal lifespan without some type of embryo adoption or surrogate motherhood. The act itself of transferring the embryo to a woman's womb is a medical procedure inherently directed at giving life to a human person who otherwise would remain frozen until no longer viable (or until purposefully destroyed). Thus, the second font is good since the moral object is a particular fulfillment of the commandment to love your neighbor. Note also that, as with surrogate motherhood, the Congregation did not condemn embryo adoption as intrinsically evil. In fact, in this case the Congregation did not specifically state that embryo adoption is morally illicit.

An important circumstance (in the third font) to consider is that the number of frozen embryos worldwide is very large, and most are not planned for later implantation in the biological mother. They are stored in case the couple wishes an additional child, but usually none are planned. This results in storage occurring for many years, even indefinitely. But it is not reasonable to assume that such storage can continue indefinitely, without a substantial and continual decrease in the chances of successful thawing and implantation in the womb. Thus, if an embryo remains in storage indefinitely, he or she certainly dies, sooner or later. Remaining in cryopreservation is similar to a prisoner being on death row; he may be on death row for a longer or shorter period of time, but sooner or later he will die. This presents a very weighty consequence in favor of embryo adoption or surrogate motherhood: that a human person is given life who otherwise would die at a very young age, in a very innocent state.

Another circumstance is that parents of frozen embryos are charge storage fees of hundreds of dollars per year (in the future these fees might increase further). The parents are therefore pressured by economics to agree to the destruction of these embryos. Many couples unfortunately do not acknowledge that the deliberate destruction of human embryos is a form of murder. So as a result of ignorance about morality combined with economic pressure, frozen embryos are subject to a continuous danger of a parental decision to be deliberately killed.

Abandonment is another circumstance to consider; adoption and implantation in another woman, an adoptive mother, would be the only path to continued life for the abandoned frozen embryo. Another consideration is the age of the biological mother. When a frozen embryo is implanted in a woman over 35 years of age, and even more so if she is over 40, the chance of survival of the embryo drops dramatically. The bad consequence of a substantial increase in risk of death to the human embryo (who is in truth a prenatal child) would outweigh the good consequence of being carried to birth by the biological mother; implantation in a surrogate mother would carry a substantially lessened risk of death. Surrogate motherhood is not intrinsically evil, and is only immoral if the bad consequences outweigh the good consequences (or with bad intention). The risk of death to the very young human person, and the chance for development and birth, are the most weighty consequences. And so surrogate motherhood could be morally used to decrease the risk of death to the embryo, even if the embryo has not been abandoned by the mother.

Other circumstances include avoiding formal cooperation in the sin of artificial procreation. The woman who carries a child from a frozen embryo must not be involved in any type of agreement, in some way resulting in additional embryos being created for that woman. And the sin of scandal must be avoided, so that the woman who agrees to carry the child, and her husband, make it clear that they do not approve of, and will not formally cooperate with, artificial procreation or any other immoral ART procedure. There can be no 'embryo reduction' whereby several embryos are implanted, and if more than one or two survive, some are directly killed; this is a type of direct abortion. The number of embryos implanted should perhaps be one, since a higher number of embryos transferred to the womb means a greater risk of death to each. However, if the circumstances are such that there is an overwhelming number of frozen embryos in need of life, and few women who are willing to attempt to give them birth, two embryos might be implanted at a time. But if both develop successfully, then certainly both must be given life.

.296. However, it was because of very grave problems in the current circumstances regarding frozen embryos that the CDF stated the need to recognize that the situation of frozen embryos, especially those that have been abandoned by their parents, represent a situation of injustice which has no satisfactory moral resolution at the present time. These circumstances require a discussion of certain facts, as follows.

Some research into the current situation regarding frozen embryos reveals a very grave injustice that seems unable to be made right in the vast majority of cases. A 2003 survey in the United States found over 390,000 frozen embryos stored at 340 fertility clinics (called assisted reproductive technology or ART clinics), plus several thousand more stored in off-site facilities, plus an estimate of over 50,000 more in clinics that did not participate in the survey, but had participated in a 1999 survey, plus an unknown additional number from over 30 clinics which declined to provide any information. The same article cited other estimates in other surveys: over 50,000 frozen embryos in the United Kingdom (in 1996), and over 70,000 in Australia and New Zealand (in 2000).[318] The result is well over one half million frozen embryos. This figure does not include many nations known to have these same kind of clinics and services, and does not include additional embryos frozen since that time. Other statistics available indicate an increase in the use of fertility clinics since those surveys, implying a substantial and continued increase in the number of frozen embryos worldwide.[319] It is

---

[318] Hoffman, Cryopreserved embryos..., May 2003.
[319] See the U.S. Centers for Disease Control Assisted Reproductive Technology Report 2006, Section 5: ART Trends, 1996–2006; http://www.cdc.gov/ART/

entirely possible that the current number of frozen embryos worldwide (as of late 2009) has exceeded one million.

The chance of death to a frozen embryo is very high. The 2006 U.S. Centers for Disease Control ART Report, based on data reported by all U.S. ART clinics as required by law, states that the percentage of live births (at least one live infant born) for each transfer (embryos transferred to the womb) ranges from 20.0% to 27.4% for frozen embryos from non-donor eggs for women 40 years of age or less (the percentages are worse for women over 40). But this does not take into account the fact that the number of embryos transferred averages 2 or more. So in the best case of 27.4% live births for women under 35, the 72.6% without a live birth represents 2 or more deaths, and the 27.4% may include one or more deaths (since a live birth may be only one child, even though more than one embryo was transferred). And this also does not take into account the conservative estimate that at least 35% of frozen embryos do not survive thawing.[320] Nor does it account for the fact that about 5% of frozen embryos are awaiting destruction, or use in medical research (necessarily also resulting in destruction).[321]

If there is an attempt to give 100 frozen embryos development and birth, about 35 die in thawing (a conservative estimate).[322] Then of the 65 remaining, in the best case of women under 35 using non-donor eggs, 72.4% (again a conservative estimate) die after transfer to the womb, which is about 47 more deaths. Then the 18 embryos remaining (from the original 100) are within the 27.4% of transfers that result in at least one live birth. The number of embryos transferred averages at least 2. So the 18 remaining from the original 100 represent about 9 'transfers' (and therefore 9 women). Of those 9 transfers (of frozen embryos from non-donor eggs that resulted in live births), approx. 75.8% were single infants, 22.6% were two infants, 1.6% were three or more. So of those 9 transfers, about 6.8 have only one infant born, even though the average number of embryos implanted is over 2; so the 6.8 represents the death of at least 6.8 more embryos (out of every 100). The remaining 2.2 transfers had multiple births (2 or more infants born), but even in a percentage of these cases there may have been deaths, since three or more embryos may have been transferred, but only 1.6% of live births included three or more infants. There is not enough information given in the report to find the exact number of frozen embryo that died in all cases. However, the 2.2 transfers with multiple live births represents about 4.5 infants (average just over two) added to the 6.8 when only one infant is born. [Numbers do not add to 100 due to rounding.] Even if we assume that there were no deaths in cases of multiple births (which is sometimes not the case), the number of live infants surviving from the original 100 frozen embryos may be calculated very conservatively at about 11.3%.[323]

---

[320] Hoffman, Cryopreserved embryos..., May 2003.
[321] Hoffman, Cryopreserved embryos..., May 2003.
[322] Hoffman, Cryopreserved embryos..., May 2003.
[323] Data is from the U.S. Centers for Disease Control Assisted Reproductive Technology Report 2006, Section 5: ART Trends, 1996-2006; http://www.cdc.gov/ART/

Of the 100 frozen embryos, 35 die in thawing, 47 die in transfers that have no live births, and at least 6.8 die in transfers with multiple embryos but resulting in only one live birth. The result is 11.3% of frozen embryos that survived until birth. These numbers are very conservative estimates, based on the best case scenario, which is when the embryo is from non-donor eggs, and is implanted in the biological mother's womb, and she is under 35 years of age. The survival rates for frozen embryos transferred to older women are lower. The actual average survival rate for all frozen embryos that are thawed in an attempt to give them development and birth is almost certainly significantly lower, since in many cases the woman is either over 35 or donor eggs are used. And this does not account for the reasonable assumption that the longer an embryo is frozen, the more likely it will not survive thawing. Therefore, the actual chance that a frozen embryo will die during an attempt to bring that human person to further development and birth is most probably over 90%.

The ethical implications of this situation are immense. When the CDF stated that the situation of frozen embryos may be morally irresolvable, they were accounting for many different factors within the third font of morality. If the embryos remain frozen, the chance of successful thawing drops; eventually, any frozen embryo stored for a long enough period of time will not be able to be saved. But if we attempt to give those embryos life by either implanting in the biological mother, or in a surrogate mother, the chances of death are very likely over 90%. And if we allow them to remain frozen on the hope that science may find a method to reduce the 90% risk of death, such a method might not be found. And as we wait, the immoral use of ART continues, with many resultant deaths, even apart from the situation of frozen embryos. So it is likely that for 90% of frozen embryos, there is no path to life.

However, given that death is a near certainty if no attempt is made to save the lives of frozen embryos, weighing all of the circumstances, especially the good consequence of a chance at further development and birth, a faithful and reasonable Catholic might judge that the third font is good, and that the overall act of embryo adoption is moral, when done with good intention in order to attempt to save a life that otherwise would almost certainly be lost. The Sacred Congregation for the Doctrine of the Faith has not condemned either embryo adoption or surrogate motherhood as intrinsically evil. These acts have a good moral object because each is inherently directed at protecting and defending the life of a human embryo who, although unfortunately brought to life by artificial procreation, is made in the image of God and has the same right to life as all conceived human persons. Therefore, with good intention, and after carefully weighing the good and bad circumstances (as discussed in detail above), a faithful and reasonable Catholic married couple might morally choose to adopt an abandoned embryo and attempt to give that human person development in the womb, birth, and a chance at a normal lifespan.

.297. The Right to Life

Pope John Paul II: "As far as the right to life is concerned, every innocent human being is absolutely equal to all others. This equality is the basis of all authentic social relationships which, to be truly such, can only be founded on truth and justice, recognizing and protecting every man and woman as a person and not as an object to be used."[324]

Pope John Paul II: "…the Church has always taught and continues to teach that the result of human procreation, from the first moment of its existence, must be guaranteed that unconditional respect which is morally due to the human being in his or her totality and unity as body and spirit: 'The human being is to be respected and treated as a person from the moment of conception; and therefore from that same moment his rights as a person must be recognized, among which in the first place is the inviolable right of every innocent human being to life' "[325]

The most weighty circumstance in considering the morality of embryo adoption and surrogate motherhood is the right to life of the human person. Even when a human person is created by the immoral means of artificial procreation, once procreated, that human person has the same right to life as all other innocent human persons. Therefore, the parents of a frozen embryo (or of a procreated human person in any state or at any stage of life) have a grave moral obligation to attempt to give that human person continued development and birth.

Certainly, it is a mortal sin of omission to deny a seriously ill human person ordinary and necessary medical treatment; euthanasia is a type of murder which can be committed either by commission, or by omission.[326] Similarly, if the parents of frozen embryos refuse to attempt to save the lives of those very young human persons, allowing them to die by remaining frozen indefinitely, they commit the sin of murder by omission. But if the parents give permission for the frozen embryos to be directly destroyed in any way, they commit the sin of murder by commission.

This obligation to avoid committing the sin of murder by omission outweighs the bad consequences that occur from surrogate motherhood and embryo adoption, as well as from the risks of implanting the frozen embryo in the womb of the natural mother. Since no other path to continued life for frozen embryos is available, and since the acts involved are not intrinsically evil, the overall act is moral of implanting the frozen embryo in the womb of the natural mother, or, in grave circumstances, the womb of a surrogate mother.

Other members of society also have a grave obligation not to morally abandon frozen embryos, but instead to support laws and lawful acts that give these very young human persons the best chance for life. It would be a sin of omission to deny any available moral path to life for the many frozen embryos, who will almost certainly perish if kept frozen indefinitely. Society should pass laws outlawing all artificial procreation, outlawing the freezing of human embryos, and making it easier for the existing frozen embryos to have a path to life (such as by permitting embryo adoption, and by acknowledging in law the moral right to life already possessed by all human persons, even frozen embryos).

---

[324] Pope John Paul II, Evangelium Vitae, n. 57.
[325] Pope John Paul II, Evangelium Vitae, n. 60; inner quote from Donum Vitae, I. 1.
[326] Pope John Paul II, Evangelium Vitae, n. 65.

.298. Abortion and ART

The World Report on ART 2003 estimated "240,000 ART babies were born in the world in 2003" and "more than three million ART babies have been born since the first ART baby" (since 1978).[327] But the ratio of human embryos that are killed to those that are born, when ART (assisted reproductive technology) is used may be as high as 10 to 1 (or even higher). Even if the embryos are not frozen, it is apparently a common procedure to create more embryos in vitro than are needed, to select some for implantation, perhaps also to select some for cryopreservation, but then the remainder are apparently destroyed. The exact number or percentage killed is difficult to determine as ART clinics do not report the number of embryos created in vitro; they report the number of procedures, not the number of human lives. If we also take into account the high rate of failure of transferred embryos to form a placenta, and the high miscarriage rate for those that do form a placenta, the ratio of the number of embryos created by artificial procreation to the number that survive to be born is appallingly high. Most human persons created by artificial procreation are never born. If they are not directly destroyed, they are subject to very high risk of death. Therefore, if three million ART babies have been born from 1978 to 2003, the number who died would certainly be in the tens of millions. When we consider that the use of artificial procreation has increased steadily since 2003, ART begins to rival surgical abortions and abortifacient contraceptives as one of the top killers of prenatal human persons.

There are two types of abortion, direct and indirect; both types are associated with artificial procreation and assisted reproductive technology (ART). Direct abortion is intrinsically evil and always gravely immoral. ART uses direct abortion in various forms and under various disingenuous terms. When human persons are procreated by in vitro fertilization (IVF), it is apparently common to create more embryos than will be transferred to the womb; those that are not selected for transfer or freezing are summarily destroyed. (I say 'apparently' because, as far as I know, fertility clinics do not report or even keep track of these deaths. They do not consider or treat the human person at this early stage of development as a human being in any sense of the word. They treat these human persons as mere objects to be used, misused, or destroyed.) The direct destruction of a conceived human being, from the single cell zygote and in any stage of development thereafter, constitutes a type of murder, specifically a type of abortion when the murdered human person is prenatal. Every direct abortion is intrinsically evil and always gravely immoral, regardless of intention or circumstances.

Pope John Paul II: "But no word has the power to change the reality of things: procured abortion is the deliberate and direct killing, by whatever means it is

---

[327] World Report on ART 2003, International Committee for Monitoring Assisted Reproductive Technologies; http://www.medicalnewstoday.com/articles/75985.php

carried out, of a human being in the initial phase of his or her existence, extending from conception to birth."[328]

ART also uses direct abortion by a procedure disingenuously called embryo reduction. ART often transfers more than one embryo at a time to the mother's womb. If only one child is desired, and yet more than one embryo forms a placenta and begins to develop, one or more of these very young human persons will be directly killed by so-called embryo reduction.

Sacred Congregation for the Doctrine of the Faith: "Some techniques used in artificial procreation, above all the transfer of multiple embryos into the mother's womb, have caused a significant increase in the frequency of multiple pregnancy. This situation gives rise in turn to the practice of so-called embryo reduction, a procedure in which embryos or fetuses in the womb are directly exterminated.... From the ethical point of view, embryo reduction is an intentional selective abortion. It is in fact the deliberate and direct elimination of one or more innocent human beings in the initial phase of their existence and as such it always constitutes a grave moral disorder."[329]

ART also uses direct abortion on frozen embryos. If the parents of a frozen embryo decide to have those embryos destroyed, the fertility clinic carries out the direct destruction of these human embryos. This act by the parents constitutes the procuring of a direct abortion; the act by the clinic is the carrying out of a direct abortion. In such cases, both the parents and the persons at the clinic are guilty of direct homicide, i.e. murder.

Pope John Paul II: "No circumstance, no purpose, no law whatsoever can ever make licit an act which is intrinsically illicit, since it is contrary to the Law of God which is written in every human heart, knowable by reason itself, and proclaimed by the Church. This evaluation of the morality of abortion is to be applied also to the recent forms of intervention on human embryos...."[330]

.299. All acts of direct abortion, including the direct killing of any human person from conception to birth, are not only intrinsically evil and always gravely immoral, but are also subject to the penalty of excommunication.

Code of Canon Law: "A person who procures a completed abortion incurs a latae sententiae excommunication."[331]

Parents who give permission for their frozen embryos to be destroyed, or used for research (which inevitably results in their destruction), or used in any other way that results in their direct destruction, are guilty of the sin of abortion and fall under the penalty of automatic excommunication. Any one who directly and deliberately destroys a human being, from the single cell zygote stage and anytime thereafter, is also guilty of the sin of abortion, and also falls under the penalty of automatic excommunication. The sin of abortion includes destruction

---

[328] Pope John Paul II, Evangelium Vitae, n. 58.
[329] Sacred Congregation for the Doctrine of the Faith, Dignitas Personae, n. 21.
[330] Pope John Paul II, Evangelium Vitae, n. 62-63.
[331] Code of Canon Law for the Latin Church, 1983, Canon 1398.

of human beings at the time of their creation by artificial procreation, destruction of frozen embryos, use of frozen embryos for 'quality assurance activities' (which inevitably results in their destruction), use of embryos for medical research of any kind for any reason (again resulting in their destruction), so-called embryo reduction, induced abortion, and any other direct and voluntary killing of any human being from conception to birth, for any purpose, in any circumstance. All such acts are the sin of abortion. And all such sins of abortion fall under the penalty of excommunication.

Pope John Paul II: "…these techniques have a high rate of failure: not just failure in relation to fertilization but with regard to the subsequent development of the embryo, which is exposed to the risk of death, generally within a very short space of time."[332]

ART also results in many indirect abortions. Although indirect abortions are not intrinsically evil under the second font of morality, they may well be immoral under the first or third fonts of morality (intention and circumstances). As ART is generally practiced, these indirect abortions of prenatal human persons are gravely immoral. First, the artificial procreation of human embryos in vitro is not a flawless technique; human beings may be procreated who do not develop normally into embryos, resulting in their indirect death. These deaths are in addition to those viable embryos that are promptly and directly destroyed because they are not needed for transfer to the womb or for freezing. Second, an average of two or more embryos are transferred to the womb, but very often one or more embryos does not successfully implant (in that no placenta is formed). The result is that these embryos die; they cannot survive for long without a placenta. For those embryos who do form a placenta, the miscarriage rate is also very high.[333] In a majority of cases, even using so-called 'fresh' embryos (non-frozen), which have a higher success rate, and despite the transfer of an average of 2 or more embryos at a time, most transfers result in not even one live birth. The risk of death to a human person created by artificial procreation, regardless of which of several techniques is used, is much higher than for natural procreation. The choice of artificial procreation is a choice not only of an act that is intrinsically evil (second font), but which also has grave bad consequences in the third font, chiefly the high risk of death to the procreated human person. These deaths are indirect, since they are in the third font, not the second font. But there is no good consequence to an act of artificial procreation that can outweigh such a high risk of death to innocent human persons. Thus, the use of artificial procreation is gravely immoral under the third font of morality, as well as under the second font of morality.

---

[332] Pope John Paul II, Evangelium Vitae, n. 14.
[333] U.S. CDC ART Report 2006, p. 21.

Chapter 24
Sexual Sins

.300.
You will not be able to avoid serious sexual sin, unless you practice all the virtues, in cooperation with grace, every day.

[Matthew]
{12:43} "Now when an unclean spirit departs from a man, he walks through dry places, seeking rest, and he does not find it.
{12:44} Then he says, 'I will return to my house, from which I departed'. And arriving, he finds it vacant, swept clean, and decorated.
{12:45} Then he goes and takes with him seven other spirits more wicked than himself, and they enter in and live there. And in the end, the man becomes worse than he was at first. So, too, shall it be with this most wicked generation."

You will not be able to free your life from sin, unless you fill your life with virtue. If you merely learn a list of sins, and try to avoid those acts, you will not be able. For when you will seem to have rid yourself of one serious sin or another, you will soon find that the same sin returns, along with several other serious sins. You cannot remove darkness from a room, except by adding light. You cannot remove the darkness of sin from your soul, except by adding the light of virtue.

.301. The Three Theological Virtues

[1 Corinthians]
{13:13} But for now, these three continue: faith, hope, and charity. And the greatest of these is charity.

Pope John Paul II: " 'God has sent the Spirit of his Son into our hearts, crying, "Abba! Father!" ' (Gal 4:6). 'All who are led by the Spirit are children of God... It is that very Spirit bearing witness to our spirit that we are children of God' (Rom 8:14, 16). The words of the Apostle Paul remind us that the fundamental gift of the Spirit is sanctifying grace (gratia gratum faciens), with which we receive the theological virtues -- faith, hope and charity -- and all the infused virtues (virtutes infusae), which enable us to act under the influence of the Holy Spirit."[334]

At Baptism, we receive the three theological virtues, so called because they are infused by God and directed toward God. Charity is also called love. But this is not emotional love. Charity is the true spiritual love of God above all else, and also of our neighbor as ourselves. This threefold love of God, neighbor, self is the basis for the moral law, and the basis for the life of grace in the soul. Charity, the true spiritual love of God, neighbor, and self, is the greatest of all virtues. All who are in a state of grace have charity; all who are not in a state of grace do not have charity. (Those who are not in a state of grace can still cooperate with grace, in a limited way, from time to time, but not in the continual and full manner of those who are in a state of grace.)

---

[334] Pope John Paul II, Letter to Priests, Holy Thursday, 1998.

Faith is not human confidence, nor human faithfulness, nor the mere adherence to intellectual assertions. Faith is the true spiritual adherence to God who is Truth, and to the truths taught by God. Faith is assisted in its work by reason. But a true living faith believes beyond what reason can comprehend.

Hope is not human trust, nor the human anticipation of temporal goods. Hope is the true spiritual desire for, and trust in, God and our eternal life with God in Heaven. All three theological virtues are ordered toward God directly and immediately.

The infused theological virtues of love, faith, hope are given to us at our baptism. Those who have a state of grace by a baptism of desire also have these three infused virtues. No one can possess all three of these virtues without being in a state of sanctifying grace. The daily practice of the virtues of love, faith, hope, by means of prayer, self-denial, works of mercy, is the only path to a holy and moral life, free from serious sins of every kind, including sexual sins. This is the sole path to purity in this life and to the complete purity found in eternal life. There is no other way to avoid sexual sin.

.302. The Three Intellectual Virtues

The intellectual virtues are wisdom, understanding, and knowledge. Wisdom as an infused virtue is right judgment in accord with the eternal moral law.[335] And this virtue of "wisdom is not merely speculative, but also practical."[336] As this virtue pertains to sexuality, wisdom assists us in judging moral matters in the light of faith, so as to avoid sexual sin.

Understanding as an infused virtue is the sound intellectual grasp of truths, even those beyond the reach of reason, such as the revealed truths of the Faith. Understanding purifies the mind from false doctrines and foolish ideas. Understanding assists us in avoiding sexual sins. For although the whole moral law is accessible to reason, it is more easily and more firmly attained through faith in Divine Revelation. This infused virtue of understanding allows us to more fully perceive right from wrong than fallen reason alone.

Knowledge as an infused virtue is not the mere knowledge of facts; knowledge is the intellectual grasp of all that is good as distinguished from all that is evil. This gift includes knowledge of our sins and of the punishment due for sin. Thus the gift of knowledge also assists us in knowing what is and what is not a sexual sin, and in knowing which of our past acts were sexual sins.

.303. The Four Moral Virtues

Catechism of the Catholic Church: "To live well is nothing other than to love God with all one's heart, with all one's soul and with all one's efforts; from this it comes about that love is kept whole and uncorrupted (through temperance). No misfortune can disturb it (and this is fortitude). It obeys only God (and this is

---

[335] Saint Thomas Aquinas, Summa Theologica, II-II, Q. 45, A. 2.
[336] Saint Thomas Aquinas, Summa Theologica, II-II, Q. 45, A. 3.

justice), and is careful in discerning things, so as not to be surprised by deceit or trickery (and this is prudence)."[337]

The four moral virtues (also called cardinal virtues) are prudence, fortitude, temperance, justice. All four moral virtues have a pivotal role in helping us avoid sexual sin, as well as all other types of sin. (Virtue is a vast topic. For now, we will consider the usefulness of the moral virtues in avoiding sexual sins.)

Prudence is needed to choose the course of our life, and to avoid sin, and to select the acts that are more pleasing to God. Prudence is needed to judge complex circumstances in accord with reason and justice, so as to do good and to avoid doing harm. As an infused virtue, prudence is not merely the use of reason, but the use of reason and grace, in order to act wisely in particular circumstances. Prudence also assists us in avoiding occasions of sexual sins.

Fortitude helps us to stand firm in the Faith, and to resist temptation, and to persevere in the just and prudent path illuminated by faith and reason. Fortitude is especially important in avoiding sexual sins because the sexual drive found in fallen human nature makes us susceptible to sexual sins. As an infused virtue, fortitude extends beyond reason, to stand firm in doing the will of God despite all opposition.

Temperance as an infused virtue is not moderation and restraint for the sake of life in this world (e.g. when one refrains from certain foods in order to lose weight). Temperance in the faithful is moderation, restraint, and self-control for the sake of eternal life. We practice temperance not merely to act in accord with reason, but also to act in accord with grace, and with the perfect will of God.

The practice of temperance is found not only in avoiding what is sinful, but also in avoiding excess in what is not sinful. Temperance applies to all areas of life, but particular aspects of temperance are important in order to avoid sexual sins. Although sexual desire itself is not inherently evil, much self-restraint, exercised through the virtue of temperance, is required by the moral law, so as to give sexuality its proper place in human life.

The severe sins and great abuses that are possible when sexuality is expressed without any restraint are well-known to everyone who is aware of the sins and crimes of modern society. The three theological virtues always have the primary role when we cooperate with grace to avoid any sin. But the three intellectual virtues and the four moral virtues and are next in importance. The lack of temperance eventually leads to sinful self-indulgences of every kind, including many sexual sins.

Justice pertains to all areas of human life, including sexuality. All illicit sexual sins are inherently unjust; the moral nature of all such acts is gravely contrary to justice. The virtue to treat others justly requires us to refrain from every illicit sexual act, as well as from all sin. "Everyone who commits a sin, also commits

---

[337] Catechism of the Catholic Church, n. 1809.

iniquity. For sin is iniquity." (1 John 3:4). Iniquity means injustice. To be entirely just, a person must cooperate with grace and obey the moral law.

.304. For the unmarried, justice requires avoiding all sexual acts (i.e. all deliberate use of the genital sexual faculty). The only moral sexual act is found within marriage: natural marital relations open to life. Temperance assists the unmarried by enabling the person to avoid near occasions of sexual sins (interior sins and exterior sins). A dating relationship with a person of the opposite sex cannot include sexual acts of any kind. But neither would excessive indulgence in acts of mere physical affection be moral. Expressions of physical affection by unmarried couples are not intrinsically evil, but must be limited, because the couple must avoid occasions for serious sexual sins, including lust and any sexual acts at all outside of marriage. Temperance assists the faithful in making restrained use of what is moral, so as to avoid what is immoral.

For the married, justice requires avoiding all sexual acts other than natural marital relations open to life. But temperance is needed to avoid excessive indulgence in moral acts, such as moral foreplay, and natural marital relations. The married faithful must not only avoid objective mortal sin, they must strive to live holy lives, filled with virtue. The lack of temperance eventually leads to a marriage marred by selfishness and discord.

For both the married and the unmarried, temperance assists the faithful in making prudent and just, but limited use of modern forms of media. These forms of media often contain a degree of objectionable material (misrepresentations of what is moral, immodest or sensual material, excessive violence, and various influences toward immorality of every kind). Although use of such material is generally not intrinsically evil, temperance is needed so as to do good and to avoid doing evil. The virtue of temperance is needed by both the married and the unmarried in order to avoid both mortal sin and venial sin, and in order to live holy lives of self-restraint and devotion to God.

All the infused virtues (theological virtues, intellectual virtues, moral virtues) allow our free will to be more easily moved by grace, to more easily continue in grace, and to more easily avoid obstacles to grace. All these virtues assist us in avoiding sexual sin, in avoiding occasions for sexual sin, and in choosing those acts that are more perfect over those acts that are moral but less perfect.

.305. Modesty

Modesty can refer to self-restraint in every area of life.

Saint Thomas Aquinas: "Augustine says (De Morib. Eccl. xxi): 'In both Testaments the temperate man finds confirmation of the rule forbidding him to love the things of this life, or to deem any of them desirable for its own sake, and commanding him to avail himself of those things with the moderation of a user, not the attachment of a lover, in so far as they are requisite for the needs of this life and of his station.' "[338]

---

[338] Saint Thomas Aquinas, Summa Theologica, II-II, Q. 141, A. 6.

Or modesty can refer specifically to self-restraint in the area of sexuality.

Catechism of the Catholic Church: "Purity requires modesty, an integral part of temperance. Modesty protects the intimate center of the person. It means refusing to unveil what should remain hidden. It is ordered to chastity to whose sensitivity it bears witness. It guides how one looks at others and behaves toward them in conformity with the dignity of persons and their solidarity."[339]

Modesty in the area of sexuality includes all that is related to sexuality even generally, such as clothing, speech, behavior, etc. For married Christians, the self-restraint of modesty includes the moderate use of the only moral sexual act, which is natural marital relations open to life. As a part of the infused virtue of temperance, modesty is moderation, restraint, and self-control for the sake of eternal life, not only so as to act in accord with reason, but also so as to act in accord with the perfect will of God. The modest Christian avoids not only illicit sexual acts, but all sexual sins (even interior sins), all occasions for sexual sin, and any excessive use even of what is moral.

Modesty is temperance concerning all that is related to sexuality, and includes avoiding what is sinful, and limiting what is not sinful. Chastity is found in avoiding all objectively grave sexual sins. If anyone avoids all mortal sexual sins, he is certainly chaste. He might not be modest or pure, but he at least has chastity. The chaste Christian avoids all objective mortal sexual sins, including interior lust and exterior illicit sexual acts. And chaste married Christians do the same, but they may engage in natural marital relations open to life.

Purity includes modesty and chastity. If anyone is chaste, but immodest, he is not entirely pure. Pure Christians are not only chaste and modest, they also strive to avoid even venial sexual sins. Now all this pertains to sexuality.

But when purity is at its fullest, not only sexual sins, but all sins are avoided. All sin sullies the soul. All sin is impurity before God. All sin is unfaithfulness to God. So when the ancient Israelites strayed from the true Faith given to them by Divine Revelation, they were compared to an adulterous spouse (e.g. Jer 3:6-10). Therefore, perfect purity must include both bodily purity and spiritual purity. But within the human race, only Jesus and Mary are absolutely free from all sin (original sin and personal sin), and so only Jesus and Mary are absolutely perfect in purity. Though many a faithful Christian is properly called a chaste and pure virgin, no one who has any type of sin is truly a Virgin in the fullest sense of the word. The only two perfect Virgins are Jesus and Mary.

.306. Immodesty

Immodesty is the first step along a path that eventually leads to all the other, more serious, sexual sins. If someone is free from all sexual sins, he or she is also modest. Modesty protects against every kind of sexual sin. A person who perseveres in modesty in thought, word, and deed, in body and soul, cannot commit a sexual sin. All sexual sins are based upon immodesty.

---

[339] Catechism of the Catholic Church, n. 2521.

[Genesis]
{9:18} And so the sons of Noah, who came out of the ark, were Shem, Ham, and Japheth. Now Ham himself is the father of Canaan.
{9:19} These three are the sons of Noah. And from these all the family of mankind was spread over the whole earth.
{9:20} And Noah, a good farmer, began to cultivate the land, and he planted a vineyard.
{9:21} And by drinking its wine, he became inebriated and was naked in his tent.
{9:22} Because of this, when Ham, the father of Canaan, had indeed seen the privates of his father to be naked, he reported it to his two brothers outside.
{9:23} And truly, Shem and Japheth put a cloak upon their arms, and, advancing backwards, covered the privates of their father. And their faces were turned away, so that they did not see their father's manhood.
{9:24} Then Noah, awaking from the wine, when he had learned what his younger son had done to him,
{9:25} he said, "Cursed be Canaan, a servant of servants will he be to his brothers."
{9:26} And he said: "Blessed be the Lord God of Shem, let Canaan be his servant.
{9:27} May God enlarge Japheth, and may he live in the tents of Shem, and let Canaan be his servant."

What was the sin of Ham, that he would be cursed by his own father? Although some theologians have speculated that Ham committed one serious sexual sin or another, Sacred Scripture says only that Ham saw the nakedness of his father. Ham was immodest. He looked on his father's nakedness, and next he spoke about it to his brothers; he was immodest in what he saw and in what he said.

But this passage is not merely about the immodesty of one man, Ham. It is about the people of whom he was the father, Canaan. Now a man can be a father in two ways, either by literally (by blood) or figuratively (by some similarity). And so Abraham is said to have many descendents, both literally, in the Hebrew people, and figuratively, by similarity in way of life, in his spiritual descendents (Mt 3:9; Lk 1:55; 19:9; Rom 4:16).

Therefore, this passage from Genesis is not merely about the particular sin of immodesty committed by Ham on one occasion. Rather, it is about all the many serious sexual sins committed by the people of Canaan. The sin of immodesty committed by Ham in this particular case is used by Scripture as an example in order to teach that immodesty is the beginning of all sexual sins.

[Matthew]
{5:29} And if your right eye causes you to sin, root it out and cast it away from you. For it is better for you that one of your members perish, than that your whole body be cast into Hell.

Christ taught that immodesty of the eye leads to other sexual sins. To avoid those other sins, begin by 'rooting out' the immodesty in your eye, by no longer looking with immodesty at the things of this passing life. Christ was speaking figuratively; the body was created by God and is good, so we must not harm or maim our bodies, such as by rooting out an eye or cutting off a limb. But we should rid ourselves of sin, by 'rooting out' or 'cutting off' any knowing choice in our lives that is sin, or that leads to sin.

[1 Timothy]
{6:10} For desire is the root of all evils. Some persons, hungering in this way, have strayed from the faith and have entangled themselves in many sorrows.

.307. This teaching also applies to sexual sins. Inordinate sexual desire is the root of all sexual sins. Inordinate desire often begins with the eye (literally or figuratively). A person first gazes on the object of desire, either literally, with his eyes, or figuratively, with his heart and mind. Inordinate desire is the root of all sin. A person steals because he first desires the goods that belong to another. A person murders because he first desires to do harm to his neighbor. A person commits sexual sins because he first consents to inordinate desire in the heart, presented by the eye (literally or figuratively).

{6:22} The lamp of your body is your eye. If your eye is wholesome, your entire body will be filled with light.
{6:23} But if your eye has been corrupted, your entire body will be darkened. If then the light that is in you is darkness, how great will that darkness be!

Christ taught that the eye is the lamp of the body. God is Truth. And truth is comparable to light, not only because truth shows us the path to God, but also because all falsehood and ignorance is a deprivation of truth, just as darkness is a deprivation of light. The eye is used as a figure to indicate any means that a person uses to take in truth, to enlighten the mind and heart, including listening, reading, observing nature, observing other persons, watching television, using a computer, etc. All of the means by which a person learns can be a source of enlightenment. Christ is instructing us to make use of these means to bring light, that is, truth into our hearts and minds.

However, these same means can be used to take in immorality of every kind. If the eyes and ears are used to see and hear immorality, then these may influence us to sin. We should use prudent temperate judgment in what we read and watch, in every form of media (print, television, internet, any other media), so as not to sin, and so as not to be led into sin.

[Sirach]
{9:4} You should not be continually in need of entertainment, nor should you be persuaded by it, lest perhaps you may perish by its effectiveness.

How is it that the entertainers of today consider themselves to be sages? They make use of their positions in the media to presume to teach and to correct on every subject, yet without understanding. The ability to entertain is not the ability to understand. Such persons often promote ideas that are directly contrary to Catholic teaching. Some even openly attack the Church and the Faith. Their words are immodest in every way, and they have no fear of God. But they have great influence because modern society gives great importance to entertainment.

The inordinate desire to be entertained is a type of sinful self-indulgence, which may lead to many other sins.

{9:5} You should not stare at a virgin, lest perhaps you may be scandalized by her beauty.

By the grace of God, we may look upon our fellow human beings and see them as they truly are, as children of God like ourselves. This verse warns against a particular type of looking, i.e. with inordinate desire. The beauty of the human form may be admired without sin. But excessive attention to this lesser good can lead to sin. For we sin whenever we seek a lesser good in contradiction to a greater good.

{9:6} You should not give your soul, in any way, to fornicators, lest you destroy yourself and your inheritance.

Forms of entertainment that are filled with immodesty, or, what is far worse, with sexually-explicit material, are harmful to the soul. Such material can have a negative influence on our understanding and on our behavior, leading even to serious sin. The practice of modesty with the eyes and ears leads to modesty in the heart and mind. Every form of immodesty leads to every form of sin.

.308. Intrinsic Evil

Is immodesty intrinsically evil? Immodesty is a matter of degree. For example, consider the length of a woman's skirt. If it reaches to the ankles, it is not immodest in length. A shorter skirt does not, at some point, suddenly go from being modest at one length to sinfully immodest at a slightly shorter length. By degrees, a shorter skirt becomes first immodest as a matter of imperfection, and thereafter as a matter of venial sin. Intrinsically evil acts are never moral in one degree and immoral in another degree. Also, modesty and immodesty depend on circumstances. The same attire that is modest for the beach is sinfully immodest for the church. But intrinsically evil acts never change from moral to immoral solely by a change in circumstances. Therefore, immodesty is not intrinsically evil. Some acts are immodest to such a limited degree that the immodesty is an imperfection, not a sin.

If a form of media (television show, movie, book, etc.) is objectionable merely because of some limited immodesty, it is not intrinsically evil to watch that show. The immodesty in the show is in the circumstances of the act, not the moral object. Some bad circumstances can be tolerated in the third font without sin, as long as the good in the third font outweighs the bad. However, the consequences of watching an excessive amount of entertainment containing immodesty (and various other sins) should not be disregarded or underestimated. Many Catholics have fallen into heresy by believing the false teachings explicitly or implicitly expressed in various forms of modern media. And many Catholics have been led into serious sin, in part by various types of sin integrated into the entertainment shows found in modern forms of media.

.309. Chastity and Purity

[Wisdom]
{4:1} O how beautiful is the chaste fruit of purity! For its remembrance is immortal, because it is observed both with God and with men.

The chaste person avoids every objectively grave sexual sin, interior and exterior. The modest person practices self-restraint and self-denial in all that pertains to sexuality, in thought, word, and deed. Modesty in heart, mind, body, and soul, leads to chastity in heart, mind, body, and soul. But chastity and modesty are only the beginning of purity. True purity is freedom from every sexual sin, interior and exterior. And purity in the fullest sense is freedom from sin of every kind. Every modest and chaste life is pleasing to God. But every pure life is a reflection of the very Nature of God.

{4:9} and an immaculate life is a generation of sages.

If anyone is wise in words only, and not also in deeds, then he is not truly wise. An immaculate life, a life of modesty, chastity, and purity, a life unstained by sexual sins, is a life of great wisdom. This true wisdom is not confined to words. It is the wisdom of a life lived in cooperation with grace. A modest, chaste, and pure life offers more wisdom than a generation of sages.

{4:12} For fascination with entertainment obscures good things, and the unfaithfulness of desire subverts the mind without malice.

Christ warned us that the eye is the lamp of the body. But if anyone is fascinated with entertainment, especially the modern forms of entertainment that are so thoroughly tainted by sin, his eye is obscured. The more that we immerse ourselves in mere entertainment, especially sinful entertainment, the more difficult it becomes for us to understand what is truly good. Right and wrong become obscured; and this is all the more true for those poor souls who lack the light of the Church's teaching so as to distinguish right from wrong.

Entertainment itself is not intrinsically evil. Good entertainment can refresh the mind and heart, can be a respite from the difficulties of daily life, and can even give examples (in both fiction and non-fiction) of the goods found in humanity and in human relationships. Therefore, certainly, the faithful may morally make use of entertainment in their lives.

However, the warning of Sacred Scripture against the misuse of entertainment is true for all generations. The faithful must avoid the worst examples in various types of media, while distinguishing between good and evil even in the better examples of entertainment. And so, if a book or movie has some good and some bad in it, the faithful may judge whether reading that book or watching that movie will do more harm or more good. If making use of any example of entertainment is good under all three fonts (good intention, good moral object, the good consequences outweigh the bad), then its use is moral. Unfortunately, as society moves ever further from God, what is immoral in various forms of media increases, and what is good and useful decreases. The faithful must not be subverted by sinful desire or false teachings (implicit or explicit) when making moderate use of various forms of entertainment. In using modern forms of entertainment, the faithful must be careful to guard not only their eyes and ears, but also their hearts and minds, by means of that grace-filled restraint called modesty (a type of temperance). Sometimes modesty is exercised by self-restraint, by the moderate use of the things of the world, and other times by self-denial.

[1 John]
{2:15} Do not choose to love the world, nor the things that are in the world. If anyone loves the world, the charity of the Father is not in him.
{2:16} For all that is in the world is the desire of the flesh, and the desire of the eyes, and the arrogance of a life which is not of the Father, but is of the world.
{2:17} And the world is passing away, with its desire. But whoever does the will of God abides unto eternity.

While living in the world and making temperate use of worldly things, we must always remember that we are not of the world, but of God. The virtue of modesty assists us in loving God by guarding us against the impure desire for the things of this world, the desires of the flesh, the love of worldly passing things. Thus modesty opposes the false love of lesser things, freeing us to love the higher things of life. And this true love of the higher things in life is always ultimately directed at, and guided by, the love of God, who is the greatest Good.

.310. Marriage and Modesty

[Sirach]
{7:21} Do not choose to depart from a good and understanding wife, whom you have been allotted in the fear of the Lord. For the grace of her modesty is above gold.

A wife should be modest even before her husband, and a husband should be modest even before his wife. Whoever teaches immodesty to married couples, leads them away from Christ, and harms the Sacrament of Marriage. For the relationship between a husband and wife is a reflection of the relationship between Christ and His Church. Should Christ be immodest with His Bride, the Church? Should the Church be immodest before Christ? So then, neither should a husband and wife be immodest with one another, neither in thought, nor in word, nor in deed. For immodesty leads to every sexual sin.

Marriage is not an exception to the eternal moral law. Natural marital relations is morally good only when it is practiced in accord with morality. Lust within marriage is gravely immoral. If the spouses use one another for mere sexual pleasure, apart from love, faith, hope, apart from the primary goods of marital relations (found in the unitive, procreative, and marital meanings), then they sin seriously against God. And all unnatural sexual acts are intrinsically evil and always gravely immoral, even within marriage.

But lesser sins are also possible concerning sexuality within marriage. Even for a husband and wife, it is a sin to speak or act in a licentious manner, to speak or act as if marital relations were base or were merely for pleasure, to speak or act with immodesty and impurity. Certainly, modesty depends in part on intention and circumstances. Modest clothing in public differs from modest clothing before one's spouse at home. Modesty for a husband and wife differs from modesty for a man and woman who are dating but unmarried. Yet even spouses must have respect for the dignity of the body and of sexuality, and a holy fear of God, in order to avoid various misuses of the body and of sexuality.

A just war does not justify all acts of violence within that war. And a holy marriage does not justify all sexual acts within that marriage. The eternal moral law prohibits intrinsically evil and gravely immoral sexual acts, as well as acts that are not intrinsically evil, but are sinful due to intention or circumstances. So the thoughts, words, and deeds of immodesty are not justified by marriage.

Immodesty is not intrinsically evil, but is a matter of degree. And so, if the spouses fall into some limited degree of immodesty, this is an imperfection in a lesser degree, and a venial sin in a greater degree. However, whoever continues along this path of ever increasing immodesty eventually will fall into various mortal sexual sins. And severe immodesty itself may reach to the extent of a mortal sin, since immodestly concerns the important good of sexuality.

.311. Concupiscence

The husband and wife, joined in the holy Sacrament of Matrimony, remain nevertheless in the fallen state. Although baptism entirely wipes away original sin, there remains an effect of original sin in the human person called concupiscence, which is a tendency toward personal sin. Even the holiest of persons, if they were conceived with original sin, have concupiscence. Only Jesus and the Virgin Mary were conceived without original sin, and never had concupiscence. (Adam and Eve were created without original sin, but they later fell from grace, and as a result they had concupiscence.) We mere weak and mortal sinners must always struggle against this tendency toward selfishness, toward valuing lesser goods over greater goods, toward the disorder of values that is the basis for sin.

Therefore, throughout any marriage, both spouses must continually struggle against the misuse of sexuality. For sexuality has great power to do good within marriage (uniting the spouses, procreating children, strengthening the marriage) and yet great power to do harm within marriage. Its potential for harm is in proportion to its potential for benefit. There is an intrinsic danger to sexuality.[340]

The potential of sexuality to unite the spouses has a counterpart when sexuality is misused within marriage, even if only by immodest thoughts, words, and deeds. The spouses can be pushed apart by this misuse of the gift of sexuality, resulting in disunity. Sin of any kind, mortal or venial, does not cooperate with grace and does not benefit any relationship. Although there might seem to be some short-term benefits if the spouses behave in a licentious or immodest

---

[340] Cf. Dietrich von Hildebrand, In Defense of Purity, An analysis of the Catholic ideals of purity and virginity, Part III: The Attitude of the Pure in Marriage, I. The Intrinsic Dangers of Sex; (New York: Sheed and Ward, 1935) p. 89.

manner, the spiritual harm, and the harm to the marriage relationship in the long term, is much weightier.

Modesty within marriage requires the spouses to treat one another as whole persons, with respect and affection, and with a holy fear of sin. Modesty within marriage requires the spouses to view sexuality as integral to the Sacrament of Marriage, and not as a mere source of entertainment or pleasure. Modesty within marriage requires the spouses to subjugate the lesser goods of sexuality (pleasure, emotions), to the higher goods of sexuality (the unitive, procreative, and marital meanings), and to the marriage as a whole. Respect for the human body as a gift from God requires the spouses to act with self-restraint or even self-denial, and to avoid excessive indulgence in even lawful acts.

.312. Chrysostom on Modesty in Marriage

Saint John Chrysostom: "Beginning on their wedding night, let him be an example of gentleness, temperance, and self-control; and she will be likewise."[341]

When St. John says "beginning on their wedding night," he is not unaware that the wedding night is the first time that the spouses have marital relations. And yet it is at this point that he recommends "gentleness, temperance, and self-control." The marital bedroom is not an excuse for sexual excess. The spouses are bound by the moral law not only to reject all intrinsically evil acts, but also to choose acts that are moral in intention and in circumstances. Moreover, merely avoiding sin is not the aim of a Christian life. We are called to holiness and to continually strive for more perfect behavior. The spouses cannot use the marital bedroom as an excuse for any sin, nor for behaving in any manner that would be unbecoming of disciples of Christ.

If anyone teaches that a husband and wife in any marriage, but most especially in the Sacrament of holy Matrimony, are free, within the marital bedroom, from modesty and self-restraint, from shame and a holy fear of sin, it is proof that he has gone astray from the true Gospel of Jesus Christ, in order to teach the false gospel of sexual self-indulgence, the false freedom of unrestrained sexuality, and the false right to misuse the gifts of marriage that God gave to men and women. All such teachers will be punished by God, with their willing students.

St. John Chrysostom: "If the bridegroom shows his wife that he takes no pleasure in worldly excess, and will not stand for it, their marriage will remain free from the evil influences that are so popular these days. Let them shun the immodest music and dancing [i.e. all forms of immodest entertainment] that are currently so fashionable. I am aware that many people think me ridiculous for giving such advice; but if you listen to me, you will understand the advantages of a sober life-style more and more as time goes on.... Remove from your lives shameful, immodest, and Satanic music, and don't associate with people who enjoy such profligate [i.e. utterly shameless] entertainment."[342]

---

[341] St. John Chrysostom, On Marriage and Family Life, Popular Patristic Series, trans. Roth and Anderson, Homily 20, p. 60.
[342] St. John Chrysostom, On Marriage and Family Life, p. 60.

Although St. John mentions music and dancing, he is certainly condemning every example of shameful entertainment, and also advising temperance in the use of entertainment that is not shameful. Again, this advice is given specifically to married persons, clearly showing that what is shameful or immodest is not justified merely by occurring within marriage.

Now I know that many Catholics will read these words of St. John, and the words of this book also, and respond with ridicule. For the power of modern media is such that many Catholics have been seduced into believing ideas about sexuality and freedom and rights that are incompatible with the Gospel of Christ. Therefore, when even a Saint criticizes the way that they live their daily lives, they do not listen. But those faithful Catholics who are sincerely seeking moral truth are well-advised to listen to those sober voices within the Church which are calling them to modesty and self-restraint, even in the marital bedroom.

St. Chrysostom: "Will this sort of life be distasteful for a young bride? Only perhaps for the shortest time, and soon she will discover how delightful it is to live this way. She will retain her modesty if you retain yours."[343]

A husband and wife must be mindful that their actions, especially concerning sexuality, affect one another. If one spouse is immodest, this may tempt the other spouse not only toward immodesty, but also toward more serious sins, such as lust. The consequences of our choices affect the morality of our acts. Although we must avoid all intrinsically evil acts, our knowingly chosen acts must be good under all three fonts in order to be moral. Also, the harm that can be done to the spouses and to the marriage by a disregard for lesser sexual sins (immodesty, excessive indulgence in natural marital relations, licentious speech, etc.) should not be underestimated. Those spouses who strive only to avoid mortal sin, will not only commit many fully deliberate venial sins, but will also be likely to fall into some mortal sins. If any married couple wishes to please God, they must daily strive to avoid, not only mortal sin, but also venial sin, especially that which is fully deliberate.

St. Chrysostom: "Remind one another that nothing in life is to be feared, except offending God. If you marriage is like this, your perfection will rival the holiest of monks. If you are inclined to entertain and give dinner parties, there should be nothing immodest or excessive about them."[344]

Marriage is not for immorality. The spouses should not fear that their marriage will not have sexual pleasure, or that their marriage will not be exciting, or that they will fall out of emotional love, which is not truly of the heart and mind, not truly of the soul. Instead, the spouses should fear that they might sin against God within the holy Sacrament of Matrimony, and so be deserving of even greater punishment than those who commit the same sins, but within only a natural marriage. Fear of the Lord is the beginning of a happy marriage. And this

---

[343] St. John Chrysostom, On Marriage and Family Life, p. 61.
[344] St. John Chrysostom, On Marriage and Family Life, p. 61-62.

happiness is not a worldly, superficial, and fleeting happiness, but rather that true happiness which bears fruit in eternal life.

.313. Notice that St. John considers some entertainment to be good and moral. He suggests that a married couple might entertain guests and have dinner parties. He does not condemn all entertainment, nor does he equate all entertainment with what is shameful or immodest or excessive. Some entertainment is useful to the human person, refreshing the mind and heart, benefiting both body and soul. It is only the misuse of entertainment to which this wise Saint objects. There is no offense to God in gathering with some friends for companionship, food, drink, humor, conversation, and the like.

[1 Corinthians]
{6:13} Food is for the stomach, and the stomach is for food. But God shall destroy both the stomach and food. And the body is not for fornication, but rather for the Lord; and the Lord is for the body.
{6:14} Truly, God has raised up the Lord, and he will raise us up by his power.
{6:15} Do you not know that your bodies are a part of Christ? So then, should I take a part of Christ and make it a part of a harlot? Let it not be so!
{6:16} And do you not know that whoever is joined to a harlot becomes one body? "For the two," he said, "shall be as one flesh."
{6:17} But whoever is joined to the Lord is one spirit.
{6:18} Flee from fornication. Every sin whatsoever that a man commits is outside of the body, but whoever fornicates, sins against his own body.
{6:19} Or do you not know that your bodies are the Temple of the Holy Spirit, who is in you, whom you have from God, and that you are not your own?
{6:20} For you have been bought at a great price. Glorify and carry God in your body.

Fornication can be defined narrowly, to refer to sexual acts outside of marriage, or it can be defined broadly, to include all illicit sexual acts. In this verse, the Holy Spirit is speaking through St. Paul against every kind of immoral sexual act. The teaching that "the body is not for fornication, but rather for the Lord" is general, referring to the holy use of every human person's body, not only to the unmarried. And this becomes clearer as the passage continues. The resurrection of the body by the Lord is given to all persons, not only to the unmarried. So when the Holy Spirit teaches that "your bodies are a part of Christ," He includes all human persons. Even within marriage, sexual immorality of every kind remains immoral, including unnatural sexual acts, lust, licentiousness, self-indulgence, and every kind of shameful behavior. And opposing all these sins is the virtue of modesty. For the person who practices modesty thereby guards himself against every kind of sexual sin.

As this passage continues, the teaching remains general, directed at all the faithful. And so the term 'harlot' not only condemns sexual acts with prostitutes, but every illicit sexual act. Whoever commits any illicit sexual act, even within marriage, is acting as if he or she were a harlot, trading away sexual purity in exchange for the gain of pleasure. A prostitute commits sexual sins, trading away the graces of the soul for the lesser goods of this world. Anyone who commits an illicit sexual act of any kind similarly trades away the graces of the soul in exchange for some lesser good, such as sexual pleasure (or whatever lesser good or apparent good might be sought).

Whoever commits fornication of any kind, even within marriage, sins against his or her own body, and against the Lord. And whoever commits any illicit sexual act within the Sacrament of Marriage sins also against the Sacrament. For the Sacrament of Marriage continues every day; the Sacrament, its graces and its obligations, are not limited to the day of the wedding ceremony.

Finally, the Holy Spirit concludes this passage by teaching that our bodies are His temples. Yet again, it is clear that this passage is general, for it is not only the unmarried who have the Holy Spirit. Therefore, the teaching that we must flee from fornication applies to all the faithful, married and unmarried. Whoever uses sacred Matrimony as an excuse for sexual sins commits both sexual sins and a sacrilege. For natural marriage joins husband and wife, but the Sacrament of Marriage joins husband and wife and God.

.314. Pope Pius XII, Address to Midwives

"The same Creator, Who in His bounty and wisdom willed to make use of the work of man and woman, by uniting them in matrimony, for the preservation and propagation of the human race, has also decreed that in this function the parties should experience pleasure and happiness of body and spirit. Husband and wife, therefore, by seeking and enjoying this pleasure do no wrong whatever. They accept what the Creator has destined for them. Nevertheless, here also, husband and wife must know how to keep themselves within the limits of a just moderation. As with the pleasure of food and drink so with the sexual they must not abandon themselves without restraint to the impulses of the senses."[345]

This teaching, that the husband and wife may seek and enjoy pleasure in body and spirit, by natural marital relations, must be understood in union with all the teachings of the Faith. Such a teaching cannot be interpreted to mean that the married couple may make use of sexuality solely for pleasure, nor that they may ignore or reject the greater goods of marital relations, nor that they may seek sexual pleasure by any means whatsoever. For the same Pope also taught, in his encyclical Casti Connubii: "For in matrimony as well as in the use of the matrimonial rights there are also secondary ends, such as mutual aid, the cultivating of mutual love, and the quieting of concupiscence which husband and wife are not forbidden to consider so long as they are subordinated to the primary end and so long as the intrinsic nature of the act is preserved."[346] The pleasure that is found in natural marital relations open to life is a secondary end; it is not the primary threefold end of the sexual act, but rather is that type of end found in the good consequences of a knowingly chosen act. The secondary ends of marital relations must be subordinated to the primary ends of marital relations. Now the intrinsic nature of the marital act is due to its moral object. Therefore,

---

[345] Pope Pius XII, Address to participants in the Conference of the Italian Catholic Union of Obstetricians (October 29, 1951), commonly called 'Address to Midwives.'
[346] Pope Pius XII, Casti Connubii, n. 59.

any sexual act that is non-procreative, or non-unitive, or non-marital is contrary to the intrinsic nature of the sexual act. The enjoyment of sexual pleasure cannot be used as an excuse to engage in acts which do not preserve the intrinsic nature of the unitive, procreative, marital act.

In addition, Pope Pius XII taught that even when a married couple are making proper use of the matrimonial rights (by natural sexual relations), they must show restraint. For at no time and in no circumstance should sexual desire and sexual pleasure be allowed to draw the couple away from living a moral life. These lesser goods must be kept in their proper, limited, well-ordered place within married life. For it is always a sin to seek a lesser good in contradiction to a greater good, or to place a lesser good above a greater good.

And this restraint in marital relations is included under the term modesty. For modesty is temperance concerning all that pertains to sexuality. And marital relations is not an exception to the negative precepts of the moral law, which forbid immoral acts, nor is it an exception to the positive precepts of the moral law, which require us to exercise all the virtues by what we do, not only by what we refrain from doing.

"The right rule is this: the use of the natural procreative disposition is morally lawful in matrimony only, in the service of and in accordance with the ends of marriage itself. Hence it follows that only in marriage with the observing of this rule is the desire and fruition of this pleasure and of this satisfaction lawful. For the pleasure is subordinate to the law of the action whence it derives, and not vice versa -- the action to the law of pleasure. And this law, so very reasonable, concerns not only the substance but also the circumstances of the action, so that, even when the substance of the act remains morally safe, it is possible to sin in the way it is performed."[347]

.315. Pope Pius XII taught that the desire for, and the fruition (attainment) of, sexual pleasure is only lawful (morally licit) within the unitive procreative marital act. All sexual acts which lack the unitive or the procreative or the marital meaning are immoral due to the substance, i.e. the nature, of the act. But even when the substance of the sexual act remains morally safe, so that all unnatural sexual acts are avoided, the natural marital act must be good under all three fonts. The way that the natural marital act is performed can be a sin by intention or by circumstances. The moderation of the natural marital act by temperance protects against this type of sin by the way that the marital act is performed.

Although God intends the natural marital act to be enjoyable, this pleasure is not the primary purpose of marital relations. The primary purpose is that threefold significance which is unitive, procreative, and marital. The mere fact that an act gives sexual pleasure to a husband and wife does not justify that act as morally licit. The benefit of pleasure is subordinate to the eternal moral law and to the higher purposes of marriage and the marital act. Furthermore, the fact that the natural marital act has the proper threefold moral object does not imply that the

---

[347] Pope Pius XII, Address to Midwives, 29 October 1951.

act is good under intention or circumstances. A husband and wife might sin by intention, or by excessive indulgence (a circumstance), even when the act itself is a moral act of natural marital relations open to life.

"The transgression of this law is as old as original sin. But in our times there is the risk that one may lose sight of the fundamental principle itself. At present, in fact, it is usual to support in words and in writing (and this by Catholics in certain circles) the necessary autonomy, the proper end, and the proper value of sexuality and of its realization, independently of the purpose of procreating a new life. There is a tendency to subject to a new examination and to a new norm the very order established by God and not to admit any other restraint to the way of satisfying the instinct than by considering the essence of the instinctive act. In addition there would be substituted a license to serve blindly and without restraint the whims and instincts of nature in the place of the moral obligations to dominate passions; and this sooner or later cannot but turn out to be a danger to morals, conscience and human dignity."[348]

.316. This distortion of sexuality, about which Pope Pius XII laments, continues to be found among many Catholics today. Certain false teachers claim that God created the marital act for the end of pleasure, and therefore the married couple may seek and obtain this pleasure through acts that are non-procreative or non-unitive. But this transgression is not the teaching of the Church. Pleasure in marital relations is not intrinsically evil. But neither does this pleasure justify acts that are intrinsically evil, nor acts that are immoral under any font. This pleasure can never justify acts that are non-unitive, or non-procreative, or non-marital. These false teachings about marital sexual ethics endanger the morals, conscience, and dignity of all married persons, and also endanger the sanctity of the Sacrament of Marriage itself.

"If nature had aimed exclusively, or at least in the first place, at a reciprocal gift and possession of the married couple in joy and delight, and if it had ordered that act only to make happy in the highest possible degree their personal experience, and not to stimulate them to the service of life, then the Creator would have adopted another plan in forming and constituting the natural act. Now, instead, all this is subordinated and ordered to that unique, great law of the 'generatio et educatio prolis,' [the generation and education of offspring] namely the accomplishment of the primary end of matrimony as the origin and source of life."[349]

Although the natural marital act has pleasure among its good consequences, Pope Pius XII taught that pleasure is neither the exclusive, nor the primary meaning of the marital act. The natural marital act, by its very nature, is ordered by the Creator toward union, procreation, and marriage. And of these three meanings, the greatest place is given to procreation. For without procreation, the human race would cease to exist. Yet this procreative meaning is not limited merely to the conception of new life, but rather it includes the entire process of

---

[348] Pope Pius XII, Address to Midwives, 29 October 1951.
[349] Pope Pius XII, Address to Midwives, 29 October 1951.

development that naturally follows after conception, and even after birth. And so the good of procreation includes the raising and education of children, not merely their conception. Marriage is not ordained solely or mainly for the enjoyment of the married couple, but rather for the conception and raising of offspring, to the great benefit of the family and of the human race.

"Unfortunately, unceasing waves of hedonism invade the world and threaten to submerge in the swelling tide of thoughts, desires and acts the whole marital life, not without serious dangers and grave prejudice to the primary duty of husband and wife."[350]

Hedonism considers the pursuit of pleasure to be the path to happiness in this life. This error of giving excessive importance to mere enjoyment has had a strong influence on attitudes and behaviors in secular society. Even many Catholic Christians have been influenced, to one extent or another, by the distorted place given to pleasure by secular society. As a result, many Catholics imagine that the purpose of their marriage is to provide self-fulfillment or happiness, in the secular sense of these words. This error harms Christian marriage in many ways. Selfishness, which is the path to many sorrows, is mistaken for the path to true happiness. Sexual sins are said to be justified on the grounds that sex within married has enjoyment as its main purpose. The result is that many marriages are no longer pleasing to God, and some marriages have become thoroughly offensive to God.

"This anti-Christian hedonism too often is not ashamed to elevate itself to a doctrine, inculcating the ardent desire to make always more intense the pleasure in the preparation and in the performance of the conjugal union, as if in matrimonial relations the whole moral law were reduced to the normal performance of the act itself, and as if all the rest, in whatever way it is done, were to be justified by the expression of mutual affection, sanctified by the Sacrament of Matrimony, worthy of praise and reward before God and conscience. There is no thought at all of the dignity of man and of the Christian -- a dignity which restrains the excess of sensuality."[351]

This hedonism is anti-Christian because the pursuit of pleasure and self-centered personal fulfillment is contrary to the most fundamental Christian values: to love God above all else, and to love your neighbor as yourself. When hedonism invades the thinking of married Christians, they commit various immoral acts in the pursuit of sexual pleasure, and even when they engage in natural marital relations, they fail to restrain the excess of sensuality. Notice that the Pope rejects the idea that, as long as the acts of the spouses include 'the normal performance of the act itself' (i.e. natural marital relations) that all else is justified on the grounds of expressing affection or achieving pleasure. This common false idea lacks a proper understanding of the dignity of the human person, and of the dignity of the Sacrament of Marriage, and of the necessity to act in accord with all the virtues. In particular, the true spiritual love of God, neighbor, and self

---

[350] Pope Pius XII, Address to Midwives, 29 October 1951.
[351] Pope Pius XII, Address to Midwives, 29 October 1951.

must always be given the first place in human life, far above mere physical or emotional expressions of love. The marital bedroom is no exception to this rule.

"No; the gravity and sanctity of the Christian moral law do not admit an unchecked satisfaction of the sexual instinct tending only to pleasure and enjoyment; they do not permit rational man to let himself be mastered to such an extent, neither as regards the substance nor the circumstances of the act."[352]

The substance of the sexual act refers to the second font. Unnatural sexual acts have a different essential moral nature from natural marital relations; the substance of the act differs. Unnatural sexual acts are always gravely immoral, regardless of intention or circumstances, because the substance of the act is inherently contrary to natural law. But even when the sexual act is natural marital relations open to life, intention and circumstances must be good. So if the married couple intend to use natural marital relations for mere pleasure, or if, in intention and circumstances, they show no degree of restraint (temperance), then they sin. Sexual relations and the sanctity of marriage are always under the eternal moral law.

.317. Now Pope Pius XII clearly and unequivocally taught that the spouses do not sin in taking some degree of pleasure and enjoyment in natural marital relations. However, they may not give pleasure the first place in the order of goods in marital relations. Nor may they indulge in unrestrained pleasure and sensuality on the excuse that natural marital relations is inherently good. When the second font is good, the other two fonts must also be good in order to avoid sin. And this pleasure, naturally found in sexual relations, does not justify any act that is inherently unnatural, i.e. inherently contrary to natural law.

However, if the spouses sin by intention or circumstances, while the substance of the act is good (natural marital relations), then they might sin only venially. A bad intention is not necessarily a grave matter; it depends on what is intended. And if the bad consequences outweigh the good, but to a limited extent, not to a grave extent, then the matter again might not be grave. Unnatural sexual acts are always objective mortal sins, because the matter of the act is grave. But when the act is natural marital relations, some degree of sin in intention or circumstances is not necessarily grave. Such a sin might be venial, or might be mortal.

"There are some who would allege that happiness in marriage is in direct proportion to the reciprocal enjoyment in conjugal relations. It is not so: indeed, happiness in marriage is in direct proportion to the mutual respect of the partners, even in their intimate relations; not that they regard as immoral and refuse what nature offers and what the Creator has given, but because this respect, and the mutual esteem which it produces, is one of the strongest elements of a pure love, and for this reason all the more tender."[353]

The Pope rejects the idea that happiness in marriage is due solely or mainly to the enjoyment of sexual relations. This erroneous idea is often found implicitly

---

[352] Pope Pius XII, Address to Midwives, 29 October 1951.
[353] Pope Pius XII, Address to Midwives, 29 October 1951.

even in Catholic texts on marriage. Although such authors usually do not state that sexual enjoyment in marriage is the basis for happiness, they overemphasize the role and importance of marital relations within the overall marriage. In effect, they are saying that the enjoyment of marital relations is fundamental to happiness in marriage. But the Pontiff states otherwise; the foundation of a happy marriage is not sexual pleasure, but "the mutual respect of the partners, even in their intimate relations." The foundation of enjoyment of every kind in marriage and in marital relations is not sexual pleasure, but mutual respect. The true and pure spiritual love of the spouses for one another is the basis for a happy marriage, and is even the basis for the mutual enjoyment of marital relations -- not sexual pleasure, and not mere emotional love.

"In the performance of your profession, do your utmost to repel the attack of this refined hedonism void of spiritual values and thus unworthy of Christian married couples. Show how nature has given, truly, the instinctive desire for pleasure and sanctions it in the lawful marriage, not as an end in itself, but rather for the service of life. Banish from your heart that cult of pleasure, and do your best to prevent the spreading of a literature which considers as its duty the description in full of the intimacies of married life under the pretext of instructing, guiding and reassuring. In general, common sense, natural instinct and a brief instruction on the clear and simple maxims of Christian moral law, are sufficient to give peace to the tender conscience of married people. If, in certain circumstances, a fiancée or a young married woman were in need of further enlightenment on some particular point, it is your duty to give them tactfully an explanation in conformity with natural law and with a healthy Christian conscience."[354]

A married couple sins whenever they give sexual pleasure the first place, above the higher values in marital relations and in the marriage as a whole. Notice that the Pope shows concern for banishing every kind of sin from marriage. He even rejects immodesty in literature intended to give sexual instruction to spouses. For no marriage is exempt from any provision of the eternal moral law. Modesty is necessary to avoid sexual sin, even in marriage. And the good intentions of "instructing, guiding and reassuring" do not justify immodesty or other sins. Overly-detailed 'instruction,' even to marriage or engaged couples, about the marital act is immodest, even to the extent of sin. Some instruction to the married and unmarried is moral and useful, but sexuality is not exempt from the virtue of temperance (modesty).

.318. Immodesty in Art

There are no exceptions to the eternal moral law. Art is not exempt from the moral law. A particular work may be art and moral, or art and immoral, or moral and not art, or immoral and not art. It is false to assume that, if a work is truly a type of art, then the moral law does not apply, or that any type and degree of immodesty would somehow become moral. The artist must strive to avoid sin in all areas of his life, including in his artwork. Good art is a reflection

---

[354] Pope Pius XII, Address to Midwives, 29 October 1951.

of the glory of God, and of His Creation, especially humanity. Immoral art offends God and harms humanity.

As previously explained, immodesty is not intrinsically evil, but is a matter of degree. Since matters of degree are in the third font, a judgment of the prudential order is needed to determine if an act (of making a work of art) is imperfect, or a venial sin, or even a mortal sin. Some limited immodesty in art would be imperfect but moral. A greater degree of immodesty in art would be immoral, but only a venial sin. If the immodesty is particularly extensive, the act of making such art might be a mortal sin. All this pertains to immodesty, exclusive of other types of sin, which may be intrinsically evil and inherently gravely immoral.

Nudity in art is not necessarily immoral, and is not necessarily even imperfect. The Vatican museum includes artworks with some limited nudity. Though nudity in art is not justified merely because it is art, neither is nudity in art necessarily immoral. Whether an act is modest or immodest depends on intention and circumstances. Some nudity of a husband and wife who are alone would not necessarily be immodest. And some limited discrete nudity in art would not necessarily be immodest.

However, modern artists sometimes show no concern for morality and no degree of modesty or temperance in their work. They speak and act as if art were exempt from the moral law. To the contrary, no area of human life, and no type of human endeavor, is beyond the eternal moral law. The artist cannot disregard the moral law, nor can he disregard, in particular, the consequences that any immodesty or immorality in his art may have on persons who view his art.

Second Vatican Council: "…there is no human activity which can be withdrawn from God's dominion."[355]

.319. Pope Paul VI Address to Artists

"We now address you, artists, who are taken up with beauty and work for it: poets and literary men, painters, sculptors, architects, musicians, men devoted to the theater and the cinema. To all of you, the Church of the council declares to you through our voice: if you are friends of genuine art, you are our friends."[356]

The work done by artists of every kind is generally morally good. However, works of art and of entertainment are not above the moral law. Every artist is a person subject to the same laws of good and evil as every other person. The good that is done for the Church and the world through art does not justify even a single venial sin. Artists must strive to be both good artists and moral persons.

"The Church has long since joined in alliance with you. You have built and adorned her temples, celebrated her dogmas, enriched her liturgy. You have aided her in translating her divine message in the language of forms and figures, making the invisible world palpable. Today, as yesterday, the Church needs you

---

[355] Second Vatican Council, Lumen Gentium, n. 36.
[356] Pope Paul VI, Address to Artists at the Second Vatican Council, December 8th, 1965.

and turns to you. She tells you through our voice: Do not allow an alliance as fruitful as this to be broken. Do not refuse to put your talents at the service of divine truth. Do not close your mind to the breath of the Holy Spirit."[357]

From the time when Divine Revelation was first entrusted to the Israelites, and throughout the entire history of the Church, artists have used their work to assist the rest of the faithful in worship and in learning and in life. But the influence of sinful secular society on the artists of today is all too apparent. Those artists who are also faithful Christians must continually strive to avoid sin, to cooperate with all the graces of the Holy Spirit, and to find a way to use their artistic talents to do good for the Church and the world.

"This world in which we live needs beauty in order not to sink into despair. It is beauty, like truth, which brings joy to the heart of man and is that precious fruit which resists the wear and tear of time, which unites generations and makes them share things in admiration. And all of this is through your hands. May these hands be pure and disinterested. Remember that you are the guardians of beauty in the world. May that suffice to free you from tastes which are passing and have no genuine value, to free you from the search after strange or unbecoming expressions. Be always and everywhere worthy of your ideals and you will be worthy of the Church which, by our voice, addresses to you today her message of friendship, salvation, grace and benediction."[358]

.320. Pornography

The term pornography refers to various kinds of sexuality-explicit depictions. But since morality pertains to knowingly chosen acts, not to tangible or intangible items, it is useful to distinguish between the pornographic material and the various sinful acts related to that material. Even if an item is commonly used to commit objective mortal sins, the item itself is not a sin; it is the knowingly chosen acts of human persons that are sins. And a number of different types of sins are related to pornographic material.

Some commentators on modern society, wishing to strongly condemn all sexual immorality, have used the term pornography in a rhetorical and overly-broad manner. They apply the term to condemn any type or degree of immodest depiction. Under this approach, a commercial with scantily-clad women, or a movie scene with a limited portrayal of sensuality, are each condemned as pornography. This merely rhetorical use of the term pornography is not theologically sound. It is harmful to the proper understanding of moral and immoral acts to apply such a strong term to relatively limited moral transgressions. Although the intention to condemn all sexual immorality is good, this approach does harm to the proper understanding of ethics in the minds of the faithful. Secular society can be rightly criticized for many various sins and errors, but to do so with mere rhetoric, apart from sound ethical distinctions, does more harm than good. The term pornography should be reserved for sexually-explicit material which severely harms God's plan for sexuality in

---

[357] Pope Paul VI, Address to Artists, December 8th, 1965.
[358] Pope Paul VI, Address to Artists, December 8th, 1965.

human life. Other terms, such as immodest or indecent, can then be used for non-explicit material which constitutes only a limited departure from God's plan for sexuality in human life.

For example, a movie scene depicting explicit sexual acts is pornographic material. But a movie scene depicting some immodest sensuality, or some limited degree of nudity, should not be placed in the same category. Even when the latter immodest material is rightly faulted for doing some harm to a proper understanding of God's plan for sexuality, the type of material and the degree of harm is substantially different. A merely rhetorical or overly-broad use of the term pornography tends to lack any distinction as to the type of material or degree of severity. The result is that many different degrees and types of sin are categorized together and equally condemned, even though some of these sins are substantially more sinful and more harmful than others.

A narrower definition of pornography is more useful, because it allows for a stronger and clearer condemnation of what is most harmful. When the definition used is overly-broad, the condemnation of pornography becomes less effective and less meaningful, because many lesser sins are included in the term. It is contrary to reason to condemn with equal force and without distinction, both severe sins and lesser sins, both mortal sins and venial sins. Therefore, the term pornography should be used narrowly, rather than broadly. Then other terms (e.g. immodesty, excessive sensuality, etc.) can be used to condemn harmful material of a substantially different type or of a substantially lesser degree. In this way, lesser sins are still understood to be sinful, but are given a terminology fitting to the degree and type of sinfulness, and the more severe term is reserved for the more severe sins.

.321. Pornographic Material

Catechism of the Catholic Church: "Pornography consists in removing real or simulated sexual acts from the intimacy of the partners, in order to display them deliberately to third parties. It offends against chastity because it perverts the conjugal act, the intimate giving of spouses to each other. It does grave injury to the dignity of its participants (actors, vendors, the public), since each one becomes an object of base pleasure and illicit profit for others. It immerses all who are involved in the illusion of a fantasy world. It is a grave offense. Civil authorities should prevent the production and distribution of pornographic materials."[359]

Pornographic material may be considered to include: explicit depictions of sexual acts; depictions of strong or perverse sensuality, even when per se sexual acts are not depicted; explicit depictions of the genitals, for the purpose of committing sexual sins; other depictions, even those that are not overtly sexual, for the purpose of committing sexual sins; and any similar material. These depictions might be found in movies or videos, still photos, written words (e.g. books or magazines), audio recordings, live conversations (e.g. 'phone sex'), live performances (e.g. a pornographic play or stage show), or other live or recorded

---

[359] Catechism of the Catholic Church, n. 2354.

material. When strong sensuality is depicted, even without per se sexual acts, the material may still be categorized as pornographic, especially if the material is closely related to gravely immoral sexual acts (homosexual acts, adulterous acts, sexual acts with minors, et cetera).

In some cases, the material is pornographic because the content is objectively gravely disordered. Explicit depictions of sexual acts, and depictions of strong or perverse sensuality, are rightly categorized as pornographic regardless of the intentions of the persons who create, distribute, and use this material. The material itself is morally disordered because it conflicts, to a grave extent, with the plan of God for human sexuality by removing "sexual acts from the intimacy of the partners" or by depicting gravely disordered sexual acts.

The only moral sexual act is natural marital relations open to life. But even if a married couple were to video tape their sexual acts for their own use, without distribution to third parties, such creation and use of pornographic material would not be moral. The marital act is inherently intimate and private, and should not be recorded for any purpose. The material itself is also morally disordered when the contents contain explicit depictions of unnatural sexual acts, or explicit depictions of any type of perverse sexuality. Such acts are inherently gravely contrary to God's plan for sexuality in human life.

In other cases, the purpose or usage of the material is the basis for the moral disorder. This type of material does not contain explicit depictions, but is pornographic by usage rather than content. For example, some limited nudity may be moral in art, but the same depiction might be used to commit gravely immoral sexual sins. Depictions of nudity are not necessarily pornographic. For example, explicit depictions of body parts are needed in medical training and medical texts. When the material is not inherently gravely disordered, but is put to the same use as pornography, it is the act that is disordered, not the material. Such material may be said to be pornographic by usage, rather than by objective content.

In certain cases, it may be difficult to categorize the material. Explicitness in any depiction of sexuality is a matter of degree. For example, a movie scene might merely imply that immoral sexual acts are occurring between two characters, or a scene might depict a sexual act in a non-explicit manner, or a scene might depict strong sensuality, but without per se sexual acts. The degree of sensuality and the degree of explicitness may be greater or lesser. Therefore, the material might be pornographic to a degree, or immodest to a degree.

In all cases, what is most important is not the exact categorization of the material, but avoiding sin. The three fonts of morality apply to each and every knowingly chosen act. If you are not certain whether the material is pornographic or merely immodest, you must still avoid every kind of sin. And since it is possible to commit objective mortal sins by the usage of material that is not pornographic, the avoidance of every kind of sin is more important than the categorization of the material.

.322. Sinful Acts Related to Pornography

Sin is nothing else but a knowingly chosen immoral act. Pornographic material is not itself a sin, but it is related to various serious sins. The Catechism of the Catholic Church summarizes the "participants" in the sins of pornography as "actors, vendors, the public." In other words, those who commit the sins related to pornographic material fall into three categories: (1) those who create pornography, such as actors, performers, photographers, writers, and other persons, (2) those who distribute pornography, such as vendors and other persons, and (3) those who use pornography, such as members of the public. Therefore, the sins related to pornography can be divided into three types: (1) creation, (2) distribution, (3) use.

The sins involved in the creation, distribution, and use of pornography are various. A sin related to pornography is not one single type of act. Lying is one type of act, with one particular evil moral object. Although there are a myriad of ways to tell a lie, they all have the same essential moral nature, because they have the same moral object. Similarly, theft is one type of act. There are innumerable ways to commit theft, yet each has the very same moral object and therefore is essentially the same type of act. The same is true of murder, and of any other intrinsically evil act. However, the acts related to pornography have various moral objects. Some of these acts are intrinsically evil and always gravely immoral, and other acts are immoral without being intrinsically evil. Each act must be considered on its own as to its morality, under all three fonts.

.323. Immodest Material

Not every depiction of sensuality, immodesty, or nudity is immoral. Some forms of art or entertainment may possibly contain some limited sensuality or nudity without sin on the part of the creators of the material, and without sin on the part of the audience. The depictions of scenes from the Bible in the Sistine Chapel contain some nudity.

Nevertheless, art is not exempt from the moral law. And so it is possible for a work of art to be either pornographic, or at least sinfully immodest. The fact or claim that a work is a type of art does not imply that its creation, distribution, and use is necessarily moral.

It is possible for a work of art or entertainment to be sinfully immodest without being pornographic. For example, excessive nudity or sensuality in a movie may be sinful, to one degree or another, but perhaps not to such an extent as to be properly called pornographic. A limited depiction of sensuality, especially if the relationship depicted is not gravely immoral, may be immodest or even sinful, but without being pornographic. Not every depiction of sensuality or nudity is accurately called pornography.

It is difficult to give an exact definition of pornographic material, because portrayals of sexual acts, sensuality, immodesty, and nudity vary by degree and type. But if, in a particular case, it is unclear whether the material should be categorized as pornographic, the three fonts of morality must still be applied to

Sexual Sins

each knowingly chosen act to determine whether that act is moral or immoral. Avoid all sinful acts, especially objective mortal sin, and any mistakes in the exact categorization or definition of such material will do little or no harm. Therefore, the remainder of this section will emphasis the sinful acts, rather than the material.

.324. The Creation of Pornography

Perhaps the most harmful type of pornographic material is video recordings of persons committing various explicit sexual acts. The creation of this type of material necessarily includes numerous gravely immoral sexual acts, including unnatural sexual acts and extra-marital sexual acts. These acts are gravely immoral under each and all of the three fonts of morality. Under the first font, the intention to create this material for display to others is gravely immoral. And the intention to create material that will assist other persons in committing intrinsically evil and gravely immoral sexual sins is also gravely immoral. Under the second font, unnatural sexual acts as well as any extra-marital natural sexual acts are intrinsically evil and always gravely immoral. Committing such acts for any purpose is always an objective mortal sin. Under the third font, the creation of pornographic material is gravely immoral, because much harm is done to individuals and to society in the consequences.

The deliberate choice to create a work of pornographic material of any kind, even if no sexual acts are committed in its creation, is a grave matter. When pornography is defined narrowly, such that the material is gravely contrary to the plan of God for sexuality, then the creation of pornographic material is always an objective mortal sin. The entire team of persons who deliberately work together to create any work of pornography are guilty of objective mortal sin.

Even when the pornographic material does not involve any real sexual acts by performers, the creation of pornographic material is objectively gravely immoral because the material is intended for use in committing sexual sins, such as lust, masturbation, fornication, adultery, and unnatural sexual acts, and because the consequences do grave harm to many persons. Therefore, even if the creation of pornographic material does not include the commission of gravely immoral sexual acts, the acts pertaining to its creation are nevertheless gravely immoral by intention and circumstances, if not also by intrinsically evil acts.

.325. The Distribution of Pornography

The deliberate distribution of pornography is an objective mortal sin. The intention to distribute this inherently gravely disordered material is a gravely immoral intention. And any intention to assist other persons, by distributing this material, in committing sexual sins, is also a gravely immoral intention. In addition, the distribution of pornography is gravely immoral because of the objectively grave harm done as a consequence of this distribution.

In the present situation in secular society, a number of large corporations make substantial sums of money distributing explicit pornographic material by cable and satellite television, and by other means. A number of large hotel and motel chains make money distributing pornography by pay television services to rented rooms. Many small independent video stores sell pornographic movies out of 'adults only' backrooms. Worldwide revenue from pornography is estimated to be in the tens of billions of dollars (at least). In addition, the use of pornography is becoming more and more acceptable to the ever-changing baseless norms of sinful secular society. And this acceptance is making the distribution of pornography easier. The distribution of pornography is a widespread and serious problem in the world today.

Children are harmed by the distribution of pornography to adults because there is no 100% effective means for distributing this material solely to adults. Any material that is sought by children, and especially by teenagers, is able to be obtained, in part because of the many electronic means of distribution available in modern society. Those who create and distribute pornography know that they cannot keep this material, which is sinful even for adults, from falling into the hands of minors.

.326. The Use of Pornography

The claim that a pornographic work is art or entertainment does not justify the grave moral disorders in that work, nor the associated sins. Neither works of art, nor works of entertainment are exempt from the eternal moral law. Just as there are objective mortal sins in the creation and distribution of pornography, so also there are objective mortal sins in the use of pornography. The creation of pornography often involves the commission of gravely immoral sexual acts. Similarly, the use of pornography often involves the commission of gravely immoral sexual acts. Immoral sexual acts, such as masturbation, fornication, adultery, and unnatural sexual acts, are intrinsically evil and always gravely immoral. The use of pornography in committing these sins makes these acts even more gravely immoral because of the greater moral disorder and greater harm.

The use of pornography makes sexual sins more likely. Those who use pornography are harmed in their souls by the loss of grace when they commit actual mortal sins. Their understanding of God's plan for sexuality in human life, and their understanding of sexual ethics are harmed. Their understanding of the proper relationships between human persons is harmed. Their ability to persevere in chastity and modesty is harmed. Married persons who use pornography harm their marriage relationship. Unmarried persons who use pornography harm their relationships with any future spouse, and with other persons in general.

Children are harmed when pornography is used by adults. A society which accepts and uses pornography as if it were moral will not be able to teach children right from wrong on the topic of sexual ethics. Adults who use pornography are setting a bad example for children and teenagers. Children and teens eventually become aware of the existence and use of pornography by adults. Therefore, this usage by adults includes the sin of scandal. Also, when adults in society accept and use pornography, committing many gravely immoral sexual sins, some of those adults might also commit other sexual sins, such as the sexual abuse of children. A society that accepts pornography as if it were moral will not be able to rid itself of the sexual abuse of children, nor of other crimes such as rape and spousal abuse. The human person is harmed by pornography, and as a result the whole of society is also harmed.

.327. Pornography and Marriage

[Hebrews]
{13:4} May marriage be honorable in every way, and may the marriage bed be immaculate. For God will judge fornicators and adulterers.

All sexual acts outside of marriage are immoral because they lack the marital meaning in the moral object of the sexual act. All non-marital sexual acts are intrinsically evil and gravely immoral. Even natural sexual relations open to life is intrinsically evil and gravely immoral when it is non-marital. However, the marital bedroom is not exempt from the eternal moral law. There are other types of sexual sins aside from extra-marital sexual acts. The only moral sexual act is natural marital relations open to life. To be moral, each and every sexual act must be marital and unitive and procreative.

The use of pornography, even within marriage, is often associated with various sexual sins. Masturbation is intrinsically evil and always gravely immoral. An unnatural sexual act is any type of sexual act that is non-procreative or non-unitive, such as oral, anal, or manipulative sexual acts. Unnatural sexual acts are intrinsically evil and always gravely immoral, even within marriage. The use of pornography may make these sins of masturbation or unnatural sexual acts more likely, with gravely harmful consequences for the person and the marriage. The use of pornography to facilitate gravely immoral sexual acts of any kind is a grave sin. The use of pornography may also make the interior sin of lust more likely. The sin of lust is immoral under all three fonts of morality; it includes an evil intention, an evil moral object, and only bad consequences.

But even apart from particular intrinsically evil sexual acts that may accompany the use of pornography, this usage is also immoral, even when used (viewed, read, etc.) by a married couple. The holy Sacrament of Marriage, or even a merely natural marriage, does not justify any sin. If an act is immoral under one or more of the three fonts of morality, then the act is a sin. God did not establish marriage as a pretext for sin, nor is the marital bedroom exempt from sexual morality.

Neither is the use of pornography justified as a means to achieve arousal and subsequent natural marital relations. Although natural marital relations open to life is good and moral, a good end does not justify an evil means. Both the means and the end must be good for the person to avoid sin. Even if the pornographic material is not used to commit gravely immoral sexual sins, the use of this material (e.g. by watching a pornographic movie, or reading a pornographic magazine, etc.) harms the human person. The acts portrayed in this material are often gravely immoral types of acts: fornication, adultery, masturbation, unnatural sexual acts. Viewing pornographic material harms the soul, the mind, and the heart, and causes the human person to be more likely to commit various sexual sins. Therefore, the use of pornography, even within marriage and even apart from particular intrinsically evil sexual sins, is immoral due to bad consequences of grave moral weight.

.328. Child Pornography

The use of children or teenagers in pornographic movies, photos, and other material is even more gravely immoral than the same sins committed in adult pornography. Any immoral sexual act is more gravely immoral, more offensive to God, and has greater culpability, when the act is done with a minor (a person too young to give a full and meaningful consent to the acts). All sexual acts outside of marriage are intrinsically evil and always gravely immoral; the same acts with a minor are even more sinful. All unnatural sexual acts are intrinsically evil and always gravely immoral; the same acts with a minor are even more sinful. And as the age of the minor decreases, the gravity of these offenses increases. The use of minors in the creation of pornography is such a grievous offense against God and humanity, that even persons who are blind to all manner of objective mortal sin nevertheless condemn this type of sin.

However, the sins of adult pornography and of child pornography are not unrelated. The progressive acceptance of adult pornography in secular society will inevitably lead to greater sexual sins of every kind, including the severe sins of child pornography. As the conscience becomes blind to one sin after another of any kind, eventually no act is regarded as sinful. Similarly, as the conscience becomes blind to one sexual sin after another, eventually no sexual act is regarded as sinful. The increased acceptance of pornography in secular society will eventually lead to every kind of sexual sin being accepted, even those involving children.

.329. Eradicating Pornography

[Matthew]
{6:22} The lamp of your body is your eye. If your eye is wholesome, your entire body will be filled with light.
{6:23} But if your eye has been corrupted, your entire body will be darkened. If then the light that is in you is darkness, how great will that darkness be!

If everyone avoided all objectively grave sexual sins, there would be little or no pornographic material. Pornography exists in society because grave sexual sins exist in society. The creation and the use of pornography often involves the commission of various intrinsically evil gravely immoral sexual sins. Without these sins, most pornography would not exist. And if everyone avoided all objective mortal sins, pornography could not be created, distributed, or used. The path to the eradication of pornography is for people to give up all gravely immoral sexual sins of every kind. A chaste people would not create, distribute, or use pornography. The extent to which a population commits sexual sins is related to the extent to which they use pornography. An unchaste people will have every kind of sexual sin, including the many sins related to pornographic material.

Every government has a responsibility to protect and promote the common good. But the creation, distribution, and use of pornography is gravely harmful to the common good. Therefore, every government should outlaw the creation, distribution, and use of pornography. Just laws are necessary. For every large population will have some persons who are willing to commit mortal sins. But just laws are not sufficient. For if the laws are just but the people are wicked, the nation will destroy itself by its own sins. And every group of persons who persevere in mortal sin will find ways to circumvent any set of just laws, in order to commit the sins that they desire. Therefore, in order to eradicate pornography, the laws must be just, prohibiting the creation, distribution, and use of pornography, but the people must also be just, choosing to reject pornographic material and all the many grave sins associated with it.

.330. The Sin of Lust

[Matthew]
{5:27} You have heard that it was said to the ancients: 'You shall not commit adultery.'
{5:28} But I say to you, that anyone who will have looked at a woman, so as to lust after her, has already committed adultery with her in his heart.

Lust is an interior sin; it is committed in the mind and heart. But lust pertains to sexual acts, which are committed with the body, exterior to the mind and heart. The relationship between interior sins of lust and exterior sexual sins is implied by the teaching of our Lord. He gives the example of a man who lusts after a woman, and He explains that such a man has, in a sense, already committed the sin of adultery with her, in his heart. For he has consented with his will to the act of adultery. Even if this consent remains in the heart and mind, and is not followed by any bodily sexual sins, he has sinned gravely. For every act of lust is a gravely disordered sin against God and neighbor.

The sin of lust is an act whereby the human person interiorly consents to the disordered desire for a sexual act that he knows to be gravely immoral, such as adultery. In this sin, the person is truly willing to commit the exterior act, if there were an opportunity. But this interior act is substantially different from merely fantasizing about a sexual act. Lust is essentially consent to the sinful sexual act itself (though in desire), not merely consent to thoughts about the act. (See the chapter on Interior and Exterior Acts for more on this point.)

When a person commits an exterior sin of adultery, he has sinned with the will and intellect by knowingly choosing a gravely immoral bodily act. Lust is substantially the same type of interior act, but by consent to disordered desire, independent of the exterior act. Lust may occur by itself, with no exterior sinful sexual act, but with consent to the desire for any sexual act known to be gravely immoral. Or lust may occur along with an exterior sexual act. When the sin of lust occurs along with an exterior sexual sin, the two choices are two distinct sins, even if they occur at the same time. The knowing choice of the bodily sexual sin is a mortal sin. And the consent to the interior inordinate enjoyment of that sexual act is also a sin, the sin of lust. And this type of consent, too, is an adultery of the heart. Therefore, the interior sin of lust may occur in either of two ways: (1) the disordered desire for a sexual act, or (2) the inordinate enjoyment of a sexual act.

Catechism of the Catholic Church: "Lust is disordered desire for, or inordinate enjoyment of, sexual pleasure. Sexual pleasure is morally disordered when sought for itself, isolated from its procreative and unitive purposes."[360]

Although Jesus mentions looking at a woman when describing lust, He then adds "so as to lust after her." For the sin of lust does not consist merely in looking at an attractive body, but in consenting to disordered desire for, or inordinate enjoyment of, a sexual act. Although Scripture gives the example of adultery, any gravely immoral sexual act might be the object of this disordered desire. The grave immorality of the sexual act causes the desire for that act to be gravely disordered. An unmarried man might lust after an unmarried woman, thereby consenting to the sin of fornication. Any gravely immoral sexual sin of any type can be the object of lust, including adultery, fornication, masturbation, unnatural sexual acts (not only homosexual acts, but also unnatural sexual acts between a man and woman), and any other gravely immoral sexual acts.

When a person commits an objective mortal sexual sin, such as pre-marital sex, but with invincible ignorance, the chosen act does not necessarily include the sin of lust. If the person is a non-Catholic and sincerely believes that the act in question is moral, he or she might avoid the intrinsically evil sin of lust. His desire is not gravely disordered because of a lack of knowledge that the desired act is gravely contrary to the love of God and neighbor. An act is not the sin of lust unless it is deliberately chosen, either with the knowledge that the act is gravely immoral, or without concern for whether the act is gravely immoral.

.331. Lust and Marriage

Pope John Paul II: "The moral evaluation of lust (of looking lustfully), which Christ called adultery committed in the heart, seems to depend above all on the personal dignity itself of man and of woman. This holds true both for those who are not united in marriage, and -- perhaps even more -- for those who are husband and wife."[361]

Lust may occur even within marriage. Now the desire that a husband and wife have for sexual relations with one another is good and moral, and the act of natural marital relations open to life is also good and moral. But lust may occur in marriage in either of its two forms.

(1) Lust may be directed at a desired illicit sexual act. Either or both spouses might desire and consent interiorly to an act of adultery, or to an unnatural sexual act within marriage, or to an act of masturbation. Either or both spouses might desire and consent interiorly to a contracepted act of marital relations (because they desire the pleasure of sex without openness to life).

---

[360] Catechism of the Catholic Church, n. 2351.
[361] Pope John Paul II, Theology of the Body lecture series, 8 October 1980, n. 1.

Sexual Sins

(2) Lust may be directed at an inordinately desired, but in itself licit, act of natural marital relations. If a husband desires to have natural marital relations with his wife, but with consent to inordinate desire for, or inordinate enjoyment of, that sexual act, then he commits the sin of lust. A husband might lust after his wife, desiring her as a sexual object, not caring whether he satisfies his sexual desire morally or immorally. And the same applies to the wife's inordinate desire or inordinate enjoyment.

To understand how sexual desire can be inordinate even within marriage, we must understand the moral object of lust. Lust is an intrinsically evil act, and so lust always has an evil moral object, i.e. a moral object deprived of some good required by the eternal moral law. The only moral sexual act is natural marital relations open to life; this act is marital and unitive and procreative. Lust seeks to deprive the sexual act of this threefold moral object that is required by the love of God and neighbor. The different types of lust are each defined by an interior consent to the deprivation of one or more of these three meanings.

(1) So a person who desires and consents interiorly to an adulterous act commits lust because the object of his desire and consent is a sexual act deprived of the marital meaning; such a desire is inherently gravely disordered. And the husband who desires and consents interiorly to contracepted sexual relations with his wife commits lust because the object of his desire and consent is a sexual act deprived of the procreative meaning. Similarly, a person who desires and consents interiorly to an act of masturbation, or to an unnatural sexual act, or to an act of fornication, also commits lust because the object of his desire and consent is a sexual act deprived of one or more of the three meanings required by the moral law: the marital meaning, the unitive meaning, the procreative meaning. The desire is gravely disordered because of the deprivation of a good required by the eternal moral law in the moral object of the desire.

(2) But when a husband commits lust by inordinate desire for his spouse (or she for him), then he desires and consents interiorly to the sexual pleasure sought for itself (as its own end), separate from, or in direct contradiction to, the proper threefold moral object. He does not care is the act is marital or not, procreative or not, unitive or not. He desires and consents to the pleasure just as if the act were non-marital, or non-unitive, or non-procreative. When the act itself that he commits exteriorly has all three meanings, then that act is not intrinsically evil. But this exterior act may be accompanied by an interior act of lust, which is deprived of this same moral object. For the inherent moral meaning of the act itself is determined by the moral object, good or evil, toward which that act is inherently directed, not by the attainment of that moral object. If a contracepted (non-procreative) sexual act accidentally attains procreation, the act was nevertheless intrinsically evil because it was not inherently ordered toward procreation.

Similarly, a husband might commit the sin of lust, in regard to an act of natural marital relations open to life, by an interior act which is not inherently ordered toward the marital, unitive, procreative meanings, but which instead seeks sexual pleasure as an end, in and of itself, with thorough disregard for, or in direct contradiction to, that threefold good. Although such an interior act of lust, in the case of natural marital relations, fails to deprive the act of that threefold meaning, it is nevertheless ordered toward that deprivation. And so the interior act of lust remains intrinsically evil and gravely immoral, even though it may occur within marriage, or in conjunction with an act of natural marital relations open to life.

.332. Moral Sexual Thoughts and Desires

If the intention is good, and the act is not intrinsically evil, and the good consequences outweigh any bad consequences, then the act is certainly moral. Thoughts and desires pertaining to sexuality do not necessarily have a bad intention, nor an evil moral object, nor bad consequences that outweigh the good consequences. Therefore, interior thoughts and desire concerning sexuality are not necessarily a sin.

A passing sexual thought to which one does not consent is not a sin. Such thoughts are merely a temptation. Only knowingly chosen acts can possibly be sins. We have such thoughts because we are in a fallen state, that is, because of concupiscence. But without consent, no passing thought is a sin.

Admiration for the beauty of the human form, in an ordered way and to a limited extent, is not a sin. Attraction to members of the opposite sex is natural and good, when kept within the bounds of love of God and neighbor. If there were no such attraction, then there would be no marriage, and no propagation of the human race. This ordinary natural attraction is not lust and is not in itself a sin.

Consideration of sexual acts, in an ordered way, to a limited extent, and without lustful desire, for any good purpose is moral, if all three fonts are good. For example, a person who is studying morality must consider which acts are moral and which are immoral in the realm of sexuality. And a person who is considering married life may morally consider, in an ordered way, to a limited extent, and without lustful desire, what marital relations might be like, and what constitutes an ordered sexual relationship in marriage.

.333. Venial Sexual Thoughts and Desires

Even when interior thoughts or desires are sinful in some way, to some extent, the sin may be venial, or it may be mortal. The usual conditions for a sin to be an actual sin, or an actual mortal sin, always apply. So the following discussion will focus on whether or not the matter is grave for sexual thoughts and desires.

Lust is always an objective mortal sin because the moral object is gravely immoral (as explained previously). But not every sexual thought or desire, even when sinful, is lust. Some sexual thoughts or desires might be sinful under the first font of intention, without sin in the second font of moral object. Other sexual thoughts or desires might be sinful under the third font, or under both the first and third fonts, but not the second. Therefore, some sexual thoughts and desires may be sinful, without being the objective mortal sin of lust.

Some limited sexual fantasies, without consent to the act itself (i.e. without a willingness to commit an illicit sexual act), but with consent to thoughts about sexual acts and sexuality, would not constitute the sin of lust, and would generally not be objective mortal sins. The intention may be somewhat selfish or self-indulgent, but not necessarily to such an extent as to be entirely incompatible with the love of God and neighbor, and with the state of grace in the soul. Similarly, some consent to sexual thoughts and desires might have some limited bad consequences, which outweigh the good consequences, but not to a grave extent. Such a sin is venial because the chosen act is not entirely incompatible with the love of God and neighbor. Lust is always a grave matter, and is always an objective mortal sin. But there are numerous possible interior acts in the mind and heart, which pertain to sexuality in some way and to some extent, but without grave matter. These acts are not objective mortal sins, but may well be objective venial sins.

.334. The Epistles of Paul

[2 Corinthians]
{12:21} If so, then, when I have arrived, God may again humble me among you. And so, I mourn for the many who sinned beforehand, and did not repent, over the lust and fornication and homosexuality, which they have committed.

Notice the progression of sins that Saint Paul describes: from the interior sin of lust, to the exterior sexual sin of fornication, to the more grievous exterior sin of homosexual acts. When a person commits the sin of lust and does not repent, he is led to ever worse sins. When a person repeatedly commits grave sins, and continues to refuse to repent, his sins become worse and worse. Sexual sins generally begin as interior sins, and then progress to exterior sins, and next the exterior sins become progressively worse. The faithful disciple of Christ must guard his heart and mind from even the lesser interior sexual sins, so that he may remain far from the interior sin of lust, and far from all the exterior sexual sins.

[Galatians]
{5:19} Now the works of the flesh are manifest; they are: fornication, lust, homosexuality, self-indulgence,
{5:20} the serving of idols, drug use, hostility, contentiousness, jealousy, wrath, quarrels, dissensions, divisions,
{5:21} envy, murder, inebriation, carousing, and similar things. About these things, I continue to preach to you, as I have preached to you: that those who act in this way shall not obtain the kingdom of God.
{5:22} But the fruit of the Spirit is charity, joy, peace, patience, kindness, goodness, forbearance,
{5:23} meekness, faith, modesty, abstinence, chastity. There is no law against such things.

Recall that this chapter on sexual sins began with a discussion of virtue. If you wish to avoid sins of lust and other interior sexual sins, you must practice all the virtues in cooperation with the Holy Spirit. The infused and acquired virtues are like a close-knit holy family, who each and all support and assist one another in every good work. But the vices are like a close-knit wicked family, who each and all support and assist one another in every evil work. Therefore, every actual mortal sin, and even venial sins, have a tendency to lead the human person into ever more serious sins of the same type, and into sins of every type. Practice all the virtues in order to avoid all the vices.

[Ephesians]
{5:1} Therefore, as most beloved sons, be imitators of God.
{5:2} And walk in love, just as Christ also loved us and delivered himself for us, as an oblation and a sacrifice to God, with a fragrance of sweetness.
{5:3} But let not any kind of fornication, or impurity, or rapacity so much as be named among you, just as is worthy of the saints,
{5:4} nor any indecent, or foolish, or abusive talk, for this is without purpose; but instead, give thanks.
{5:5} For know and understand this: no one who is a fornicator, or lustful, or rapacious (for these are a kind of service to idols) holds an inheritance in the kingdom of Christ and of God.
{5:6} Let no one seduce you with empty words. For because of these things, the wrath of God was sent upon the sons of unbelief.
{5:7} Therefore, do not choose to become participants with them.
{5:8} For you were darkness, in times past, but now you are light, in the Lord. So then, walk as sons of the light.

True love of God and neighbor is entirely incompatible with lust. If we imitate Christ, and strive to please God in lives of prayer, self-denial, works of mercy, then we will be willing and able to avoid all objective mortal sins, including the interior and exterior sexual sins. Notice that Paul is concerned not only with prohibiting mortal sins, such as fornication and lust, but also lesser sins that might lead to greater sins, such as "indecent, or foolish, or abusive talk." For the continued unrepentant commission of lesser sins will inevitably lead to serious sins of every kind. And anyone who commits even one actual mortal sin, if he does not repent before death, loses the inheritance of eternal life, and will be punished in the darkness of Hell forever.

[Colossians 3]
{3:1} Therefore, if you have risen together with Christ, seek the things that are above, where Christ is seated at the right hand of God.
{3:2} Consider the things that are above, not the things that are upon the earth.
{3:3} For you have died, and so your life is hidden with Christ in God.
{3:4} When Christ, your life, appears, then you also will appear with him in glory.
{3:5} Therefore, mortify your body, while it is upon the earth. For because of fornication, impurity, lust, evil desires, and avarice, which are a kind of service to idols,
{3:6} the wrath of God has overwhelmed the sons of unbelief.

In order to avoid sexual sins, both interior and exterior, we must practice the imitation of Christ with every virtue, in every kind of good work. Prayer and self-denial are also essential to strengthen the soul against every kind of interior and exterior sin, including "fornication, impurity, lust...." Not only exterior sexual sins, such as fornication, but also interior sexual sins, such as lust, must be avoided.

Scripture uses the word 'fornication' in this verse in the broader sense, to include all illicit sexual acts. And lust is mentioned because it is the worst of the interior sexual sins; but a rejection of other lesser interior sexual sins is also implied. Impurity is placed between fornication and lust because impurity can be either exterior or interior. Also, while fornication and lust are each objective mortal sins, impurity can be venial or mortal. There are various exterior impure acts, which are not per se sexual acts and which may be venial or mortal, e.g. viewing a movie with excessive sensuality or nudity. And there are various interior impure thoughts and desires, which are not lust and which may be venial or mortal. Thus, with only three words, Sacred Scripture indicates all sexual sins, from exterior to interior, and from mortal to venial.

Sexual sins can become a form of idolatry, figuratively speaking. True worship of God involves a giving over of one's self to an infinitely good God, to believe His teachings and to do what is good in His sight. But idolatry involves giving one's self over to that which is finite, which has only limited goodness. Sexual sins can lead a person to a false worship of pleasure, which is essentially just a way of worshiping one's self. And every form of idolatry is objective mortal sin.

[1 Thessalonians 4]
{4:1} Therefore, concerning other things, brothers, we ask and beg you, in the Lord Jesus, that, just as you have received from us the way in which you ought to walk and to please God, so also may you walk, in order that you may abound all the more.
{4:2} For you know what precepts I have given to you through the Lord Jesus.
{4:3} For this is the will of God, your sanctification: that you should abstain from fornication,
{4:4} that each one of you should know how to possess his vessel in sanctification and honor,
{4:5} not in passions of lust, like the Gentiles who do not know God,
{4:6} and that no one should overwhelm or circumvent his brother in business. For the Lord is the vindicator of all these things, just as we have preached and testified to you.
{4:7} For God has not called us to impurity, but to sanctification.
{4:8} And so, whoever despises these teachings, does not despise man, but God, who has even provided his Holy Spirit within us.

In verse four, the term 'vessel' refers to the genital sexual faculty. The various intrinsically evil sexual sins (adultery, fornication, masturbation, unnatural sexual acts) all represent different ways to deliberately misuse the genital sexual faculty. But Sacred Scripture instructs each person to abstain from fornication (used broadly to refer to any illicit sexual act) by knowing how to possess his or her vessel (the sexual faculty) in sanctification and honor, without sexual sins of any kind. This holy understanding of human sexuality contradicts the beliefs and practices of sinful secular society, a society which promotes self-indulgence in the passions of lust. They despise and ridicule this teaching on purity and sanctification. In its place, they teach an idolatry which exalts sexuality above all else, above even the eternal moral law.

.335. Adultery

The sin of adultery is intrinsically evil and always gravely immoral because the moral object of the sexual act is deprived of the marital meaning. In this regard, the second font of adultery is like the second font of any extra-marital sexual act. However, adultery also has a second gravely immoral object, which is the breaking of the marital vows. So for this reason, an act of adultery is more gravely immoral than an act of pre-marital sex. All this concerns the second font.

In the third font, every intrinsically evil gravely immoral sexual act does some grave harm. But adultery is more grave than many other illicit sexual acts because of the additional harm done to the marriage, and possibly to the children. So the harm done in the third font makes the act of adultery even more grave. In the first font, the intentions of the sinner may vary, but no intention can justify an act that is gravely immoral under the second font, and no intention can justify an act that is gravely immoral under the third font. Adultery is always gravely immoral, and has grave bad consequences for the individuals, the marriage, the family, and society. Marriage is the basis for the family, and is one of the fundamental building blocks of civilized society. Whatever harms the institution of marriage, harms the family and society.

Adultery can occur in a number of different forms. A married man might have sexual relations with an unmarried woman, or with a woman who is married to someone else. A married woman might have sexual relations with an unmarried man, or with a man who is married to someone else. Whenever a married person commits sexual acts of any kind (including homosexual acts) with anyone other than his or her spouse, the act is the sin of adultery.

Catechism of the Catholic Church: "Adultery refers to marital infidelity. When two partners, of whom at least one is married to another party, have sexual relations -- even transient ones -- they commit adultery."[362]

The phrase 'even transient ones' [French: *même éphémère;* Latin: *etiam fugacem*] refers to a brief sexual relationship, which might consist of even one sexual act. Any sexual act between a married person and someone other than his or her spouse is the sin of adultery. Sometimes the term adultery refers to an on-going adulterous relationship, which might include a number of extra-marital sexual acts. But even one sexual act outside of marriage and in violation of the marriage vows is adultery.

Adultery can be narrowly defined by its moral object, as a sexual act that lacks the marital meaning and violates the marriage vows. Masturbation lacks the marital meaning, and is always gravely immoral, but is not a per se violation of the marital vows. However, all intrinsically evil sexual acts, including adultery, masturbation, and any unnatural sexual acts that occur between the husband and

---

[362] Catechism of the Catholic Church, n. 2380.

the wife, harm the marriage and offend against both natural marriage and the Sacrament of Marriage. And any offense against the Sacrament of Marriage is more grave than the same offense against a marriage that is only natural, because greater harm is done when the good is greater.

Adultery can also be used broadly to refer to any illicit sexual act by married persons. Every illicit sexual act offends against the marriage vows, because the vows are not only a mutual promise between husband and wife, but also vows made before God. So any intrinsically evil gravely immoral sexual act committed by one or both spouses is a type of adultery, broadly defined. All such acts lack one or more of the three meanings required by God: unitive, procreative, marital, and all such acts offend against the marriage vows made before God. Saint Thomas uses the term adultery to refer, in a sense, even to sexual sins between a husband and wife.

Saint Thomas Aquinas: "And since the man who is too ardent a lover of his wife acts counter to the good of marriage if he use her indecently, although he be not unfaithful, he may in a sense be called an adulterer; and even more so than he that is too ardent a lover of another woman."[363]

[Hebrews 13]
{13:4} May marriage be honorable in every way, and may the marriage bed be immaculate. For God will judge fornicators and adulterers.

In this verse, 'fornicators' is used to refer to all sexual sins by unmarried persons, and 'adulterers' is used to refer to all sexual sins by married persons. Thus, in only two words, Sacred Scripture sums up all illicit sexual acts. Every person who commits any objective mortal sexual sin will be judged by God, whether the sexual sin occurred within marriage or outside of marriage, whether the sexual sin was committed by a married person or an unmarried person. Being married is not an excuse for committing sexual sins. Being unmarried is not an excuse for committing sexual sins.

[Matthew]
{15:19} For from the heart go out evil thoughts, murders, adulteries, fornications, thefts, false testimonies, blasphemies.

.336. Divorce and Adultery

[Luke]
{16:18} Everyone who divorces his wife and marries another commits adultery. And whoever marries her who has been divorced by her husband commits adultery.

It is not the purpose of this work to consider every possible situation regarding natural marriage, Old Testament practices, the Sacrament of Marriage, validity, licitness, annulments, separation of a validly married couple, or cases of uncertainty as to validity. A consideration of the complexities of these various possible situations would fill a book of its own.

---

[363] Saint Thomas Aquinas, Summa Theologica, II-II, Q. 154, A. 8.

However, on the question of adultery, when a Christian man and woman are validly married in the Sacrament of holy Matrimony, the bond of the Sacrament remains until the death of one of the spouses. And a second valid marriage cannot occur while the bond remains. When one spouse dies, the other spouse may validly remarry. But a civil divorce while both spouses are living does not break the Sacramental bond. Therefore, if a validly married couple obtain a civil divorce, they remain married in the eyes of God and His Church. And if one or both of them remarries, any second marriage is not a valid Sacrament of Marriage and is not even a merely natural marriage. The couple in the 'second marriage' are both committing the sin of adultery. Although every valid Sacrament of Marriage is also a natural marriage, a baptized couple cannot validly contract a marriage that is only a natural marriage, and is not also the true valid Sacrament of holy Matrimony.[364]

In such cases, the sexual acts of the couple in the 'second marriage' are deprived of the marital meaning because no true marriage can exist while the bond of the Sacrament remains between either person and a living spouse from a previous and valid Sacrament of Marriage. Any attempted second marriage would be necessarily always invalid. And this is why our Lord equates adultery with divorce and remarriage.

An annulment does not break the bond of a valid Sacrament of Marriage. An annulment is merely a declaration of the temporal authority of the Church, after diligent examination, that no valid Sacrament of Marriage exists between two persons. If the decision to grant an annulment was in error, then the bond of the Sacrament remains. Even the Church does not have the authority to break the bond of a valid Sacrament of Marriage.

[Matthew]
{5:31} And it has been said: 'Whoever would dismiss his wife, let him give her a bill of divorce.'
{5:32} But I say to you, that anyone who will have dismissed his wife, except in the case of fornication, causes her to commit adultery; and whoever will have married her who has been dismissed commits adultery.

The previous passage on divorce and adultery in Luke considered the sin itself of adultery; each spouse who divorces and remarries commits the sin of adultery. But now we are considering the effect on other persons of one spouse's decision to obtain a divorce. Often, one spouse chooses divorce against the will of the other spouse. In such cases, the divorcing spouse commits other sins, in addition to the sin of adultery if he or she remarries. The divorcing spouse commits the sin of scandal (leading other persons into sin) by giving a bad example to the rest of the faithful by initiating a divorce (without a grave reason). But a more serious type of scandal is also implied in many cases.

---

[364] Pope Pius XI, Casti Connubii, n. 39, "there can be no true marriage between baptized persons 'without it being by that very fact a sacrament.' " Inner quote from Codex Iuris Canonici (1917) Canon 1012, n. 2; cf. Code of Canon Law (1983), Canon 1055, n. 2.

For Jesus taught that, in a sense, the divorcing spouse 'causes' the other spouse to commit adultery. Of course, no one can cause someone else to sin, since sin is by definition an act of the free will. What Jesus means is that the divorcing spouse causes the other spouse to be in a situation in which many persons would be tempted to commit grave sexual sins, particularly the sin of adultery, either by invalid remarriage, or by sexual relations without remarriage. The divorcing spouse is committing a grave sin of scandal, since his or her act of divorcing the other spouse places that person in a situation where avoiding sexual sins is more difficult, and perhaps in some cases much more difficult. The gravity of this sin of scandal is determined, in part, by the degree of likelihood that the other spouse will sin in this situation. As is true in all cases of scandal, this degree of likelihood is weighed in the third font.

The phrase 'the case of fornication' refers to grave sexual sins by one spouse. The term fornication is used here very broadly, to include any intrinsically evil and gravely immoral sexual sin (contraception, adultery, masturbation, spousal rape, child sexual abuse, homosexual acts and any other unnatural sexual acts). Every grave sexual sin committed by a married person not only offends God due to the lack of the marital, unitive, or procreative meanings, but also offends gravely against the holy Sacrament of Marriage. Therefore, our Lord and His Church permit separation of the spouses for these sins (and for some other grave sins), but with the bond of the Sacrament remaining. The separated persons may not remarry, and may not have sexual relations outside of marriage; they must each remain chaste, just as if they were single persons.

And if the spouse who offends in 'the case of fornication' continues to commit grave sexual sins after separation, the other spouse is not guilty of having led that person into grave sin, regardless of who initiated the divorce. For the offending spouse decided to commit these grave sexual sins in marriage, sins that are gravely harmful to the marriage. The innocent spouse may obtain this separation as a type of self-defense of the soul against grave and unrepentant sins. For the continued grave sexual sins of one spouse are likely to cause grave harm to the soul of the other spouse.

Otherwise, in cases where both spouses agree to divorce, neither one is guilty of leading the other person into sin. But each one is guilty of whatever sins he or she commits, such as the sin of adultery (in cases of divorce and remarriage), or the sin of scandal (in divorce and remarriage, or in divorce without grave cause), or the sin of contempt for the Sacrament of Marriage. The teaching that divorcing a spouse without grave cause causes him or her to commit adultery does not apply if both spouses willingly divorce one another. Each is then responsible for his or her own sins, because each chose to be in the state of divorce with the bond of the Sacrament remaining.

The last point made in Matthew 5:32 concerns a person who might not have been previously married. Even when he or she, as a first marriage, marries a divorced person (one who is still validly married to another), he or she commits adultery. This type of merely civil marriage includes the sin of adultery for both persons, even if only one of them has a living spouse from a previous valid marriage. Similarly, when an unmarried person has sexual relations with a married person, both persons are committing adultery. And this type of civil marriage, when one or both spouses are still validly married in the eyes of the Church, is neither a true natural marriage, nor a valid Sacrament of Marriage; mere civil marriage is not a true type of marriage at all. But as our Lord clearly taught, the relationship is adulterous, not marital. And so all sexual acts within that remarriage lack the marital meaning and are gravely immoral.

[1 Corinthians]
{7:10} But to those who have been joined in matrimony, it is not I who commands you, but the Lord: a wife is not to separate from her husband.
{7:11} But if she has separated from him, she must remain unmarried, or be reconciled to her husband. And a husband should not divorce his wife.

.337. Fornication

Catechism of the Catholic Church: "Fornication is carnal union between an unmarried man and an unmarried woman. It is gravely contrary to the dignity of persons and of human sexuality which is naturally ordered to the good of spouses and the generation and education of children. Moreover, it is a grave scandal when there is corruption of the young."[365]

The term 'fornication' can be defined in a number of different ways. The narrowest definition includes only natural intercourse between an unmarried man and an unmarried woman; this may be referred to as simple fornication, since it is the simplest case. The moral object of simple fornication lacks only the marital meaning, and does not lack the unitive and procreative meanings.

But this is not the only possible useful definition of fornication. The use of contraception would deprive the act of the procreative meaning also, and would harm the unitive meaning, making the sin more grave than the simplest case. And this, too, is a type of fornication. Sometimes the term fornication is used very broadly, as in Matthew 5:32, which includes any grave sexual sin, even by a married person. A number of intermediate definitions of fornication are also possible. Sins such as masturbation, homosexual acts, and unnatural sexual acts between a man and woman (even if they are married) may be accurately called types of fornication.

As in adultery, the sexual act of simple fornication lacks the marital meaning in its moral object. Some types of fornication also lack the unitive and procreative meanings in the moral object. In every case, fornication is intrinsically evil and always gravely immoral. But the evil moral object particular to adultery, the breaking of the marital vows, is not found in a narrower definition of fornication. Therefore, under the second font, simple fornication is a somewhat less serious sin than adultery, but nevertheless is an objective mortal sin. Some mortal sins are more serious than other mortal sins. However, for any particular act of fornication or adultery, the first and third fonts may make the act a more or less serious sin. So it is possible for a particular act of fornication to be more grave

---

[365] Catechism of the Catholic Church, n. 2353.

than a particular act of adultery. But in every case, each and every act of adultery or fornication is an objective mortal sin. Whenever one font is gravely immoral, the other two fonts cannot make the act less than an objective mortal sin.

Sacred Scripture sometimes uses the term 'fornication' narrowly, and other times broadly.

[Sirach]
{23:33} For first, she was unbelieving of the law of the Most High. Second, she offended against her husband. Third, she fornicated by adultery, and so established her children by another man.

In the above verse, the verb referring to fornication [Latin: *fornicata est*] is used to describe an act of adultery. In this example, fornication is used so broadly as to include every illicit sexual act, whether in marriage or out of marriage. Whenever any sexual act lacks one of more of the three meanings required by the love of God and neighbor -- the marital, unitive, and procreative meanings -- then the sexual act is intrinsically evil and gravely immoral, and may be termed a type of fornication (using the broad term).

This same broad definition is used in Matthew 5:32, which refers to sexual sins by a spouse as cause for separation (as previously discussed). 1 Corinthians uses the term fornication when referring to a man having sexual relations with 'the wife of his father' [i.e. his stepmother], which is a type of adultery (and a type of incest). The same Epistle later uses 'fornication' to refer to any illicit sexual act.

[1 Corinthians]
{5:1} Above all else, it is being said that there is fornication among you, even fornication of a such kind that is not among the Gentiles, so that someone would have the wife of his father.
...
{6:13} Food is for the stomach, and the stomach is for food. But God shall destroy both the stomach and food. And the body is not for fornication, but rather for the Lord; and the Lord is for the body.
...
{6:18} Flee from fornication. Every sin whatsoever that a man commits is outside of the body, but whoever fornicates, sins against his own body.

Every type of illicit sexual act is a sin against the body, which is the Temple of the Holy Spirit. Therefore, every type of fornication, whether out of marriage or in marriage, even between a husband and wife, is always gravely immoral. This use of the word 'fornication' includes every illicit sexual act.

But Sacred Scripture also uses 'fornication' more narrowly, as distinct from adultery and other grave sexual sins. In 1 Corinthians 6:9-10, fornication is distinguished from other gravely immoral sexual sins, such as adultery and homosexual acts. But in 1 Corinthians 7:1-2, the term 'fornication' refers to any sexual acts outside of marriage, without any other distinction.

[1 Corinthians]
{6:9} Do you not know that the iniquitous will not possess the kingdom of God? Do not choose to wander astray. For neither fornicators, nor servants of idolatry, nor adulterers,
{6:10} nor the effeminate, nor males who sleep with males, nor thieves, nor the avaricious, nor the inebriated, nor slanderers, nor the rapacious shall possess the kingdom of God.
...
{7:1} Now concerning the things about which you wrote to me: It is good for a man not to touch a woman.
{7:2} But, because of fornication, let each man have his own wife, and let each woman have her own husband.

This difference in the way that the word 'fornication' is used in Scripture is not an indication of a difference in doctrine. Terminology is not dogma. Various terms may be used to describe the same doctrine, or the same term may be used variously when explaining different points of doctrine in different ways. It would be the error of Pharisaism to unthinkingly require each term to be used only in one specific way, regardless of the truths being taught. And neither is it correct to claim that Scripture necessarily intends the same meaning wherever the same word is used.

.338. Secular Norms

Fornication (sexual acts between unmarried persons) is very common in modern society. This sin is so widespread that it has become the accepted social norm. Couples do not even consider whether sexual relations before marriage is moral. It is assumed to be moral because so many persons hold that opinion. However, the moral law is eternal and unchanging because the Just Nature of God is eternal and unchanging. All sexual acts outside of marriage are always gravely immoral because they are intrinsically evil; they lack the marital meaning that is required by the love of God, neighbor, self.

Part of the reason that pre-marital sexual relations is so widely practiced and accepted may be because a large segment of society is sexually mature, and yet unmarried. In recent decades, men and women have married at a progressively later time in life. In many nations, men and women wait until their mid to late 20's, or even their early 30's, before marrying. From their teens through much of their 20's, a large proportion of the population is sexually mature, but unmarried. Society teaches them, in subtle and not so subtle ways, that it is good to have sexual relations before marriage, and that it is not good to marry until later in life.

A related problem, also seen in recent decades, is a progressive decrease in the average age at the onset of puberty. These two trends, earlier puberty and later marriage, cause the number of years from the age of sexual maturity (of the body) to the age of marriage to have increased substantially. This age gap is one of many factors which has influenced secular society to approve of pre-marital sexual relations, despite the ethical mores of previous generations.

.339. Masturbation

Sacred Congregation for the Doctrine of the Faith: "in fact both the Magisterium of the Church -- in the course of a constant tradition -- and the moral sense of the faithful have declared without hesitation that masturbation is an intrinsically and seriously disordered act. The main reason is that, whatever the motive for acting this way, the deliberate use of the sexual faculty outside normal conjugal relations essentially contradicts the finality of the faculty. For it lacks the sexual relationship called for by the moral order, namely the relationship which realizes 'the full sense of mutual self-giving and human procreation in the context of true love.' All deliberate exercise of sexuality must be reserved to this regular relationship. Even if it cannot be proved that Scripture condemns this sin by name, the tradition of the Church has rightly understood it to be condemned in the New Testament when the latter speaks of 'impurity,' 'unchasteness' and other vices contrary to chastity and continence."[366]

The Magisterium teaches that masturbation is an intrinsically evil and gravely immoral act. An act is intrinsically evil only when it has an evil moral object. The moral object in the case of masturbation is the deliberate use of the sexual faculty without the marital, unitive, or procreative meanings. In moral terms, the sin of masturbation is much like all the other intrinsically evil sexual sins. They each lack one or more of the three meanings intended by God for sexual acts.

Since acts of masturbation are intrinsically evil, such acts are never justified by intention (purpose) or circumstances. Therefore, masturbation cannot morally be used for the purpose of obtaining a specimen for medical analysis. Neither does an act of masturbation become moral by association with an act of natural marital relations. Whether this act is committed on one's self or on another person (also called manipulate sex), the act is intrinsically evil and always gravely immoral. The good end of natural marital relations does not justify the evil means of masturbation (or manipulative sex). All such acts remain intrinsically evil and always gravely immoral, regardless of whether these acts occur in marriage or out of marriage, regardless of whether these acts occur before, during, or after an act of natural marital relations, and regardless of whether or not sexual climax occurs.

Masturbation is intrinsically evil for the same reason that other illicit sexual acts are intrinsically evil: because the act does not have all three goods required by the moral law in its moral object: the procreative, marital, and unitive meanings. The absence of sexual climax does not add the unitive, or procreative, or marital meaning to an intrinsically evil sexual act. The commission of an act of natural marital relations before, during, or after an act of masturbation (or other illicit sexual act) does not change the moral object of that illicit sexual act. Therefore, even within marriage, the act of masturbation, whether on one's self or one one's spouse, with or without sexual climax, is intrinsically evil and always gravely immoral.

---

[366] CDF, Persona Humana, IX; inner quote from Second Vatican Council, Gaudium et Spes, n. 51.

Sexual Sins

Catechism of the Catholic Church: "By masturbation is to be understood the deliberate stimulation of the genital organs in order to derive sexual pleasure."[367]

A sexual act is any deliberate use of the genital sexual faculty. The sin of masturbation includes a person stimulating himself or herself, or a person similarly stimulating another person. Although the Catechism states the usual purpose (intended end) of this sin, the purpose is in the first font, and the definition of every intrinsically evil act, in its inherent moral meaning, is in the second font. So even if a person were to use masturbation for another purpose, such as to obtain a sample for medical testing, or such as to prepare for natural marital relations, the act remains intrinsically evil and always gravely immoral. Intrinsically evil acts are always defined, in their essential moral nature, by their moral object, not by their purpose.

The intention to derive sexual pleasure is in the first font. The result called sexual climax is a consequence in the third font. Neither a change in intention nor a change in consequences has any effect on the moral object of an act. The absence of sexual climax, or the presence of a different intention, does not justify any act of masturbation, nor any other intrinsically evil sexual act.

The same reasoning applies to masturbation before, during, or after an act of natural marital relations. The purpose, in the first font, to facilitate the natural marital act, does not change the moral object, in the second font. The absence of sexual climax, in the third font, does not change the moral object, in the second font. The act itself of masturbation, whether of one's self or of another person is intrinsically evil because of its moral object. Any deliberate sexual stimulation of the genitals by manipulation (or by devices, or by other means) is a use of the genital sexual faculty without the marital, unitive, and procreative meanings, and is intrinsically evil and gravely immoral. Such acts are not justified by any intention or circumstance, nor by any prior, concurrent, or subsequent act.

It is difficult to judge how widespread the sin of masturbation might be in the world today. This sin is probably widespread even among Catholic Christians. The sin of masturbation is often committed where no one can see. But Sacred Scripture has an insightful rebuke of this sin. For God not only created all things, He continues to behold all things, including sins committed in darkness, or behind walls and closed doors.

[Sirach]
{23:22} A desirous soul is like a burning fire, it will not be quenched, until it devours something.
{23:23} And a man who is wicked in the desires of his flesh will not desist until he has kindled a fire.
{23:24} To a man of fornication, all bread is sweet; he will not tire of transgression, to the very end.
{23:25} Every man who transgresses his own bed has contempt for his own soul. And so he says: "Who can see me?

---
[367] Catechism of the Catholic Church, n. 2352.

Sexual Sins

{23:26} Darkness surrounds me, and the walls enclose me, and no one catches sight of me. Whom should I fear? The Most High will not remember my offenses."

{23:27} And he does not understand that God's eye sees all things. For fear within a man such as this drives away from him both the fear of God and the eyes of those men who fear God.

{23:28} And he does not acknowledge that the eyes of the Lord are much brighter than the sun, keeping watch over all the ways of men, even to the depths of the abyss, and gazing into the hearts of men, even to the most hidden parts.

{23:29} For all things, before they were created, were known to the Lord God. And even after their completion, he beholds all things.

The sin of masturbation is an objective mortal sin. Some theologians are quick to claim a reduction in culpability, due to various psychological or social factors, to that of an actual venial sin. Now it is true that any objective mortal sin might be reduced, by any of the previously discussed factors that affect culpability, to an actual venial sin. This is particularly true for children, who might not have sufficient maturity or understanding to be able to give a true and full consent to sexual acts. Both full consent and full knowledge are required for an objective mortal sin to be also an actual mortal sin.

However, due to the natural law, and the clear definitive teaching of the Church, many persons (including youths) have sufficient understanding to know that masturbation is gravely immoral. And while psychological factors can reduce culpability, a minor reduction in culpability does not cause an objective mortal sin to be anything other than an actual mortal sin. Only a substantial reduction in the exercise of free will, or in the knowledge of the grave immorality of the act, can cause an objective mortal sin to be less than an actual mortal sin. Many sexual sins in the world today are not only objective mortal sins, but also actual mortal sins. For the world in which we live is very sinful.

.340. Homosexual Acts

Catechism of the Catholic Church: "Basing itself on Sacred Scripture, which presents homosexual acts as acts of grave depravity, tradition has always declared that 'homosexual acts are intrinsically disordered.' They are contrary to the natural law. They close the sexual act to the gift of life. They do not proceed from a genuine affective and sexual complementarity. Under no circumstances can they be approved."[368]

All unnatural sexual acts are intrinsically evil and always gravely immoral, regardless of the gender of the persons committing those acts. Such acts are deprived of the procreative meaning, and are also not truly unitive, and not truly marital. Sexual acts of any kind between two persons of the same gender are always unnatural, intrinsically evil, and gravely immoral. All such acts lack the marital meaning, and the unitive meaning, and the procreative meaning. There is no more thorough deprivation of the good moral object intended by God for sexual acts than sexual acts between persons of the same gender. All three

---

[368] Catechism of the Catholic Church, n. 2357; inner quote: CDF, Persona Humana, VIII.

meanings are entirely absent from all such acts. There is no genuine affective complementarity and no genuine sexual complementarity. And no type of sexual act could ever be moral between two persons of the same gender. The grave immorality of any and all sexual acts between persons of the same gender is due to an evil moral object, under the second font.

Under the first font of intention, some persons might claim to have a good intended end. But a good intended end cannot justify the use of a gravely immoral intrinsically evil act as the intended means to that end. Whenever anyone intends to use an intrinsically evil means to achieve a good end, the intended means, and therefore the first font, is immoral.

Under the third font of consequences, homosexual acts are also gravely immoral, due to the grave harm necessarily found in the consequences of such acts. All illicit sexual acts are intrinsically evil and gravely immoral, and therefore they do grave harm. It is not possible for a grave sin under the second font to do no harm in the third font because all of our actions, even those hidden in the heart and mind, have consequences, both interior and exterior. Even an interior mortal sin does grave harm to the soul of the sinner, grave harm to persons near and far who would have received important graces if he had not sinned, and grave harm to the Church and to the world.

In particular, grave sexual sins of any kind harm marriage and the family by distorting the proper understanding of sexuality and its place in humanity. All such sins harm the progress of the plan of God to form a holy people, and these sins generally include the sin of scandal. Grave sexual sins committed with other persons do grave harm to the souls and lives of those other persons. All sexual sins do grave harm, but the sins of homosexual acts do far more harm by being far more thoroughly contrary to all that God intends for men and women, human sexuality, marriage, family, society, and the Church.

Sacred Congregation for the Doctrine of the Faith: "Sacred Scripture condemns homosexual acts…. This same moral judgment is found in many Christian writers of the first centuries and is unanimously accepted by Catholic Tradition."[369]

[Romans]
{1:22} For, while proclaiming themselves to be wise, they became foolish.

This verse is still true today. Many persons in secular society speak vehemently against the teaching of the Church on morals, and in favor of all manner of sin. They consider their own arguments to be common sense, or even wisdom, but in truth, their ideas are corrupt and their arguments are foolish.

---

[369] Cardinal Ratzinger, CDF, Considerations Regarding Proposals to Give Legal Recognition to Unions between Homosexual Persons, n. 4. Cf. St. Polycarp, Letter to the Philippians, V, 3; St. Justin Martyr, First Apology, 27, 1-4; Athenagoras, Supplication for the Christians, 34.

{1:23} And they exchanged the glory of the incorruptible God for the likeness of an image of corruptible man, and of flying things, and of four-legged beasts, and of serpents.
{1:24} For this reason, God handed them over to the desires of their own heart for impurity, so that they afflicted their own bodies with indignities among themselves.
{1:25} And they exchanged the truth of God for a lie. And they worshipped and served the creature, rather than the Creator, who is blessed for all eternity. Amen.

In one sense, Paul is speaking about the pagan religions, which lacked both a proper understanding of God, and a proper understanding of morality. But all of Sacred Scripture is Christ speaking to us. And so, in another sense, this verse condemns every form of idolatry, including the worship of money, technology, culture, drugs and alcohol, sexual sins, and whatever else people substitute for the worship of God.

All idolatry is a form of self-worship. As a result, this idolatry often leads to self-indulgences of every kind, and then to the disuse of conscience and a deprivation of moral truth in the mind, and finally to every serious sins. Immersed in self-indulgence, and lacking a true understanding of good and evil, many persons fall into various types of serious sin, including sexual sins. All this is a consequence of abandoning the true worship of God, just as Sacred Scripture teaches.

{1:26} Because of this, God handed them over to shameful passions. For example, their females have exchanged the natural use of the body for a use which is against nature.
{1:27} And similarly, the males also, abandoning the natural use of females, have burned in their desires for one another: males doing with males what is disgraceful, and receiving within themselves the recompense that necessarily results from their error.

This entire passage from Romans supports the distinction between the natural sexual act, and various unnatural sexual acts. The natural law condemns all homosexual acts and also any unnatural sexual acts between a man and woman. God 'hands them over,' in the sense of permitting these sins and their grave consequences. These persons are acting contrary to the eternal moral law, which can be known, even apart from Divine Revelation, by reason from nature. These truths can also be understood, even more clearly, from Tradition and Scripture.

Notice the language used by Sacred Scripture, throughout this passage, to condemn homosexual acts: impurity, indignities, shameful, against nature, disgraceful, morally depraved. And the result of this grave moral error is called a recompense. For all gravely immoral acts have grave consequences, and gravely immoral sexual acts are no exception. All persons who commit any type of unnatural sexual act are harmed in their souls and in their lives by these sins.

{1:28} And since they did not prove to have God by knowledge, God handed them over to a morally depraved way of thinking, so that they might do those things which are not fitting:

Sexual Sins

{1:29} having been completely filled with all iniquity, malice, fornication, avarice, wickedness; full of envy, murder, contention, deceit, spite, gossiping;
{1:30} slanderous, hateful toward God, abusive, arrogant, self-exalting, devisers of evil, disobedient to parents,
{1:31} foolish, disorderly; without affection, without fidelity, without mercy.

God does not force anyone to do good. When persons commit one mortal sin after another, without repentance, continuing to reject grace, God permits them not only to sin by choices of their free will, but to suffer the consequences of those sins. And one of the consequences of grave sin without repentance is that the person continues to commit gravely immoral acts, advancing from one type of sin to another, to another. And this result is due, not to a rejection of them by God, but to their continuing rejection of God's grace, which is always available.

{1:32} And these, though they had known the justice of God, did not understand that those who act in such a manner are deserving of death, and not only those who do these things, but also those who consent to what is done.

They understood that these acts are sins, by natural law, but their understanding was limited. They did not realize that such acts are deserving of the death of the soul in mortal sin, and the eternal death of Hell. For natural law contains all teachings on morals, but not all teachings on faith.

Both those who commit these unnatural sexual acts and those who consent to such acts are committing objective mortal sins. And this condemnation of all unnatural sexual acts includes not only homosexual acts, but the same type of acts committed between a man and woman, or a husband and wife. If one spouse commits such an act, and the other spouse consents, both have committed objective mortal sin.

[1 Corinthians]
{6:9} Do you not know that the iniquitous will not possess the kingdom of God? Do not choose to wander astray. For neither fornicators, nor servants of idolatry, nor adulterers,
{6:10} nor the effeminate, nor males who sleep with males, nor thieves, nor the avaricious, nor the inebriated, nor slanderers, nor the rapacious shall possess the kingdom of God.

Sacred Scripture teaches that certain kinds of acts, regardless of intention or circumstances, are inherently gravely immoral, and deserve eternal punishment. No intention or purpose, and no set of circumstances or desired consequences can justify an intrinsically evil act. Such acts include fornication, adultery, and idolatry, which are each always gravely immoral. The term 'males who sleep with males' is used to condemn, by example, all homosexual acts, including those of women who sleep with women. Scripture often condemns a set of sins or a type of sin by giving a few specific examples; this approach is more easily understood by the reader than a solely abstract explanation.

.341. The term 'effeminate' refers to the violation of the roles given to each gender by God (apart from particular sexual sins). Men who knowingly choose

Sexual Sins

to dress or behave like women, or to take roles reserved for women, and women who knowingly choose to dress or behave like men, or to take roles reserved for men, sin against the plan of God for men and women. Although not all of the sins given as examples in this passage are always gravely immoral, they are all sins that can be committed to the extent of an objective mortal sin.

{6:11} And some of you were like this. But you have been absolved, but you have been sanctified, but you have been justified: all in the name of our Lord Jesus Christ and in the Spirit of our God.

Sacred infallible Scripture condemns all sinful acts, especially those that are gravely immoral. But persons are not condemned unless they commit actual mortal sin and refuse, through the last moment of life, to repent. Therefore, some persons have committed these strongly condemned acts, but they repented and were absolved (forgiven), and now they lead holy and just lives as faithful Christians. Condemn the sin; pray for the sinner.

[2 Corinthians]
{12:21} If so, then, when I have arrived, God may again humble me among you. And so, I mourn for the many who sinned beforehand, and did not repent, over the lust and fornication and homosexuality, which they have committed.

Those persons who commit gravely immoral sexual sins, and who do not repent, will be condemned by God. But the faithful do not condemn such persons; instead, they mourn over them, over their sins, and over their refusal to repent.

.342. Homosexual Orientation

[Mark]
{7:20} "But," he said "the things which go out from a man, these pollute a man.
{7:21} For from within, from the heart of men, proceed evil thoughts, adulteries, fornications, murders,
{7:22} thefts, avarice, wickedness, deceitfulness, homosexuality, an evil eye, blasphemy, self-exaltation, foolishness.
{7:23} All these evils procede from within and pollute a man."

Our Lord condemned all gravely immoral acts, interior and exterior, and gave us a few specific examples: sinful thoughts, adulteries, fornications, murders, thefts. But he also condemned even tendencies directed toward sin, such as greed, a deceitful attitude, and a homosexual orientation. Next he sums up all other such tendencies toward evil by the general expression: 'an evil eye.' For all such inner evil inclinations are like an eye looking in the direction of evil. Even though an inner tendency is not a sin, since it is not itself an act, it is nevertheless inherently disordered because it is directed toward sinful acts. Similarly, the homosexual orientation is inherently gravely disordered because it is an inner tendency toward homosexual acts. The acts are gravely immoral sins; the orientation is an inclination toward those sins. The sexual attraction between a man and woman has a proper expression in natural marital relations open to life. But a sexual attraction between persons of the same gender has no moral expression. All sexual acts between persons of the same gender (same sex) are intrinsically evil and always gravely immoral. The homosexual orientation is inherently ordered toward acts that are objective mortal sins.

Sacred Congregation for the Doctrine of the Faith: "In the pastoral field, these homosexuals must certainly be treated with understanding and sustained in the hope of overcoming their personal difficulties and their inability to fit into society. Their culpability will be judged with prudence. But no pastoral method can be employed which would give moral justification to these acts on the grounds that they would be consonant with the condition of such people. For according to the objective moral order, homosexual relations are acts which lack an essential and indispensable finality. In Sacred Scripture they are condemned as a serious depravity and even presented as the sad consequence of rejecting God. This judgment of Scripture does not of course permit us to conclude that all those who suffer from this anomaly are personally responsible for it, but it does attest to the fact that homosexual acts are intrinsically disordered and can in no case be approved of."[370]

Only an act can possibly be a sin. An orientation or tendency or inclination of any kind is not an act, and therefore is not itself a sin. A tendency to eat or drink too much is not the sin of gluttony. A tendency to be selfish is not a sin against your neighbor. A tendency to commit any particular kind of sin is not itself a sin. But neither is such a tendency good or natural or approved by God. Any tendency toward a gravely immoral act is an inherently disordered tendency. The act is immoral, therefore the tendency toward the commission of that act is morally disordered. This type of disorder is physical evil, not moral evil.

A homosexual orientation is an inherently disordered tendency; it is a sexual attraction to persons of the same gender. This attraction is not itself a sin, but it directs the person toward sin. There is no moral expression of such a sexual attraction. The natural sexual attraction between a man and a woman (heterosexual orientation) has a moral sexual expression in natural marital relations open to life. A homosexual orientation has no moral sexual expression. However, regardless of orientation, all sexual acts between persons of the same gender, and all unnatural sexual acts even between a man and woman, remain intrinsically evil and always gravely immoral. Even if homosexual acts do not proceed from a homosexual orientation, the acts are gravely immoral.

Though this tendency or orientation is not itself a sin, it is the result of sin. No tendency toward any sin would occur in anyone if we were not in a fallen state. Adam and Eve, before the fall from grace, had no sin and no tendency toward sin of any kind. Only after the fall, when men and women began to be conceived with original sin, did both sin and the tendency toward sin begin. Although original sin is entirely wiped away by baptism, concupiscence, which is a general tendency toward sin, remains. However, concupiscence does not directly result in any particular tendency toward any particular type of sin.

Some persons have a tendency toward one particular type of sin or another because of their own particular sins and the influence of the sins of other persons,

---

[370] Sacred Congregation for the Doctrine of the Faith, Persona Humana, VIII.

both of particular individuals and of society in general. The same is true of the homosexual orientation. No tendency toward any sin is part of human nature as created by God. All sin is contrary to the will and plan of God. Therefore, this type of tendency or orientation, like all inclinations toward sin, is neither of nature, nor of grace. A tendency toward sin can only be of sin.

A person who has a homosexual orientation may or may not be culpable, to one extent or another, for being in that state. All culpability is a matter of degree. If a person lacks the light of truth found in Catholic teaching, and was influenced to a great extent by the sins of other persons, then his or her culpability for having a homosexual orientation is lessened. But because of the light of natural law, human persons are able to know that homosexual acts are immoral, and that the homosexual orientation is a disorder. And so, rarely would the culpability for the orientation be reduced essentially to zero. Such is the case with the sinful acts in question, and with any gravely immoral acts at all. Even when certain factors reduce culpability substantially, so that the acts committed are not actual mortal sins, there is usually at least some culpability, to the extent of venial sin.

On the other hand, it is possible for someone who has a homosexual orientation to be culpable to the extent of an actual mortal sin, not for the orientation itself, but for the acts that led to that state. For example, if a person rejects the search for moral truth, and rejects all religion, having no concern for whether his acts are moral or not, he commits an actual mortal sin. And if he then engages in whatever sexual acts, interior and exterior, pleases him, either knowing that such acts are gravely immoral, or not caring if they are gravely immoral, then he again commits actual mortal sin. And if the end result of this process is to arrive at the state of a homosexual orientation, or some other gravely disordered orientation, then he is culpable for that disorder within himself because it is the result of his knowingly chosen immoral acts.

Sacred Congregation for the Doctrine of the Faith: "Moral conscience requires that, in every occasion, Christians give witness to the whole moral truth, which is contradicted both by approval of homosexual acts and unjust discrimination against homosexual persons. Therefore, discreet and prudent actions can be effective; these might involve: unmasking the way in which such tolerance might be exploited or used in the service of ideology; stating clearly the immoral nature of these unions; reminding the government of the need to contain the phenomenon within certain limits so as to safeguard public morality and, above all, to avoid exposing young people to erroneous ideas about sexuality and marriage that would deprive them of their necessary defenses and contribute to the spread of the phenomenon."[371]

The Catholic Faith condemns all sin, and seeks the repentance and conversion and salvation of all persons. Persons who have any type of disordered tendency, whether the homosexual orientation or some other tendency toward sin, must be treated with the same respect due to all human persons. Unjust discrimination,

---

[371] Cardinal Ratzinger, CDF, Considerations Regarding Proposals to Give Legal Recognition to Unions between Homosexual Persons, n. 5.

violence, hatred, and any other treatment unbefitting of human persons is to be rejected by all Christians. But neither do such persons deserve special rights within society, apart from the rights belonging to all human persons.

Secular society sometimes claims discrimination or hatred or 'homophobia' merely because a belief on morality is contrary to the prevailing norm. True justice does not demand that homosexuals or other persons known to have committed grave offenses be treated as if they were holy and chaste. The Church rightly judges that persons with a homosexual orientation are not fit for the priesthood or religious life. Certain positions of authority, teaching, or leadership in the Church, or in organizations closely associated with the Church, should not be given to anyone whose beliefs or actions are in grave conflict with the clear and definitive teaching of the Catholic Faith. This type of good judgment is based on the eternal moral law, and is not a type of spiritual or mental disorder (or phobia). The Faith does not condemn homosexual acts out of fear, but out of love for truth and justice, for God and neighbor. All such sins are contrary to the Just Nature of God, contrary to the natural law, and harmful to human persons. Any inherent tendency toward serious sin is a grave matter, which requires prudent judgment when considering such persons for position of authority, teaching, or leadership in the Church.

.343. Other Disordered Tendencies

Various gravely disordered tendencies exist among the members of sinful society, including many in the area of sexuality. The faithful of the Church know that all such tendencies and the acts associated with them are contrary to the will and plan of God. It is not necessary to name every such disorder, nor every possible sexual perversion. A few widely discussed examples should be sufficient.

Bisexuality is a tendency to be sexually attracted to the members of both sexes. As is true in homosexuality, any sexual attraction to members of the same sex is inherently gravely disordered. The condemnation of homosexuality found in Tradition, Scripture, Magisterium also applies to bisexuality. In addition, any attraction to persons, even of the opposite sex, which seeks to treat the human person as a sexual object, or which treats sexual acts as merely a source of pleasure, apart from marriage, love, and procreation, is a grave disorder.

Transgender is a term used to describe persons who have obtained, or who wish to obtain an attempted change of gender by any of various means. The claim is made that such persons are one gender in their inner self, contrary to the gender of their physical body. Such a perception on the part of any individual is a result of sin, since God created two genders, and only one gender is given to each person from conception. Whatever might be the cause of such a state of perception, any attempt to change from one gender to another, either by mere change of appearances (e.g. dress, grooming, etc.), or by physical changes to the body (e.g. by surgery and drugs), is a grave sin, and is contrary to natural law and Divine Revelation. For Scripture repeatedly condemns effeminacy, the sin in which a person attempts, by one means or another, to take upon himself or herself what is proper only to the other gender.

[Deuteronomy]
{22:5} A woman shall not be clothed with manly apparel, nor shall a man make use of feminine apparel. For whoever does these things is abominable with God.

The above verse condemns any grave violation against the distinctions between men and women ordained by God within the very fabric of human nature and the human race. Apparel is a symbol of behavior and roles. Deuteronomy is not here presenting a rule of mere discipline concerning changeable customs of dress and grooming. Instead, Scripture is using clothing as a symbol to teach an eternal truth about the distinctions between men and women, of which clothing is an outward sign. Any deliberate grave violation of this distinction between the genders is abominable to God. For God established this distinction when He created the human race. But as always, a lesser violation is a lesser sin.

[1 Kings]
{14:24} Moreover, the effeminate were in the land, and they committed all the abominations of the peoples that the Lord had destroyed before the face of the sons of Israel....
{15:11} And Asa did what was right before the sight of the Lord, just as his father David did.
{15:12} And he took away the effeminate from the land. And he purged all the filth of the idols, which his fathers had made.

Homosexual, bisexual, and transgender persons do not deserve special rights within society, apart from the rights due to all human persons. No human person attains to any special rights or privileges by committing objective mortal sins, or by having an inherent inclination to commit such sins. But all human persons, even those who commit serious sin, have the same fundamental human rights because they have the very same human nature.

[1 Corinthians]
{6:9} Do you not know that the iniquitous will not possess the kingdom of God? Do not choose to wander astray. For neither fornicators, nor servants of idolatry, nor adulterers,
{6:10} nor the effeminate, nor males who sleep with males, nor thieves, nor the avaricious, nor the inebriated, nor slanderers, nor the rapacious shall possess the kingdom of God.

Although fornication, idolatry, adultery, and homosexual acts are always gravely immoral, some of the other acts listed and condemned by Scripture are grave or not, depending on intention and circumstances, which includes degree. So a man or woman whose behavior is somewhat affected, so as to act like the other gender, might be guilty of only venial sin. But any grave violation of the distinctions between male and female ordained by God would be a grave sin.

.344. Pedophilia

[Proverbs 23]
{23:10} Do not touch the boundaries of little ones, and do not enter into the field of the fatherless.

{23:11} For their close relative is strong, and he will judge their case against you.

Pedophilia is a tendency to be sexually attracted to children, of one or both sexes. The disorder of homosexuality is distinct from pedophilia. An adult who seeks to have sexual relations with a child of the same gender is not necessarily attracted to adults of the same gender. Pedophilia is even more gravely disordered than homosexuality. Any person who commits a sexual act of any kind with a child commits a very grave sin. Such an act is not truly marital, or unitive, or procreative, and is a type of rape, since it is done without consent. For children do not have the maturity to be able to give a true and full consent to sexual acts. Under the moral law, any sexual act done without the true and full consent of the other person is a type of rape, but the rape of a child is even more serious than the forcible rape of an adult. It should also be noted that sexual acts with children are always gravely immoral, regardless of whether or not the abuser has the disorder of pedophilia. Some abusers are pedophiles, and others merely seek sexual pleasure however they might obtain it.

[Matthew 18]
{18:1} In that hour, the disciples drew near to Jesus, saying, "Whom do you consider to be greater in the kingdom of heaven?"
{18:2} And Jesus, calling to himself a little child, placed him in their midst.
{18:3} And he said: "Amen I say to you, unless you change and become like little children, you shall not enter into the kingdom of heaven.
{18:4} Therefore, whoever will have humbled himself like this little child, such a one is greater in the kingdom of heaven.
{18:5} And whoever shall accept one such little child in my name, accepts me.
{18:6} But whoever will have led astray one of these little ones, who trust in me, it would be better for him to have a great millstone hung around his neck, and to be submerged in the depths of the sea."

.345. Priests and Religious Who Abuse Children

Some sexual sins are more grave than other sexual sins. A man and woman who have premarital sexual relations commit a grave sin. A husband who commits adultery commits an even graver sin, for he offends also against the Sacrament of Marriage. And the sin of adultery is made more grave if the sexual act is also unnatural. Though rape is a very grave sexual sin, rape by an unnatural sexual act is even more grave, and rape by a man who is married is still more grave. So if the same act is adultery, an unnatural sexual act, and a sexual act with a minor, which is a type of rape, the sexual act is extremely grave. But a sexual act by an ordained Bishop, priest, or deacon against a child is substantially more sinful than all of the aforementioned sins combined. Anathema sint.

The Sacrament of Holy Orders is greater than the Sacrament of Marriage. For without priests to dispense the Sacraments and Bishops also to exercise the Magisterium, the faithful would be lost. So a sexual sin by a priest with a child offends against the Sacrament of Holy Orders, causes one of the gravest types of scandal imaginable, and does immense harm to the ability of the Church to bring salvation to the world. For the very grave sexual sins of only a small percentage of priests are sufficient to cause the world to proclaim that the Church and the

Catholic Faith itself is corrupt. Although this exaggerated claim ignores the innumerable selfless deeds of chaste spiritual love done by the majority of priests, religious, and the faithful, the damage done by these sexual sins and by the scandal that ensues is immense. It would be better for a priest or religious to have a great millstone hung around his neck and be thrown into the sea, than to commit a single sexual sin against any child.

And although monks and nuns do not have the Sacrament of Holy Orders, they are nevertheless consecrated to God, and are representatives of the Church and of the Catholic Faith, more so than the ordinary laity. So if they commit these types of sexual sins against children, they also do grave harm to the Church and to the Faith, endangering many souls. And all of this very great harm is in addition to the very great harm done by the sexual sins themselves.

[Revelation]
{20:11} And I saw a great white throne, and One sitting upon it, from whose sight earth and heaven fled, and no place was found for them.
{20:12} And I saw the dead, great and small, standing in view of the throne. And books were opened. And another Book was opened, which is the Book of Life. And the dead were judged by those things that had been written in the books, according to their works.
{20:13} And the sea gave up the dead who were in it. And death and Hell gave up their dead who were in them. And they were judged, each one according to his works.
{20:14} And Hell and death were cast into the pool of fire. This is the second death.
{20:15} And whoever was not found written in the Book of Life was cast into the pool of fire.

.346. False Types of Marriage

Secular society has invented various false types of marriage. There is the civil marriage in which any two persons legally permitted to do so are given a legal union by a government official or by a person designated by the government. Secular society generally permits both divorce (for little or no cause) and any number of remarriages. Some civil marriages are not even true natural marriages. Most governments have taken upon themselves an ability, not given to them by God or the Church, to conduct marriages. A marriage that is merely civil is not a true type of marriage, but is an offense against God. It is fornication under the guise of legal marriage.

It is acceptable for Christian married couples to comply with government laws on marriage, within reason, so as to be also legally married under civil law. But it is never acceptable for any two baptized persons to attempt to have any type of marriage apart from the true Sacrament of Marriage. Those baptized couples who seem to be married, but do not have the Sacrament of Marriage, are living in the sin of fornication; they are living in sin. They do not have even a merely natural marriage, and so their civil marriage is not a marriage in the eyes of God.

USCCB Catechism: "There are attempts by some in contemporary society to change the definition or understanding of what exactly constitutes marriage. Efforts to gain approval for and acceptance of same-sex unions as marriages are examples. While the Church clearly teaches that discrimination against any group of people is wrong, efforts to make cohabitation, domestic partnerships, same-sex unions, and polygamous unions equal to marriage are misguided and also wrong. The Church and her members need to continue to be a strong and clear voice in protecting an understanding of marriage, which is rooted in natural law and revealed in God's law."[372]

When a couple lives together without marriage, they are cohabitating. This form of relationship is a poor imitation of marriage. Any sexual acts between such a couple lack the marital meaning and so are intrinsically evil and gravely immoral. Although some persons claim that cohabitation is a preparation for marriage, the end does not justify the means. Even an engaged couple, who are certain that they will marry soon, may not have sexual relations before marriage.

The exact meaning of the terms 'domestic partnership' and 'civil union' varies. These are legal forms, established by human law, and the laws vary greatly from one place to another. Generally, these forms of union are legal constructs similar to marriage, without life-long commitment, and without any acknowledgement of God. Sometimes these legal forms of union are designed to give certain legal rights to the members of the union. Sometimes these unions are designed primarily for same-sex civil unions. But in any case, regardless of the particulars of the legal form, they are not a true type of marriage, and they do not confer any of the rights and privileges reserved to married persons and the married state of life. All such attempts to construct a legal substitute for true marriage are offensive to natural law and to God, who created man and woman for each other, to be joined in a life-long commitment to one another and before God, in holy matrimony, for the good of the children, the family, and society.

.347. Same-sex Unions

USCCB Catechism: "The political pressure for the legalization of same-sex unions is yet another step in the erosion of God's plan for marriage and the understanding of marriage in the natural moral order of creation."[373]

"Attempts to justify same-sex unions or relationships or to give them matrimonial status also contradict God's plan -- as revealed from the beginning both in nature and in Revelation -- for marriage to be a life-long union of a man and a woman."[374]

Another false type of marriage is called 'same-sex marriage' or 'gay marriage.' Neither a natural marriage, nor the Sacrament of Marriage, is possible between two persons of the same sex (a man with another man, or a woman with another

---

[372] United States Conference of Catholic Bishops, United States Catholic Catechism for Adults, p. 280.
[373] USCCB, United States Catholic Catechism for Adults, p. 286.
[374] USCCB, United States Catholic Catechism for Adults, p. 411.

woman). God created human nature with two genders, so as to unite one man and one woman in holy matrimony for the benefit of the family, society, the Church, and humanity. The harmonious union of husband and wife in love before God depends partly on the complementarity of this union, and partly on the distinct roles given to each spouse, all of which is based on the difference in gender. The natural procreation of children is one of the greatest goods of marriage, and this good is not possible between persons of the same gender.

Second Vatican Council: "By their very nature, the institution of matrimony itself and conjugal love are ordained for the procreation and education of children, and find in them their ultimate crown."[375]

Sacred Congregation for the Doctrine of the Faith: "The Church's teaching on marriage and on the complementarity of the sexes reiterates a truth that is evident to right reason and recognized as such by all the major cultures of the world. Marriage is not just any relationship between human beings. It was established by the Creator with its own nature, essential properties and purpose. No ideology can erase from the human spirit the certainty that marriage exists solely between a man and a woman, who by mutual personal gift, proper and exclusive to themselves, tend toward the communion of their persons. In this way, they mutually perfect each other, in order to cooperate with God in the procreation and upbringing of new human lives."[376]

A domestic partnership, civil union, or any type of claimed marriage between persons of the same gender is neither a marriage, nor its near equivalent. Two persons of the same gender who live together in the same home is not a marriage. The fact that these two persons commit sexual sins with one another does not cause their relationship to be in any way similar to a marriage. Such grave sexual sins make their relationship less like a marriage, rather than more like one.

Civil unions or same-sex marriages have been proposed by some legislators as a way to give health insurance, or inheritance rights, or other benefits to persons with a homosexual orientation. But the end does not justify the means. It is the sin of scandal for a legislator to promote legalized same-sex marriages. Such laws harm true marriage and the family, upon which civilization is based.

Sacred Congregation for the Doctrine of the Faith: "There are absolutely no grounds for considering homosexual unions to be in any way similar or even remotely analogous to God's plan for marriage and family. Marriage is holy, while homosexual acts go against the natural moral law."[377]

Homosexual acts are intrinsically evil and always gravely immoral. Therefore, a sexual relationship between two persons of the same gender cannot be the basis for a marriage. True marriage is a source of grace and holiness for both spouses

---

[375] Second Vatican Council, Gaudium et Spes, n. 48.
[376] Cardinal Ratzinger, CDF, Considerations Regarding Proposals to Give Legal Recognition to Unions between Homosexual Persons, n. 2 in its entirety.
[377] Cardinal Ratzinger, CDF, Considerations Regarding Proposals to Give Legal Recognition to Unions between Homosexual Persons, n. 4.

and for the whole family. A mutual grave sin between two persons does not establish a basis for marriage, nor for any type of holy relationship whatsoever.

Sacred Congregation for the Doctrine of the Faith: "Those who would move from tolerance to the legitimization of specific rights for cohabiting homosexual persons need to be reminded that the approval or legalization of evil is something far different from the toleration of evil. In those situations where homosexual unions have been legally recognized or have been given the legal status and rights belonging to marriage, clear and emphatic opposition is a duty. One must refrain from any kind of formal cooperation in the enactment or application of such gravely unjust laws and, as far as possible, from material cooperation on the level of their application. In this area, everyone can exercise the right to conscientious objection."[378]

We Catholic Christians live in a world of people who do not share our faith. And so we must be tolerant of the objectively sinful choices of other persons. We are not called to force our faith upon others, but to teach by word and example. Though we are called to speak out against all sin, we are also called to act with charity toward those who are living sinful lives. Toleration is a duty of charity for all those who live in a sinful world.

But toleration does not include sinful cooperation. When acts are gravely contrary to the moral law, human law should never approve or encourage such acts. And when acts are not only gravely immoral, but harmful to marriage, children, family, and society, human law should stand against those acts. The legalization of objective mortal sins harmful to society is not an act of charity or toleration or fairness or equality. The granting of legal status of any kind to same-sex unions is contrary to the natural law, since those unions are based on gravely immoral sexual acts and the inherently disordered orientation toward those acts. Faithful Catholics are morally obligated to oppose any attempt to establish any kind of false marriage, or its near equivalent, in custom, law, or constitution.

Both a merely natural marriage and the Sacrament of Marriage include moral acts of sexual relations between the husband and wife. But a same-sex 'marriage' includes immoral sexual acts between the homosexual couple, acts that are intrinsically evil and always gravely immoral. Therefore, the ceremony itself of a same-sex 'marriage' (or 'civil union') constitutes a type of public approval for homosexual acts. Any approval for an intrinsically evil act is a type of formal cooperation. (See the chapter on Cooperation with Evil.) Formal cooperation is itself an intrinsically evil act. And the public nature of the approval adds the sin of scandal.

.348. Prostitution

Catechism of the Catholic Church: "Prostitution does injury to the dignity of the person who engages in it, reducing the person to an instrument of sexual

---

[378] Cardinal Ratzinger, CDF, Considerations Regarding Proposals to Give Legal Recognition to Unions between Homosexual Persons, n. 5.

pleasure. The one who pays sins gravely against himself: he violates the chastity to which his Baptism pledged him and defiles his body, the temple of the Holy Spirit. Prostitution is a social scourge. It usually involves women, but also men, children, and adolescents (The latter two cases involve the added sin of scandal.). While it is always gravely sinful to engage in prostitution, the imputability of the offense can be attenuated by destitution, blackmail, or social pressure."[379]

There are numerous grave sins associated with prostitution. Each person is morally responsible for his or her own knowingly chosen immoral acts. When a person willingly exchanges a sexual act for remuneration, this knowingly chosen act is the sin of prostitution. Some persons work in prostitution as a type of gravely immoral employment. But even if a man or woman is not employed as a prostitute, he or she might still commit the sin of prostitution by having sexual relations in exchange for something of value. The type of remuneration varies, but may include money, drugs, or goods. If an employee has sexual relations with a boss in order to obtain a raise or a promotion or some other advantage in the workplace, the chosen act is a type of prostitution.

The sexual acts associated with prostitution might include adultery, fornication, unnatural sexual acts, or any other intrinsically evil and gravely immoral sexual acts. Each of these acts is an objective mortal sin for each person who knowingly chooses such an act. Both the person who chooses to exchange sexual relations in exchange for money, and the person who pays for and receives this service, commit gravely immoral sexual acts.

In addition to the sinful sexual acts, they also sin by the exchange of money (or other remuneration) for sexual acts, since sexual relations is ordained by God for the good of marriage, procreation, and the expression of love. Anyone who buys or sells this special good, which is given by God to humanity as a gift, commits a grave sin. So if a third person pays for the prostitution services, but does not participate in any sexual acts, he nevertheless commits the gravely immoral sin of prostitution because he has paid for an act which is reserved by God for the good of marriage, and the unity of the spouses, and the procreation of children. All illicit sexual acts are gravely immoral, but the selling or buying of any sexual act is also gravely immoral, even considered apart from the sexual acts. In this way, a mortal sin becomes an even more serious mortal sin. Prostitution treats sexuality as a commodity, treats the human body as something to be bought and sold, and treats prostitutes in an inhumane manner. Prostitution also spreads diseases, harms marriages and families, and does grave harm to society in general.

Those persons who knowingly choose, even under duress, to sell sexual acts commit gravely immoral sins. Some very poor persons turn to prostitution as a last resort in order to earn money to pay for food and the necessities of life. But the sexual acts they commit are intrinsically evil and always gravely immoral, even in dire circumstances. And the act itself of exchanging sexual acts for remuneration is also intrinsically evil and always gravely immoral, since the

---

[379] Catechism of the Catholic Church, n. 2355.

moral object is to sell or buy what the eternal moral law reserves for a loving marital relationship. Intention and circumstances can cause an intrinsically evil and gravely immoral act to be a more or less grave mortal sin. But whenever any one font causes an act to be an objective mortal sin, the other two fonts cannot reduce the act to an objective venial sin. The goodness of one font cannot reform a grave immorality in another font. Good intentions and dire circumstances cannot cause any act that is intrinsically evil and gravely immoral under the second font to be anything less than an objective mortal sin. Severe duress, such as dire circumstances of poverty, may reduce the objective gravity of the act, under all three fonts, to a somewhat less serious mortal sin. The objective gravity of any sin may be attenuated by one or two good fonts, but never to less than an objective mortal sin if the other font is gravely immoral.

The culpability of the person who commits a sin of selling sexual acts might be less than that of an actual mortal sin. If the person does not have full knowledge of the grave immorality of prostitution, or if the person does not act with full freedom of will, then the act would not be an actual mortal sin. A lack of full knowledge might occur for a person who incorrectly believes that prostitution to obtain food for her family is not gravely immoral due to that dire circumstance. This lack of knowledge is more likely for a non-Christian, for a poorly educated person, or for someone misled by sinful secular society for many years. A lack of full freedom might occur if the person is forced into prostitution at a young age, or is kept addicted to drugs. The acts involved in prostitution are objectively gravely immoral, but in some cases these acts might be less than actual mortal sins, due to a reduction in knowledge or in the use of free will.

In any case, it is reprehensible when any person uses the dire circumstances of a fellow human being in order to obtain sexual acts. The buyer of sexual acts in this case (or even in cases where no remuneration is given) commits an even more grievous mortal sin. In such a case, the person is treating the unwilling prostitute like a slave, using severe poverty or other circumstances in order to subjugate another human person to an inhumane role as a mere sexual object. His punishment in Hell is worse than for most other serious sins. The humane response to seeing another person in severe poverty is to give the person money and to ask nothing in return, or to give the person moral work and fitting payment for that work, or to provide whatever other type of help is needed.

Now if any person is raped, even if the rapist paid someone for the sexual acts, that person has not committed any knowingly chosen immoral act, and so there is not even a mere objective sin for the victim of the rape. This situation might occur with the trafficking of women and children for purposes of sexual slavery. And this sin is not so much prostitution as it is rape in exchange for money as well as a severe form of slavery.

.349. Rape

Catechism of the Catholic Church: "Rape is the forcible violation of the sexual intimacy of another person. It does injury to justice and charity. Rape deeply wounds the respect, freedom, and physical and moral integrity to which every person has a right. It causes grave damage that can mark the victim for life. It is

Sexual Sins

always an intrinsically evil act. Graver still is the rape of children committed by parents (incest) or those responsible for the education of the children entrusted to them."[380]

USCCB Catechism: "Rape is an act of violence in which a person forces a sexual act on an unwilling partner."[381]

Both of the above definitions of rape refer to force, with the words "forcible violation" and "an act of violence...forces." However, the concepts of violence and force in moral theology include, but extend beyond, physical force. An unjust law is a type of violence, i.e. moral violence, a violence to the just exercise of the free will of the human person. And so rape can occur with or without physical violence.

For example, if an adult convinces a child to commit a sexual act, the act is a type of rape because the child is unable to give full and free consent to the sexual act. Similarly, if an adult convinces a child to sign a contractual agreement, the child's signature is not true consent and so there exists no contract between them at all. In another example, if a woman is unconscious, or is so inebriated that she cannot properly exercise her free will, then she is unable to consent to sexual relations, and a man who has sexual relations with her, taking advantage of that state (or any similar state where consent is not possible), commits the sin of rape. In all of these examples, as well as in any similar example, even when physical violence is absent, the acts are a type of violence against the free will, and are acts of rape.

To be moral, each and every sexual act must have that threefold moral object intended by God, which is procreative, unitive, and marital. If a husband rapes his wife, in an act of natural intercourse, are any of these three meanings absent?

As previously discussed, an unnatural sexual act between husband and wife is certainly not procreative, and is also not truly unitive, and not truly marital. For such acts do not fulfill the will and plan of God for sexual acts within the marital state of life. Unnatural sexual acts are not inherently ordered toward the proper union of the husband and wife in holiness before God. Unnatural sexual acts are also not inherently ordered toward the proper expression and strengthening of the marital relationship. All such acts harm union and marriage.

Similarly, if rape occurs between husband and wife, the sexual act, even if it is the natural act, is not truly marital, and is not truly unitive, as God intends union and marriage between husband and wife. And so, all such acts are intrinsically evil and always gravely immoral. The violence done by rape to the just exercise of the free will of the victim necessarily implies that the sexual act is not truly marital, and not truly unitive, even if it is (in some sense) procreative.

---

[380] Catechism of the Catholic Church, n. 2356.
[381] United States Conference of Catholic Bishops, United States Catholic Catechism for Adults, p. 407.

And just as adultery has an additional evil moral object, the breaking of the marital vows, so also does rape of a spouse have the evil moral object of the breaking of the marital vows. And every rape also has another evil moral object, that of violence to the innocent. For all rapes are a type of violent act, a violence to the free will, even if no force at all is used. Therefore, in terms of the moral object, under the second font of morality, rape has multiple evil moral objects, causing the act to be not only intrinsically evil, but also more wicked than many other intrinsically evil sexual acts.

Under the first font, there is no good intended end that could ever justify an act of rape. And it is to be observed that rapists generally have gravely immoral intentions. Furthermore, an intention to use an intrinsically evil act as a means to any end causes the intention to be immoral.

Under the third font, there are gravely harmful consequences to any gravely immoral sexual act. But because rape is even more gravely immoral than many other illicit sexual acts, the consequences are even more harmful. And this greater harm causes the third font to be even more gravely immoral. No intention and no set of circumstances can cause any intrinsically evil act to become moral.

USCCB Catechism: "Sexual abuse of any kind harms the victim on many more levels than only the physical. Forcing sexual intimacy of any type on a child or minor is an even graver evil (cf. CCC, no. 2356), which often scars the victim for life (cf. CCC, no. 2389)."[382]

Rape is very gravely immoral because of the lack of the proper threefold moral object required for any sexual act to be moral, and because every rape is a type of violence against the innocent. If the victim of the rape is a child, the act of rape becomes even more gravely immoral. The rape of a child is one of the most wicked acts that one human person can commit against another human person. But this act becomes even more sinful when the person committing the rape is a priest or religious. For then the breaking of the vow of chastity and the grave harm done to the Church due to scandal are added to all the other reasons that the rape of a child is gravely immoral and gravely harmful, causing the act to be extremely wicked, even beyond expression in words.

.350. Incest

Incest is sexual relations between persons who are related, by blood or marriage. Sexual relations outside of marriage is intrinsically evil and always gravely immoral, because the act is deprived of the marital aspect of the moral object. And so, the term incest, as it is used in moral theology, is more often applied to the question of whom one may marry.

In common language, the term incest refers to an adult having sexual relations with a child within the same family. Such acts are intrinsically evil and always

---

[382] United States Conference of Catholic Bishops, United States Catholic Catechism for Adults, p. 407.

gravely immoral. Sexual relations with a child is a type of rape, since the child is unable to consent due to a lack of maturity; rape is intrinsically evil and always gravely immoral. All sexual relations outside of marriage is intrinsically evil and always gravely immoral. And the harm done to the child is very grave.

But in moral theology, the question of incest also considers (separately) various possible marriages between adults, in order to discern who may marry whom. Since all human beings are descendents of Adam and Eve, we are all at least distantly related. Therefore, the morality of incest, defined as a marriage between adults who are related, depends on the type and degree of relation. There are three categories of incest:

1. Incest in the direct line occurs in a marriage between adults who are related by blood and by direct descent, e.g. parent-child, grandparent-grandchild, etc. This type of incest is intrinsically evil and always gravely immoral. For Christ said:

[Matthew]
{19:5} "For this reason, a man shall separate from father and mother, and he shall cling to his wife, and these two shall become one flesh."

[Mark]
{10:6} "But from the beginning of creation, God made them male and female.
{10:7} Because of this, a man shall leave behind his father and mother, and he shall cling to his wife.
{10:8} And these two shall be one in flesh. And so, they are now, not two, but one flesh.
{10:9} Therefore, what God has joined together, let no man separate."

The marital meaning of sexual relations includes the command to separate from father and mother, to be joined to a spouse. Therefore, what God has separated, let no man join. Sexual relations within an attempted marriage in the direct line lacks the true marital meaning, and is therefore intrinsically evil and always gravely immoral. An incestuous marriage in the direct line is not a valid Sacrament of Marriage, and not a valid natural marriage. For from the beginning of the creation of humanity, inherent to the human race, there is a command to separate from father and mother, in order to be joined to a spouse.

2. Incest in the collateral line occurs in a marriage between adults who are related by blood, but not by direct descent, e.g. siblings, cousins, other relatives of blood. This type of marriage is not intrinsically evil, but the morality depends upon the other fonts, particularly the circumstance as to the closeness of the relation. All descendents of Adam and Eve, the entire human race, are related at least distantly; therefore, this type of marriage cannot be intrinsically evil. God established marriage from the beginning, within the human race, and all human persons are related to one another, to some extent.

In the circumstance of the origins of the human race, the children of Adam and Eve, of necessity and without sin, procreated the human race by marriage to one another. Since this type of marriage was not in the direct line, it was not intrinsically evil. Very soon afterward, such a close marriage was not necessary, and so the circumstances would then make a marriage between siblings generally immoral (but not intrinsically so).

Abraham married his half-sister (Gen 20:12), and yet this marriage is not condemned anywhere in Scripture. Christ himself calls God the "God of Abraham" (Mk 12:26) and He says that the Blessed shall "sit at table with Abraham, and Isaac, and Jacob in the kingdom of heaven." (Mt 8:11). The Virgin Mary says about Abraham in the Magnificat: "He has taken up his servant Israel, mindful of his mercy, just as he spoke to our fathers: to Abraham and to his offspring forever. (Lk 1:54-55)" Her prayer was inspired by the Holy Spirit, and this prayer speaks well of Abraham and his offspring. But if the offspring of Abraham were of an intrinsically evil union, then neither Jesus nor Mary would speak well of him and his offspring. Therefore, marriages in the collateral line are not intrinsically evil; it depends on the circumstances whether or not the marriage is moral.

Also, in Sacred Scripture, the brother of Abraham (Abram), whose name was Nahor, married the daughter of their brother Haran:

[Genesis]
{11:27} And these are the generations of Terah. Terah conceived Abram, Nahor, and Haran. Next Haran conceived Lot.
{11:28} And Haran died before his father Terah, in the land of his nativity, in Ur of the Chaldeans.
{11:29} Then Abram and Nahor took wives. The name of Abram's wife was Sarai. And the name of Nahor's wife was Milcah, the daughter of Haran, the father of Milcah, and the father of Iscah.

Again, there is no condemnation of this marriage, as would be expected in Sacred Scripture if this marriage in the collateral line were intrinsically evil.

The degree in the collateral line is determined by counting the number of persons from each intended spouse back to the common ancestor; but only one count, whichever is longest, gives the number of the degree. A brother and sister are each one degree from the common ancestor of their parents, so siblings are related in the first degree of the collateral line (half-siblings are also still related in the first degree). First cousins are related in the second degree; second cousins in the third degree; third cousins in the fourth degree, etc.

In the present-day circumstances, Canon Law, and the practice of the Church, wisely forbid marriages in the first and second degree of the collateral line (e.g. siblings, first cousins, nieces and nephews); such marriages are invalid and dispensation is not generally available.[383] Marriages in the third and fourth degree (e.g. second and third cousins), are prohibited by Canon Law and are invalid, unless there is a dispensation from the Bishop. However, the ancient practice of the Church includes occasions of dispensation for marriages in any

---

[383] Code of Canon Law for the Latin Church, 1983, Canon 1078 n. 3: "A dispensation is never given from the impediment of consanguinity in the direct line or in the second degree of the collateral line."

degree of the collateral line, even the first or second.[384] Examples of valid natural marriages in the first or second degree occur in Sacred Scripture (as cited above). Also, despite the Canon that forbids it, the Holy See may validly and licitly dispense from Canons that are not either articles of faith, or requirements of the moral law. Therefore, a dispensation might be granted, so as to allow for a valid Sacrament of Marriage, in any degree of the collateral line. For example, if a couple, related in the first or second degree, and married according to another religion or culture, were both to convert and seek the Sacrament of Marriage (cf. 2 Samuel 13:13).

3. Incest by affinity occurs in a marriage between adults who are related by marriage or adoption, and not by blood (neither by direct descent, nor any close blood relation). This affinity can be either in the direct line, as with a step-parent and step-child, or in the collateral line, as with a step-brother and step-sister, or as with an adopted child and a natural child of the same family. Any family relationship that is not by blood is a type of affinity. If there is a relationship between two persons of affinity in one line, and of blood in another line, both relationships must be permissible for the marriage to be valid and licit. Incest by affinity is not intrinsically evil; the act depends upon the circumstances.

Canon Law and the practice of the Church wisely forbid marriages when there is affinity in any degree of the direct line.[385] Dispensations from Bishops are not generally available for affinity in the direct line. Affinity in the collateral line does not generally require a dispensation for a valid marriage. In the Old Testament, marriages were permitted, and even required, between a man and his widowed and childless sister-in-law. Jesus is asked about this practice, and He does not object (Mt 22:24-30). Therefore, such marriages are not intrinsically evil. Furthermore, dispensations can and have been given by the Holy See, even for affinity in the first degree of the direct line.[386] An example would be a man and woman, related by affinity in a different religion and culture, who convert and seek the Sacrament of Marriage.

Summary: Incest in marriage is of three types: by blood in the direct line, by blood in the collateral line, and by affinity (in either the direct or collateral line). The direct and collateral types of affinity are one type because, with a lack of blood relations, the affinity is essentially the same, as concerns the second font. Incest in the direct line is intrinsically evil; incest in the collateral line is not intrinsically evil, but depends on the circumstances as to whether or not it is moral. Circumstances also determine whether or not a dispensation may be granted. Incest by affinity is not intrinsically evil, neither in the direct nor in the

---

[384] Burtsell, Richard. "Affinity (in Canon Law)." The Catholic Encyclopedia. Vol. 1. New York: Robert Appleton Company, 1907. http://www.newadvent.org/cathen/01178a.htm
[385] Code of Canon Law for the Latin Church, 1983, Canon 1092 "Affinity in the direct line in any degree invalidates a marriage."
[386] Burtsell, Richard. "Affinity (in Canon Law)." The Catholic Encyclopedia. Vol. 1. New York: Robert Appleton Company, 1907. http://www.newadvent.org/cathen/01178a.htm

collateral line, because in neither line is there any blood relation. Thus there is no absolute prohibition against marriages with affinity; again, it depends on the circumstances.

Terminology: Since the term incest is commonly used to describe what is gravely immoral, the term incest could be applied solely to those relationships that are immoral, so that any valid marriages, in the collateral line or by affinity, would not be termed incest despite a close relationship. However, when used more broadly, incest technically includes both moral and immoral (as well as valid and invalid) marriage relationships.

Notice that this definition of incest is divided into a type that is intrinsically evil, and a type that is moral or immoral depending on the circumstances. The same kind of division and distinction occurs in usury: one type is intrinsically evil and the other depends on circumstances.

.351. True Marriage

There are only two types of true marriage before the eyes of God, a merely natural marriage, and the Sacrament of holy Matrimony. Natural marriage was established when Adam and Eve were created, that is, at the beginning of the human race. And natural marriage prevailed as the only true marriage from that time until Christ. So during Old Testament times, the Israelites had only natural marriages, though they had the benefit of the beginning of Divine Revelation. The Jewish Law concerning marriage only pertained to natural marriage. And natural marriage still prevails today among the unbaptized.

Christ established the holy Sacrament of Marriage at the time of the wedding at Cana. When He changed water into wine, this miracle was symbolic of a greater, yet hidden, miraculous event, occurring at the same time. Christ elevated natural marriage to the dignity of a Sacrament. He gave the outward sign of this elevation by changing water into wine. The water symbolizes natural marriage and the wine symbolizes the Sacrament of Marriage. This is a fitting symbol, because wine includes water, just as the Sacrament of Marriage includes natural marriage. Every valid Sacrament of holy Matrimony is also a natural marriage. All the goods of natural marriage are present within this Sacrament, but in a higher form. For the entire marriage bestows grace on the husband and wife, the children, the extended family, the Church, and all humanity, grace upon grace, through this Sacrament.

When the Virgin Mary told her Divine Son Jesus that they had no wine, she understood that the human race had only natural marriage, and that they needed a Sacrament for married life. Mary was asking Jesus to establish a Sacrament of Marriage based upon the Sacrament of Baptism that He had already established when He Himself was baptized in the Jordan by John. Since the Sacrament of Marriage is based upon the Sacrament of Baptism, only the baptized can receive the valid Sacrament of Marriage. No other type of marriage is possible for two baptized Christians, other than the Sacrament of holy Matrimony.

Pope Pius XI: "And since the valid matrimonial consent among the faithful was constituted by Christ as a sign of grace, the sacramental nature is so intimately bound up with Christian wedlock that there can be no true marriage between baptized persons 'without it being by that very fact a sacrament.' "[387]

.352. Reciprocal and Asymmetrical

The relationship between husband and wife is a figure of the relationship between Christ and His Church. In one sense, Christ and His Church have a reciprocal relationship. The mutual love between Christ and His Bride, the Church, is not two different types of love, nor two different meanings of the word 'love'. Christ loves His Church, and the Church loves Christ. This love is reciprocal; it is the same type of love in both directions, Christ to the Church, and the Church to Christ. Although Christ as God has greater love for the Church than the Church has for Christ, the type of act is the same: a true and pure spiritual love.

Certainly, Christ is not only man, but also God, and as God He is infinitely greater than all Creation, including the Church. But here we are considering Christ and His Church only to the extent that their relationship is a figure for the marriage relationship. So any point that pertains to Christ as God would not pertain to the husband, and any point that pertains to the powers of the Church (the Sacraments, the Magisterium, etc.) would not pertain to the wife.

But the role of Christ in this blessed relationship is not the same as the role of the Church. And so this relationship is not entirely reciprocal; it is not an entirely mutual relationship. Christ is the head of the Church, but the Church is not the head of Christ. Christ leads the Church, and the Church follows. Christ has a role of authority, teaching, and leadership over the Church, and the Church has the role of subjection (submission, obedience) to Christ. This role of headship is asymmetrical. Christ and His Church do not have the same roles.

The obedience between Christ and His Church is asymmetrical. The Church must obey Christ, her Lord and Savior. Christ does not obey the Church, as if She were leading Him, as if She had authority over Him, as if He were required to be submissive to Her. And yet, when the Church asks Christ for anything good, He grants the Church her request, which is a type of obedience. Similarly, Mary (a figure of the Church) is obedient to God, but God grants to her all that she requests; and this, too, is a type of obedience. So there is a type of obedience in both directions, but it is fundamentally unequal, that is, asymmetrical.

The relationship between husband and wife in the Sacrament of holy Matrimony is reciprocal, that is, mutual. The husband should love his wife, and the wife should love her husband. Both are equally subject to the eternal moral law, and both follow the same path to salvation (though the particulars will vary from one person to another). Their relationship is mutual in many ways, just as the relationship between Christ and the Church is mutual in many ways -- but not in

---

[387] Pope Pius XI, Casti Connubii, n. 39; inner quote from Codex Iuris Canonici (1917) Canon 1012, n. 2; cf. Code of Canon Law (1983), Canon 1055, n. 2.

every way. And this is the great lie that sinful secular society tells everyone who will listen about the marriage relationship: that a husband and wife have exactly the same role in every way, and that they are exactly equal in every way. For sinful secular society is ignorant of Christ and His Church.

Like the relationship between Christ and His Church, the relationship between a husband and wife is asymmetrical. The husband is the head of his wife, but the wife is not the head of her husband. A marriage cannot have two heads, for then it would be a monster, and not a figure of the Church.[388] The wife should be submissive to her husband, but he should not be submissive to her. For the Church is submissive to Christ, but Christ is not submissive to the Church. The wife should be obedient to her husband, but he should not be obedient to her. However, as is true also for Christ and His Church, when the Church is obedient to Christ, He gives Her all that She asks.

.353. The husband has a role of authority, teaching, and leadership over his wife, just as Christ has a role of authority, teaching, and leadership over the Church. The wife does not have the role to give orders to the husband, or to teach him (1 Cor 14:35), or to lead him. The wife does not have the role to be a co-leader of the family, if by co-leader is indicated a role that is the same for both spouses. For the husband and wife are both types of leaders of the family, but the husband has the higher station. Sinful secular society teaches a type of false equality, in which gender is irrelevant to marriage. But Sacred Scripture teaches the truth.

[Esther]
{3:22} and he sent letters to all the provinces of his kingdom, so that every nation was able to hear and to read, in various languages and letters, that husbands are to be the greater rulers in their own houses, and that this should be published to every people.[389]

Saint John Chrysostom: "The wife is a second authority. She should not demand equality, for she is subject to the head; neither should the husband belittle her subjection, for she is the body.... Where there is equal authority, there is never peace. A household cannot be a democracy, ruled by everyone, but the authority must necessarily rest in one person. The same is true for the Church...."[390]

Whenever a wife usurps the role proper to her husband, she sins (Esther 3:1-22). And if she does so to a grave extent, or in a grave matter, then she sins gravely. A wife who attempts to make her husband subject to her, as if to authority, offends Christ, who created Eve from the side of Adam in order to be a helper to him, and who created the Church from His own side, on the Cross, in order to be a helper to Him.

Now because of sin and imperfection, some husbands are lacking, to one degree or another, in their ability to fulfill this role. In such cases, the husband and wife

---

[388] cf. Pope Boniface VIII, Unam Sanctam, n. 3; author's translation of the Latin: "And so, the one and only Church is one body, one head, (not two heads like a monster)...."
[389] Chapter and verse numbering from the Catholic Public Domain Version.
[390] Saint John Chrysostom, On Marriage and Family Life, Homily 20, p. 53.

should strive to avoid all sin, and to conform their marriage as much as possible to the perfect plan of God. But some degree of failure to conform to this perfect plan is not sin, but imperfection. So if her husband is lacking, she should support and assist him, so that with her help he will no longer be lacking. And if he is still unable, or is obstinately unwilling, she may do whatever is necessary for the family, even tasks that her husband ought to be doing. But in no case is she to take the role itself of the head of the family. For the Church does many great and selfless deeds to assist the work of Christ, but She never usurps His role as the head of the Church, neither on the excuse of necessity, nor for any reason.

But if the husband sins gravely, or attempts to cause his wife to sin gravely, he has lost his authority in one of two ways. First, if his grave sin is only in one particular matter or only on a few occasions, he has no authority to cause his wife to sin, nor to cooperate sinfully with his acts, at those times or in those matters. She need not obey him in anything that pertains to sin. All persons are always under the moral law, above all other authorities, because the moral law is the authority of God. Second, if the husband has gone so far astray from truth and justice that he no longer guards the common good of the family, no longer takes his proper role as husband and father at all, then he has lost his authority over his wife. She must still obey the moral law, and do whatever she can for the good of the family. But she need not be obedient or submissive to him. However, a wife should never exaggerate the sins and faults of her husband in order to remove herself from her proper role, subordinate to him, within the family.

.354.
[Ephesians]
{5:21} Be subject to one another in the fear of Christ.

Sacred Scripture teaches us to be subject to one another in the fear of Christ. This fear of Christ is not the emotion of fear, but a holy acceptance of Christ's role over each of us. We are each mutually subject to one another, under Christ, to love one another and to assist one another in Christ's work of salvation. The fear of Christ is not an emotion, but is our subjection to Christ. We are all subject to Christ. We must all be submissive and obedient to Christ. We are all equal in this role of subjection. And we must all practice the fear of the Lord. (See the Book of Sirach, and numerous other passages in the Bible, on the fear of the Lord.)

But this verse (5:21) does not refer specifically to the role of husband and wife. Rather, it is a general command to the whole Church to be subject to one another in Christ. And since the submission of the Church to Christ is the basis for the submission of the wife to her husband, the Apostle next discusses subjection in marital roles. The husband and wife are both mutually subject to Christ, but not mutually subject to one another; for each has a unique role.

{5:22} Wives should be submissive to their husbands, as to the Lord.

Since the Lord has ordained a different role for the wife than for the husband, her submissiveness to her husband is a submission to the plan and will of the Lord. And when she rejects this role, she rejects the will of God. Whoever rejects the teaching that wives should be submissive to their husbands, rejects the teaching of Christ.

{5:23} For the husband is the head of the wife, just as Christ is the head of the Church. He is the Savior of his body.

The state of holy Matrimony is a living figure of the relationship between Christ and His Church. Christ is the Savior of His Body the Church. The husband is not the savior of his wife, but he does have a role in his wife's salvation, and his role in her salvation is different from her role in his salvation. For marriage and family are an integral part of God's plan for salvation, and the husband, as the head of his wife and of the family, has the role to lead the family in works pertaining to salvation. Very many graces are poured out to the Church and the world through each holy marriage and each holy family. But the wife's role in the salvation of the family is not to lead, but to assist, just as Mary's role in our salvation is not to save, but to assist Christ in saving.

{5:24} Therefore, just as the Church is subject to Christ, so also should wives be subject to their husbands in all things.

God created the human race and human nature, and He so ordered natural marriage and the Sacrament of marriage, so that men and women, husbands and wives, would have different roles in the family. And this order is a reflection of the order in all Creation. For just as Creation is subject to Christ (1 Cor 15:26-28), so also is the wife subject to her husband. And Eve was created from the side of Adam, but Adam was not created from the side of Eve.

{5:25} Husbands, love your wives, just as Christ also loved the Church and handed himself over for her,
{5:26} so that he might sanctify her, washing her clean by water and the Word of life,
{5:27} so that he might offer her to himself as a glorious Church, not having any spot or wrinkle or any such thing, so that she would be holy and immaculate.

The husband has a different role in God's plan of salvation for the family than the wife has. The husband leads the family, to guard the common good, so that each member of the family may more easily seek, obtain, and keep the salvation of Christ. The wife's role in the salvation of the family in some ways is the same, in that both pray, both fast, both do good works, but in other ways is different. For she is not the head of the family, but the heart of the family. Both head and heart cooperate, in their respective tasks, to lead the whole body, the whole family, closer to Christ, the one and only Savior.

{5:28} So, too, husbands should love their wives as their own bodies. He who loves his wife loves himself.
{5:29} For no man has ever hated his own flesh, but instead he nourishes and cherishes it, as Christ also does to the Church.
{5:30} For we are a part of his body, of his flesh and of his bones.
{5:31} "For this reason, a man shall leave behind his father and mother, and he shall cling to his wife; and the two shall be as one flesh."

The husband and wife must each love one another, mutually. But the ways that this love is expressed differs according to the proper role for each spouse. For the love between Christ and His Church is mutual; it is the same type of love. But the ways in which Christ expresses that love differs from the ways in which the Church expresses that love. For example, He expresses that love by leading, and She expresses that love by following. So this union of two as one is a reciprocal, and yet asymmetrical union.

{5:32} This is a great Sacrament. And I am speaking in Christ and in the Church.

The word Sacrament means mystery. If anyone tells you that the Sacrament of marriage is simple, that it only means this and that, nothing more, do not be led astray. Each and every Sacrament is a great mystery, including the Sacrament of holy Matrimony. And when sinful secular society tells you that marriage is merely a 50-50 partnership, or some similar claim, do not be led astray. If marriage is a 50-50 partnership, which 50 is God's role? The true Sacrament of Marriage is a mystery beyond complete human comprehension. For God participates in the marriage in a way which is part of His plan of salvation for the human family, and in a way which is beyond description in words.

{5:33} Yet truly, each and every one of you should love his wife as himself. And a wife should fear her husband.

This passage (Ephesians 5:21-33) began by calling every one to the fear of Christ; that fear is respectful submission to the authority of Christ. Similarly, the fear that a wife should have for her husband is not the emotion of fear; instead, it is respectful submission to the authority of her husband, which is an authority ordained by Christ. If any wife does not fear her husband, then she does not fear Christ. But all this refers to holy fear, not to being afraid of someone. A wife should fear her husband, but she should not be afraid of him.

Although some translations of the Bible have cast aside the word 'fear,' Sacred Scripture uses the same word (in the Latin and in the Greek) in verse 5:33 as in verse 5:21. Both verses refer to the same type of fear, the holy fear of Christ. A wife should fear her husband because his authority is of Christ. In doing so, she is fearing Christ and a role that is a figure of Christ, but she is not fearing the person of her husband. Whoever rejects the fear of the Lord, rejects the Lord.

This same word 'fear' is used in the Old and New Testaments to refer to the fear of the Lord. But certainly, this fear is not the emotion of fear. Even so, the word 'fear' is fitting, because the same type of respectful submission required of us all toward Christ the Lord, is also required of the wife toward her husband. If anyone still does not understand what this means, let him or her meditate on the meaning of the fear of the Lord. "The fear of the Lord is the beginning of wisdom." (Proverbs 1:7; Sirach 1:16; Psalms 110:10).

.355. Casti Connubii

The mutual nature of the marriage relationship is widely accepted. But the asymmetrical nature of the relationship between husband and wife is often denied or ignored or distorted. But this asymmetry is the teaching of Tradition,

Sexual Sins

Scripture, and the Magisterium. It is only the influence of secular society that has caused this doctrine to be so widely rejected. Pope Pius XI, in the encyclical Casti Connubii (Chaste Marriage), taught both the reciprocal (mutual) and the asymmetrical nature of the marriage relationship.

Pope Pius XI: "This mutual molding of husband and wife, this determined effort to perfect each other, can in a very real sense, as the Roman Catechism teaches, be said to be the chief reason and purpose of matrimony, provided matrimony be looked at not in the restricted sense as instituted for the proper conception and education of the child, but more widely as the blending of life as a whole and the mutual interchange and sharing thereof."[391]

The mutual love between the husband and wife results in a mutual responsibility to act for the good of one another. And this reciprocal nature of the relationship unfolds in many ways in daily life, according to the circumstances of the moment. The whole of marriage life is characterized by this mutual interchange and sharing of life, based on mutual love.

However, this mutual love, which thoroughly permeates their entire married life, must not be misrepresented as if it extinguishes the difference in roles between the husband and the wife within the family. Sacred Scripture could not be more clear on this truth, as previously discussed. But the Magisterium has also taught this doctrine, clearly and definitively.

Pope Pius XI: "Domestic society being confirmed, therefore, by this bond of love, there should flourish in it that 'order of love,' as St. Augustine calls it. This order includes both the primacy of the husband with regard to the wife and children, the ready subjection of the wife and her willing obedience, which the Apostle commends in these words: 'Let women be subject to their husbands as to the Lord, because the husband is the head of the wife, and Christ is the head of the Church.' "[392]

The Magisterium clearly teaches that the husband is the head of his wife, and his wife should be subject to him in obedience. Some commentators on Scripture, attempting to nullify this teaching, have tried to reinterpret subjection, as if it were mutual submission, or mutual obedience. This approach is half right. There is a mutual aspect to submission and to obedience. But it is a serious doctrinal error to claim that the marriage relationship is entirely mutual and equal in every way. Whoever adheres to this error, commits material heresy. Whoever teaches this error, harms the Sacrament of Marriage. God has ordained, in natural marriage, and all the more so in the Sacrament of holy Matrimony, a distinction in roles between the husband and wife, such that the husband has a role of primacy in regard to the wife and children, and the wife has a role of subjection and obedience to him.

Pope Pius XI: "This subjection, however, does not deny or take away the liberty which fully belongs to the woman both in view of her dignity as a human person,

---

[391] Pope Pius XI, Casti Connubii, n. 24.
[392] Pope Pius XI, Casti Connubii, n. 26.

and in view of her most noble office as wife and mother and companion; nor does it bid her obey her husband's every request if not in harmony with right reason or with the dignity due to wife; nor, in fine, does it imply that the wife should be put on a level with those persons who in law are called minors, to whom it is not customary to allow free exercise of their rights on account of their lack of mature judgment, or of their ignorance of human affairs. But it forbids that exaggerated liberty which cares not for the good of the family; it forbids that in this body which is the family, the heart be separated from the head to the great detriment of the whole body and the proximate danger of ruin. For if the man is the head, the woman is the heart, and as he occupies the chief place in ruling, so she may and ought to claim for herself the chief place in love."[393]

.356. Obedience and subjection to human persons is always limited. Only obedience and subjection to God is inherently unlimited. For example, Mary's holiness is based on her obedience to God, not to Joseph. Also, the husband and wife are equal as concerns their nature. Each has the same human nature and the dignity of that nature. Each is made in the image of God. The inequality between husband and wife is not of nature, but of roles. Each has his and her own function and place in the family. And this was true even for Joseph and Mary.

During their chaste and pure marriage, Mary was obedient to Joseph; he exercised his proper role as the head of the family. When it was the will of God for the holy family to flee to Egypt, an angel was sent to Joseph in a dream, not to Mary or the Child Jesus. Joseph then decided to flee to Egypt, with his family. When it was time for them to return from Egypt, Joseph was again told that the family should return, and where they should settle (Mt 2:13-23). And Joseph held this role as head of the family despite the fact that Mary is much holier than Joseph, and that the Child Jesus is not only holier still, but is their God and Savior. Therefore, the leader of the family is the husband and father, and not whichever person is said to be most fit. Neither are the tasks of headship in the family to be dispensed to whomever has the greatest ability. God has ordained that there would be a certain structure to the family, just as to the Church. The pastor is the head of the parish, and the Bishop is the head of the diocese, and the Roman Pontiff is the head of the entire Church on earth.

Although the husband is ordained by God to be the head of the family, and the head of his wife, she must be obedient, first and foremost, to God. If his will is contrary to the will of God, she may decline to obey. If his will is contrary to the will of God and contrary to the moral law, she must decline to obey. Similarly, even a person who has taken a vow of obedience must always and without exception decline to obey any order to sin, and any order to commit sinful cooperation with evil.

Obedience in the family, and any type of holy obedience at all, is not primarily the giving and receiving of orders. Rather, true obedience is fulfilled mainly by a cooperative attitude, in which the wife assists the husband in his good plans and

---

[393] Pope Pius XI, Casti Connubii, n. 27.

Sexual Sins

good works. Eve was created to be a helper and companion to Adam, not his slave or servant. And there are examples in Sacred Scripture in which a person with a lower station gives good advice to a person of a higher station. Sometimes this good advice is followed (2 Kings 5:12-14), and sometimes it is not followed (Acts 27:9-11).

Pope Pius XI: "Again, this subjection of wife to husband in its degree and manner may vary according to the different conditions of persons, place and time. In fact, if the husband neglect his duty, it falls to the wife to take his place in directing the family. But the structure of the family and its fundamental law, established and confirmed by God, must always and everywhere be maintained intact."[394]

The authority of the husband over his wife is a figure for the authority of Christ over His Church. But the more the husband sins, the less he is like Christ, the less he has authority, and the less his wife must be subject to him. If he fails utterly in his God-given role as the head of the family, his wife may take up his duties, as necessity requires. However, she takes his place only in the sense of doing the necessary tasks that should have been done by him. She does not become the head of the family, for "the structure of the family...must always and everywhere be maintained intact."[395] Similarly, when one Pope dies, and before his successor is elected, a Cardinal or group of Cardinals will take over the necessary tasks that would have been done by the Pope. But this Cardinal or group of Cardinals does not thereby become the head of the Church on earth. They take up the necessary tasks, but they cannot claim to have the role itself.

.357. The Marriage Debt

Pope Pius XI: "By this same love it is necessary that all the other rights and duties of the marriage state be regulated as the words of the Apostle: 'Let the husband render the debt to the wife, and the wife also in like manner to the husband,' express not only a law of justice but of charity."[396]

The term 'marriage debt' refers to the mutual obligation between the husband and wife to engage in natural marital relations open to life. This obligation is mutual because it is a requirement of the moral law, that is the law of justice. The husband and wife are equal under the moral law. The reasons for the marriage debt, i.e. the obligation of the spouses to engage in sexual relations with one another, are several. First, the human race would not continue without sexual relations leading to the procreation of children. And children are best served by being conceived and born into a family with a father and mother. The emphasis in modern secular society on sexual relations for pleasure has led to a decline in the birth rate in many nations below what is needed to sustain the population.

---

[394] Pope Pius XI, Casti Connubii, n. 28.
[395] Pope Pius XI, Casti Connubii, n. 28.
[396] Pope Pius XI, Casti Connubii, n. 25.

Second, marital relations offers the goods of expressing and strengthening the marriage, and of binding and keeping the couple united in mind and heart by an outward expression of the body. The marital and unitive meanings offer goods to the marriage in addition to the good of the procreation of children.

Third, the aforementioned goods, by benefiting the husband and wife, also benefit the whole family. For when the spouses regularly express and strengthen their love, even in this bodily manner, the benefits to their souls and spirits then also benefit the whole family.

Fourth, marital relations quiets concupiscence, thereby protecting the spouses from the danger of sexual sins, including sins in the mind and heart, as well as bodily sins, such as masturbation or adultery. This purpose to marital relations, though certainly secondary to the primary threefold end of the marital, unitive, and procreative meaning, is nevertheless so important (for us poor sinners living in a sinful world) that the Apostle Paul emphasizes it when speaking about the marriage debt in Sacred Scripture.

[1 Corinthians]
{7:1} Now concerning the things about which you wrote to me: It is good for a man not to touch a woman.
{7:2} But, because of fornication, let each man have his own wife, and let each woman have her own husband.
{7:3} A husband should fulfill his obligation to his wife, and a wife should also act similarly toward her husband.
{7:4} It is not the wife, but the husband, who has power over her body. But, similarly also, it is not the husband, but the wife, who has power over his body.
{7:5} So, do not fail in your obligations to one another, except perhaps by consent, for a limited time, so that you may empty yourselves for prayer. And then, return together again, lest Satan tempt you by means of your abstinence.

Scripture begins this passage by asserting the truth, also infallibly taught by the Council of Trent, that virginity and celibacy are better than marriage. But as our Lord also taught (Mt 19:12), some persons are called to the lower state of marriage, and other persons are called to the higher state of chastity as a single person.

Within the married state, natural sexual relations is not only a right and privilege given to married persons, it is also a duty. The husband and wife have a mutual obligation to one another, sometimes represented under the figure of a debt that is to be paid, to engage in marital relations for the good of the other person. The reason for this marriage debt is not to make certain that both spouses have ample sexual pleasure in their life, but rather so that all the goods of natural marital relations will benefit both spouses, and the family, and humanity.

Notice that the modern idea of sex for pleasure is absent from this passage about natural marital relations. Even some misguided Catholics today are loudly proclaiming that sexual relations in marriage is for the purpose of pleasure, is guided by that purpose, and is justified (even in unnatural acts) by that purpose. They even claim, by misuse of the term 'theology of the body', that their errors are merely the teachings of the personal theology of Pope John Paul II. They are like the Nicolaitans in this regard (Rev 2:6).[397] But the teaching of Tradition, Scripture, Magisterium contains no such assertions. And truly, neither did Pope John Paul II teach any of those errors, neither in his private theology, nor in any act of the Magisterium.

[1 Corinthians]
{7:6} But I am saying this, neither as an indulgence, nor as a commandment.
{7:7} For I would prefer it if you were all like myself. But each person has his proper gift from God: one in this way, yet another in that way.
{7:8} But I say to the unmarried and to widows: It is good for them, if they would remain as they are, just as I also am.
{7:9} But if they cannot restrain themselves, they should marry. For it is better to marry, than to be burned.

No one can be compelled to choose the married state; it is not a commandment that any particular person marry. Neither is the married state, and marital relations in particular, ordained for the purpose of self-indulgence, so that each person will have the pleasures that they desire. Paul would prefer, and Christ is also speaking to us through Paul, in the Holy Spirit, that the faithful choose the higher state of virginity and celibacy over the lower state of holy matrimony. But this gift is not given to all persons. Each person has their own gifts and their own calling, some to marriage and some to virginity and celibacy.

If any persons, due to their own sinfulness, find virginity and celibacy too difficult, then they should marry. For it is better to be married, i.e. to be in a lower but still holy state of life, than to burn with desire, which leads to sin, and which finally may lead to being burned in Hell. Illicit sexual acts are always gravely immoral, and so the danger of Hellfire should caution us in this area of life. Whoever preaches unrestrained sexual practices even within marriage, sins by formal cooperation with evil, harms the holy Sacrament of Marriage, and endangers many souls.

.358. Virginity and Celibacy

The Council of Trent: "If any one says that the marriage state is to be placed above the state of virginity, or of celibacy, and that it is not better and more blessed to remain in virginity, or in celibacy, than to be united in matrimony; let him be anathema."[398]

It is a heresy against the holy Catholic Faith to claim that the state of matrimony is greater than, or equal to, the state of virginity, or of celibacy. Although this type of explicit heretical statement, condemned by the Council of Trent, is rare today, the very same heretical idea is implicit in the attitudes and words of many Catholics. For example, they bewail the fact that most priests in the Church, and almost all priests in the Latin Rite, are celibate. If they truly believed the

---

[397] Nicolaitans preached and practiced utter sexual immorality; they falsely attributed this severe moral error to Nicolas, one of the first deacons of the Church (Acts 6:5).
[398] The Council of Trent, 24th Session, On The Sacrament of Matrimony, Canon X.

infallible teaching that celibacy is a better state than holy matrimony, then they would not plead for a married priesthood and speak of celibacy with contempt. In another example, the holy state of virginity is often denigrated, not only by secular society, but also by some members of the faithful. If a man or woman refrains from sexual relations prior to marriage, he or she is treated as an oddity, or as a Saint, rather than as an ordinary member of the Church following the ordinary path of the faithful.

Virginity is better than marriage. For Jesus Christ our Savior, perfect man and perfect God, was a perfect virgin. He never married, even though nearly all Jews married, and He was a faithful Jew. The Jewish Faith did not have a celibate priesthood or a celibate religious life; the priests and Levites married. And yet Christ not only chose to be celibate Himself, He also chose celibacy as the main and ordinary state of life for priests and bishops. If anyone says that the Church would be better served by a married priesthood, than by a priesthood that is mostly celibate, he contradicts the example of Christ and of Sacred Tradition.

The plan of God for our salvation included choosing a woman, the Virgin Mary, to conceive and give birth to Jesus, who is God Incarnate, and to raise Him within a holy family led by Mary's husband, Joseph. And even though this holy plan included that Mary be married and bear a child, it was also God's will, and her will in harmony with God's will, that she be a perfect virgin, and that she have a celibate marriage, entirely without sexual relations. Although natural marital relations is good and is part of the Sacrament of Marriage, Joseph and Mary remained celibate, thereby proving that virginity and celibacy are the greater good. God chose a virgin, and kept her by His grace as a virgin forever, despite the fact that she was chosen to bear a child. Therefore, virginity and celibacy are better than marital relations.

.359. Some married men are permitted to become priests, because no Sacrament contradicts any other Sacrament. All the Sacraments are one harmonious whole. But when an unmarried man becomes a priest, he is not permitted to seek a wife. For it is not right to move from a higher calling to a lower calling. A priest who seeks a wife is seeking to spend much of his time in a lower calling instead of his present higher calling. Whereas a married man who becomes a priest moves from a lower calling to a higher calling. Jesus was an unmarried virgin, and Mary was a married virgin. Therefore, it is established by their examples, which are among the deeds of infallible Sacred Tradition, that the priesthood must always consist mainly of unmarried celibate men, and that the religious life must always consist of celibate men and women as well.

Chapter 25
Marital Sexual Ethics

.360.
[Hebrews 13]
{13:4} May marriage be honorable in every way, and may the marriage bed be immaculate. For God will judge fornicators and adulterers.

The eternal moral law is universal, applying to all persons, at all times, in all places. There is no exemption from the moral law for sexuality, or for the marital bedroom. Every knowingly chosen act must be good in all three fonts in order to be moral. The same basic principles of morality apply to sexual ethics as to all other areas of human life. As is true for all knowingly chosen acts, a sexual act is immoral if any one or more of the fonts is bad. Now certainly, when considering any particular act, the particular intention (first font), the particular act with its inherent moral meaning determined by its moral object (second font), and the particular circumstances, must be evaluated in order to determine the morality of the overall act. These particulars will vary from one act to another, and from one type of act to another. But the basic principles are always the same, without any exception, for each and every knowingly chosen act. If anyone states or implies that the basic principles of morality do not apply to sexuality, or that there are exceptions to the basic principles of morality for sexuality, or that a different set of basic principles of morality apply to sexuality, then he has gone astray from the true Catholic Faith. Marital sexual acts are not exempt from the eternal moral law.

Second Vatican Council: "…there is no human activity which can be withdrawn from God's dominion."[399]

.361. THE FIRST AND THIRD FONTS

Sexual acts are always a grave matter.[400] Therefore, whenever a sexual act is immoral under the second font, the act itself is not only intrinsically evil and always immoral, but also always objectively gravely immoral. Every intrinsically evil sexual act is always an objective mortal sin. However, if a sexual act is inherently good, having all three meanings (marital, unitive, procreative), the act may still be a sin under the first or third fonts. And if it is a sin under the first or the third fonts, but not under the second font, then the sin may be venial or mortal, depending on the gravity of the intention and the circumstances.

A sexual act might possibly be done with good or bad intention, or in good or bad circumstances. Even if a sexual act is moral under the second font, the person nevertheless sins if the first or third fonts are bad. A husband and wife are not exempt from the requirement of the eternal moral law that every intention (both the intended end and the intended means) must be good in order to avoid sin. If a husband and wife have natural marital relations open to life, which is

---

[399] Second Vatican Council, Lumen Gentium, n. 36.
[400] Cardinal Seper, CDF, Persona Humana, n. X.

moral under the second font, with bad intention, or in circumstances when the bad consequences outweigh the good, then they sin.

Sexual ethics often focuses on intrinsically evil acts, i.e. acts that are immoral under the second font. But as is true for all knowingly chosen acts, even when an act is not intrinsically evil, the first and third fonts must also be good for the overall act to be moral. It is false to say that, if a husband and wife are having natural marital relations open to life, they are certainly not sinning. The act itself of natural marital relations open to life is not intrinsically evil. But, as is always the case, the first font (intention) and the third font (circumstances) must also be good in order to avoid sin.

.362. THE SECOND FONT

As is true for all knowingly chosen acts, a sexual act is intrinsically evil whenever its moral object is bad. A moral object is bad whenever the act itself is inherently ordered toward the direct and voluntary deprivation of a good required to be present by true love of God, neighbor, self. Every good moral object is a particular fulfillment of true love of God, neighbor, self. Every bad moral object is a direct and voluntary deprivation that is in some particular way contrary to true love of God, neighbor, self. And this one threefold love is the basis for all morality. Any act that is contrary to love of God, or love of neighbor, or a true ordered love of self, is contrary to all three.

A. Marital

All sexual acts outside of marriage are intrinsically evil. The lack of the marital meaning in any sexual act is sufficient to cause that act to be intrinsically evil. All non-marital sexual acts are intrinsically evil. To be moral, a sexual act must be marital.

Pope Leo XIII: "Marriage has God for its Author, and was from the very beginning a kind of foreshadowing of the Incarnation of His Son; and therefore there abides in it something holy and religious; not extraneous, but innate; not derived from men, but implanted by nature."[401]

Pope Pius XI: "Nor must We omit to remark, in fine, that since the duty entrusted to parents for the good of their children is of such high dignity and of such great importance, every use of the faculty given by God for the procreation of new life is the right and the privilege of the married state alone, by the law of God and of nature, and must be confined absolutely within the sacred limits of that state."[402]

Sacred Congregation for the Doctrine of the Faith: "This same principle, which the Church holds from Divine Revelation and from her authentic interpretation of the natural law, is also the basis of her traditional doctrine, which states that

---

[401] Pope Leo XIII, Arcanum (On Christian Marriage), n. 19.
[402] Pope Pius XI, Casti Connubii, n. 18.

the use of the sexual function has its true meaning and moral rectitude only in true marriage."[403]

Sacred Congregation for the Doctrine of the Faith: "Through marriage, in fact, the love of married people is taken up into that love which Christ irrevocably has for the Church, while dissolute sexual union [16] defiles the temple of the Holy Spirit which the Christian has become. Sexual union therefore is only legitimate if a definitive community of life has been established between the man and the woman. This is what the Church has always understood and taught, and she finds a profound agreement with her doctrine in men's reflection and in the lessons of history. Experience teaches us that love must find its safeguard in the stability of marriage, if sexual intercourse is truly to respond to the requirements of its own finality and to those of human dignity." Footnote 16 states: "Sexual intercourse outside marriage is formally condemned I Cor 5:1; 6:9; 7:2; 10:8 Eph. 5:5; I Tim 1:10; Heb 13:4; and with explicit reasons I Cor 6:12-20."[404] The term 'dissolute sexual union' refers to sexual acts without the marital bond.

Numerous other texts could be cited, from Tradition, Scripture, Magisterium, all of which teach that any type of sexual act outside of marriage is always inherently gravely immoral. But the faithful already know and live by this truth, that sexual relations is only moral within marriage.

The marital meaning is not the physical sexual act itself. The marital meaning is one part of the threefold moral object that determines the essential moral nature of the sexual act. The full moral meaning of the sexual act is found only within a marriage relationship. The act of natural intercourse is inherently directed at expressing and strengthening the marriage relationship. For the act of natural intercourse is inherently ordered toward the marriage itself, as ordained by God. The physical sexual act is the concrete act (the act itself), but every concrete act has an inherent moral meaning as determined by its moral object. Thus the marital meaning of the sexual act is based upon the physical act, but is itself of the moral order. The marital meaning of the sexual act is based upon, but also transcends, the mere physical act.

B. Unitive

All non-unitive sexual acts are intrinsically evil. The lack of the unitive meaning in any sexual act is sufficient to cause that act to be intrinsically evil. To be moral, a sexual act must be unitive.

Pope Paul VI: "This particular doctrine, often expounded by the magisterium of the Church, is based on the inseparable connection, established by God, which man on his own initiative may not break, between the unitive significance and the procreative significance which are both inherent to the marriage act. The reason is that the fundamental nature of the marriage act, while uniting husband and wife in the closest intimacy, also renders them capable of generating new life -- and this as a result of laws written into the actual nature of man and of

---

[403] Cardinal Seper, CDF, Persona Humana, n. V.
[404] Cardinal Seper, CDF, Persona Humana, n. VII.

woman. And if each of these essential qualities, the unitive and the procreative, is preserved, the use of marriage fully retains its sense of true mutual love and its ordination to the supreme responsibility of parenthood to which man is called."[405]

The unitive significance (or meaning) of the marital act is found in that type of intimate physical union, between husband and wife, which is inherently capable of procreation (genital-to-genital intercourse, i.e. natural intercourse). The marital act is intended by God to unite two whole persons, and to express and strengthen their union in love. The unitive significance is "the expression and strengthening of the union of husband and wife."[406] The unitive meaning achieves its fullest realization only when united with the procreative and marital meanings. An act of natural intercourse apart from marriage, or with the use of contraception, or both, is not fully unitive, as God intends. For this unitive meaning is more than the mere natural physical union that occurs during the act; it also implies the continuous union of the man and woman in marriage, with openness to the procreation of children. The unitive meaning is not sexual climax, nor sexual pleasure, nor mere physical unity.

The unitive meaning is not the physical sexual act itself. The unitive meaning is one part of the threefold moral object that determines the essential moral nature of the sexual act. This moral object determines the essential moral nature of the natural marital act, so that the act itself is inherently ordered toward the union of a man and a woman, in marriage, with openness to new life, as ordained by God. The physical union of the natural sexual act is the concrete act (the act itself), but every concrete act has an inherent moral meaning as determined by its moral object. Thus the unitive meaning is based upon a particular physical act, but is itself of the moral order. The unitive meaning of the sexual act is based upon, but also transcends, the mere physical act.

C. Procreative

All non-procreative sexual acts are intrinsically evil. The lack of the procreative meaning in any sexual act is sufficient to cause that act to be intrinsically evil. Therefore, all non-procreative sexual acts are intrinsically evil. To be moral, a sexual act must be procreative.

Pope Paul VI: "The Church, nevertheless, in urging men to the observance of the precepts of the natural law, which it interprets by its constant doctrine, teaches that each and every marital act must of necessity retain its intrinsic relationship to the procreation of human life."[407]

Pope Paul VI: "Consequently, it is a serious error to think that a whole married life of otherwise normal relations can justify sexual intercourse which is deliberately contraceptive and so intrinsically wrong."[408]

---

[405] Pope Paul VI, Humanae Vitae, n. 12.
[406] Pope Paul VI, Humanae Vitae, n. 11.
[407] Pope Paul VI, Humanae Vitae, n. 11.
[408] Pope Paul VI, Humanae Vitae, n. 14.

Pope John Paul II: "With regard to intrinsically evil acts, and in reference to contraceptive practices whereby the conjugal act is intentionally rendered infertile, Pope Paul VI teaches: 'Though it is true that sometimes it is lawful to tolerate a lesser moral evil in order to avoid a greater evil or in order to promote a greater good, it is never lawful, even for the gravest reasons, to do evil that good may come of it (cf. Rom 3:8) -- in other words, to intend directly something which of its very nature contradicts the moral order, and which must therefore be judged unworthy of man, even though the intention is to protect or promote the welfare of an individual, of a family or of society in general'."[409]

Even though each sexual act within marriage does not produce new life, only natural intercourse is that type of act inherently ordered toward the procreation of new life. And so, even if the couple is infertile, as long as each sexual act within marriage is the natural type (genital-to-genital intercourse), the sexual act remains inherently ordered toward procreation. For it is not the attainment of the moral object that makes the act moral, but rather the inherent ordering of the act itself toward that moral object. The act of natural marital relations open to life by a married couple who are infertile has the procreative meaning in its moral object, even if no child is conceived. A contracepted act of natural marital relations lacks the procreative meaning in its moral object, even if by chance a child is conceived. For the contracepted sexual act is not inherently ordered toward procreation. But the infertile natural sexual act is inherently ordered toward procreation.

The procreative meaning is not the physical sexual act itself. The procreative meaning is one part of the threefold moral object that determines the essential moral nature of the sexual act. For the act of natural intercourse is inherently ordered toward the procreation of children, within marriage, as ordained by God. The physical sexual act is the concrete act (the act itself), but every concrete act has an inherent moral meaning as determined by its moral object. Thus the procreative meaning is based upon the physical act, but is itself of the moral order. The procreative meaning of the sexual act is based upon, but also transcends, the mere physical act.

.363. The Threefold Moral Object

To be moral, each and every sexual act must be unitive and procreative and marital. The absence of any one or more of these meanings is a deprivation of a good required by true love of God, neighbor, self. The eternal moral law requires each and every sexual act to have all three meanings within the moral object. The lack of any one or more of these meanings results in an evil moral object. For evil is properly defined as a deprivation of good, and moral evil is properly defined as the deprivation of a good required by the moral law. True love of God, neighbor, self is the single threefold principle upon which the entire moral law rests.

When the moral object is deprived of a good required by the moral law, the act itself is intrinsically evil. Non-marital sexual acts are intrinsically evil, because

---

[409] Pope John Paul II, Veritatis Splendor, n. 80; inner quote from Humanae Vitae, n. 14.

the moral object is deprived of the marital meaning. Non-unitive sexual acts are intrinsically evil, because the moral object is deprived of the unitive meaning. Non-procreative sexual acts are intrinsically evil, because the moral object is deprived of the procreative meaning. Without any exception at all, the moral object of each and every sexual act must have all three meanings in order to be good. The deprivation of any one or more of these three meanings makes the act itself intrinsically evil and always gravely immoral. A sexual act is never moral unless its moral object possesses all three meanings: unitive, procreative, marital. These three meanings are truly one threefold moral object. For God has ordained that these three distinct meanings be always united and never separated, in each and every sexual act.

.364. The Unitive Procreative Marital Act

The only sexual act that is unitive and procreative and marital is natural marital relations open to life. Only natural marital relations open to life possesses all three meanings by being inherently ordered toward this threefold moral object. Therefore, the only moral sexual act is natural marital relations open to life.

Natural marital relations is inherently ordered toward a threefold moral object that is unitive, procreative, and marital. Any knowingly chosen sexual act that is deprived of any one or more of these three meanings is an intrinsically evil sexual act. Every sexual act must be inherently ordered toward these three meanings, which are truly one threefold meaning (or significance). Every sexual act must have this same threefold moral object. Only natural marital relations open to life has the fullness of all three meanings.

This single statement by Pope Paul VI includes all three meanings of the moral sexual act [with my notations]:

Pope Paul VI: "The sexual activity, in which husband and wife [marital] are intimately and chastely united with one another [unitive], through which human life is transmitted [procreative], is, as the recent Council recalled, 'noble and worthy.' "[410]

This type of sexual act alone is noble, worthy, chaste, and moral. The concrete act of natural marital relations open to life is inherently good because it is inherently ordered toward its proper threefold moral object. This moral object, like all good moral objects, is a particular fulfillment of true love of God, neighbor, self.

The marital act is no mere physical union, but involves an intimate union of the whole person; it is a chaste union in accord with the plan of God for man and woman. This union is not only an expression of the love of the husband and wife for each other, but also of their love for God. The expression of this love is good for both one's self and one's spouse. And so the union is a particular way of fulfilling the commandment to love God, and to love your neighbor as yourself.

---

[410] Pope Paul VI, Humanae Vitae, n. 11; inner quote from Second Vatican Council, Gaudium et Spes, n. 49.

Marital Sexual Ethics

The marital act is procreative, not merely in terms of biology, for a child is not conceived as a result of each sexual act, but in terms of morality. The human race continues to exist, in each successive generation, only because men and women are willing to commit themselves, not only to one another, but to their whole family, including to the procreation and raising of children.

The marital act is aptly named, for sexual intercourse outside of marriage is a lie, a false promise, in which the couple give their bodies to one another, but they refuse to give their whole selves and their lives to one another. Natural law is the promulgation of the eternal moral law within the very nature of created things, and within the proper relationship of created things, especially created persons, including their relationship with God. The plan of God is for men and women to unite in sexual intercourse only within marriage, through that particular sexual act in which both the unitive and the procreative meanings are inseparably combined, for the benefit of the marriage.

Canon Law 1061 n. 1: "A valid marriage between the baptized is called ratum tantum if it has not been consummated; it is called ratum et consummatum if the spouses have performed between themselves in a human fashion a conjugal act which is suitable in itself for the procreation of offspring, to which marriage is ordered by its nature and by which the spouses become one flesh."[411]

This paragraph of Canon Law also incorporates and expresses the three meanings of the moral sexual act. The act must be marital: "to which marriage is ordered by its nature." The act must be unitive: "a conjugal act...by which the spouses become one flesh." The act must be procreative, i.e. the type of act "which is suitable in itself for the procreation of offspring."

Second Vatican Council: "Marriage and conjugal love are by their nature ordained toward the begetting and educating of children.... Parents should regard as their proper mission the task of transmitting human life and educating those to whom it has been transmitted.... Marriage to be sure is not instituted solely for procreation; rather, its very nature as an unbreakable compact between persons, and the welfare of the children, both demand that the mutual love of the spouses be embodied in a rightly ordered manner, that it grow and ripen.... But where the intimacy of married life is broken off, its faithfulness can sometimes be imperiled and its quality of fruitfulness ruined, for then the upbringing of the children and the courage to accept new ones are both endangered."[412]

The Second Vatican Council's teaching on marriage refers to the three meanings of the moral sexual act: (1) unitive: "conjugal love...the intimacy of married life," (2) procreative: "ordained toward the begetting and educating of children.... the task of transmitting human life," (3) marital: "its very nature as an unbreakable compact between persons." The three meanings required for any sexual act to be moral is the definitive teaching of the Roman Catholic Church, and is required belief for all the faithful.

---

[411] Code of Canon Law for the Latin Church, 1983, Canon 1061 n. 1.
[412] Second Vatican Council, Gaudium et Spes, n. 50-51.

.365. Secondary Ends of Natural Marital Relations

Pope Pius XI: "For in matrimony as well as in the use of the matrimonial rights there are also secondary ends, such as mutual aid, the cultivating of mutual love, and the quieting of concupiscence which husband and wife are not forbidden to consider so long as they are subordinated to the primary end and so long as the intrinsic nature of the act is preserved."[413]

The moral object of natural marital relations determines the intrinsic moral nature of the act; the proper moral object is procreative, unitive, and marital. This intrinsic nature of the act is its inherent moral meaning, i.e. its essential moral nature, which is in the second font. But there exist good ends of natural marital relations that are found in the third font. No matter how good the consequences (i.e. the effects) of an act may be, in the third font, these can never justify an act that is intrinsically evil, in the second font. So in the quote above, the Pope cautions that the intrinsic nature of the act must be preserved in order for it to be moral; the act must be unitive, procreative, and marital. But given a good act of natural marital relations open to life, there exist licit secondary ends, i.e. good consequences, which may also be sought by the husband and wife within natural marital relations. These good ends include comforting one another, assisting one another in avoiding sexual sins (1 Cor 7:1-5), expressing affection, and enjoying the companionship of one another in body and soul.

The quieting of concupiscence refers to the effect that natural marital relations has in quenching sexual desire, so that neither the husband nor the wife is tempted to commit a sexual sin (such as masturbation, adultery, or unnatural sexual acts with a spouse). This secondary end of natural marital relations is mentioned in Sacred Scripture:

[1 Corinthians]
{7:1} Now concerning the things about which you wrote to me: It is good for a man not to touch a woman.
{7:2} But, because of fornication, let each man have his own wife, and let each woman have her own husband.
{7:3} A husband should fulfill his obligation to his wife, and a wife should also act similarly toward her husband.
{7:4} It is not the wife, but the husband, who has power over her body. But, similarly also, it is not the husband, but the wife, who has power over his body.
{7:5} So, do not fail in your obligations to one another, except perhaps by consent, for a limited time, so that you may empty yourselves for prayer. And then, return together again, lest Satan tempt you by means of your abstinence.
{7:6} But I am saying this, neither as an indulgence, nor as a commandment.
{7:7} For I would prefer it if you were all like myself. But each person has his proper gift from God: one in this way, yet another in that way.
{7:8} But I say to the unmarried and to widows: It is good for them, if they would remain as they are, just as I also am.

---

[413] Pope Pius XI, Casti Connubii, n. 59.

{7:9} But if they cannot restrain themselves, they should marry. For it is better to marry, than to be burned.

.366. Virginity and celibacy are better than marriage.[414] But many persons would frequently fall into mortal sexual sins (fornication) if they remained unmarried. Therefore, Sacred Scripture states that one of the purposes of natural marital relations is to avoid sins of fornication. The husband and wife each have an obligation toward the other to engage in natural marital relations, so as to assist one another in avoiding sexual sins. But this good consequence of natural marital relations is found in the third font, not the second font; it does not determine the morality of the act itself. Therefore, no one can justify an intrinsically evil sexual act (such as masturbation or unnatural sexual acts) on the basis of a claim that it quiets concupiscence. Intrinsically evil acts are never justified by any good consequence, nor by any good intention.

Another good consequence of natural marital relations, again in the third font, is that in this way the husband and wife comfort one another after all of the difficulties of the day. Throughout most of human history, most married couples struggled merely to survive in this world. They comforted one another in body, spirit, and soul by natural marital relations open to life. Only in recent times have persons, even married couples, begun to sinfully place the search for self-indulgence first in their lives. And this exaltation of selfishness and pleasure has led many persons to claim that sexual relations within marriage is primarily for pleasure, as if the good consequences (in the third font) of the pleasure found in sexual acts would somehow justify acts that are intrinsically evil and always gravely immoral.

Still another good consequence of natural marital relations is the cultivating of mutual love, in that the husband and wife express and increase their loving affection, in heart and mind, for one another, by the physical act of natural marital relations. The husband and wife may seek this good end, as long as the act itself is unitive, procreative, and marital. For the primary purpose of natural marital relations is found in the inherent moral meaning of the act itself. All the good consequences in the third font are of lesser importance, even the expression of loving affection. However, the expression of true spiritual love by the couple in natural marital relations is found in the second font, under the unitive moral object. Certainly, the moral object of every good act includes true spiritual love of God, neighbor, and self; for the entire moral law is based on that threefold commandment. But true spiritual love is of the soul, whereas affective love (emotional love; loving affection) is of the spirit (i.e. the mind and heart). The expression of affective love is a good consequences of natural marital relations in the third font. But the expression of true spiritual love is in the moral object of the second font. Yet both are expressed by the same physical act of natural

---

[414] Council of Trent, Decree on the Sacrament of Matrimony, Canon X. "If any one says, that the marriage state is to be placed above the state of virginity, or of celibacy, and that it is not better and more blessed to remain in virginity, or in celibacy, than to be united in matrimony; let him be anathema."

marital relations, which is of the body. Thus, body, spirit, and soul together cooperate in the act of natural marital relations open to life.

Now there is nothing to prevent many other good consequences from resulting, in the third font, from an act of natural marital relations open to life. But perhaps the most commonly-sought good consequence is pleasure. Though the pleasure of sexual relations is a physical pleasure, in a good marriage the enjoyment of natural marital relations will be not merely physical (of the body), but also of the heart and mind. So this secondary end is best referred to as enjoyment. The husband and wife enjoy companionship, emotion, intimacy, as well as physical pleasure. And the physical pleasure is not limited to sexual climax, but is the full range of feelings and sensations that accompany moral acts of natural marital relations open to life. The married couple may seek this secondary end of enjoyment, as long as it is subordinate to the primary end of the threefold meaning ordained by God, which is unitive, procreative, and marital.

The couple that seeks mere physical pleasure, as if this were the greatest purpose of sexuality, has been deluded by the false teachings of sinful secular society. And anyone who claims that the primary purpose of marital relations is pleasure has gone astray from the clear and definitive teachings of the Church on sexuality. But worse still is the claim that this secondary end of pleasure somehow justifies all manner of sexual acts, without regard to the intrinsic nature of the act itself. Such a claim abandons the most basic principles of morality in Catholic teaching, not only on sexuality, but on ethics in general. For the end never justifies the means. And the human person was not created to seek and find physical pleasure. The pleasure that God intends for natural marital relations is not the primary purpose of sexuality, and is not in the threefold moral object, and so it does not determine the inherent moral meaning of any sexual act. This pleasure is only a secondary end in the third font. Therefore, pleasure in marital relations should never be exalted as if it were the primary purpose, nor as if this secondary purpose justified any and all acts.

When a good act, such as natural marital relations open to life, is done with good intention, many good consequences naturally result. But these good consequences must be subordinated to the primary purpose of marital relations, found in its single threefold moral object, which is unitive, procreative, marital. But if any married couple engage in natural marital relations solely or mainly for the purpose of pleasure, they sin by placing their own pleasure above the will and plan of God for marriage. Worse still is the sin of those married persons who commit intrinsically evil unnatural sexual acts, which are always gravely immoral under the second font of morality, on the excuse of seeking good consequences, such as pleasure or the quieting of concupiscence. They fail to preserve the intrinsic nature of the act, as Pope Pius XI taught they must, and they refuse to subordinate secondary ends, such as pleasure, to the primary end of the use of the sexual faculty. And that primary end must always be unitive and procreative and marital.

.367. Non-unitive, Non-procreative, Non-marital Acts

The three meanings of this one moral object are interrelated. Whenever any one meaning is absent, the other meanings are harmed, because all three meanings are closely connected, and because together they constitute one threefold moral object.

Each and every non-unitive sexual act is intrinsically evil and always gravely immoral. A sexual act is only moral when it is inherently unitive, because this particular physical sexual act, by its very nature, is ordered toward the expression and the strengthening of the union of the spouses in love. This unitive meaning is no mere physical union, but neither is it separate from the particular physical union of natural intercourse. The concrete physical act of natural intercourse is inherently ordered toward the union of the man and woman who engage in that particular act. Natural marital relations is good because it is the loving union of two whole persons, within the natural plan of God for men and women, and for humanity, and not merely the physical union of body parts. The unitive meaning of the act is an expression of the love that the couple have for one another and for God. The unitive meaning is the most fundamental meaning of the marital act. The unitive meaning is related to the theological virtue of love.

Each and every non-procreative sexual act is intrinsically evil and always gravely immoral. A sexual act is only moral when it is inherently procreative because the sexual act, by its very nature, is ordered toward the procreation of children. Without the procreative meaning of the sexual act, the human race would not survive. The procreation of children by means of the marital act also expresses and strengthens the faithfulness of the couple. The procreative meaning of the act is an expression of the faith the couple have in one another and in God. The procreative meaning proceeds from the unitive meaning, in that the expression of love in this unitive marital act results in procreation and strengthens faithfulness. The procreative meaning is related to the theological virtue of faith.

Each and every non-marital sexual act is intrinsically evil and always gravely immoral. A sexual act is only moral when it is inherently marital, because the sexual act, by its very nature, is ordered toward the continued union of the man and woman in marriage. From the love and faithfulness of the spouses proceeds hope for the future of the marriage relationship, and of the family, and of the human race. Marriage is not only a current state, but also a continuation of that state: "from this day forward, for better, for worse, for richer, for poorer, in sickness and in health, until death do us part." Thus the marital meaning not only requires that the man and woman be married, but also that the marriage continue. Marriage is not merely a current relationship between a man and a woman, but also a continuing commitment to that relationship. The marriage relationship is the foundation of the family and of society, and is necessary for the continuation and welfare of the entire human race.

The marital meaning proceeds primarily from the unitive meaning, and secondarily from the procreative meaning. The union of the spouses, first in vows and next in consummation, is the beginning of the marriage. The husband and wife express their love and faithfulness to one another in marriage by the marital act. Procreation follows after this union of consummation. Both this loving union of natural marital relations and the procreation of children result in a continued expression and strengthening of the marriage relationship. Thus, union and procreation naturally result in the continuation of the marriage, and in hope for the future of each family and of the whole human family. The marital meaning is related to the theological virtue of hope.

The procreative and marital meanings contribute to the unitive meaning. The ordering of the act toward procreation and toward the good of marriage give the unitive meaning its fullest sense. When a man and woman unite in natural intercourse, with love for one another, but outside of marriage and with contraception, the unitive meaning is harmed because this union is non-marital and non-procreative. The plan of God for humanity is such that sexual union should strengthen the marriage and contribute to the procreation of the human race. The absence of any one or more meanings has the effect of harming the other meanings that are present. Only with the procreative and marital meanings does the unitive meaning have the fullness intended by God for sexual acts.

The unitive and marital meanings contribute to the procreative meaning. God intends not only that men and women procreate children, but that the children be conceived, born, and raised within the marriage of one man and one woman. God intends that procreation occur as a result of that natural act which is unitive, and which is inherent to human nature as created by God. Only with the unitive and marital meanings does the procreative meaning have the fullness intended by God for sexual acts.

The unitive and procreative meanings contribute to the marital meaning. The marital act expresses and strengthens the union of the couple in love. And from this expression of love proceeds one of the greatest goods of marriage, the procreation of children. Only with the unitive and procreative meanings does the marital meaning have the fullness intended by God for sexual acts.

The direct and voluntary deprivation of the unitive meaning from any sexual act necessarily causes that act to be intrinsically evil and always gravely immoral. The direct and voluntary deprivation of the procreative meaning from any sexual act necessarily causes that act to be intrinsically evil and always gravely immoral. The direct and voluntary deprivation of the marital meaning from any sexual act necessarily causes that act to be intrinsically evil and always gravely immoral.

.368. Artificial Procreation

The procreation intended by God is not merely any act that can conceive a child. Unfortunately, science has provided the human race with the possibility of the procreation of new human life apart from the unitive act of natural relations. The gravely sinful acts of artificial insemination, in vitro fertilization, in vivo fertilization, and human cloning, and any other types of artificial procreation, separate procreation from natural intercourse. Such acts are intrinsically evil and always gravely immoral because they are deprived of the unitive meaning. Artificial procreation, by definition, takes place apart from the natural unitive sexual act.

But such acts of artificial procreation are not only non-unitive, they are also not truly and fully procreative. For procreation is not merely of the physical order, but also of the moral order. Only the procreation of new human life as intended by God, in the natural manner and within marriage, only this sexual act with its threefold moral object, truly fulfills the procreative meaning in accord with human nature and the will of God. Artificial procreation not only lacks the unitive meaning, it contradicts the manner of procreation intended by God for the human race. Even when both husband and wife contribute gametes to this type of procreation, artificial procreation harms the marriage because the new life that is created is not the result of the unitive procreative marital act. In this way, science intervenes and disrupts the marriage relationship, conceiving a child, not by the natural human act of husband and wife, but by an artificial act of science and technology.

Worse still is any method of procreation that makes use of gametes from persons other than husband and wife. Such an approach further harms and disrupts the marriage by the intervention of another man or woman as the father or mother of the procreated child. This sin is analogous to adultery, where another person enters into the intimacy of the marriage relationship. Even worse is any method, such as human cloning, that does not make use of the gametes from one man and one woman. Any and all such methods of procreation fundamentally contradict the plan of God for procreation, for the union of husband and wife in marriage, and for the propagation of the human race in accord with natural law.

.369. Contraception

The direct and voluntary deprivation of the procreative meaning from any sexual act necessarily causes that act to be intrinsically evil and always gravely immoral.

Second Vatican Council: "Relying on these principles, sons of the Church may not undertake methods of birth control which are found blameworthy by the teaching authority of the Church in its unfolding of the divine law."[415]

Pope Pius XI: "But no reason, however grave, may be put forward by which anything intrinsically against nature may become conformable to nature and morally good. Since, therefore, the conjugal act is destined primarily by nature for the begetting of children, those who, in exercising it, deliberately frustrate its natural power and purpose, sin against nature and commit a deed which is shameful and intrinsically vicious.

"Small wonder, therefore, if Holy Writ bears witness that the Divine Majesty regards with greatest detestation this horrible crime and at times has punished it with death. As St. Augustine notes, 'Intercourse even with one's legitimate wife is unlawful and wicked where the conception of the offspring is prevented. Onan, the son of Judah, did this and the Lord killed him for it.' [St. Augustine, De Adulterinis Coniugiis, Book II, n. 12; Genesis 38:8-10]

---

[415] Second Vatican Council, Gaudium et Spes, n. 51.

"Since, therefore, openly departing from the uninterrupted Christian tradition, some recently have judged it possible solemnly to declare another doctrine regarding this question, the Catholic Church, to whom God has entrusted the defense of the integrity and purity of morals, standing erect in the midst of the moral ruin which surrounds her, in order that she may preserve the chastity of the nuptial union from being defiled by this foul stain, raises her voice in token of her divine ambassadorship and through Our mouth proclaims anew: any use whatsoever of matrimony exercised in such a way that the act is deliberately frustrated in its natural power to generate life is an offense against the law of God and of nature, and those who indulge in such are branded with the guilt of a grave sin."[416]

Pope Paul VI: "Neither is it valid to argue, as a justification for sexual intercourse which is deliberately contraceptive, that a lesser evil is to be preferred to a greater one, or that such intercourse would merge with procreative acts of past and future to form a single entity, and so be qualified by exactly the same moral goodness as these. Though it is true that sometimes it is lawful to tolerate a lesser moral evil in order to avoid a greater evil or in order to promote a greater good, it is never lawful, even for the gravest reasons, to do evil that good may come of it (cf. Romans 3:8) -- in other words, to intend directly something which of its very nature contradicts the moral order, and which must therefore be judged unworthy of man, even though the intention is to protect or promote the welfare of an individual, of a family, or of society in general. Consequently, it is a serious error to think that a whole married life of otherwise normal relations can justify sexual intercourse which is deliberately contraceptive and so intrinsically wrong."[417]

Pope John Paul II: "Paul VI affirmed that the teaching of the Church 'is founded upon the inseparable connection, willed by God and unable to be broken by man on his own initiative, between the two meanings of the conjugal act: the unitive meaning and the procreative meaning.' And he concluded by re-emphasizing that there must be excluded as intrinsically immoral 'every action which, either in anticipation of the conjugal act, or in its accomplishment, or in the development of its natural consequences, proposes, whether as an end or as a means, to render procreation impossible.' "[418]

Pope John Paul II: "When couples, by means of recourse to contraception, separate these two meanings that God the Creator has inscribed in the being of man and woman and in the dynamism of their sexual communion, they act as arbiters of the divine plan and they manipulate and degrade human sexuality -- and with it themselves and their married partner -- by altering its value of total self-giving. Thus the innate language that expresses the total reciprocal self-giving of husband and wife is overlaid, through contraception, by an objectively contradictory language, namely, that of not giving oneself totally to the other.

---

[416] Pope Pius XI, Casti Connubii, n. 54-56.
[417] Pope Paul VI, Humanae Vitae, n. 14.
[418] Pope John Paul II, Familiaris Consortio, 32; inner quote is from Humanae Vitae, n. 12, 14.

This leads not only to a positive refusal to be open to life but also to a falsification of the inner truth of conjugal love, which is called upon to give itself in personal totality."[419]

Notice that the above teaching of the Magisterium is clear and unequivocal. Each and every contracepted sexual act is intrinsically evil and always gravely immoral, because the act is deliberately deprived of the procreative meaning. No matter how good the intention, and no matter how dire the circumstances, every non-procreative sexual act is an objective mortal sin. This prohibition against non-procreative acts includes the contracepted natural sexual act as well as every type of unnatural sexual act, since these acts too are inherently incapable of procreation.

.370. Natural Family Planning (NFP)

Natural family planning refers to any method of determining natural increases or decreases in fertility, in order to decide whether or not to engage in sexual relations. NFP can be used to determine when a woman is most fertile, so that the couple may have sexual relations at that time and increase the chances of conception. NFP can be used to determine when a woman is less fertile, so that the couple can limit sexual relations to that time and decrease the chances of conception. Natural Family Planning is sometimes used strictly, in order to attempt to avoid all conception. Natural Family Planning is sometimes used more loosely, in order to space out the births of the children.

The morality of NFP is based on the teaching that a husband and wife may cease from marital relations, for a determinate period of time, for a variety of different reasons. This principle was taught infallibly by an Ecumenical Council.

The Council of Trent: "If anyone says, that the Church errs, in that she declares that, for many causes, a separation may take place between husband and wife, in regard of bed, or in regard of cohabitation, for a determinate or for an indeterminate period; let him be anathema."[420]

This teaching of Trent includes periodic abstinence (separation...in regard of bed... for a determinate...period) as well as other types of separation. Therefore, the rejection of natural family planning on the basis of a claim that the husband and wife may not periodically abstain from marital relations for a determinate period of time is a heresy against the Catholic Faith. Similarly, the claim that natural family planning may only be used morally for one reason, or for few reasons, or in rare circumstances, contradicts the teaching that there are "many causes" for such a separation in regard of bed. (The other types of separation possible under this Canon of Trent would include a spouse separating in regard of cohabitation because of infidelity, or abuse, or some other grave reason. The spouses may also abstain from marital relations for a period of time, if both spouses consent to abstinence for the sake of prayer and holiness. They may also abstain for a period of time, or even indefinitely, if a spouse is seriously ill.)

---

[419] Pope John Paul II, Familiaris Consortio, 32.
[420] Council of Trent, 24th Session, On the Sacrament of Matrimony, Canon VIII.

When a husband and wife have natural marital relations while using NFP, the sexual act is unitive, procreative, and marital. None of the methods of NFP are contraceptive; there is no barrier, chemical, or other interference with conception. NFP permits each and every marital act to be both unitive and procreative, as required by the natural law. Natural family planning makes use of natural increases and decreases in fertility to permit the husband and wife to have some influence, but not complete control, over the likelihood of conception. Natural family planning is not intrinsically evil.

Pope Paul VI: "God has wisely ordered laws of nature and the incidence of fertility in such a way that successive births are already naturally spaced through the inherent operation of these laws."[421]

Pope John Paul II: "When, instead, by means of recourse to periods of infertility, the couple respect the inseparable connection between the unitive and procreative meanings of human sexuality, they are acting as ministers of God's plan and they benefit from their sexuality according to the original dynamism of total self-giving, without manipulation or alteration."

"The choice of the natural rhythms involves accepting the cycle of the person, that is the woman, and thereby accepting dialogue, reciprocal respect, shared responsibility and self-control. To accept the cycle and to enter into dialogue means to recognize both the spiritual and corporal character of conjugal communion and to live personal love with its requirement of fidelity. In this context the couple comes to experience how conjugal communion is enriched with those values of tenderness and affection which constitute the inner soul of human sexuality, in its physical dimension also. In this way sexuality is respected and promoted in its truly and fully human dimension, and is never used as an object that, by breaking the personal unity of soul and body, strikes at God's creation itself at the level of the deepest interaction of nature and person."[422]

Pope Paul VI: "If therefore there are well-grounded reasons for spacing births, arising from the physical or psychological condition of husband or wife, or from external circumstances, the Church teaches that married people may then take advantage of the natural cycles immanent in the reproductive system and engage in marital intercourse only during those times that are infertile, thus controlling birth in a way which does not in the least offend the moral principles which We have just explained.

"Neither the Church nor her doctrine is inconsistent when she considers it lawful for married people to take advantage of the infertile period but condemns as always unlawful the use of means which directly prevent conception, even when the reasons given for the latter practice may appear to be upright and serious. In reality, these two cases are completely different. In the former the married couple rightly use a faculty provided them by nature. In the latter they obstruct the

---

[421] Pope Paul VI, Humanae Vitae, n. 11.
[422] Pope John Paul II, Familiaris Consortio, 32.

natural development of the generative process. It cannot be denied that in each case the married couple, for acceptable reasons, are both perfectly clear in their intention to avoid children and wish to make sure that none will result. But it is equally true that it is exclusively in the former case that husband and wife are ready to abstain from intercourse during the fertile period as often as for reasonable motives the birth of another child is not desirable. And when the infertile period recurs, they use their married intimacy to express their mutual love and safeguard their fidelity toward one another. In doing this they certainly give proof of a true and authentic love."[423]

Pope Paul VI: "The teaching of the Church regarding the proper regulation of birth is a promulgation of the law of God Himself."[424]

The Magisterium has clearly and definitively taught that married couples may use natural family planning either "for spacing births" or even when the couple has an "intention to avoid children and wish to make sure that none will result." However, the couple may use NFP to decrease the likelihood of conception only for "well-grounded reasons" or "reasonable motives."[425]

When a husband and wife have natural marital relations open to life, whether during the time when she is most fertile or during the time when she is least fertile, the act itself is inherently unitive, procreative, and marital. And so the use of NFP does not cause a deprivation in the moral object of natural marital relations open to life. Natural family planning is not intrinsically evil. Natural marital relations open to life is not intrinsically evil. Refraining from sexual relations is not intrinsically evil. Therefore, when a husband and wife use NFP, either refraining from, or engaging in, natural marital relations open to life, the second font of morality is good.

.371. However, all three fonts must be good for an act to be moral. The use of NFP is only moral when all three fonts are good. The husband and wife must not intend to use NFP with a contraceptive mentality, or with selfishness, or with disregard for the will of God concerning procreation. If a husband and wife use NFP in order to avoid all conception for selfish reasons, then they sin seriously against God. For the procreation of children is one of the highest goods of marriage. The use of NFP is not inherently immoral, but the intention for its use might be good or evil.

Similarly, a husband and wife must not use NFP to avoid conception if the bad consequences outweigh the good consequences. If using NFP strictly for many years will result in few, if any, children in the marriage, then this deprivation of children from the family is a bad consequence. On the other hand, if the husband and wife procreate more children than they are able to care for, resulting in harm to the children and the family, then this is also a bad consequence in the third font. As always, the good and bad consequences must be weighed, and whenever the bad consequences outweigh the good, the act is immoral. The

---

[423] Pope Paul VI, Humanae Vitae, n. 16.
[424] Pope Paul VI, Humanae Vitae, n. 20.
[425] Pope Paul VI, Humanae Vitae, n. 16.

husband and wife must sincerely consider whether it is better to have more children, or fewer children, in the eyes of God. And a mere calculation as to the selfish benefits and detriments does not result in a moral choice.

Marriage is ordained by God for the procreation of children, for the good of the family, the Church, and the human race. The procreation of children by a husband and wife is not optional; the couple cannot choose to be childless, unless they have a grave reason. If they are able to do so, a husband and wife fulfill a grave moral obligation when they procreate children for God, for their family, and for humanity.

The number of children that a family should have depends on the circumstances, which varies from one couple to another. A couple need only have a just reason (a reason of moderate moral weight) in order to limit their family to a few children. But a couple would need a grave reason to attempt to have no children at all. Similarly, a couple should have a just reason if they decide to have very many children in their family. They should not procreate children irresponsibly, without considering the will of God and the good of the whole family.

Pontifical Council For The Family: "However, profoundly different from any contraceptive practice is the behavior of married couples, who, always remaining fundamentally open to the gift of life, live their intimacy only in the unfruitful periods, when they are led to this course by serious motives of responsible parenthood. This is true both from the anthropological and moral points of view, because it is rooted in a different conception of the person and of sexuality. The witness of couples who for years have lived in harmony with the plan of the Creator, and who, for proportionately serious reasons, licitly use the methods rightly called 'natural,' confirms that it is possible for spouses to live the demands of chastity and of married life with common accord and full self-giving."[426]

The Holy See teaches that "serious motives," that is "proportionately serious reasons," are needed in order to use NFP to avoid, or to decrease the likelihood of, conception. The degree of moral weight for the reason depends on the degree of moral weight of the act being considered. Children are the primary good of marriage. A grave reason is needed to use NFP to attempt to have no children at all. A less grave but still serious reason is needed to choose to have only one child. Similarly, for a large or very large number of children, a proportionately serious reason is needed, because the family has limited resources for raising the children. But even when choosing to have an ordinary number of children, a couple must make this moral decision based on faith and reason, not on their own selfish desires, and not arbitrarily or irresponsibly. The use of NFP, whether to conceive or to avoid conception, must always have at least "well-grounded reasons" or "reasonable motives."

For the husband and wife do not create children, but rather they procreate children. The married couple participates with God in the creation of new

---

[426] Pontifical Council for the Family, Vademecum ['Go with me'] for Confessors concerning some Aspects of the Morality of Conjugal Life, n. 2-6.

human life. The body of the human person is created by natural reproduction. But God creates the soul of each and every human person directly. The husband and wife should understand that they are not acting on their own in creating new life. For they are participants with God, in the plan of God, to the benefit of the Church and the human race, when children are procreated by the husband and wife, and by God. Therefore, the husband and wife must always have at least a just reason for using NFP, whether to avoid or to seek conception.

Pope Pius XI: Thus amongst the blessings of marriage, the child holds the first place. And indeed the Creator of the human race Himself, Who in His goodness wishes to use men as His helpers in the propagation of life, taught this when, instituting marriage in Paradise, He said to our first parents, and through them to all future spouses: "Increase and multiply, and fill the earth." (Gen 1:28). As St. Augustine admirably deduces from the words of the holy Apostle Saint Paul to Timothy (1 Tim 5:14) when he says: "The Apostle himself is therefore a witness that marriage is for the sake of generation: 'I wish,' he says, 'young girls to marry.' And, as if someone said to him, 'Why?,' he immediately adds: 'To bear children, to be mothers of families'."[427]

[1 Timothy]
{5:14} Therefore, I want the younger women to marry, to procreate children, to be mothers of families, to provide no ready opportunity for the adversary to speak evil.

Pope John Paul II: "According to the plan of God, marriage is the foundation of the wider community of the family, since the very institution of marriage and conjugal love are ordained to the procreation and education of children, in whom they find their crowning."[428]

.372. As the first and highest blessing of marriage, the procreation and education of children cannot be cast aside for no reason, nor for a light reason, nor even for a reason with only moderate weight. The obligation of a husband and wife to procreate children is a grave obligation within the plan of God for the family, for the Church, and for humanity. Only a grave reason can entirely exempt a husband and wife, who are able to do so, from the grave obligation to bear children for God. Therefore, a husband and wife are not free to use NFP to attempt to avoid all conception, so that their marriage bears no children at all, except for a grave reason.

A husband and wife may use NFP to space out the births of their children, and to limit the size of their family in accord with reason and the particular circumstances of their lives (such as limited resources). They need only have a just reason ("well-grounded reasons," "reasonable motives") to use NFP in this way. For they are not using NFP to avoid all conception for the entire length of their marriage; they are not using NFP so that their marriage will never procreate children. The use of natural family planning to keep the total number of children within reasonable limits, given the particular circumstances, requires

---

[427] Pope Pius XI, Casti Connubii, n. 11.
[428] Pope John Paul II, Familiaris Consortio, n. 14.

only a reason of moderate moral weight. Similarly, the use of NFP to allow for some length of time between one birth and another require only a just reason (i.e. a moderate reason), not a grave reason.

A husband and wife who are older, and who already have procreated children for God, may elect, for well-grounded reasons, to use NFP with the intention of avoiding the conception of more children. Although they intend to avoid all further procreation of children, they do not need a grave reason, since they have already met their grave obligation before God to procreate children. But as always, the husband and wife must be open to life, not only in the sexual act itself, but also in their hearts and minds, so as to accept any new life that God might choose to give to them, regardless of whether or not they had planned for additional children.

NFP is not used with moral intention, regardless of the circumstances, if it is used with the intention to exclude God from the decision to procreate children. There are three fonts of morality; all three fonts, including intention, must be good for the overall act to be moral. If any husband or wife uses NFP with the intention of gaining complete control over procreation, such that the will of God is deliberately thwarted, or is ignored, or is paid only lip service, such a person sins grievously by using NFP with a contraceptive intent. Although NFP is not a type of contraception under the second font, any type of contraceptive intent is a sin under the first font. Pope John Paul II has repeatedly spoken against the "contraceptive mentality" that is so prevalent in the world today.[429] This mentality sometimes influences Catholics, so that they use NFP as if it were a form of contraception, as if it were a way to gain selfish control over procreation apart from God.

But even if a married couple uses NFP with good intention, in order to conceive many children, they nevertheless sin if they act with disregard for the will of God and the good of the family within the particular circumstances of their lives. There are three fonts of morality; all three fonts, including the circumstances, must be good for the overall act to be moral. It is not sufficient that NFP is good under the second font; intention and circumstances must also be good. The procreation of children is the greatest good of marriage, yet this does not justify a selfish intention, nor a disregard for the moral weight of the consequences of one's actions. In some circumstances, a couple may be morally obligated to space the births of their children, or to limit the overall size of their family, or both. Each particular family, and the human family worldwide, has limited resources to be shared by all its members.

Examples: (1) A married couple are in difficult financial circumstances, either unemployed or under-employed, such that they cannot provide adequately for the basic needs of any new child. If they are able to use NFP, but refuse to do so,

---

[429] Pope John Paul II, Evangelium Vitae, n. 13; Familiaris Consortio, n. 6; Address to the Bishops of Thailand, August 1996. See also Pope Benedict XVI, Address to the Bishops of South Africa, June 2005.

and they continue to procreate more children, they sin under the third font of morality, since the bad consequences outweigh the good.

(2) A married and childless couple uses NFP strictly, with the intention of avoiding all procreation, without a grave reason. They sin under both the first and third fonts: under the first font, because their intention is contraceptive in that they attempt to gain selfish control over procreation; and under the third font, because the bad consequence of a childless marriage is not outweighed by any good consequence. Bearing children for God is the highest good of marriage.

(3) A married couple wishes to avoid all conception because, due to medical problems, a pregnancy would endanger the life of the mother. For this grave reason, they may morally use NFP very strictly, so as to attempt to avoid all conception. Alternatively, they may refrain from all marital relations, if they are mutually willing and are able to do so without falling into serious sin.

(4) A married couple are in their early 40's, and have already procreated several children. They prayerfully decide that it would be best to dedicate their time, efforts, and resources to raising their existing children. They use NFP strictly, attempting to avoid all conception. But they are willing to accept a new child from the Providence of God. They have good intention (first font), and they judge that the good consequences of limiting the size of their family outweighs any bad consequences (third font). The use of NFP, even strictly, is good under the second font. And so they are not sinning by using NFP in this way.

.373. The Sexual Faculty

A sexual act is any deliberate use of the sexual faculty.

Sacred Congregation for the Doctrine of the Faith: "the deliberate use of the sexual faculty outside normal conjugal relations essentially contradicts the finality of the faculty. For it lacks the sexual relationship called for by the moral order, namely the relationship which realizes 'the full sense of mutual self-giving and human procreation in the context of true love.' "[430]

Sacred Congregation for the Doctrine of the Faith: "every genital act must be within the framework of marriage."[431]

The first quote above not only condemns any non-marital use of the sexual faculty, but also any use that is non-unitive ("the full sense of mutual self-giving") or non-procreative ("human procreation"). The second quote above, from the same document, uses a different wording, which has the effect of clarifying that the use of the sexual faculty refers to genital acts. Therefore, acts which are only peripherally-related to sexual acts, such as flirting, kissing, hugging, would not be sexual acts per se. These peripheral acts are not a use of the genital sexual faculty.

---

[430] Cardinal Seper, CDF, Persona Humana, n. IX; inner quote is from Second Vatican Council, Gaudium et Spes, n. 51.
[431] Cardinal Seper, CDF, Persona Humana, n. VII.

.374. Moral Use of the Sexual Faculty

Sacred Congregation for the Doctrine of the Faith: "Marriage is instituted by the Creator as a form of life in which a communion of persons is realized involving the use of the sexual faculty. 'That is why a man leaves his father and mother and clings to his wife and they become one flesh' (Gen 2:24)."[432]

Sacred Congregation for the Doctrine of the Faith: "It is only in the marital relationship that the use of the sexual faculty can be morally good."[433]

Pope Paul VI: "The Church, nevertheless, in urging men to the observance of the precepts of the natural law, which it interprets by its constant doctrine, teaches that each and every marital act must of necessity retain its intrinsic relationship to the procreation of human life. This particular doctrine, often expounded by the magisterium of the Church, is based on the inseparable connection, established by God, which man on his own initiative may not break, between the unitive significance and the procreative significance which are both inherent to the marriage act."[434]

The first two quotes above specifically condemn sexual acts outside of marriage, using the term 'sexual faculty' to refer to sexual acts per se. The third quote above addresses not only the marital meaning of the sexual faculty, but also the unitive and procreative meanings. For all sexual acts must be unitive and procreative and marital. This truth is taught by the Magisterium of the Church, not only from Sacred Tradition and Sacred Scripture, but from the natural law, as Pope Paul VI points out in the quote above. Therefore, the only moral use of the sexual faculty is in that type of sexual act with a threefold moral object which is unitive, procreative, and marital. All other uses of the sexual faculty are contrary to the eternal moral law, contrary to natural law, and contrary to the teaching of the Church.

.375. Natural Intercourse

Natural intercourse refers to that type of sexual act which is genital-to-genital, between one man and one woman, and which is inherently capable of procreation. Natural intercourse includes both the unitive and procreative meanings of the sexual act. Even if the man or the woman is infertile, due to old age, or injury, or illness, the act of natural intercourse retains the procreative meaning as long as it is the type of act that is inherently directed at procreation. For the act itself is moral or immoral based on the inherent ordering of the act toward its moral object, regardless of whether or not that moral object is attained. An act of attempted murder is intrinsically evil and always immoral, even though the attempt fails, because the chosen act is inherently ordered toward the killing of an innocent human being. An act of natural marital relations open to

---

[432] Cardinal Ratzinger, CDF, Considerations Regarding Proposals To Give Legal Recognition To Unions Between Homosexual Persons, n. 3.
[433] Cardinal Ratzinger, CDF, Letter To The Bishops Of The Catholic Church On The Pastoral Care Of Homosexual Persons, n. 7.
[434] Pope Paul VI, Humanae Vitae, n. 11-12.

life is inherently moral, even if the couple is infertile, because the act itself is inherently ordered toward procreation, even if such procreation happens not to occur.

Natural intercourse within marriage is called natural marital relations. The term 'natural marital relations' implies that no contraception is used, for the use of contraception is contrary to the natural procreative meaning of sexual relations. However, to emphasize the necessity of the procreative meaning in all moral sexual acts, sometimes the explanatory term 'natural marital relations open to life' is used. Both terms have essentially the same meaning. Natural marital relations open to life is the only moral sexual act. Natural sexual intercourse is the type of sexual act which has served to propagate the human race since after its inception, and which has served as an essential part of the Sacrament of Marriage since its inception.

This type of sexual act alone is properly called natural, as understood from natural law, i.e. from the expression of the eternal moral law inherent to human nature and to the proper order among human persons, as intended by God, the Creator. For, in terms of morality and natural law, the term 'natural' refers solely to nature as created and intended by God, and not to what might seem natural to the fallen sinner, or to any of the sciences (whether the physical sciences or the social sciences). The natural sexual act within marriage is unitive, procreative, and marital, as those terms are properly understood within the moral order. All other sexual acts are contrary to the eternal moral law, as it is expressed in natural law and in the teaching of the Church.

.376. Unnatural Sexual Acts

Any sexual act other than natural intercourse is an unnatural sexual act. Although some persons might claim that various non-procreative, non-unitive sexual acts are somehow natural, nothing contrary to the eternal moral law is truly natural. For the natural law is a direct expression of the eternal moral law, within creation, as intended by God. And God never intends anything contrary to the eternal moral law, which is the Justice inherent to His very Nature. The absence of the procreative meaning in a sexual act always necessarily makes that knowingly chosen act an intrinsically evil objective mortal sin.

Only natural marital relations open to life is fully unitive and fully procreative. Sexual acts other than natural (genital-to-genital) intercourse are not procreative, and also not truly unitive. For the unitive meaning is not merely of the physical order, but also of the moral order. The union of the natural marital act is that union ordained by God for the expression and strengthening of the love of husband and wife, and also for procreation. Unnatural sexual acts are both non-procreative and non-unitive. The only truly unitive sexual act is that act of natural intercourse established by God as integral to human nature and to the propagation of the human race. The absence of the unitive meaning in a sexual act always necessarily makes that knowingly chosen act an intrinsically evil objective mortal sin.

An unnatural sexual act is any sexual act, i.e. any use of the genital sexual faculty, which is not in and of itself capable of procreation. An unnatural sexual act accompanied by a natural sexual act is two distinct acts; the unnatural sexual act is not inherently capable of procreation and is not justified by being accompanied by another act, one that is capable of procreation.

Unnatural sexual acts include masturbation, manipulative sexual acts, anal sexual acts, oral sexual acts, and sexual acts using devices. Even though some unnatural sexual acts may have a certain mere physical union, such acts are not the type of union ordained by God for the use of the sexual faculty by men and women. Therefore, all unnatural sexual acts are both non-procreative and non-unitive.

If a man and a woman have natural intercourse, the type of act inherently capable of procreation, but they use contraception, the act itself is unitive, but not procreative. In some sense, even contracepted natural intercourse is unnatural, since the natural tendency of the act toward procreation is contravened. However, in order to maintain a clear distinction between different types of sexual acts, the term unnatural sexual act refers to any sexual act which is not that genital-to-genital sexual act between one man and one woman which, as a type of act, is inherently capable of procreation. And the term natural intercourse (or natural sexual act, or natural relations) refers to that genital-to-genital sexual act between one man and one woman which is the type of act inherently capable of procreation. Contracepted natural intercourse is intrinsically evil and always gravely immoral, because the procreative meaning is absent, but the act may still called natural intercourse because it is that same type of act, despite the contraception. Unnatural sexual acts are not the natural type of act, and so they necessarily lack both the unitive and procreative meanings; as a result, unnatural sexual acts are intrinsically evil and always gravely immoral.

An act of masturbation is the solitary use of the sexual faculty; it is the direct and voluntary use of the sexual faculty without the unitive, procreative, and marital meanings. Masturbation is intrinsically evil and always gravely immoral. Whenever the term 'direct' is used to describe an intrinsically evil act, the meaning is moral directness, not necessarily physical directness. Thus, even if a person is able to use the sexual faculty in a seemingly indirect manner, any such use is nevertheless morally direct. Whenever the term 'voluntary' is used to describe an intrinsically evil act, the meaning is the deliberate choice of the act itself (the concrete act), regardless of intention or circumstances.

A manipulative sexual act is similar to masturbation, except that one person performs the act on another; it is the direct and voluntary use of the sexual faculty without the unitive and procreative meanings. The term masturbation is sometimes used to describe this act. Such acts are performed with the hand, or with another body part, or with an object or device. Even if such an act occurs between husband and wife, the act is deprived of the marital meaning in its moral object because this type of act, within the moral order, is not inherently directed at the expression and strengthening of the marriage as ordained by God.

Intrinsically evil acts between a husband and wife are never truly marital. For all such acts are inherently contrary to the will of God for the marriage relationship.

An oral sexual act is the use of the genital sexual faculty by oral stimulation; it is the direct and voluntary use of the sexual faculty without the unitive and procreative meanings. An anal sexual act is the use of the genital sexual faculty by anal stimulation; it is the direct and voluntary use of the sexual faculty without the unitive and procreative meanings. Even if such acts occur between husband and wife, these acts are deprived of the marital meaning in the moral object because these types of acts, within the moral order, are not inherently directed at the expression and strengthening of the marriage as ordained by God.

Since sexual climax is a use of the genital sexual faculty, any deliberate stimulation to sexual climax, other than by natural marital relations, is intrinsically evil and always immoral, even if the means does not involve the genitals. If a person is able to be stimulated to sexual climax by physical stimulation of a non-genital body part, or by a non-physical stimulation (such as by word or thought), such a deliberate act constitutes a morally direct and voluntary use of the sexual faculty which is not procreative, not truly unitive, not truly marital, and therefore intrinsically evil and always gravely immoral.

A physically indirect stimulation of the genital sexual faculty can occur in a number of different ways, each of which is intrinsically evil and always gravely immoral, since the unitive and procreative meanings are absent. A person might stimulate themselves or another person to sexual climax by touching parts of the body other than the genitals; any such deliberate act is morally direct and intrinsically evil, even though there is only an indirect physical stimulation. This type of stimulation of the genital sexual faculty is physically indirect, but morally direct.

A non-physical stimulation of the genital sexual faculty can occur in a number of different ways, each of which is intrinsically evil and always gravely immoral, since the unitive and procreative meanings are absent. A person might stimulate themselves to sexual climax by means of mere thought; any such deliberate act is morally-direct and intrinsically evil, even though there is no direct or indirect physical stimulation. A person might stimulate themselves or another person to sexual climax by sight or sound, apart from any physical touching; any such deliberate act is morally direct and intrinsically evil, even though there is no direct or indirect physical stimulation. Examples would include the use of pornographic movies or photographs, or so-called phone sex (use of another persons' voice on the phone for stimulation to climax), or any similar act.

Any such act, and any combination of such acts, and any similar types of acts (which are inherently non-unitive, or non-procreative, or non-marital) are necessarily always intrinsically evil and gravely immoral. All sexual acts are an objectively grave matter, and so, in addition to being intrinsically evil, every immoral use of the genital sexual faculty is an objective mortal sin. No intention or purpose, no set of circumstances, no motive however compelling, no situation however dire, can justify an act that is intrinsically evil.

Any deliberate and morally direct use of the genital sexual faculty, whether by a physically direct means, or by a physically indirect means, or by a non-physical means, or by any means whatsoever, is intrinsically evil and always gravely immoral whenever any one or more of the three meanings are absent (unitive, procreative, marital). The only sexual act that is unitive and procreative and marital is natural marital relations open to life. The only moral type of sexual act is natural marital relations open to life. All other sexual acts are intrinsically evil and always gravely immoral.

All these various unnatural sexual acts have the same evil moral object: the direct and deliberate use of the genital sexual faculty deprived of the threefold moral object intended by God for human nature and for relationships between human persons. All unnatural sexual acts are essentially the same under the second font of morality. There may be differences between these acts in the intention or in the circumstances. But intrinsically evil acts are always immoral, regardless of the intention and circumstances. Therefore, each and every unnatural sexual act is intrinsically evil and always gravely immoral, due to the lack of the unitive and procreative meanings.

.377. Unnatural sexual acts within Marriage

Unnatural sexual acts remain immoral, even within marriage, because all three meanings (unitive, procreative, marital) must be present for a sexual act to be moral. Extra-marital sexual acts are immoral because they lack the marital meaning. Contracepted sexual acts are immoral because they lack the procreative meaning. Unnatural sexual acts are immoral because they lack both the unitive and procreative meanings. Unnatural sexual acts are also not truly marital, even if these acts occur between husband and wife, because intrinsically evil sexual acts are not a part of God's plan for the expression and strengthening of marriage. The lack of even one meaning (unitive, procreative, marital) is sufficient to make any sexual act intrinsically evil and always gravely immoral. But unnatural sexual acts, even between husband and wife, lack all three meanings required by the natural law. Therefore, unnatural sexual acts are not justified by being done by a husband and wife within marriage.

The basic principles of morality are the same for all areas of human life, for each and every knowingly chosen act. There are no exceptions from the eternal moral law for the marital bedroom. The husband and wife cannot do any acts whatsoever to one another, nor can they disregard the eternal moral law, on the excuse that these acts are within marriage. There are no situations within human life that are exempt from morality. Each and every knowingly chosen act must be good under all three fonts of morality; otherwise, the act is a sin before God, who is all-knowing and who punishes every kind of sin. His mercy is not unjust. His love is not unjust. Therefore, He does not permit a husband and wife to engage in inherently unjust acts, on the basis of a claim that such acts are loving, or merciful, or mutually-pleasing.

Unnatural sexual acts before, during, or after natural marital relations:

In all areas of life, each and every knowingly chosen act must be moral under all three fonts of morality. In all areas of life, whenever two or more acts are chosen, either one after the other or at the same time, each chosen act must be good on its own, as the three fonts of morality apply to that particular act. A good act does not justify a prior, concurrent, or subsequent bad act. If a good act occurs before or after a bad act, the good act remains good and the bad act remains bad. If a good act and a bad act occur at the same time, the good act remains good and the bad act remains bad. A immoral means is never justified by a good intended end, nor by the circumstances of the chosen act.

Intrinsically evil acts are always immoral, regardless of intention or circumstance. Whoever says or implies otherwise has abandoned the true moral teachings of the Roman Catholic Faith. Nothing whatsoever can justify an intrinsically evil act. If any act is intrinsically evil when done by itself, then it remains intrinsically evil when done before, during, or after another act, one that is good. Therefore, unnatural sexual acts remain intrinsically evil and always gravely immoral, even when such acts are done before, during, or after a good act of natural marital relations open to life.

Any use of the sexual faculty is immoral when the act lacks the unitive, or the procreative, or the marital meaning. Each and every sexual act that lacks the unitive or the procreative or the marital meaning has an evil moral object. Each and every sexual act, other than natural marital relations open to life, is intrinsically evil and always immoral. Each and every intrinsically evil act is the direct and voluntary deprivation of a particular good required by love of God, neighbor, self. The good required of each and every sexual act is the threefold good of the unitive, procreative, and marital meanings.

Therefore, if a sexual act within marriage lacks the unitive or procreative meanings, that act is intrinsically evil and always gravely immoral. Furthermore, unnatural sexual acts within marriage are not truly marital, since this type of act is contrary to the plan of God for marriage. All unnatural sexual acts are inherently contrary to the meaning of marriage as intended by God, which is inherent to human nature and to the human race, male and female, as created by God. And so no one can justify an unnatural sexual act by saying that God permits such acts between a husband and wife.

[Ephesians]
{5:5} For know and understand this: no one who is a fornicator, or lustful, or rapacious (for these are a kind of service to idols) holds an inheritance in the kingdom of Christ and of God.
{5:6} Let no one seduce you with empty words. For because of these things, the wrath of God was sent upon the sons of unbelief.
{5:7} Therefore, do not choose to become participants with them.
{5:8} For you were darkness, in times past, but now you are light, in the Lord. So then, walk as sons of the light.
{5:9} For the fruit of the light is in all goodness and justice and truth,
{5:10} affirming what is well-pleasing to God.

{5:11} And so, have no fellowship with the unfruitful works of darkness, but instead, refute them.
{5:12} For the things that are done by them in secret are shameful, even to mention.

If anyone teaches that an unnatural sexual act is not intrinsically evil, or is not always objectively gravely immoral, or is moral between a husband and wife, or is moral before, during, or after natural marital relations, or is moral for any particular intention or purpose, or is moral in any particular circumstance, then he is teaching heresy, and promoting grave immorality, and doing serious harm to souls and to marriage, and he has gone astray from the true moral teachings of Jesus Christ and His Church.

[James]
{3:1} My brothers, not many of you should choose to become teachers, knowing that you shall receive a stricter judgment.

.378. Saints and Doctors of the Church

Saint John Chrysostom: "To this end every marriage should be set up so that it may work together with us for chastity. This will be the case if we marry such brides as are able to bring great piety, chastity, and goodness to us. The beauty of the body, if it is not joined with virtue of the soul, will be able to hold the husband for twenty or thirty days, but will go no farther before it shows its wickedness and destroys all its attractiveness. As for those who radiate the beauty of the soul, the longer time goes by and tests their proper nobility, the warmer they make their husband's love and the more they strengthen their affection for him. Since this is so, and since a warm and genuine friendship holds between them, every kind of immorality is driven out. Not even any thought of wantonness ever enters the mind of the man who truly loves his own wife, but he continues always content with her. By his chastity he attracts the good will and protection of God for his whole household."[435]

A married couple must still practice chastity. The virtue of chastity is sexual purity according to one's state of life. For married persons, this does not refer merely to refraining from adultery. Every kind of sexual immorality must be driven out of the holy matrimonial bond, so that even unchaste thoughts do not enter the mind of the husband or the wife. The chastity of husband and wife should extend to their entire selves, body and soul, even reaching to the inner thoughts of the heart and mind. There are no exceptions to the positive precept of chastity. No one is exempt from the requirement of the eternal moral law to practice chastity according to one's state of life. Even when a husband and wife have marital relations, the conjugal act cannot be lustful in heart or mind, nor can it be morally disordered in the particulars of the act itself.

The idea that unnatural sexual acts can be used in the service of natural marital relations open to life is fundamentally incompatible with the holiness and

---

[435] Saint John Chrysostom, On Marriage and Family Life, St. Vladimir's Seminary Press: 1986, trans. Roth and Anderson, p. 100.

chastity required of all married couples. Unnatural sexual acts are intrinsically evil, and so they cannot be used as the servants of natural marital relations open to life. No good employer would knowingly choose to hire employees entirely lacking in what is good and necessary to the task at hand. No holy king and queen would choose advisors or assistants who were fundamentally opposed to every good upon which their kingdom depends. No married Christian couple can morally choose to use unnatural sexual acts, with or without sexual climax, even if the intention is to use these acts in the service of natural marital relations open to life. Evil cannot be used in the service of good, because good and evil are fundamentally incompatible.

Saint Jerome, Doctor and Father of the Church

Saint Jerome: "And it makes no difference how honorable may be the cause of a man's insanity. Hence Xystus in his Sentences tells us that 'He who too ardently loves his own wife is an adulterer.' It is disgraceful to love another man's wife at all, or one's own too much. A wise man ought to love his wife with judgment, not with passion. Let a man govern his voluptuous impulses, and not rush headlong into intercourse. There is nothing blacker than to love a wife as if she were an adulteress."[436]

Jerome states that "it makes no difference how honorable may be the cause of a man's insanity." In other words, the intention which motivates a man cannot justify an intrinsically evil act. Intrinsically evil acts are inherently contrary to reason and justice, and so St. Jerome refers to the choice of such acts as a type of insanity, figuratively speaking. Thus, if a sexual act is a sin, it does not matter how honorable a person's intentions are, or what his intended end (or purpose) may be, the act is inherently gravely contrary to the moral law.

Jerome plainly taught that there are sexual sins within marriage. The idea that no sexual act is immoral as long as the natural marital act occurs at some point in time is plainly rejected by St. Jerome. It is contrary to wisdom and good judgment for a man to have sexual relations with his wife in an inordinate manner. Though St. Jerome does not, like modern-day moral theologians, give explicit descriptions of various sexual acts, it is clear that he rejects the idea that the mere deposit of semen in the correct location justifies all other acts.

Saint Thomas Aquinas, Doctor of the Church

In the quote below, St. Thomas teaches that grave sexual sins within marriage are comparable to adultery, because the acts offend against the good of marriage. He does not teach that all sexual acts within marriage are moral. He does not teach that all sexual acts occurring before or after the natural act are moral.

Saint Thomas Aquinas: "And since the man who is too ardent a lover of his wife acts counter to the good of marriage if he use her indecently, although he be not

---

[436] St. Jerome, Against Jovinianus, Bk 1, n. 49.

unfaithful, he may in a sense be called an adulterer; and even more so than he that is too ardent a lover of another woman."[437]

The phrasing 'if he use her indecently' refers to unnatural sexual acts within marriage. This is clear because the good of marriage emphasized by St. Thomas is the procreation of children (Summa Theologica, II-II, Q. 154, article 2). St. Thomas could not be referring to natural marital relations when he says 'if he use her indecently' because even natural marital relations done with some disorder of desire still retains the unitive and procreative meanings. But unnatural sexual acts lack both meanings, and so they are contrary to the good of marriage. The use of unnatural sexual acts within marriage is therefore worse than adultery. St. Thomas again condemns this same type of act later in the same question.

Saint Thomas Aquinas: "Lastly comes the sin of not observing the right manner of copulation, which is more grievous if the abuse regards the 'vas' than if it affects the manner of copulation in respect of other circumstances."[438]

First, the word 'vas' is Latin for 'vessel,' referring to the use of bodily parts or orifices, other than the genitals, for sexual acts. If a husband treats his wife lustfully during natural marital relations, he sins. But he commits an even more grievous offense, which St. Thomas calls an abuse, if he sins by committing unnatural sexual acts (i.e. using a non-genital body part or orifice for sexual intercourse). Here St. Thomas explicitly, but in discrete language, condemns the sin of unnatural sexual acts within marriage.

Second, as is clear from the quotes above, St. Thomas taught that not every sexual act is justified within marriage. Otherwise, he would not have taught that a man who is too ardent a lover of his wife commits a sin that is like adultery, which is an intrinsically evil and gravely immoral sexual sin.

Third, St. Thomas does not even consider the absurd claim that acts which are intrinsically evil and gravely immoral by themselves could become good and moral when combined in some way with natural marital relations open to life. If this were the case, then St. Thomas could not have compared a man who is too ardent a lover of his wife to an adulterer. For if he took such a position, then he would have to say that a husband's ardent love would be entirely justified, as long as 'the semen is not misdirected' (as some claim). Saint Thomas does not consider any and all sexual acts to be justified merely because, at some point in time, a completed act of natural marital relations also occurs.

The popular idea, that a husband and wife can commit any kind of sexual act toward one another as long as the husband climaxes during the natural act, is false, is contrary to the teaching of the Saints, is a serious doctrinal error, and is entirely incompatible with the teaching of the Magisterium on the marital, unitive, procreative meaning of natural marital relations, and on the grave immorality of intrinsically evil sexual sins.

---

[437] Saint Thomas Aquinas, Summa Theologica, II-II, Q. 154, A. 8.
[438] Saint Thomas Aquinas, Summa Theologica, II-II, Q. 154, A. 12.

Saints Joachim and Anna

Saint Joseph and the Blessed Virgin Mary never had marital relations. So perhaps the holiest example of a marriage that includes natural marital relations is the marriage of the Virgin Mary's parents: Joachim and Anna. They were chosen by God to be the parents of our Lord's mother. They had two children: the Virgin Mary, and her sister, who is mentioned in Sacred Scripture.

[John]
{19:25} And standing beside the cross of Jesus were his mother, and his mother's sister, and Mary of Cleophas, and Mary Magdalene.

Concerning their married life, Joachim and Anna certainly engaged in natural marital relations. But does any faithful and reasonable Catholic believe that these two very holy Saints would make use of unnatural sexual acts within their holy marriage, or that they would advise any married couple to do so? Certainly not! The very idea is incompatible not only with the holiness of Saints, but with the ordinary holiness required by Christ of every married couple. All married persons are required by God to refrain from every kind of immoral act, from all sexual sins, from actual mortal sins as well as objective mortal sins. We are all called to imitate the Saints, even the least worthy among us.

.379. The Sacrament of Marriage

The Sacrament of Marriage confers grace on the husband and wife throughout their marriage, not only at the wedding ceremony, when the marriage vows are taken. The whole of married life, each and every day, continues to be a part of the Sacrament and a source of grace. And the consummation of the marriage in natural marital relations is a part of the Sacrament, not only once, but each time.

Therefore, whenever any gravely immoral sexual sin of any type occurs within holy Matrimony, there is an additional offense against the Sacrament. If a man rapes a woman, he commits a serious sin. If a man rapes his own wife, the sin is even more serious because it is also an offense against the Sacrament of Marriage. If two unmarried persons commit an unnatural sexual act, they commit a serious sin. But if a husband and wife commit an unnatural sexual act, the sin is even more serious because it is also an offense against the Sacrament of Marriage.

Worse still is the sin of anyone who encourages married persons to commit unnatural sexual acts, or who teaches them that such acts are not immoral within marriage, for such a one as this is responsible for much harm to many souls and to many marriages. This false teaching does grave harm to the Sacrament of Marriage and to the Church and to the faithful. Such a one as this has gone astray from the true love taught by Christ, and is teaching a false gospel, not the true Gospel taught by Christ and His Church.

[Galatians]
{1:6} I wonder that you have been so quickly transferred, from him who called you into the grace of Christ, over to another gospel.

{1:7} For there is no other, except that there are some persons who disturb you and who want to overturn the Gospel of Christ.

{1:8} But if anyone, even we ourselves or an Angel from Heaven, were to preach to you a gospel other than the one that we have preached to you, let him be anathema.

{1:9} Just as we have said before, so now I say again: If anyone has preached a gospel to you, other than that which you have received, let him be anathema.

The Absence of Sexual Climax

The moral use of the sexual faculty may occur even in the absence of sexual climax.

Examples: (1) A husband and wife begin to have natural marital relations open to life. They are interrupted, and as a result neither the husband or wife attains sexual climax. In this case, the use of the sexual faculty was moral because the act of natural marital relations open to life is inherently ordered toward its proper moral object (the unitive, procreative, and marital meanings), even though the act was, in some sense, incomplete.

(2) A husband and wife have natural marital relations open to life. The husband climaxes, but the wife does not. In this case, the use of the sexual faculty was moral because all three meanings were present in the act. Neither the unitive meaning, nor the procreative meaning, nor the marital meaning depend on the occurrence of sexual climax. The natural sexual act remains inherently ordered toward procreation, even if climax happens not to occur.

And it would be contrary to reason to claim that the spouses have not had sexual relations in this case. For the wife might even become pregnant, proving that sexual relations did occur. Or if by chance she does not become pregnant, it would be absurd to claim that whether or not sexual relations occurred depends on whether or not conception occurred.

(3) A husband and wife have natural marital relations open to life. The wife climaxes, but the husband does not. In this case, the use of the sexual faculty was moral because all three meanings were present in the act. Even though the lack of sexual climax in the husband makes procreation an unlikely result, the act itself was still the type of act inherently directed toward procreation. It is not the attainment of the moral object that makes an act moral or immoral, but the inherent ordering of the act toward its moral object. The morality of the second font never depends on the attainment of the moral object (in this case procreation), but on the inherent ordering of the act toward its moral object.

The immoral use of the sexual faculty may occur even in the absence of sexual climax.

Examples: (1) A man rapes a woman, and neither person reaches sexual climax. The act is not only immoral as an act of violence, it is immoral as a sexual act. It would be absurd to claim that no sexual act occurred merely because climax was absent.

(2) A young man and young woman decide to commit the sin of premarital natural intercourse. If neither the man or the woman reaches sexual climax, the chosen act still has the same inherent moral meaning, and the same moral object, i.e. use of the sexual faculty without the marital meaning. The lack of sexual climax does not affect the immorality of the chosen act.

(3) A man or woman is masturbating, and is interrupted, so that sexual climax never occurs. The person still chose an act that is inherently non-procreative, non-unitive, and non-marital. Therefore, the sexual act remains intrinsically evil and gravely immoral, despite the lack of sexual climax.

(4) A husband and wife use an unnatural sexual act as a type of so-called foreplay, in order to become aroused for a subsequent act of natural marital relations. The good end of natural marital relations does not justify the intrinsically evil means of an unnatural sexual act. Even if sexual climax does not occur during the unnatural sexual act, the act itself is still inherently non-procreative and inherently non-unitive and inherently non-marital; therefore, the act itself is intrinsically evil. A lack of sexual climax does not cause an unnatural sexual act to become moral.

Also, the mere use of a different terminology, by calling an intrinsically evil unnatural sexual act 'foreplay,' does not justify the act. It is still the same immoral act, no matter which words are used to describe it. "Woe to you who call evil good, and good evil; who substitute darkness for light, and light for darkness; who exchange bitter for sweet, and sweet for bitter!" (Isaiah 5:20).

.380. The immoral use of the sexual faculty may occur with or without sexual climax.

(1) A husband and wife engage in natural marital relations open to life. In order for one or the other spouse, or both spouses, to achieve sexual climax, or to achieve greater enjoyment of the act, they make use of one or another unnatural sexual act during the very act of natural marital relations. The act of natural marital relations open to life remains a good act. But the accompanying unnatural sexual act remains intrinsically evil and always gravely immoral. The purpose of the evil act, i.e. to facilitate a good act, does not justify the evil act. Nothing whatsoever can justify that which is inherently immoral. It is never the case under the eternal moral law that a good act could justify an evil act, regardless of whether the evil act occurs before, during, or after the good act. Even if sexual climax occurs during natural marital relations, and as a result of natural marital relations, the intrinsically evil unnatural sexual act remains intrinsically evil and always immoral. The inherent moral meaning of an unnatural sexual act is not changed by a prior, concurrent, or subsequent act of natural marital relations. The morality of a sexual act does not depend on the absence or presence of sexual climax, but on the absence or presence of the proper threefold moral object: the unitive, procreative, and marital meanings.

(2) A husband and wife have natural marital relations, and the husband reaches climax, but the wife does not. The husband then performs an unnatural sexual act on his wife to bring her to sexual climax. In this case, the chosen act is a

completed unnatural sexual act (including sexual climax). Such acts are intrinsically evil and always gravely immoral. The husband's intention to satisfy his wife does not justify the intrinsically evil sexual act, because intrinsically evil acts are always immoral, regardless of intention. The circumstance that the wife is unable to achieve sexual climax without one type of unnatural sexual act or another does not justify the intrinsically evil sexual act, because intrinsically evil acts are always immoral, regardless of circumstances. The lack of sexual climax for the wife during natural marital relations does not justify committing an intrinsically evil sexual act. The end does not justify the means. Neither good intention, nor dire circumstances, can justify an intrinsically evil act of any kind.

Sexual climax occurs as a consequence of a moral or immoral sexual act; and so climax is in the third font, not the second font. The completion of a sexual act in sexual climax does not determine the morality of the second font. Even if the consequence of sexual climax is lacking, the inherent moral meaning of the act itself, as determined by the moral object, remains the same. Regardless of whether or not sexual climax occurs, such acts remain a use of the genital sexual faculty. Therefore, even if sexual climax does not occur as a result of an unnatural sexual act, the act itself remains intrinsically evil and always gravely immoral because unnatural sexual acts are not inherently ordered to the proper threefold moral object: the unitive, procreative, and marital meanings.

.381. Which Sexual Positions Are Permitted?

Any sexual position which includes an unnatural sexual act is prohibited because all such acts are inherently gravely contrary to the moral law. However, every solely natural position is permitted. A natural position allows the marital act to be both unitive and procreative; then the moral object is good and the sexual act is not intrinsically evil, but intrinsically good. As is always the case, intention and circumstances must also be good. A number of different physical positions of the bodies of the husband and wife permit the act to be unitive and procreative (so that the husband's penis enters his wife's vagina for copulation).

.382. Marital Foreplay

Foreplay is a means to an end; it is a means to prepare for sexual relations. The end does not justify the means. Therefore, each and every act of foreplay must be morally good. No act of foreplay is justified merely by being foreplay. Moral foreplay within marriage is not devoid of morality. Each and every knowingly chosen act must be good under all three fonts of morality, as each font springs up from, and applies to, that particular act. An act of foreplay can never borrow its morality from a prior, concurrent, or subsequent act of natural marital relations (nor from any other act). Each act must stand on its own as to its morality. Natural marital relations open to life is good, but the foreplay that prepares for this good act must also be good in itself. Knowingly chosen acts are never morally indifferent. Each and every knowingly chosen act is either moral or immoral. And God hates all immorality.

Each and every knowingly chosen act is under the eternal moral law. Each act of foreplay must be good, as the three fonts of morality apply to that particular act, regardless of the fonts of other acts. Foreplay is not an exception to the moral law. There are no exceptions to the eternal moral law. If anyone says or implies that there are exceptions to the eternal moral law, let him be anathema.

Unnatural sexual acts are not morally licit, even if used as so-called foreplay, i.e. as a means to prepare for natural marital relations. Intrinsically evil sexual acts are never moral, not for any purpose, not in any circumstance, regardless of whether or not sexual climax occurs. Other intrinsically evil acts (non-sexual acts) are also not moral to use as foreplay, for the same reason. Sexual acts are not an exception to the moral law. Intrinsically evil acts are never moral, regardless of whether or not those acts are in the realm of sexuality or not.

But not every immoral act is intrinsically evil. Any act that is immoral due to the second font is intrinsically evil. But an act may have a good second font, and still be immoral under the first or third fonts. All immorality is offensive to God. If a particular act used as foreplay is not intrinsically evil, but is immoral under the first or third font, then that act of foreplay is a sin against God.

Moral acts of foreplay remain moral even if the end of natural marital relations open to life is not achieved. The same is true for any good means to a good end. If, for any reason, the good end is not achieved, the good means remains good. The end does not justify the means because the means takes its morality from the three fonts as these apply to that particular act (the chosen act of the means). A good means may stand on its own and remain moral because it does not take its morality from the end. And this is the same reason why the end does not justify the means. Each and every knowingly chosen act must be good on its own, i.e. according to the three fonts of morality as these spring up from, and apply to, each chosen act. A good means to a good end never becomes immoral when the good end is absent, because good acts remain good regardless of other acts. Under the eternal moral law, each and every knowingly chosen act stands on its own before God.

A husband and wife may engage in acts of moral foreplay (such as hugging and kissing), without subsequently engaging in natural marital relations open to life. In one case, they might intend to have marital relations, but then change their minds or be interrupted. In another case, they might wish to use moral acts of foreplay in order to express their affection for one another. Such acts are perhaps more accurately termed acts of affection, rather than acts of foreplay, when they are not being used as a means to the end of natural marital relations. But because the types of acts are generally the same, the term foreplay may also be used.

Moral acts of foreplay are not sexual acts per se because they are not genital sexual acts. Moral acts of foreplay are never sexual acts per se, because the only moral sexual act is natural marital relations open to life. And natural marital relations is not foreplay; it is not a preparation for a sexual act, because it is a sexual act. Neither is any per se sexual act properly called a type of foreplay. Moral acts of foreplay do not involve the deliberate or morally-direct use of the genital sexual faculty.

Moral acts of foreplay between a husband and wife include various acts that are moral under all three fonts of morality. A moral act of foreplay cannot be a use of the genital sexual faculty. A use of the genital sexual faculty is either a physically direct act, or a physically indirect act, or a non-physical act, that tends to stimulate the genitals to sexual climax. All such deliberate uses of the sexual faculty (physically direct, physically indirect, non-physical) are morally direct and are intrinsically evil whenever any one or more of the three meanings are lacking (unitive, procreative, marital). All such deliberate uses of the sexual faculty are immoral, even if sexual climax does not occur, because the use of the genital sexual faculty is only moral when these three meanings are present.

Sexual climax is a consequence of the use of the sexual faculty, but consequences are in the third font. And so, even when that consequence is not present, the sexual act is still moral or immoral based on the presence or absence of that threefold moral object, which is unitive, procreative, and marital. If an act is a genital sexual act, then the act must be unitive, procreative, and marital. Any use of the sexual faculty is only justified if each such act is unitive, procreative, and marital.

Immoral acts of foreplay include any and all unnatural sexual acts, regardless of whether or not sexual climax occurs. Such acts are intrinsically evil and always gravely immoral, because they are not unitive and procreative and marital. The use of an unnatural sexual act as a way to prepare for natural marital relations is not moral because the end does not justify the means. In addition to unnatural sexual acts, immoral acts of foreplay include any act that is immoral under any one or more of the three fonts of morality.

Sexual arousal by itself is not an act. Sexual arousal by itself is a consequence; consequences are in the third font. Sexual arousal by itself might be intended, as an end, or as a means to an end; intention is in the first font. The three fonts of morality always apply to every knowingly chosen act; all three fonts must be good for a knowingly chosen act to be good. However, arousal by itself is not an act, and so it cannot be intrinsically evil. The act that causes arousal might be intrinsically evil (under the second font), or the act that causes arousal might be immoral under the first or third fonts.

Illicit sexual acts are intrinsically evil because the moral object is deprived of one or more of the three meanings of sexual relations: unitive, procreative, marital. All unnatural sexual acts are intrinsically evil and always gravely immoral, regardless of whether or not sexual climax occurs, even if used as a form of foreplay in marriage.

.383. Is All Touching Prohibited?

Is every type of touching of the spouse's genitals prohibited by the moral law? No, but any type of touching that is masturbatory is prohibited. A husband may not masturbate himself, nor may he masturbate (perform manipulative sex on) his wife. A wife may not masturbate herself, nor may she masturbate her husband. All such acts are intrinsically evil and always gravely immoral, with or without sexual climax, because these acts are non-unitive and non-procreative sexual acts. Neither are such acts, even within marriage, truly marital, since they are contrary to God's plan for holy matrimony. Every sexual act must be unitive, procreative, and marital.

A masturbatory or other unnatural sexual act cannot be used, even without climax, to prepare for a subsequent act of natural marital relations, as a type of foreplay. Foreplay is a means to the end of natural marital relations. The end does not justify the means. Some acts of foreplay are moral, and other acts of foreplay are immoral. No act is justified merely because it is used as a type of foreplay. Unnatural sexual acts are contrary to the moral law because they lack the procreative meaning. (Neither are such acts truly unitive or truly marital.) The lack of sexual climax does not change the fact that the moral object is deprived of the procreative meaning. And a different act, an act of natural marital relations, cannot contribute its procreative meaning to the unnatural act because each knowingly chosen act must stand on its own as to its morality. Each and every marital act must have both the unitive and procreative meanings.

Unnatural sexual acts, with or without sexual climax, are intrinsically evil and always gravely immoral, and such acts do not become moral by being done within marriage, nor by being done before, during, or after natural marital relations. The only moral sexual act is natural marital relations open to life. Every use of the genital sexual faculty must be marital, unitive, procreative.

Caressing, stroking, or otherwise directly stimulating the genitals of one's spouse is a non-unitive and non-procreative use of the genital sexual faculty. This type of stimulation remains non-unitive and non-procreative even if climax does not occur (as a consequence in the third font) or is not intended (as the purpose in the first font). This act is morally no different than masturbation without climax, and so is intrinsically evil and gravely immoral.

Kissing, embracing, and caressing the body of one's spouse, but not the private areas, is generally not ordered toward climax. This might include touching of the hands, face, neck, back, breasts, abdomen, legs, or feet. This type of sensual touching, done to excess, might cause sexual climax in some persons. Even married persons must avoid any act that results in sexual climax outside of natural marital relations open to life. However, this type of act is not a use of the genital sexual faculty, and so, as long as climax is not likely for a particular married couple, these acts are moral. These are not per se sexual acts, and so they need not be unitive or procreative, as long as there is no danger of sexual climax.

.384. Foreplay Prior to Marriage

The absence of the marital meaning from acts of foreplay (when those acts are not a use of the genital sexual faculty) does not, by itself, make these acts immoral. Each act in every area of human life must be moral on its own. So even if the means of foreplay is not followed by the end of natural marital relations, the morality of the means stands on its own. If all three fonts of morality are good, then the chosen act is good. If an unmarried man and woman express affection for one another, with good intention, without any unnatural sexual acts, and without any deliberate or morally-direct use of the genital sexual faculty at all (since they are unmarried), and such that the good consequences outweigh the bad, then these acts of affection are moral. Whenever all three fonts are good, the act is moral, without exception.

The use of some limited sensual acts (similar to moral foreplay in marriage) by an unmarried man and woman as a way to express affection is not intrinsically evil, as long as such acts do not include any type of unnatural sexual act, nor natural sexual relations outside of marriage, nor any genital sexual act at all, even without climax. Each and every sexual act must have all three meanings in its moral object: marital, unitive, procreative. But when physical acts expressing affection are not any type of sexual act at all, then these acts do not need to be marital, unitive, and procreative. For an unmarried man and woman, all per se sexual acts are immoral, including natural intercourse, masturbation, and all unnatural sexual acts, such as oral, anal, or manipulative 'stimulation', with or without climax. However, other acts, those that are not per se sexual acts (not a use of the genital sexual faculty), are moral if all three fonts are good.

.385. Passionate Kissing Prior to Marriage

Many moralists claim that 'passionate' kissing is always an objective mortal sin for any unmarried man and woman, regardless of intention or circumstances, even if the couple is engaged. But they allow that non-passionate kissing is moral. There are several doctrinal problems with this claim.

First, only intrinsically evil acts are always immoral regardless of intention or circumstances. There are three fonts of morality, if an act is immoral regardless of two fonts, it must be immoral under the remaining font. Intrinsically evil acts have an evil moral object; the moral nature of the act is inherently disordered. But the addition of the adjective 'passionate' does not signify a different moral nature, nor a different moral object. So if the type of act and the moral object have not changed, then the act cannot be intrinsically evil. For the moral object always is the sole determinant of the moral nature (or species) of an act.

We are not here discussing lust, which is intrinsically evil, because lust is a type of act, not an adjective describing an act. Although, in secular terms, any act might be described as lustful, such a phrasing does not necessarily signify the objective mortal sin of lust. If kissing, or any other act, even the mere act of looking at a person, is accompanied by an interior act of lust, it is that interior act which is always gravely immoral, not the kissing or the looking.

Second, passion refers to emotion. But emotions, even strong emotions, do not necessarily imply sin. For example, Jesus became angry in the Temple, when He drove out the buyers and the sellers: "Zeal for your house consumes me." (John 2:17). And He experienced the emotions of sorrow and fear in the garden at the beginning of His Passion: "My soul is sorrowful, even unto death." (Mt 26:38), and, "And he began to be afraid…" (Mk 14:33).

Now the emotion of sexual passion is a result of the fallen state, and so neither Jesus nor Mary experienced sexual passion or sexual arousal. But this emotion which results from being in the fallen state is not itself a sin, and when it is accompanied by sin, the sin is not necessarily mortal. Emotions are not knowingly chosen acts. Only knowingly chosen immoral acts are sins. A knowingly chosen immoral act might result in one emotion or another, or a person might knowingly make a sinful choice in response to an emotion, but emotions are not themselves sins. So the idea that kissing becomes a mortal sin merely because an emotion occurs during kissing is absurd.

Third, kissing does not have an evil moral object. "Greet one another with a holy kiss." (Romans 16:16). A kiss might be accompanied by a sin of one type or another. "And he who betrayed him gave them a sign, saying: 'Whomever I will kiss, it is he. Take hold of him.' " (Mt 26:48). But the act itself of kissing is not intrinsically evil.

Neither does any emotion, even emotions resulting from the fallen state, have an evil moral object. Although certain interior sins, such as lust, or hatred, or envy, etc., are often confused with the associated emotions (feelings), morally there is a very sharp distinction between experiencing an emotion, and knowingly choosing an immoral act. The emotion of anger is not the sin of hatred. The feeling of jealousy is not the sin of envy. The emotion (or feelings of) passion are not the sin of lust. No emotion has an evil moral object, because feelings are not knowingly chosen acts.

An excess of anger might occur if a person is harmed by another person, and he sins by choosing to dwell on that harm, and he sins by choosing not to forgive the injury, and he sins by choosing various acts that result in excessive anger. And in experiencing this excess of anger caused by his sins, he might next choose the sin of revenge. But the initial anger is not a sin. And the subsequent excessive anger is a bad consequence of his knowingly chosen acts, but it is not itself a sin. (Excessive anger is 'physical evil', not moral evil.)

An excess of passion may be the result of sinful acts, such as unmarried persons choosing acts of excessive physical affection or excessive sensuality. And the resultant feelings may make it difficult for the unmarried couple to remain chaste. In this case, if the acts of physical affection or sensuality do not include any intrinsically evil acts, then the morality would depend on intention and circumstances. But the fact that the emotion of passion occurs during kissing (or similar acts) does not cause the act to become an objective mortal sin.

Fourth, when an unmarried man and woman kiss, the fonts of intention or circumstances might be gravely immoral: such as an intention to induce the other person to commit an intrinsically evil sexual act, or a circumstance in which the kissing can reasonably be anticipated to have gravely harmful bad consequences (such as a near occasion of mortal sin). Or a related but distinct act might be gravely immoral, such as an interior act of lust. But the use the term 'passionate' to describe the kissing does not imply that any of the three fonts is gravely immoral, nor does it imply an accompanying gravely immoral act.

Fifth, kissing and similar acts of limited sensuality (but always non-genital acts) assist a couple who are considering marriage, or who are engaged, in preparing for later acts of natural marital relations open to life. This good consequence can certainly outweigh some bad consequences of limited moral weight. And the intention to express affection, or to prepare for moral sexual acts at a later time, within marriage, are moral intentions.

Sixth, the usual approach to this question lacks any consideration of degrees of sin. Kissing is said to be moral, but when it becomes, at some point, passionate, it is said to be suddenly gravely immoral. There is no acknowledgement of degrees of sin. But without any gravely immoral intention, or a gravely immoral object, or bad consequences that outweigh good consequences to a grave extent, there is no basis for this claim of mortal sin.

Seventh, under the three fonts approach to morality, none of the fonts is gravely immoral merely because the kissing has become passionate. Some degree of selfishness might be present in the intention of one or both persons, but this would be a venial sin. There may be some limited bad consequences to excessive sensuality in that the persons are aroused and chastity becomes somewhat more difficult, but not necessarily gravely so. And there is no gravely immoral object in such acts, since all genital sexual acts are absent from mere kissing and similar limited expressions of affection and sensuality.

Therefore, passionate kissing and similar acts of affection between an unmarried man and woman are not necessarily objective mortal sin. The mere emotion of sexual passion is not a knowingly chosen immoral act. And the acts that lead to this emotion may be moral, or may be venial sins. Kissing with passion may have some degree of disorder in intention or circumstances, but not so that this knowingly chosen act would be always entirely incompatible with the love of God and neighbor, and with the state of grace in the soul.

.386. The Gravity of Sexual Sins

Sacred Congregation for the Doctrine of the Faith: "Now according to Christian tradition and the Church's teaching, and as right reason also recognizes, the moral order of sexuality involves such high values of human life that every direct violation of this order is objectively serious."[439]

Sexual sins are always objective mortal sins. Each and every deliberate and morally-direct sexual act that is deprived of the unitive, or procreative, or marital meaning is necessarily and objectively a mortal sin, and is also intrinsically evil. Objective mortal sexual sins include masturbation, premarital sexual acts, homosexual acts, adultery, contracepted sexual acts, and all unnatural sexual acts, even within marriage. The use of the sexual faculty is a serious matter, and so any use, other than natural marital relations open to life, is a grave sin. However, this refers to sexual acts per se, not to acts that are peripherally-related to sexuality. If an act is sexual in the broader sense of being related to sexuality, without including any kind of sexual act whatsoever, then the act might not be an objective mortal sin.

---

[439] Cardinal Seper, CDF, Persona Humana, n. X.

Examples: (1) A married man has sexual relations with someone other than his wife. He has committed the objective mortal sin of adultery. (2) A married man flirts, but does nothing more, with a woman other than his wife. In this case, perhaps he has not sinned seriously, but only venially. However, even a venial act of flirting becomes a mortal sin if done with lustful intent. (3) An unmarried man and woman have sexual relations prior to marriage. They have sinned seriously. Their subsequent marriage does not justify the sexual sins committed prior to the marriage. (4) An unmarried man and woman, refraining from all sexual acts prior to marriage, indulge, to some degree of excess, in acts of physical affection. In this case, perhaps they have only sinned venially (as long as there was no interior sin of lust).

But again, the three fonts of morality always apply. Even if an act is related to sexuality without being a sexual act per se, that act must be good under all three fonts in order to avoid sin. If any one font is bad, the overall act is immoral, even if the act is not intrinsically evil. And if any one font of such an act is so disordered as to be gravely contrary to the eternal moral law, then the act would be an objective mortal sin, even if the act is not a sexual act per se.

.387. Chastity in Marriage

The Encyclical of Pope Pius XI on Chaste Marriage (in Latin: Casti Connubii) enlightens us on marital sexual ethics. The word 'chaste' refers to sexual purity according to one's state of life. For each and every unmarried person, chastity requires refraining from all sexual acts. For each and every married husband and wife, chastity requires that they have sexual relations only in natural marital relations open to life. Both the husband and wife must refrain from adultery, masturbation, and every kind of unnatural sexual act between themselves. The only morally licit sexual act is natural marital relations open to life.

Pope Pius XI: "But no reason, however grave, may be put forward by which anything intrinsically against nature may become conformable to nature and morally good. Since, therefore, the conjugal act is destined primarily by nature for the begetting of children, those who, in exercising it, deliberately frustrate its natural power and purpose, sin against nature and commit a deed which is shameful and intrinsically vicious."[440]

This passage condemns not only contraception, but also all unnatural sexual acts, even within marriage. Unnatural sexual acts are non-procreative, and therefore are intrinsically evil. No reason, no matter how serious, can justify any intrinsically evil act. Nothing can cause an act that is intrinsically unnatural to become natural and moral. Unnatural sexual acts are inherently contrary to nature, because the natural law requires that "each and every marital act must of necessity retain its intrinsic relationship to the procreation of human life."[441] Those who deliberately exercise the sexual faculty in a manner that is non-procreative, sin against nature and commit a shameful and inherently unjust act.

---

[440] Pope Pius XI, Casti Connubii, n. 54.
[441] Pope Paul VI, Humanae Vitae, n. 11.

Marital Sexual Ethics

Pope Pius XI: "Since, therefore, openly departing from the uninterrupted Christian tradition some recently have judged it possible solemnly to declare another doctrine regarding this question, the Catholic Church, to whom God has entrusted the defense of the integrity and purity of morals, standing erect in the midst of the moral ruin which surrounds her, in order that she may preserve the chastity of the nuptial union from being defiled by this foul stain, raises her voice in token of her divine ambassadorship and through Our mouth proclaims anew: any use whatsoever of matrimony exercised in such a way that the act is deliberately frustrated in its natural power to generate life is an offense against the law of God and of nature, and those who indulge in such are branded with the guilt of a grave sin."[442]

This teaching of the Church, that "any use whatsoever of matrimony in such a way that the act is deliberately frustrated in its natural power to generate life is an offense against the law of God and of nature," must be understood to condemn not only contracepted sexual acts, but also any and all non-procreative sexual acts, even within marriage, including unnatural sexual acts. For all sexual acts are a type of use of the sexual faculty, and all unnatural sexual acts are non-procreative. If the Pope had wished to narrow his statements to only contraception, he would not have said "any use whatsoever," or if he had wished to allow unnatural sexual acts only within marriage, he would not have said "any use whatsoever of matrimony." Instead, he unequivocally proclaimed the Magisterium's definitive teaching, which is also found in natural law, that "each and every" marital sexual act must include both the unitive and procreative meanings. This teaching necessarily prohibits the married couple from engaging in any kind of unnatural sexual act (consummated or non-consummated), because all such acts lack the procreative meaning.

Pope Paul VI: "The Church, nevertheless, in urging men to the observance of the precepts of the natural law, which it interprets by its constant doctrine, teaches that each and every marital act must of necessity retain its intrinsic relationship to the procreation of human life. This particular doctrine, often expounded by the magisterium of the Church, is based on the inseparable connection, established by God, which man on his own initiative may not break, between the unitive significance and the procreative significance which are both inherent to the marriage act."[443]

The Magisterium has never taught that non-procreative sexual acts are justified within marriage, or are justified by being combined in some way with acts of natural marital relations. The Magisterium has definitively taught that each and every sexual act must be unitive and procreative and marital in order to be moral, and that non-procreative sexual acts, even within marriage, remain intrinsically immoral. There are no exceptions to the moral law for the marital bedroom. Unnatural sexual acts are never justified by being combined in some way with natural marital relations. Non-procreative sexual acts are never justified by being

---

[442] Pope Pius XI, Casti Connubii, n. 55.
[443] Pope Paul VI, Humanae Vitae, n. 11-12.

combined in some way with procreative sexual acts. Each act must stand on its own as to its morality.

Pope Paul VI: "Neither is it valid to argue, as a justification for sexual intercourse which is deliberately contraceptive...that such intercourse would merge with procreative acts of past and future to form a single entity, and so be qualified by exactly the same moral goodness as these."[444]

Contracepted sexual intercourse is intrinsically evil because such acts are non-procreative. All unnatural sexual acts are also non-procreative, therefore all such acts are intrinsically evil. Non-procreative acts cannot be justified by being merged with procreative acts (i.e. acts of natural marital relations) of the past or future. The eternal moral law requires that each and every act be good under all three fonts of morality, as those fonts spring up from, and apply to, each particular act. Therefore, even if two acts occur at the same time, each act stands on its own as to its morality. It is never the case, in any area of morality, that a good and bad act could be combined, as if to form a single moral entity, such that the good act would justify the bad act. It is never the case, in any area of morality, that an intrinsically evil act could be somehow transformed to have the same moral goodness as another act, one that is good under all three fonts of morality.

Pope John Paul II: "Consequently, circumstances or intentions can never transform an act intrinsically evil by virtue of its object into an act 'subjectively' good or defensible as a choice."[445]

The intention to perform an act of natural marital relations after an unnatural sexual act does not justify that unnatural act. The circumstance that an unnatural sexual act occurs before, during, or after an act of natural marital relations does not justify that unnatural act. The circumstance that an unnatural sexual act lacks sexual climax does not justify that unnatural act. Unnatural sexual acts are intrinsically evil and always gravely immoral because all such acts lack the procreative meaning required by the natural law for each and every sexual act. And in truth, unnatural sexual acts lack all three meanings, for such acts are not truly unitive, nor are they truly marital, in the way that God intends for human nature and for a husband and wife in holy matrimony.

.388. Summary

Like all knowingly chosen acts, moral sexual acts must be good under all three fonts. The good moral object which must be present for any sexual act to be moral under the second font is threefold: unitive, procreative, marital. The unitive, procreative, and marital meanings are interrelated as one threefold moral object. Any sexual act that lacks one or more of these three meanings is an intrinsically evil sexual act.

---

[444] Pope Paul VI, Humanae Vitae, n. 15.
[445] Pope John Paul II, Veritatis Splendor, n. 81.

The completion of the act in sexual climax does not determine the morality of the second font. As is true for all knowingly chosen acts, the inherent ordering of the act itself toward its moral object determines the morality of the second font. A contracepted sexual act that is not completed in sexual climax is nevertheless an intrinsically evil sexual act, since it lacks the procreative meaning. An unnatural sexual act that is not completed in sexual climax is nevertheless an intrinsically evil sexual act, since it lacks the procreative meaning. The lack of sexual climax does not allow the couple to claim that no sinful sexual act occurred. Even without sexual climax on the part of either or both persons, the couple knowingly chose a sexual act that is deprived of the procreative meaning.

In order to be moral, each and every sexual act must be good under all three fonts of morality. In order to be good under the second font, each and every use of the sexual faculty must have that threefold moral object which determines the inherent moral meaning of the sexual act itself, so that the essential nature of the act is unitive, procreative, and marital. This threefold meaning of natural marital relations, which is unitive, procreative, and marital, is a reflection of the threefold gifts to humanity of love, faith, and hope. The plan of God for human sexuality is written into our very nature, and so every sexual act that is not unitive and procreative and marital is contrary to the natural law and is a serious sin before God.

Each and every sexual act that is non-unitive, or non-procreative, nor non-marital is intrinsically evil and always gravely immoral. Intrinsically evil sexual acts are not justified by being done within marriage, since all three meanings must be present for a sexual act to be moral. Unnatural sexual acts are neither procreative, nor truly unitive, nor even truly marital, and so such acts are intrinsically evil and always gravely immoral. A good intention, or dire circumstances, cannot justify an intrinsically evil act in any area of human life. All of the basic principles of morality apply to sexuality just as they apply to every other area of life. Marital sexual acts are not exempt from the eternal moral law, nor are marital sexual acts subject to a different set of basic principles, such that an intrinsically evil act might become good, or be considered morally neutral, by being done for the sake of the marriage.

.389. Sexual acts other than natural intercourse are not truly unitive, because these acts depart from the plan of God for the union of husband and wife. Only natural intercourse is truly unitive in the moral sense of the word. Sexual acts other than natural intercourse are not truly procreative, because these acts depart from the plan of God for the procreation of new life within a marriage and a family. Only natural intercourse is both unitive and procreative, in the full moral sense of these words. And only natural marital relations includes all three meanings required by the natural law for each and every sexual act.

Artificial contraception, in all of its forms, is intrinsically evil and always gravely immoral, because the use of contraception deprives the sexual act of its procreative meaning. Natural intercourse within marriage, but with contraception, is unitive and marital, but not procreative. Even so, when any one meaning is absent, the other meanings are harmed. The lack of the procreative meaning in contracepted sexual acts harms the unitive and marital meanings.

Artificial procreation seems to include a type of union (of male and female gametes) and a type of procreation. But this type of union is not union as intended by God for a man and a woman within marriage. And this type of procreation is not procreation as intended by God for marriages, and for families, and for the human race. Artificial procreation is contrary to the natural law, and so it is intrinsically evil and always gravely immoral. Artificial procreation of every type is not truly procreative and not truly unitive, in the moral sense of these words.

Only natural marital relations open to life is truly and fully: unitive, procreative, and marital. Natural marital relations open to life is the only act ordained by God to fulfill His will in human nature: for sexual union, for procreation, and for marriage. The only moral sexual act is natural marital relations open to life. All other uses of the genital sexual faculty are intrinsically evil and always gravely immoral.

[1 Corinthians]
{3:16} Do you not know that you are the Temple of God, and that the Spirit of God lives within you?
{3:17} But if anyone violates the Temple of God, God will destroy him. For the Temple of God is holy, and you are that Temple.
{3:18} Let no one deceive himself. If anyone among you seems to be wise in this age, let him become foolish, so that he may be truly wise.
{3:19} For the wisdom of this world is foolishness with God. And so it has been written: "I will catch the wise in their own astuteness."
{3:20} And again: "The Lord knows the thoughts of the wise, that they are vain."

[2 Corinthians]
{7:1} Therefore, having these promises, most beloved, let us cleanse ourselves from all defilement of the flesh and of the spirit, perfecting sanctification in the fear of God.

Chapter 26
Sets of Acts

.390.
An immoral act is not justified by a prior, concurrent, or subsequent good act. An immoral means is not justified by a good end, nor is an immoral end justified by a good means. The end never justifies the means.[446] Both the end and the means to that end must be moral for a person to avoid sin. A good act cannot cause a bad act to become good. A bad act cannot cause a good act to become bad. If a person commits two acts, one good and the other bad, the good act remains good, and the bad act remains bad.

Two or more knowingly chosen acts cannot be grouped together such that any act takes its morality, in part or in whole, from another act. Such an approach would contradict and effectively nullify the three fonts of morality, because the morality of an act would no longer be based on the three fonts as they apply to that act, but as they apply to a different act. The end result of this approach would be to justify an immoral act by using one or more fonts from a different act. To the contrary, immorality is never justified. The three fonts that are used to evaluate the morality of any act must be the fonts that spring from, and apply to, that same act. Whenever there is even one bad font, there is sin. Each knowingly chosen act must be good in all three fonts for the act to be moral.

Each and every knowingly chosen act must be good before God in order to avoid sin. An act that is good before God remains good, even if the same person commits many bad acts before, during, or after the good act. An act that is evil before God remains evil, even if the same person performs many good acts before, during, or after the evil act. A thousand good acts do not justify one bad act, and a thousand bad acts do not corrupt one good act. The moral law is universal and unchanging because God is universal and unchanging. The moral law applies everywhere at all times because God is everywhere at all times. If an act is immoral, it does not become moral by being done before, during, or after another act, no matter how good and moral that other act may be.

Two or more knowingly chosen acts cannot be grouped together such that any act takes its morality from the set of acts. Such an approach would contradict and effectively nullify the three fonts of morality, because the morality of an act would no longer be based on the three fonts as they apply to that act, but as they are taken selectively from within the set of acts. The end result of this approach would be to justify an immoral act by finding at least one good example of each of the three fonts within the entire set of acts, ignoring any and all immorality in any of the other fonts within the set of acts. An immoral act cannot be justified by finding a different act with good intent, and one with a good moral object, and one with good circumstances, within the same set of acts. Such an approach in effect would permit some moral evil (iniquity) on the excuse that some good was also done. To the contrary, all moral evil is sin before the eyes of God.

---

[446] CCC, n. 1753; cf. Romans 3:8

[Judith]
{5:21} And, as long as they did not sin in the sight of their God, it was well with them. For their God hates iniquity.

[Proverbs]
{8:13} The fear of the Lord hates evil. I detest arrogance, and pride, and every wicked way, and a mouth with a double tongue.

[1 John]
{5:17} All that is iniquity is sin.

.391. All evil is always abhorrent to God, and therefore the moral law applies universally, to all acts, by all persons, at all times, in all places, within all situations. There are no exceptions to the moral law. There is no situation or context or circumstance or intention or act which is beyond the moral law, or which falls under a different set of moral principles, or which is exempt from some or all of the requirements of the moral law. Each and every knowingly chosen act must be moral, under all three fonts, in order to avoid sin.

Within any set of acts, each act must be evaluated individually, under all three fonts, to determine if that particular act is good or evil. Two or more knowingly chosen acts cannot be grouped together such that any act, or any font of any act, is treated as if it were devoid of morality, or exempt from the moral law, or justifiable under a different set of moral principles. For the moral law is universal. Each and every knowingly chosen act must be good, under all three fonts, for the act to be morally licit.

Even if two acts occur at the same time, each knowingly chosen act must be moral, under all three fonts of morality, as these fonts spring from, and apply to, each particular act. Two or more knowingly chosen acts cannot be grouped together such that the set of acts is morally evaluated as if it were one continuous act, or as one so-called context, or as one set of acts, ignoring the immorality of certain acts or certain fonts, for several reasons.

The three fonts of morality apply whenever a knowing choice is made. But as a human person continues to act over the course of time, every voluntary action is under the direction of will and intellect, and so more than one knowing choice is made. It is manifestly false to claim that a set of knowingly chosen acts, whether interior or exterior acts, can be considered as a single knowingly chosen act, when in fact the individual is continuing to choose from various different possible acts over the course of time. Each knowingly chosen act must be good under all three fonts of morality, and therefore a set of acts cannot be morally evaluated as if it were one act.

When a set of acts, some good and some bad, are said to form one continuous act, the morality of the so-called continuous act is selectively taken from only one act, or from a subset of the acts, or from a subset of the fonts of the acts chosen selectively. The result of this approach is to exempt certain acts and their fonts from the moral law, and to justify certain immoral acts, both acts that are intrinsically evil (under the second font), and acts that are evil (under the first or third fonts) but not intrinsically evil. In this approach, any font that would make any act immoral is ignored. Despite the obvious fact that the set of acts includes a number of different intentions, for the purposes of moral evaluation the intention is taken only from one good act. Despite the obvious fact that the set of acts includes a number of different acts, each with its own moral object, for the purposes of moral evaluation the moral object is taken only from one good act with a good moral object. Despite the obvious fact that the set of acts includes a number of different acts with different consequences, for the purposes of moral evaluation the consequences are taken only from one good act. Some have taken this dishonest approach to such an extreme that numerous intrinsically evil acts are said to be justified by combination with only a single good act.

.392. It is obvious to reason alone that two or more acts are not one continuous act if each act is capable of being knowingly chosen on its own. When each act in a set can be done on its own, or when two or more acts can be done in any order, or when any act can be omitted from the set, then these acts are not one continuous act, and cannot be morally evaluated as if they were one continuous act. Each act is knowingly chosen, and so each act must be moral under all three fonts of morality as those fonts apply to each particular act. To say otherwise is to exempt some acts from the eternal moral law.

If any act is intrinsically evil, it cannot be justified by being combined with other good acts, because that which is intrinsically evil is necessarily immoral by the very nature of the act. Nothing whatsoever can justify that which is inherently contrary to the moral law. But an approach that groups two or more acts together, claiming that they are one continuous act, would result in some intrinsically evil acts being supposedly justified. Intrinsically evil acts are immoral under the second font of morality. But when the so-called continuous act is evaluated as to its morality, one good act within the set is used to justify the moral object, and the corrupt moral object of every intrinsically evil act is ignored (or they claim that the moral object of the good act now belongs also to the intrinsically evil act). This approach has the effect of denying the absolute immorality of intrinsically evil acts, since intrinsically evil acts within the so-called continuous act (which is in truth a set of diverse acts) are not distinguished as distinct acts, and are utterly ignored as to their immorality. This approach contradicts and effectively nullifies the teaching that intrinsically evil acts are always immoral. Therefore, such an approach is contrary to the moral truths taught by the Catholic Christian Faith.

Pope John Paul II: "Consequently, without in the least denying the influence on morality exercised by circumstances and especially by intentions, the Church teaches that 'there exist acts which per se and in themselves, independently of circumstances, are always seriously wrong by reason of their object.' "[447]

The moral law is absolutely universal. But by combining a set of acts into one continuous act for the purpose of moral evaluation, the moral law is not applied

---

[447] Pope John Paul II, Veritatis Splendor, n. 80; inner quote is from Pope John Paul II, Reconciliation and Penance, n. 17.

Sets of Acts

to every font of every knowingly chosen act. The so-called continuous act is evaluated as to its morality based on only some of the choices made, and other choices are treated as if they are beyond the reach of the moral law. This error is particularly clear when an act that is admitted to be intrinsically evil when done by itself is nevertheless claimed to become moral by being part of a set, or by being part of a so-called continuous act, or by being part of a so-called context, merely because one morally good act is also done at about the same time. And this approach also errs by justifying acts that are immoral under the first or third font, i.e. acts that are evil, but not intrinsically evil. In effect, this approach denies the universality of the moral law.

.393. At times, this approach is used to claim that the moral object of an intrinsically evil act can change and become good by being combined with a good act. An act that is admitted to be intrinsically evil and always immoral, with a particular intention and circumstance, is said to have a new moral object, one that is good, merely due to a change in intention or a change in circumstance. To the contrary, each and every knowingly chosen act is inherently ordered toward its moral object, independent of intention and circumstance. The moral object is by definition inherent to the act, which is why an act with a bad moral object is called intrinsically evil, and not merely evil. Therefore, a change in intention or in circumstances can never change the moral object of the act itself. If an act is intrinsically evil, such an act is immoral by the very nature of the act itself, and no change in intention or in circumstances can ever change the nature of that act. Neither can a different knowingly chosen act, whether prior, concurrent, or subsequent, change the moral object of an act, because each act has its own moral object, and, as a result, its own inherent moral meaning. To say otherwise is to justify immorality.

Pope John Paul II: "Consequently, circumstances or intentions can never transform an act, intrinsically evil by virtue of its object, into an act 'subjectively' good or defensible as a choice."[448]

This approach of evaluating the morality of acts as a set, and not individually, is often used to justify one or more bad acts on the basis that these acts occur in the context of a good act. But if that were true, then there would be nothing to limit the application of this approach to an ever larger context. Any suggested time limit for the good act to justify a prior or subsequent bad act would be arbitrary. Any suggested limit to the number or kind of bad acts that are justified by the good act would be arbitrary. The end result would be to justify any number or kind of evil acts, no matter how much evil were done, if only one good act were also done.

This approach also makes it impossible to judge the morality of an act until the entire set of acts is completed. The approach admits that certain acts are intrinsically evil and gravely immoral when done by themselves, but then goes on to claim that adding a subsequent good act would make the prior act moral. But if a subsequent good act could justify a prior bad act, then what is the

---

[448] Pope John Paul II, Veritatis Splendor, n. 81.

morality of the bad act before the subsequent good act occurs? All of the possible answers are absurd: the act would be bad and then change to become good, or would have no morality until the subsequent act occurs, or would be moral based on the mere intention to commit a subsequent good act. And if the set of acts is interrupted, so that the subsequent moral act never occurs, the intrinsically evil act stands on its own and must be admitted to be gravely immoral. Therefore, the claim that a subsequent good act justifies one or more prior evil acts is contrary to reason, and is incompatible with Catholic moral teaching. The only correct approach is to admit the truth that a bad act is never justified by a subsequent, concurrent, or prior good act, nor by the intention to perform a good act.

Concerning sets of acts such as slavery or war, even when the set of acts is said to be immoral, as in the case of slavery, or is said to be moral, as in the case of just war, each act within the set remains moral or immoral based on the three fonts of morality as they apply to each particular act. If a good act is done toward a slave, the intrinsically evil acts that are essential to the definition of slavery remain immoral, and the good act remains moral. If an unjust act occurs during a just war, the just acts that are essential to the definition of just war remain moral, and the unjust act remains immoral. Even when a set of acts is considered as a whole, each act remains moral or immoral based on the three fonts of morality, regardless of the morality of the other acts in the set.

.394. If every act within a set of acts is intrinsically evil, then the set of acts may be called intrinsically evil. Nevertheless, each act is good or evil as the three fonts of morality spring from, and apply to, that particular act. If every act within a set of acts is moral, then the set of acts may be called moral. Nevertheless, each act is good or evil as the three fonts of morality spring from, and apply to, that particular act. If some acts within a set of acts are good and others are evil, each act stands on its own as to its morality.

Each and every knowingly chosen act stands on its own as to its morality. And we shall all answer to God for each and every knowingly chosen immoral act throughout our entire lives.

[Revelation]
{20:11} And I saw a great white throne, and One sitting upon it, from whose sight earth and heaven fled, and no place was found for them.
{20:12} And I saw the dead, great and small, standing in view of the throne. And books were opened. And another Book was opened, which is the Book of Life. And the dead were judged by those things that had been written in the books, according to their works.
{20:13} And the sea gave up the dead who were in it. And death and Hell gave up their dead who were in them. And they were judged, each one according to his works.
{20:14} And Hell and death were cast into the pool of fire. This is the second death.
{20:15} And whoever was not found written in the Book of Life was cast into the pool of fire.

.395. There are no knowingly chosen acts that are devoid of morality, or morally neutral, or beyond the moral law. There are no knowingly chosen acts that are contrary to the moral law and yet not also contrary to the will and the Nature of God. The morality of each and every knowingly chosen act stands or falls on its own, as to whether or not it is an act that offends God. The morality of each knowingly chosen act does not change by being combined, in any way at all, with other acts. All knowingly chosen acts are subject to the moral law. No knowingly chosen acts are morally neutral. Acts that are good before God are always good, and acts that are evil before God are always evil.

Examples: (1) A man robs a bank. During the robbery, he repents from this sin. These are two separate acts. The act of robbery is intrinsically evil and always immoral. He chose the act of robbery, and next he chose to repent. The act of repentance is good. But this subsequent good act of repentance does not justify the prior bad act of robbery.

(2) A man goes for a walk with his wife, and during the walk he lies to her. Taking a recreational walk with someone is a good act. Lying is intrinsically evil and always immoral. The act of lying occurs at the same time as the walking, yet these are two distinct acts. The walking remains good, and the lying remains evil. Afterwards, when his wife realizes that he lied, she will condemn the act of lying, but she will not condemn the act of taking a walk. She will not ask him never to take a walk with her again, but rather never to lie to her again.

(3) A man works hard all day for his employer, but he is underpaid, and so, at the end of the work day, he steals some money from his employer. The good act of doing difficult but honest work does not justify the subsequent bad act of theft.

(4) An engaged man and woman have natural sexual relations, and subsequently they marry. In order to be moral, each and every sexual act must be marital, unitive, and procreative. The immoral act of pre-marital sex is not justified by the subsequent good act of marrying.

(5) A married man and woman have natural marital relations on several occasions, sometimes with contraception and other times without contraception. This is a set of sexual acts in which some acts are contraceptive and others are open to life. These acts cannot be morally evaluated as a set, such that the entire set would be justified by the openness to life of only some of the acts within the set. Each and every sexual act must marital, unitive and procreative.

(6) A married man and woman have natural marital relations open to life, an act which is marital, unitive, and procreative. Prior to this moral marital act, the husband and wife commit one or more unnatural sexual acts, such as oral, anal, or manipulative sex. Unnatural sexual acts are not inherently procreative, nor are they truly unitive, nor are they truly marital. These prior unnatural sexual acts are not justified by the subsequent good act of natural marital relations. Although some have attempted to justify unnatural sexual acts when used as a type of so-called foreplay, the end of natural marital relations does not justify the means of unnatural sexual acts. An unnatural sexual act does not become inherently procreative by being followed by, preceded by, or accompanied by a

procreative act of natural marital relations. Unnatural sexual acts inherently lack the procreative meaning, and so all such acts are intrinsically evil and always gravely immoral. Combining one or more unnatural sexual acts in a set with one or more acts of natural marital relations does not cause the unnatural sexual acts to cease from being intrinsically evil and always gravely immoral.

(7) Subsequent to an act of natural marital relations, the husband performs an unnatural sexual act on his wife, in order to bring her to sexual climax. The prior good act of natural marital relations does not justify the subsequent unnatural sexual act. The subsequent unnatural sexual act is not inherently directed at procreation, and cannot take its moral object from the prior procreative act. A set of sexual acts cannot be justified if only some of the acts are marital, unitive, and procreative.

(8) During an act of natural marital relations, one spouse also performs an unnatural sexual act. These are two distinct sexual acts. The act of natural marital relations can be performed without the unnatural sexual act, and the unnatural sexual act (though gravely immoral) can be performed without the act of natural marital relations. The act of natural marital relations is marital, unitive, and procreative, and so it is a moral sexual act. The unnatural sexual act is not, in and of itself, procreative or unitive or even truly marital, despite being accompanied by a unitive, procreative, marital act. The act of natural marital relations is good, but the unnatural sexual act remains intrinsically evil and always immoral. An intrinsically evil act does not become moral by being done at the same time as a good act.

.396. Pope Paul VI considered the so-called principle of totality, which proposed grouping together a set of sexual acts, some procreative and some non-procreative, and which justified the non-procreative sexual acts by being part of a set of acts, some of which are procreative: "Could it not be admitted, in other words, that procreative finality applies to the totality of married life rather than to each single act?"[449] But the Pope rejected this idea as being contrary to the definitive teaching of the Catholic Faith: "The Church, nevertheless, in urging men to the observance of the precepts of the natural law, which it interprets by its constant doctrine, teaches that each and every marital act must of necessity retain its intrinsic relationship to the procreation of human life. This particular doctrine, often expounded by the magisterium of the Church, is based on the inseparable connection, established by God, which man on his own initiative may not break, between the unitive significance and the procreative significance which are both inherent to the marriage act."[450]

The Magisterium of the Church teaches that each sexual act between a husband and wife must be evaluated on its own, without regard to the morality of other sexual acts. Pope Paul VI considered whether the morality of sexual acts might be based on a set of acts, or on "each single act." He concluded and definitively taught that "each and every marital act," i.e. each and every sexual act between

---

[449] Pope Paul VI, Humanae Vitae, n. 3.
[450] Pope Paul VI, Humanae Vitae, n. 11-12.

a husband and wife, must be both unitive and procreative. Unnatural sexual acts are neither procreative, nor truly unitive; therefore, all unnatural sexual acts are intrinsically evil, even when these acts occur between a husband and wife, even when these acts occur before, during, or after an act of natural marital relations. This teaching is the constant doctrine of the Church, based on the precepts of the natural law.

Similarly, when considering acts of artificial procreation, which, like unnatural sexual acts, are neither truly unitive, nor truly procreative (in the moral sense of those words), the Magisterium rejected the idea that acts of artificial procreation can be justified by combination with the set of acts of conjugal life as a whole. Each act must be judged in itself, and no act can borrow its morality from other acts. This is true in all areas of morality; there are no exceptions to the moral law for sexuality.

Sacred Congregation for the Doctrine of the Faith: "The process of IVF and ET must be judged in itself and cannot borrow its definitive moral quality from the totality of conjugal life of which it becomes part, nor from the conjugal acts which may precede or follow it."[451]

It is never the case, in any area of morality, that an intrinsically evil act could become moral by being part of a set of acts. The basic principle of morality that each and every act must be good under all three fonts in order to be moral also applies to sexual acts. Unnatural sexual acts are non-procreative, and so they are intrinsically evil. Using one or more unnatural sexual acts in a set with one or more acts of natural marital relations does not justify the unnatural sexual acts. Each and every sexual act must be unitive, procreative, and marital.

Pope John Paul II: "No circumstance, no purpose, no law whatsoever can ever make licit an act which is intrinsically illicit, since it is contrary to the Law of God which is written in every human heart, knowable by reason itself, and proclaimed by the Church."[452]

---

[451] Cardinal Ratzinger, CDF, Donum Vitae, II. n. 5.
[452] Pope John Paul II, Evangelium Vitae, n. 62.

Chapter 27
Incomplete Acts

.397.
A knowingly chosen act may be incomplete, in a certain sense, in any of three ways, each of which corresponds to one of the three fonts of morality. However, in no case is any knowingly chosen act ever morally incomplete. Once an act has been knowingly chosen, it is either moral or immoral before God. Once an act has been knowingly chosen, each of the three fonts is morally complete, in that each of the three fonts is either morally good, or morally bad. To say otherwise is to deny the universality of the moral law.

FIRST FONT: Under the first font, if the intended end is not achieved, then the font is, in some sense, incomplete. But this does not change the morality of the intention. If the intended end is not obtained, the morality of the first font is unaffected because that end was nevertheless intended. If a person intends an evil end, but then fails to achieve that evil end, the morality of the intention is the same as if the end was achieved. For the sin of intention is based on what is intended, and not on whether than intention is fulfilled (or completed).

And if someone were to intend to use an immoral means, and then fail even to make use of that evil intended means, the intention would remain immoral. The intention of either an immoral means or an immoral end is a sin, even if what is intended is not used or attained. For whoever intends evil, offends God, even if he does not succeed in his evil intention.

SECOND FONT: All knowingly chosen acts have a moral object. The moral object is the end, in terms of morality, toward which the chosen act is directed. An act that is inherently directed toward an evil moral object is intrinsically evil and always immoral. The inherent ordering of the act toward its moral object determines the moral meaning of the act. But even if the moral object is not achieved, the act remains inherently ordered toward that same moral object. Therefore, morality of the second font remains the same, regardless of whether or not the act achieves its moral object.

Under the second font, if an act does not achieve its moral object, then the act is, in some sense, incomplete. But as long as the act is inherently ordered toward that same moral object, then the inherent moral meaning of the act is the same; it is morally the same type of act, regardless of whether or not the moral object is attained. An act that is incomplete, in the sense that it does not obtain the moral object that it inherently seeks, nevertheless possesses the same moral object because it remains inherently ordered toward that end. The essential moral nature of any act is determined by the inherent ordering of that act toward its moral object, not by the achievement of that moral object. If the completed act has an evil moral object, then the act is intrinsically evil. If the same act is not completed, then the act remains intrinsically evil because it remains inherently ordered toward the same moral object that it failed to attain. Intrinsically evil acts are always immoral because the act itself is inherently ordered toward an evil end, regardless of whether or not the end is reached.

If incomplete acts had no moral object, then some acts would have no second font of morality, and would be exempt from the eternal moral law, despite being knowingly chosen acts. But there are no exceptions to the moral law. The eternal moral law is the infinite Justice of God, and all knowingly chosen acts are under that law. Therefore, even if a knowingly chosen act is, in one sense or another, incomplete, the act nevertheless has three fonts, and the act must be moral under all three fonts in order to avoid sin. To say otherwise is to exempt some knowingly chosen acts from the moral law. But the moral law is universal, for God is all-knowing and all-powerful and ever-present and infinitely Just.

Therefore, even if the moral object is not obtained, the morality of the second font is unaffected because the chosen act remains inherently ordered toward that good or evil moral object. An act that is inherently ordered toward a good moral object is an intrinsically good act; and act that is inherently ordered toward an evil moral object is an intrinsically evil act.

Every knowingly chosen act has an inherent moral nature, independent of intention and circumstance, and that nature is determined by the moral object, which is the end toward which the act itself is inherently ordered. The moral nature of an act is not defined by the attainment of that end, but by the inherent ordering of the act toward that end, its moral object. An act has a particular moral object because that act, by its very nature, is directed toward that moral object; this inherent ordering constitutes the moral meaning (or moral nature, or moral 'species') of the act. The knowingly chosen acts of human persons are never without a moral meaning before God, who is the eternal moral law. The moral object determines the moral meaning of the act before the eyes of God. Therefore, all knowingly chosen acts have a moral object. Each and every good moral object is capable of being ordered toward God as our final end. Each and every evil moral object is incapable of being ordered toward God as our final end.

Even if an act does not attain the moral object (the 'proximate end') toward which it is directed, the inherent moral nature of the act remains the same, because the act remains inherently ordered toward that same moral object, and remains either capable or incapable of being ordered toward God as our ultimate end. It is this inherent ordering of the act toward its moral object that makes the nature of the act good or evil. When an act is intrinsically ordered toward an evil moral object, the act is intrinsically evil. When an act is intrinsically ordered toward a good moral object, that act is intrinsically good. (Although even when an act is 'intrinsically good,' all three fonts of morality must be good for the overall act to be moral.) Although in one sense an act might be said to be incomplete if it does not attain its moral object, this incompleteness has no effect on the inherent ordering of the act toward that moral object. Therefore, an act that is incomplete, in the sense that the moral object is not attained, has the same moral meaning under the second font as if the moral object had been attained.

.398.
THIRD FONT: The third font is the circumstances pertaining to the morality of the chosen act, especially the anticipated good and bad consequences. The past and present circumstances inform us as to the likely good and bad consequences.

Incomplete Acts

If we reasonably anticipate that the bad consequences will outweigh the good consequences, then the third font is immoral.

Under the third font, the act is, in some sense, incomplete if some of the good or bad consequences that were anticipated are not achieved. However, the morality of the third font is not based on the actual outcome of the good and bad consequences, but on the reasonable anticipation of those consequences. So if a person chooses a good act, with good intention, but also with the reasonable anticipation that the consequences will do more harm than good, then the person sins. Whenever the bad consequences are reasonably anticipated to outweigh the good consequences, then the third font and the overall act is immoral. It is always immoral to knowingly choose an act that one reasonably anticipates will do more harm than good.

[Romans]
{13:10} The love of neighbor does no harm. Therefore, love is the plenitude of the law.

Even if some or all of the reasonably foreseeable good or bad consequences do not occur, the morality of the third font is unaffected because the moral weight of the third font is based on the reasonable anticipation of good or bad consequences at the time that the act was chosen, not on the subsequent attainment of those consequences. Therefore, even if the act is in some sense incomplete, because some reasonably anticipated good or bad consequences did not occur, the morality of the third font and of the act is unchanged.

As is also true for the first and second fonts, the morality of the third font does not depend on the attainment of the end toward which the font is directed, but on the fact that the font is directed toward that end. And this is true regardless of whether the end is the intended end, the moral object, or the consequences (the end result). Each font is directed toward a type of end. But the morality of each font is not based on the attainment of those ends, but on the very fact that each font is directed toward each type of end. Therefore, the failure to attain any one or more of those ends does not affect the morality of the act at all.

This principle is particularly clear when we consider that, in many circumstances, the good and bad consequences are a matter of likelihood. There is a degree of possibility, not a certainty, that each consequence will occur as an end result of the chosen act. Consider two acts: in one act, the good consequences are unlikely, and the bad consequences are likely; in the other act, the good consequences are likely, and the bad are unlikely. The morality of the third font for each of these two acts is obviously not the same. A reasonable person would choose the act with likely good consequences and unlikely bad consequences, over the act with unlikely good consequences and likely bad consequences. The likelihood that each consequence will occur affects its moral weight (along with the gravity of each consequence). A consequence with a greater likelihood has greater moral weight, and a consequence with a lesser likelihood has a lesser moral weight.

But suppose that a person chooses a good act, with good intention, and the good consequences of that act outweigh the bad consequences, because the good are likely and the bad are unlikely. Such an act is good under all three fonts, and so it is a moral act. But if, by chance, the unlikely bad consequences occur, and the likely good consequences do not occur, the morality of the act has not changed. The morality of the third font is based on the reasonable anticipation of good and bad consequences, not on the later outcome.

.399. Human persons are not all-knowing, and we do not have complete or absolute or certain knowledge of the future. We can reasonably anticipate certain future consequences to our actions, based on our knowledge of the past circumstances and the present situation. And we are morally bound to refrain from acts that we reasonably anticipate will result in more harm than good. But it would be unreasonable for God to expect us to know the exact outcome of every decision, so that the morality of the third font would be based on the actual future outcome, rather than on our limited knowledge at the time of the act. Therefore, even if a knowingly chosen act is in some sense incomplete, because some expected good or bad consequences were not attained or did not occur, the morality of the third font is unchanged.

Examples: (1) A man attempts to murder an innocent person, but fails. Although legally his crime is called attempted murder, under the moral law he has committed the mortal sin of murder. He knowingly chose an act inherently ordered toward the evil moral object of murder (the killing of an innocent human being). Although the act did not achieve its moral object, the act remains intrinsically evil because the inherent moral meaning of the act consists in being ordered toward the moral object, not in achieving the moral object. Therefore, both attempted murder and completed murder are intrinsically evil. The moral object (and the entire second font) is exactly the same for attempted murder as for completed murder. The lack of completion in attempted murder does not change the moral object or the inherent moral meaning at all. Neither does this lack of completion reduce the gravity of the second font at all.

(2) A man attempts to steal from his neighbor's house, but he fails. Under the moral law, his sin is theft, not merely attempted theft. He knowingly chose an act inherently ordered toward the evil moral object of taking what belongs to another. And although the act did not achieve its moral object, the act remains intrinsically evil because the inherent moral meaning of the act is due to its ordering toward the moral object, not to its achievement of the moral object. Therefore, both attempted theft and completed theft are intrinsically evil. The moral object (second font) is the same for attempted theft as for completed theft. The lack of completion in attempted theft does not change the moral object, nor the inherent moral meaning, nor the gravity of the second font, at all.

Human acts do not always attain the moral object toward which they inherently aim. However, the inherent moral meaning of the act itself remains the same, regardless of whether or not that moral object was achieved. This basic principle of morality is no less true for sexual acts. Natural marital relations open to life remains good, even when the moral object of procreation is not obtained, as long as the act is of the type inherently ordered toward procreation. And intrinsically evil sexual acts remain intrinsically evil and always gravely immoral, regardless

Incomplete Acts

of whether or not the intended end is achieved, regardless of whether or not certain consequences occur.

(3) A husband and wife have natural marital relations, while using contraception. Contracepted sexual acts are intrinsically evil because the act itself is inherently ordered toward a moral object deprived of the procreative meaning. If this non-procreative (contracepted) sexual act happens to result in procreation, the act remains intrinsically evil and always gravely immoral. Despite the attainment of procreation, the contracepted sexual act remains inherently directed at a moral object deprived of the procreative meaning. For the attainment of procreation, in this case, was not the result of an act inherently directed to procreation, in the second font, but rather was a consequence in the third font. The third font does not change the moral meaning of the second font.

(4) A husband and wife have natural marital relations open to life, but they are unable to conceive (e.g. due to illness, injury, advanced age). The act of natural marital relations is still inherently ordered toward the moral object of procreation, even though this moral object cannot be attained, and so the act is good. The failure to achieve procreation is a bad consequence in the third font. The chosen act remains inherently ordered toward its good moral object. The third font cannot change the second font. Natural intercourse is inherently directed to the procreation of new life. And so, even when this procreation cannot occur, the natural marital act remains inherently ordered toward its good moral object, and the act remains intrinsically good.

(5) A husband and wife engage in an unnatural sexual act prior to an act of natural marital relations open to life. The unnatural sexual act does not reach sexual climax. The moral object of the unnatural sexual act is deprived of the procreative, unitive, and marital meanings. The intention to use this intrinsically evil act as a means to the good end of natural marital relations does not affect the moral object. And the absence of sexual climax does not restore the procreative, unitive, and marital meanings. The moral object of natural marital relations is not sexual climax, nor sexual pleasure, but the threefold moral object of the procreative, unitive, and marital meanings. Sexual climax and pleasure are consequences in the third font. The absence of climax and pleasure in the third font does not change the inherent moral meaning of an unnatural sexual act in the second font. The presence or absence of certain consequences never changes the moral object or the inherent moral meaning. An unnatural sexual act that is not completed in climax remains intrinsically evil and always gravely immoral.

.400. Certainly, it is the inherent ordering of the act itself toward the moral object that makes the act good or evil, not the attainment of that moral object. If a completed act, that is, an act that attains its intended end, or attains its moral object, or attains certain consequences, is immoral under any one or more fonts, then the same act remains immoral even if the act is not completed by attaining one or more of these ends. Furthermore, any knowingly chosen act that is inherently ordered toward an evil moral object remains intrinsically evil and always immoral, regardless of whether or not the act is completed by the attainment of the moral object, and regardless of intention and consequences.

Incomplete Acts

On the other hand, if an act has a good intended end, and a good moral object, and good consequences, then the same act remains good, even when the act is not completed by attaining one or more of these good ends.

.401. The Three Fonts

All knowingly chosen acts are subject to the moral law. Once an act has been knowingly chosen, it is either morally good or morally evil under the moral law. Each and every knowingly chosen act has three fonts of morality, and each and every knowingly chosen act is moral only if all three fonts are good. All knowingly chosen acts are subject to the moral law, even if the individual fails to achieve his intended end (first font), even if the chosen act fails to achieve its moral object (second font), even if some or all of the reasonably anticipated good or bad consequences are not achieved (third font).

If the intended end is evil, but that end is not achieved, the intention remains evil and the overall act is immoral. It is not the achievement of the intended end that makes the first font immoral, but rather the intention to achieve that end. And the same is true for an immoral intended means. The intention itself makes the first font good or evil, not the success or failure of that intention.

If the moral object is evil, but the moral object is not achieved, the act remains intrinsically evil and the overall act is immoral. It is not the achievement of the moral object that makes the second font immoral, but rather the inherent ordering of the act itself toward that moral object.

If, at the time the act is knowingly chosen, the reasonably anticipated bad consequences outweigh the reasonably anticipated good consequences, the third font is bad and the overall act is immoral, even if those anticipated bad consequences happen not to occur, even if weighty unanticipated good consequences occur instead. It is not the achievement of the consequences that makes the third font moral or immoral, but rather the moral weight of those consequences, as they are reasonably anticipated.

Therefore, if any knowingly chosen act is incomplete, in the sense that the act fails to attain the intended end, or the moral object, or the reasonably anticipated consequences, this same knowingly chosen act remains just as moral or immoral as it would be if the intended end, or the moral object, or the consequences had been attained. All knowingly chosen acts are subject to the moral law, and so each act is either morally good or morally bad, and the person who chose the act is either innocent or guilty of sin. All morally good acts are licit, and therefore can be done without sin. All morally bad acts are illicit, and therefore cannot be done without sin. All knowingly chosen acts are either morally licit or morally illicit, even if the chosen act is in some sense incomplete or partial because the act fails to achieve its intended end, or its moral object, or the reasonably anticipated good or bad consequences.

All knowingly chosen acts are always under the full force of the moral law. Knowingly chosen acts are never devoid of morality, never morally neutral, and never take their morality from other acts. Even when a knowingly chosen act is in some sense incomplete, if that same act, having been completed, would be a sin, then the incomplete act is also a sin, because the same knowing choice was made. Every knowingly chosen immoral act is a sin.

Whenever an individual knowingly chooses an immoral act, he sins; and this sin is morally the same, regardless of whether or not the moral object is fulfilled, because the moral object is inherent to the knowingly chosen act. When an individual knowingly chooses an immoral act, he is necessarily choosing both the act itself and its inherent ordering toward its moral object, because the inherent ordering of an act is inseparable from that act. If the inherent ordering of the act toward its moral object could be separated from the act itself, then intrinsically evil acts would not be always immoral. The reason that intrinsically evil acts are always immoral is that the ordering of an act toward its moral object is intrinsic to, and therefore inseparable from, the act itself. If this ordering toward the moral object could be separated from the act, then acts with an evil moral object would not be intrinsically evil, for the ordering of an act toward its moral object constitutes the essential moral nature of the act. Therefore, whenever an act is chosen, the inherent ordering of the act toward is moral object is also chosen, even if the moral object is never achieved.

Each and every knowingly chosen act must be good, under all three fonts of morality, otherwise the act is sinful. There are no exceptions to the moral law. All knowingly chosen acts, whether complete or in some way incomplete, are subject to the moral law and must be good under all three fonts. If an act is, in some sense, incomplete under any of its fonts, the act nevertheless has all three fonts. A knowingly chosen act never has less than three fonts of morality. Every knowingly chosen act has three and only three fonts of morality.

Even if an act is, in some sense, incomplete, the act is nevertheless morally complete, because the act was knowingly chosen and has three fonts of morality. The incompleteness of an act does not change its intended purpose, nor its inherent ordering toward a moral object, nor its anticipated good and bad consequences. Therefore, the incompleteness of an act, in the sense of its failure to achieve any of the ends in any of the fonts, does not change its morality under those three fonts. If an act is immoral, under one or more of the three fonts, then the same act remains immoral even if the act does not obtain the end intended by the person, or the moral object toward which the act is inherently ordered, or any of the reasonably anticipated good or bad consequences.

.402. Incomplete Sexual Acts

The basic principles of morality are no different for sexual acts than for other types of acts. Sexual acts are not an exception to the eternal moral law, such that any knowingly chosen sexual act would be exempt from the moral law, or would be evaluated under a different set of basic principles, or would be moral despite one or more bad fonts of morality. Many persons speak and act as if the moral law did not apply, or did not apply in the same way, to sexuality. Such is not the case. The universality of the eternal moral law means that the same basic principles of ethics apply in all areas of human life, including sexuality.

Incomplete Acts

Incomplete acts, acts in which either the intended purpose, or the moral object, or any good or bad anticipated consequences, are not achieved, have the same moral value as the same act which is completed by achieving its intended purpose, or moral object, or anticipated consequences. The failure to attain an immoral intention does not cause the intention to become moral. The failure to attain an evil moral object does not cause the inherent ordering of that act toward that evil moral object to become moral. The failure to attain some or all of the reasonably anticipated consequences does not change the moral weight of those consequences as they were reasonably anticipated at the time that the act was knowingly chosen.

The moral object of natural marital relations is a threefold meaning that is unitive, procreative, marital. The moral object of sexual relations is not sexual climax, which is a consequence in the third font. The moral object of sexual relations is not the intention of the persons involved, which is in the first font. Even if a husband and wife fail to achieve a good intended end, such as to conceive a child or to give one another pleasure, the morality of the sexual act, under all three fonts, does not change. Even if the husband and wife fail to achieve an anticipated consequence of sexual relations, such as sexual climax, or pregnancy, the morality of the sexual act, under all three fonts, does not change. Even if a husband and wife have the best of intentions (first font), and even if they judge that the good consequences outweigh the bad (third font), each and every sexual act must be unitive, procreative, and marital in order to be moral under the second font.

If an unnatural sexual act is in some sense incomplete, because it does not achieve sexual climax, the act has the same moral value as when it is completed in sexual climax. The failure to attain a particular consequence (sexual climax) in the third font does not change the moral object in the second font. All unnatural sexual acts, whether consummated or non-consummated, are intrinsically evil and always gravely immoral, due to the deprivation of the required threefold good in the moral object.

Therefore, a husband and wife are not justified in using unnatural sexual acts as a type of foreplay, even if the unnatural sexual act does not reach sexual climax. The moral object of every unnatural sexual act remains the same, regardless of whether or not the act is completed in climax. Each and every marital act must have both the unitive and procreative meanings. Unnatural sexual acts by definition are not procreative. And these acts are neither truly unitive, nor truly marital, in the eyes of God. Therefore, all unnatural sexual acts are intrinsically evil, and always gravely immoral, and are not justified by being used as a type of foreplay, regardless of whether or not sexual climax occurs.

For each and every sexual act, including natural marital relations open to life as well as all intrinsically evil sexual acts, the moral object (good or evil) remains the same, regardless of whether or not the sexual act is completed in sexual climax, regardless of the attainment or failure to attain the intended end or any reasonably anticipated consequences. Intrinsically evil acts are always immoral and can never be justified by intention, nor by circumstances, nor by the fonts of

Incomplete Acts

other acts. Intrinsically evil sexual acts are not an exception to the teaching of the Church that intrinsically evil acts are always immoral. Failure to attain a particular intended end, or the moral object, or particular consequences does not change an intrinsically evil act into a good act.

If a wife does not achieve sexual climax during natural marital relations, this failure to achieve a consequence in the third font of one sexual act does not justify the choice of an unnatural sexual act to seek and attain that same consequence. Each act has its own fonts, and therefore its own moral object. An unnatural sexual act, which is intrinsically evil due to its lack of the unitive, procreative, and marital meanings, does not become justified in order to obtain a good intended end or a good consequence, which a different act, a moral act of natural marital relations, failed to attain.

Under the third font, a completed act, such as murder, would seem to have more bad consequences than an incomplete act, such as attempted murder. However, the moral weight of the consequences of any knowingly chosen act is entirely due to those consequences that are reasonably anticipated, and not to those consequences that actually occur (after the knowing choice). The person who chooses the intrinsically evil act of murder reasonably anticipates severe harm in the third font, as a result of the death. Even if the harm happens not to occur because the attempted murder fails, he is nevertheless guilty of choosing an act with this same anticipated severe harm. The same is true for lying under oath, theft, adultery, unnatural sexual acts, and all other immoral acts (whether intrinsically evil or not). The third font is not the good and bad consequences that actually occur, but only the reasonably foreseen good and bad consequences. The morality of any knowingly chosen act, good or evil, does not change when the intended purpose, or the moral object, or any good or bad anticipated consequences, are not achieved.

.403. Examples: (1) On a particular occasion, a husband and wife intended to conceive a child, by natural marital relations open to life, with the good consequences of starting a family. Even if the intended end, the conception of a child, does not occur, the intention remains good. Even if the couple later discover that they are infertile, and so the moral object of procreation cannot be attained, the act of natural marital relations remains inherently ordered toward its good moral object. Even if the husband and wife begin natural marital relations, but are interrupted, so that the sexual act does not achieve the anticipated consequence of sexual climax, the third font and the act remain good.

(2) An act of pre-marital sex between a young man and young woman remains intrinsically evil and always gravely immoral, even if neither person achieves sexual climax. For the moral object of sexual acts is not determined by the presence or absence of sexual climax, nor of any other consequences in the third font, nor of any intention in the first font. Pre-marital sexual relations is intrinsically evil, regardless of whether or not sexual climax is achieved, because the act itself is inherently non-marital; it is ordered toward a moral object deprived of the marital meaning. Even when the consequence of sexual climax is

not achieved (in the third font), the act remains inherently ordered toward an evil moral object (in the second font), and so the act remains immoral.

Whenever any moral object lacks a good required by the moral law, that moral object is evil. Each and every sexual act is required by the eternal moral law to be unitive and procreative and marital. Each and every sexual act must be inherently unitive, inherently procreative, inherently marital. Each and every sexual act that lacks any of these three meanings is a gravely immoral and intrinsically evil sexual act, regardless of whether or not sexual climax occurs, regardless of whether or not another act, one that is prior or concurrent or subsequent, is moral. Each and every knowingly chosen act stands on its own as to its morality.

(3) An unnatural sexual act between a man and a women remains intrinsically evil and always gravely immoral, even if the man and woman are married, even if the unnatural sexual act occurs before, during, or after an act of natural marital relations, even if the unnatural sexual act does not result in sexual climax. Each and every unnatural sexual act is intrinsically evil because this type of sexual act is inherently non-procreative, inherently non-unitive (despite some mere physical union), and inherently non-marital (since the act is contrary to the will of God for marriage and for married persons). The lack of sexual climax does not cause the act to become moral.

God is equally offended by any sinful act, regardless of whether or not the act is completed, because none of the three fonts of morality are affected by the failure to obtain what was intended, or by the failure of the act itself to achieve the moral object toward which it is inherently ordered, or by the failure to achieve a good or bad consequence. The intention, the essential moral nature of the act itself, and the reasonably anticipated consequences at the time that the knowing choice was made, are all unaffected by the subsequent outcome as to whether or not the intention, the moral object, or the consequences were attained. Therefore, the morality of any knowingly chosen act remains the same, even if the act is, in some sense, incomplete under any of the three fonts.

Chapter 28
Cooperation with Evil

.404.
[2 Corinthians]
{6:14} Do not choose to bear the yoke with unbelievers. For how can justice be a participant with iniquity? Or how can the fellowship of light be a participant with darkness?
{6:15} And how can Christ join together with Belial? Or what part do the faithful have with the unfaithful?
{6:16} And what consensus does the temple of God have with idols? For you are the temple of the living God, just as God says: "I will dwell with them, and I will walk among them. And I will be their God, and they shall be my people.
{6:17} Because of this, you must depart from their midst and be separate, says the Lord. And do not touch what is unclean.
{6:18} Then I will accept you. And I will be a Father to you, and you shall be sons and daughters to me, says the Lord Almighty."

In some ways, we Christians must be separate from the world. We are called to live in imitation of Christ, not in imitation of worldly society. We must not imitate the unfaithful, nor behave as if we were in the dark about good and evil. No worship of God is true worship unless it is accompanied by a love of good and a hatred of evil.

Yet most faithful Christians are not called to be entirely separate from the world, not called to live in a strict cloister, not called to be a hermit in the desert. Instead, we are called to live among the unfaithful in a sinful world, in order to begin to transform the world to become more pleasing to God. And so, most Christians live and work in societies of various kinds, such as nations, states, cities, towns, neighborhoods, extended families, schools, businesses, etc. And though our fellow human beings in these societies are sometimes also fellow Catholics, they are always fellow sinners.

We are sinners living among other sinners, and so it is inevitable that we will have to make choices that are related to the sinful choices of other persons. Our knowingly chosen acts often have some relationship to the sinful acts of other persons. Moral theology uses the term 'cooperation with evil' when considering whether or not we sin, if our knowingly chosen acts are related to the sins of other persons. Cooperation with evil refers to any situation in which one person is sinning, and a second person must decide whether or not to commit a related act. Despite the term 'cooperation with evil,' our acts are not always sinful merely by being related to the sins of other persons. If that were so, then nearly all acts would be sins, for we live as members of one human family, in one world, and all our acts are in some way at least distantly related to the acts, even the sinful acts, of other persons. So it is true that sometimes we act without sin, even though our act is related to the sin of another person.

It is absolutely certain, with no exceptions whatsoever, that the morality of each and every knowingly chosen act depends solely on the three fonts of morality.

Therefore, just as the principle of double effect is merely the application of the three fonts to a particular class of acts, so also the principle of cooperation with evil is merely the application of the three fonts to a particular class of acts. This principle concerns a class of acts in which one person is considering committing an act that is related to the sinful act of another person. When in doubt about these principles and their application, merely applying the three fonts of morality properly will result in a correct determination as to whether or not the proposed act is sinful. These principles of cooperation with evil are designed to assist in the application of the three fonts, but they in no way alter the three fonts. All of the basic principles of morality still apply in cases of cooperation with evil, in cases of the principle of double effect, and in all cases whatsoever.

.405. Persons versus Acts

As Christians, we are called to judge acts, but not persons. We should not judge the person, neither so as to condemn, nor so as to exonerate. The judgment of each person, and of each person's life, is reserved to the particular judgment and the general judgment. However, we can, should, and must judge acts. Otherwise, we could neither live a moral life ourselves, nor assist others in living a moral life. Our salvation and the salvation of others would be lost if we could not judge acts, as to whether they are good or evil.

[Matthew 7]
{7:1} "Do not judge, so that you may not be judged.
{7:2} For with whatever judgment you judge, so shall you be judged; and with whatever measure you measure out, so shall it be measured back to you.
{7:3} And how can you see the splinter in your brother's eye, and not see the board in your own eye?
{7:4} Or how can you say to your brother, 'Let me take the splinter from your eye,' while, behold, a board is in your own eye?
{7:5} Hypocrite, first remove the board from your own eye, and then you will see clearly enough to remove the splinter from your brother's eye."

Christ taught that we should not judge persons: "Do not judge, so that you may not be judged." But He also taught that we must judge acts, even the acts of other persons. Otherwise, we would be unable to remove a 'board' (a mortal sin) from our own lives, and unable to remove a 'splinter' (a venial sin) from the lives of others.

[Luke]
{6:37} Do not judge, and you will not be judged. Do not condemn, and you will not be condemned. Forgive, and you will be forgiven.
...
{12:57} And why do you not, even among yourselves, judge what is just?

Christ teaches that we should not judge or condemn persons. However, in order to forgive, we must first recognize that a sinful act has occurred. And in order to judge what is just, we must judge whether an act is moral or immoral. So again, we should not judge persons, but we must judge acts.

This teaching has an implication for cooperation with evil. The mere fact that you are cooperating with a person who is a sinner does not constitute cooperation with evil. Only cooperation with an act, with whatever is evil in that act, falls under the principle of cooperation with evil. If you knowingly choose a good act, and if that act cooperates with the good act of another person, but someone guilty of serious sin, you are not cooperating with evil. For example, a priest might visit, teach, counsel, and otherwise act with kindness toward prisoners who have been convicted of serious crimes. These acts are good under all three fonts, and so they are moral. The mere fact that these acts pertain to persons who have committed serious sins does not cause the acts to fall under cooperation with evil. If you are not cooperating with whatever is evil in an act, you are not cooperating with evil.

Therefore, cooperation is based on the act of the other person, not on the person himself. Cooperation with moral evil is cooperation with sinful acts, not with sinful persons. Cooperation with a sinner, in acts that are entirely moral, is not cooperation with evil.

The same distinction applies to groups of persons. If a group is involved in committing some immoral acts, you are cooperating with evil if your act cooperates with the sinful acts of that group. But you would not be cooperating with evil by committing an act that is merely related to the group. For example, a town government provides services to all persons and groups in the town (trash collection, water, sewage, police protection, ambulance service). The town is not cooperating with evil by providing these general services to all persons and groups in the town. The decision of the town's leaders to provide these services without distinction to everyone does not fall under any type of cooperation with evil. These acts provide assistance to the persons in that town, but they do not provide assistance to the sins of those persons.

On the other hand, suppose that a power company finds out that some persons are using the power that they supply in order to grow plants (indoors) for use in making illegal drugs. The decision to continue to provide power is related to the sinful act. The persons who run the power company would be morally obligated not to provide this material cooperation with an immoral act. In this case, the act is cooperation with evil because it is an act that cooperates with a sinful act, not because it is an act that cooperates with a sinful person or a sinful group.

A group of persons who are known to have committed serious sins enter a restaurant in order to have dinner together. The owner of the restaurant is not committing any type of cooperation with evil by providing them with dinner. He is not cooperating with any sinful act. For cooperation with evil is always and only cooperation with whatever is evil in an act, not merely cooperation with persons or groups known to have committed immoral acts.

.406. Perpetration

Before we consider acts that cooperate with the sin of another person, we must distinguish cooperation from perpetration. If your act, in terms of morality, is essentially the same as the sin of another person, you are not cooperating with

Cooperation with Evil

that sin, you are committing that same sin. Cooperation occurs when your chosen act is a different but related act as compared to the sin of the other person. To commit the same sinful act, even in a somewhat different manner, is not cooperation, but perpetration. In such a case, you are not a cooperator, but a fellow perpetrator, a co-perpetrator, of that sin.

Germaine Grisez: "Formal cooperation usually is distinguished from the full involvement of two or more people in the same wrongful action -- for example, a couple's joining in fornication or a gang's collaboration in robbing a bank. So, cooperator is used to refer to someone involved in another's wrongdoing by an act more or less distinct from it."[453]

Pope John Paul II: "To concur with the intention of another person to commit suicide and to help in carrying it out through so-called 'assisted suicide' means to cooperate in, and at times to be the actual perpetrator of, an injustice which can never be excused, even if it is requested."[454]

Suppose that two persons work together so that one of them may commit suicide. They commit a series of acts, and these acts generally have the same intention, the same moral object (the death of an innocent person), and the same bad consequences. The man who commits suicide, and the man who works with him toward that same evil moral object, are committing the same type of sin. This is an example of perpetration, not cooperation. They are both guilty of murder.

Even if these two men have somewhat different intentions, the evil moral object of their acts is the same. Even though the circumstances are somewhat different, in that one man is suffering, and the other man is not suffering, the moral object of their acts has the same deprivation: the loss of life of an innocent human person. Despite some difference in intention and circumstance, the one who is committing 'assisted suicide' and the one who is committing suicide are often perpetrators of the same moral species of sin. And this is why Pope John Paul II teaches that sometimes assisted suicide is not cooperation, but perpetration.

However, it is also possible that the person who assists in the suicide is a cooperator, not a perpetrator. Suppose that a man is suffering and wishes to commit suicide. His physician is unwilling to commit 'physician assisted suicide;' he does not want his patient to commit suicide. But knowing that his patient is suffering and wishes to die, he changes the man's medication. He chooses a medication that more easily and more promptly results in death by overdose, with little suffering. He lets the patient know of this fact. He also discourages the patient from committing suicide, and offers to work with him to manage his pain. In this example, the physician is cooperating with the moral evil of suicide, but he is not perpetrating that same sin. His sin is classified as formal cooperation. His sin is intrinsically evil and always gravely immoral, but it is a sin of cooperation; it is not the perpetration of the same sin as the patient.

---

[453] Germaine Grisez, The Way of the Lord Jesus, Difficult Moral Questions, Appendix 2.
[454] Pope John Paul II, Evangelium Vitae, n. 66; inner quote from Augustine, Epistulae, Corpus Scriptorum Ecclesiasticorum Latinorum, vol. 57, n. 320.

His knowingly chosen act cooperates with the sinful act of his patient, without perpetrating that same act.

.407. Perpetration can occur by any of the three fonts of morality. If two persons sin by having the same immoral intention, then they are each perpetrators of an act that is sinful due to an intention in the first font. If two persons sin by committing acts with the same evil moral object, then they are each perpetrators of the same species of act, one that is sinful due to the moral object in the second font. If two persons sin by committing acts with the same bad consequences, then they are each perpetrators of an act that is sinful due to the consequences in the third font. Perpetration can also occur with acts that are sinful due to two or three bad fonts. If two persons are committing the same sin, then they are each perpetrators, not cooperators. Although, in the secular sense of the word, they may be 'cooperating' (working together) to commit these sins, this is not the meaning of the theological term 'cooperation with evil.'

Examples: (1) Four men decide to work together to commit a crime. They drive to a bank; three of the men enter the bank and rob it. The fourth man does not enter the bank at all; he merely drives the other three men to and from the bank. The driver knowingly chose to perpetrate the sin of bank robbery; his knowingly chosen act was deliberate and morally direct. The moral object of his act was the same as the moral object of the other three men, to rob a bank. Therefore, all four men committed the same intrinsically evil act of bank robbery. The driver is not guilty of cooperation, but of perpetration.

(2) Suppose that the three men who enter and rob the bank also commit murder of the bank guard. Morally, the driver is guilty of bank robbery, since he knowingly chose an act with that moral object. Is he morally guilty of murder? If the four robbers planned to kill the bank guard, or even if they planned to kill him as a contingency ("If such and such happens, then we will kill the bank guard."), then all four are guilty of murder under the moral law. But if they did not plan to kill anyone, then only the person or persons who committed the murder are guilty of that sin. Every intrinsically evil act is intentionally chosen. If the driver did not intentionally choose murder, but only robbery, then he is only guilty of the sin that he intentionally chose.

(3) A young woman is pregnant and is considering procuring an abortion. She informs the father of the child, and together they decide what to do. If they both decide to abort the child, then they are both guilty of the sin of abortion. Even if the father does not take her to the abortion clinic, does not pay for the abortion, and does not sign any paperwork, he is still guilty of the sin of abortion itself, not merely of cooperation. With the mother, he was in a position to decide whether or not the abortion occurred. He shared responsibility for that decision with the mother of the child, and although he had no further involvement in the abortion, his act of deciding on abortion is morally-direct and deliberate, and its moral object is the death of an innocent human person. The mother is also guilty of abortion, even though she does not perform the abortion on herself, but merely authorizes someone else to perform the abortion. This man and woman have each committed the same type of act, with the same moral object, the direct and

voluntary killing of an innocent human person. So they are each perpetrators of an intrinsically evil and gravely immoral act, not merely cooperators.

However, suppose in the same situation that the mother of the child informs the father, but does not allow him to participate in the decision of abortion. If he has no ability to cause the abortion to occur by making the decision with the mother, then he is not a perpetrator. However, he would be a formal cooperator in the sin of abortion if he advises or encourages her to commit this sin, or even if he merely approves of her decision to obtain an abortion.

(4) Abortion is broadly illegal in a particular city or state or nation. A group of legislators vote a bill into law which makes abortion broadly legal. These legislators are not merely cooperating in the subsequent sins of abortion that will occur; they are committing the sin of procuring many abortions. For like the mother and father of the prenatal child in the previous example, they authorize someone else to perform abortion. The moral object of their act of voting is the deprivation of life from innocent human persons.

Even if, after passing the law, no one actually obtains an abortion, because the law is vetoed and never takes effect, the legislators are nevertheless guilty of the sin of many abortions. For the second font is not determined by the attainment of the moral object, but by the inherent ordering of the chosen act toward that moral object. The legislators deliberately chose an act, the passing of a law legalizing abortion, which was inherently directed at the deaths of many innocent human persons. The act of voting for such a law is not merely cooperation with evil, but the intrinsically evil and gravely immoral sin itself of procuring many abortions. In such cases, the legislators are perpetrators of abortion, not merely cooperators. For they had the ability to decide whether or not the abortions occurred.

.408. Cooperation: the Usual Approach

The usual approach is to divide cooperation with evil into formal and material cooperation. Formal cooperation occurs when your act participates in the sin itself of the other person. Material cooperation occurs when your act participates in the circumstances of the sin of the other person. Formal cooperation is then divided into explicit and implicit. Explicit formal cooperation occurs when you share the same sinful intention as the other sinner. Implicit formal cooperation occurs when you do not share his sinful intention. Material cooperation is divided into immediate material cooperation and mediate material cooperation. Immediate material cooperation occurs when you participate in circumstances essential to the commission of the other sin. Mediate material cooperation occurs when you participate in circumstances that are not essential to the commission of the other sin. This is the usual approach to cooperation. (In addition, there are numerous disputed points on cooperation among theologians. This summary states only what is generally common on the topic.)

But the usual approach has a number of problems and failings, which at times results in an incorrect determination as to which acts are moral and which are immoral. The solution to these problems is to base the distinctions used in the principle of cooperation with evil on the three fonts of morality. This results in more precise conclusions as to which acts are moral and which are immoral, greater clarity as to why any cooperative act is moral or immoral, and greater surety. The use of the three fonts of morality to analyze cooperation with evil also resolves numerous disputed points on the topic.

The usual approach places too much emphasis on the distinction between immediate material cooperation and mediate material cooperation. Some sources even claim that immediate material cooperation is always immoral, or that immediate material cooperation with an intrinsically evil act is always immoral, or that immediate material cooperation with a gravely immoral act is always immoral, (or even that immediate material cooperation is the same as implicit formal cooperation). But as will be shown below, the Magisterium does not teach that immediate material cooperation, in any form, is always immoral. Immediate material cooperation is more likely to be immoral, especially when the sin of the other person is grave, but it is not always or necessarily immoral.

The usual approach only applies the distinction of explicit versus implicit cooperation to formal cooperation, not also to material cooperation. But it is obvious that the first font of intention may be immoral in any knowingly chosen act, regardless of whether the act is classified as formal or material cooperation. Therefore, the distinction as to whether an act of cooperation is explicit or implicit should be applied to both formal and material cooperation.

.409. The Three Fonts Approach

When the principle of cooperation with evil is analyzed and understood in terms of the three fonts of morality, the distinctions and conclusions are in complete accord with all of the other basic principles of morality. The three fonts are the sole determinant of the morality of each and every knowingly chosen act. And so it is necessary to apply these fonts to acts of cooperation as well. But when we do so, certain errors and insufficiencies in the usual approach become clear, and are promptly corrected. Also, as the section below on Cooperation in Magisterial Documents demonstrates, the three fonts approach is in complete accord with magisterial teaching on cooperation.

.410. Explicit Cooperation

Explicit cooperation refers to the sinful intention to cooperate with something that is evil in the act of the other person. Now any bad intention by itself causes any act to be a sin, even if the other two fonts are good. However, a bad intention by itself cannot cause an act to be a type of cooperation with evil. Each and every knowingly chosen act has all three fonts. So if an intention is explicit cooperation with evil, it is necessarily accompanied by the other two fonts. If one person sins, and you intend to cooperate with that sin, the intention must be accompanied by the other two fonts, the chosen act itself and its consequences. And so your intention also includes at least an interior act, such as approving in your heart of the other person's sin. The result is that the chosen act itself, or the consequences of the chosen act, are part of the explicit cooperation. Therefore, intention does not stand on its own as a type of cooperation.

Suppose that you commit an exterior act with a good moral object and only good consequences (the second and third fonts are good). If your intention is to somehow cooperate with the sin of another person, the chosen act and its consequences are not ordered to that end. The intention is sinful, but there is no cooperation in that particular exterior act. Thus, explicit cooperation does not stand on its own as a type of cooperation. It cannot be the case that the act and the consequences are good, but the intention is a type of cooperation with evil. However, if you intend to cooperate with the sin of another person, you also have chosen an interior act that is sinful cooperation, regardless of the exterior act. You have chosen the act of consenting interiorly to the sin of the other person. Explicit cooperation is always also either formal cooperation, or material cooperation.

If another person sins by an immoral intention, and if you have the same sinful intention, you are perpetrating that same sin. But an act of cooperation is always a different act from the sin of the other person. If the act is the same, then it is merely another example of the same type of sin. This type of act is perpetration, not cooperation. Similarly, if another person sins by an immoral intention, and if you have a different but still sinful intention, you are perpetrating a different sin. But without some type of cooperation under the second or third fonts, the intention by itself may be a sin, but it is not cooperation.

Now suppose that another person sins solely by an immoral intention in the first font, but with a good moral object in the second font, and good consequences in the third font. As is always true, if your act is good under all three fonts, you are not sinning. If you cooperate in that good act of the second font, or if you cooperate in the good circumstances of the third font, with good intention, then you are not sinning. The immoral intention of the other person is his own sin, not your sin. Saint Paul the Apostle encountered this type of situation.

[Philippians]
{1:14} And many from among the brothers in the Lord, becoming confident through my chains, are now much bolder in speaking the Word of God without fear.
{1:15} Certainly, some do so even because of envy and contention; and others, too, do so because of a good will to preach Christ.
{1:16} Some act out of charity, knowing that I have been appointed for the defense of the Gospel.
{1:17} But others, out of contention, announce Christ insincerely, claiming that their difficulties lift them up to my chains.
{1:18} But what does it matter? As long as, by every means, whether under pretext or in truthfulness, Christ is announced. And about this, I rejoice, and moreover, I will continue to rejoice.

Some of Paul's fellow preachers of the Gospel were committing the good act of preaching, with the good consequence that Christ was announced, but with the bad intention of self-exaltation. They were sinning, but their sin did not affect the good acts of Saint Paul in preaching the Gospel with good intent. His acts were not a type of cooperation with evil because he was cooperating only with the good acts of preaching and the good consequences. In other words, he was only cooperating with what was good in their acts. He was not cooperating with the sinful intention of those self-exalting preachers.

In a different case involving intention, suppose that you intend that someone else should sin as a means to accomplish your intended end. Even if your intended end is good, your intended means is immoral. Physical evil can be tolerated in the intended means, to a limited extent, but moral evil cannot be tolerated in the intended means to any extent. Whatever is immoral must be entirely unintended. Anyone who intends immorality, sins against God. And this is true even if the sinful act of another person is the intended means. Your intention remains immoral, even if you do not commit any sinful exterior act, but instead you intend to make use of the sinful act of another person as an immoral means to your own good end.

Suppose that another person is sinning by an intrinsically evil act; the second font of his act has an evil moral object. Regardless of the other two fonts, he is committing an objective sin. If you intend to assist the other person to attain his moral object, your intention is immoral. You are sinning by explicit formal cooperation. And this is true regardless of whether or not the other person realizes that his chosen act is intrinsically evil, and regardless of his intention.

Now suppose that the other person is committing a good act, with good intention, but with bad consequences that outweigh any good consequences. If you intend to assist the other person to attain those bad consequences, then you are sinning by explicit material cooperation. Even if the act of the other person is good under all three fonts, including a good intention, but with some lesser bad consequences in the third font, you are sinning by explicit material cooperation if you intend those bad consequences as an end. It is always immoral to intend any type of bad consequence (harm or disorder) as an end. Explicit cooperation does not depend on the sinful intention of the other person, but on your sinful intention to cooperate with whatever is evil in the act of the other person.

In summary, a person can sin by a bad intention alone (first font), but a person cannot commit a sin of cooperation with evil by intention alone. At least one of the other two fonts must be involved in any explicit cooperation with evil. Therefore, explicit cooperation with evil is always also either formal cooperation (second font), or material cooperation (third font). Explicit cooperation with evil never stands on its own. An immoral intention by itself is a sin, but the intention does not cooperate with the sin of another person unless the second or third font is related to the sin of that person.

Explicit cooperation pertains to the first font. Formal cooperation pertains to the second font. Material cooperation pertains to the third font. Explicit formal cooperation is a sin under the first and second fonts. Explicit material cooperation is a sin under the first and third fonts, if the material cooperation by itself is objectively a sin. Explicit material cooperation is a sin only under the first font, if the material cooperation by itself is objectively moral.

.411. Implicit Cooperation

Implicit cooperation refers to any type of cooperation with evil in which the cooperator does not intend to assist the other person in whatever is evil in his act. All knowingly chosen acts have an intention. The intention in cases of implicit cooperation might be moral or immoral, but it is not the particular immoral intention to cooperate with whatever is evil in the act of another person. Since implicit cooperation occurs when a cooperative intention is absent, it should be obvious that implicit cooperation cannot occur apart from some aspect of the other two fonts that would constitute cooperation, either formal or material.

The mere absence of a particular immoral intention by itself is not a cooperation with evil. The absence of all immoral intentions is required of all human persons by the eternal moral law. Therefore, implicit cooperation only exists as either implicit formal cooperation or implicit material cooperation. When a person is objectively cooperating, under the second font, with another person's act, but without the intention to assist in attaining the evil moral object, then the cooperation is implicit formal cooperation. When a person is objectively cooperating, under the third font, with another person's act, but without the intention to assist in attaining the bad consequences, then the cooperation is implicit material cooperation.

.412. Explicit versus Implicit Cooperation

It is always true that a single bad font is sufficient to cause the overall act to be immoral. However, if an act is immoral under the second or third fonts, the addition of an immoral intention always makes the act a more serious sin. So an act that is a venial sin, due to the second or third font, becomes at least a more serious venial sin, or perhaps even a mortal sin, if the intention is also immoral. Similarly, an act that is a mortal sin, due to the second or third font, becomes a more serious mortal sin, if the intention is also immoral.

Therefore, if a person sins by either formal cooperation or material cooperation, the act becomes a more serious sin (either venial or mortal) if the cooperation is also explicit. For explicit cooperation implies that the person has an immoral intention, specifically, to cooperate with what is evil in the act of another person. So for the same cooperative act, explicit formal cooperation is always more sinful than implicit formal cooperation, and explicit material cooperation is always more sinful than implicit material cooperation. But this applies only when comparing two sins that are the same except for the intention. The addition of an immoral intention always makes a sin more offensive to God.

.413. Formal Cooperation

Pope John Paul II: "To refuse to take part in committing an injustice is not only a moral duty; it is also a basic human right."[455]

Formal cooperation is usually distinguished from material cooperation by saying that formal cooperation participates in the sin itself of the other person, whereas

---

[455] Pope John Paul II, Evangelium Vitae, n. 74.

material cooperation participates in the circumstances of the other person's sin. This correct distinction becomes clearer, and more easily applied to particular cases, if we view the same distinction in terms of the three fonts of morality. Formal cooperation pertains to the second font, the act itself with its moral object. Material cooperation pertains to the third font, the circumstances, especially the consequences.

Formal cooperation, by definition, is always cooperation with an intrinsically evil act. Formal cooperation is distinct from perpetration, though both types of acts are intrinsically evil (second font). If your act has the same evil moral object as the intrinsically evil act of another person, then you are both committing the same type of act; you are each committing an act with the same inherent moral meaning (essential moral nature). In such a case, you are not cooperating with the sin of the other person, you are perpetrating that same sin. For the essential moral nature of any act is entirely determined by its moral object. So even if your act seems, to all appearances, to be a different type of act, it is morally the same type of act if it has the same moral object.

Your act is formal cooperation, not perpetration, only when your act has the moral object of assisting the other person in attaining the moral object of his intrinsically evil act. Formal cooperation is always intrinsically evil because it has the evil moral object of assisting another person in attaining his evil moral object. In formal cooperation, the cooperative act is related to the evil moral object of the other person indirectly, by assisting the chosen act of the other person to attain that moral object. But if your chosen act has the same evil moral object as the act of another person, then your act is related to that moral object directly; you have made that moral object your own by choosing an act directly related (inherently ordered) to that same evil moral object. In this case, you are a perpetrator of the intrinsically evil act, not merely a cooperator.

Suppose that another person is committing an intrinsically evil act; such acts are inherently ordered toward an evil moral object. The relationship between any intrinsically evil act and its moral object is direct. If you are committing an act that is directly related to that same evil moral object, then you are committing essentially the same type of sin; this is perpetration, not cooperation. The direct relationship of your act to the same evil moral object found in the other person's act makes your act perpetration, not cooperation.

Only when your chosen act is indirectly related to the evil moral object of the sin of the other person are you a cooperator, not a perpetrator. When the sin of the other person is an intrinsically evil act (having an evil moral object), your act is formal cooperation if it has the moral object of assisting the other person in attaining that evil moral object. An act of formal cooperation assists, in a way that is morally direct (but may be physically indirect), the other person in committing the sinful act itself. All acts of formal cooperation are intrinsically evil, and all acts of formal cooperation have an evil moral object (to which the cooperative act is directly related). But the moral object of a cooperative act is not the same as the moral object of the other person's act. Your act is perpetration if your act is directed, not at the moral object of assisting the other person in his act, but at the very same evil moral object that his act also seeks to attain.

Suppose that another person commits an intrinsically evil act. Your act is perpetration if your act is directly related to that same moral object. You have made his intrinsically evil act your own by choosing an act, even a very different act, that has the same moral object. But your act is formal cooperation, not perpetration, if your act has the evil moral object of assisting his act in attaining his evil moral object. In such a case, your act is indirectly related to his moral object, through your cooperation with his intrinsically evil act. So the distinction between perpetration and formal cooperation is based on whether your act is related to his evil moral object directly or indirectly.

.414. Every act of formal cooperation is always intrinsically evil and therefore always immoral. Explicit formal cooperation adds an immoral intention, making the act even more sinful. And there is nothing to prevent the third font of circumstances from being also sinful. If an act of explicit formal cooperation also has a bad third font, then the act is sinful under all three fonts. Formal cooperation is always an objectively immoral act, but the same act becomes more sinful if the first font of intention is bad; and this can occur in two ways. Explicit formal cooperation occurs when the bad intention is specifically to assist the act of the other person in attaining its moral object. But an act of implicit formal cooperation, which lacks that particular bad intention, might have a different bad intention, so that the first font would still be immoral. Any immoral intention that accompanies an act of formal cooperation makes the act more sinful.

The same is true for formal cooperation and the third font. The addition of a bad third font (when the bad consequences outweigh the good consequences) makes any intrinsically evil act even more sinful. And the third font can be bad in either of two ways: either by a sin that is material cooperation, or by a sin that is not material cooperation. Nothing prevents a sin of cooperation from being also a sin apart from cooperation. One act can be sinful for more than one reason.

Sinful cooperation can occur by the second font, or by the third font, or by both together. A single knowingly chosen act can be both formal cooperation and material cooperation. And each type of cooperation can be explicit or implicit. A person might intend the formal cooperation, but not the material cooperation, or vice versa, or both. In any case, the addition of another bad font always makes an act a more serious sin. For example, lying is an intrinsically evil act, immoral under the second font. The addition of a bad intention makes the lie a more serious sin; the addition of bad consequences that outweigh any good consequences makes the act a more serious sin. The act of lying might still be venial, but it is a more serious venial sin if the first or third fonts are also bad.

All acts of formal cooperation are intrinsically evil acts. And since they take as their moral object the intrinsically evil act of another person, if that act is an objective mortal sin, then the act of formal cooperation is a mortal sin. The act of the other person is gravely immoral due to its moral object. The cooperative act is gravely immoral because it assists the act of the other person in attaining its gravely immoral object. But even if that evil moral object is never attained, both the act of the other person and the cooperative act remain intrinsically evil and always gravely immoral. For both acts remain inherently directed at gravely immoral objects.

However, if the act of the other person is intrinsically evil but only venial (e.g. a lie), then the act of formal cooperation is also only venial. For each act takes its morality from that same moral object, the one act directly and the other act indirectly (by assisting the act of the other person). However, the evaluation of the three fonts of morality always applies. Suppose that the moral object of the other person's act is only venial, but his intention, or the grave weight of the bad consequences, makes the overall act a mortal sin. Your act of formal cooperation with the act that seeks to attain that venial moral object would be only venial, as long as your act does not similarly add a gravely immoral intention, or gravely immoral consequences.

.415. But now suppose that the other person's intrinsically evil act is venial, without any mortal sin in any font. Your cooperative act is a venial sin under the second font, unless you add a gravely immoral first or third font; in which case you would be committing a mortal sin, even though the other person is only committing a venial sin. So the gravity of the second font of the other person's act determines the gravity of the act of formal cooperation. But the three fonts of morality still apply to each person's act to determine the gravity of the overall act.

If one font makes an act a mortal sin, nothing in the other fonts can reduce the act to less than a mortal sin. If the act of the other person is intrinsically evil and gravely immoral, then the other fonts can make his act more or less serious as a mortal sin, but nothing can cause that act to become venial, rather than mortal. And the same is true of the cooperative act. Formal cooperation with a gravely immoral act is itself always gravely immoral. And nothing in the other two fonts of the cooperative act can cause the act to be less than a mortal sin.

However, an act can have more than one moral object. If the other person's single intrinsically evil act has two moral objects, one venial and the other mortal, and if you are cooperating with his single act, your act of formal cooperation is a mortal sin. For the gravely evil moral object makes the act itself inherently gravely immoral, and the addition of another moral object, one that is venial or even one that is not a sin, does not reform the inherent ordering of the act toward the gravely immoral object. Your act of formal cooperation is directed toward assisting the inherently gravely disordered act; that act is a mortal sin, therefore your cooperative act is also a mortal sin.

Similarly, your act of formal cooperation with an intrinsically evil venial sin is itself a venial sin. But your own act might have a second moral object, one not related to the act of the other person. And if that second moral object is gravely immoral, then your act is a mortal sin. In this case, it is not the cooperative act per se that is gravely immoral, but rather the second moral object. So your sin is gravely immoral, not because of the cooperation, but because of what is found in your act alone, not in the act of the other person. In this way, an act of formal cooperation can also be an act of perpetration.

Formal cooperation need not include physical participation in the sinful deed. Verbal participation, by the spoken or written word, may also fall under formal cooperation. For example, if a suicidal person is on a ledge, and the crowd below encourages him to jump, their acts constitute formal cooperation with the intrinsically evil and gravely immoral sin of suicide. Or if a group of voters conduct a letter writing campaign to encourage a legislator to vote for a law legalizing abortion, their acts constitute formal cooperation. Germaine Grisez gives this example of formal cooperation: "when a misguided counselor encourages a person to commit embarrassing sins, imagining that this will lead to his or her spiritual growth...."[456]

.416. Formal cooperation need not be an exterior act. Consider what great good can be done with interior acts, such as prayer and self-denial. But great harm can also be done with interior acts. For example, if a citizen in one State learns that the legislators in another State are thinking of legalizing euthanasia, the citizen might do great good by praying that the law will not pass. But a citizen might also do great harm by interiorly approving of that law, hoping that it will pass. This interior act is certainly a grave sin, and all grave sins harm the Church and the world, even if this harm is not readily apparent. In physical terms, this interior approval is not a participation in the sin of the other person, but in moral terms, and before the eyes of God, it is a type of participation, and it is directed toward the intrinsically evil act itself as to a moral object. Therefore, an interior or exterior act of approval is a type of formal cooperation.

Formal cooperation can be an interior decision to omit an exterior act. For example, an employee might decide not to report an act of theft by his friend and co-worker; this act of formal cooperation is interior. An interior act of approval for the intrinsically evil sin of another person is formal cooperation just as an interior decision to omit an exterior act can be formal cooperation. The interior act of approval is inherently directed toward the intrinsically evil act of the other person as to a moral object; and this is precisely what makes an act of formal cooperation intrinsically evil. So even an interior act of approval for someone else's intrinsically evil sin is formal cooperation.

In summary, formal cooperation assists the intrinsically evil act of another person in attaining its evil moral object. The cooperative act is therefore related to the evil moral object of the other act through the other act itself. When your cooperative act is directly related to the other act itself, and thereby indirectly related to the evil moral object of that other act, then your act is formal cooperation. But if your act is related to the evil moral object, not indirectly through the act of the other person, but directly (such that your chosen act is inherently ordered toward that end), then your act is perpetration, not cooperation. In such a case, both acts have the same evil moral object and the same inherent moral meaning; both acts are the same type of sin.

---

[456] Germaine Grisez, The Way of the Lord Jesus, Living a Christian Life, 7-F.

.417. Material Cooperation: the Usual Approach

Some sources consider the distinction between immediate and mediate material cooperation to be based on whether the cooperative act is essential or non-essential to the sin of the other person. However, in the complex circumstances of this life, the relationship between the cooperative act and the sinful act of the other person is a matter of degree. Rarely is a cooperative act essential in an absolute sense, so that the cooperator could entirely prevent the sin from occurring merely by inaction, i.e. by refusing to cooperate. And even if this were so, inaction is not necessarily the only moral choice; material cooperation might still be moral. This is proven by the fact that God could have prevented all sins whatsoever from occurring, merely by His own inaction, by not creating any persons with free will. Yet He chose to act and to create, and He did not sin by immediate material cooperation in this choice. Therefore, neither do we necessarily sin when our material cooperation is essential or immediate.

On the other hand, the mere fact that the other person could conceivably find another way to accomplish his sinful act without your cooperation is not sufficient to cause your cooperative act to be mediate and moral. So if the usual approach determines that the cooperation is mediate, that determination is not sufficient to determine if the cooperation is moral. And if the usual approach determines that the cooperation is immediate, that determination is not sufficient to determine if the cooperation is immoral.

The distinction between immediate and mediate material cooperation is of some use, as a matter of degree. But this distinction is not sufficient to determine the morality of any material cooperation. However, the degree to which the cooperative act is essential to the sinful act does partially determine the moral weight of the bad consequences of the cooperative act. If the cooperative act has a greater participation in the sin, which we might characterize as being more essential or more proximate, then the bad consequences resulting from the sin are more closely related, morally, to the cooperative act; the result is that the bad consequences of that cooperation have a greater moral weight. But this is a matter of degree. There is no absolute distinction between essential and non-essential material cooperation; there is no absolute separation between immediate material cooperation and mediate material cooperation. Rather, this distinction indicates the degree of remoteness of the cooperation, which affects the moral weight of the bad consequences of the cooperative act.

Another problem with the usual approach to material cooperation is the claimed distinction between material cooperation with an intrinsically evil act and material cooperation with an act that is immoral only due to bad consequences. Formal cooperation with an intrinsically evil act is always immoral because the cooperative act has an evil moral object, causing the cooperative act to be also intrinsically evil and always immoral. But the same cannot be said for material cooperation. The morality of material cooperation depends on the moral weight of the good and bad consequences of the cooperative act. As a result, material cooperation is not always immoral. The fact that the sin of the other person is intrinsically evil does not determine the overall weight of the consequences of the cooperative act, and therefore material cooperation with an intrinsically evil act may or may not be moral. When the cooperation is material, not formal, the evil moral object of the other person's act does not affect the moral object of the cooperative act, and therefore cannot cause the cooperative act to be intrinsically evil and always immoral.

.418. Now if we assert that immediate material cooperation is always immoral, in order for this to be true the term immediate would have to be defined such that the bad consequences would always outweigh the good consequences; but this is not the meaning of the term immediate. It is often the case that, with immediate material cooperation, the bad consequences outweigh the good, but this is not always or necessarily the case. The usual approach does not define the term immediate in such a way that immediate material cooperation would be always immoral.

Example: A soldier is ordered to attack a military target during a just war (good moral object), in circumstances when the bad consequences of likely civilian casualties would outweigh the good consequences. Such a soldier's cooperation is immediate and material to the sinful act of the other person (the commander who gives such an order). But his cooperative act might also be moral, because the circumstances of his act differ substantially from the circumstances of the commanding officer's act. The soldier is less certain than his commanding officer as to what the civilian casualties will be, because the commander has more information. This reduced certitude reduces the weight of that consequence. The more certain that a bad consequence is, the greater its moral weight. If he refuses to obey the order, his act also has the bad consequence of scandal (due to disobeying an order), and of harm to the defense of the nation (since if soldiers judge every order and frequently disobey, the entire war effort is endangered). Since the act that he is ordered to carry out is not intrinsically evil, it may be the case that the good consequences outweigh the bad consequences in his act, but not in the act of the commanding officer. Therefore, immediate material cooperation is not always immoral.

It is possible for immediate material cooperation, with an act that is immoral only due to the circumstances, to be moral because the fonts of the cooperative act spring up from that act, not from the related sinful act of the other person. Immediate material cooperation is usually immoral, but only because any progressive decrease in remoteness between the cooperative act and the sinful act of the other person causes the bad consequences to have greater moral weight for the cooperative act. A more immediate (more proximate) act of cooperation has greater participation in the bad consequences of the sinful act of the other person. A more remote act of cooperation has less participation in the bad consequences of the sinful act of the other person.

If we assert that immediate material cooperation with an intrinsically evil act is always immoral, several problems arise. First, when the cooperative act is not intrinsically evil, then the act is not formal cooperation. Formal cooperation is always immoral because its morality is based on the second font, and when the second font is bad, the act is always intrinsically evil. But material cooperation is not always immoral because its morality is based on the third font, which tolerates some bad consequences. The fact that the sin of the other person is intrinsically evil does not necessarily cause the bad consequences of the cooperative act to outweigh the good consequences. Some intrinsically evil acts have good consequences that outweigh the bad; therefore, some acts of cooperation with an intrinsically evil act may have good consequences that outweigh the bad.

Some sources, as alleged proof that immediate material cooperation with an intrinsically evil act is always immoral, present examples of intrinsically evil acts which are gravely immoral and which have grave bad consequences that far outweigh any good consequences. They are correct that, in those examples, any immediate (i.e. proximate, not remote) material cooperation would be immoral, but only because the bad consequences of the cooperative act gravely outweigh any good consequences. However, this alleged proof cannot be generalized to all intrinsically evil acts because not all intrinsically evil acts are gravely immoral, and not all intrinsically evil acts have a bad third font.

Suppose that a venial lie is told with the consequence that many innocent persons are protected from murder. The lie is intrinsically evil and always immoral, but it is only a venial sin. And in those circumstances, the good consequences outweigh the bad consequences. In such a case, if you were to cooperate materially, without lying or committing any intrinsically evil act yourself, the good consequences of your cooperative act would outweigh any bad consequences, even if your cooperation was proximate (immediate).

Therefore, immediate material cooperation with intrinsically evil acts, and immediate material cooperation in general, is not always immoral. As is always the case, the morality of the third font depends on the moral weight of the good and bad consequences. Since the sin of the other person does not determine the moral weight of the third font in the cooperative act in an absolute way, material cooperation with the sin of the other person cannot be said to be always immoral, at least not before the moral weight of the good and bad consequences of the cooperative act itself has been determined.

.419. In the usual approach, mediate material cooperation with the sin of another person is said to be moral if three basic conditions are met:

1. "If there is a proportionately serious reason for the cooperation (i.e., for the sake of protecting an important good or for avoiding a worse harm); the graver the evil the more serious a reason required for the cooperation;"

2. "The importance of the reason for cooperation must be proportionate to the causal proximity of the cooperator's action to the action of the principal agent (the distinction between proximate and remote);"

3. "The danger of scandal (i.e., leading others into doing evil, leading others into error, or spreading confusion) must be avoided."[457]

---

[457] AscensionHealth.org Principles of Formal and Material Cooperation,

These conditions of the usual approach are sound. However, all this is merely an expression of the proper evaluation of the third font. The first point, the proportion between the reason for the cooperation and the potential harm, is merely a consideration of the good consequences, e.g. "protecting an important good" or "avoiding a worse harm," compared to the bad consequences. The more grave the sin of the other person, the more grave the consequences of that sin, and this gives greater weight to the bad consequences in the third font of the cooperative act. The requirement that the good consequences be proportionate is merely another way of saying that the good consequences must outweigh the bad.

The second point, "the distinction between proximate and remote," is also a matter of degree, as the use of the term 'proportionate' indicates. And this degree of remoteness affects the weight of the bad consequences. Although the bad consequences in the sinful act of the other person may be of grave moral weight, the bad consequences of the cooperative act are reduced in moral weight in so far as the cooperative act is remote from the sinful act. A very remote cooperation with a sin that has grave consequences has a relatively light moral weight because of this degree of remoteness. Similarly, if any act at all (not necessarily a cooperative act) has only a slight likelihood of grave bad consequences, those bad consequences have only a slight moral weight. And this is also true for cooperation because the cooperative act is distinct from the sinful act of the other person. The fact that the other person's act is gravely immoral does not necessarily cause an act of material cooperation to be gravely immoral. A very remote act of material cooperation with grave evil has only a slight moral weight.

The third point in the usual approach is to consider the danger of scandal. But the danger of scandal is merely another possible bad consequence in the third font. If any act at all might present a bad example that would lead others into sin, then that danger of scandal weighs in the bad consequences of the third font.

So the usual approach to mediate material cooperation is correct, but we should understand that all these considerations are merely an evaluation of the third font. In every case without exception, every knowingly chosen act is moral if all three fonts of morality are good. The principle of cooperation with evil is no exception to this fundamental truth of the eternal moral law. Therefore, every point of the principle of cooperation with evil can be correctly understood in the light of the three fonts of morality.

.420. Material Cooperation: the Three Fonts Approach

A better approach to material cooperation is to understand these distinctions in terms of the three fonts of morality, and to apply the three fonts whenever we are evaluating a cooperative act, an act that is related to the sinful act of another person. This approach systematically evaluates each font of any proposed cooperative act, including its relationship, or lack thereof, to the sin of the other person. If all three fonts are good, then the act is moral. If any one font is bad, then the act is immoral. If it is unclear to which category of cooperation the

---

http://www.ascensionhealth.org/index.php?option=com_content&view=article&id=82

proposed act belongs, this evaluation of the three fonts nevertheless results in a correct determination as to whether or not the act is moral. In all cases whatsoever, if each font is properly evaluated as to its morality, then the correct determination can be made as to whether or not the act is moral.

Material cooperation, in the three fonts approach, is based on the third font of morality. In the second font, if your knowingly chosen act is inherently directed at the moral object of assisting the act of another person in attaining an evil moral object, then your chosen act is formal cooperation (and is therefore intrinsically evil and always immoral). In the third font, if the consequences of your act assist the act of the other person in attaining its bad consequences (in the third font of that other act), then your act is material cooperation. In the first font, if your intention is to assist the act of the other person, either in attaining an evil moral object, or in attaining the bad consequences of the other act, then your intention is either explicit formal cooperation, or explicit material cooperation.

In order to determine if an act of material cooperation is moral, the three fonts must each be evaluated. If your intention is good, then the first font is good and the act is at least not explicit cooperation. If the second font is good, then the act is not intrinsically evil, and is not formal cooperation. The weight of the good and bad consequences in the third font then determines if the act of material cooperation is moral or immoral. In cases of material cooperation, there are several types of consequences that need to be considered.

Certainly, your knowingly chosen act, even when it is material cooperation, takes its fonts only from your act. In this sense, the sin of the other person is their sin alone. But if your act assists the other person in attaining anything evil in his act, then your act does have that particular moral evil or physical evil in its fonts. In material cooperation, by definition, your act assists in attaining at least some of the bad consequences of the other person's act. But your cooperative act might also assist in attaining some of the good consequences of that act as well. An act often has both good and bad consequences, so your cooperative act might assist in attaining both the good and the bad in the third font of the other person's act.

Therefore, you must weigh, in the third font of your act, any portion of the good and bad consequences of the other person's act that are attributable to your cooperation. If you are partly responsible for the good results of his act as well as the bad, then the good is weighed in the morality of your third font along with the bad. This consideration includes the gravity of each of the reasonably anticipated good and bad consequences, the likelihood that each will actually occur, and the degree of remoteness (or proximity) of these consequences to your act. In addition, your act is likely to have its own good and bad consequences, not indirectly, by assisting the act of the other person in attaining its consequences, but directly, as a result of your act alone. The possibility of scandal (of leading others into sin) may occur either as a result of the other person's act, or as a result of your act, or both. This consideration also weighs in the third font of your act of material cooperation.

.421. The considerations needed to evaluate the third font of an act of material cooperation can be summarized and listed as follows:

1. Which good and bad consequences of the other person's act does your act assist in attaining?

2. What is the moral weight of those good and bad consequences? This consideration includes the degree of benefit or harm, and the degree of likelihood that each will occur.

3. To what extent does each consequence result from your act? The more remote each is from your act, the less its moral weight; the more proximate each is to your act, the greater its moral weight. This remoteness or proximity affects your degree of responsibility for those good and bad consequences. In material cooperation, you are only partly responsible, since those consequences occur directly because of the other person's act, and only indirectly because of your act. Thus, your responsibility is less than that of the other person.

4. Does the act of the other person have the bad consequence of scandal (leading others into sin)? Does your cooperative act have the bad consequence of scandal?

5. What are the good and bad consequences, and their moral weight, that result directly from your act? These are in addition to the good and bad consequences resulting from your cooperation with the act of the other person.

The above considerations include all of the reasonably anticipated good and bad consequences of your act, those that occur directly as a result of your act, and those that occur indirectly, through the other person's act by your cooperation. As always, if the good consequences outweigh the bad, then the third font is good. But if the bad consequences outweigh the good, then the third font is bad, and the overall act is a sin.

.422. Explicit versus Implicit Material Cooperation

The usual approach to cooperation with evil does not apply the distinction between explicit and implicit cooperation to material cooperation. There is no apparent justification for this omission. Every knowingly chosen act has all three fonts of morality, including an intention. And the three fonts are independent of one another. Therefore, an act of material cooperation could possibly have either a good or bad intention. However, the term explicit cooperation implies not merely an immoral intention, but an immoral intention specifically related to the cooperative act.

As is true also for formal cooperation, in material cooperation, an immoral intention can occur in either of two ways, either the specific intention to assist in attaining the bad consequences of the other person's act, or any other immoral intention, not related to the cooperation. In the former case, the cooperation is rightly called explicit material cooperation. In the latter case, and in any case in which the intention is moral, any material cooperation would be implicit, not explicit.

.423. Material Cooperation with Intrinsically Evil Acts

Material cooperation with an intrinsically evil act is not necessarily immoral. If the cooperative act has a good intention and a good moral object, then the morality of the cooperative act is based on the moral weight of the good and bad consequences. If the act of the other person is an intrinsically evil act, this might affect the bad consequence of scandal, since some degree of scandal is possible in cooperating with an intrinsically evil act. Intrinsically evil acts are always immoral and therefore always to be avoided. But material cooperation with an intrinsically evil act may be moral, and so scandal is not necessarily implied. An intrinsically evil act does not necessarily have greater bad consequences than an act that has a good second font, but an immoral third font. The three fonts are independent of one another. And so, some intrinsically evil acts have a good first or third font (e.g. lying to save innocent persons from death). Since material cooperation pertains to the consequences, not to the moral object, of the sin of the other person, material cooperation with an intrinsically evil act is not always immoral. In material cooperation, the morality of the cooperative act depends on the weight of the good and bad consequences.

Immediate material cooperation with an intrinsically evil act is not necessarily immoral. If the intrinsically evil act is a venial sin, and if the good consequences of the venial sin outweigh the bad consequences (so that the third font is good), then even proximate cooperation with the circumstances of that venial sin would not be immoral. This is true because material cooperation assists the sinful act only in attaining consequences, not in attaining the evil moral object (in which case the cooperation would be formal). Assisting another person in attaining consequences, when the good outweighs the bad, is not immoral, even if the other person is sinning by intention or by an intrinsically evil act. In material cooperation, the other person's sinful act does not affect the moral object of the cooperative act. Only the third font of circumstances is affected, and the third font may tolerate some bad consequences without being immoral.

However, if the other person's act is both intrinsically evil and gravely immoral, his act necessarily has some weighty bad consequences. And if the cooperation is proximate or 'immediate', the cooperative act will necessarily share in these weighty bad consequences. However, in such a case, it is still possible for the good consequences of the cooperative act to outweigh the bad. Your act adds its own good consequences to the moral weight of the third font, along with the bad consequences (and any good consequences) in the act of the other person. Nothing prevents your cooperative act from having sufficient good consequences to outweigh the bad consequences resulting from cooperation.

But as the weight of the bad consequences in the sinful act of the other person increases, and as the degree of proximity of your cooperative act increases, much weightier good consequences would be necessary in your act to make your cooperation moral. The moral weight of the possibility of scandal also increases. And it is always possible, in cases of immediate material cooperation with a gravely immoral intrinsically evil act, to propose a hypothetical in which the bad consequences outweigh the good consequences. But in advance of weighing these consequences, one cannot say that an act of material cooperation is necessarily moral or immoral, regardless of whether the cooperation is immediate or mediate, regardless of whether the act of the other person is intrinsically evil or not, and regardless of whether the act of the other person is gravely immoral or not.

Another reason that immediate material cooperation, even with an intrinsically evil and gravely immoral act, is not necessarily always immoral is that cooperative acts are never absolutely immediate. If so, then the act would not be an act of cooperation, but of perpetration. If the bad consequences are directly and immediately the result of your act, not by means of your assistance to the act of the other person, then those consequences are not a type of cooperation. They are directly and immediately attributable, in terms of morality, to your act. Therefore, acts of material cooperation are always mediate to some degree; for that is the meaning of the term 'cooperation.' So even when the terminology uses the word 'immediate,' this should be understood as a matter of degree, as being relatively less mediate, not absolutely immediate. Any absolutely immediate act of 'cooperation' is actually perpetration, and this is true for the second font as well as for the third font.

.424. Material Cooperation with a Good Third Font

Even if the act of the other person is good under all three fonts, but with some lesser bad consequences in the third font, you are sinning by explicit material cooperation, if you intend those bad consequences as an end. It is always immoral to intend any type of harm or bad consequence as an end. Also, if your act cooperates with the good act of another person, but so that your act enables or increases the bad consequences of that act, your cooperative act might be a sin, even though the act of the other person is not a sin. The evaluation of the third font of your act is always independent of the fonts and acts of other persons. The principle of cooperation with evil is no exception to the three fonts of morality. Even if the act of the other person is not a sin, if you are cooperating with any evil in his act (i.e. the 'physical evil' of bad consequences), your cooperative act may be a sin.

Your act is material cooperation if your act assists the other person in attaining the bad consequences of his act. He might avoid sin, if the good consequences of his act outweigh the bad consequences of his act. But your cooperative act will generally not have the same consequences, with the same moral weight. Your cooperative act might have fewer good consequences than the other act, so that the bad consequences outweigh the good. Therefore, it is possible to sin by material cooperation with an act that is not itself a sin.

Some authors might not call this type of relationship between two acts a cooperation with evil, since the act of the other person is not moral evil. But, in truth, your act is a cooperation with the physical evil of the bad consequences in the act of the other person, and that is the basis for material cooperation. And so, strictly speaking, such an act is a type of cooperation with evil. But it is important to understand that your act, in order to be moral, must always be good under all three fonts. Even if you are cooperating with the moral act of another person, your act does not necessarily have the same three fonts, and so your act is not necessarily moral merely because his act is moral.

Suppose that your act has some of the same bad consequences as the moral act of another person. His act has good consequences of greater moral weight than the bad consequences. But this is not necessarily also true of your act. Perhaps your act is related to the bad consequences, but not to the good. Or perhaps your act has its own additional bad consequences, such as scandal. If you are Catholic and the other person is not, there may be more scandal from an apparent bad example on your part than on his part. So the fact that you are cooperating with an entirely moral act by another person does not prove that your act is moral.

.425. Combined Formal and Material Cooperation

Any knowingly chosen act is immoral if even one of the three fonts is bad. But in some cases, an act may have two or three bad fonts. An intrinsically evil act (second font) might also have an immoral intention (first font), or bad consequences that outweigh any good consequences (third font). An act that is immoral under the third font of consequences might also be immoral under the first font of intention, even if the second font is good. And a sinful act might even have three bad fonts.

Similarly, an act of material cooperation might also be an act of formal cooperation. If the second font of your cooperative act is directed at assisting the act of the other person in attaining an evil moral object, then you are committing the sin of formal cooperation. But nothing prevents this same act, in its consequences, from also assisting the act of the other person in attaining the bad consequences of that sin. And an act that is both formal cooperation and material cooperation might also be explicit cooperation. The formal cooperation might be explicit and the material cooperation implicit, or vice versa, or both types of cooperation might be explicit, or both types might be implicit.

.426. Summary

An act is formal cooperation only if it assists the intrinsically evil act of another person in attaining an evil moral object. Otherwise, an act of cooperation pertains, not to the moral object in the second font, but to the circumstances in the third font. This type of cooperation is termed material cooperation because the cooperative act pertains to the circumstances, not to the essential moral nature, of the other person's act. An act of formal cooperation is, by definition, a type of intrinsically evil act. All acts of formal cooperation are therefore always immoral. An act that is good under the second font is never formal cooperation. But even if an act is good under all three fonts, that act might still be a type of material cooperation (which is sometimes moral).

An act of material cooperation with the sin of another person is moral if done with good intention and a good moral object, and in circumstances where the good consequences outweigh the bad. The evaluation of the morality of any act of material cooperation depends especially on the third font of consequences. Any act of material cooperation is moral if all three fonts are good. But since material cooperation by definition cooperates with the bad consequences in the act of the other person, the third font is of particular concern. When the bad consequences in any act, including acts of material cooperation, outweigh the good consequences, then that act is immoral. Cooperative acts are no exception to this requirement of the moral law.

As always, a judgment of the prudential order is needed in order to evaluate the moral weight of the consequences of any act. As a result, when the third font of an act of material cooperation is evaluated, the prudential judgments of faithful and reasonable Catholics may differ. However, the basic principles of morality do not change from one person to another, nor from one act to another. Three good fonts cause any act to be moral, even if the act is material cooperation. Even one bad font causes any act to be immoral, regardless of whether the act is categorized as cooperation with evil, or not.

.427. Cooperation by Omission

Germaine Grisez: "Formal cooperation with others' sinful acts can be by means of an omission. For instance, a police officer who ignores criminal activities in order to obtain a percentage of the proceeds intends the success of the criminal acts; thus, he or she formally cooperates with them by omitting the police work that would impede them."[458]

Concerning sins in general, any font can be immoral due to a knowingly chosen omission. For example, in the first font, if you omit the intention to do good to your neighbor in your acts of almsgiving, then your intention is sinful by omission. This is true even if you have no particular evil intent. For the eternal moral law requires good intentions in the fulfillment of positive precepts.

In the second font, even a grave sin such as euthanasia can be committed by omission.[459] In the third font, a positive precept may well require that our acts have certain good consequences. The most startling example of this requirement is found in the adult who fails to attain to the state of grace in his life, either by a formal baptism or by a non-formal baptism (e.g. a baptism of desire), so that he dies in a state of original sin; he is punished with eternal Hellfire. For he has committed the actual mortal sin of omission of not having obtained sanctifying grace in his life.[460] The state of sanctifying grace is a consequence of receiving some type of baptism (formal or non-formal). Therefore, any font can be bad, making the overall act immoral, by a culpable omission.

Similarly, a sin of omission in any font can cause that act to be either explicit cooperation (first font), or formal cooperation (second font), or material

---

[458] Germaine Grisez, The Way of the Lord Jesus, Living a Christian Life, 7-F.
[459] Pope John Paul II, Evangelium Vitae, n. 65: "Euthanasia in the strict sense is understood to be an action or omission which of itself and by intention causes death, with the purpose of eliminating all suffering."
[460] Council of Florence, Sixth Session, 6 July 1439: "But the souls of those who depart this life in actual mortal sin, or in original sin alone, go down straightaway to hell to be punished, but with unequal pains."

cooperation (third font). Of course, explicit cooperation with evil only occurs in conjunction with either formal cooperation or material cooperation. But the omission of an intention required by the moral law can cause formal or material cooperation to be also explicit cooperation. (Some sources call cooperation by omission 'passive cooperation,' and they call cooperation by commission 'active cooperation.' This is a difference in terminology, not doctrine.)

In formal cooperation, suppose that a nurse is caring for a terminally ill patient, and she knows that the patient plans to commit suicide (which is also euthanasia in this example). The patient has obtained a pain medication that he can use to commit suicide by overdose. The nurse might cooperate formally with the suicide of that patient by deciding to omit a scheduled visit to the patient's room, so that the overdose will not be detected until the patient is dead. This act of omission is directed at assisting the patient in attaining the moral object of an intrinsically evil act of suicide. Therefore, the nurse is committing an intrinsically evil and gravely immoral act of formal cooperation by omission.

In this same example, the nurse might have the intention to assist the patient in committing suicide. This intention would cause the act of formal cooperation to be explicit formal cooperation. But suppose instead that she omits the scheduled visit, knowing that the omission helps the patient commit suicide, not because she intends to assist in his suicide, but because she lacks an intention required by the moral law, in this case to intend the protection of innocent human life. She does not care if the patient dies; this is the omission of an intention required by the moral law. (She still must have some type of intention of commission, since every knowingly chosen act has all three fonts. But the immorality of the first font is found in what is omitted.) In such a case, her sin of formal cooperation is also explicit cooperation, both by omission.

Suppose that a voter is able to vote for or against a constitutional amendment outlawing all direct abortions. If he omits voting at all, he cooperates with the sin of abortion by omission. In this case, his sin is material cooperation by omission because his act has the bad consequence of making the failure of the amendment more likely. His sin would also be explicit cooperation by omission if he does not care whether abortion remains legal or not. His lack of the intention to protect his innocent neighbor from an unjust death is a sin of omission.

Suppose that a voter is able to vote for a politician, who campaigns on a promise to protect innocent human life from abortion and euthanasia, or for his opponent, who promises to broaden the legality of abortion and euthanasia. But the voter does not care about his fellow human being; he lacks an intention required by the moral law. And so, in the voting booth, he votes on other political races, but he omits voting at all in the race with those candidates. His knowing choice to omit voting for a candidate is the sin of material cooperation by omission. His act of omission has the bad consequence that the candidate might be elected who would do grave harm to the innocent. And this material cooperation is explicit cooperation because his intention is sinful, due to the omission of a required intention, and this sinful omission makes the attainment of that bad consequence more likely.

Cooperation with Evil

Suppose that another voter lacks an intention required by the moral law: to do good, and to avoid harm, to others by his acts. Such an omission is sinful, and is in the first font. His intention might be to support his political party, or to improve his personal finances. These particular intentions of commission are not immoral. What is immoral is his lack of intention to do good, and to avoid doing harm, to other human persons. His intention is sinful by omission. Now if this same sinful intention pertains to an act of formal or material cooperation in a one vote or another, then that sin of formal cooperation, or that sin of material cooperation, would also be explicit cooperation by omission.

So from the above examples it is clear that a sin of omission in any of the three fonts can make a cooperative act a sin. Explicit formal cooperation is sinful under both the first and second fonts; and either or both fonts might be sinful by omission or by commission. Implicit formal cooperation is a sin of omission or of commission, under the second font.

When material cooperation is sinful, it is a sin under the third font. Explicit material cooperation may be sinful under both the first and third fonts; and if so, either or both fonts might be sinful by omission or by commission. It is also possible for an act of material cooperation to be moral, because the good consequences outweigh the bad, but to become a sin if the intention is to assist the other person in attaining bad consequences. In this case, the explicit material cooperation would be sinful, by omission or by commission, under the first font. Implicit material cooperation, when sinful, is a sin of omission or of commission, under the third font.

.428. Forced Formal Cooperation

The term 'forced' can have two meanings, either when a person is compelled by duress to knowingly choose an act, or when a person is forced without any knowing choice. The latter case occurs, for example, if a woman is forcibly raped, or if a person is physically-restrained and dragged away in a kidnapping. In such cases, the victim does not commit any knowingly chosen act, and so there is no sin on the part of the victim. Sin is a knowingly chosen immoral act.

In the former case, the person is said to be forced because he is under the threat of violence or other harm if he does not choose to comply. In such cases, the person either commits the act of deciding not to comply, which is an act of omission (not necessarily a sin of omission), or he knowingly chooses to commit the act that he is under duress to perform. Since both choices are types of knowingly chosen acts, it is possible for either choice to be a sin. Any knowingly chosen act might be a sin, according to the proper evaluation of the three fonts of that act.

Since every act of formal cooperation is itself an intrinsically evil act, being forced by duress to commit formal cooperation is morally the same as being forced by duress to commit an intrinsically evil act (apart from any cooperation).

Every intrinsically evil act, by definition, is both morally direct and deliberate. Being under duress does not make an act indirect or non-deliberate. However, some acts done under duress are not intrinsically evil because the act has a good moral object. It is never the case that the same act, with the same moral object and therefore the same essential moral nature, becomes a different type of act by being done under duress. The circumstance of duress does not change the moral object of the chosen act. However, the essential moral nature of any chosen act is not determined by appearances, but by the moral object.

Examples: (1) You are in a bank and a robber compels you at gunpoint to hand a note to the bank teller demanding money. Your intended end is good, to avoid death. The moral object of your act is to relay a communication from one person to another. Your act of handing the note from the robber to the teller does not have the moral object of robbing the bank. So your act is not intrinsically evil, even though the act of the robber is intrinsically evil. Your act has the bad consequence of assisting in the circumstances of the robbery, which is material cooperation. But the good consequence of avoiding death outweighs the bad consequence of material cooperation in the robbery.

Notice that this material cooperation is morally 'remote' even though physically you are immediately involved in the robbery. The terms proximate and remote, in the principle of cooperation with evil, must be understood in terms of morality: whether a knowingly chosen act is morally proximate or morally remote.

If you knowingly choose to rob a bank by handing a note to a teller, the act is intrinsically evil. But if you are compelled to hand the same note to a teller, with the same consequence that the bank is robbed, your act is not intrinsically evil because you are not robbing the bank. The two similar exterior acts have very different inherent moral meanings, due to different moral objects.

However, duress never causes an intrinsically evil act, or any formal cooperation with an intrinsically evil act, to become mere material cooperation. Duress is a matter of degree and is in the third font; it is a circumstance. The moral object in the second font is unaffected by the circumstances in the third font. To understand if an act is intrinsically evil, we must determine the moral object; but nothing can change that moral object, except choosing a different type of act.

(2) A person threatens to kill you and your family unless you commit, or assist in committing, an intrinsically evil act, such as murder. You are being pressured, under grave duress, to commit either the perpetration of, or formal cooperation in, an intrinsically evil act. It would not be moral for you to commit murder, even if you and your family are under the threat of death if you refuse. Murder is intrinsically evil and always gravely immoral. Formal cooperation with murder is also intrinsically evil and always gravely immoral.

The same moral analysis holds true for any intrinsically evil act, even a venial sin. If a person threatens to kill you and your family unless you commit an intrinsically evil, but not gravely immoral, act of lying or theft, it is a venial sin if you comply. Intrinsically evil acts are always immoral, by the very nature of the act itself. Acts of formal cooperation are a type of intrinsically evil act. Even extreme duress cannot cause such acts to become moral.

.429. Forced Material Cooperation

Even when material cooperation is immediate (proximate), the act is not immoral unless one or more of the three fonts of morality is bad. Even when material cooperation is immediate material cooperation with an intrinsically evil and gravely immoral act, the cooperative act is only immoral if one or more fonts is bad. All material cooperation, including immediate material cooperation, pertains to the morality of the third font. And the third font is only immoral if the bad consequences outweigh the good. Some bad consequences can be tolerated in the third font, if the good consequences have a greater moral weight. Therefore, immediate material cooperation with an intrinsically evil and gravely immoral act is not necessarily always immoral. And the circumstance of duress might cause the good consequences to outweigh the bad consequences in the cooperative act.

Examples: (1) A gravely immoral and intrinsically evil act of robbery cannot occur unless you enter the code (or combination) to open the store safe. You are compelled at gunpoint to give this code to the robber. This act of giving the code is immediate material cooperation with an intrinsically evil and gravely immoral act. The act of robbery will not occur without your cooperative act; and so your act is essential and is immediate material cooperation (as the usual approach would say). Theft of a large sum of money from a store is intrinsically evil and gravely immoral. The threat of deadly force is used to commit this theft, making the act an even more serious sin (robbery).

The usual approach to cooperation with evil would consider this act to be always objectively immoral. Some theologians would add the claim that the person acts with diminished freedom of will, so that his act is an objective mortal sin, but not an actual mortal sin; but this claim is doctrinally false. If acting under duress (e.g. at gunpoint) caused a knowingly chosen act to be only an objective sin, and not also an actual sin, then a person who commits murder under duress (e.g. under threat to the lives of his family) would not be committing an actual sin, despite having knowingly chosen an act of murder. Such a conclusion is contrary to the teaching of the Catholic Faith on morals. A knowingly chosen and intrinsically evil act committed under duress is still an actual sin.

Each and every knowingly chosen immoral act is a sin. The person who fully realizes that an act is gravely immoral, and who freely chooses to commit that act with full consent, is guilty of actual mortal sin. Severe duress, such as the threat of death, may have an affect on judgment that would reduce culpability, or some persons might mistakenly believe that a particular act is not gravely immoral if they are under severe duress. But duress does not take away free will, and does not take away the knowledge that the act is gravely immoral. A person who knows that an act is intrinsically evil, and who chooses to commit the act, even under severe duress, is guilty of actual sin. This is the teaching of Pope John Paul II in Veritatis Splendor, and this is the teaching of the Catholic Faith.

Pope John Paul II: "The Church proposes the example of numerous Saints who bore witness to and defended moral truth even to the point of enduring martyrdom, or who preferred death to a single mortal sin. In raising them to the honor of the altars, the Church has canonized their witness and declared the truth of their judgment, according to which the love of God entails the obligation to respect his commandments, even in the most dire of circumstances, and the refusal to betray those commandments, even for the sake of saving one's own life."[461]

Therefore, even severe duress does not transform a knowingly chosen gravely immoral act from an actual sin into a merely objective sin.

Returning to the consideration of the robbery at gunpoint of a store safe, your act of giving the codes (or combination) to open the safe is immediate material cooperation with an intrinsically evil and gravely immoral act. But the analysis of this act under the three fonts approach proves that the act is moral. Your intended end is good, to avoid death. Your act is not intrinsically evil, because you are in effect being robbed of the safe codes at gunpoint. Your act does not have the moral object of theft; reason does not consider a person to be a thief or robber when he acts in material cooperation under severe duress. But your act materially assists the robber in stealing the money, and the robbery cannot occur without your act. Therefore, this is an example of moral immediate material cooperation with an intrinsically evil and gravely immoral act.

Your immediate material cooperation with this intrinsically evil and gravely immoral act of robbery is moral because the good consequence of saving your own innocent life outweighs the bad consequence of the loss of money to the store. But even in this very clear case of immediate material cooperation, the harm done is not a direct consequence of your act, but is only indirect, through the sinful act of the other person. Therefore, even when immediate material cooperation is essential to the commission of an intrinsically evil and gravely immoral act, such that the sinful act could not occur without that cooperation, the cooperative act is still only indirectly related to the bad consequences of the sinful act, and is still truly mediate. The term 'immediate' material cooperation is merely a type of mediate material cooperation in which the cooperative act is proximate, or even essential, to the sinful act. But all material cooperation is by definition related to the bad consequences of the other person's act mediately, i.e. indirectly, through that other act.

Again, we see that the three fonts of morality always apply. Despite the claim of some theologians that immediate material cooperation with an intrinsically evil and gravely immoral act is always immoral, a proper analysis of each of the three fonts shows that all three fonts may be moral. The cooperative act may have more good consequences, such as saving innocent life, than bad consequences, such as the loss of a large sum of money. And reason also attests to this conclusion, since no reasonable person would hold the store manager to be guilty of theft because he gave the safe codes to the robber at gunpoint.

In the example above, the material cooperation of the store manager with the act of theft by the robber is certainly moral. However, just as material cooperation is not always moral, so also forced material cooperation is not always moral. The

---

[461] Pope John Paul II, Veritatis Splendor, n. 91.

degree of force used may be greater or lesser. If a thief pressures a store manager to provide the combination to the store safe by threatening to reveal a past act of adultery committed by the manager, the manager could not morally cooperate. For the harm done by the theft outweighs the harm of a past sin coming to light. The bad consequences resulting from that sin being revealed are directly caused by the sin of adultery itself, and are only remotely caused by the decision of the manager not to cooperate; this factor reduces the moral weight of those bad consequences with regard to the cooperative act.

The circumstance of duress weighs in the bad consequences of the third font in any cooperative act. But the morality of the third font is always determined by the total moral weight of all the good and bad consequences combined. So the mere fact that duress is present does not determine whether or not the cooperative act is moral. Duress admits of varying degrees, and so its reasonably anticipated bad consequences admit of varying degrees. Material cooperation under duress is sometimes moral, and sometimes immoral, depending on the moral weight of the consequences. The first two fonts must also be good for the person to avoid sin (since other types of sin are possible aside from the sin of cooperation).

.430. Explicit Material Cooperation

Explicit cooperation occurs when you intend your chosen act to assist in attaining an evil moral object (second font), or in attaining bad consequences (third font). Since explicit cooperation always involves intending evil as an end, explicit cooperation, by definition, is always immoral. If you do not intend to assist the other person in attaining an evil moral object or bad consequences, then your intention is not explicit cooperation. Explicit cooperation is defined such that the cooperation is only explicit if the intention is sinful. Implicit cooperation lacks this particular evil intention, but the intention might still be immoral on some other basis. With implicit cooperation, the intention might be moral or immoral; with explicit cooperation, the intention is always immoral. When implicit cooperation is immoral, the immorality is not due to the cooperation; it is independent of the cooperation.

In cases of material cooperation, it is never moral for you to intend the bad consequences that result from your act as an end, neither those that result directly from your act, nor those that result indirectly from your act through your cooperation with the act of the other person. Otherwise the cooperation would be explicit material cooperation and would be a sin under the first font. And this is true even if the good consequences of the cooperative act objectively outweigh the bad consequences; the fact that the bad consequences are intended makes the act a sin under the first font. But such is always the case in any act; the first font is immoral if any evil is an intended end. Therefore, if a case of material cooperation (third font) is objectively moral, but you intend (first font) the bad consequences as your intended end, then your act of cooperation is immoral, though solely under the first font. Such an act is objectively moral, except for the intention. So an act of explicit material cooperation is either immoral under both the first and third fonts, if the bad consequences outweigh the good, or immoral only under the first font, if the good consequences outweigh the bad, but those bad consequences are intended.

Implicit material cooperation may be entirely moral, if all three fonts are good. The bad consequences in the third font, which cause the act to be a type of material cooperation with evil, might be outweighed by the good consequences. And there is no intention to cooperate with whatever is evil in the act of the other person; otherwise the act would be explicit cooperation, not implicit. So if the cooperator does not add any sin in any font, aside from the cooperation, and if the cooperation is entirely moral, then all three fonts are good and the act of implicit material cooperation is moral. Of course, if an act of implicit material cooperation has bad consequences that outweigh the good, then the cooperative act is objectively a sin, despite the lack of bad intention.

.431. Culpability and Cooperation

It is possible for the cooperator to be sinning more seriously than the perpetrator of an act. Suppose that a person is committing an intrinsically evil act, but with invincible ignorance. The act is an objective sin, but not an actual sin; there is no culpability. But if you knowingly choose to commit an act of formal cooperation with the objective sin of the other person, your sin is an actual sin; and there is culpability for you. Invincible ignorance only applies to the person who has the sincere ignorance, not to someone who knows that the act is intrinsically evil and yet freely chooses to cooperate. Therefore, you do not need to know if the other person realizes that his act is a sin. It is enough for you to know that the other person is committing an objective sin, in order for you to determine if your cooperation is sinful or not.

Every act of formal cooperation is intrinsically evil and always immoral. But if you do not know that your act of formal cooperation is a sin, your act is an objective sin, but not an actual sin. Every act of material cooperation is either objectively moral or objectively immoral. But if you do not know that your act of material cooperation is a sin, your act is an objective sin, but not an actual sin.

The same principles which apply to culpability in general also apply to the culpability of cooperative acts, whether formal or material. Only actual sin includes culpability; mere objective sin is not culpable. An objective mortal sin might be reduced in culpability to a minor extent, so that the act is still an actual mortal sin, or to a substantial extent, so that the act is an actual venial sin, or to a full extent, so that the objective mortal sin is not culpable at all (as occurs in invincible ignorance). These same truths about culpability also apply to sins of cooperation.

Formal cooperation in any objective mortal sin is itself an objective mortal sin. The reason is that the act of the cooperator has the moral object of assisting the act of the other person in attaining its evil moral object. And that moral object is the sole determinant of the objective gravity of the second font. So when that other act is gravely immoral, the act of formal cooperation is gravely immoral. Formal cooperation with an intrinsically evil venial sin is a venial sin, unless the cooperator adds another factor in any of the three fonts that would make his act gravely immoral. Suppose that the other person is committing an objective venial sin, and you are committing the sin of formal cooperation. Your sin could be either venial or mortal. If you do nothing more serious than cooperate with a venial sin, then your sin is venial. But if your sin of cooperation adds a gravely immoral intention, or a second gravely immoral object, or gravely immoral consequences, then your sin would be mortal, even though the sin of the other person is only a venial sin.

Germaine Grisez: "Formal cooperation in a gravely sinful act is always excluded as gravely sinful; material cooperation is sometimes, but not always, permissible."[462]

Pope John Paul II: "And when through sin, the soul commits a disorder that reaches the point of turning away from its ultimate end, God, to which it is bound by charity, then the sin is mortal; on the other hand, whenever the disorder does not reach the point of a turning away from God, the sin is venial. For this reason venial sin does not deprive the sinner of sanctifying grace, friendship with God, charity and therefore eternal happiness, whereas just such a deprivation is precisely the consequence of mortal sin."[463]

A mortal sin is a different type of act from a venial sin. No sin is mortal unless at least one font is gravely disordered in such a way that the person who chooses that act thereby turns himself away from God as the highest Good. One gravely immoral font is sufficient to cause the entire act to be a mortal sin. And there is no exception to this rule for cooperation with the sin of another person. Whether or not your knowingly chosen act is moral or immoral, venial or mortal, depends only on the three fonts of your act.

.432. Morally-required Cooperation with Evil

In some circumstances, material cooperation with evil may be a moral obligation. Explicit cooperation of any kind is always immoral, and is never required by the moral law. Formal cooperation of any kind is always immoral, and is never required by the moral law. Implicit material cooperation is sometimes permitted by the moral law, and is even at times required by the moral law.

A store manager is threatened with death if he does not give the combination to the store safe to a robber. His cooperation with the intrinsically evil and gravely immoral act of the robber is both material and moral. The good consequence of saving his own life outweighs the bad consequence of the loss of a large amount of money from the store. But can the manager morally refuse to cooperate, even if he loses his own life? Morally, he cannot refuse his cooperation, because the chosen act of refusal results in greater harm, by the loss of innocent human life, than good, in preventing a robbery. He would be committing a sin of omission, under the third font, if he refuses his material cooperation. This material cooperation is both moral and morally-required. A decision to refrain from

---

[462] Germaine Grisez, The Way of the Lord Jesus, Christian Moral Principles, 12-G-2.
[463] Pope John Paul II, Reconciliation and Penance, n. 17; he cites St. Thomas Aquinas, Summa Theologica, I-II, Q. 72, A. 5.

cooperating would be a sinful decision because the third font makes the act immoral. And since the bad consequence of the loss of innocent human life gravely outweighs the good consequence of preventing the loss of money, the refusal to cooperate would be an objective mortal sin.

In a different example, a legislator is able to vote for a bill placing substantial restrictions on abortion, but not outlawing all direct abortion. The bill has both good and bad consequences; it restricts abortion, but it also restricts protests at abortion clinics. A vote for this law would be material cooperation with evil. The vote not only does good by restricting abortion, but also materially cooperates with abortion by restricting protests. The legislator may vote for the bill, with good intention, because the act of voting for this bill is not intrinsically evil, and the good consequences outweigh the bad. And depending on the particular circumstances, he may even be morally required to vote for the bill, since to vote against it, or to abstain from voting, would result in a greater likelihood that the bill would not pass, and that more abortions would occur without the proposed restrictions.

Some acts of material cooperation are moral, but not required. Other acts of material cooperation are both moral and morally-required. At times, it would be a sin of omission not to act in material cooperation with evil, because the harm done by the decision to omit cooperation would be greater than the good done by that omission.

.433.
COOPERATION IN MAGISTERIAL DOCUMENTS

This section examines the application of the principles of cooperation with evil in magisterial documents. There is currently no complete exposition of the principles of cooperation with evil in any magisterial document of the Holy See (of which I am aware). It often happens that theology develops a set of ideas based on Sacred Tradition and Sacred Scripture, and then subsequently the Magisterium makes some use of that theology, without answering every question on the same topic. This section compares the use of cooperation with evil in magisterial documents to the three fonts approach.

Evangelium Vitae

Pope John Paul II: "To concur with the intention of another person to commit suicide and to help in carrying it out through so-called 'assisted suicide' means to cooperate in, and at times to be the actual perpetrator of, an injustice which can never be excused, even if it is requested.... The height of arbitrariness and injustice is reached when certain people, such as physicians or legislators, arrogate to themselves the power to decide who ought to live and who ought to die."[464]

Suicide is an intrinsically evil and gravely immoral act. Therefore, formal cooperation with suicide, whether as a type of euthanasia or not, is also an

---

[464] Pope John Paul II, Evangelium Vitae, n. 66.

intrinsically evil and gravely immoral act. Notice that the Pontiff does not even consider the possibility that such formal cooperation could be moral. Formal cooperation is always immoral; only material cooperation is sometimes moral.

And such formal cooperation is not limited to the acts of a physician or other person who is physically present to assist with the suicide. Those legislators who pass laws making such intrinsically evil acts easier to commit are guilty of formal cooperation. But, as the Pope also points out, such acts might extend beyond mere cooperation, to become acts of perpetration. And this is true not only for a person who is physically present for a suicide, but also for persons, such legislators, who, though not physically present, commit acts with the same evil moral object. Those legislators who pass a bill legalizing suicide or euthanasia are committing an act that has the death of many innocent persons as its moral object. Such an act is not merely formal cooperation, but perpetration.

Pope John Paul II: "Christians, like all people of good will, are called upon under grave obligation of conscience not to cooperate formally in practices which, even if permitted by civil legislation, are contrary to God's law. Indeed, from the moral standpoint, it is never licit to cooperate formally in evil."[465]

The Magisterium teaches that formal cooperation is never morally licit. In the three fonts approach, formal cooperation, by definition, always has an evil moral object, is always intrinsically evil, and is always immoral. The magisterial teaching that formal cooperation is never morally licit is based on the magisterial teaching that intrinsically evil acts are always immoral. The Pontiff then goes on to talk about the various types of cooperation.

Pope John Paul II: "Such cooperation occurs when an action, either by its very nature or by the form it takes in a concrete situation, can be defined as a direct participation in an act against innocent human life or a sharing in the immoral intention of the person committing it. This cooperation can never be justified either by invoking respect for the freedom of others or by appealing to the fact that civil law permits it or requires it. Each individual in fact has moral responsibility for the acts which he personally performs; no one can be exempted from this responsibility, and on the basis of it everyone will be judged by God himself (cf. Rom 2:6; 14:12)."[466]

Here the Pontiff considers all the types of cooperation: explicit, formal, and material. The term "by its very nature" refers to the second font, the act itself with its essential moral nature (or moral species) as determined by the moral object. In another document on ethics, Pope John Paul II uses the same term, "its very nature," to refer to intrinsically evil acts.[467] The "very nature" of any act is determined by its moral object. An act is cooperative "by its very nature" when the cooperative act has the moral object of assisting the other person in attaining an evil moral object. In other words, an act of formal cooperation, by

---

[465] Pope John Paul II, Evangelium Vitae, n. 74.
[466] Pope John Paul II, Evangelium Vitae, n. 74.
[467] Pope John Paul II, Veritatis Splendor, n. 80.

its very nature, assists another act, one that is intrinsically evil, in attaining its evil moral object. All this pertains to the second font of morality.

Next, the Pope refers to material cooperation, which he describes as an action that participates in the sin of another person "by the form it takes in a concrete situation," in other words, by the circumstances surrounding the act itself. So this point refers now to material cooperation, relating it to the third font of circumstances. He uses the example of a sin against human life because this explanation is given in his encyclical Evangelium Vitae (the Gospel of Life). The USCCB Catechsim uses the same phrase, "concrete situation," to refer to the third font of morality:

USCCB Catechism: "Every moral act consists of three elements: the objective act (what we do), the subjective goal or intention (why we do the act), and the concrete situation or circumstances in which we perform the act...."[468]

Thus, Pope John Paul II distinguishes formal from material cooperation by implicitly referring to the three fonts. In his explanation, formal cooperation pertains to the very nature of the act, which is the second font. When the second font is bad, the act is always immoral; formal cooperation is always immoral. But he considers material cooperation to refer only to the concrete situation, i.e. to the circumstances, which is the third font. Material cooperation is not always immoral because the evaluation of the circumstances allows for some bad consequences, if these are outweighed by the good consequences.

Next, the Pontiff describes explicit cooperation, calling it a "sharing in the immoral intention of the person committing it."[469] The three fonts approach considers explicit cooperation to be always immoral because the cooperator has the immoral intention to assist the act of the other person to attain what is evil. The cooperator, by this intention, shares in the immorality of the intentionally chosen act of the other person; it is in this sense that he shares in the intention of the other person. But he need not share in the specific intention of the other person. For the other person might have a good intention, through invincible ignorance; or the other person might have a different immoral intention from the cooperator. Yet explicit cooperation could still occur, if the cooperator intends either the evil moral object, or whatever is evil in the consequences, of the other person's act.

Therefore, this 'sharing' of intention need not be specific, so that the two persons have the same exact intention. Such an overly-narrow definition would make explicit cooperation very unlikely, since any two persons generally have some differences in their intentions, and since the full and exact intention of each person is generally not known to others. To constitute explicit cooperation with evil, it is sufficient for the cooperator to have any evil intention related to the intentionally chosen act of the other person, either intending to assist in attaining the evil moral object of the act itself in formal cooperation, or intending to assist

---

[468] United States Catholic Catechism for Adults, U.S. Conference of Catholic Bishops, July 2006, p. 311-312.
[469] Pope John Paul II, Evangelium Vitae, n. 74.

Cooperation with Evil

in attaining any of the bad consequences in material cooperation. This basis for determining explicit cooperation is in accord with Pope John Paul II's description of a sharing by immoral intention, without interpreting his words in an overly-literal fashion.

.434. Notice that the three fonts approach to the principle of cooperation with evil is in accord with this succinct explanation given by the Magisterium. The Pope does not make the claim, found in the usual approach, that immediate material cooperation with an intrinsically evil act is always immoral. He teaches that formal cooperation is always immoral, but not that any type of material cooperation is always immoral. Neither does the Pontiff find it necessary to distinguish between immediate and mediate material cooperation. Only three types of cooperation are distinguished, and each is described in terms of one of the three fonts of morality.

Next, we consider Pope John Paul II's application of these general principles of cooperation with evil to the morality of laws pertaining to abortion.

Pope John Paul II: "In the case of an intrinsically unjust law, such as a law permitting abortion or euthanasia, it is therefore never licit to obey it, or to 'take part in a propaganda campaign in favor of such a law, or vote for it.' "[470]

It is never licit to obey a law that requires you either to commit an intrinsically evil act, especially one that is gravely immoral such as abortion or euthanasia, or to cooperate formally with an intrinsically evil act. For formal cooperation is itself a type of intrinsically evil act. The Pontiff gives three examples of such intrinsically evil acts: promoting the law, voting for the law, and obeying the law. Now these examples do not refer to every law that is in any way, or to any extent, unjust. Many laws have some limited injustice in the consequences of the law. The absolute prohibition against such cooperation must refer either to formal cooperation with, or to the perpetration of, an intrinsically evil act, and not to the much broader, and sometimes moral, material cooperation.

The knowingly chosen acts that are part of a campaign to pass a pro-abortion law, or a pro-euthanasia law, have a moral object; these acts are inherently directed toward attaining an end. The moral object of such acts is to assist in passing the law, and the act of passing the law has the moral object of the death of innocent human persons. Notice that these acts of formal cooperation are not assisting in the act of abortion, but in the act of passing a pro-abortion (or pro-euthanasia) law. Such acts are formal cooperation, not merely material cooperation. These intentionally chosen acts are, by their very nature, directed toward the end of assisting the intrinsically evil acts of other persons, acts that have the death of innocents as an end.

Is the act of passing of an intrinsically unjust law intrinsically evil, or is it formal cooperation with the intrinsically evil act which the law permits or requires? Either answer gives the result that the passing of such a law is always immoral,

---

[470] Pope John Paul II, Evangelium Vitae, n. 73; inner quote from Sacred Congregation for the Doctrine of the Faith, Declaration on Procured Abortion, n. 22.

since formal cooperation is itself a type of intrinsically evil act. If the law assists by protecting an abortion clinic from protests, or by reducing restrictions on the circumstances of the abortion (such as a waiting period), then the passing of the law pertains to the circumstances and is material cooperation. If the law assists in the act itself of abortion, such as by paying for the abortions, or requiring health care plans to include coverage for abortions, then the law is formal cooperation. But when a law simply legalizes, or broadly extends the legalization, of abortion, the passing of such a law constitutes a perpetration of the sin of procuring abortion.

But even when the passing of a law is formal cooperation, cooperative acts that seek to assist in passing the law, such as taking part in a campaign to pass the law, are cooperating with an intrinsically evil act. For every act of formal cooperation is itself an intrinsically evil act. Therefore, if your cooperative act has the moral object of assisting another person in his intrinsically evil act of formal cooperation, though not in an act of perpetration itself, then your cooperative act is still an act of formal cooperation, and is intrinsically evil. For your act has the evil moral object of assisting in the intrinsically evil act of formal cooperation by another person. Formal cooperation with an act of formal cooperation by another person is also intrinsically evil and always immoral. Ultimately, any act of formal cooperation, by its very nature, is ordered toward an evil moral object, and so is always immoral.

The Pope also refers to voting for a pro-abortion or pro-euthanasia law as being never morally licit. Voting for such a law is either an act of formal cooperation with abortion, or an act of perpetration (procuring abortion or euthanasia for all those persons who will make use of the law). In either case, the act of voting for a law making abortion or euthanasia legal, or substantially broadening its legality, is intrinsically evil and always gravely immoral. But this question is similar to the question as to whether a women who signs a paper authorizing an abortion to be performed on her commits formal cooperation, or perpetration, of abortion. Although she does not perform the abortion, she has committed an act of perpetration, not merely cooperation, because she has procured an abortion.[471] Her chosen act is inherently directed to the death of the innocent prenatal as its moral object. Similarly, if a legislator or citizen votes for a law that legalizes abortion, the act of voting passes the law, thereby authorizing (or procuring) many abortions. Therefore, the act of voting for such a law is an act of perpetration, not merely formal cooperation.

.435. The above quote from Pope John Paul II in Evangelium Vitae includes a quote from the CDF document 'Declaration on Procured Abortion.' The full passage sheds further light on the topic of cooperation with evil.

Sacred Congregation for the Doctrine of the Faith: "It must in any case be clearly understood that whatever may be laid down by civil law in this matter, man can never obey a law which is in itself immoral, and such is the case of a

---

[471] cf. Canon 1398: "A person who procures a completed abortion incurs a latae sententiae excommunication."

law which would admit in principle the liceity of abortion. Nor can he take part in a propaganda campaign in favor of such a law, or vote for it. Moreover, he may not collaborate in its application. It is, for instance, inadmissible that doctors or nurses should find themselves obliged to cooperate closely in abortions and have to choose between the law of God and their professional situation."[472]

Any act that is 'in itself immoral' is intrinsically evil. If a law requires anyone to commit an act that is intrinsically evil, that law must not be obeyed. And since every act of formal cooperation is necessarily an intrinsically evil act, if a law requires anyone to commit an act of formal cooperation, that law must not be obeyed. Collaboration in the application of such a law is a type of cooperation. So if a doctor or nurse is obliged by the law to cooperate closely in an abortion, the moral law obliges them to refuse any and all such acts of perpetration or formal cooperation. The law of God prevails over all human law. An unjust law is not a law, but a type of violence. A human law that contradicts the eternal moral law is not a law, and must not be obeyed.

Pope John Paul II: "A particular problem of conscience can arise in cases where a legislative vote would be decisive for the passage of a more restrictive law, aimed at limiting the number of authorized abortions, in place of a more permissive law already passed or ready to be voted on.... In a case like the one just mentioned, when it is not possible to overturn or completely abrogate a pro-abortion law, an elected official, whose absolute personal opposition to procured abortion was well known, could licitly support proposals aimed at limiting the harm done by such a law and at lessening its negative consequences at the level of general opinion and public morality. This does not in fact represent an illicit cooperation with an unjust law, but rather a legitimate and proper attempt to limit its evil aspects."[473]

Here the Pontiff gives an example of moral material cooperation. The elected official's position against abortion should be well-known; this is to avoid the sin of scandal, which is a possible bad consequence in cases of material cooperation. Such a politician's support for the proposed law is moral because the good consequences of enacting further restrictions on abortion outweigh the negative consequences (the harm done). But if a more restrictive law could be passed, the elected official must support the more restrictive law. Since laws can be complex, having many possible good and bad consequences, which may be difficult to determine in advance, a judgment of the prudential order is used to weigh all the possible good and bad consequences of material cooperation. The result determines if the material cooperation is moral or immoral.

But notice that the Pope does not consider any cases of immediate material cooperation, nor does he even refer to this distinction used by so many authors. The only basis for determining the morality of material cooperation is the three

---

[472] Sacred Congregation for the Doctrine of the Faith, Declaration on Procured Abortion, 18 November 1974, n. 22.
[473] Pope John Paul II, Evangelium Vitae, n. 73.

fonts of morality. So if the act is done with good intention, and the act is not intrinsically evil, then the totality of the moral weight of the good and bad consequences determines if the material cooperation is licit or illicit. A more immediate (less remote) act of material cooperation gives the bad consequences of the other person's act more moral weight in the cooperative act. But immediate material cooperation, even with an intrinsically evil act, is not necessarily always immoral. The Magisterium teaches that formal cooperation is always immoral, and that material cooperation is sometimes moral. There is no magisterial teaching that any type of immediate material cooperation is necessarily always immoral. The morality of every type of material cooperation depends on an evaluation of the third font.

.436. The Address of John Paul II to the Roman Rota

The Roman Rota deals with appeals concerning cases of Church law. In the quotes below, the Pope relates unjust laws on divorce and civil unions to the concept of cooperation with evil.

"The essential witness to the value of indissolubility is given through the married life of the spouses, in their fidelity to the bond, through all the joys and trials of life. However the value of indissolubility cannot be held to be just the object of a private choice: it concerns one of the cornerstones of all society. Therefore, while all the initiatives that Christians, along with other persons of good will, promote for the good of the family (for example, the celebrations of wedding anniversaries) are to be encouraged, one must avoid the risk of permissiveness on fundamental issues concerning the nature of marriage and the family (cf. Letter to Families, n. 17)."[474]

Christians have a moral obligation to promote true marriage over false ideas about marriage, and to guard the goods of marriage and family.

"Among the initiatives should be those that aim at obtaining the public recognition of indissoluble marriage in the civil juridical order (cf. ibid., n. 17). Resolute opposition to any legal or administrative measures that introduce divorce or that equate de facto unions -- including those between homosexuals -- with marriage must be accompanied by a pro-active attitude, acting through juridical provisions that tend to improve the social recognition of true marriage in the framework of legal orders that unfortunately admit divorce."[475]

Civil divorce, for spouses who have the valid Sacrament of Marriage, is permitted under Church teaching, only in cases of grave necessity, and even then, the bond of the Sacrament of Marriage remains.

Catechism of the Catholic Church: "The separation of spouses while maintaining the marriage bond can be legitimate in certain cases provided for by canon law. If civil divorce remains the only possible way of ensuring certain

---

[474] Address of Pope John Paul II to the Prelate Auditors, Officials and Advocates of the Tribunal of the Roman Rota, 28 January 2002, n. 9.
[475] Pope John Paul II to the Tribunal of the Roman Rota, 28 January 2002, n. 9.

legal rights, the care of the children, or the protection of inheritance, it can be tolerated and does not constitute a moral offense."[476]

The couple is divorced only under secular law; in the eyes of God they are still married. Such a separation and its legal recognition is only moral for a grave reason, such as to protect one spouse against abuse by the other spouse, or to protect the right of one spouse to continue to worship God as a Catholic Christian.

"On the other hand, professionals in the field of civil law should avoid being personally involved in anything that might imply a cooperation with divorce. For judges this may prove difficult, since the legal order does not recognize a conscientious objection to exempt them from giving sentence."[477]

Civil divorce is not intrinsically evil, and so cooperation with civil divorce is material cooperation, not formal cooperation. The Pontiff does not state that involvement in divorce cases, by a lawyer or judge, is never licit, since material cooperation is sometimes moral, depending on the circumstances. This position contrasts sharply with what the Pope says on cooperation with intrinsically unjust laws (e.g. on abortion or euthanasia), since that cooperation is formal cooperation and is always immoral.

"For grave and proportionate motives they may therefore act in accord with the traditional principles of material cooperation. But they too must seek effective means to encourage marital unions, especially through a wisely handled work of reconciliation."[478]

.437. The morality of material cooperation depends on the comparative moral weight of the good and bad consequences. If the good consequences are proportionately grave (weighty), so that they outweigh the bad consequences, then material cooperation is moral. Again, there is no question raised of whether the material cooperation is immediate or mediate. Only the proportionality of the good and bad consequences is considered. A judge who hears a divorce case, and a lawyer who has a client in a divorce case, are engaging in a type of cooperation that is categorized, in the usual approach, as immediate material cooperation; their acts are essential to the sin of the married couple in obtaining a divorce when the circumstances would not justify a divorce (a sin under the third font, not the second font). Yet the Pontiff does not teach that, in such a case of immediate material cooperation, the cooperation is always immoral. Again, there is no magisterial teaching asserting that immediate material cooperation of any type is always immoral. In fact, some magisterial documents, such as this Address, imply that immediate material cooperation is not always immoral, and that the morality of all material cooperation depends on the proportional weight of the consequences.

---

[476] Catechism of the Catholic Church, n. 2383.
[477] Pope John Paul II to the Tribunal of the Roman Rota, 28 January 2002, n. 9.
[478] Pope John Paul II to the Tribunal of the Roman Rota, 28 January 2002, n. 9.

"Lawyers, as independent professionals, should always decline the use of their profession for an end that is contrary to justice, as is divorce. They can only cooperate in this kind of activity when, in the intention of the client, it is not directed to the break-up of the marriage, but to the securing of other legitimate effects that can only be obtained through such a judicial process in the established legal order (cf. Catechism of the Catholic Church, n. 2383). In this way, with their work of assisting and reconciling persons who are going through a marital crises, lawyers truly serve the rights of the person and avoid becoming mere technicians at the service of any interest whatever."[479]

In this section, the Pontiff teaches that we should always decline to cooperate with any end contrary to justice, "as is divorce." Now all three fonts are directed each to its own type of end: the intended end, the moral object, and the end results (consequences) of the act. So we must determine the type of end that he means. The Church permits some recourse to civil divorce, even while the bond of the Sacrament remains, yet he gives the example of divorce as an end contrary to justice. And his next statement allows for cooperation with divorce in certain circumstances. Therefore, the Pontiff was not referring to intrinsically evil acts, but instead to intention and circumstances, both of which are types of ends. This interpretation is confirmed by the subsequent statement that the intention of the client must not be against marriage, but in favor of justice, such as the equitable distribution of goods, and that the divorce may morally seek certain good effects (i.e. consequences) that cannot be obtained outside the legal process.

But understood more generally, the Pope is teaching that we "should always decline" any type of cooperation in which any end, the intended end (explicit cooperation), the moral object (formal cooperation), or the end results (the moral weight of the consequences), is "an end that is contrary to justice." In other words, we must refuse to commit acts of explicit cooperation, acts of formal cooperation, and any acts of material cooperation in which the consequences, in the totality of their moral weight, are immoral. So if any one font is "contrary to justice," then that act of cooperation is immoral.

Again, this confirms the three fonts approach. Cooperation in cases of divorce requires a good intention in the first font. Any act done with a bad intention is a sin. And if a cooperative act intends either an evil moral object in the second font, or the bad consequences in the third font, then the cooperation is explicit cooperation and is immoral. The Pope indicates this truth when he states the requirement of good intention on the part of the client, and therefore also on the part of the lawyer. Then, concerning the circumstances, the good consequences of securing legitimate ends, such as obtaining goods needed for a livelihood or obtaining the return of personal possessions, must outweigh any bad consequences. Here the third font applies, making this act material cooperation, not formal cooperation. For these reasons, the Pope permits lawyers and judges to cooperate in divorces, under the principle of material cooperation.

---

[479] Pope John Paul II to the Tribunal of the Roman Rota, 28 January 2002, n. 9.

However, we should bear in mind the words of our Savior: "Everyone who divorces his wife and marries another commits adultery. And whoever marries her who has been divorced by her husband commits adultery." (Luke 16:18). If a divorce is directed at the end of enabling a subsequent marriage to another, while the bond of the Sacrament remains, then the act of obtaining a divorce is intrinsically evil because it is formal cooperation with adultery. If an attorney were to formally cooperate with such formal cooperation, he also would be committing an intrinsically evil act of formal cooperation with adultery.

Moral cooperation with an intrinsically evil act is only possible if the cooperation is material, not formal, meaning that the cooperation does not assist the other person in obtaining an evil moral object, but only assists in attaining the consequences of the act. In such cases, the good consequences must outweigh the bad for the act of material cooperation to be moral.

.438. Cardinal Ratzinger

Pope Benedict XVI, prior to becoming the Roman Pontiff, also referred to the principle of cooperation with evil.

Cardinal Ratzinger: "Regarding the grave sin of abortion or euthanasia, when a person's formal cooperation becomes manifest (understood, in the case of a Catholic politician, as his consistently campaigning and voting for permissive abortion and euthanasia laws), his Pastor should meet with him, instructing him about the Church's teaching, informing him that he is not to present himself for Holy Communion until he brings to an end the objective situation of sin, and warning him that he will otherwise be denied the Eucharist."[480]

Campaigning for pro-abortion or pro-euthanasia laws is formal cooperation, not merely material cooperation. Voting for such laws is also categorized by the Cardinal as formal cooperation. But whether voting for a law is perpetration or formal cooperation depends on the substance of the law. If a law has the effect of procuring abortion for many persons, voting for such a law is perpetration, rather than formal cooperation. Such a vote has the moral object of procuring abortions. By comparison, if a law does not have the direct effect of procuring abortion, but only assists in obtaining abortions, as when a law provides government money for abortions or reduces some minor restrictions, then the vote for that law is formal cooperation, not perpetration. However, both perpetration of, and formal cooperation with, abortion is intrinsically evil and always gravely immoral.

Cardinal Ratzinger: "In those situations where homosexual unions have been legally recognized or have been given the legal status and rights belonging to marriage, clear and emphatic opposition is a duty. One must refrain from any kind of formal cooperation in the enactment or application of such gravely

---

[480] Cardinal Joseph Ratzinger, Worthiness to Receive Holy Communion, General Principles (sent by Cardinal Ratzinger to Cardinal McCarrick, Archbishop of Washington, D.C., and made public in July, 2004), n. 5; http://www.priestsforlife.org/magisterium/bishops/04-07ratzingerommunion.htm

unjust laws and, as far as possible, from material cooperation on the level of their application. In this area, everyone can exercise the right to conscientious objection."[481]

The Cardinal teaches the positive precept that opposition to grave immorality within society is a moral obligation. Then he states the duty to refrain from formal cooperation "in the enactment or application" of these inherently unjust laws. He permits no exception to this prohibition from formal cooperation.

Formal cooperation applies only to cooperation with intrinsically evil acts. Yet Cardinal Ratzinger allows that cooperation with an intrinsically evil act can instead be material. First he states that cooperation with the application of such a law can be formal cooperation. Next he states that such cooperation can instead be material cooperation. This difference depends on whether the cooperative act assists in attaining the moral object, or the bad consequences, of the intrinsically evil act. But concerning this material cooperation, he uses the phrase "as far as possible" to indicate that material cooperation, even with acts that are intrinsically evil and gravely immoral, is not always immoral.

.439. Pope Innocent XI

Under Pope Innocent XI, a decree of the Holy Office (now called the Sacred Congregation for the Doctrine of the Faith), on 4 March 1679, **condemned** the claim that: "A male servant who knowingly by offering his shoulders assists his master to ascend through windows to ravage a virgin, and many times serves the same by carrying a ladder, by opening a door, or by cooperating in something similar, does not commit a mortal sin, if he does this through fear of considerable damage, for example, lest he be treated wickedly by his master, lest he be looked upon with savage eyes, or, lest he be expelled from the house."[482]

If the servant were guilty of drugging or tying the woman, so that she could be raped, he would (at least) be guilty of formal cooperation, because such acts assist in attaining the moral object of the intrinsically evil act. But the set of examples given in the above decree pertain to the circumstances of the intrinsically evil act, not to the moral object, so these are examples of material cooperation. This servant is doing various tasks related to the circumstances, not to the inherent moral meaning of the act itself. He opens a door, or he carries a ladder, or he permits his shoulder to be used to ascend to a window; these acts pertain to the circumstances surrounding the intrinsically evil act. This is an example of immoral material cooperation with an intrinsically evil and gravely immoral act.

However, the main point of the decree is to condemn the idea that duress makes an act of material cooperation either entirely moral, or reduced to only an actual venial sin. Despite this decision by the Holy Office, some sources continue to claim that duress reduces an act of material cooperation to less than an actual

---

[481] Congregation for the Doctrine of the Faith, Considerations Regarding Proposals to Give Legal Recognition to Unions between Homosexual Persons, n. 5.
[482] Decree of the Holy Office, 4 March 1679, n. 51; Denzinger, n. 1201.

mortal sin, no matter what the moral weight of the bad consequences may be, because of 'diminished freedom.' Such a position is contrary to the above decree, which finds that, when the sinful act of the other person is very grave, moderate duress is not sufficient to cause the act to become moral, nor to cause the act to be less than a mortal sin, even though the cooperation is material.

The above decree does not state the need for proportionality in weighing the good and bad consequences. But this proportionality, explicitly stated in other magisterial documents already reviewed above, is implicit in this decree. The sin of the other person is severe, "to ravage a virgin," which is an expression used to refer to rape. This is not a man who is secretly entering his lover's bedroom for consensual premarital sexual relations (which is still a mortal sin), but rather for the even more serious sin of rape. The woman is a virgin, so, in the particular social context of this decree, she is young and unmarried; it was always, until modern times, common for women to marry at a young age. And the man has a servant, and has the ability to expel this servant from the household, so he is older and is likely, given the same social context, married. This is the severe sin of an older married man who rapes a young woman.

But the examples of duress given in the decree are not proportionately severe. None of the examples of duress include death, or maiming, or imprisonment. The examples of duress are not light, but are "considerable" or moderate: "lest he be treated wickedly by his master, lest he be looked upon with savage eyes, or, lest he be expelled from the house." The example of being expelled is the most severe, and the other two examples refer either to being treated with bias ("savage eyes") or to being mistreated openly.

The good consequence of this material cooperation is that harm (of moderate weight) is avoided. But the bad consequence of the material cooperation is that a young woman is raped. Even though proportionality in the consequences is not stated, it is plainly implied. A set of circumstances is given as an example in which the bad consequences plainly and substantially outweigh the good consequences. The harm done to the woman by this intrinsically evil mortal sin is grave, and so the act of material cooperation is also grave.

We can draw several conclusions from this decree, understood in the light of other magisterial documents. First, not every cooperation with an intrinsically evil act is formal cooperation. Material cooperation can occur with a sinful act regardless of whether the sin is immoral under the second or third font. When the cooperative act assists in the circumstances of a sinful act, it is material cooperation, not formal cooperation, even if the sin is intrinsically evil. Second, material cooperation is moral or immoral based on the proportionality of the good and bad consequences in the third font of the cooperative act.

Third, duress, in and of itself, does not constitute a reduction in freedom of the chosen act. Even if a perpetrator threatens you with death, you are still able to exercise free will in your decision as to whether or not you will cooperate. The duress might result in poor judgment, which would reduce culpability, but duress itself does not directly reduce culpability. Fourth, when the third font has bad consequences which gravely outweigh the good consequences, the act cannot be less than a mortal sin. For mortal sin differs from venial sin not merely by degree, but also by type. If one font is gravely immoral, making the act a mortal sin, the other two fonts cannot reduce the act to less than an objective mortal sin.

.440. Pope Pius XI

Pope Pius XI wrote, in 1932, on the principle of cooperation with evil in order to address the persecution of Catholics in Mexico. At that time, the Mexican government was attempting to control the Catholic Faith: by exiling all Bishops, restricting the number and activities of priests, closing seminaries, imprisoning dissenters, and requiring permission for public worship. There was a concern among some of the faithful that any compliance with these unjust laws might constitute immoral cooperation. But the Pontiff, while condemning these laws, taught that not all cooperation with unjust laws is immoral.

Pope Pius XI: "Certainly, the laws are iniquitous that are impious, as We have already said, and condemned by God for everything that they iniquitously and impiously derogate from the rights of God and of the Church in the government of souls. Nevertheless, it would be a vain and unfounded fear to think that one is cooperating with these iniquitous legislative ordinances which oppress him, were he to ask the Government which imposes these things for permission to carry out public worship, and hence to hold that it is one's duty to refrain absolutely from making such a request. Such an erroneous opinion and conduct might lead to a total suspension of public worship, and would, without doubt, inflict grievous harm on the entire flock of the faithful."[483]

When laws are unjust, not all cooperation with those laws is unjust. Although the Pontiff terms certain acts of cooperation with these unjust laws as being not truly cooperative, such acts are considered, in the commonly used terminology, to be a type of material cooperation. The person who asks for permission to worship, even though it is unjust for the law to require such permission, is not cooperating with the evil moral object of the law to restrict the worship of God; this is not formal cooperation. Rather, the person is cooperating with the circumstances of that unjust law; this is material cooperation. As the Pope notes, the refusal to give such material cooperation results in the very harmful consequences of the "total suspension of public worship" and "grievous harm on the entire flock of the faithful." But some limited material cooperation results in fewer bad consequences, and the good consequences of permitting public worship and broadening access to the Sacraments. So again, we see that material cooperation is sometimes moral, when the good consequences outweigh the bad. And the Pope, in this same document, encourages the faithful to continue to protest these unjust laws, so in this way the sin of scandal (appearing to approve of the law through material cooperation) is avoided. Even though these laws are intrinsically evil and gravely immoral, implicit material cooperation is not necessarily immoral, but depends on the weight of the good and bad consequences.

---

[483] Pope Pius XI, Acerba Animi, On the Persecution of the Church in Mexico, n. 16-17.

Pope Pius XI: "It is well to observe that to approve such an iniquitous law, or spontaneously to give to it true and proper cooperation, is undoubtedly illicit and sacrilegious."[484]

In the quote above, Pope Pius XI refers to formal cooperation by the term "true and proper cooperation." The Pontiff implies that even the mere approval of an intrinsically evil law constitutes a true and proper cooperation that is undoubtedly morally illicit. Therefore, an interior act of approval for any intrinsically evil act of another person constitutes a type of formal cooperation, which is itself intrinsically evil and always immoral. Just as some sins are exterior and other sins are interior, so also some sins of cooperation are exterior and other sins of cooperation are interior. The interior knowingly chosen act of approval for the intrinsically evil act of another person is formal cooperation, and is itself intrinsically evil and always immoral. Exterior acts of approval for intrinsically evil acts are likewise formal cooperation, intrinsically evil, and always immoral.

Previously, the Pope described acts of moral material cooperation as not truly a cooperation with evil; this is correct in the sense that any moral material cooperation is not a cooperation with sin itself (moral evil), but rather a cooperation with the bad consequences (physical evil) of a sinful act. Next, the Pope describes this moral material cooperation in greater detail.

Pope Pius XI: "But absolutely different is the case of one who yields to such unjust regulations solely against his will and under protest, and who besides does everything he can to lessen the disastrous effects of the pernicious law. In fact, the priest finds himself compelled to ask for that permission without which it would be impossible for him to exercise his sacred ministry for the good of souls; it is an imposition to which he is forced to submit in order to avoid a greater evil. His behavior, consequently, is not very different from that of one who having been robbed of his belongings is obliged to ask his unjust despoiler for at least the use of them."[485]

In order to be moral, material cooperation must always be implicit, not explicit cooperation. If the cooperator intends the evil moral object, or if he intends the bad consequences as an end, then his cooperation is explicit and is always sinful, at least due to a bad intention. The Pontiff teaches that moral cooperation must always be done, in a sense, "against his will and under protest." In other words, the cooperator must have no immoral intention, despite the sinfulness of the act of the other person or persons. The fact that a cooperator knowingly chooses an act of material cooperation does not imply that the cooperation is explicit, since he does not intend anything evil in the act of the other person.

In order to be moral, material cooperation must also have good consequences that outweigh the bad consequences. This principle is clearly expressed by the Pontiff in the case of this real life example. He requires his priests to materially cooperate with a law that the Church has strongly condemned, because the good

---

[484] Pope Pius XI, Acerba Animi, On the Persecution of the Church in Mexico, n. 16-17.
[485] Pope Pius XI, Acerba Animi, On the Persecution of the Church in Mexico, n. 16-17.

done to souls by the exercise of the priestly ministry, and the avoidance of a great evil (the loss of many spiritual benefits to souls), outweigh any bad consequences of cooperating with the law. Here the Pope is not only teaching about cooperation, but also acting based on that teaching. Nothing makes a teaching clearer than putting that teaching into practice.

.441. These laws are intrinsically evil and gravely immoral. The Pope describes this set of laws as iniquitous, sacrilegious, and a "manifestation of the will to destroy the Catholic Church itself." These laws are a grievous and clear example of intrinsically evil and gravely immoral law. Yet the Pope permits a type of material cooperation with these laws, even though this cooperation is not very remote. Again, it is clear that the Magisterium permits material cooperation whenever the good consequences outweigh the bad. The Magisterium does not teach that any type of material cooperation, even with an intrinsically evil and gravely immoral act, is always immoral.

In material cooperation, whether the cooperation is remote or proximate is a matter of degree. Therefore, even 'immediate' material cooperation is somewhat mediate and somewhat remote; it is not absolutely proximate. But if any act of material cooperation is not at all mediate, then the consequences in question would have to proceed directly from the act of the cooperator. In such a case, the act would not be cooperation, but perpetration. Therefore, the morality of material cooperation always depends on the moral weight of the good and bad consequences in the third font. No type of material cooperation is absolutely immediate. No type of material cooperation is necessarily always immoral, unless it is also formal cooperation, or also explicit cooperation, or also an act of perpetration of some sin.

Pope Pius XI: "In truth, the danger of formal cooperation, or of any approval whatever of the present law, is removed, as far as is necessary, by the protests energetically expressed by this Apostolic See, by the whole Episcopate and the people of Mexico. To these are added the precautions of the priest himself, who, although already appointed to the sacred ministry by his own Bishop, is obliged to ask the Government for the possibility of holding divine service; and, far from approving the law that unjustly imposes such a request, submits to it materially, as the saying is, and only in order to remove an obstacle to the exercise of the sacred ministry: an obstacle that would lead, as We have said, to a total cessation of worship, and hence to exceedingly great harm to innumerable souls. In much the same manner the faithful and the sacred ministers of the early Church, as history relates, sought permission, by means of gifts even, to visit and comfort the martyrs detained in prison and to administer the Sacraments to them; yet surely no one could have thought that by so doing they in some way approved or justified the conduct of the persecutors."[486]

Previously in this document, the Pontiff used terminology such that formal cooperation was called "true and proper" cooperation and moral material cooperation was presented as not truly and properly a type of cooperation. Now

---

[486] Pope Pius XI, Acerba Animi, On the Persecution of the Church in Mexico, n. 16-17.

he changes terminology to the more common terms: formal and material. Pope Pius XI explains that material cooperation is moral when the good consequences outweigh the bad, as in this particular case.

But on the topic of formal cooperation, again, the Pope implies that the mere approval of an inherently unjust law is always immoral. An interior act of approval for any intrinsically evil act does not seek the same moral object, and so it is not perpetration, but formal cooperation. However, if any type of interior act, whether it is called or seems to be a type of approval, has the same evil moral object as another act, then that interior act is the perpetration of that intrinsically evil act, and not merely a type of cooperation. But if we consider that an act of interior approval extends only to approving of the act itself, which is a type of assistance to that act, then this cooperative act is related to the evil moral object of the other person's act only indirectly, through the act itself of the other person, causing this type of approval to be formal cooperation, not perpetration. The mere approval of any intrinsically evil act is a type of formal cooperation.

.442. United States Conference of Catholic Bishops

USCCB: "Formal cooperation in the grave evil of contraceptive sterilization, either by approving or tolerating it for medical reasons, is forbidden and totally alien to the mission entrusted by the Church to Catholic health care facilities."[487]

Direct sterilization is intrinsically evil; if the moral object of the chosen act is sterilization, then the act is always gravely immoral, regardless of the intended end, or the good and bad consequences. Indirect sterilization is an act that has a good moral object, such as treating a medical condition, but also has the unintended bad consequence of infertility. The term contraceptive sterilization refers to direct sterilization. The intentional approval of any intrinsically evil act, including direct sterilization, is explicit formal cooperation, and is therefore intrinsically evil and always immoral.

But the phase "tolerating it for medical reasons" requires some explanation. This does not refer to indirect sterilization, in which sterility is an unintended consequence (in the third font) tolerated for the sake of a morally good medical treatment (in the second font). Rather, the phrase refers to a Catholic health care facility, whose leaders willfully permit acts of direct sterilization in their facility, which they are able to prevent. This is an example of formal cooperation by omission. When persons having the ability and authority to prevent intrinsically evil and gravely immoral acts from occurring decide to do nothing, they effectively cooperate formally with the act itself, assisting the act (by means of a willful omission) in attaining its evil moral object.

An exterior or interior act of approval for any intrinsically evil act constitutes formal cooperation and is always immoral. Also, even if formal cooperation occurs by a willful act of omission, it is intrinsically evil and always immoral.

---

[487] National Conference of Catholic Bishops (now called the U.S. Conference of Catholic Bishops), Statement on Tubal Ligation, 3 July 1980, n. 3.

USCCB: "A Catholic cannot vote for a candidate who takes a position in favor of an intrinsic evil, such as abortion or racism, if the voter's intent is to support that position. In such cases a Catholic would be guilty of formal cooperation in grave evil. At the same time, a voter should not use a candidate's opposition to an intrinsic evil to justify indifference or inattentiveness to other important moral issues involving human life and dignity."[488]

Anyone who acts with immoral intent, sins under the first font of morality. And this is also true for acts of voting, whether by a citizen or a legislator. If a voter intends to assist a candidate in attaining an evil moral object, such as the legalization of abortion or euthanasia, then the voter commits the sin of explicit formal cooperation, which is a sin under the first and second fonts. If a voter intends to cooperate with a candidate in the circumstances of an intrinsically evil act, then the voter commits the sin of explicit material cooperation. But if the voter's act is inherently ordered toward the evil moral object itself, not through the act of another person, but in a way that is morally direct and deliberate, such as a vote in favor of an inherently unjust constitutional amendment, then the act of voting is perpetration, not merely cooperation.

If racism is defined as a bias or a tendency toward discrimination, then only the knowingly chosen immoral acts based on that bias would be sins. The bias itself is a type of harm or disorder ('physical evil'). If a legislator seeks to deprive some group of persons of fundamental human rights, because of their race, ethnicity, religion, gender, age, or even because of sinful behavior, then the act that seeks such a deprivation as its moral object is intrinsically evil and gravely immoral. Formal cooperation with such an act by any means is also intrinsically evil and gravely immoral. Explicit formal cooperation adds a sinful intention to the objectively immoral act, making the act even more gravely immoral.

.443. The Catechism and the Compendium

Compendium of the Catechism: "What is forbidden by the fifth commandment? The fifth commandment forbids as gravely contrary to the moral law:
 * direct and intentional murder and cooperation in it;
 * direct abortion, willed as an end or as a means, as well as cooperation in it. Attached to this sin is the penalty of excommunication because, from the moment of his or her conception, the human being must be absolutely respected and protected in his integrity;
 * direct euthanasia, which consists in putting an end to the life of the handicapped, the sick, or those near death by an act or by the omission of a required action;
 * suicide and voluntary cooperation in it, insofar as it is a grave offense against the just love of God, of self, and of neighbor. One's responsibility may be aggravated by the scandal given; one who is psychologically disturbed or is experiencing grave fear may have diminished responsibility."[489]

---

[488] USCCB, 'Forming Consciences for Faithful Citizenship,' 14 November 2007, n. 34.
[489] Compendium of the Catechism of the Catholic Church, n. 470.

Cooperation with Evil

The Compendium teaches that cooperation in murder is a sin. Abortion, euthanasia, and suicide are types of murder. Even though the Compendium happens not to mention cooperation in discussing euthanasia, cooperation in any type of murder is a sin. Notice that the Compendium distinguishes direct and intentional killing from indirect and unintentional killing. Murder is intrinsically evil, and so it is always direct and intentional. Direct abortion, and any other type of direct and voluntary killing of the innocent, is intrinsically evil.

The type of cooperation referred to here is formal cooperation. Although the Compendium uses only the term 'cooperation,' the unequivocal condemnation of this cooperation with intrinsically evil acts implies that the type of cooperation is formal, not material. Formal cooperation is always immoral; material cooperation is not always immoral. Indirect abortion, and any other indirect and unintended killing of the innocent, may be moral or immoral, depending on the circumstances. Cooperation with such an act may also be moral or immoral, depending on the circumstances; this is material cooperation, not formal cooperation. It is also possible for an act of material cooperation to occur in relation to an intrinsically evil act, such as abortion. But the above passage from the Compendium refers only to direct and voluntary immoral acts (intrinsically evil acts) and to formal cooperation with those acts.

Catechism of the Catholic Church: "Formal cooperation in an abortion constitutes a grave offense."[490]

The Catechism explicitly states that formal cooperation with abortion is a grave offense (an objective mortal sin). Abortion is gravely immoral because it is a type of murder, and this implies that formal cooperation with any type of murder, and with any type of gravely immoral intrinsically evil act, is also a grave offense.

.444. Summary

So from all of the above uses of the term 'cooperation' in magisterial documents, several points are clear. Formal cooperation refers to cooperation with the second font of an intrinsically evil act. Formal cooperation takes its gravity, mortal or venial, from the gravity of the second font of the other person's act, because the moral object of an act of formal cooperation is to assist the other act in attaining that evil moral object. Formal cooperation is always immoral, not merely because it is cooperation with an intrinsically evil act, but because it is an intrinsically evil type of cooperation with an intrinsically evil act. Participation in attaining an evil moral object makes formal cooperation intrinsically evil.

Explicit cooperation occurs as either explicit formal cooperation, or explicit material cooperation. All explicit cooperation is always immoral, at least due to a sinful intention. Explicit formal cooperation is more sinful than implicit formal cooperation, due to the addition of an immoral intention to an act of cooperation that is already intrinsically evil. Explicit material cooperation is always immoral because of the intention, but the material cooperation itself may or may not be objectively immoral under the third font.

---

[490] Catechism of the Catholic Church, n. 2272.

The Magisterium does not teach that immediate material cooperation is always immoral, nor that immediate material cooperation with an intrinsically evil act is always immoral, nor that immediate material cooperation with a gravely immoral intrinsically evil act is always immoral. All of the examples of moral or immoral material cooperation given in magisterial documents are plainly based on the weight of the good and bad consequences of the chosen act. No principle is stated, and no example from which a general principle might be drawn is given, which would indicate that any type of immediate material cooperation is always immoral. Material cooperation is sometimes moral, and other times immoral, depending on the moral weight of the good and bad consequences.

Finally, the Magisterium has explicitly rejected the idea that a person who is under duress commits no actual mortal sin, even if he knowingly chooses a gravely immoral act of cooperation. Duress can reduce culpability by adversely affecting judgment, as the Compendium points out in cases of suicide. But the decree of the Holy Office under Pope Pius XI gives an example of duress that is still a mortal sin, despite being only material cooperation, and despite duress of moderate moral weight.

.445.
EXAMPLES OF COOPERATION

Please understand that these examples of cooperation depend in part on the application of general principles to particular concrete acts, and in part on a judgment of the particular circumstances of the acts in question. Faithful and reasonable Catholics may sometimes disagree in the application of the teachings of the Church to particular cases, especially when a judgment of the prudential order is needed to weigh complex circumstances. These examples are presented to assist the reader in better understanding the general principles of cooperation, not as a definitive judgment as to which type of cooperation applies to each hypothetical case.

Direct Abortion

Direct abortion is intrinsically evil and always gravely immoral. Formal cooperation with direct abortion is also intrinsically evil and always gravely immoral.

(1) A pregnant woman goes to a hospital to obtain an abortion. She signs the permission form, and a physician performs the abortion. Both the physician and the woman are guilty of the sin of abortion; this is the perpetration of sin, not merely cooperation with sin. The woman's act is not cooperation because her knowingly chosen act has, as its moral object, the death of the innocent prenatal. The physician's act is not cooperation because his act is also directed to the same evil moral object. Both are guilty of perpetrating the same intrinsically evil and gravely immoral sin of abortion.

(2) A nurse assists a physician in performing an abortion. Formal cooperation is defined as an act that assists the act of another person in attaining an evil moral object. But the term 'assists' must be understood according to the moral meaning

of the term. Although in secular terms the nurse may be 'assisting' the physician, morally her act will be either perpetration or formal cooperation, depending on the nature of her act. This truth is clear from the teaching of Pope John Paul II on assisted suicide. He plainly taught that sometimes an act of 'assisted' suicide is perpetration, and other times it is cooperation.

Pope John Paul II: "To concur with the intention of another person to commit suicide and to help in carrying it out through so-called 'assisted suicide' means to cooperate in, and at times to be the actual perpetrator of, an injustice which can never be excused, even if it is requested."[491]

When, in secular terms, a person is committing an act of 'assisted' suicide, in moral terms he might be either a perpetrator or a cooperator. Similarly, when a nurse is assisting a physician in performing an abortion, her act may be either perpetration or formal cooperation, depending on the nature of the act. Now formal cooperation is itself an intrinsically evil act, since its moral object is to assist the act of the other person in attaining an evil moral object. If the nurse's acts are directed at the evil moral object of killing an innocent prenatal, then she is a perpetrator; if her acts are directed at the evil moral object of assisting the act of another person in attaining that moral object, then she is a formal cooperator.

Suppose that a nurse assists directly in the procedure of abortion. She hands the physician the instruments used to kill the prenatal. She physically assists him throughout the procedure. She is part of a team of two or more persons, and the purpose of that team is to abort a prenatal. In such a case, she is a perpetrator, not merely a cooperator. The nurse's act is directed at the same moral object as the physician's act, to kill an innocent person. Her act is essentially the same type of act under the moral law. Even though the nurse has a subordinate role, her act is still directed at the same moral object. Her act has the same moral object as the act of the physician because she is part of a team, whose knowingly chosen acts are each and all directed at the evil moral object of the death of the prenatal. The fact that a person has a subordinate role is not sufficient to reduce the sin from perpetration to cooperation.

Similarly, if two men work together to accomplish the suicide of one of them, both are guilty of perpetration. Even though the one man's act is, in secular terms, an act of 'assisted suicide,' the two men work together to accomplish the same evil moral object. And so both are perpetrators, regardless of which one of them actually commits the final physical act that results in death.

This role of perpetration is particularly clear when a nurse works at an abortion clinic, since it is the purpose of her job there to accomplish abortions. Her acts are directed at the end of abortion. The moral meaning of her acts is to bring about the death of prenatals. Her acts might not be physically direct, but they are morally direct. The inherent moral meaning of her acts, as part of a team that performs abortions, is the direct and voluntary killing of innocent human persons, which is perpetration, not cooperation.

---

[491] Pope John Paul II, Evangelium Vitae, n. 66; inner quote from Augustine, Epistulae, Corpus Scriptorum Ecclesiasticorum Latinorum, vol. 57, n. 320.

On the other hand, suppose that, in a case of assisted suicide, the two men do not work together toward the evil moral object of the death of one of them. But instead, the one man provides the ability to the other man to commit suicide. His act is directed at enabling the other man to commit an intrinsically evil act; such an act is formal cooperation, not perpetration. An example of formal cooperation would be a man who obtains and provides a drug to another man so that he will be able to commit suicide.

Now suppose that a nurse works in a hospital, and her job is generally moral and not involved in abortion. Then, on a particular occasion, she is required to provide assistance to a direct abortion. Her act might still be one of perpetration, if she is part of a team that works together to achieve a particular moral object, to abort a child. She is not exonerated merely because her job is usually moral. The circumstances of an act never affect the moral object. Both the nurse who works in an abortion clinic and the nurse who works in a hospital commit the same sin when each is part of a team performing an abortion.

But in some instances, her acts might be formal cooperation, not perpetration. For example, if she prepares the patient for the abortive operation, she is formally cooperating, because her act is directed at assisting the act of the physician in performing the abortion. But if she 'assists' in the procedure itself, she is a perpetrator. A cooperative act is always substantially different from an act of perpetration, not merely in exterior terms, but in its essential moral nature. In another example, if a worker at an abortion clinic never 'assists' in the abortions, but works at the front desk, taking information from women who want an abortion, giving them permission forms to sign, entering their names into the schedule for the procedure, and conducting each to a room for an initial examination, then the worker is committing the sin of formal cooperation with abortion, not perpetration. These acts all assist the act of the physician (or of the team) in attaining the moral object of the death of a prenatal.

.446. To the secular mind, it might seem as if these acts of formal cooperation are merely material cooperation, since they are somewhat distant, in physical terms, from the abortive act. Handing someone a form to fill out, and getting their signature seems far removed from the actual abortion. But the true inherent moral meaning of any act is determined by its moral object. Such acts have as their moral object to assist someone else's act in attaining the moral object of abortion. Therefore, it is formal cooperation, not merely material cooperation. And this is all the more clear when we recall the teaching of the Magisterium that formal cooperation includes even a mere act of approval of an intrinsically evil act, such as approving of an inherently unjust law, or approving of an act of euthanasia. And this is true for persons not directly involved, in any exterior way, in the sinful act. For even an interior act of approval for an intrinsically evil act is a type of formal cooperation. Therefore, we must judge whether an act is perpetration, or formal cooperation, or material cooperation in terms of morality, not in terms of mere appearances.

(3) Some acts related to the intrinsically evil act of abortion are material cooperation. A worker who cleans operating rooms before and after all kinds of

procedures, including some abortions, provides only material cooperation. To provide such a service to a clinic that only performs abortions would be much less remote than to provide such a service to a hospital that performs many different types of procedures. But in any case the moral weight of the good and bad consequences would determine whether or not the material cooperation was moral. A person who provides the service of cleaning the exterior windows of buildings might morally provide that service even to an abortion clinic.

A physician or nurse in a hospital emergency room who admits a pregnant woman to the hospital due to injury or illness, knowing that eventually another physician and the woman might decide that a direct abortion would be done, still commits only material cooperation. The act of admitting the injured or ill woman is directed at treating an illness or injury; such an act is not intrinsically evil, and so cannot be formal cooperation (which is always intrinsically evil). Whether a cooperative act is formal or material can always be determined by ascertaining the moral object of the chosen act. Every act of formal cooperation has an evil moral object, that of assisting another person in attaining an evil moral object. Every act of mere material cooperation (if it is not both formal cooperation and material cooperation) pertains to the circumstances, particularly the bad consequences, of the other person's act, not to the moral object. Material cooperation assists in attaining the bad consequences of the other person's act, but not in attaining the moral object of the other person's act.

(4) Consider the case of a woman who becomes pregnant, and of the father who wants her to abort their child. Suppose that the father, to one degree or another, pressures the mother to abort the child. If he compels her to have the abortion, he is guilty of perpetration. It may seem as if his act is mediate or indirect, since he attains the abortion through the act of the mother. But his knowingly chosen act seeks the end of abortion in a way that is morally direct and deliberate. His act does not merely seek to assist the mother in getting an abortion. Therefore, morally, his act is directly related to the moral object, as an act of perpetration, not cooperation.

If the father strongly pressures her, but does not compel her, his act still attempts to attain the moral object of abortion itself. The attempt to strongly pressure someone to commit an intrinsically evil act, even if the attempt fails to attain its moral object, is still directed toward the same moral object as the sinful act of the other person. For a person who strongly pressures another is not merely assisting the act of the other person. So in order for his act to be cooperation, not perpetration, she must have a willingness to commit the intrinsically evil act apart from his pressure. But what was said previously about duress still applies. Even if she is pressured into the abortion, if she knowingly chooses the sin of abortion, she is a perpetrator and is guilty of an actual mortal sin (under the usual conditions for a mortal sin to be actual).

.447. Now if we consider successive cases in which his pressuring of her decreases by degrees, and her willingness increases by degrees, at some point he becomes merely a cooperator, not a perpetrator. But the problem of distinguishing between perpetration and formal cooperation is merely academic.

Both types of acts are intrinsically evil. And if the perpetration of an intrinsically evil act is gravely immoral, then formal cooperation with that same act is gravely immoral. If, in a particular case, it is unclear as to whether an act is perpetration or formal cooperation, it will nevertheless be clear that the proposed act is a sin, of similar gravity, and must be avoided.

(5) A taxi driver is asked to drive a woman to an abortion clinic. She states during the trip that she is going there for an abortion. If he refuses to take her to the clinic, he will lose his job. His cooperation is material cooperation. And if he does not take her, she will still be able to get to the clinic and obtain the abortion, so if he decides not to cooperation, the bad consequence of losing his job is not outweighed by any good consequence (e.g. that the abortion would not occur). If he takes her to the clinic, the good consequence is that he retains his job, and the bad consequence of abortion is unaffected. So the good consequences outweigh the bad consequences, and the act of material cooperation is moral.

(6) However, the same cannot be said for the taxi driver who approves of the abortion. If she reveals that she is getting an abortion, and he expresses approval for this grave sin in his mind and heart, or in his words or actions, then he commits the sin of formal cooperation with a gravely immoral act. And if he then takes her to the clinic with the intention of helping her to obtain the abortion, his act is also explicit material cooperation. The material cooperation is objectively moral, if the good consequences outweigh the bad, but the immoral intention makes the act a sin. The exterior acts in the above two cases (n. 5 and 6) are similar, but the morality of any act is not based on exterior appearances, but on the three fonts of morality.

(7) A military law prohibits female soldiers from becoming pregnant, and punishes any pregnancy with a penalty, up to and including court martial. Even if this law is limited to pregnancy outside of marriage (and in which a mortal sin was committed), the law has the reasonably foreseeable consequence that a female soldier who becomes pregnant might seek and obtain an abortion in order to avoid the penalty. Such a law constitutes material cooperation with abortion because the law can be reasonably anticipated to have a bad consequence in the act of another person. This example of material cooperation is gravely immoral because the harm done by abortion far outweighs the good done in decreasing pregnancies outside of marriage among female soldiers. The law is not formal cooperation because the law does not have an evil moral object.

(8) An abortion clinic attempts to rent space in a shopping mall. If the owner of the mall rents the space, what type of sin it is? If he commits explicit cooperation by intending to assist the clinic in its work of abortion, then he sins mortally; his intention is gravely contrary to the love of God and neighbor. But if he lacks the intention of explicit cooperation, is his act formal cooperation or material? Two situations are possible.

(a) The owner is compelled by law and the threat of long imprisonment to rent to the abortion clinic. In such a case, his implicit cooperation is not formal. His intention and his act have the same end, the intended end and the moral object of avoiding imprisonment. His act is not formal cooperation because his act does not seek to assist in attaining the death of prenatals. His cooperation is like the person who is robbed at gunpoint (or by some other grave threat); his act does not seek to assist the robber, but to avoid grave harm. And the deaths of the prenatals that occur are not the moral object of his chosen act. In this case, his cooperation is material, and will be moral if the good consequences outweigh the bad. If his refusal to cooperate results in the abortion clinic being established in the shopping mall anyway, and results in grave harm to him, then he may morally cooperate. The bad consequences are unavoidable.

(b) The owner is free to allow or disallow the abortion clinic to be established in his shopping mall. If he permits the clinic to be established there, he commits the sin of formal cooperation. His act assists the clinic in attaining the moral object of the deaths of innocent prenatals. This act is also material cooperation, since his act also assists in attaining the bad consequences of the other persons' acts. It is often the case that formal cooperation includes material cooperation, because intrinsically evil acts always have some bad consequences, and gravely immoral intrinsically evil acts always have some bad consequences of grave moral weight. Any act that assists in attaining an evil moral object also likely assists in attaining some or all of the bad consequences of that intrinsically evil act.

(9) A physician is threatened with long imprisonment or death if he does not perform direct abortions. This case is unlike the case of the shopping mall owner (n. 8 above). The sin of direct abortion is intrinsically evil. Severe duress never changes the moral object of any intrinsically evil act. The act of the owner who rents space under severe duress is not inherently directed toward the killing of any innocent person. But the act of the physician who performs an abortion is inherently directed at killing the innocent. If he performs the abortion, even under severe duress, he commits an intrinsically evil and gravely immoral act. And severe duress does not reduce the sin to anything less than an actual mortal sin (but the usual conditions for actual mortal sin always apply).

.448. Does automatic excommunication apply to formal cooperation?

Canon 18: "Laws which establish a penalty, restrict the free exercise of rights, or contain an exception from the law are subject to strict interpretation."

The laws of the Church, given under the temporal authority, especially when they include a strict penalty, are to be interpreted narrowly (i.e. strictly). If the penalty is strict, the interpretation must be narrow. When interpreting Sacred Scripture, the literal meaning can be extended to many different similar cases. So when Scripture forbids adultery, we understand that all sexual sins are prohibited by that same text. And Scripture also has a spiritual level of meaning, whereby the literal or figurative meaning of the text also refers to another type of meaning, one not explicitly stated. But not so with Canon Law. In the laws of the Church, especially when a penalty is given, only what is explicitly stated as forbidden is forbidden. Perhaps the eternal moral law also forbids and punishes numerous other related acts. But Canon Law per se only forbids what it explicitly forbids, and only punishes what is explicitly punishes.

Canon 751: "Heresy is the obstinate denial or obstinate doubt after the reception of baptism of some truth which is to be believed by divine and Catholic faith; apostasy is the total repudiation of the Christian faith; schism is the refusal of submission to the Supreme Pontiff or of communion with the members of the Church subject to him."

Canon 1364 n. 1: "an apostate from the faith, a heretic, or a schismatic incurs a latae sententiae excommunication."

Canon 1398: "A person who procures a completed abortion incurs a latae sententiae excommunication."

Only formal apostasy, formal heresy, and formal schism carry the penalty of automatic excommunication. The penalty of excommunication is strict, so the interpretation must be narrow. Therefore, also, if the person did not know that a particular sin carried the penalty of excommunication, then he or she is not automatically excommunicated.[492] And so, if a woman procures a completed abortion, but she did not know that the sin included the penalty of automatic excommunication, then she is not automatically excommunicated. Any severe penalty of Church law requires a strict interpretation and a narrow application.

Therefore, if a person does not procure a completed abortion, he or she is not automatically excommunicated, even if the sin committed is an actual mortal sin. (A man can procure a completed abortion for a woman, by performing the procedure, or by compelling her to obtain an abortion, or by enacting a law that authorizes legal direct abortions, or in other ways.) A person who commits even an actual mortal sin of explicit cooperation, or of formal cooperation, or of sinful material cooperation, with abortion, is not excommunicated (as the Code of Canon Law currently stands).

However, if a person obstinately denies or obstinately doubts that direct abortion is always gravely immoral, he or she is guilty of material heresy. And if that person knows that the Church definitively teaches that direct abortion is always gravely immoral, and yet he or she persists in obstinate denial or obstinate doubt, then he or she is guilty of formal heresy, and is automatically excommunicated.

.449. Embryonic Stem Cells

(1) Can a medical researcher make use of embryonic stem cells (ESCs), or the cell line derived from them, if he is not involved in obtaining the cells? The persons who obtained the ESCs did so by destroying living human embryos. Such an act is essentially no different than abortion; the morally-direct destruction of human embryos is the murder of prenatal human persons. Making use of those cells in research is not formal cooperation with the act of destroying the embryos, since the acts involved in research do not seek to assist in attaining that moral object.

---

[492] This conclusion is also based on Canon 1323: "The following are not subject to a penalty when they have violated a law or precept ... a person who without negligence was ignorant that he or she violated a law or precept...."

However, the embryos are killed in order to result in a line of stem cells for the researchers to use.[493] So any use of ESCs might have the bad consequence of making further acts of killing human embryos more likely, in order to provide more ESC lines for further research. This bad consequence is not the moral object of the research; it is in the third font, not the second. So this type of research is material cooperation, not formal cooperation. However, the good consequences of doing medical research are greatly outweighed by the deaths of innocent very young human persons. Therefore, the material cooperation in this case is immoral. This sin of cooperation is an objective mortal sin because the deaths of these innocents gravely outweighs any good consequences. Catholic medical researchers may not participate in embryonic stem cell research.

(2) Under the second font, the moral object of this research is good: to seek an understanding of human biology, and to seek treatments and cures for disease. Such an understanding might result in a treatment or cure that is not based on the need for an ESC line. But more likely, if the research results in a treatment or cure, additional ESC lines would be needed to produce such a treatment or cure. Then there would be a much stronger inducement toward killing more human embryos. The research does not seek this result as a moral object, but it is a grave and sufficiently-likely consequence, which, in this case, proceeds directly from the research, as well as from cooperation with the production of the ESC line. So in addition to the sin of material cooperation with the deaths of the innocents used to produce the embryonic stem cell line, this type of research is also sinful as a type of perpetration of a sin under the third font. This research has possible grave bad consequences, that a treatment may result that will promote further killing of human embryos, which outweigh the possible good consequences.

(3) If a cure is developed from ESCs, would it be moral to use that cure? If the cure or treatment requires an embryo to be killed for that patient, then it would not be moral to take that cure or treatment because the patient would in effect be ordering the death of the embryo. Such an act would be the sin itself of abortion, not merely cooperation, because the moral object of the chosen act is the death of an innocent prenatal.

However, if the cure or treatment made use of an existing stem cell line, the act would not be intrinsically evil; the moral object would be the healing of the patient. The morality of the act would depend on intention and consequences. Supposing good intention, the good consequences would have to outweigh the bad consequences. There is some material cooperation in using such a cure or treatment, but if the good consequences outweigh the bad, then the cure or treatment could be used. The danger of scandal must be avoided, so that people do not think that ESC research is moral. The treatment cannot be highly experimental, nor offer only limited benefits, for then the harm done by the cooperation would outweigh the good. And the use of such a treatment must not cause the death of further embryos (which would make the act formal cooperation, not material cooperation). Neither can the use of such a treatment

---

[493] Embryonic stem cells are kept alive in a culture medium, and they divide to produce generation after generation of cells; these successive generations are called a cell line.

make the deaths of more human embryos more likely, for then the harm done by the material cooperation would outweigh the good done. The death of an innocent prenatal has greater moral weight than the cure or treatment of the patient. In addition, there must be no other moral way to obtain a treatment or cure; if an alternative treatment is less effective, it might still be preferable if it lacks the bad consequences of the material cooperation. Therefore, if the person is acting with good intention, and if the chosen act is not intrinsically evil, and if all the good and bad consequences are weighed, and the good outweighs the bad, then the act of material cooperation would be moral. In general, in many cases, the result of this moral evaluation would be that the use of such a cure or treatment would be immoral.

.450. Contraception

(1) Is it moral for a physician to prescribe, or for a pharmacist to dispense, birth control pills? The use of any type of artificial contraception is intrinsically evil and always gravely immoral. Chemical contraceptives (birth control pills; BCPs) are generally also abortifacient; they are capable of causing a very early abortion, usually by preventing implantation of the conceived prenatal.

If a physician prescribes contraceptives to a sexually-active woman, the moral object of his act is to prevent conception, depriving the sexual act of the procreative meaning. Artificial contraception is intrinsically evil and always gravely immoral. His act is a sin of perpetration, not of formal cooperation, because his act has the moral object of preventing conception. But if a physician prescribes abortifacient contraception, his act is a sin of perpetration of both contraception and abortion. His act has two moral objects, to prevent conception and to abort a conceived prenatal. The reason that the physician's act is not formal cooperation is that he is not merely assisting the contraceptive act of the patient. He is authorizing, and therefore procuring, contraception. A prescription does not merely provide a product or service, it authorizes a particular act, such as taking a pill, or using a medical device. From a secular point of view, it seems as if the physician 'assists' the woman in contraception. But from a moral point of view, his act is directed at the end of contraception.

(2) The pharmacist who dispenses contraception is committing the sin of formal cooperation. He does not have the role of authorizing the use of a medication or device. He assists the patient in attaining the evil moral object by providing the means. His act is not merely material cooperation because he provides the whole (or at least a substantial) means to that moral object; the contraceptive that he provides is the means to the end of contraception (or abortifacient contraception). Therefore, his act does not pertain merely to the circumstances. If he provided information on the safe use of a birth control pill, such as which medications might conflict with the BCP, then his act would be material cooperation.

(3) The store clerk who takes payment for the contraceptive commits an act of material cooperation. He does not provide authorization for the contraceptive, nor does he dispense the contraceptive. His act pertains to the circumstances, i.e. accepting payment for the contraceptive. And the money received does not go to

him personally, but to the store. In such a case, the evaluation of the good and bad consequences applies.

(4) Is it moral for a physician to prescribe contraceptives to a woman who is either not sexually-active, or post-menopausal, for a medical purpose? In this case, the moral object is not contraception, but the treatment of a medical problem (such as painful irregular periods, or post-menopausal symptoms). So if the good consequences outweigh the bad, then his act is moral.

However, he cannot morally prescribe a contraceptive, even for a medical purpose, to a woman who is fertile and sexually-active. His intention to treat a medical condition is good. But the act itself has two moral objects, the good end of treating a medical condition and the evil end of preventing conception. His intention does not change the moral object. And the one good moral object does not reform the other evil moral object. Therefore, the act is intrinsically evil and always gravely immoral.

.451. Sexual Acts Outside of Marriage

How should faithful Catholics respond to the situation of family or friends who are living together outside of marriage?

(1) Suppose that an adult visits with her parents, and she brings her boyfriend with her. If the parents permit them to sleep in the same bedroom, is this sinful cooperation? This is a case of material cooperation, not perpetration, and not formal cooperation. The parents do not have authority over an adult child to decide what that adult may do. Their chosen act to permit the couple to stay in the same bedroom does not have the moral object of sexual relations outside of marriage. The act of permitting them to decide their own sleeping arrangements does not have an evil moral object. However, as an act of material cooperation, the good consequences would still need to outweigh the bad consequences, including scandal. The parents might decide to require the two to sleep in separate rooms, or to find overnight accommodations elsewhere.

(2) The same analysis does not apply if the child is minor, or, from a Biblical point of view, is under 20 years (cf. Exodus 30:14; Leviticus 27:3-4). In such a case, the parents have the authority (and usually the ability) to prevent their teenager and her boyfriend (or his girlfriend) from sleeping in the same bedroom. If they permit them to sleep in the same bedroom, they are at least committing the sin of formal cooperation with a gravely immoral act. In the case of minors, the parents might be guilty of perpetration if they authorize the young couple to have sexual relations as minors and outside of marriage. The moral object of the act would determine whether is was formal cooperation or perpetration.

(3) Is it a sin of cooperation by omission to refrain from objecting to adult family members or friends who are living together outside of marriage? It may be a sin of material cooperation by omission, depending on the circumstances. The omission of an objection is not intrinsically evil, because there is no requirement of the moral law that each person object to every sin by every person around him. Each person is responsible for his or her own acts. However, Christians are

required by the moral law to spread the Gospel, in accord with the circumstances of their lives, and this includes the teachings of Christ on morality as well as on faith and salvation. If a decision to omit speaking up against a sin, such as premarital sex, makes that act more likely to continue to occur, the omission may be material cooperation. But an evaluation as to the good and bad consequences of raising the objection is needed. If the persons are unlikely to respond the objection by avoiding the sin, if more harm is done than good by objecting, then the omission would not be material cooperation. And in some circumstances silence might be morally required, if it is clear that speaking would do more harm than good.

(4) Should family members attend the wedding of a Catholic who is marrying outside the Church, by divorce and remarriage? In this case, merely attending such a ceremony is not formal cooperation. The act of attending does not have the moral object of assisting the couple in marrying outside the Church, nor of sexual relations without the true marital meaning, and does not necessarily imply approval. However, as is always the case, any type of approval for an intrinsically evil act would be formal cooperation. The person who is attending must not approve of the sin of marrying outside the Church.

The Catholic who attends such a ceremony may do so with good intention, such as to avoid harm to his relationship with that family member. And he must not be attending as a type of approval; to that end, he should probably avoid being a part of the ceremony itself. To avoid scandal, he should voice his objection to marrying outside the Church, unless his objection is already well-known. He should not disrupt the ceremony, nor speak words of malice, nor utterly reject that family member; such acts would be sinful. The sin of another person does not justify your own knowingly chosen act.

In some circumstances, declining to attend such a ceremony may be a moral obligation. Although custom and secular society pressure family members to attend such events, the moral law is above custom and above popular opinion. If more harm is done by attending than by declining to attend, then the person must not attend. Otherwise, it is a sin under the third font.

(5) How should a Catholic treat a family member who engages in a homosexual relationship? Homosexual acts are intrinsically evil and always gravely immoral. Therefore, any approval for such acts would be formal cooperation and also gravely immoral. Furthermore, grave harm is done to the Church by the sin of scandal when a Catholic expresses approval for such behavior, which is inherently and gravely disordered. Catholics should not attend gay marriage ceremonies, even of close family members, because of the danger of scandal, and because such a 'marriage' or 'civil union' is neither a true natural marriage, nor a valid Sacrament of Marriage. Also, the ceremony itself is intrinsically evil, since it constitutes a type of approval for homosexual acts. The approval of any type of intrinsically evil act is always the sin of formal cooperation.

On the other hand, the moral law does not require us to utterly reject all persons who continue committing objective mortal sin. We are required to judge acts, so that we can avoid sin and help others avoid sin, but we are also required not to judge persons. Some persons who commit objective mortal sin might have a reduction in culpability so that they might still be in a state of grace. Therefore, a family member or other person who is known to be committing one type of objective mortal sin or another should still be treated with the respect due to all human persons, regardless of their sins. Catholics must be careful never to cooperate formally with any intrinsically evil act, and to avoid scandal and any sinful or unnecessary material cooperation with sin. But cooperation with evil applies to sins, not to persons who are sinners.

(6) Suppose that a wife refuses to have sexual relations with her husband, for a long time and without a grave reason. She is guilty of a mortal sin against the grave obligation to render the marriage debt (1 Cor 7:5). Now suppose that her husband, because he is denied marital relations for a long time falls into some serious sexual sin, such as masturbation or adultery. Is she guilty of cooperation by her omission? Her refusal is intrinsically evil as a sin of perpetration, since the moral object of her act is to deprive the marriage of the good of marital relations. But nothing prevents an act from having more than one moral object. Scripture teaches (1 Cor 7:5) that refusing to have relations with one's spouse may cause the spouse to fall into temptation and sin. Therefore, unless she knows that her husband's character is such that he will not be tempted, her decision to omit marital relations makes her husband's sin more likely. But degree of probability pertains to the circumstances, but not to the moral object. So her refusal is sinful material cooperation under the third font of circumstances, because her decision makes it more difficult for her husband to avoid mortal sin. If she does not intend that he sin, her cooperation is implicit, not explicit. But objectively, her refusal is sinful cooperation with intrinsically evil and gravely immoral acts.

.452. Cooperation with the Evil of Pornography

The sins associated with pornographic material can be divided into three types: (1) those associated with its creation, (2) with its distribution, and (3) with its use. In each category, there are certainly sins of perpetration, but also some sins of cooperation. The creation of pornography cooperates with the sins of distribution and use. The distribution of pornography cooperates with the sins of creation and use. The use of pornography cooperates with the sins of creation and distribution.

(1) The persons who create pornography generally intend that the material be distributed and used. They also realize, and might even intend, that this material be used to commit various gravely immoral sexual sins. The acts involved in creating pornography assist the intrinsically evil acts of other persons to attain evil moral objects. In addition, the creation of pornography assists other persons (distributors and users) in committing various sins with bad consequences of grave moral weight. Therefore, the creation of pornography often includes sins of explicit formal cooperation and of explicit material cooperation, in addition to the various sins of perpetration.

(2) The distribution of pornography includes sinful cooperation with the evils of creating and using pornography. Both the creation and the use of pornography include many various serious sins. The distribution of pornography cooperates

with those sins explicitly, formally, and materially. Those who distribute pornography generally intend that this material continue to be created, and continue to be used, so that it can continue to be distributed. The distributors commit the sin of explicit formal cooperation by approving of the commission of various intrinsically evil sexual sins. And if the distributors intend that the material be used to commit sexual sins (since this is known to be one of the main uses of pornography), they also commit the sin of explicit formal cooperation.

The sexual sins associated with pornographic material are intrinsically evil and gravely immoral acts, and so any formal cooperation with these sins is also intrinsically evil and gravely immoral. The distribution of pornography may include some acts of explicit formal cooperation with the sins of the creators, as well as some acts of explicit formal cooperation with the sins of the users. Distribution is also explicit material cooperation, since the acts of distribution pertain to the circumstances of the creation and use of pornography. Therefore, the distribution of pornography includes various sins of cooperation in addition to the sins of perpetration.

(3) The use of pornography includes a number of different types of sins, as explained previously (in the chapter on Sexual Sins). In addition, the use of pornography is a type of sinful cooperation with the evils of creating and distributing pornography. The use of pornography makes it more likely that pornography will continue to be created and distributed. If no one used pornography, most pornography would never be created or distributed, since creation and distribution is directed toward use. Therefore, anyone who uses pornography is also cooperating materially with the sins of creation and distribution. When money is used to buy pornography, this sin also includes material cooperation with creation and distribution. Explicit cooperation would apply whenever the user intends that this material continue to be created and distributed. And the cooperation would be explicit formal cooperation if the user approves of the intrinsically evil sexual acts displayed in the material. The intentional approval of any intrinsically evil act is the sin of explicit formal cooperation.

.453. Theft

(1) A man knows that a fellow employee at work is stealing a significant amount of money or merchandise. He decides not to report this theft to anyone because the thief is his friend. His decision is a sin of omission, but it is also a type of cooperation. His decision to omit a morally-required act assists the other person in attaining the moral object of his intrinsically evil act, the theft of goods owned by another. Therefore, his sin is formal cooperation by omission.

(2) In a different case, a man is under the threat of death to himself and his family if he reports a similar theft. In such a case, he does not sin by omission, since his act is directed at the moral object of protecting the lives of himself and his family. His act of omission is a type of material cooperation, but the good consequence of protecting innocent life outweigh the bad consequence of the loss of money to the employer.

Although in both cases the exterior act, or rather the omission of the same exterior act, is the same from a secular point of view. From a moral point of view, the act in both cases is interior, but each act has a different moral meaning. The act in the first example is a decision to assist another person in attaining the moral object of an intrinsically evil act. This interior act is the sin of explicit formal cooperation; and since the theft is a grave matter, so is the cooperation. But the act in the second example is a decision to protect the lives of himself and his family; the cooperation is neither explicit, nor formal. But since the omission assists the thief in attaining the consequences of his sin, the second example is material cooperation with a gravely immoral intrinsically evil act. This material cooperation is also essential to the act of the other person, in that the theft cannot continue to occur without the silence of the cooperator. And so, here again is an example of immediate material cooperation (with an intrinsically evil and gravely immoral act) that is moral, since the good consequences outweigh the bad consequences in the third font (and the other two fonts are good).

.454. Lying

Lying is an intrinsically evil act; cooperation with lying may be either formal or material cooperation. If the cooperation has the moral object of assisting the act of the other person in making a false assertion, then the cooperative act is formal cooperation. But if the cooperative act assists the lie in attaining any type of bad consequences, then it is material cooperation.

(1) Suppose that a co-worker lies (in a venial matter) to his employer to avoid being fired. If the employer asks you if the co-worker's statement is true, you may not lie; lying is always immoral. If you use mental reservation, you assist the other person in attaining the good and bad consequences of his lie. But if the good of retaining his job outweighs the bad (that the employer's understanding is not corrected), then your act of cooperation is moral. However, circumstances in such cases can be more complex than in this hypothetical example. As always, all the good and bad consequences for all persons affected by the chosen act must be weighed, and every immoral intention must be avoided, and every chosen act must have a good moral object.

(2) A person lies to prevent innocent persons from being apprehended by an unjust government and put to death without cause. Your silence or your act of mental reservation is needed for his lie to succeed. Your chosen act is material cooperation, because it seeks to assist the act of the other person in attaining its consequences, especially saving the lives of the innocent. You do not intend to assist the other person's act in depriving an assertion of truth, nor to assist the other person's act in attaining any bad consequences. Therefore, your act is not explicit cooperation. Your act does not have the moral object of assisting the other person's act in depriving an assertion of truth (e.g. by suggesting the most effective lie). You do not approve of lying per se. Therefore, your act is not formal cooperation.

Notice here that the morality of a cooperative act is based on whether or not your act assists the act of the other person to do evil; it is not based on whether you as a person are assisting another person. Morality concerns acts chosen by persons, but not persons per se. In one sense, you are assisting another person, and that other person is sinning. But this has no effect on the morality of your act. Only if your act assists the other act in attaining evil are you cooperating with evil, and only if one or more of the fonts of your act are bad are you sinning by your cooperation. Your chosen act is good under all three fonts. Your silence or mental reservation has good intention, is not intrinsically evil, and the good consequence of saving innocent lives outweighs the bad consequence that some persons believe what is false. This is an example of moral material cooperation.

(3) Another person lies, out of malice, in order to cause serious harm to the reputation of another person. His lie is a mortal sin. If you are in a position to refute that lie, so that the grave harm that he intends is avoided, you are morally obligated to do so. Your silence would result in grave harm in the consequences, and there is no greater good consequence that would also result. But if you refute the lie, much good and little or no harm is done. To remain silent would be a mortal sin of omission. You would also be cooperating with the grave lie of the other person, assisting him in attaining gravely harmful consequences, which would be gravely immoral material cooperation.

(4) A man is in danger of losing his health insurance, unless he lies to his employer or health insurance company. The man decides to lie. If you approve of his lie, or encourage him to lie, or suggest the most effective lie, then you are committing the sin of formal cooperation. Lying is always immoral. Even when the good consequences of a lie outweigh the bad, the lie is immoral, and any formal cooperation with any lie is also immoral.

.455. Paying Taxes

Governments generally require their citizens to pay taxes, and the tax money is used for many different types of works, including perhaps some that are immoral. So the question of cooperation with evil arises with regard to taxation.

(1) A particular government is thoroughly unjust, does not protect or promote the common good, and uses tax money for grave immorality and for the gain of its leaders, not for the benefit of the nation and its people. However, if a citizen does not pay the tax, he is put to death without a fair trial. Is it moral to pay taxes to such a government? The first consideration is intention. The citizen must not intend to assist the government in attaining any evil moral object or any bad consequences that result from the act of cooperation. By avoiding this type of immoral intention, he avoids explicit cooperation.

The second consideration is the moral object of the chosen act. The act itself of paying taxes under threat of death or long imprisonment is like a man who is robbed at gunpoint, and so he hands over the money demanded by the robber. The act of the victim is not formal cooperation with the robbery, because his chosen act has the moral object of self-defense. This type of act is like the man who uses deadly force in self-defense. His act is directed at the protection of innocent life; the death of the attacker is a bad consequence in the third font, not the moral object in the second font. Similarly, the man who pays taxes to an unjust government under threat of death or long imprisonment chooses an act that has the protection of innocent life in the second font; the resultant usage of the money is a consequence in the third font. Therefore, his act of paying taxes is not formal cooperation.

The third consideration is the consequences of the chosen act. Clearly the protection of innocent life has greater moral weight than the payment of money to an unjust government. But the citizen also has an obligation to avoid the sin of scandal, by speaking out against the injustice of such a government. This act of paying taxes is moral under all three fonts, and is an example of moral material cooperation.

(2) A particular government is generally just, elected by the people, and guarding the common good. However, some of the money paid in taxes to the government is used to pay for abortions. Again, the taxpayer must not have any cooperative intention. He can intend that his taxes be used for any and all good purposes, but he must not intend any cooperation with whatever is evil in the use of that money. His act of paying taxes is not directed at assisting in the sin of abortion, but is directed at the general support of a just government and its just acts. And since the just government does more good than harm, the good consequences of paying taxes outweigh the bad consequences. Also falling into the third font is the fact that if he refuses to pay taxes, he may be imprisoned. So paying taxes avoids the harm that results from the crime of not paying taxes.

(3) Jesus was asked whether it was moral to pay taxes to the Roman government. At that time, Israel has been conquered and was being occupied by the Roman empire. The tax money went to a government that had undertaken and won an unjust war against Israel. Yet Jesus states that the tax should be paid.

[Luke]
{20:20} And being attentive, they sent traitors, who would pretend that they were just, so that they might catch him in his words and then hand him over to the power and authority of the procurator.
{20:21} And they questioned him, saying: "Teacher, we know that you speak and teach correctly, and that you do not consider anyone's status, but you teach the way of God in truth.
{20:22} Is it lawful for us to pay the tribute to Caesar, or not?"
{20:23} But realizing their deceitfulness, he said to them: "Why do you test me?
{20:24} Show me a denarius. Whose image and inscription does it have?" In response, they said to him, "Caesar's."
{20:25} And so, he said to them: "Then repay the things that are Caesar's, to Caesar, and the things that are God's, to God."
{20:26} And they were not able to contradict his word before the people. And being amazed at his answer, they were silent.

This is an example from Sacred Scripture of moral material cooperation. The citizen must give to God what God requires, including living a moral life. Thus, any type of immoral cooperation is excluded by this teaching of Jesus in the Gospel of Luke. But paying taxes is not an intrinsically evil act, and so it is moral, if the intention and the circumstances are good.

.456.
VOTING AND COOPERATION WITH EVIL

As is also true in the previous examples, a person might sin in voting either by perpetration of a sin apart from any cooperation, or by cooperation with evil. The eternal moral law requires that each and every human person avoid every kind of sin at all times. There is no exception from the moral law for voting. Although many persons believe in freedom in political discussions and in voting, the faithful and reasonable Catholic exercises this freedom in its truest form, by a conscience formed in the light of Tradition, Scripture, Magisterium, by acts that are entirely in accord with the will of God for the common good, and never by any act that is contrary to the eternal moral law. Freedom in politics does not extend to sin, nor to cooperation with sin.

Certain acts are sins against the eternal moral law. Certain sins are intrinsically evil acts that are always immoral, regardless of intention or circumstances. Voting cannot change the eternal moral law. A majority vote or an amendment to a constitution cannot turn good into evil, or evil into good. Political leaders and voters must acknowledge that immutable truths of justice exist, and that these truths cannot be changed by politics.

Pope Benedict XVI: "The just ordering of society and the State is a central responsibility of politics. As Augustine once said, a State which is not governed according to justice would be just a bunch of thieves...."[494]

When a government involves its citizens, through voting, in its decision-making, every voter must have in mind the common good, the just ordering of the nation, and the eternal moral law of God. For if each voter merely votes according to his own self-interest, or according to his own baseless opinions, the nation will not be governed by justice, but by sin and foolishness.

Pope Benedict XVI: "Justice is both the aim and the intrinsic criterion of all politics. Politics is more than a mere mechanism for defining the rules of public life: its origin and its goal are found in justice, which by its very nature has to do with ethics. The State must inevitably face the question of how justice can be achieved here and now."[495]

When politics is not based on truth and justice, then neither is it based on rights and freedoms, but on a clever violence to the human person masquerading as a benefit. Without ethics, politics is thievery, robbery, and murder. The faithful and reasonable Catholic is morally obligated to avoid sins of commission, sins of omission, and all sinful cooperation when exercising his legal and moral right to participate in government by voting. Justice is the basis of all good politics. An unjust vote is not a right or a freedom, but an offense against God and man.

Pope Benedict XVI: "Here politics and faith meet. Faith by its specific nature is an encounter with the living God -- an encounter opening up new horizons extending beyond the sphere of reason. But it is also a purifying force for reason

---

[494] Pope Benedict XVI, God is Love, n. 28.
[495] Pope Benedict XVI, God is Love, n. 28.

itself. From God's standpoint, faith liberates reason from its blind spots and therefore helps it to be ever more fully itself. Faith enables reason to do its work more effectively and to see its proper object more clearly."[496]

In a sinful world, a world in which every politician and voter is a sinner, reason alone is not sufficient to properly guide leaders and citizens. For reason has been injured by original sin and by personal sin. Faith purifies reason from the blind spots caused by sin. Faith provides ethical insights, which should be reachable by reason alone, but which sin prevents reason from achieving. Faith provides truth, and does so with greater depth, breadth, and surety than reason alone. Therefore, the Catholic voter must inform his conscience by the teachings of the Faith, and not by fallen sinful human reason alone.

Pope Benedict XVI: "the Church wishes to help form consciences in political life and to stimulate greater insight into the authentic requirements of justice as well as greater readiness to act accordingly, even when this might involve conflict with situations of personal interest. Building a just social and civil order, wherein each person receives what is his or her due, is an essential task which every generation must take up anew."[497]

Every Catholic must form his conscience in the light of Catholic teaching. And every Catholic voter must vote in accord with Catholic moral teaching. It is an objective mortal sin for any Catholic to intentionally disregard Catholic teaching when voting on any grave matter of justice and the common good. It is an objective mortal sin for any Catholic to vote so as to enact, or formally cooperate with the enactment of, any gravely immoral law. Even the intention to vote, in a grave matter, in contradiction to Catholic moral teaching, is an objective mortal sin. And the interior approval for a gravely immoral intrinsically evil law is formal cooperation and is an objective mortal sin. Politics is not exempt from the moral law.

.457. Abortion and Voting

Suppose that a voter is able to vote for or against a constitutional amendment outlawing all direct abortions. If he omits voting at all, he cooperates with the sin of abortion by omission. In this case, his sin is material cooperation because his act has the bad consequence of making the failure of the amendment more likely. His sin is also explicit cooperation by omission if he does not care whether abortion remains legal or not. His culpable lack of the intention to protect the innocent and helpless from death is a mortal sin of omission under the first font.

If he votes against the amendment, he is guilty of formal cooperation with abortion because his act assists other persons in attaining the moral object of abortion. If he votes against the amendment with the intention of keeping abortion broadly legal, he sins by explicit formal and explicit material cooperation because his act is intended to assist other persons in attaining the

---

[496] Pope Benedict XVI, God is Love, n. 28.
[497] Pope Benedict XVI, God is Love, n. 28.

moral object of abortion, and that same act is intended to assist in attaining the bad consequence that the amendment fails and abortion remains legal.

When there is a law or amendment that will further restrict or generally outlaw direct abortion, legislators and citizens are morally obligated to vote for and support that law. The love of neighbor required by the moral law requires us to act, when we are able to do so, to save the lives of our innocent neighbors, whether they are prenatals, infants, children, or adults; to refuse to act is a sin of omission.

In some cases of voting and abortion, the legislator or citizen is not merely guilty of cooperation with evil, but of perpetration of the sin of procuring abortion. If he votes for an amendment or a law legalizing direct abortion, he is guilty of procuring very many abortions. When a law or amendment has the direct effect of making direct abortion legal, or of substantially broadening access to direct abortion, then a vote for such a law or amendment procures abortion. The voter, whether a legislator or a citizen, is in a position to authorize abortions. Morally, this act is the same as a woman who signs a paper authorizing someone to perform an abortion on her, or a parent who authorizes an abortion on a child who is a minor, or a judge who authorizes an abortion in a particular case.

If the legislature passes a law legalizing or substantially broadening access to direct abortion, and if the president or governor is able to veto the law, or to otherwise prevent the law from taking effect, he is morally obligated to do so. If he signs the bill into law, he commits the sin of procuring abortion.

If abortion was already legal, and the law either pays for abortions, or reduces restrictions on abortions, then any vote for that law is formal cooperation with abortion. Such a law assists other persons in attaining the moral object of abortion. And the final approval of that law by a president or governor is also formal cooperation with abortion.

When a national or local court, either one judge or a panel of judges, decides that direct abortion is legal, they are guilty of objective mortal sin. Even if the nation's constitution and law clearly allow for direct abortion, and even if the judge's role is strictly limited to interpreting and applying constitution and law, the judge is morally obligated not to do so. Every unjust law is not a law. No unjust law is morally binding. The moral law requires the judge not to commit the sin of procuring abortion by in effect making direct abortion legal by his judgment or interpretation of constitution, law, or the particulars of a case. The moral law also requires the judge not to commit the sin of formal cooperation, by commission or omission, by assisting other persons in the sin of abortion, regardless of whether it is a particular case or a question of general law.

In the U.S. Supreme Court case of Roe versus Wade, seven of the nine Justices voted to the effect that direct abortion would essentially become broadly legal, and that State laws prohibiting abortion would generally become null and void. By doing so, these Justices committed the objective mortal sin of procuring countless abortions.

If a judge is not able to change law or the interpretation of constitution, then he is still morally obligated not to formally cooperate with abortion by authorizing an abortion, or by rendering a judgment that permits someone to obtain an abortion, or by obeying a law requiring him to authorize or permit a direct abortion. The moral law binds every judge, in every case, regardless of human law, constitution, and precedent.

Material cooperation with abortion would occur in cases where a law pertains to the circumstances of abortion. For example, a vote for a law that restricts protests at abortion clinics would be material cooperation with abortion. Such a law might be moral material cooperation, if the protests had become increasingly violent, so that the good of preventing the violence outweighed the harm of restricting protests.

.458. Material cooperation might apply in cases of a complex set of laws, such as in a bill that annually authorizes the government to spend money. Such a set of laws may have many indirect effects, some of which might have a likelihood to increase or decrease abortions indirectly. Or material cooperation could apply to a particular law that has a reasonably foreseeable bad consequence of increasing abortions. For example, eliminating tax deductions for children might lead some couples who have a pregnancy to abort the child. Adding a new tax deduction for children born after a certain date (when the law takes effect) might lead some parents to abort a child who would have been born prior to that date. Eliminating social safety net payments (such as welfare) might lead some pregnant women to obtain an abortion due to financial constraints. Enacting, in military law, punishments for women soldiers who become pregnant might lead some women soldiers to abort a pregnancy. Such laws have an indirect effect that has a certain degree of likelihood to increase abortions. The usual principles of cooperation with evil in cases of material cooperation would apply to this type of law. The likelihood and gravity of the bad consequences must be weighed against the good consequences of such a law.

Voting for a law that procures or formally cooperates with abortion is an intrinsically evil and gravely immoral act. All intrinsically evil acts are always immoral. Suppose that a law has many consequences (third font), and that the good consequences outweigh the bad. But if voting for the law is intrinsically evil, whether as perpetration or cooperation, then the act of voting for that law is not justified by a good third font. As is always the case, if any one font is bad, the other fonts cannot justify that act.

But in the case of a complex proposed law (a bill) with many effects, one that neither procures, nor formally cooperates with, abortion, all the good and bad consequences of the bill must be weighed. When the vote is merely material cooperation, the totality of the good and bad consequences in their moral weight must be considered. It would be unjust and immoral to ignore all the good consequences of a law, merely because that law cooperates materially with abortion or euthanasia or another serious sin. The teaching of the Catholic Faith is that material cooperation is not always immoral. And this was made all the more clear when Pope Pius XI permitted and even instructed priests in Mexico to cooperate with a gravely immoral and intrinsically evil set of laws, because the cooperation was merely material (it was not also explicit cooperation or formal cooperation) and the good consequences outweighed the bad. Similarly, in cases where explicit cooperation and formal cooperation are absent, the Catholic legislator or citizen is morally obligated to consider all the good and bad consequences in the third font of his act of voting. To do otherwise is to act contrary to Catholic teaching of the basic principles of morality.

.459. Voting and Euthanasia

Euthanasia is a type of murder. Therefore, any law that authorizes euthanasia authorizes murder. The moral analysis of laws permitting euthanasia, suicide, and assisted suicide is essentially the same as for abortion. Every act of murder, whether by perpetration or by formal cooperation, is intrinsically evil and always gravely immoral. A legislator or citizen who enacts, or who cooperates with the enactment of, a law legalizing or broadening access to any type of murder commits a gravely immoral act. All that is said above on voting and abortion also applies to these other types of murder. If it is not clear whether an act is perpetration of, or formal cooperation with, some type of murder, the question is academic. Both perpetration of, and formal cooperation with, any type of murder would be intrinsically evil and always gravely immoral.

Murder can occur by commission or by omission. In the case of a human person who is in a coma, or in a state of reduced mental capacity (a so-called vegetative state), or any other state, the withholding (omission) of food or water is an act of murder. A hospital or hospice or nursing home is not morally obligated to provide every possible extraordinary medical intervention to keep a person alive. But food and water are not extraordinary and are not medical acts per se, even when food or water is provided by an artificial means.

Pope John Paul II: "I feel the duty to reaffirm strongly that the intrinsic value and personal dignity of every human being do not change, no matter what the concrete circumstances of his or her life. A man, even if seriously ill or disabled in the exercise of his highest functions, is and always will be a man, and he will never become a 'vegetable' or an 'animal'. Even our brothers and sisters who find themselves in the clinical condition of a 'vegetative state' retain their human dignity in all its fullness."[498]

The use of the term 'vegetative state' to refer to any human person is never fitting and is always contrary to reason. Human persons are not fittingly compared to vegetables, nor even to the lower animals, since human persons have free will, reason, and an immortal soul. In particular, a person who is awake and somewhat responsive to stimuli is not reasonably said to be in a 'vegetative' state, even if his or her ability to exercise free will and reason is substantially reduced. To make matters worse, this dehumanizing term is sometimes used to justify the

---

[498] Address of Pope John Paul II to The International Congress on Life-sustaining Treatments and the Vegetative State, 20 March 2004, n. 3;
http://www.vatican.va/holy_father/john_paul_ii/speeches/2004/march/documents/hf_jp-ii_spe_20040320_congress-fiamc_en.html

killing of an innocent human person. But according to the teaching of the Catholic Faith, all human persons from conception to natural death retain their full human dignity as persons created in the image of God. Even a severe reduction in the exercise of normal functioning, due to injury or illness, does not reduce the right to life of that person.

"I should like particularly to underline how the administration of water and food, even when provided by artificial means, always represents a natural means of preserving life, not a medical act. Its use, furthermore, should be considered, in principle, ordinary and proportionate, and as such morally obligatory, insofar as and until it is seen to have attained its proper finality, which in the present case consists in providing nourishment to the patient and alleviation of his suffering."[499]

Here again is an example where exterior appearances differ from the inherent moral meaning of the act. The administration of food and water by medical means, such as intravenous and nasogastric tubes, seems like a medical act. But because food and water are ordinary and necessary to human life, the provision of these goods, even by medical devices in a hospital, is, in moral terms, neither a medical act, nor an extraordinary act. Therefore, the withdrawal or withholding of this or any other ordinary and necessary care is a type of murder by omission.

"The obligation to provide the 'normal care due to the sick in such cases' (Congregation for the Doctrine of the Faith, Iura et Bona, p. IV) includes, in fact, the use of nutrition and hydration (cf. Pontifical Council 'Cor Unum', Dans le Cadre, 2, 4, 4; Pontifical Council for Pastoral Assistance to Health Care Workers, Charter of Health Care Workers, n. 120). The evaluation of probabilities, founded on waning hopes for recovery when the vegetative state is prolonged beyond a year, cannot ethically justify the cessation or interruption of minimal care for the patient, including nutrition and hydration. Death by starvation or dehydration is, in fact, the only possible outcome as a result of their withdrawal. In this sense it ends up becoming, if done knowingly and willingly, true and proper euthanasia by omission. In this regard, I recall what I wrote in the Encyclical Evangelium Vitae, making it clear that 'by euthanasia in the true and proper sense must be understood an action or omission which by its very nature and intention brings about death, with the purpose of eliminating all pain'; such an act is always 'a serious violation of the law of God, since it is the deliberate and morally unacceptable killing of a human person' (n. 65)."[500]

Any knowingly chosen act that procures euthanasia or suicide, even by means of the omission of ordinary and necessary care (such as food and water), is an intrinsically evil and gravely immoral act of murder. Any knowingly chosen act that formally cooperates with euthanasia or suicide is an intrinsically evil and gravely immoral act of formal cooperation with murder. Political leaders and voters also have a moral obligation not to cooperate with any type of intrinsically

---

[499] Pope John Paul II, International Congress on Life-sustaining Treatments, n. 4.
[500] Pope John Paul II, International Congress on Life-sustaining Treatments, n. 4.

evil and gravely immoral act by means of voting, campaigning, or other types of political acts. The just laws of every nation must include protection for human life from conception to natural death. The omission of such just laws is a serious offense against God.

.460. Intrinsic Evil and Voting

An act of voting can possibly be an intrinsically evil act. For example, a citizen who votes for a constitutional amendment legalizing abortion or euthanasia commits an intrinsically evil act, since the act of voting for that amendment is inherently directed at the moral object of depriving innocent persons of life. Or an act of voting might be an act of formal cooperation, which is a type of intrinsically evil act. For example, a legislator who votes for a law that provides government money for abortion commits the sin of formal cooperation.

An act of voting can possibly be explicit cooperation. If the vote constitutes formal cooperation with an intrinsically evil act, and the voter has the intention of assisting in attaining the evil moral object of that other act, then the vote is explicit formal cooperation. If the vote constitutes an act of material cooperation, even if the material cooperation is moral, and the voter has the intention of assisting in attaining the bad consequences of the other act, then the vote is explicit material cooperation. Material cooperation can occur with intrinsically evil acts as well as other types of acts.

If the vote is not itself an intrinsically evil act, and if the voter has good intention, then the act of voting is not a sin under the first or second fonts of morality. Also, if the first and second fonts are good, the act is certainly not explicit cooperation or formal cooperation. In such cases, it falls to the third font of circumstances to determine if the chosen act (voting) is moral or immoral. Only when an act of voting is intrinsically evil, either by perpetration or by formal cooperation, is that act always immoral regardless of intention and circumstances.

.461. Voting for Persons

Voting for a political candidate is a different type of act than voting for a law or constitutional amendment. A law is said to be intrinsically evil when the law requires or authorizes acts that are intrinsically evil. The act of voting for an intrinsically evil law has the same moral object as the intrinsically evil act authorized or required by that law; such a vote is itself intrinsically evil. However, a person cannot be intrinsically evil. The acts of a person may be intrinsically evil, but the person himself is not. The human nature of every human person is good, and is created in the image of God. Therefore, voting for a person is never, in and of itself, an intrinsically evil act. (If some system of politics were devised whereby a voter seemingly votes for a person, but in truth votes for a law or a constitutional amendment, then such a vote could be intrinsically evil, depending on the moral object of the law or amendment.)

However, if a voter, by his vote for a pro-abortion candidate, is expressing his approval for the intrinsically evil act of abortion, or for laws permitting direct abortion, then his act is formal cooperation and is gravely immoral. In such a case, the immorality of the vote is based on the act of expressing approval for an intrinsically evil act. On the other hand, if the intention of the voter in any vote is to attain the evil moral object of an intrinsically evil act, such as abortion, or to attain the bad consequences of any act, then the act of that vote would be explicit cooperation with evil, and would be always immoral (since the first font is bad). But in both these cases, the immorality of the vote is not based on the views, voting record, or character of the candidate. Such immoral votes are not immoral because of the candidate, but because of the chosen act of the voter.

A voter who votes for a candidate precisely because he is pro-abortion commits the sin of formal cooperation with abortion, by expressing approval for that intrinsically evil act. And the same is true for other intrinsically evil acts. And he commits the sin of explicit formal cooperation, if his intention is to assist in attaining the moral object of the intrinsically evil act. Then if his intention is to assist in attaining the bad consequences of any act, whether intrinsically evil or not, he commits the sin of explicit material cooperation. Although voting for a person (a candidate) is not per se a sinful act, the intention may make the act a sin, even a grave sin. Although voting for a person (a candidate) is not an intrinsically evil act, the voter might commit an intrinsically evil act in his heart and mind by his interior approval for, or cooperation with, some intrinsically evil sin that the candidate promotes.

A Catholic voter must form his conscience in accord with Catholic teaching, must have only good intentions in his acts of voting, and must avoid committing any intrinsically evil acts, including formal cooperation. If he does so in his voting decisions, then he can and should cast his vote so that the act of voting does the most good and the least harm. In such a case, the fonts of intention and moral object are good, and the third font of consequences determines the morality of the act of voting. If so, then only when the bad consequences of his vote outweigh the good consequences would the act of voting be immoral.

Consequently, a Catholic voter is not morally obligated to vote exclusively for pro-life candidates, or to refrain from voting for any pro-abortion candidate. The act of voting for a pro-abortion candidate is not an intrinsically evil act because such a vote is not inherently directed at procuring, or assisting in procuring, abortion. Some political offices have no ability to affect the abortion issue. In some nations, the issue of abortion is not likely to come up for a vote during the term of office of that candidate. In some circumstances, a vote for a pro-abortion candidate might give more political power to his party, which might be generally a pro-life party.

Therefore, a Catholic voter may morally vote for a pro-abortion candidate, or a pro-euthanasia candidate, or a candidate who is in favor of some other type of gravely immoral legislation (even if it is not intrinsically evil), but only if all three fonts of morality are good. The intentions of the voter must be good, the act of voting itself must not be intrinsically evil, and the good consequences must outweigh the bad. If the candidate is in favor of legalizing, or keeping legal, abortion or euthanasia or any gravely immoral act that ought to be outlawed by every nation, then certainly there are some weighty bad consequences in voting for that candidate. But the truth about whether that vote is moral includes the total moral weight of all the consequences of the vote, not merely the consequences from one or a few issues, and not merely the consequences related to intrinsically evil acts.

The fact that a candidate has a political position that would make legal, or keep legal, an intrinsically evil act does not necessarily prohibit a Catholic voter from voting for him. The reason is that the act of voting for a person is not an intrinsically evil act. Therefore, if the voter's intention is good, and the good consequences of the vote outweigh the bad, then the vote is moral. The voter is not voting for or against abortion, but for a particular person. The morality of any act of voting is based solely on the three fonts of morality, as these fonts spring up from, and apply to, that particular act of voting.

.462. Some sources claim that if a candidate supports legalizing, or keeping legal, any intrinsically evil act, then a Catholic voter cannot vote for him. This position is erroneous for several reasons. First, not every intrinsically evil act is gravely immoral. The voter must weigh the good and bad consequences of his act of voting, and if he gives excessive weight to a consequence merely because it proceeds from an intrinsically evil act, then he errs in his evaluation of the third font. For example, a candidate might favor decriminalizing lying to federal law enforcement officers because he believes that the current law is being misused. Lying is intrinsically evil, but not always gravely immoral.

Second, the vote for a person who favors legalization of an intrinsically evil act is not an intrinsically evil vote. Voting for a person does not necessarily have an evil moral object, since persons are not intrinsically evil.

Third, human law need not and should not include laws against every sin.[501] For example, if a law prohibits public expressions of blasphemy, the law cannot be enforced without the secular government and court system deciding what is and is not blasphemy, thereby usurping the role of the Church, and the role of God. The temporal authority given to secular governments and courts does not extend to deciding spiritual matters, such as what constitutes blasphemy.

Fourth, while some intrinsically evil acts are only venial sins, some gravely immoral acts are not intrinsically evil. Human law must prohibit some acts that are gravely immoral under the third font, because the consequences of such acts do grave harm to the common good. Such acts might not be intrinsically evil under the second font. It would be immoral for a voter to vote solely based on the morality of acts under the second font (intrinsically evil acts) and ignore the grievous harm that can occur in the consequences of acts that are not intrinsically evil.

Fifth, the idea that a voter should only vote based on a candidate's positions on intrinsically evil acts ignores the teaching of the Church that all our acts must be good under all three fonts in order to avoid sin. Our intentions must be good, our

---

[501] Saint Thomas Aquinas, Summa Theologica, I-II, Q. 96, A. 2. "Should human law repress all vices?" Saint Thomas answers in the negative.

acts must not be intrinsically evil, and the good done must outweigh any harm done. If we vote based solely on a candidate's stated positions, sometimes the act of voting will result in grave harm. If we vote solely based on one or a few issues, sometimes the act of voting will result in grave harm due to other issues. It is always immoral to knowingly choose an act that can be reasonably anticipated to do more harm than good in the consequences of that act.

Sixth, some candidates for political office lie to the voters. The mere fact that a candidate publicly claims to be opposed to abortion should not be sufficient to establish a moral certitude in the mind of a sincere voter as to the consequences of electing that politician. The assumption that a candidate who claims to be pro-life will act against abortion once he is elected is contrary to reason and contrary to observable facts.

Seventh, often a candidate is said to be pro-life, but he in fact publicly states that he believes direct abortion should be legal in cases of rape, incest, and danger to the life of the mother. His position is openly contrary to the definitive teaching of the Church on direct abortion; his position is material heresy. His position may be closer to Catholic teaching than the position of his opponent, and some moral weight should be given to that degree of conformity. But unfortunately most candidates have only a limited degree of conformity with Catholic teaching on abortion, euthanasia, and other grave matters. It is an oversimplification, contrary to manifest truth, to divide all candidates into only two categories, either for or against abortion (or for or against some other issue). Politicians often have varying degrees of conformity with Catholic teaching on grave issues.

Examples: (1) Two candidates are running for a political office, one is pro-life and the other is pro-abortion. If the office in question has no likely substantial effect on laws or government acts pertaining to abortion, then the moral weight of this circumstance (each one's position on abortion) is reduced. There is some moral weight in the fact that one candidate perceives the truth that abortion is gravely immoral, and the other does not. But other factors might outweigh this circumstance. A faithful and reasonable Catholic might vote for either candidate, in accord with his prudential judgment as to which vote will do the most good and the least harm.

(2) Two candidates are running for a political office, one is pro-life (but a member of a party that is generally pro-abortion) and the other is pro-abortion (but a member of a party that is generally pro-life). If voting for the pro-abortion candidate will give more power to the pro-life party, such as by giving that party control of a house of the legislature, then a faithful and reasonable Catholic might vote for that pro-abortion candidate, in order to do the most good and the least harm with his vote.

(3) Two candidates are running for a political office, one is pro-life and the other is pro-abortion. However, the voter judges that the pro-life candidate is not likely to take any action against abortion, because the candidate has been in office for many years and has done nothing substantial on the issue of abortion. And he judges that the pro-abortion candidate is also not likely to make any changes to the current laws on abortion. Then if there is another grave issue, about which

both candidates are likely to take action, such as war, or severe unemployment and poverty, the voter might judge that the most good and the least harm is done by voting for the pro-abortion candidate.

(4) Two candidates are running for a political office, both are pro-abortion, but one has a position on abortion that is closer to the teaching of the Church, in that he would increase restrictions on abortion. In such a case, the Catholic voter is not obligated by the moral law to refrain from voting. Neither is he obligated to vote for the candidate with the better position on the abortion issue. As long as he has good intention and avoids any intrinsically evil act, the morality of his voting decision falls to the third font: the good consequences of his vote must outweigh the bad consequences. The moral weight of all the issues, and the likelihood that any issue would be affected by a particular vote must be weighed. He may vote for either candidate, if he judges that all three fonts are good for that vote.

.463. However, when any candidate has a sincere position on any issue that is closer to Church teaching, the voter should give that position its proper moral weight. On that issue, that candidate should be favored. But the voter also has a moral obligation, and this is not merely an option, to evaluate the moral weight of all the reasonably anticipated good and bad consequences of his act of voting. The moral weight of all the consequences of a vote, including the likelihood that each consequence will occur, determines the morality of the third font.

(5) Two candidates are running for a political office, both are pro-abortion. The voter judges that a vote for either candidate will do more harm than good. Therefore, in order to avoid a sin under the third font of morality (when the bad consequences of an act outweigh the good consequences), he refrains from voting for either candidate. Perhaps he votes in other political races, but not in that race. Or perhaps he votes for a candidate with no chance of being elected, as a protest vote, to express his disapproval for abortion and for the other candidates. But in any case, he must refrain from any act of voting that would be a sin against God.

(6) A candidate is pro-life, but because of his position on other issues the voter judges that a vote for this candidate will do more harm than good. If the bad outweighs the good in the third font, then the voter is morally obligated, under pain of sin, not to vote for that candidate. And it is possible that such a candidate, for whom in a particular circumstance it would be a sin to vote, might be pro-life or might have a position in agreement with Church teaching on another issue. If the voter judges that a vote for a particular candidate will have bad consequences that will outweigh any good consequences, and will do so to a grave extent, it would be a mortal sin to vote for that candidate.

(7) Three candidates are running for the same office. Two of the candidates have a good chance of being elected, but the third is very unlikely to be elected. Even if the third candidate has the best stated positions on every issue, the voter must consider not only the stated positions, but the likelihood that a vote for that candidate will do good or will do harm. If the voter's evaluation of the third font determines that a vote for this third candidate is unlikely to do any good, he may

vote for one of the other candidates. Although the other candidate's position on issues may be less in conformity with Catholic teaching, more moral weight must be given to any good or bad consequence when it is likely to occur, and less moral weigh when it is less likely to occur.

(8) Two candidates are both pro-life; one candidate's stated position on that issue is the same as the teaching of the Church, and the other candidate's position is generally pro-life, but departs from Church teaching to some extent. However, the candidate with the better stated position has never accomplished anything for the pro-life cause, and the other candidate has passed legislation restricting abortion. So if the voter judges that the candidate with the better stated position will likely do less good than the other candidate, he may morally vote for the candidate with the worse stated position. Perhaps the other candidate states a particular position disingenuously, in order to get more votes. The voter is not morally obligated to believe every statement made by every politician.

The claim that a Catholic voter must blindly vote for every pro-life candidate, or for every candidate whose position on abortion is closest to Church teaching, regardless of the harm done in the consequences of the act, is a claim that contradicts the fundamental teachings of the Catholic Church on morality.

Furthermore, in addition to avoiding sin in any voting decisions, the faithful and reasonable Catholic should do more. He should be attempting to do the most good and the least harm, and he should have in mind the will of God and the common good. For our discipleship in Christ is not only to strive to avoid sin, but also to strive to do the whole will of God, as much as is possible for us poor sinners living in a sinful world. In this way, we strive to become ever more like Christ, our Savior, and ever more like the Virgin Mary, His perfect disciple.

.464. Summary of Cooperation with evil

If these many examples seem too complex to the reader, remember that your act is always moral if all three fonts are good. If you have only good intentions, and commit only morally good acts, in which the reasonably anticipated good consequences outweigh any reasonably anticipated, but unintended, bad consequences, then you are not sinning. The principle of cooperation with evil can sometimes assist us in discerning good from evil in complex situations. But if it is not helpful for a particular circumstance, you can always rely on the three fonts of morality by themselves. All that is said in this chapter is merely an application of the three fonts of morality to certain kinds of situations.

The morality of every knowingly chosen act, without any exception at all, is determined entirely and solely by the three fonts of morality. The morality of the type acts considered under the term 'cooperation with evil' is also determined by the three fonts. All the terminology used to describe the morality of cooperative acts is simply an expression of the three fonts as they apply to particular types of acts and circumstances. There are no exceptions to the eternal moral law. The teachings and terminology on the morality of cooperative acts is nothing other than a particular way of expressing and applying the eternal moral law to this particular type of act.

Chapter 29
Temptation

.465.

Ever since Adam and Eve fell from grace, humanity has been in a fallen state and subject to various types and degrees of temptation to sin. Life in a sinful world is complex, and as a result, there are many different possible temptations. But there are also many different ways to avoid temptation. Catholic moral theology often focuses on identifying sin. But in order to avoid sin, we should understand what temptation is and how we should respond.

What Is Temptation?

Temptation is related to sin. Sin is a knowingly chosen immoral act. Sin is an act of the will and intellect. The intellect knows that the act is immoral, but the free will chooses the act despite this knowledge. Sin is moral evil, and moral evil is a deprivation of moral good, of some good required by the eternal moral law, required by the love of God, neighbor, self. However, no one who sins chooses evil, in and of itself. Evil is an absence of good, just as darkness is an absence of light. The person who sins chooses either a lesser good or an apparent good.[502] This lesser or apparent good is chosen in contradiction to a greater good, as a type of rejection, in part or in full, of the command to love God above all else, and to love your neighbor as yourself. A partial rejection, in any particular act, is a venial sin. A full rejection, in any particular act, is a mortal sin.

Temptation is of the will and intellect, just as sin is of the will and intellect. The intellect presents, to the will, knowledge of a particular good; this in itself is not temptation. There are many goods in this life, and many of these goods may be obtained by acts that are entirely moral. However, it is inevitable that the intellect will notice that some goods may be obtained by acts that are not entirely moral. This is the basis for temptation. Temptation is the understanding that a particular good may be obtained if the free will chooses a particular immoral act.

All temptation is therefore based upon good, not evil. Temptation does not seek evil as an end; temptation does not offer evil for its own sake. For evil is an absence; it is a deprivation. Evil is essentially emptiness. A sinful act is not directed at evil, but at a true or apparent lesser good, in contradiction to a greater good. And this greater good, of which sin is deprived, is always some particular fulfillment of the love of God, neighbor, self. So temptation offers what is good, but at a price. And the price is sin.

Temptation is not itself a sin; it is an inducement toward sin. Temptation is like a vendor selling a faulty product, disguising its harm under the cover of some true or apparent good. The product looks shiny and new; it may or may not be shiny and new. But it is also broken in some way. The product may be truly good in some way, to some extent, but, in another way, it is also truly harmful, to some

---

[502] cf. Saint Thomas Aquinas, Summa Theologica, I-II, Q. 34, A. 2; see also, Compendium of the Catechism, n. 367.

extent. Temptation is like an apple that looks good, but is rotten inside, to some extent. The apple is truly good in some way; it offers good nutrition and good taste. But this particular good is accompanied by some particular evil, by a certain rottenness. And you cannot have the one without the other. Temptation is some type of goodness combined with some type of moral evil.

.466. How Should We Respond?

When the intellect understands that a good can be obtained at the price of sin, the free will has not yet chosen. Temptation is only the opportunity to sin. If the free will chooses not to act, or chooses to act only in a way that is morally good, then the temptation did not lead to sin. Often, a good that is available at the price of sin can also be obtained in some other way, at some other time, or in some other circumstance, and without any sin. So the will and intellect might seek to obtain the same good, or a similar good, but without sin.

For example, sexual relations outside of marriage is gravely immoral, but natural sexual relations within marriage is moral. The free will must choose not to obtain the good of sexual relations at the price of mortal sin. But the free will can instead choose to seek marriage, and all of its many goods, including natural marital relations open to life.

If a vendor is offering a product with some good feature, but which is also defective or harmful in some way, the astute buyer will refrain from buying that product. But he may well seek and obtain a similar product, having the same or better good features, and without the harm or defect. If a vendor is selling an apple with a certain rottenness, so that its good is accompanied by evil, the astute buyer will refrain from buying that apple. But he may well decide to seek and obtain an entirely good apple, or some similar good food, in some other place or time, in some other circumstance.

But it sometimes happens that a particular good cannot be obtained, except at the price of sin. Even so, the human person is not justified in sinning in order to obtain a good that is otherwise unobtainable. In such cases, the only moral course is to refrain from sin, and to give up seeking that good. But the loss of such a good, no matter how great that loss might seem, is small compared to the great good of eternal life in Heaven, where all losses are repaid many times over. Nothing of true and lasting value is ever lost to those who obtain eternal life.

[Philippians]
{3:7} But the things which had been to my gain, the same have I considered a loss, for the sake of Christ.
{3:8} Yet truly, I consider everything to be a loss, because of the preeminent knowledge of Jesus Christ, my Lord, for whose sake I have suffered the loss of everything, considering it all to be like dung, so that I may gain Christ....

[Mark]
{8:36} For how does it benefit a man, if he gains the whole world, and yet causes harm to his soul?
{8:37} Or, what will a man give in exchange for his soul?

.467. Sources of Temptation

The three sources of temptation were summarized succinctly by the theologian Peter Abelard, in his commentary on the Our Father prayer.

Peter Abelard: "For there are three things which tempt us: the flesh, the world, the devil. The flesh tempts us by appetite and by indulgence. The world [tempts us] by prosperity and adversity: by prosperity so that it may deceive, by adversity so that it may dishearten. The devil attempts, in every way, to assail us and to lead us into every wickedness."[503]

There is only one source of sin: free will. By definition, sin is a knowing choice of the free will. The three sources of temptation are not sources of sin, but only of temptation to sin. Nothing can cause a human person to sin, except the free will of that person. An act not freely chosen is not a sin. Although the valley of tears in which we all live has many inducements to sin, nothing can compel anyone to commit even a single venial sin. But there are three sources of temptation toward sin: (1) the flesh, (2) the world, (3) the devil.

(1) The term 'the flesh' is a way of referring to the fallen state of humanity. All the descendents of Adam and Eve, other than Jesus and Mary, are conceived with original sin. Even after Baptism entirely wipes away original sin, there remains a tendency toward personal sin, called concupiscence. This inner tendency toward sin is described by the Apostle Paul in Sacred Scripture.

[Romans]
{7:15} For I do things that I do not understand. For I do not do the good that I want to do. But the evil that I hate is what I do.
...
{7:19} For I do not do the good that I want to do. But instead, I do the evil that I do not want to do.
...
{7:23} But I perceive another law within my body, fighting against the law of my mind, and captivating me with the law of sin which is in my body.
{7:24} Unhappy man that I am, who will free me from this body of death?
{7:25} The grace of God, by Jesus Christ our Lord! Therefore, I serve the law of God with my own mind; but with the flesh, the law of sin.

Within each of us is a tendency to be selfish, to seek what we desire without regard for other persons, to act without regard for morality. Now this is merely tendency, and so it is not itself a sin. But it is the main influence on human persons toward sin. For we might not be constantly among sinners, and we are certainly not constantly tempted by fallen angels. But you cannot get away from yourself. The temptations that come from within are the greatest influence toward personal sins of every kind.

---

[503] Peter Abelard, Expositio Orationis Dominicae, Petitio Sexta; author's translation of the Latin. Pope Benedict XVI recently spoke favorably about Peter Abelard's work, even crediting him as "the very person who introduced the term 'theology' in the sense in which we understand it today...." General Audience, 4 November 2009.

Peter Abelard tells us that: "The flesh tempts us by appetite and by indulgence." In other words, we are tempted by our desire, our appetite, for what we do not possess. We desire what we do not have, and we sin to obtain it (James 4:2). And this inner disordered desire is of the flesh, that is, of concupiscence due to our fallen state. But we are also tempted by indulgence in what we already possess. For we can easily fall into sins of various kinds by self-indulgence, by misusing what we already possess (2 Peter 2:13; Ecclesiastes 10:17).

(2) The term 'the world' is a way of referring to temptations that come to us from other human persons, either from particular individuals around us, or from the influence of society in general. Another individual (or more than one individual) might influence you toward sin by word or deed, by a bad example, by offering an inducement toward sin or assistance in committing a sin. An individual might advise, encourage, approve, or reward you for committing a sin. An individual might discourage, disapprove, threaten, or punish you for refusing to sin. No one can force you to sin, but other persons can make it easier for you to sin, and harder for you to avoid sin.

And the same applies to groups of individuals, small and large, and to society in general. We live in a world in which everyone was conceived with original sin. We live in a world filled with innumerable personal sins, many of them mortal sins. The very thorough influence that sin has had on the world has caused the world itself to be an influence toward personal sins. Sinful secular society has a tendency to encourage and even reward sin, and to discourage and even punish the refusal to sin. In addition, society often inculcates us with false teachings on morals, making it more difficult to know right from wrong. The result is that very many persons commit objective mortal sins without realizing it.

Next, Peter Abelard says: "The world [tempts us] by prosperity and adversity: by prosperity so that it may deceive, by adversity so that it may dishearten." Both prosperity and adversity can present temptations. Our prosperity might deceive us, so that we think that material success is happiness, or that material goods are the greatest goods. Prosperity might lead us into the temptations associated with self-indulgences of every kind, that is, by the misuse of what we possess. Also, prosperity might include the temptation toward pride (self-exaltation) due to any notoriety, social status, or accomplishments that we might obtain due to our prosperity.

But the opposite state, adversity, can also present temptations. For life in this world includes many difficulties. And some circumstances might offer the temptation of reduced difficulties in exchange for the commission of some sin. A person who is tested by poverty may be tempted to steal. A person who is in danger of losing his job may be tempted to lie. When adversity arises, it becomes more difficult to do good and to avoid doing evil. Some persons might lose heart because the search for truth and the attempt to live a moral life is difficult, even at times very difficult, within this sinful world.

(3) The term 'the devil' is a way to refer to the temptation toward sin arising, at times, from the limited influence of one or another fallen angel. The particular fallen angel named 'Satan' does not provide every temptation. There are many

fallen angels, and each is very limited in what he can do to tempt anyone toward sin. The fallen angel named Satan is not all knowing or all powerful -- far from it. So he cannot know what each person is doing, nor can he personally tempt each person. The fallen angels have limited abilities, because they are creatures, not gods. Moreover, God limits what the fallen angels can do to interfere in human affairs. This principle is clear from the book of Job, in which God permits Satan to commit certain harmful acts, but within clear limits (Job 1:12; 2:6).

Peter Abelard says: "The devil attempts, in every way, to assail us and to lead us into every wickedness." There are numerous different ways that the fallen angels attempt to influence us toward sin. They can briefly offer temptation to the mind or to the emotions. They can tempt one person, in this same way, in order to present some harmful influence to another person. But fallen angels are not permitted to tempt continually (cf. Mt 4:11; Mk 1:13; Lk 4:13). They tempt only intermittently. Good persons, even Saints, are sometimes tempted by fallen angels. But the fallen angels mainly tempt those who are most susceptible to influence, due to the number and severity of their sins.

.468. Protection from the influence of fallen angels, and from the temptations that they might occasionally offer, can be obtained by prayer, by self-denial, and by works of mercy toward others. For the more we grow in grace, the less we are susceptible to temptation. Prayer for the intercession of the Virgin Mary and the holy Saints and martyrs is very useful to keep away temptations of every kind. In particular, the following prayer can be used against fallen angels:

August Queen of Heaven!
Sovereign Directress of the Angels!
You received from God, from the beginning,
the power and mission to crush the head of Satan.
Therefore, we humbly beg you
to send forth your legions of holy Angels,
so that, under your direction and by your virtue,
they may pursue the fallen angels,
engage them on every side,
resist their arrogant attacks,
and drive them from here
into the abyss of eternal woe. Amen.

Sacramentals are also useful against the influence of fallen angels. Examples of sacramentals include holy water, the scapular, rosary beads, pictures of Jesus, pictures of Mary, pictures of Saints, a crucifix, any relics of Saints, and the holy Bible. But all these physical items have no real power of their own. They obtain their effectiveness from their devout usage. Rosary beads on which one prays devoutly every day are a powerful Sacramental. But rosary beads on which one never prayers are just beads. And the same is true of the other Sacramentals; they obtain their effectiveness from devout and faithful usage.

The three sources of temptation may be listed in order from greatest to least as follows: the flesh, the world, the devil. The greatest temptation comes from within yourself. The influence of other persons, as a temptation toward sin, is clearly secondary. For sin is always fundamentally interior; it is of the heart and mind. Other persons are exterior to your heart and mind, and so their ability to offer temptation is substantially limited. The influence of fallen angels as a temptation toward sin is a distant third. The influence of our own fallen nature is with us continually. And the influence of other persons, though less extensive, is still pervasive and daily. But the influence of fallen angels is intermittent, and is limited by the power of God, by grace, by the intercession of the Virgin Mary and the Saints, and by the intercession and intervention of the holy Angels.

These three sources of temptation may be phrased as:

(1) the flesh, our own fallen human nature (concupiscence),
(2) the world, other fallen human persons as well as sinful society in general,
(3) the devil, any of the fallen angels, in their limited ability to offer temptation.

.469. The First Temptation

[Genesis]
{3:6} And so the woman saw that the tree was good to eat, and beautiful to the eyes, and delightful to consider. And she took from its fruit, and she ate. And she gave to her husband, who ate.

Within the human race, the first temptation occurred when Eve was tempted by Satan in the Garden of Paradise. The second temptation occurred when Adam was subsequently tempted by Eve. First Eve, and next Adam, freely chose to sin in response to temptation. The temptation of Eve was based on the goodness of the fruit of that tree; the fruit was not evil. God created the tree and its fruit. But God commanded Adam and Eve not to eat from that tree; that particular good fruit could not be obtained by them without sin. For not every created good is available to every person. Adam and Eve were permitted to eat from every other tree in Paradise (Gen 2:16), and the tree of life was a tree in Paradise (Gen 3:22). They could have eaten good fruit from these many trees, even the excellent fruit of the tree of life. Similarly, when we cannot obtain a particular good except by sin, we certainly are able to obtain many other types of goods without sin, especially the excellent good of eternal life.

Many persons wrongly assume that the first sin was a sexual sin; such is not the case. The verses on the temptation and fall of Adam and Eve do not mention sexual sin. Also, Eve was tempted first, and so she fell from grace first, just as Sacred Scripture explicitly states: "And Adam was not seduced, but the woman, having been seduced, was in transgression." (1 Timothy 2:14). So the claim that Adam and Eve fell from grace by have sexual relations with one another cannot be true.

Saint Thomas Aquinas: "It is written (Sirach 10:15): 'Pride is the beginning of all sin.' Now man's first sin is the beginning of all sin, according to Romans 5:12, 'By one man sin entered into this world.' Therefore man's first sin was pride."[504]

---

[504] Saint Thomas Aquinas, Summa Theologica, II-II, Q. 163, A. 1.

Pride is the beginning of all sin because in order to sin, one must depart from the moral law, which is based on the love of God above all else. All sin is a type of disorder whereby the love of something less than God is placed above God. All sin is a type of selfishness whereby pride in one's self permits one to act contrary to the will and plan of God. Pride was the first sin of Eve, and next of Adam, not some sexual sin. Pride is the foundation of all sin; therefore, pride must have been the first sin. For a house cannot be built before its foundation has been laid.

Saint Thomas Aquinas: "Now man was so appointed in the state of innocence, that there was no rebellion of the flesh against the spirit. Wherefore it was not possible for the first inordinateness in the human appetite to result from his coveting a sensible good, to which the concupiscence of the flesh tends against the order of reason. It remains therefore that the first inordinateness of the human appetite resulted from his coveting inordinately some spiritual good. Now he would not have coveted it inordinately by desiring it according to his measure, as established by the Divine rule. Hence it follows that man's first sin consisted in his coveting some spiritual good above his measure: and this pertains to pride. Therefore it is evident that man's first sin was pride."[505]

Adam and Eve were not, before the fall from grace, in a fallen state; they did not have concupiscence. Therefore, they were not prone to sexual sins, nor to any sins of rebellion of the flesh against the spirit. For fallen humanity, temptation is from three sources: the flesh, the world, and the devil. But Adam and Eve were not yet fallen, and so they were not tempted by the flesh. And they did not live in a sinful fallen world, but in Paradise, so they were not tempted by the world. They were tempted by a fallen angel; he did not tempt them with sins of the flesh, because they were not susceptible to such sins. Satan tempted them to pride because his own first sin was the sin of pride, in his rebellion against God, and because pride is the beginning of all sin.

.470. Were Jesus or Mary Tempted?

Temptation, properly defined, does not imply that any sin has occurred. If you are tempted, you should respond by refusing to sin; then you will be blameless. Both Jesus and Mary were tempted; both never sinned at all; both are entirely blameless. Like Adam and Eve before the Fall, Jesus and Mary did not have any concupiscence, for they were each conceived without original sin. So they were not tempted by the flesh. But Jesus and Mary both lived in a sinful world, and so they were surrounded by temptations to sin. They were tempted by the world.

When a person says that he or she was tempted, sometimes a different meaning of the word is intended, one which includes some degree of interior sin. A person might say that he was tempted, meaning not only that temptation presented itself, but that he interiorly consented (often only partially) to that temptation; therefore he committed at least a venial sin interiorly. This common use of the term differs from the proper definition of temptation. So when Sacred Scripture states that Jesus was tempted (Mt 4:1; Mk 1:13; Lk 4:13), the meaning is only that temptations were presented to Him, not that he interiorly consented,

---

[505] Saint Thomas Aquinas, Summa Theologica, II-II, Q. 163, A. 1.

Temptation

not even to the slightest extent. Any interior consent to temptation is a sin. But temptation itself does not include sin. Both Jesus and Mary were tempted, but neither Jesus or Mary ever sinned in the least.

.471. Sacred Scripture on Temptation

There are many passages in Sacred Scripture on temptation and its relationship to sin. A full consideration of this topic would fill a book of its own. This section examines a few select passages in order to arrive at a better understanding of what temptation is and how we should respond.

[James]
{1:12} Blessed is the man who suffers temptation. For when he has been proven, he shall receive the crown of life which God has promised to those who love him.
{1:13} No one should say, when he is tempted, that he was tempted by God. For God does not entice toward evils, and he himself tempts no one.
{1:14} Yet truly, each one is tempted by his own desires, having been enticed and drawn away.

God never tempts anyone. God permits temptation to occur, but it is never His will for anyone to sin in response to temptation. Even Jesus was tempted, and so we mere weak and mortal sinners cannot expect to be exempt from temptation. But when we are tempted, it is our own disordered desire that results in a sinful response to temptation, rather than a holy response.

God permits much suffering and disorder in this world, including the disorder of various temptations, because there is much sin in this world. God permits sin because free will (in this life) includes the possibility to choose evil or good. God gave us the gift of free will and reason so that we could be like Him by choosing to love. No one is able to love without free will. Love requires free will, and free will allows for the possibility of sin, and sin results in various types of sufferings and disorder in this life, including temptation.[506]

Even though temptation results from sin, temptation can be a blessing. For it is an opportunity to cooperate with grace, and to provide a good example to our fellow human persons. When we are tempted and yet turn aside from sin, we benefit the Church and the world, and we store up a reward in Heaven.

[1 Corinthians]
{10:13} Temptation should not take hold of you, except what is human. For God is faithful, and he will not permit you to be tempted beyond your ability. Instead, he will effect his Providence, even during temptation, so that you may be able to bear it.

Temptation is only said to take hold of us when we consent to that temptation, in some way, to some extent, even if only interiorly. It is human to be tested by some temptations in life. But we are able, through free will and grace, to say 'no' to temptation. And God never permits anyone to be tempted beyond his or her

---

[506] In Heaven, we have free will without the possibility of sin, because our intellect knows God directly, in the Beatific Vision of God.

ability to refuse to sin. And therein lies the culpability of sin: you were able to choose good over evil, but instead you freely chose the moral evil of sin. Free will has been weakened by original sin and by personal sins, making us more susceptible to various temptations. But grace strengthens free will, making us able to turn away from temptation and to live virtuous lives.

Providence also assists us in avoiding temptation, in enduring temptation, and in avoiding sin. Providence is the often subtle, and sometimes not so subtle, work of God guiding the events of our lives in one direction or another. God exercises His Providence both directly and indirectly: directly by His own power, and indirectly by the work of holy Angels. The Virgin Mary and the Saints also have a role in Providence, since their intercession results not only in grace, but also in the guidance of Providence, as well as in powerful miracles. By guiding events so that fewer temptations are presented to us, or so that we have various helps during times of temptation, God effects His Providence, even in the midst of the worst temptations, so that we may be able to bear it.

[1 Timothy]
{6:6} But piety with sufficiency is great gain.
{6:7} For we brought nothing into this world, and there is no doubt that we can take nothing away.
{6:8} But, having nourishment and some kind of covering, we should be content with these.
{6:9} For those who want to become rich fall into temptation and into the snare of the devil and into many useless and harmful desires, which submerge men in destruction and in perdition.
{6:10} For desire is the root of all evils. Some persons, hungering in this way, have strayed from the faith and have entangled themselves in many sorrows.

.472. The Greek text of "desire is the root of all evils" has "love of silver" (i.e. love of money), instead of the more general Latin term 'cupiditas' (desire). The word cupiditas is closely related to the word concupiscence. Both the Greek and the Latin terms refer to inordinate desire of any kind (not only greed). Money is not desired for itself, but for all the things that it might obtain. Thus, the love of money is a figure for inordinate desire of every kind.[507] And so, with either text, the meaning is the same.

The desire for sufficiency, so as to meet the needs of this life, is not inordinate desire, and is neither temptation, nor sin. However, both wealth and the desire for wealth can tempt persons into many different kinds of other desires, and into every kind of sin. Temptation is resisted by turning away from inordinate desire. And so a proper response to temptation, even a preemptive response, is to have a pure heart. For the pure heart desires only good, and always places spiritual goods above temporal goods.

[Hebrews]
{4:14} Therefore, since we have a great High Priest, who has pierced the heavens, Jesus the Son of God, we should hold to our confession.

---

[507] Saint Thomas Aquinas, Summa Theologica, I-II, Q. 84, A. 1.

{4:15} For we do not have a high priest who is unable to have compassion on our infirmities, but rather one who was tempted in all things, just as we are, yet without sin.
{4:16} Therefore, let us go forth with confidence toward the throne of grace, so that we may obtain mercy, and find grace, in a helpful time.

Jesus was tempted in all things, so that He could be like us in all things but sin. For temptation is not sin. He was born into a very sinful world, full of every temptation. He grew up in that sinful world. He lived His adult life in that sinful world. Yet He did not sin, and He abounded in grace in His human nature. He was even tempted directly by Satan. But He never sinned in the least.

Jesus did not have concupiscence, and so He did not have the type of temptation that comes from a fallen human nature. This inner tendency toward sin, called concupiscence, is a type of darkness. Such darkness could not be present in Him who is the Light (John 1:9). Concupiscence is a disorder that tends toward personal sin. But Jesus was unable to sin, because His human nature is united, continually and irrevocably, to His Divine Nature, as one Person. All sin is a denial of God. Jesus was unable to sin because God cannot deny Himself (2 Timothy 2:13).

[Matthew]
{4:7} Jesus said to him, "Again, it has been written: 'You shall not tempt the Lord your God.'"

God cannot sin, and nothing in His Creation is a temptation to Him toward sin. So the phrase 'to tempt God' does not refer to temptation per se; it is a figure of speech. God puts us to the test by permitting temptations. Our response in grace can be a great blessing. But we should not treat God as someone who needs to be tested, who needs to prove Himself to us by His response to a difficult situation.

{6:13} "And lead us not into temptation. But free us from evil. Amen."

In the Our Father prayer, Jesus teaches us to ask God the Father not to lead us into temptation. God Himself tempts no one, but He does guide events through Providence, permitting temptations of various kinds from time to time, in accord with His will. Prayer can assist us in responding to temptation without sin. But prayer can also obtain the Providence of God in order to avoid some temptations altogether. Certainly, no one living in this sinful world is free from temptation, especially we poor fallen sinners afflicted with concupiscence. But by God's Providence, some temptations can be avoided, and by God's grace, any temptation can be endured without sin, especially without mortal sin.

{18:7} "Woe to a world that leads people astray! Although it is necessary for temptations to arise, nevertheless: Woe to that man through whom temptation arises!"

God does nothing wrong in permitting temptation. And we do nothing wrong in merely enduring temptation. Temptation is necessary, in the sense that living a holy life in a sinful world necessarily results in conflicts and temptations for any faithful Christian. Temptation is not necessary, in the sense of being required for salvation, but it will necessarily occur as we progress toward salvation.

.473. Nevertheless, a knowingly chosen act, which presents a temptation to sin to other persons, may itself be a sin; this sin is called scandal (as previously discussed). Scandal is in the third font; whether or not an act which has the consequence of scandal is a sin depends on an evaluation of the good and bad consequences.

Since one person cannot literally cause another person to sin, the essence of the sin of scandal is to present a temptation toward sin. Though it might seem as if merely offering a temptation toward sin is a lesser offense, Jesus condemns this sin of scandal, of tempting others to sin, with strong words. The term 'woe' is not used lightly in Sacred Scripture. Why such strong words for this sin? Consider how many fewer mortal sins would be in the world if individuals and society did not lead anyone toward sin. Very many souls are lost to Hell forever because individuals, groups of individuals, and society in general lead people into serious sin. The ways in which this scandalizing occurs are myriad. But regardless of the exact form of the temptation, very much harm is done to countless souls. And this is why Jesus says "Woe to that man through whom temptation arises!"

{26:41} "Be vigilant and pray, so that you may not enter into temptation. Indeed, the spirit is willing, but the flesh is weak."

Prayer is a means both to endure temptation without sin, and at times even to avoid temptation all together. The weakness of the flesh is a result of original sin. Both soul and body were damaged by the Fall of Adam and Eve. As a result, the soul is not given sanctifying grace at conception; this salvific grace must be sought and obtained in this life. The stain and guilt of original sin is entirely wiped away by Baptism, but concupiscence remains. And so fallen human nature does not have the harmonious obedience of body to soul as was true before the Fall. The flesh is in conflict with the spirit; that which is bodily is in conflict with that which is spiritual. The heart and mind are obscured by concupiscence. The soul must struggle against temptations of the body. So even when a human person is willing to avoid sin, the disorder of the fallen state, particularly in the weakness of the flesh, makes avoiding sin more difficult.

.474. Occasions of Sin

An occasion of sin is a situation in which a particular person might be tempted to commit a particular type of sin. The occasion itself (situation, circumstance) is not an act, and so it is not a sin. And no situation or circumstance can cause a person to sin, because sin is an act of the free will. An occasion of sin offers a substantial temptation toward sin, but it is not itself a sin, and it does not compel a person to sin.

The types of situations that might represent a substantial temptation to sin vary, and are dependent upon the temptations that any particular person finds difficult to resist. This susceptibility to a particular temptation is what causes a situation to be an occasion for sin for that person. But another person might not find the same situation to be a substantial temptation toward sin. What is an occasion for sin for one person is not an occasion for sin for another person. In this regard, the saying is true: "What is food to one, may be bitter poison to others."[508] A situation that one person finds to be a difficult temptation, another person might find to be helpful, or at least not a substantial temptation to sin.

If a situation presents a temptation to a particular person, one to which he or she is susceptible (so that there is a certain likelihood that the person will sin), then that situation is called an occasion for sin. And this is true even if the person does not happen to sin in a particular instance of that situation. The likelihood that the person will sin, as a result of being in that situation, is what constitutes an occasion for sin. This likelihood is a matter of degree. No situation can compel someone to sin, and therefore a likelihood of sin is only a possibility, not a certainty.

Sometimes a situation that represents an occasion for sin may occur without any decision by that person to enter that situation. Other times, the person decides to enter a particular situation, knowing that the situation includes a temptation to which he or she is susceptible. But the mere fact that the person is present in a situation of temptation does not constitute a sin. The situation itself is not a sin, but only a circumstance in which the person is likely, to some extent, to sin in some particular way.

When a particular situation represents an occasion for sin for a particular person, the decision to enter that situation may or may not be a sin. The fact that the person is in that situation is not a sin. The likelihood that the person will sin is a matter of degree. The sin that might be committed is also a matter of degree; it might be a more or less serious venial sin, or a more or less serious mortal sin. Therefore, the decision to enter that situation may or may not be a sin, depending on an evaluation of the three fonts of morality.

.475. Occasions of Sin and the Three Fonts

If an occasion of sin arises without any knowingly chosen act, then so far no sin has been committed. If the person enters a situation which is an occasion for sin by committing a knowingly chosen act, either an interior act (e.g. a decision) or an exterior act (e.g. going to a place where a particular temptation is present), then the knowingly chosen act might possibly be a sin. Whether or not any knowingly chosen act is a sin always depends on the three fonts of morality.

First Font: Intention

If a person chooses to enter a situation, one which is an occasion for sin, with the intention of committing a sin, then he has sinned by his immoral intention. Any act done with an immoral intention is a sinful act. If he then also commits the particular sin that pertains to the situation, he has sinned again. But even if

---

[508] Lucretius, De Rerum Natura (On the Nature of Things), book 4, n. 637; author's translation of the Latin: "quod ali cibus est aliis fuat [i.e. sit] acre venenum...."

he changes his mind, and does not commit the sin that pertains to the situation, he nevertheless did sin previously by the act of choosing, with an immoral intention, to enter the situation.

Second Font: Moral Object

If a person enters a situation, one which is an occasion for sin, by committing an intrinsically evil act, then he has already sinned by deliberately choosing an act with an evil moral object. Intrinsically evil acts are always immoral. If he then also commits the particular sin that pertains to the situation, he has sinned again. If he does not commit that particular sin, he nevertheless did sin previously by choosing an intrinsically evil act. Each and every knowingly chosen act stands on its own as to its morality.

Third Font: Circumstances

In general, the term 'occasion of sin' is used for situations where the person has no intention to sin, and can enter that situation (can place himself in that circumstance which is an occasion of sin) without committing an intrinsically evil act. In this case, the act that the person commits in order to place himself in an occasion of sin is not sinful under the first or second fonts. Whether or not this decision (to enter a circumstance which is an occasion of sin) is moral depends on the third font. The good and bad consequences of that act, of the decision to enter that situation, are weighed. And if the good consequences have greater moral weight than the bad consequences, then the act is moral. But if the bad consequences have greater moral weight than the good consequences, then the act is immoral. The decision to place one's self in circumstances which are an occasion for sin is moral or immoral depending on the weight of the third font. (Of course, this only applies when the intention is good, and no intrinsically evil act is committed, in order to enter that situation.)

As is true for the third font of any knowingly chosen act, when there is a possible occasion of sin, all of the good and bad consequences for all persons affected by the act must be weighed. The moral weight of the totality of the reasonably anticipated good and bad consequences then determines if the decision to enter that situation is moral. However, there are certain anticipated consequences that apply particularly to occasions of sin. In deciding whether or not to enter a particular situation in which there is an occasion of sin, the most important considerations are: (1) the likelihood that you will commit the sin, and (2) the gravity of the sin.

(1) This likelihood is never certain. Free will is always able to decide not to sin. Also, in order to determine future possible consequences, one must always consider the past circumstances and the present situation. Reason can only anticipate the future based on knowledge from the past and present. You must consider how you have responded in the past to similar circumstances. If you have frequently fallen into a particular sin in that circumstance, then the likelihood is greater. You must also consider your current spiritual state. Perhaps you have changed since those past circumstances occurred, being now in a weaker state, or being now in a stronger state. When you are spiritually weaker,

then you are more likely to sin. When you are spiritually stronger, then you are less likely to sin.

(2) The degree of sin is subject to the usual considerations, as explained at length in the other chapters of this book. Some sins are venial, and other sins are mortal. The venial sins deserve punishment, but not eternal punishment. The mortal sins deserve eternal punishment, if the person does not repent. Some venial sins are more serious than other venial sins. Some mortal sins are more serious than other mortal sins. All the usual considerations as to degree of sin and degree of culpability apply when considering occasions of sin.

Many texts distinguish between proximate and remote occasions of sin. By these terms, they indicate the likelihood that a particular person will sin when faced with the temptations offered by a particular situation. A proximate occasion of sin offers a greater likelihood of sin; a remote occasion of sin offers a lesser likelihood of sin. But as is true also for material cooperation, proximate and remote are a matter of degree. In addition, the degree of the sin that might be committed must also be weighed. A great likelihood that a person will commit a fully deliberate venial sin has greater moral weight than a very remote possibility that a person will commit a mortal sin. A likelihood that a person will commit a mortal sin has greater moral weight than the same degree of likelihood that a person will commit a venial sin.

Both the likelihood that a sin will occur, and the moral weight of the sin, must be weighed in the third font. Once you understand the likelihood and degree of the possible sin, then you can begin to evaluate the third font of morality concerning that occasion of sin.

.476. Occasions of Venial Sin

If the degree of likelihood that you will sin is small, and the degree of sin is venial, then the moral weight of this bad consequence is light. You only need a reason of relatively modest weight to enter a situation that has a small likelihood of venial sin, especially a venial sin that is not fully deliberate, or that is relatively less serious when compared to other venial sins.

If there is no good reason to enter a situation, and you will likely commit some significant venial sin because of the influence of that situation, then you should avoid that occasion of venial sin. In such a case, there are no significant good consequences, even of light weight, to entering the situation. And we are always morally obligated to avoid sin, even venial sin.

Therefore, if you decide to enter a situation, despite the reasonable anticipation that the bad consequences, found in the likelihood of an occasion of venial sin, will outweigh the good, your decision is a sin under the third font, but it is only a venial sin. An occasion of venial sin does not have grave moral weight in the third font of circumstances, and so it can never, by itself, cause the third font, or the act as a whole, to be gravely immoral.

Now a problem occurs with occasions of venial sin, in that most persons commit some venial sins, even many venial sins, every day. For many persons, almost any situation has a certain likelihood of some venial sin. Often, these objective venial sins are lacking in full knowledge and/or lacking in full deliberation, but they are sins with some degree of culpability nonetheless. If the anticipated venial sins are not a result of the situation, but instead result from the spiritual state of the individual (lack of holiness), then there is no occasion of sin. The person is subject to possible venial sins in any situation. Therefore, his response to this daily possibility of venial sin should be prayer, self-denial, works of mercy, and the continual practice of all the virtues, and frequent recourse to Confession and Communion.

.477. Occasions of Mortal Sin

Good consequences of relatively modest weight can justify entering a situation that is an occasion for venial sin, even a likely (proximate) occasion for venial sin. The third font of morality is always good if the good consequences outweigh the bad. Good consequences of relatively modest weight can also justify entering a situation that is an occasion for mortal sin, but only if the likelihood of mortal sin is small (remote).

No situation in this life is entirely and necessarily free from even the possibility of mortal sin. Any person is able to freely choose to commit an actual mortal sin, especially by an interior act (e.g. lust, greed, envy), at any time, in any situation. We are never in a situation with no possibility of mortal sin. And so it is not necessary for a situation to be entirely free from all possibility of mortal sin, or free from all temptation toward mortal sin, in order for entering that situation to be moral. All that is required, in every case, is three good fonts: good intention, good moral object, and the good consequences must outweigh the bad.

The moral law requires us to avoid all sin, but does not require us to avoid all occasions of sin. Rather, if the intention and moral object are good (in the act by which we enter that situation), then the only additional requirement is that the good consequences outweigh the bad. When there is a likelihood that a mortal sin might be committed, we are not always, regardless of circumstances, obliged to avoid that situation. For this likelihood of mortal sin is a matter of degree, and the degree is limited. The likelihood of mortal sin is always substantially limited by the gift of free will, enlightened and strengthened by reason and grace. No situation can compel anyone to sin, and no situation can increase the likelihood of sin to such a high degree that the commission of an actual mortal sin is a near certainty. Through prayer and grace, our free will is able to endure and resist any temptation to any sin, especially actual mortal sin. Therefore, the act by which we enter an occasion of sin cannot be said to be moral or immoral until all three fonts have been evaluated, including both the good and the bad consequences in the third font. But if you have evaluated only the bad consequences, and not the good, then you do not yet know the moral weight of the third font.

Furthermore, the moral weight of the bad consequence of possibly committing a mortal sin is reduced with any reduction in the possibility that the sin will be committed. So a small likelihood that you will commit a mortal sin has relatively modest moral weight. And this weight, for any sin, can be reduced by acts of prayer and self-denial, before and during that situation of temptation. Every increase in grace decreases sin, and makes any sin less likely to occur.

The gravity of the mortal sin that one might commit in any situation can be greater or lesser. If there is a likelihood that a person might commit an objective mortal sin, but without full knowledge or full consent, then this type of mortal sin has less weight in the consequences than the same likelihood of an actual mortal sin. And even among actual mortal sins, some sins are more serious than other sins. The more disorder that there is in a sin, the more thoroughly it is contrary to the love of God, and the more it harms your neighbor. Some mortal sins are substantially more sinful than other mortal sins. Both the degree of sin, and the degree of likelihood that the sin will occur, weigh in the third font.

.478. Leaving an Occasion of Sin

When an occasion of sin occurs without any decision or act on the part of the person, then that person has not yet sinned. But he is obligated to refrain from sin while in that situation. And he may also be obligated to find a way to leave that situation, if and when he is able to do so. Whether or not a person is obligated to depart from a situation that presents a temptation to sin is subject to the same conditions for entering an occasion for sin. If the gravity of the possible sin and its degree of likelihood outweigh any good consequences, then the person is obligated to free himself from the situation, if and when it is possible. If he is able and does not do so, then he would be guilty of a sin of omission.

Similarly, a person might enter a situation which is an occasion for sin, because he judges that the good consequences outweigh the bad. And he might then find that the danger of sin, or the seriousness of the sin, is greater than he realized before, so great as to cause the bad consequences to outweigh the good. If so, then he is obligated to free himself from that situation, if and when he is able. If he does not do so, then he would be guilty of a sin of omission. And the same applies even if the person sinned (under any font) in entering the situation. Once he is in a situation of temptation to sin, if the bad consequences of remaining in that situation outweigh the good, then he is morally obligated to free himself from that situation, if he can do so without sin.

In all situations, at all times, all persons are obligated to avoid all sin, especially mortal sin. The obligation to avoid occasions of sin is due to the application of the three fonts of morality to a particular type of situation, one in which there is a temptation to sin. But the proper evaluation of this type of situation is solely based on the three fonts. If all three fonts are good, the act is moral. Both sins of commission and sins of omission must also be avoided. We are obligated, not only to avoid situations of temptation to sin in which the bad consequences outweigh the good, but also to free ourselves from any situation in which the bad consequences of temptation to sin outweigh the good.

.479. EXAMPLES OF OCCASIONS OF SIN

Examples: (1) A man considers whether or not he should go to a party where he knows that there will be drinking. He is prone to drinking to excess, and he reasonably anticipates that, for himself in that particular situation, he will be likely to sin by drinking to excess, and also perhaps by committing other serious sins while inebriated. For him, that situation represents a temptation to commit one or more mortal sins. If he decides to go to the party, without any intention to sin, his decision is moral under the first two fonts (intention, moral object). However, the third font has the weighty bad consequence of a likelihood of mortal sin, and no weighty good consequences. Therefore, it is a sin under the third font for him to attend that party.

(2) A second man considers attending the same party, and he is not susceptible to the sin of drinking to excess. But he is susceptible to sexual sins, and he reasonably anticipates that, if he attends the party, he might face substantial temptation to commit sexual sins. Even if he attends the party with the intention of resisting temptation, so that the first font is good, he must also evaluate the third font, as to whether any good consequences would outweigh the danger of mortal sin. In this example, the danger of mortal sin is likely, and there is no good consequence of greater weight, and so the decision to attend the party is a sin, in addition to any sins that he might commit at the party. But even if it happens that he resists temptation and does not sin during the party, the decision to attend was still a sin because he reasonably anticipated that the bad consequences would outweigh the good consequences.

(3) A third man considers attending the same party. He is not susceptible to sins of drinking to excess, nor to sexual sins. He reasonably anticipates that the party will not present any occasion of serious sin for him. He also anticipates that he will be able to enjoy spending time with his friends, and will be refreshed in heart and mind, despite the presence at that party of some persons who are sinning. This man does not sin in deciding to attend the party. All three fonts of morality are good. There are good consequences to attending the party, and, for him, there are no substantial bad consequences that would outweigh the good.

(4) A religious nun living in a strict cloister might attain to a relatively high degree of holiness and be free from most venial sins. She might commit only a few semi-deliberate venial sins, once in a while. But she knows that her relative freedom from most sin is due to the benefits of living in a strict community, away from much of the world. She reasonably anticipates that if she transfers to a different order, an order active in doing good works within the sinful world, that she will commit more venial sins. The increased proximity to the secular world, and the absence of the benefits of a strict cloister, might result in significantly more venial sins in her life, if she makes this change.

But these considerations fall into the third font of morality. She has a good intention, to do works of mercy in the active life, and it is not intrinsically evil to make the transfer. The great likelihood that she will commit more venial sins if she changes to the active life has moderate moral weight; it is not of great moral weight because the sins are only venial. The good consequences of doing works of mercy in the active life would generally outweigh the bad consequences of a likely increase in venial sins (unless there are other considerations). For holiness is not based solely on committing as few sins as possible, but on doing the will of God as much as possible.

(5) The same cannot be said for this nun if she reasonably anticipates, based on her understanding of her own weaknesses and of her life before she joined her religious order, that there is a moderate likelihood that she will commit mortal sins. The moral weight of the lightest actual mortal sin is much heavier than the weight of the heaviest actual venial sin. For mortal sins deserve eternal punishment, and venial sins do not. If she must stay in the cloister in order to avoid likely occasions of actual mortal sin, then she should not transfer to the active life, not even if she anticipates doing many works of mercy there. If she anticipates the likelihood of objective mortal sins that are not also actual mortal sins, the moral weight, due to the grave matter of any objective mortal sin, is substantially greater than any objective venial sin. As always, the morality of the third font is determined by weighing all the good and bad consequences. The more serious the sin, and the more likely the sin, the heavier its moral weight in the third font.

(6) A soldier is compelled by orders to enter a difficult situation, such as to battle insurgents among the general population in a city. His close friends were killed in that same area, and he anticipates that he will have difficulty avoiding certain sins, such as unjust anger against the population, and the sin of revenge. But he cannot refuse to follow his orders without grave consequences, including that he will be jailed and court-martialed, as well as harm to the war effort due to his disobedience to a lawful order. For this occasion of sin, the likelihood of sin is moderate, and the degree of sin is mortal. But he might still judge that the good consequences outweigh the bad. This judgment is strengthened if he also reduces the weight of these bad consequences by reducing the likelihood of mortal sin through prayer, self-denial, and works of mercy (e.g. acts of kindness to persons in the general population). Therefore, he may morally obey that order, despite a significant likelihood of mortal sin.

.480. EXAMPLES FROM SCRIPTURE

[Sirach]
{9:11} Many, by admiring the beauty of the wife of another, have become reprobate. For familiarity with her flares up like a fire.
{9:12} You should not sit down at all with another man's wife, nor recline with her on a couch.
{9:13} And you should not argue with her over wine, lest perhaps your heart may turn toward her, and by your emotion, you would be toppled into perdition.

The acts that are being discussed in this passage from Sirach are not condemned because of a bad intention. And these are not intrinsically evil acts: admiring the beauty of a woman who is married, sitting down with her, reclining on a couch with her, arguing with her over wine. But Sacred Scripture warns us against these acts because of the likely bad consequences. It may be an occasion of sin, even mortal sin, to do these acts. By admiring her beauty, and then spending time alone with her, and then arguing and drinking wine, they might both fall into the mortal sin of adultery. (Arguing with her enflames the emotion of anger, which can then enflame other emotions, such as passion, especially when under the influence of alcohol.) Scripture is here discussing the moral obligation to avoid occasions of mortal sin.

[1 Corinthians 8]
{8:7} But knowledge is not in everyone. For some persons, even now, with consent to an idol, eat what has been sacrificed to an idol. And their conscience, being infirm, becomes polluted.
{8:8} Yet food does not commend us to God. For if we eat, we will not have more, and if we do not eat, we will not have less.
{8:9} But be careful not to let your liberty become a cause of sin to those who are weak.
{8:10} For if anyone sees someone with knowledge sitting down to eat in idolatry, will not his own conscience, being infirm, be emboldened to eat what has been sacrificed to idols?
{8:11} And should an infirm brother perish by your knowledge, even though Christ died for him?
{8:12} So when you sin in this way against the brothers, and you harm their weakened conscience, then you sin against Christ.
{8:13} Because of this, if food leads my brother to sin, I will never eat meat, lest I lead my brother to sin.

Saint Paul the Apostle is discussing the sin of scandal, when one person presents an occasion of sin to another person. We should generally avoid occasions of sin, and avoid presenting occasions of sin to other persons. However, either of these types of acts may be moral, depending on the three fonts. If your act is done with good intention, and a good moral object, you nevertheless sin if you reasonably anticipate that your act will lead your neighbor into sin, and if, as a result, the bad consequences of your act outweigh the good. The example given by Paul concerns a Christian who knows that pagan gods do not exist, and that food sacrificed to them is merely ordinary food. This Christian can eat foods from the marketplace in good conscience, even though the food may have been sacrificed to idols. He does not sin because he knows that this is merely ordinary food. But if his example of eating food sacrificed to idols will likely lead another Christian into thinking that pagan gods and pagan religion is true, then he sins by leading his fellow Christian into an occasion of mortal sin.

.481. Forgiveness and Punishment

Occasions of temptation to sin are not themselves sins, but they may lead to sin. We avoid temptation in order to avoid sin, especially mortal sin. Every mortal sin is thoroughly contrary to the will of God, is a grave violation of the moral law, and does serious harm to neighbor and self. But only actual mortal sin deserves eternal punishment. The punishment that all other types and degrees of sin deserve is limited; this is called temporal punishment. Any temporal punishment can be satisfied (completed) within a finite period of time. Eternal punishment is satisfied only by eternal damnation in Hell. Temporal punishment is satisfied by penance in this life (prayer, self-denial, works of mercy), by various sufferings in this life, and by sufferings in Purgatory. Therefore, for the sake of our eternal salvation, our primary obligation under the eternal moral law is to avoid every actual mortal sin, including sins of commission and sins of omission, and to repent and seek forgiveness in the Sacrament of Confession if we ever do commit an actual mortal sin.

If any person is living a sinful life and desires to change, he should first strive to rid his life of every actual mortal sin, and to obtain forgiveness through the Sacrament of Confession. For his eternal salvation depends on avoiding, or at least repenting from, every actual mortal sin. No sin is justified, not even the smallest sin. But venial sins are not so thoroughly contrary to the love of God and neighbor as to be incompatible with the state of grace in the soul, nor so as to deserve eternal punishment. After freeing himself from every actual mortal sin, he should free himself from every merely objective mortal sin, even if there is reduced culpability due to a lack of full knowledge or a lack of full deliberation. Lastly, he should strive to avoid, as much as possible, venial sins, especially those that are fully deliberate.

We are each always able to avoid every actual mortal sin. It is entirely possible to live a life free from all actual mortal sin. However, it is not possible, in this life, for human persons to avoid all venial sin, except by a special grace of God.

The Council of Trent: "If anyone says that a man, once justified, can sin no more, nor lose grace, and that therefore he that falls and sins was never truly justified; or, on the other hand, that he is able, during his whole life, to avoid all sins, even those that are venial, except by a special privilege from God, as the Church holds in regard of the Blessed Virgin: let him be anathema."[509]

Human persons are not able to avoid all venial sins, except by a special privilege from God. And so we should not be disheartened if we still have a number of venial sins in our lives, despite our belief and practice of the holy Catholic Faith, and our many acts of prayer, self-denial, and works of mercy. And we can always obtain forgiveness from any and all sins, mortal and venial, without any exception, if we repent and receive the Sacrament of Confession (also called the Sacrament of Penance, or the Sacrament of Reconciliation).

In addition to forgiveness from the sin itself, we must also make satisfaction for the punishment that is justly deserved because of the sin. All sins deserve some punishment, because all sins offend God, and harm neighbor and self. If we do not sufficiently satisfy the punishment due for sin in this life, but we die in a state of grace, then that satisfaction must be completed in the sufferings of Purgatory. But whoever dies not in a state of grace will suffer eternal punishment in Hell.

A valid Confession, with full repentance, forgives all sins, mortal and venial. A devout reception of holy Communion forgives all venial sin. Any devout act of prayer, self-denial, or mercy toward others also forgives venial sin. Venial sins also require satisfaction by temporal punishment, but venial sins do not deserve eternal punishment. And the temporal punishment justly due for venial sin is partially, even at times completely, forgiven by the devout reception of any

---

[509] Council of Trent, Decree on Justification, Sixth Session, Canon XXIII.

Sacrament, including Confession itself. And when Confession is followed by devout attendance at Mass and devout reception of Communion, it is even more likely that all temporal punishment due for all venial sins is forgiven. In addition, various types of devout penance, such as prayer, self-denial, works of mercy, also readily satisfy the punishment due for venial sin, even in its entirety.

A valid Confession, with full repentance, forgives all sins, including any and all actual mortal sins without exception. Although the punishment due for actual mortal sin is eternal punishment in Hell, when an actual mortal sin is forgiven, that punishment is always reduced from eternal to temporal. And this temporal punishment can be fully satisfied in this life, partly by devout reception of the Sacraments (especially Confession and holy Communion), and partly by various acts of penance. The Sacrament of Confession itself, validly received, always forgives at least some of the punishment due for any sins, mortal and venial.

Compendium of the Catechism: "The effects of the sacrament of Penance are: reconciliation with God and therefore the forgiveness of sins; reconciliation with the Church; recovery, if it has been lost, of the state of grace; remission of the eternal punishment merited by mortal sins, and remission, at least in part, of the temporal punishment which is the consequence of sin; peace, serenity of conscience and spiritual consolation; and an increase of spiritual strength for the struggle of Christian living."[510]

.482. The Sin That Cannot Be Forgiven

[Matthew]
{12:31} For this reason, I say to you: Every sin and blasphemy shall be forgiven men, but blasphemy against the Spirit shall not be forgiven.
{12:32} And anyone who will have spoken a word against the Son of man shall be forgiven. But whoever will have spoken against the Holy Spirit shall not be forgiven, neither in this age, nor in the future age.

[Mark]
{3:28} Amen I say to you, that all sins will be forgiven the sons of men, and the blasphemies by which they will have blasphemed.
{3:29} But he who will have blasphemed against the Holy Spirit shall not have forgiveness in eternity; instead he shall be guilty of an eternal offense."

[Luke]
{12:10} And everyone who speaks a word against the Son of man, it will be forgiven of him. But of him who will have blasphemed against the Holy Spirit, it will not be forgiven.

The sin called blasphemy against the Holy Spirit is nothing other than the sin of final impenitence. Anyone who commits an actual mortal sin, and who remains unrepentant through the last moment of his life, has committed the sin of final impenitence, and will be punished forever in the fires of Hell. This sin is called blasphemy against the Holy Spirit because the graces offered by the Holy Spirit bring about the repentance of sinners. The refusal to repent of actual mortal sin,

---
[510] Compendium of the Catechism of the Catholic Church, n. 310.

even through the last moment of life, is the worst offense against the Holy Spirit. This sin cannot be forgiven because it is not possible to be forgiven of an unrepentant actual mortal sin after death. Whoever dies in a state of unrepentant actual mortal sin is certainly condemned to Hell forever.

The gift of final perseverance is opposed to the sin of final impenitence. This gift is the companion of the gift of salvific grace. At Baptism, each person is given salvific (sanctifying) grace. The gift of the graces needed to persevere in that state of grace, even though the last moment of life, completes the gift of salvific grace. All who die in a state of grace have eternal salvation.

.483. Helps against Temptation

Any good act, freely and knowingly chosen in cooperation with grace, advances a person in holiness and strengthens that person against temptation. Advancing in holiness, by practicing all the virtues in cooperation with grace, is the best way to avoid temptation. We advance in holiness by the reception of the Sacraments, especially the devout and frequent reception of Confession and Communion. We advance in holiness by three types of acts: prayer, self-denial, works of mercy. And we advance in holiness by the ordinary deeds of our state of life, done in love, faith, hope, wisdom, knowledge, understanding, prudence, temperance, fortitude, and justice.

The Rosary and Divine Mercy Chaplet

There are numerous different types and examples of prayer. Only a few will be mentioned here. The Rosary is a very powerful prayer, used and recommended by many Popes and Saints, and by countless ordinary faithful souls of the Church. This prayer combines a recitation of the Our Father, the Hail Mary, and the Glory Be, with a meditation on various mysteries in the lives of Jesus and Mary, mysteries pertaining to the plan of God for our salvation.

The Divine Mercy Chaplet was given to the Church through Saint Faustina much more recently than the Rosary, but it has quickly become a favorite of the faithful throughout the world. This prayer is recited using rosary beads, but with a different set of prayers. Both of these prayers are very powerful at obtaining every kind of grace, including grace for the conversion of hardened sinners, grace to avoid any kind of sin and any temptation toward sin, and grace to increase in virtue and holiness.

Brief Prayers

There is an ancient practice in the Church of using very brief recited prayers, spontaneously expressed many times throughout each day, in addition to times set aside specifically for longer recited prayers and other forms of prayer. Any devout brief prayer can be used for this purpose. The same prayer can be said repeatedly throughout the day, or a selection of different prayers can be used alternately. A few suggestions follow.

Jesus, Mary, I love you, save souls.

Most Sacred Heart of Jesus, have mercy on us.

Most Holy Trinity, have mercy on me, a sinner.

Lord, have mercy on my soul.

O Mary, conceived without sin, pray for us who have recourse to thee.

Any brief recited prayer, or any spontaneously composed prayer, can be used for the same purpose, which is to raise the heart and mind to God, even while immersed in the various tasks of daily life.

It is also an ancient and sacred form of prayer to make the Sign of the Cross, either in the usual manner across the head, heart, and shoulders, or a small Sign of the Cross over one place (e.g. the head, or the heart). The Sign of the Cross can be made while reciting the words, "In the name of the Father, and of the Son, and of the Holy Spirit," or with some other recited or spontaneous prayer. Or the Sign of the Cross can be made without any words.

Prayer Without Words

Recited prayers are memorized forms of prayer with words. The faithful have always made use of recited prayer. Jesus Himself taught us the Our Father prayer (Mt 6:9-13; Lk 11:2-4). The faithful have always made use of spontaneous prayer also, whereby a person prays with words, but according to his or her own mind and heart at the time. When the Virgin Mary prayed her Magnificant, she was not reciting a memorized prayer, but was praying spontaneously, in words from her heart and mind (Lk 1:46-55).

But prayer is also possible without any words: "For we do not know how to pray as we ought, but the Spirit himself asks on our behalf with ineffable sighing." (Romans 8:26). Our free will and intellect, cooperating with the grace of God, can seek and find God in prayer without words. This prayer can take the form of a wordless expression (like the Sign of the Cross), or an ineffable silent sighing of the soul, or listening to the grace of God in silence: "And she had a sister, named Mary, who, while sitting beside the Lord's feet, was listening to his word." (Lk 10:39). In addition, there is a higher form of silent prayer, called contemplative prayer, such as Thomas Merton practiced and discussed.

Lectio Divina (Divine Reading) is a form of prayer consisting of a devout meditation on any passage in Sacred Scripture. The person reads the passage, consisting of a brief set of verses, or even one verse alone. The passage is read slowly and repeatedly. The person mediates on these verses, with or without interior words, but always allowing the truths of Divine Revelation to rest upon and enliven the soul.

The truths of the Catholic Faith include mysteries beyond complete human comprehension, and beyond complete expression in words. Therefore, our prayers must sometimes be without words. Jesus Christ has saved us; we have not saved ourselves. Therefore, in our prayers, we should place listening to Christ above talking to Christ. Prayer should not be mainly a list of requests to

God. The true depth and breadth of prayer is found in silence, in listening to God, and in meditating on the Word of God.

Whoever does not pray, does not avoid sin. Whoever prays little, sins much.

.484. Self-denial

Fasting is one type of self-denial. Fasting is the archetype of all self-denial. We can understand any type of self denial by comparing it to fasting. Fasting is the most fundamental type of self-denial because the human person needs food, every day, a number of times a day. By the practice of fasting, the human person learns to show self-restraint and self-denial in what is a fundamental necessity of life, thereby also learning to show self-restraint and self-denial in every other area of human life.

Fasting includes any reduction in the type or amount of food or drink, chosen freely out of devotion to God. A strict fast might include only bread and water, or only rice with some vegetable oil and water. But not every fast need be strict. The circumstances of each person's life should play a role in this decision concerning fasting. No one should endanger his or her health by fasting too strictly. Fasting has its effectiveness from the love, faith, hope and other virtues exercised by fasting. Fasting is only a means to an end, the end of cooperating more effectively with grace. When fasting is an end in itself, then fasting is a sin. Fasting is a type of physical evil, and so it can never be morally sought as an end. And it is not the strictness of the fast, but the devotion accompanying the fast, which causes the fast to be spiritually effective. A person may fast merely by reducing the quantity of food at each meal, or by changing the types of food to those that are still healthy, but less palatable, or by doing both. A person can also fast by giving up particular beverages, such as alcohol or soda. There are countless ways to fast that are pleasing to God. Do not believe anyone who claims that every fast must be the same.

Self-denial is important for avoiding sin, and for enduring temptation without committing sin. By the practice of self-denial in all things, exterior and interior, the person learns to choose a path based on faith and reason, rather than on emotion and selfish desire. All temptation becomes much less tempting when the soul learns to choose the higher things by denying itself the lower things.

Self-denial is found either (a) in refraining from, or reducing, any activities that are pleasant, moral, and not necessary to one's duties in life, or (b) in performing, or increasing, any activities that are moral, unpleasant, and not contrary to one's duties in life. In acts of self-denial, we choose little crosses for ourselves in order to become more detached from the things of this life, freeing us to love God and neighbor with a pure spiritual love. These crosses should be small sufferings done with great love, and not great sufferings done with pride in how much we are suffering. The smallest deed done out of pure love is better in the eyes of God than any great deed done with little or no love.

Also, these acts of self-denial must not include any sins of commission or omission. We must not ignore the requirements of our state of life, nor do any harm to self or neighbor. It is the love, faith, hope and other virtues with which the act is done that provides the benefits. All suffering, by itself, is merely physical evil. Only when this physical evil is directed toward a higher purpose, such as holiness and salvation, is the act of taking suffering upon ourselves moral and beneficial.

If you still have some sins in your life, mortal or venial, refraining from these sins is not so much an act of self-denial as it is an absolute requirement of the eternal moral law. In refraining from sin, we deny ourselves certain true or apparent goods. But the term self-denial is mainly used to refer to acts of denial that are not required in order to avoid sin. A person may not merely reduce, or merely refrain temporarily, from sin, on the excuse that is it self-denial.

Examples of self-denial: (1) fasting, (2) giving up alcohol, (3) eating fewer sweet foods or fewer unhealthy foods, (4) making less use of various forms of entertainment (television, games, novels, magazine, movies), (5) refraining from idle conversation, (6) refraining from self-indulgent thoughts, (7) reducing any activities that waste time or money, (8) eating foods that are plain or even unpleasant tasting, (9) wearing less comfortable clothing, (10) sleeping less, or sleeping with less comfort, (11) taking cold showers, (12) enduring various small discomforts that occur in daily life, rather than immediately seeking to remedy them (e.g. not immediately satisfying hunger or thirst) -- as well as many other similar acts.

.485. In the practice of self-denial, we are not required to permanently refrain from any activity that is not a sin. Usually self-denial is exercised by decreasing the frequency of activities that are pleasant, but also moral, and not by abandoning all pleasant or entertaining activities. Most of the faithful are not called to live as hermits in a cave, in continual severe self-denial. The pleasant activities of life in this world, those that are moral, can relax the body and refresh the mind. Self-denial should not treat the goods of this life as if they were evil, but only as lesser goods that must sometimes be set aside, even if only temporarily, in favor of the higher goods of the soul. Also, self-denial should never be done in any way, or at any time, if it will result in harm to self or neighbor. Self-denial is only a means to a greater and purer love for God, neighbor, self. When self-denial becomes its own end, it becomes moral evil.

However, if a person has sinful activities in his life, he is morally obligated to refrain from all such sinful activities. This type of self-denial takes precedence over a denial of what is not sinful. Neither can self-denial of this type (if it can even be called self-denial) be intermittent or temporary. For we are always required by the moral law to refrain from sins of every kind. Acts of self-denial must never include any type or degree of sin. Self-denial is sometimes justified if it is merely a type of limited physical evil for a higher purpose; but self-denial is never justified if it includes any knowingly chosen immoral act, regardless of the purpose or the circumstances.

.486. Self-indulgence Leads To Sin

[Deuteronomy]
{21:20} And they shall say to them: 'This our son is reckless and disobedient. He shows contempt when listening to our admonitions. He occupies himself with carousing, and self-indulgence, and feasting.'

[Ecclesiastes]
{10:17} Blessed is the land whose king is noble, and whose princes eat at the proper time, for refreshment and not for self-indulgence.

The opposite of self-denial is self-indulgence. Just as self-denial strengthens us against temptation and sin, so also does self-indulgence weaken us to temptation and sin. The more self-indulgent you are, the harder it is to resist temptation and the more likely you are to sin. Self-restraint and self-denial are opposed to self-indulgence.

[Numbers]
{11:31} Then a wind, going out from the Lord and moving forcefully across the sea, brought quails and cast them into the camp, across a distance of one day's journey, in every part of the camp all around, and they flew in the air two cubits high above the ground.
{11:32} Therefore, the people, rising up, gathered quails all that day and night, and the next day; he who did least well gathered ten homers. And they dried them throughout the camp.
{11:33} The flesh was still between their teeth, neither had this kind of food ceased, and behold, the fury of the Lord was provoked against the people, and he struck them with an exceedingly great scourge.
{11:34} And that place was called, 'The Graves of Lust.' For there, they buried the people who had desired. Then, departing from the Graves of Lust, they arrived in Hazeroth, and they stayed there.

The ancient Israelites were given good food, in the form of quails, but they ate with self-indulgence, not with self-restraint. They were not required to deny themselves this good food provided by the Lord. But they were morally required to exercise that partial self-denial which is called self-restraint. They should have shown moderation in their use of material things (temperance). Instead, they were self-indulgent, and this lack of self-restraint led to other self-indulgent acts, especially sexual sins. One vice leads to another. One virtue leads to another. Choose any virtue, and you move away from every vice. Choose any vice, and you move away from every virtue.

.487. Works of Mercy

Catechism of the Catholic Church: "The works of mercy are charitable actions by which we come to the aid of our neighbor in his spiritual and bodily necessities. Instructing, advising, consoling, comforting are spiritual works of mercy, as are forgiving and bearing wrongs patiently. The corporal works of mercy consist especially in feeding the hungry, sheltering the homeless, clothing the naked, visiting the sick and imprisoned, and burying the dead."[511]

A work of mercy is any morally good act that benefits your neighbor, in body or in soul. A sinful act is never a work of mercy, despite any apparent benefits to your neighbor. To whatever extent an act is sinful, it harms and does not benefit your neighbor. The term 'works of mercy' uses the word 'mercy' because these good acts should be done for the benefit of any and all human persons, even unrepentant sinners. For while we were yet unrepentant sinners, Christ died for us. Our works of mercy should especially benefit sinners, since the more one sins, the more one is in need of God's mercy. Acts of mercy toward sinners can cause those sinners to repent, and ultimately to obtain eternal life in Heaven, rather than eternal punishment in Hell.

[Matthew 6]
{6:1} "Pay attention, lest you perform your justice before men, in order to be seen by them; otherwise you shall not have a reward with your Father, who is in heaven.
{6:2} Therefore, when you give alms, do not choose to sound a trumpet before you, as the hypocrites do in the synagogues and in the towns, so that they may be honored by men. Amen I say to you, they have received their reward.
{6:3} But when you give alms, do not let your left hand know what your right hand is doing,
{6:4} so that your almsgiving may be in secret, and your Father, who sees in secret, will repay you.

These various works that benefit our neighbor must be done in cooperation with grace, accompanied by interior acts of love, faith, hope and all the virtues. If not, then no matter how much your neighbor benefits, your act is not pleasing to God and you will not be rewarded by God. So if you donate a large sum of money to a charity, not with the intention of helping others, but with the intention of obtaining the praise and approval of others, then it is not truly a work of mercy. Or if you preach the Gospel in order to exalt yourself (Philippians 1:17), it is not truly a work of mercy.

There are two commonly used lists of works of mercy, the corporal works of mercy and the spiritual works of mercy. But these are merely examples of types of works; any work that is moral, and is good for your neighbor, is a work of mercy, especially when the act is done out of a pure and selfless love. In fact, the greatness of a work of mercy is not measured by the apparent consequences of the work, but by the purity of love, faith, hope, and all the virtues with which the act of mercy is done. Christ's salvific act of mercy on the Cross was so very effective, not because of His great suffering, but because of His great Love. We must imitate the works of mercy of Christ.

---

[511] Catechism of the Catholic Church, n. 2447.

.488. The Corporal Works of Mercy

The corporal works of mercy are primarily directed at assisting the bodily needs of our neighbor. These works can be listed as follows:

> [1] feed the hungry,
> [2] give drink to the thirsty,
> [3] shelter the homeless,
> [4] clothe the naked,
> [5] visit the sick,
> [6] visit prisoners,
> [7] bury the dead.

This list of corporal works is based on Sacred Scripture:

[Matthew]
{25:35} For [1] I was hungry, and you gave me to eat; [2] I was thirsty, and you gave me to drink; [3] I was a stranger, and you took me in;
{25:36} [4] naked, and you covered me; [5] sick, and you visited me; [6] I was in prison, and you came to me.'

The seventh corporal work of mercy is also taught in Sacred Scripture, by the example of Tobit, who buried the bodies of the Jewish martyrs (Tobit 1:21-2:7), by the example of the disciples of John, who buried the Baptist's body (Mt 14:12), and by the example of the disciples of Jesus, who prepared and buried His Body in a new tomb (John 19:40-41).

But these seven examples of corporal works of mercy need not be taken as a limit, nor as an exclusive list; they should be interpreted and applied broadly. Feeding the hungry can include assisting the needy with agriculture, so that they can grow food, and assisting the unemployed to find work, so that they can buy food. Giving drink to the thirsty can include efforts to provide clean water to a community. Sheltering the homeless can include any type of hospitality to strangers, even if it does not include literal shelter. Sheltering the homeless can also include helping the poor to obtain land and land rights, helping orphans find a home, and helping widows live in dignity and security. Clothing the naked can include providing clothing, blankets, beds and bedding, as well as providing work gloves for manual labor. Clothing the naked can also include donations of money, or assistance in finding employment, so that those in need may buy these various necessities.

Visiting the sick can also include providing medical care and supplies for a person or a community, providing access to health insurance, and establishing hospitals and hospices. Visiting prisoners can also include helping the innocent to be freed from unjust sentences, helping prisoners to reform, helping former prisons to find work and housing, and similar acts of kindness. Notice that these works of mercy include acts even toward persons convicted of serious crimes. Any human person who is willing to accept mercy, can benefit from a work of mercy. Burying the dead includes visiting the dying to comfort them with words and with companionship, giving the deceased and destitute a dignified burial, reforming customs and laws that do not respect the dignity of the dying human person and of the deceased human body, and any similar acts of mercy.

In addition, some acts assist the needy across several different types of works of mercy. Helping the needy with donations of money, so that they can buy what they need, helping a person find work, helping a community develop more jobs, and any truly beneficial economic development for a community, would fall under more than one of the corporal works of mercy. Such efforts benefit the body in many ways, assisting persons in obtaining what the body needs for a healthy life.

But all these deeds must be done with true selfless spiritual love of God and neighbor. And all these deeds must be done in a way that is moral and is truly beneficial. Those who do works of mercy must continually strive to find the most effective way to provide assistance, according to the specific needs of particular circumstances. Wisdom and prudence are necessary; good intentions are not sufficient. Much harm can be done, despite the intention to do good works, if attention is not paid to the particular needs and the most fitting way to meet those needs. An act is not moral merely because it has a good intention. The act itself must have a good moral object, and the good done must outweigh any harm that might result. When persons attempt works of mercy, corporal or spiritual, without evaluating all the possible good and bad consequences that can be reasonably anticipated to occur, they sin against God, and they harm their neighbor.

.489. The Spiritual Works of Mercy

The spiritual works of mercy are directed primarily at assisting the spiritual needs of our neighbor. These works can be listed as follows:

>[1] teach the ignorant,
>[2] counsel the doubtful,
>[3] correct sinners,
>[4] forbear wrongs patiently,
>[5] forgive offenses,
>[6] comfort the afflicted,
>[7] pray for the living and the dead.

This list of spiritual works is based on Sacred Scripture:

[Colossians]
{1:28} We are announcing him, correcting every man and teaching every man, with all wisdom, so that we may offer every man perfect in Christ Jesus.

There are many passages in Scripture clearly showing by word and example that teaching is a good work, and that correcting sinners is also a good work. Each of us needs to be taught, for we are not all knowing, and we are not born with knowledge. This teaching may include any useful knowledge on any good subject. But the preeminent need of this world is for teaching on matters of faith, morals, and salvation, so that we may offer Christ Jesus to everyone who is willing to accept Him.

[Matthew]
{9:10} And it happened that, as he was sitting down to eat in the house, behold, many tax collectors and sinners arrived, and they sat down to eat with Jesus and his disciples.
{9:11} And the Pharisees, seeing this, said to his disciples, "Why does your Teacher eat with tax collectors and sinners?"
{9:12} But Jesus, hearing this, said: "It is not those who are healthy who are in need of a physician, but those who have maladies.
{9:13} So then, go out and learn what this means: 'I desire mercy and not sacrifice.' For I have not come to call the just, but sinners."

Jesus ate with sinners in order to heal their souls by correcting their sins. The correction of sinners is a work of mercy. Each of us needs correction, from time to time, for we are all sinners. The works of teaching the ignorant and of correcting sinners are required by the positive precept to love your neighbor. The failure to do these works can be a sin of omission. We should not ignore the sins of our neighbors, nor act as if their sins were of no consequence. We have a moral obligation, in fitting circumstances and in a virtuous manner, to correct the sins of those who go astray from good morals. This moral obligation requires us to judge acts, but not persons.

Catechism of the Catholic Church: "However, although we can judge that an act is in itself a grave offense, we must entrust judgment of persons to the justice and mercy of God."[512]

It is perhaps due to the influence of sinful secular society that many Christians have turned aside from this duty to correct sinners, on the excuse that we cannot judge. Although we should not judge persons, we certainly should judge acts, as to which acts are moral and which are immoral. And when some persons commit immoral acts, especially objective mortal sins, we have a Christian duty to correct them.

[2 Corinthians]
{8:10} And about this, I give my counsel. For this is useful to those of you who, only a year earlier, had just begun to act, or even to be willing to act.

In one letter, the Apostle Saint Paul gives his counsel (his advice) in order to help those who were in doubt to make the best decision. Those who are new to the Faith, or those who have suddenly encountered a new difficulty, often have a greater need for counsel. However, our counsel as disciples of Christ should not be in accord with the continually changing and baseless norms of sinful secular society, but rather in accord with the teaching of the Church and the examples of the Saints.

[Philemon]
{1:14} But I was willing to do nothing without your counsel, so as not to make use of your good deed as if out of necessity, but only willingly.

---

[512] Catechism of the Catholic Church, n. 1861.

In another letter, Paul seeks counsel Himself, even though he is a holy Apostle. Even the Pope will seek counsel from other persons, not only from Cardinals and Bishops, but from priests, deacons, religious, theologians, and the laity in general. None of us is above the need for sound advice from time to time. But no one should offer advice lightly, or without a firm basis in wisdom, knowledge, and understanding. Good advice can do much good, and bad advice can do much harm.

.490. Forbear and Forgive

The spiritual works of mercy include two related types of acts:

[4] forbear wrongs patiently
[5] forgive offenses

Forbearance is patient endurance in the midst of the difficulties caused by the sins of other persons. When we have been wronged, but we steadfastly persevere in grace, without repaying harm for harm, then we are exercising forbearance. If a person has sinned, and their sin has harmed us, even if he is unrepentant, we must patiently endure these sufferings, offering them to Christ on the Cross to obtain the repentance of sinners.

Our forgiveness of persons who have committed sins, sins which also cause us injury or harm in some way, is like the forgiveness of Christ on the Cross, who, while patiently enduring great suffering, obtained forgiveness for every kind of sin, for all persons who are willing to repent from sin. We forgive others because Christ taught us forgiveness by His example toward us.

[Sirach]
{2:3} Endure steadfastly for God. Join yourself to God, and persevere, so that your life may increase in the very end.
{2:4} Accept everything that will happened to you, and persevere in your sorrow, and have patience in your humiliation.
{2:5} For gold and silver are tested in fire, yet truly, acceptable men are tested in the furnace of humiliation.
...
{28:2} Forgive your neighbor, if he has harmed you, and then your sins will be forgiven you when you pray.

[Romans]
{12:17} Render to no one harm for harm. Provide good things, not only in the sight of God, but also in the sight of all men.
{12:18} If it is possible, in so far as you are able, be at peace with all men.

[Matthew]
{6:14} For if you will forgive men their sins, your heavenly Father also will forgive you your offenses.
{6:15} But if you will not forgive men, neither will your Father forgive you your sins.

When a person sins in some way so as to cause you suffering, and is unrepentant, you should forbear the offense, and seek the repentance of that sinner by acts of prayer and self-denial. For small offenses, you can both forbear and forgive. God forgives venial sins even without a specific act of repentance for each venial offense. Any act of love, faith, hope, or other virtues, done in cooperation with grace, forgives venial sins by implicit repentance. Similarly, we should forgive minor offenses by other persons without requiring anything from them but continued good will. But if the other person has not sinned against God in any way, we should not consider them to have offended us either.

For greater offenses though, especially objective mortal sins, we must consider that the repentance of that sinner may be necessary to his or her salvation. It may be a sin of omission not to seek the repentance and conversion of someone whom we know has committed an objective mortal sin. We should forbear, i.e. patiently endure, the sufferings that result in our lives from the sins of other persons. We should also seek their repentance. And when they do repent, we should forgive them. For we might be spending eternity in Heaven with that person. But even God does not forgive persons who are unrepentant from actual mortal sin. And so it is not correct to say that we should 'forgive and forget' serious and unrepentant sin. Instead, we should do what Christ does in response to such sins: seek their repentance, and forgive them when they repent.

[Luke]
{17:3} Be attentive to yourselves. If your brother has sinned against you, correct him. And if he has repented, forgive him.
{17:4} And if he has sinned against you seven times a day, and seven times a day has turned back to you, saying, 'I am sorry,' then forgive him."

Notice what our Lord instructs us to do when someone has sinned in such a way as to do us harm. He does not tell us to forgive that person immediately. First, He instructs us to correct the person for his sin; this correction benefits the soul, and is a particular fulfillment of the love of neighbor. Next, He commands us to forgive him if he is repentant. Jesus did not teach us to forgive unrepentant mortal sins. He Himself does not forgive unrepentant mortal sins. And He did not give the Church the authority to forgive unrepentant mortal sin. If anyone is unrepentant, and yet he goes to Confession, and recites his sins, and is told by the priest that all his sins were forgiven, in truth and according to the teaching of the Catholic Faith, his sins were not forgiven. Repentance is required for a valid confession.[513] The Church does not forgive unrepentant actual mortal sin. So if someone commits mortal sins that cause us serious harm, and he is unrepentant, we should correct him, and forbear the injury, and continue to practice the love of neighbor toward him. But we should not scandalize him and others by acting as if the forgiveness of serious sins can be obtained without repentance.

---

[513] Council of Trent, 14th Session, On the Most Holy Sacraments of Penance and Extreme Unction, Chapter IV, On Contrition: "This movement of contrition was at all times necessary for obtaining the pardon of sins...."

.491. Comfort and Pray for Others

> [6] comfort the afflicted
> [7] pray for the living and the dead

There are innumerable ways that a person might be afflicted with sufferings of various kinds. And there are innumerable ways that we might comfort them. All of the other corporal and spiritual works can be a type of comfort for persons who are suffering. Examples of ways that we might comfort those who are suffering include kind words, helping them with a task, offering them companionship during their suffering, relieving their suffering (to some extent, if we are able), and praying for them.

Christ offers salvation to everyone, without exception. But each human person has free will, and so some person, even many persons, freely choose not to accept that offer of salvation. Similarly, we should pray for every living person, even though we know that some persons, even many persons, will freely choose to reject the grace of God that our prayers will obtain. But our prayers for such persons are not wasted, since, if they refuse the benefits of our prayers, God will apply those benefits to other persons, to those who will accept it.

The deceased in Hell cannot benefit from our prayers; they suffer unending punishment. The blessed in Heaven have no need of our prayers; they enjoy eternal happiness. Only the holy souls in Purgatory, who are suffering the temporal punishment due for their sins (a punishment not satisfied in this life by sufferings or penances), can benefit from our prayers. When we pray for any deceased soul, if they are in Purgatory, they will benefit from our prayers. If they are not in Purgatory, God will apply the benefits of our prayers to other souls, to those who are in Purgatory, and to those on earth.

.492. Summary of the Works of Mercy

The corporal works primarily benefit the body, and the spiritual works of mercy primarily benefit the soul. And both types of works benefit the human spirit, since the human spirit (i.e. mind and heart) is a result of the close cooperation of body and soul. The corporal works comfort and strengthen the soul. And the spiritual works, in benefiting the soul, also benefit the body. Health in soul assists health in mind and heart, and health in mind and heart assists health in body. Thus, all the works of mercy are interrelated.

Pope John Paul II: "the fact that only the negative commandments oblige always and under all circumstances does not mean that in the moral life prohibitions are more important than the obligation to do good indicated by the positive commandments. The reason is this: the commandment of love of God and neighbor does not have in its dynamic any higher limit...."[514]

Every work of mercy is a particular fulfillment of the commandment to love God, and to love your neighbor as yourself. The negative precepts have a limit. The most that you can do is to entirely refrain from whatever the negative precept

---

[514] Pope John Paul II, Veritatis Splendor, n. 52.

forbids. But the positive precepts have no upper limit. You cannot love God too much, nor can you love your neighbor as yourself too much (as long as every expression of this love is moral and is set in good order by the greater love of God). There is no practical limit to the number and kind of good works that we may do in order to fulfill the requirement of the moral law that we love our neighbor.

Pope John Paul II: "Jesus shows that the commandments must not be understood as a minimum limit not to be gone beyond, but rather as a path involving a moral and spiritual journey towards perfection, at the heart of which is love (cf. Col 3:14)."[515]

The works of mercy are not optional. Although "prudence always has the task of verifying that they apply in a specific situation, for example, in view of other duties which may be more important or urgent,"[516] we are required by the moral law, by the positive precepts, to assist other human persons in works that are good for body and soul. Anyone who refuses to do any works of mercy for other human persons, commits a mortal sin of omission. Some souls are sentenced to eternal punishment in Hell solely for the actual mortal sin of omitting good works toward neighbors in need. Jesus taught this doctrine in His parable of the rich man and Lazarus (Luke 16:19-31).

.493. Idleness and Temptation

[Sirach]
{33:29} For idleness has taught much evil.

[Proverbs]
{10:16} The work of the just is unto life. But the fruit of the impious is unto sin.

Temptation is found not only in what we choose to do, such as choosing to enter an occasion of sin, but also in what we choose not to do. Idleness is a great source of temptation. When we are idle, sinful thoughts and desires are more likely to occur. When we are busy in prayer and good works, sinful thoughts and desires are less likely to occur. In order to dispel the darkness within yourself, you must let in the light of God. You cannot dispel darkness without light. And you cannot avoid temptation without prayer and good works. The fruit of prayer and good works, all done in cooperation with grace, is unto eternal life. But the fruit of idleness is sinful thoughts and desires, and sinful exterior acts, all of which can lead to the eternal death of Hell.

.494. Grace Against Temptation

God always gives each person sufficient grace for his or her current needs. This does not mean that we receive, at every moment, grace to resist temptations that we are not currently facing. We are given at least as much grace as we need for the current circumstances. God could not expect us to do good and to avoid evil if we did not have the graces needed go choose good over evil. God gives each

---

[515] Pope John Paul II, Veritatis Splendor, n. 15.
[516] Pope John Paul II, Veritatis Splendor, n. 67.

person all that he needs for the present time. What is needed in the future to resist a particular temptation will at least be given at that future time. Whenever temptation arises, then God provides the grace needed to resist. No one can say that he sinned because God did not give him the grace to avoid the sin. We are always given sufficient grace to freely choose not to sin.

Now it might seem to you, when facing a particular temptation, that you lack the grace you need; this is merely the mistaken perception of a sinner. Cooperation with grace is not always accompanied by good feelings and easy decisions. Sometimes cooperation with grace occurs in the midst of great difficulty, through trying emotions and difficult decisions. When tempted, first pray and then choose; resolve to do good, and to avoid evil. You do not need to worry whether or not you have sufficient grace. Faith teaches that grace is always available. Faith perceives truths that are beyond reason and emotion. In times of difficulty and temptation, trust your faith more than your own reasonings, and trust faith and reason above emotion.

.495. Repeated Failure to Resist Temptation

If you have moral certitude that you have committed an actual mortal sin, then you should say an act of contrition, expressing sorrow and repentance for your sin out of love for God. This type of contrition is called perfect contrition because it is based on the most perfect motive for contrition: love of God. But your expression of contrition need not be perfect in every way. Any sincere act of perfect contrition immediately forgives any actual mortal sin, without exception, as long as the desire to receive the Sacrament of Confession is included therein.[517] But the sinner who repents with perfect contrition is still morally obligated to go to Confession. Here is one example of an act of perfect contrition:

> My God, I am sorry for having offended you and for having harmed my neighbor. I regret all of my sins, because I fear the loss of Heaven and the pains of Hell, but most of all out of love for you, my Savior, who is perfect in Love and Mercy. I firmly resolve, with the help of your grace, to confess my sins, to do penance, and to amend my life. Amen.

Then, you should go to confession at your next opportunity. For example, if Confession is offered in your parish every Saturday, then you may wait to go to confession on that day. Examine your conscience thoroughly, confess your sins to the priest, follow his advice, and do the penances assigned by him.

What should you do if you find that you repeatedly fall to a particular type of temptation, especially one that includes mortal sins? On each occasion, you should repent promptly, pray an act of perfect contrition, and go to confession at your next opportunity. You need not rush to confession anxiously. Trust in the grace and providence of God. If your sin was an actual mortal sin, an act of perfect contrition restores you to the state of grace immediately. Resolve to go to confession at your next opportunity, and do not worry.

---

[517] Council of Trent, Fourteenth Session, On Penance, Chapter IV, On Contrition.

[Luke]
{12:32} Do not be afraid, little flock; for it has pleased your Father to give you the kingdom.

If you find that you fall into the same sin again and again, remember that to dispel darkness, you must add light. You will not be able to avoid sin merely by your own efforts to refrain from sin. You must add light to your life by prayer, self-denial, and works of mercy. You must strive to practice all the virtues: love, faith, hope, wisdom, knowledge, understanding, prudence, temperance, fortitude, and justice. The more you advance in holiness and virtue, the less you will be tempted to sin. If your sin pertains to a particular area of life, increase your efforts to practice self-denial in that area. And then offer your self-denial as a sacrifice to God.

.496. One underlying problem can be the temptation to do only the minimum, to strive only to avoid mortal sin. But if you only try to avoid mortal sin, you will often fall into mortal sin. Mortal sin is like a cliff; in order to avoid falling off that cliff, keep far away from it. In order to avoid mortal sin, you must strive to avoid mortal sins, and strive to avoid venial sins, and strive to grow in holiness. Otherwise, you will continue to fall repeatedly into the same serious sins. When someone falls repeatedly into mortal sins, there is a temptation to turn aside from striving to avoid venial sin, and striving to do the whole will of God. But the only way to avoid sin, is to become holy. Sin is darkness, and holiness is light.

The eternal moral law requires us not only to avoid doing evil, but to actively strive to do good. Many persons mistakenly think that they have only sinned if they have acted in violation of a negative precept. To the contrary, a person can also sin by refusing to act in accordance with a positive precept. And the positive precepts are more fundamental, since every precept is based on that threefold positive precept to love God, neighbor, self. Therefore, in order to avoid falling repeatedly into sins against negative precepts, we must strive to grow in holiness by an ever more perfect fulfillment of the positive precepts.

Holiness is more than avoiding sin. But the avoidance of sin is the foundation of holiness. Temptation to sin is one of the main obstacles to a holy life. Advancing in holiness is one of the main ways to avoid temptation and sin. If you find yourself falling again and again into the same sins, seek holiness. Trying to avoid sin without advancing in holiness is like trying to remove darkness from a room without adding any light. Only light can dispel darkness, for darkness is an absence of light. And only holiness can dispel sin. Holiness is found in prayer, self-denial, and works of mercy. Holiness is found in the exercise of love, faith, hope, and all the virtues. Holiness is found in a continual cooperation with the grace of God, obtained for us all by Jesus Christ through His Sacrifice on the Cross.

Chapter 30
Grace and Salvation

.497.

It is difficult to live a moral life in an immoral world. It is difficult to live a chaste life in an unchaste world. It is difficult to live a selfless life in a selfish world. It is difficult to live a peaceful life in a world of violence and false peace. This unloving and unmerciful world cannot teach you how to live a loving and merciful life. This unbelieving world cannot teach you how to live a life of faith in God. Only Christ can teach you the path to live a moral life, a life of grace. He does so through the teachings of Sacred Tradition, Sacred Scripture, and the Magisterium. He does so through the life of worship of the Church.

No matter how well you understand moral theology, no matter how adept you are at distinguishing moral acts from immoral acts, you will not be able to avoid sin unless you are cooperating with grace in the practice of all the virtues. Only light can dispel darkness. Only virtue can overcome vice. Only holiness can vanquish sin. Only by living a life of grace, a life filled with the love of God and neighbor, a life of prayer, self-denial, works of mercy, only in this way -- which is truly the Way of Christ -- can we avoid evil, and do good. The only moral life is a life filled with grace, love, virtue, prayer, self-denial, mercy. If you find yourself unable to remove sin from your life, it is because you are not cooperating with grace in acts of prayer, self-denial, works of mercy, in acts of love, faith, hope, and all the virtues.

"an immaculate life is a generation of sages." (Wisdom 4:9).

An immaculate life is a life of greater wisdom than an entire generation of sages. The truest form of wisdom is found in living a life in imitation of Christ. The truly immaculate life is a life which is both lacking in sinful deeds, and filled with virtuous deeds. The Virgin Mary is Immaculate, not only because she was always free from all sin, but also because she filled her life with good works, works of prayer, self-denial, mercy, in full cooperation with every grace, and in the full exercise of every virtue. Spiritual purity consists in avoiding sin, and in doing good, out of love for God and neighbor, in harmony with the will of God. Cooperation with grace brings forth every virtue and every good work. The path of cooperation with grace leads us, in the end, to a life of eternal grace with God.

Whoever does not cooperate with grace, does not love God. Whoever does not love God, cannot avoid committing many sins. Catholic moral theology often focuses on sin, on determining which acts are immoral. But the mere knowledge that an act is immoral is not sufficient for us to be able to avoid that sin. We must cooperate with grace by practicing the virtues. A life of grace is a life of virtue. The practice of any virtue is the practice of every virtue. All the virtues are closely related; each virtue supports and complements every other virtue. No virtue is ever in conflict with any other virtue. All the virtues work together, in grace, to accomplish the will of God.

.498. Grace and Morality

The grace of God is absolutely essential to living a moral life. Some knowingly chosen acts can be moral, in the sense of morally permissible, without grace. Acts that are merely natural, such as eating a meal, exercising, going to sleep, etc. are moral because human nature is good. Even without grace, such acts are morally permissible. However, any act that is meritoriously good must be done in cooperation with grace. Every act that contributes to holiness, pleases God, contributes to salvation, and merits a reward in Heaven requires grace. Every act done in cooperation with grace contributes to holiness, pleases God, contributes to salvation, and merits a reward in Heaven. Other acts can be moral, but only acts that cooperate with grace are both moral and holy.

All immoral acts deserve punishment. But not all morally permissible acts deserve reward. Knowingly chosen acts are never morally neutral. Every act is either moral or immoral. However, some moral acts deserve neither reward nor punishment; such acts are morally permissible, but they do not cooperate with grace, and so they do not deserve a reward. Even so, if a merely natural act, such as eating a meal, is done in cooperation with grace, for example, with grace-filled thanks to God, the act is both morally good and meritorious.

Every cooperation with grace deserves a reward. Every sinful failure to cooperate with grace deserves a punishment. However, some failures to cooperate with grace are merely imperfections, and not sins. The human nature of Jesus Christ always fully cooperated with all graces from His Divine Nature. The Blessed Virgin Mary always fully cooperated with all graces given to her by her Divine Son Jesus. Everyone else falls short, sometimes to the extent of imperfection, other times to the extent of sin. Not every failure to cooperate with grace is immoral. But every act of cooperation with grace is not only moral, but also holy and salvific (in the sense of contributing to salvation) and meritorious. Every act of the free will cooperating with the supernatural grace of God merits both an increase in grace and a reward in Heaven. The final full payment of that meritorious reward is eternal life. So be careful that you do not fall into actual mortal sin, and thereby lose your eternal reward.

.499. What is Grace?

Baltimore Catechism: "Grace is a supernatural gift of God bestowed on us through the merits of Jesus Christ for our salvation."[518]

Catechism of the Catholic Church: "Grace is favor, the free and undeserved help that God gives us to respond to his call to become children of God, adoptive sons, partakers of the divine nature and of eternal life. Grace is a participation in the life of God.... It surpasses the power of human intellect and will, as [well as] that of every other creature."[519]

---

[518] Baltimore Catechism, Lesson 9, Q. 109, What is grace?
[519] Catechism of the Catholic Church, n. 1996-1998.

Saint Thomas Aquinas: "grace is a light of the soul.... when a man is said to have the grace of God, there is signified something bestowed on man by God"[520]

The human person has a number of natural abilities, such as the use of the body, and the use of will and intellect. These abilities are of human nature, which is created by God. But grace is supernatural; it is a gift bestowed on man by God beyond what human nature can accomplish. The power of grace surpasses the power of every created thing. Grace is an act of God, directly affecting the soul, enabling the human person to be good and to do good. The grace of God changes the human person to be and to do more than what human nature allows. Grace moves and enables the will, and enlightens and guides the intellect, so that the person may choose, carry out, and complete good and holy acts of every kind. Grace directs the soul and its acts continually toward God.

Grace is not necessary for each and every morally permissible act. But grace is necessary to live a moral life because the human person has free will and reason. The natural use of free will and reason is inherently ordered toward a search for truth and goodness, not only the natural limited truths and goods of temporal life (e.g. food, other necessities, the affection of others), but even more so the higher goods, such as moral truth, true spiritual love, and the single highest good: God.

Free will and reason naturally seek moral truth, true spiritual love, God, and eternal happiness. But the use of free will and reason to seek these higher things requires grace. Therefore, human nature is designed so as to require grace in order to fulfill its innermost needs and longings. Even though grace is a gift of God beyond what is natural, human nature is inherently ordered toward receiving and using that gift, in order to fulfill its inherent purpose: to find truth and love, and to find the Eternal God and eternal happiness. So when God's grace moves, enables, and cooperates with the will, there is no conflict between the freedom of will and the gift of grace. The use of grace by free will and reason is as natural to the human person as the use of water is to a fish. The water is not part of the nature of the fish, and yet the nature of the fish requires the use of water. And this necessity to make use of grace is inherent to human nature, as created by God.

Fallen human persons are not created with sanctifying grace from conception. And so this life is a journey, by means of grace, to find God and eternal salvation. But the journey cannot begin, cannot continue, and cannot succeed, without grace at every step and at every turn. If you never use your free will and reason to seek the higher things of life, you cannot find and obtain eternal happiness. If you never use your free will and reason to seek the higher things of life, then you have committed an actual mortal sin of omission, for which you will be condemned to Hell forever, unless you repent.

Grace is absolutely necessary to live a Christian life and to attain eternal life. No one can hear the Word of God and keep it without the grace of God (cf. Luke 11:28). No one can obey the commandment to love God above all else without grace. No one can obey the commandment to love your neighbor and to love

---

[520] Saint Thomas Aquinas, Summa Theologica, I-II, Q. 110, A. 1.

even your enemies, without grace. No one has true spiritual love without grace. No one can avoid sin without grace. And no one can have eternal salvation unless they die in a state of grace.

.500. Types of Grace

Grace is divided into two main types:

1. Sanctifying grace -- also called: justifying grace, the grace of justification, the state of grace, the state of sanctifying grace, salvific grace, or habitual grace;

2. Actual grace -- also called gratuitous grace by St. Thomas.

According to St. Thomas, actual grace is "a movement of the soul" and sanctifying grace is "a quality of the soul."[521]

Catholic Encyclopedia: "Actual grace…is granted by God for the performance of salutary acts and is present and disappears with the action itself. Its opposite, therefore, is…habitual grace, which causes a state of holiness, so that the mutual relations between these two kinds of grace are the relation between action and state…."[522]

Sanctifying grace is continuous, and actual grace is intermittent. Actual grace is the help of God for particular knowingly chosen acts of the human person. Sanctifying grace is the help of God for the soul of the human person. Particular acts occur from time to time, and so actual grace is not continuous. But the soul is continually in need of the presence of God, our highest Good, and so sanctifying grace is continuous.

God is not merely loving, He is Love. Love is His very Nature. God is not merely just, He is Justice. God is not merely truthful, He is Truth. And so on. In God, being and doing are exactly the same. God is good, and God does good, are exactly the same in God. For God is not a Nature that does good acts. God is the good that He does. All that God is/does is One Divine Eternal Act.[523]

But created persons are divided into being and doing. We are divided into what we are, and what we do. Human persons have a nature, and that nature can then commit various acts, which are either good or evil. Therefore, we need two types of grace, one for being good, and the other for doing good. Although human nature is naturally good, sanctifying grace makes us supernaturally good.

By actual grace, we do good. By sanctifying grace, we are good. The difference between actual grace and sanctifying grace is the difference between doing and being. Each act done in cooperation with grace is a good act. To whatever extent your acts cooperate with grace, your acts are truly good. And each person who has sanctifying grace is truly good, and therefore is rightly said to be a child of God. Only God is infinitely Good; only God is Goodness itself by His very

---

[521] Saint Thomas Aquinas, Summa Theologica, I-II, Q. 100, A. 2.
[522] Joseph Pohle, 'Actual Grace', The Catholic Encyclopedia, Vol. 6, (New York: Robert Appleton Company, 1909); http://www.newadvent.org/cathen/06689x.htm
[523] For more on this point, see the author's book: *New Insights into the Deposit of Faith*.

Nature. But all who are in a state of sanctifying grace are good, in a lesser but true sense.

Baltimore Catechism: "Grace is a supernatural gift of God bestowed on us through the merits of Jesus Christ for our salvation. There are two kinds of grace: sanctifying grace and actual grace. Sanctifying grace is that grace which confers on our souls a new life, that is, a sharing in the life of God Himself.... Actual grace is a supernatural help of God which enlightens our mind and strengthens our will to do good and to avoid evil."[524]

Grace is supernatural; it is beyond what human nature can do, it is beyond what any created thing can do. Grace is a direct effect on the soul of the power of God. Sanctifying grace orders (i.e. directs) our soul toward God, giving the soul a life beyond nature, to share in the good life of God. Actual grace is a direct effect on the soul of the power of God, giving the soul the ability to act beyond nature, to share in the good acts of God. Both types of grace were merited for us by Jesus Christ on the Cross. His death gives us a supernatural gift of life, a life of being good and of doing good, a life in imitation of God, who is and does only good.

.501. Sanctifying Grace

Sanctifying grace is a continuous effect in the soul caused directly by the Divine Nature of God. This effect orders the soul toward God as our highest good and final end. And this ordering implies that the goods of Creation also have their proper place, especially concern for the good of our neighbor. The state of sanctifying grace is a continuous ordering of the soul, first, toward the highest good, who is God, and second, toward the good of our fellow human persons. The state of grace continuously directs the soul toward the love of God above all else, and the love of neighbor as self. By the state of grace, the commandments to love God above all, and to love your neighbor as yourself, become inherent to the ordering of the soul.

Sanctifying grace is analogous to prayer. In prayer, we lift up and direct our mind and heart toward God. In sanctifying grace, our soul is continually lifted up and directed toward God. The state of sanctifying grace is like a continual prayer of the soul brought about by the free gift of God, obtained for us by Jesus Christ through his Passion and Crucifixion. Through sanctifying grace, the soul is lifted up and directed toward God, and remains with God in that state, as if praying without ceasing.

Sanctifying grace is analogous to the three fonts of a morally good act. Every morally good font is directed toward a good end, an end that fulfills the precept to love of God above all else, and to love your neighbor as yourself. The state of sanctifying grace directs the soul to God as the highest good, and to an ordered love of neighbor and self. The human person is in a state of grace when the soul is directed toward God as our final end, with a proper ordering of all the goods of Creation, especially human persons.

---

[524] Baltimore Catechism, Lesson 9, Q. 109-111, 113.

Why does an actual mortal sin cause the immediate loss of the state of grace? The answer is found in the definition of sanctifying grace and in the definition of actual mortal sin. The state of grace directs the human person toward God as our highest Good and final end. By choosing to commit any actual mortal sin, the human person chooses to turn away from God as our highest Good and final end. The state of grace directs the soul toward the threefold good of the love of God, neighbor, self, with each in its proper order. But every actual mortal sin is entirely incompatible with the love of God, neighbor, self. Every actual mortal sin is a grave violation of that proper ordering of goods.

The state of grace and the choice of actual mortal sin are entirely incompatible. By choosing to commit an actual mortal sin, the human person freely chooses to reject this inherent ordering of his own soul, of his intellect and free will, toward truth and goodness and the proper ordering of values, with God above all else. A soul that chooses an act entirely incompatible with love of God and neighbor, thereby necessarily loses the state of grace. For by definition the state of grace is a continuous ordering of the soul, first toward the good who is God, and second toward the good of our fellow human persons. Whoever chooses to commit an actual mortal sin is thereby choosing to remove his soul from that good order.

.502. Sanctifying grace is salvific.

Pope Pius XII: "Above all, the state of grace is absolutely necessary at the moment of death; without it, salvation and supernatural happiness -- the beatific vision of God -- are impossible."[525]

Sanctifying grace is the beginning of eternal salvation. Sanctifying grace is salvific because all who die in the state of grace will certainly receive eternal life in Heaven (perhaps after a temporary stay in Purgatory). All who have sanctifying grace have the promise of eternal life, and also the beginning eternal life, within them. For all the blessed souls in Heaven have sanctifying grace. In this life, however, sanctifying grace can be lost, if the person commits an actual mortal sin. In order to receive the fullness of eternal life, which can never be lost, we must die in a state of grace.

Sanctifying grace is a state of the soul, which begins with Baptism, and which continues without ceasing, unless the person commits an actual mortal sin. Upon receiving forgiveness from God for actual mortal sin, the person is immediately returned to this state of sanctifying grace. "For God forsakes not those who have been once justified by His grace, unless he be first forsaken by them."[526]

Catholic Encyclopedia: "From this it follows that the grace must be as distinct from the Holy Spirit as the gift from the giver and the seed from the sower...."[527]

---

[525] Pope Pius XII, Address to participants in the Conference of the Italian Catholic Union of Obstetricians (October 29, 1951), commonly called 'Address to Midwives.'
[526] Council of Trent, Sixth Session, Decree on Justification, Chapter XI.
[527] Joseph Pohle, 'Sanctifying Grace,' The Catholic Encyclopedia, Vol. 6, (New York: Robert Appleton Company, 1909).

Grace is not identical to God.

Sanctifying grace is not God, but an effect wrought by God in the soul. All who are in a state of grace have the presence of God in their souls. But sanctifying grace itself is not the presence of God, but rather an effect of that presence. Grace is a gift from God, but grace is not the Giver of that gift.

All graces were merited for us by the salvific death of Christ. But if grace were God, then we would be left with the absurd position that Christ merited God. Therefore, grace is not God, but a gift from God, a gift merited for us by Christ. Grace is an effect that God Himself directly causes in the soul.

.503. By sanctifying grace, we share in the Divine Nature.

Saint Thomas Aquinas: "Now the gift of grace surpasses every capability of created nature, since it is nothing short of a partaking of the Divine Nature, which exceeds every other nature."[528]

We are finite, but God is infinite. Therefore, our sharing (partaking) in the Divine Nature is finite. For the finite cannot contain the infinite. We share in the Divine Nature because sanctifying grace orders our soul continually toward God. We share in the Divine Nature because sanctifying grace makes us like God. We become like God by receiving and living His gift of sanctifying grace. Therefore, all who are in a state of sanctifying grace have a type of participation in the Divine Nature.

Even so, until we receive eternal life in Heaven, this participation is limited. We still can commit sins; we can possibly commit an actual mortal sin and lose the state of sanctifying grace. We are on a journey, but we have not yet arrived at the destination. There are difficulties found in the journey which are not found in the destination. The destination is greater than the journey. And so the participation in the Divine Nature that we will have in Heaven is greater than the participation that we have in this life through the state of sanctifying grace.

Sanctifying grace makes us like God.

[Matthew]
{5:48} "Therefore, be perfect, even as your heavenly Father is perfect."

[Ephesians]
{5:1} Therefore, as most beloved sons, be imitators of God.

The free gift of sanctifying grace transforms the human person, from the merely natural good found in human nature, to the higher good of a person who uses free will and reason to knowingly choose to live a life in imitation of God. By sanctifying grace, we are good, and by actual grace, we do good. In both these ways, by both types of grace, we are like God, who is and does only good.

Sanctifying grace makes us children of God.

---

[528] Saint Thomas Aquinas, Summa Theologica, I-II, Q. 112, A. 1.

[Romans]
{8:14} For all those who are led by the Spirit of God are the sons of God.
{8:15} And you have not received, again, a spirit of servitude in fear, but you have received the Spirit of the adoption of sons, in whom we cry out: "Abba, Father!"
{8:16} For the Spirit himself renders testimony to our spirit that we are the sons of God.
{8:17} But if we are sons, then we are also heirs: certainly heirs of God, but also co-heirs with Christ, yet in such a way that, if we suffer with him, we shall also be glorified with him.

Christ is the Son of God. By sanctifying grace, we become sons of God. A son is an heir to a father; he inherits from what the father has. Christ is the Son of God. He receives all that He is and has from the Father. When we receive and live by sanctifying grace, we become adoptive sons of God and co-heirs with Christ, inheriting a share in the eternal kingdom of God.

.504. Baptism bestows sanctifying grace, justifying the soul.

Council of Trent: "in that new birth [of Baptism], there is bestowed upon them, through the merit of His passion, the grace whereby they are made just."[529]

Baltimore Catechism: "Baptism is the sacrament that gives our souls the new life of sanctifying grace by which we become children of God and heirs of heaven."[530]

A person who is in a state of grace is just and good. A person who is in a state of grace has been justified (made just) by Christ, and therefore this grace is also called the grace of justification or justifying grace. Jesus Christ obtained both justifying grace and actual grace for us, by His loving and merciful sacrifice on the Cross, so that we could both be just, and do what is just. By His death, we each receive that inner life of grace called justification, whereby we become true children of God, sons of light, and members of the Body of Christ (the Church). And this inner life of sanctifying grace, along with all the acts of our life done in cooperation with actual grace, lead us eventually to the eternal life of grace in Heaven. Everyone who dies in a state of grace certainly will have eternal life.

Roman Catechism of Trent: "Now according to the definition of the Council of Trent, which under pain of anathema we are bound to believe, grace not only remits sin, but is also a divine quality inherent in the soul, and, as it were, a brilliant light that effaces all those stains which obscure the luster of the soul, investing it with increased brightness and beauty."[531]

When we receive sanctifying grace at Baptism, all our sins and all punishment due for our sins is remitted (forgiven, taken away). And our soul is then free from the guilt of original sin, free from the guilt of all past personal sins, and free

---

[529] Council of Trent, Sixth Session, Decree on Justification, chap. 3.
[530] Baltimore Catechism, Lesson 24, Q. 315, What is Baptism?
[531] The Catechism of Trent, Part II, chapter 2, On Baptism, n. 50.

from any punishment for past sins. The soul is then bright and beautiful, with an inherent and divine quality, whereby we are like God in goodness and in virtue. The soul of a newly Baptized Christian, whether an adult, child, or infant, is a pure and beautiful reflection of the Most Holy Trinity.

.505. By sanctifying grace, we live in the presence of God.

Pope Pius XI: "it is not enough to be a member of the Church of Christ, one needs to be a living member, in spirit and in truth, i.e., living in the state of grace and in the presence of God, either in innocence or in sincere repentance."[532]

God is present everywhere. The presence and knowledge and power of God is throughout all Time and Place, and is beyond Time and Place. But those who have sanctifying grace have the presence of God within them in higher sense. For by sanctifying grace, the human person and God are united in love. The gift of sanctifying grace directs the soul, and therefore the whole person, to God continuously, and thereby unites the person to God in love. This union is not yet the full union of eternal life in Heaven. This presence is not yet the full presence of the Beatific Vision in Heaven. But sanctifying grace grants to the soul a type of presence of God, and a type of union with God, to assist us in our journey to the eternal presence of God, and to eternal union with God.

By the state of grace, we have the indwelling of the Holy Spirit, and God is truly present within us. However, what is finite, our soul, cannot contain what is infinite, God. The presence of God by sanctifying grace is a limited presence, the purpose of which is to bring us to the full presence of God found in eternal life in Heaven. Then we will see God face-to-face, in the unceasing Beatific Vision. For now, sanctifying grace gives us a true presence of God, but one that is limited by our fallen state and by our journey in this world. We are on a journey to God. We have God by means of sanctifying grace and actual grace. And yet the grace of God within us is not yet the full gift of eternal life, but only its beginning and its promise.

Sanctifying grace is of the Holy Spirit.

The Holy Spirit dwells in the Church, as the source of Her life, and He sanctifies souls through the gift of grace.[533]

Whenever one Person of the Most Holy Trinity acts, all Three act. For the Three Persons are the One Nature. But we attribute certain acts to one Person, rather than to another Person, because of the distinctions between the Persons due to procession. The Son proceeds from the Father. The Father sent the Son to merit the gift of grace for us by dying on the Cross. The Spirit proceeds from the Father and the Son. The Father and the Son sent the Spirit into the Church in order to dispense salvation through sanctifying grace and actual grace. This gift of grace is willed by the Father, obtained by the Son, and applied by the Spirit, for the sake of our salvation. The Spirit pours out this grace, in and through the

---

[532] Pope Pius XI, Mit Brennender Sorge, n. 19.
[533] Baltimore Catechism, Lesson 9, Q. 108.

Church, which is the Body of Christ. All graces, both sanctifying grace and actual grace, are given to us by the Most Holy Trinity, so that we may obtain eternal salvation and eternal life with the Most Holy Trinity.

.506. Actual Grace

Actual grace is the assistance of God, to our will and intellect, so that we may knowingly choose good acts. Actual grace is caused directly by God. Actual grace is an act of God, which moves and enables our free will, and which enlightens and guides our intellect, so that we may act beyond what is merely natural, so that we may act with a supernatural goodness, in meritorious fulfillment of the precepts to love God and neighbor.

Actual grace is supernatural.

The human person cannot make a proper and full use of the natural abilities of intellect and free will without supernatural grace. Human nature is designed to desire, seek, and obtain goods that require supernatural grace, not only to obtain, but even to desire and seek. The human person uses the natural abilities of free will and intellect, in cooperation with supernatural grace, in order to act beyond human nature, in imitation of God.

The human person naturally desires happiness. But free will and intellect cannot seek and obtain true happiness, cannot understand and desire true happiness, without grace. God has designed human nature so that supernatural grace is required in order to fulfill the inherent purpose of that nature. We were created by God to understand good from evil, and to freely choose good; we were created by God to know and to choose love. But all this requires supernatural grace.

An intellect capable of distinguishing between good and evil, and a free will capable of choosing between good and evil, naturally seek to know what is good, and to choose what is good; this requires actual grace. The human person, understanding this distinction between good and evil, naturally seeks to become a good person; this requires sanctifying grace. These good acts by actual grace, and this good state in sanctifying grace, are the beginning of true happiness; they are the path to eternal happiness. The human person naturally uses free will and intellect to seek happiness, but the path to true happiness is supernatural, requiring actual grace and sanctifying grace.

All grace is supernatural; grace is beyond what human nature can achieve on its own. And yet human nature was designed by God to seek and to live a life filled with grace and ordered by grace. Therefore, in order to save fallen humanity, in order to offer us all eternal salvation, the Father sent the Son to obtain the supernatural gift of grace, which we could never obtain on our own, since it is beyond our nature. And the Son then sent the Spirit to offer the supernatural gift of grace, which we cannot accept, or even desire, without the assistance of that same grace. Human nature is entirely dependent on the undeserved gift of supernatural grace from God in order to do good, to be good, and to be happy forever.

.507. Actual grace is salvific.

Every person who dies in a state of sanctifying grace will have eternal life in Heaven. And so sanctifying grace is certainly salvific. However, actual grace is also salvific, in a lesser sense, since actual grace works with sanctifying grace toward our salvation. A person who is in a state of grace, but who thereafter refuses to cooperate with actual grace, will eventually commit one or more actual mortal sins, either by omission or by commission. A person who is in a state of grace remains in that state by cooperation with actual graces, in various particular acts, as he fulfills the commandment to love God, neighbor, self, through both the positive and the negative precepts.

If any baptized adult commits no mortal sins of commission, but lives an entirely self-centered life, when he dies, he will be sent by God to Hell forever. For he has committed the actual mortal sin of omission of failing to love God and neighbor by cooperation with actual grace. Our cooperation with actual grace, after receiving sanctifying grace, is essential to our salvation. For actual grace is absolutely necessary in order to fulfill the commandments to love God above all else, and to love your neighbor as yourself. No one can avoid mortal sins of commission and omission without cooperating with actual grace.

Some merely natural acts, of limited goodness, are moral even without grace. However, such acts are not meritorious; they do not deserve a reward in Heaven; they do not contribute to salvation. All acts done in cooperation with actual grace are good and meritorious. All acts done in cooperation with actual grace contribute to salvation. Whether or not you eventually obtain salvation, depends on whether or not you die in a state of grace. But all acts of cooperation with actual grace lead toward salvation.

Acts done in grace are holy acts.

Only God is HOLY, in the truest and fullest sense of the word. But every act done in cooperation with actual grace is a holy act. I repeat, every act done in cooperation with actual grace is a holy act, even if the person is not in a state of grace at the time. Every knowingly chosen act with three good fonts is a moral act. Every knowingly chosen moral act, done in the love God and neighbor, is certainly done in cooperation with grace, and is therefore a holy act. Each act stands on its own as to its morality. If a person commits a thousand good acts, and one bad act, the good acts remain good, and the bad act remains bad. If a person commits a thousand bad acts, and one good act, the bad acts remain bad, and the good act remains good. If a person in a state of sanctifying grace commits a sin, the act is still a sin. If a person who is not in a state of sanctifying grace cooperates with actual grace in a good act, the act is still good. Every human person alive, good or evil, is able to cooperate with the grace of God. And all such acts of cooperation with grace are holy acts, which move the person closer to eternal salvation. Nothing of true and lasting value can ever be done by any created person without grace.

508. Prevenient Grace

Operating grace is distinguished from cooperating grace. Operating grace occurs when God acts on the soul without any cooperation by our free will. This type of grace is also called prevenient (from the Latin: 'to go before') because it occurs prior to even the possibility of an act of cooperation by our free will. Whenever we knowingly choose a holy act, an act of cooperation with grace (such as prayer or a kind deed), our act is preceded by the grace of God, acting without any possible cooperation on our part. God first touches our soul with grace, enabling us subsequently to cooperate with grace, if we freely choose to do so. This 'first grace' of God is before every holy act of every human person, including the Virgin Mary, and the human nature of Christ.

For example, the Virgin Mary freely chose to say 'Yes' to the plan of God at the Annunciation; this is called her 'fiat' (from the Latin: 'let it be done'). Her fiat was a knowingly chosen holy act, done in cooperation with grace (a very full cooperation in this case). However, she would have been entirely unable to cooperate with grace at that time, and at any time, without the prevenient grace of God. Before Mary said 'Yes' to God, He first gave her His grace so that she would be moved and enabled to respond subsequently, in free cooperation with His grace.

This 'first grace' is called prevenient or operating grace, and the next grace is called subsequent or cooperating grace. Prevenient grace is called operating, rather than cooperating, because this first grace is not at all accompanied by our cooperation. At that point, the grace of God is acting (i.e. operating or working) alone. Only subsequently may we then respond to this first grace, by our free will, so as to cooperate with subsequent grace.

Prevenient grace is certainly always logically prior to subsequent grace, and it is often also chronologically prior to subsequent grace. Sometimes the sinner refuses to cooperate with prevenient grace, and so there is no subsequent grace. But the prevenient grace is given nevertheless. Even the most wicked persons on earth have frequently received prevenient grace. They are wicked not because of a lack of prevenient grace, but because they refuse to cooperate with subsequent grace. It is not the case that the wicked have turned away prevenient grace. It would be impossible to do so, because prevenient grace is first, and the refusal of grace is second. So even the worst sinners have often received prevenient grace.

Although grace is sometimes described as if God offers grace, and sinners refuse the offer, this description is not theologically accurate. When God acts in prevenient grace, it is not possible for us to refuse prevenient grace. Any response by the sinner, either refusing or accepting grace, occurs after the prevenient grace was first received. And therein lies the culpability. The sinner was truly touched by the grace of God, and subsequently the sinner refused to cooperate. The first grace of God truly affected the soul, and next the sinner refused to cooperate. All sinners have received and been affected by prevenient grace. If a refusal to cooperate with grace occurs, this refusal is always subsequent to the prevenient act of God. The human person is not able to refuse prevenient grace; he can only refuse subsequent (cooperating) grace from God. Prevenient grace always occurs without cooperation and without consent.

To use an analogy, prevenient grace is like the water in which a fish is immersed. The water surrounds him. He moves in it, and it is even within him. The fish has no choice at this point. He is immersed in the water, whether he likes it or not. The fish can then choose to swim, or not to swim in the water. But he cannot refuse to be in the water. Similarly, all human persons have prevenient grace, not merely as an offer of grace, by as an actual effect in their soul, moving and enabling them to do good. They can refuse, subsequently, to cooperate with grace, but they have already been touched by grace in this way.

.509. This concept is absolutely essential to a proper understanding of grace. Consider what the alternative position would be. If God merely makes an offer of grace, which we must first accept before we can receive any grace, then we would have no grace with which to make that good choice to accept the offer. We would then be unable to accept any grace. For without prevenient grace, the grace that goes before, we would have no grace, and therefore no ability to accept any grace. Accepting grace from God is an act of love for God. But grace is necessary whenever the free will commits any act fulfilling the command to love God, or to love your neighbor as yourself. So this alternative position fails. The idea of prevenient grace is necessary to the concept of grace as a free gift from God. We make no choice prior to, or concurrent with, this first grace, because a previous grace would be required in order to do so. In prevenient grace, God acts alone, entirely before any act of our free will. No one ever cooperates with prevenient grace; to do so is entirely impossible. Only subsequent grace allows for cooperation.

God is morally obligated (in a manner of speaking) to give everyone prevenient grace, because He designed human nature so that it cannot function properly without grace and cannot avoid sin without grace. God cannot deny prevenient grace to any human person, not even to the worst of sinners, for He cannot act contrary to His own plan for human nature. Therefore, prevenient grace is not merely offered to all sinners; prevenient grace affects all sinners. Prevenient grace never fails to affect each and every soul, even those that are very sinful, even if they are in a state of actual mortal sin. It is the refusal to consent to, and cooperate with, subsequent grace that distinguishes the sinful person from the holy person. Prevenient grace occurs without consent or cooperation; subsequent grace requires consent and cooperation.

Catechism of the Catholic Church: "Every time we begin to pray to Jesus it is the Holy Spirit who draws us on the way of prayer by his prevenient grace."[534]

Consider the example of a woman who begins to pray to Jesus. Before she can pray, before she can decide to pray, before she can even consider perhaps praying, God first acts to move and enable her intellect and will with prevenient grace. Every act of cooperation with actual grace, and every refusal to cooperate with actual grace, was preceded by an act of God touching the soul with

---

[534] Catechism of the Catholic Church, n. 2670.

Grace and Salvation

prevenient grace, moving and enabling the soul to do good. Therefore, the sinner has no excuse. All sinners, no matter how wicked, have prevenient grace. They are culpable for their sins because they were moved and enabled by God to do good, and to avoid doing evil, and subsequently they refused. They did not lack for grace. They were affected by grace, and subsequently they turned away.

To use an analogy, grace and the human person are like electricity and a radio. The radio can do nothing, prior to receiving the electricity, to cooperate with the electricity. Once the electricity is received, the radio and the electricity work together to produce beautiful music. The first event is not a cooperative event of electricity and radio working together. The first event is the electricity enlivening the radio. Only subsequent events are cooperative; the initial event 'goes before' (prevenient) any cooperation.

.510. Grace is before, during, after every holy act. Grace initiates the act, assists it in continuing, and guides it to its end. Our every cooperation with grace is always preceded by the free gift of prevenient grace. And every cooperation with grace merits an increase in grace. We cannot cooperate with prevenient grace (as soon as we cooperate, it is no longer prevenient). But we can cooperate with, and even merit an increase in, subsequent grace.

Is prevenient grace continuous? No, it is not. For example, there is no reason for God to give prevenient grace while we are asleep, or while we are cooperating with subsequent grace (unless God wills a new good act concurrent with that act). Prevenient actual grace, like subsequent actual grace, is intermittent. The more you cooperate with subsequent grace, the more you will receive both prevenient grace and subsequent grace. For prevenient grace not only allows us at least to avoid sin, it also allows us to do the will of God in virtuous acts beyond the minimum required by the moral law.

Therefore, even the most wicked of sinners has received prevenient grace frequently. For whenever the moral law requires a person to do good, or to avoid doing evil, prevenient grace is necessarily granted. Otherwise a sinner would not be guilty of sin, if he did not have the prevenient grace to avoid the sin. Therefore, every actual sin is preceded by prevenient grace; the sinner received the grace to avoid the sin, and yet he freely chose to sin, and thereby chose not to cooperate with subsequent grace.

Cooperation with actual grace does not require the state of grace.

Suppose that an adult is unbaptized and not in a state of grace. He can be baptized and receive the state of grace. But what will move him to choose Baptism? Why would he even consider receiving this Sacrament? The answer is actual grace. Although he lacks sanctifying grace, he certainly frequently receives prevenient actual grace. And in so far as he cooperates with subsequent actual grace, he necessarily moves closer and closer to salvation. By cooperation with actual grace, he reaches the point of deciding to be baptized. And so, by cooperation with actual grace, he is led to the state of sanctifying grace. Therefore, even a person who is not in a state of grace due to a lack of baptism still receives actual graces.

Suppose that an adult was baptized, and later he commits an actual mortal sin, thereby losing the state of sanctifying grace. He can return to the state of grace by repentance and confession, by what will move him to choose repentance and confession? The answer is actual grace. Although he lacks sanctifying grace, and he is in a state of mortal sin, he certainly still receives prevenient actual grace. And if he chooses to cooperate with subsequent actual grace, he can be brought by grace to repentance from his actual mortal sin. This repentance can occur all at once, as if in a single step, if he cooperates fully. Or this repentance can be sought and found, as if by a journey, through a series of acts of partial cooperation with actual grace. Therefore, even a person who is not in a state of grace due to actual mortal sin still receives actual graces.

Cooperation with actual grace can be partial or full.

Suppose that a person is tempted to commit a mortal sin. All persons always have sufficient grace, especially prevenient grace, to avoid every sin. However, the human person may cooperate with subsequent grace to a greater or lesser degree. He might cooperate to the extent of avoiding the mortal sin, but at the same time fall into venial sin. He might avoid sin, but cooperate imperfectly, so that he does not do the whole will of God. Or, he might cooperate, on a particular occasion, fully, so that he does the whole will of God concerning that particular act. Sinners are not perfect. But some acts of sinners can be perfect, fulfilling the whole will of God for that individual act. Therefore, cooperation with grace is a matter of degree.

.511. The initial gift of sanctifying grace is prevenient.

Actual grace is divided into operating prevenient grace and cooperating subsequent grace, and sanctifying grace is divided the same way. Our initial reception of sanctifying grace, by which our souls are justified, is prevenient; it occurs by an act of God working alone, operating, not cooperating. Our initial reception of sanctifying grace is also an undeserved free gift. Everyone who is in a state of grace was first given that state of grace by God as a free gift. The act of God whereby our soul is placed in a state of justification does not occur with our cooperation. This initial act of God is prevenient sanctifying grace. This grace is given to the soul in Baptism. Therefore, Baptism may be given even to infants. For no cooperating act of free will and intellect is involved in an act of God's prevenient sanctifying grace.

This principle becomes particularly clear in the unique case of the Virgin Mary's justification. She received the state of sanctifying grace in the first moment of her existence, at her Immaculate Conception. What did she do prior to that moment in order to merit or to cooperate, so as to subsequently obtain the state of sanctifying grace? Nothing at all. She did not exist before her Immaculate Conception. She could not possibly have merited, or cooperated, or acted in any way, prior to her justification, since it occurred in the first moment of her existence. And what did she do in that first moment of her existence to cooperate with the act of God simultaneously creating and justifying her soul? Nothing at all. Like all human persons, she could not effectively use her free will and intellect until later in life. The Immaculate Conception is the preeminent example of prevenient sanctifying grace.

But even if Mary had been created and justified in the same moment as an adult, as Eve was, she would still have had no role of cooperation in her justification. Both Mary and Eve were created justified; neither Mary, nor Eve cooperated with the initial grace whereby each soul is justified in sanctifying grace. The initial act of God whereby any soul is given sanctifying grace, whenever that grace may be given, is without any cooperative act on the part of the free will and intellect. The initial act is prevenient; it occurs before any possibility of cooperation by the human person with sanctifying grace.

In some ways, the justification of the Blessed Virgin Mary was like every sinner's justification in Baptism: an undeserved free gift that is not accompanied by any merit or cooperation on the part of the recipient of that gift. Even when an adult prepares for Baptism, and cooperates with actual grace in that preparation, and consents to receive the Sacrament, his actual reception of sanctifying grace (the grace of justification) is entirely passive on his part. He does not cooperate with the act of God that justifies his soul with sanctifying grace. His free will and intellect play no role at all in that justification, even though he freely chose to prepare and to receive the Sacrament. The act of God whereby he is justified is an operating act, not a cooperating act.

.512. The continuing gift of sanctifying grace involves cooperation.

After the initial act of justification, sanctifying grace is a type of cooperating subsequent grace. The initial act of God whereby we receive sanctifying grace is operating prevenient grace; God acts, and we do not act. But as the state of sanctifying grace continues, we are able to cooperate. For the baptized infant, who does not yet have sufficient use of free will and intellect, the soul continues in a state of justification. No act is needed to cause this state to continue in the infant or young child. Even in an adult, the state of justification continues without any particular act. Your soul is ordered toward God, and it remains so ordered unless you commit an actual mortal sin. However, some cooperation is required of an adult in a state of sanctifying grace.

Any single actual mortal sin causes the loss of the state of grace. An adult can lose the state of grace by failing to cooperate with actual grace to the extent of an actual mortal sin. An actual mortal sin can occur by omission. So if you are in a state of grace, but you refuse to cooperate with actual grace to the extent of an actual mortal sin of omission, then you lose the state of grace. A type of cooperation with the state of grace is required, but only in the sense that we must fulfill the commandments to love God and neighbor, or else we lose that state.

This type of cooperation differs from cooperation with actual grace. The state of sanctifying grace continues without any particular act on our part from one moment to the next. However, the state of grace can be lost if we fail, to the extent of actual mortal sin, to live out the love of God and neighbor which is made inherent to our souls by sanctifying grace. So a type of cooperation is required of the human person. The gifts of free will and intellect can be misused, in an actual mortal sin of commission, or in an actual mortal sin of omission, resulting in the loss of sanctifying grace. Sanctifying grace is given to us both to make us holy, and to make holy acts easier and fuller.

.513. Sanctifying grace and actual grace complement one another.

A person who is not in a state of grace still receives prevenient actual grace, and still may cooperate with subsequent actual grace. But until and unless the person receives sanctifying grace, he is not in a state of grace (either he is unbaptized, or he is unrepentant from actual mortal sin). While he is not in a state of grace, his cooperation with actual grace is partial.

Every act of full cooperation with actual grace is always an act of full true selfless spiritual love. Every act done in cooperation with grace is a holy act. Every holy act is a particular fulfillment of the commandment to love God above all else, and to love your neighbor as yourself. Therefore, every act of full cooperation with grace is a full act of love of God and neighbor. Such a full cooperation with grace allows a person who is not in a state of grace to be brought into a state of grace, either by a Baptism of desire, or by an act of perfect contrition (including at least the implicit desire for Confession). For every act of full cooperation with actual grace, by a person who is unbaptized, constitutes at least an implicit Baptism of desire, in which God grants the state of grace to the soul. And every act of full cooperation with actual grace, by a person in a state of mortal sin, constitutes at least an implicit act of perfect contrition, in which God restores the state of grace to the soul. Therefore, a person who is not in a state of sanctifying grace only cooperates partially with actual grace. Once his cooperation is full, he is brought by God into the state of grace.

A person who is in a state of grace can fully cooperate with actual grace, and the state of grace itself makes such full cooperation easy.

[Matthew]
{11:28} Come to me, all you who labor and have been burdened, and I will refresh you.
{11:29} Take my yoke upon you, and learn from me, for I am meek and humble of heart; and you shall find rest for your souls.
{11:30} For my yoke is sweet and my burden is light."

The person who is not in a state of sanctifying grace labors to cooperate with actual grace, and he finds this cooperation burdensome. A person who is not in a state of grace, who then cooperates with actual grace, is acting contrary to the state of his own soul. He is like a fish swimming against the current. Such cooperation is a burdensome labor. But the person who receives the yoke of sanctifying grace finds cooperation with actual grace sweet and light. He is like a fish swimming with the current. The state of sanctifying grace allows the intellect to understand the path of cooperation with actual grace more easily, and the free will to follow that path of cooperation with actual grace more easily, so easily, at times, that this cooperation seems like rest, rather than labor.

Grace and Salvation

The justified soul is ordered toward the love God above all else, and toward the love of neighbor as self. Thus every act of cooperation with actual grace is in harmony with the state of grace of the soul. Sanctifying grace makes cooperation with actual grace easy because both the state of sanctifying grace and particular acts done in cooperation with actual grace are ordered toward the love of God and neighbor. When a soul which is not in a state of grace acts in cooperation with actual grace, the disorder of that soul is contrary to the order of the cooperative act. Every act of cooperation with actual grace is ordered toward the love of God and neighbor. But every soul lacking in the state of grace lacks such an inherent order. The selfishness of a soul without sanctifying grace causes cooperation with actual grace to be a laborious and burdensome journey.

.514. Baptism provides sanctifying grace.

The formal Sacrament of Baptism confers sanctifying grace on the soul of the baptized person. A Christian receives the state of sanctifying grace at Baptism. However, the state of grace can also be obtained by a Baptism of desire, or by a Baptism of blood. A Baptism by desire or by blood is a non-formal Baptism.

Council of Trent: "If anyone says that the sacraments of the New Law are not necessary unto salvation, but are superfluous; and that without them, or without the desire thereof, men may obtain from God, through faith alone, the grace of justification -- though all [the Sacraments] are not indeed necessary for every individual, let him be anathema."[535]

All seven Sacraments are necessary to salvation in the sense that the Church requires all seven in order to bring salvation to the world. But for an individual fallen human person, Baptism is the only Sacrament absolutely necessary to salvation. Baptism confers the state of sanctifying grace. All who die in a state of grace receive eternal life. All who die without the state of grace do not receive eternal life. Now if anyone falls into actual mortal sin, he loses the state of grace. But he can be returned to the state of grace by contrition and Confession. And so the Sacrament of Confession is necessary to salvation for those who have fallen into actual mortal sin.

But in cases of necessity, the desire for certain Sacraments can suffice. The Council of Trent infallibly taught that Baptism may be received by desire alone, and that Confession may be received by desire alone.[536]

A person may receive sanctifying grace from God by means of an explicit desire for the Sacrament of Baptism. For example, suppose a man is preparing to receive Baptism, but he dies in a car accident. He dies in a state of grace, having been granted sanctifying grace because of his explicit desire for Baptism. When does he receive sanctifying grace as a result of this explicit desire? We cannot be certain, but he receives sanctifying grace at least in the last moment of life. No

---

[535] Council of Trent, Seventh Session, On the Sacraments, Canon IV.
[536] Council of Trent, Sixth Session, Decree on Justification, Chapter IV refers to Baptism of desire; Chapter XIV refers to Confession: "the eternal punishment...together with the guilt, [is] remitted either by the Sacrament, or by the desire of the Sacrament...."

one receives sanctifying grace after death. Perhaps this man received sanctifying grace before the last moment of life. But it is certain that, if he truly desired Baptism in cooperation with actual grace, he did not die without the state of sanctifying grace.

A person may receive sanctifying grace from God by means of an implicit desire for the Sacrament of Baptism. For example, suppose that a person is a non-Christian, who has rejected the Christian Faith, but without the culpability of an actual mortal sin. Perhaps he was misled by secular society about the true nature of the Christian Faith, or perhaps his reduction in culpability is due to other factors. In any case, he is unbaptized; he has not received sanctifying grace through the formal Sacrament of Baptism. How can he be saved? He must receive sanctifying grace, and must die in the state of sanctifying grace, in order to have eternal life. But he has no explicit desire for the Sacrament of Baptism. Nevertheless, if he has an implicit desire for the Sacrament of Baptism, he can receive sanctifying grace, and therefore he can be saved.

.515. Non-Christians and the State of Grace

Only God is HOLY, in the truest and fullest sense of the word. But every person who is in a state of grace is a holy person. I repeat, every human person, including Catholics, non-Catholic Christians, Jews, Muslims, adherents of other religions, agnostics, and atheists, everyone and anyone who is in a state of grace is a holy person. And every person who dies in a state of grace will have eternal life in Heaven, including Catholics, non-Catholic Christians, Jews, Muslims, adherents of other religions, agnostics, and atheists, if in truth they die in a state of grace. It is an objective mortal sin to reject the Catholic Christian Faith, or to reject belief in God. But for some persons, harmed and deceived by this sinful world, this rejection might not be an actual mortal sin. Some person have committed the objective mortal sin of rejecting the true Faith, without the full culpability of an actual mortal sin. And so they might still receive the state of sanctifying grace, despite not being Catholic Christian, by means of an implicit Baptism of desire.

Pope John Paul II: "For those, however, who have not received the Gospel proclamation, as I wrote in the Encyclical 'Redemptoris Missio,' salvation is accessible in mysterious ways, inasmuch as divine grace is granted to them by virtue of Christ's redeeming sacrifice, without external membership in the Church, but nonetheless always in relation to her (cf. Redemptoris Missio, n. 10). It is a mysterious relationship. It is mysterious for those who receive the grace, because they do not know the Church and sometimes even outwardly reject her. It is also mysterious in itself, because it is linked to the saving mystery of grace, which includes an essential reference to the Church the Savior founded. In order to take effect, saving grace requires acceptance, cooperation, a 'yes' to the divine gift. This acceptance is, at least implicitly, oriented to Christ and the Church."[537]

---

[537] Pope John Paul II, All Salvation Comes through Christ, General Audience, 31 May 1995.

Grace and Salvation

The holy Pontiff considers two types of cases of persons who receive saving grace, i.e. sanctifying grace, without formal Baptism: 1) those who do not know the Church, either because they have never heard of Christianity, or because they have receive little or no accurate information about the Faith, and 2) those who have outwardly rejected the Church, but with substantially reduced culpability, that is, without committing an actual mortal sin. Both types of cases allow for the possibility of sanctifying grace by an implicit Baptism, which has its effectiveness from its mystical connection to Christ on the Cross, and to the Church created from the side of Christ on the Cross.

.516. How does implicit Baptism occur? The reception of sanctifying grace by a formal Baptism relies on a ceremony with water and words. But the reception of sanctifying grace by an implicit Baptism of desire relies on a full cooperation with actual grace by the human person.

This full cooperation is analogous, as a type of negative image, to the type of full rejection of grace that causes the loss of sanctifying grace: an actual mortal sin. When a gravely immoral act is chosen with full knowledge in the intellect that the act is gravely immoral, and with full consent to that act by the free will, then the act is an actual mortal sin. Such an act always constitutes a full rejection of the grace of God, and is always an act gravely contrary to the love of God and neighbor. A person who is in a state of grace, and who then commits an actual mortal sin, loses the state of grace.

Conversely, a person who is not in a state of grace (because he is unbaptized) must commit an act of full cooperation with grace, with both intellect and free will, in order to receive sanctifying grace by an implicit Baptism of desire. Such an act, like every cooperation with actual grace, is always a particular fulfillment of the commandment to love God and to love your neighbor as yourself. Although in secular terms, the chosen act might not seem like an act of love, every act of full cooperation with actual grace is a full true selfless act of love.

Pope Pius XII: "Above all, the state of grace is absolutely necessary at the moment of death without it salvation and supernatural happiness -- the beatific vision of God -- are impossible. An act of love is sufficient for the adult to obtain sanctifying grace and to supply the lack of baptism...."[538]

An act of love is sufficient for an unbaptized adult to obtain sanctifying grace. This act must be done in full cooperation with grace. This love must be a true selfless spiritual love of God and neighbor. However, any selfless act of love toward one's neighbor is implicitly an act of love for God also. And so even an atheist or an agnostic might receive sanctifying grace by an implicit Baptism of desire -- but only by full cooperation with actual grace in a truly substantially selfless act of spiritual love for neighbor. Why does such an act of love result in God conferring sanctifying grace on the person? It is because any selfless act of love, done in full cooperation with actual grace, unites the person to Christ dying on the Cross, which is the preeminent selfless act of love, and which is the source of all Baptism, formal and non-formal.

---

[538] Pope Pius XII, Address to Midwives, 29 October 1951.

In my article on mystical Baptism (non-formal Baptism), I explain: "Any sincere act of the soul which fundamentally resembles the salvific act of Christ dying for our salvation on the Cross is capable of obtaining salvific grace for that soul in a mystical Baptism through the Holy Spirit. A mystical Baptism is a true Baptism because all Baptism unites the person being baptized with Christ on the Cross. That is why it is aptly said that in Baptism we die with Christ. It is Christ's salvific suffering and death on the Cross which effects all true Baptisms....

"Although mystical Baptism is often connected to external acts (acts of heroic virtue, acts of mercy toward others, enduring severe suffering, etc.), such external acts do not, in and of themselves, obtain salvific grace. Internal acts in response to grace are capable of opening the soul to salvific grace from God in a mystical Baptism. These internal acts of the soul are often accompanied by external acts of mercy or virtue, but (unlike formal Baptism) these external acts guarantee nothing."[539]

.517. Baptism of Blood

A baptism of blood typically occurs when a person dies for the sake of the Christian Faith. During times of severe persecution of the Church, some catechumens (persons preparing to receive Baptism) died as martyrs, prior to Baptism. The Church has always taught that these persons receive a Baptism of blood, whereby they receive sanctifying grace, without the formal Sacrament, by their selfless act of love for Christ in the face of death. There are two types of non-formal Baptism: a Baptism of desire, and a Baptism of blood. In each, the human person receives sanctifying grace, without the water and words of formal Baptism. Sanctifying grace is always salvific, no matter how it is attained. Therefore, persons who have not received the formal Sacrament of Baptism may still be saved by a Baptism of desire, or of blood.

The Blessed Virgin Mary

The Immaculate Conception of the Virgin Mary, in the first moment of her existence, preserved her from every effect of original sin. Usually, Baptism is given to someone who was conceived in original sin, and one of the effects of Baptism is to completely take away original sin, and to restore the sanctifying grace that was lost by the sin of Adam and Eve (the sin at the origins of the human race). However, in her Immaculate Conception, the Virgin Mary was preserved from original sin. She was given the same type of sanctifying grace that we all receive in Baptism, but without ever having been touched by original sin. Now the Immaculate Conception is greater than the Baptism given to us poor sinners; for after our Baptism, we are still affected by concupiscence. Mary never had original sin, and so she never had concupiscence. But she still received what we also each receive: sanctifying grace. For sanctifying grace is absolutely required for salvation, even for the sinless Virgin Mary, the Mother of God. And she would not have been able to be sinless if not for sanctifying grace, along with actual grace in great abundance throughout her life.

---

[539] Conte, Treatise on Mystical Baptism, n. 8.

It is a dogma of the Faith that the Virgin Mary received sanctifying grace at her Immaculate Conception. For the Immaculate Conception preserved her from all of the effects of original sin, including certainly the worst effect, which is the lack of sanctifying grace. The Immaculate Conception was a type of Baptism. For in that event, the Virgin Mary received the sanctifying grace that we all receive in Baptism. Although Mary's Baptism at her Conception was in some ways unique, the gift of sanctifying grace that she received was not unique; it is the same gift that we all receive at Baptism. Her Immaculate Conception was both a type of Baptism, and a gift much greater than any Baptism.

Second Vatican Council: " 'For there is one God, and one mediator between God and men, Himself a man, Jesus Christ, who gave Himself as a ransom for all' (1 Tim. 2:45), 'neither is there salvation in any other' (Acts 4:12). Therefore, all must be converted to Him, made known by the Church's preaching, and **all must be incorporated into Him by baptism** and into the Church which is His body. For Christ Himself 'by stressing in express language the necessity of faith and baptism (cf. Mark 16:16; John 3:5), at the same time confirmed the **necessity** of the Church, into which men enter by baptism, as by a door.' "[540]

The Council's teaching on the necessity of Baptism is not new. The Church has always taught that Baptism is required for salvation. Baptism also makes us children of God, and members of the Church. Certainly, the Blessed Virgin Mary is a child of God, a member of the Church, and saved by Christ. Therefore, it is also certain that Mary's Immaculate Conception was a type of Baptism.

But the Immaculate Conception did not occur by a formal ceremony of water and words, so it was not a formal Baptism. And Mary could not have had any implicit or explicit desire in order to receive a Baptism of desire. Her Immaculate Conception occurred in the first moment of her existence. She could not have had any prior desire which would have resulted in her being granted sanctifying grace. And she could not have had a desire for Baptism concurrent with her conception. It is only later in life that human persons are able to use intellect and free will in order to know and to desire Baptism, even implicitly. Also, the initial reception of sanctifying grace is always prevenient, so it is not granted in a cooperative act with the human person, but in an operative act of God alone. Therefore, Mary's Baptism at her Immaculate Conception was neither a formal Baptism, nor a Baptism of desire.

There are only three types of Baptism: by water, in the formal Sacrament; by desire, explicit or implicit; and by blood. Mary received a Baptism, but without water or desire; therefore, she must have received a Baptism of blood. The Immaculate Conception of the Virgin Mary was a type of Baptism of blood.

Ordinarily a Baptism of blood is received when a person who has not received a formal Baptism dies as a martyr for Christ. This Baptism of blood grants sanctifying grace. However, sanctifying grace cannot be received after death; it

---

[540] Second Vatican Council, Ad Gentes, n. 7; inner quote from Lumen Gentium, n. 14; my emphasis added in bold.

can only be received in this life. These martyrs must receive sanctifying grace prior to death. The latest that they could receive sanctifying grace would be in the last moment of life. The Virgin Mary received sanctifying grace in the first moment of her life, so there is nothing to prevent a person from receiving sanctifying grace in the last moment of life. But since these martyrs need grace in order to accept martyrdom, it is probable that God gives them sanctifying grace well before the last moment of life. Therefore, it is not the death itself of the recipient of a Baptism of blood that grants sanctifying grace. Rather, as with all Baptism, it is the salvific death of Christ on the Cross that grants the graces of Baptism. The impending death of the martyr unites that person with Christ dying for our salvation on the Cross, and thereby grants sanctifying grace directly from Christ on the Cross.

This understanding leads to the conclusion that a person might receive a Baptism of blood without dying, as was the case with the Virgin Mary. She received her Baptism of blood in her Immaculate Conception, without water, without desire, and without dying, by the Blood of Christ. Her impending life as a living martyr for Christ was like the impending death of those martyrs who receive a Baptism of blood. However, neither the Virgin Mary, nor anyone else who receives a Baptism of blood, merits sanctifying grace at all. Though God grants sanctifying grace to martyrs who are about to die for Christ, and to Mary who was about to live for Christ, this great gift is undeserved by all, and is merited only by the merits of Christ on the Cross.

Such a Baptism of blood, without any desire or act on the part of the recipient, is possible because salvation is a free gift; it is not merited by us. Even Mary did not merit her own salvation. Jesus Christ merited salvation for all persons. That is why infants are able to be baptized and to receive sanctifying grace, without a preceding cooperative act on their part. That is why Mary could be saved, by sanctifying grace, in the first moment of her life. The gift of sanctifying grace only occurs by a prevenient act of God. He can give sanctifying grace to a soul without a prior desire or act on the part of that soul because salvation is a free undeserved gift.

.518. Prenatals and Infants Who Die without Baptism

This particular point of theology is currently speculative; the Magisterium has not yet decided the question. But it is absolutely clear to my mind that prenatals, infants, and young children, who die without having received a formal Baptism, nevertheless die in a state of sanctifying grace, because they receive a non-formal Baptism (a mystical Baptism) at least in the last moment of life, perhaps sooner. They therefore die in a state of grace and will have eternal life. All Baptism is effective because Jesus Christ obtained sanctifying grace (and actual grace) for us by his death on the Cross. When an innocent human person, who has never committed actual mortal sin, dies at a very young age, prior to an age when he could reasonably be expected to have obtained the state of grace at least by desire, the impending death of this person unites him to Jesus dying on the Cross, who is the source of all Baptism and all grace.

[Romans 6]
{6:3} Do you not know that those of us who have been baptized in Christ Jesus have been baptized into his death?
{6:4} For through baptism we have been buried with him into death, so that, in the manner that Christ rose from the dead, by the glory of the Father, so may we also walk in the newness of life.

[John]
{12:24} Amen, amen, I say to you, unless the grain of wheat falls to the ground and dies,
{12:25} it remains alone. But if it dies, it yields much fruit. Whoever loves his life, will lose it. And whoever hates his life in this world, preserves it unto eternal life.

The concept of unbaptized prenatals and infants receiving sanctifying grace prior to death has only one major theological problem, which is the lack of a desire on the part of the free will and intellect. In an adult, Baptism by desire occurs either explicitly, when the adult desires Baptism but dies before receiving it, or at least implicitly, when the adult, by choosing a selfless act of love in full cooperation with grace, is implicitly desiring and choosing the good order of the soul that is granted by Baptism, i.e. sanctifying grace. But very young persons, especially prenatals, are not able to know and to choose with sufficient fullness. They cannot know and choose with sufficient fullness to commit an actual mortal sin. They cannot know and choose with sufficient fullness to receive an implicit Baptism of desire.

The solution to this problem is found in Sacred Tradition and Sacred Scripture, in three events of salvation history: the Immaculate Conception, the Visitation, and the death of the Holy Innocents.

.519. The Immaculate Conception

The Virgin Mary received sanctifying grace, in the first moment of her existence, without any explicit or implicit desire from her free will. Although the gift of the Immaculate Conception is greater than ordinary Baptism, it also includes all that Baptism includes. The Immaculate Conception gave the Virgin Mary sanctifying grace; the same type and degree of sanctifying grace that we all have. Mary's degree of actual grace in her life is greater than that of any other mere human person; only the human nature of Christ had a greater degree of actual grace. But sanctifying grace is essentially the same in all persons, because it is not a matter of degree; it is all or nothing. You are either in a state of grace, or you are not. Your soul is either ordered toward God, or not. Therefore, the Immaculate Conception is a type of Baptism, given as a free gift without the formal Sacrament, and without any explicit or implicit desire, by which the soul of the Virgin Mary was given sanctifying grace. She received a Baptism of blood, but by the blood of Christ, the source of all Baptism.

Pope Pius XI: "We declare, pronounce, and define that the doctrine, which holds that the most Blessed Virgin Mary, in the first instant of her conception, by a singular grace and privilege of Almighty God, in view of the merits of Jesus

Christ, the Savior of the human race, was preserved immune from every stain of original sin, is revealed by God, and therefore is to be believed firmly and constantly by all the faithful."[541]

The Immaculate Conception preserved the Virgin Mary from every stain of original sin, that is, from every effect of the sin at the origins of humanity, the sin of Adam and Eve. One of the effects of original sin is that the descendents of Adam and Eve are not given sanctifying grace at conception. Mary was preserved from this effect, and so she did have sanctifying grace from conception. The other descendents of Adam and Eve, other than Jesus and Mary, are have original sin from conception, and at Baptism original sin is entirely taken away, and they receive sanctifying grace. Although there are substantial differences between the Immaculate Conception and the Baptism of a person conceived with original sin, the gift of sanctifying grace is the same.

The Immaculate Conception conferred sanctifying grace on the Virgin Mary, at the first moment of her existence, without any prior or concurrent, explicit or implicit desire for Baptism on her part. This free gift is possible because Jesus merited all grace for all persons by shedding his blood on the Cross. It is the infallible teaching of the Church that the Immaculate Conception was granted to the Virgin Mary by virtue of the merits of Christ, and that the Immaculate Conception preserved her from all effects of original sin, which must include the worst effect of original sin, the lack of sanctifying grace.

The gift of sanctifying grace to the Virgin Mary was prevenient, occurring before any good act or any response to grace by her. The same is true for any Baptism. Although an adult who receives Baptism may have cooperated with many actual graces prior to Baptism, the gift of sanctifying grace itself, which orders the soul toward God, is prevenient; it is not preceded or accompanied by any act of the human person cooperating with sanctifying grace itself.

Therefore, the theological problem of a lack of implicit desire for Baptism in the very young is solved. Such an implicit desire is rightly required of an adult, since adults have a moral responsibility, just as the Council of Trent taught, to prepare for Baptism by cooperating with actual grace.[542] However, the Council did not require such preparation even of older children, and it would be absurd to require such preparation or cooperation from infants or prenatals. Therefore, prenatals, infants, and young children are free from the general requirement of having at least an implicit desire for Baptism in order to receive sanctifying grace. Nevertheless, they are not given sanctifying grace merely because of their youth, but because they are about to die in their youth, and so will be unable to seek and find sanctifying grace later in life. The Justice of God requires that they be given sanctifying grace, at least in the last moment of life, by virtue of the shedding of the blood of Jesus on the Cross, which is the source of all grace. Therefore, they receive a Baptism of blood, not entirely unlike the Baptism of blood given to the Virgin Mary as part of her Immaculate Conception.

---

[541] Pope Pius XI, Ineffabilis Deus; translated from the Latin by the author.
[542] Council of Trent, Sixth Session, Decree on Justification, Chapters V and VI.

Grace and Salvation

The implicit desire for Baptism is not required of them for yet another reason. No one merits sanctifying grace, except Jesus Christ. Even the Virgin Mary did not merit sanctifying grace. And so, the requirement that the recipient of sanctifying grace have at least an implicit desire for Baptism is not an absolute necessity. Jesus obtained sanctifying grace for us as a free gift. The recipient need not commit any particular prior or concurrent act in order to obtain this free gift. For baptized adults, justice requires that we cooperate with grace in order to attain to eternal salvation. For unbaptized adults, justice requires that they cooperate with grace by at least an implicit desire for Baptism. But justice never requires anyone to do what is impossible. Therefore, unbaptized prenatals, infants, and young children, who die at such a young age, are not required to have even an implicit desire for Baptism. They are baptized by the blood of Christ, due to their impending untimely deaths. They are much like those holy martyrs who died before they could receive formal Baptism; they receive a Baptism of blood prior to death.

.520. The Visitation

Further support for this merciful act of God is found, not only in the Immaculate Conception, but also in the Visitation, when John the Baptist was given sanctifying grace while he was still in the womb of Elizabeth. The Immaculate Conception was a singular grace and privilege. No other human person was conceived of fallen parents, and yet preserved from original sin. Therefore, John the Baptist did not have an immaculate conception; he was conceived with original sin. And yet he was sanctified in the womb. He certainly could not have had an implicit desire for Baptism while still in the womb; prenatals are too young to exercise free will and intellect in such a full manner. And yet he was given sanctifying grace. Therefore, prenatals, infants, and young children, who die at such a young age, without having received a formal Baptism, are given sanctifying grace without even an implicit desire for Baptism.

Sacred Scripture infallibly teaches that John the Baptist was filled with the Holy Spirit beginning in the womb (when he was a prenatal).

[Luke]
{1:13} But the Angel said to him: "Do not be afraid, Zechariah, for your prayer has been heard, and your wife Elizabeth shall bear a son to you. And you shall call his name John.
{1:14} And there will be joy and exultation for you, and many will rejoice in his nativity.
{1:15} For he will be great in the sight of the Lord, and he will not drink wine or strong drink, and he will be filled with the Holy Spirit, even from his mother's womb.

No one can be filled with the Holy Spirit unless he is in a state of sanctifying grace. For being filled with the Holy Spirit does not indicate the type of partial cooperation with actual grace that might be found even in a person who lacks sanctifying grace. Being filled with the Holy Spirit implies that the soul of the person is holy, and therefore in a state of grace. For no one can be filled with the grace of the Holy Spirit, and yet lack the grace required for salvation, which is sanctifying grace. Therefore, John the Baptist received a non-formal Baptism (also called a mystical Baptism) while he was still in the womb. And this event in salvation history, found in Sacred Tradition and described by Sacred Scripture, implies that other prenatals, despite being conceived in original sin, and despite the lack of even an implicit desire for Baptism, can nevertheless receive sanctifying grace. For the impending death of the prenatal (or of the unbaptized infant or young child) unites the person to Jesus Christ shedding His blood on the Cross, and from that singular wellspring of all graces, draws out sanctifying grace for the salvation of these very young souls.

Does this theological position contradict the teaching of the Council of Trent that Baptism or its desire is required to receive sanctifying grace? Not at all. The Council taught no absolute requirement of a desire for Baptism. This is clear because the Council infallibly condemned the idea that infants cannot receive Baptism.[543] And yet infants do not have a desire for Baptism. So in allowing for a Baptism of desire, the Council did not imply that such desire is an absolute requirement of all persons, not even of all persons who do not receive a formal Baptism. And this is further supported by the acknowledgement of the Council that the Virgin Mary was not subject to the effects of original sin, which include the deprivation of sanctifying grace found in the unbaptized. The Council's teachings therefore allow the possibility that prenatals and infants may receive sanctifying grace, without any explicit or implicit desire for Baptism. For by their deaths at such a young age, they are united to Christ dying on the Cross, which is the only source of grace. For in every Baptism, all who are justified "are truly buried together with Christ by baptism into death."[544]

Furthermore, Pope Innocent III taught that since original sin is contracted without consent, it can be removed by Baptism without consent, and therefore even infants may be baptized.

"We say that a distinction must be made, that sin is twofold: namely, original and actual: original, which is contracted without consent; and actual, which is committed with consent. Original, therefore, which is committed without consent, is remitted without consent through the power of the sacrament...."[545]

Although the Pontiff was here defending infant Baptism, the same principle applies to prenatals, infants, and even young children who die without the formal Sacrament of Baptism. It is not contrary to the teaching of the Faith for original sin to be remitted without any act of the free will (consent) by the human person. Therefore, a non-formal Baptism is possible even without an explicit or implicit desire of the will, but only in the case of the very young, who die without the opportunity to use free will and intellect to obtain some form of Baptism with consent.

Saint Thomas Aquinas taught that there are three types of Baptism: (1) Baptism of water (i.e. the formal Sacrament), (2) Baptism of repentance, or 'of the Spirit,'

---

[543] Council of Trent, Fifth Session, Decree on Original sin, n. 4.
[544] Council of Trent, Fifth Session, Decree on Original sin, n. 5.
[545] Pope Innocent III, Denzinger, n. 410.

(i.e. a Baptism of desire), and (3) Baptism of blood. And this threefold division of Baptism has been the teaching of the Church also, since the beginning. But the Virgin Mary and John the Baptist each received sanctifying grace without desire, and without the formal Sacrament, and yet they did not die at about the time of their Baptism. Since there are only three types of Baptism, they each must have received the Baptism of blood, but without dying. This is possible because the blood of any Baptism of blood is primarily the blood of Christ on the Cross.

Similarly, prenatals, infants, and young children who die at that young age have neither the formal Sacrament, nor even an implicit desire for Baptism. But by their impending death they are given the Baptism of blood from the Cross of Christ. For it is established beyond doubt by the examples of Mary and John that the Baptism of blood does not depend essentially on the choice of the free will to die for Christ, but on the choice of Christ to die for us.

.521. The Holy Innocents

[Matthew]
{2:16} Then Herod, seeing that he had been fooled by the Magi, was very angry. And so he sent to kill all the boys who were in Bethlehem, and in all its borders, from two years of age and under, according to the time that he had learned by questioning the Magi.
{2:17} Then what was spoken through the prophet Jeremiah was fulfilled, saying:
{2:18} "A voice has been heard in Ramah, great weeping and wailing: Rachel crying for her sons. And she was not willing to be consoled, because they were no more."

Now as a third witness to this truth, we have the holy Innocents. The Church has always called them holy, and yet if they died without Baptism they would have died in sin and would not be holy. Only persons in a state of sanctifying grace are holy. By actual grace, our acts are holy; by sanctifying grace our selves are holy. Therefore, the holy Innocents must have been in a state of grace. But since they had no Baptism of water, and they were too young to have had a Baptism of desire, they must have received a Baptism of blood.

In one sense, the holy Innocents died for Christ, since Herod killed them in an attempt to kill the Christ-child. But in another sense, their deaths are more like that of all prenatals, infants, and young children, who die in youth. For they did not knowingly choose to die for Christ; they died without any act of the free will and intellect in cooperation with actual grace. Yet they are called holy, and so they must have received sanctifying grace prior to death. Therefore, all prenatals, infants, and young children, who die without formal Baptism, nevertheless die in a state of grace, having been given sanctifying grace, just as the holy Innocents were given sanctifying grace, just as John the Baptist and the Virgin Mary were given sanctifying grace, by a Baptism into the blood of Christ on the Cross.

.522. Concupiscence and Grace

Council of Trent: "But this holy synod confesses and is sensible that in the baptized there remains concupiscence, or an incentive [to sin] which, whereas it is left for our exercise, cannot injure those who consent not, but resist manfully by the grace of Jesus Christ: 'Yea, he who shall have striven lawfully shall be crowned [2 Tim 2:5].' This concupiscence, which the Apostle sometimes calls sin, the holy Synod declares that the Catholic Church has never understood it to be called sin, as being truly and properly sin in those born again, but because it is of sin, and inclines to sin."[546]

Baptism takes away original sin in its entirety, including the guilt of original sin, and the lack of sanctifying grace, so that the whole person is justified in the eyes of God. However, something remains after original sin is taken away, which is not any part of original sin, but which is of original sin and which tends toward personal sin; this is called concupiscence. The word 'concupiscence' is derived from the Latin 'concupiscere,' meaning 'to desire eagerly.' But as a theological term, concupiscence is not any desire of the human will, but rather a tendency toward inordinate desire. For the body is still in a fallen state, even after Baptism gives the soul justifying grace. "Indeed, the spirit is willing, but the flesh is weak." (Mt 26:41). The fallen body is the source of this tendency toward sin. For sanctifying grace causes the soul to be holy and to be ordered toward doing good, but grace affects the body only indirectly (since body and soul are one person).

Concupiscence and grace are opposed to one another. For concupiscence directs the human person toward what is selfish, but sanctifying grace and actual grace direct the human person to love of God above all else, and to love of neighbor as self. But grace is more powerful than concupiscence. Concupiscence certainly affects the whole person, including the soul. But concupiscence is of the body. Grace certainly affects the whole person, including the body. But grace is of the soul. The soul is greater than the body; therefore, grace is greater than concupiscence. When a human person is not in a state of grace, concupiscence has a much stronger affect on the soul because there is only intermittent actual grace to oppose the selfish tendency that is concupiscence. When a human person is in a state of grace, both the state itself and actual grace oppose concupiscence. And cooperation with actual grace is generally fuller and more frequent in those who are in a state of grace. Those who are in a state of grace resist concupiscence much more easily than those who are in a state of mortal sin.

When a person in a state of grace dies, the body and the soul are separated. Death is the separation of body and soul. The soul is then no longer affected by concupiscence, whose source in the human person is the fallen body. After death, whether in the particular judgment, or in Purgatory, or in Heaven, or even in Hell, the human person is not affected by concupiscence; for the body is gone. And after the general Resurrection, the resurrected body is not fallen. The resurrected Just will have no personal sin, no original sin, and no concupiscence.

.523. Merit and Grace

All graces, both sanctifying grace and actual grace, were merited for us by the sacrifice of Jesus Christ on the Cross. If not for the meritorious death of Christ,

---

[546] Council of Trent, Fifth Session, Decree on Original Sin, n. 5.

nothing that we do would be at all meritorious, nor would we have grace at all. But Christ has died and risen. Therefore, we mere weak and mortal sinners can receive grace, and can cooperate with grace, and can even merit an increase in grace and a reward in Heaven. But all of our merits with our entire reward are only possible through Christ and in Christ. Our merits are entirely dependent on, and proceed solely from, the merits of Christ. If Christ had not died and risen, then we would have neither sanctifying grace, nor actual grace, nor merit, nor reward, nor eternal life in Heaven.

Council of Trent: "If anyone asserts that this sin of Adam...is taken away either by the powers of human nature, or by any other remedy than the merit of the one mediator, our Lord Jesus Christ, who has reconciled us to God in his own blood, made unto us justice, sanctification, and redemption; or if he denies that the said merit of Jesus Christ is applied, both to adults and to infants, by the sacrament of baptism rightly administered in the form of the church; let him be anathema...."[547]

Sanctifying grace is bestowed on us by the formal Sacrament of Baptism, or by a non-formal (mystical) Baptism. This sanctifying grace is given to us because of the merits of Jesus Christ, who reconciles us to God, through His sacrifice on the Cross, by giving us sanctifying grace. And this sanctifying grace makes us children of God and members of the Church. Since we do not merit this grace given to us by Baptism, even infants may be baptized.

All grace is merited for us by Jesus Christ on the Cross, both sanctifying grace and actual grace.

Council of Trent: "If any one says that the good works of one that is justified are in such manner the gifts of God, as that they are not also the good merits of him that is justified; or, that the said justified, by the good works which he performs through the grace of God and the merit of Jesus Christ, whose living member he is, does not truly merit increase of grace, eternal life, and the attainment of that eternal life, -- if so be, however, that he depart in grace, -- and also an increase of glory; let him be anathema."[548]

When an act is done in cooperation with grace, actual grace is given to us by the Holy Spirit before, during, and after that good act. For example, suppose that a Christian prays to God for grace. First, the Holy Spirit gives grace, merited by Christ, to move that person to prayer. Second, the Holy Spirit gives grace, during the prayer, graces with which the person cooperates while praying. Third, the person receives an increase in grace from the Holy Spirit. The grace of God is before, during, and after every holy act. But all of these graces were first merited by Christ. The increase in grace granted during and after the good act is merited by the individual by his freely chosen acts of cooperation with subsequent grace, but only in a manner that is entirely dependent upon the preeminent merits of Christ. All graces without exception were merited by Christ. But some actual graces are also merited by us, secondarily, through our cooperation with grace.

---

[547] Council of Trent, Fifth Session, Decree on Original Sin, n. 3.
[548] Council of Trent, Sixth Session, On Justification, Canon XXXII.

All graces were obtained for us by Jesus Christ. These graces are a gift from God. Even those actual graces that we merit are a gift, since Christ first merited them for us. Our merit is secondary and is entirely dependent on Christ. Christ's merit is primary and is not dependent on us.

.524. Virtue and Grace

The reception of sanctifying grace and the continuation of the state of grace is always accompanied by virtue: the three theological virtues (love, faith, hope) and the four moral virtues (prudence, temperance, fortitude, justice) and the three intellectual virtues (wisdom, knowledge, understanding). All these virtues are infused by God at Baptism (whether the Baptism is formal or non-formal). An infused virtue is an ability given to the soul by an act of the Holy Spirit. The theological virtues are infused and are only able to be obtained as a supernatural gift from God.

Although it may seem by appearances that a particular person is exercising love, or a living faith, or hope, such is not always the case. The Lord beholds the soul. True spiritual love is supernatural and is substantially different from mere natural love, mere emotional love, affection, loving feelings, 'being in love,' and the like. Only persons in a state of sanctifying grace are truly loving persons, in the highest and truest sense of the word 'love.' Only persons in a state of sanctifying grace have a soul that is continually and inherently ordered toward the love of God above all else, and the love of neighbor as self.

[Matthew]
{16:15} Jesus said to them, "But who do you say that I am?"
{16:16} Simon Peter responded by saying, "You are the Christ, the Son of the living God."
{16:17} And in response, Jesus said to him: "Blessed are you, Simon son of Jonah. For flesh and blood has not revealed this to you, but my Father, who is in heaven."

By supernatural faith, Peter believed that Jesus was the Messiah and the Son of God. The natural abilities of the human person, by reason and free will, are not able to exercise the theological virtues apart from grace. And so flesh and blood, i.e. natural ability, was not the source of Peter's response in faith. God the Father gave Peter the graces of love, faith, hope, which Peter then freely chose to exercise in this profession of faith in Jesus.

The theological virtue of faith is obtained at Baptism. And this virtue continues while the person is in a state of grace. If the state of grace is lost by an actual mortal sin against faith, by apostasy, then the virtue of faith is also lost. For an apostate by definition no longer has faith. But otherwise, when an actual mortal sin causes the loss of the state of grace, the true living faith that is a theological virtue is lost, but a type of true faith remains. And by this true but dead faith, the person continues to believe the truths of the Faith, such as that certain acts are mortal sins, that actual mortal sin causes the loss of the state of grace, that contrition and Confession can return him to a state of grace (and many other beliefs). Therefore, faith continues to be of use to the person, guiding him back to a state of grace. And yet this true type of faith that occurs even in the state of mortal sin is not enlivened by love and hope. Not until the person repents and is forgiven are love, hope, and the fullness of faith returned to the soul.

A person who is not in a state of grace may have a true type of faith, limited in its abilities, not enlivened by love and hope, which adheres to the teachings of the Faith: "If any one says, that, grace being lost through sin, faith also is always lost with it; or, that the faith which remains, though it be not a lively faith, is not a true faith; or, that he, who has faith without charity, is not a Christian; let him be anathema."[549]

Although it might seem as if a particular person has hope, appearances can be deceiving. "The Lord beholds the ways of man, and he considers all his steps." (Proverbs 5:21). The infused virtue of hope is found solely in those persons who are in a state of grace. The virtue of hope is not the mere anticipation of good results, or the mere human hope for good consequences. The infused virtue of hope proceeds from love of God, and from faith in God, giving the person a hope that is both reasonable and beyond reason, beyond what can be known or reasonably expected by the intellect. Ultimately, the virtue of hope is directed at the salvation of sinners and eternal life with God.

The three theological virtues are only possessed by those persons who have received sanctifying grace. They are infused and may only be obtained by being infused. Therefore, any person who is not in a state of grace, either due to the lack of Baptism, or due to unrepented actual mortal sin, does not possess true spiritual love, or a living faith, or true spiritual hope.

.525. Love and Grace

If you love your enemies, then you love God and neighbor. If you only love your friends and family, then you might not have the true virtue of love; you might only have the worldly version of love: affection for one's own. True love of neighbor is seen in love for those who treat you badly, love for those who persecute you, love for those who annoy or displease you, love for those whose political and social views are contrary to your own, love for those who religious views are contrary to your own, love for those who are the outcasts of society, love for acquaintances and strangers, love for the needy (any kind of true need in body or in soul), and love for humanity as a whole.

Many people think that they have love, even though they are not in a state of grace. They love those who agree with them, who please them in some way, who are like themselves. Such a person only loves what he sees of himself in other persons; this is a disordered self-love, and not a selfless love of others. True love of neighbor is ordered under the love of God above all else. And since God is Truth, a person in a state of grace will love truth. And since God is Justice, a person in a state of grace will love justice. And since God is Mercy, a person in a state of grace will love mercy.

---

[549] Council of Trent, Sixth Session, Decree on Justification, Canon XXVIII.

An adult who never knowingly chooses selfless acts of true detached spiritual love is not in a state of grace. He has at least committed the actual mortal sin of omission of not cooperating with actual grace in acts of true selfless love. A person who is not in a state of grace, either due to the lack of baptism, or due to the loss of that state by actual mortal sin, cannot perform any truly substantially selfless acts of love for God or neighbor. For he does not have habitual grace (sanctifying grace). He can cooperate with grace partially, haltingly, now and then. But if he were ever to cooperate fully with grace, that grace with his full cooperation would result in God bringing him into the state of grace, either for the first time, or again, by means of an act of at least implicit perfect contrition.

A person who knowingly chooses any selfless act of true detached spiritual love, in full cooperation with actual grace, is certainly in a state of grace. If he was not in a state of grace before such a substantial deed of selfless love, the grace that accompanies that deed allows him to be given the state of grace by God. If he was never baptized, then his selfless act of love in full cooperation with actual grace results in God bestowing on him sanctifying grace, through a non-formal Baptism (a Baptism of desire).

Pope Pius XII: "An act of love is sufficient for the adult to obtain sanctifying grace and to supply the lack of baptism...."[550]

Otherwise, if he was once baptized and in a state of grace, and he lost that state due to actual mortal sin, then his selfless act of love in full cooperation with actual grace constitutes an implicit act of perfect contrition, by which he is returned to the state of grace.

The only true spiritual love is the theological virtue of love. Sin and love are incompatible; they cannot coexist. In so far as you love God above all else, and love your neighbor as yourself, then to that same extent you do not sin. In so far as you lack the love of God and neighbor, then to that same extent you do sin. Love is light and sin is darkness. Shine the light of love and the darkness of sin is gone. Where did it go? Nowhere. Sin does not have existence or being; it is an absence. You can only rid your life of sin by being in a state of grace, which always includes the three theological virtues (love, faith, hope), the four moral virtues, and the three intellectual virtues, and by exercising these virtues, especially and above all else the virtue of love. When you love, you do not sin; and when you sin, you do not love. Although many persons will claim that they love, what they are referring to is at best an emotional love, and at worst a type of selfishness under the guise of love.

Many people who are living very sinful lives perceive a certain emptiness in their lives. But they do not know how to fill that emptiness. Sin is moral evil, and all evil is a deprivation of good. Moral evil is always a deprivation of the single threefold love of God, neighbor, self. Moral evil is a deprivation of love. Their lives are empty because they lack the theological virtue of love. They do not lack emotional love, or physical expressions of affection, or worldly relationships of various kinds (which are often confused with true love). They lack that type of

---

[550] Pope Pius XII, Address to Midwives.

love which alone is worthy to be called 'love,' the true spiritual selfless love of God and neighbor. That is why their lives feel empty. That is why all their attempts to fill that emptiness with false kinds of love ultimately fail. The emptiness that they perceive is a deprivation of true love, caused by their lack of the theological virtue of love, and caused by their many selfish sins. Unless they repent of their sins, receive the infused virtues of love, faith, hope, and choose acts of selfless love for other persons, they will continue to feel this emptiness, this darkness, this absence of the true love that is the light of truth -- until they die and are sent to Hell, where they will have the deprivation of the light and love of God forever.

.526. The Seven Cardinal Virtues

The intellectual virtues are primarily of the intellect: wisdom, understanding, knowledge. The moral virtues are primarily of the will: prudence, fortitude, temperance, justice. The free will is greater than the intellect. By the intellect, we know what is good; by the free will, we love what is good. Love is greater than knowledge (cf. 1 Cor 13). Yet a person cannot love what he does not know (cf. 1 Cor 8:3). We may love God only in so far as we know Him. That is why the Beatific Vision of God includes the intellect knowing God, in unfailing certainty, as well as the free will loving God, in unceasing unity, all of which results in unfailing and unceasing happiness. Therefore, the moral virtues are greater than the intellectual virtues, but the intellectual virtues are necessary to the moral virtues. Moral acts are greater than the knowledge of what is moral. Yet a person cannot choose moral acts without that knowledge.

The four moral virtues (prudence, fortitude, temperance, justice) are traditionally called cardinal (meaning 'hinge') because they are pivotal virtues in any moral life. The term cardinal indicates the fundamental importance of the moral virtues. However, the three intellectual virtues (wisdom, understanding, knowledge) are of lesser but still fundamental importance to living a moral life. For the moral virtues are not able to be exercised without the intellectual virtues. Without wisdom, understanding, and knowledge, no one can exercise prudence, fortitude, temperance, or justice. For the proper exercise of the free will is dependent upon the proper exercise of the intellect. Therefore, all seven virtues deserve the name cardinal: the four moral virtues and the three intellectual virtues. All seven virtues are interdependent; each virtue assists every other virtue in its task. And together they form one cooperative set of seven virtues, which function as the primary servants of the three theological virtues.

Under this expanded use of the term 'cardinal virtue,' the seven cardinal virtues would consist of the four moral virtues, which are of the will, and the three intellectual virtues, which are of the intellect. Although the free will is of greater importance to the human person than the intellect, the will cannot decide what to choose without knowledge provided by the intellect. Similarly, the moral virtues cannot know what to choose without the wisdom, knowledge, and understanding provided by the intellectual virtues. Both will and intellect are the basis for virtue, and so, when God infuses us with these seven virtues, His grace strengthens and guides both will and intellect. The moral virtues are greater than

Grace and Salvation

the intellectual virtues, but the former cannot function without the latter, and so all seven are cardinal.

This change in terminology contradicts the view of some of the ancient pagan philosophers, whose good work on virtue was used to the great benefit of the Church by Saint Thomas and other theologians. But if we look for guidance to Sacred Scripture, we find that the intellectual virtues are nearly as fundamental as the moral virtues. Consider how closely the seven cardinal virtues correspond to the seven gifts of the Holy Spirit. But no one would dare to separate these seven gifts into those that are cardinal and those that are supposedly not cardinal. Though we may rightly make a number of distinctions between each of these seven gifts, they are one cooperative set of gifts, and each is of more or less equal importance to the life of faith.

.527. Infused versus Acquired

"A virtue is an habitual and firm disposition to do the good."[551]

But the good toward which virtue is directed is any true and lasting good, not any mere temporal good. And so, if a person seeks and obtains food, in order to satisfy hunger, his act is good, but not virtuous. Virtue pertains to the higher spiritual goods, such as love, justice, moral truth, etc. When a knowingly chosen act has nothing of the spiritual goods, even implicitly, in the act, then the act is has nothing of virtue. All virtue is directed toward true and lasting good over temporal good. Even the lower animals, though they entirely lack grace and virtue, still seek food, and shelter, and base companionship with their own.

A virtuous act is always done in cooperation with actual grace. Every human person receives prevenient grace, and every human person is made capable, by that prevenient grace, of next cooperating with subsequent grace, in a virtuous act. Even a person who is not in a state of sanctifying grace can cooperate with actual grace, and can commit some virtuous acts, to a limited extent.

For an individual virtuous act does not imply that the person possesses the virtue associated with that act. A virtuous act is distinguished from virtue itself, which is a disposition of the person who acts. This distinction is similar to the distinction between being good, by sanctifying grace, and doing good, by actual grace. A virtuous act is the doing of good by actual grace. A virtue is a state whereby the person is disposed to do these same types of acts. A person may arrive at this state in either of two ways, actively, by acquiring the virtue through repeated virtuous acts of cooperation with actual grace, or passively, by being infused with the virtue through Baptism (formal or non-formal).

At Baptism, we receive the three theological virtues, and the three intellectual virtues, and the four moral virtues. At Confirmation, all these virtues are increased and strengthened and perfected. Confirmation perfects Baptism. All these ten virtues are supernaturally infused at Baptism, and supernaturally strengthened at Confirmation.

---

[551] Catechism of the Catholic Church, n. 1803.

The theological virtues of love, faith, hope are solely obtained by being infused by the Holy Spirit. They are not acquired by habit, not even in cooperation with actual grace. Only a person in a state of sanctifying grace possesses all three of these theological virtues.

A person who is not in a state of grace can cooperate partially with actual grace in particular virtuous acts of limited love, of limited faith, or of limited hope. But an act of full cooperation with actual grace, in an act of true selfless spiritual love, would be accompanied by sanctifying grace in a Baptism of desire (at least implicitly), or by a return to sanctifying grace by perfect contrition and the desire for Confession (at least implicitly). So a person who is not in a state of grace can knowingly choose particular virtuous acts of love, faith, or hope. But all such acts are partial, imperfect, transient, halting, and do not cause the person to acquire the virtue expressed in the act. Only when the person receives or returns to sanctifying grace does he obtain and possess the three theological virtues of love, faith, hope. Otherwise, these three virtues are not possessed at all.

We must distinguish the theological virtues and the related virtuous acts from natural acts of mere affective love, or of mere belief that a particular proposition is true, or of mere anticipation of good results in a situation. These latter acts and dispositions are not virtues and do not require sanctifying grace or actual grace; they merely resemble, superficially, the theological virtues. These merely human acts may occur in anyone, even persons not in a state of grace.

The seven cardinal virtues (three intellectual and four moral) can be either acquired or infused. They are infused at Baptism, and strengthened at Confirmation, by a supernatural act of God. However, these seven virtues can also be acquired, to a limited extent, by the unbaptized. What is acquired is a disposition to do the associated virtuous acts, acts of wisdom, understanding, knowledge, prudence, fortitude, temperance, and justice. The way that these virtues are acquired, apart from sanctifying grace, is by cooperation with actual grace. As the human person repeatedly chooses to cooperate with actual grace in these virtuous acts, the person gradually becomes disposed to perform the same type of act. This disposition makes subsequent virtuous acts of the same type easier to knowingly choose. Thus, the virtue is said to be acquired by repetition, but this is always by repetition of virtuous acts in cooperation with grace.

Even the unbaptized and those in a state of unrepentant actual mortal sin, despite their lack of sanctifying grace, can cooperate with actual grace, partially and intermittently, in the virtuous acts of the seven cardinal virtues. These acts of cooperation with actual grace are virtuous, since each of these seven virtues is directed toward a higher spiritual good (not merely to temporal goods). But it is important to note that, until the person cooperates fully with grace so as to obtain or return to sanctifying grace, only a partial cooperation with actual grace occurs. Such persons cooperate with actual grace, partially and intermittently, in acts of limited virtue, and without possessing any of these virtues in their fullest and truest form. By such acts of partial cooperation with grace, the person is said to acquire any or all of the seven cardinal virtues. But until the person has sanctifying grace and the supernatural infusion of these virtues, he has not truly and fully acquired them. So the term 'acquired virtue' is something of a misnomer. Only when the virtues are infused at Baptism (formal or non-formal) are these virtues possessed in full by the person. Otherwise, the exercise of these seven cardinal virtues is imperfect and intermittent, and they are acquired only partially.

The seven cardinal virtues can be acquired, in some sense, by virtuous acts in cooperation with grace, but they are not fully possessed, nor fully exercised, until they are infused at Baptism. By comparison, the three theological virtues cannot be acquired, but only infused. A person may knowingly choose virtuous acts, by cooperating with actual grace, acts pertaining to any of the seven cardinal virtues, or any of the three theological virtues. But the theological virtues are not acquired or possessed in any sense except by being infused at Baptism.

.528. The Seven Gifts of the Holy Spirit

[Isaiah]
{11:2} And the Spirit of the Lord will rest upon him: the spirit of wisdom and understanding, the spirit of counsel and fortitude, the spirit of knowledge and piety.
{11:3} And he will be filled with the spirit of the fear of the Lord. He will not judge according to the sight of the eyes, nor reprove according to the hearing of the ears.

In my theological opinion, the seven gifts of the Holy Spirit are the same as the seven infused cardinal virtues. At Baptism, when sanctifying grace is received, the Holy Spirit infuses the baptized person with the three theological virtues and the seven cardinal virtues. The seven gifts of the Holy Spirit are also given at Baptism. But some of these gifts are given the same name as some of the virtues:

Catechism of the Catholic Church: "The seven gifts of the Holy Spirit are wisdom, understanding, counsel, fortitude, knowledge, piety, and fear of the Lord."[552]

The three intellectual virtues (wisdom, understanding, knowledge) are the same as three of the seven gifts of the Spirit. And there is no tradition or magisterial teaching defining wisdom, understanding, and knowledge as gifts of the Spirit in a way that would distinguish them from the same three virtues as they are infused by the same Spirit. Wisdom as a gift of the Spirit is the same as the virtue of wisdom infused by the Spirit. The same is true for understanding and knowledge. There is no distinction, neither in wording, nor in the meaning of the words. Therefore, the gifts of the Spirit called wisdom, understanding, and knowledge, which are given at Baptism and strengthened at Confirmation, are the three infused intellectual virtues.

Since these three gifts of the Spirit are each virtues, it follows that the other four gifts would also be virtues. Fortitude as a gift of the Spirit is the same as one of the infused cardinal virtues; and again there is no distinction between fortitude as a gift of the Spirit and fortitude as a virtue infused by the Spirit.

---

[552] Catechism of the Catholic Church, n. 1831.

Counsel is a gift of the Spirit, and prudence is one of the cardinal virtues. Saint Thomas Aquinas asks the question: "Does the gift of counsel correspond to prudence?" And he answers by affirming that "the gift of counsel corresponds to prudence, as helping and perfecting it."[553]

Now Saint Thomas distinguishes counsel from prudence by saying that counsel helps and perfects prudence. But this is exactly the relationship between an infused virtue and the same virtue in its acquired form. A person may obtain and exercise all of the cardinal virtues, without sanctifying grace, but only in their acquired form, by the use of intellect and free will. Such an exercise of virtue is always done in cooperation with actual grace, but when sanctifying grace is lacking, this cooperation is limited, and therefore the exercise of the acquired virtue is limited. The infused form of each cardinal virtue given with sanctifying grace allows each virtue to be exercised in a more perfect manner, even in full cooperation with actual grace. Therefore, the gift of the Spirit called 'counsel' is nothing other than the infused form of the virtue called prudence.

The remaining gifts of the Spirit are piety and fear of the Lord, and the remaining infused cardinal virtues are temperance and justice. Now temperance is often described as moderation. But moderation is only a virtue, even in its limited acquired form, when a person restricts or denies himself the use of temporal goods in order to pursue spiritual goods. So not all moderation is a virtuous act done in cooperation with grace. A person might moderate eating, for the sake of vanity, or might moderate leisure activities in order to obtain more money by working. Only when moderation is practiced for the sake of higher spiritual goods is moderation the virtue of temperance. And this type of temperance, in its fullest and truest form as an infused virtue, is identical to piety. For piety refers to acts of a spiritual nature, to acts which order spiritual goods above temporal goods. A person who places temporal goods above spiritual goods is not pious. A person who places one temporal good above another is not necessarily pious. A person who places spiritual goods above temporal goods is pious, by definition. This piety is identical to the infused virtue of temperance, which places spiritual goods above temporal goods, resulting in moderation. Therefore, the gift of the Spirit called piety is the same as the infused cardinal virtue called temperance.

The remaining gift of the Spirit is fear of the Lord, and the remaining infused cardinal virtue is justice. The virtue of justice considered here is not merely the acquired virtue of justice, which includes only limited cooperation with grace, and which is based more on reason than on faith. The infused virtue of justice does what is good and right out of fear of the Lord. But this fear of the Lord is not fear as a human emotion, nor is it the worldly fear of punishment. Perfect love casts out worldly fear. But the fear of the Lord is found even in the sinless and perfect Virgin Mary. This fear of the Lord is a virtue whereby the person does what is just for the sake of God, not for the sake of self, and not merely for the sake of family or friends.

---

[553] Saint Thomas Aquinas, Summa Theologica, II-II, Q. 52, A. 2.

[Psalm 33]
{33:12} Come forward, sons. Listen to me. I will teach you the fear of the Lord.
{33:13} Which is the man who wills life, who chooses to see good days?
{33:14} Prohibit your tongue from evil and your lips from speaking deceit.
{33:15} Turn away from evil, and do good. Inquire about peace, and pursue it.
{33:16} The eyes of the Lord are on the just, and his ears are with their prayers.
{33:17} But the countenance of the Lord is upon those who do evil, to perish the remembrance of them from the earth.
{33:18} The just cried out, and the Lord heard them, and he freed them from all their tribulations.

This Psalm teaches us that the fear of the Lord is exercised in just acts, in doing good and in avoiding evil because the Lord is just. And this is identical to the exercise of the infused virtue of justice.

[Proverbs]
{15:27} Whoever pursues avarice disturbs his own house. But whoever hates bribes shall live. Through mercy and faith, sins are purged. But through the fear of the Lord, each one turns aside from evil.

The fear of the Lord is a gift of the Spirit whereby each person does good and avoids doing evil because God is and does only good. Again, this describes the infused cardinal virtue of justice.

And so, for all the seven cardinal virtues and the corresponding gifts of the Spirit, the infused form of each cardinal virtue is the same as the corresponding gift of the Spirit. However, the acquired form of each cardinal virtue is merely related to the corresponding gift of the Spirit, in that the gift helps and perfects the acquired virtue. So the only distinction that needs to be made between the seven cardinal virtues and the seven gifts of the Spirit is that the cardinal virtues may be infused or acquired. These seven virtues are identical to the gifts of the Spirit when we are considering them in their infused form. But when we are considering them as merely acquired virtues, they are only related to the gifts of the Spirit.

.529. The Practice of Virtue

A few examples will suffice, because the faithful are capable of determining how to apply the teachings of the Faith to the particular circumstances of their lives. Although certain virtues are particularly prominent in certain types of acts, all the theological and cardinal virtues work together at all times. An act of love is never a faithless act. An act of faith is never a hopeless act. An act of love, faith, hope is never without wisdom, understanding, knowledge, prudence, fortitude, temperance, and justice. All the virtues work together at all times.

Love is practiced by prayer, self-denial, the spiritual and corporal works of mercy, and by devout reception of Confession and Communion.

Faith is practiced by learning and accepting the teachings of Tradition, Scripture, Magisterium, and by believing those teachings in contradiction to popular opinion and even in contradiction to one's own reasonings.

Hope is practiced by continuing to practice love and faith despite the small and great difficulties of this life, and by continuing to pray, and to fast, and to do works of mercy, even when it seems as if these acts are not effective.

Wisdom, understanding, and knowledge are practiced by continually seeking an ever better knowledge of the Faith, an ever better understanding of the will of God, and ever better choices in life between good and evil, between perfect and imperfect. Wisdom, understanding, and knowledge are practiced by learning and teaching the Faith, by correcting sinners, and by rebuking heretics.

Prudence, fortitude, temperance, and justice are practiced by applying wisdom, understanding, and knowledge to the acts of our daily life. Prudence is practiced by using wisdom to decide the right path to take in particular circumstances. Prudence is a spirit of counsel. Fortitude is practiced by persevering in the right path by an understanding of the will of God. Temperance is practiced in any and all acts of piety, whereby spiritual goods are ordered above temporal goods. Temperance is piety. Justice is practiced in all of the other virtues. Justice is practiced by applying the love of God and neighbor to particular circumstances, in faith and hope, with wisdom, understanding, knowledge, prudence, fortitude, and temperance. Justice is the fear of the Lord. And the culmination of the practice of all the virtues is a life that is just before God and man, a life that avoids sin and repents from sin.

.530. Contrition, Confession, Satisfaction

Council of Trent: "But the acts of the penitent himself, namely, contrition, confession and satisfaction, are as it were the matter of this sacrament. Which acts, in as much as they are, by God's institution, required in the penitent for the integrity of the sacrament, and for the full and perfect remission of sins, are for this reason called the parts of penance."[554]

Three things are required for the full forgiveness of an actual mortal sin and the punishment due for that sin: contrition, Confession, and satisfaction. However, if anyone has the first two (he is repentant from his actual mortal sin and he receives Confession), but he fails to do the penances needed to make satisfaction for the punishment that is justly due for his sins, then he is still forgiven and has been returned to the state of grace. But he will be required to do penance to make satisfaction for his sins either in this life, or in Purgatory.

Council of Trent: "Contrition, which holds the first place amongst the aforesaid acts of the penitent, is a sorrow of mind, and a detestation for sin committed, with the purpose of not sinning for the future. This movement of contrition was at all times necessary for obtaining the pardon of sins...."[555]

If anyone goes to Confession, and recites his sins in full, and yet is not contrite (not repentant), then he is not forgiven. Even if the priest tells you that all your sins have been forgiven, if you are not repentant, then it is certain that you are

---

[554] Council of Trent, Fourteenth Session, On Penance and Extreme Unction, Chap. III.
[555] Council of Trent, Fourteenth Session, On Penance and Extreme Unction, Chap. IV.

not forgiven. Contrition is at all times necessary in order to receive forgiveness for actual mortal sin, even in the confessional.

Council of Trent: "The Synod teaches moreover, that, although it sometimes happen that this contrition is perfect through charity, and reconciles man with God before this sacrament be actually received, the said reconciliation, nevertheless, is not to be ascribed to that contrition, independently of the desire of the sacrament which is included therein."[556]

Perfect contrition is repentance from sin out of charity, that is, out of love for God and neighbor. This contrition need not be perfect in every way; it is called perfect contrition because love is the most perfect motive for contrition. Imperfect contrition, also called attrition, is repentance out of an ordered love of self, such as the desire to be a better person, or the desire to avoid Hell and obtain Heaven. A disordered 'love of self,' i.e. selfishness, e.g. a motive of pride, does not constitute contrition or attrition; it is false repentance.

Even a person who is not a believer in God could possibly have perfect contrition, because his true selfless charity for his neighbor implicitly includes a love for God, despite his explicit rejection of the idea of God. Therefore, even an unbeliever can obtain sanctifying grace by implicit desire for Baptism, and can return to a state of grace after an actual mortal sin by perfect contrition, by sorrow for his sins out of love for his neighbor, whom he has harmed by sinning seriously.

But in order for any perfect contrition to be true and full, and to bring about the forgiveness of sin needed for the sinner to be reconciled to God, the Council of Trent taught that the contrition must include a desire for the Sacrament of Confession: "the said reconciliation, nevertheless, is not to be ascribed to that contrition, independently of the desire of the sacrament which is included therein."[557]

Again, the concept of implicit desire applies. In order for a person to be repentant from actual mortal sin with perfect contrition, his contrition must include at least an implicit desire for Confession. This principle still allows for a non-Catholic to be forgiven from actual mortal sin, and to be returned to a state of grace, since this desire (like the desire for Baptism) can be implicit. The person is sorrowful for his sins out of love for neighbor; he desires a type of forgiveness that is found in the Sacrament of Confession; but he does not realize that the forgiveness that he desires is found therein. So perfect contrition always includes love of God and a desire for Confession, but both the desire for Confession and the love of God may be implicit. And implicit perfect contrition is sufficient to forgive actual mortal sin, and to return a repentant sinner to a state of sanctifying grace, even if the penitent is not a Catholic, or not a Christian.

A Catholic who is repentant from actual mortal sin, even with perfect contrition, must still go to Confession and confess his sin. If his contrition does not include

---

[556] Council of Trent, Fourteenth Session, On Penance and Extreme Unction, Chap. IV.
[557] Council of Trent, Fourteenth Session, On Penance and Extreme Unction, Chap. IV.

at least the implicit desire for Confession, then it is not truly perfect contrition. If his contrition does include at least the implicit desire for Confession, then his actual mortal sin is immediately forgiven him, and he is immediately returned to a state of grace. He is still morally obligated to confess his sin in Confession, but if he dies before being able to go to Confession, he dies in a state of grace.

Just as the desire for Baptism may be implicit, and the desire for Confession may be implicit, so also perfect contrition as a whole may be implicit. An explicit perfect contrition consists in calling to mind a sin and choosing to repent from that sin out of love for God and neighbor, with explicit desire for Confession. Or the love for God and the desire for Confession may be implicit. Or the entire perfect contrition may be implicit. Just as an act of selfless love, in full cooperation with grace, can grant the initial state of sanctifying grace (in an implicit Baptism of desire), so also an act of selfless love, in full cooperation with grace, can return a person to the state of sanctifying grace, after that state was lost by actual mortal sin.

For example, suppose that a person is in a state of mortal sin, and has not yet repented and been forgiven. Then, as the last act of his life, he commits an act of true selfless love of neighbor, in full cooperation with grace, sacrificing his own life to save his neighbor's life. In this case, his act of love in full cooperation with grace constitutes an act of implicit perfect contrition, including an implicit desire for Confession, and he is thereby forgiven for all his past actual mortal sins. He has not explicitly called to mind each actual mortal sin, and he has not explicitly repented of each sin. But his full cooperation with grace in an act of selfless love constitutes an act of implicit perfect contrition, and so God forgives his sins and returns him to a state of grace. He therefore dies in a state of grace and obtains eternal life.

And the same type of implicit perfect contrition can possibly occur with other true and full acts of selfless love for neighbor, even without the sacrifice of the person's life. Therefore, a non-Catholic, a non-Christian, even an unbeliever, having obtained the state of grace by an implicit Baptism, and having fallen into actual mortal sin, can obtain forgiveness and return to a state of grace by means of an implicit perfect contrition. In this way, the Mercy of God makes grace and salvation available to all persons. No souls are ever sent to Hell, except those who deserve eternal punishment because of unrepentant actual mortal sin.

.531. Anointing of the Sick
also called Last Rites or Extreme Unction

Catechism of the Catholic Church: "The special grace of the sacrament of the Anointing of the Sick has as its effects: -- the uniting of the sick person to the passion of Christ, for his own good and that of the whole Church; -- the strengthening, peace, and courage to endure in a Christian manner the sufferings of illness or old age; -- the forgiveness of sins, if the sick person was not able to obtain it through the sacrament of Penance; -- the restoration of health, if it is conducive to the salvation of his soul; -- the preparation for passing over to eternal life."

Only Baptism (or a non-formal Baptism of desire) can confer sanctifying grace for the first time to the soul. Baptism can only be received once. If subsequently the person falls into actual mortal sin, then contrition and Confession (or perfect contrition including a desire for Confession) can return the soul to sanctifying grace. However, the Sacrament of Last Rites (also called Extreme Unction), in some cases, can also return the soul to a state of grace.

[James]
{5:14} Is anyone ill among you? Let him bring in the priests of the Church, and let them pray over him, anointing him with oil in the name of the Lord.
{5:15} And a prayer of faith will save the infirm, and the Lord will alleviate him. And if he has sins, these will be forgiven him.

Council of Trent: "If any one says, that the sacred unction of the sick does not confer grace, nor remit sin, nor comfort the sick; but that it has already ceased, as though it were of old only the grace of working cures; let him be anathema."[558]

The valid reception of any Sacrament, including holy Communion, forgives venial sins and remits at least some temporal punishment. Baptism forgives all sins, mortal and venial, and remits all punishment due for those sins. The Sacrament of Confession, with at least the imperfect contrition of the penitent, forgives all sins, mortal and venial, and remits at least some temporal punishment.

The Sacrament of Extreme Unction forgives venial sins and remits at least some temporal punishment. But in some cases, this Sacrament also can forgive actual mortal sin, even without perfect contrition. If a person has fallen out of the state of grace by an actual mortal sin, and if he is unable to receive the Sacrament of Confession (also called the Sacrament of Reconciliation, or the Sacrament of Penance), and if he had at least implicit imperfect contrition for his actual mortal sin, then when he receives the Sacrament of Extreme Unction, his sin is forgiven and he is returned to the state of grace.

The Sacrament of Extreme Unction can only be administered by a priest. So in what circumstances would a person be unable to receive Confession, yet able to receive Extreme Unction, since a priest is needed for each Sacrament? If the person is ill to the extent of being either unconscious, or affected by dementia or the like, and so is unable to use reason, then he could not confess his sins, but a priest could still administer the Sacrament of Extreme Unction. This is perhaps the most common example.

Now suppose that there is a severe persecution of Christians in a particular place and time, so that priests are not allowed to administer the Sacraments. If the person is near death, whether he is ill or is about to be executed, and a priest is present in disguise, he might be able to administer the Sacrament of Extreme Unction surreptitiously, but not the Sacrament of Confession. In this case, too, even actual mortal sin could be forgiven, with imperfect contrition.

---

[558] Council of Trent, 14th Session, On Extreme Unction, Canon II.

.532. Punishment from God

Each and every actual mortal sin deserves eternal punishment in Hell. But when a sinner repents from an actual mortal sin, the punishment due is lessened, from eternal punishment to temporal punishment. Each and every actual venial sin also deserves temporal punishment, which is a type and degree of punishment that can be entirely satisfied and remitted in a limited period of time.

Some persons in this life commit actual mortal sins and do not repent. No matter how much they suffer in this life, the punishment due for these sins is not satisfied or remitted. Only after repentance can the punishment due for actual mortal sin begin to be remitted, because only then is it reduced from eternal punishment to temporal punishment.

But for the repentant sinner, temporal punishment may be satisfied in this life by our penances (prayer, self-denial, works of mercy), by devout reception of the Sacraments, by any holy acts that we do in cooperation with grace, as well as by the various sufferings given to us in life under the Providence of God. Whenever we suffer and accept that suffering as a punishment for sin, that suffering remits some or all of the temporal punishment still due for our sins. And often the repentant sinner will suffer more than his sins deserve, and so, to that same extent, he suffers innocently, like Christ on the Cross. These innocent sufferings, beyond what is deserved to satisfy temporal punishment, are meritorious. These sufferings deserve an eternal reward in Heaven; they merit grace for self and others; they merit additional assistance from God's Providence. Even miracles can be obtained from God by the merits of our innocent sufferings united to the suffering of Christ.

Therefore, we should offer all our sufferings to Christ on the Cross. For our sufferings would have no value if not for His Suffering. Whenever a repentant sinner suffers severely, some of that suffering is likely a punishment for past sins, but the rest of that suffering, beyond what is deserved as temporal punishment, is meritorious. The more that a person repents and does penance (prayer, self-denial, works of mercy), the less his sufferings in life are a punishment, and the more they are meritorious, for self and others.

.533. Baptism Forgives All Sin

The Church has always taught that Baptism forgives all sin and all punishment due for sin.

Saint Clement of Alexandria: "This ceremony is often called 'free gift,' 'enlightenment,' 'perfection,' and 'cleansing' -- 'cleansing,' because through it we are completely purified in our sins; 'free gift,' because by it the punishments due to our sins are remitted; 'enlightenment,' since by it we behold the wonderful holy light of salvation, that is, it enables us to see God clearly; finally, we call it 'perfection' as needing nothing further, for what more does he need who possesses the knowledge of God? It would indeed be out of place to call something that was not fully perfect a gift of God."[559]

Saint Cyril of Jerusalem: "For you go down into the water, bearing your sins, but the invocation of grace, having sealed your soul, suffers you not afterwards to be swallowed up by the terrible dragon. Having gone down dead in sins, you come up quickened in righteousness"[560]

Saint Thomas Aquinas: "As the Apostle says (Romans 6:3), 'all we, who are baptized in Christ Jesus, are baptized in His death.' And further on he concludes (Romans 6:11): 'So do you also reckon that you are dead to sin, but alive unto God in Christ Jesus our Lord.' Hence it is clear that by Baptism man dies unto the oldness of sin, and begins to live unto the newness of grace. But every sin belongs to the primitive oldness. Consequently every sin is taken away by Baptism."[561]

Saint Thomas Aquinas: "Consequently he who is baptized, is freed from the debt of all punishment due to him for his sins, just as if he himself had offered sufficient satisfaction for all his sins."[562]

What if an adult has committed actual mortal sins prior to Baptism, and at the time of Baptism, he has neither imperfect, nor perfect contrition? There are only two possibilities, either the Sacrament is valid and all sins are forgiven, or the Sacrament is not valid.

If the adult accepts the Sacrament of Baptism willingly, then his willingness to receive the Sacrament is a type of implicit perfect contrition. For Baptism is the foundation of the whole Faith, and by accepting Baptism, the person implicitly accepts all that is of the Faith, including repentance from sin. Although perfect contrition, to be truly perfect, must also include the desire for Confession, in this case, the explicit desire for Baptism substitutes for the desire for Confession, since Baptism forgives sins even more thoroughly than Confession. Therefore, the adult who willingly receives Baptism is forgiven for all his sins, including any actual mortal sins from which he has not explicitly repented, and all venial sins, and all punishment due for all sin, and also he is cleansed of original sin.

If the adult receives the Sacrament of Baptism unwillingly, if either it is forced upon him, or if he has no sincere intention to receive a Sacrament (but perhaps just to attend a ceremony to please a friend or loved one), then he does not receive the Sacrament validly. For every Sacrament requires he who dispenses the Sacrament to intend to do what the Church does. But when a Sacrament requires the participation of an adult, such as in Marriage, or in Confession, the recipient of the Sacrament must also intend to do what the Church does. A couple who do not intend to bind themselves in a lifelong commitment, in a marriage as a Sacrament, not merely as a human custom, do not receive the

---

[559] John R. Willis, S.J., The Teachings of the Church Fathers, n. 625.
[560] Willis, The Teachings of the Church Fathers, n. 834.
[561] Saint Thomas Aquinas, Summa Theologica, III, Q. 69, A. 1.
[562] Saint Thomas Aquinas, Summa Theologica, III, Q. 69, A. 2.

Sacrament validly. A man who goes to Confession unrepentant does not receive the Sacrament validly, for he does not intend to do what the Church does: contrition and Confession. Thus, an adult who accepts the water of Baptism without intending to do what the Church does, in that he is insincere and does not truly consent to the Sacrament, does not receive Baptism validly, and he is not forgiven.

These are the only two possibilities for the Sacrament of Baptism, either it is valid and all sins are forgiven without exception, or it is not valid and no sins are forgiven.

Some theologians have tried to construct a third possibility, whereby the Baptism is not effective, if the person is in a state of mortal sin, until he subsequently repents and goes to Confession. But this approach undermines and essentially nullifies the ancient and unchanging teaching of the Church that Baptism forgives all sins. For it is claimed that the person's sins are not forgiven, until he subsequently goes to Confession. But under this approach, the sins are forgiven by Confession, not by Baptism. So Baptism becomes dependent on Confession. And this approach also undermines the teaching that only the Baptized may receive the other Sacraments, including Confession. Therefore, this theological claim is not correct.

.534. The Particular Judgment

[Sirach]
{11:28} For it is easy, in the sight of God, on the day of one's passing, to repay each one according to his ways.
{11:29} The affliction of an hour causes one to forget great delights, and in the end of a man is the uncovering of his works.

[Romans]
{14:12} And so, each one of us shall offer an explanation of himself to God.

Immediately after death, the soul is judged by God. The works of the person are uncovered, so that the soul then knows the good and evil in his life in the light of truth from God. For God is the Just Judge over all Creation and over all created persons. It is false to say that each person judges his own life, and makes his own decision as to whether or not he goes to Hell or to Heaven. God shows the soul the truth about good and evil in that person's life. And the soul cannot deny this truth. But whether or not the person's life was good or evil depends on the truth about love of God and neighbor, moral truth, virtue, vice, sin and imperfection. And this truth is understood in the light of Jesus Christ, the perfect man, who is the only Way, the only Truth, and the only Life.

Catechism of the Catholic Church: "Each man receives his eternal retribution in his immortal soul at the very moment of his death, in a particular judgment that refers his life to Christ: either entrance into the blessedness of heaven -- through a purification or immediately, -- or immediate and everlasting damnation."[563]

---

[563] Catechism of the Catholic Church, n. 1022.

Grace and Salvation

Christ is the judge of each person's life, in the sense that the truth of your life is made clear by comparison with the Truth that is Christ. And after the life of that person is shown to him by God, the person knows whether he deserves eternal life in Heaven (immediately or by way of Purgatory) or eternal death in Hell. The soul does not choose Heaven or Hell. The choices that the person made in his life constitute that person's choice of Heaven or Hell. If you chose a life of love of God and neighbor, and your choices culminated with your death in a state of grace, then at the particular judgment, when your life is compared to Christ, you will know that you deserve Heaven. If you chose a life of selfishness and sin without repentance, or even a life with only one unrepented actual mortal sin, then at the particular judgment, when your life is compared to Christ, you will know that you deserve Hell. But you have no choice in this matter after death, only knowledge of the truth of your life in the light of Christ.

[Romans]
{2:13} For it is not the hearers of the law who are just before God, but rather it is the doers of the law who shall be justified.
{2:14} For when the Gentiles, who do not have the law, do by nature those things which are of the law, such persons, not having the law, are a law unto themselves.
{2:15} For they reveal the work of the law written in their hearts, while their conscience renders testimony about them, and their thoughts within themselves also accuse or even defend them,
{2:16} unto the day when God shall judge the hidden things of men, through Jesus Christ, according to my Gospel.

Even the unbelievers will be judged by God at the particular judgment. For though they do not know the moral law by Divine Revelation, they still know the moral law, though less perfectly, by the natural law written in their hearts. Therefore, God will judge every human person after death, and He will judge even the hidden things of men, both hidden sins and hidden holy acts, and He will judge through the Gospel of Jesus Christ. For the very same moral law has been promulgated in the Gospel as well as in natural law.

There is an absurd idea, found among some of the faithful, that at the particular judgment the individual soul chooses Heaven or Hell, and therefore that God never sends any soul to Hell, but the souls sends itself to Hell. This claim was refuted by our Lord:

[Luke 12]
{12:5} But I will reveal to you whom you should fear. Fear him who, after he will have killed, has the power to cast into Hell. So I say to you: Fear him.

.535. The General Judgment

[Revelation]
{20:12} And I saw the dead, great and small, standing in view of the throne. And books were opened. And another Book was opened, which is the Book of Life. And the dead were judged by those things that had been written in the books, according to their works.

Grace and Salvation

Since there is a particular judgment immediately after death for all persons, what is the purpose of the general judgment? The human person is body and soul. When the soul is judged in the particular judgment, it receives the punishment in Hell, or the reward in Heaven, that the whole person deserves. Later, both the just and the unjust are given the general Resurrection.

[Acts]
{24:15} having a hope in God, which these others themselves also expect, that there will be a future resurrection of the just and the unjust.

At that time, the reward and punishment that is due to the body is measured out. For body and soul are one person. The human person commits sinful acts in body and soul, and commits good acts in body and soul. Therefore, the reward or punishment that the person deserves is for body and soul, not only for the soul. The general Resurrection is appointed by God for the purpose of returning the body to the soul, and the general Judgment is appointed by God to reward or punish the person, in body also, in accord with the life of each one. The souls from Hell are given horrific resurrected bodies, like their horrific sinful acts. The souls from Heaven are given glorious resurrected bodies, like their glorious holy acts, in the glory of Christ.

The human person is both a unique individual before God, and also a member of the whole human family. Therefore, reward and punishment are first singular, when the soul is alone with God at the particular judgment, and then corporate (in the sense of a group of persons), when all the just and unjust are resurrected and given bodies befitting of their lives, in the sight of all. For our sinful acts harm everyone, and our holy acts benefit everyone. Therefore, in the very end, all is brought to light.

Pope Benedict XII: "Nevertheless, on the day of judgment all men will appear with their bodies 'before the judgment seat of Christ' to give an account of their personal deeds, 'so that each one may receive good or evil, according to what he has done in the body' (2 Cor. 5.10)."[564]

The body participates in acts of virtue and in acts of vice, in holy acts and in evil acts, and so the body also participates in the reward or punishment given to each person. The souls in Heaven are given glorious resurrected bodies. The wicked in Hell are given horrific resurrected bodies. Thereafter, the Just are rewarded in body and soul in the timelessness of Eternity in a new Heaven, one fit to reward body and soul. But the unjust are punished in body and soul in the endless time of a new Hell, one fit to punish body and soul.

The glorious new body of the resurrected Just is fitting to the holiness of the soul and fitting to the place of each blessed person as a child of God. The resurrected glorified bodies of the Just share in the glory of Jesus Christ, and are like the resurrected glorified bodies of Jesus and Mary. The Beatific Vision, which began when the soul entered Heaven, continues through the general Resurrection and

---

[564] Pope Benedict XII, On the Beatific Vision of God, Constitution issued in 1336.

Judgment, and thereafter forever. The happiness of the person is not increased by being given a resurrected body. But the quality of that happiness changes, since the happiness of the resurrected Just is now that of a whole person, body and soul.

.536. Original Sin

All the descendents of Adam and Eve, other than Jesus and Mary, are in a fallen state. We are all conceived without sanctifying grace. When the soul is created by God at the moment of conception, it is merely natural, and lacks the supernatural gift of sanctifying grace. It is the will of God that we seek and obtain sanctifying grace in our lives, through formal or non-formal Baptism.

Original sin is the sin at the origins of the human race. Adam and Eve were two real historical persons, the first two human persons. They each were created, in body and in soul, by a miracle of God. They each had sanctifying grace from the first moment of their existence. Adam and Eve are like Jesus and Mary in that each of these four human natures was given sanctifying grace from conception. Adam and Eve each fell from sanctifying grace, by committing actual mortal sin. All of their descendents, other than Jesus and Mary, do not have sanctifying grace from conception, and therefore they are subsequently in need of a formal or non-formal Baptism.

The historical existence of Adam and Eve, their fall from sanctifying grace by the commission of sin, and their place as the first parents of the whole human race is the infallible teaching of Sacred Tradition, Sacred Scripture, and the Magisterium. Whoever rejects this teaching commits the objective mortal sin of heresy.

The Virgin Mary was preserved from original sin at her conception. The dogma of the Immaculate Conception depends upon the dogma of original sin. If there was no sin at the origins of humanity, then there was no Immaculate Conception. So if Adam and Eve did not exist, or if they did not fall from grace by sin, or if they were not the first parents of humanity, then there would be no original sin to be inherited, and there would be no need for an Immaculate Conception to preserve Mary from inheriting original sin. Therefore, whoever denies original sin, denies the Immaculate Conception. And whoever denies Adam and Eve, denies the Virgin Mary.

The Council of Trent infallibly taught that Adam existed, and that he fell from grace, and that we inherit, in body and soul, the effects of his fall from grace. The denial of the existence of Adam and Eve, or the denial of their fall from sanctifying grace, or the denial that all human persons are descendents of Adam and Eve, constitutes a direct rejection of the infallible teaching of the Council of Trent, and is abject heresy and an objective mortal sin.

The Council of Trent: "If any one does not confess that the first man, Adam, when he had transgressed the commandment of God in Paradise, immediately lost the holiness and justice wherein he had been constituted; and that he incurred, through the offence of that prevarication, the wrath and indignation of

God, and consequently death, with which God had previously threatened him, and, together with death, captivity under his power who thenceforth had the empire of death, that is to say, the devil, and that the entire Adam, through that offence of prevarication, was changed, in body and soul, for the worse; let him be anathema."[565]

Therefore, the denial of any of the following: -- the existence of Adam as an historical person, his place as the first man, his transgression of the commandment of God in Paradise, or his loss of sanctifying grace by that transgression -- constitutes a rejection of an infallible teaching of an Ecumenical Council and is the objective mortal sin of heresy. And whoever teaches this heresy to others adds the mortal sin of teaching heresy to the mortal sin of adhering to heresy.

The Council of Trent: "If any one asserts, that the prevarication of Adam injured himself alone, and not his posterity; and that the holiness and justice, received of God, which he lost, he lost for himself alone, and not for us also; or that he, being defiled by the sin of disobedience, has only transfused death, and pains of the body, into the whole human race, but not sin also, which is the death of the soul; let him be anathema: -- whereas he contradicts the apostle who says; 'By one man sin entered into the world, and by sin death, and so death passed upon all men, in whom all have sinned.' "[566]

.537. The denial that Adam and Eve are the first parents of the whole human race, so that we are each and all descendents of Adam and Eve, constitutes a rejection of this teaching of Trent that the human race as a whole is in a fallen state due to the sin of our first parents. Whoever claims that we do not inherit original sin from Adam and Eve commits the objective mortal sin of heresy. And whoever teaches this heresy to others adds the mortal sin of teaching heresy to the mortal sin of adhering to heresy.

The Council of Trent: "If any one asserts, that this sin of Adam, -- which in its origin is one, and being transfused into all by propagation, not by imitation, is in each one as his own, -- is taken away either by the powers of human nature, or by any other remedy than the merit of the one mediator, our Lord Jesus Christ, who has reconciled us to God in his own blood, made unto us justice, sanctification, and redemption; or if he denies that the said merit of Jesus Christ is applied, both to adults and to infants, by the sacrament of baptism rightly administered in the form of the church; let him be anathema."[567]

The infallible teaching of the Magisterium is that Adam sinned, and that the effects of this sin is "transfused into all by propagation," and is inherited at conception by the descendents of Adam and Eve. The Council also infallibly teaches that the Sacrament of Baptism is absolutely necessary for salvation, in order to take away original sin, and to make us just, and holy, and redeemed by the merits of Christ. But if there were no original sin, then Baptism would not be

---

[565] Council of Trent, Fifth Session, Decree on Original Sin, n. 1.
[566] Council of Trent, Fifth Session, Decree on Original Sin, n. 2.
[567] Council of Trent, Fifth Session, Decree on Original Sin, n. 3.

Grace and Salvation

necessary, and the Sacrifice of Jesus would not be necessary. Therefore, whoever denies original sin, denies Baptism and the Sacrifice of Christ on the Cross. And if anyone distorts the meaning of original sin, so that it is not the sin of Adam and Eve, or is not inherited, or does not need to be remedied in order to obtain eternal salvation, then he thereby distorts the meaning of Baptism and of the Sacrifice of Christ on the Cross.

The Council of Trent: "If any one denies, that infants, newly born from their mothers' wombs, even though they be sprung from baptized parents, are to be baptized; or says that they are baptized indeed for the remission of sins, but that they derive nothing of original sin from Adam, which has need of being expiated by the laver [washing] of regeneration for the obtaining life everlasting, -- whence it follows as a consequence, that in them the form of baptism, for the remission of sins, is understood to be not true, but false, -- let him be anathema."[568]

The connection between Adam and Eve, original sin, and the need for Baptism is essential to a proper understanding of the Catholic Faith. The idea that human persons do not derive original sin from Adam, which then requires expiation by Baptism, is an abject heresy, explicitly and infallibly condemned by the Council of Trent. Everyone who rejects the literal historical existence of Adam and Eve, or their sin and fall from grace, or their place as the first parents of the whole human race, thereby rejects several infallible teachings of the Council of Trent, and commits the objective mortal sin of heresy. Whoever teaches the same error, teaches heresy, and sins even more gravely.

The Council of Trent: "For that which the apostle has said, By one man sin entered into the world, and by sin death, and so death passed upon all men in whom all have sinned, is not to be understood otherwise than as the Catholic Church spread everywhere has always understood it."[569]

This teaching of the Council refutes those who call for a reinterpretation of original sin, otherwise than as the Catholic Church has understood it and has taught it everywhere (by the Universal Magisterium, in addition to the teaching of this Council). The teaching of the Catholic Church on original sin cannot be changed such that sin did not enter the world by one man, Adam, or such that sin and death did not pass into all human persons (other than Jesus and Mary) by being the descendents of Adam and Eve after the fall from grace. For the Council taught that "all men had lost their innocence in the prevarication of Adam...."[570] Therefore, the rejection of the historical existence of Adam and Eve, and any redefinition of original sin, is nothing other than abject heresy, which rejects the infallible teaching Tradition, Scripture, Magisterium.

"For as in truth men, if they were not born propagated of the seed of Adam, would not be born unjust, -- seeing that, by that propagation, they contract

---

[568] Council of Trent, Fifth Session, Decree on Original Sin, n. 4.
[569] Council of Trent, Fifth Session, Decree on Original Sin, n. 4.
[570] Council of Trent, Sixth Session, Decree on Justification, Chapter I.

through him, when they are conceived, injustice as their own, -- so, if they were not born again in Christ, they never would be justified...."[571]

The teaching of the Council of Trent could not be more clear on this point. Adam fell from grace, and we are all biological descendents of Adam; therefore, we are conceived with original sin, and therefore, we need Baptism into the death of Christ in order to have salvation. So the denial that Adam and Eve ever existed, is a denial of original sin, of the need for Baptism, and of the need for sanctifying grace from Christ on the Cross.

Pope Pius XII: "For the faithful cannot embrace that opinion which maintains that either after Adam there existed on this earth true men who did not take their origin through natural generation from him as from the first parent of all, or that Adam represents a certain number of first parents. Now it is in no way apparent how such an opinion can be reconciled with that which the sources of revealed truth and the documents of the Teaching Authority of the Church propose with regard to original sin, which proceeds from a sin actually committed by an individual Adam and which, through generation, is passed on to all and is in everyone as his own."[572]

.538. The Magisterium clearly and definitively teaches that all human persons on earth are descendents of Adam and Eve. There exist no human beings on this earth who do not take their origin, by natural generation as biological descendents, from Adam, the first parent of all. "This is he, who was formed first by God, the father of the world, who was alone when created...." (Wisdom 10:1). Neither is it possible to reinterpret Adam and Eve as a figure for a set of first parents. For then the verse of Sacred Scripture would be false which states that sin and death are in all from one man, Adam. "Therefore, just as through one man sin entered into this world, and through sin, death; so also death was transferred to all men, to all who have sinned." (Romans 5:12). But "Scripture cannot be broken" (John 10:35); therefore, Adam is one man, at the beginning of human history, the biological father of all mankind.

Second Vatican Council: "The truth is that only in the mystery of the incarnate Word does the mystery of man take on light. For Adam, the first man, was a figure of Him Who was to come, namely Christ the Lord. Christ, the final Adam, by the revelation of the mystery of the Father and His love, fully reveals man to man himself and makes his supreme calling clear.... To the sons of Adam He restores the divine likeness which had been disfigured from the first sin onward."[573]

Vatican II also taught that Adam was the first man, and that we are all descendents of Adam. Therefore, it is foolish and false to say that the teachings of the Council of Trent are archaic, or that older Catholic teachings have been changed or overruled by the teachings of Vatican II, or that the teaching of any

---

[571] Council of Trent, Sixth Session, Decree on Justification, Chapter III.
[572] Pope Pius XII, Humani Generis, n. 37.
[573] Second Vatican Council, Gaudium et Spes, n. 22.

past Council was due to a lack of scientific or historical knowledge. The solemn teaching of every Ecumenical Council is the teaching of the Holy Spirit.

Second Vatican Council: "At the same time, however, because she belongs to the offspring of Adam she is one with all those who are to be saved.... Thus Mary, a daughter of Adam, consenting to the divine Word, became the mother of Jesus, the one and only Mediator."[574]

The Second Vatican Council also taught that the Virgin Mary is a descendent of Adam. Even though Mary was saved by Christ in the first moment of her existence, in her Immaculate Conception, she in fact needed to be saved because she, like all of us, is a descendent of Adam. The Catholic Faith teaches that all of us, including the Virgin Mary, are descendents of Adam and Eve.

Pope John Paul II: "The plan of life given to the first Adam finds at last its fulfillment in Christ. Whereas the disobedience of Adam had ruined and marred God's plan for human life and introduced death into the world, the redemptive obedience of Christ is the source of grace poured out upon the human race, opening wide to everyone the gates of the kingdom of life (cf. Rom 5:12-21). As the Apostle Paul states: 'The first man Adam became a living being; the last Adam became a life-giving spirit' (1 Cor 15:45)."

The holy Pope John Paul II also taught that Adam was one real historical man, whose sin introduced death into the world, so that all human persons required redemption through Christ. Adam was the first man, a real living human being, and a foreshadowing of Jesus Christ.

Pope John Paul II: "In creating the human race 'male and female,' God gives man and woman an equal personal dignity, endowing them with the inalienable rights and responsibilities proper to the human person. God then manifests the dignity of women in the highest form possible, by assuming human flesh from the Virgin Mary, whom the Church honors as the Mother of God, calling her the new Eve and presenting her as the model of redeemed woman."[575]

Jesus is the new Adam, and Mary is the new Eve. Just as sin and death were brought into the human race through Adam and Eve, so also are sin and death taken away by Jesus, the new Adam, and Mary, the new Eve. The denial that Adam and Eve existed, and fell from grace, and became the first parents of us all, is essentially a denial of the need for redemption through Christ, with the assistance of the Virgin Mary.

.539. Interpretation of the Adam and Eve Story

Many people assume that the story of Adam and Eve in the Bible must be either entirely literal, or entirely figurative. They also notice that certain elements in the story are figurative, such as the serpent, which represents Satan, and the choice to eat fruit from a certain tree, which represents the sin of pride. And so they incorrectly conclude that the whole story must be figurative. But there is nothing

---

[574] Second Vatican Council, Lumen Gentium, n. 53, 56.
[575] Pope John Paul II, Familiaris Consortio, n. 22.

to prevent a story from containing both literal elements and figurative elements. The teaching of the Council of Trent, and other teachings of Tradition, Scripture, Magisterium, require the belief that certain elements of the story of Adam and Eve are literally true. Other elements of the story have always been understood as figures, such as the talking serpent and the fruit that is sinful to eat.

Another error is to begin with science and history, and to reject any elements of the story of Adam and Eve that cannot be reconciled with those disciplines. But this approach places science and reason above faith, and above the infallible teachings of Tradition, Scripture, Magisterium. However, science and reason are fallible, and the reasoning of sinners is not only fallible, but includes a certain likelihood of error. As a result, any approach that places reason above faith is not a reliable path to truth. If Faith teaches a truth, then Faith should be believed above and beyond what seems reasonable to a sinful human person or to sinful secular society.

Other stories in Sacred Scripture, especially in the Old Testament, also may be interpreted as containing some literal historical elements and some figurative elements. For example, the story of Noah and the Flood need not be understood as either entirely literal or entirely figurative. We need not deny the existence of Noah and the occurrence of a great Flood merely because some elements in the story are figures, such as the extent of the Flood and the depth of the water. The extent to which all animal life on earth was represented on the Ark may be a figure. A relatively small number of animals would be sufficient to be a living figure representing all life on earth. We need not hold that every species without exception was represented. We need not hold that all human persons not in the Ark perished. For this, too, is a figure, such that the Ark represents the Church as the sole source of salvation. We need not hold that the Flood covered every area of land. The extent of the Flood is a figure for the extent of sin, and for the extent of the offer of salvation though the waters of Baptism. But neither do we need to deny that Noah existed, and that he built an Ark, that a great Flood occurred, and that he saved his family by this Ark.

.540. Membership in the Church

All who are in a state of sanctifying grace are members of the Church. Some are formal members of the Catholic Church, because they received a formal Baptism, and because they believe and practice the Catholic Faith. Some are members because they received a formal Baptism from a Christian community separated from the Catholic Church, such as a Protestant denomination. These Christians are also members of the Church, which is the Body of Christ and the Ark of Salvation, even though they lack the full communion with the Church possessed by believing and practicing Catholics.

Many other human persons are also members of the Church, but in a hidden way and to a limited extent. For they received a Baptism of desire, giving them the gift of sanctifying grace. These mystical members of the Church might be members of Judaism or Islam, or members of some other religion, or they might be agnostics, or atheists. Although they lack formal membership in the Church, they are members of the Church in a mystical way, by the state of sanctifying grace in their souls, which they obtained by an implicit Baptism of desire. Outside the Church, there is no salvation. But some persons who lack formal membership in the Church are nevertheless within the Church. They are non-formal members of the Church, which is the Ark of Salvation for the whole human race.

.541. The State of Actual Mortal Sin

The state of sanctifying grace is analogous to light filling a room, the light of the grace of God is continually within any soul in a state of grace. When a person in a state of grace commits an actual mortal sin (which is a gravely immoral act done with full knowledge that the act is gravely immoral, and with full consent), as a direct and immediate result of that freely chosen actual mortal sin, he loses the state of grace. This new state of his soul is called the state of mortal sin; it is analogous to a dark room. The light of sanctifying grace is suddenly gone from the soul.

The person in a state of mortal sin, even though he completely lacks sanctifying grace, still receives prevenient actual grace, and is still able to cooperate with subsequent actual grace. Therefore, he is still culpable for his sins. Even in a state of mortal sin, the soul is given graces by God, and therefore is able to avoid additional sins, is able to repent from any and all past sins, and is able to cooperate with grace in the Confessional, in order to return to a state of grace. Actual graces, both operating and cooperating, are still available to the person in the state of mortal sin. Otherwise, he would be unable to repent and to return to God.

If a person is in a state of actual mortal sin, and he also refuses to repent from the actual mortal sin that he has committed, his cooperation with actual grace is necessarily limited. If he decides to cooperate fully with actual grace, that grace, with his full cooperation, immediately moves him to contrition and to the desire for Confession. So if he continues to refuse to repent, he is thereby refusing to cooperate fully with actual grace. He then cooperates with actual grace either not at all, or only partially from time to time. As a result, for as long as he resists full cooperation with actual grace, he is not able to commit any true and substantial selfless acts of love of God and neighbor.

A person who is unrepentant and in a state of mortal sin does not fulfill the commandments to love God, and to love your neighbor as yourself. There may be some limited goodness, by partial cooperation with grace, in some of his acts. But none of his acts are truly selfless acts of love for anyone. None of his good acts involve full cooperation with grace. Even his good acts are tainted with selfishness. A substantially selfless act of true spiritual love requires full cooperation with grace. A person in a state of mortal sin still receives prevenient grace, and he still is able to cooperate fully with subsequent grace; but he has not yet done so. If and when he does fully cooperate with grace, the very same grace of God immediately brings him to contrition and to the desire for Confession, at least implicitly through an act of love for God and neighbor.

There are two types of people in the world: those who are in a state of grace, and those who are not. Only those who are in a state of grace can perform substantially selfless acts of true spiritual love for God and neighbor. Those who are not in a state of grace (either through the lack of Baptism or because they are unrepentant from actual mortal sin) are unable to perform these same selfless acts of love -- or rather, they are able, but they have not yet done so. For such a full cooperation with actual grace would result in God granting to that person the gift of sanctifying grace, either by at least an implicit Baptism of desire, or by at least implicit perfect contrition.

A person in a state of mortal sin may seem good and loving. He may seem to love family and friends. He may have an affective love and loving feelings for other persons. But he lacks a true and full selfless love. For the state of grace is the state of loving God above all else, and of loving your neighbor as yourself. A person in a state of mortal sin can be charming, and agreeable, and can believe what the Church teaches (for faith is not necessarily lost by actual mortal sin). He might even seem holy and loving; but this is by way of appearances only. The person who truly loves God and neighbor is the person who keeps the commandments, who loves everyone selflessly, who loves even his enemies. A person in a state of mortal sin will generally treat enemies with contempt and derision and malice. A person in a state of grace might not be charming or agreeable; he might not seem loving and holy. "For man sees those things that are apparent, but the Lord beholds the heart." (1 Samuel 16:7).

.542. Why is there so much suffering in the world? Why are there so many crimes and serious sins? Why are so many people unfaithful and unreasonable? Why is the world such a cold and difficult place in which to live? Why are there so many selfish and cruel people, who are unwilling to change? Why does secular society reject the true Faith? Why is truth trampled to the ground? All this occurs mainly because there are so many people who are not in a state of grace, so many people who have committed actual mortal sins and have refused to repent. The lack of the state of sanctifying grace, as well as the lack of cooperation with actual grace, is the reason for all the sin and suffering in the world.

But if anyone is not in a state of grace, and next he cooperates fully with actual grace in an act of true spiritual love for God and neighbor, he is given sanctifying grace by God, either by at least an implicit Baptism of desire, or by at least an act of implicit perfect contrition. If sanctifying grace is given to him for the first time, due to an act of love in full cooperation with grace, then he has received a Baptism of desire. If instead he is returned to a state of grace from a state of mortal sin, due to an act of love in full cooperation with grace, then he has received forgiveness by at least implicit perfect contrition (which always includes at least an implicit desire for Confession).

The state of mortal sin consists in the lack of sanctifying grace in a soul that previously had sanctifying grace. A human person may only receive sanctifying grace for the first time by a formal or non-formal Baptism. Any actual mortal sin committed subsequent to either type of Baptism places the soul in a state of mortal sin. But since Baptism cannot be received more than once, the remedy for this state of mortal sin, the only way to return to a state of grace, is contrition and Confession. But this contrition may be implicit, and this Confession may be the implicit desire for Confession. Just as there is a Baptism of desire that can confer the state of sanctifying grace, so also there is a 'contrition and Confession of desire' that can return the person to a state of sanctifying grace, from a state of mortal sin.

However, if a person commits one or more actual mortal sins, and if that person refuses, through the last moment of his life, to cooperate with grace in order to be forgiven (by imperfect contrition and Confession, or by perfect contrition and Confession, or by at least implicit perfect contrition with the implicit desire for Confession), then that person dies in a state of unrepentant actual mortal sin, and will certainly be condemned to Hell forever.

Pope Benedict XII: "Moreover we define that according to the general disposition of God, the souls of those who die in actual mortal sin go down into hell immediately after death and there suffer the pain of hell."[576]

.543. The Punishments of Hell

Hell includes three categories of punishment: (1) what is absent, (2) what is present, and (3) the character of what is present.

(1) What is absent

[2 Thessalonians]
{1:9} These shall be given the eternal punishment of destruction, apart from the face of the Lord and apart from the glory of his virtue....

The primary suffering of Hell is the deprivation of the Beatific Vision of God. But the sufferings of Hell also include the deprivation of the communion of the saints, and the deprivation of all the joys and blessings of Heaven. These are passive punishments; the soul is punished by what is not given to the soul. All the souls in Hell suffer these deprivations equally, in that all are completely deprived of each of these absent blessings.

Pope Innocent III: "The punishment of original sin is deprivation of the vision of God, but the punishment of actual sin is the torments of everlasting Hell...."[577]

Those who die in a state of original sin only, are given the passive punishments of deprivation, but not the active punishments (torments). These souls were sent to Hell by God for the actual mortal sin of omission of never having found sanctifying grace in their lives. But if they have not committed any other actual mortal sins, then their sufferings are only of the first type, deprivation. This punishment is fitting to their sin, for they chose to deprive their souls of sanctifying grace, and to deprive their lives of the true love of God and neighbor.

---

[576] Pope Benedict XII, On the Beatific Vision of God, Constitution issued in 1336.
[577] Pope Innocent III, Denzinger, n. 410.

Grace and Salvation

Therefore, in Hell they are deprived of the goods of Heaven that are based upon sanctifying grace and the love of God and neighbor.

.544.
(2) What is present

[Jude]
{1:7} And also Sodom and Gomorrah, and the adjoining cities, in similar ways, having given themselves over to fornication and to the pursuing of other flesh, were made an example, suffering the punishment of eternal fire.

For most souls in Hell, their sufferings include active punishments. These are properly and accurately referred to as torments or tortures. And these torments are directly inflicted by the will of God, in just and measured proportion to the kind and degree of the sin being punished. Only the all-powerful and all-knowing God can dispense punishment that is perfectly just, and yet perfectly merciful, and also perfectly fitting to the sins that the person made in life.

Those who claim that the damned in Hell punish themselves cannot explain how a soul entirely lacking grace could measure out a punishment that is just and merciful, or how a soul that is so thoroughly imperfect, so thoroughly damaged by sin, could dispense a punishment that is perfect in its fittingness to the sins that are being punished. To the contrary, the damned in Hell are punished by God.

But even more absurd is the claim that the punishments in Hell are somehow dispensed by fallen angels. The wicked fallen angels cannot possibly dispense the just and merciful punishments of Hell. And our Lord Himself refuted this type of claim when He taught that Hell is a place of punishment, not only for human souls, but also for the devil and his fellow fallen angels. "Depart from me, you accursed ones, into the eternal fire, which was prepared for the devil and his angels." (Mt 25:41).

[Sirach]
{19:6} Whoever sins against his own soul will be punished. And whoever rejoices in malice will be condemned.

Sacred Scripture does not say that the sinner condemns himself, but that he will be punished. Sacred Scripture does not say that the sinner punishes himself, but that he will be punished. And the only power and authority capable of punishing all fallen angels and all condemned souls in Hell, and all the holy souls in Purgatory, with perfect justice and mercy, is God, who is infinitely just and merciful, who is Justice and Mercy. Therefore, the condemned angels and souls in Hell, and the holy souls in Purgatory, are punished by Justice Himself.

[Lamentations]
{3:64} THAU. You shall pay a recompense to them, O Lord, according to the works of their hands.
{3:65} THAU. You shall give them a heavy shield of the heart: your hardship.

{3:66} THAU. You shall pursue them in fury, and you shall destroy them under the heavens, O Lord.

These three verses, labeled with the last letter of the Hebrew alphabet (thau), describe the three places that the sinner may be punished: in this life, in Purgatory, or in Hell. Sacred Scripture teaches that God pays a recompense to sinners in this life (verse 64), and a hardship in Purgatory (verse 65), but fury and destruction in Hell (verse 66). Notice the increase in the severity of the sufferings. Sufferings and penances in this life are relatively light; they are a recompense for sin from God, and we can even make this recompense lighter by taking penances upon ourselves. But the punishments of Purgatory are more severe. They are described as 'a heavy shield of the heart': heavy, because they are severe; a shield, because they are a help to the soul, not a harm. They are described as 'your hardship' (with 'your' referring to God) because these difficult sufferings are inflicted by God.

Then the final verse describes the punishments of Hell. These torments are also inflicted by God, since He is the One who pursues and destroys them. The punishments of Hell are described under the figure of a fury of the Lord because the sufferings in Hell are severe, and because they are the result of the conflict between the sins of the person's life and the Justice of God. The soul in Hell is destroyed by God, meaning that God inflicts an eternal punishment, an unending destruction.

.545. First among the active punishments inflicted by God in Hell is the knowledge given as a gift to all human persons after death in the particular judgment. Each and every condemned soul in Hell knows the sins of his life, especially the unrepentant actual mortal sins. Each soul knows that these acts were sinful, were unjustifiable, and were harmful. Each soul knows that the actual mortal sins he committed, from which he refused to repent, caused him to be justly condemned to Hell. And this knowledge remains with him, so that the souls in Hell are tormented by their own sins. But this torment is due to the act of God both giving the soul that knowledge, and keeping the soul in that knowledge. God inflicts this active punishment indirectly, by way of the knowledge of sin.

Second among the active punishments in Hell is the communion of the damned. The holy souls in Heaven enjoy knowledge of God in the intellect, and union with God in love in the will, and the happiness that results from knowledge and love. The damned in Hell are deprived of this vision and love of God. But the holy souls in Heaven also enjoy the company of the holy angels and of the other holy souls. For Heaven is a community which perfectly fulfills the commandment to love God and neighbor. The damned in Hell are not only deprived of this community of love, they also are tormented by the perverse companionship of fallen angels and damned souls. The sins of these wicked devils and damned souls are a source of torment to each condemned person. However, this punishment is also of God. For God Himself must inflict this suffering, indirectly through the communion of the damned, in order that the suffering be just and merciful and fitting to the type and degree of sins of each person. The number of fallen angels and damned souls in Hell is very great. If anyone were given an unrestricted communion with all those condemned persons, the punishment would be excessive and unjust. Therefore, God, by His power, directly limits this active punishment. The punishment is indirectly of God, by way of the communion of the damned, but it is also directly limited by God, so that Justice rules in Hell, not sin.

Third among the active punishments in Hell is what is figuratively called the fires of Hell. This type of punishment is an active punishment directly inflicted by God. It is the suffering deserved due to the unrepentant actual mortal sins of the person in Hell, in addition to the passive punishments (deprivation of Heaven), and in addition to the knowledge of one's sins, and the communion of the damned. Now the Magisterium teaches that the punishments of Hell are unequal, and that those who die in original sin only, have the passive punishments only, not the active ones.

Pope Innocent III: "The punishment of original sin is deprivation of the vision of God, but the punishment of actual sin is the torments of everlasting Hell…."[578]

Council of Florence: "But the souls of those who depart this life in actual mortal sin, or in original sin alone, go down straightaway to hell to be punished, but with unequal pains."[579]

Therefore, not all souls in Hell suffer this third type of active punishment, whereby God inflicts pains on the damned. This active punishment is necessary because of the gravity of certain actual mortal sins. The actual mortal sin of choosing to live a life deprived of sanctifying grace deserves the passive punishment of deprivation, as well as the mere knowledge of the sin and its just consequences.

.546. Other actual mortal sins deserve additional punishment, that of the communion of the damned, because of the grave harm done to other souls by actual mortal sin. All sin harms other persons, but actual mortal sin does grave harm, even to the extent of leading other persons into actual mortal sin and into Hell. Therefore, it is a just punishment for the damned to have to suffer from the company of other damned souls. For their sins were partly responsible for the damnation of other persons.

But some actual mortal sins are so severe as to deserve more punishment still, in the form of an active infliction of suffering. And this active punishment is represented under the figure of fire.

[Matthew]
{3:12} His winnowing fan is in his hand. And he will thoroughly cleanse his threshing floor. And he will gather his wheat into the barn. But the chaff he will burn with unquenchable fire." …

---

[578] Pope Innocent III, Denzinger, n. 410.
[579] Council of Florence, Sixth Session, 6 July 1439.

{5:22} But I say to you, that anyone who becomes angry with his brother shall be liable to judgment. But whoever will have called his brother, 'Idiot,' shall be liable to the council. Then, whoever will have called him, 'Worthless,' shall be liable to the fires of Hell....
{7:19} Every tree which does not produce good fruit shall be cut down and cast into the fire....
{13:41} The Son of man shall send out his Angels, and they shall gather from his kingdom all who lead astray and those who work iniquity.
{13:42} And he shall cast them into the furnace of fire, where there shall be weeping and gnashing of teeth....
{25:41} Then he shall also say, to those who will be on his left: 'Depart from me, you accursed ones, into the eternal fire, which was prepared for the devil and his angels.

The truth that certain sins deserve not only the passive deprivation of Heaven, but active punishments as well, was taught plainly by our Lord Jesus Christ:

[Mark]
{9:41} And whoever will have scandalized one of these little ones who believe in me: it would be better for him if a great millstone were placed around his neck and he were thrown into the sea.
{9:42} And if your hand causes you to sin, cut it off: it is better for you to enter into life disabled, than having two hands to go into Hell, into the unquenchable fire,
{9:43} where their worm does not die, and the fire is not extinguished.
{9:44} But if your foot causes you to sin, chop it off: it is better for you to enter into eternal life lame, than having two feet to be cast into the Hell of unquenchable fire,
{9:45} where their worm does not die, and the fire is not extinguished.
{9:46} But if your eye causes you to sin, pluck it out: it is better for you to enter into the kingdom of God with one eye, than having two eyes to be cast into the Hell of fire,
{9:47} where their worm does not die, and the fire is not extinguished.

Under the figure of 'worm' and 'fire', our Lord taught two types of active punishments. In Hell, there are pains proper to the soul (since worms devour the interior of dead bodies, 'worm' signifies pain of the soul) and there are pains proper to the body (since fire causes pain to the body from the outside).[580] The interior sufferings include knowledge of one's own sins, and the knowledge of the sins of other persons (the communion of the damned), and whatever additional interior active suffering is due for the person's unrepentant actual mortal sins. These punishments are of the soul.

Then, in addition, there is a type of exterior active suffering, which inflicts a pain like that of bodily pain. Just as Heaven includes joys in addition to love, so also Hell includes pains in addition to the deprivation of love. And these pains

---

[580] Saint Augustine held this interpretation, and his view is cited in the supplement to the Summa Theologica: Augustine, City of God, XX, 22; Summa, Suppl. Q. 97, A. 2.

continue forever, for "their worm does not die and the fire is not extinguished." How can these pains be like that of the body, while the soul in Hell is without a body? When a person in this life suffers in body, these pains affect the soul; for body and soul are one person. Then, in Purgatory as well as in Hell, a soul that deserves additional punishment is given the same type of pains in the soul that would have resulted from pains in the body in this life. And the reason that this punishment is just and fitting is that we sin in this life in both body and soul, we do harm to our neighbor's bodies and souls; therefore, we deserve to suffer the pains of the body as well as of the soul.

This active infliction of suffering is not inflicted by means of holy angels, since the holy angels and all the blessed are enjoying eternal rest in Heaven. It is not inflicted by the fallen angels, since those wicked things cannot distribute a perfectly just and perfectly merciful punishment, exactly fitting to the sins of each soul. Only God can and does, in some cases, inflict interior and/or exterior active punishments, in addition to the passive punishment (loss of Heaven). But not every soul deserves these additional active punishments. Only certain souls in Hell (and only certain souls in Purgatory) are given this type of punishment.

.547. That some sins deserve a greater, and other sins a lesser punishment is clear from Sacred Scripture.

[Luke]
{10:10} But into whatever city you have entered and they have not received you, going out into its main streets, say:
{10:11} 'Even the dust which clings to us from your city, we wipe away against you. Yet know this: the kingdom of God has drawn near.'
{10:12} I say to you, that in that day, Sodom will be forgiven more than that city will be.
{10:13} Woe to you, Chorazin! Woe to you, Bethsaida! For if the miracles that have been wrought in you, had been wrought in Tyre and Sidon, they would have repented long ago, sitting in haircloth and ashes.
{10:14} Yet truly, Tyre and Sidon will be forgiven more in the judgment than you will be.
{10:15} And as for you, Capernaum, who would be exalted even up to Heaven: you shall be submerged into Hell.

All the sexual sins symbolized by the cities of Sodom (homosexual sins) and Gomorrah (heterosexual sins) deserve eternal Hellfire. But the sins of those who culpably reject the true Faith and its true ministers are greater still. The sins greed and material excess, symbolized by the merchant cities of Tyre and Sidon, deserve eternal Hellfire. But sins against the true Faith, symbolized by Chorazin (schism), Bethsaida (heresy), and Capernaum (apostasy), are worse still. And worse sins deserve greater punishment. The more severe sins of this life can only be justly (and yet mercifully) punished by the infliction of eternal suffering. The mere deprivation of Heaven would not be sufficient to satisfy the justice of God.

After the general Resurrection, these active punishments include sufferings in the body as well as in the soul. For both the just and the unjust are given the general Resurrection (Acts 24:15). And thereafter they suffer in a new Hell, one fitting for the punishment of both soul and body: "And death and Hell gave up their dead who were in them. And they were judged, each one according to his works. And Hell and death were cast into the pool of fire. This is the second death." (Rev 20:13-14). The second death is the new Hell, after the general Resurrection.

.548.
(3) The character of what is present

The third type of punishment in Hell is the character of the aforementioned sufferings, which is in accord, not merely with the degree of the sins being punished, but with the kind of sin. Thus, two sinners in Hell might suffer the same degree of punishment, but with different types of punishment according to the type of sin. The character of the sufferings in Hell is also affected by the other persons in Hell, both human and angelic. Now the joys of Heaven have a certain character, in addition to the degree of happiness, which flows both from the particular virtues and good deeds of each one's life, as well as from the particular unique individuals, human and angelic, who share those joys in the communion of the saints. But the torments of Hell also have a certain character, which flows both from the particular vices and wicked deeds of each one's life, as well as from the particular unique individuals, human and angelic, who share those torments within the communion of the damned.

This character of the sufferings, in addition to degree, is necessary so that each and every devil and soul in Hell will be punished both to an extent and in a manner that is exactly fitting to the sins that each committed. The justice and knowledge and power of God punish each one in the exact way that is most fitting to the exact sins that each chose to commit. Anything less would not be the perfect justice of a place prepared by God for just punishment. For the domain of Hell is not of the devil, but of God. Hell is like a prison prepared by God for the just punishment and internment of the wicked.

.549. False Ideas about Hell

Some sources describe Hell as if it were a place of extreme punishment, without any relationship between the type and degree of suffering and the type and degree of the sins being punished. This idea is certainly and absolutely false. Jesus taught that Hell is a place of just punishment. It is a place prepared by God for those who deserve eternal punishment.

[Matthew]
{25:41} Then he shall also say, to those who will be on his left: 'Depart from me, you accursed ones, into the eternal fire, which was prepared for the devil and his angels.
{25:42} For I was hungry, and you did not give me to eat; I was thirsty, and you did not give me to drink;
{25:43} I was a stranger and you did not take me in; naked, and you did not cover me; sick and in prison, and you did not visit me.'
{25:44} Then they will also answer him, saying: 'Lord, when did we see you hungry, or thirsty, or a stranger, or naked, or sick, or in prison, and did not minister to you?'

{25:45} Then he shall respond to them by saying: 'Amen I say to you, whenever you did not do it to one of these least, neither did you do it to me.'
{25:46} And these shall go into eternal punishment, but the just shall go into eternal life."

Saint Thomas Aquinas: "Punishment is proportionate to sin."[581]

And as noted above, both Pope Innocent III and the Council of Florence taught that the punishments of Hell are not the same for all souls. Sacred Scripture teaches, and St. Thomas further explains, that the punishments of Hell are a just punishment, and are therefore proportionate to the sins committed. Different persons have committed sins which differ by type and degree. Therefore, it is false to portray the sufferings of Hell as either the same for all souls, or without proportion to the sins committed. This error usually occurs in one of two forms: either Hell is portrayed as a place of extreme suffering for all, or Hell is portrayed as having no suffering for anyone, other than the deprivation of Heaven. Both approaches err by describing the punishments of Hell as if they were the same for all persons, without any just relationship between the sufferings and the mortal sins being punished by those sufferings.

Some souls in Hell suffer only the deprivation of Heaven (but this also implies the suffering of the knowledge of that deprivation). However, other souls suffer additionally, because their greater sins deserve greater punishment. And this teaching is not only of faith, but also of reason. For it would be unreasonable to punish crimes that vary in type and in degree of severity in the same manner and to the same extent. Even the justice system of civil society recognizes the need for different types and degrees of punishment for various offenses.

.550. Another false idea about Hell portrays the sufferings there as uniform, as if they were unchanging. To the contrary, the persons in Hell have will and intellect; and therefore, they have thoughts, which change from one moment to the next. They suffer from the consideration of one sin (or one aspect of a sin) in one moment, and from a consideration of another sin (or aspect of sin) in the next moment. And those souls who suffer additional pains have first one pain, and then a different pain. For the damned in Hell do not have the timeless Eternity of Heaven, but rather are trapped in a type of time, in which one moment of pain follows after another. Their pains are changing and unceasing.

[Psalm 10]
{10:7} He will rain down snares upon sinners. Fire and brimstone and windstorms will be the portion of their cup.
{10:8} For the Lord is just, and he has chosen justice. His countenance has beheld equity.

[Job]
{24:19} May he cross from the snowy waters to excessive heat, and his sin, all the way to hell.

---

[581] Saint Thomas Aquinas, Summa Theologica, I-II, Q. 87, A. 4.

Grace and Salvation

The Summa Theologica, in the Supplement (not written by St. Thomas, but based on his work), cites these verses from Scripture (Ps 10:7; Job 24:19) to teach that the sufferings of Hell change, from fire to ice, and back to fire again.[582] Thus, the punishments of Hell are not only different from one person to another, but also vary from one moment to the next for each person.

Another false idea about Hell, often found in secular descriptions of Hell, is the portrayal of Satan and his fallen angels as either in charge of Hell, or in charge of dispensing punishments to the souls there. Neither claim is true. In the parable of the Just King, our Lord said: "Depart from me, you accursed ones, into the eternal fire, which was prepared for the devil and his angels." (Mt 25:41). God prepared Hellfire to punish both the fallen angels and human persons who die unrepentant from actual mortal sin. God created all that exists; only God is uncreated. Hell exists. Therefore, God also created Hell.

.551. In one sense, God is not present in Hell; for no one in Hell has the Beatific Vision of God. But in another sense, God is present in Hell. For the knowledge and power and essence of God is everywhere without limits. God holds all things in existence: "in him all things continue." (Colossians 1:17). God is present to all creation: " 'For in him we live, and move, and exist.' " (Acts 17:28). All things are subject to Christ (Philippians 3:21), and this must include Hell. God created Hell as a place of just punishment (Mt 15:41). And no one but God could dispense the perfectly just, perfectly merciful, and perfectly fitting punishments of Hell. But in order to punish in Hell, God must be present in Hell. Therefore, God is even present in Hell.

Hell is like a prison, in which the most severe crimes, unrepentant actual mortal sins, are punished. But the fallen angels are not like wardens or prison guards; they are prisoners. Hell was originally created to punish the fallen angels (Mt 25:41); and that purpose still remains. The fallen angels in Hell have no power to punish anyone. The denizens of Hell are punished by God, some indirectly, by deprivation, and others both indirectly and directly, by the additional pains that are inflicted. For God is both a just judge and a just avenger.

"The Lord judges the people....
"God is a just judge, strong and patient." (Psalm 7:9, 12).

"For the Lord, the powerful revenger, will certainly repay." (Jer 51:56).

"And the Lord said to me.... 'But against anyone who is not willing to listen to his words, which he will speak in my name, I will stand forth as the avenger.' " (Deut 18:17, 19).

.552. Another common false idea about Hell portrays the fallen angels and the souls in Hell as continuing to commit one mortal sin after another. Even some Saints have described visions of Hell that portray the souls there as continually uttering blasphemies. But this type of vision must be interpreted as a figure. The sin of final impenitence is called blasphemy against the Holy Spirit. All the souls

---

[582] Saint Thomas Aquinas, Summa Theologica, Suppl. Q. 97, A. 1.

in Hell have committed this type of blasphemy. For no matter what their sins were in life, if they had repented before death, they would not be in Hell. These souls do not continue to blaspheme against God forever. Rather, they forever suffer punishment for their blasphemy against the Spirit. For they are in Hell because they refused to cooperate with grace from the Holy Spirit so as to repent from actual mortal sin.

It is not possible for the devils and souls in Hell to continue sinning in that place, for several reasons. First, it would be contrary to the infinite justice of God if He permitted the innumerable persons in Hell to continue committing innumerable grave sins every moment unceasingly forever. Second, it would be impossible to punish such sins, since every moment would add ever more grave sins, and the sinning would not cease forever. Third, if the devils and souls in Hell continue to sin, and if they are then given additional punishments in Hell for the grave sins committed in Hell, then their sufferings in Hell would continually increase. But Hell continues forever. So the sufferings of all persons in Hell would increase to an extreme degree, and would continue to increase without limit. But a punishment that increases forever without limit is contrary to justice.

Fourth, the Magisterium teaches that some souls in Hell suffer only the punishment of deprivation of Heaven (and the knowledge, from the particular judgment, as to why they are so deprived). But if the souls in Hell are permitted by God to sin, they would certainly all commit grave sins continually. For they all completely lack both sanctifying grace and actual grace. But then the souls that suffer only the deprivation of Heaven would commit sins that require further punishment. Then either they would not be punished, which is contrary to justice, or they would be punished with active punishments, which is contrary to the teaching that some souls suffer only the punishment of deprivation. So for all of these reasons, it is clear that the devils and the souls in Hell are entirely prevented by God from sinning any more.

.553. Another error is the idea that the damned in Hell suffer punishment only for their unrepented actual mortal sins. There are two types of punishment required by the Justice of God, eternal punishment for unrepented actual mortal sin, and temporal punishment for all other sin. The souls in Hell suffer eternal punishment for their unrepented actual mortal sins. But the Justice of God also requires that they suffer any unremitted punishment due for actual mortal sins from which they repented in life, and for venial sins. This temporal punishment occurs when the person is first sent to Hell, along side the punishment for unrepented actual mortal sin. Once the temporal punishment is remitted, only the eternal punishment continues, forever.

Justice requires temporal punishment for actual venial sins, repented or unrepented, if insufficient suffering and penance was completed in life. Justice also requires temporal punishment for repented actual mortal sin. This requirement even applies to those who are destined for Heaven, so much so that God created a separate place, Purgatory, to meet this requirement. Therefore, the same requirement applies to the damned. They too must remit the temporal punishment due for actual venial sin, and for repented actual mortal sin, to whatever extent that punishment was not remitted sufficiently in life. And this temporal punishment takes place in Hell (for only holy souls are admitted to Purgatory). But once this punishment is remitted, it ends. Then only the eternal punishment due for unrepented actual mortal sin continues forever.

Ss. Augustine and Aquinas: "God is truly and absolutely simple."[583]

Yet another common error holds that Hell is of the Justice of God, but not of His Mercy. This claim is certainly false, because God is truly and absolutely simple. All that God is and does is One. God is not divided so that He is part mercy, part Justice, part Love, etc. Neither are the acts of God divided so that some acts are merciful, but other acts are just, and other acts are loving. God is not merely loving; He is Love. God is not merely merciful; He is Mercy. God is not merely just; He is Justice. And the love and mercy and justice that is God is One. In God, love is mercy is justice. Therefore, it is not possible for any of His acts to be without love and justice and mercy (and all that is God). For the acts of God are one with His Nature, and His Nature is truly and absolutely simple. Therefore, an act of God's justice is an act of His mercy is an act of His love, even in Hell.

The fallen angels and damned souls are in Hell because God is Just. But they are also there because God is Mercy, and is Love. Infinite Love could never permit the devils and sinful souls to remain among the community of believers. Infinite Justice requires that these fallen angels and sinful souls be given the punishment that fits their sins. And infinite Mercy punishes their sins less than they truly deserve. For they have sinned against God who is infinitely Good, yet he tempers His punishment of them. Yes, God not only tempers the just punishments that He dispenses in this life, and in Purgatory, He also tempers the just punishments that He dispenses in Hell. Although their punishment is unending, the type and degree of punishment is less than their sins deserve.

.554. One of the more grievous errors about Hell is the claim that Hell might perhaps be empty. To the contrary, very many serious sins are committed throughout the world, by countless persons, and often without any sign of repentance prior to death. Now while some of these persons might have repented, and some might have had a reduction in culpability, it is unreasonable to conclude that they all died in a state of grace. Furthermore, Sacred Scripture clearly teaches that Hell is not empty:

[Luke]
{10:15} And as for you, Capernaum, who would be exalted even up to Heaven: you shall be submerged into Hell.

Capernaum symbolizes the sins of apostasy prevalent in that place. Jesus states unequivocally that these persons will be sent to Hell. He uses the figure of a populous and sinful town to show that the number sent to Hell is not small.

---

[583] Saint Thomas Aquinas, Summa Theologica, I, Q. 3, A. 7. "On the contrary, Augustine says (De Trin. iv, 6,7): 'God is truly and absolutely simple.' I answer that, the absolute simplicity of God may be shown in many ways."

{12:5} But I will reveal to you whom you should fear. Fear him who, after he will have killed, has the power to cast into Hell. So I say to you: Fear him.

If Hell were empty, then there would be no reason to fear being cast into Hell by God. Many souls are sent to Hell to be punished forever, and so, in the grace of God, exercising both faith and reason, we should fear Hell.

{16:22} Then it happened that the beggar died, and he was carried by the Angels into the bosom of Abraham. Now the wealthy man also died, and he was entombed in Hell.

Again, Jesus speaks unequivocally of some persons being sent to Hell. And by this story Jesus warns other persons not to commit the same sins, and be sent to the same place. But if Hell were empty, such a warning would be needless.

[Matthew]
{5:20} For I say to you, that unless your justice has surpassed that of the scribes and the Pharisees you shall not enter into the kingdom of heaven.

Jesus implies that many of the scribes and Pharisees have not entered the kingdom of heaven, and that therefore they were sent to Hell.

{7:13} Enter through the narrow gate. For wide is the gate, and broad is the way, which leads to perdition, and many there are who enter through it.
{7:14} How narrow is the gate, and how straight is the way, which leads to life, and few there are who find it!

Jesus taught that the way to perdition (meaning Hell) is wide, and that many persons follow that path. If Hell were empty, then this teaching would be false. There are also many passages in the Old Testament referring to Hell, and plainly stating that there are souls in Hell. Therefore, the claim that Hell does not exist, or that it exists but it is empty or it may be empty, is false and heretical.

.555. Yet another grievous and heretical error is the claim that no one is sent to Hell by God, that after death each person chooses whether he will go to Heaven or to Hell. This claim is contradicted by the teaching of Sacred Scripture.

"And when the hearts of the sons of men are filled with malice and contempt in their lives, afterwards they shall be dragged down to hell." (Ecclesiastes 9:3).

Now if anyone is dragged down to Hell, then he did not go there of his own free will; he was sent to Hell against his wishes. Therefore, the damned in Hell did not literally send themselves to Hell, nor did they literally decide, after death, to go to Hell. In a sense, they decided to go to Hell by deciding to commit actual mortal sin and by deciding not to repent. In a sense, they sent themselves to Hell by the way that they lived their lives. And at the particular judgment, each soul realizes and cannot deny the truth as to whether he belongs in Hell, or in Purgatory, or in Heaven. But it would be a serious doctrinal error to claim that God does not have the role of a Just Judge, who judges each soul after death, and who sends each soul to its proper destination.

And about the punishment of Hell, our Lord said: "Then, whoever will have called him, 'Worthless,' shall be liable to the fires of Hell." (Mt 5:22).

But whoever is liable to something is judged, and perhaps found guilty, and then his punishment is not of his own choosing. For though he chose the act that resulted in judgment and conviction, he does not choose his punishment.

And our Lord also said: "And if your right eye causes you to sin, root it out and cast it away from you. For it is better for you that one of your members perish, than that your whole body be cast into Hell." (Mt 5:29).

The soul of a person is "cast into Hell" because of his sins; therefore, he does not go into Hell willingly. And Jesus says "your whole body," even though the soul alone is sent to Hell, because, after the Resurrection, the damned in Hell have body and soul united, and they suffer in body and soul.

Jesus also said: "And do not be afraid of those who kill the body, but are not able to kill the soul. But instead fear him who is able to destroy both soul and body in Hell." (Mt 10:28).

If a person only goes to Hell by his own choosing, then he would have no need to fear Hell. But Jesus taught that sinners should be afraid of being destroyed in Hell, in both body and soul. For though the sinner can decided to avoid sin, and so avoid Hell, if he commits actual mortal sin and does not repent, then after death he has no further choice; he will be sent to Hell.

The teaching of the Magisterium also refutes the claim that persons who die are able, after death, to choose whether or not they go to Hell.

Pope Benedict XII: "By this Constitution which is to remain in force for ever, we, with apostolic authority, define the following.... Moreover, we define that according to the general disposition of God, the souls of those who die in actual mortal sin go down into hell immediately after death and there suffer the pain of hell."

Council of Florence: "But the souls of those who depart this life in actual mortal sin, or in original sin alone, go down straightaway to hell to be punished, but with unequal pains."

Therefore, the claim is false and heretical which says that, after death, a person chooses whether he will go to Heaven or to Hell. Instead, it is the choices that a person makes in this life, especially those pertaining to sanctifying grace and actual mortal sin, which result in the person either dying in a state of grace, and being sent to Heaven (perhaps by way of Purgatory), or dying in a state of actual mortal sin and being sent to Hell.

.556. Did Jesus literally descend to Hell?

The Apostles' Creed states, "descendit ad inferna," meaning, "he descended to hell." Although modern forms of this Creed have changed the wording to "he descended to the dead," the Latin form of this Creed has been accepted and used for many centuries. The Latin 'inferna' refers to Hell, since it literally means 'a lower place.' Furthermore, the word 'descended' also implies a lower place. But Purgatory is close to Heaven, and therefore is not accurately referred to as a lower place to which one descends. Therefore, Jesus did, in some sense, descend to Hell.

Saint Thomas Aquinas asks the question: "Whether Christ went down into the hell of the lost?" He then uses the word 'hell' in two senses: the hell of the lost, by which he means Hell, and also Purgatory.

Saint Thomas Aquinas: "I answer that, A thing is said to be in a place in two ways. First of all, through its effect, and in this way Christ descended into each of the hells, but in different manner. For going down into the hell of the lost He wrought this effect, that by descending thither He put them to shame for their unbelief and wickedness: but to them who were detained in Purgatory He gave hope of attaining to glory...."[584]

Next, Saint Thomas says that Jesus visited the souls in Purgatory "interiorly by grace," but he did not visit the souls in Hell in this same manner. So Jesus did visit both Hell and Purgatory, in His soul, after His death, but in different ways. We might distinguish between these two types of visits by saying that the soul of Jesus went into Purgatory, but went only to the gates of Hell. For He was present to the souls in Purgatory by the close union of grace. But to the souls in Hell, He was only present in that they knew what they had lost, and in that they were compelled by truth to acknowledge that Jesus is Lord. He was present in Hell by His power, but not by His grace, since the damned there lack all grace.

Jesus descended to the gates of Hell for several reasons. First, He went so as to make himself known, in a limited manner, to the souls there, so that they would know what they had lost. Second, He went "so that, at the name of Jesus, every knee would bend, of those in heaven, of those on earth, and of those in hell, and so that every tongue would confess that the Lord Jesus Christ is in the glory of God the Father." (Philippians 2:10-11; cf. Romans 14:11) For even the fallen angels and the damned souls in Hell know and admit that Jesus is the Son of God Incarnate, and that they each sinned against Him by their own free will. Third, He went so that He would "hold the keys of death and of Hell." (Rev 1:18). Fourth, He went in order to exercise His power, so that the gates of Hell could never prevail over the Church (Mt 16:18), and so that He could break "the sorrows of Hell" (Acts 2:24). For Jesus is Lord of Heaven and earth, and He is even Lord over Hell, in that Hell is a place of just punishment for those who rejected Christ by means of unrepentant actual mortal sin.

Hell is a place created by God, where the devils and the damned are punished by God. God is not present in Hell as He is present in Heaven, in the sense of the Beatific Vision. But God is present in Hell by His unlimited knowledge, and by His power to punish, and because He is present everywhere. And Jesus is God. Therefore, we must hold that Jesus is present in Hell, by His Divine Nature. And so that even the damned in Hell would know that Jesus, the Son of God, became Incarnate, lived, taught, and even died, in order to offer salvation to all -- an offer

---

[584] Saint Thomas Aquinas, Summa Theologica, III, Q. 52, A. 2.

that the damned rejected -- the human soul of Jesus went to the gates of Hell, after His death, though without any detriment to Himself. For He went to Hell not as a prisoner, but as Lord of all Creation, including Hell. For Hell is the domain of the Justice of God. And Jesus is God.

Blessed Anne Catherine Emmerich, in the book *The Dolorous Passion of Our Lord Jesus Christ*, describes the descent of Jesus to Hell, based on a vision she received from God. Although the visions of Blesseds and Saints are not a source of definitive teaching, her description of the descent is in accord with Scripture and the teaching of the Church, and is accepted by many of the faithful.

"I saw our Saviour perform many other actions.... Finally, I beheld him approach to the centre of the great abyss, that is to say, to Hell itself; and the expression of his countenance was most severe.... when the gates of Hell were thrown open by the angels ... our Lord spoke first to the soul of Judas, and the angels then compelled all the demons to acknowledge and adore Jesus. They would have infinitely preferred the most frightful torments to such a humiliation; but all were obliged to submit."[585]

.557. Did Jesus visit Purgatory?

[1 Peter]
{3:18} For Christ also died once for our sins, the Just One on behalf of the unjust, so that he might offer us to God, having died, certainly, in the flesh, but having been enlivened by the Spirit.
{3:19} And in the Spirit, he preached to those who were in prison, going to those souls
{3:20} who had been unbelieving in past times, while they waited for the patience of God, as in the days of Noah, when the ark was being built. In that ark, a few, that is, eight souls, were saved by water.

After His death, Jesus made Himself and His Gospel known to the souls in prison, that is, in Purgatory. For no one enters Heaven except through Christ. These souls were waiting patiently in Purgatory, after having completed any temporal punishment that was due for sin, because Jesus had to die on the Cross in order to open the gates of Heaven. Some of these souls had been unbelieving in past times, but they were saved by an implicit Baptism of desire (for formal Baptism, and even the explicit desire for it, were not available before Christ).

.558. Purgatory

Those souls who die in a state of grace receive eternal life in Heaven, no matter how many unrepentant actual venial sins they have on their consciences, and no matter how much temporal punishment for the sins of their life is still owed. But how can a soul with unrepented actual venial sins on the conscience, and with unremitted temporal punishment, immediately enter into Heaven? Or how can a soul that does not know Jesus Christ enter into Heaven? In Purgatory, the soul

---

[585] Blessed Anne Catherine Emmerich, The Dolorous Passion of Our Lord Jesus Christ, Chapter LIX, 'A Detached Account of the Descent into Hell.'

that dies in a state of sanctifying grace, but in need of further purification (from venial sin and from temporal punishment), is given all that is needed in order to become pure and holy, and ready to be received into eternal happiness.

The souls in Purgatory know that they are saved; they know that they will eventually have eternal life in Heaven. They suffer for their sins, but they suffer willingly, in cooperation with grace. None of the souls in Purgatory are able to sin any more. They no longer have concupiscence, which is of the body. And they died in a state of sanctifying grace, so their souls are holy. Although they have free will, by the grace of God they no longer sin.

[Matthew]
{5:25} "Be reconciled with your adversary quickly, while you are still on the way with him, lest perhaps the adversary may hand you over to the judge, and the judge may hand you over to the officer, and you will be thrown in prison.
{5:26} Amen I say to you, that you shall not go forth from there, until you have repaid the last quarter."

[Hebrews]
{13:3} Remember those who are prisoners, just as if you were imprisoned with them, and those who endure hardships, just as if you were in their place.

Immediately after death, every soul is judged by God; this is called the particular judgment. Everyone who dies in a state of unrepentant actual mortal sin, and therefore not in a state of grace, will be punished forever in Hell. Everyone who dies in a state of sanctifying grace will be rewarded forever in Heaven. There are only two final destinations, Heaven and Hell. However, many souls arrive in Heaven only after a temporary stay in Purgatory. Dying in a state of grace necessarily implies that the person did not have any unrepentant actual mortal sins on his conscience at the time of death. But a person might have unrepentant venial sins, and also unremitted temporal punishment due for past sins.

Every sin deserves punishment. Temporal punishment can be satisfied in a limited period of time, either in this life or in Purgatory. Eternal punishment can only be satisfied by eternal Hellfire. Every actual mortal sin deserves eternal punishment. But when a sinner repents and is forgiven for an actual mortal sin, the punishment is reduced from eternal punishment to temporal punishment. All other sins, every sin other than actual mortal sin, deserves only temporal punishment. If an objective mortal sin is reduced in culpability to an actual venial sin, due to less than full knowledge or less than full consent, then the punishment that is deserved is temporal punishment. All venial sins deserve only temporal punishment.

Every person who dies in a state of unrepentant actual mortal sin is sent to Hell forever to suffer the eternal punishment due for his sin. Every Christian who dies in a state of grace, with no unforgiven sins on his conscience and no unremitted temporal punishment, goes directly to Heaven. But many persons die in a state of grace, so that they do not deserve eternal punishment, but with unrepented venial sins or unremitted temporal punishment on their conscience. These persons will have eternal life, because they died in a state of grace. But they must repent of any venial sins still on their conscience. And they must suffer any temporal punishment still due for their sins. When a sin is forgiven by God, the temporal punishment due for that sin must still be satisfied. This remission of the punishment due occurs in this life by penance. Penance is cooperation with grace in enduring suffering, and in works of prayer, self-denial, and mercy. But if a repentant sinner has not done sufficient penance for his sins, he completes this penance by enduring suffering and by praying in Purgatory.

The souls in Purgatory suffer punishment for the sins of their lives, but only for those sins for which they did not suffer or do penance on earth. Some persons have suffered little in this life, and have done little penance in the form of prayer, self-denial, and works of mercy. Souls such as these spend a long time in Purgatory. Time in Purgatory is not the same as time on earth. However, there is a type of passing of time in Purgatory, not based on the change from one day to the next, or from one year to the next, but based on the changes in the soul of each person. A soul who enters Purgatory needing much change in order to be fit for Heaven spends what seems to that soul like a long time there. A soul needing less change, spends less time there.

[Matthew]
{18:34} And his lord, being angry, handed him over to the torturers, until he repaid the entire debt.

.559. The sufferings of Purgatory are very severe; much greater than any bodily sufferings here on earth. Our Lord even describes these sufferings as torture. For the sufferings of Purgatory are of the soul, and the soul, being greater in power than the body, can also suffer more than the body. The sufferings of the soul are sufferings at the very core of the being of the human person. The light of the particular judgment fully exposes the sins of their lives and the harm done by those sins. And the light of grace given to the souls in Purgatory is a bright light, by which these souls continue to consider their sins and the harm done by those sins. This knowledge and consideration of one's own sins is the main suffering of Purgatory. This type of spiritual suffering is severe, even being fittingly described as torture, because sin is severely contrary to the Goodness of God, and because the harm done by sin is severe.

Immediately after death, at the particular judgment, each soul is shown his or her whole life by God, especially in terms of morality. By the gift of the particular judgment, each person is given the knowledge of his sins and of his holy acts throughout his life. For the souls in Purgatory, this knowledge of sins committed, and of the harm done, including the sin of omitting sufficient penance, becomes the main source of suffering for the soul. Although Purgatory includes sufferings analogous to bodily sufferings, sometimes described as the fires of Purgatory, the most important and most severe suffering is the knowledge that each soul has of his own sins and the harm caused by his sins. The soul realizes that each sinful act was freely chosen despite the knowledge that it was immoral. The soul realizes and regrets both the sin and the harm done by that sin. This type of suffering of the soul is much more severe than the other pains in Purgatory. Sufferings of the soul reach to the innermost depths of the human person. But the sufferings of the soul due to knowledge of one's own sins is a very instructive type of suffering. The soul is not merely suffering, but is learning and changing and becoming holy. And as is often true in this life also, change hurts. These souls are changing for the better, and so they are suffering.

The souls in Purgatory are holy, because they are in a state of grace. And so they have love, faith, hope, and all the virtues. They know with certainty that they are saved and will eventually enter Heaven. They are suffering due to the sins of their lives, and yet they are consoled by the knowledge of the holy acts of their lives, especially that they died in a state of grace.

The souls in Purgatory who did not know Christ explicitly in this life learn about Christ in Purgatory. The purpose of Purgatory is not only suffering, but also learning. And the souls there not only learn the mistakes of their lives, but also the goodness of Christ, who is the sole source of salvation, and whom they offended by their many sins. Those souls who died in a state of grace, but without knowing Christ, including those who died before Christ, those who died after Christ but without hearing of Him, and those who heard of Christ but knew very little of Him, are instructed in Purgatory, so that they will know their Savior. And this instruction is not a punishment, but a blessing and a fitting preparation for eternal life with Christ in Heaven.

The souls in Purgatory do penance by suffering and by prayer, especially prayers for other persons. They cannot merit anything for themselves by their own sufferings and prayers. Their sufferings and prayers are part of the punishment that is justly due to them; it is not meritorious. A person who spends a longer time in Purgatory does not have a greater place in Heaven, as if he had greater merits from greater suffering, but rather a lower place in Heaven, because he did not suffer and do penance in this life. But because these souls are part of the Communion of Saints, their prayers can benefit us on earth, and our prayers can benefit their souls.

When each soul has completed repenting from all venial sins, and suffering the temporal punishment still due for sin, and thereby has been changed to become holier and more fit for Heaven, and when each soul has been instructed about Jesus Christ, the Savior of all, then the soul leaves Purgatory and enters eternal life in Heaven. Every soul in Purgatory will eventually, sooner or later, have eternal life in Heaven. The souls in Purgatory all died in a state of sanctifying grace, and they all remain in a state of sanctifying grace in Purgatory. None of the souls in Purgatory can sin at all, neither by mortal sin, nor by venial sin. Hence, these souls are called the holy souls of Purgatory. For they have sanctifying grace, and they are without sin.

.560. Dying in a State of Grace

[Matthew]
{22:11} Then the king entered to see the guests. And he saw a man there who was not clothed in a wedding garment.
{22:12} And he said to him, 'Friend, how is it that you have entered here without having a wedding garment?' But he was dumbstruck.

{22:13} Then the king said to the ministers: 'Bind his hands and feet, and cast him into the outer darkness, where there will be weeping and gnashing of teeth. {22:14} For many are called, but few are chosen.' "

The kingdom of Heaven is like a wedding feast. For Christ is the groom and the Church is His bride. And the state of sanctifying grace is like a wedding garment for the soul. Everyone who dies without the state of grace will be cast by God into the outer darkness of Hell, where those who tried to be good but failed will weep, and where those who tried to be evil and succeeded will gnash their teeth.

Baptism, either formal or non-formal, grants the state of sanctifying grace. If any person obtains Baptism, and later loses that state of grace by actual mortal sin, and does not repent before death, then that person is judged by God immediately after death, and is sent to Hell. If any person obtains Baptism and dies in a state of grace, no matter how many actual mortal sins he committed, as long as he repented from all actual mortal sins, then that person is judged by God immediately after death, and is sent to Heaven, perhaps by way of Purgatory.

Suppose that an adult never commits any actual mortal sins, but he also never obtains a formal or non-formal Baptism. He dies without the state of grace, and is judged by God immediately after death. In this case, though it may seem as if he has never committed any actual mortal sins, and therefore would not deserve Hell, he has in truth committed an actual mortal sin. He has committed the actual mortal sin of omission of never finding even an implicit Baptism of desire in his life. He had prevenient grace many times in his life, but he never freely chose to cooperate fully with actual grace in even a single selfless act of love for God or neighbor. He lived a thoroughly selfish life, and even though he might have seemed to other persons to be a good person, he has sinned gravely by refusing to love selflessly. His actual mortal sin of omission, from which he never repented, is the reason that he will be sent to Hell forever.

Whoever dies with the wedding garment of the state of sanctifying grace will have eternal life in Heaven. Whoever dies without the wedding garment of the state of sanctifying grace will have eternal death in Hell, where there will be weeping and gnashing of teeth. There are no exceptions to this moral truth.

.561. The Communion of the Saints

[Ephesians]
{2:13} But now, in Christ Jesus, you, who were in times past far away, have been brought near by the blood of Christ....
{2:18} For by him, we both have access, in the one Spirit, to the Father.
{2:19} Now, therefore, you are no longer visitors and new arrivals. Instead, you are citizens among the saints in the household of God,
{2:20} having been built upon the foundation of the Apostles and of the Prophets, with Jesus Christ himself as the preeminent cornerstone.
{2:21} In him, all that has been built is framed together, rising up into a holy temple in the Lord.
{2:22} In him, you also have been built together into a habitation of God in the Spirit.

By the sacrifice of Christ on the Cross, in sanctifying grace, we have been joined together in the Holy Spirit as one household of God, as one foundation of the Church, as one holy temple in the Lord, as one habitation of God in the Spirit. This union of all the faithful, of all those who are in a state of grace, is called the communion of the saints.

All those who are in a state of grace are called saints because they are truly holy. Although only the holiest among the faithful are called Saints in the sense of canonized Saints, all persons who are in a state of sanctifying grace are saints (with a small letter 's') also. For sanctifying grace causes us to be holy. And since it is the continued presence of the Holy Spirit that effects this grace and holiness, all those in a state of grace are one Body of Christ in the Spirit.

[Ephesians]
{4:3} Be anxious to preserve the unity of the Spirit within the bonds of peace.
{4:4} One body and one Spirit: to this you have been called by the one hope of your calling:
{4:5} one Lord, one faith, one baptism,
{4:6} one God and Father of all, who is over all, and through all, and in us all.

All those who are in a state of grace, on earth, in Purgatory, and in Heaven, are united to God in a holy and pure love, and are also united to one another in love. This love is no mere human affection, but the true selfless spiritual love that is only possible by the grace of God. This union is a type of community, closer than any mere human relationship of family or friends. And all the members of this communion of love contribute to, and benefit from, the prayers, holy sufferings, and works of mercy of each other. If you have any need, you can rely on your fellow members of the Body of Christ to assist you by this mystical union of all who are in a state of grace.

The souls in Purgatory are in particular need of our prayers and merits through the communion of saints. These souls cannot merit anything for themselves; their sufferings are a just recompense for their sins. When any of the faithful suffer in this life, some of that suffering is temporal punishment for sin (if any temporal punishment remains unremitted at that time). But the rest of the suffering is meritorious, and is of benefit to the communion of the saints, to souls in this life and in Purgatory. When any of the faithful in this life pray or perform works of mercy, these acts are a penance for any temporal punishment due for past sins. But if no further temporal punishment is due, then these acts contribute to the merits available to the communion of the saints.

The souls in Purgatory participate in the communion of the saints by their prayers for us, and by our prayers, sufferings, and works of mercy offered to God for their benefit. Our prayers for our fellow saints, both those in this life and those in Purgatory, are made more effective by our sufferings, acts of self-denial, and works of mercy. Our prayers are made more effective by being part of the communion of the saints. But what is the ultimate source of this effectiveness and of all these merits?

The communion of the saints is the Body of Christ, with Christ as its Head, and the Spirit as its Life. Our holy acts are meritorious only when we cooperate with the graces of the Holy Spirit, and only because Christ first merited all grace for us on the Cross. We merit nothing that Christ did not first merit for us. All of our merits are secondary to, and entirely dependent upon, His merits.

.562. The Treasury of Merits

[Acts]
{2:42} Now they were persevering in the doctrine of the Apostles, and in the communion of the breaking of the bread, and in the prayers.
{2:43} And fear developed in every soul. Also, many miracles and signs were accomplished by the Apostles in Jerusalem. And there was a great awe in everyone.
{2:44} And then all who believed were together, and they held all things in common.
{2:45} They were selling their possessions and belongings, and dividing them to all, just as any of them had need.
{2:46} Also, they continued, daily, to be of one accord in the temple and to break bread among the houses; and they took their meals with exultation and simplicity of heart,
{2:47} praising God greatly, and holding favor with all the people. And every day, the Lord increased those who were being saved among them.

After the Ascension of Christ, the faithful held all things in common, and they distributed from those who had more, to those who had less. This practice was a figure of the communion of the saints. All of the merits of the members of the communion of the saints are like a single treasury, to which all contribute who are able, and from which all draw who have need. There are three types of members of this communion:

1. The angels and souls in Heaven, who contributed to the treasury of by the holy acts of their lives, but who no longer need to receive merits.
2. The souls in Purgatory, who draw from, but can no longer contribute to, the treasury of merits.
3. All persons in this life who are in a state of grace, who can both contribute to, and draw from, the treasury of merits.

Those in need of merits draw from this treasury of merits. Those who merit more than they need contribute to this treasury of merits. From this treasury, the Church Herself both contributes and draws merits, applying them to all those who are in spiritual need. Even those sinners who are not in a state of grace can benefit from the treasury of merits, since they receive actual grace, and may cooperate with actual grace, and are under the Providence of God. Merits are applied by means of grace, providence, and even miracles. All merits are from Christ on the Cross, and so all grace, all providence, and all miracles are from Christ on the Cross. Persons who are not in a state of grace benefit from our merits by grace and providence, and especially by being led to the state of grace. All this occurs due to the merits of Christ on the Cross. But our merits also participate in the redemptory merits of Christ. Jesus Christ is the sole Redeemer, without whom no one would be redeemed. But the entire communion of saints participates in His salvific work through the merits of our prayers, sufferings, and works of mercy, in so far as these occur in cooperation with grace.

.563. The merits from this treasury are obtained, for ourselves and for other souls, by our prayers, sufferings, acts of self-denial, works of mercy, and by participation in the Sacraments and worship of the Church. But the Church Herself can apply these merits, not only by the aforementioned means, but also by a special means called an indulgence. The Church has the authority to forgive sins, and to forgive the punishment due for sin. When the Church draws on the treasury of merits of all the saints and applies those merits in order to forgive the punishment due for repented forgiven sins, this application is called an indulgence. In this way, the merits of Christ on the Cross are applied by His Body, the Church, in order to forgive the punishment due for sin.

This application of the merits of the Church through an indulgence requires cooperation with grace on the part of the penitent, as well as certain works, such as certain prayers, or prayer for certain intentions, or almsgiving, or a pilgrimage to a particular location, or other good works. If a person performs all the works required by the indulgence, but if he is not repentant from the sin that deserves the punishment, or if he did not perform these acts in cooperation with grace, then no remission of the punishment occurs; the indulgence is ineffective.

Pope Paul VI: "An indulgence is the remission before God of the temporal punishment due sins already forgiven as far as their guilt is concerned, which the follower of Christ with the proper dispositions and under certain determined conditions acquires through the intervention of the Church which, as minister of the Redemption, authoritatively dispenses and applies the treasury of the satisfaction won by Christ and the saints."[586]

All indulgences are merely a particular formal means of obtaining merits from the Church's treasury of merits. And these same merits are able to be obtained by other means. Once forgiveness from sin is obtained, any penitent may obtain the remission of the temporal punishment due for sin, in whole or in part, by the Sacraments, by prayer, self-denial, and works of mercy, done in cooperation with grace, at any time, in innumerable different ways. The fruits of an indulgence may be obtained without an indulgence. The benefit of using an indulgence to obtain the remission of punishment more easily, by the assistance of our brothers and sisters in the state of grace.

When we are forgiven for our sins in Confession, the Sacrament itself also forgives some, at times all, of the temporal punishment due for sin. But since we cannot know with certitude if all the temporal punishment due has been remitted, we do penance after Confession in order to pay the debt of the punishment due. Penance can include any sincere acts of prayer, or self-denial, or works of mercy. And since we are all members of the communion of the saints, when we do penance, we also benefit from their penances, and they also benefit from our penances. For the faithful contribute to the treasury of the merits of the saints,

---

[586] Pope Paul VI, Indulgentiarum Doctrina, n. 1.

and the faithful draw from that same treasury. Indulgences are merely particular forms of performing penance, thereby drawing from that treasury, which was established by the merits of Christ on the Cross.

A plenary ('full') indulgence remits all temporal punishment due. A partial indulgence remits a portion of the temporal punishment due. However, if little temporal punishment remains, even a partial indulgence can remit all remaining temporal punishment. There are numerous ways to obtain indulgences. And from time to time the temporal authority of the Church offers a new indulgence, or retires a former indulgence. The Church received this ability from Christ.

[John]
{20:21} Therefore, he said to them again: "Peace to you. As the Father has sent me, so I send you."
{20:22} When he had said this, he breathed on them. And he said to them: "Receive the Holy Spirit.
{20:23} Those whose sins you shall forgive, they are forgiven them, and those whose sins you shall retain, they are retained."

The Church has the ability and the authority to forgive sin and the punishment due for sin. Therefore, the Church has the authority to issue indulgences, and to require certain conditions to obtain those indulgences, as a means of forgiving the punishment due for sin.

Pope Paul VI: "To acquire a plenary indulgence it is necessary to perform the work to which the indulgence is attached and to fulfill three conditions: sacramental confession, Eucharistic Communion and prayer for the intentions of the Supreme Pontiff. It is further required that all attachment to sin, even to venial sin, be absent."[587]

These four acts: 1) Confession, 2) Communion, 3) prayers for the Pope, and 4) performance of the work (e.g. prayer, self-denial, kind deeds) should be carried out either all on the same day, or within a few days. However, for a just reason, a person may extend this length of time as necessary. The requirement that the person be detached from even venial sin does not imply that the person must have a high degree of holiness in order to obtain a plenary indulgence. Freedom from attachment to sin does not require the sinner to be free from all venial sin. The sinner need only be repentant from all sin, even venial sin, and be resolved to try to avoid all sin. This full contrition is within the reach of every sinner, and is required for a full indulgence. Otherwise, an attempted plenary indulgence will remit only some of the punishment due for sin.

.564. The Rewards of Heaven

The Council of Florence: "Also, [1] the souls of those who have incurred no stain of sin whatsoever after baptism, as well as souls who after incurring the stain of sin have been cleansed whether [2] in their bodies or [3] outside their bodies, as was stated above, are straightaway received into heaven and clearly

---

[587] Pope Paul VI, Indulgentiarum Doctrina, n. 7.

behold the triune God as he is, yet one person more perfectly than another according to the difference of their merits."[588]

[1] If a person is baptized as an infant, and dies before reaching an age when he is able to sin (by the use of reason in knowingly chosen acts), then he incurs no stain of sin after baptism, and he is sent to Heaven. [2] If a person is baptized and subsequently sins, but is entirely cleansed of that sin in this life ('in their bodies') by contrition, Confession, and satisfaction, then he is sent to Heaven when he dies. [3] If a person is baptized and subsequently sins, and he is cleansed of that sin, in this life at least by repenting and being forgiven for any actual mortal sins, and yet he dies with unrepented actual venial sins or unremitted temporal punishment on his conscience, then he is sent to Heaven after being cleansed in Purgatory ('outside their bodies').

But all those persons and only those persons who die unrepentant from actual mortal sin are sent to Hell after death. Although the Council of Florence also taught that persons who die in a state of original sin only are sent to Hell, this should be interpreted to refer only to persons who had ample opportunity in their lives to obtain sanctifying grace, either by a formal or non-formal Baptism, and who committed the actual mortal sin of omission of not obtaining sanctifying grace. Therefore, only persons who die unrepentant from actual mortal sin are sent to Hell. And since there is no possibility of repentance from actual mortal sin after death, all persons who die unrepentant from actual mortal sin are certainly sent to Hell, after the particular judgment.

Those souls who are sent to Heaven "clearly behold the triune God as he is." They have the Beatific Vision of God, which is threefold. First, the intellect directly knows God, with absolute certainty. God is infinite, and the created intellect is finite, therefore this knowledge is limited. The intellect knows God to the fullest possible extent, given its own natural ability combined with the gift of grace. This extent is greater than what the intellect can naturally obtain on its own, but is nevertheless a finite knowledge of the infinite God.

Second, the free will is united to God by a true profound selfless spiritual love. Again, the extent of this love is limited, since the created person is finite. But the extent of the love reaches to the fullest possible extent, given the soul's own natural ability combined with the gift of grace. The extent of this love is greater than what the person could naturally possess in this life, but is nevertheless a finite love of the infinite God. The will remains free, but can no longer choose sin. The light of God makes the darkness of sin impossible for all the souls in Heaven.

Third, as a direct result of this knowledge and love, the person is entirely filled with happiness, even beyond the soul's own natural ability. For the gift of supernatural grace extends the rewards of Heaven beyond what is naturally possible, to an extent only possible by a continuous act of God. And every act of God is the presence of God, since God is His acts.

---

[588] Council of Florence, Sixth Session, 6 July 1439.

Thus, the knowledge and love and happiness of Heaven is like a cup overflowing. For the soul has these benefits to an extent greater than naturally possible, due to the fullness of grace continually given in the Beatific Vision. God grants to every soul in Heaven an ability to know, and to love, and to be happy beyond even what a perfect soul could naturally possess. In Heaven, the natural soul is forever filled with the supernatural grace of God.

.565. In Heaven the person is entirely filled with grace, just as the Virgin Mary is entirely filled with grace, just as the human nature of Christ is entirely filled with grace. However, the Council also states, about the benefits of the Beatific Vision of God: "yet one person more perfectly than another according to the difference of their merits." A bucket entirely filled with water, and a thimble entirely filled with water are each entirely filled, but one more so than the other due to the differences in capacity between the two. Similarly, all the souls in Heaven are filled with grace, just as Jesus and Mary are filled with grace, but each to a different measure, according to the capacity obtained by their merits.

Why should the soul have knowledge, love, and happiness each to a different measure? Only God is infinite. And finite created persons are not all the same. The differences between each person result in differences in the benefits of Heaven, both in quantity (so to speak) and quality. Although the Council taught that these differences are due to merit, the meaning is that each person has benefits in Heaven in accord with the way that each person lived his life. Those who cooperated with grace so as to become very holy in this life thereby became persons who were able to love more than other persons. In Heaven, this difference continues. When one Saint is holier than another Saint in this life, that difference continues in Heaven.

[1 Corinthians]
{3:8} Now he who plants, and he who waters, are one. But each shall receive his proper reward, according to his labors.

The meritorious acts of our life are the acts that are knowingly chosen in cooperation with grace. These acts are not merely good in the sense of morally permissible (e.g. eating a meal, going for a walk), but are holy acts. They deserve reward in Heaven. All of our holy acts in this life, from the smallest to the greatest, even those that were applied to satisfy temporal punishment, are rewarded in Heaven. "And whoever shall give, even to one of the least of these, a cup of cold water to drink, solely in the name of a disciple: Amen I say to you, he shall not lose his reward." (Mt 10:42).

But suppose that an infant dies in infancy, after Baptism. What reward does he have? He is a member of the Body of Christ, a member of the household of God, and so he shares in the reward of the whole Body, of the whole household. And the same is true for adults. Our reward in Heaven is partly due to our own merits. But all that we merit is first merited by Christ. And much of the gifts in our life are unmerited gifts from Christ. And so our reward in Heaven is not limited to whatever we merited. We share in the glorious reward that is a free gift from Christ to all who die in a state of grace.

[Romans]
{6:3} Do you not know that those of us who have been baptized in Christ Jesus have been baptized into his death?
...
{8:16} For the Spirit himself renders testimony to our spirit that we are the sons of God.
{8:17} But if we are sons, then we are also heirs: certainly heirs of God, but also co-heirs with Christ, yet in such a way that, if we suffer with him, we shall also be glorified with him.
{8:18} For I consider that the sufferings of this time are not worthy to be compared with that future glory which shall be revealed in us.

All persons who receive sanctifying grace by Baptism (formal or non-formal) are baptized into the death of Jesus. There are purified by the blood of Christ, and so, if they remain in a state of grace until death, they will share in His glory. Therefore, our reward in Heaven is not only due to the merits of this life, but also, much more so, to the merits of Christ. He labored to sow a field, and yet we reap the reward. We gather the fruits of a field that we did not sow.

[John]
{4:36} For he who reaps, receives wages and gathers fruit unto eternal life, so that both he who sows and he who reaps may rejoice together.
{4:37} For in this the word is true: that it is one who sows, and it is another who reaps.
{4:38} I have sent you to reap that for which you did not labor. Others have labored, and you have entered into their labors."

But as for the reward that we each do merit, each created person is unique. The benefits of Heaven are the same type for each person: knowledge, love, happiness. But the quality of knowledge, love, and happiness for each is unique. For the benefits of Heaven are like a finely tailored suit, exactly fitting to the uniqueness of each person. The benefits of Heaven are like a sumptuous meal, prepared by a chef who knows exactly which foods to prepare and how to prepare them for each person. The benefits of Heaven are unique to the individual because of his or her unique qualities as a person, and because part of the happiness of Heaven is found in the particular relationships of family and friends, those that continue in Heaven, which as a set are unique to each person. This uniqueness was developed in this life, and continues in the afterlife.

.566. Love, Faith, and Hope in Heaven

Pope Benedict XII: "Such a vision and enjoyment of the divine essence do away with the acts of faith and hope in these souls, inasmuch as faith and hope are properly theological virtues. And after such intuitive and face-to-face vision and enjoyment has or will have begun for these souls, the same vision and enjoyment has continued and will continue without any interruption and without end until the last Judgment and from then on forever."[589]

---

[589] Pope Benedict XII, On the Beatific Vision of God, Constitution issued in 1336.

Faith is "the substance of things hoped for, the evidence of things not apparent." (Hebrews 11:1). Faith is the choice of the will to adhere to truths presented by the intellect, but not known and understood solely and entirely by the intellect. The intellect has some limited knowledge ("the evidence of things"), which then points to greater truths, beyond what is "apparent," beyond what is known with certainty, beyond what is comprehended in its entirety. The will chooses to adhere to these truths by cooperation with grace, not by reason alone. If anyone believes only what he knows and understands with his own reason, then he does not have the theological virtue of faith. Only when a person chooses, in cooperation with grace, beyond reason, to believe that certain ideas are truths, only then is he exercising the true virtue of faith.

In one sense, when the Beatific Vision begins, faith ends. For the Beatific Vision gives each person direct knowledge and absolute certainty of the truths that formerly were known, partially and imperfectly, by the virtue of faith. But in another sense, faith continues in a higher form. For all the blessed in Heaven are faithful; they are not apostates. They have not lost their faith, but rather it has been transfigured into the true pure direct knowledge of God.

Hope is the anticipation of the enjoyment of things not yet obtained. In this life, by sanctifying grace, we have a hope that is both reasonable and beyond the reach of reason. By this hope, the holy martyrs were able to suffer and die, rather than abandon the Faith, rather than commit even a single mortal sin. By this hope, we place spiritual goods above temporal goods, love of God above love of neighbor, and love of neighbor above love of self.

In one sense, when the Beatific Vision begins, hope ends. For the Beatific Vision gives each person the full enjoyment of God, neighbor, and self, in a type and degree of happiness that formerly was only hoped for. But in another sense, hope continues in a higher form. For all the blessed in Heaven are joyful; they are not in despair. They have not lost their hope, but rather it has been transfigured into the enjoyment of Heaven. They have not lost the ordering of values that is based not only on love, but on faith and hope.

.567. Love

Love is the reason that God created the universe, and the angels, and humanity. Love is the reason that God gave the gift of free will to created persons, even though He knew that they would freely choose to sin. For He also knew that they would freely choose to love. The meaning and purpose of human life is to love, and to be loved, and to love and be loved eternally in Heaven. Love is the requirement and fulfillment of every commandment and of the whole moral law.

Love is the greatest of the virtues. The virtue of love does not end in any sense in Heaven. The virtue of love continues forever in Heaven, in its highest and most perfect form, for all those who die in a state of grace. The state of grace is the state of loving God above all else, and of loving your neighbor as yourself. And this description of the state of grace is also a description of Heaven. In Heaven, all the elect continually fulfill the commandment to love God above all else, and to love your neighbor as yourself.

Our eternal reward is to love God and neighbor, and to be loved by God and neighbor, perfectly and fully, forever. And this eternal love is always entirely full of the grace of God, so that we love not only with our whole human nature, but in the supernatural grace of God, in a manner and to a degree currently unimaginable, far beyond the capability of nature. Our love in Heaven is more than the perfect fulfillment of human nature; by grace it is also supernatural.

Selfless love on earth often includes suffering. Our love in Heaven is even more selfless, and yet is entirely without suffering. The willingness to suffer in this life for God and neighbor is a proof of love and an expression of love. But in Heaven, no proof is needed, and every expression of love for God and neighbor is full and perfect. Our eternal love in Heaven is like the love of Christ as he was dying on the Cross for our eternal salvation. His love obtained our salvation, and this salvation is to love and to be loved forever in Heaven.

Salvation by Crucifixion

The Crucifixion was an act of salvific love. In His human nature, Jesus fulfilled the commandment to love God above all else, and to love your neighbor as yourself, by dying on the Cross. Why should Jesus, who is God, fulfill any commandments? All the commandments are an expression of the Nature of God, who is Love and Mercy and Justice and all that is Good. Jesus was obeying His own Divine Nature when He died out of love for us; he was being true to His Divine Nature, and true to His perfect human nature. Therefore, the commandment to love your neighbor as yourself is also stated, in its fullest and most perfect form: to love as Christ loves. And to love as Christ loves is also a description of our reward in Heaven. Love is the commandment of Christ, and love is our reward in Heaven.

[John]
{13:34} I give you a new commandment: Love one another. Just as I have loved you, so also must you love one another.

This commandment is new, in the sense that, by His Crucifixion, Christ newly reveals the highest form of the eternal commandment of love and its most perfect expression. In the single act of dying on the Cross for our salvation, Jesus Christ reveals the fullness of the love of God for us all, and the fullness of the love of neighbor to which we all are called, and which we all will live in Heaven.

By His Crucifixion, Jesus Christ obtained for us: all grace and all salvation. All salvation is through Christ alone. Even those persons who are not Christians may obtain salvation, but only through Christ and His Church (at least implicitly). If Christ had not died for us on the Cross, we would have neither actual grace, nor sanctifying grace; we would not be able to choose holy deeds, and we would not be holy. If Christ had not died for us on the Cross, we would not love God, and we would not love neighbor, and we would not even truly love ourselves. If Christ had not died for us on the Cross, none of us would be saved, and none of us would have true spiritual love.

The Crucifixion is the love of God. The moral law is the love of God. The Crucifixion is the moral law. The entire moral law is implicit in the single act of Christ dying on the Cross for our salvation.

If you are having difficulty deciding whether or not an act is moral, meditate on the Crucifixion. If you are having difficulty accepting that an act is immoral, meditate on the Crucifixion. A life lived in sincere imitation of the death of Christ is a moral life. Every teaching of the Catholic Church on faith and morals is implicit in the Crucifixion.

"For even if our heart reproaches us, God is greater than our heart, and he knows all things." (1 John 3:20).

"You should not say, 'I sinned, and what grief has befallen me?' For the Most High is a patient recompensor…. You should not delay being converted to the Lord, and you should not set it aside from day to day." (Sirach 5:4, 8)

"Be merciful to me, O God, according to your great mercy. And, according to the plentitude of your compassion, wipe out my iniquity. Wash me once again from my iniquity, and cleanse me from my sin. For I know my iniquity, and my sin is ever before me. Against you only have I sinned, and I have done evil before your eyes. And so, you are justified in your words, and you will prevail when you give judgment." (Psalm 50:3-6)

"Then, to him who has the power to keep you free from sin and to present you, immaculate, with exultation, before the presence of his glory at the advent of our Lord Jesus Christ, to the only God, our Savior, through Jesus Christ our Lord: to him be glory and magnificence, dominion and power, before all ages, and now, and in every age, forever. Amen." (Jude 1:24-25).

God alone is good.

Afterword

.568.
Pope John Paul II, in his encyclical Veritatis Splendor, discusses a grave problem in the Church on the subject of morality. The holy Pontiff wrote this landmark encyclical about the basic principles of morality in order to address a serious problem, which he describes as follows. (My emphasis is added in bold.)

"Today, however, it seems necessary to reflect on the whole of the Church's moral teaching, with the precise goal of recalling certain fundamental truths of Catholic doctrine which, in the present circumstances, risk being distorted or denied. In fact, a new situation has come about **within the Christian community itself**, which has experienced the spread of numerous doubts and objections of a human and psychological, social and cultural, religious and even properly theological nature, with regard to the Church's moral teachings. **It is no longer a matter of limited and occasional dissent, but of an overall and systematic calling into question of traditional moral doctrine**, on the basis of certain anthropological and ethical presuppositions."[590]

Still today, the teaching of the Catholic Church on morality, especially certain fundamental truths of Catholic doctrine, are being distorted, doubted, denied, and rejected by many Catholics. Sometimes their objections use the same approach as secular society, relying on psychological, social, cultural, or merely human (natural) elements in order to argue against Catholic moral teaching. Other times their objections take the form of faulty religious or theological arguments. But this dissent is no longer limited to a few persons, nor to a few points in the application of moral teaching. This dissent has become a widespread and systematic attack on the foundations of Catholic moral teaching, an attack launched from within the Church.

"At the root of these presuppositions is the more or less obvious influence of currents of thought which end by detaching human freedom from its essential and constitutive relationship to truth. Thus **the traditional doctrine regarding the natural law, and the universality and the permanent validity of its precepts, is rejected**; certain of the Church's moral teachings are found simply unacceptable; and the Magisterium itself is considered capable of intervening in matters of morality only in order to 'exhort consciences' and to 'propose values', in the light of which each individual will independently make his or her decisions and life choices."[591]

Part of the reason for this rejection of Catholic teaching, not only on particular points, but in its most basic principles, is the influence of modern society, which teaches false ideas about rights and freedoms. But this error, which has secular society as its source, has been adopted by many Catholic teachers of ethics, who use various arguments, some clever and some absurd, to undermine the universal and unchanging nature of the eternal moral law, and its expression in

---

[590] Pope John Paul II, Veritatis Splendor, n. 4.
[591] Pope John Paul II, Veritatis Splendor, n. 4.

the natural law. The teachings of the Magisterium are sometimes rejected openly, and other times are cleverly reinterpreted so as to arrive at the desired conclusion. In addition, some Catholics simply reject Catholic teaching on morality without any reasoning; the teachings of the Church have become entirely unacceptable to them because they have taken in and made their own the many false ideas of modern society. They are not even willing to consider whether the changing and baseless norms of secular society might be incorrect.

.569.
"In particular, note should be taken of the lack of harmony between the traditional response of the Church and certain theological positions, **encountered even in Seminaries and in Faculties of Theology**, with regard to questions of the greatest importance for the Church and for the life of faith of Christians, as well as for the life of society itself."[592]

Most disturbingly, this problem has put down deep roots in schools of theology, in seminaries, even in those institutions once considered bastions of orthodox thinking. Many theologians, priests, and religious adhere to and promote serious errors on morality. In addition, similar problems are often found in various dioceses, in religious education programs for children, in RCIA and adult continuing education programs, in marriage preparation classes, and in the responses to particular ethical questions given by some priests and religious.

To make matters worse, some lay Catholics misuse the internet by spreading similar errors on ethics even more widely. They use the anonymity of the internet to pretend to teach and to correct on matters of faith and morals, when in fact they are teaching heresy or serious doctrinal error. And while similar errors in the case of priests and theologians are usually limited by a basic understanding theology, some of these lay persons, due to a combination of ignorance and arrogance, have distorted these errors even further, making them more harmful and more absurd. But all false teachers will suffer a strict judgment from God (cf. James 3:1).

As a result, the faithful do not know whom they should believe. If they try to learn from the Magisterium, they have numerous seemingly credible teachers distorting and misinterpreting magisterial teachings, so that grave error is presented as if it were the true teaching and required belief of the Magisterium. If they try to learn from Sacred Tradition and Sacred Scripture, again, they have many teachers distorting and misinterpreting Tradition and Scripture. Even many theologians whose teaching is generally sound have been affected by this problem, and have fallen into serious error on particular points of ethics.

As a result of this widespread problem, many of the faithful have little or no understanding of the basic principles of ethics. If the Magisterium teaches that a particular act is immoral, some will believe it is immoral, and some will not, but even those who believe do not understand why the act is immoral. They are unable to apply the basic principles of ethics to a variety of different acts and circumstances in order to determine what is moral. They make decisions in their

---

[592] Pope John Paul II, Veritatis Splendor, n. 4.

Afterword

lives based on what seems right to them, and based on explicit teachings of the Magisterium about particular acts. But if the Magisterium has not specifically decided a particular question, they are left with only what seems right to them. For they have no understanding of the foundations of morality, because so many different teachers are presenting contrary and incompatible explanations. And without this foundation, they are often unable even to properly interpret and understand the explicit teachings of the Magisterium on particular acts.

.570.
"Given these circumstances, which still exist, I came to the decision…to write an Encyclical with the aim of treating 'more fully and more deeply the issues regarding the very foundations of moral theology', **foundations which are being undermined by certain present day tendencies**."[593]

Veritatis Splendor was published in 1993. But so many years later, the same problems that the holy Pontiff addressed in that encyclical are still prevalent in the Church. This book, the Catechism of Catholic Ethics, was written to address the same problem: the dire need in the Church for correct teaching and sound theology on the basic principles of Catholic ethics. I pray that the grace and providence of God will use this book to assist the faithful in understanding the true teachings of the Catholic Faith on morality, especially in its fundamental principles, and to guide the faithful out of the current confusion, and into the light of the teaching of Christ found in Tradition, Scripture, Magisterium.

May God have mercy on the Church.

---

[593] Pope John Paul II, Veritatis Splendor, n. 5.

Afterword

www.ingramcontent.com/pod-product-compliance
Lightning Source LLC
Chambersburg PA
CBHW080718230426
43665CB00020B/2555